Classes Not Derived

Internet Server API
- CHtmlStream
- CHttpFilter
- CHttpFilterContext
- CHttpServer
- CHttpServerContext

Runtime Object Model Support
- CArchive
- CDumpContext
- CRuntimeClass

Simple Value Types
- CPoint
- CRect
- CSize
- CString
- CTime
- CTimeSpan

Structures
- CCreateContext
- CMemoryState
- COleSafeArray
- CPrintInfo

Support
- CCmdUI
  - COleCmdUI
- CDaoFieldExchange
- CDataExchange
- CDBVariant
- CFieldExchange
- COleDataObject
- COleDispatchDriver
- CPropExchange
- CRectTracker
- CWaitCursor

Typed Template Collections
- CTypedPtrArray
- CTypedPtrList
- CTypedPtrMap

OLE Type Wrappers
- CFontHolder
- CPictureHolder

OLE Automation Types
- COleCurrency
- COleDateTime
- COleDateTimeSpan
- COleVariant

Synchronization
- CMultiLock
- CSingleLock

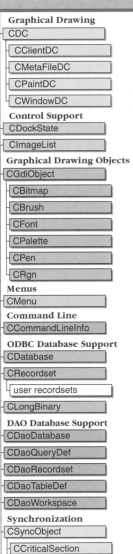

Graphical Drawing
- CDC
  - CClientDC
  - CMetaFileDC
  - CPaintDC
  - CWindowDC

Control Support
- CDockState
- CImageList

Graphical Drawing Objects
- CGdiObject
  - CBitmap
  - CBrush
  - CFont
  - CPalette
  - CPen
  - CRgn

Menus
- CMenu

Command Line
- CCommandLineInfo

ODBC Database Support
- CDatabase
- CRecordset
  - user recordsets
- CLongBinary

DAO Database Support
- CDaoDatabase
- CDaoQueryDef
- CDaoRecordset
- CDaoTableDef
- CDaoWorkspace

Synchronization
- CSyncObject
  - CCriticalSection
  - CEvent
  - CMutex
  - CSemaphore

Windows Sockets
- CAsyncSocket
  - CSocket

Arrays
- CArray (template)
- CByteArray
- CDWordArray
- CObArray
- CPtrArray
- CStringArray
- CUIntArray
- CWordArray
- arrays of user types

Lists
- CList (template)
- CPtrList
- CObList
- CStringList
- lists of user types

Maps
- CMap (template)
- CMapWordToPtr
- CMapPtrToWord
- CMapPtrToPtr
- CMapWordToOb
- CMapStringToPtr
- CMapStringToOb
- CMapStringToString
- maps of user types

Internet Services
- CInternetSession
- CInternetConnection
  - CFtpConnection
  - CGopherConnection
  - CHttpConnection
- CFileFind
  - CFtpFileFind
  - CGopherFileFind
- CGopherLocator

Programming

Microsoft®
Visual C++®

Fifth Edition

David J. Kruglinski,
Scot Wingo, and George Shepherd

***Microsoft** Press*

PUBLISHED BY
Microsoft Press
A Division of Microsoft Corporation
One Microsoft Way
Redmond, Washington 98052-6399

Copyright © 1998 by David J. Kruglinski

Library of Congress Cataloging-in-Publication Data
Kruglinski, David.
      Programming Microsoft Visual C++ / David J. Kruglinski, Scot Wingo, George Shepherd. -- 5th ed.
          p.   cm.
      Rev. ed. of: Inside Visual C++.
      Includes index.
      ISBN 1-57231-857-0
      1. C++ (Computer program language)   2. Microsoft Visual C++.
I. Wingo, Scot.   II. Shepherd, George, 1962– .   III. Kruglinski,
David.   Inside Visual C++.   IV. Title.
QA76.73.C153K78 1998
005.13'3--dc21
                                                                      98-27329
                                                                      CIP

Printed and bound in the United States of America.

2 3 4 5 6 7 8 9   WCWC   3 2 1 0 9 8

Distributed in Canada by ITP Nelson, a division of Thomson Canada Limited.

A CIP catalogue record for this book is available from the British Library.

Microsoft Press books are available through booksellers and distributors worldwide. For further information about international editions, contact your local Microsoft Corporation office or contact Microsoft Press International directly at fax (425) 936-7329. Visit our Web site at mspress.microsoft.com.

Acquisitions Editor: Eric Stroo
Project Editor: Rebecca McKay
Technical Editor: Jean Ross

TABLE OF CONTENTS

CHAPTER FOURTEEN

Toolbars and Status Bars **323**

CHAPTER FIFTEEN

A Reusable Frame Window Base Class **349**

CHAPTER SIXTEEN

Separating the Document from Its View **367**

CHAPTER TWENTY-SIX

Uniform Data Transfer—Clipboard Transfer and OLE Drag and Drop   **687**

CHAPTER TWENTY-SEVEN

Structured Storage   **717**

CHAPTER TWENTY-EIGHT

OLE Embedded Components and Containers   **745**

CHAPTER TWENTY-NINE

Introducing the Active Template Library **799**

CHAPTER THIRTY

ATL and ActiveX Controls **849**

PART V: DATABASE MANAGEMENT

CHAPTER THIRTY-ONE

Database Management with Microsoft ODBC **897**

CHAPTER THIRTY-TWO

Database Management with Microsoft Data Access Objects **929**

CHAPTER THIRTY-THREE

The OLE DB Templates **955**

PART VI: PROGRAMMING FOR THE INTERNET

ACKNOWLEDGMENTS

I first met David Kruglinski at a software development conference. I had just quit my job and started a new company, and I approached David at an author signing for an earlier edition of this book. Our new company was going to focus on Microsoft Foundation Class (MFC)/Microsoft Visual C++ class libraries. I hoped that David would listen to our ideas and maybe provide some feedback on our products and their usefulness to the Visual C++ development community—a community that he had both helped to build and understood like the back of his own hand.

Much to my surprise, David was very excited about the product ideas and asked if I could send him evaluation copies of our products. I did, and we started a long e-mail conversation about our products and ideas for improvements. David gave his time, expertise, and great opinions freely, without ever asking for any compensation—he genuinely wanted to help us make products for the Visual C++ developer that would make MFC/Visual C++ better.

I first heard about David's fatal paragliding accident via a posting on a newsgroup and initially thought it was some kind of cruel hoax. I called David's agent, who checked into the story, and much to my shock it was true. With David's passing, the Visual C++ community has lost one of its brightest and most giving stars. Talk to any Visual C++ developers about how they first learned Visual C++ and invariably they will say, "The Kruglinski book!" The Visual C++ community owes David greatly for what he gave us and taught us about Visual C++ over the years. It goes without saying that he should receive special acknowledgment for this book, and our thoughts go out to his family and friends for their loss.

It is a great honor to carry on the Kruglinski tradition with this fifth edition of *Inside Visual C++* (now called *Programming Microsoft Visual C++*). We have done our best to stay true to David's vision of this book, following his format and style as closely as possible.

Thanks to my wife, Kris, and to my son, Sean, for putting up with all of the late nights and weekends of writing. Many thanks also go to my coauthor, George Shepherd, who always helps me get motivated for a late night of book writing with his upbeat, wacky, and great personality. Thanks to Claire Horne, our agent, for helping us get on board with the project.

Visual C++, and therefore this book, wouldn't exist if not for the many members of the Visual C++ team. Special thanks to Mike Blaszczak, Walter Sullivan, Dean McCrory, Rick Laplante, Marie Huwe, Christian Gross, and Jim Springfield for all of the help they have provided over the years.

Finally, but not least, thanks to the folks at Microsoft Press who worked on this project—especially Kathleen Atkins, Jim Fuchs, Becka McKay, John Pierce, Jean Ross, Eric Stroo, and the entire production team who worked extremely hard to get this large book out and into your hands with the highest quality possible.

—Scot Wingo

Much work goes into writing books—even revisions of existing work. I'd like to acknowledge the following people for helping me get this work out the door: First I'd like to thank my wife, Sandy, for sticking with me while I worked to get the pages and chapters out. Sandy has been an invaluable source of encouragement throughout my software endeavors. Thanks to my son, Teddy, for being patient with me as I bowed out on various activities every once in a while. I wish to thank my mother, Betsy, for engendering in me a desire to write and my twin brother, Patrick, for being a great Java foil for me—and for arguing cogently with me about various hardware and software platform issues.

Thanks to Claire Horne of the Moore Literary Agency for helping to get this project rolling with Microsoft Press.

To Scot Wingo, thanks for taking on another writing project with me. And thanks to the folks at Stingray—you all are a great bunch to work with. Thanks to all the folks at DevelopMentor for providing a great training and learning environment. And thanks to Don Box for continuing to explain COM in a way that makes sense.

Getting a book out involves more than just authors. I wish to thank everyone at Microsoft Press who helped kick *Programming Microsoft Visual C++, Fifth Edition* out the door, especially Eric Stroo for his kindness and patience, Kathleen Atkins and Becka McKay for sifting through our text and making it ever more readable, Jean Ross for balancing out the technical review to catch even the most minute error, and John Pierce for keeping everything on track.

Finally, thanks to David Kruglinski for starting this project. While I never had the opportunity to meet David, his writing had a considerable impact on me when I was first learning MFC. I hope Scot and I did justice to his achievements.

—George Shepherd

INTRODUCTION

The 6.0 release of Visual C++ shows Microsoft's continued focus on Internet technologies and COM, which are key components of the new Windows Distributed interNet Application Architecture (DNA). In addition to supporting these platform initiatives, Visual C++ 6.0 also adds an amazing number of productivity-boosting features such as Edit And Continue, IntelliSense, AutoComplete, and code tips. These features take Visual C++ to a new level. We have tried to make sure that this book keeps you up to speed on the latest technologies being introduced into Visual C++.

MFC, ATL, and WFC—Is MFC Dead?

Ever since Microsoft released the Active Template Library (ATL) as part of Visual C++, Windows developers have speculated that the Microsoft Foundation Class Library (MFC) was no longer "en vogue" at Microsoft and that future efforts would focus on newer libraries such as ATL. Recently, Microsoft released another class library, Windows Foundation Classes (WFC), for Java Windows developers, which has unfortunately helped to fan the rumors that "MFC is dead."

The rumors of MFC's demise are definitely premature. Visual C++ 6.0 has added significant functionality to MFC and ATL in parallel, which indicates that both libraries will receive equal attention moving forward. Part of the problem is that the <u>design goals</u> of each library are sometimes not clearly stated and therefore are not clearly understood by the Visual C++ developer. MFC is designed to be a great class library for creating graphically rich, sophisticated Windows applications. ATL is designed to make it easy to create extremely lightweight COM objects and ActiveX controls. Each of these design goals has resulted in a different library to empower the developer.

Another common misconception is that MFC and ATL are mutually exclusive. This is definitely not the case! In fact, it is very easy to create ATL-based COM objects that use MFC. The only issue is that since many developers choose ATL for its lightweight nature, using MFC, which is feature-rich and "heavy," seems to contradict the reason for choosing ATL. While this might be the case for some developers, it doesn't make ATL and MFC mutually exclusive.

While ATL does not replace MFC, we do think it is an important part of Visual C++, so in this edition of *Programming Microsoft Visual C++* we have added two chapters that cover the ATL class libraries.

C++ vs. Java

In the last couple of years, there has been a great deal of interest in the Java programming language. Why should you choose C++ over Java? In the first place, a compiled program will always be faster than an interpreted program. Think about a high-performance spreadsheet program with cell formulas and macros. Now imagine the Java virtual machine interpreting the code that, in turn, interprets the formulas and macros. Not pretty, is it? With just-in-time compilation, it's necessary to compile the program every time you load it. Will that code be as good as the optimized output from a C++ compiler?

Execution speed is one factor; access to the operating system is another. For security reasons, Java applets can't perform such tasks as writing to disk and accessing serial ports. In order to be platform-independent, Java application programs are limited to the "lowest common denominator" of operating system features. A C++ program for Microsoft Windows is more flexible because it can call any Win32 function at any time.

Java will be an important language, but we believe it's just another language, not a revolution. If you need an Internet applet or a truly platform-independent application, choose Java. If you need efficiency and flexibility, choose C++.

Who Can Use This Book

The product name "Visual C++" misleads some people. They think they've bought a pure visual programming system similar to Microsoft Visual Basic, and for the first few days the illusion persists. However, people soon learn that they must actually read and write C++ code. The Visual C++ wizards save time and improve accuracy, but programmers must understand the <u>code</u> that the wizards generate and, ultimately, the structure of the MFC library and the inner workings of the Windows operating system.

Visual C++, with its sophisticated application framework, is for professional programmers, and so is this book. We assume that you're proficient in the C language—you can write an *if* statement without consulting the manual. And we assume that you've been exposed to the C++ language—you've at least taken a course or read a book, but maybe you haven't written much code. Compare learning C++ to learning the French language. You can study French in school, but you won't be able to speak fluently unless you go to France and start talking to people. Reading this book is like taking your trip to France!

We won't assume, however, that you already know Windows programming. We're sure that proficient C programmers can learn Windows the MFC way. It's more important to know C++ than it is to know the Win32 application programming interface (API). You should, however, know how to run Windows and Windows-based applications.

What if you're already experienced with the Win32 API or with the MFC library? There's something in this book for you too. First you'll get some help making the transition to Win32 programming. Then you'll learn about new features such as Data Access Objects (DAO), ActiveX control container support, and the controls introduced with Windows 95. If you haven't already figured out the Component Object Model (COM), this book presents some important theory that will get you started on understanding ActiveX Controls. You'll also learn about the ATL class library, the new Microsoft Internet Explorer 4.0 common controls, and OLE/DB database programming. Finally, you'll learn C++ programming for the Internet (including the hot new topic Dynamic HTML). We've even included coverage on how to make your Visual C++ programs work on the new Windows CE operating system.

What's Not Covered

It's not possible to cover every aspect of Windows-based programming in a single book. We exclude topics that depend on special-purpose hardware and software, such as MAPI, TAPI, and communications port access. We do cover using ActiveX controls in an application, but we'll defer the subject of writing ActiveX controls to Adam Denning and his *ActiveX Controls Inside Out* (Microsoft Press, 1997). We get you started with 32-bit memory management, DLL theory, and multithreaded programming techniques, but you need to get the third edition of Jeffrey Richter's *Advanced Windows* (Microsoft Press, 1997) if you're serious about these subjects. Another useful book is *MFC Internals* by George Shepherd and Scot Wingo (Addison-Wesley, 1996).

How to Use This Book

When you're starting with Visual C++, you can use this book as a tutorial by going through it sequentially. Later you can use it as a reference by looking up topics in the table of contents or in the index. Because of the tight interrelationships among many application framework elements, it wasn't possible to cleanly isolate each concept in its own chapter, so the book really isn't an encyclopedia. When you use this book, you'll definitely want to keep the online help available for looking up classes and member functions.

If you're experienced with the Win16 version of Visual C++, scan Part I for an overview of new features. Then skip the first three chapters of Part II, but read Chapters 6 through 12, which cover elements specific to Win32.

The Organization of This Book

As the table of contents shows, this book has six parts and an appendix section.

Part I: Windows, Visual C++, and Application Framework Fundamentals

In this part, we try to strike a balance between abstract theory and practical application. After a quick review of Win32 and the Visual C++ components, you'll be introduced, in a gentle way, to the MFC application framework and the document–view architecture. You'll look at a simple "Hello, world!" program, built with the MFC library classes, that requires only 30 lines of code.

Part II: The MFC Library View Class

The MFC library documentation presents all the application framework elements in quick succession, with the assumption that you know the original Windows API. In Part II, you're confined to one major application framework component—the <u>view</u>, which is really a window. You'll learn here what experienced Windows programmers know already, but in the context of C++ and the MFC library classes. You'll use the Visual C++ tools that eliminate much of the coding drudgery that early Windows programmers had to endure.

Part II covers a lot of territory, including graphics programming with bitmaps, dialog data exchange, ActiveX control usage, 32-bit memory management, and multithreaded programming. The exercises will help you to write reasonably sophisticated Windows-based programs, but those programs won't take advantage of the advanced application framework features.

Part III: The Document–View Architecture

This part introduces the real core of application framework programming—the document–view architecture. You'll learn what a <u>document</u> is (something much more general than a word processing document), and you'll see how to connect the document to the view that you studied in Part II. You'll be amazed, once you have written a document class, at how the MFC library simplifies file I/O and printing.

Along the way, you'll learn about command message processing, toolbars and status bars, splitter frames, and context-sensitive help. You'll also be introduced to the Multiple Document Interface (MDI), the current standard for Windows-based applications.

Part III also contains a discussion of dynamic link libraries (DLLs) written with the MFC library. You'll learn the distinction between an extension DLL and a regular DLL. If you're used to Win16 DLLs, you'll notice some changes in the move to Win32.

Part IV: ActiveX: COM, Automation, and OLE

COM by itself deserves more than one book. Part IV will get you started in learning fundamental COM theory from the MFC point of view. You'll progress to Automation, which is the link between C++ and Visual Basic for Applications (VBA). You'll also become familiar with uniform data transfer and structured storage, and you'll learn the basics of compound documents and embedded objects.

Part V: Database Management

Windows-based programs often need access to information in large databases. Visual C++ now supports two separate database management options: Open Database Connectivity (ODBC) and Data Access Objects (DAO). Part V offers a chapter on each option. You'll learn about the extensive MFC and wizard support for both options, and you'll see the differences between and similarities of ODBC and DAO. We'll also cover a new data access technology, OLE/DB, which is supported by ATL OLE/DB consumer and providers.

Part VI: Programming for the Internet

This part starts with a technical Internet tutorial that covers the TCP/IP protocol plus the Winsock and WinInet APIs. You'll learn how to write C++ server and client programs for the Internet and the intranet, you'll learn how to write ISAPI DLLs that extend the Microsoft Internet Information Server, and you'll learn how to program for Dynamic HTML. We've also included coverage on Windows CE in this section.

Appendixes

Appendix A contains a list of message map macros and their corresponding handler function prototypes. ClassWizard usually generates this code for you, but sometimes you must make manual entries.

Appendix B offers a description of the MFC application framework's runtime class information and dynamic creation system. This is independent of the RTTI (runtime type information) feature that is now a part of ANSI C++.

Win32 vs. Win16

Lots of old computers out there are still running Windows 3.1. However, there's not much point in spending money writing new programs for obsolete technology. This edition of *Programming Microsoft Visual C++* is about 32-bit programming for Microsoft Windows 95, Microsoft Windows 98, and Microsoft Windows NT using the Win32 API. If you really need to do 16-bit programming, find an old copy of the second edition of this book.

Windows 95 and Windows 98 vs. Windows NT

Visual C++ version 6.0 requires either Windows 95, Windows 98, or Windows NT version 4.0 or later, all of which have the same user interface. We recommend that you use Windows NT as your development platform because of its stability—you can often go for months without rebooting your computer. If you use only the MFC programming interface, your compiled programs will run under Windows 95, Windows 98, and Windows NT, but a program can include Win32 calls that use specific Windows 98 or Windows NT features.

Going Further with Windows:
The "For Win32 Programmers" Sidebars

This book can't offer the kind of detail, tricks, and hidden features found in the newer, specialized books on Win32. Most of those books are written from the point of view of a C-language programmer: in order to use them, you'll have to understand the underlying Win32 API and its relationship to the MFC library. In addition, you'll need to know about the Windows message dispatch mechanism and the role of <u>window</u> <u>classes</u>.

This book's "For Win32 Programmers" sidebars, scattered throughout the text, help you make the connection to low-level programming for Windows. These specially formatted boxes help experienced C programmers relate new MFC library concepts to principles they're already familiar with. If you're unfamiliar with low-level programming, you should skip these notes the first time through, but you should read them on your second pass through the book. Even though you may never write a low-level Windows-based program with a

WinMain function, for example, you eventually need to know how the Windows operating system interacts with your program.

Using the Companion CD-ROM

The companion CD-ROM bound inside the back cover of this book contains the source code files for all the sample programs. The executable program files are included, so you won't have to build the samples that you're interested in. To install the companion CD-ROM's files, insert the disc in your CD-ROM drive and run the Setup program. Follow the on-screen instructions.

> NOTE: The Setup program copies about 30 MB of files to your hard disk. If you prefer, you can manually install only the files for individual projects. Simply tree-copy the corresponding subdirectories from the CD-ROM to c:\vcpp32. Because each project is self-contained, no additional files from other projects are needed. (You'll need to remove the read-only attribute from these files if you copy them using Windows Explorer or File Manager.)

> NOTE: Many of the files on the companion CD-ROM have long filenames. If you use Windows 95 and your CD-ROM drive uses a real-mode driver, you'll see truncated names for these files and you might not see all of the files or directories. The Setup program will still work correctly, however, by copying files from a special \SETUP directory on the CD-ROM and renaming them with their proper long filenames. You can then browse the files on your hard disk. Alternatively, you can browse the files using the 8.3 aliases in the \SETUP directory on the CD-ROM.

With a conventional C-language program using the Windows API, the source code files tell the whole story. With the MFC library application framework, things are not so simple. AppWizard generates much of the C++ code, and the resources originate in the resource editors. The examples in the early chapters of this book include step-by-step instructions for using the tools to generate and customize the source code files. You'd be well advised to walk through those instructions for the first few examples; there's very little code to type. For the middle chapters, use the code from the companion CD-ROM but read through the steps in order to appreciate the role of the resource editors and the wizards. For the final chapters, not all the source code is listed. You'll need to examine the companion CD-ROM's files for those examples.

For Win32 Programmers: Unicode

Until recently, Windows-based programs have used only the ANSI character set, which consists of 256 single-byte characters. Developers targeting the Asian software market are moving to the Unicode character set, which consists of 65,536 characters, each 2 bytes (wide). A third option, the double-byte character set (DBCS), includes both 1-byte characters and 2-byte characters, but DBCS is falling out of favor.

The MFC library and the runtime library both support Unicode applications. If you define the constant _UNICODE and follow the steps described in the online documentation, all your character variables and constant strings will be wide and the compiler will generate calls to the wide-character versions of the Win32 functions. This assumes that you use certain macros when you declare character pointers and arrays—for example, *TCHAR* and _T.

You'll hit a snag, though, if you try to run your MFC Unicode applications under Windows 95 or Windows 98, because they don't support Unicode internally. Even though Windows 95 and Windows 98 have wide-character versions of Win32 functions, those functions return a failure code. Windows NT, on the other hand, uses Unicode internally and has two versions of the Win32 functions that deal with characters. If you call a single-byte version, Windows NT makes the necessary conversions to and from wide characters.

None of the sample programs in this book are configured for Unicode. All the programs use single-byte types such as *char* and single-byte string constants, and they <u>do</u> <u>not</u> define _UNICODE. If you run the samples under Windows NT, the operating system will do the necessary single-to-wide conversions; if you run them under Windows 95 or Windows 98, the interface is pure single-byte.

One area in which you're forced to deal with wide characters is COM. All non-MFC COM functions (except DAO functions) that have string and character parameters require wide (*OLECHAR*) characters. If you write a non-Unicode program, you must do the conversions yourself with the help of the MFC *CString* class and various MFC macros.

If you want to write Unicode applications, read the Unicode chapter in Jeffrey Richter's *Advanced Windows*. You should also read the Unicode material in the Visual C++ online documentation.

Technical Notes and Sample Programs

The MSDN Library for Visual Studio 6.0 contains technical notes and sample programs that are referenced in this book. The technical notes, identified by number, are available from the Contents tab under the heading:

MSDN Library Visual Studio 6.0
  Visual C++ Documentation Reference
    Microsoft Foundation Class Library and Templates
      Microsoft Foundation Class Library
        MFC Technical Notes

The MSDN CD-ROM also contains a number of MFC sample programs also referenced in the book and identified by name. These sample programs are documented under the heading:

MSDN Library Visual Studio 6.0
  Visual C++ Documentation
    Samples
      MFC Samples

Support

Every effort has been made to ensure the accuracy of this book and the contents of the companion disc. Microsoft Press provides corrections for books through the Web at: *http://mspress.microsoft.com/mspress/support/*

If you have comments, questions, or ideas regarding this book or the companion disc, please send them to Microsoft Press using postal mail or e-mail:

Microsoft Press
Attn: Programming Microsoft Visual C++ Editor
One Microsoft Way
Redmond, WA 98052-6399

MSPINPUT@MICROSOFT.COM

Please note that product support is not offered through the above mail addresses. For support information regarding Microsoft Visual C++, you can call the technical support line at (425) 635-7007 weekdays between 6 a.m. and 6 p.m. Pacific time. Microsoft also provides information about Visual C++ at *http://www.microsoft.com/visualc/* and about the Microsoft Developer Network at *http://www.microsoft.com/MSDN/*

PART I

WINDOWS,
VISUAL C++,
AND APPLICATION
FRAMEWORK
FUNDAMENTALS

CHAPTER ONE

Microsoft Windows and Visual C++

Enough has already been written about the acceptance of Microsoft Windows and the benefits of the graphical user interface (GUI). This chapter summarizes the Windows programming model (Win32 in particular) and shows you how the Microsoft Visual C++ components work together to help you write applications for Windows. Along the way, you might learn some new things about Windows.

The Windows Programming Model

No matter which development tools you use, programming for Windows is different from old-style batch-oriented or transaction-oriented programming. To get started, you need to know some Windows fundamentals. As a frame of reference, we'll use the well-known MS-DOS programming model. Even if you don't currently program for plain MS-DOS, you're probably familiar with it.

Message Processing

When you write an MS-DOS–based application in C, the only absolute requirement is a function named *main*. The operating system calls *main* when the user runs the program, and from that point on, you can use any programming structure you want. If your program needs to get user keystrokes or otherwise use operating system services, it calls an appropriate function, such as *getchar*, or perhaps uses a character-based windowing library.

When the Windows operating system launches a program, it calls the program's *WinMain* function. Somewhere your application must have *WinMain*, which performs some specific tasks. Its most important task is creating the application's main window, which must have its own code to process messages that Windows sends it. An essential difference between a program written for MS-DOS and a program written for Windows is that an MS-DOS–based

3

program calls the operating system to get user input, but a Windows-based program processes user input via messages from the operating system.

NOTE: Many development environments for Windows, including Microsoft Visual C++ version 6.0 with the Microsoft Foundation Class (MFC) Library version 6.0, simplify programming by hiding the *WinMain* function and structuring the message-handling process. When you use the MFC library, you need not write a *WinMain* function but it is essential that you understand the link between the operating system and your programs.

Most messages in Windows are strictly defined and apply to all programs. For example, a WM_CREATE message is sent when a window is being created, a WM_LBUTTONDOWN message is sent when the user presses the left mouse button, a WM_CHAR message is sent when the user types a character, and a WM_CLOSE message is sent when the user closes a window. All messages have two 32-bit parameters that convey information such as cursor coordinates, key code, and so forth. Windows sends WM_COMMAND messages to the appropriate window in response to user menu choices, dialog button clicks, and so on. Command message parameters vary depending on the window's menu layout. You can define your own messages, which your program can send to any window on the desktop. These user-defined messages actually make C++ look a little like Smalltalk.

Don't worry yet about how these messages are connected to your code. That's the job of the application framework. Be aware, though, that the Windows message processing requirement imposes a lot of structure on your program. Don't try to force your Windows programs to look like your old MS-DOS programs. Study the examples in this book, and then be prepared to start fresh.

The Windows Graphics Device Interface

Many MS-DOS programs wrote directly to the video memory and the printer port. The disadvantage of this technique was the need to supply driver software for every video board and every printer model. Windows introduced a layer of abstraction called the Graphics Device Interface (GDI). Windows provides the video and printer drivers, so your program doesn't need to know the type of video board and printer attached to the system. Instead of addressing the hardware, your program calls GDI functions that reference a data structure called a device context. Windows maps the device context structure to a physical device and issues the appropriate input/output instructions. The GDI is almost as fast as direct video access, and it allows different applications written for Windows to share the display.

Resource-Based Programming

To do data-driven programming in MS-DOS, you must either code the data as initialization constants or provide separate data files for your program to read. When you program for Windows, you store data in a resource file using a number of established formats. The linker combines this binary resource file with the C++ compiler's output to generate an executable program. Resource files can include bitmaps, icons, menu definitions, dialog box layouts, and strings. They can even include custom resource formats that you define.

You use a text editor to edit a program, but you generally use <u>wysiwyg</u> (what you see is what you get) tools to edit resources. If you're laying out a dialog box, for example, you select elements (buttons, list boxes, and so forth) from an array of icons called a <u>control palette</u>, and you position and size the elements with the mouse. Microsoft Visual C++ 6.0 has graphics resource editors for all standard resource formats.

Memory Management

With each new version of Windows, memory management gets easier. If you've heard horror stories about locking memory handles, thunks, and burgermasters, don't worry. That's all in the past. Today you simply allocate the memory you need, and Windows takes care of the details. Chapter 10 describes current memory management techniques for Win32, including virtual memory and memory-mapped files.

Dynamic Link Libraries

In the MS-DOS environment, all of a program's object modules are statically linked during the build process. Windows allows dynamic linking, which means that specially constructed libraries can be loaded and linked at runtime. Multiple applications can share dynamic link libraries (DLLs), which saves memory and disk space. Dynamic linking increases program modularity because you can compile and test DLLs separately.

Designers originally created DLLs for use with the C language, and C++ has added some complications. The MFC developers succeeded in combining all the application framework classes into a few ready-built DLLs. This means that you can statically or dynamically link the application framework classes into your application. In addition, you can create your own <u>extension DLLs</u> that build on the MFC DLLs. Chapter 22 includes information about creating MFC extension DLLs and regular DLLs.

The Win32 Application Programming Interface

Early Windows programmers wrote applications in C for the Win16 application programming interface (API). Today, if you want to write 32-bit applications, you must use the new Win32 API, either directly or indirectly. Most Win16 functions have Win32 equivalents, but many of the parameters are different—16-bit parameters are often replaced with 32-bit parameters, for example. The Win32 API offers many new functions, including functions for disk I/O, which was formerly handled by MS-DOS calls. With the 16-bit versions of Visual C++, MFC programmers were largely insulated from these API differences because they wrote to the MFC standard, which was designed to work with either Win16 or Win32 underneath.

The Visual C++ Components

Microsoft Visual C++ is two complete Windows application development systems in one product. If you so choose, you can develop C-language Windows programs using only the Win32 API. C-language Win32 programming is described in Charles Petzold's book *Programming Windows 95* (Microsoft Press, 1996). You can use many Visual C++ tools, including the resource editors, to make low-level Win32 programming easier.

Visual C++ also includes the ActiveX Template Library (ATL), which you can use to develop ActiveX controls for the Internet. ATL programming is neither Win32 C-language programming nor MFC programming, and it's complex enough to deserve its own book.

This book is not about C-language Win32 programming or ATL programming (although Chapters 29 and 30 provide an introduction to ATL). It's about C++ programming within the MFC library application framework that's part of Visual C++. You'll be using the C++ classes documented in the *Microsoft Visual C++ MFC Library Reference* (Microsoft Press, 1997), and you'll also be using application framework–specific Visual C++ tools such as AppWizard and ClassWizard.

> NOTE: Use of the MFC library programming interface doesn't cut you off from the Win32 functions. In fact, you'll almost always need some direct Win32 calls in your MFC library programs.

A quick run-through of the Visual C++ components will help you get your bearings before you zero in on the application framework. Figure 1-1 shows an overview of the Visual C++ application build process.

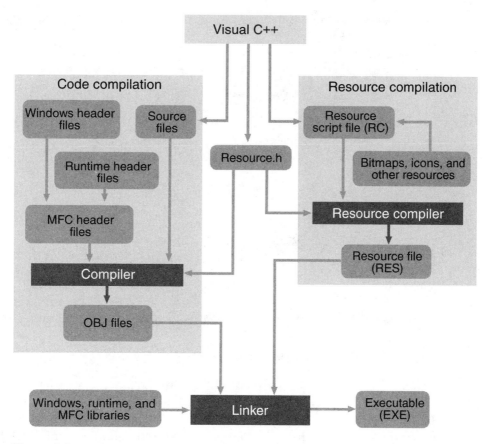

Figure 1-1.
The Visual C++ application build process.

Microsoft Visual C++ 6.0 and the Build Process

Visual Studio 6.0 is a suite of developer tools that includes Visual C++ 6.0. The Visual C++ IDE is shared by several tools including Microsoft Visual J++. The IDE has come a long way from the original Visual Workbench, which was based on QuickC for Windows. Docking windows, configurable toolbars, plus a customizable editor that runs macros, are now part of Visual Studio. The online help system (now integrated with the MSDN Library viewer) works like a Web browser. Figure 1-2 on the following page shows Visual C++ 6.0 in action.

Workspace window

WizardBar

Source code

Build target

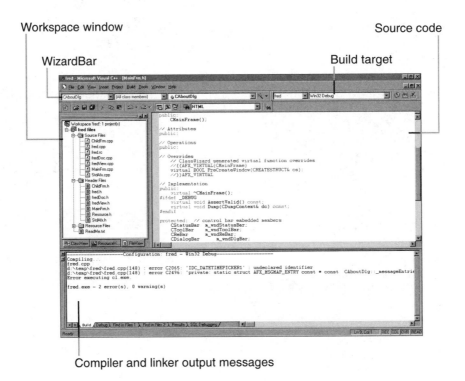

Compiler and linker output messages

Figure 1-2.
Visual C++ 6.0 windows.

If you've used earlier versions of Visual C++ or another vendor's IDE, you already understand how Visual C++ 6.0 operates. But if you're new to IDEs, you'll need to know what a project is. A project is a collection of interrelated source files that are compiled and linked to make up an executable Windows-based program or a DLL. Source files for each project are generally stored in a separate subdirectory. A project depends on many files outside the project subdirectory too, such as include files and library files.

Experienced programmers are familiar with makefiles. A makefile stores compiler and linker options and expresses all the interrelationships among source files. (A source code file needs specific include files, an executable file requires certain object modules and libraries, and so forth.) A make program reads the makefile and then invokes the compiler, assembler, resource compiler, and linker to produce the final output, which is generally an executable file. The make program uses built-in inference rules that tell it, for example, to invoke the compiler to generate an OBJ file from a specified CPP file.

In a Visual C++ 6.0 project, there is no makefile (with an MAK extension) unless you tell the system to export one. A text-format <u>project file</u> (with a DSP extension) serves the same purpose. A separate text-format <u>workspace file</u> (with a DSW extension) has an entry for each project in the workspace. It's possible to have multiple projects in a workspace, but all the examples in this book have just one project per workspace. To work on an existing project, you tell Visual C++ to open the DSW file and then you can edit and build the project.

Visual C++ creates some intermediate files too. The following table lists the files that Visual C++ generates in the workspace.

File Extension	Description
APS	Supports ResourceView
BSC	Browser information file
CLW	Supports ClassWizard
DEP	Dependency file
DSP	Project file*
DSW	Workspace file*
MAK	External makefile
NCB	Supports ClassView
OPT	Holds workspace configuration
PLG	Builds log file

*Do not delete or edit in a text editor.

The Resource Editors—Workspace ResourceView

When you click on the ResourceView tab in the Visual C++ Workspace window, you can select a resource for editing. The main window hosts a <u>resource editor</u> appropriate for the resource type. The window can also host a wysiwyg editor for menus and a powerful graphical editor for dialog boxes, and it includes tools for editing icons, bitmaps, and strings. The dialog editor allows you to insert ActiveX controls in addition to standard Windows controls and the new Windows common controls (which have been further extended in Visual C++ 6.0). Chapter 3 shows pictures of the ResourceView page and one of the resource editors (the dialog editor).

Each project usually has one text-format resource script (RC) file that describes the project's menu, dialog, string, and accelerator resources. The RC file also has *#include* statements to bring in resources from other subdirectories.

These resources include project-specific items, such as bitmap (BMP) and icon (ICO) files, and resources common to all Visual C++ programs, such as error message strings. Editing the RC file outside the resource editors is not recommended. The resource editors can also process EXE and DLL files, so you can use the clipboard to "steal" resources, such as bitmaps and icons, from other Windows applications.

The C/C++ Compiler

The Visual C++ compiler can process both C source code and C++ source code. It determines the language by looking at the source code's filename extension. A C extension indicates C source code, and CPP or CXX indicates C++ source code. The compiler is compliant with all ANSI standards, including the latest recommendations of a working group on C++ libraries, and has additional Microsoft extensions. Templates, exceptions, and runtime type identification (RTTI) are fully supported in Visual C++ version 6.0. The C++ Standard Template Library (STL) is also included, although it is not integrated into the MFC library.

The Source Code Editor

Visual C++ 6.0 includes a sophisticated source code editor that supports many features such as dynamic syntax coloring, auto-tabbing, keyboard bindings for a variety of popular editors (such as VI and EMACS), and pretty printing. In Visual C++ 6.0, an exciting new feature named AutoComplete has been added. If you have used any of the Microsoft Office products or Microsoft Visual Basic, you might already be familiar with this technology. Using the Visual C++ 6.0 AutoComplete feature, all you have to do is type the beginning of a programming statement and the editor will provide you with a list of possible completions to choose from. This feature is extremely handy when you are working with C++ objects and have forgotten an exact member function or data member name—they are all there in the list for you. You no longer have to memorize thousands of Win32 APIs or rely heavily on the online help system, thanks to this new feature.

The Resource Compiler

The Visual C++ resource compiler reads an ASCII resource script (RC) file from the resource editors and writes a binary RES file for the linker.

The Linker

The linker reads the OBJ and RES files produced by the C/C++ compiler and the resource compiler, and it accesses LIB files for MFC code, runtime library code, and Windows code. It then writes the project's EXE file. An incremental link option minimizes the execution time when only minor changes have been made to the source files. The MFC header files contain *#pragma* statements (special compiler directives) that specify the required library files, so you don't have to tell the linker explicitly which libraries to read.

The Debugger

If your program works the first time, you don't need the debugger. The rest of us might need one from time to time. The Visual C++ debugger has been steadily improving, but it doesn't actually fix the bugs yet. The debugger works closely with Visual C++ to ensure that breakpoints are saved on disk. Toolbar buttons insert and remove breakpoints and control single-step execution. Figure 1-3 illustrates the Visual C++ debugger in action. Note that the Variables and Watch

Debug toolbar   Call stack

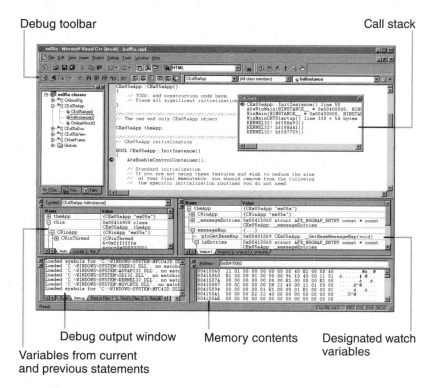

Debug output window   Memory contents   Designated watch
                                                  variables
Variables from current
and previous statements

Figure 1-3.
The Visual C++ debugger window.

windows can expand an object pointer to show all data members of the derived class and base classes. If you position the cursor on a simple variable, the debugger shows you its value in a little window. To debug a program, you must build the program with the compiler and linker options set to generate debugging information.

Visual C++ 6.0 adds a new twist to debugging with the Edit And Continue feature. Edit And Continue lets you debug an application, change the application, and then continue debugging with the new code. This feature dramatically reduces the amount of time you spend debugging because you no longer have to manually leave the debugger, recompile, and then debug again. To use this feature, simply edit any code while in the debugger and then hit the continue button. Visual C++ 6.0 automatically compiles the changes and restarts the debugger for you.

AppWizard

AppWizard is a code generator that creates a working skeleton of a Windows application with features, class names, and source code filenames that you specify through dialog boxes. You'll use AppWizard extensively as you work through the examples in this book. Don't confuse AppWizard with older code generators that generate all the code for an application. AppWizard code is minimalist code; the functionality is inside the application framework base classes. AppWizard gets you started quickly with a new application.

Advanced developers can build custom AppWizards. Microsoft Corporation has exposed its macro-based system for generating projects. If you discover that your team needs to develop multiple projects with a telecommunications interface, you can build a special wizard that automates the process.

ClassWizard

ClassWizard is a program (implemented as a DLL) that's accessible from Visual C++'s View menu. ClassWizard takes the drudgery out of maintaining Visual C++ class code. Need a new class, a new virtual function, or a new message-handler function? ClassWizard writes the prototypes, the function bodies, and (if necessary) the code to link the Windows message to the function. ClassWizard can update class code that you write, so you avoid the maintenance problems common to ordinary code generators. Some ClassWizard features are available from Visual C++'s WizardBar toolbar, shown in Figure 1-2 on page 8.

The Source Browser

If you write an application from scratch, you probably have a good mental picture of your source code files, classes, and member functions. If you take over someone else's application, you'll need some assistance. The Visual C++ Source Browser (the browser, for short) lets you examine (and edit) an application from the class or function viewpoint instead of from the file viewpoint. It's a little like the "inspector" tools available with object-oriented libraries such as Smalltalk. The browser has the following viewing modes:

- **Definitions and References**—You select any function, variable, type, macro, or class and then see where it's defined and used in your project.

- **Call Graph/Callers Graph**—For a selected function, you'll see a graphical representation of the functions it calls or the functions that call it.

- **Derived Classes and Members/Base Classes and Members**— These are graphical class hierarchy diagrams. For a selected class, you see the derived classes or the base classes plus members. You can control the hierarchy expansion with the mouse.

- **File Outline**—For a selected file, the classes, functions, and data members appear together with the places in which they're defined and used in your project.

A typical browser window is shown on page 37 in Chapter 3.

NOTE: If you rearrange the lines in any source code file, Visual C++ regenerates the browser database when you rebuild the project. This increases the build time.

In addition to the browser, Visual C++ has a ClassView option that does not depend on the browser database. You get a tree view of all the classes in your project, showing member functions and data members. Double-click on an element, and you see the source code immediately. The ClassView does not show hierarchy information, whereas the browser does.

Online Help

In Visual C++ 6.0, the help system has been moved to a separate application named the MSDN Library Viewer. This help system is based on HTML. Each topic is covered in an individual HTML document; then all are combined into indexed files. The MSDN Library Viewer uses code from Microsoft Internet Explorer 4.0, so it works like the Web browser you already know. MSDN Library can access the help files from the Visual C++ CD-ROM (the default installation option) or from your hard disk, and it can access HTML files on the Internet.

Visual C++ 6.0 allows you to access help in four ways:

- **By book**—When you choose Contents from Visual C++'s Help menu, the MSDN Library application switches to a contents view. Here Visual Studio, Visual C++, Win32 SDK documentation, and more is organized hierarchically by books and chapters.

- **By topic**—When you choose Search from Visual C++'s Help menu, it automatically opens the MSDN Library Viewer. You can then select the Index tab, type a keyword, and see the topics and articles included for that keyword.

- **By word**—When you choose Search from Visual C++'s Help menu, it invokes the MSDN Library with the Search tab active. With this tab active, you can type a combination of words to view articles that contain those words.

- **F1 help**—This is the programmer's best friend. Just move the cursor inside a function, macro, or class name, and then press the F1 key and the help system goes to work. If the name is found in several places—in the MFC and Win32 help files, for example—you choose the help topic you want from a list window.

Whichever way you access online help, you can copy any help text to the clipboard for inclusion in your program.

Windows Diagnostic Tools

Visual C++ 6.0 contains a number of useful diagnostic tools. SPY++ gives you a tree view of your system's processes, threads, and windows. It also lets you view messages and examine the windows of running applications. You'll find PVIEW (PVIEW95 for Windows 95) useful for killing errant processes that aren't visible from the Windows 95 task list. (The Windows NT Task Manager, which you can run by right-clicking the toolbar, is an alternative to PVIEW.) Visual C++ also includes a whole suite of ActiveX utilities, an ActiveX control test program (now with full source code in Visual C++ 6.0), the help workshop (with compiler), a library manager, binary file viewers and editors, a source code profiler, and other utilities.

Source Code Control

During development of Visual C++ 5.0, Microsoft bought the rights to an established source code control product named SourceSafe. This product has since been included in the Enterprise Edition of Visual C++ and Visual Studio Enterprise, and it is integrated into Visual C++ so that you can coordinate large software projects. The master copy of the project's source code is stored in a central place on the network, and programmers can check out modules for updates. These checked-out modules are usually stored on the programmer's local hard disk. After a programmer checks in modified files, other team members can synchronize their local hard disk copies to the master copy. Other source code control systems can also be integrated into Visual C++.

The Gallery

The Visual C++ Components and Controls Gallery lets you share software components among different projects. The Gallery manages three types of modules:

- **ActiveX controls**—When you install an ActiveX control (OCX— formerly OLE control), an entry is made in the Windows Registry. All registered ActiveX controls appear in the Gallery's window, so you can select them in any project.

- **C++ source modules**—When you write a new class, you can add the code to the Gallery. The code can then be selected and copied into other projects. You can also add resources to the Gallery.

- **Visual C++ components**—The Gallery can contain tools that let you add features to your project. Such a tool could insert new classes, functions, data members, and resources into an existing project. Some component modules are supplied by Microsoft (Idle time processing, Palette support, and Splash screen, for example) as part of Visual C++. Others will be supplied by third-party software firms.

TIP: If you decide to use one of the prepackaged Visual C++ components, try it out first in a dummy project to see if it's what you really want. Otherwise, it might be difficult to remove the generated code from your regular project.

All user-generated Gallery items can be imported from and exported to OGX files. These files are the distribution and sharing medium for Visual C++ components.

The Microsoft Foundation Class Library Version 6.0

The Microsoft Foundation Class Library version 6.0 (the MFC library, for short) is really the subject of this book. It defines the application framework that you'll be learning intimately. Chapter 2 gets you started with actual code and introduces some important concepts.

The Microsoft Active Template Library

ATL is a tool, separate from MFC, for building ActiveX controls. You can build ActiveX controls with either MFC or ATL, but ATL controls are much smaller and quicker to load on the Internet. Chapters 29 and 30 provide a brief overview of ATL and creating ActiveX controls with ATL.

CHAPTER TWO

The Microsoft Foundation Class Library Application Framework

This chapter introduces the Microsoft Foundation Class Library version 6.0 (the MFC library) application framework by explaining its benefits. Starting on page 23, you'll see a stripped-down but fully operational MFC library program for Microsoft Windows that should help you understand what application framework programming is all about. Theory is kept to a minimum here, but the sections on message mapping and on documents and views contain important information that will help you with the examples in later chapters.

Why Use the Application Framework?

If you're going to develop applications for Windows, you've got to choose a development environment. Assuming that you've already rejected non-C options such as Microsoft Visual Basic and Borland Delphi, here are some of your remaining options:

- Program in C with the Win32 API
- Write your own C++ Windows class library that uses Win32
- Use the MFC application framework
- Use another Windows-based application framework such as Borland's Object Windows Library (OWL)

If you're starting from scratch, any option involves a big learning curve. If you're already a Win16 or Win32 programmer, you'll still have a learning curve with the MFC library. Since its release, MFC has become the dominant Windows class library. But even if you're familiar with it, it's still a good idea to step through the features of this programming choice.

The MFC library is the C++ Microsoft Windows API. If you accept the premise that the C++ language is now the standard for serious application development, you'd have to say that it's natural for Windows to have a C++ programming interface. What better interface is there than the one produced by Microsoft, creator of Windows? That interface is the MFC library.

Application framework applications use a standard structure. Any programmer starting on a large project develops some kind of structure for the code. The problem is that each programmer's structure is different, and it's difficult for a new team member to learn the structure and conform to it. The MFC library application framework includes its own application structure—one that's been proven in many software environments and in many projects. If you write a program for Windows that uses the MFC library, you can safely retire to a Caribbean island, knowing that your minions can easily maintain and enhance your code back home.

Don't think that the MFC library's structure makes your programs inflexible. With the MFC library, your program can call Win32 functions at any time, so you can take maximum advantage of Windows.

Application framework applications are small and fast. Back in the 16-bit days, you could build a self-contained Windows EXE file that was less than 20 kilobytes (KB) in size. Today, Windows programs are larger. One reason is that 32-bit code is fatter. Even with the large memory model, a Win16 program used 16-bit addresses for stack variables and many globals. Win32 programs use 32-bit addresses for everything and often use 32-bit integers because they're more efficient than 16-bit integers. In addition, the new C++ exception-handling code consumes a lot of memory.

That old 20-KB program didn't have a docking toolbar, splitter windows, print preview capabilities, or control container support—features that users expect in modern programs. MFC programs are bigger because they do more and look better. Fortunately, it's now easy to build applications that dynamically link to the MFC code (and to C runtime code), so the size goes back down again—from 192 KB to about 20 KB! Of course, you'll need some big support DLLs in the background, but those are a fact of life these days.

As far as speed is concerned, you're working with machine code produced by an optimizing compiler. Execution is fast, but you might notice a startup delay while the support DLLs are loaded.

The Visual C++ tools reduce coding drudgery. The Visual C++ resource editors, AppWizard, and ClassWizard significantly reduce the time needed to write code that is specific to your application. For example, the resource editor creates a header file that contains assigned values for *#define* constants. App-Wizard generates skeleton code for your entire application, and ClassWizard generates prototypes and function bodies for message handlers.

The MFC library application framework is feature rich. The MFC library version 1.0 classes, introduced with Microsoft C/C++ version 7.0, included the following features:

- A C++ interface to the Windows API
- General-purpose (non-Windows-specific) classes, including:
  - Collection classes for lists, arrays, and maps
  - A useful and efficient string class
  - Time, time span, and date classes
  - File access classes for operating system independence
  - Support for systematic object storage and retrieval to and from disk
- A "common root object" class hierarchy
- Streamlined Multiple Document Interface (MDI) application support
- Some support for OLE version 1.0

The MFC library version 2.0 classes (in Visual C++ version 1.0) picked up where the version 1.0 classes left off by supporting many user interface features that are found in current Windows-based applications, plus they introduced the application framework architecture. Here's a summary of the important new features:

- Full support for File Open, Save, and Save As menu items and the most recently used file list
- Print preview and printer support
- Support for scrolling windows and splitter windows
- Support for toolbars and status bars
- Access to Visual Basic controls
- Support for context-sensitive help
- Support for automatic processing of data entered in a dialog box

- An improved interface to OLE version 1.0

- DLL support

The MFC library version 2.5 classes (in Visual C++ version 1.5) contributed the following:

- Open Database Connectivity (ODBC) support that allows your application to access and update data stored in many popular databases such as Microsoft Access, FoxPro, and Microsoft SQL Server

- An interface to OLE version 2.01, with support for in-place editing, linking, drag and drop, and OLE Automation

Visual C++ version 2.0 was the first 32-bit version of the product. It included support for Microsoft Windows NT version 3.5. It also contained MFC version 3.0, which had the following new features:

- Tab dialog (property sheet) support (which was also added to Visual C++ version 1.51, included on the same CD-ROM)

- Docking control bars that were implemented within MFC

- Support for thin-frame windows

- A separate Control Development Kit (CDK) for building 16-bit and 32-bit OLE controls, although no OLE control container support was provided

A subscription release, Visual C++ 2.1 with MFC 3.1, added the following:

- Support for the new Microsoft Windows 95 (beta) common controls

- A new ODBC Level 2 driver integrated with the Access Jet database engine

- Winsock classes for TCP/IP data communication

Microsoft decided to skip Visual C++ version 3.0 and proceeded directly to 4.0 in order to synchronize the product version with the MFC version. MFC 4.0 contains these additional features:

- New OLE-based Data Access Objects (DAO) classes for use with the Jet engine

- Use of the Windows 95 docking control bars instead of the MFC control bars

- Full support for the common controls in the released version of Windows 95, with new tree view and rich-edit view classes

- New classes for thread synchronization

- OLE control container support

Visual C++ 4.2 was an important subscription release that included MFC version 4.2. The following new features were included:

- WinInet classes

- ActiveX Documents server classes

- ActiveX synchronous and asynchronous moniker classes

- Enhanced MFC ActiveX Control classes, with features such as windowless activation, optimized drawing code, and so forth

- Improved MFC ODBC support, including recordset bulk fetches and data transfer without binding

Visual C++ 5.0 included MFC version 4.21, which fixed some 4.2 bugs. Visual C++ 5.0 introduced some worthwhile features of its own as well:

- A redesigned IDE, Developer Studio 97, which included an HTML-based online help system and integration with other languages, including Java

- The Active Template Library (ATL) for efficient ActiveX control construction for the Internet

- C++ language support for COM (Component Object Model) client programs with the new *#import* statement for type libraries, as described in Chapter 25

The latest edition of Visual C++, 6.0, includes MFC 6.0. (Notice that the versions are now synchronized again.) Many of the features in MFC 6.0 enable the developer to support the new Microsoft Active Platform, including the following:

- MFC classes that encapsulate the new Windows common controls introduced as part of Internet Explorer 4.0

- Support for Dynamic HTML, which allows the MFC programmer to create applications that can dynamically manipulate and generate HTML pages

- Active Document Containment, which allows MFC-based applications to contain Active Documents

- OLE DB Consumers and Providers Template support and Active Data Objects (ADO) data binding, which help database developers who use MFC or ATL

The Learning Curve

All the listed benefits sound great, don't they? You're probably thinking, "You don't get something for nothing." Yes, that's true. To use the application framework effectively, you have to learn it thoroughly, and that takes time. If you have to learn C++, Windows, and the MFC library (without OLE) all at the same time, it will take at least six months before you're really productive. Interestingly, that's close to the learning time for the Win32 API alone.

How can that be if the MFC library offers so much more? For one thing, you can avoid many programming details that C-language Win32 programmers are forced to learn. From our own experience, we can say that an object-oriented application framework makes programming for Windows easier to learn—that is, once you understand object-oriented programming.

The MFC library won't bring real Windows programming down to the masses. Programmers of applications for Windows have usually commanded higher salaries than other programmers, and that situation will continue. The MFC library's learning curve, together with the application framework's power, should ensure that MFC library programmers will continue to be in strong demand.

What's an Application Framework?

One definition of <u>application framework</u> is "an integrated collection of object-oriented software components that offers all that's needed for a generic application." That isn't a very useful definition, is it? If you really want to know what an application framework is, you'll have to read the rest of this book. The application framework example that you'll familiarize yourself with later in this chapter is a good starting point.

An Application Framework vs. a Class Library

One reason that C++ is a popular language is that it can be "extended" with class libraries. Some class libraries are delivered with C++ compilers, others are sold by third-party software firms, and still others are developed in-house. A class library is a set of related C++ classes that can be used in an application. A mathematics class library, for example, might perform common mathematics operations, and a communications class library might support the transfer of data over a serial link. Sometimes you construct objects of the supplied classes; sometimes you derive your own classes—it all depends on the design of the particular class library.

An application framework is a superset of a class library. An ordinary library is an isolated set of classes designed to be incorporated into any program, but an application framework defines the structure of the program itself. Microsoft didn't invent the application framework concept. It appeared first in the academic world, and the first commercial version was MacApp for the Apple Macintosh. Since MFC 2.0 was introduced, other companies, including Borland, have released similar products.

An Application Framework Example

Enough generalizations. It's time to look at some code—not pseudocode but real code that actually compiles and runs with the MFC library. Guess what? It's the good old "Hello, world!" application, with a few additions. (If you've used version 1.0 of the MFC library, this code will be familiar except for the frame window base class.) It's about the minimum amount of code for a working MFC library application for Windows. (Contrast it with an equivalent pure Win32 application such as you would see in a Petzold book!) You don't have to understand every line now. Don't bother to type it in and test it, because EX23B on the CD-ROM is quite similar. Wait for the next chapter, where you'll start using the "real" application framework.

NOTE: By convention, MFC library class names begin with the letter *C*.

Following is the source code for the header and implementation files for our MYAPP application. The classes *CMyApp* and *CMyFrame* are each derived from MFC library base classes. First, here is the MyApp.h header file for the MYAPP application:

```
// application class
class CMyApp : public CWinApp
{
public:
    virtual BOOL InitInstance();
};
```

(continued)

```
// frame window class
class CMyFrame : public CFrameWnd
{
public:
    CMyFrame();
protected:
    // "afx_msg" indicates that the next two functions are part
    //  of the MFC library message dispatch system
    afx_msg void OnLButtonDown(UINT nFlags, CPoint point);
    afx_msg void OnPaint();
    DECLARE_MESSAGE_MAP()
};
```

And here is the MyApp.cpp implementation file for the MYAPP application:

```
#include <afxwin.h> // MFC library header file declares base classes
#include "myapp.h"

CMyApp theApp; // the one and only CMyApp object

BOOL CMyApp::InitInstance()
{
    m_pMainWnd = new CMyFrame();
    m_pMainWnd->ShowWindow(m_nCmdShow);

    m_pMainWnd->UpdateWindow();
    return TRUE;
}

BEGIN_MESSAGE_MAP(CMyFrame, CFrameWnd)
    ON_WM_LBUTTONDOWN()
    ON_WM_PAINT()
END_MESSAGE_MAP()

CMyFrame::CMyFrame()
{
    Create(NULL, "MYAPP Application");
}

void CMyFrame::OnLButtonDown(UINT nFlags, CPoint point)
{
    TRACE("Entering CMyFrame::OnLButtonDown - %lx, %d, %d\n",
            (long) nFlags, point.x, point.y);
}

void CMyFrame::OnPaint()
{
    CPaintDC dc(this);
    dc.TextOut(0, 0, "Hello, world!");
}
```

Here are some of the program elements:

The *WinMain* function—Remember that Windows requires your application to have a *WinMain* function. You don't see *WinMain* here because it's hidden inside the application framework.

The *CMyApp* class—An object of class *CMyApp* represents an application. The program defines a single global *CMyApp* object, *theApp*. The *CWinApp* base class determines most of *theApp*'s behavior.

Application startup—When the user starts the application, Windows calls the application framework's built-in *WinMain* function, and *WinMain* looks for your globally constructed application object of a class derived from *CWinApp*. Don't forget that in a C++ program global objects are constructed <u>before</u> the main program is executed.

The *CMyApp::InitInstance* member function—When the *WinMain* function finds the application object, it calls the virtual *InitInstance* member function, which makes the calls needed to construct and display the application's main frame window. You must override *InitInstance* in your derived application class because the *CWinApp* base class doesn't know what kind of main frame window you want.

The *CWinApp::Run* member function—The *Run* function is hidden in the base class, but it dispatches the application's messages to its windows, thus keeping the application running. *WinMain* calls *Run* after it calls *InitInstance*.

The *CMyFrame* class—An object of class *CMyFrame* represents the application's main frame window. When the constructor calls the *Create* member function of the base class *CFrameWnd*, Windows creates the actual window structure and the application framework links it to the C++ object. The *ShowWindow* and *UpdateWindow* functions, also member functions of the base class, must be called in order to display the window.

The *CMyFrame::OnLButtonDown* function—This function is a sneak preview of the MFC library's message-handling capability. We've elected to "map" the left mouse button down event to a *CMyFrame* member function. You'll learn the details of the MFC library's message mapping in Chapter 4. For the time being, accept that this function gets called when the user presses the left mouse button. The function invokes the MFC library *TRACE* macro to display a message in the debugging window.

The **CMyFrame::OnPaint** function—The application framework calls this important mapped member function of class *CMyFrame* every time it's necessary to repaint the window: at the start of the program, when the user resizes the window, and when all or part of the window is newly exposed. The *CPaintDC* statement relates to the Graphics Device Interface (GDI) and is explained in later chapters. The *TextOut* function displays "Hello, world!"

Application shutdown—The user shuts down the application by closing the main frame window. This action initiates a sequence of events, which ends with the destruction of the *CMyFrame* object, the exit from *Run*, the exit from *Win-Main*, and the destruction of the *CMyApp* object.

Look at the code example again. This time try to get the big picture. Most of the application's functionality is in the MFC library base classes *CWinApp* and *CFrameWnd*. In writing MYAPP, we've followed a few simple structure rules and we've written key functions in our derived classes. C++ lets us "borrow" a lot of code without copying it. Think of it as a partnership between us and the application framework. The application framework provided the structure, and we provided the code that made the application unique.

Now you're beginning to see why the application framework is more than just a class library. Not only does the application framework define the application structure but it also encompasses more than C++ base classes. You've already seen the hidden *WinMain* function at work. Other elements support message processing, diagnostics, DLLs, and so forth.

MFC Library Message Mapping

Refer to the *OnLButtonDown* member function in the previous example application. You might think that *OnLButtonDown* would be an ideal candidate for a virtual function. A window base class would define virtual functions for mouse event messages and other standard messages, and derived window classes could override the functions as necessary. Some Windows class libraries do work this way.

The MFC library application framework doesn't use virtual functions for Windows messages. Instead, it uses macros to "map" specified messages to derived class member functions. Why the rejection of virtual functions? Suppose MFC used virtual functions for messages. The *CWnd* class would declare virtual functions for more than 100 messages. C++ requires a virtual function dispatch table, called a <u>vtable</u>, for each derived class used in a program. Each vtable needs one 4-byte entry for each virtual function, regardless of whether the functions are actually overridden in the derived class. Thus, for each distinct type of window or control, the application would need a table consisting of over 400 bytes to support virtual message handlers.

What about message handlers for menu command messages and messages from button clicks? You couldn't define these as virtual functions in a window base class because each application might have a different set of menu commands and buttons. The MFC library message map system avoids large vtables, and it accommodates application-specific command messages in parallel with ordinary Windows messages. It also allows selected nonwindow classes, such as document classes and the application class, to handle command messages. MFC uses macros to connect (or map) Windows messages to C++ member functions. No extensions to the C++ language are necessary.

An MFC message handler requires a function prototype, a function body, and an entry (macro invocation) in the message map. ClassWizard helps you add message handlers to your classes. You select a Windows message ID from a list box, and the wizard generates the code with the correct function parameters and return values.

Documents and Views

The previous example used an application object and a frame window object. Most of your MFC library applications will be more complex. Typically, they'll contain application and frame classes plus two other classes that represent the "document" and the "view." This document–view architecture is the core of the application framework and is loosely based on the Model/View/Controller classes from the Smalltalk world.

In simple terms, the document–view architecture separates data from the user's view of the data. One obvious benefit is multiple views of the same data. Consider a document that consists of a month's worth of stock quotes stored on disk. Suppose a table view and a chart view of the data are both available. The user updates values through the table view window, and the chart view window changes because both windows display the same information (but in different views).

In an MFC library application, documents and views are represented by instances of C++ classes. Figure 2-1 on the next page shows three objects of class *CStockDoc* corresponding to three companies: AT&T, IBM, and GM. All three documents have a table view attached, and one document also has a chart view. As you can see, there are four view objects—three objects of class *CStockTable-View* and one of class *CStockChartView*.

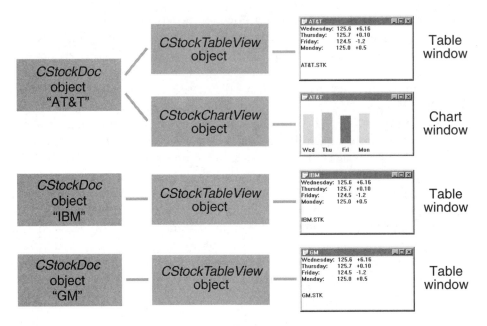

Figure 2-1.
The document–view relationship.

The document base class code interacts with the File Open and File Save menu items; the derived document class does the actual reading and writing of the document object's data. (The application framework does most of the work of displaying the File Open and File Save dialog boxes and opening, closing, reading, and writing files.) The view base class represents a window contained inside a frame window; the derived view class interacts with its associated document class and does the application's display and printer I/O. The derived view class and its base classes handle Windows messages. The MFC library orchestrates all interactions among documents, views, frame windows, and the application object, mostly through virtual functions.

Don't think that a document object must be associated with a disk file that is read entirely into memory. If a "document" were really a database, for example, you could override selected document class member functions and the File Open menu item would bring up a list of databases instead of a list of files.

PART II

THE MFC
LIBRARY
VIEW CLASS

CHAPTER THREE

Getting Started with AppWizard—"Hello, world!"

Chapter 2 sketched the MFC library version 6.0 document–view architecture. This hands-on chapter shows you how to build a functioning MFC library application, but it insulates you from the complexities of the class hierarchy and object interrelationships. You'll work with only one document–view program element, the "view class" that is closely associated with a window. For the time being, you can ignore elements such as the application class, the frame window, and the document. Of course, your application won't be able to save its data on disk, and it won't support multiple views, but Part III of this book provides plenty of opportunity to exploit those features.

Because resources are so important in Microsoft Windows–based applications, you'll use ResourceView to visually explore the resources of your new program. You'll also get some hints for setting up your Windows environment for maximum build speed and optimal debugging output.

> **REQUIREMENTS:** To compile and run the examples presented in this chapter and in the following chapters, you must have successfully installed the released version of Microsoft Windows 95 or Microsoft Windows NT version 4.0 or later, plus all the Microsoft Visual C++ version 6.0 components. Be sure that Visual C++'s executable, include, and library directories are set correctly. (You can change the directories by choosing Options from the Tools menu.) If you have any problems with the following steps, please refer to your Visual C++ documentation and Readme files for troubleshooting instructions.

What's a View?

From a user's standpoint, a <u>view</u> is an ordinary window that the user can size, move, and close in the same way as any other Windows-based application window. From the programmer's perspective, a view is a C++ object of a class derived from the MFC library *CView* class. Like any C++ object, the view object's behavior is determined by the member functions (and data members) of the class—both the application-specific functions in the derived class and the standard functions inherited from the base classes.

With Visual C++, you can produce interesting applications for Windows by simply adding code to the derived view class that the AppWizard code generator produces. When your program runs, the MFC library application framework constructs an object of the derived view class and displays a window that is tightly linked to the C++ view object. As is customary in C++ programming, the view class code is divided into two source modules—the header file (H) and the implementation file (CPP).

Single Document Interface vs. Multiple Document Interface

The MFC library supports two distinct application types: Single Document Interface (SDI) and Multiple Document Interface (MDI). An SDI application has, from the user's point of view, only one window. If the application depends on disk-file "documents," only one document can be loaded at a time. The original Windows Notepad is an example of an SDI application. An MDI application has multiple <u>child</u> <u>windows</u>, each of which corresponds to an individual document. Microsoft Word is a good example of an MDI application.

When you run AppWizard to create a new project, MDI is the default application type. For the early examples in this book, you'll be generating SDI applications because fewer classes and features are involved. Be sure you select the Single Document option (on the first AppWizard screen) for these examples. Starting with Chapter 18, you'll be generating MDI applications. The MFC library application framework architecture ensures that most SDI examples can be upgraded easily to MDI applications.

The "Do-Nothing" Application—EX03A

The AppWizard tool generates the code for a functioning MFC library application. This working application simply brings up an empty window with a menu attached. Later you'll add code that draws inside the window. Follow these steps to build the application:

1. Run AppWizard to generate SDI application source code. Choose New from Visual C++'s File menu, and then click the Projects tab in the resulting New dialog box, as shown here.

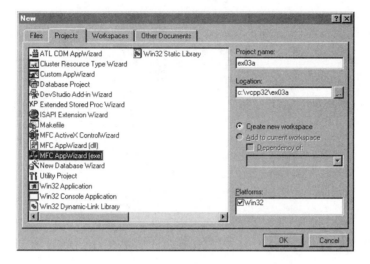

Make sure that MFC AppWizard (exe) is highlighted, and then type *C:\vcpp32* in the Location edit box. Type *ex03a* as shown in the Project Name edit box, and then click the OK button. Now you will step through a sequence of AppWizard screens, the first of which is shown here.

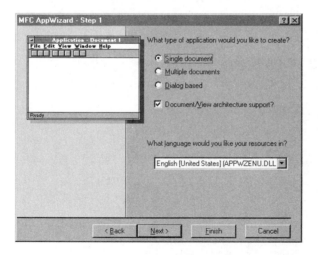

Be sure to select the Single Document option. Accept the defaults in the next four screens. The last screen should look like the following illustration.

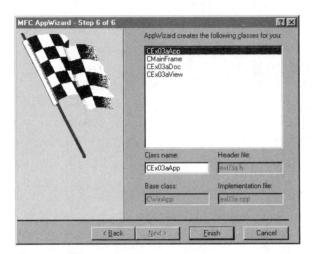

Notice that the class names and source-file names have been generated based on the project name EX03A. You could make changes to these names at this point if you wanted to. Click the Finish button. Just before AppWizard generates your code, it displays the New Project Information dialog box, shown here.

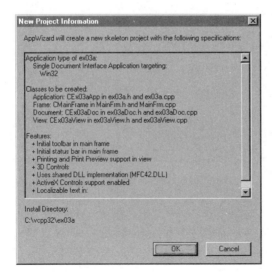

When you click the OK button, AppWizard begins to create your application's subdirectory (ex03a under \vcpp32) and a series of files in that subdirectory. When AppWizard is finished, look in the application's subdirectory. The following files are of interest (for now).

File	Description
ex03a.dsp	A project file that allows Visual C++ to build your application
ex03a.dsw	A workspace file that contains a single entry for ex03a.dsp
ex03a.rc	An ASCII resource script file
ex03aView.cpp	A view class implementation file that contains *CEx03aView* class member functions
ex03aView.h	A view class header file that contains the *CEx03aView* class declaration
ex03a.opt	A binary file that tells Visual C++ which files are open for this project and how the windows are arranged (This file is not created until you save the project.)
ReadMe.txt	A text file that explains the purpose of the generated files
resource.h	A header file that contains *#define* constant definitions

Open the ex03aView.cpp and ex03aView.h files and look at the source code. Together these files define the *CEx03aView* class, which is central to the application. An object of class *CEx03aView* corresponds to the application's view window, where all the "action" takes place.

2. **Compile and link the generated code.** AppWizard, in addition to generating code, creates custom project and workspace files for your application. The project file, ex03a.dsp, specifies all the file dependencies together with the compile and link option flags. Because the new project becomes Visual C++'s current project, you can now build the application by choosing Build Ex03a.exe from the Build menu or by clicking the Build toolbar button, shown here.

If the build is successful, an executable program named ex03a.exe is created in a new Debug subdirectory underneath \vcpp32\ex03a. The OBJ files and other intermediate files are also stored in Debug. Compare the file structure on disk with the structure in the Workspace window's FileView page shown here.

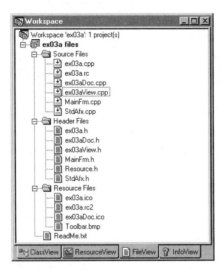

The FileView page contains a logical view of your project. The header files show up under Header Files, even though they are in the same subdirectory as the CPP files. The resource files are stored in the \res subdirectory.

3. **Test the resulting application.**   Choose Execute Ex03a.exe from the Build menu. Experiment with the program. It doesn't do much, does it? (What do you expect for no coding?) Actually, as you might guess, the program has a lot of features—you simply haven't activated them yet. Close the program window when you've finished experimenting.

4. **Browse the application.**   Choose Source Browser from the Tools menu. If your project settings don't specify browser database creation, Visual C++ will offer to change the settings and recompile the program for you. (To change the settings yourself, choose Settings from the Project menu. On the C/C++ page, click Generate Browse Info, and on the Browse Info page, click Build Browse Info File.)

When the Browse window appears, choose Base Classes And Members and then type *CEx03aView*. After you expand the hierarchy, you should see output similar to this.

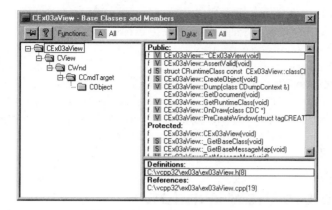

Compare the browser output to ClassView in the Workspace window.

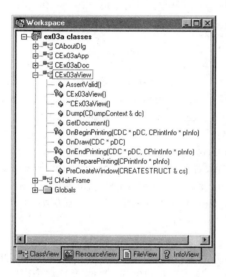

ClassView doesn't show the class hierarchy, but it also doesn't involve the extra overhead of the browser. If ClassView is sufficient for you, don't bother building the browser database.

The *CEx03aView* View Class

AppWizard generated the *CEx03aView* view class, and this class is specific to the EX03A application. (AppWizard generates classes based on the project name you entered in the first AppWizard dialog box.) *CEx03aView* is at the bottom of a long inheritance chain of MFC library classes, as illustrated previously in the Browse window. The class picks up member functions and data members all along the chain. You can learn about these classes in the *Microsoft Foundation Class Reference* (online or printed version), but you must be sure to look at the descriptions for every base class because the descriptions of inherited member functions aren't generally repeated for derived classes.

The most important *CEx03aView* base classes are *CWnd* and *CView*. *CWnd* provides *CEx03aView*'s "windowness," and *CView* provides the hooks to the rest of the application framework, particularly to the document and to the frame window, as you'll see in Part III of this book.

Drawing Inside the View Window—The Windows Graphics Device Interface

Now you're ready to write code to draw inside the view window. You'll be making a few changes directly to the EX03A source code.

The *OnDraw* Member Function

Specifically, you'll be fleshing out *OnDraw* in ex03aView.cpp. *OnDraw* is a virtual member function of the *CView* class that the application framework calls every time the view window needs to be repainted. A window needs to be repainted if the user resizes the window or reveals a previously hidden part of the window, or if the application changes the window's data. If the user resizes the window or reveals a hidden area, the application framework calls *OnDraw*, but if a function in your program changes the data, it must inform Windows of the change by calling the view's inherited *Invalidate* (or *Invalidate-Rect*) member function. This call to *Invalidate* triggers a later call to *OnDraw*.

Even though you can draw inside a window at any time, it's recommended that you let window changes accumulate and then process them all together in the *OnDraw* function. That way your program can respond both to program-generated events and to Windows-generated events such as size changes.

The Windows Device Context

Recall from Chapter 1 that Windows doesn't allow direct access to the display hardware but communicates through an abstraction called a "device context" that is associated with the window. In the MFC library, the device context is a C++ object of class *CDC* that is passed (by pointer) as a parameter to *OnDraw*. After you have the device context pointer, you can call the many *CDC* member functions that do the work of drawing.

Adding Draw Code to the EX03A Program

Now let's write the code to draw some text and a circle inside the view window. Be sure that the project EX03A is open in Visual C++. You can use the Workspace window's ClassView to locate the code for the function (double-click on *On-Draw*), or you can open the source code file ex03aView.cpp from FileView and locate the function yourself.

1. Edit the *OnDraw* function in ex03aView.cpp. Find the AppWizard-generated *OnDraw* function in ex03aView.cpp:

```
void CEx03aView::OnDraw(CDC* pDC)
{
    CEx03aDoc* pDoc = GetDocument();
    ASSERT_VALID(pDoc);

    // TODO: add draw code for native data here
}
```

The following boldface code (which you type in) replaces the previous code:

```
void CEx03aView::OnDraw(CDC* pDC)
{
    pDC->TextOut(0, 0, "Hello, world!");   // prints in default font
                                           //  & size, top left corner
    pDC->SelectStockObject(GRAY_BRUSH);    // selects a brush for the
                                           //  circle interior
    pDC->Ellipse(CRect(0, 20, 100, 120));  // draws a gray circle
                                           //  100 units in diameter
}
```

You can safely remove the call to *GetDocument* because we're not dealing with documents yet. The functions *TextOut*, *SelectStockObject*, and *Ellipse* are all member functions of the application framework's device context class *CDC*. The *Ellipse* function draws a circle if the bounding rectangle's length is equal to its width.

The MFC library provides a handy utility class, *CRect*, for Windows rectangles. A temporary *CRect* object serves as the bounding rectangle argument for the ellipse drawing function. You'll see more of the *CRect* class in quite a few of the examples in this book.

2. Recompile and test EX03A. Choose Build from the Project menu, and, if there are no compile errors, test the application again. Now you have a program that visibly does something!

For Win32 Programmers

Rest assured that the standard Windows *WinMain* and window procedure functions are hidden away inside the application framework. You'll see those functions later in this book, when the MFC library frame and application classes are examined. In the meantime, you're probably wondering what happened to the WM_PAINT message, aren't you? You would expect to do your window drawing in response to this Windows message, and you would expect to get your device context handle from a *PAINTSTRUCT* structure returned by the Windows *BeginPaint* function.

It so happens that the application framework has done all the dirty work for you and served up a device context (in object pointer form) in the virtual function *OnDraw*. As explained in Chapter 2, true virtual functions in window classes are an MFC library rarity. MFC library message map functions dispatched by the application framework handle most Windows messages. MFC version 1.0 programmers always defined an *OnPaint* message map function for their derived window classes. Beginning with version 2.5, however, *OnPaint* was mapped in the *CView* class, and that function made a polymorphic call to *OnDraw*. Why? Because *OnDraw* needs to support the printer as well as the display. Both *OnPaint* and *OnPrint* call *OnDraw*, thus enabling the same drawing code to accommodate both the printer and the display.

A Preview of the Resource Editors

Now that you have a complete application program, it's a good time for a quick look at the resource editors. Although the application's resource script, ex03a.rc, is an ASCII file, modifying it with a text editor is not a good idea. That's the resource editors' job.

The Contents of ex03a.rc

The resource file determines much of the EX03A application's "look and feel." The file ex03a.rc contains (or points to) the Windows resources listed here.

Resource	Description
Accelerator	Definitions for keys that simulate menu and toolbar selections.
Dialog	Layout and contents of dialog boxes. EX03A has only the About dialog box.
Icon	Icons (16-by-16-pixel and 32-by-32-pixel versions), such as the application icon you see in Microsoft Windows Explorer and in the application's About dialog box. EX03A uses the MFC logo for its application icon.
Menu	The application's top-level menu and associated pop-up menus.
String table	Strings that are not part of the C++ source code.
Toolbar	The row of buttons immediately below the menu.
Version	Program description, version number, language, and so on.

In addition to the resources listed above, ex03a.rc contains the statements

```
#include  "afxres.h"
#include  "afxres.rc"
```

which bring in some MFC library resources common to all applications. These resources include strings, graphical buttons, and elements needed for printing and OLE.

N O T E :   If you're using the shared DLL version of the MFC library, the common resources are stored inside the MFC DLL.

The ex03a.rc file also contains the statement

```
#include  "resource.h"
```

This statement brings in the application's three *#define* constants, which are *IDR_MAINFRAME* (identifying the menu, icon, string list, and accelerator table), *IDR_EX03ATYPE* (identifying the default document icon, which we won't use in this program), and *IDD_ABOUTBOX* (identifying the About dialog box). This same resource.h file is included indirectly by the application's source code files. If you use a resource editor to add more constants (symbols), the definitions ultimately show up in resource.h. Be careful if you edit this file in text mode because your changes might be removed the next time you use a resource editor.

Running the Dialog Resource Editor

1. **Open the project's RC file.** Click the ResourceView button in the Workspace window. If you expand each item, you will see the following in the resource editor window.

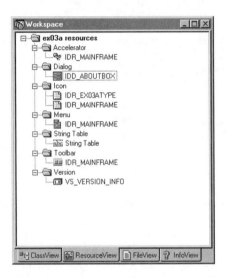

2. **Examine the application's resources.** Now take some time to explore the individual resources. When you select a resource by double-clicking on it, another window opens with tools appropriate for the selected resource. If you open a dialog resource, the control palette should appear. If it doesn't, right-click inside any toolbar, and then check Controls.

3. **Modify the IDD_ABOUTBOX dialog box.** Make some changes to the About Ex03a dialog box, shown here.

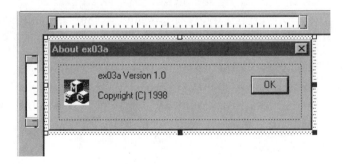

You can change the size of the window by dragging the right and bottom borders, move the OK button, change the text, and so forth. Simply click on an element to select it, and then right-click to change its properties.

4. **Rebuild the project with the modified resource file.** In Visual C++, choose Build Ex03a.exe from the Build menu. Notice that no actual C++ recompilation is necessary. Visual C++ saves the edited resource file, and then the Resource Compiler (rc.exe) processes ex03a.rc to produce a compiled version, ex03a.res, which is fed to the linker. The linker runs quickly because it can link the project incrementally.

5. **Test the new version of the application.** Run the EX03A program again, and then choose About from the application's Help menu to confirm that your dialog box was changed as expected.

Win32 Debug Target vs. Win32 Release Target

If you open the drop-down list on the Build toolbar, you'll notice two items: Win32 Debug and Win32 Release. (The Build toolbar is not present by default, but you can choose Customize from the Tools menu to display it.) These items are targets that represent distinct sets of build options. When AppWizard generates a project, it creates two default targets with different settings. These settings are summarized in the following table.

Option	Release Build	Debug Build
Source code debugging	Disabled	Enabled for both compiler and linker
MFC diagnostic macros	Disabled (NDEBUG defined)	Enabled (_DEBUG defined)
Library linkage	MFC Release library	MFC Debug libraries
Compiler optimization	Speed optimization (not available in Learning Edition)	No optimization (faster compile)

You develop your application in Debug mode, and then you rebuild in Release mode prior to delivery. The Release build EXE will be smaller and faster, assuming that you have fixed all the bugs. You select the configuration from the build target window in the Build toolbar, as shown in Figure 1-2 in Chapter 1.

By default, the Debug output files and intermediate files are stored in the project's Debug subdirectory; the Release files are stored in the Release sub-directory. You can change these directories on the General tab in the Project Settings dialog box.

You can create your own custom configurations if you need to by choosing Configurations from Visual C++'s Build menu.

Enabling the Diagnostic Macros

The application framework *TRACE* macros are particularly useful for monitoring program activity. They require that tracing be enabled, which is the default setting. If you're not seeing *TRACE* output from your program, first make sure that you are running the debug target from the debugger and then run the TRACER utility. If you check the Enable Tracing checkbox, TRACER will insert the statement

```
TraceEnabled = 1
```

in the [Diagnostics] section of a file named Afx.ini. (No, it's not stored in the Registry.) You can also use TRACER to enable other MFC diagnostic outputs, including message, OLE, database, and Internet information.

Understanding Precompiled Headers

When AppWizard generates a project, it generates switch settings and files for precompiled headers. You must understand how the make system processes precompiled headers in order to manage your projects effectively.

> NOTE: Visual C++ has two precompiled header "systems:" auto-matic and manual. Automatic precompiled headers, activated with the /Yx compiler switch, store compiler output in a "database" file. Manual precompiled headers are activated by the /Yc and /Yu switch settings and are central to all AppWizard-generated projects.

Precompiled headers represent compiler "snapshots" taken at a particu-lar line of source code. In MFC library programs, the snapshot is generally taken immediately after the following statement:

```
#include   "StdAfx.h"
```

The file StdAfx.h contains *#include* statements for the MFC library header files. The file's contents depend on the options that you select when you run App-Wizard, but the file always contains these statements:

```
#include <afxwin.h>
#include <afxext.h>
```

If you're using compound documents, StdAfx.h also contains the statement

```
#include <afxole.h>
```

and if you're using Automation or ActiveX Controls, it contains

```
#include <afxdisp.h>
```

If you're using Internet Explorer 4 Common Controls, StdAfx.h contains the statement

```
#include <afxdtctl.h>
```

Occasionally you will need other header files—for example, the header for template-based collection classes that is accessed by the statement

```
#include <afxtempl.h>
```

The source file StdAfx.cpp contains only the statement

```
#include  "StdAfx.h"
```

and is used to generate the precompiled header file in the project directory. The MFC library headers included by StdAfx.h never change, but they do take a long time to compile. The compiler switch /Yc, used only with StdAfx.cpp, causes <u>creation</u> of the precompiled header (PCH) file. The switch /Yu, used with all the other source code files, causes <u>use</u> of an existing PCH file. The switch /Fp specifies the PCH filename that would otherwise default to the project name (with the PCH extension) in the target's output files subdirectory. Figure 3-1 on the following page illustrates the whole process.

AppWizard sets the /Yc and /Yu switches for you, but you can make changes if you need to. It's possible to define compiler switch settings for individual source files. On the C/C++ tab in the Project Settings dialog box, if you select only StdAfx.cpp, you'll see the /Yc setting. This overrides the /Yu setting that is defined for the target.

Be aware that PCH files are big—5 MB is typical. If you're not careful, you'll fill up your hard disk. You can keep things under control by periodically cleaning out your projects' Debug directories, or you can use the /Fp compiler option to reroute PCH files to a common directory.

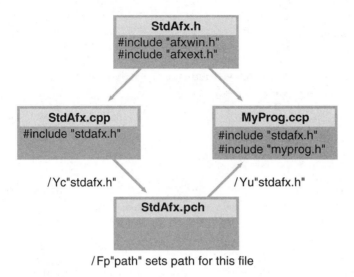

Figure 3-1.
The Visual C++ precompiled header process.

Two Ways to Run a Program

Visual C++ lets you run your program directly (by pressing Ctrl-F5) or through the debugger (by pressing F5). Running your program directly is much faster because Visual C++ doesn't have to load the debugger first. If you know you don't want to see diagnostic messages or use breakpoints, start your program by pressing Ctrl-F5 or use the "exclamation point" button on the Build toolbar.

CHAPTER FOUR

Basic Event Handling, Mapping Modes, and a Scrolling View

In Chapter 3, you saw how the Microsoft Foundation Class (MFC) Library application framework called the view class's virtual *OnDraw* function. Take a look at the online help for the MFC library now. If you look at the documentation for the *CView* class and its base class, *CWnd*, you'll see several hundred member functions. Functions whose names begin with *On*—such as *OnKeyDown* and *OnLButtonUp*—are member functions that the application framework calls in response to various Windows "events" such as keystrokes and mouse clicks.

Most of these application framework–called functions, such as *OnKey-Down*, aren't virtual functions and thus require more programming steps. This chapter explains how to use the Visual C++ ClassWizard to set up the message map structure necessary for connecting the application framework to your functions' code. You'll see the practical application of message map functions.

The first two examples use an ordinary *CView* class. In EX04A, you'll learn about the interaction between user-driven events and the *OnDraw* function. In EX04B, you'll see the effects of different Windows mapping modes.

More often than not, you'll want a scrolling view. The last example, EX04C, uses *CScrollView* in place of the *CView* base class. This allows the MFC library application framework to insert scroll bars and connect them to the view.

Getting User Input—Message Map Functions

Your EX03A application from Chapter 3 did not accept user input (other than the standard Microsoft Windows resizing and window close commands). The window contained menus and a toolbar, but these were not "connected" to the view code. The menus and the toolbar won't be discussed until Part III of this book because they depend on the frame class, but plenty of other Windows input sources will keep you busy until then. Before you can process any Windows event, even a mouse click, however, you must learn how to use the MFC message map system.

The Message Map

When the user presses the left mouse button in a view window, Windows sends a message—specifically WM_LBUTTONDOWN—to that window. If your program needs to take action in response to WM_LBUTTONDOWN, your view class must have a member function that looks like this:

```
void CMyView::OnLButtonDown(UINT nFlags, CPoint point)
{
    // event processing code here
}
```

Your class header file must also have the corresponding prototype:

```
afx_msg void OnLButtonDown(UINT nFlags, CPoint point);
```

The *afx_msg* notation is a "no-op" that alerts you that this is a prototype for a message map function. Next, your code file needs a message map macro that connects your *OnLButtonDown* function to the application framework:

```
BEGIN_MESSAGE_MAP(CMyView, CView)
    ON_WM_LBUTTONDOWN() // entry specifically for OnLButtonDown
    // other message map entries
END_MESSAGE_MAP()
```

Finally, your class header file needs the statement

```
DECLARE_MESSAGE_MAP()
```

How do you know which function goes with which Windows message? Appendix A (and the MFC library online documentation) includes a table that lists all standard Windows messages and corresponding member function prototypes. You can manually code the message-handling functions—indeed, that is still necessary for certain messages. Fortunately, Visual C++ provides a tool, ClassWizard, that automates the coding of most message map functions.

Saving the View's State—Class Data Members

If your program accepts user input, you'll want the user to have some visual feedback. The view's *OnDraw* function draws an image based on the view's current "state," and user actions can alter that state. In a full-blown MFC application, the document object holds the state of the application, but you're not to that point yet. For now, you'll use two view class data members, *m_rectEllipse* and *m_nColor*. The first is an object of class *CRect*, which holds the current bounding rectangle of an ellipse, and the second is an integer that holds the current ellipse color value.

> **NOTE:** By convention, MFC library nonstatic class data member names begin with *m_*.

You'll make a message-mapped member function toggle the ellipse color (the view's state) between gray and white. (The toggle is activated by pressing the left mouse button.) The initial values of *m_rectEllipse* and *m_nColor* are set in the view's constructor, and the color is changed in the *OnLButtonDown* member function.

> **TIP:** Why not use a global variable for the view's state? Because if you did, you'd be in trouble if your application had multiple views. Besides, encapsulating data in objects is a big part of what object-oriented programming is all about.

Initializing a View Class Data Member

The most efficient place to initialize a class data member is in the constructor, like this:

```
CMyView::CMyView() : m_rectEllipse(0, 0, 200, 200) {...}
```

You could initialize *m_nColor* with the same syntax. Because we're using a built-in type (integer), the generated code is the same if you use an assignment statement in the constructor body.

Invalid Rectangle Theory

The *OnLButtonDown* function could toggle the value of *m_nColor* all day, but if that's all it did, the *OnDraw* function wouldn't get called (unless, for example, the user resized the view window). The *OnLButtonDown* function must call the *InvalidateRect* function (a member function that the view class inherits from *CWnd*). *InvalidateRect* triggers a Windows WM_PAINT message, which is mapped in the *CView* class to call to the virtual *OnDraw* function. If necessary, *OnDraw* can access the "invalid rectangle" parameter that was passed to *InvalidateRect*.

There are two ways to optimize painting in Windows. First of all, you must be aware that Windows updates only those pixels that are inside the invalid rectangle. Thus, the smaller you make the invalid rectangle (in the *OnLButtonDown* handler, for instance), the quicker it can be repainted. Second, it's a waste of time to execute drawing instructions outside the invalid rectangle. Your

OnDraw function could call the *CDC* member function *GetClipBox* to determine the invalid rectangle, and then it could avoid drawing objects outside it. Remember that *OnDraw* is being called not only in response to your *InvalidateRect* call but also when the user resizes or exposes the window. Thus, *OnDraw* is responsible for all drawing in a window, and it has to adapt to whatever invalid rectangle it gets.

For Win32 Programmers

The MFC library makes it easy to attach your own state variables to a window through C++ class data members. In Win32 programming, the *WNDCLASS* members *cbClsExtra* and *cbWndExtra* are available for this purpose, but the code for using this mechanism is so complex that developers tend to use global variables instead.

The Window's Client Area

A window has a rectangular client area that excludes the border, caption bar, menu bar, and any docking toolbars. The *CWnd* member function *GetClientRect* supplies you with the client-area dimensions. Normally, you're not allowed to draw outside the client area, and most mouse messages are received only when the mouse cursor is in the client area.

CRect, *CPoint*, and *CSize* Arithmetic

The *CRect*, *CPoint*, and *CSize* classes are derived from the Windows *RECT*, *POINT*, and *SIZE* structures, and thus they inherit public integer data members as follows:

CRect	*left, top, right, bottom*
CPoint	*x, y*
CSize	*cx, cy*

If you look in the *Microsoft Foundation Class Reference,* you will see that these three classes have a number of overloaded operators. You can, among other things, do the following:

- Add a *CSize* object to a *CPoint* object
- Subtract a *CSize* object from a *CPoint* object
- Subtract one *CPoint* object from another, yielding a *CSize* object

■ Add a *CPoint* or *CSize* object to a *CRect* object

■ Subtract a *CPoint* or *CSize* object from a *CRect* object

The *CRect* class has member functions that relate to the *CSize* and *CPoint* classes. For example, the *TopLeft* member function returns a *CPoint* object, and the *Size* member function returns a *CSize* object. From this, you can begin to see that a *CSize* object is the "difference between two *CPoint* objects" and that you can "bias" a *CRect* object by a *CPoint* object.

Is a Point Inside a Rectangle?

The *CRect* class has a member function *PtInRect* that tests a point to see whether it falls inside a rectangle. The second *OnLButtonDown* parameter (*point*) is an object of class *CPoint* that represents the cursor location in the client area of the window. If you want to know whether that point is inside the *m_rectEllipse* rectangle, you can use *PtInRect* in this way:

```
if (m_rectEllipse.PtInRect(point)) {
    // point is inside rectangle
}
```

As you'll soon see, however, this simple logic applies only if you're working in device coordinates (which you are at this stage).

The *CRect LPCRECT* Operator

If you read the *Microsoft Foundation Class Reference* carefully, you will notice that *CWnd::InvalidateRect* takes an *LPCRECT* parameter (a pointer to a *RECT* structure), not a *CRect* parameter. A *CRect* parameter is allowed because the *CRect* class defines an overloaded operator, *LPCRECT()*, that returns the address of a *CRect* object, which is equivalent to the address of a *RECT* object. Thus, the compiler converts *CRect* arguments to *LPCRECT* arguments when necessary. You call functions as though they had *CRect* reference parameters. The view member function code

```
CRect rectClient;
GetClientRect(rectClient);
```

retrieves the client rectangle coordinates and stores them in *rectClient*.

Is a Point Inside an Ellipse?

The EX04A code determines whether the mouse hit is inside the rectangle. If you want to make a better test, you can find out whether the hit is inside the ellipse. To do this, you must construct an object of class *CRgn* that corresponds to the ellipse and then use the *PtInRegion* function instead of *PtInRect*. Here's the code:

```
CRgn rgn;
rgn.CreateEllipticRgnIndirect(m_rectEllipse);
if (rgn.PtInRegion(point)) {
    // point is inside ellipse
}
```

Note that the *CreateEllipticRgnIndirect* function is another function that takes an *LPCRECT* parameter. It builds a special region structure within Windows that represents an elliptical region inside a window. That structure is then attached to the C++ *CRgn* object in your program. (The same type of structure can also represent a polygon.)

The EX04A Example

In the EX04A example, an ellipse (which happens to be a circle) changes color when the user presses the left mouse button while the mouse cursor is inside the rectangle that bounds the ellipse. You'll use the view class data members to hold the view's state, and you'll use the *InvalidateRect* function to cause the view to be redrawn.

In the Chapter 3 example, drawing in the window depended on only one function, *OnDraw*. The EX04A example requires three customized functions (including the constructor) and two data members. The complete *CEx04aView* header and source code files are listed in Figure 4-1. (The steps for creating the program are shown after the program listings.) All changes to the original App-Wizard and OnLButtonDown ClassWizard output are in boldface.

EX04AVIEW.H

```
// ex04aView.h : interface of the CEx04aView class
//
/////////////////////////////////////////////////////////////////////

#if !defined(AFX_EX04AVIEW_H__B188BE41_6377_11D0_8FD4_00C04FC2A0C2__INCLUDED_)
#define AFX_EX04AVIEW_H__B188BE41_6377_11D0_8FD4_00C04FC2A0C2__INCLUDED_

#if _MFC_VER > 1000
#pragma once
#endif // _MFC_VER > 1000
class CEx04aView : public CView
```

Figure 4-1. *(continued)*

The CEx04aView *header and source code files.*

```
{
protected: // create from serialization only
    CEx04aView();
    DECLARE_DYNCREATE(CEx04aView)

// Attributes
public:
    CEx04aDoc* GetDocument();

// Operations
public:

// Overrides
    // ClassWizard generated virtual function overrides
    //{{AFX_VIRTUAL(CEx04aView)
    public:
    virtual void OnDraw(CDC* pDC);  // overridden to draw this view
    virtual BOOL PreCreateWindow(CREATESTRUCT& cs);
    protected:
    virtual BOOL OnPreparePrinting(CPrintInfo* pInfo);
    virtual void OnBeginPrinting(CDC* pDC, CPrintInfo* pInfo);
    virtual void OnEndPrinting(CDC* pDC, CPrintInfo* pInfo);
    //}}AFX_VIRTUAL

// Implementation
public:
    virtual ~CEx04aView();
#ifdef _DEBUG
    virtual void AssertValid() const;
    virtual void Dump(CDumpContext& dc) const;
#endif

protected:

// Generated message map functions
protected:
    //{{AFX_MSG(CEx04aView)
    afx_msg void OnLButtonDown(UINT nFlags, CPoint point);
    //}}AFX_MSG
    DECLARE_MESSAGE_MAP()
private:
    int m_nColor;
    CRect m_rectEllipse;
};
```

(continued)

Figure 4-1. *continued*

```
#ifndef _DEBUG  // debug version in ex04aView.cpp
inline CEx04aDoc* CEx04aView::GetDocument()
    { return (CEx04aDoc*)m_pDocument; }
#endif


/////////////////////////////////////////////////////////////////////////

//{{AFX_INSERT_LOCATION}}
// Microsoft Visual C++ will insert additional declarations
//   immediately before the previous line.

#endif // !defined(AFX_EX04AVIEW_H__B188BE41_6377_  →
                   11D0_8FD4_00C04FC2A0C2__INCLUDED_)
```

EX04AVIEW.CPP

```
// ex04aView.cpp : implementation of the CEx04aView class
//

#include "stdafx.h"
#include "ex04a.h"

#include "ex04aDoc.h"
#include "ex04aView.h"

#ifdef _DEBUG
#define new DEBUG_NEW
#undef THIS_FILE
static char THIS_FILE[] = __FILE__;
#endif


/////////////////////////////////////////////////////////////////////////
// CEx04aView

IMPLEMENT_DYNCREATE(CEx04aView, CView)

BEGIN_MESSAGE_MAP(CEx04aView, CView)
    //{{AFX_MSG_MAP(CEx04aView)
    ON_WM_LBUTTONDOWN()
    //}}AFX_MSG_MAP
    // Standard printing commands
    ON_COMMAND(ID_FILE_PRINT, CView::OnFilePrint)
    ON_COMMAND(ID_FILE_PRINT_DIRECT, CView::OnFilePrint)
    ON_COMMAND(ID_FILE_PRINT_PREVIEW, CView::OnFilePrintPreview)
END_MESSAGE_MAP()
```

```
/////////////////////////////////////////////////////////////////////
// CEx04aView construction/destruction

CEx04aView::CEx04aView() : m_rectEllipse(0, 0, 200, 200)
{
    m_nColor = GRAY_BRUSH;
}

CEx04aView::~CEx04aView()
{
}

BOOL CEx04aView::PreCreateWindow(CREATESTRUCT& cs)
{
    // TODO: Modify the Window class or styles here by modifying
    //   the CREATESTRUCT cs

    return CView::PreCreateWindow(cs);
}

/////////////////////////////////////////////////////////////////////
// CEx04aView drawing

void CEx04aView::OnDraw(CDC* pDC)
{
    pDC->SelectStockObject(m_nColor);
    pDC->Ellipse(m_rectEllipse);
}

/////////////////////////////////////////////////////////////////////
// CEx04aView printing

BOOL CEx04aView::OnPreparePrinting(CPrintInfo* pInfo)
{
    // default preparation
    return DoPreparePrinting(pInfo);
}

void CEx04aView::OnBeginPrinting(CDC* /*pDC*/, CPrintInfo* /*pInfo*/)
{
    // TODO: add extra initialization before printing
}

void CEx04aView::OnEndPrinting(CDC* /*pDC*/, CPrintInfo* /*pInfo*/)
{
```

(continued)

Figure 4-1. *continued*

```
    // TODO: add cleanup after printing
}


/////////////////////////////////////////////////////////////////////
// CEx04aView diagnostics

#ifdef _DEBUG
void CEx04aView::AssertValid() const
{
    CView::AssertValid();
}

void CEx04aView::Dump(CDumpContext& dc) const
{
    CView::Dump(dc);
}

CEx04aDoc* CEx04aView::GetDocument() // non-debug version is inline
{
    ASSERT(m_pDocument->IsKindOf(RUNTIME_CLASS(CEx04aDoc)));
    return (CEx04aDoc*)m_pDocument;
}
#endif //_DEBUG


/////////////////////////////////////////////////////////////////////
// CEx04aView message handlers

void CEx04aView::OnLButtonDown(UINT nFlags, CPoint point)
{
    if (m_rectEllipse.PtInRect(point)) {
        if (m_nColor == GRAY_BRUSH) {
            m_nColor = WHITE_BRUSH;
        }
        else {
            m_nColor = GRAY_BRUSH;
        }
        InvalidateRect(m_rectEllipse);
    }
}
```

Using ClassWizard with EX04A

Look at the following ex04aView.h source code:

```
//{{AFX_MSG(CEx04aView)
afx_msg void OnLButtonDown(UINT nFlags, CPoint point);
//}}AFX_MSG
```

Now look at the following ex04aView.cpp source code:

```
//{{AFX_MSG_MAP(CEx04aView)
ON_WM_LBUTTONDOWN()
//}}AFX_MSG_MAP
```

AppWizard generated the funny-looking comment lines for the benefit of ClassWizard. ClassWizard adds message handler prototypes between the *AFX_MSG* brackets and message map entries between the *AFX_MSG_MAP* brackets. In addition, ClassWizard generates a skeleton *OnLButtonDown* member function in ex04aView.cpp, complete with the correct parameter declarations and return type.

Notice how the AppWizard–ClassWizard combination is different from a conventional code generator. You run a conventional code generator only once and then edit the resulting code. You run AppWizard to generate the application only once, but you can run ClassWizard as many times as necessary, and you can edit the code at any time. You're safe as long as you don't alter what's inside the *AFX_MSG* and *AFX_MSG_MAP* brackets.

Using AppWizard and ClassWizard Together

The following steps show how you use AppWizard and ClassWizard together to create this application:

1. **Run AppWizard to create EX04A.** Use AppWizard to generate an SDI project named EX04A in the \vcpp32\ex04a subdirectory. The options and the default class names are shown here.

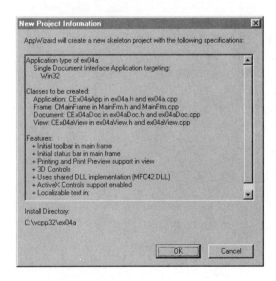

2. **Add the *m_rectEllipse* and *m_nColor* data members to *CEx04aView*.**
With the Workspace window set to ClassView, right-click the *CEx04aView* class, select Add Member Variable, and then insert the following two data members:

```
private:
    CRect m_rectEllipse;
    int m_nColor;
```

If you prefer, you could type the above code inside the class declaration in the file ex04aView.h.

3. **Use ClassWizard to add a *CEx04aView* class message handler.**
Choose ClassWizard from the View menu of Visual C++, or right-click inside a source code window and choose ClassWizard from the context menu. When the MFC ClassWizard dialog appears, be sure that the *CEx04aView* class is selected, as shown in the illustration below. Now click on *CEx04aView* at the top of the Object IDs list box, and then scroll down past the virtual functions in the Messages list box and double-click on WM_LBUTTONDOWN. The *OnLButtonDown* function name should appear in the Member Functions list box, and the message name should be displayed in bold in the Messages list box. Here's the ClassWizard dialog box.

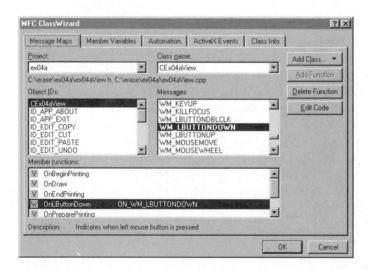

NOTE: Instead of using ClassWizard, you can map the function from the Visual C++ WizardBar (shown in Figure 1-2 in Chapter 1).

4. **Edit the *OnLButtonDown* code in ex04aView.cpp.** Click the Edit Code button. ClassWizard opens an edit window for ex04aView.cpp in Visual C++ and positions the cursor on the newly generated *OnLButton-Down* member function. The following boldface code (that you type in) replaces the previous code:

```
void CEx04aView::OnLButtonDown(UINT nFlags, CPoint point)
{
    if (m_rectEllipse.PtInRect(point)) {
        if (m_nColor == GRAY_BRUSH) {
            m_nColor = WHITE_BRUSH;
        }
        else {
            m_nColor = GRAY_BRUSH;
        }
        InvalidateRect(m_rectEllipse);
    }
}
```

5. **Edit the constructor and the *OnDraw* function in ex04aView.cpp.** The following boldface code (that you type in) replaces the previous code:

```
CEx04aView::CEx04aView() : m_rectEllipse(0, 0, 200, 200)
{
    m_nColor = GRAY_BRUSH;
}
    ⋮
void CEx04aView::OnDraw(CDC* pDC)
{
    pDC->SelectStockObject(m_nColor);
    pDC->Ellipse(m_rectEllipse);
}
```

6. **Build and run the EX04A program.** Choose Build Ex04a.exe from the Build menu, or, on the Build toolbar, click the button shown here.

Then choose Execute Ex04a.exe from the Build menu. The resulting program responds to presses of the left mouse button by changing the color of the circle in the view window. (Don't press the mouse's left button quickly in succession; Windows interprets this as a double click rather than two single clicks.)

For Win32 Programmers

A conventional Windows-based application registers a series of <u>window</u> <u>classes</u> (not the same as C++ classes) and, in the process, assigns a unique function, known as a <u>window</u> <u>procedure</u>, to each class. Each time the application calls *CreateWindow* to create a window, it specifies a window class as a parameter and thus links the newly created window to a window procedure function. This function, called each time Windows sends a message to the window, tests the message code that is passed as a parameter and then executes the appropriate code to handle the message.

The MFC application framework has a single window class and window procedure function for most window types. This window procedure function looks up the window handle (passed as a parameter) in the MFC <u>handle</u> <u>map</u> to get the corresponding C++ window object pointer. The window procedure function then uses the MFC <u>runtime</u> <u>class</u> system (see Appendix B) to determine the C++ class of the window object. Next it locates the handler function in static tables created by the dispatch map functions, and finally it calls the handler function with the correct window object selected.

Mapping Modes

Up to now, your drawing units have been display pixels, also known as <u>device</u> <u>coordinates</u>. The EX04A drawing units are pixels because the device context has the default <u>mapping</u> <u>mode</u>, *MM_TEXT*, assigned to it. The statement

```
pDC->Rectangle(CRect(0, 0, 200, 200));
```

draws a square of 200-by-200 pixels, with its top-left corner at the top left of the window's client area. (Positive *y* values increase as you move down the window.) This square would look smaller on a high-resolution display of 1024-by-768 pixels than it would look on a standard VGA display that is 640-by-480 pixels, and it would look tiny if printed on a laser printer with 600-dpi resolution. (Try EX04A's Print Preview feature to see for yourself.)

What if you want the square to be 4-by-4 centimeters (cm), regardless of the display device? Windows provides a number of other mapping modes, or coordinate systems, that can be associated with the device context. Coordinates in the current mapping mode are called <u>logical</u> <u>coordinates</u>. If you assign the *MM_HIMETRIC* mapping mode, for example, a logical unit is $1/100$ millimeter (mm) instead of 1 pixel. In the *MM_HIMETRIC* mapping mode, the *y* axis runs in the opposite direction to that in the *MM_TEXT* mode: *y* values decrease as you move down. Thus, a 4-by-4-cm square is drawn in logical coordinates this way:

```
pDC->Rectangle(CRect(0, 0, 4000, -4000));
```

Looks easy, doesn't it? Well, it isn't, because you can't work only in logical coordinates. Your program is always switching between device coordinates and logical coordinates, and you need to know when to convert between them. This section gives you a few rules that could make your programming life easier. First you need to know what mapping modes Windows gives you.

The *MM_TEXT* Mapping Mode

At first glance, *MM_TEXT* appears to be no mapping mode at all, but rather another name for device coordinates. Almost. In *MM_TEXT*, coordinates map to pixels, values of *x* increase as you move right, and values of *y* increase as you move down, but you're allowed to change the origin through calls to the *CDC* functions *SetViewportOrg* and *SetWindowOrg*. Here's some code that sets the window origin to (100, 100) in logical coordinate space and then draws a 200-by-200-pixel square offset by (100, 100). (An illustration of the output is shown in Figure 4-2.) The logical point (100, 100) maps to the device point (0, 0). A scrolling window uses this kind of transformation.

```
void CMyView::OnDraw(CDC* pDC)
{
    pDC->SetMapMode(MM_TEXT);
    pDC->SetWindowOrg(CPoint(100, 100));
    pDC->Rectangle(CRect(100, 100, 300, 300));
}
```

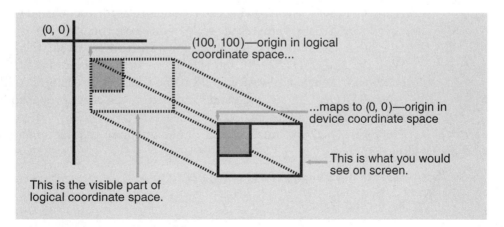

Figure 4-2.
A square drawn after the origin has been moved to (100, 100).

61

The Fixed-Scale Mapping Modes

One important group of Windows mapping modes provides fixed scaling. You have already seen that, in the *MM_HIMETRIC* mapping mode, *x* values increase as you move right and *y* values decrease as you move down. All fixed mapping modes follow this convention, and you can't change it. The only difference among the fixed mapping modes is the actual scale factor, listed in the table shown here.

Mapping Mode	Logical Unit
MM_LOENGLISH	0.01 inch
MM_HIENGLISH	0.001 inch
MM_LOMETRIC	0.1 mm
MM_HIMETRIC	0.01 mm
MM_TWIPS	$1/_{1440}$ inch

The last mapping mode, *MM_TWIPS*, is most often used with printers. One <u>twip</u> unit is $1/_{20}$ point. (A <u>point</u> is a type measurement unit. In Windows it equals exactly $1/_{72}$ inch.) If the mapping mode is *MM_TWIPS* and you want, for example, 12-point type, set the character height to 12 × 20, or 240, twips.

The Variable-Scale Mapping Modes

Windows provides two mapping modes, *MM_ISOTROPIC* and *MM_ANISO-TROPIC*, that allow you to change the scale factor as well as the origin. With these mapping modes, your drawing can change size as the user changes the size of the window. Also, if you invert the scale of one axis, you can "flip" an image about the other axis and you can define your own arbitrary fixed-scale factors.

With the *MM_ISOTROPIC* mode, a 1:1 aspect ratio is always preserved. In other words, a circle is always a circle as the scale factor changes. With the *MM_ANISOTROPIC* mode, the *x* and *y* scale factors can change independently. Circles can be squished into ellipses.

Here's an *OnDraw* function that draws an ellipse that fits exactly in its window:

```
void CMyView::OnDraw(CDC* pDC)
{
    CRect rectClient;
```

```
GetClientRect(rectClient);
pDC->SetMapMode(MM_ANISOTROPIC);
pDC->SetWindowExt(1000, 1000);
pDC->SetViewportExt(rectClient.right, -rectClient.bottom);
pDC->SetViewportOrg(rectClient.right / 2, rectClient.bottom / 2);

    pDC->Ellipse(CRect(-500, -500, 500, 500));
}
```

What's going on here? The functions *SetWindowExt* and *SetViewportExt* work together to set the scale, based on the window's current client rectangle returned by the *GetClientRect* function. The resulting window size is exactly 1000-by-1000 logical units. The *SetViewportOrg* function sets the origin to the center of the window. Thus, a centered ellipse with a radius of 500 logical units fills the window exactly, as illustrated in Figure 4-3.

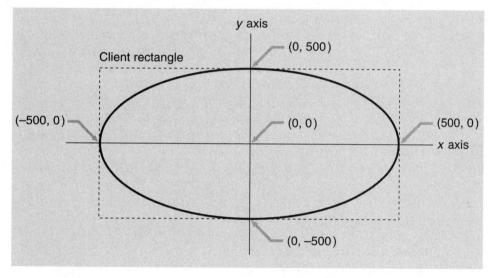

Figure 4-3.
A centered ellipse drawn in the MM_ANISOTROPIC *mapping mode.*

Here are the formulas for converting logical units to device units:

x scale factor = x viewport extent / x window extent
y scale factor = y viewport extent / y window extent
device x = logical $x \times x$ scale factor + x origin offset
device y = logical $y \times y$ scale factor + y origin offset

Suppose the window is 448 pixels wide (*rectClient.right*). The right edge of the ellipse's client rectangle is 500 logical units from the origin. The *x* scale factor is $^{448}/_{1000}$, and the *x* origin offset is $^{448}/_2$ device units. If you use the formulas shown on the previous page, the right edge of the ellipse's client rectangle comes out to 448 device units, the right edge of the window. The *x* scale factor is expressed as a ratio (viewport extent/window extent) because Windows device coordinates are integers, not floating-point values. The extent values are meaningless by themselves.

If you substitute *MM_ISOTROPIC* for *MM_ANISOTROPIC* in the preceding example, the "ellipse" is always a circle, as shown in Figure 4-4. It expands to fit the smallest dimension of the window rectangle.

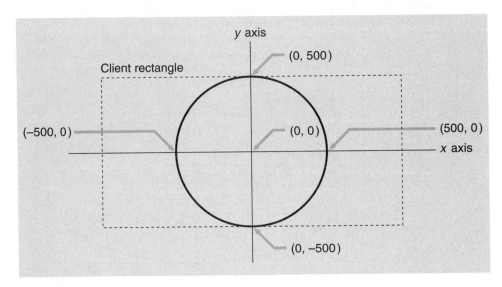

Figure 4-4.
A centered ellipse drawn in the MM_ISOTROPIC *mapping mode.*

Coordinate Conversion

Once you set the mapping mode (plus the origin) of a device context, you can use logical coordinate parameters for most *CDC* member functions. If you get the mouse cursor coordinates from a Windows mouse message (the *point* parameter in *OnLButtonDown*), for example, you're dealing with device coordinates. Many other MFC functions, particularly the member functions of class *CRect*, work correctly only with device coordinates.

NOTE: The *CRect* arithmetic functions use the underlying Win32 *RECT* arithmetic functions, which assume that *right* is greater than *left* and *bottom* is greater than *top*. A rectangle (0, 0, 1000, –1000) in *MM_HIMETRIC* coordinates, for example, has *bottom* less than *top* and cannot be processed by functions such as *CRect::PtInRect* unless your program first calls *CRect::NormalizeRect*, which changes the rectangle's data members to (0, –1000, 1000, 0).

Furthermore, you're likely to need a third set of coordinates that we will call physical coordinates. Why do you need another set? Suppose you're using the *MM_LOENGLISH* mapping mode in which a logical unit is 0.01 inch, but an inch on the screen represents a foot (12 inches) in the real world. Now suppose the user works in inches and decimal fractions. A measurement of 26.75 inches translates to 223 logical units, which must be ultimately translated to device coordinates. You will want to store the physical coordinates as either floating-point numbers or scaled long integers to avoid rounding-off errors.

For the physical-to-logical translation you're on your own, but the Windows GDI takes care of the logical-to-device translation for you. The *CDC* functions *LPtoDP* and *DPtoLP* translate between the two systems, assuming the device context mapping mode and associated parameters have already been set. Your job is to decide when to use each system. Here are a few rules of thumb:

■ Assume that the *CDC* member functions take logical coordinate parameters.

■ Assume that the *CWnd* member functions take device coordinate parameters.

■ Do all hit-test operations in device coordinates. Define regions in device coordinates. Functions such as *CRect::PtInRect* work best with device coordinates.

■ Store long-term values in logical or physical coordinates. If you store a point in device coordinates and the user scrolls through a window, that point is no longer valid.

Suppose you need to know whether the mouse cursor is inside a rectangle when the user presses the left mouse button. The code is on the following page.

```
// m_rect is CRect data member of the derived view class with MM_LOENGLISH
// logical coordinates

void CMyView::OnLButtonDown(UINT nFlags, CPoint point)
{
    CRect rect = m_rect; // rect is a temporary copy of m_rect.
    CClientDC dc(this);  // This is how we get a device context
                         //   for SetMapMode and LPtoDP
                         //   -- more in next chapter
    dc.SetMapMode(MM_LOENGLISH);
    dc.LPtoDP(rect);        // rect is now in device coordinates
    if (rect.PtInRect(point)) {
        TRACE("Mouse cursor is inside the rectangle.\n");
    }
}
```

Notice the use of the *TRACE* macro (covered in Chapter 3).

NOTE: As you'll soon see, it's better to set the mapping mode in the virtual *CView* function *OnPrepareDC* instead of in the *OnDraw* function.

The EX04B Example—
Converting to the *MM_HIMETRIC* Mapping Mode

EX04B is EX04A converted to *MM_HIMETRIC* coordinates. The EX04B project on the companion CD-ROM uses new class names and filenames, but the instructions here take you through modifying the EX04A code. Like EX04A, EX04B performs a hit-test so that the ellipse changes color only when you click inside the bounding rectangle.

1. Use ClassWizard to override the virtual *OnPrepareDC* function.
ClassWizard can override virtual functions for selected MFC base classes, including *CView*. It generates the correct function prototype in the class's header file and a skeleton function in the CPP file. Select the class name *CEx04aView* in the Object IDs list, and then double-click on the *OnPrepareDC* function in the Messages list. Edit the function as shown here:

```
void CEx04aView::OnPrepareDC(CDC* pDC, CPrintInfo* pInfo)
{
    pDC->SetMapMode(MM_HIMETRIC);
    CView::OnPrepareDC(pDC, pInfo);
}
```

The application framework calls the virtual *OnPrepareDC* function just before it calls *OnDraw*.

2. Edit the view class constructor. You must change the coordinate values for the ellipse rectangle. That rectangle is now 4-by-4 centimeters instead of 200-by-200 pixels. Note that the *y* value must be negative; otherwise, the ellipse will be drawn on the "virtual screen" right above your monitor! Change the values as shown here:

```
CEx04aView::CEx04aView() : m_rectEllipse(0, 0, 4000, -4000)
{
    m_nColor = GRAY_BRUSH;
}
```

3. Edit the *OnLButtonDown* function. This function must now convert the ellipse rectangle to device coordinates in order to do the hit-test. Change the function as shown in the following code:

```
void CEx04aView::OnLButtonDown(UINT nFlags, CPoint point)
{
    CClientDC dc(this);
    OnPrepareDC(&dc);
    CRect rectDevice = m_rectEllipse;
    dc.LPtoDP(rectDevice);
    if (rectDevice.PtInRect(point)) {
        if (m_nColor == GRAY_BRUSH) {
            m_nColor = WHITE_BRUSH;
        }
        else {
            m_nColor = GRAY_BRUSH;
        }
        InvalidateRect(rectDevice);
    }
}
```

4. Build and run the EX04B program. The output should look similar to the output from EX04A, except that the ellipse size will be different. If you try using Print Preview again, the ellipse should appear much larger than it did in EX04A.

A Scrolling View Window

As the lack of scroll bars in EX04A and EX04B indicates, the MFC *CView* class, the base class of *CEx04bView*, doesn't directly support scrolling. Another MFC library class, *CScrollView*, does support scrolling. *CScrollView* is derived from *CView*. We'll create a new program, EX04C, that uses *CScrollView* in place of *CView*. All the coordinate conversion code you added in EX04B sets you up for scrolling.

The *CScrollView* class supports scrolling from the scroll bars but not from the keyboard. It's easy enough to add keyboard scrolling, so we'll do it.

A Window Is Larger than What You See

If you use the mouse to shrink the size of an ordinary window, the contents of the window remain anchored at the top left of the window, and items at the bottom and/or on the right of the window disappear. When you expand the window, the items reappear. You can correctly conclude that a window is larger than the <u>viewport</u> that you see on the screen. The viewport doesn't have to be anchored at the top left of the window area, however. Through the use of the *CWnd* functions *ScrollWindow* and *SetWindowOrg*, the *CScrollView* class allows you to move the viewport anywhere within the window, including areas above and to the left of the origin.

Scroll Bars

Microsoft Windows makes it easy to display scroll bars at the edges of a window, but Windows by itself doesn't make any attempt to connect those scroll bars to their window. That's where the *CScrollView* class fits in. *CScrollView* member functions process the WM_HSCROLL and WM_VSCROLL messages sent by the scroll bars to the view. Those functions move the viewport within the window and do all the necessary housekeeping.

Scrolling Alternatives

The *CScrollView* class supports a particular kind of scrolling that involves one big window and a small viewport. Each item is assigned a unique position in this big window. If, for example, you have 10,000 address lines to display, instead of having a window 10,000 lines long, you probably want a smaller window with scrolling logic that selects only as many lines as the screen can display. In that case, you should write your own scrolling view class derived from *CView*.

> NOTE: Microsoft Windows NT uses 32-bit numbers for logical coordinates, so your logical coordinate space is almost unlimited. Microsoft Windows 95, however, still has some 16-bit components, so it uses 16-bit numbers for logical coordinates, limiting values to the range −32,768 to 32,767. Scroll bars send messages with 16-bit values in both operating systems. With these facts in mind, you probably want to write code to the lowest common denominator, which is Windows 95.

The *OnInitialUpdate* Function

You'll be seeing more of the *OnInitialUpdate* function when you study the document–view architecture, starting in Chapter 16. The virtual *OnInitial-Update* function is important here because it is the first function called by the framework after your view window is fully created. The framework calls *On-InitialUpdate* before it calls *OnDraw* for the first time, so *OnInitialUpdate* is the natural place for setting the logical size and mapping mode for a scrolling view. You set these parameters with a call to the *CScrollView::SetScrollSizes* function.

Accepting Keyboard Input

Keyboard input is really a two-step process. Windows sends WM_KEYDOWN and WM_KEYUP messages, with <u>virtual key codes</u>, to a window, but before they get to the window they are translated. If an ANSI character is typed (resulting in a WM_KEYDOWN message), the translation function checks the keyboard shift status and then sends a WM_CHAR message with the proper code, either uppercase or lowercase. Cursor keys and function keys don't have codes, so there's no translation to do. The window gets only the WM_KEYDOWN and WM_KEYUP messages.

You can use ClassWizard to map all these messages to your view. If you're expecting characters, map WM_CHAR; if you're expecting other keystrokes, map WM_KEYDOWN. The MFC library neatly supplies the character code or virtual key code as a handler function parameter.

The EX04C Example—Scrolling

The goal of EX04C is to make a logical window 20 centimeters wide by 30 centimeters high. The program draws the same ellipse that it drew in the EX04B project. You could edit the EX04B source files to convert the *CView* base class to a *CScrollView* base class, but it's easier to start over with AppWizard. AppWizard generates the *OnInitialUpdate* override function for you. Here are the steps:

1. **Run AppWizard to create EX04C.** Use AppWizard to generate a program named EX04C in the \vcpp32\ex04c subdirectory. In AppWizard Step 6, set the *CEx04cView* base class to *CScrollView*, as shown on the following page.

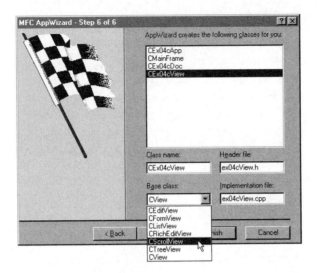

2. **Add the *m_rectEllipse* and *m_nColor* data members in ex04c-View.h.** Insert the following code by right-clicking the *CEx04cView* class in the Workspace window or by typing inside the *CEx04cView* class declaration:

```
private:
    CRect m_rectEllipse;
    int m_nColor;
```

These are the same data members that were added in the EX04A and EX04B projects.

3. **Modify the AppWizard-generated *OnInitialUpdate* function.** Edit *OnInitialUpdate* in ex04cView.cpp as shown here:

```
void CEx04cView::OnInitialUpdate()
{
    CScrollView::OnInitialUpdate();
    CSize sizeTotal(20000, 30000); // 20 by 30 cm
    CSize sizePage(sizeTotal.cx / 2, sizeTotal.cy / 2);
    CSize sizeLine(sizeTotal.cx / 50, sizeTotal.cy / 50);
    SetScrollSizes(MM_HIMETRIC, sizeTotal, sizePage, sizeLine);
}
```

4. **Use ClassWizard to add a message handler for the WM_KEYDOWN message.** ClassWizard generates the member function *OnKeyDown* along with the necessary message map entries and prototypes. Edit the code as follows:

```
void CEx04cView::OnKeyDown(UINT nChar, UINT nRepCnt, UINT nFlags)
{
    switch (nChar) {
    case VK_HOME:
        OnVScroll(SB_TOP, 0, NULL);
        OnHScroll(SB_LEFT, 0, NULL);
        break;
    case VK_END:
        OnVScroll(SB_BOTTOM, 0, NULL);
        OnHScroll(SB_RIGHT, 0, NULL);
        break;
    case VK_UP:
        OnVScroll(SB_LINEUP, 0, NULL);
        break;
    case VK_DOWN:
        OnVScroll(SB_LINEDOWN, 0, NULL);
        break;
    case VK_PRIOR:
        OnVScroll(SB_PAGEUP, 0, NULL);
        break;
    case VK_NEXT:
        OnVScroll(SB_PAGEDOWN, 0, NULL);
        break;
    case VK_LEFT:
        OnHScroll(SB_LINELEFT, 0, NULL);
        break;
    case VK_RIGHT:
        OnHScroll(SB_LINERIGHT, 0, NULL);
        break;
    default:
        break;
    }
}
```

5. **Edit the constructor and the *OnDraw* function.** Change the AppWizard-generated constructor and the *OnDraw* function in ex04cView.cpp as follows:

```
CEx04cView::CEx04cView() : m_rectEllipse(0, 0, 4000, -4000)
{
    m_nColor = GRAY_BRUSH;
}
⋮
void CEx04cView::OnDraw(CDC* pDC)
{
    pDC->SelectStockObject(m_nColor);
    pDC->Ellipse(m_rectEllipse);
}
```

These functions are identical to those used in the EX04A and EX04B projects.

6. **Map the WM_LBUTTONDOWN message and edit the handler.** Make the following changes to the ClassWizard-generated code:

```
void CEx04cView::OnLButtonDown(UINT nFlags, CPoint point)
{
    CClientDC dc(this);
    OnPrepareDC(&dc);
    CRect rectDevice = m_rectEllipse;
    dc.LPtoDP(rectDevice);
    if (rectDevice.PtInRect(point)) {
        if (m_nColor == GRAY_BRUSH) {
            m_nColor = WHITE_BRUSH;
        }
        else {
            m_nColor = GRAY_BRUSH;
        }
        InvalidateRect(rectDevice);
    }
}
```

This function is identical to the *OnLButtonDown* handler in the EX04B project. It calls *OnPrepareDC* as before, but there is something different. The *CEx04bView* class doesn't have an overridden *OnPrepareDC* function, so the call goes to *CScrollView::OnPrepareDC*. That function sets the mapping mode based on the first parameter to *SetScrollSizes*, and it sets the window origin based on the current scroll position. Even if your scroll view used the *MM_TEXT* mapping mode, you'd still need the coordinate conversion logic to adjust for the origin offset.

7. **Build and run the EX04C program.** Check to be sure the mouse hit logic is working even if the circle is scrolled partially out of the window. Also check the keyboard logic. The output should look like this.

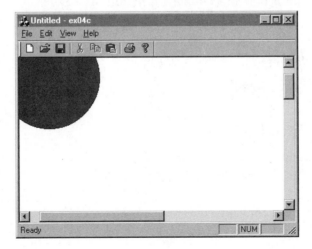

Other Windows Messages

The MFC library directly supports hundreds of Windows message-handling functions. In addition, you can define your own messages. You will see plenty of message-handling examples in later chapters, including handlers for menu items, child window controls, and so forth. In the meantime, five special Windows messages deserve special attention: WM_CREATE, WM_CLOSE, WM__QUERYENDSESSION, WM_DESTROY, and WM_NCDESTROY.

The WM_CREATE Message

This is the first message that Windows sends to a view. It is sent when the window's *Create* function is called by the framework, so the window creation is not finished and the window is not visible. Therefore, your *OnCreate* handler cannot call Windows functions that depend on the window being completely alive. You can call such functions in an overridden *OnInitialUpdate* function, but you must be aware that in an SDI application *OnInitialUpdate* can be called more than once in a view's lifetime.

The WM_CLOSE Message

Windows sends the WM_CLOSE message when the user closes a window from the system menu and when a parent window is closed. If you implement the *OnClose* message map function in your derived view class, you can control the closing process. If, for example, you need to prompt the user to save changes to a file, you do it in *OnClose*. Only when you have determined that it is safe to close the window do you call the base class *OnClose* function, which continues the close process. The view object and the corresponding window are both still active.

> TIP: When you're using the full application framework, you probably won't use the WM_CLOSE message handler. You can override the *CDocument::SaveModified* virtual function instead, as part of the application framework's highly structured program exit procedure.

The WM_QUERYENDSESSION Message

Windows sends the WM_QUERYENDSESSION message to all running applications when the user exits Windows. The *OnQueryEndSession* message map function handles it. If you write a handler for WM_CLOSE, write one for WM_QUERYENDSESSION too.

The WM_DESTROY Message

Windows sends this message after the WM_CLOSE message, and the *OnDestroy* message map function handles it. When your program receives this message, it should assume that the view window is no longer visible on the screen but that it is still active and its child windows are still active. Use this message handler to do cleanup that depends on the existence of the underlying window. Be sure to call the base class *OnDestroy* function. You cannot "abort" the window destruction process in your view's *OnDestroy* function. *OnClose* is the place to do that.

The WM_NCDESTROY Message

This is the last message that Windows sends when the window is being destroyed. All child windows have already been destroyed. You can do final processing in *OnNcDestroy* that doesn't depend on a window being active. Be sure to call the base class *OnNcDestroy* function.

> TIP: Do not try to destroy a dynamically allocated window object in *OnNcDestroy*. That job is reserved for a special *CWnd* virtual function, *PostNcDestroy*, that the base class *OnNcDestroy* calls. MFC Technical Note #17 in the online documentation gives hints on when it's appropriate to destroy a window object.

CHAPTER FIVE

The Graphics Device Interface, Colors, and Fonts

You've already seen some elements of the Graphics Device Interface (GDI). Anytime your program draws to the display or the printer, it must use the GDI functions. The GDI provides functions for drawing points, lines, rectangles, polygons, ellipses, bitmaps, and text. You can draw circles and squares intuitively once you study the available functions, but text programming is more difficult. This chapter gives you the information you need to start using the GDI effectively in the Microsoft Visual C++ environment. You'll learn how to use fonts on both the display and the printer. You must wait until Chapter 19, however, for details on how the framework controls the printer.

The Device Context Classes

In Chapters 3 and 4, the view class's *OnDraw* member function was passed a pointer to a device context object. *OnDraw* selected a brush and then drew an ellipse. The Microsoft Windows <u>device</u> <u>context</u> is the key GDI element that represents a physical device. Each C++ device context object has an associated Windows device context, identified by a 32-bit handle of type HDC.

Microsoft Foundation Class (MFC) Library version 6.0 provides a number of device context classes. The base class *CDC* has all the member functions (including some virtual functions) that you'll need for drawing. Except for the oddball *CMetaFileDC* class, derived classes are distinct only in their constructors and destructors. If you (or the application framework) construct an object of a derived device context class, you can pass a *CDC* pointer to a function such as *OnDraw*. For the display, the usual derived classes are *CClientDC* and *CWindowDC*. For other devices, such as printers or memory buffers, you construct objects of the base class *CDC*.

The "virtualness" of the *CDC* class is an important feature of the application framework. In Chapter 19, you'll see how easy it is to write code that works with both the printer and the display. A statement in *OnDraw* such as

```
pDC->TextOut(0, 0, "Hello");
```

sends text to the display, the printer, or the Print Preview window, depending on the class of the object referenced by the *CView::OnDraw* function's *pDC* parameter.

For display and printer device context objects, the application framework attaches the handle to the object. For other device contexts, such as the memory device context that you'll see in Chapter 11, you must call a member function after construction in order to attach the handle.

The Display Context Classes *CClientDC* and *CWindowDC*

Recall that a window's client area excludes the border, the caption bar, and the menu bar. If you create a *CClientDC* object, you have a device context that is mapped only to this client area—you can't draw outside it. The point (0, 0) usually refers to the upper-left corner of the client area. As you'll see later, an MFC *CView* object corresponds to a child window that is contained inside a separate frame window, often along with a toolbar, a status bar, and scroll bars. The client area of the view, then, does not include these other windows. If the window contains a docked toolbar along the top, for example, (0, 0) refers to the point immediately under the left edge of the toolbar.

If you construct an object of class *CWindowDC*, the point (0, 0) is at the upper-left corner of the nonclient area of the window. With this whole-window device context, you can draw in the window's border, in the caption area, and so forth. Don't forget that the view window doesn't have a nonclient area, so *CWindowDC* is more applicable to frame windows than it is to view windows.

Constructing and Destroying *CDC* Objects

After you construct a *CDC* object, it is important to destroy it promptly when you're done with it. Microsoft Windows limits the number of available device contexts, and if you fail to release a Windows device context object, a small amount of memory is lost until your program exits. Most frequently, you'll construct a device context object inside a message handler function such as *OnLButtonDown*. The easiest way to ensure that the device context object is destroyed (and that the underlying Windows device context is released) is to construct the object on the stack in the following way:

```
void CMyView::OnLButtonDown(UINT nFlags, CPoint point)
{
    CRect rect;

    CClientDC dc(this);  // constructs dc on the stack
    dc.GetClipBox(rect); // retrieves the clipping rectangle
} // dc automatically released
```

Notice that the *CClientDC* constructor takes a window pointer as a parameter. The destructor for the *CClientDC* object is called when the function returns. You can also get a device context pointer by using the *CWnd::GetDC* member function, as shown in the following code. You must be careful here to call the *ReleaseDC* function to release the device context.

```
void CMyView::OnLButtonDown(UINT nFlags, CPoint point)
{
    CRect rect;

    CDC* pDC = GetDC();     // a pointer to an internal dc
    pDC->GetClipBox(rect); // retrieves the clipping rectangle
    ReleaseDC(pDC);         // Don't forget this
}
```

> **WARNING:** You must not destroy the *CDC* object passed by the pointer to *OnDraw*. The application framework handles the destruction for you.

The State of the Device Context

You already know that a device context is required for drawing. When you use a *CDC* object to draw an ellipse, for example, what you see on the screen (or on the printer's hard copy) depends on the current "state" of the device context. This state includes the following:

- Attached GDI drawing objects such as pens, brushes, and fonts
- The mapping mode that determines the scale of items when they are drawn (You've already experimented with the mapping mode in Chapter 4.)
- Various details such as text alignment parameters and polygon filling mode

You have already seen, for example, that choosing a gray brush prior to drawing an ellipse results in the ellipse having a gray interior. When you create a device context object, it has certain default characteristics, such as a black pen for shape boundaries. All other state characteristics are assigned through *CDC* class member functions. GDI objects are selected into the device context by means of the overloaded *SelectObject* functions. A device context can, for example, have one pen, one brush, or one font selected at any given time.

The *CPaintDC* Class

You'll need the *CPaintDC* class only if you override your view's *OnPaint* function. The default *OnPaint* calls *OnDraw* with a properly set up device context, but sometimes you'll need display-specific drawing code. The *CPaintDC* class is special because its constructor and destructor do housekeeping unique to drawing to the display. Once you have a *CDC* pointer, however, you can use it as you would any other device context pointer.

Here's a sample *OnPaint* function that creates a *CPaintDC* object:

```
void CMyView::OnPaint()
{
    CPaintDC dc(this);
    OnPrepareDC(&dc); // explained later
    dc.TextOut(0, 0, "for the display, not the printer");
    OnDraw(&dc);      // stuff that's common to display and printer
}
```

> ### For Win32 Programmers
>
> The *CPaintDC* constructor calls *BeginPaint* for you, and the destructor calls *EndPaint*. If you construct your device context on the stack, the *EndPaint* call is completely automatic.

GDI Objects

A Windows GDI object type is represented by an MFC library class. *CGdiObject* is the abstract base class for the GDI object classes. A Windows GDI object is represented by a C++ object of a class derived from *CGdiObject*. Here's a list of the GDI derived classes:

- *CBitmap*—A bitmap is an array of bits in which one or more bits correspond to each display pixel. You can use bitmaps to represent images, and you can use them to create brushes.

- *CBrush*—A brush defines a bitmapped pattern of pixels that is used to fill areas with color.

- ■ *CFont*—A font is a complete collection of characters of a particular typeface and a particular size. Fonts are generally stored on disk as resources, and some are device-specific.

- ■ *CPalette*—A palette is a color mapping interface that allows an application to take full advantage of the color capability of an output device without interfering with other applications.

- ■ *CPen*—A pen is a tool for drawing lines and shape borders. You can specify a pen's color and thickness and whether it draws solid, dotted, or dashed lines.

- ■ *CRgn*—A region is an area whose shape is a polygon, an ellipse, or a combination of polygons and ellipses. You can use regions for filling, clipping, and mouse hit-testing.

Constructing and Destroying GDI Objects

You never construct an object of class *CGdiObject*; instead, you construct objects of the derived classes. Constructors for some GDI derived classes, such as *CPen* and *CBrush*, allow you to specify enough information to create the object in one step. Others, such as *CFont* and *CRgn*, require a second creation step. For these classes, you construct the C++ object with the default constructor and then you call a create function such as the *CreateFont* or *CreatePolygonRgn* function.

The *CGdiObject* class has a virtual destructor. The derived class destructors delete the Windows GDI objects that are attached to the C++ objects. If you construct an object of a class derived from *CGdiObject*, you must delete it prior to exiting the program. To delete a GDI object, you must first separate it from the device context. You'll see an example of this in the next section.

NOTE: Failure to delete a GDI object was a serious offense with Win16. GDI memory was not released until the user restarted Windows. With Win32, however, the GDI memory is owned by the process and is released when your program terminates. Still, an unreleased GDI bitmap object can waste a significant amount of memory.

Tracking GDI Objects

OK, so you know that you have to delete your GDI objects and that they must first be disconnected from their device contexts. How do you disconnect them? A member of the *CDC::SelectObject* family of functions does the work of selecting a GDI object into the device context, and in the process it returns a pointer to the previously selected object (which gets deselected in the process).

Trouble is, you can't deselect the old object without selecting a new object. One easy way to track the objects is to "save" the original GDI object when you select your own GDI object and "restore" the original object when you're finished. Then you'll be ready to delete your own GDI object. Here's an example:

```
void CMyView::OnDraw(CDC* pDC)
{
    CPen newPen(PS_DASHDOTDOT, 2, (COLORREF) 0);   // black pen,
                                                   //  2 pixels wide
    CPen* pOldPen = pDC->SelectObject(&newPen);

    pDC->MoveTo(10, 10);
    pDC->Lineto(110, 10);
    pDC->SelectObject(pOldPen);                    // newPen is deselected
} // newPen automatically destroyed on exit
```

When a device context object is destroyed, all its GDI objects are deselected. Thus, if you know that a device context will be destroyed before its selected GDI objects are destroyed, you don't have to deselect the objects. If, for example, you declare a pen as a view class data member (and you initialize it when you initialize the view), you don't have to deselect the pen inside *OnDraw* because the device context, controlled by the view base class's *OnPaint* handler, will be destroyed first.

Stock GDI Objects

Windows contains a number of stock GDI objects that you can use. Because these objects are part of Windows, you don't have to worry about deleting them. (Windows ignores requests to delete stock objects.) The MFC library function *CDC::SelectStockObject* selects a stock object into the device context and returns a pointer to the previously selected object, which it deselects. Stock objects are handy when you want to deselect your own nonstock GDI object prior to its destruction. You can use a stock object as an alternative to the "old" object you used in the previous example, as shown here:

```
void CMyView::OnDraw(CDC* pDC)
{
    CPen newPen(PS_DASHDOTDOT, 2, (COLORREF) 0);   // black pen,
                                                   //  2 pixels wide

    pDC->SelectObject(&newPen);
    pDC->MoveTo(10, 10);
    pDC->Lineto(110, 10);
    pDC->SelectStockObject(BLACK_PEN);             // newPen is deselected
} // newPen destroyed on exit
```

The Microsoft Foundation Class Reference lists, under *CDC::SelectStock-Object*, the stock objects available for pens, brushes, fonts, and palettes.

The Lifetime of a GDI Selection

For the <u>display</u> device context, you get a "fresh" device context at the beginning of each message handler function. No GDI selections (or mapping modes or other device context settings) persist after your function exits. You must, therefore, set up your device context from scratch each time. The *CView* class virtual member function *OnPrepareDC* is useful for setting the mapping mode, but you must manage your own GDI objects.

For other device contexts, such as those for printers and memory buffers, your assignments can last longer. For these long-life device contexts, things get a little more complicated. The complexity results from the temporary nature of GDI C++ object pointers returned by the *SelectObject* function. (The temporary "object" will be destroyed by the application framework during the idle loop processing of the application, sometime after the handler function returns the call. See MFC Technical Note #3 in the online documentation.) You can't simply store the pointer in a class data member; instead, you must convert it to a Windows handle (the only permanent GDI identifier) with the *GetSafeHdc* member function. Here's an example:

```
// m_pPrintFont points to a CFont object created in CMyView's constructor
// m_hOldFont is a CMyView data member of type HFONT, initialized to 0

void CMyView::SwitchToCourier(CDC* pDC)
{
    m_pPrintFont->CreateFont(30, 10, 0, 0, 400, FALSE, FALSE,
                            0, ANSI_CHARSET, OUT_DEFAULT_PRECIS,
                            CLIP_DEFAULT_PRECIS, DEFAULT_QUALITY,
                            DEFAULT_PITCH | FF_MODERN,
                            "Courier New"); // TrueType
    CFont* pOldFont = pDC->SelectObject(m_pPrintFont);

    // m_hOldFont is the CGdiObject public data member that stores
    //   the handle
    m_hOldFont = (HFONT) pOldFont->GetSafeHandle();
}

void CMyView:SwitchToOriginalFont(CDC* pDC)
{
    // FromHandle is a static member function that returns an
    //   object pointer
```

(continued)

```
    if (m_hOldFont) {
        pDC->SelectObject(CFont::FromHandle(m_hOldFont));
    }
}

// m_pPrintFont is deleted in the CMyView destructor
```

> **NOTE:** Be careful when you delete an object whose pointer is returned by *SelectObject*. If you've allocated the object yourself, you can delete it. If the pointer is temporary, as it will be for the object initially selected into the device context, you won't be able to delete the C++ object.

Windows Color Mapping

The Windows GDI provides a hardware-independent color interface. Your program supplies an "absolute" color code, and the GDI maps that code to a suitable color or color combination on your computer's video display. Most programmers of applications for Windows try to optimize their applications' color display for a few common video card categories.

Standard Video Graphics Array Video Cards

A standard Video Graphics Array (VGA) video card uses 18-bit color registers and thus has a palette of 262,144 colors. Because of video memory constraints, however, the standard VGA board accommodates 4-bit color codes, which means it can display only 16 colors at a time. Because Windows needs fixed colors for captions, borders, scroll bars, and so forth, your programs can use only 16 "standard" pure colors. You cannot conveniently access the other colors that the board can display.

Each Windows color is represented by a combination of 8-bit "red," "green," and "blue" values. The 16 standard VGA "pure" (nondithered) colors are shown in the table on the facing page.

Color-oriented GDI functions accept 32-bit *COLORREF* parameters that contain 8-bit color codes each for red, green, and blue. The Windows RGB macro converts 8-bit red, green, and blue values to a *COLORREF* parameter. The following statement, when executed on a system with a standard VGA board, constructs a brush with a dithered color (one that consists of a pattern of pure-color pixels):

```
CBrush brush(RGB(128, 128, 192));
```

Red	Green	Blue	Color
0	0	0	Black
0	0	255	Blue
0	255	0	Green
0	255	255	Cyan
255	0	0	Red
255	0	255	Magenta
255	255	0	Yellow
255	255	255	White
0	0	128	Dark blue
0	128	0	Dark green
0	128	128	Dark cyan
128	0	0	Dark red
128	0	128	Dark magenta
128	128	0	Dark yellow
128	128	128	Dark gray
192	192	192	Light gray

The following statement (in your view's *OnDraw* function) sets the text background to red:

```
pDC->SetBkColor(RGB(255, 0, 0));
```

The *CDC* functions *SetBkColor* and *SetTextColor* don't display dithered colors as the brush-oriented drawing functions do. If the dithered color pattern is too complex, the closest matching pure color is displayed.

256-Color Video Cards

Most video cards can accommodate 8-bit color codes at all resolutions, which means they can display 256 colors simultaneously. This 256-color mode is now considered to be the "lowest common denominator" for color programming.

If Windows is configured for a 256-color display card, your programs are limited to 20 standard pure colors unless you activate the Windows color palette system as supported by the MFC library *CPalette* class and the Windows API, in which case you can choose your 256 colors from a total of more than 16.7 million. Windows color palette programming is discussed in Chapter 11. In this chapter, we'll assume that the Windows default color mapping is in effect.

With an SVGA 256-color display driver installed, you get the 16 VGA colors listed in the previous table plus 4 more, for a total of 20. The following table lists the 4 additional colors.

Red	Green	Blue	Color
192	220	192	Money green
166	202	240	Sky blue
255	251	240	Cream
160	160	164	Medium gray

The RGB macro works much the same as it does with the standard VGA. If you specify one of the 20 standard colors for a brush, you get a pure color; otherwise, you get a dithered color. If you use the *PALETTERGB* macro instead, you don't get dithered colors; you get the closest matching standard pure color as defined by the current palette.

16-Bit–Color Video Cards

Most modern video cards support a resolution of 1024-by-768 pixels, and 1 MB of video memory can support 8-bit color at this resolution. If a video card has 2 MB of memory, it can support 16-bit color, with 5 bits each for red, green, and blue. This means that it can display 32,768 colors simultaneously. That sounds like a lot, but there are only 32 shades each of pure red, green, and blue. Often, a picture will look better in 8-bit–color mode with an appropriate palette selected. A forest scene, for example, can use up to 236 shades of green. Palettes are not supported in 16-bit–color mode.

24-Bit–Color Video Cards

High-end cards (which are becoming more widely used) support 24-bit color. This 24-bit capability enables the display of more than 16.7 million pure colors. If you're using a 24-bit card, you have direct access to all the colors. The RGB macro allows you to specify the exact colors you want. You'll need 2.5 MB of video memory, though, if you want 24-bit color at 1024-by-768-pixel resolution.

Fonts

Old-fashioned character-mode applications could display only the boring system font on the screen. Windows provides multiple device-independent fonts in variable sizes. The effective use of these Windows fonts can significantly energize an application with minimum programming effort. TrueType fonts, first introduced with Windows version 3.1, are even more effective and are easier to program than the previous device-dependent fonts. You'll see several example programs that use various fonts later in this chapter.

Fonts Are GDI Objects

Fonts are an integral part of the Windows GDI. This means that fonts behave the same way other GDI objects do. They can be scaled and clipped, and they can be selected into a device context as a pen or a brush can be selected. All GDI rules about deselection and deletion apply to fonts.

Choosing a Font

Choosing a Windows font used to be like going to a fruit stand and asking for "a piece of reddish-yellow fruit, with a stone inside, that weighs about 4 ounces." You might have gotten a peach or a plum or even a nectarine, and you could be sure that it wouldn't have weighed exactly 4 ounces. Once you took possession of the fruit, you could weigh it and check the fruit type. Now, with True-Type, you can specify the fruit type, but you still can't specify the exact weight.

Today you can choose between two font types—device-independent True-Type fonts and device-dependent fonts such as the Windows display System font and the LaserJet LinePrinter font—or you can specify a font category and size and let Windows select the font for you. If you let Windows select the font, it will choose a TrueType font if possible. The MFC library provides a font selection dialog box tied to the currently selected printer, so there's little need for printer font guesswork. You let the user select the exact font and size for the printer, and then you approximate the display the best you can.

Printing with Fonts

For text-intensive applications, you'll probably want to specify printer font sizes in points (1 point = $\frac{1}{72}$ inch). Why? Most, if not all, built-in printer fonts are defined in terms of points. The LaserJet LinePrinter font, for example, comes in one size, 8.5 point. You can specify TrueType fonts in any point size. If you work in points, you need a mapping mode that easily accommodates points.

That's what *MM_TWIPS* is for. An 8.5-point font is 8.5 × 20, or 170, twips, and that's the character height you'll want to specify.

Displaying Fonts

If you're not worried about the display matching the printed output, you have a lot of flexibility. You can choose any of the scalable Windows TrueType fonts, or you can choose the fixed-size system fonts (stock objects). With the TrueType fonts, it doesn't much matter what mapping mode you use; simply choose a font height and go for it. No need to worry about points.

Matching printer fonts to make printed output match the screen presents some problems, but TrueType makes it easier than it used to be. Even if you're printing with TrueType fonts, however, you'll never quite get the display to match the printer output. Why? Characters are ultimately displayed in pixels (or dots), and the width of a string of characters is equal to the sum of the pixel widths of its characters, possibly adjusted for kerning. The pixel width of the characters depends on the font, the mapping mode, and the resolution of the output device. Only if both the printer and the display were set to *MM_TEXT* mode (1 pixel or dot = 1 logical unit) would you get an exact correspondence. If you're using the *CDC::GetTextExtent* function to calculate line breaks, the screen breakpoint will occasionally be different from the printer breakpoint.

> **NOTE:** In the MFC Print Preview mode, which we'll examine closely in Chapter 19, line breaks occur exactly as they do on the printer, but the print quality in the preview window suffers in the process.

If you're matching a printer-specific font on the screen, TrueType again makes the job easier. Windows substitutes the closest matching TrueType font. For the 8.5-point LinePrinter font, Windows comes pretty close with its Courier New font.

Logical Inches and Physical Inches on the Display

The *CDC* member function *GetDeviceCaps* returns various display measurements that are important to your graphics programming. The six described below provide information about the display size. The values listed are for a typical display card configured for a resolution of 640-by-480 pixels with Microsoft Windows NT 4.0.

Index	Description	Value
HORZSIZE	Physical width in millimeters	320
VERTSIZE	Physical height in millimeters	240
HORZRES	Width in pixels	640
VERTRES	Height in raster lines	480
LOGPIXELSX	Horizontal dots per logical inch	96
LOGPIXELSY	Vertical dots per logical inch	96

The indexes *HORZSIZE* and *VERTSIZE* represent the physical dimensions of your display. (These indexes might not be true since Windows doesn't know what size display you have connected to your video adapter.) You can also calculate a display size by multiplying *HORZRES* and *VERTRES* by *LOGPIXELSX* and *LOGPIXELSY*, respectively. The size calculated this way is known as the <u>logical size</u> of the display. Using the values above and the fact that there are 25.4 millimeters per inch, we can quickly calculate the two display sizes for a 640-by-480 pixel display under Windows NT 4.0. The physical display size is 12.60-by-9.45 inches, and the logical size is 6.67-by-5.00 inches. So the physical size and the logical size need not be the same.

For Windows NT 4.0, it turns out that *HORZSIZE* and *VERTSIZE* are independent of the display resolution, and *LOGPIXELSX* and *LOGPIXELSY* are always 96. So the logical size changes for different display resolutions, but the physical size does not. For Windows 95, the logical size and the physical size are equal, so both change with the display resolution. (At a resolution of 640-by-480 pixels with Windows 95, *HORZSIZE* is 169 and *VERTSIZE* is 127.)

Whenever you use a fixed mapping mode such as *MM_HIMETRIC* or *MM_TWIPS*, the display driver uses the physical display size to do the mapping.

So, for Windows NT, text is smaller on a small monitor; but that's not what you want. Instead, you want your font sizes to correspond to the logical display size, not the physical size.

You can invent a special mapping mode, called <u>logical twips</u>, for which one logical unit is equal to $\frac{1}{1440}$ logical inch. This mapping mode is independent of the operating system and display resolution and is used by programs such as Microsoft Word. Here is the code that sets the mapping mode to logical twips:

```
pDC->SetMapMode(MM_ANISOTROPIC);
pDC->SetWindowExt(1440, 1440);
pDC->SetViewportExt(pDC->GetDeviceCaps(LOGPIXELSX),
                    -pDC->GetDeviceCaps(LOGPIXELSY));
```

NOTE: From the Windows Control Panel, you can adjust both the display font size and the display resolution. If you change the display font size from the default 100 percent to 200 percent, *HORZSIZE* becomes 160, *VERTSIZE* becomes 120, and the dots-per-inch value becomes 192. In that case, the logical size is divided by 2, and all text drawn with the logical twips mapping mode is doubled in size.

Computing Character Height

Five font height measurement parameters are available through the *CDC* function *GetTextMetrics*, but only three are significant. Figure 5-1 shows the important font measurements. The *tmHeight* parameter represents the full height of the font, including descenders (for the characters g, j, p, q, and y) and any diacritics that appear over capital letters. The *tmExternalLeading* parameter is the distance between the top of the diacritic and the bottom of the descender from the line above. The sum of *tmHeight* and *tmExternalLeading* is the total character height. The value of *tmExternalLeading* can be 0.

You would think that *tmHeight* would represent the font size in points. Wrong! Another *GetTextMetrics* parameter, *tmInternalLeading*, comes into play. The point size corresponds to the difference between *tmHeight* and

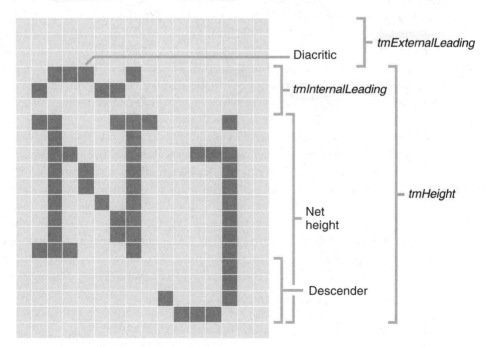

Figure 5-1.
Font height measurements.

tmInternalLeading. With the *MM_TWIPS* mapping mode in effect, a selected 12-point font might have a *tmHeight* value of 295 logical units and a *tmInternalLeading* value of 55. The font's net height of 240 corresponds to the point size of 12.

The EX05A Example

This example sets up a view window with the logical twips mapping mode. A text string is displayed in 10 point sizes with the Arial TrueType font. Here are the steps for building the application:

1. **Run AppWizard to generate the EX05A project.**   Start by choosing New from the File menu, and then select MFC AppWizard (exe) on the Project tab. Select Single Document and deselect Printing And Print Preview; accept all the other default settings. The options and the default class names are shown in the following illustration.

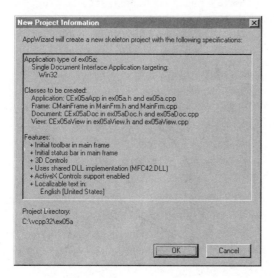

2. **Use ClassWizard to override the *OnPrepareDC* function in the *CEx05aView* class.**   Edit the code in ex05aView.cpp as follows:

```
void CEx05aView::OnPrepareDC(CDC* pDC, CPrintInfo* pInfo)
{
    pDC->SetMapMode(MM_ANISOTROPIC);
    pDC->SetWindowExt(1440, 1440);
    pDC->SetViewportExt(pDC->GetDeviceCaps(LOGPIXELSX),
                        -pDC->GetDeviceCaps(LOGPIXELSY));
}
```

3. Add a private *ShowFont* helper function to the view class. Add the prototype shown below in ex05aView.h:

```
private:
    void ShowFont(CDC* pDC, int& nPos, int nPoints);
```

Then add the function itself in ex05aView.cpp:

```
void CEx05aView::ShowFont(CDC* pDC, int& nPos, int nPoints)
{
    TEXTMETRIC  tm;
    CFont       fontText;
    CString     strText;
    CSize       sizeText;

    fontText.CreateFont(-nPoints * 20, 0, 0, 0, 400, FALSE, FALSE, 0,
                        ANSI_CHARSET, OUT_DEFAULT_PRECIS,
                        CLIP_DEFAULT_PRECIS, DEFAULT_QUALITY,
                        DEFAULT_PITCH | FF_SWISS, "Arial");
    CFont* pOldFont = (CFont*) pDC->SelectObject(&fontText);
    pDC->GetTextMetrics(&tm);
    TRACE("points = %d, tmHeight = %d, tmInternalLeading = %d,"
        " tmExternalLeading = %d\n", nPoints, tm.tmHeight,
        tm.tmInternalLeading, tm.tmExternalLeading);
    strText.Format("This is %d-point Arial", nPoints);
    sizeText = pDC->GetTextExtent(strText);
    TRACE("string width = %d, string height = %d\n", sizeText.cx,
        sizeText.cy);
    pDC->TextOut(0, nPos, strText);
    pDC->SelectObject(pOldFont);
    nPos -= tm.tmHeight + tm.tmExternalLeading;
}
```

4. Edit the *OnDraw* function in ex05aView.cpp. AppWizard always generates a skeleton *OnDraw* function for your view class. Find the function, and replace the code with the following:

```
void CEx05aView::OnDraw(CDC* pDC)
{
    int nPosition = 0;

    for (int i = 6; i <= 24; i += 2) {
        ShowFont(pDC, nPosition, i);
    }
    TRACE("LOGPIXELSX = %d, LOGPIXELSY = %d\n",
        pDC->GetDeviceCaps(LOGPIXELSX),
        pDC->GetDeviceCaps(LOGPIXELSY));
    TRACE("HORZSIZE = %d, VERTSIZE = %d\n",
```

```
                pDC->GetDeviceCaps(HORZSIZE),
                pDC->GetDeviceCaps(VERTSIZE));
        TRACE("HORZRES = %d, VERTRES = %d\n",
                pDC->GetDeviceCaps(HORZRES),
                pDC->GetDeviceCaps(VERTRES));
}
```

5. **Build and run the EX05A program.** You must run the program from the debugger if you want to see the output from the TRACE statements. You can choose Go from the Start Debug submenu of the Build menu in Visual C++, or click the following button on the Build toolbar.

The resulting output (assuming the use of a standard VGA card) looks like the screen shown here.

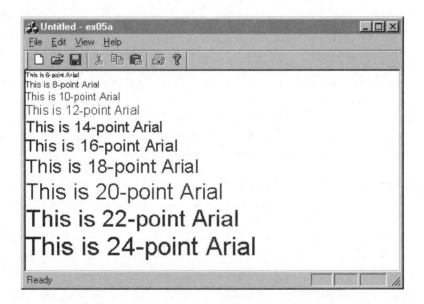

Notice that the output string sizes don't quite correspond to the point sizes. This discrepancy results from the font engine's conversion of logical units to pixels. The program's trace output, partially shown on the following page, shows the printout of font metrics. (The numbers depend on your display driver and your video driver.)

```
points = 6, tmHeight = 150, tmInternalLeading = 30, tmExternalLeading = 4
string width = 990, string height = 150
points = 8, tmHeight = 210, tmInternalLeading = 45, tmExternalLeading = 5
string width = 1380, string height = 210
points = 10, tmHeight = 240, tmInternalLeading = 45, tmExternalLeading = 6
string width = 1770, string height = 240
points = 12, tmHeight = 270, tmInternalLeading = 30, tmExternalLeading = 8
string width = 2130, string height = 270
```

The EX05A Program Elements

Following is a discussion of the important elements in the EX05A example.

Setting the Mapping Mode in the *OnPrepareDC* Function

The application framework calls *OnPrepareDC* prior to calling *OnDraw*, so the *OnPrepareDC* function is the logical place to prepare the device context. If you had other message handlers that needed the correct mapping mode, those functions would have contained calls to *OnPrepareDC*.

The *ShowFont* Private Member Function

ShowFont contains code that is executed 10 times in a loop. With C, you would have made this a global function, but with C++ it's better to make it a private class member function, sometimes known as a helper function.

This function creates the font, selects it into the device context, prints a string to the window, and then deselects the font. If you choose to include debug information in the program, *ShowFont* also displays useful font metrics information, including the actual width of the string.

Calling *CFont::CreateFont*

This call includes lots of parameters, but the important ones are the first two— the font height and width. A width value of 0 means that the aspect ratio of the selected font will be set to a value specified by the font designer. If you put a nonzero value here, as you'll see in the next example, you can change the font's aspect ratio.

> TIP: If you want your font to be a specific point size, the *Create-Font* font height parameter (the first parameter) must be negative. If you're using the *MM_TWIPS* mapping mode for a printer, for example, a height parameter of −240 ensures a true 12-point font, with *tmHeight − tmInternalLeading* = 240. A +240 height parameter gives you a smaller font, with *tmHeight* = 240.

The last *CreateFont* parameter specifies the font name, in this case the Arial TrueType font. If you had used *NULL* for this parameter, the *FF_SWISS* specification (which indicates a proportional font without serifs) would have caused Windows to choose the best matching font, which, depending on the specified size, might have been the System font or the Arial TrueType font. The font name takes precedence. If you had specified *FF_ROMAN* (which indicates a proportional font with serifs) with Arial, for example, you would have gotten Arial.

The EX05B Example

This program is similar to EX05A except that it shows multiple fonts. The mapping mode is *MM_ANISOTROPIC*, with the scale dependent on the window size. The characters change size along with the window. This program effectively shows off some TrueType fonts and contrasts them with the old-style fonts. Here are the steps for building the application:

1. Run AppWizard to generate the EX05B project. The options and the default class names are shown here.

2. Use ClassWizard to override the *OnPrepareDC* function in the *CEx05bView* class. Edit the code in ex05bView.cpp as shown on the following page.

93

```
void CEx05bView::OnPrepareDC(CDC* pDC, CPrintInfo* pInfo)
{
    CRect clientRect;

    GetClientRect(clientRect);
    pDC->SetMapMode(MM_ANISOTROPIC); // +y = down
    pDC->SetWindowExt(400, 450);
    pDC->SetViewportExt(clientRect.right, clientRect.bottom);
    pDC->SetViewportOrg(0, 0);
}
```

3. **Add a private *TraceMetrics* helper function to the view class.**   Add the following prototype in ex05bView.h:

```
private:
    void TraceMetrics(CDC* pDC);
```

Then add the function itself in ex05bView.cpp:

```
void CEx05bView::TraceMetrics(CDC* pDC)
{
    TEXTMETRIC tm;
    char       szFaceName[100];

    pDC->GetTextMetrics(&tm);
    pDC->GetTextFace(99, szFaceName);
    TRACE("font = %s, tmHeight = %d, tmInternalLeading = %d,"
          " tmExternalLeading = %d\n", szFaceName, tm.tmHeight,
          tm.tmInternalLeading, tm.tmExternalLeading);
}
```

4. **Edit the *OnDraw* function in ex05bView.cpp.**   AppWizard always generates a skeleton *OnDraw* function for your view class. Find the function, and edit the code as follows:

```
void CEx05bView::OnDraw(CDC* pDC)
{
    CFont fontTest1, fontTest2, fontTest3, fontTest4;

    fontTest1.CreateFont(50, 0, 0, 0, 400, FALSE, FALSE, 0,
                         ANSI_CHARSET, OUT_DEFAULT_PRECIS,
                         CLIP_DEFAULT_PRECIS, DEFAULT_QUALITY,
                         DEFAULT_PITCH | FF_SWISS, "Arial");
    CFont* pOldFont = pDC->SelectObject(&fontTest1);
    TraceMetrics(pDC);
    pDC->TextOut(0, 0, "This is Arial, default width");
```

```
      fontTest2.CreateFont(50, 0, 0, 0, 400, FALSE, FALSE, 0,
                           ANSI_CHARSET, OUT_DEFAULT_PRECIS,
                           CLIP_DEFAULT_PRECIS, DEFAULT_QUALITY,
                           DEFAULT_PITCH | FF_MODERN, "Courier");
                           // not TrueType
  pDC->SelectObject(&fontTest2);
  TraceMetrics(pDC);
  pDC->TextOut(0, 100, "This is Courier, default width");

      fontTest3.CreateFont(50, 10, 0, 0, 400, FALSE, FALSE, 0,
                           ANSI_CHARSET, OUT_DEFAULT_PRECIS,
                           CLIP_DEFAULT_PRECIS, DEFAULT_QUALITY,
                           DEFAULT_PITCH | FF_ROMAN, NULL);
  pDC->SelectObject(&fontTest3);
  TraceMetrics(pDC);
  pDC->TextOut(0, 200, "This is generic Roman, variable width");

      fontTest4.CreateFont(50, 0, 0, 0, 400, FALSE, FALSE, 0,
                           ANSI_CHARSET, OUT_DEFAULT_PRECIS,
                           CLIP_DEFAULT_PRECIS, DEFAULT_QUALITY,
                           DEFAULT_PITCH | FF_MODERN, "LinePrinter");
  pDC->SelectObject(&fontTest4);
  TraceMetrics(pDC);
  pDC->TextOut(0, 300, "This is LinePrinter, default width");
  pDC->SelectObject(pOldFont);
}
```

5. **Build and run the EX05B program.**   Run the program from the debug-ger to see the TRACE output. The program's window is shown here.

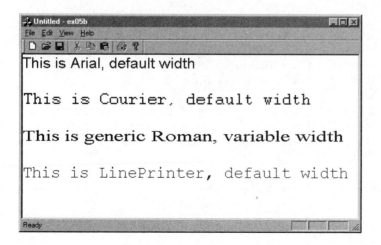

95

Resize the window to make it smaller, and watch the font sizes change. Compare this window with the previous one.

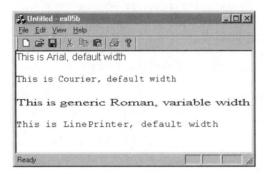

If you continue to downsize the window, notice how the Courier font stops shrinking after a certain size and how the Roman font width changes.

The EX05B Program Elements

Following is a discussion of the important elements in the EX05B example.

The *OnDraw* Member Function

The *OnDraw* function displays character strings in four fonts, as follows:

- *fontTest1*—The TrueType font Arial with default width selection.

- *fontTest2*—The old-style font Courier with default width selection. Notice how jagged the font appears in larger sizes.

- *fontTest3*—The generic Roman font for which Windows supplies the TrueType font Times New Roman with programmed width selection. The width is tied to the horizontal window scale, so the font stretches to fit the window.

- *fontTest4*—The LinePrinter font is specified, but because this is not a Windows font for the display, the font engine falls back on the *FF_MODERN* specification and chooses the TrueType Courier New font.

The *TraceMetrics Helper* Function

The *TraceMetrics* helper function calls *CDC::GetTextMetrics* and *CDC::GetTextFace* to get the current font's parameters, which it prints in the Debug window.

The EX05C Example—*CScrollView* Revisited

You saw the *CScrollView* class in Chapter 4 (in EX04C). The EX05C program allows the user to move an ellipse with a mouse by "capturing" the mouse, using a scrolling window with the *MM_LOENGLISH* mapping mode. Keyboard scrolling is left out, but you can add it by borrowing the *OnKeyDown* member function from EX04C.

Instead of a stock brush, we'll use a pattern brush for the ellipse—a real GDI object. There's one complication with pattern brushes: you must reset the origin as the window scrolls; otherwise, strips of the pattern don't line up and the effect is ugly.

As with the EX04C program, this example involves a view class derived from *CScrollView*. Here are the steps to create the application:

1. **Run AppWizard to generate the EX05C project.** Be sure to set the view base class to *CScrollView*. The options and the default class names are shown here.

2. **Edit the *CEx05cView* class header in the file ex05cView.h.** Add the following lines in the class *CEx05cView* declaration:

```
private:
    const CSize m_sizeEllipse; // logical
    CPoint m_pointTopLeft; // logical, top left of ellipse rectangle
    CSize  m_sizeOffset; // device, from rect top left
                    //   to capture point
    BOOL   m_bCaptured;
```

3. **Use ClassWizard to add three message handlers to the *CEx05cView* class.** Add the message handlers as follows:

Message	Member Function
WM_LBUTTONDOWN	*OnLButtonDown*
WM_LBUTTONUP	*OnLButtonUp*
WM_MOUSEMOVE	*OnMouseMove*

4. **Edit the *CEx05cView* message handler functions.** ClassWizard generated the skeletons for the functions listed in the preceding step. Find the functions in ex05cView.cpp, and code them as follows.

```
void CEx05cView::OnLButtonDown(UINT nFlags, CPoint point)
{
    CRect rectEllipse(m_pointTopLeft, m_sizeEllipse); // still logical
    CRgn  circle;

    CClientDC dc(this);
    OnPrepareDC(&dc);
    dc.LPtoDP(rectEllipse); // Now it's in device coordinates
    circle.CreateEllipticRgnIndirect(rectEllipse);
    if (circle.PtInRegion(point)) {
        // Capturing the mouse ensures subsequent LButtonUp message
        SetCapture();
        m_bCaptured = TRUE;
        CPoint pointTopLeft(m_pointTopLeft);
        dc.LPtoDP(&pointTopLeft);
        m_sizeOffset = point - pointTopLeft; // device coordinates
        // New mouse cursor is active while mouse is captured
        ::SetCursor(::LoadCursor(NULL, IDC_CROSS));
    }
}

void CEx05cView::OnLButtonUp(UINT nFlags, CPoint point)
{
    if (m_bCaptured) {
        ::ReleaseCapture();
        m_bCaptured = FALSE;
    }
}

void CEx05cView::OnMouseMove(UINT nFlags, CPoint point)
{
    if (m_bCaptured) {
```

```
            CClientDC dc(this);
            OnPrepareDC(&dc);
            CRect rectOld(m_pointTopLeft, m_sizeEllipse);
            dc.LPtoDP(rectOld);
            InvalidateRect(rectOld, TRUE);
            m_pointTopLeft = point - m_sizeOffset;
            dc.DPtoLP(&m_pointTopLeft);
            CRect rectNew(m_pointTopLeft, m_sizeEllipse);
            dc.LPtoDP(rectNew);
            InvalidateRect(rectNew, TRUE);
        }
    }
```

5. **Edit the *CEx05cView* constructor, the *OnDraw* function, and the *OnInitialUpdate* function.** AppWizard generated these skeleton functions. Find them in ex05cView.cpp, and code them as follows:

```
CEx05cView::CEx05cView() : m_sizeEllipse(100, -100),
                           m_pointTopLeft(0, 0),
                           m_sizeOffset(0, 0)
{
    m_bCaptured = FALSE;
}


void CEx05cView::OnDraw(CDC* pDC)
{
    CBrush brushHatch(HS_DIAGCROSS, RGB(255, 0, 0));
    CPoint point(0, 0);                       // logical (0, 0)

    pDC->LPtoDP(&point);                      // In device coordinates,
    pDC->SetBrushOrg(point);                  //   align the brush with
                                              //   the window origin
    pDC->SelectObject(&brushHatch);
    pDC->Ellipse(CRect(m_pointTopLeft, m_sizeEllipse));
    pDC->SelectStockObject(BLACK_BRUSH); // Deselect brushHatch
    pDC->Rectangle(CRect(100, -100, 200, -200)); // Test invalid rect
}


void CEx05cView::OnInitialUpdate()
{
    CScrollView::OnInitialUpdate();

    CSize sizeTotal(800, 1050); // 8-by-10.5 inches
    CSize sizePage(sizeTotal.cx / 2, sizeTotal.cy / 2);
    CSize sizeLine(sizeTotal.cx / 50, sizeTotal.cy / 50);
    SetScrollSizes(MM_LOENGLISH, sizeTotal, sizePage, sizeLine);
}
```

6. **Build and run the EX05C program.** The program allows an ellipse to be dragged with the mouse, and it allows the window to be scrolled through. The program's window should look like the one shown here. As you move the ellipse, observe the black rectangle. You should be able to see the effects of invalidating the rectangle.

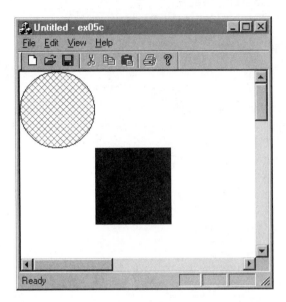

The EX05C Program Elements

Following is a discussion of the important elements in the EX05C example.

The *m_sizeEllipse* and *m_pointTopLeft* Data Members

Rather than store the ellipse's bounding rectangle as a single *CRect* object, the program separately stores its size (*m_sizeEllipse*) and the position of its top left corner (*m_pointTopLeft*). To move the ellipse, the program merely recalculates *m_pointTopLeft*, and any round-off errors in the calculation won't affect the size of the ellipse.

The *m_sizeOffset* Data Member

When *OnMouseMove* moves the ellipse, the relative position of the mouse within the ellipse must be the same as it was when the user first pressed the left mouse button. The *m_sizeOffset* object stores this original offset of the mouse from the top left corner of the ellipse rectangle.

The *m_bCaptured* Data Member

The *m_bCaptured* Boolean variable is set to TRUE when mouse tracking is in progress.

The *SetCapture* and *ReleaseCapture* Functions

SetCapture is the *CWnd* member function that "captures" the mouse, such that mouse movement messages are sent to this window even if the mouse cursor is outside the window. An unfortunate side effect of this function is that the ellipse can be moved outside the window and "lost." A desirable and necessary effect is that all subsequent mouse messages are sent to the window, including the WM_LBUTTONUP message, which would otherwise be lost. The Win32 *ReleaseCapture* function turns off mouse capture.

The *SetCursor* and *LoadCursor* Win32 Functions

The MFC library does not "wrap" some Win32 functions. By convention, we use the C++ scope resolution operator (::) when calling Win32 functions directly. In this case, there is no potential for conflict with a *CView* member function, but you can deliberately choose to call a Win32 function in place of a class member function with the same name. In that case, the :: operator ensures that you call the globally scoped Win32 function.

When the first parameter is *NULL*, the *LoadCursor* function creates a cursor resource from the specified predefined mouse cursor that Windows uses. The *SetCursor* function activates the specified cursor resource. This cursor remains active as long as the mouse is captured.

The *CScrollView::OnPrepareDC* Member Function

The *CView* class has a virtual *OnPrepareDC* function that does nothing. The *CScrollView* class implements the function for the purpose of setting the view's mapping mode and origin, based on the parameters that you passed to *SetScrollSizes* in *OnCreate*. The application framework calls *OnPrepareDC* for you prior to calling *OnDraw*, so you don't need to worry about it. You must call *OnPrepareDC* yourself in any other message handler function that uses the view's device context, such as *OnLButtonDown* and *OnMouseMove*.

The *OnMouseMove* Coordinate Transformation Code

As you can see, this function contains several translation statements. The logic can be summarized by the following steps:

1. Construct the previous ellipse rectangle and convert it from logical to device coordinates.

2. Invalidate the previous rectangle.

3. Update the top left coordinate of the ellipse rectangle.

4. Construct the new rectangle and convert it to device coordinates.

5. Invalidate the new rectangle.

The function calls *InvalidateRect* twice. Windows "saves up" the two invalid rectangles and computes a new invalid rectangle that is the union of the two, intersected with the client rectangle.

The *OnDraw* Function

The *SetBrushOrg* call is necessary to ensure that all of the ellipse's interior pattern lines up when the user scrolls through the view. The brush is aligned with a reference point, which is at the top left of the logical window, converted to device coordinates. This is a notable exception to the rule that *CDC* member functions require logical coordinates.

The *CScrollView SetScaleToFitSize* Mode

The *CScrollView* class has a stretch-to-fit mode that displays the entire scrollable area in the view window. The Windows *MM_ANISOTROPIC* mapping mode comes into play, with one restriction: positive y values always increase in the down direction, as in *MM_TEXT* mode.

To use the stretch-to-fit mode, make the following call in your view's function in place of the call to *SetScrollSizes*:

```
SetScaleToFitSize(sizeTotal);
```

You can make this call in response to a Shrink To Fit menu command. Thus, the display can toggle between scrolling mode and shrink-to-fit mode.

Using the Logical Twips Mapping Mode in a Scrolling View

The MFC *CScrollView* class allows you to specify only standard mapping modes. The EX19A example in Chapter 19 shows a new class *CLogScrollView* that accommodates the logical twips mode.

The Modal Dialog and Windows Common Controls

Almost every Windows-based program uses a dialog window to interact with the user. The dialog might be a simple OK message box, or it might be a complex data entry form. Calling this powerful element a dialog "box" is an injustice. A dialog is truly a window that receives messages, that can be moved and closed, and that can even accept drawing instructions in its client area.

The two kinds of dialogs are <u>modal</u> and <u>modeless</u>. This chapter explores the most common type, the modal dialog. In the first of this chapter's two examples, you'll use all the familiar "old" controls, such as the edit control and the list box, inherited from Win16. In the second example, you'll use the Windows common controls, which Microsoft Windows 95 introduced. In Chapter 7 we'll take a look at the modeless dialog and the special-purpose Windows common dialogs for opening files, selecting fonts, and so forth. In Chapter 8 we'll examine ActiveX Controls. Then Chapter 9 discusses the new Internet Explorer control classes, introduced in MFC 6.0

Modal vs. Modeless Dialogs

The *CDialog* base class supports both modal and modeless dialogs. With a modal dialog, such as the Open File dialog, the user cannot work elsewhere in the same application (more correctly, in the same user interface thread) until the dialog is closed. With a modeless dialog, the user can work in another window in the application while the dialog remains on the screen. Microsoft Word's Find and Replace dialog is a good example of a modeless dialog; you can edit your document while the dialog is open.

Your choice of a modal or a modeless dialog depends on the application. Modal dialogs are much easier to program, which might influence your decision.

FYI: The 16-bit versions of Windows support a special kind of modal dialog called a system modal dialog, which prevents the user from switching to another application. Win32 also supports system modal dialogs but with weird results: the user can switch to another application, but the dialog remains as the top window. You probably don't want to use system modal dialogs in Win32 applications.

Resources and Controls

So now you know a dialog is a window. What makes the dialog different from the *CView* windows you've seen already? For one thing, a dialog window is almost always tied to a Windows resource that identifies the dialog's elements and specifies their layout. Because you can use the dialog editor (one of the resource editors) to create and edit a dialog resource, you can quickly and efficiently produce dialogs in a visual manner.

A dialog contains a number of elements called controls. Dialog controls include edit controls (aka text boxes), buttons, list boxes, combo boxes, static text (aka labels), tree views, progress indicators, sliders, and so forth. Windows manages these controls using special grouping and tabbing logic, and that relieves you of a major programming burden. The dialog controls can be referenced either by a *CWnd* pointer (because they are really windows) or by an index number (with an associated *#define* constant) assigned in the resource. A control sends a message to its parent dialog in response to a user action such as typing text or clicking a button.

The Microsoft Foundation Class (MFC) Library and ClassWizard work together to enhance the dialog logic that Windows provides. ClassWizard generates a class derived from *CDialog* and then lets you associate dialog class data members with dialog controls. You can specify editing parameters such as maximum text length and numeric high and low limits. ClassWizard generates statements that call the MFC data exchange and data validation functions to move information back and forth between the screen and the data members.

Programming a Modal Dialog

Modal dialogs are the most frequently used dialogs. A user action (a menu choice, for example) brings up a dialog on the screen, the user enters data in the dialog, and then the user closes the dialog. Here's a summary of the steps to add a modal dialog to an existing project:

1. Use the dialog editor to create a dialog resource that contains various controls. The dialog editor updates the project's resource script (RC) file to include your new dialog resource, and it updates the project's resource.h file with corresponding *#define* constants.

2. Use ClassWizard to create a dialog class that is derived from *CDialog* and attached to the resource created in step 1. ClassWizard adds the associated code and header file to the Microsoft Visual C++ project.

   N O T E :   When ClassWizard generates your derived dialog class, it generates a constructor that invokes a *CDialog* modal constructor, which takes a resource ID as a parameter. Your generated dialog header file contains a class enumerator constant *IDD* that is set to the dialog resource ID. In the CPP file, the constructor implementation looks like this:

   ```
   CMyDialog::CMyDialog(CWnd* pParent /*=NULL*/)
       : CDialog(CMyDialog::IDD, pParent)
   {
       // initialization code here
   }
   ```

   The use of *enum IDD* decouples the CPP file from the resource IDs that are defined in the project's resource.h file.

3. Use ClassWizard to add data members, exchange functions, and validation functions to the dialog class.

4. Use ClassWizard to add message handlers for the dialog's buttons and other event-generating controls.

5. Write the code for special control initialization (in *OnInitDialog*) and for the message handlers. Be sure the *CDialog* virtual member function *OnOK* is called when the user closes the dialog (unless the user cancels the dialog). (Note: *OnOK* is called by default.)

6. Write the code in your view class to activate the dialog. This code consists of a call to your dialog class's constructor followed by a call to the *DoModal* dialog class member function. *DoModal* returns only when the user exits the dialog window.

Now we'll proceed with a real example, one step at a time.

The Dialog That Ate Cincinnati— The EX06A Example

Let's not mess around with wimpy little dialogs. We'll build a monster dialog that contains almost every kind of control. The job will be easy because Visual C++'s dialog editor is there to help us. The finished product is shown in Figure 6-1.

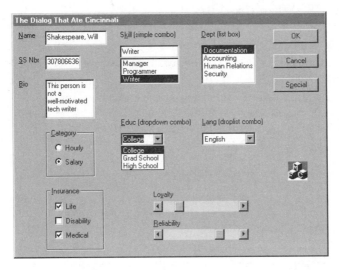

Figure 6-1.
The finished dialog in action.

As you can see, the dialog supports a human resources application. These kinds of business programs are fairly boring, so the challenge is to produce something that could not have been done with 80-column punched cards. The program is brightened a little by the use of scroll bar controls for "Loyalty" and "Reliability." Here is a classic example of direct action and visual representation of data! ActiveX controls could add more interest, but you'll have to wait until Chapter 8 for details on ActiveX.

Building the Dialog Resource

Here are the steps for building the dialog resource:

1. Run AppWizard to generate a project called EX06A. Choose New from Visual C++'s File menu, and then click the Projects tab and select MFC AppWizard (exe). Accept all the defaults but two: select Single

Document and deselect Printing And Print Preview. The options and the default class names are shown here.

As usual, AppWizard sets the new project as the current project.

2. **Create a new dialog resource with ID *IDD_DIALOG1*.** Choose Resource from Visual C++'s Insert menu. The Insert Resource dialog appears. Click on Dialog, and then click New. Visual C++ creates a new dialog resource, as shown here.

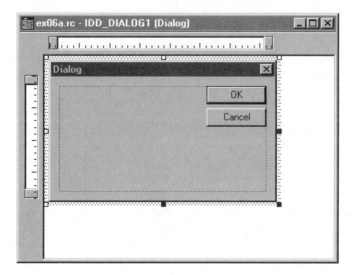

The dialog editor assigns the resource ID *IDD_DIALOG1* to the new dialog. Notice that the dialog editor inserts OK and Cancel buttons for the new dialog.

3. **Size the dialog and assign a caption.**   Enlarge the dialog box to about 5-by-7 inches.

When you right-click on the new dialog and choose Properties from the pop-up menu, the Dialog Properties dialog appears. Type in the caption for the new dialog as shown in the screen below. The state of the pushpin button in the upper-left corner determines whether the Dialog Properties dialog stays on top of other windows. (When the pushpin is "pushed," the dialog stays on top of other windows.) Click the Toggle Grid button (on the Dialog toolbar) to reveal the grid and to help align controls.

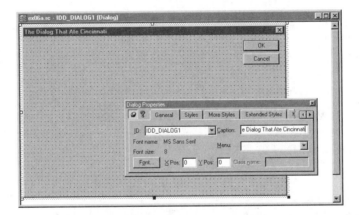

4. **Set the dialog style.**   Click on the Styles tab at the top of the Dialog Properties dialog, and then set the style properties as shown in the following illustration.

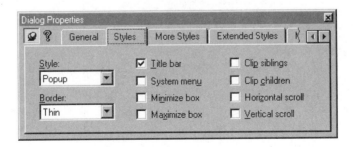

5. Set additional dialog styles.   Click on the More Styles tab at the top of the Dialog Properties dialog, and then set the style properties as shown here.

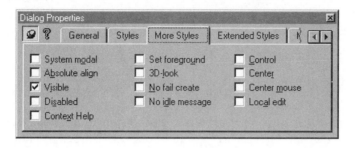

6. Add the dialog's controls.   Use the control palette to add each control. (If the control palette is not visible, right-click any toolbar and choose Controls from the list.) Drag controls from the control palette to the new dialog, and then position and size the controls, as shown in Figure 6-1 on page 106. Here are the control palette's controls.

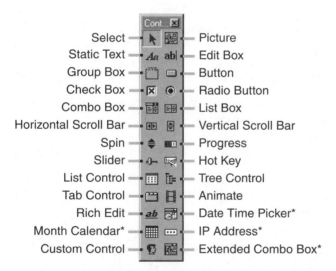

*Indicates a new Internet Explorer 4 common control introduced in Visual C++ 6.0. These are covered in Chapter 9.

NOTE: The dialog editor displays the position and size of each control in the status bar. The position units are special "dialog units," or DLUs, <u>not</u> device units. A horizontal DLU is the average width of the dialog font divided by 4. A vertical DLU is the average height of the font divided by 8. The dialog font is normally 8-point MS Sans Serif.

Here's a brief description of the dialog's controls:

❑ **The static text control for the Name field.** A static text control simply paints characters on the screen. No user interaction occurs at runtime. You can type the text after you position the bounding rectangle, and you can resize the rectangle as needed. This is the only static text control you'll see listed in text, but you should also create the other static text controls as shown earlier in Figure 6-1. Follow the same procedure for the other static text controls in the dialog. All static text controls have the same ID, but that doesn't matter because the program doesn't need to access any of them.

❑ **The Name edit control.** An edit control is the primary means of entering text in a dialog. Right-click the control, and then choose Properties. Change this control's ID from *IDC_EDIT1* to *IDC-_NAME*. Accept the defaults for the rest of the properties. Notice that the default sets Auto HScroll, which means that the text scrolls horizontally when the box is filled.

❑ **The SS Nbr (social security number) edit control.** As far as the dialog editor is concerned, the SS Nbr control is exactly the same as the Name edit control. Simply change its ID to *IDC_SSN*. Later you will use ClassWizard to make this a numeric field.

❑ **The Bio (biography) edit control.** This is a multiline edit control. Change its ID to *IDC_BIO*, and then set its properties as shown here.

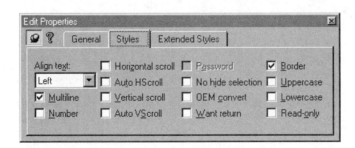

❑ **The Category group box.** This control serves only to group two radio buttons visually. Type in the caption *Category*. The default ID is sufficient.

❑ **The Hourly and Salary radio buttons.** Position these radio buttons inside the Category group box. Set the Hourly button's ID to *IDC_CAT* and set the other properties as shown here.

Be sure that both buttons have the Auto property (the default) on the Styles tab set and that only the Hourly button has the Group property set. When these properties are set correctly, Windows ensures that only one of the two buttons can be selected at a time. The Category group box has no effect on the buttons' operation.

❑ **The Insurance group box.** This control holds three check boxes. Type in the caption *Insurance*.

> N O T E :   Later, when you set the dialog's tab order, you'll ensure that the Insurance group box follows the last radio button of the Category group. Set the Insurance control's Group property now in order to "terminate" the previous group. If you fail to do this, it isn't a serious problem, but you'll get several warning messages when you run the program through the debugger.

❏ **The Life, Disability, and Medical check boxes.** Place these controls inside the Insurance group box. Accept the default properties, but change the IDs to *IDC_LIFE*, *IDC_DIS*, and *IDC_MED*. Unlike radio buttons, check boxes are independent; the user can set any combination.

❏ **The Skill combo box.** This is the first of three types of combo boxes. Change the ID to *IDC_SKILL*, and then click on the Styles tab and set the Type option to Simple. Click on the Data tab, and add three skills (terminating each line with Ctrl-Enter) in the Enter Listbox Items box.

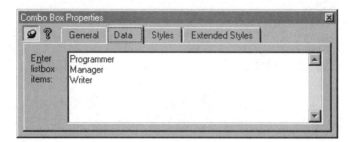

This is a combo box of type Simple. The user can type anything in the top edit control, use the mouse to select an item from the attached list box, or use the Up or Down direction key to select an item from the attached list box.

❏ **The Educ (education) combo box.** Change the ID to *IDC-_EDUC*; otherwise, accept the defaults. Add the three education levels in the Data page, as shown in Figure 6-1 on page 106. In this Dropdown combo box, the user can type anything in the edit box, click on the arrow, and then select an item from the drop-down list box or use the Up or Down direction key to select an item from the attached list box.

Aligning Controls

To align two or more controls, select the controls by clicking on the first control and then Shift-clicking on the other controls you want to align. Next choose one of the alignment commands (Left, Horiz-.Center, Right, Top, Vert.Center, or Bottom) from the Align submenu on the dialog editor's Layout menu.

NOTE: To set the size for the drop-down portion of a combo box, click on the box's arrow and drag down from the center of the bottom of the rectangle.

❑ **The Dept (department) list box.**   Change the ID to *IDC_DEPT*; otherwise, accept all the defaults. In this list box, the user can select only a single item by using the mouse, by using the Up or Down direction key, or by typing the first character of a selection. Note that you can't enter the initial choices in the dialog editor. You'll see how to set these choices later.

❑ **The Lang (language) combo box.**   Change the ID to *IDC- _LANG*, and then click on the Styles tab and set the Type option to Drop List. Add three languages (English, French, and Spanish) in the Data page. With this Drop List combo box, the user can select only from the attached list box. To select, the user can click on the arrow and then select an entry from the drop-down list, or the user can type in the first letter of the selection and then refine the selection using the Up or Down direction key.

❑ **The Loyalty and Reliability scroll bars.**   Do not confuse scroll bar controls with a window's built-in scroll bars as seen in scrolling

Selecting a Group of Controls

To quickly select a group of controls, position the mouse cursor above and to the left of the group. Hold down the left mouse button and drag to a point below and to the right of the group, as shown here.

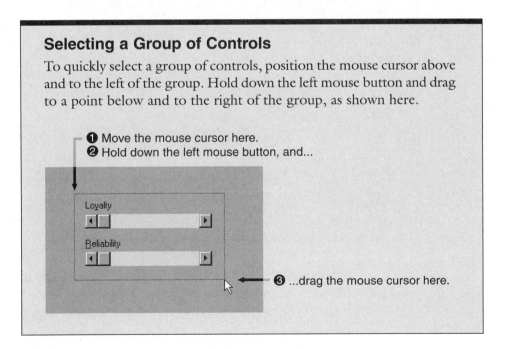

❶ Move the mouse cursor here.
❷ Hold down the left mouse button, and...

Loyalty

Reliability

❸ ...drag the mouse cursor here.

views. A scroll bar control behaves in the same manner as do other controls and can be resized at design time. Position and size the horizontal scroll bar controls as shown previously in Figure 6-1, and then assign the IDs *IDC_LOYAL* and *IDC_RELY*.

❏ **The OK, Cancel, and Special pushbuttons.** Be sure the button captions are *OK*, *Cancel*, and *Special*, and then assign the ID *IDC_SPECIAL* to the Special button. Later you'll learn about special meanings that are associated with the default IDs *IDOK* and *IDCANCEL*.

❏ **Any icon. (The MFC icon is shown as an example.)** You can use the Picture control to display any icon or bitmap in a dialog, as long as the icon or bitmap is defined in the resource script. We'll use the program's MFC icon, identified as *IDR_MAINFRAME*. Set the Type option to Icon, and set the Image option to *IDR_MAIN-FRAME*. Leave the ID as *IDC_STATIC*.

7. **Check the dialog's tabbing order.** Choose Tab Order from the dialog editor's Layout menu. Use the mouse to set the tabbing order shown below. Click on each control in the order shown, and then press Enter.

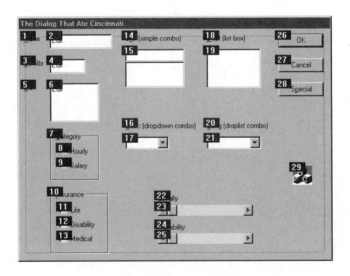

TIP: If you mess up the tab sequence partway through, you can re-cover with a Ctrl-left mouse click on the <u>last</u> <u>correctly</u> <u>sequenced</u> control. Subsequent mouse clicks will start with the next sequence number.

NOTE: A static text control (such as Name or Skill) has an ampersand (&) embedded in the text for its caption. At runtime, the ampersand will appear as an underscore under the character that follows. (See Figure 6-1 on page 106.) This enables the user to jump to selected controls by holding down the Alt key and pressing the key corresponding to the underlined character. (The related control must immediately follow the static text in the tabbing order.) Thus, Alt-N jumps to the Name edit control and Alt-K jumps to the Skill combo box. Needless to say, designated jump characters should be unique within the dialog. The Skill control uses Alt-K because the SS Nbr control uses Alt-S.

8. **Save the resource file on disk.** For safety, choose Save from the File menu or click the Save button on the toolbar to save ex06a.rc. Keep the dialog editor running, and keep the newly built dialog on the screen.

ClassWizard and the Dialog Class

You have now built a dialog resource, but you can't use it without a corresponding dialog class. (The section titled "Understanding the EX06A Application" beginning on page 121 explains the relationship between the dialog window and the underlying classes.) ClassWizard works in conjunction with the dialog editor to create that class as follows:

1. **Choose ClassWizard from Visual C++'s View menu (or press Ctrl-W).** Be sure that you still have the newly built dialog, *IDD_DIALOG1*, selected in the dialog editor and that EX06A is the current Visual C++ project.

2. **Add the *CEx06aDialog* class.** ClassWizard detects the fact that you've just created a dialog resource without an associated C++ class. It politely asks whether you want to create a class, as shown below.

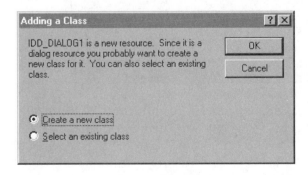

115

Accept the default selection of Create A New Class, and click OK. Fill in the top field of the New Class dialog, as shown here.

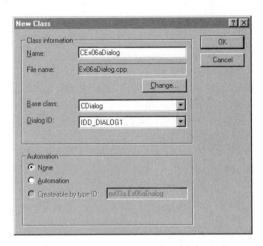

3. **Add the *CEx06aDialog* variables.** After ClassWizard creates the *CEx-06aDialog* class, the MFC ClassWizard dialog appears. Click on the Member Variables tab, and the Member Variables page appears, as shown here.

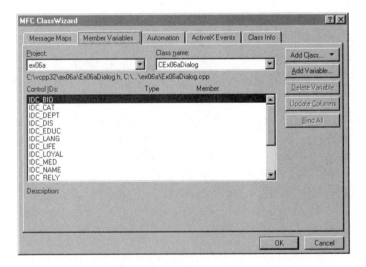

You need to associate data members with each of the dialog's controls. To do this, click on a control ID and then click the Add Variable button. The Add Member Variable dialog appears, as shown in the following illustration.

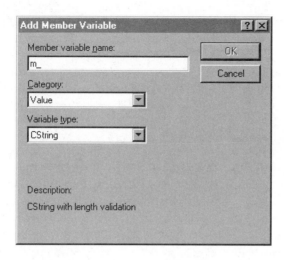

Type in the member variable name, and choose the variable type according to the following table. Be sure to type in the member variable name exactly as shown; the case of each letter is important. When you're done, click OK to return to the MFC ClassWizard dialog. Repeat this process for each of the listed controls.

Control ID	Data Member	Type
IDC_BIO	m_strBio	CString
IDC_CAT	m_nCat	int
IDC_DEPT	m_strDept	CString
IDC_DIS	m_bInsDis	BOOL
IDC_EDUC	m_strEduc	CString
IDC_LANG	m_nLang	int
IDC_LIFE	m_bInsLife	BOOL
IDC_LOYAL	m_nLoyal	int
IDC_MED	m_bInsMed	BOOL
IDC_NAME	m_strName	CString
IDC_RELY	m_nRely	int
IDC_SKILL	m_strSkill	CString
IDC_SSN	m_nSsn	int

As you select controls in the MFC ClassWizard dialog, various edit boxes appear at the bottom of the dialog. If you select a *CString* variable, you can set its maximum number of characters; if you select a numeric variable, you can set its high and low limits. Set the minimum value for *IDC_SSN* to 0 and the maximum value to 999999999.

Most relationships between control types and variable types are obvious. The way in which radio buttons correspond to variables is not so intuitive, however. The *CDialog* class associates an integer variable with each radio button *group,* with the first button corresponding to value 0, the second to 1, and so forth.

4. Add the message-handling function for the Special button.
CEx06aDialog doesn't need many message-handling functions because the *CDialog* base class, with the help of Windows, does most of the dialog management. When you specify the ID *IDOK* for the OK button (ClassWizard's default), for example, the virtual *CDialog* function *OnOK* gets called when the user clicks the button. For other buttons, however, you need message handlers.

Click on the Message Maps tab. The ClassWizard dialog should contain an entry for *IDC_SPECIAL* in the Object IDs list box. Click on this entry, and double-click on the BN_CLICKED message that appears in the Messages list box. ClassWizard invents a member function name, *OnSpecial*, and opens the Add Member Function dialog, as shown here.

You could type in your own function name here, but this time accept the default and click OK. Click the Edit Code button in the MFC Class-Wizard dialog. This opens the file ex06aDialog.cpp and moves to the *OnSpecial* function. Insert a *TRACE* statement in the *OnSpecial* function by typing in the boldface code, shown below, which replaces the existing code:

```
void CEx06aDialog::OnSpecial()
{
    TRACE("CEx06aDialog::OnSpecial\n");
}
```

5. Use ClassWizard to add an *OnInitDialog* message-handling function.
As you'll see in a moment, ClassWizard generates code that initializes a dialog's controls. This DDX (Dialog Data Exchange) code won't initialize the list-box choices, however, so you must override the *CDialog::OnInit-Dialog* function. Although *OnInitDialog* is a virtual member function, ClassWizard generates the prototype and skeleton if you map the WM-_INITDIALOG message in the derived dialog class. To do so, click on *CEx06aDialog* in the Object IDs list box and then double-click on the WM_INITDIALOG message in the Messages list box. Click the Edit Code button in the MFC ClassWizard dialog to edit the *OnInitDialog* function. Type in the boldface code, which replaces the existing code:

```
BOOL CEx06aDialog::OnInitDialog()
{
    // Be careful to call CDialog::OnInitDialog
    //   only once in this function
    CListBox* pLB = (CListBox*) GetDlgItem(IDC_DEPT);
    pLB->InsertString(-1, "Documentation");
    pLB->InsertString(-1, "Accounting");
    pLB->InsertString(-1, "Human Relations");
    pLB->InsertString(-1, "Security");

    // Call after initialization
    return CDialog::OnInitDialog();
}
```

You could also use the same initialization technique for the combo boxes, in place of the initialization in the resource.

Connecting the Dialog to the View

Now we've got the resource and the code for a dialog, but it's not connected to the view. In most applications, you would probably use a menu choice to activate a dialog, but we haven't studied menus yet. Here we'll use the familiar mouse-click message WM_LBUTTONDOWN to start the dialog. The steps are as follows:

1. In ClassWizard, select the *CEx06aView* class. At this point, be sure that EX06A is Visual C++'s current project.

2. Use ClassWizard to add the *OnLButtonDown* member function.
You've done this in the examples in earlier chapters. Simply select the *CEx06aView* class name, click on the *CEx06aView* object ID, and then double-click on WM_LBUTTONDOWN.

3. **Write the code for *OnLButtonDown* in file ex06aView.cpp.** Add the boldface code below. Most of the code consists of *TRACE* statements to print the dialog data members after the user exits the dialog. The *CEx06aDialog* constructor call and the *DoModal* call are the critical statements, however:

```
void CEx06aView::OnLButtonDown(UINT nFlags, CPoint point)
{
    CEx06aDialog dlg;
    dlg.m_strName  = "Shakespeare, Will";
    dlg.m_nSsn     = 307806636;
    dlg.m_nCat     = 1;  // 0 = hourly, 1 = salary
    dlg.m_strBio   = "This person is not a well-motivated tech writer";
    dlg.m_bInsLife = TRUE;
    dlg.m_bInsDis  = FALSE;
    dlg.m_bInsMed  = TRUE;
    dlg.m_strDept  = "Documentation";
    dlg.m_strSkill = "Writer";
    dlg.m_nLang    = 0;
    dlg.m_strEduc  = "College";
    dlg.m_nLoyal   = dlg.m_nRely = 50;
    int ret = dlg.DoModal();
    TRACE("DoModal return = %d\n", ret);
    TRACE("name = %s, ssn = %d, cat = %d\n",
        dlg.m_strName, dlg.m_nSsn, dlg.m_nCat);
    TRACE("dept = %s, skill = %s, lang = %d, educ = %s\n",
        dlg.m_strDept, dlg.m_strSkill, dlg.m_nLang, dlg.m_strEduc);
    TRACE("life = %d, dis = %d, med = %d, bio = %s\n",
        dlg.m_bInsLife, dlg.m_bInsDis, dlg.m_bInsMed, dlg.m_strBio);
    TRACE("loyalty = %d, reliability = %d\n",
        dlg.m_nLoyal, dlg.m_nRely);
}
```

4. **Add code to the virtual *OnDraw* function in file ex06aView.cpp.** To prompt the user to press the left mouse button, code the *CEx06a-View::OnDraw* function. (The skeleton was generated by AppWizard.) The following boldface code (which you type in) replaces the existing code:

```
void CEx06aView::OnDraw(CDC* pDC)
{
    pDC->TextOut(0, 0, "Press the left mouse button here.");
}
```

5. **To ex06aView.cpp, add the dialog class include statement.** The *OnLButtonDown* function above depends on the declaration of class *CEx06aDialog*. You must insert the include statement

```
#include "ex06aDialog.h"
```

at the top of the *CEx06aView* class source code file (ex06aView.cpp), after the statement

```
#include "ex06aView.h"
```

6. **Build and test the application.** If you have done everything correctly, you should be able to build and run the EX06A application through Visual C++. Try entering data in each control, and then click the OK button and observe the *TRACE* results in the Debug window. Notice that the scroll bar controls don't do much yet; we'll attend to them later. Notice what happens when you press Enter while typing in text data in a control: the dialog closes immediately.

Understanding the EX06A Application

When your program calls *DoModal*, control is returned to your program only when the user closes the dialog. If you understand that, you understand modal dialogs. When you start creating modeless dialogs, you'll begin to appreciate the programming simplicity of modal dialogs. A lot happens "out of sight" as a result of that *DoModal* call, however. Here's a "what calls what" summary:

```
CDialog::DoModal
    CEx06aDialog::OnInitDialog
        …additional initialization…
        CDialog::OnInitDialog
            CWnd::UpdateData(FALSE)
                CEx06aDialog::DoDataExchange
    user enters data…
    user clicks the OK button
    CEx06aDialog::OnOK
        …additional validation…
        CDialog::OnOK
            CWnd::UpdateData(TRUE)
                CEx06aDialog::DoDataExchange
            CDialog::EndDialog(IDOK)
```

OnInitDialog and *DoDataExchange* are virtual functions overridden in the *CEx06aDialog* class. Windows calls *OnInitDialog* as part of the dialog initialization process, and that results in a call to *DoDataExchange*, a *CWnd* virtual function that was overridden by ClassWizard. Here is a listing of that function:

```
void CEx06aDialog::DoDataExchange(CDataExchange* pDX)
{
    CDialog::DoDataExchange(pDX);
    //{{AFX_DATA_MAP(CEx06aDialog)
    DDX_Text(pDX, IDC_BIO, m_strBio);
    DDX_Radio(pDX, IDC_CAT, m_nCat);
    DDX_LBString(pDX, IDC_DEPT, m_strDept);
    DDX_Check(pDX, IDC_DIS, m_bInsDis);
    DDX_CBString(pDX, IDC_EDUC, m_strEduc);
    DDX_CBIndex(pDX, IDC_LANG, m_nLang);
    DDX_Check(pDX, IDC_LIFE, m_bInsLife);
    DDX_Scroll(pDX, IDC_LOYAL, m_nLoyal);
    DDX_Check(pDX, IDC_MED, m_bInsMed);
    DDX_Text(pDX, IDC_NAME, m_strName);
    DDX_Scroll(pDX, IDC_RELY, m_nRely);
    DDX_CBString(pDX, IDC_SKILL, m_strSkill);
    DDX_Text(pDX, IDC_SSN, m_nSsn);
    DDV_MinMaxInt(pDX, m_nSsn, 0, 999999999);
    //}}AFX_DATA_MAP
}
```

The *DoDataExchange* function and the *DDX_* (exchange) and *DDV_* (validation) functions are "bidirectional." If *UpdateData* is called with a *FALSE* parameter, the functions transfer data from the data members to the dialog controls. If the parameter is *TRUE*, the functions transfer data from the dialog controls to the data members. *DDX_Text* is overloaded to accommodate a variety of data types.

The *EndDialog* function is critical to the dialog exit procedure. *DoModal* returns the parameter passed to *EndDialog*. *IDOK* accepts the dialog's data, and *IDCANCEL* cancels the dialog.

> TIP: You can write your own "custom" DDX function and wire it into Visual C++. This feature is useful if you're using a unique data type throughout your application. See MFC Technical Note #26 in the online documentation.

Enhancing the Dialog Program

The EX06A program required little coding for a lot of functionality. Now we'll make a new version of this program that uses some hand-coding to add extra features. We'll eliminate EX06A's rude habit of dumping the user in response to a press of the Enter key, and we'll hook up the scroll bar controls.

Taking Control of the *OnOK* Exit

In the original EX06A program, the *CDialog::OnOK* virtual function handled the OK button, which triggered data exchange and the exit from the dialog. Pressing the Enter key happens to have the same effect, and that might or might not be what you want. If the user presses Enter while in the Name edit control, for example, the dialog closes immediately.

What's going on here? When the user presses Enter, Windows looks to see which pushbutton has the <u>input focus</u>, as indicated on the screen by a dotted rectangle. If no button has the focus, Windows looks for the <u>default pushbutton</u> that the program or the resource specifies. (The default pushbutton has a thicker border.) If the dialog has no default button, the virtual *OnOK* function is called, even if the dialog does not contain an OK button.

You can disable the Enter key by writing a do-nothing *CEx06aDialog-::OnOK* function and adding the exit code to a new function that responds to clicking the OK button. Here are the steps:

1. **Use ClassWizard to "map" the IDOK button to the virtual *OnOK* function.**   In ClassWizard, choose *IDOK* from the *CEx06aDialog* Object IDs list, and then double-click on BN_CLICKED. This generates the prototype and skeleton for *OnOK*.

2. **Use the dialog editor to change the OK button ID.**   Select the OK button, change its ID from *IDOK* to *IDC_OK*, and then uncheck its Default Button property. Leave the *OnOK* function alone.

3. **Use ClassWizard to create a member function called *OnClickedOk*.** This *CEx06aDialog* class member function is keyed to the BN_CLICKED message from the newly renamed control *IDC_OK*.

4. **Edit the body of the *OnClickedOk* function in ex06aDialog.cpp.** This function calls the base class *OnOK* function, as did the original *CEx06aDialog::OnOK* function. Here is the code:

```
void CEx06aDialog::OnClickedOk()
{
    TRACE("CEx06aDialog::OnClickedOk\n");
    CDialog::OnOK();
}
```

123

5. **Edit the original *OnOK* function in ex06aDialog.cpp.** This function is a "leftover" handler for the old *IDOK* button. Edit the code as shown here:

```
void CEx06aDialog::OnOK()
{
    // dummy OnOK function -- do NOT call CDialog::OnOK()
    TRACE("CEx06aDialog::OnOK\n");
}
```

6. **Build and test the application.** Try pressing the Enter key now. Nothing should happen, but *TRACE* output should appear in the Debug window. Clicking the OK button should exit the dialog as before, however.

For Win32 Programmers

Dialog controls send WM_COMMAND notification messages to their parent dialogs. For a single button click, for example, the bottom 16 bits of *wParam* contain the button ID, the top 16 bits of *wParam* contain the BN_CLICKED notification code, and *lParam* contains the button handle. Most window procedure functions process these notification messages with a nested switch statement. MFC "flattens out" the message processing logic by "promoting" control notification messages to the same level as other Windows messages.

For a Delete button (for example), ClassWizard generates notification message map entries similar to these:

```
ON_BN_CLICKED(IDC_DELETE, OnDeleteClicked)
ON_BN_DOUBLECLICKED(IDC_DELETE, OnDeleteDblClicked)
```

Button events are special because they generate command messages if your dialog class doesn't have notification handlers like the ones above. As Chapter 13 explains, the application framework "routes" these command messages to various objects in your application. You could also map the control notifications with a more generic *ON_COMMAND* message-handling entry like this:

```
ON_COMMAND(IDC_DELETE, OnDelete)
```

In this case, the *OnDelete* function is unable to distinguish between a single click and a double click, but that's no problem because few Windows-based programs utilize double clicks for buttons.

OnCancel Processing

Just as pressing the Enter key triggers a call to *OnOK*, pressing the Esc key triggers a call to *OnCancel*, which results in an exit from the dialog with a *DoModal* return code of *IDCANCEL*. EX06A does no special processing for *IDCANCEL*; therefore, pressing the Esc key (or clicking the Close button) closes the dialog. You can circumvent this process by substituting a dummy *OnCancel* function, following approximately the same procedure you used for the OK button.

Hooking Up the Scroll Bar Controls

The dialog editor allows you to include scroll bar controls in your dialog, and ClassWizard lets you add integer data members. You must add code to make the Loyalty and Reliability scroll bars work.

Scroll bar controls have position and range values that can be read and written. If you set the range to (0, 100), for example, a corresponding data member with a value of 50 positions the scroll box at the center of the bar. (The function *CScrollBar::SetScrollPos* also sets the scroll box position.) The scroll bars send the WM_HSCROLL and WM_VSCROLL messages to the dialog when the user drags the scroll box or clicks the arrows. The dialog's message handlers must decode these messages and position the scroll box accordingly.

Each control you've seen so far has had its own individual message handler function. Scroll bar controls are different because all horizontal scroll bars in a dialog are tied to a single WM_HSCROLL message handler and all vertical scroll bars are tied to a single WM_VSCROLL handler. Because this monster dialog contains two horizontal scroll bars, the single WM_HSCROLL message handler must figure out which scroll bar sent the scroll message.

Here are the steps for adding the scroll bar logic to EX06A:

1. **Add the class *enum* statements for the minimum and maximum scroll range.** In ex06aDialog.h, add the following lines at the top of the class declaration:

```
enum { nMin = 0 };
enum { nMax = 100 };
```

2. **Edit the *OnInitDialog* function to initialize the scroll ranges.** In the *OnInitDialog* function, we'll set the minimum and the maximum scroll values such that the *CEx06aDialog* data members represent percentage values. A value of 100 means "Set the scroll box to the extreme right"; a value of 0 means "Set the scroll box to the extreme left."

Add the following code to the *CEx06aDialog* member function *OnInitDialog* in the file ex06aDialog.cpp:

```
CScrollBar* pSB = (CScrollBar*) GetDlgItem(IDC_LOYAL);
pSB->SetScrollRange(nMin, nMax);

pSB = (CScrollBar*) GetDlgItem(IDC_RELY);
pSB->SetScrollRange(nMin, nMax);
```

3. **Use ClassWizard to add a scroll bar message handler to *CEx06a-Dialog*.** Choose the WM_HSCROLL message, and then add the member function *OnHScroll*. Enter the following boldface code:

```
void CEx06aDialog::OnHScroll(UINT nSBCode, UINT nPos,
                             CScrollBar* pScrollBar)
{
    int nTemp1, nTemp2;

    nTemp1 = pScrollBar->GetScrollPos();
    switch(nSBCode) {
    case SB_THUMBPOSITION:
        pScrollBar->SetScrollPos(nPos);
        break;
    case SB_LINELEFT: // left arrow button
        nTemp2 = (nMax - nMin) / 10;
        if ((nTemp1 - nTemp2) > nMin) {
            nTemp1 -= nTemp2;
        }
        else {
            nTemp1 = nMin;
        }
        pScrollBar->SetScrollPos(nTemp1);
        break;
    case SB_LINERIGHT: // right arrow button
        nTemp2 = (nMax - nMin) / 10;
        if ((nTemp1 + nTemp2) < nMax) {
            nTemp1 += nTemp2;
        }
        else {
            nTemp1 = nMax;
        }
        pScrollBar->SetScrollPos(nTemp1);
        break;
    }
}
```

> NOTE: The scroll bar functions use 16-bit integers for both range and position.

4. **Build and test the application.** Build and run EX06A again. Do the scroll bars work this time? The scroll boxes should "stick" after you drag them with the mouse, and they should move when you click the scroll bars' arrows. (Notice that we haven't added logic to cover the user's click on the scroll bar itself.)

Identifying Controls: *CWnd* Pointers and Control IDs

When you lay out a dialog resource in the dialog editor, you identify each control by an ID such as *IDC_SSN*. In your program code, however, you often need access to a control's underlying window object. The MFC library provides the *CWnd::GetDlgItem* function for converting an ID to a *CWnd* pointer. You've seen this already in the *OnInitDialog* member function of class *CEx06aDialog*. The application framework "manufactured" this returned *CWnd* pointer because there never was a constructor call for the control objects. This pointer is temporary and should not be stored for later use.

> TIP: If you need to convert a *CWnd* pointer to a control ID, use the MFC library *GetDlgCtrlID* member function of class *CWnd*.

Setting the Color for the Dialog Background and for Controls

You can change the background color of individual dialogs or specific controls in a dialog, but you have to do some extra work. The parent dialog is sent a WM_CTLCOLOR message for each control immediately before the control is displayed. A WM_CTLCOLOR message is also sent on behalf of the dialog itself. If you map this message in your derived dialog class, you can set the foreground and background text colors and select a brush for the control or dialog non-text area.

Following is a sample *OnCtlColor* function that sets all edit control backgrounds to yellow and the dialog background to red. The *m_hYellowBrush* and *m_hRedBrush* variables are data members of type *HBRUSH*, initialized in the dialog's *OnInitDialog* function. The *nCtlColor* parameter indicates the type of control, and the *pWnd* parameter identifies the specific control. If you wanted to set the color for an individual edit control, you would convert *pWnd* to a child window ID and test it.

```
HBRUSH CMyDialog::OnCtlColor(CDC* pDC, CWnd* pWnd, UINT nCtlColor)
{
    if (nCtlColor == CTLCOLOR_EDIT) {
        pDC->SetBkColor(RGB(255, 255, 0));  // yellow
        return m_hYellowBrush;
    }
    if (nCtlColor == CTLCOLOR_DLG) {
        pDC->SetBkColor(RGB(255, 0, 0));    // red
        return m_hRedBrush;
    }
    return CDialog::OnCtlColor(pDC, pWnd, nCtlColor);
}
```

> **NOTE:** The dialog does not post the WM_CTLCOLOR message in the message queue; instead, it calls the Win32 *SendMessage* function to send the message immediately. Thus the message handler can return a parameter, in this case a handle to a brush. This is not an MFC *CBrush* object but rather a Win32 *HBRUSH*. You can create the brush by calling the Win32 functions *CreateSolidBrush*, *CreateHatchBrush*, and so forth.

For Win32 Programmers

Actually, Win32 no longer has a WM_CTLCOLOR message. It was replaced by control-specific messages such as WM_CTLCOLORBTN, WM_CTLCOLORDLG, and so on. MFC and ClassWizard process these messages invisibly, so your programs look as though they're mapping the old 16-bit WM_CTLCOLOR messages. This trick makes debugging more complex, but it makes portable code easier to write. Another option would be to use the *ON_MESSAGE* macro to map the real Win32 messages.

If your dialog class (or other MFC window class) doesn't map the WM_CTLCOLOR message, the framework reflects the message back to the control. When you study window subclassing in Chapter 16, you'll learn how to write your own control window classes that can process these reflected messages.

Painting Inside the Dialog Window

You can paint directly in the client area of the dialog window, but you'll avoid overwriting dialog elements if you paint only inside a control window. If you want to display text only, use the dialog editor to create a blank static control with a unique ID and then call the *CWnd::SetDlgItemText* function in a dialog member function such as *OnInitDialog* to place text in the control.

Displaying graphics is more complicated. You must use ClassWizard to add an *OnPaint* member function to the dialog; this function must convert the static control's ID to a *CWnd* pointer and get its device context. The trick is to draw inside the control window while preventing Windows from overwriting your work later. The *Invalidate/UpdateWindow* sequence achieves this. Here is an *OnPaint* function that paints a small black square in a static control:

```
void CMyDialog::OnPaint()
{
    CWnd* pWnd = GetDlgItem(IDC_STATIC1);       // IDC_STATIC1 specified
                                                //  in the dialog editor
    CDC* pControlDC = pWnd->GetDC();

    pWnd->Invalidate();
    pWnd->UpdateWindow();
    pControlDC->SelectStockObject(BLACK_BRUSH);
    pControlDC->Rectangle(0, 0, 10, 10);        // black square bullet
    pWnd->ReleaseDC(pControlDC);
}
```

As with all windows, the dialog's *OnPaint* function is called only if some part of the dialog is invalidated. You can force the *OnPaint* call from another dialog member function with the following statement:

```
Invalidate();
```

Adding Dialog Controls at Runtime

You've seen how to use the resource editor to create dialog controls at build time. If you need to add a dialog control at runtime, here are the programming steps:

1. Add an embedded control window data member to your dialog class. The MFC control window classes include *CButton*, *CEdit*, *CListBox*, and *CComboBox*. An embedded control C++ object is constructed and destroyed along with the dialog object.

2. Choose Resource Symbols from Visual C++'s View menu. Add an ID constant for the new control.

3. Use ClassWizard to map the WM_INITDIALOG message, thus overriding *CDialog::OnInitDialog*. This function should call the embedded control window's *Create* member function. This call displays the new control in the dialog. Windows will destroy the control window when it destroys the dialog window.

4. In your derived dialog class, manually add the necessary notification message handlers for your new control.

In Chapter 13, you'll be adding a rich edit control to a view at runtime.

Using Other Control Features

You've seen how to customize the control class *CScrollBar* by adding code in the dialog's *OnInitDialog* member function. You can program other controls in a similar fashion. In the *Microsoft Visual C++ MFC Library Reference*, or in the online help under "Microsoft Foundation Class Library and Templates," look at the control classes, particularly *CListBox* and *CComboBox*. Each has a number of features that ClassWizard does not directly support. Some combo boxes, for example, can support multiple selections. If you want to use these features, don't try to use ClassWizard to add data members. Instead, define your own data members and add your own exchange code in *OnInitDialog* and *OnClickedOK*.

For Win32 Programmers

If you've programmed controls in Win32, you'll know that parent windows communicate to controls via Windows messages. So what does a function such as *CListBox::InsertString* do? (You've seen this function called in your *OnInitDialog* function.) If you look at the MFC source code, you'll see that *InsertString* sends an LB_INSERTSTRING message to the designated list-box control. Other control class member functions don't send messages because they apply to all window types. The *CScrollView::SetScrollRange* function, for example, calls the Win32 *SetScrollRange* function, specifying the correct *hWnd* as a parameter.

Windows Common Controls

The controls you used in EX06A are great learning controls because they're easy to program. Now you're ready for some more "interesting" controls. We'll take a look at some important new Windows controls, introduced for Microsoft Windows 95 and available in Microsoft Windows NT. These include the progress indicator, trackbar, spin button control, list control, and tree control.

The code for these controls is in the Windows COMCTL32.DLL file. This code includes the window procedure for each control, together with code that registers a window class for each control. The registration code is called when the DLL is loaded. When your program initializes a dialog, it uses the symbolic class name in the dialog resource to connect to the window procedure in the DLL. Thus your program owns the control's window, but the code is in the DLL. Except for ActiveX controls, most controls work this way.

Example EX06B uses the aforementioned controls. Figure 6-2 shows the dialog from that example. Refer to it when you read the control descriptions that follow.

Be aware that ClassWizard offers no member variable support for the common controls. You'll have to add code to your *OnInitDialog* and *OnOK* functions to initialize and read control data. ClassWizard will, however, allow you to map notification messages from common controls.

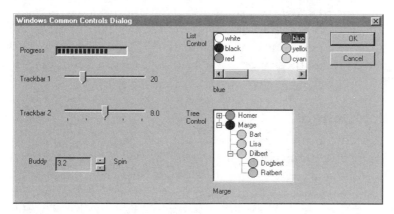

Figure 6-2.
The Windows Common Controls Dialog example.

The Progress Indicator Control

The progress indicator is the easiest common control to program and is represented by the MFC *CProgressCtrl* class. It is generally used only for output. This

131

control, together with the trackbar, can effectively replace the scroll bar controls you saw in the previous example. To initialize the progress indicator, call the *SetRange* and *SetPos* member functions in your *OnInitDialog* function, and then call *SetPos* anytime in your message handlers. The progress indicator shown in Figure 6-2 on the previous page has a range of 0 to 100, which is the default range.

The Trackbar Control

The trackbar control (class *CSliderCtrl*), sometimes called a slider, allows the user to set an "analog" value. (Trackbars would have been more effective than sliders for Loyalty and Reliability in the EX06A example.) If you specify a large range for this control—0 to 100 or more, for example—the trackbar's motion appears continuous. If you specify a small range, such as 0 to 5, the tracker moves in discrete increments. You can program tick marks to match the increments. In this discrete mode, you can use a trackbar to set such items as the display screen resolution, lens f-stop values, and so forth. The trackbar does not have a default range.

The trackbar is easier to program than the scroll bar because you don't have to map the WM_HSCROLL or WM_VSCROLL messages in the dialog class. As long as you set the range, the tracker moves when the user slides it or clicks in the body of the trackbar. You might choose to map the scroll messages anyway if you want to show the position value in another control. The *GetPos* member function returns the current position value. The top trackbar in Figure 6-2 operates continuously in the range 0 to 100. The bottom trackbar has a range of 0 to 4, and those indexes are mapped to a series of double-precision values (4.0, 5.6, 8.0, 11.0, and 16.0).

The Spin Button Control

The spin button control (class *CSpinButtonCtrl*) is an itsy-bitsy scroll bar that's most often used in conjunction with an edit control. The edit control, located just ahead of the spin control in the dialog's tabbing order, is known as the spin control's <u>buddy</u>. The idea is that the user holds down the left mouse button on the spin control to raise or lower the value in the edit control. The spin speed accelerates as the user continues to hold down the mouse button.

If your program uses an integer in the buddy, you can avoid C++ programming almost entirely. Just use ClassWizard to attach an integer data member to the edit control, and set the spin control's range in the *OnInitDialog* function. (You probably won't want the spin control's default range, which runs backward from a minimum of 100 to a maximum of 0.) Don't forget to select Auto

Buddy and Set Buddy Integer in the spin control's Styles property page. You can call the *SetRange* and *SetAccel* member functions in your *OnInitDialog* function to change the range and the acceleration profile.

If you want your edit control to display a noninteger, such as a time or a floating-point number, you must map the spin control's WM_VSCROLL (or WM_HSCROLL) messages and write handler code to convert the spin control's integer to the buddy's value.

The List Control

Use the list control (class *CListCtrl*) if you want a list that contains images as well as text. Figure 6-2 shows a list control with a "list" view style and small icons. The elements are arranged in a grid, and the control includes horizontal scrolling. When the user selects an item, the control sends a notification message, which you map in your dialog class. That message handler can determine which item the user selected. Items are identified by a zero-based integer index.

Both the list control and the tree control get their graphic images from a common control element called an <u>image list</u> (class *CImageList*). Your program must assemble the image list from icons or bitmaps and then pass an image list pointer to the list control. Your *OnInitDialog* function is a good place to create and attach the image list and to assign text strings. The *InsertItem* member function serves this purpose.

List control programming is straightforward if you stick with strings and icons. If you implement drag and drop or if you need custom owner-drawn graphics, you've got more work to do.

The Tree Control

You're already familiar with tree controls if you've used Microsoft Windows Explorer or Visual C++'s Workspace view. The MFC *CTreeCtrl* class makes it easy to add this same functionality to your own programs. Figure 6-2 on page 131 illustrates a tree control that shows a modern American combined family. The user can expand and collapse elements by clicking the + and - buttons or by double-clicking the elements. The icon next to each item is programmed to change when the user selects the item with a single click.

The list control and the tree control have some things in common: they can both use the same image list, and they share some of the same notification messages. Their methods of identifying items are different, however. The tree control uses an *HTREEITEM* handle instead of an integer index. To insert an item, you call the *InsertItem* member function, but first you must build up a *TV_INSERTSTRUCT* structure that identifies (among other things) the string, the image list index, and the handle of the parent item (which is null for top-level items).

As with list controls, infinite customization possibilities are available for the tree control. For example, you can allow the user to edit items and to insert and delete items.

The WM_NOTIFY Message

The original Windows controls sent their notifications in WM_COMMAND messages. The standard 32-bit *wParam* and *lParam* message parameters are not sufficient, however, for the information that a common control needs to send to its parent. Microsoft solved this "bandwidth" problem by defining a new message, WM_NOTIFY. With the WM_NOTIFY message, *wParam* is the control ID and *lParam* is a pointer to an *NMHDR* structure, which is managed by the control. This C structure is defined by the following code:

```
typedef struct tagNMHDR {
    HWND hwndFrom;  // handle to control sending the message
    UINT idFrom;    // ID of control sending the message
    UINT code;      // control-specific notification code
} NMHDR;
```

Many controls, however, send WM_NOTIFY messages with pointers to structures larger than *NMHDR*. Those structures contain the three members above plus appended control-specific members. Many tree control notifications, for example, pass a pointer to an *NM_TREEVIEW* structure that contains *TV_ITEM* structures, a drag point, and so forth. When ClassWizard maps a WM_NOTIFY message, it generates a pointer to the appropriate structure.

The EX06B Example

I won't try to contrive a business-oriented example that uses all the custom controls. I'll just slap the controls in a modal dialog and trust that you'll see what's going on. The steps are shown below and on the following pages. After step 3, the instructions are oriented to the individual controls rather than to the Visual C++ components you'll be using.

1. **Run AppWizard to generate the EX06B project.** Choose New from Visual C++'s File menu, and then select Microsoft AppWizard (exe) from the Projects page. Accept all the defaults but two: select Single Document and deselect Printing And Print Preview. The options and the default class names are shown here.

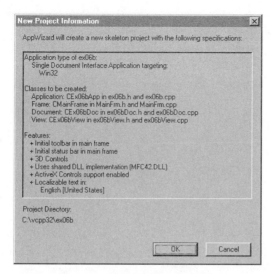

2. Create a new dialog resource with ID *IDD_DIALOG1*. Place the controls as shown back in Figure 6-2.

You can select the controls from the control palette that is shown on page 109. The following table lists the control types and their IDs.

Don't worry about the other properties now—you'll set those in the following steps. (Some controls might look different than they do in Figure 6-2 until you set their properties.) Set the tab order as shown next.

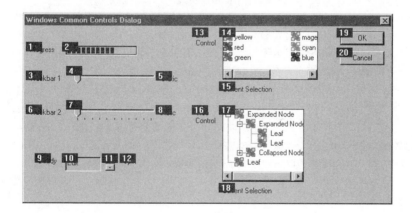

Tab Sequence	Control Type	Child Window ID
1	Static	IDC_STATIC
2	Progress	IDC_PROGRESS1
3	Static	IDC_STATIC
4	Trackbar (Slider)	IDC_TRACKBAR1
5	Static	IDC_STATIC_TRACK1
6	Static	IDC_STATIC
7	Trackbar (Slider)	IDC_TRACKBAR2
8	Static	IDC_STATIC_TRACK2
9	Static	IDC_STATIC
10	Edit	IDC_BUDDY_SPIN1
11	Spin	IDC_SPIN1
12	Static	IDC_STATIC
13	Static	IDC_STATIC
14	List control	IDC_LISTVIEW1
15	Static	IDC_STATIC_LISTVIEW1
16	Static	IDC_STATIC
17	Tree control	IDC_TREEVIEW1
18	Static	IDC_STATIC_TREEVIEW1
19	Pushbutton	IDOK
20	Pushbutton	IDCANCEL

3. **Use ClassWizard to create a new class, *CEx06bDialog*, derived from *CDialog*.** ClassWizard will automatically prompt you to create this class because it knows that the *IDD_DIALOG1* resource exists without an associated C++ class. Map the WM_INITDIALOG message, the WM-_HSCROLL message, and the WM_VSCROLL message.

4. **Program the progress control.** Because ClassWizard won't generate a data member for this control, you must do it yourself. Add a public integer data member named *m_nProgress* in the *CEx06bDialog* class header, and set it to 0 in the constructor. Also, add the following code in the *OnInitDialog* member function:

```
CProgressCtrl* pProg =
    (CProgressCtrl*) GetDlgItem(IDC_PROGRESS1);
pProg->SetRange(0, 100);
pProg->SetPos(m_nProgress);
```

5. Program the "continuous" trackbar control. Add a public integer data member named *m_nTrackbar1* to the *CEx06bDialog* header, and set it to 0 in the constructor. Next add the following code in the *OnInitDialog* member function to set the trackbar's range, to initialize its position from the data member, and to set the neighboring static control to the tracker's current value.

```
CString strText1;
CSliderCtrl* pSlide1 =
    (CSliderCtrl*) GetDlgItem(IDC_TRACKBAR1);
pSlide1->SetRange(0, 100);
pSlide1->SetPos(m_nTrackbar1);
strText1.Format("%d", pSlide1->GetPos());
SetDlgItemText(IDC_STATIC_TRACK1, strText1);
```

To keep the static control updated, you need to map the WM_HSCROLL message that the trackbar sends to the dialog. Here is the code for the handler:

```
void CEx06bDialog::OnHScroll(UINT nSBCode, UINT nPos,
                            CScrollBar* pScrollBar)
{
    CSliderCtrl* pSlide = (CSliderCtrl*) pScrollBar;
    CString strText;
    strText.Format("%d", pSlide->GetPos());
    SetDlgItemText(IDC_STATIC_TRACK1, strText);
}
```

Finally, you need to update the trackbar's *m_nTrackbar1* data member when the user clicks OK. Your natural instinct would be to put this code in the *OnOK* button handler. You would have a problem, however, if a data exchange validation error occurred involving any other control in the dialog. Your handler would set *m_nTrackbar1* even though the user might choose to cancel the dialog. To avoid this problem, add your code in the *DoDataExchange* function as shown below. If you do your own validation and detect a problem, call the *CDataExchange::Fail* function, which alerts the user with a message box.

```
if (pDX->m_bSaveAndValidate) {
    TRACE("updating trackbar data members\n");
    CSliderCtrl* pSlide1 =
        (CSliderCtrl*) GetDlgItem(IDC_TRACKBAR1);
    m_nTrackbar1 = pSlide1->GetPos();

}
```

6. Program the "discrete" trackbar control. Add a public integer data member named *m_nTrackbar2* to the *CEx06bDialog* header, and set it to 0 in the constructor. This data member is a zero-based index into the *dValue*, the array of numbers (4.0, 5.6, 8.0, 11.0, and 16.0) that the trackbar can represent. Define *dValue* as a private static double array member variable in ex06bDialog.h, and add to ex06bDialog.cpp the following line:

```
double CEx06bDialog::dValue[5] = {4.0, 5.6, 8.0, 11.0, 16.0};
```

Next add code in the *OnInitDialog* member function to set the trackbar's range and initial position.

```
CString strText2;
CSliderCtrl* pSlide2 =
    (CSliderCtrl*) GetDlgItem(IDC_TRACKBAR2);
pSlide2->SetRange(0, 4);
pSlide2->SetPos(m_nTrackbar2);
strText2.Format("%3.1f", dValue[pSlide2->GetPos()]);
SetDlgItemText(IDC_STATIC_TRACK2, strText2);
```

If you had only one trackbar, the WM_HSCROLL handler in step 5 would work. But because you have two trackbars that send WM_H-SCROLL messages, the handler must differentiate. Here is the new code:

```
void CEx06bDialog::OnHScroll(UINT nSBCode, UINT nPos,
                             CScrollBar* pScrollBar)
{
    CSliderCtrl* pSlide = (CSliderCtrl*) pScrollBar;
    CString strText;

    // Two trackbars are sending
    //   HSCROLL messages (different processing)
    switch(pScrollBar->GetDlgCtrlID()) {
    case IDC_TRACKBAR1:
        strText.Format("%d", pSlide->GetPos());
        SetDlgItemText(IDC_STATIC_TRACK1, strText);
        break;
    case IDC_TRACKBAR2:
        strText.Format("%3.1f", dValue[pSlide->GetPos()]);
        SetDlgItemText(IDC_STATIC_TRACK2, strText);
        break;
    }
}
```

This trackbar needs tick marks, so you must check the control's Tick Marks and Auto Ticks properties back in the dialog editor. With Auto

Ticks set, the trackbar will place a tick at every increment. The same data exchange considerations applied to the previous trackbar apply to this trackbar. Add the following code in the dialog class *DoDataExchange* member function inside the block for the *if* statement you added in the previous step:

```
CSliderCtrl* pSlide2 =
    (CSliderCtrl*) GetDlgItem(IDC_TRACKBAR2);
m_nTrackbar2 = pSlide2->GetPos();
```

Use the dialog editor to set the Point property of both trackbars to Bottom/Right. Select Right for the Align Text property of both the *IDC_STATIC_TRACK1* and *IDC_STATIC_TRACK2* static controls.

7. **Program the spin button control.**   The spin control depends on its buddy edit control, located immediately before it in the tab order. Use ClassWizard to add a double-precision data member called *m_dSpin* for the *IDC_BUDDY_SPIN1* edit control. We're using a *double* instead of an *int* because the *int* would require almost no programming, and that would be too easy. We want the edit control range to be 0.0 to 10.0, but the spin control itself needs an integer range. Add the following code to *OnInitDialog* to set the spin control range to 0 to 100 and to set its initial value to *m_dSpin * 10.0*:

```
CSpinButtonCtrl* pSpin =
    (CSpinButtonCtrl*) GetDlgItem(IDC_SPIN1);
pSpin->SetRange(0, 100);
pSpin->SetPos((int) (m_dSpin * 10.0));
```

To display the current value in the buddy edit control, you need to map the WM_VSCROLL message that the spin control sends to the dialog. Here's the code:

```
void CEx06bDialog::OnVScroll(UINT nSBCode, UINT nPos,
                             CScrollBar* pScrollBar)
{
    if (nSBCode == SB_ENDSCROLL) {
        return; // Reject spurious messages
    }
    // Process scroll messages from IDC_SPIN1 only
    if (pScrollBar->GetDlgCtrlID() == IDC_SPIN1) {
        CString strValue;
        strValue.Format("%3.1f", (double) nPos / 10.0);
        ((CSpinButtonCtrl*) pScrollBar)->GetBuddy()
                                    ->SetWindowText(strValue);
    }
}
```

There's no need for you to add code in *OnOK* or in *DoDataExchange* because the dialog data exchange code processes the contents of the edit control. In the dialog editor, select the spin control's Auto Buddy property and the buddy's Read-only property.

8. **Set up an image list.**   Both the list control and the tree control need an image list, and the image list needs icons.

First use the graphics editor to add icons to the project's RC file. On the companion CD-ROM, these icons are circles with black outlines and different-colored interiors. Use fancier icons if you have them. You can import an icon by choosing Resource from the Insert menu and then clicking the Import button. For this example, the icon resource IDs are as follows.

Resource ID	Icon File
IDI_BLACK	Icon1
IDI_BLUE	Icon3
IDI_CYAN	Icon5
IDI_GREEN	Icon7
IDI_PURPLE	Icon6
IDI_RED	Icon2
IDI_WHITE	Icon0
IDI_YELLOW	Icon4

Next add a private *CImageList* data member called *m_imageList* in the *CEx06bDialog* class header, and then add the following code to *OnInitDialog*:

```
HICON hIcon[8];
int n;
m_imageList.Create(16, 16, 0, 8, 8); // 32, 32 for large icons
hIcon[0] = AfxGetApp()->LoadIcon(IDI_WHITE);
hIcon[1] = AfxGetApp()->LoadIcon(IDI_BLACK);
hIcon[2] = AfxGetApp()->LoadIcon(IDI_RED);
hIcon[3] = AfxGetApp()->LoadIcon(IDI_BLUE);
hIcon[4] = AfxGetApp()->LoadIcon(IDI_YELLOW);
hIcon[5] = AfxGetApp()->LoadIcon(IDI_CYAN);
hIcon[6] = AfxGetApp()->LoadIcon(IDI_PURPLE);
hIcon[7] = AfxGetApp()->LoadIcon(IDI_GREEN);
for (n = 0; n < 8; n++) {
    m_imageList.Add(hIcon[n]);
}
```

About Icons

You probably know that a bitmap is an array of bits that represent pixels on the display. (You'll learn more about bitmaps in Chapter 11.) In Windows, an icon is a "bundle" of bitmaps. First of all, an icon has different bitmaps for different sizes. Typically, small icons are 16-by-16 pixels and large icons are 32-by-32 pixels. Within each size are two separate bitmaps: one 4-bit-per-pixel bitmap for the color image and one monochrome (1-bit-per-pixel) bitmap for the "mask." If a mask bit is 0, the corresponding image pixel represents an opaque color. If the mask bit is 1, an image color of black (0) means that the pixel is transparent and an image color of white (0xF) means that the background color is inverted at the pixel location. Windows 95 and Windows NT seem to process inverted colors a little differently than Windows 3.x does—the inverted pixels show up transparent against the desktop, black against a Windows Explorer window background, and white against list and tree control backgrounds. Don't ask me why.

Small icons were new with Windows 95. They're used in the task bar, in Windows Explorer, and in your list and tree controls, if you want them there. If an icon doesn't have a 16-by-16-pixel bitmap, Windows manufactures a small icon out of the 32-by-32-pixel bitmap, but it won't be as neat as one you draw yourself.

The graphics editor lets you create and edit icons. Look at the color palette shown here.

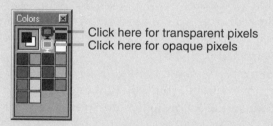

Click here for transparent pixels
Click here for opaque pixels

The top square in the upper-left portion shows you the main color for brushes, shape interiors, and so on, and the square under it shows the border color for shape outlines. You select a main color by left-clicking on a color, and you select a border color by right-clicking on a color. Now look at the top center portion of the color palette. You click on the upper "monitor" to paint transparent pixels, which are drawn in dark cyan. You click on the lower monitor to paint inverted pixels, which are drawn in red.

9. **Program the list control.** In the dialog editor, set the list control's style attributes as shown in the next illustration.

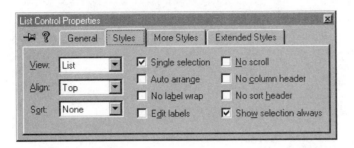

Make sure the Border style on the More Styles page is set. Next add the following code to *OnInitDialog*:

```
static char* color[] = {"white", "black", "red",
                        "blue", "yellow", "cyan",
                        "purple", "green"};
CListCtrl* pList =
    (CListCtrl*) GetDlgItem(IDC_LISTVIEW1);
pList->SetImageList(&m_imageList, LVSIL_SMALL);
for (n = 0; n < 8; n++) {
    pList->InsertItem(n, color[n], n);
}
pList->SetBkColor(RGB(0, 255, 255)); // UGLY!
pList->SetTextBkColor(RGB(0, 255, 255));
```

As the last two lines illustrate, you don't use the WM_CTLCOLOR message with common controls; you just call a function to set the background color. As you'll see when you run the program, however, the icons' inverse-color pixels look shabby.

If you use ClassWizard to map the list control's LVN_ITEM-CHANGED notification message, you'll be able to track the user's selection of items. The code in the following handler displays the selected item's text in a static control:

```
void CEx06bDialog::OnItemchangedListview1(NMHDR* pNMHDR,
                                          LRESULT* pResult)
{
    NM_LISTVIEW* pNMListView = (NM_LISTVIEW*)pNMHDR;
    CListCtrl* pList =
        (CListCtrl*) GetDlgItem(IDC_LISTVIEW1);
    int nSelected = pNMListView->iItem;
    if (nSelected >= 0) {
        CString strItem = pList->GetItemText(nSelected, 0);
```

```
        SetDlgItemText(IDC_STATIC_LISTVIEW1, strItem);
    }
    *pResult = 0;
}
```

The *NM_LISTVIEW* structure has a data member called *iItem* that contains the index of the selected item.

10. Program the tree control. In the dialog editor, set the tree control's style attributes as shown here.

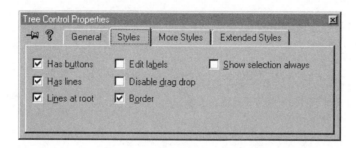

Next, add the following lines to *OnInitDialog*:

```
CTreeCtrl* pTree = (CTreeCtrl*) GetDlgItem(IDC_TREEVIEW1);
pTree->SetImageList(&m_imageList, TVSIL_NORMAL);
// tree structure common values
TV_INSERTSTRUCT tvinsert;
tvinsert.hParent = NULL;
tvinsert.hInsertAfter = TVI_LAST;
tvinsert.item.mask = TVIF_IMAGE | TVIF_SELECTEDIMAGE |
                     TVIF_TEXT;
tvinsert.item.hItem = NULL;
tvinsert.item.state = 0;
tvinsert.item.stateMask = 0;
tvinsert.item.cchTextMax = 6;
tvinsert.item.iSelectedImage = 1;
tvinsert.item.cChildren = 0;
tvinsert.item.lParam = 0;
// top level
tvinsert.item.pszText = "Homer";
tvinsert.item.iImage = 2;
HTREEITEM hDad = pTree->InsertItem(&tvinsert);
tvinsert.item.pszText = "Marge";
HTREEITEM hMom = pTree->InsertItem(&tvinsert);
// second level
tvinsert.hParent = hDad;
```

(continued)

```
tvinsert.item.pszText = "Bart";
tvinsert.item.iImage = 3;
pTree->InsertItem(&tvinsert);
tvinsert.item.pszText = "Lisa";
pTree->InsertItem(&tvinsert);
// second level
tvinsert.hParent = hMom;
tvinsert.item.pszText = "Bart";
tvinsert.item.iImage = 4;
pTree->InsertItem(&tvinsert);
tvinsert.item.pszText = "Lisa";
pTree->InsertItem(&tvinsert);
tvinsert.item.pszText = "Dilbert";
HTREEITEM hOther = pTree->InsertItem(&tvinsert);
// third level
tvinsert.hParent = hOther;
tvinsert.item.pszText = "Dogbert";
tvinsert.item.iImage = 7;
pTree->InsertItem(&tvinsert);
tvinsert.item.pszText = "Ratbert";
pTree->InsertItem(&tvinsert);
```

As you can see, this code sets TV_INSERTSTRUCT text and image indexes and calls *InsertItem* to add nodes to the tree.

Finally, use ClassWizard to map the TVN_SELCHANGED notification for the tree control. Here is the handler code to display the selected text in a static control:

```
void CEx06bDialog::OnSelchangedTreeview1(NMHDR* pNMHDR,
                                         LRESULT* pResult)
{
    NM_TREEVIEW* pNMTreeView = (NM_TREEVIEW*)pNMHDR;
    CTreeCtrl* pTree = (CTreeCtrl*) GetDlgItem(IDC_TREEVIEW1);
    HTREEITEM hSelected = pNMTreeView->itemNew.hItem;
    if (hSelected != NULL) {
        char text[31];
        TV_ITEM item;
        item.mask = TVIF_HANDLE | TVIF_TEXT;
        item.hItem = hSelected;
        item.pszText = text;
        item.cchTextMax = 30;
        VERIFY(pTree->GetItem(&item));
        SetDlgItemText(IDC_STATIC_TREEVIEW1, text);
    }
    *pResult = 0;
}
```

The *NM_TREEVIEW* structure has a data member called *itemNew* that contains information about the selected node; *itemNew.hItem* is the handle of that node. The *GetItem* function retrieves the node's data, storing the text using a pointer supplied in the *TV_ITEM* structure. The *mask* variable tells Windows that the *hItem* handle is valid going in and that text output is desired.

11. Add code to the virtual *OnDraw* function in file ex06bView.cpp.
The following boldface code replaces the previous code:

```
void CEx06bView::OnDraw(CDC* pDC)
{
    pDC->TextOut(0, 0, "Press the left mouse button here.");
}
```

12. Use ClassWizard to add the *OnLButtonDown* member function.
Edit the AppWizard-generated code as follows:

```
void CEx06bView::OnLButtonDown(UINT nFlags, CPoint point)
{
    CEx06bDialog dlg;

    dlg.m_nTrackbar1 = 20;
    dlg.m_nTrackbar2 = 2; // index for 8.0
    dlg.m_nProgress = 70; // write-only
    dlg.m_dSpin = 3.2;

    dlg.DoModal();
}
```

Add a statement to include ex06bDialog.h in file ex06bView.cpp.

13. Compile and run the program. Experiment with the controls to see how they work. We haven't added code to make the progress indicator functional; we'll cover that in Chapter 12.

Other Windows Common Controls

You've seen most of the common controls that appear on the dialog editor control palette. We've skipped the animation control because this book doesn't cover multimedia, and we've skipped the hot key control because it isn't very interesting. The tab control is interesting, but you seldom use it inside another dialog. Chapter 13 shows you how to construct a tabbed dialog, sometimes known as a property sheet. In Chapter 13, you'll also see an application that is built around the *CRichEditView* class, which incorporates the Windows rich edit control.

The Modeless Dialog and Windows Common Dialogs

In Chapter 6, you saw the ordinary modal dialog and most of the controls for Microsoft Windows. Now you'll move on to the modeless dialog and to the common dialogs for Microsoft Windows 95 and Microsoft Windows NT versions 4.0 and later. Modeless dialogs, as you'll remember, allow the user to work elsewhere in the application while the dialog is active. The common dialog classes are the C++ programming interface to the group of Windows utility dialogs that include File Open, Page Setup, Color, and so forth and that are supported by the dynamic link library COMDLG32.DLL.

In this chapter's first example, you'll build a simple modeless dialog that is controlled from a view. In the second example, you'll derive from the COMDLG32 *CFileDialog* class a class that allows file deletion.

Modeless Dialogs

In the Microsoft Foundation Class (MFC) Library version 6.0, modal and modeless dialogs share the same base class, *CDialog*, and they both use a dialog resource that you can build with the dialog editor. If you're using a modeless dialog with a view, you'll need to know some specialized programming techniques.

Creating Modeless Dialogs

For modal dialogs, you've already learned that you construct a dialog object using a *CDialog* constructor that takes a resource template ID as a parameter, and then you display the modal dialog window by calling the *DoModal* member function. The window ceases to exist as soon as *DoModal* returns. Thus, you can construct a modal dialog object on the stack, knowing that the dialog window has been destroyed by the time the C++ dialog object goes out of scope.

Modeless dialogs are more complicated. You start by invoking the *CDialog* default constructor to construct the dialog object, but then to create the dialog window you need to call the *CDialog::Create* member function instead of *DoModal*. *Create* takes the resource ID as a parameter and returns immediately with the dialog window still on the screen. You must worry about exactly when to construct the dialog object, when to create the dialog window, when to destroy the dialog, and when to process user-entered data.

Here's a summary of the differences between creating a modal dialog and a modeless dialog.

	Modal Dialog	Modeless Dialog
Constructor used	Constructor with resource ID param	Default constructor (no params)
Function used to create window	*DoModal*	*Create* with resource ID param

User-Defined Messages

Suppose you want the modeless dialog window to be destroyed when the user clicks the dialog's OK button. This presents a problem. How does the view know that the user has clicked the OK button? The dialog could call a view class member function directly, but that would "marry" the dialog to a particular view class. A better solution is for the dialog to send the view a user-defined message as the result of a call to the OK button message-handling function. When the view gets the message, it can destroy the dialog window (but not the object). This sets the stage for the creation of a new dialog.

You have two options for sending Windows messages: the *CWnd::SendMessage* function or the *PostMessage* function. The former causes an immediate call to the message-handling function, and the latter posts a message in the Windows message queue. Because there's a slight delay with the *PostMessage* option, it's reasonable to expect that the handler function has returned by the time the view gets the message.

Dialog Ownership

Now suppose you've accepted the dialog default pop-up style, which means that the dialog isn't confined to the view's client area. As far as Windows is concerned, the dialog's "owner" is the application's main frame window (introduced in

Chapter 13), not the view. You need to know the dialog's view to send the view a message. Therefore, your dialog class must track its own view through a data member that the constructor sets. The *CDialog* constructor's *pParent* parameter doesn't have any effect here, so don't bother using it.

A Modeless Dialog Example—EX07A

We could convert the Chapter 6 monster dialog to a modeless dialog, but starting from scratch with a simpler dialog is easier. Example EX07A uses a dialog with one edit control, an OK button, and a Cancel button. As in the Chapter 6 example, pressing the left mouse button while the mouse cursor is inside the view window brings up the dialog, but now we have the option of destroying it in response to another event—pressing the <u>right</u> mouse button when the mouse cursor is inside the view window. We'll allow only one open dialog at a time, so we must be sure that a second left button press doesn't bring up a duplicate dialog.

To summarize the upcoming steps, the EX07A view class has a single associated dialog object that is constructed on the heap when the view is constructed. The dialog window is created and destroyed in response to user actions, but the dialog object is not destroyed until the application terminates.

Here are the steps to create the EX07A example:

1. Run AppWizard to produce \vcpp32\ex07a\ex07a. Accept all the defaults but two: select Single Document and deselect Printing And Print Preview. The options and the default class names are shown here.

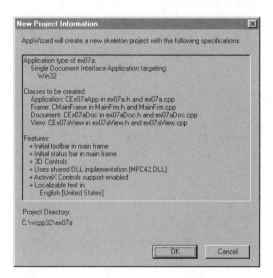

2. Use the dialog editor to create a dialog resource. Choose Resource from Visual C++'s Insert menu, and then select Dialog. The dialog editor assigns the ID *IDD_DIALOG1* to the new dialog. Change the dialog caption to *Modeless Dialog*. Accept the default OK and Cancel buttons with IDs *IDOK* and *IDCANCEL*, and then add a static text control and an edit control with the default ID *IDC_EDIT1*. Change the static text control's caption to *Edit 1*. Here is the completed dialog.

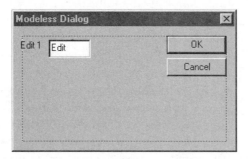

NOTE: Be sure to select the dialog's Visible property.

3. Use ClassWizard to create the *CEx07aDialog* class. Choose Class-Wizard from Microsoft Visual C++'s View menu. Fill in the New Class dialog as shown here, and then click the OK button.

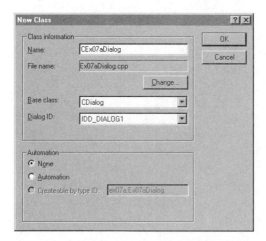

Add the message-handling functions shown next. To add a message-handling function, click on an object ID, click on a message, and then click the Add Function button. The Add Member Function dialog box appears. Edit the function name if necessary, and click the OK button.

Object ID	Message	Member Function
IDCANCEL	BN_CLICKED	*OnCancel*
IDOK	BN_CLICKED	*OnOK*

4. **Add a variable to the *CEx07aDialog* class.** While in ClassWizard, click on the Member Variables tab, choose the *IDC_EDIT1* control, and then click the Add Variable button to add the *CString* variable *m_strEdit1*.

5. **Edit ex07aDialog.h to add a view pointer and function prototypes.** Type in the following boldface code in the *CEx07aDialog* class declaration:

```
private:
    CView* m_pView;
```

Also, add the function prototypes as follows:

```
public:
    CEx07aDialog(CView* pView);
    BOOL Create();
```

NOTE: Using the *CView* class rather than the *CEx07aView* class allows the dialog class to be used with any view class.

6. **Edit ex07aDialog.h to define the WM_GOODBYE message ID.** Add the following line of code:

```
#define WM_GOODBYE    WM_USER + 5
```

The Windows constant WM_USER is the first message ID available for user-defined messages. The application framework uses a few of these messages, so we'll skip over the first five messages.

NOTE: Visual C++ maintains a list of symbol definitions in your project's resource.h file, but the resource editor does not understand constants based on other constants. Don't manually add WM_GOOD-BYE to resource.h because Visual C++ might delete it.

7. **Add the modeless constructor in the file ex07aDialog.cpp.** You could modify the existing *CEx07aDialog* constructor, but if you add a separate one, the dialog class can serve for both modal and modeless dialogs. Add the lines on the following page.

```
CEx07aDialog::CEx07aDialog(CView* pView)  // modeless constructor
{
    m_pView = pView;
}
```

You should also add the following line to the AppWizard-generated modal constructor:

```
m_pView = NULL;
```

The C++ compiler is clever enough to distinguish between the modeless constructor *CEx07aDialog(CView*)* and the modal constructor *CEx07a-Dialog(CWnd*)*. If the compiler sees an argument of class *CView* or a derived *CView* class, it generates a call to the modeless constructor. If it sees an argument of class *CWnd* or another derived *CWnd* class, it generates a call to the modal constructor.

8. **Add the *Create* function in ex07aDialog.cpp.** This derived dialog class *Create* function calls the base class function with the dialog resource ID as a parameter. Add the following lines:

```
BOOL CEx07aDialog::Create()
{
    return CDialog::Create(CEx07aDialog::IDD);
}
```

> NOTE: *Create* is not a virtual function. You could have chosen a different name if you had wanted to.

9. **Edit the *OnOK* and *OnCancel* functions in ex07aDialog.cpp.** These virtual functions generated by ClassWizard are called in response to dialog button clicks. Add the following boldface code:

```
void CEx07aDialog::OnCancel()  // not really a message handler
{
    if (m_pView != NULL) {
        // modeless case -- do not call base class OnCancel
        m_pView->PostMessage(WM_GOODBYE, IDCANCEL);
    }
    else {
        CDialog::OnCancel(); // modal case
    }
}

void CEx07aDialog::OnOK()        // not really a message handler
{
    if (m_pView != NULL) {
        // modeless case -- do not call base class OnOK
        UpdateData(TRUE);
```

```
            m_pView->PostMessage(WM_GOODBYE, IDOK);
    }
    else {
        CDialog::OnOK(); // modal case
    }
}
```

If the dialog is being used as a modeless dialog, it sends the user-defined message WM_GOODBYE to the view. We'll worry about handling the message later.

> **NOTE:** For a modeless dialog, be sure you do <u>not</u> call the *CDialog::OnOK* or *CDialog::OnCancel* function. This means you <u>must</u> override these virtual functions in your derived class; otherwise, using the Esc key, the Enter key, or a button click would result in a call to the base class functions, which call the Windows *EndDialog* function. *EndDialog* is appropriate only for modal dialogs. In a modeless dialog, you must call *DestroyWindow* instead, and if necessary, you must call *UpdateData* to transfer data from the dialog controls to the class data members.

10. **Edit the ex07aView.h header file.** You need a data member to hold the dialog pointer:

```
private:
    CEx07aDialog* m_pDlg;
```

If you add the forward declaration

```
class CEx07aDialog;
```

at the beginning of ex07aView.h, you won't have to include ex07aDialog.h in every module that includes ex07aView.h.

11. **Modify the *CEx07aView* constructor and destructor in the file ex07aView.cpp.** The *CEx07aView* class has a data member *m_pDlg* that points to the view's *CEx07aDialog* object. The view constructor constructs the dialog object on the heap, and the view destructor deletes it. Add the following boldface code:

```
CEx07aView::CEx07aView()
{
    m_pDlg = new CEx07aDialog(this);
}

CEx07aView::~CEx07aView()
{
    delete m_pDlg; // destroys window if not already destroyed
}
```

12. **Add code to the virtual *OnDraw* function in the ex07aView.cpp file.**
The *CEx07aView OnDraw* function (whose skeleton was generated by AppWizard) should be coded as follows in order to prompt the user to press the mouse button:

```
void CEx07aView::OnDraw(CDC* pDC)
{
    pDC->TextOut(0, 0, "Press the left mouse button here.");
}
```

13. **Use ClassWizard to add *CEx07aView* mouse message handlers.**
Add handlers for the WM_LBUTTONDOWN and WM_RBUTTON-DOWN messages. Now edit the code in file ex07aView.cpp as follows:

```
void CEx07aView::OnLButtonDown(UINT nFlags, CPoint point)
{
    // creates the dialog if not created already
    if (m_pDlg->GetSafeHwnd() == 0) {
        m_pDlg->Create(); // displays the dialog window
    }
}

void CEx07aView::OnRButtonDown(UINT nFlags, CPoint point)
{
    m_pDlg->DestroyWindow();
    // no problem if window was already destroyed
}
```

For most window types except main frame windows, the *DestroyWindow* function does not destroy the C++ object. We want this behavior because we'll take care of the dialog object's destruction in the view destructor.

14. **Add the dialog header include statement to file ex07aView.cpp.**
While you're in ex07aView.cpp, add the following dialog header include statement after the view header include statement:

```
#include "ex07aView.h"
#include "ex07aDialog.h"
```

15. **Add your own message code for the WM_GOODBYE message.**
Because ClassWizard does not support user-defined messages, you must write the code yourself. This task makes you appreciate the work Class-Wizard does for the other messages.

❑ In ex07aView.cpp, add the following line after the *BEGIN_MES-SAGE_MAP* statement but outside the *AFX_MSG_MAP* brackets:

```
ON_MESSAGE(WM_GOODBYE, OnGoodbye)
```

❑ Also in ex07aView.cpp, add the message handler function itself:

```
LRESULT CEx07aView::OnGoodbye(WPARAM wParam, LPARAM lParam)
{
    // message received in response to modeless dialog OK
    //  and Cancel buttons
    TRACE("CEx07aView::OnGoodbye %x, %lx\n", wParam, lParam);
    TRACE("Dialog edit1 contents = %s\n",
        (const char*) m_pDlg->m_strEdit1);
    m_pDlg->DestroyWindow();
    return 0L;
}
```

❑ In ex07aView.h, add the following function prototype before the *DECLARE_MESSAGE_MAP()* statement but outside the *AFX_ MSG* brackets:

```
afx_msg LRESULT OnGoodbye(WPARAM wParam, LPARAM lParam);
```

With Win32, the *wParam* and *lParam* parameters are the usual means of passing message data. In a mouse button down message, for example, the mouse *x* and *y* coordinates are packed into the *lParam* value. With the MFC library, message data is passed in more meaningful parameters. The mouse position is passed as a *CPoint* object. User-defined messages must use *wParam* and *lParam*, so you can use these two variables however you want. In this example, we've put the button ID in *wParam*.

16. **Build and test the application.**   Build and run EX07A. Press the left mouse button, and then press the right button. (Be sure the mouse cursor is outside the dialog window when you press the right mouse button.) Press the left mouse button again and enter some data, and then click the dialog's OK button. Does the view's *TRACE* statement correctly list the edit control's contents?

> NOTE: If you use the EX07A view and dialog classes in an MDI application, each MDI child window can have one modeless dialog. When the user closes an MDI child window, the child's modeless dialog is destroyed because the view's destructor calls the dialog destructor, which, in turn, destroys the dialog window.

The *CFormView* Class—
A Modeless Dialog Alternative

If you need an application based on a single modeless dialog, the *CFormView* class will save you a lot of work. You'll have to wait until Chapter 16, however, because the *CFormView* class is most useful when coupled with the *CDocument* class, and we haven't progressed that far in our exploration of the application framework.

The Windows Common Dialogs

Windows provides a group of standard user interface dialogs, and these are supported by the MFC library classes. You are probably familiar with all or most of these dialogs because so many Windows-based applications, including Visual C++, already use them. All the common dialog classes are derived from a common base class, *CCommonDialog*. A list of the COMDLG32 classes is shown in the following table.

Class	Purpose
CColorDialog	Allows the user to select or create a color
CFileDialog	Allows the user to open or save a file
CFindReplaceDialog	Allows the user to substitute one string for another
CPageSetupDialog	Allows the user to input page measurement parameters
CFontDialog	Allows the user to select a font from a list of available fonts
CPrintDialog	Allows the user to set up the printer and print a document

Here's one characteristic that all common dialogs share: they gather information from the user, but they don't do anything with it. The file dialog can help the user select a file to open, but it really just provides your program with the pathname—your program must make the call that opens the file. Similarly, a font dialog fills in a structure that describes a font, but it doesn't create the font.

Using the *CFileDialog* Class Directly

Using the *CFileDialog* class to open a file is easy. The following code opens a file that the user has selected through the dialog:

```
CFileDialog dlg(TRUE, "bmp", "*.bmp");
if (dlg.DoModal() == IDOK) {
    CFile file;
    VERIFY(file.Open(dlg.GetPathName(), CFile::modeRead));
}
```

The first constructor parameter (*TRUE*) specifies that this object is a "File Open" dialog instead of a "File Save" dialog. The default file extension is *bmp*, and **.bmp* appears first in the filename edit box. The *CFileDialog::GetPath-Name* function returns a *CString* object that contains the full pathname of the selected file.

Deriving from the Common Dialog Classes

Most of the time, you can use the common dialog classes directly. If you derive your own classes, you can add functionality without duplicating code. Each COMDLG32 dialog works a little differently, however. The next example is specific to the file dialog, but it should give you some ideas for customizing the other common dialogs.

> **N O T E :** In the early editions of this book, the EX07B example dynamically created controls inside the standard file dialog. That technique doesn't work in Win32, but the nested dialog method described here has the same effect.

Nested Dialogs

Win32 provides a way to "nest" one dialog inside another so that multiple dialogs appear as one seamless whole. You must first create a dialog resource template with a "hole" in it—typically a group box control—with the specific child window ID *stc32 (=0x045f)*. Your program sets some parameters that tell COMDLG32 to use your template. In addition, your program must hook into the COMDLG32 message loop so that it gets first crack at selected notifications. When you're done with all of this, you'll notice that you have created a dialog window that is a child of the COMDLG32 dialog window, even though your template wraps COMDLG32's template.

This sounds difficult, and it is unless you use MFC. With MFC, you build the dialog resource template as described above, derive a class from one of the common dialog base classes, add the class-specific connection code in *OnInit-Dialog*, and then happily use ClassWizard to map the messages that originate from your template's new controls.

NOTE: Windows NT 3.51 uses an earlier version of the common dialogs DLL that does not support the new Windows namespace feature. The nested dialog technique illustrated in the EX07B example won't work with the Windows NT 3.51 version of the file dialog.

A *CFileDialog* Example—EX07B

In this example, you will derive a class *CEx07bDialog* that adds a working Delete All Matching Files button to the standard file dialog. It also changes the dialog's title and changes the Open button's caption to Delete (to delete a single file). The example illustrates how you can use nested dialogs to add new controls to standard common dialogs. The new file dialog is activated as in the previous examples—by pressing the left mouse button when the mouse cursor is in the view window. Because you should be gaining skill with Visual C++, the following steps won't be as detailed as those for the earlier examples. Figure 7-1 shows what the dialog looks like.

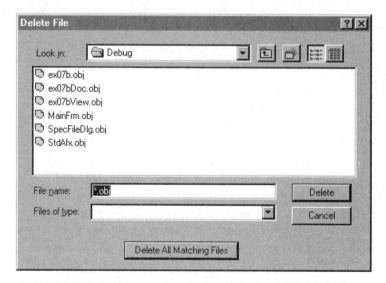

Figure 7-1.
The Delete File dialog in action.

Follow these steps to build the EX07B application:

1. **Run AppWizard to produce \vcpp32\ex07b\ex07b.** Accept all the defaults but two: select Single Document and deselect Printing And Print Preview. The options and the default class names are shown in the next graphic.

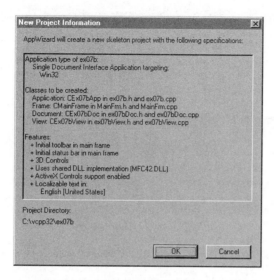

2. **Use the dialog editor to create a dialog resource.**   Make the dialog box
   about 3-by-5 inches, and use the ID *IDD_FILESPECIAL*. Set the dialog's
   Style property to Child, its Border property to None, and select its Clip
   Siblings and Visible properties. Create the template with a button with ID
   IDC_DELETE and a group box with ID *stc32=0x045f*, as shown here.

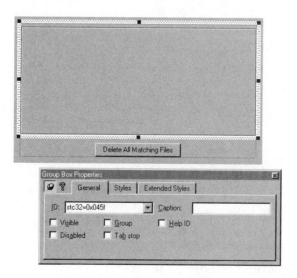

   Check your work by choosing Resource Symbols from the Visual C++ View
   menu. You should see a symbol list like the one shown in the graphic on
   the following page.

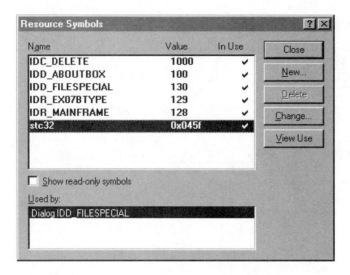

3. **Use ClassWizard to create the *CSpecialFileDialog* class.** Fill in the
New Class dialog, as shown here, and then click the Change button.

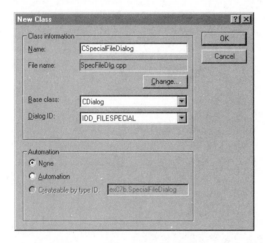

Change the names to SpecFileDlg.h and SpecFileDlg.cpp. Unfortunately,
we cannot use the Base Class drop-down list to change the base class to
CFileDialog, as that would decouple our class from the *IDD_FILESPECIAL*
template. We have to change the base class by hand.

4. **Edit the file SpecFileDlg.h.** Change the line

```
class CSpecialFileDialog : public CDialog
```

to

```
class CSpecialFileDialog : public CFileDialog
```

Add the following two public data members:

```
CString m_strFilename;
BOOL m_bDeleteAll;
```

Finally, edit the constructor declaration:

```
CSpecialFileDialog(BOOL bOpenFileDialog,
    LPCTSTR lpszDefExt = NULL,
    LPCTSTR lpszFileName = NULL,
    DWORD dwFlags = OFN_HIDEREADONLY | OFN_OVERWRITEPROMPT,
    LPCTSTR lpszFilter = NULL,
    CWnd* pParentWnd = NULL);
```

5. **Replace *CDialog* with *CFileDialog* in SpecFileDlg.h.** Choose Replace from Visual C++'s Edit menu, and replace this name globally.

6. **Edit the *CSpecialFileDialog* constructor in SpecFileDlg.cpp.** The derived class destructor must invoke the base class constructor and initialize the *m_bDeleteAll* data member. In addition, it must set some members of the *CFileDialog* base class data member *m_ofn*, which is an instance of the Win32 *OPENFILENAME* structure. The *Flags* and *lpTemplateName* members control the coupling to your *IDD_FILESPECIAL* template, and the *lpstrTitle* member changes the main dialog box title. Edit the constructor as follows:

```
CSpecialFileDialog::CSpecialFileDialog(BOOL bOpenFileDialog,
        LPCTSTR lpszDefExt, LPCTSTR lpszFileName, DWORD dwFlags,
        LPCTSTR lpszFilter, CWnd* pParentWnd)
    : CFileDialog(bOpenFileDialog, lpszDefExt, lpszFileName,
        dwFlags, lpszFilter, pParentWnd)
{
    //{{AFX_DATA_INIT(CSpecialFileDialog)
        // NOTE: the ClassWizard will add member initialization here
    //}}AFX_DATA_INIT
    m_ofn.Flags |= OFN_ENABLETEMPLATE;
    m_ofn.lpTemplateName = MAKEINTRESOURCE(IDD_FILESPECIAL);
    m_ofn.lpstrTitle = "Delete File";
    m_bDeleteAll = FALSE;
}
```

7. **Map the WM_INITDIALOG message in the *CSpecialDialog* class.** The *OnInitDialog* member function needs to change the common dialog's Open button caption to Delete. The child window ID is *IDOK*.

```
BOOL bRet = CFileDialog::OnInitDialog();
if (bRet == TRUE) {
    GetParent()->GetDlgItem(IDOK)->SetWindowText("Delete");
}
return bRet;
```

161

8. **Map the new IDC_DELETE button (Delete All Matching Files) in the *CSpecialDialog* class.** The *OnDelete* member function sets the *m_bDeleteAll* flag and then forces the main dialog to exit as if the Cancel button had been clicked. The client program (in this case, the view) gets the *IDCANCEL* return from *DoModal* and reads the flag to see whether it should delete all files. Here is the function:

```
void CSpecialFileDialog::OnDelete()
{
    m_bDeleteAll = TRUE;
    // 0x480 is the child window ID of the File Name edit control
    //    (as determined by SPYXX)
    GetParent()->GetDlgItem(0x480)->GetWindowText(m_strFilename);
    GetParent()->SendMessage(WM_COMMAND, IDCANCEL);
}
```

9. **Add code to the virtual *OnDraw* function in file ex07bView.cpp.** The *CEx07bView OnDraw* function (whose skeleton was generated by AppWizard) should be coded as follows to prompt the user to press the mouse button:

```
void CEx07bView::OnDraw(CDC* pDC)
{
    pDC->TextOut(0, 0, "Press the left mouse button here.");
}
```

10. **Add the OnLButtonDown message handler to the *CEx07bView* class.** Use ClassWizard to create the message handler for WM_LBUTTON-DOWN, and then edit the code as follows:

```
void CEx07bView::OnLButtonDown(UINT nFlags, CPoint point)
{
    CSpecialFileDialog dlgFile(TRUE, NULL, "*.obj");
    CString strMessage;
    int nModal = dlgFile.DoModal();
    if ((nModal == IDCANCEL) && (dlgFile.m_bDeleteAll)) {
        strMessage.Format(
            "Are you sure you want to delete all %s files?",
            dlgFile.m_strFilename);
        if (AfxMessageBox(strMessage, MB_YESNO) == IDYES) {
            HANDLE h;
            WIN32_FIND_DATA fData;
            while((h = ::FindFirstFile(dlgFile.m_strFilename, &fData))
                    != (HANDLE) 0xFFFFFFFF) { // no MFC equivalent
                if (::DeleteFile(fData.cFileName) == FALSE) {
                    strMessage.Format("Unable to delete file %s\n",
                        fData.cFileName);
```

```
                AfxMessageBox(strMessage);
                break;
            }
        }
    }
}
else if (nModal == IDOK) {
    CString strSingleFilename = dlgFile.GetPathName();
    strMessage.Format(
        "Are you sure you want to delete %s?", strSingleFilename);
    if (AfxMessageBox(strMessage, MB_YESNO) == IDYES) {
        CFile::Remove(strSingleFilename);
    }
}
}
```

Remember that common dialogs just gather data. Since the view is the client of the dialog, the view must call *DoModal* for the file dialog object and then figure out what to do with the information returned. In this case, the view has the return value from *DoModal* (either *IDOK* or *IDCANCEL*) and the value of the public *m_bDeleteAll* data member, and it can call various *CFileDialog* member functions such as *GetPathName*. If *DoModal* returns *IDCANCEL* and the flag is *TRUE*, the function makes the Win32 file system calls necessary to delete all the matching files. If *DoModal* returns *IDOK*, the function can use the MFC *CFile* functions to delete an individual file.

Using the global *AfxMessageBox* function is a convenient way to pop up a simple dialog that displays some text and then queries the user for a Yes/No answer. The *Microsoft Foundation Classes And Templates* section in the online help describes all of the message box variations and options.

Of course, you'll need to include the statement

```
#include "SpecFileDlg.h"
```

after the line

```
#include "ex07bView.h"
```

11. **Build and test the application.** Build and run EX07B. Pressing the left mouse button should bring up the Delete File dialog, and you should be able to use it to navigate through the disk directory and to delete files. Be careful not to delete your important source files!

Other Customization for *CFileDialog*

In the EX07B example, you added a pushbutton to the dialog. It's easy to add other controls too. Just put them in the resource template, and if they are standard Windows controls such as edit controls or list boxes, you can use ClassWizard to add data members and DDX/DDV code to your derived class. The client program can set the data members before calling *DoModal*, and it can retrieve the updated values after *DoModal* returns.

> NOTE: Even if you don't use nested dialogs, two windows are still associated with a *CFileDialog* object. Suppose you have overridden *OnInitDialog* in a derived class and you want to assign an icon to the file dialog. You must call *CWnd::GetParent* to get the top-level window, just as you did in the EX07B example. Here's the code:

```
HICON hIcon = AfxGetApp()->LoadIcon(ID_MYICON);
GetParent()->SetIcon(hIcon, TRUE);        // Set big icon
GetParent()->SetIcon(hIcon, FALSE);       // Set small icon
```

CHAPTER EIGHT

Using ActiveX Controls

Microsoft Visual Basic (VB) was introduced in 1991 and has proven to be a wildly popular and successful application development system for Microsoft Windows. Part of its success is attributable to its open-ended nature. The 16-bit versions of VB (versions 1 through 3) supported Visual Basic controls (VBXs), ready-to-run software components that VB developers could buy or write themselves. VBXs became the center of a whole industry, and pretty soon there were hundreds of them. At Microsoft, the Microsoft Foundation Class (MFC) team figured out a way for Microsoft Visual C++ programmers to use VBXs in their programs, too.

The VBX standard, which was highly dependent on the 16-bit segment architecture, did not make it to the 32-bit world. Now ActiveX Controls (formerly known as OLE controls, or OCXs) are the industrial-strength replacement for VBXs based on Microsoft COM technology. ActiveX controls can be used by application developers in both VB and Visual C++ 6.0. While VBXs were written mostly in plain C, ActiveX controls can be written in C++ with the help of the MFC library or with the help of the ActiveX Template Library (ATL).

This chapter is not about writing ActiveX controls; it's about using them in a Visual C++ application. The premise here is that you can learn to use ActiveX controls without knowing much about the Component Object Model (COM) on which they're based. After all, Microsoft doesn't require that VB programmers be COM experts. To effectively write ActiveX controls, however, you need to know a bit more, starting with the fundamentals of COM. Consider picking up a copy of Adam Denning's *ActiveX Controls Inside Out* (Microsoft Press, 1997) if you're serious about creating ActiveX controls. Of course, knowing more ActiveX Control theory won't hurt when you're using the controls in your programs. Chapters 24, 25, and 30 of this book are a good place to start.

ActiveX Controls vs. Ordinary Windows Controls

An ActiveX control is a software module that plugs into your C++ program the same way a Windows control does. At least that's the way it seems at first. It's worthwhile here to analyze the similarities and differences between ActiveX controls and the controls you already know.

Ordinary Controls—A Frame of Reference

In Chapter 6, you used ordinary Windows controls such as the edit control and the list box, and you saw the Windows common controls that work in much the same way. These controls are all child windows that you use most often in dialogs, and they are represented by MFC classes such as *CEdit* and *CTreeCtrl*. The client program is always responsible for the creation of the control's child window.

Ordinary controls send notification command messages (standard Windows messages), such as BN_CLICKED, to the dialog. If you want to perform an action on the control, you call a C++ control class member function, which sends a Windows message to the control. The controls are all windows in their own right. All the MFC control classes are derived from *CWnd*, so if you want to get the text from an edit control, you call *CWnd::GetWindowText*. But even that function works by sending a message to the control.

Windows controls are an integral part of Windows, even though the Windows common controls are in a separate DLL. Another species of ordinary control, the so-called <u>custom</u> <u>control</u>, is a programmer-created control that acts as an ordinary control in that it sends WM_COMMAND notifications to its parent window and receives user-defined messages. You'll see one of these in Chapter 22.

How ActiveX Controls Are Similar to Ordinary Controls

You can consider an ActiveX control to be a child window, just as an ordinary control is. If you want to include an ActiveX control in a dialog, you use the dialog editor to place it there, and the identifier for the control turns up in the resource template. If you're creating an ActiveX control on the fly, you call a *Create* member function for a class that represents the control, usually in the WM_CREATE handler for the parent window. When you want to manipulate an ActiveX control, you call a C++ member function, just as you do for a Windows control. The window that contains a control is called a <u>container</u>.

How ActiveX Controls Are Different from Ordinary Controls—Properties and Methods

The most prominent ActiveX Controls features are properties and methods. Those C++ member functions that you call to manipulate a control instance all revolve around properties and methods. Properties have symbolic names that are matched to integer indexes. For each property, the control designer assigns a property name, such as BackColor or GridCellEffect, and a property type, such as string, integer, or double. There's even a picture type for bitmaps and icons. The client program can set an individual ActiveX control property by specifying the property's integer index and its value. The client can get a property by specifying the index and accepting the appropriate return value. In certain cases, ClassWizard lets you define data members in your client window class that are associated with the properties of the controls the client class contains. The generated Dialog Data Exchange (DDX) code exchanges data between the control properties and the client class data members.

ActiveX Controls methods are like functions. A method has a symbolic name, a set of parameters, and a return value. You call a method by calling a C++ member function of the class that represents the control. A control designer can define any needed methods, such as *PreviousYear*, *LowerControlRods*, and so forth.

An ActiveX control doesn't send WM_ notification messages to its container the way ordinary controls do; instead, it "fires events." An event has a symbolic name and can have an arbitrary sequence of parameters—it's really a container function that the control calls. Like ordinary control notification messages, events don't return a value to the ActiveX control. Examples of events are Click, KeyDown, and NewMonth. Events are mapped in your client class just as control notification messages are.

In the MFC world, ActiveX controls act just like child windows, but there's a significant layer of code between the container window and the control window. In fact, the control might not even have a window. When you call *Create*, the control's window isn't created directly; instead, the control code is loaded and given the command for "in-place activation." The ActiveX control then creates its own window, which MFC lets you access through a *CWnd* pointer. It's not a good idea for the client to use the control's *hWnd* directly, however.

A DLL is used to store one or more ActiveX controls, but the DLL often has an OCX filename extension instead of a DLL extension. Your container program loads the DLLs when it needs them, using sophisticated COM techniques that rely on the Windows Registry. For the time being, simply accept the fact that once you specify an ActiveX control at design time, it will be loaded for you at runtime. Obviously, when you ship a program that requires special ActiveX controls, you'll have to include the OCX files and an appropriate setup program.

Installing ActiveX Controls

Let's assume you've found a nifty ActiveX control that you want to use in your project. Your first step is to copy the control's DLL to your hard disk. You could put it anywhere, but it's easier to track your ActiveX controls if you put them in one place, such as in the system directory (typically \Windows\System for Microsoft Windows 95 or \Winnt\System32 for Microsoft Windows NT). Copy associated files such as help (HLP) or license (LIC) files to the same directory.

Your next step is to register the control in the Windows Registry. Actually, the ActiveX control registers itself when a client program calls a special exported function. The Windows utility Regsvr32 is a client that accepts the control name on the command line. Regsvr32 is suitable for installation scripts, but another program, RegComp, in the project REGCOMP on the companion CD-ROM for this book, lets you find your control by browsing the disk. Some controls have licensing requirements, which might involve extra entries to the Registry. (See Chapters 15, 17, 24, and 25 for information about how the Windows Registry works.) Licensed controls usually come with setup programs that take care of those details.

After you register your ActiveX control, you must install it <u>in</u> <u>each</u> <u>project</u> that uses it. That doesn't mean that the OCX file gets copied. It means that ClassWizard generates a copy of a C++ class that's specific to the control, and it means that the control shows up in the dialog editor control palette for that project.

To install an ActiveX control in a project, choose Add To Project from the Project menu and then choose Components And Controls. Select Registered ActiveX Controls, as shown in the following illustration.

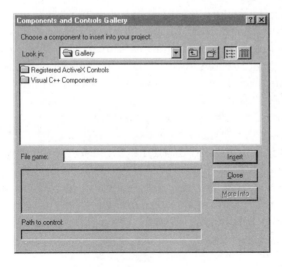

This gets you the list of all the ActiveX controls currently registered on your system. A typical list is shown here.

The Calendar Control

The MSCal.ocx control is a popular Microsoft ActiveX Calendar control that's probably already installed and registered on your computer. If it isn't there, don't worry. It's on the CD-ROM that comes with this book.

Figure 8-1 shows the Calendar control inside a modal dialog.

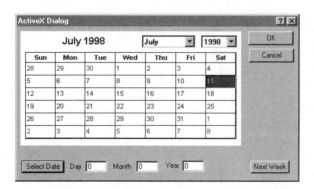

Figure 8-1.
The Calendar control in use.

The Calendar control comes with a help file that lists the control's properties, methods, and events shown here.

Properties	Methods	Events
BackColor	AboutBox	AfterUpdate
Day	NextDay	BeforeUpdate
DayFont	NextMonth	Click
DayFontColor	NextWeek	DblClick
DayLength	NextYear	KeyDown
FirstDay	PreviousDay	KeyPress
GridCellEffect	PreviousMonth	KeyUp
GridFont	PreviousWeek	NewMonth
GridFontColor	PreviousYear	NewYear
GridLinesColor	Refresh	
Month	Today	
MonthLength		
ShowDateSelectors		
ShowDays		
ShowHorizontalGridlines		
ShowTitle		
ShowVerticalGridlines		
TitleFont		
TitleFontColor		
Value		
ValueIsNull		
Year		

You'll be using the BackColor, Day, Month, Year, and Value properties in the EX08A example later in this chapter. BackColor is an unsigned long, but it is used as an *OLE_COLOR*, which is almost the same as a *COLORREF*. Day, Month, and Year are short integers. Value's type is the special type *VARIANT*, which is described in Chapter 25. It holds the entire date as a 64-bit value.

Each of the properties, methods, and events listed above has a corresponding integer identifier. Information about the names, types, parameter sequences, and integer IDs is stored inside the control and is accessible to ClassWizard at container design time.

ActiveX Control Container Programming

MFC and ClassWizard support ActiveX controls both in dialogs and as "child windows." To use ActiveX controls, you must understand how a control grants access to properties, and you must understand the interactions between your DDX code and those property values.

Property Access

The ActiveX control developer designates certain properties for access at design time. Those properties are specified in the property pages that the control displays in the dialog editor when you right-click on a control and choose Properties. The Calendar control's main property page looks like the one shown next.

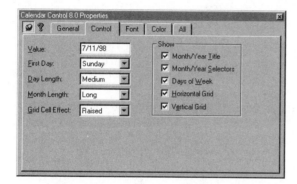

When you click on the All tab, you will see a list of all the design-time–accessible properties, which might include a few properties not found on the Control tab. The Calendar control's All page looks like this.

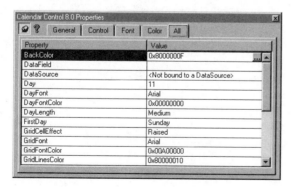

171

All the control's properties, including the design-time properties, are accessible at runtime. Some properties, however, might be designated as read-only.

ClassWizard's C++ Wrapper Classes for ActiveX Controls

When you insert an ActiveX control into a project, ClassWizard generates a C++ wrapper class, derived from *CWnd*, that is tailored to your control's methods and properties. The class has member functions for all properties and methods, and it has constructors that you can use to dynamically create an instance of the control. (ClassWizard also generates wrapper classes for objects used by the control.) Following are a few typical member functions from the file Calendar.cpp that ClassWizard generates for the Calendar control:

```
unsigned long CCalendar::GetBackColor()
{
    unsigned long result;
    InvokeHelper(DISPID_BACKCOLOR, DISPATCH_PROPERTYGET,
            VT_I4, (void*)&result, NULL);
    return result;
}

void CCalendar::SetBackColor(unsigned long newValue)
{
    static BYTE parms[] =
        VTS_I4;
    InvokeHelper(DISPID_BACKCOLOR, DISPATCH_PROPERTYPUT,
            VT_EMPTY, NULL, parms, newValue);
}

short CCalendar::GetDay()
{
    short result;
    InvokeHelper(0x11, DISPATCH_PROPERTYGET, VT_I2,
            (void*)&result, NULL);
    return result;
}

void CCalendar::SetDay(short nNewValue)
{
    static BYTE parms[] =
        VTS_I2;
    InvokeHelper(0x11, DISPATCH_PROPERTYPUT, VT_EMPTY,
            NULL, parms, nNewValue);
}
```

```
COleFont CCalendar::GetDayFont()
{
    LPDISPATCH pDispatch;
    InvokeHelper(0x1, DISPATCH_PROPERTYGET, VT_DISPATCH,
                 (void*)&pDispatch, NULL);
    return COleFont(pDispatch);
}

void CCalendar::SetDayFont(LPDISPATCH newValue)
{
    static BYTE parms[] =
        VTS_DISPATCH;
    InvokeHelper(0x1, DISPATCH_PROPERTYPUT, VT_EMPTY,
                 NULL, parms, newValue);
}

VARIANT CCalendar::GetValue()
{
    VARIANT result;
    InvokeHelper(0xc, DISPATCH_PROPERTYGET, VT_VARIANT,
                 (void*)&result, NULL);
    return result;
}

void CCalendar::SetValue(const VARIANT& newValue)
{
    static BYTE parms[] =
        VTS_VARIANT;
    InvokeHelper(0xc, DISPATCH_PROPERTYPUT, VT_EMPTY,
                 NULL, parms, &newValue);
}

void CCalendar::NextDay()
{
    InvokeHelper(0x16, DISPATCH_METHOD, VT_EMPTY, NULL, NULL);
}

void CCalendar::NextMonth()
{
    InvokeHelper(0x17, DISPATCH_METHOD, VT_EMPTY, NULL, NULL);
}
```

You don't have to concern yourself too much with the code inside these functions, but you can match up the first parameter of each *InvokeHelper* function with the dispatch ID for the corresponding property or method in the Calendar control property list. As you can see, properties always have separate *Set* and *Get* functions. To call a method, you simply call the corresponding function. For example, to call the NextDay method from a dialog class function, you write code such as this:

```
m_calendar.NextDay();
```

In this case, *m_calendar* is an object of class *CCalendar*, the wrapper class for the Calendar control.

AppWizard Support for ActiveX Controls

When the AppWizard ActiveX Controls option is checked (the default), AppWizard inserts the following line in your application class *InitInstance* member function:

```
AfxEnableControlContainer();
```

It also inserts the following line in the project's StdAfx.h file:

```
#include <afxdisp.h>
```

If you decide to add ActiveX controls to an existing project that doesn't include the two lines above, you can simply add the lines.

ClassWizard and the Container Dialog

Once you've used the dialog editor to generate a dialog template, you already know that you can use ClassWizard to generate a C++ class for the dialog window. If your template contains one or more ActiveX controls, you can use ClassWizard to add data members and event handler functions.

Dialog Class Data Members vs. Wrapper Class Usage

What kind of data members can you add to the dialog for an ActiveX control? If you want to set a control property before you call *DoModal* for the dialog, you can add a dialog data member for that property. If you want to change properties inside the dialog member functions, you must take another approach: you add a data member that is an object of the wrapper class for the ActiveX control.

Now is a good time to review the MFC DDX logic. Look back at the Cincinnati dialog in Chapter 6. The *CDialog::OnInitDialog* function calls *CWnd::UpdateData(FALSE)* to read the dialog class data members, and the *CDialog::OnOK* function calls *UpdateData(TRUE)* to write the members. Suppose you added a data member for each ActiveX control property and you needed to get the Value property value in a button handler. If you called *UpdateData(FALSE)* in the button handler, it would read <u>all</u> the property values from <u>all</u> the dialog's controls—clearly a waste of time. It's more effective to avoid using a data member and to call the wrapper class *Get* function instead. To call that function, you must first tell ClassWizard to add a wrapper class object data member.

Suppose you have a Calendar wrapper class *CCalendar* and you have an *m_calendar* data member in your dialog class. If you want to get the Value property, you do it like this:

```
COleVariant var = m_calendar.GetValue();
```

> **N O T E :** The *VARIANT* type and *COleVariant* class are described in Chapter 25.

Now consider another case: you want to set the day to the 5th of the month before the control is displayed. To do this by hand, add a dialog class data member *m_sCalDay* that corresponds to the control's short integer Day property. Then add the following line to the *DoDataExchange* function:

```
DDX_OCShort(pDX, ID_CALENDAR1, 0x11, m_sCalDay);
```

The third parameter is the Day property's integer index (its DispID), which you can find in the *GetDay* and *SetDay* functions generated by ClassWizard for the control. Here's how you construct and display the dialog:

```
CMyDialog dlg;
dlg.m_sCalDay = 5;
dlg.DoModal();
```

The DDX code takes care of setting the property value from the data member before the control is displayed. No other programming is needed. As you would expect, the DDX code sets the data member from the property value when the user clicks the OK button.

> **N O T E :** Even when ClassWizard correctly detects a control's properties, it can't always generate data members for all of them. In particular, no DDX functions exist for *VARIANT* properties like the Calendar's Value property. You'll have to use the wrapper class for these properties.

Mapping ActiveX Control Events

ClassWizard lets you map ActiveX control events the same way you map Windows messages and command messages from controls. If a dialog class contains one or more ActiveX controls, ClassWizard adds and maintains an <u>event sink map</u> that connects mapped events to their handler functions. It works something like a message map. You can see the code in Figure 8-2 beginning on page 180.

NOTE: ActiveX controls have the annoying habit of firing events before your program is ready for them. If your event handler uses windows or pointers to C++ objects, it should verify the validity of those entities prior to using them.

Locking ActiveX Controls in Memory

Normally, an ActiveX control remains mapped in your process as long as its parent dialog is active. That means it must be reloaded each time the user opens a modal dialog. The reloads are usually quicker than the initial load because of disk caching, but you can lock the control into memory for better performance. To do so, add the following line in the overridden *OnInitDialog* function after the base class call:

```
AfxOleLockControl(m_calendar.GetClsid());
```

The ActiveX control remains mapped until your program exits or until you call the *AfxOleUnlockControl* function.

The EX08A Example—
An ActiveX Control Dialog Container

Now it's time to build an application that uses a Calendar control in a dialog. Here are the steps to create the EX08A example:

1. **Verify that the Calendar control is registered.** If the control does not appear in the Visual C++ Gallery's Registered ActiveX Controls page, copy the files MSCal.ocx, MSCal.hlp, and MSCal.cnt to your system directory and register the control by running the REGCOMP program.

2. **Run AppWizard to produce \vcpp32\ex08a\ex08a.** Accept all of the default settings but two: select Single Document and deselect Printing And Print Preview. In the AppWizard Step 3 dialog, make sure the ActiveX Controls option is selected, as shown on the next page.

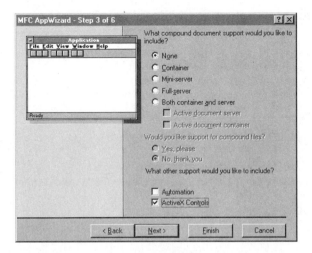

3. Install the Calendar control in the EX08A project. Choose Add To Project from Visual C++'s Project menu, and then choose Components And Controls. Choose Registered ActiveX Controls, and then choose Calendar Control 8.0. ClassWizard generates two classes in the EX08A directory, as shown here.

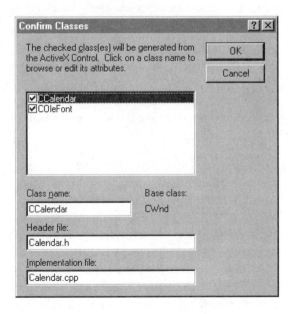

4. Edit the Calendar control class to handle help messages. Add Calendar.cpp to the following message map code:

```
BEGIN_MESSAGE_MAP(CCalendar, CWnd)
    ON_WM_HELPINFO()
END_MESSAGE_MAP()
```

In the same file, add the *OnHelpInfo* function:

```
BOOL CCalendar::OnHelpInfo(HELPINFO* pHelpInfo)
{
    // Edit the following string for your system
    ::WinHelp(GetSafeHwnd(), "c:\\winnt\\system32\\mscal.hlp",
            HELP_FINDER, 0);
    return FALSE;
}
```

In Calendar.h, add the function prototype and declare the message map:

```
protected:
    afx_msg BOOL OnHelpInfo(HELPINFO* pHelpInfo);
    DECLARE_MESSAGE_MAP()
```

The *OnHelpInfo* function is called if the user presses the F1 key when the Calendar control has the input focus. We have to add the message map code by hand because ClassWizard doesn't modify generated ActiveX classes.

> NOTE: The *ON_WM_HELPINFO* macro maps the WM_HELP message, which is new to Microsoft Windows 95 and Microsoft Windows NT 4.0. You can use *ON_WM_HELPINFO* in any view or dialog class and then code the handler to activate any help system. Chapter 21 describes the MFC context-sensitive help system, some of which predates the WM_HELP message.

5. Use the dialog editor to create a new dialog resource. Choose Resource from Visual C++'s Insert menu, and then choose Dialog. The dialog editor assigns the ID *IDD_DIALOG1* to the new dialog. Next change the ID to *IDD_ACTIVEXDIALOG*, change the dialog caption to *ActiveX Dialog*, and set the dialog's Context Help property (on the More Styles page). Accept the default OK and Cancel buttons with the IDs *IDOK* and *IDCANCEL*, and then add the other controls as shown in Figure 8-1 on page 169. Make the Select Date button the default button. Drag the Calendar control from the control palette. Then set an appropriate tab order. Assign control IDs as shown in the following table.

Control	ID
Calendar control	*IDC_CALENDAR1*
Select Date button	*IDC_SELECTDATE*
Edit control	*IDC_DAY*
Edit control	*IDC_MONTH*
Edit control	*IDC_YEAR*
Next Week button	*IDC_NEXTWEEK*

6. Use ClassWizard to create the *CActiveXDialog* class. If you run ClassWizard directly from the dialog editor window, it will know that you want to create a *CDialog*-derived class based on the *IDD_ACTIVEX-DIALOG* template. Simply accept the default options, and name the class *CActiveXDialog*.

Click on the ClassWizard Message Maps tab, and then add the message handler functions shown in the table below. To add a message handler function, click on an object ID, click on a message, and click the Add Function button. If the Add Member Function dialog box appears, type the function name and click the OK button.

Object ID	Message	Member Function
CActiveXDialog	WM_INITDIALOG	*OnInitDialog* (virtual function)
IDC_CALENDAR1	NewMonth (event)	*OnNewMonthCalendar1*
IDC_SELECTDATE	BN_CLICKED	*OnSelectDate*
IDC_NEXTWEEK	BN_CLICKED	*OnNextWeek*
IDOK	BN_CLICKED	*OnOK* (virtual function)

7. Use ClassWizard to add data members to the *CActiveXDialog* class. Click on the Member Variables tab, and then add the data members as shown in the illustration on the following page.

> NOTE: You might think that the ClassWizard ActiveX Events tab is for mapping ActiveX control events in a container. That's not true: it's for ActiveX control developers who are <u>defining</u> events for a control.

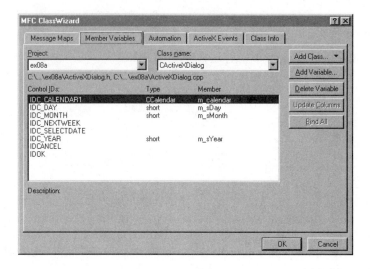

8. **Edit the *CActiveXDialog* class.**   Add the *m_varValue* and *m_BackColor*
   data members, and then edit the code for the five handler functions
   OnInitDialog, *OnNewMonthCalendar1*, *OnSelectDate*, *OnNextWeek*, and
   OnOK. Figure 8-2 shows all the code for the dialog class, with new code
   in boldface.

ACTIVEXDIALOG.H

```
//{{AFX_INCLUDES()
#include "calendar.h"
//}}AFX_INCLUDES
#if !defined(AFX_ACTIVEXDIALOG_H__1917789D_6F24_        ➙
            11D0_8FD9_00C04FC2A0C2__INCLUDED_)
#define AFX_ACTIVEXDIALOG_H__1917789D_6F24_             ➙
        11D0_8FD9_00C04FC2A0C2__INCLUDED_

#if _MSC_VER > 1000
#pragma once
#endif // _MSC_VER > 1000

// ActiveXDialog.h : header file
//

//////////////////////////////////////////////////////////////////
// CActiveXDialog dialog
class CActiveXDialog : public CDialog
```

Figure 8-2.   *(continued)*
Code for the CActiveXDialog *class.*

```
{
// Construction
public:
    CActiveXDialog(CWnd* pParent = NULL);    // standard constructor

// Dialog Data
    //{{AFX_DATA(CActiveXDialog)
    enum { IDD = IDD_ACTIVEXDIALOG };
    CCalendar    m_calendar;
    short    m_sDay;
    short    m_sMonth;
    short    m_sYear;
    //}}AFX_DATA
    COleVariant m_varValue;
    unsigned long m_BackColor;

// Overrides
    // ClassWizard generated virtual function overrides
    //{{AFX_VIRTUAL(CActiveXDialog)
    protected:
    virtual void DoDataExchange(CDataExchange* pDX); // DDX/DDV
                                                     //  support

    //}}AFX_VIRTUAL

// Implementation
protected:

    // Generated message map functions
    //{{AFX_MSG(CActiveXDialog)
    virtual BOOL OnInitDialog();
    afx_msg void OnNewMonthCalendar1();
    afx_msg void OnSelectDate();
    afx_msg void OnNextWeek();
    virtual void OnOK();
    DECLARE_EVENTSINK_MAP()
    //}}AFX_MSG
    DECLARE_MESSAGE_MAP()
};

//{{AFX_INSERT_LOCATION}}
// Microsoft Visual C++ will insert additional
//   declarations immediately before the previous line.

#endif // !defined(AFX_ACTIVEXDIALOG_H__1917789D_6F24_      ⟶
                 11D0_8FD9_00C04FC2A0C2__INCLUDED_)
```

(continued)

Figure 8-2. *continued*

ACTIVEXDIALOG.CPP

```cpp
// ActiveXDialog.cpp : implementation file
//

#include "stdafx.h"
#include "ex08a.h"
#include "ActiveXDialog.h"

#ifdef _DEBUG
#define new DEBUG_NEW
#undef THIS_FILE
static char THIS_FILE[] = __FILE__;
#endif


/////////////////////////////////////////////////////////////////////////
// CActiveXDialog dialog


CActiveXDialog::CActiveXDialog(CWnd* pParent /*=NULL*/)
    : CDialog(CActiveXDialog::IDD, pParent)
{
    //{{AFX_DATA_INIT(CActiveXDialog)
    m_sDay = 0;
    m_sMonth = 0;
    m_sYear = 0;
    //}}AFX_DATA_INIT
    m_BackColor = 0x8000000F;
}

void CActiveXDialog::DoDataExchange(CDataExchange* pDX)
{
    CDialog::DoDataExchange(pDX);
    //{{AFX_DATA_MAP(CActiveXDialog)
    DDX_Control(pDX, IDC_CALENDAR1, m_calendar);
    DDX_Text(pDX, IDC_DAY, m_sDay);
    DDX_Text(pDX, IDC_MONTH, m_sMonth);
    DDX_Text(pDX, IDC_YEAR, m_sYear);
    //}}AFX_DATA_MAP
    DDX_OCColor(pDX, IDC_CALENDAR1, DISPID_BACKCOLOR, m_BackColor);
}

BEGIN_MESSAGE_MAP(CActiveXDialog, CDialog)
    //{{AFX_MSG_MAP(CActiveXDialog)
    ON_BN_CLICKED(IDC_SELECTDATE, OnSelectDate)
    ON_BN_CLICKED(IDC_NEXTWEEK, OnNextWeek)
```

```
    //}}AFX_MSG_MAP
END_MESSAGE_MAP()

/////////////////////////////////////////////////////////////////////
// CActiveXDialog message handlers

BEGIN_EVENTSINK_MAP(CActiveXDialog, CDialog)
    //{{AFX_EVENTSINK_MAP(CActiveXDialog)
    ON_EVENT(CActiveXDialog, IDC_CALENDAR1, 3 /* NewMonth */,        ⇁
            OnNewMonthCalendar1, VTS_NONE)
    //}}AFX_EVENTSINK_MAP
END_EVENTSINK_MAP()

BOOL CActiveXDialog::OnInitDialog()
{
    CDialog::OnInitDialog();
    m_calendar.SetValue(m_varValue); // no DDX for VARIANTs
    return TRUE;  // return TRUE unless you set the focus to a control
                  // EXCEPTION: OCX Property Pages should return FALSE

}
void CActiveXDialog::OnNewMonthCalendar1()
{
    AfxMessageBox("EVENT:  CActiveXDialog::OnNewMonthCalendar1");
}


void CActiveXDialog::OnSelectDate()
{
    CDataExchange dx(this, TRUE);
    DDX_Text(&dx, IDC_DAY, m_sDay);
    DDX_Text(&dx, IDC_MONTH, m_sMonth);
    DDX_Text(&dx, IDC_YEAR, m_sYear);
    m_calendar.SetDay(m_sDay);
    m_calendar.SetMonth(m_sMonth);
    m_calendar.SetYear(m_sYear);
}


void CActiveXDialog::OnNextWeek()
{
    m_calendar.NextWeek();
}


void CActiveXDialog::OnOK()
{
    CDialog::OnOK();
    m_varValue = m_calendar.GetValue(); // no DDX for VARIANTs
}
```

The *OnSelectDate* function is called when the user clicks the Select Date button. The function gets the day, month, and year values from the three edit controls and transfers them to the control's properties. ClassWizard can't add DDX code for the BackColor property, so you must add it by hand. In addition, there's no DDX code for *VARIANT* types, so you must add code to the *OnInitDialog* and *OnOK* functions to set and re-trieve the date with the control's Value property.

9. **Connect the dialog to the view.** Use ClassWizard to map the WM_L-BUTTONDOWN message, and then edit the handler function as follows:

```
void CEx08aView::OnLButtonDown(UINT nFlags, CPoint point)
{
    CActiveXDialog dlg;
    dlg.m_BackColor = RGB(255, 251, 240); // light yellow
    COleDateTime today = COleDateTime::GetCurrentTime();
    dlg.m_varValue = COleDateTime(today.GetYear(), today.GetMonth(),
                                  today.GetDay(), 0, 0, 0);
    if (dlg.DoModal() == IDOK) {
        COleDateTime date(dlg.m_varValue);
        AfxMessageBox(date.Format("%B %d, %Y"));
    }
}
```

The code sets the background color to light yellow and the date to today's date, displays the modal dialog, and reports the date returned by the Calendar control. You'll need to include ActiveXDialog.h in ex08aView.cpp.

10. **Edit the virtual *OnDraw* function in the file ex08aView.cpp.** To prompt the user to press the left mouse button, replace the code in the view class *OnDraw* function with this single line:

```
pDC->TextOut(0, 0, "Press the left mouse button here.");
```

11. **Build and test the EX08A application.** Open the dialog, enter a date in the three edit controls, and then click the Select Date button. Click the Next Week button. Try moving the selected date directly to a new month, and observe the message box that is triggered by the NewMonth event. Watch for the final date in another message box when you click OK. Press the F1 key for help on the Calendar control.

For Win32 Programmers

If you use a text editor to look inside the ex08a.rc file, you might be quite mystified. Here's the entry for the Calendar control in the ActiveX Dialog template:

```
CONTROL          "",IDC_CALENDAR1,
                 "{8E27C92B-1264-101C-8A2F-040224009C02}",
                 WS_TABSTOP,7,7,217,113
```

There's a 32-digit number sequence where the window class name should be. What's going on? Actually, the resource template isn't the one that Windows sees. The *CDialog::DoModal* function "preprocesses" the resource template before passing it on to the dialog box procedure within Windows. It strips out all the ActiveX controls and creates the dialog window without them. Then it loads the controls (based on their 32-digit identification numbers, called CLSIDs) and activates them in place, causing them to create their own windows in the correct places. The initial values for the properties you set in the dialog editor are stored in binary form inside the project's custom DLGINIT resource.

When the modal dialog runs, the MFC code coordinates the messages sent to the dialog window both by the ordinary controls and by the ActiveX controls. This allows the user to tab between all the controls in the dialog, even though the ActiveX controls are not part of the actual dialog template.

When you call the member functions for the control object, you might think you're calling functions for a child window. The control window is quite far removed, but MFC steps in to make it seem as if you're communicating with a real child window. In ActiveX terminology, the container owns a <u>site</u>, which is not a window. You call functions for the site, and ActiveX and MFC make the connection to the underlying window in the ActiveX control.

The container window is an object of a class derived from *CWnd*. The control site is also an object of a class derived from *CWnd*—the ActiveX control wrapper class. That means that the *CWnd* class has built-in support for both containers and sites.

What you're seeing here is MFC ActiveX control support grafted onto regular Windows. Maybe some future Windows version will have more direct support for ActiveX Controls. As a matter of fact, ActiveX versions of the Windows common controls already exist.

ActiveX Controls in HTML Files

You've seen the ActiveX Calendar control in an MFC modal dialog. You can use the same control in a Web page. The following HTML code will work (assuming the person reading the page has the Calendar control installed and registered on his or her machine):

```
<OBJECT
    CLASSID="clsid:8E27C92B-1264-101C-8A2F-040224009C02"
    WIDTH=300 HEIGHT=200 BORDER=1 HSPACE=5 ID=calendar>
<PARAM NAME="Day" VALUE=7>
<PARAM NAME="Month" VALUE=11>
<PARAM NAME="Year" VALUE=1998>
</OBJECT>
```

The CLASSID attribute (the same number that was in the EX08A dialog resource) identifies the Calendar control in the Registry. A browser can download an ActiveX control.

Creating ActiveX Controls at Runtime

You've seen how to use the dialog editor to insert ActiveX controls at design time. If you need to create an ActiveX control at runtime without a resource template entry, here are the programming steps:

1. Insert the component into your project. ClassWizard will create the files for a wrapper class.

2. Add an embedded ActiveX control wrapper class data member to your dialog class or other C++ window class. An embedded C++ object is then constructed and destroyed along with the window object.

3. Choose Resource Symbols from Visual C++'s View menu. Add an ID constant for the new control.

4. If the parent window is a dialog, use ClassWizard to map the dialog's WM_INITDIALOG message, thus overriding *CDialog::OnInitDialog*. For other windows, use ClassWizard to map the WM_CREATE message. The new function should call the embedded control class's *Create* member function. This call indirectly displays the new control in the dialog. The control will be properly destroyed when the parent window is destroyed.

5. In the parent window class, manually add the necessary event message handlers and prototypes for your new control. Don't forget to add the event sink map macros.

TIP: ClassWizard doesn't help you with event sink maps when you add a dynamic ActiveX control to a project. Consider inserting the target control in a dialog in another temporary project. After you're finished mapping events, simply copy the event sink map code to the parent window class in your main project.

The EX08B Example—
The Web Browser ActiveX Control

Microsoft Internet Explorer 4.x has become a leading Web browser. I was surprised to find out that most of its functionality is contained in one big ActiveX control, Shdocvw.dll. When you run Internet Explorer, you launch a small shell program that loads this Web Browser control in its main window.

NOTE: You can find complete documentation for the Web Browser control's properties, methods, and events in the Internet SDK, downloadable from http://www.microsoft.com. This documentation is in HTML form, of course.

Because of this modular architecture, you can write your own custom browser program with very little effort. EX08B creates a two-window browser that displays a search engine page side-by-side with the target page, as shown here.

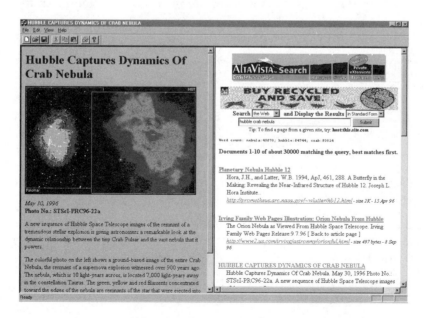

This view window contains two Web Browser controls that are sized to occupy the entire client area. When the user clicks an item in the search (right-hand) control, the program intercepts the command and routes it to the target (left-hand) control.

Here are the steps for building the example:

1. **Make sure the Web Browser control is registered.** You undoubtedly have Microsoft Internet Explorer 4.x installed, since Visual C++ 6.0 requires it, so the Web Browser control should be registered. You can download Internet Explorer from http://www.microsoft.com if necessary.

2. **Run AppWizard to produce \vcpp32\ex08b\ex08b.** Accept all the default settings but two: except select Single Document and deselect Printing And Print Preview. Make sure the ActiveX Controls option is checked as in EX08A.

3. **Install the Web Browser control in the EX08B project.** Choose Add To Project from Visual C++'s Project menu, and choose Components And Controls from the submenu. Select Registered ActiveX Controls, and then choose Microsoft Web Browser. Visual C++ will generate the wrapper class *CWebBrowser* and add the files to your project.

4. **Add two *CWebBrowser* data members to the *CEx08bView* class.** Click on the ClassView tab in the Workspace window, and then right-click the *CEx08bView* class. Choose Add Member Variable, and fill in the dialog as shown here.

Repeat for *m_target*. ClassWizard adds an *#include* statement for the webbrowser.h file.

5. **Add the child window ID constants for the two controls.** Select Resource Symbols from Visual C++'s View menu, and then add the symbols *ID_BROWSER_SEARCH* and *ID_BROWSER_TARGET*.

6. **Add a static character array data member for the AltaVista URL.** Add the following static data member to the class declaration in ex08bView.h:

```
private:
    static const char s_engineAltavista[];
```

Then add the following definition in ex08bView.cpp, outside any function:

```
const char CEx08bView::s_engineAltavista[] =
    "http://altavista.digital.com/";
```

7. **Use ClassWizard to map the view's WM_CREATE and WM_SIZE messages.** Edit the handler code in ex08bView.cpp as follows:

```
int CEx08bView::OnCreate(LPCREATESTRUCT lpCreateStruct)
{
    if (CView::OnCreate(lpCreateStruct) == -1)
        return -1;

    DWORD dwStyle = WS_VISIBLE | WS_CHILD;
    if (m_search.Create(NULL, dwStyle, CRect(0, 0, 100, 100),
                        this, ID_BROWSER_SEARCH) == 0) {
        AfxMessageBox("Unable to create search control!\n");
        return -1;
    }
    m_search.Navigate(s_engineAltavista, NULL, NULL, NULL, NULL);

    if (m_target.Create(NULL, dwStyle, CRect(0, 0, 100, 100),
                        this, ID_BROWSER_TARGET) == 0) {
        AfxMessageBox("Unable to create target control!\n");
        return -1;
    }
    m_target.GoHome(); // as defined in Internet Explorer 4 options

    return 0;
}

void CEx08bView::OnSize(UINT nType, int cx, int cy)
{
    CView::OnSize(nType, cx, cy);

    CRect rectClient;
    GetClientRect(rectClient);
    CRect rectBrowse(rectClient);
    rectBrowse.right = rectClient.right / 2;
    CRect rectSearch(rectClient);
    rectSearch.left = rectClient.right / 2;

    m_target.SetWidth(rectBrowse.right - rectBrowse.left);
    m_target.SetHeight(rectBrowse.bottom - rectBrowse.top);
```

(continued)

```
    m_target.UpdateWindow();

    m_search.SetLeft(rectSearch.left);
    m_search.SetWidth(rectSearch.right - rectSearch.left);
    m_search.SetHeight(rectSearch.bottom - rectSearch.top);
    m_search.UpdateWindow();
}
```

The *OnCreate* function creates two browser windows inside the view window. The right-hand browser displays the top-level AltaVista page, and the left-hand browser displays the "home" page as defined through the Internet icon in the Control Panel. The *OnSize* function, called whenever the view window changes size, ensures that the browser windows completely cover the view window. The *CWebBrowser* member functions *SetWidth* and *SetHeight* set the browser's Width and Height properties.

8. **Add the event sink macros in the *CEx08bView* files.** ClassWizard can't map events from a dynamic ActiveX control, so you must do it manually. Add the following lines inside the class declaration in the file ex08bView.h:

```
protected:
    afx_msg void OnBeforeNavigateExplorer1(LPCTSTR URL,        ⟶
        long Flags, LPCTSTR TargetFrameName,                   ⟶
        VARIANT FAR* PostData, LPCTSTR Headers, BOOL FAR* Cancel);
    afx_msg void OnTitleChangeExplorer2(LPCTSTR Text);
    DECLARE_EVENTSINK_MAP()
```

Then add the following code in ex08bView.cpp:

```
BEGIN_EVENTSINK_MAP(CEx08bView, CView)
    ON_EVENT(CEx08bView, ID_BROWSER_SEARCH, 100,               ⟶
        OnBeforeNavigateExplorer1, VTS_BSTR VTS_I4 VTS_BSTR ⟶
        VTS_PVARIANT VTS_BSTR VTS_PBOOL)
    ON_EVENT(CEx08bView, ID_BROWSER_TARGET, 113,               ⟶
        OnTitleChangeExplorer2, VTS_BSTR)
END_EVENTSINK_MAP()
```

9. **Add two event handler functions.** Add the following member functions in ex08bView.cpp:

```
void CEx08bView::OnBeforeNavigateExplorer1(LPCTSTR URL,
    long Flags, LPCTSTR TargetFrameName,
    VARIANT FAR* PostData, LPCTSTR Headers, BOOL FAR* Cancel)
{
    TRACE("CEx08bView::OnBeforeNavigateExplorer1 -- URL = %s\n", URL);
```

```
    if (!strnicmp(URL, s_engineAltavista, strlen(s_engineAltavista))) {
        return;
    }
    m_target.Navigate(URL, NULL, NULL, PostData, NULL);
    *Cancel = TRUE;
}

void CEx08bView::OnTitleChangeExplorer2(LPCTSTR Text)
{
    // Careful!  Event could fire before we're ready.
    CWnd* pWnd = AfxGetApp()->m_pMainWnd;
    if (pWnd != NULL) {
        if (::IsWindow(pWnd->m_hWnd)) {
            pWnd->SetWindowText(Text);
        }
    }
}
```

The *OnBeforeNavigateExplorer1* handler is called when the user clicks on a link in the search page. The function compares the clicked URL (in the *URL* string parameter) with the search engine URL. If they match, the navigation proceeds in the search window; otherwise, the navigation is cancelled and the Navigate method is called for the target window. The *OnTitleChangeExplorer2* handler updates the EX08B window title to match the title on the target page.

10. **Build and test the EX08B application.**   Search for something on the AltaVista page, and then watch the information appear in the target page.

> NOTE: At the time this edition of this book was written, Visual C++ 6.0 had not been released. Examples EX08B and EX08C could not be created in the prerelease version to run correctly. The code on the companion CD was created with Visual C++ 5.0 and then compiled with version 6.0. We're hopeful that these examples can be created successfully in the release version of Visual C++ 6.0.

The EX08C Example—
A Complete Dual-Window Web Browser

I deliberately kept the EX08B example simple to clearly illustrate the use of the Web Browser control. However, I couldn't resist upgrading the program so that I could use it as my primary Internet browser. The result is EX08C, which uses MFC features described in later chapters of this book—in particular the features on the following page.

- A splitter window with moveable vertical bar browser windows

- Use of the Registry to "remember" the search and target pages

- Printing of both search and target pages

- Support for multiple search engines

- Toolbar buttons for navigation, printing, and search engine selection

- Status bar display of activity and the selected URL

If EX08B runs, \vcpp32\Debug\ex08c should run also. I'm sure you'll have your own ideas for further customization. Once you've studied the rest of the book, you'll be able to take control of this project from the CD-ROM.

Picture Properties

Some ActiveX controls support picture properties, which can accommodate bitmaps, metafiles, and icons. If an ActiveX control has at least one picture property, ClassWizard generates a *CPicture* class in your project during the control's installation. You don't need to use this *CPicture* class, but you must use the MFC class *CPictureHolder*. To access the *CPictureHolder* class declaration and code, you need the following line in StdAfx.h:

```
#include <afxctl.h>
```

Suppose you have an ActiveX control with a picture property named Picture. Here's how you set the Picture property to a bitmap in your program's resources:

```
CPictureHolder pict;
pict.CreateFromBitmap(IDB_MYBITMAP); // from project's resources
m_control.SetPicture(pict.GetPictureDispatch());
```

NOTE: If you include the AfxCtl.h file, you can't statically link your program with the MFC library. If you need a stand-alone program that supports picture properties, you'll have to borrow code from the *CPictureHolder* class, located in the \Program Files\Microsoft Visual Studio\VC98\mfc\src\ctlpict.cpp file.

Bindable Properties—Change Notifications

If an ActiveX control has a property designated as <u>bindable</u>, the control will send an *OnChanged* notification to its container when the value of the property changes inside the control. In addition, the control can send an *OnRequestEdit* notification for a property whose value is about to change but has not yet changed. If the container returns *FALSE* from its *OnRequestEdit* handler, the control should not change the property value.

MFC fully supports property change notifications in ActiveX control containers, but as of Visual C++ version 6.0, no ClassWizard support was available. That means you must manually add entries to your container class's event sink map.

Suppose you have an ActiveX control with a bindable property named Note with a dispatch ID of *4.* You add an *ON_PROPNOTIFY* macro to the *EVENTSINK* macros in this way:

```
BEGIN_EVENTSINK_MAP(CAboutDlg, CDialog)
    //{{AFX_EVENTSINK_MAP(CAboutDlg)
    // ClassWizard places other event notification macros here
    //}}AFX_EVENTSINK_MAP
    ON_PROPNOTIFY(CAboutDlg, IDC_MYCTRL1, 4, OnNoteRequestEdit, ⇥
                  OnNoteChanged)
END_EVENTSINK_MAP()
```

You must then code the *OnNoteRequestEdit* and *OnNoteChanged* functions with return types and parameter types exactly as shown here:

```
BOOL CMyDlg::OnNoteRequestEdit(BOOL* pb)
{
    TRACE("CMyDlg::OnNoteRequestEdit\n");
    *pb = TRUE; // TRUE means change request granted
    return TRUE;
}

BOOL CMyDlg::OnNoteChanged()
{
    TRACE("CMyDlg::OnNoteChanged\n");
    return TRUE;
}
```

You'll also need corresponding prototypes in the class header, as shown here:

```
afx_msg BOOL OnNoteRequestEdit(BOOL* pb);
afx_msg BOOL OnNoteChanged();
```

193

Other ActiveX Controls

You'll probably notice that your disk fills up with ActiveX controls, especially if you accept controls from Web sites. Most of these controls are difficult to use unless you have the documentation on hand, but you can have fun experimenting. Try the Marquee.ocx control that is distributed with Visual C++ 6.0. It works fine in both MFC programs and HTML files. The trick is to set the szURL property to the name of another HTML file that contains the text to display in the scrolling marquee window.

Many ActiveX controls were designed for use by Visual Basic programmers. The SysInfo.ocx control that comes with Visual C++, for example, lets you retrieve system parameters as property values. This isn't of much use to a C++ programmer, however, because you can make the equivalent Win32 calls anytime. Unlike the many objects provided by MFC, ActiveX controls are binary objects that are not extensible. For example, you cannot add a property or event to an ActiveX control. Nor can you use many C++ object-oriented techniques like polymorphism with ActiveX controls. Another downside of ActiveX controls is they are not compatible with many advanced MFC concepts such as the document/view architecture, which we will cover later.

Internet Explorer 4 Common Controls

When Microsoft developers released Internet Explorer 4 (IE4), they included a new and improved version of the COMCTL32.DLL, which houses Microsoft Windows Common Controls. Since this update to the common controls was not part of an operating system release, Microsoft calls the update Internet Explorer 4 Common Controls. IE4 Common Controls updates all of the existing controls and adds a variety of advanced new controls. Microsoft Visual C++ 6.0 and Microsoft Foundation Class (MFC) 6.0 have added a great deal of support for these new controls. In this chapter, we'll look at the new controls and show examples of how to use each one. If you haven't worked with Windows controls or Windows Common Controls, be sure you read Chapter 6 before proceeding with IE4 Common Controls.

> **NOTE:** While Microsoft Windows 95 and Microsoft Windows NT 4.0 do not include the new COMCTL32.DLL, future versions of Windows will. To be safe, you will need to redistribute the COMCTL32.DLL for these existing operating systems as part of your installation. Currently you must ship a "developer's edition" of Internet Explorer to be able to redistribute these controls. However, this might change once a version of Windows ships with the updated controls. Be sure you check *www.microsoft.com/msdn* for the latest news on this subject.

An Introduction to the New Internet Explorer 4 Common Controls

Example EX09A uses each of the new IE4 common controls. Figure 9-1 on the following page shows the dialog from that example. Refer to it when you read the control descriptions that follow.

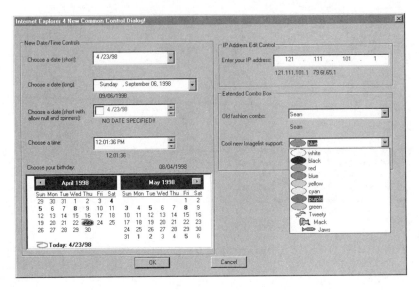

Figure 9-1.
The new Internet Explorer 4 Common Controls dialog.

The Date and Time Picker

A common field on a dialog is a place for the user to enter a date and time. Before IE4 controls provided the date and time picker, developers had to either use a third-party control or subclass an MFC edit control to do significant data validation to ensure that the entered date was valid. Fortunately, the new date and time picker control is provided as an advanced control that prompts the user for a date or time while offering the developer a wide variety of styles and options. For example, dates can be displayed in short formats (8/14/68) or long formats (August 14, 1968). A time mode lets the user enter a time using a familiar hours/minutes/seconds AM/PM format.

The control also lets you decide if you want the user to select the date via in-place editing, a pull-down calendar, or a spin button. Several selection options are available including single and multiple select (for a range of dates) and the ability to turn on and off the "circling" in red ink of the current date. The control even has a mode that lets the user select "no date" via a check box. In Figure 9-1, the first four controls on the left illustrate the variety of configurations available with the date and time picker control.

The new MFC 6.0 class *CDateTimeCtrl* provides the MFC interface to the IE4 date and time picker common control. This class provides a variety of notifications that enhance the programmability of the control. *CDateTimeCtrl* provides member functions for dealing with either *CTime* or *COleDateTime* time structures.

You set the date and time in a *CDateTimeCtrl* using the *SetTime* member function. You can retrieve the date and time via the *GetTime* function. You can create custom formats using the *SetFormat* member function and change a variety of other configurations using the *CDateTimeCtrl* interface.

CTime vs. *COleDateTime*

Most "longtime" MFC developers are accustomed to using the *CTime* class. However, since *CTime*'s valid dates are limited to dates between January 1, 1970, and January 18, 2038, many developers are looking for an alternative. One popular alternative is *COleDateTime*, which is provided for OLE automation support and handles dates from 1 January 100 through 31 December 9999. Both classes have various pros and cons. For example, *CTime* handles all the issues of daylight savings time, while *COleDateTime* does not.

With the Year 2000 crisis looming ahead, many developers choose *COleDateTime* because of its much larger range. Any application that uses *CTime* will need to be reworked in approximately 40 years, since the maximum value is the year 2038. To see this limitation in action, select a date outside the *CTime* range in EX09A. The class you decide to use will depend on your particular needs and the potential longevity of your application.

The Month Calendar

The large display at the bottom left of Figure 9-1 is a Month Calendar. Like the date and time picker control, the month calendar control lets the user choose a date. However, the month calendar control can also be used to implement a small Personal Information Manager (PIM) in your applications. You can show as many months as room provides—from one month to a year's worth of months, if you want. EX09A uses the month calendar control to show only two months.

The month calendar control supports single or multiple selection and allows you to display a variety of different options such as numbered months and a circled "today's date." Notifications for the control let the developer specify which dates are in boldface. It is entirely up to the developer to decide what boldface dates might represent. For example, you could use the bold feature to indicate holidays, appointments, or unusable dates. The MFC 6.0 class *CMonthCalCtrl* implements this control.

To initialize the *CMonthCalCtrl* class, you can call the *SetToday()* member function. *CMonthCalCtrl* provides members that deal with both *CTime* and *COleDateTime*, including *SetToday()*.

The Internet Protocol Address Control

If you write an application that uses any form of Internet or TCP/IP functionality, you might need to prompt the user for an Internet Protocol (IP) Address. The IE4 common controls include an IP address edit control as shown in the top right of Figure 9-1. In addition to letting the user enter a 4-byte IP address, this control performs an automatic validation of the entered IP address. *CIPAddressCtrl* provides MFC support for the IP address control.

An IP address consists of four "fields" as shown in Figure 9-2. The fields are numbered from left to right.

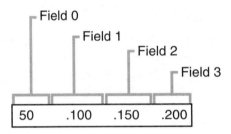

Figure 9-2.
The fields of an IP address control.

To initialize an IP address control, you call the *SetAddress* member function in your *OnInitDialog* function. *SetAddress* takes a DWORD, with each BYTE in the DWORD representing one of the fields. In your message handlers, you can call the *GetAddress* member function to retrieve a DWORD or a series of BYTES to retrieve the various values of the four IP address fields.

The Extended Combo Box

The "old-fashioned" combo box was developed in the early days of Windows. Its age and inflexible design have been the source of a great deal of developer confusion. With the IE4 controls, Microsoft has decided to release a much more flexible version of the combo box called the extended combo box.

The extended combo box gives the developer much easier access to and control over the edit-control portion of the combo box. In addition, the extended combo box lets you attach an image list to the items in the combo box. You can display graphics in the extended combo box easily, especially when compared with the old days of using owner-drawn combo boxes. Each item in the extended combo box can be associated with three images: a selected image, an unselected image, and an overlay image. These three images can be used to provide a variety of graphical displays in the combo box, as we'll see in the EX09A sample. The bottom two combo boxes in Figure 9-1 are both extended combo boxes. The MFC *CComboBoxEx* class provides comprehensive extended combo box support.

Like the list control introduced in Chapter 6, *CComboBoxEx* can be attached to a *CImageList* that will automatically display graphics next to the text in the extended combo box. If you are already familiar with *CComboBox*, *CComboBoxEx* might cause some confusion: instead of containing strings, the extended combo box contains items of type *COMBOBOXEXITEM*, a structure that consists of the following fields:

- **UINT *mask***—A set of bit flags that specify which operations are to be performed using the structure. For example, set the *CBEIF_IMAGE* flag if the image field is to be set or retrieved in an operation.

- **int *iItem***—The extended combo box item number. Like the older style of combo box, the extended combo box uses zero-based indexing.

- **LPSTR *pszText***—The text of the item.

- **int *cchTextMax***—The length of the buffer available in pszText.

- **int *iImage***—Zero-based index into an associated image list.

- **int *iSelectedImage***—Index of the image in the image list to be used to represent the "selected" state.

- **int *iOverlay***—Index of the image in the image list to be used to overlay the current image.

- **int *iIndent***—Number of 10-pixel indentation spaces.

- **LPARAM *lParam***—32-bit parameter for the item.

You will see first-hand how to use this structure in the EX09A example.

The EX09A Example

To illustrate how to take advantage of the new Internet Explorer 4 Common Controls, we'll build a dialog that demonstrates how to create and program each control type. The steps required to create the dialog are shown on the following pages.

1. **Run AppWizard to generate the EX09A project.** Choose New from the Visual C++ File menu, and then select Microsoft AppWizard (exe) from the Projects page. Accept all the defaults but one: choose Single Document Interface (SDI). The options and the default class names are shown here.

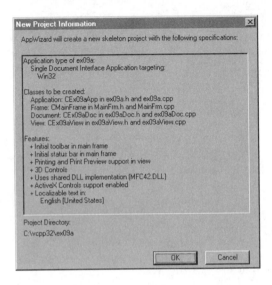

2. **Create a new dialog resource with ID _IDD_DIALOG1_.** Place the controls as shown in Figure 9-1.

   You can drag the controls from the control palette, shown on page 109 in Chapter 6. Remember that IE4 Common Controls are at the bottom of the palette. The following table lists the control types and their IDs.

Tab Sequence	Control Type	Child Window ID
1	Group Box	IDC_STATIC
2	Static	IDC_STATIC
3	Date Time Picker	IDC_DATETIMEPICKER1
4	Static	IDC_STATIC1
5	Static	IDC_STATIC
6	Date Time Picker	IDC_DATETIMEPICKER2
7	Static	IDC_STATIC2
8	Static	IDC_STATIC
9	Date Time Picker	IDC_DATETIMEPICKER3
10	Static	IDC_STATIC3

Tab Sequence	Control Type	Child Window ID
11	Static	*IDC_STATIC*
12	Date Time Picker	*IDC_DATETIMEPICKER4*
13	Static	*IDC_STATIC4*
14	Static	*IDC_STATIC*
15	Month Calendar	*IDC_MONTHCALENDAR*
16	Static	*IDC_STATIC5*
17	Group Box	*IDC_STATIC*
18	Static	*IDC_STATIC*
19	IP Address	*IDC_IPADDRESS1*
20	Static	*IDC_STATIC6*
21	Group Box	*IDC_STATIC*
22	Static	*IDC_STATIC*
23	Extended Combo Box	*IDC_COMBOBOXEX1*
24	Static	*IDC_STATIC7*
25	Static	*IDC_STATIC*
26	Extended Combo Box	*IDC_COMBOBOXEX2*
27	Static	*IDC_STATIC8*
28	Pushbutton	*IDOK*
29	Pushbutton	*IDCANCEL*

The following figure shows each control and its appropriate tab order.

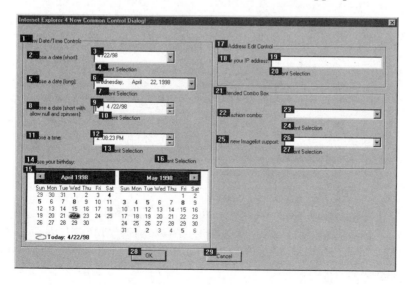

Until we set some properties, your dialog will not look exactly like the one in Figure 9-1.

3. **Use ClassWizard to create a new class, *CDialog1*, derived from *CDialog*.** ClassWizard will automatically prompt you to create this class because it knows that the *IDD_DIALOG1* resource exists without an associated C++ class. Go ahead and create a message handler for the WM_INITDIALOG message.

4. **Set the properties for the dialog's controls.** To demonstrate the full range of controls, we will need to set a variety of properties on each of the IE4 common controls in the example. Here is a brief overview of each property you will need to set:

❑ **The Short Date and Time Picker.** To set up the first date and time picker control to use the short format, select the properties for *IDC_DATETIMEPICKER1,* as shown in the following figure.

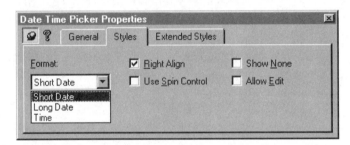

❑ **The Long Date and Time Picker.** Now configure the second date and time picker control (*IDC_DATETIMEPICKER2*) to use the long format as shown below.

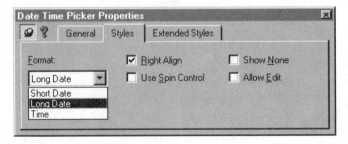

❑ **The Short and NULL Date and Time Picker.** This is the third date and time picker control, *IDC_DATETIMEPICKER3*. Configure this third date and time picker to use the short format and the styles shown here.

❑ **The Time Picker**. The fourth date and time picker control, *IDC_DATETIMEPICKER4*, is configured to let the user choose time. To configure this control, select Time from the Format combo box on the Styles tab as shown.

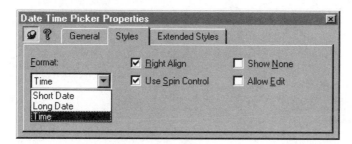

❑ **The Month View.** To configure the month view, you will need to set a variety of styles. First, from the Styles tab, choose Day States, as shown here.

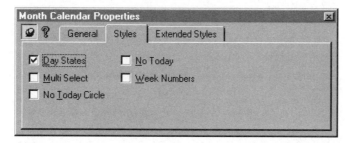

If we leave the default styles, the month view does not look like a control on the dialog. There are no borders drawn at all. To make the control fit in with the other controls on the dialog, select Client Edge and Static Edge from the Extended Styles tab, as shown on the following page.

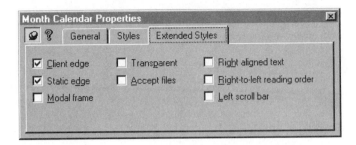

❏ **The IP Address.** This control (*IDC_IPADDRESS1*) does not require any special properties.

❏ **The First Extended Combo Box.** Make sure that you enter some items, as shown here, and also make sure the list is tall enough to display several items.

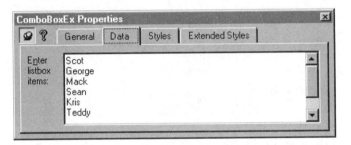

❏ **The Second Extended Combo Box.** Enter three items: Tweety, Mack, and Jaws. Later in the example, we will use these items to show one of the ways to draw graphics in an extended combo box.

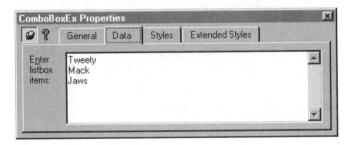

5. Add the *CDialog1* variables. Start ClassWizard and click on the Member Variables tab to view the Member Variables page. Enter the following member variables for each control listed.

Control ID	Data Member	Type
IDC_DATETIMEPICKER1	m_MonthCal1	CDateTimeCtrl
IDC_DATETIMEPICKER2	m_MonthCal2	CDateTimeCtrl
IDC_DATETIMEPICKER3	m_MonthCal3	CDateTimeCtrl
IDC_DATETIMEPICKER4	m_MonthCal4	CDateTimeCtrl
IDC_IPADDRESS1	m_ptrIPCtrl	CIPAddressCtrl
IDC_MONTHCALENDAR1	m_MonthCal5	CMonthCalCtrl
IDC_STATIC1	m_strDate1	CString
IDC_STATIC2	m_strDate2	CString
IDC_STATIC3	m_strDate3	CString
IDC_STATIC4	m_strDate4	CString
IDC_STATIC5	m_strDate5	CString
IDC_STATIC6	m_strIPValue	CString
IDC_STATIC7	m_strComboEx1	CString
IDC_STATIC8	m_strComboEx2	CString

6. Program the short date time picker. In this example, we don't mind if the first date time picker starts with the current date, so we don't have any *OnInitDialog* handling for this control. However, if we wanted to change the date, we would make a call to *SetTime* for the control in *OnInitDialog*. At runtime, when the user selects a new date in the first date and time picker, the companion static control should be automatically updated. To achieve this, we need to use ClassWizard to add a handler for the DTN_DATETIMECHANGE message. Start ClassWizard (CTRL-W) and choose *IDC_DATETIMEPICKER1* from the Object IDs list and DTN_DATETIMECHANGE from the Messages list. Accept the default message name and click OK. Repeat this step for each of the other three *IDC_DATETIMEPICKER* IDs. Your ClassWizard should look like the illustration on the following page.

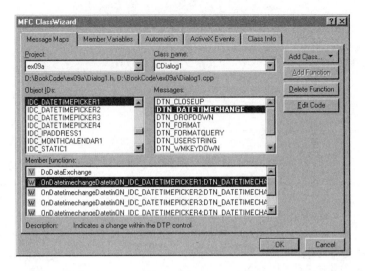

Next add the following code to the handler for Datetimepicker1 created by ClassWizard:

```
void CDialog1::OnDatetimechangeDatetimepicker1(NMHDR* pNMHDR,
    LRESULT* pResult)
{
    CTime ct;
    m_MonthCal1.GetTime(ct);
    m_strDate1.Format(_T("%02d/%02d/%2d"),
                      ct.GetMonth(),ct.GetDay(),ct.GetYear());
    UpdateData(FALSE);
    *pResult = 0;
}
```

This code uses the *m_MonthCal1* data member that maps to the first date time picker to retrieve the time into the *CTime* object variable *ct*. It then calls the *CString::Format* member function to set the companion static string. Finally the call to *UpdateData(FALSE)* triggers MFC's DDX and causes the static to be automatically updated to *m_strDate1*.

7. Program the long date time picker. Now we need to provide a similar handler for the second date time picker.

```
void CDialog1::OnDatetimechangeDatetimepicker2(NMHDR* pNMHDR,
    LRESULT* pResult)
{
    CTime ct;
    m_MonthCal2.GetTime(ct);
    m_strDate2.Format(_T("%02d/%02d/%2d"),
                      ct.GetMonth(),ct.GetDay(),ct.GetYear());
    UpdateData(FALSE);
```

```
            *pResult = 0;
    }
```

8. **Program the third date time picker.** The third date time picker needs a similar handler, but since we set the Show None style in the dialog properties, it is possible for the user to specify a NULL date by checking the inline check box. Instead of blindly calling *GetTime*, we have to check the return value. If the return value of the *GetTime* call is nonzero, the user has selected a NULL date. If the return value is zero, a valid date has been selected. As in the previous two handlers, when a *CTime* object is returned, it is converted into a string and automatically displayed in the companion static control.

```
void CDialog1::OnDatetimechangeDatetimepicker3(NMHDR* pNMHDR,
    LRESULT* pResult)
{
    //NOTE: this one can be null!
    CTime ct;
    int nRetVal = m_MonthCal3.GetTime(ct);
    if (nRetVal) //If not zero, it's null; and if it is,
                 // do the right thing.
    {
        m_strDate3 = "NO DATE SPECIFIED!!";
    }
    else
    {
        m_strDate3.Format(_T("%02d/%02d/%2d"),ct.GetMonth(),
                        ct.GetDay(),ct.GetYear());
    }
    UpdateData(FALSE);
    *pResult = 0;
}
```

9. **Program the time picker.** The time picker needs a similar handler, but this time the format displays hours/minutes/seconds instead of months/days/years:

```
void CDialog1::OnDatetimechangeDatetimepicker4(NMHDR* pNMHDR,
    LRESULT* pResult)
{
    CTime ct;
    m_MonthCal4.GetTime(ct);
    m_strDate4.Format(_T("%02d:%02d:%2d"),
                    ct.GetHour(),ct.GetMinute(),ct.GetSecond());
    UpdateData(FALSE);
    *pResult = 0;
}
```

10. **Program the Month Selector.** You might think that the month selector handler is similar to the date time picker's handler, but they are actually somewhat different. First of all, the message you need to handle for detecting when the user has selected a new date is the MCN_SELCHANGE message. Select this message in the ClassWizard, as shown here.

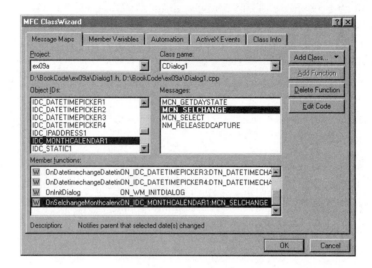

In addition to the different message handler, this control uses *GetCurSel* as the date time picker instead of *GetTime*. The code below shows the MCN_SELCHANGE handler for the month calendar control.

```
void CDialog1::OnSelchangeMonthcalendar1(NMHDR* pNMHDR,
    LRESULT* pResult)
{
    CTime ct;
    m_MonthCal5.GetCurSel(ct);
    m_strDate5.Format(_T("%02d/%02d/%2d"),
                      ct.GetMonth(),ct.GetDay(),ct.GetYear());
    UpdateData(FALSE);
    *pResult = 0;
}
```

11. **Program the IP control.** First we need to make sure the control is initialized. In this example, we initialize the control to 0 by giving it a 0 DWORD value. If you do not initialize the control, each segment will be blank. To initialize the control, add this call to the *CDialog1::OnInitDialog* function:

```
m_ptrIPCtrl.SetAddress(0L);
```

Now we need to add a handler to update the companion static control whenever the IP address control changes. First we need to add a handler for the IPN_FIELDCHANGED notification message using ClassWizard, as shown here.

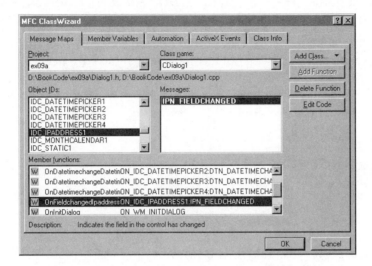

Next we need to implement the handler as follows:

```
void CDialog1::OnFieldchangedIpaddress1(NMHDR* pNMHDR,
    LRESULT* pResult)
{
    DWORD dwIPAddress;
    m_ptrIPCtrl.GetAddress(dwIPAddress);

    m_strIPValue.Format("%d.%d.%d.%d   %x.%x.%x.%x",
        HIBYTE(HIWORD(dwIPAddress)),
        LOBYTE(HIWORD(dwIPAddress)),
        HIBYTE(LOWORD(dwIPAddress)),
        LOBYTE(LOWORD(dwIPAddress)),
        HIBYTE(HIWORD(dwIPAddress)),
        LOBYTE(HIWORD(dwIPAddress)),
        HIBYTE(LOWORD(dwIPAddress)),
        LOBYTE(LOWORD(dwIPAddress)));
    UpdateData(FALSE);
    *pResult = 0;
}
```

The first call to *CIPAddressCtrl::GetAddress* retrieves the current IP address into the local *dwIPAddress DWORD* variable. Next we make a fairly complex call to *CString::Format* to deconstruct the *DWORD* into the various fields. This call uses the *LOWORD* macro to first get to the bottom word of the *DWORD* and the *HIBYTE/LOBYTE* macros to further deconstruct the fields in order from field 0 to field 3.

12. **Add a handler for the first extended combo box.**   No special initialization is required for the extended combo box, but we do need to handle the CBN_SELCHANGE message. The following code shows the extended combo box handler. Can you spot the ways that this differs from a "normal" combo box control?

```
void CDialog1::OnSelchangeComboboxex1()
{
    COMBOBOXEXITEM cbi;
    CString str ("dummy_string");
    CComboBoxEx * pCombo = (CComboBoxEx *)GetDlgItem(IDC_COMBOBOXEX1);

    int nSel = pCombo->GetCurSel();
    cbi.iItem = nSel;
    cbi.pszText = (LPTSTR)(LPCTSTR)str;
    cbi.mask = CBEIF_TEXT;
    cbi.cchTextMax = str.GetLength();
    pCombo->GetItem(&cbi);
    SetDlgItemText(IDC_STATIC7,str);
    return;
}
```

The first thing you probably noticed is the use of the *COMBOBOXEXITEM* structure for the extended combo box instead of the plain integers used for items in an older combo box. Once the handler retrieves the item, it extracts the string and calls *SetDlgItemText* to update the companion static control.

13. **Add Images to the Items in the second extended combo box.**   The first extended combo box does not need any special programming. It is used to demonstrate how to implement a simple extended combo box very similar to the older, nonextended combo box. The second combo box requires a good bit of programming. First we created six bitmaps and eight icons that we need to add to the resources for the project, as shown in the following illustration.

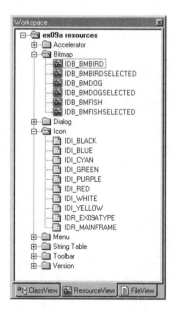

Of course, you are free to grab these images from the companion CD instead of recreating them all by hand, or you can choose to use any bitmaps and icons.

There are two ways to add our graphics to an extended combo box. The first method is to attach images to existing combo box items. (Remember that we used the dialog editor to add the Tweety, Mack, and Jaws items to the combo box.) The second method is to add new items and specify their corresponding images at the time of addition.

Before we start adding graphics to the extended combo box, let's create a public *CImageList* data member in the *CDialog1* class named *m_imageList*. Be sure you add the data member to the header file (Dialog1.h) for the class.

Now we can add some of the bitmap images to the image list and then "attach" the images to the three items already in the extended combo box. Add the following code to your *CDialog1*'s *OnInitDialog* method to achieve this:

```
//Initialize the IDC_COMBOBOXEX2
CComboBoxEx* pCombo =
    (CComboBoxEx*) GetDlgItem(IDC_COMBOBOXEX2);
//First let's add images to the items there.
//We have six images in bitmaps to match to our strings:
```

(continued)

211

```
//CImageList * pImageList = new CImageList();
m_imageList.Create(32,16,ILC_MASK,12,4);

CBitmap bitmap;

bitmap.LoadBitmap(IDB_BMBIRD);
m_imageList.Add(&bitmap, (COLORREF)0xFFFFFF);
bitmap.DeleteObject();

bitmap.LoadBitmap(IDB_BMBIRDSELECTED);
m_imageList.Add(&bitmap, (COLORREF)0xFFFFFF);
bitmap.DeleteObject();

bitmap.LoadBitmap(IDB_BMDOG);
m_imageList.Add(&bitmap, (COLORREF)0xFFFFFF);
bitmap.DeleteObject();

bitmap.LoadBitmap(IDB_BMDOGSELECTED);
m_imageList.Add(&bitmap, (COLORREF)0xFFFFFF);
bitmap.DeleteObject();

bitmap.LoadBitmap(IDB_BMFISH);
m_imageList.Add(&bitmap, (COLORREF)0xFFFFFF);
bitmap.DeleteObject();

bitmap.LoadBitmap(IDB_BMFISHSELECTED);
m_imageList.Add(&bitmap, (COLORREF)0xFFFFFF);
bitmap.DeleteObject();

//Set the imagelist
pCombo->SetImageList(&m_imageList);
//Now attach the images to the items in the list.
COMBOBOXEXITEM    cbi;
cbi.mask = CBEIF_IMAGE|CBEIF_SELECTEDIMAGE|CBEIF_INDENT;
CString strTemp;
int nBitmapCount = 0;
for (int nCount = 0;nCount < 3;nCount++)
{
    cbi.iItem = nCount;
    cbi.pszText = (LPTSTR)(LPCTSTR)strTemp;
    cbi.cchTextMax = 256;
    pCombo->GetItem(&cbi);
    cbi.iImage = nBitmapCount++;
    cbi.iSelectedImage = nBitmapCount++;
    cbi.iIndent = (nCount & 0x03);
    pCombo->SetItem(&cbi);

}
```

First the extended combo box initialization code creates a pointer to the control using *GetDlgItem*. Next it calls *Create* to create memory for the images to be added and to initialize the image list. The next series of calls loads each bitmap, adds them to the image list, and then deletes the resource allocated in the load.

CComboBoxEx::SetImageList is called to associate the *m_imageList* with the extended combo box. Next a *COMBOBOXEXITEM* structure is initialized with a mask, and then the *for* loop iterates from 0 through 2, setting the selected and unselected images with each pass through the loop. The variable *nBitmapCount* increments through the image list to ensure that the correct image ID is put into the *COMBOBOXEXITEM* structure. The *for* loop makes a call to *CComboBoxEx::GetItem* to retrieve the *COMBOBOXEXITEM* structure for each item in the extended combo box. Then the loop sets up the images for the list item and finally calls *CComboBoxEx::SetItem* to put the modified *COMBOBOXEXITEM* structure back into the extended combo box and complete the association of images with the existing items in the list.

14. **Add Items to the Extended Combobox.**   The other technique available for putting images into an extended combo box is to add them dynamically, as shown in the code added to *OnInitDialog* below:

```
    HICON hIcon[8];
    int n;
//Now let's insert some color icons
    hIcon[0] = AfxGetApp()->LoadIcon(IDI_WHITE);
    hIcon[1] = AfxGetApp()->LoadIcon(IDI_BLACK);
    hIcon[2] = AfxGetApp()->LoadIcon(IDI_RED);
    hIcon[3] = AfxGetApp()->LoadIcon(IDI_BLUE);
    hIcon[4] = AfxGetApp()->LoadIcon(IDI_YELLOW);
    hIcon[5] = AfxGetApp()->LoadIcon(IDI_CYAN);
    hIcon[6] = AfxGetApp()->LoadIcon(IDI_PURPLE);
    hIcon[7] = AfxGetApp()->LoadIcon(IDI_GREEN);
    for (n = 0; n < 8; n++) {
        m_imageList.Add(hIcon[n]);
    }

    static char* color[] = {"white", "black", "red",
                            "blue", "yellow", "cyan",
                            "purple", "green"};

    cbi.mask = CBEIF_IMAGE|CBEIF_TEXT|CBEIF_OVERLAY|
               CBEIF_SELECTEDIMAGE;
```

(continued)

```
for (n = 0; n < 8; n++) {
    cbi.iItem = n;
    cbi.pszText = color[n];
    cbi.iImage = n+6; //6 is the offset into the image list from
    cbi.iSelectedImage = n+6; // the first six items we added...
    cbi.iOverlay = n+6;
    int nItem = pCombo->InsertItem(&cbi);
    ASSERT(nItem == n);
}
```

The addition of the icons above is similar to the EX06B list control example in Chapter 6. The *for* loop fills out the *COMBOBOXEXITEM* structure and then calls *CComboBoxEx::InsertItem* with each item to add it to the list.

15. **Add a handler for the second extended combo box.**   The second extended combo box handler is essentially the same as the first:

```
void CDialog1::OnSelchangeComboboxex2()
{
    COMBOBOXEXITEM cbi;
    CString str ("dummy_string");
    CComboBoxEx * pCombo = (CComboBoxEx *)GetDlgItem(IDC_COMBOBOXEX2);
    int nSel = pCombo->GetCurSel();
    cbi.iItem = nSel;
    cbi.pszText = (LPTSTR)(LPCTSTR)str;
    cbi.mask = CBEIF_TEXT;
    cbi.cchTextMax = str.GetLength();
    pCombo->GetItem(&cbi);
    SetDlgItemText(IDC_STATIC8,str);

    return;
}
```

16. **Connect the view and the dialog.**   Add code to the virtual *OnDraw* function in ex09aView.cpp. The following boldface code replaces the previous code:

```
void CEx09aView::OnDraw(CDC* pDC)
{
    pDC->TextOut(0, 0, "Press the left mouse button here.");
}
```

17. **Use ClassWizard to add the *OnLButtonDown* member function to the CEx09aView class.**   Edit the AppWizard-generated code as follows:

```
void CEx09aView::OnLButtonDown(UINT nFlags, CPoint point)
{
    CDialog1 dlg;
    dlg.DoModal();
}
```

Add a statement to include Dialog1.h in file ex09aView.cpp.

18. Compile and run the program.   Now you can experiment with the various IE4 common controls to see how they work and how you can apply them in your own applications.

CHAPTER TEN

Win32 Memory Management

Forget everything you ever knew about Win16 memory management. Some of theWin16 memory management functions, such as *GlobalAlloc*, were carried forward into Win32, but this was done to enable developers to port source code quickly. Underneath, the original functions work very differently, and many new ones have been added.

This chapter starts out with a dose of Win32 memory management theory, which includes coverage of the fundamental heap management functions. Then you'll see how the C++ *new* and *delete* operators connect with the underlying heap functions. Finally, you'll learn how to use the memory-mapped file functions, and you'll get some practical tips on managing dynamic memory. In no way is this chapter intended to be a definitive description of Win32 memory management. For that, you'll have to read Jeffrey Richter's *Advanced Windows* (Microsoft Press, 1997). (Be sure you have the latest edition—a new version may be in the works that covers Microsoft Windows 98/NT 5.0.)

NOTE: At the time this edition was written, both Windows 98 and Windows NT 5.0 were in beta and not released. Our examination of these betas indicates that the memory management has not changed significantly.

Processes and Memory Space

Before you learn how Microsoft Windows manages memory, you must first understand what a process is. If you already know what a <u>program</u> is, you're on your way. A program is an EXE file that you can launch in various ways in Windows. Once a program is running, it's called a <u>process</u>. A process owns its memory, file handles, and other system resources. If you launch the same program twice in a row, you have two separate processes running simultaneously. Both the Microsoft Windows NT Task Manager (right-click the taskbar) and the Microsoft Windows 95 PVIEW95 program give you a detailed list of processes that are currently running, and they allow you to kill processes that are not responding. The SPYXX program shows the relationships among processes, tasks, and windows.

> **NOTE:** The Windows taskbar shows main windows, not processes. A single process (such as Windows Explorer) might have several main windows, each supported by its own thread, and some processes don't have windows at all. (See Chapter 12 for a discussion of threads.)

The important thing to know about a process is that it has its own "private" 4-gigabyte (GB) virtual address space (which I'll describe in detail in the next section). For now, pretend that your computer has hundreds of gigabytes of RAM and that each process gets 4 GB. Your program can access any byte of this space with a single 32-bit linear address. Each process's memory space contains a variety of items, including the following:

- Your program's EXE image
- Any nonsystem DLLs that your program loads, including the MFC DLLs
- Your program's global data (read-only as well as read/write)
- Your program's stack
- Dynamically allocated memory, including Windows and C runtime library (CRT) heaps
- Memory-mapped files
- Interprocess shared memory blocks
- Memory local to specific executing threads
- All sorts of special system memory blocks, including virtual memory tables
- The Windows kernel and executive, plus DLLs that are part of Windows

The Windows 95 Process Address Space

In Windows 95, only the bottom 2 GB (0 to 0x7FFFFFFF) of address space is truly private, and the bottom 4 MB of that is off-limits. The stack, heaps, and read/write global memory are mapped in the bottom 2 GB along with application EXE and DLL files.

The top 2 GB of space is the same for all processes and is shared by all processes. The Windows 95 kernel, executive, virtual device drivers (VxDs), and file system code, along with important tables such as page tables, are mapped to the top 1 GB (0xC0000000 to 0xFFFFFFFF) of address space. Windows DLLs and memory-mapped files are located in the range 0x80000000 to 0xBFFFFFFF. Figure 10-1 shows a memory map of two processes using the same program.

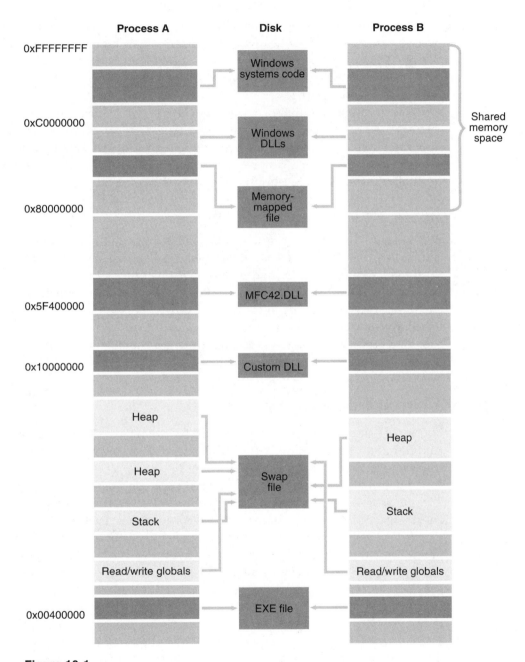

Figure 10-1.
*A typical Windows 95 virtual memory map for two processes linked to
the same EXE file.*

How safe is all this? It's next to impossible for one process to overwrite another process's stack, global, or heap memory because this memory, located in the bottom 2 GB of virtual address space, is assigned only to that specific process. All EXE and DLL code is flagged as read-only, so there's no problem if the code is mapped in several processes.

However, because important Windows read/write data is mapped there, the top 1 GB of address space is vulnerable. An errant program could wipe out important system tables located in this region. In addition, one process could mess up another process's memory-mapped files in the range 0x80000000 through 0xBFFFFFFF because this region is shared by all processes.

The Windows NT Process Address Space

A process in Windows NT can access only the bottom 2 GB of its address space, and the lowest and highest 64 KB of that is inaccessible. The EXE, the application's DLLs and Windows DLLs, and memory-mapped files all reside in this space between 0x00010000 and 0x7FFEFFFF. The Windows NT kernel, executive, and device drivers all reside in the upper 2 GB, where they are completely protected from any tampering by an errant program. Memory-mapped files are safer, too. One process cannot access another's memory-mapped file without knowing the file's name and explicitly mapping a view.

How Virtual Memory Works

You know that your computer doesn't really have hundreds of gigabytes of RAM. And it doesn't have hundreds of gigabytes of disk space either. Windows uses some smoke and mirrors here.

First of all, a process's 4-GB address space is going to be used sparsely. Various programs and data elements will be scattered throughout the 4-GB address space in 4-KB units starting on 4-KB boundaries. Each 4-KB unit, called a page, can hold either code or data. When a page is being used, it occupies physical memory, but you never see its physical memory address. The Intel microprocessor chip efficiently maps a 32-bit virtual address to both a physical page and an offset within the page, using two levels of 4-KB page tables, as shown in Figure 10-2. Note that individual pages can be flagged as either read-only or read/write. Also note that each process has its own set of page tables. The chip's CR3 register holds a pointer to the directory page, so when Windows switches from one process to another, it simply updates CR3.

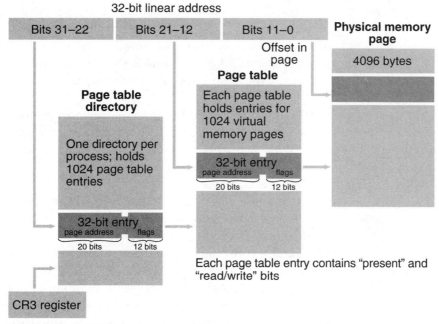

Figure 10-2.
Win32 virtual memory management (Intel).

So now our process is down from 4 GB to maybe 5 MB—a definite improvement. But if we're running several programs, along with Windows itself, we'll still run out of RAM. If you look at Figure 10-2 again, you'll notice that the page table entry has a "present" bit that indicates whether the 4-KB page is currently in RAM. If we try to access a page that's not in RAM, an interrupt fires and Windows analyzes the situation by checking its internal tables. If the memory reference was bogus, we'll get the dreaded "page fault" message and the program will exit. Otherwise, Windows reads the page from a disk file into RAM and updates the page table by loading the physical address and setting the present bit. This is the essence of Win32 virtual memory.

The Windows virtual memory manager figures out how to read and write 4-KB pages so that it optimizes performance. If one process hasn't used a page for a while and another process needs memory, the first page is swapped out or discarded and the RAM is used for the new process's page. Your program isn't normally aware that this is going on. The more disk I/O that happens, however, the worse your program's performance will be, so it stands to reason that more RAM is better.

I mentioned the word "disk," but I haven't talked about files yet. All processes share a big systemwide <u>swap</u> <u>file</u> that's used for all read/write data and some read-only data. (Windows NT supports multiple swap files.) Windows determines the swap file size based on available RAM and free disk space, but there are ways to fine-tune the swap file's size and specify its physical location on disk.

The swap file isn't the only file used by the virtual memory manager, however. It wouldn't make sense to write code pages back to the swap file, so instead of using the swap file, Windows maps EXE and DLL files directly to their files on disk. Because the code pages are marked read-only, there's never a need to write them back to disk.

If two processes use the same EXE file, that file is mapped into each process's address space. The code and constants never change during program execution, so the same physical memory can be mapped for each process. The two processes cannot share global data, however, and Windows 95 and Windows NT handle this situation differently. Windows 95 maps separate copies of the global data to each process. In Windows NT, both processes use the same copy of each page of global data until one process attempts to write to that page. At that point the page is copied; as a result, each process has its own private copy stored at the same virtual address.

> **NOTE:** A dynamic link library can be mapped directly to its DLL file only if the DLL can be loaded at its designated base address. If a DLL were statically linked to load at, say, 0x10000000 but that address range is already occupied by another DLL, Windows must "fix up" the addresses within the DLL code. Windows NT copies the altered pages to the swap file when the DLL is first loaded, but Windows 95 can do the fixup "on the fly" when the pages are brought into RAM. Needless to say, it's important to build your DLLs with nonoverlapping address ranges. If you're using the MFC DLLs, set the base address of your own DLLs outside the range 0x5F400000 through 0x5FFFFFFF. Chapter 22 provides more details on writing DLLs.

Memory-mapped files, which I'll talk about later, are also mapped directly. These can be flagged as read/write and made available for sharing among processes.

For Win32 Programmers: Segment Registers in Win32

If you've experimented with the debugger in Win32, you may have noticed the segment registers, particularly CS, DS, and SS. These 16-bit relics haven't gone away, but you can mostly ignore them. In 32-bit mode, the Intel microprocessor still uses segment registers, which are 16 bits long, to translate addresses prior to sending them through the virtual memory system. A table in RAM, called the descriptor table, has entries that contain the virtual memory base address and block size for code, data, and stack segments. In 32-bit mode, these segments can be up to 4 GB in size and can be flagged as read-only or read/write. For every memory reference, the chip uses the selector, the contents of a segment register, to look up the descriptor table entry for the purpose of translating the address.

Under Win32, each process has two segments—one for code and one for data and the stack. You can assume that both have a base value of 0 and a size of 4 GB, so they overlap. The net result is no translation at all, but Windows uses some tricks that exclude the bottom 16 KB from the data segment. If you try to access memory down there, you get a protection fault instead of a page fault, which is useful for debugging null pointers.

Some future operating system might someday use segments to get around that annoying 4-GB size limitation, but by then we'll have Win64 to worry about!

The *VirtualAlloc* Function— Committed and Reserved Memory

If your program needs dynamic memory, sooner or later the Win32 *VirtualAlloc* function will be called. Chances are that your program will never call *VirtualAlloc*; instead you'll rely on the Windows heap or the CRT heap functions to call it directly. Knowing how *VirtualAlloc* works, however, will help you better understand the functions that call it.

First you must know the meanings of reserved and committed memory. When memory is reserved, a contiguous virtual address range is set aside. If, for example, you know that your program is going to use a single 5-MB memory block (known as a region) but you don't need to use it all right away, you call *VirtualAlloc* with a *MEM_RESERVE* allocation type parameter and a 5-MB size parameter. Windows rounds the start address of the region to a 64-KB boundary and prevents your process from reserving other memory in the same range. You can specify a start address for your region, but more often you'll let Windows assign it for you. Nothing else happens. No RAM is allocated, and no swap file space is set aside.

When you get more serious about needing memory, you call *VirtualAlloc* again to commit the reserved memory, using a *MEM_COMMIT* allocation type parameter. Now the start and end addresses of the region are rounded to 4-KB boundaries, and corresponding swap file pages are set aside together with the required page table. The block is designated either read-only or read/write. Still no RAM is allocated, however; RAM allocation occurs only when you try to access the memory. If the memory was not previously reserved, no problem. If the memory was previously committed, still no problem. The rule is that memory must be committed before you can use it.

You call the *VirtualFree* function to "decommit" committed memory, thereby returning the designated pages back to reserved status. *VirtualFree* can also free a reserved region of memory, but you have to specify the base address you got from a previous *VirtualAlloc* reservation call.

The Windows Heap and the *GlobalAlloc* Function Family

A heap is a memory pool for a specific process. When your program needs a block of memory, it calls a heap allocation function, and it calls a companion function to free the memory. There's no assumption about 4-KB page boundaries; the heap manager uses space in existing pages or calls *VirtualAlloc* to get more pages. First we'll look at Windows heaps. Next we'll consider heaps managed by the CRT library for functions like *malloc* and *new*.

Windows provides each process with a default heap, and the process can create any number of additional Windows heaps. The *HeapAlloc* function allocates memory in a Windows heap, and *HeapFree* releases it.

You might never need to call *HeapAlloc* yourself, but it will be called for you by the *GlobalAlloc* function that's left over from Win16. In the ideal 32-bit world, you wouldn't have to use *GlobalAlloc*, but in this real world, we're stuck with a lot of code ported from Win16 that uses "memory handle" (*HGLOBAL*) parameters instead of 32-bit memory addresses.

GlobalAlloc uses the default Windows heap. It does two different things, depending on its attribute parameter. If you specify *GMEM_FIXED*, *GlobalAlloc* simply calls *HeapAlloc* and returns the address cast as a 32-bit *HGLOBAL* value. If you specify *GMEM_MOVEABLE*, the returned *HGLOBAL* value is a pointer to a <u>handle</u> <u>table</u> entry in your process. That entry contains a pointer to the actual memory, which is allocated with *HeapAlloc*.

Why bother with "moveable" memory if it adds an extra level of indirection? You're looking at an artifact from Win16, in which, once upon a time, the operating system actually moved memory blocks around. In Win32, moveable blocks exist only to support the *GlobalReAlloc* function, which allocates a new memory block, copies bytes from the old block to the new, frees the old block, and assigns the new block address to the existing handle table entry. If nobody called *GlobalReAlloc*, we could always use *HeapAlloc* instead of *GlobalAlloc*.

Unfortunately, many library functions use *HGLOBAL* return values and parameters instead of memory addresses. If such a function returns an *HGLOBAL* value, you should assume that memory was allocated with the *GMEM_MOVE-ABLE* attribute, and that means you must call the *GlobalLock* function to get the memory address. (If the memory was fixed, the *GlobalLock* call just returns the handle as an address.) Call *GlobalUnlock* when you're finished accessing the memory. If you're required to supply an *HGLOBAL* parameter, to be absolutely safe you should generate it with a *GlobalAlloc(GMEM_MOVEABLE, ...)* call in case the called function decides to call *GlobalReAlloc* and expects the handle value to be unchanged.

The Small-Block Heap, the C++ *new* and *delete* Operators, and _*heapmin*

You can use the Windows *HeapAlloc* function in your programs, but you're more likely to use the *malloc* and *free* functions supplied by the CRT. If you write C++ code, you won't call these functions directly; instead, you'll use the *new* and *delete* operators, which map directly to *malloc* and *free*. If you use *new* to allocate a block larger than a certain threshold (480 bytes is the default), the CRT passes the call straight through to *HeapAlloc* to allocate memory from a Windows heap created for the CRT. For blocks smaller than the threshold, the CRT manages a <u>small-block</u> <u>heap</u>, calling *VirtualAlloc* and *VirtualFree* as necessary. Here is the algorithm:

1. Memory is reserved in 4-MB regions.

2. Memory is committed in 64-KB blocks (16 pages).

3. Memory is decommitted 64 KB at a time. As 128 KB becomes free, the last 64 KB is decommitted.

4. A 4-MB region is released when every page in that region has been decommitted.

As you can see, this small-block heap takes care of its own cleanup. The CRT's Windows heap doesn't automatically decommit and unreserve pages, however. To clean up the larger blocks, you must call the CRT *_heapmin* function, which calls the windows *HeapCompact* function. (Unfortunately, the Windows 95 version of *HeapCompact* doesn't do anything—all the more reason to use Windows NT.) Once pages are decommitted, other programs can reuse the corresponding swap file space.

NOTE: In previous versions of the CRT, the free list pointers were stored inside the heap pages. This strategy required the *malloc* function to "touch" (read from the swap file) many pages to find free space, and this degraded performance. The current system, which stores the free list in a separate area of memory, is faster and minimizes the need for third-party heap management software.

If you want to change or access the block size threshold, use the CRT functions *_set_sbh_threshold* and *_get_sbh_threshold*.

A special debug version of *malloc*, *_malloc_dbg*, adds debugging information inside allocated memory blocks. The *new* operator calls *_malloc_dbg* when you build an MFC project with *_DEBUG* defined. Your program can then detect memory blocks that you forgot to free or that you inadvertently overwrote.

Memory-Mapped Files

In case you think you don't have enough memory management options already, I'll toss you another one. Suppose your program needs to read a DIB (device-independent bitmap) file. Your instinct would be to allocate a buffer of the correct size, open the file, and then call a read function to copy the whole disk file into the buffer. The Windows memory-mapped file is a more elegant tool for handling this problem, however. You simply map an address range directly to the file. When the process accesses a memory page, Windows allocates RAM and reads the data from disk. Here's what the code looks like:

```
HANDLE hFile = ::CreateFile(strPathname, GENERIC_READ,
    FILE_SHARE_READ, NULL, OPEN_EXISTING, FILE_ATTRIBUTE_NORMAL, NULL);
ASSERT(hFile != NULL);
HANDLE hMap = ::CreateFileMapping(hFile, NULL, PAGE_READONLY,
    0, 0, NULL);
ASSERT(hMap != NULL);
LPVOID lpvFile = ::MapViewOfFile(hMap, FILE_MAP_READ,
    0, 0, 0); // Map whole file
DWORD dwFileSize = ::GetFileSize(hFile, NULL);  // useful info
// Use the file
```

```
::UnmapViewOfFile(lpvFile);
::CloseHandle(hMap);
::CloseHandle(hFile);
```

Here you're using virtual memory backed by the DIB file. Windows determines the file size, reserves a corresponding address range, and commits the file's storage as the physical storage for this range. In this case, *lpvFile* is the start address. The *hMap* variable contains the handle for the file mapping object, which can be shared among processes if desired.

The DIB in the example above is a small file that you could read entirely into a buffer. Imagine a larger file for which you would normally issue seek commands. A memory-mapped file works for such a file, too, because of the underlying virtual memory system. RAM is allocated and pages are read when you access them, and not before.

> **NOTE:** By default, the entire file is committed when you map it, although it's possible to map only part of a file.

If two processes share a file mapping object (such as *hMap* in the sample code above), the file itself is, in effect, shared memory, but the virtual addresses returned by *MapViewOfFile* might be different. Indeed, this is the preferred Win32 method of sharing memory. (Calling the *GlobalAlloc* function with the *GMEM_SHARE* flag doesn't create shared memory as it did in Win16.) If memory sharing is all you want to do and you don't need a permanent disk file, you can omit the call to *CreateFile* and pass 0xFFFFFFFF as the *CreateFileMapping hFile* parameter. Now the shared memory will be backed by pages in the swap file. Consult Richter for details on memory-mapped files. The EX35B and EX35C sample programs in Chapter 35 illustrate sharing of memory-mapped files.

> **NOTE:** If you intend to access only a few random pages of a file mapping object that is backed by the swap file, you can use a technique that Jeffrey Richter describes in *Advanced Windows* under the heading "Sparsely Committed Memory-Mapped Files." In this case, you call *CreateFileMapping* with a special flag and then you commit specific address ranges later with the *VirtualAlloc* function.

> **NOTE:** You might want to look carefully at the Windows message WM_COPYDATA. This message lets you transfer data between processes in shared memory without having to deal with the file mapping API. You must send this message rather than post it, which means the sending process has to wait while the receiving process copies and processes the data.

Unfortunately, there's no direct support for memory-mapped files or shared memory in MFC. The *CSharedFile* class supports only clipboard memory transfers using *HGLOBAL* handles, so the class isn't as useful as its name implies.

Accessing Resources

Resources are contained inside EXEs and DLLs and thus occupy virtual address space that doesn't change during the life of the process. This fact makes it easy to read a resource directly. If you need to access a bitmap, for example, you can get the DIB address with code like this:

```
LPVOID lpvResource = (LPVOID) ::LoadResource(NULL,
    ::FindResource(NULL, MAKEINTRESOURCE(IDB_REDBLOCKS),
    RT_BITMAP));
```

The *LoadResource* function returns an *HGLOBAL* value, but you can safely cast it to a pointer.

Some Tips for Managing Dynamic Memory

The more you use the heap, the more fragmented it gets and the more slowly your program runs. If your program is supposed to run for hours or days at a time, you have to be careful. It's better to allocate all the memory you need when your program starts and then free it when the program exits, but that's not always possible. The *CString* class is a nuisance because it's constantly allocating and freeing little bits of memory. Fortunately, MFC developers have recently made some improvements.

Don't forget to call *_heapmin* every once in a while if your program allocates blocks larger than the small-block heap threshold. And be careful to remember where heap memory comes from. You'd have a big problem, for instance, if you called *HeapFree* on a small-block pointer you got from *new*.

Be aware that your stack can be as big as it needs to be. Because you no longer have a 64-KB size limit, you can put large objects on the stack, thereby reducing the need for heap allocations.

As in Win16, your program doesn't run at full speed and then suddenly throw an exception when Windows runs out of swap space. Your program just slowly grinds to a halt, making your customer unhappy. And there's not much you can do except try to figure out which program is eating memory and why. Because the Windows 95 USER and GDI modules still have 16-bit components, there is some possibility of exhausting the 64-KB heaps that hold GDI objects and window structures. This possibility is pretty remote, however, and if it happens, it probably indicates a bug in your program.

Optimizing Storage for Constant Data

Remember that the code in your program is backed not by the swap file but directly by its EXE and DLL files. If several instances of your program are running, the same EXE and DLL files will be mapped to each process's virtual address space. What about constant data? You would want that data to be part of the program rather than have it copied to another block of address space that's backed by the swap file.

You've got to work a little bit to ensure that constant data gets stored with the program. First consider string constants, which often permeate your programs. You would think that these would be read-only data, but guess again. Because you're allowed to write code like this:

```
char* pch = "test";
*pch = 'x';
```

"*test*" can't possibly be constant data, and it isn't.

If you want "*test*" to be a constant, you must declare it as an initialized *const* static or global variable. Here's the global definition:

```
const char g_pch[] = "test";
```

Now *g_pch* is stored with the code, but where, specifically? To answer that, you must understand the "data sections" that the Visual C++ linker generates. If you set the link options to generate a map file, you'll see a long list of the sections (memory blocks) in your program. Individual sections can be designated for code or data, and they can be read-only or read/write. The important sections and their characteristics are listed here.

Name	Type	Access	Contents
.text	Code	Read-only	Program code
.rdata	Data	Read-only	Constant initialized data
.data	Data	Read/write	Nonconstant initialized data
.bss	Data	Read/write	Nonconstant uninitialized data

The .rdata section is part of the EXE file, and that's where the linker puts the *g_pch* variable. The more stuff you put in the .rdata section, the better. The use of the *const* modifier does the trick.

You can put built-in types and even structures in the .rdata section, but you can't put C++ objects there if they have constructors. If you write a statement like the following one:

```
const CRect g_rect(0, 0, 100, 100);
```

the linker puts the object into the .bss section, and it will be backed separately to the swap file for each process. If you think about it, this makes sense because the compiler must invoke the constructor function after the program is loaded.

Now suppose you wanted to do the worst possible thing. You'd declare a *CString* global variable (or static class data member) like this:

```
const CString g_str("this is the worst thing I can do");
```

Now you've got the *CString* object (which is quite small) in the .bss section, and you've also got a character array in the .data section, neither of which can be backed by the EXE file. To make matters worse, when the program starts, the *CString* class must allocate heap memory for a copy of the characters. You would be much better off using a *const* character array instead of a *CString* object.

Bitmaps

Without graphics images, Microsoft Windows–based applications would be pretty dull. Some applications depend on images for their usefulness, but any application can be spruced up with the addition of decorative clip art from a variety of sources. Windows <u>bitmaps</u> are arrays of bits mapped to display pixels. That might sound simple, but you have to learn a lot about bitmaps before you can use them to create professional applications for Windows.

This chapter starts with the "old" way of programming bitmaps—creating the device-dependent GDI bitmaps that work with a memory device context. You need to know these techniques because many programmers are still using them and you'll also need to use them on occasion.

Next you'll graduate to the modern way of programming bitmaps—creating device-independent bitmaps (DIBs). If you use DIBs, you'll have an easier time with colors and with the printer. In some cases you'll get better performance. The Win32 function *CreateDIBSection* gives you the benefits of DIBs combined with all the features of GDI bitmaps.

Finally, you'll learn how to use the MFC *CBitmapButton* class to put bitmaps on pushbuttons. (Using *CBitmapButton* to put bitmaps on pushbuttons has nothing to do with DIBs, but it's a useful technique that would be difficult to master without an example.)

GDI Bitmaps and Device-Independent Bitmaps

There are two kinds of Windows bitmaps: <u>GDI</u> <u>bitmaps</u> and <u>DIBs</u>. GDI bitmap objects are represented by the Microsoft Foundation Class (MFC) Library version 6.0 *CBitmap* class. The GDI bitmap object has an associated Windows data structure, maintained inside the Windows GDI module, that is device-dependent. Your program can get a copy of the bitmap data, but the bit arrangement depends on the display hardware. GDI bitmaps can be freely transferred among programs on a single computer, but because of their device dependency, transferring bitmaps by disk or modem doesn't make sense.

NOTE: In Win32, you're allowed to put a GDI bitmap handle on the clipboard for transfer to another process, but behind the scenes Windows converts the device-dependent bitmap to a DIB and copies the DIB to shared memory. That's a good reason to consider using DIBs from the start.

DIBs offer many programming advantages over GDI bitmaps. Because a DIB carries its own color information, color palette management is easier. DIBs also make it easy to control gray shades when printing. Any computer running Windows can process DIBs, which are usually stored in BMP disk files or as a resource in your program's EXE or DLL file. The wallpaper background on your monitor is read from a BMP file when you start Windows. The primary storage format for Microsoft Paint is the BMP file, and Visual C++ uses BMP files for toolbar buttons and other images. Other graphic interchange formats are available, such as TIFF, GIF, and JPEG, but only the DIB format is directly supported by the Win32 API.

Color Bitmaps and Monochrome Bitmaps

Now might be a good time to reread the "Windows Color Mapping" section in Chapter 5. As you'll see in this chapter, Windows deals with color bitmaps a little differently from the way it deals with brush colors.

Many color bitmaps are 16-color. A standard VGA board has four contiguous color planes, with 1 corresponding bit from each plane combining to represent a pixel. The 4-bit color values are set when the bitmap is created. With a standard VGA board, bitmap colors are limited to the standard 16 colors. Windows does not use dithered colors in bitmaps.

A monochrome bitmap has only one plane. Each pixel is represented by a single bit that is either off (0) or on (1). The *CDC::SetTextColor* function sets the "off" display color, and *SetBkColor* sets the "on" color. You can specify these pure colors individually with the Windows *RGB* macro.

Using GDI Bitmaps

A GDI bitmap is simply another GDI object, such as a pen or a font. You must somehow create a bitmap, and then you must select it into a device context. When you're finished with the object, you must deselect it and delete it. You know the drill.

There's a catch, though, because the "bitmap" of the display or printer device is effectively the display surface or the printed page itself. Therefore, you can't select a bitmap into a display device context or a printer device context.

You have to create a special <u>memory device context</u> for your bitmaps, using the *CDC::CreateCompatibleDC* function. You must then use the *CDC* member function *StretchBlt* or *BitBlt* to copy the bits from the memory device context to the "real" device context. These "bit-blitting" functions are generally called in your view class's *OnDraw* function. Of course, you mustn't forget to clean up the memory device context when you're finished.

Loading a GDI Bitmap from a Resource

The easiest way to use a bitmap is to load it from a resource. If you look in ResourceView in the Workspace window, you'll find a list of the project's bitmap resources. If you select a bitmap and examine its properties, you'll see a filename.

Here's an example entry in an RC (resource script) file, when viewed by a text editor:

```
IDB_REDBLOCKS               BITMAP  DISCARDABLE     "res\\Red Blocks.bmp"
```

IDB_REDBLOCKS is the resource ID, and the file is Red Blocks.bmp in the project's \res subdirectory. (This is one of the Microsoft Windows 95 wallpaper bitmaps, normally located in the \WINDOWS directory.) The resource compiler reads the DIB from disk and stores it in the project's RES file. The linker copies the DIB into the program's EXE file. You know that the Red Blocks bitmap must be in device-independent format because the EXE can be run with any display board that Windows supports.

The *CDC::LoadBitmap* function converts a resource-based DIB to a GDI bitmap. Below is the simplest possible self-contained *OnDraw* function that displays the Red Blocks bitmap:

```
CMyView::OnDraw(CDC* pDC)
{
    CBitmap bitmap; // Sequence is important
    CDC dcMemory;
    bitmap.LoadBitmap(IDB_REDBLOCKS);
    dcMemory.CreateCompatibleDC(pDC);
    dcMemory.SelectObject(&bitmap);
    pDC->BitBlt(100, 100, 54, 96, &dcMemory, 0, 0, SRCCOPY);
    // CDC destructor deletes dcMemory; bitmap is deselected
    // CBitmap destructor deletes bitmap
}
```

The *BitBlt* function copies the Red Blocks pixels from the memory device context to the display (or printer) device context. The bitmap is 54 bits wide by 96 bits high, and on a VGA display it occupies a rectangle of 54-by-96 logical units, offset 100 units down and to the right of the upper-left corner of the window's client area.

NOTE: The code on the previous page works fine for the display. As you'll see in Chapter 19, the application framework calls the *On-Draw* function for printing, in which case *pDC* points to a printer device context. The bitmap here, unfortunately, is configured specifically for the display and thus cannot be selected into the printer-compatible memory device context. If you want to print a bitmap, you should look at the *CDib* class described later in this chapter.

The Effect of the Display Mapping Mode

If the display mapping mode in the Red Blocks example is *MM_TEXT*, each bitmap pixel maps to a display pixel and the bitmap fits perfectly. If the mapping mode is *MM_LOENGLISH*, the bitmap size is 0.54-by-0.96 inch, or 52-by-92 pixels for Windows 95, and the GDI must do some bit crunching to make the bitmap fit. Consequently, the bitmap might not look as good with the *MM_LOENGLISH* mapping mode. Calling *CDC::SetStretchBltMode* with a parameter value of *COLORONCOLOR* will make shrunken bitmaps look nicer.

Stretching the Bits

What if we want Red Blocks to occupy a rectangle of exactly 54-by-96 pixels, even though the mapping mode is not *MM_TEXT*? The *StretchBlt* function is the solution. If we replace the *BitBlt* call with the following three statements, Red Blocks is displayed cleanly, whatever the mapping mode:

```
CSize size(54, 96);
pDC->DPtoLP(&size);
pDC->StretchBlt(0, 0, size.cx, -size.cy,
                &dcMemory, 0, 0, 54, 96, SRCCOPY);
```

With either *BitBlt* or *StretchBlt*, the display update is slow if the GDI has to actually stretch or compress bits. If, as in the case above, the GDI determines that no conversion is necessary, the update is fast.

The EX11A Example

The EX11A example displays a resource-based bitmap in a scrolling view with mapping mode set to *MM_LOENGLISH*. The program uses the *StretchBlt* logic described above, except that the memory device context and the bitmap are created in the view's *OnInitialUpdate* member function and last for the life of the program. Also, the program reads the bitmap size through a call to the *CGdiObject* member function *GetObject*, so it's not using hard-coded values as in the preceding examples.

Here are the steps for building the example:

1. **Run AppWizard to produce \vcpp32\ex11a\ex11a.** Accept all the default settings but two: select Single Document, and select the *CScrollView* view base class, as shown in Chapter 4 on page 70, for *CEx11aView*. The options and the default class names are shown here.

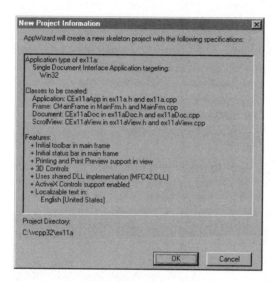

2. **Import the Gold Weave bitmap.** Choose Resource from Visual C++'s Insert menu. Import the bitmap Gold Weave.bmp from the \WINDOWS directory. (If your version of Windows doesn't have this bitmap, load it from this book's companion CD-ROM.) Visual C++ will copy this bitmap file into your project's \res subdirectory. Assign the ID *IDB_GOLDWEAVE*, and save the changes.

3. **Add the following private data members to the class *CEx11aView*.** Edit the file ex11aView.h or use ClassView. The bitmap and the memory device context last for the life of the view. The *CSize* objects are the source (bitmap) dimensions and the destination (display) dimensions.

```
CDC*     m_pdcMemory;
CBitmap* m_pBitmap;
CSize    m_sizeSource, m_sizeDest;
```

4. **Edit the following member functions in the class *CEx11aView*.** Edit the file ex11aView.cpp. The constructor and destructor do C++ house-keeping for the embedded objects. You want to keep the constructor as simple as possible because failing constructors cause problems.

The *OnInitialUpdate* function sets up the memory device context and the bitmap, and it computes output dimensions that map each bit to a pixel. The *OnDraw* function calls *StretchBlt* twice—once by using the special computed dimensions and once by mapping each bit to a 0.01-by-0.01-inch square. Add the following boldface code:

```
CEx11aView::CEx11aView()
{
    m_pdcMemory = new CDC;
    m_pBitmap = new CBitmap;
}


CEx11aView::~CEx11aView()
{
    // cleans up the memory device context and the bitmap
    delete m_pdcMemory; // deselects bitmap
    delete m_pBitmap;
}
void CEx11aView::OnDraw(CDC* pDC)
{
    pDC->SetStretchBltMode(COLORONCOLOR);
    pDC->StretchBlt(20, -20, m_sizeDest.cx, -m_sizeDest.cy,
        m_pdcMemory, 0, 0,
        m_sizeSource.cx, m_sizeSource.cy, SRCCOPY);

    pDC->StretchBlt(350, -20, m_sizeSource.cx, -m_sizeSource.cy,
        m_pdcMemory, 0, 0,
        m_sizeSource.cx, m_sizeSource.cy, SRCCOPY);
}


void CEx11aView::OnInitialUpdate()
{
    CScrollView::OnInitialUpdate();
    CSize sizeTotal(800, 1050); // 8-by-10.5 inches
    CSize sizeLine = CSize(sizeTotal.cx / 100, sizeTotal.cy / 100);
    SetScrollSizes(MM_LOENGLISH, sizeTotal, sizeTotal, sizeLine);

    BITMAP bm; // Windows BITMAP data structure; see Win32 help
    if (m_pdcMemory->GetSafeHdc() == NULL) {
        CClientDC dc(this);
        OnPrepareDC(&dc); // necessary
        m_pBitmap->LoadBitmap(IDB_GOLDWEAVE);
        m_pdcMemory->CreateCompatibleDC(&dc);
        m_pdcMemory->SelectObject(m_pBitmap);
        m_pBitmap->GetObject(sizeof(bm), &bm);
        m_sizeSource.cx = bm.bmWidth;
        m_sizeSource.cy = bm.bmHeight;
```

```
        m_sizeDest = m_sizeSource;
        dc.DPtoLP(&m_sizeDest);
    }
}
```

5. Build and test the EX11A application. Your screen should look like this.

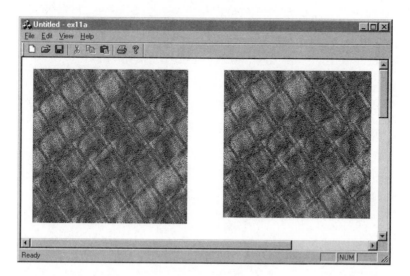

6. Try the Print Preview and Print features. The bitmap prints to scale because the application framework applies the *MM_LOENGLISH* mapping mode to the printer device context just as it does to the display device context. The output looks great in Print Preview mode, but (depending on your print drivers) the printed output will probably be either blank or microscopic! We'll fix that soon.

Using Bitmaps to Improve the Screen Display

You've seen an example program that displays a bitmap that originated outside the program. Now you'll see an example program that generates its own bitmap to support smooth motion on the screen. The principle is simple: you draw on a memory device context with a bitmap selected, and then you zap the bitmap onto the screen.

The EX11B Example

In the EX05C example in Chapter 5, the user dragged a circle with the mouse. As the circle moved, the display flickered because the circle was erased and re-drawn on every mouse-move message. EX11B uses a GDI bitmap to correct this problem. The EX05C custom code for mouse message processing carries over almost intact; most of the new code is in the *OnPaint* and *OnInitialUpdate* functions.

In summary, the EX11B *OnInitialUpdate* function creates a memory device context and a bitmap that are compatible with the display. The *OnPaint* function prepares the memory device context for drawing, passes *OnDraw* a handle to the memory device context, and copies the resulting bitmap from the memory device context to the display.

Here are the steps to build EX11B from scratch:

1. **Run AppWizard to produce \vcpp32\ex11b\ex11b.** Accept all the default settings but two: select Single Document and select *CScrollView* view as the base class for *CEx11bView*. The options and the default class names are shown here.

2. **Use ClassWizard to add *CEx11bView* message handlers.** Add message handlers for the following messages:

   ■ WM_LBUTTONDOWN

   ■ WM_LBUTTONUP

   ■ WM_MOUSEMOVE

   ■ WM_PAINT

3. **Edit the ex11bView.h header file.** Add the private data members shown here to the *CEx11bView* class:

```
private:
    const CSize m_sizeEllipse;
    CPoint  m_pointTopLeft;
    BOOL    m_bCaptured;
    CSize   m_sizeOffset;
    CDC*    m_pdcMemory;
    CBitmap* m_pBitmap;
```

4. Code the *CEx11bView* constructor and destructor in ex11bView.cpp.

You need a memory device context object and a bitmap GDI object. These are constructed in the view's constructor and destroyed in the view's destructor. Add the following boldface code:

```
CEx11bView::CEx11bView() : m_sizeEllipse(100, -100),
                           m_pointTopLeft(10, -10),
                           m_sizeOffset(0, 0)
{
    m_bCaptured = FALSE;
    m_pdcMemory = new CDC;
    m_pBitmap   = new CBitmap;
}

CEx11bView::~CEx11bView()
{
    delete m_pBitmap; // already deselected
    delete m_pdcMemory;
}
```

5. Add code for the *OnInitialUpdate* function in ex11bView.cpp.

The C++ memory device context and bitmap objects are already constructed. This function creates the corresponding Windows objects. Both the device context and the bitmap are compatible with the display context *dc*, but you must explicitly set the memory device context's mapping mode to match the display context. You could create the bitmap in the *OnPaint* function, but the program runs faster if you create it once here. Add the boldface code shown here:

```
void CEx11bView::OnInitialUpdate()
{
    CScrollView::OnInitialUpdate();
    CSize sizeTotal(800, 1050); // 8-by-10.5 inches
    CSize sizePage(sizeTotal.cx / 2, sizeTotal.cy / 2);
    CSize sizeLine(sizeTotal.cx / 50, sizeTotal.cy / 50);
    SetScrollSizes(MM_LOENGLISH, sizeTotal, sizePage, sizeLine);
    // creates the memory device context and the bitmap
    if (m_pdcMemory->GetSafeHdc() == NULL) {
```

(continued)

```
CClientDC dc(this);
OnPrepareDC(&dc);
CRect rectMax(0, 0, sizeTotal.cx, -sizeTotal.cy);
dc.LPtoDP(rectMax);
m_pdcMemory->CreateCompatibleDC(&dc);
// makes bitmap same size as display window
m_pBitmap->CreateCompatibleBitmap(&dc, rectMax.right,
                                    rectMax.bottom);
m_pdcMemory->SetMapMode(MM_LOENGLISH);
    }
}
```

6. Add code for the *OnPaint* function in ex11bView.cpp. Normally it isn't necessary to map the WM_PAINT message in your derived view class. The *CView* version of *OnPaint* contains the following code:

```
CPaintDC dc(this);
OnPrepareDC(&dc);
OnDraw(&dc);
```

In this example, you will be using the *OnPaint* function to reduce screen flicker through the use of a memory device context. *OnDraw* is passed this memory device context for the display, and it is passed the printer device context for printing. Thus, *OnDraw* can perform tasks common to the display and to the printer. You don't need to use the bitmap with the printer because the printer has no speed constraint.

The *OnPaint* function must perform, in order, the following three steps to prepare the memory device context for drawing:

■ Select the bitmap into the memory device context.

■ Transfer the invalid rectangle (as calculated by *OnMouseMove*) from the display context to the memory device context. There is no *SetClipRect* function, but the *CDC::IntersectClipRect* function, when called after the *CDC::SelectClipRgn* function (with a *NULL* parameter), has the same effect. If you don't set the clipping rectangle to the minimum size, the program runs more slowly.

■ Initialize the bitmap to the current window background color. The *CDC::PatBlt* function fills the specified rectangle with a pattern. In this case, the pattern is the brush pattern for the current window background. That brush must first be constructed and selected into the memory device context.

After the memory device context is prepared, *OnPaint* can call *OnDraw* with a memory device context parameter. Then the *CDC::BitBlt* function copies the updated rectangle from the memory device context to the display device context. Add the following boldface code:

```
void CEx11bView::OnPaint()
{
    CPaintDC dc(this); // device context for painting
    OnPrepareDC(&dc);
    CRect rectUpdate;
    dc.GetClipBox(&rectUpdate);
    CBitmap* pOldBitmap = m_pdcMemory->SelectObject(m_pBitmap);
    m_pdcMemory->SelectClipRgn(NULL);
    m_pdcMemory->IntersectClipRect(&rectUpdate);
    CBrush backgroundBrush((COLORREF) ::GetSysColor(COLOR_WINDOW));
    CBrush* pOldBrush = m_pdcMemory->SelectObject(&backgroundBrush);
    m_pdcMemory->PatBlt(rectUpdate.left, rectUpdate.top,
                        rectUpdate.Width(), rectUpdate.Height(),
                        PATCOPY);
    OnDraw(m_pdcMemory);
    dc.BitBlt(rectUpdate.left, rectUpdate.top,
              rectUpdate.Width(), rectUpdate.Height(),
              m_pdcMemory, rectUpdate.left, rectUpdate.top,
              SRCCOPY);
    m_pdcMemory->SelectObject(pOldBitmap);
    m_pdcMemory->SelectObject(pOldBrush);
}
```

7. **Code the *OnDraw* function in ex11bView.cpp.** Copy the code from ex05cView.cpp. In EX11B, *OnDraw* is passed a pointer to a memory device context by the *OnPaint* function. For printing, *OnDraw* is passed a pointer to the printer device context.

8. **Copy the mouse message-handling code from ex05cView.cpp.** Copy the functions shown below from ex05cView.cpp to ex11bView.cpp. Be sure to change the functions' class names from *CEx05cView* to *CEx11bView*.

   ■ *OnLButtonDown*

   ■ *OnLButtonUp*

   ■ *OnMouseMove*

9. **Change two lines in the *OnMouseMove* function in ex11bView.cpp.** Change the following two lines:

```
InvalidateRect(rectOld, TRUE);
InvalidateRect(rectNew, TRUE);
```

to

```
InvalidateRect(rectOld, FALSE);
InvalidateRect(rectNew, FALSE);
```

If the second *CWnd::InvalidateRect* parameter is *TRUE* (the default), Windows erases the background before repainting the invalid rectangle. That's what you needed in EX05C, but the background erasure is what causes the flicker. Because the entire invalid rectangle is being copied from the bitmap, you no longer need to erase the background. The *FALSE* parameter prevents this erasure.

10. **Build and run the application.** Here is the EX11B program output.

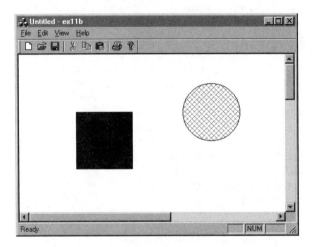

Is the circle's movement smoother now? The problem is that the bitmap is only 8-by-10.5 inches, and if the scrolling window is big enough, the circle goes off the edge. One solution to this problem is to make the bitmap as big as the largest display.

Windows Animation

EX11B is a crude attempt at Windows animation. What if you wanted to move an angelfish instead of a circle? Win32 doesn't have an *Angelfish* function (yet), so you'd have to keep your angelfish in its own bitmap and use the *StretchBlt* mask ROP codes to merge the angelfish with the background. You'd probably keep the background in its own bitmap, too. These techniques are outside the scope of this book. If you are interested in learning more about Windows Animation, run out and get Nigel Thompson's *Animation Techniques in Win32* (Microsoft Press, 1995). After you read it, you can get rich writing video games for Windows!

DIBs and the *CDib* Class

There's an MFC class for GDI bitmaps (*CBitmap*), but there's no MFC class for DIBs. Don't worry—I'm giving you one here. It's a complete rewrite of the *CDib* class from the early editions of this book (prior to the fourth edition), and it takes advantage of Win32 features such as memory-mapped files, improved memory management, and DIB sections. It also includes palette support. Before you examine the *CDib* class, however, you need a little background on DIBs.

A Few Words About Palette Programming

Windows palette programming is quite complex, but you've got to deal with it if you expect your users to run their displays in the 8-bpp (bits per pixel) mode—and many users will if they have video cards with 1 MB or less of memory.

Suppose you're displaying a single DIB in a window. First you must create a logical palette, a GDI object that contains the colors in the DIB. Then you must "realize" this logical palette into the hardware system palette, a table of the 256 colors the video card can display at that instant. If your program is the foreground program, the realization process tries to copy all your colors into the system palette, but it doesn't touch the 20 standard Windows colors. For the most part, your DIB looks just like you want it to look.

But what if another program is the foreground program, and what if that program has a forest scene DIB with 236 shades of green? Your program still realizes its palette, but something different happens this time. Now the system palette won't change, but Windows sets up a new mapping between your logical palette and the system palette. If your DIB contains a neon pink color, for example, Windows maps it to the standard red color. If your program forgot to realize its palette, your neon pink stuff would turn green when the other program went active.

The forest scene example is extreme because we assumed that the other program grabbed 236 colors. If instead the other program realized a logical palette with only 200 colors, Windows would let your program load 36 of its own colors, including, one hopes, neon pink.

So when is a program supposed to realize its palette? The Windows message WM_PALETTECHANGED is sent to your program's main window whenever a program, including yours, realizes its palette. Another message, WM_QUERYNEWPALETTE, is sent whenever one of the windows in your program gets the input focus. Your program should realize its palette in response to both these messages (unless your program generated the message). These palette messages are not sent to your view window, however. You must map them in your application's main frame window and then notify the view. Chapter 13 discusses the relationship between the frame window and the view, and Chapter 26 contains a complete palette-aware MDI application (EX26A).

You call the Win32 *RealizePalette* function to perform the realization, but first you must call *SelectPalette* to select your DIB's logical palette into the device context. *SelectPalette* has a flag parameter that you normally set to *FALSE* in your WM_PALETTECHANGED and WM_QUERYNEWPALETTE handlers. This flag ensures that your palette is realized as a foreground palette if your application is indeed running in the foreground. If you use a *TRUE* flag parameter here, you can force Windows to realize the palette as though the application were in the background.

You must also call *SelectPalette* for each DIB that you display in your *OnDraw* function. This time you call it with a *TRUE* flag parameter. Things do get complicated if you're displaying several DIBs, each with its own palette. Basically, you've got to choose a palette for one of the DIBs and realize it (by selecting it with the *FALSE* parameter) in the palette message handlers. The chosen DIB will end up looking better than the other DIBs. There are ways of merging palettes, but it might be easier to go out and buy more video memory.

DIBs, Pixels, and Color Tables

A DIB contains a two-dimensional array of elements called pixels. In many cases, each DIB pixel will be mapped to a display pixel, but the DIB pixel might be mapped to some logical area on the display, depending on the mapping mode and the display function stretch parameters.

A pixel consists of 1, 4, 8, 16, 24, or 32 contiguous bits, depending on the color resolution of the DIB. For 16-bpp, 24-bpp, and 32-bpp DIBs, each pixel represents an RGB color. A pixel in a 16-bpp DIB typically contains 5 bits each for red, green, and blue values; a pixel in a 24-bpp DIB has 8 bits for each color value. The 16-bpp and 24-bpp DIBs are optimized for video cards that can display 65,536 or 16.7 million simultaneous colors.

A 1-bpp DIB is a monochrome DIB, but these DIBs don't have to be black and white—they can contain any two colors chosen from the color table that is built into each DIB. A monochrome bitmap has two 32-bit color table entries, each containing 8 bits for red, green, and blue values plus another 8 bits for flags. Zero (0) pixels use the first entry, and one (1) pixel uses the second. Whether you have a 65,536-color video card or a 16.7-million-color card, Windows can display the two colors directly. (Windows truncates 8-bits-per-color values to 5 bits for 65,536-color displays.) If your video card is running in 256-color palettized mode, your program can adjust the system palette to load the two specified colors.

Eight-bpp DIBs are quite common. Like a monochrome DIB, an 8-bpp DIB has a color table, but the color table has 256 (or fewer) 32-bit entries. Each pixel is an index into this color table. If you have a palettized video card, your program can create a logical palette from the 256 entries. If another program (running in the foreground) has control of the system palette, Windows does its best to match your logical palette colors to the system palette.

What if you're trying to display a 24-bpp DIB with a 256-color palettized video card? If the DIB author was nice, he or she included a color table containing the most important colors in the DIB. Your program can build a logical palette from that table, and the DIB will look fine. If the DIB has no color table, use the palette returned by the Win32 *CreateHalftonePalette* function; it's better than the 20 standard colors you'd get with no palette at all. Another option is to analyze the DIB to identify the most important colors, but you can buy a utility to do that.

The Structure of a DIB Within a BMP File

You know that the DIB is the standard Windows bitmap format and that a BMP file contains a DIB. So let's look inside a BMP file to see what's there. Figure 11-1 shows a layout for a BMP file.

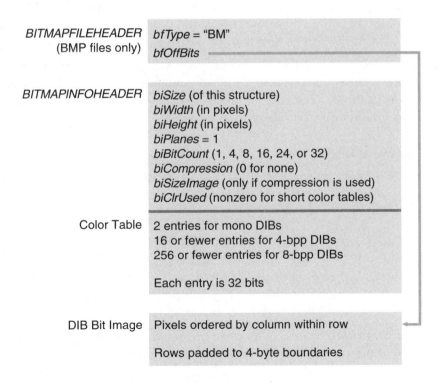

Figure 11-1.
The layout for a BMP file.

The *BITMAPFILEHEADER* structure contains the offset to the image bits, which you can use to compute the combined size of the *BITMAPINFOHEADER* structure and the color table that follows. The *BITMAPFILEHEADER* structure contains a file size member, but you can't depend on it because you don't know whether the size is measured in bytes, words, or double words.

The *BITMAPINFOHEADER* structure contains the bitmap dimensions, the bits per pixel, compression information for both 4-bpp and 8-bpp bitmaps, and the number of color table entries. If the DIB is compressed, this header contains the size of the pixel array; otherwise, you can compute the size from the dimensions and the bits per pixel. Immediately following the header is the color table (if the DIB has a color table). The DIB image comes after that. The DIB image consists of pixels arranged by column within rows, starting with the bottom row. Each row is padded to a 4-byte boundary.

The only place you'll find a *BITMAPFILEHEADER* structure, however, is in a BMP file. If you get a DIB from the clipboard, for example, there will not be a file header. You can always count on the color table to follow the *BITMAPINFOHEADER* structure, but you can't count on the image to follow the color table. If you're using the *CreateDIBSection* function, for example, you must allocate the bitmap info header and color table and then let Windows allocate the image somewhere else.

NOTE: This chapter and all the associated code are specific to Windows DIBs. There's also a well-documented variation of the DIB format for OS/2. If you need to process these OS/2 DIBs, you'll have to modify the *CDib* class.

DIB Access Functions

Windows supplies some important DIB access functions. None of these functions is wrapped by MFC, so you'll need to refer to the online Win32 documentation for details. Here's a summary:

- *SetDIBitsToDevice*—This function displays a DIB directly on the display or printer. No scaling occurs; one bitmap bit corresponds to one display pixel or one printer dot. This scaling restriction limits the function's usefulness. The function doesn't work like *BitBlt* because *BitBlt* uses logical coordinates.

- *StretchDIBits*—This function displays a DIB directly on the display or printer in a manner similar to that of *StretchBlt*.

- *GetDIBits*—This function constructs a DIB from a GDI bitmap, using memory that you allocate. You have some control over the format of the DIB because you can specify the number of color bits per pixel and the compression. If you are using compression, you have to call *GetDIBits* twice—once to calculate the memory needed and again to generate the DIB data.

■ ***CreateDIBitmap***—This function creates a GDI bitmap from a DIB. As for all these DIB functions, you must supply a device context pointer as a parameter. A display device context will do; you don't need a memory device context.

■ ***CreateDIBSection***—This Win32 function creates a special kind of DIB known as a <u>DIB</u> <u>section</u>. It then returns a GDI bitmap handle. This function gives you the best features of DIBs and GDI bitmaps. You have direct access to the DIB's memory, and with the bitmap handle and a memory device context, you can call GDI functions to draw into the DIB.

The *CDib* Class

If DIBs look intimidating, don't worry. The *CDib* class makes DIB programming easy. The best way to get to know the *CDib* class is to look at the public member functions and data members. Figure 11-2 shows the *CDib* header file. Consult the ex11c folder on the companion CD-ROM to see the implementation code.

CDIB.H

```
#ifndef _INSIDE_VISUAL_CPP_CDIB
#define _INSIDE_VISUAL_CPP_CDIB

class CDib : public CObject
{
    enum Alloc {noAlloc, crtAlloc,
                heapAlloc}; // applies to BITMAPINFOHEADER
    DECLARE_SERIAL(CDib)
public:
    LPVOID  m_lpvColorTable;
    HBITMAP m_hBitmap;
    LPBYTE  m_lpImage;  // starting address of DIB bits
    LPBITMAPINFOHEADER m_lpBMIH; // buffer containing the
                                 //   BITMAPINFOHEADER
private:
```

Figure 11-2. *(continued)*
The CDib *class declaration.*

CDIB.H *continued*

```
        HGLOBAL m_hGlobal; // for external windows we need to free;
                           //   could be allocated by this class or
                           //   allocated externally
    Alloc m_nBmihAlloc;
    Alloc m_nImageAlloc;
    DWORD m_dwSizeImage; // of bits--not BITMAPINFOHEADER
                         // or BITMAPFILEHEADER
    int m_nColorTableEntries;

    HANDLE m_hFile;
    HANDLE m_hMap;
    LPVOID m_lpvFile;
    HPALETTE m_hPalette;
public:
    CDib();
    CDib(CSize size, int nBitCount);  // builds BITMAPINFOHEADER
    ~CDib();
    int GetSizeImage() {return m_dwSizeImage;}
    int GetSizeHeader()
        {return sizeof(BITMAPINFOHEADER) +
                sizeof(RGBQUAD) * m_nColorTableEntries;}
    CSize GetDimensions();
    BOOL AttachMapFile(const char* strPathname, BOOL bShare = FALSE);
    BOOL CopyToMapFile(const char* strPathname);
    BOOL AttachMemory(LPVOID lpvMem, BOOL bMustDelete = FALSE,
        HGLOBAL hGlobal = NULL);
    BOOL Draw(CDC* pDC, CPoint origin,
        CSize size); // until we implement CreateDibSection
    HBITMAP CreateSection(CDC* pDC = NULL);
    UINT UsePalette(CDC* pDC, BOOL bBackground = FALSE);
    BOOL MakePalette();
    BOOL SetSystemPalette(CDC* pDC);
    BOOL Compress(CDC* pDC,
        BOOL bCompress = TRUE); // FALSE means decompress
    HBITMAP CreateBitmap(CDC* pDC);
    BOOL Read(CFile* pFile);
    BOOL ReadSection(CFile* pFile, CDC* pDC = NULL);
    BOOL Write(CFile* pFile);
    void Serialize(CArchive& ar);
    void Empty();
private:
    void DetachMapFile();
    void ComputePaletteSize(int nBitCount);
    void ComputeMetrics();
};
#endif // _INSIDE_VISUAL_CPP_CDIB
```

Here's a rundown of the *CDib* member functions, starting with the constructors and the destructor:

■ **Default constructor**—You'll use the default constructor in preparation for loading a DIB from a file or for attaching to a DIB in memory. The default constructor creates an empty DIB object.

■ **DIB section constructor**—If you need a DIB section that is created by the *CreateDIBSection* function, use this constructor. Its parameters determine DIB size and number of colors. The constructor allocates info header memory but not image memory. You can also use this constructor if you need to allocate your own image memory.

Parameter	Description
size	*CSize* object that contains the width and height of the DIB
nBitCount	Bits per pixel; should be 1, 4, 8, 16, 24, or 32

■ **Destructor**—The *CDib* destructor frees all allocated DIB memory.

■ *AttachMapFile*—This function opens a memory-mapped file in read mode and attaches it to the *CDib* object. The return is immediate because the file isn't actually read into memory until it is used. When you access the DIB, however, a delay might occur as the file is paged in. The *AttachMapFile* function releases existing allocated memory and closes any previously attached memory-mapped file.

Parameter	Description
strPathname	Pathname of the file to be mapped
bShare	Flag that is *TRUE* if the file is to be opened in share mode; the default value is *FALSE*
Return value	*TRUE* if successful

■ *AttachMemory*—This function associates an existing *CDib* object with a DIB in memory. This memory could be in the program's resources, or it could be clipboard or OLE data object memory. Memory might have been allocated from the CRT heap with the *new* operator, or it might have been allocated from the Windows heap with *GlobalAlloc*.

Parameter	Description
lpvMem	Address of the memory to be attached
bMustDelete	Flag that is *TRUE* if the *CDib* class is responsible for deleting this memory; the default value is *FALSE*
hGlobal	If memory was obtained with a call to the Win32 *GlobalAlloc* function, the *CDib* object needs to keep the handle in order to free it later, assuming that *bMustDelete* was set to *TRUE*
Return value	*TRUE* if successful

■ **Compress**—This function regenerates the DIB as a compressed or an uncompressed DIB. Internally, it converts the existing DIB to a GDI bitmap and then makes a new compressed or an uncompressed DIB. Compression is supported only for 4-bpp and 8-bpp DIBs. You can't compress a DIB section.

Parameter	Description
pDC	Pointer to the display device context
bCompress	*TRUE* (default) to compress the DIB; *FALSE* to uncompress it
Return value	*TRUE* if successful

■ **CopyToMapFile**—This function creates a new memory-mapped file and copies the existing *CDib* data to the file's memory, releasing any previously allocated memory and closing any existing memory-mapped file. The data isn't actually written to disk until the new file is closed, but that happens when the *CDib* object is reused or destroyed.

Parameter	Description
strPathname	Pathname of the file to be mapped
Return value	*TRUE* if successful

■ **CreateBitmap**—This function creates a GDI bitmap from an existing DIB and is called by the *Compress* function. Don't confuse this function with *CreateSection*, which generates a DIB and stores the handle.

Parameter	Description
pDC	Pointer to the display or printer device context
Return value	Handle to a GDI bitmap—*NULL* if unsuccessful. This handle is <u>not</u> stored as a public data member.

■ *CreateSection*—This function creates a DIB section by calling the Win32 *CreateDIBSection* function. The image memory will be uninitialized.

Parameter	Description
pDC	Pointer to the display or printer device context
Return value	Handle to a GDI bitmap—*NULL* if unsuccessful. This handle is also stored as a public data member.

■ *Draw*—This function outputs the *CDib* object to the display (or to the printer) with a call to the Win32 *StretchDIBits* function. The bitmap will be stretched as necessary to fit the specified rectangle.

Parameter	Description
pDC	Pointer to the display or printer device context that will receive the DIB image
origin	*CPoint* object that holds the logical coordinates at which the DIB will be displayed
size	*CSize* object that represents the display rectangle's width and height in logical units
Return value	*TRUE* if successful

■ *Empty*—This function empties the DIB, freeing allocated memory and closing the map file if necessary.

■ *GetDimensions*—This function returns the width and height of a DIB in pixels.

Parameter	Description
Return value	*CSize* object

■ *GetSizeHeader*—This function returns the number of bytes in the info header and color table combined.

Parameter	Description
Return value	32-bit integer

■ *GetSizeImage*—This function returns the number of bytes in the DIB image (excluding the info header and the color table).

Parameter	Description
Return value	32-bit integer

■ *MakePalette*—If the color table exists, this function reads it and creates a Windows palette. The *HPALETTE* handle is stored in a data member.

Parameter	Description
Return value	*TRUE* if successful

■ *Read*—This function reads a DIB from a file into the *CDib* object. The file must have been successfully opened. If the file is a BMP file, reading starts from the beginning of the file. If the file is a document, reading starts from the current file pointer.

Parameter	Description
pFile	Pointer to a *CFile* object; the corresponding disk file contains the DIB
Return value	*TRUE* if successful

■ *ReadSection*—This function reads the info header from a BMP file, calls *CreateDIBSection* to allocate image memory, and then reads the image bits from the file into that memory. Use this function if you want to read a DIB from disk and then edit it by calling GDI functions. You can write the DIB back to disk with *Write* or *CopyToMapFile*.

Parameter	Description
pFile	Pointer to a *CFile* object; the corresponding disk file contains the DIB
pDC	Pointer to the display or printer device context
Return value	*TRUE* if successful

■ ***Serialize***—Serialization is covered in Chapter 17. The *CDib::Serialize* function, which overrides the MFC *CObject::Serialize* function, calls the *Read* and *Write* member functions. See the *Microsoft Foundation Classes and Templates* section of the online help for a description of the parameters.

■ ***SetSystemPalette***—If you have a 16-bpp, 24-bpp, or 32-bpp DIB that doesn't have a color table, you can call this function to create for your *CDib* object a logical palette that matches the palette returned by the *CreateHalftonePalette* function. If your program is running on a 256-color palettized display and you don't call *SetSystemPalette*, you'll have no palette at all, and only the 20 standard Windows colors will appear in your DIB.

Parameter	Description
pDC	Pointer to the display context
Return value	*TRUE* if successful

■ ***UsePalette***—This function selects the *CDib* object's logical palette into the device context and then realizes the palette. The *Draw* member function calls *UsePalette* prior to painting the DIB.

Parameter	Description
pDC	Pointer to the display device context for realization
bBackground	If this flag is *FALSE* (the default value) and the application is running in the foreground, Windows realizes the palette as the foreground palette (copies as many colors as possible into the system palette). If this flag is *TRUE*, Windows realizes the palette as a background palette (maps the logical palette to the system palette as best it can).
Return value	Number of entries in the logical palette mapped to the system palette. If the function fails, the return value is *GDI_ERROR*.

■ **Write**—This function writes a DIB from the *CDib* object to a file. The file must have been successfully opened or created.

Parameter	Description
pFile	Pointer to a *CFile* object; the DIB will be written to the corresponding disk file.
Return value	*TRUE* if successful

For your convenience, four public data members give you access to the DIB memory and to the DIB section handle. These members should give you a clue about the structure of a *CDib* object. A *CDib* is just a bunch of pointers to heap memory. That memory might be owned by the DIB or by someone else. Additional private data members determine whether the *CDib* class frees the memory.

DIB Display Performance

Optimized DIB processing is now a major feature of Windows. Modern video cards have frame buffers that conform to the standard DIB image format. If you have one of these cards, your programs can take advantage of the new Windows DIB engine, which speeds up the process of drawing directly from DIBs. If you're still running in VGA mode, however, you're out of luck; your programs will still work, but not as fast.

If you're running Windows in 256-color mode, your 8-bpp bitmaps will be drawn very quickly, either with *StretchBlt* or with *StretchDIBits*. If, however, you are displaying 16-bpp or 24-bpp bitmaps, those drawing functions will be too slow. Your bitmaps will appear more quickly in this situation if you create a separate 8-bbp GDI bitmap and then call *StretchBlt*. Of course, you must be careful to realize the correct palette prior to creating the bitmap and prior to drawing it.

Here's some code that you might insert just after loading your *CDib* object from a BMP file:

```
// m_hBitmap is a data member of type HBITMAP
// m_dcMem is a memory device context object of class CDC
m_pDib->UsePalette(&dc);
m_hBitmap = m_pDib->CreateBitmap(&dc); // could be slow
::SelectObject(m_dcMem.GetSafeHdc(), m_hBitmap);
```

Here is the code that you use in place of *CDib::Draw* in your view's *OnDraw* member function:

```
m_pDib->UsePalette(pDC); // could be in palette msg handler
CSize sizeDib = m_pDib->GetDimensions();
pDC->StretchBlt(0, 0, sizeDib.cx, sizeDib.cy, &m_dcMem,
                0, 0, sizeToDraw.cx, sizeToDraw.cy, SRCCOPY);
```

Don't forget to call *DeleteObject* for *m_hBitmap* when you're done with it.

The EX11C Example

Now you'll put the *CDib* class to work in an application. The EX11C program displays two DIBs, one from a resource and the other loaded from a BMP file that you select at runtime. The program manages the system palette and displays the DIBs correctly on the printer. Compare the EX11C code with the GDI bitmap code in EX11A. Notice that you're not dealing with a memory device context and all the GDI selection rules!

Following are the steps to build EX11C. It's a good idea to type in the view class code, but you'll want to use the cdib.h and cdib.cpp files from the companion CD-ROM.

1. **Run AppWizard to produce \vcpp32\ex11c\ex11c.** Accept all the defaults but two: select Single Document and select the *CScrollView* view base class for *CEx11cView*. The options and the default class names are shown here.

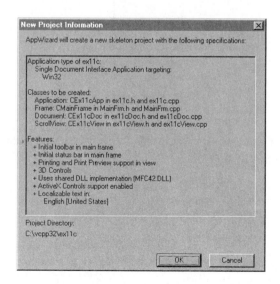

255

2. **Import the Red Blocks bitmap.** Choose Resource from Visual C++'s Insert menu. Import Red Blocks.bmp from the \WINDOWS directory. (If your version of Windows doesn't include this bitmap, load it from the companion CD-ROM.) Visual C++ will copy this bitmap file into your project's \res subdirectory. Assign *IDB_REDBLOCKS* as the ID, and save the changes.

3. **Integrate the *CDib* class with this project.** If you've created this project from scratch, copy the cdib.h and cdib.cpp files from \vcpp32\ex11c on the companion CD-ROM. Simply copying the files to disk isn't enough; you must also add the *CDib* files to the project. Choose Add To Project from Visual C++'s Project menu, and then choose Files. Select cdib.h and cdib.cpp, and click the OK button. If you now switch to ClassView in the Workspace window, you will see the class *CDib* and all of its member variables and functions.

4. **Add two private *CDib* data members to the class *CEx11cView*.** In the ClassView window, right-click the *CEx11cView* class. Choose Add Member Variable from the resulting pop-up menu, and then add the *m_dibResource* member as shown in the following illustration.

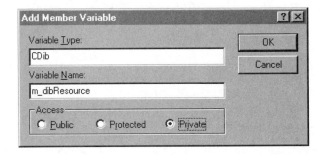

Add *m_dibFile* in the same way. The result should be two data members at the bottom of the header file:

```
CDib m_dibFile;
CDib m_dibResource;
```

ClassView also adds this statement at the top of the ex11cView.h file:

```
#include "cdib.h"   // Added by ClassView
```

5. **Edit the *OnInitialUpdate* member function in ex11cView.cpp.** This function sets the mapping mode to *MM_HIMETRIC* and loads the *m_dibResource* object directly from the *IDB_REDBLOCKS* resource. Note that we're not calling *LoadBitmap* to load a GDI bitmap as we did

in EX11A. The *CDib::AttachMemory* function connects the object to the resource in your EXE file. Add the following boldface code:

```
void CEx11cView::OnInitialUpdate()
{
    CScrollView::OnInitialUpdate();
    CSize sizeTotal(30000, 40000); // 30-by-40 cm
    CSize sizeLine = CSize(sizeTotal.cx / 100, sizeTotal.cy / 100);
    SetScrollSizes(MM_HIMETRIC, sizeTotal, sizeTotal, sizeLine);

    LPVOID lpvResource = (LPVOID) ::LoadResource(NULL,
        ::FindResource(NULL, MAKEINTRESOURCE(IDB_REDBLOCKS),
        RT_BITMAP));
    m_dibResource.AttachMemory(lpvResource); // no need for
                                           //   ::LockResource
    CClientDC dc(this);
    TRACE("bits per pixel = %d\n", dc.GetDeviceCaps(BITSPIXEL));
}
```

6. **Edit the *OnDraw* member function in the file ex11cView.cpp.** This code calls *CDib::Draw* for each of the DIBs. The *UsePalette* calls should really be made by message handlers for the WM_QUERYNEWPALETTE and WM_PALETTECHANGED messages. These messages are hard to deal with because they don't go to the view directly, so we'll take a shortcut. Add the following boldface code:

```
void CEx11cView::OnDraw(CDC* pDC)
{
    BeginWaitCursor();
    m_dibResource.UsePalette(pDC); // should be in palette
    m_dibFile.UsePalette(pDC);     //  message handlers, not here
    pDC->TextOut(0, 0,
        "Press the left mouse button here to load a file.");
    CSize sizeResourceDib = m_dibResource.GetDimensions();
    sizeResourceDib.cx *= 30;
    sizeResourceDib.cy *= -30;
    m_dibResource.Draw(pDC, CPoint(0, -800), sizeResourceDib);
    CSize sizeFileDib = m_dibFile.GetDimensions();
    sizeFileDib.cx *= 30;
    sizeFileDib.cy *= -30;
    m_dibFile.Draw(pDC, CPoint(1800, -800), sizeFileDib);
    EndWaitCursor();
}
```

7. **Map the WM_LBUTTONDOWN message in the *CEx11cView* class.** Edit the file ex11cView.cpp. *OnLButtonDown* contains code to read a DIB in two different ways. If you leave the MEMORY_MAPPED_FILES definition intact, the *AttachMapFile* code is activated to read a memory-mapped

file. If you comment out the first line, the *Read* call is activated. The *Set-SystemPalette* call is there for DIBs that don't have a color table. Add the following boldface code:

```
#define MEMORY_MAPPED_FILES
void CEx11cView::OnLButtonDown(UINT nFlags, CPoint point)
{
    CFileDialog dlg(TRUE, "bmp", "*.bmp");
    if (dlg.DoModal() != IDOK) {
        return;
    }
#ifdef MEMORY_MAPPED_FILES
    if (m_dibFile.AttachMapFile(dlg.GetPathName(),
            TRUE) == TRUE) { // share
        Invalidate();
    }
 #else
    CFile file;
    file.Open(dlg.GetPathName(), CFile::modeRead);
    if (m_dibFile.Read(&file) == TRUE) {
        Invalidate();
    }
#endif // MEMORY_MAPPED_FILES
    CClientDC dc(this);
    m_dibFile.SetSystemPalette(&dc);
}
```

8. **Build and run the application.**   The bitmaps directory on the companion CD-ROM contains several interesting bitmaps. The Chicago.bmp file is an 8-bpp DIB with 256-color table entries; the forest.bmp and clouds.bmp files are also 8-bpp, but they have smaller color tables. The balloons.bmp is a 24-bpp DIB with no color table. Try some other BMP files if you have them. Note that Red Blocks is a 16-color DIB that uses standard colors, which are always included in the system palette.

Going Further with DIBs

Each new version of Windows offers more DIB programming choices. Both Windows 95 and Microsoft Windows NT 4.0 provide the *LoadImage* and *Draw-DibDraw* functions, which are useful alternatives to the DIB functions already described. Experiment with these functions to see if they work well in your applications.

The *LoadImage* Function

The *LoadImage* function can read a bitmap directly from a disk file, returning a DIB section handle. It can even process OS/2 format DIBs. Suppose you wanted to add an *ImageLoad* member function to *CDib* that would work like *ReadSection*. This is the code you would add to cdib.cpp:

```
BOOL CDib::ImageLoad(const char* lpszPathName, CDC* pDC)
{
    Empty();
    m_hBitmap = (HBITMAP) ::LoadImage(NULL, lpszPathName,
        IMAGE_BITMAP, 0, 0,
        LR_LOADFROMFILE | LR_CREATEDIBSECTION | LR_DEFAULTSIZE);
    DIBSECTION ds;
    VERIFY(::GetObject(m_hBitmap, sizeof(ds), &ds) == sizeof(ds));
    // Allocate memory for BITMAPINFOHEADER
    //   and biggest possible color table
    m_lpBMIH = (LPBITMAPINFOHEADER) new
        char[sizeof(BITMAPINFOHEADER) + 256 * sizeof(RGBQUAD)];
    memcpy(m_lpBMIH, &ds.dsBmih, sizeof(BITMAPINFOHEADER));
    TRACE("CDib::LoadImage, biClrUsed = %d, biClrImportant = %d\n",
        m_lpBMIH->biClrUsed, m_lpBMIH->biClrImportant);
    ComputeMetrics(); // sets m_lpvColorTable
    m_nBmihAlloc = crtAlloc;
    m_lpImage = (LPBYTE) ds.dsBm.bmBits;
    m_nImageAlloc = noAlloc;
    // Retrieve the DIB section's color table
    //   and make a palette from it
    CDC memdc;
    memdc.CreateCompatibleDC(pDC);
    ::SelectObject(memdc.GetSafeHdc(), m_hBitmap);
    UINT nColors = ::GetDIBColorTable(memdc.GetSafeHdc(), 0, 256,
        (RGBQUAD*) m_lpvColorTable);
    if (nColors != 0) {
        ComputePaletteSize(m_lpBMIH->biBitCount);
        MakePalette();
    }
    // memdc deleted and bitmap deselected
    return TRUE;
}
```

Note that this function extracts and copies the *BITMAPINFOHEADER* structure and sets the values of the *CDib* pointer data members. You must do some work to extract the palette from the DIB section, but the Win32 *GetDIB-ColorTable* function gets you started. It's interesting that *GetDIBColorTable* can't tell you how many palette entries a particular DIB uses. If the DIB uses only 60 entries, for example, *GetDIBColorTable* generates a 256-entry color table with the last 196 entries set to 0.

The *DrawDibDraw* Function

Windows includes the Video for Windows (VFW) component, which is supported by Visual C++. The VFW *DrawDibDraw* function is an alternative to *StretchDIBits*. One advantage of *DrawDibDraw* is its ability to use dithered colors. Another is its increased speed in drawing a DIB with a bpp value that does not match the current video mode. The main disadvantage is the need to link the VFW code into your process at runtime.

Shown below is a *DrawDib* member function for the *CDib* class that calls *DrawDibDraw*:

```
BOOL CDib::DrawDib(CDC* pDC, CPoint origin, CSize size)
{
    if (m_lpBMIH == NULL) return FALSE;
    if (m_hPalette != NULL) {
        ::SelectPalette(pDC->GetSafeHdc(), m_hPalette, TRUE);
    }
    HDRAWDIB hdd = ::DrawDibOpen();
    CRect rect(origin, size);
    pDC->LPtoDP(rect); // Convert DIB's rectangle
                       //   to MM_TEXT coordinates
    rect -= pDC->GetViewportOrg();
    int nMapModeOld = pDC->SetMapMode(MM_TEXT);
    ::DrawDibDraw(hdd, pDC->GetSafeHdc(), rect.left, rect.top,
        rect.Width(), rect.Height(), m_lpBMIH, m_lpImage, 0, 0,
        m_lpBMIH->biWidth, m_lpBMIH->biHeight, 0);
    pDC->SetMapMode(nMapModeOld);
    VERIFY(::DrawDibClose(hdd));
    return TRUE;
}
```

Note that *DrawDibDraw* needs *MM_TEXT* coordinates and the *MM_TEXT* mapping mode. Thus, logical coordinates must be converted not to device coordinates but to pixels with the origin at the top left of the scrolling window.

To use *DrawDibDraw*, your program needs an *#include<vfw.h>* statement, and you must add vfw32.lib to the list of linker input files. *DrawDibDraw* might assume the bitmap it draws is in read/write memory, a fact to keep in mind if you map the memory to the BMP file.

Putting Bitmaps on Pushbuttons

The MFC library makes it easy to display a bitmap (instead of text) on a push-button. If you were to program this from scratch, you would set the Owner Draw property for your button and then write a message handler in your dialog class that would paint a bitmap on the button control's window. If you use the MFC *CBitmapButton* class instead, you end up doing a lot less work, but you have to follow a kind of "cookbook" procedure. Don't worry too much about how it all works (but be glad that you don't have to write much code!).

NOTE: There's also another way to put bitmaps on buttons. See Chapter 36, page 1063, for a description of the *CButton::SetBitmap* function, which associates a single bitmap with a button.

To make a long story short, you lay out your dialog resource as usual with unique text captions for the buttons you designate for bitmaps. Next you add some bitmap resources to your project, and you identify those resources by <u>name</u> rather than by numeric ID. Finally you add some *CBitmapButton* data members to your dialog class, and you call the *AutoLoad* member function for each one, which matches a bitmap name to a button caption. If the button caption is "Copy", you add two bitmaps: "COPYU" for the up state and "COPYD" for the down state. By the way, you must still set the button's Owner Draw property. (This will all make more sense when you write a program).

NOTE: If you look at the MFC source code for the *CBitmapButton* class, you'll see that the bitmap is an ordinary GDI bitmap painted with a *BitBlt* call. Thus, you can't expect any palette support. That's not often a problem because bitmaps for buttons are usually 16-color bitmaps that depend on standard VGA colors.

The EX11D Example

Here are the steps for building EX11D:

1. **Run AppWizard to produce \vcpp32\ex11d\ex11d.** Accept all the defaults but three: select Single Document, deselect Printing And Print Preview, and select Context-Sensitive Help. The options and the default class names are shown in the illustration on the next page.

   The Context-Sensitive Help option was selected for one reason only: it causes AppWizard to copy some bitmap files into your project's \hlp subdirectory. These bitmaps are supposed to be bound into your project's help file, but we won't study help files until Chapter 21.

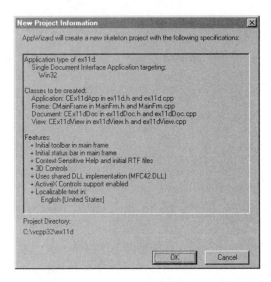

2. Modify the project's *IDD_ABOUTBOX* dialog resource. It's too much hassle to create a new dialog resource for a few buttons, so we'll use the About dialog that AppWizard generates for every project. Add three push-buttons with captions, as shown below, accepting the default IDs *IDC_BUTTON1*, *IDC_BUTTON2*, and *IDC_BUTTON3*. The size of the buttons isn't important because the framework adjusts the button size at runtime to match the bitmap size.

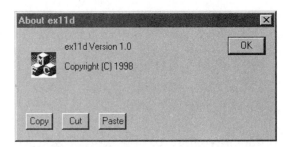

Select the Owner Draw property for all three buttons.

3. Import three bitmaps from the project's \hlp subdirectory. Choose Resource from Visual C++'s Insert menu, and then click the Import button. Start with EditCopy.bmp, as shown on the next page.

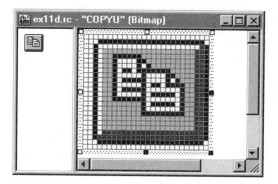

Assign the name "COPYU" as shown.

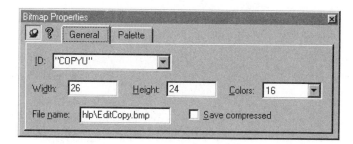

<u>Be sure to use quotes around the name</u> in order to identify the resource by name rather than by ID. This is now the bitmap for the button's up state. Close the bitmap window and, from the ResourceView window, use the clipboard (or drag and drop) to make a copy of the bitmap. Rename the copy "COPYD" (down state), and then edit this bitmap. Choose Invert Colors from the Image menu. There are other ways of making a variation of the up image, but inversion is the quickest.

Repeat the steps listed above for the EditCut and EditPast bitmaps. When you're finished, you should have the following bitmap resources in your project.

Resource Name	Original File	Invert Colors
"COPYU"	EditCopy.bmp	no
"COPYD"	EditCopy.bmp	yes
"CUTU"	EditCut.bmp	no
"CUTD"	EditCut.bmp	yes
"PASTEU"	EditPast.bmp	no
"PASTED"	EditPast.bmp	yes

4. Edit the code for the *CAboutDlg* class. Both the declaration and the implementation for this class are contained in the ex11d.cpp file. First add the three private data members shown here in the class declaration:

```
CBitmapButton m_editCopy;
CBitmapButton m_editCut;
CBitmapButton m_editPaste;
```

Then you use ClassWizard to map the WM_INITDIALOG message in the dialog class. (Be sure that the *CAboutDlg* class is selected.) The message handler (actually a virtual function) is coded as follows:

```
BOOL CAboutDlg::OnInitDialog()
{
    CDialog::OnInitDialog();
    VERIFY(m_editCopy.AutoLoad(IDC_BUTTON1, this));
    VERIFY(m_editCut.AutoLoad(IDC_BUTTON2, this));
    VERIFY(m_editPaste.AutoLoad(IDC_BUTTON3, this));
    return TRUE;  // return TRUE unless you set the focus to a control
                  // EXCEPTION: OCX Property Pages should return FALSE
}
```

The *AutoLoad* function connects each button with the two matching resources. The *VERIFY* macro is an MFC diagnostic aid that displays a message box if you didn't code the bitmap names correctly.

5. Edit the *OnDraw* function in ex11dView.cpp. Replace the AppWizard-generated code with the following line:

```
pDC->TextOut(0, 0, "Choose About from the Help menu.");
```

6. Build and test the application. When the program starts, choose About from the Help menu and observe the button behavior. The image below shows the CUT button in the down state.

Note that bitmap buttons send BN_CLICKED notification messages just as ordinary buttons do. ClassWizard can, of course, map those messages in your dialog class.

Going Further with Bitmap Buttons

You've seen bitmaps for the buttons' up and down states. The *CBitmapButton* class also supports bitmaps for the focused and disabled states. For the Copy button, the focused bitmap name would be "COPYF", and the disabled bitmap name would be "COPYX". If you want to test the disabled option, make a "COPYX" bitmap, possibly with a red line through it, and then add the following line to your program:

```
m_editCopy.EnableWindow(FALSE);
```

CHAPTER TWELVE

Windows Message Processing and Multi-threaded Programming

With its multitasking and multithreading API, Win32 revolutionized programming for Microsoft Windows. If you've seen magazine articles and advanced programming books on these subjects, you might have been intimidated by the complexity of using multiple threads. You could stick with single-threaded programming for a long time and still write useful Win32 applications. If you learn the fundamentals of threads, however, you'll be able to write more efficient and capable programs. You'll also be on your way to a better understanding of the Win32 programming model.

Windows Message Processing

To understand threads, you must first understand how 32-bit Windows processes messages. The best starting point is a single-threaded program that shows the importance of the message translation and dispatch process. You'll improve that program by adding a second thread, which you'll control with a global variable and a simple message. Then you'll experiment with events and critical sections. For heavy-duty multithreading elements such as mutexes and semaphores, however, you'll need to refer to another book, such as Jeffrey Richter's *Advanced Windows,* 3d Ed. (Microsoft Press, 1997).

How a Single-Threaded Program Processes Messages

All the programs so far in this book have been <u>single-threaded</u>, which means that your code has only one path of execution. With ClassWizard's help, you've written handler functions for various Windows messages and you've written *OnDraw* code that is called in response to the WM_PAINT message. It might seem as though Windows magically calls your handler when the message floats in, but it doesn't work that way. Deep inside the MFC code (which is linked to your program) are instructions that look something like this:

```
MSG message;
while (::GetMessage(&message, NULL, 0, 0)) {
    ::TranslateMessage(&message);
    ::DispatchMessage(&message);
}
```

Windows determines which messages belong to your program, and the *Get-Message* function returns when a message needs to be processed. If no messages are posted, your program is suspended and other programs can run. When a message eventually arrives, your program "wakes up." The *TranslateMessage* function translates WM_KEYDOWN messages into WM_CHAR messages containing ASCII characters, and the *DispatchMessage* function passes control (via the window class) to the MFC message pump, which calls your function via the message map. When your handler is finished, it returns to the MFC code, which eventually causes *DispatchMessage* to return.

Yielding Control

What would happen if one of your handler functions was a pig and chewed up 10 seconds of CPU time? Back in the 16-bit days, that would have hung up the whole computer for the duration. Only cursor tracking and a few other interrupt-based tasks would have run. With Win32, multitasking got a whole lot better. Other applications can run because of preemptive multitasking— Windows simply interrupts your pig function when it needs to. However, even in Win32, your program would be locked out for 10 seconds. It couldn't process any messages because *DispatchMessage* doesn't return until the pig returns.

There is a way around this problem, however, which works with both Win16 and Win32. You simply train your pig function to be polite and yield control once in a while by inserting the following instructions inside the pig's main loop:

```
MSG message;
if (::PeekMessage(&message, NULL, 0, 0, PM_REMOVE)) {
    ::TranslateMessage(&message);
    ::DispatchMessage(&message);
}
```

The *PeekMessage* function works like *GetMessage*, except that it returns immediately even if no message has arrived for your program. In that case, the pig keeps on chewing. If there is a message, however, the pig pauses, the handler is called, and the pig starts up again after the handler exits.

Timers

A Windows timer is a useful programming element that sometimes makes multi-threaded programming unnecessary. If you need to read a communication buffer, for example, you can set up a timer to retrieve the accumulated characters every 100 milliseconds. You can also use a timer to control animation because the timer is independent of CPU clock speed.

Timers are easy to use. You simply call the *CWnd* member function *Set-Timer* with an interval parameter, and then you provide, with the help of Class-Wizard, a message handler function for the resulting WM_TIMER messages. Once you start the timer with a specified interval in milliseconds, WM_TIMER messages will be sent continuously to your window until you call *CWnd::Kill-Timer* or until the timer's window is destroyed. If you want to, you can use multiple timers, each identified by an integer. Because Windows isn't a real-time operating system, the interval between timer events becomes imprecise if you specify an interval much less than 100 milliseconds.

Like any other Windows messages, timer messages can be blocked by other handler functions in your program. Fortunately, timer messages don't stack up. Windows won't put a timer message in the queue if a message for that timer is already present.

The EX12A Program

We're going to write a single-threaded program that contains a CPU-intensive computation loop. We want to let the program process messages after the user starts the computation; otherwise, the user couldn't cancel the job. Also, we'd like to display the percent-complete status by using a progress indicator control, as shown in Figure 12-1. The EX12A program allows message processing by yielding control in the compute loop. A timer handler updates the progress control based on compute parameters. The WM_TIMER messages could not be processed if the compute process didn't yield control.

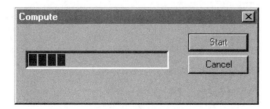

Figure 12-1.
The Compute dialog box.

Here are the steps for building the EX12A application:

1. **Run AppWizard to generate \vcpp32\ex12a\ex12a.** Accept all the default settings but two: select Single Document and deselect Printing And Print Preview. The options and the default class names are shown here.

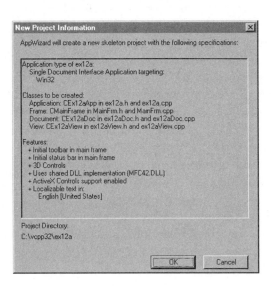

2. **Use the dialog editor to create the dialog resource *IDD_COMPUTE.*** Use the resource shown here as a guide.

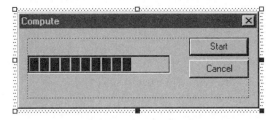

Keep the default control ID for the Cancel button, but use *IDC_START* for the Start button. For the progress indicator, accept the default ID *IDC_PROGRESS1.*

3. **Use ClassWizard to create the *CComputeDlg* class.** ClassWizard connects the new class to the *IDD_COMPUTE* resource you just created.
   After the class is generated, add a WM_TIMER message handler function. Also add BN_CLICKED message handlers for *IDC_START* and *IDCANCEL.* Accept the default names *OnStart* and *OnCancel.*

4. **Add three data members to the *CComputeDlg* class.** Edit the file
ComputeDlg.h. Add the following private data members:

```
int m_nTimer;
int m_nCount;
enum { nMaxCount = 10000 };
```

The *m_nCount* data member of class *CComputeDlg* is incremented
during the compute process. It serves as a percent complete measurement
when divided by the "constant" *nMaxCount*.

5. **Add initialization code to the *CComputeDlg* constructor in the
ComputeDlg.cpp file.** Add the following line to the constructor to
ensure that the Cancel button will work if the compute process has not
been started:

```
m_nCount = 0;
```

Be sure to add the line outside the *//{{AFX_DATA_INIT* comments
generated by ClassWizard.

6. **Code the *OnStart* function in ComputeDlg.cpp.** This code is executed
when the user clicks the Start button. Add the following boldface code:

```
void CComputeDlg::OnStart()
{
    MSG message;

    m_nTimer = SetTimer(1, 100, NULL); // 1/10 second
    ASSERT(m_nTimer != 0);
    GetDlgItem(IDC_START)->EnableWindow(FALSE);
    volatile int nTemp;
    for (m_nCount = 0; m_nCount < nMaxCount; m_nCount++) {
        for (nTemp = 0; nTemp < 10000; nTemp++) {
            // uses up CPU cycles
        }
        if (::PeekMessage(&message, NULL, 0, 0, PM_REMOVE)) {
            ::TranslateMessage(&message);
            ::DispatchMessage(&message);
        }
    }
    CDialog::OnOK();
}
```

The main *for* loop is controlled by the value of *m_nCount*. At the end of
each pass through the outer loop, *PeekMessage* allows other messages, including WM_TIMER, to be processed. The *EnableWindow(FALSE)* call
disables the Start button during the computation. If we didn't take this
precaution, the *OnStart* function could be reentered.

7. **Code the *OnTimer* function in ComputeDlg.cpp.** When the timer fires, the progress indicator's position is set according to the value of *m_nCount*. Add the following boldface code:

```
void CComputeDlg::OnTimer(UINT nIDEvent)
{
    CProgressCtrl* pBar = (CProgressCtrl*) GetDlgItem(IDC_PROGRESS1);
    pBar->SetPos(m_nCount * 100 / nMaxCount);
}
```

8. **Update the *OnCancel* function in ComputeDlg.cpp.** When the user clicks the Cancel button during computation, we don't destroy the dialog; instead, we set *m_nCount* to its maximum value, which causes *OnStart* to exit the dialog. If the computation hasn't started, it's okay to exit directly. Add the following boldface code:

```
void CComputeDlg::OnCancel()
{
    TRACE("entering CComputeDlg::OnCancel\n");
    if (m_nCount == 0) {        // prior to Start button
        CDialog::OnCancel();
    }
    else {                      // computation in progress
        m_nCount = nMaxCount; // Force exit from OnStart
    }
}
```

9. **Edit the *CEx12aView* class in ex12aView.cpp.** First edit the virtual *OnDraw* function to display a message, as shown here:

```
void CEx12aView::OnDraw(CDC* pDC)
{
    pDC->TextOut(0, 0, "Press the left mouse button here.");
}
```

Then use ClassWizard to add the *OnLButtonDown* function to handle WM_LBUTTONDOWN messages, and add the following boldface code:

```
void CEx12aView::OnLButtonDown(UINT nFlags, CPoint point)
{
    CComputeDlg dlg;
    dlg.DoModal();
}
```

This code displays the modal dialog whenever the user presses the left mouse button while the mouse cursor is in the view window.

While you're in ex12aView.cpp, add the following *#include* statement:

```
#include "ComputeDlg.h"
```

10. **Build and run the application.** Press the left mouse button while the mouse cursor is inside the view window to display the dialog. Click the Start button, and then click Cancel. The progress indicator should show the status of the computation.

On-Idle Processing

Before multithreaded programming came along, Windows developers used on-idle processing for "background" tasks such as pagination. On-idle processing is no longer as important, but it's still useful. The application framework calls a virtual member function *OnIdle* of class *CWinApp*, and you can override this function to do background processing. *OnIdle* is called from the framework's message processing loop, which is actually a little more complicated than the simple *GetMessage/TranslateMessage/DispatchMessage* sequence you've seen. Generally, once the *OnIdle* function completes its work, it is not called again until the next time the application's message queue has been emptied. If you override this function, your code will be called, but it won't be called continuously unless there is a constant stream of messages. The base class *OnIdle* updates the toolbar buttons and status indicators, and it cleans up various temporary object pointers. It makes sense for you to override *OnIdle* to update the user interface. The fact that your code won't be executed when no messages are coming is not important because the user interface shouldn't be changing.

> N O T E :   If you do override *CWinApp::OnIdle*, don't forget to call the base class *OnIdle*. Otherwise, your toolbar buttons won't be updated and temporary objects won't be deleted.

OnIdle isn't called at all if the user is working in a modal dialog or is using a menu. If you need to use background processing for modal dialogs and menus, you'll have to add a message handler function for the WM_ENTERIDLE message, but you must add it to the <u>frame</u> class rather than to the view class. That's because pop-up dialogs are always "owned" by the application's main frame window, not by the view window. Chapter 15 explores the relationship between the frame window and the view window.

Multithreaded Programming

As you'll recall from Chapter 10, a <u>process</u> is a running program that owns its own memory, file handles, and other system resources. An individual process can contain separate execution paths, called <u>threads</u>. Don't look for separate code for separate threads, however, because a single function can be called from many threads. For the most part, all of a process's code and data space is available to all of the threads in the process. Two threads, for example, can access the same global variables. Threads are managed by the operating system, and each thread has its own stack.

Windows offers two kinds of threads, <u>worker</u> <u>threads</u> and <u>user</u> <u>interface</u> <u>threads</u>. The Microsoft Foundation Class (MFC) Library supports both. A user interface thread has windows, and therefore it has its own message loop. A worker thread doesn't have windows, so it doesn't need to process messages. Worker threads are easier to program and are generally more useful. The remaining examples in this chapter illustrate worker threads. At the end of the chapter, however, an application for a user interface thread is described.

Don't forget that even a single-threaded application has one thread—the main thread. In the MFC hierarchy, *CWinApp* is derived from *CWinThread*. Back in Chapter 2, I told you that *InitInstance* and *m_pMainWnd* are members of *CWinApp*. Well, I lied. The members are declared in *CWinThread*, but of course they're inherited by *CWinApp*. The important thing to remember here is that an application <u>is</u> a thread.

Writing the Worker Thread Function and Starting the Thread

If you haven't guessed already, using a worker thread for a long computation is more efficient than using a message handler that contains a *PeekMessage* call. Before you start a worker thread, however, you must write a global function for your thread's main program. This global function should return a *UINT*, and it should take a single 32-bit value (declared *LPVOID*) as a parameter. You can use the parameter to pass anything at all to your thread when you start it. The thread does its computation, and when the global function returns, the thread terminates. The thread would also be terminated if the process terminated, but it's preferable to ensure that the worker thread terminates first, which will guarantee that you'll have no memory leaks.

To start the thread (with function name *ComputeThreadProc*), your program makes the following call:

```
CWinThread* pThread =
    AfxBeginThread(ComputeThreadProc, GetSafeHwnd(),
                   THREAD_PRIORITY_NORMAL);
```

The compute thread code looks like this:

```
UINT ComputeThreadProc(LPVOID pParam)
{
    // Do thread processing
    return 0;
}
```

The *AfxBeginThread* function returns immediately; the return value is a pointer to the newly created thread object. You can use that pointer to suspend and resume the thread (*CWinThread::SuspendThread* and *ResumeThread*), but the thread object has no member function to terminate the thread. The second parameter is the 32-bit value that gets passed to the global function, and the third parameter is the thread's priority code. Once the worker thread starts, both threads run independently. Windows divides the time between the two threads (and among the threads that belong to other processes) according to their priority. If the main thread is waiting for a message, the compute thread can still run.

How the Main Thread Talks to a Worker Thread

The main thread (your application program) can communicate with the subsidiary worker thread in many different ways. One option that will not work, however, is a Windows message; the worker thread doesn't have a message loop. The simplest means of communication is a global variable because all the threads in the process have access to all the globals. Suppose the worker thread increments and tests a global integer as it computes and then exits when the value reaches 100. The main thread could force the worker thread to terminate by setting the global variable to 100 or higher.

The code below looks as though it should work, and when you test it, it probably will:

```
UINT ComputeThreadProc(LPVOID pParam)
{
    g_nCount = 0;
    while (g_nCount++ < 100) {
        // Do some computation here
    }
    return 0;
}
```

There's a problem, however, that you could detect only by looking at the generated assembly code. The value of *g_nCount* gets loaded into a register, the register is incremented, and then the register value is stored back in *g_nCount*. Suppose *g_nCount* is 40 and Windows interrupts the worker thread just after the worker thread loads 40 into the register. Now the main thread gets control and sets *g_nCount* to 100. When the worker thread resumes, it increments the register value and stores 41 back into *g_nCount*, obliterating the previous value of 100. The thread loop doesn't terminate!

If you turn on the compiler's optimization switch, you'll have an additional problem. The compiler uses a register for *g_nCount*, and the register stays loaded for the duration of the loop. If the main thread changes the value of *g_nCount* in memory, it will have no effect on the worker thread's compute loop. (You can ensure that the counter isn't stored in a register, however, by declaring *g_nCount* as *volatile*.)

But suppose you rewrite the thread procedure as shown here:

```
UINT ComputeThreadProc(LPVOID pParam)
{
    g_nCount = 0;
    while (g_nCount < 100) {
        // Do some computation here
        ::InterlockedIncrement((long*) &g_nCount);
    }
    return 0;
}
```

The *InterlockedIncrement* function blocks other threads from accessing the variable while it is being incremented. The main thread can safely stop the worker thread.

Now you've seen some of the pitfalls of using global variables for communication. Using global variables is sometimes appropriate, as the next example illustrates, but there are alternative methods that are more flexible, as you'll see later in this chapter.

How the Worker Thread Talks to the Main Thread

It makes sense for the worker thread to check a global variable in a loop, but what if the main thread did that? Remember the pig function? You definitely don't want your main thread to enter a loop because that would waste CPU cycles and stop your program's message processing. A Windows message is the preferred way for a worker thread to communicate with the main thread because the main thread always has a message loop. This implies, however, that the main thread has a window (visible or invisible) and that the worker thread has a handle to that window.

How does the worker thread get the handle? That's what the 32-bit thread function parameter discussed on page 274 is for. You pass the handle in the *AfxBeginThread* call. Why not pass the C++ window pointer instead? Doing so would be dangerous because you can't depend on the continued existence of the object and you're not allowed to share objects of MFC classes among threads. (This rule does not apply to objects derived directly from *CObject* or to simple classes such as *CRect* and *CString*.)

Do you send the message or post it? Better to post it, because sending it could cause reentry of the main thread's MFC message pump code, and that would create problems in modal dialogs. What kind of message do you post? Any user-defined message will do.

The EX12B Program

The EX12B program looks exactly like the EX12A program when you run it. When you look at the code, however, you'll see some differences. The computation is done in a worker thread instead of in the main thread. The count value is stored in a global variable *g_nCount*, which is set to the maximum value in the dialog window's Cancel button handler. When the thread exits, it posts a message to the dialog, which causes *DoModal* to exit.

The document, view, frame, and application classes are the same except for their names, and the dialog resource is the same. The modal dialog class is still named *CComputeDlg*, but the code inside is quite different. The constructor, timer handler, and data exchange functions are pretty much the same. The following code fragment shows the global variable definition and the global thread function as given in the \ex12b\ComputeDlg.cpp file on the companion CD-ROM. Note that the function exits (and the thread terminates) when *g_nCount* is greater than a constant maximum value. Before it exits, however, the function posts a user-defined message to the dialog window.

```
int g_nCount = 0;

UINT ComputeThreadProc(LPVOID pParam)
{
    volatile int nTemp; // volatile else compiler optimizes too much

    for (g_nCount = 0; g_nCount < CComputeDlg::nMaxCount;
                        ::InterlockedIncrement((long*) &g_nCount)) {
        for (nTemp = 0; nTemp < 10000; nTemp++) {
            // uses up CPU cycles
        }
    }
    // WM_THREADFINISHED is user-defined message
    ::PostMessage((HWND) pParam, WM_THREADFINISHED, 0, 0);
    g_nCount = 0;
    return 0; // ends the thread
}
```

The *OnStart* handler below is mapped to the dialog's Start button. Its job is to start the timer and the worker thread. You can change the worker thread's priority by changing the third parameter of *AfxBeginThread*—for example, the computation runs a little more slowly if you set the priority to *THREAD_PRIORITY_LOWEST*.

```
void CComputeDlg::OnStart()
{
    m_nTimer = SetTimer(1, 100, NULL); // 1/10 second
    ASSERT(m_nTimer != 0);
    GetDlgItem(IDC_START)->EnableWindow(FALSE);
    AfxBeginThread(ComputeThreadProc, GetSafeHwnd(),
                   THREAD_PRIORITY_NORMAL);
}
```

The *OnCancel* handler below is mapped to the dialog's Cancel button. It sets the *g_nCount* variable to the maximum value, causing the thread to terminate.

```
void CComputeDlg::OnCancel()
{
    if (g_nCount == 0) { // prior to Start button
        CDialog::OnCancel();
    }
    else { // computation in progress
        g_nCount = nMaxCount; // Force thread to exit
    }
}
```

The *OnThreadFinished* handler below is mapped to the dialog's WM-_THREADFINISHED user-defined message. It causes the dialog's *DoModal* function to exit.

```
LRESULT CComputeDlg::OnThreadFinished(WPARAM wParam, LPARAM lParam)
{
    CDialog::OnOK();
    return 0;
}
```

Using Events for Thread Synchronization

The global variable is a crude but effective means of interthread communication. Now let's try something more sophisticated. We want to think in terms of thread synchronization instead of simple communication. Our threads must carefully synchronize their interactions with one another.

An event is one type of kernel object (processes and threads are also kernel objects) that Windows provides for thread synchronization. An event is identified by a unique 32-bit handle within a process. It can be identified by name, or its handle can be duplicated for sharing among processes. An event can be either in the signaled (or true) state or in the unsignaled (or false) state. Events come in two types: manual reset and autoreset. We'll be looking at autoreset events here because they're ideal for the synchronization of two processes.

Let's go back to our worker thread example. We want the main (user interface) thread to "signal" the worker thread to make it start or stop, so we'll need a "start" event and a "kill" event. MFC provides a handy *CEvent* class that's derived from *CSyncObject*. By default, the constructor creates a Win32 underset event object in the unsignaled state. If you declare your events as global objects, any thread can easily access them. When the main thread wants to start or terminate the worker thread, it sets the appropriate event to the signaled state by calling *CEvent::SetEvent*.

Now the worker thread must monitor the two events and respond when one of them is signaled. MFC provides the *CSingleLock* class for this purpose, but it's easier to use the Win32 *WaitForSingleObject* function. This function suspends the thread until the specified object becomes signaled. When the thread is suspended, it's not using any CPU cycles—which is good. The first *WaitForSingleObject* parameter is the event handle. You can use a *CEvent* object for this parameter; the object inherits from *CSyncObject* an operator *HANDLE* that returns the event handle it has stored as a public data member. The second parameter is the time-out interval. If you set this parameter to *INFINITE*, the function waits forever until the event becomes signaled. If you set the time-out to 0, *WaitForSingleObject* returns immediately, with a return value of *WAIT-_OBJECT_0* if the event was signaled.

The EX12C Program

The EX12C program uses two events to synchronize the worker thread with the main thread. Most of the EX12C code is the same as EX12B, but the *CComputeDlg* class is quite different. The StdAfx.h file contains the following line for the *CEvent* class:

```
#include <afxmt.h>
```

There are two global event objects, as shown below. Note that the constructors create the Windows events prior to the execution of the main program.

```
CEvent g_eventStart; // creates autoreset events
CEvent g_eventKill;
```

It's best to look at the worker thread global function first. The function increments *g_nCount* just as it did in EX12B. The worker thread is started by the *OnInitDialog* function instead of by the Start button handler. The first *WaitForSingleObject* call waits for the start event, which is signaled by the Start button handler. The *INFINITE* parameter means that the thread waits as long as necessary. The second *WaitForSingleObject* call is different—it has a 0 time-out value. It's located in the main compute loop and simply makes a quick test to see whether the kill event was signaled by the Cancel button handler. If the event was signaled, the thread terminates.

```
UINT ComputeThreadProc(LPVOID pParam)
{
    volatile int nTemp;

    ::WaitForSingleObject(g_eventStart, INFINITE);
    TRACE("starting computation\n");
    for (g_nCount = 0; g_nCount < CComputeDlg::nMaxCount;
                        g_nCount++) {
        for (nTemp = 0; nTemp < 10000; nTemp++) {
            // Simulate computation
        }
        if (::WaitForSingleObject(g_eventKill, 0) == WAIT_OBJECT_0) {
            break;
        }
    }
    // Tell owner window we're finished
    ::PostMessage((HWND) pParam, WM_THREADFINISHED, 0, 0);
    g_nCount = 0;
    return 0; // ends the thread
}
```

Here is the *OnInitDialog* function that's called when the dialog is initialized. Note that it starts the worker thread, which doesn't do anything until the start event is signaled.

```
BOOL CComputeDlg::OnInitDialog()
{
    CDialog::OnInitDialog();
    AfxBeginThread(ComputeThreadProc, GetSafeHwnd());
    return TRUE;  // Return TRUE unless you set the focus to a control
                  // EXCEPTION: OCX Property Pages should return FALSE
}
```

The following Start button handler sets the start event to the signaled state, thereby starting the worker thread's compute loop:

```
void CComputeDlg::OnStart()
{
    m_nTimer = SetTimer(1, 100, NULL); // 1/10 second
    ASSERT(m_nTimer != 0);
    GetDlgItem(IDC_START)->EnableWindow(FALSE);
    g_eventStart.SetEvent();
}
```

The following Cancel button handler sets the kill event to the signaled state, causing the worker thread's compute loop to terminate:

```
void CComputeDlg::OnCancel()
{
    if (g_nCount == 0) { // prior to Start button
        // Must start it before we can kill it
        g_eventStart.SetEvent();
    }
    g_eventKill.SetEvent();
}
```

Note the awkward use of the start event when the user cancels without starting the compute process. It might be neater to define a new cancel event and then replace the first *WaitForSingleObject* call with a *WaitForMultipleObjects* call in the *ComputeThreadProc* function. If *WaitForMultipleObjects* detected a cancel event, it could cause an immediate thread termination.

Thread Blocking

The first *WaitForSingleObject* call in the *ComputeThreadProc* function above is an example of thread blocking. The thread simply stops executing until an event becomes signaled. A thread could be blocked in many other ways. You could call the Win32 *Sleep* function, for example, to put your thread to "sleep" for 500 milliseconds. Many functions block threads, particularly those functions that access hardware devices or Internet hosts. Back in the Win16 days, those functions took over the CPU until they were finished. In Win32, they allow other processes and threads to run.

You should avoid putting blocking calls in your main user interface thread. Remember that if your main thread is blocked, it can't process its messages, and that makes the program appear sluggish. If you have a task that requires heavy file I/O, put the code in a worker thread and synchronize it with your main thread.

Be careful of calls in your worker thread that could block indefinitely. Check the online documentation to determine whether you have the option of setting a time-out value for a particular I/O operation. If a call <u>does</u> block forever, the thread will be terminated when the main process exits, but then you'll have some memory leaks. You could call the Win32 *TerminateThread* function from your main thread, but you'd still have the memory-leak problem.

Critical Sections

Remember the problems with access to the *g_nCount* global variable? If you want to share global data among threads and you need more flexibility than simple instructions like *InterlockedIncrement* can provide, <u>critical</u> <u>sections</u> might be the synchronization tools for you. Events are good for signaling, but critical sections (sections of code that require exclusive access to shared data) are good for controlling access to data.

MFC provides the *CCriticalSection* class that wraps the Windows critical section handle. The constructor calls the Win32 *InitializeCriticalSection* function, the *Lock* and *Unlock* member functions call *EnterCriticalSection* and *LeaveCriticalSection*, and the destructor calls *DeleteCriticalSection*. Here's how you use the class to protect global data:

```
CCriticalSection g_cs;    // global variables accessible from all threads
int g_nCount;
void func()
{
    g_cs.Lock();
    g_nCount++;
    g_cs.Unlock();
}
```

Suppose your program tracks time values as hours, minutes, and seconds, each stored in a separate integer, and suppose two threads are sharing time values. Thread A is changing a time value but is interrupted by thread B after it has updated hours but before it has updated minutes and seconds. Thread B will have an invalid time value.

If you write a C++ class for your time format, it's easy to control data access by making the data members private and providing public member functions. The *CHMS* class, shown in Figure 12-2, does exactly that. Notice that the class has a data member of type *CCriticalSection*. Thus, a critical section object is associated with each *CHMS* object.

Notice that the other member functions call the *Lock* and *Unlock* member functions. If thread A is executing in the middle of *SetTime*, thread B will be blocked by the *Lock* call in *GetTotalSecs* until thread A calls *Unlock*. The *IncrementSecs* function calls *SetTime*, resulting in nested locks on the critical section. That's okay because Windows keeps track of the nesting level.

The *CHMS* class works well if you use it to construct global objects. If you share pointers to objects on the heap, you have another set of problems. Each thread must determine whether another thread has deleted the object, and that means you must synchronize access to the pointers.

HMS.H

```
#include "StdAfx.h"

class CHMS
{
private:
    int m_nHr, m_nMn, m_nSc;
    CCriticalSection m_cs;
public:
    CHMS() : m_nHr(0), m_nMn(0), m_nSc(0) {}

    ~CHMS() {}

    void SetTime(int nSecs)
    {
        m_cs.Lock();
        m_nSc = nSecs % 60;
        m_nMn = (nSecs / 60) % 60;
        m_nHr = nSecs / 3600;
        m_cs.Unlock();
    }

    int GetTotalSecs()
    {
        int nTotalSecs;
        m_cs.Lock();
        nTotalSecs = m_nHr * 3600 + m_nMn * 60 + m_nSc;
        m_cs.Unlock();
        return nTotalSecs;
    }

    void IncrementSecs()
    {
        m_cs.Lock();
        SetTime(GetTotalSecs() + 1);
        m_cs.Unlock();
    }
};
```

Figure 12-2.
The CHMS class listing.

No sample program is provided that uses the *CHMS* class, but the file hms.h is included in the \vcpp32\ex12c subdirectory on the companion CD-ROM. If you write a multithreaded program, you can share global objects of the class. You don't need any other calls to the thread-related functions.

Mutexes and Semaphores

As I mentioned, I'm leaving these synchronization objects to Jeffrey Richter's *Advanced Windows.* You might need a mutex or a semaphore if you're controlling access to data across different processes because a critical section is accessible only within a single process. Mutexes and semaphores (along with events) are shareable by name.

User Interface Threads

The MFC library provides good support for UI threads. You derive a class from *CWinThread,* and you use an overloaded version of *AfxBeginThread* to start the thread. Your derived *CWinThread* class has its own *InitInstance* function, and most important, it has its own message loop. You can construct windows and map messages as required.

Why might you want a user interface thread? If you want multiple top-level windows, you can create and manage them from your main thread. Suppose you allow the user to run multiple instances of your application, but you want all instances to share memory. You can configure a single process to run multiple UI threads such that users think they are running separate processes. That's exactly what Windows Explorer does. Check it out with SPY++.

Starting the second and subsequent threads is a little tricky because the user actually launches a new process for each copy of Windows Explorer. When the second process starts, it signals the first process to start a new thread, and then it exits. The second process can locate the first process either by calling the Win32 *FindWindow* function or by declaring a shared data section. Shared data sections are explained in detail in Jeffrey Richter's book.

PART III

THE DOCUMENT–VIEW ARCHITECTURE

Menus, Keyboard Accelerators, the Rich Edit Control, and Property Sheets

In all the book's examples to this point, mouse clicks have triggered most program activity. Even though menu selections might have been more appropriate, you've used mouse clicks because mouse-click messages are handled simply and directly within the Microsoft Foundation Class (MFC) Library version 6.0 view window. If you want program activity to be triggered when the user chooses a command from a menu, you must first become familiar with the other application framework elements.

This chapter concentrates on menus and the <u>command</u> <u>routing</u> <u>architecture</u>. Along the way, we introduce frames and documents, explaining the relationships between these new application framework elements and the already familiar view element. You'll use the menu editor to lay out a menu visually, and you'll use ClassWizard to link document and view member functions to menu items. You'll learn how to use special update command user interface (UI) member functions to check and disable menu items, and you'll see how to use keyboard accelerators as menu shortcut keys.

Because you're probably tired of circles and dialogs, next you'll examine two new MFC building blocks. The <u>rich edit</u> common control can add powerful text editing features to your application. <u>Property sheets</u> are ideal for setting edit options.

The Main Frame Window and Document Classes

Up to now, you've been using a view window as if it were the application's only window. In an SDI application, the view window sits inside another window—the application's main frame window. The main frame window has the title bar and the menu bar. Various child windows, including the toolbar window, the view window, and the status bar window, occupy the main frame window's client area, as shown in Figure 13-1. The application framework controls the interaction between the frame and the view by routing messages from the frame to the view.

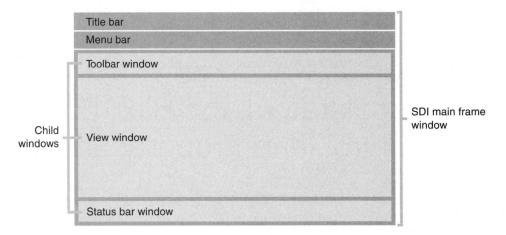

Figure 13-1.
The child windows within an SDI main frame window.

Look again at any project files generated by AppWizard. The MainFrm.h and MainFrm.cpp files contain the code for the application's main frame window class, derived from the class *CFrameWnd*. Other files, with names such as ex13aDoc.h and ex13aDoc.cpp, contain code for the application's document class, which is derived from *CDocument*. In this chapter you'll begin working with the MFC document class. You'll start by learning that each view object has exactly one document object attached and that the view's inherited *GetDocument* member function returns a pointer to that object. In Chapter 15 you'll examine frame windows, and in Chapter 16 you'll learn much more about document–view interactions.

Windows Menus

A Microsoft Windows menu is a familiar application element that consists of a top-level horizontal list of items with associated pop-up menus that appear when the user selects a top-level item. Most of the time, you define for a frame window a default menu resource that loads when the window is created. You can also define a menu resource independent of a frame window. In that case, your program must call the functions necessary to load and activate the menu.

A menu resource completely defines the initial appearance of a menu. Menu items can be grayed or have check marks, and bars can separate groups of menu items. Multiple levels of pop-up menus are possible. If a first-level menu item is associated with a subsidiary pop-up menu, the menu item carries a right-pointing arrow symbol, as shown next to the Start Debug menu item in Figure 13-2.

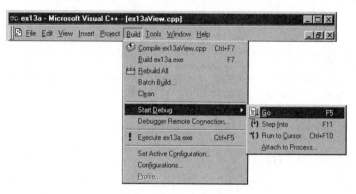

Figure 13-2.
Multilevel pop-up menus (from Microsoft Visual C++).

Visual C++ includes an easy-to-use menu-resource editing tool. This tool lets you edit menus in a wysiwyg environment. Each menu item has a properties dialog that defines all the characteristics of that item. The resulting resource definition is stored in the application's resource script (RC) file. Each menu item is associated with an ID, such as *ID_FILE_OPEN*, that is defined in the resource.h file.

The MFC library extends the functionality of the standard menus for Windows. Each menu item can have a prompt string that appears in the frame's status bar when the item is highlighted. These prompts are really Windows string resource elements linked to the menu item by a common ID. From the point of view of the menu editor and your program, the prompts appear to be part of the menu item definition.

Keyboard Accelerators

You've probably noticed that most menu items contain an underlined letter. In Visual C++ (and most other applications), pressing Alt-F followed by S activates the File Save menu item. This shortcut system is the standard Windows method of using the keyboard to choose commands from menus. If you look at an application's menu resource script (or the menu editor's properties dialog), you will see an ampersand (&) preceding the character that is underlined in each of the application's menu items.

Windows offers an alternative way of linking keystrokes to menu items. The keyboard accelerator resource consists of a table of key combinations with associated command IDs. The Edit Copy menu item (with command ID *ID_EDIT-_COPY*), for example, might be linked to the Ctrl-C key combination through a keyboard accelerator entry. A keyboard accelerator entry does not have to be associated with a menu item. If no Edit Copy menu item were present, the Ctrl-C key combination would nevertheless activate the *ID_EDIT_COPY* command.

> **NOTE:** If a keyboard accelerator is associated with a menu item or toolbar button, the accelerator key is disabled when the menu item or button is disabled.

Command Processing

As you saw in Chapter 2, the application framework provides a sophisticated routing system for command messages. These messages originate from menu selections, keyboard accelerators, and toolbar and dialog button clicks. Command messages can also be sent by calls to the *CWnd::SendMessage* or *PostMessage* function. Each message is identified by a *#define* constant that is often assigned by a resource editor. The application framework has its own set of internal command message IDs, such as *ID_FILE_PRINT* and *ID_FILE_OPEN*. Your project's resource.h file contains IDs that are unique to your application.

Most command messages originate in the application's frame window, and without the application framework in the picture, that's where you would put the message handlers. With command routing, however, you can handle a message almost anywhere. When the application framework sees a frame window command message, it starts looking for message handlers in one of the sequences listed here.

SDI Application	MDI Application
View	View
Document	Document
SDI main frame window	MDI child frame window
Application	MDI main frame window
	Application

Most applications have a particular command handler in only one class, but suppose your one-view application has an identical handler in both the view class and the document class. Because the view is higher in the command route, only the view's command handler function will be called.

What is needed to install a command handler function? The installation requirements are similar to those of the window message handlers you've already seen. You need the function itself, a corresponding message map entry, and the function prototype. Suppose you have a menu item named Zoom (with *IDM_ZOOM* as the associated ID) that you want your view class to handle. First you add the following code to your view implementation file:

```
BEGIN_MESSAGE_MAP(CMyView, CView)
    ON_COMMAND(IDM_ZOOM, OnZoom)
END_MESSAGE_MAP()

void CMyView::OnZoom()
{
    // command message processing code
}
```

Now add the following function prototype to the *CMyView* class header file (before the *DECLARE_MESSAGE_MAP* macro):

```
afx_msg void OnZoom();
```

Of course, ClassWizard automates the process of inserting command message handlers the same way it facilitates the insertion of window message handlers. You'll learn how this works in the next example, EX13A, which starts on page 295.

Command Message Handling in Derived Classes

The command routing system is one dimension of command message handling. The class hierarchy is a second dimension. If you look at the source code for the MFC library classes, you'll see lots of *ON_COMMAND* message map entries. When you derive a class from one of these base classes—for example, *CView*—the derived class inherits all the *CView* message map functions, including the command message functions. To override one of the base class message map functions, you must add both a function and a message map entry to your derived class.

Update Command User Interface Handlers

You often need to change the appearance of a menu item to match the internal state of your application. If your application's Edit menu includes a Clear All item, for example, you might want to disable that item if there's nothing to clear. You've undoubtedly seen such grayed menu items in Windows-based applications, and you've probably also seen check marks next to menu items.

With Win32 programming, it's difficult to keep menu items synchronized with the application's state. Every piece of code that changes the internal state must contain statements to update the menu. The MFC library takes a different approach by calling a special update command user interface (UI) handler function whenever a pop-up menu is first displayed. The handler function's argument is a *CCmdUI* object, which contains a pointer to the corresponding menu item. The handler function can then use this pointer to modify the menu item's appearance. Update command UI handlers apply only to items on pop-up menus, not to top-level menu items that are permanently displayed. You can't use an update command UI handler to disable a File menu item, for example.

The update command UI coding requirements are similar to those for commands. You need the function itself, a special message map entry, and of course the prototype. The associated ID—in this case, *IDM_ZOOM*—is the same constant used for the command. Here is an example of the necessary additions to the view class code file:

```
BEGIN_MESSAGE_MAP(CMyView, CView)
    ON_UPDATE_COMMAND_UI(IDM_ZOOM, OnUpdateZoom)
END_MESSAGE_MAP()

void CMyView::OnUpdateZoom(CCmdUI* pCmdUI)
{
    pCmdUI->SetCheck(m_bZoomed); // m_bZoomed is a class data member
}
```

Here is the function prototype that you must add to the class header (before the *DECLARE_MESSAGE_MAP* macro):

```
afx_msg void OnUpdateZoom(CCmdUI* pCmdUI);
```

Needless to say, ClassWizard automates the process of inserting update command UI handlers.

Commands That Originate in Dialogs

Suppose you have a pop-up dialog with buttons, and you want a particular button to send a command message. Command IDs must be in the range 0x8000 to 0xDFFF, the same ID range that the resource editor uses for your menu items.

If you assign an ID in this range to a dialog button, the button will generate a routable command. The application framework first routes this command to the main frame window because the frame window owns all pop-up dialogs. The command routing then proceeds normally; if your view has a handler for the button's command, that's where it will be handled. To ensure that the ID is in the range 0x8000 to 0xDFFF, you must use Visual C++'s symbol editor to enter the ID prior to assigning the ID to a button.

The Application Framework's Built-In Menu Items

You don't have to start each frame menu from scratch—the MFC library defines some useful menu items for you, along with all the command handler functions, as shown in Figure 13-3.

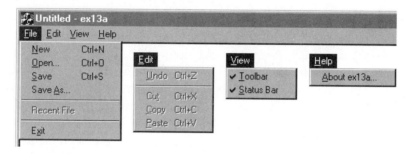

Figure 13-3.
The standard SDI frame menus.

The menu items and command message handlers that you get depend on the options you choose in AppWizard. If you deselect Printing and Print Preview, for example, the Print and Print Preview menu items don't appear. Because printing is optional, the message map entries are not defined in the *CView* class but are generated in your derived view class. That's why entries such as the following are defined in the *CMyView* class instead of in the *CView* class:

```
ON_COMMAND(ID_FILE_PRINT, CView::OnFilePrint)
ON_COMMAND(ID_FILE_PRINT_PREVIEW, CView::OnFilePrintPreview)
```

Enabling/Disabling Menu Items

The application framework can disable a menu item if it does not find a command message handler in the current command route. This feature saves you the trouble of having to write *ON_UPDATE_COMMAND_UI* handlers. You can disable the feature if you set the *CFrameWnd* data member *m_bAutoMenuEnable* to *FALSE*.

Suppose you have two views for one document, but only the first view class has a message handler for the *IDM_ZOOM* command. The Zoom item on the frame menu will be enabled only when the first view is active. Or consider the application framework-supplied Edit Cut, Copy, and Paste menu items. These will be disabled if you have not provided message handlers in your derived view or document class.

MFC Text Editing Options

Windows itself supplies two text editing tools: edit control and Windows rich edit common control. Both can be used as controls within dialogs, but both can also be made to look like view windows. The MFC library supports this versatility with the *CEditView* and *CRichEditView* classes.

The *CEditView* Class

This class is based on the Windows edit control, so it inherits all the edit control's limitations. Text size is limited to 64 KB, and you can't mix fonts. AppWizard gives you the option of making *CEditView* the base class of your view class. When the framework gives you an edit view object, it has all the functionality of both *CView* and *CEdit*. There's no multiple inheritance here, just some magic that involves window subclassing. The *CEditView* class implements and maps the clipboard cut, copy, and paste functions, so they appear active on the Edit menu.

The *CRichEditView* Class

This class uses the rich edit control, so it supports mixed formats and large quantities of text. The *CRichEditView* class is designed to be used with the *CRichEditDoc* and *CRichEditCntrItem* classes to implement a complete ActiveX container application.

The *CRichEditCtrl* Class

This class wraps the rich edit control, and you can use it to make a fairly decent text editor. That's exactly what we'll do in the EX13A example. We'll use an ordinary view class derived from *CView*, and we'll cover the view's client area with a big rich edit control that resizes itself when the view size changes. The *CRichEditCtrl* class has dozens of useful member functions, and it picks up other functions from its *CWnd* base class. The functions we'll use in this chapter are as follows.

Function	Description
Create	Creates the rich edit control window (called from the parent's WM_CREATE handler)
SetWindowPos	Sets the size and position of the edit window (sizes the control to cover the view's client area)
GetWindowText	Retrieves plain text from the control (other functions available to retrieve the text with rich text formatting codes)
SetWindowText	Stores plain text in the control
GetModify	Gets a flag that is *TRUE* if the text has been modified (text modified if the user types in the control or if the program calls *SetModify-(TRUE)*)
SetModify	Sets the modify flag to *TRUE* or *FALSE*
GetSel	Gets a flag that indicates whether the user has selected text
SetDefaultCharFormat	Sets the control's default format characteristics
SetSelectionCharFormat	Sets the format characteristics of the selected text

NOTE: If you use the dialog editor to add a rich edit control to a dialog resource, your application class *InitInstance* member function must call the function *AfxInitRichEdit*.

The EX13A Example

This example illustrates the routing of menu and keyboard accelerator commands to both documents and views. The application's view class is derived from *CView* and contains a rich edit control. View-directed menu commands, originating from a new pop-up menu named Transfer, move data between the view object and the document object, and a Clear Document menu item erases the document's contents. On the Transfer menu, the Store Data In Document item is grayed when the view hasn't been modified since the last time the data was transferred. The Clear Document item, located on the Edit menu, is grayed when the document is empty. Figure 13-4 on the following page shows the first version of the EX13A program in use.

If we exploited the document–view architecture fully, we would tell the rich edit control to keep its text inside the document, but that's rather difficult to do. Instead, we'll define a document *CString* data member named *m_strText*, the contents of which the user can transfer to and from the control. The initial

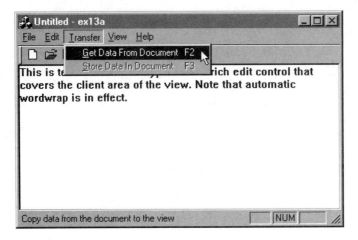

Figure 13-4.
The EX13A program in use.

value of *m_strText* is a Hello message; choosing Clear Document from the Edit menu sets it to empty. By running this example, you'll start to understand the separation of the document and the view.

The first part of the EX13A example exercises Visual C++'s wysiwyg menu editor and keyboard accelerator editor together with ClassWizard. You'll need to do very little C++ coding. Simply follow these steps:

1. **Run AppWizard to generate \vcpp32\ex13a\ex13a.** Accept all the default settings but two: select Single Document and deselect Printing and Print Preview.

2. **Use the resource editor to edit the application's main menu.**
   Click on the ResourceView tab in the Workspace window. Edit the *IDR-_MAINFRAME* menu resource to add a separator and a Clear Document item to the Edit menu, as shown here.

TIP: The resource editor's menu resource editor is intuitive, but you might need some help the first time you insert an item in the middle of a menu. A blank item is present at the bottom of each menu. Using the mouse, drag the blank item to the insertion position to define a new item. A new blank item will appear at the bottom when you're finished.

Now add a Transfer menu, and then define the underlying items.

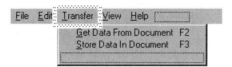

Use the following command IDs for your new menu items.

Menu	Caption	Command ID
Edit	Clear &Document	*ID_EDIT_CLEAR_ALL*
Transfer	&Get Data From Document\tF2	*ID_TRANSFER_GETDATA*
Transfer	&Store Data In Document\tF3	*ID_TRANSFER_STOREDATA*

The MFC library has defined the first item, *ID_EDIT_CLEAR_ALL*. (Note: \t is a tab character—but type \t; don't press the Tab key.)

When you add the menu items, type appropriate prompt strings in the Menu Item Properties dialog. These prompts will appear in the application's status bar window when the menu item is highlighted.

3. Use the resource editor to add keyboard accelerators. Open the *IDR-_MAINFRAME* accelerator table, and then use the insert key to add the following items.

Accelerator ID	Key
ID_TRANSFER_GETDATA	VK_F2
ID_TRANSFER_STOREDATA	VK_F3

Be sure to turn off the Ctrl, Alt, and Shift modifiers. The Accelerator edit screen and Accel Properties dialog are shown in the illustration on the following page.

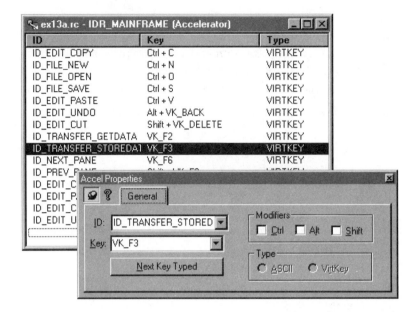

4. **Use ClassWizard to add the view class command and update command UI message handlers.** Select the *CEx13aView* class, and then add the following member functions.

Object ID	Message	Member Function
ID_TRANSFER_GETDATA	COMMAND	*OnTransferGetData*
ID_TRANSFER_STOREDATA	COMMAND	*OnTransferStoreData*
ID_TRANSFER_STOREDATA	UPDATE_COMMAND_UI	*OnUpdateTransferStoreData*

5. **Use ClassWizard to add the document class command and update command UI message handlers.** Select the *CEx13aDoc* class, and then add the following member functions.

Object ID	Message	Member Function
ID_EDIT_CLEAR_ALL	COMMAND	*OnEditClearDocument*
ID_EDIT_CLEAR_ALL	UPDATE_COMMAND_UI	*OnUpdateEditClearDocument*

6. **Add a *CString* data member to the *CEx13aDoc* class.** Edit the file ex13aDoc.h or use ClassView.

```
public:
    CString m_strText;
```

7. **Edit the document class member functions in ex13aDoc.cpp.**
The *OnNewDocument* function was generated by ClassWizard. As you'll see in Chapter 16, the framework calls this function after it first constructs the document and when the user chooses New from the File menu. Your version sets some text in the string data member. Add the following bold-face code:

```
BOOL CEx13aDoc::OnNewDocument()
{
    if (!CDocument::OnNewDocument())
        return FALSE;
    m_strText = "Hello (from CEx13aDoc::OnNewDocument)";
    return TRUE;
}
```

The Edit Clear Document message handler sets *m_strText* to empty, and the update command UI handler grays the menu item if the string is already empty. Remember that the framework calls *OnUpdateEditClearDocument* when the Edit menu pops up. Add the following boldface code:

```
void CEx13aDoc::OnEditClearDocument()
{
    m_strText.Empty();
}
```

```
void CEx13aDoc::OnUpdateEditClearDocument(CCmdUI* pCmdUI)
{
    pCmdUI->Enable(!m_strText.IsEmpty());
}
```

8. **Add a *CRichEditCtrl* data member to the *CEx13aView* class.**
Edit the file ex13aView.h or use ClassView.

```
public:
    CRichEditCtrl m_rich;
```

9. **Use ClassWizard to map the WM_CREATE and WM_SIZE messages in the *CEx13aView* class.** The *OnCreate* function creates the rich edit control. The control's size is 0 here because the view window doesn't have a size yet. The code for the two handlers is shown on the following page.

```
int CEx13aView::OnCreate(LPCREATESTRUCT lpCreateStruct)
{
    CRect rect(0, 0, 0, 0);
    if (CView::OnCreate(lpCreateStruct) == -1)
        return -1;
    m_rich.Create(ES_AUTOVSCROLL | ES_MULTILINE | ES_WANTRETURN |
                  WS_CHILD | WS_VISIBLE | WS_VSCROLL, rect, this, 1);
    return 0;
}
```

Windows sends the WM_SIZE message to the view as soon as the view's initial size is determined and again each time the user changes the frame size. This handler simply adjusts the rich edit control's size to fill the view client area. Add the following boldface code:

```
void CEx13aView::OnSize(UINT nType, int cx, int cy)
{
    CRect rect;
    CView::OnSize(nType, cx, cy);
    GetClientRect(rect);
    m_rich.SetWindowPos(&wndTop, 0, 0, rect.right - rect.left,
                        rect.bottom - rect.top, SWP_SHOWWINDOW);
}
```

10. Edit the menu command handler functions in ex13aView.cpp.
ClassWizard generated these skeleton functions when you mapped the menu commands in step 4. The *OnTransferGetData* function gets the text from the document data member and puts it in the rich edit control. The function then clears the control's modified flag. There is no update command UI handler. Add the following boldface code:

```
void CEx13aView::OnTransferGetData()
{
    CEx13aDoc* pDoc = GetDocument();
    m_rich.SetWindowText(pDoc->m_strText);
    m_rich.SetModify(FALSE);
}
```

The *OnTransferStoreData* function copies the text from the view's rich edit control to the document string and resets the control's modified flag. The corresponding update command UI handler grays the menu item if the control has not been changed since it was last copied to or from the document. Add the following boldface code:

```
void CEx13aView::OnTransferStoreData()
{
    CEx13aDoc* pDoc = GetDocument();
    m_rich.GetWindowText(pDoc->m_strText);
    m_rich.SetModify(FALSE);
}

void CEx13aView::OnUpdateTransferStoreData(CCmdUI* pCmdUI)
{
    pCmdUI->Enable(m_rich.GetModify());
}
```

11. **Build and test the EX13A application.** When the application starts, the Clear Document item on the Edit menu should be enabled. Choose Get Data From Document from the Transfer menu. Some text should appear. Edit the text, and then choose Store Data In Document. That menu item should now appear gray. Try choosing the Clear Document command, and then choose Get Data From Document again.

Property Sheets

You've already seen property sheets in Visual C++ and in many other modern Windows-based programs. A property sheet is a nice UI element that allows you to cram lots of categorized information into a small dialog. The user selects pages by clicking on their tabs. Windows offers a tab control that you can insert in a dialog, but it's more likely that you'll want to put dialogs inside the tab control. The MFC library supports this, and the result is called a property sheet. The individual dialogs are called property pages.

Building a Property Sheet

Follow these general steps to build a property sheet using the Visual C++ tools:

1. Use the resource editor to create a series of dialog templates that are all approximately the same size. The captions are the strings that you want to display on the tabs.

2. Use ClassWizard to generate a class for each template. Select *CPropertyPage* as the base class. Add data members for the controls.

3. Use ClassWizard to generate a single class derived from *CPropertySheet*.

4. To the sheet class, add one data member for each page class.

5. In the sheet class constructor, call the *AddPage* member function for each page, specifying the address of the embedded page object.

6. In your application, construct an object of the derived *CPropertySheet* class, and then call *DoModal*. You must specify a caption in the constructor call, but you can change the caption later by calling *CProperty-Sheet::SetTitle*.

7. Take care of programming for the Apply button.

Property Sheet Data Exchange

The framework puts three buttons on a property sheet. (See, for example, Figure 13-5.) Be aware that the framework calls the Dialog Data Exchange (DDX) code for a property page each time the user switches to and from that page. As you would expect, the framework calls the DDX code for a page when the user clicks OK, thus updating that page's data members. From these statements, you can conclude that all data members for all pages are updated when the user clicks OK to exit the sheet. All this with no C++ programming on your part!

NOTE: With a normal modal dialog, if the user clicks the Cancel button, the changes are discarded and the dialog class data members remain unchanged. With a property sheet, however, the data members are updated if the user changes one page and then moves to another, even if the user exits by clicking the Cancel button.

What does the Apply button do? Nothing at all if you don't write some code. It won't even be enabled. To enable it for a given page, you must set the page's modified flag by calling *SetModified(TRUE)* when you detect that the user has made changes on the page.

If you've enabled the Apply button, you can write a handler function for it in your page class by overriding the virtual *CPropertyPage::OnApply* function. Don't try to understand property page message processing in the context of normal modal dialogs; it's quite different. The framework gets a WM_NOTIFY message for all button clicks. It calls the DDX code for the page if the OK or Apply button was clicked. It then calls the virtual *OnApply* functions for all the pages, and it resets the modified flag, which disables the Apply button. Don't forget that the DDX code has already been called to update the data members in all pages, so you need to override *OnApply* in only one page class.

What you put in your *OnApply* function is your business, but one option is to send a user-defined message to the object that created the property sheet. The message handler can get the property page data members and process them. Meanwhile, the property sheet stays on the screen.

The EX13A Example Revisited

Now we'll add a property sheet to EX13A that allows the user to change the rich edit control's font characteristics. Of course, we could have used the standard MFC *CFontDialog* function, but then you wouldn't have learned how to create property sheets. Figure 13-5 shows the property sheet that you'll build as you continue with EX13A.

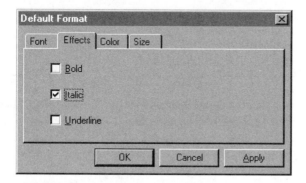

Figure 13-5.
The property sheet from EX13A.

If you haven't built EX13A, follow the instructions that begin on page 295 to build it. If you already have EX13A working with the Transfer menu commands, just continue on with these steps:

1. Use the resource editor to edit the application's main menu.
Click on the ResourceView tab in the Workspace window. Edit the *IDR-_MAINFRAME* menu resource to add a Format menu that looks like this.

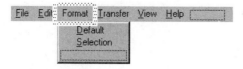

Use the following command IDs for the new Format menu items.

Caption	Command ID
&Default	*ID_FORMAT_DEFAULT*
&Selection	*ID_FORMAT_SELECTION*

Add appropriate prompt strings for the two menu items.

2. **Use ClassWizard to add the view class command and update command UI message handlers.** Select the *CEx13aView* class, and then add the following member functions.

Object ID	Message	Member Function
ID_FORMAT_DEFAULT	COMMAND	*OnFormatDefault*
ID_FORMAT_SELECTION	COMMAND	*OnFormatSelection*
ID_FORMAT_SELECTION	UPDATE_COMMAND_UI	*OnUpdateFormatSelection*

3. **Use the resource editor to add four property page dialog templates.** The templates are shown here with their associated IDs.

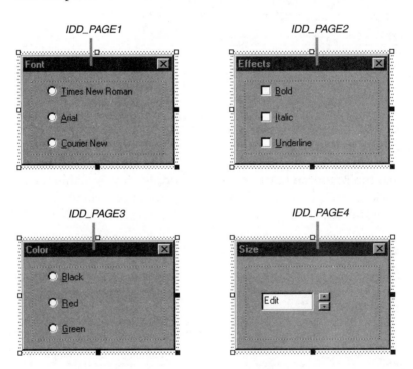

Use the IDs in the table on the facing page for the controls in the dialogs. Set the Auto Buddy and the Set Buddy Integer properties for the spin button control, and set the Group property for the *IDC_FONT* and

IDC_COLOR radio buttons. Set the minimum value of *IDC_FONTSIZE* to *8* and its maximum value to *24*.

Use ClassWizard to create the classes *CPage1*, *CPage2*, *CPage3*, and *CPage4*. In each case, select *CPropertyPage* as the base class. Click the Change button in ClassWizard's New Class dialog to generate the code for all these classes in the files Property.h and Property.cpp. Then add the data members shown here.

Dialog	Control	ID	Type	Data Member
IDD_PAGE1	First radio button	*IDC_FONT*	*int*	*m_nFont*
IDD_PAGE2	Bold check box	*IDC_BOLD*	*BOOL*	*m_bBold*
IDD_PAGE2	Italic check box	*IDC_ITALIC*	*BOOL*	*m_bItalic*
IDD_PAGE2	Underline check box	*IDC_UNDERLINE*	*BOOL*	*m_bUnderline*
IDD_PAGE3	First radio button	*IDC_COLOR*	*int*	*m_nColor*
IDD_PAGE4	Edit control	*IDC_FONTSIZE*	*int*	*m_nFontSize*
IDD_PAGE4	Spin button control	*IDC_SPIN1*		

Finally, use ClassWizard to add an *OnInitDialog* message handler function for *CPage4*.

4. Use ClassWizard to create a class derived from *CPropertySheet*.
Choose the name *CFontSheet*. Generate the code in the files Property.h and Property.cpp, the same files you used for the property page classes. Figure 13-6 shows these files with the added code in boldface.

PROPERTY.H

```
#if !defined(AFX_PROPERTY_H__CD702F99_7495_11D0_8FDC_00C04FC2A0C2__INCLUDED_)
#define AFX_PROPERTY_H_ _CD702F99_7495_11D0_8FDC_00C04FC2A0C2__INCLUDED_

#if _MSC_VER > 1000
#pragma once
#endif // _MSC_VER > 1000
// Property.h : header file
//
```

Figure 13-6.   *(continued)*
The EX13A header and implementation file listings for the property page and property sheet classes.

Figure 13-6. *continued*

```
#define WM_USERAPPLY WM_USER + 5
extern CView* g_pView;


/////////////////////////////////////////////////////////////////////
// CPage1 dialog

class CPage1 : public CPropertyPage
{
    DECLARE_DYNCREATE(CPage1)

// Construction
public:
    CPage1();
    ~CPage1();

// Dialog Data
    //{{AFX_DATA(CPage1)
    enum { IDD = IDD_PAGE1 };
    int     m_nFont;
    //}}AFX_DATA


// Overrides
    // ClassWizard generate virtual function overrides
    //{{AFX_VIRTUAL(CPage1)
    protected:
    virtual void DoDataExchange(CDataExchange* pDX); // DDX/DDV
                                                     // support
    //}}AFX_VIRTUAL
    virtual BOOL OnApply();
    virtual BOOL OnCommand(WPARAM wParam, LPARAM lParam);

// Implementation
protected:
    // Generated message map functions
    //{{AFX_MSG(CPage1)
        // NOTE: the ClassWizard will add member functions here
    //}}AFX_MSG
    DECLARE_MESSAGE_MAP()

};


/////////////////////////////////////////////////////////////////////
// CPage2 dialog
```

```
class CPage2 : public CPropertyPage
{
    DECLARE_DYNCREATE(CPage2)

// Construction
public:
    CPage2();
    ~CPage2();

// Dialog Data
    //{{AFX_DATA(CPage2)
    enum { IDD = IDD_PAGE2 };
    BOOL    m_bBold;
    BOOL    m_bItalic;
    BOOL    m_bUnderline;
    //}}AFX_DATA


// Overrides
    // ClassWizard generate virtual function overrides
    //{{AFX_VIRTUAL(CPage2)
    protected:
    virtual void DoDataExchange(CDataExchange* pDX); // DDX/DDV
                                                     // support

    //}}AFX_VIRTUAL
    virtual BOOL OnCommand(WPARAM wParam, LPARAM lParam);

// Implementation
protected:
    // Generated message map functions
    //{{AFX_MSG(CPage2)
        // NOTE: the ClassWizard will add member functions here
    //}}AFX_MSG
    DECLARE_MESSAGE_MAP()

};


//////////////////////////////////////////////////////////////////
// CPage3 dialog

class CPage3 : public CPropertyPage
{
    DECLARE_DYNCREATE(CPage3)

// Construction
public:
```

(continued)

Figure 13-6. *continued*

```
    CPage3();
    ~CPage3();

// Dialog Data
    //{{AFX_DATA(CPage3)
    enum { IDD = IDD_PAGE3 };
    int     m_nColor;
    //}}AFX_DATA


// Overrides
    // ClassWizard generate virtual function overrides
    //{{AFX_VIRTUAL(CPage3)
    protected:
    virtual void DoDataExchange(CDataExchange* pDX); // DDX/DDV
                                                     // support

    //}}AFX_VIRTUAL
    virtual BOOL OnCommand(WPARAM wParam, LPARAM lParam);

// Implementation
protected:
    // Generated message map functions
    //{{AFX_MSG(CPage3)
        // NOTE: the ClassWizard will add member functions here
    //}}AFX_MSG
    DECLARE_MESSAGE_MAP()

};

/////////////////////////////////////////////////////////////////
// CPage4 dialog

class CPage4 : public CPropertyPage
{
    DECLARE_DYNCREATE(CPage4)

// Construction
public:
    CPage4();
    ~CPage4();

// Dialog Data
    //{{AFX_DATA(CPage4)
    enum { IDD = IDD_PAGE4 };
    int     m_nFontSize;
    //}}AFX_DATA
```

```
// Overrides
    // ClassWizard generate virtual function overrides
    //{{AFX_VIRTUAL(CPage4)
    protected:
    virtual void DoDataExchange(CDataExchange* pDX); // DDX/DDV
                                                     // support

    //}}AFX_VIRTUAL
    virtual BOOL OnCommand(WPARAM wParam, LPARAM lParam);

// Implementation
protected:
    // Generated message map functions
    //{{AFX_MSG(CPage4)
    virtual BOOL OnInitDialog();
    //}}AFX_MSG
    DECLARE_MESSAGE_MAP()

};

/////////////////////////////////////////////////////////////////////
// CFontSheet

class CFontSheet : public CPropertySheet
{
    DECLARE_DYNAMIC(CFontSheet)

public:
    CPage1 m_page1;
    CPage2 m_page2;
    CPage3 m_page3;
    CPage4 m_page4;

// Construction
public:
    CFontSheet(UINT nIDCaption, CWnd* pParentWnd = NULL,
               UINT iSelectPage = 0);
    CFontSheet(LPCTSTR pszCaption, CWnd* pParentWnd = NULL,
               UINT iSelectPage = 0);

// Attributes
public:

// Operations
public:
// Overrides
    // ClassWizard generated virtual function overrides
```

(continued)

Figure 13-6. *continued*

```
    //{{AFX_VIRTUAL(CFontSheet)
    //}}AFX_VIRTUAL

// Implementation
public:
    virtual ~CFontSheet();

    // Generated message map functions
protected:
    //{{AFX_MSG(CFontSheet)
        // NOTE - the ClassWizard will add and remove      ↵
                    member functions here.
    //}}AFX_MSG
    DECLARE_MESSAGE_MAP()
};


/////////////////////////////////////////////////////////////////////
//{{AFX_INSERT_LOCATION}}
// Microsoft Visual C++ will insert additional declarations
//   immediately before the previous line.

#endif // !defined(AFX_PROPERTY_H_ _CD702F99_7495_      ↵
                    11D0_8FDC_00C04FC2A0C2__INCLUDED_)
```

PROPERTY.CPP

```
// Property.cpp : implementation file
//

#include "stdafx.h"
#include "ex13a.h"
#include "Property.h"

#ifdef _DEBUG
#define new DEBUG_NEW
#undef THIS_FILE
static char THIS_FILE[] = __FILE__;
#endif

CView* g_pView;

/////////////////////////////////////////////////////////////////////
// CPage1 property page

IMPLEMENT_DYNCREATE(CPage1, CPropertyPage)
```

```
CPage1::CPage1() : CPropertyPage(CPage1::IDD)
{
    //{{AFX_DATA_INIT(CPage1)
    m_nFont = -1;
    //}}AFX_DATA_INIT
}

CPage1::~CPage1()
{
}

BOOL CPage1::OnApply()
{
    TRACE("CPage1::OnApply\n");
    g_pView->SendMessage(WM_USERAPPLY);
    return TRUE;
}

BOOL CPage1::OnCommand(WPARAM wParam, LPARAM lParam)
{
    SetModified(TRUE);
    return CPropertyPage::OnCommand(wParam, lParam);
}

void CPage1::DoDataExchange(CDataExchange* pDX)
{
    TRACE("Entering CPage1::DoDataExchange -- %d\n",
        pDX->m_bSaveAndValidate);
    CPropertyPage::DoDataExchange(pDX);
    //{{AFX_DATA_MAP(CPage1)
    DDX_Radio(pDX, IDC_FONT, m_nFont);
    //}}AFX_DATA_MAP
}


BEGIN_MESSAGE_MAP(CPage1, CPropertyPage)
    //{{AFX_MSG_MAP(CPage1)
        // NOTE: the ClassWizard will add message map macros here
    //}}AFX_MSG_MAP
END_MESSAGE_MAP()

/////////////////////////////////////////////////////////////////
// CPage1 message handlers

/////////////////////////////////////////////////////////////////
// CPage2 property page
```

(continued)

Figure 13-6. *continued*

```
IMPLEMENT_DYNCREATE(CPage2, CPropertyPage)

CPage2::CPage2() : CPropertyPage(CPage2::IDD)
{
    //{{AFX_DATA_INIT(CPage2)
    m_bBold = FALSE;
    m_bItalic = FALSE;
    m_bUnderline = FALSE;
    //}}AFX_DATA_INIT
}

CPage2::~CPage2()
{
}

BOOL CPage2::OnCommand(WPARAM wParam, LPARAM lParam)
{
    SetModified(TRUE);
    return CPropertyPage::OnCommand(wParam, lParam);
}

void CPage2::DoDataExchange(CDataExchange* pDX)
{
    TRACE("Entering CPage2::DoDataExchange -- %d\n",
        pDX->m_bSaveAndValidate);
    CPropertyPage::DoDataExchange(pDX);
    //{{AFX_DATA_MAP(CPage2)
    DDX_Check(pDX, IDC_BOLD, m_bBold);
    DDX_Check(pDX, IDC_ITALIC, m_bItalic);
    DDX_Check(pDX, IDC_UNDERLINE, m_bUnderline);
    //}}AFX_DATA_MAP
}


BEGIN_MESSAGE_MAP(CPage2, CPropertyPage)
    //{{AFX_MSG_MAP(CPage2)
        // NOTE: the ClassWizard will add message map macros here
    //}}AFX_MSG_MAP
END_MESSAGE_MAP()

///////////////////////////////////////////////////////////////////
// CPage2 message handlers

///////////////////////////////////////////////////////////////////
// CPage3 property page
```

```
IMPLEMENT_DYNCREATE(CPage3, CPropertyPage)

CPage3::CPage3() : CPropertyPage(CPage3::IDD)
{
    //{{AFX_DATA_INIT(CPage3)
    m_nColor = -1;
    //}}AFX_DATA_INIT
}

CPage3::~CPage3()
{
}

BOOL CPage3::OnCommand(WPARAM wParam, LPARAM lParam)
{
    SetModified(TRUE);
    return CPropertyPage::OnCommand(wParam, lParam);
}

void CPage3::DoDataExchange(CDataExchange* pDX)
{
    TRACE("Entering CPage3::DoDataExchange -- %d\n",
        pDX->m_bSaveAndValidate);
    CPropertyPage::DoDataExchange(pDX);
    //{{AFX_DATA_MAP(CPage3)
    DDX_Radio(pDX, IDC_COLOR, m_nColor);
    //}}AFX_DATA_MAP
}


BEGIN_MESSAGE_MAP(CPage3, CPropertyPage)
    //{{AFX_MSG_MAP(CPage3)
        // NOTE: the ClassWizard will add message map macros here
    //}}AFX_MSG_MAP
END_MESSAGE_MAP()

/////////////////////////////////////////////////////////////////////
// CPage3 message handlers

/////////////////////////////////////////////////////////////////////
// CPage4 property page

IMPLEMENT_DYNCREATE(CPage4, CPropertyPage)

CPage4::CPage4() : CPropertyPage(CPage4::IDD)
{
```

(continued)

Figure 13-6. *continued*

```
    //{{AFX_DATA_INIT(CPage4)
    m_nFontSize = 0;
    //}}AFX_DATA_INIT
}

CPage4::~CPage4()
{
}

BOOL CPage4::OnCommand(WPARAM wParam, LPARAM lParam)
{
    SetModified(TRUE);
    return CPropertyPage::OnCommand(wParam, lParam);
}

void CPage4::DoDataExchange(CDataExchange* pDX)
{
    TRACE("Entering CPage4::DoDataExchange -- %d\n",
        pDX->m_bSaveAndValidate);
    CPropertyPage::DoDataExchange(pDX);
    //{{AFX_DATA_MAP(CPage4)
    DDX_Text(pDX, IDC_FONTSIZE, m_nFontSize);
    DDV_MinMaxInt(pDX, m_nFontSize, 8, 24);
    //}}AFX_DATA_MAP
}


BEGIN_MESSAGE_MAP(CPage4, CPropertyPage)
    //{{AFX_MSG_MAP(CPage4)
    //}}AFX_MSG_MAP
END_MESSAGE_MAP()

/////////////////////////////////////////////////////////////////
// CPage4 message handlers

BOOL CPage4::OnInitDialog()
{
    CPropertyPage::OnInitDialog();
    ((CSpinButtonCtrl*) GetDlgItem(IDC_SPIN1))->SetRange(8, 24);
    return TRUE;  // return TRUE unless you set the focus to a control
                  //  EXCEPTION: OCX Property Pages should return FALSE
}
```

```
/////////////////////////////////////////////////////////////////
// CFontSheet

IMPLEMENT_DYNAMIC(CFontSheet, CPropertySheet)

CFontSheet::CFontSheet(UINT nIDCaption, CWnd* pParentWnd,
                       UINT iSelectPage)
    :CPropertySheet(nIDCaption, pParentWnd, iSelectPage)
{
}

CFontSheet::CFontSheet(LPCTSTR pszCaption, CWnd* pParentWnd,
                       UINT iSelectPage)
    :CPropertySheet(pszCaption, pParentWnd, iSelectPage)
{
    AddPage(&m_page1);
    AddPage(&m_page2);
    AddPage(&m_page3);
    AddPage(&m_page4);
}

CFontSheet::~CFontSheet()
{
}


BEGIN_MESSAGE_MAP(CFontSheet, CPropertySheet)
    //{{AFX_MSG_MAP(CFontSheet)
        // NOTE - the ClassWizard will add and remove        ⌐
                  mapping macros here.
    //}}AFX_MSG_MAP
END_MESSAGE_MAP()

/////////////////////////////////////////////////////////////////
// CFontSheet message handlers
```

5. Add two data members and two prototypes to the *CEx13aView* class.
If you use ClassView for the data members, the #*include* for Property.h
will be added automatically.

```
private:
    CFontSheet m_sh;
    BOOL m_bDefault; // TRUE default format, FALSE selection
```

Now add the prototype for the private function *Format*:

```
void Format(CHARFORMAT &cf);
```

Insert the prototype for the protected function *OnUserApply* before the *DECLARE_MESSAGE_MAP* macro.

```
afx_msg LRESULT OnUserApply(WPARAM wParam, LPARAM lParam);
```

6. **Edit and add code in the file ex13aView.cpp.** Map the user-defined WM_USERAPPLY message, as shown here:

```
ON_MESSAGE(WM_USERAPPLY, OnUserApply)
```

Add the following lines to the *OnCreate* function, just before the *return 0* statement:

```
CHARFORMAT cf;
Format(cf);
m_rich.SetDefaultCharFormat(cf);
```

Edit the view constructor to set default values for the property sheet data members, as follows:

```
CEx13aView::CEx13aView() : m_sh("")
{
    m_sh.m_page1.m_nFont = 0;
    m_sh.m_page2.m_bBold = FALSE;
    m_sh.m_page2.m_bItalic = FALSE;
    m_sh.m_page2.m_bUnderline = FALSE;
    m_sh.m_page3.m_nColor = 0;
    m_sh.m_page4.m_nFontSize = 12;
    g_pView = this;
    m_bDefault = TRUE;
}
```

Edit the format command handlers, as shown here:

```
void CEx13aView::OnFormatDefault()
{
    m_sh.SetTitle("Default Format");
    m_bDefault = TRUE;
    m_sh.DoModal();
}

void CEx13aView::OnFormatSelection()
{
    m_sh.SetTitle("Selection Format");
    m_bDefault = FALSE;
    m_sh.DoModal();
}

void CEx13aView::OnUpdateFormatSelection(CCmdUI* pCmdUI)
{
```

```
    long nStart, nEnd;
    m_rich.GetSel(nStart, nEnd);
    pCmdUI->Enable(nStart != nEnd);
}
```

Add the following handler for the user-defined WM_USERAPPLY message:

```
LRESULT CEx13aView::OnUserApply(WPARAM wParam, LPARAM lParam)
{
    TRACE("CEx13aView::OnUserApply -- wParam = %x\n", wParam);
    CHARFORMAT cf;
    Format(cf);
    if (m_bDefault) {
        m_rich.SetDefaultCharFormat(cf);
    }
    else {
        m_rich.SetSelectionCharFormat(cf);
    }
    return 0;
}
```

Add the *Format* helper function, as shown below, to set a *CHARFORMAT* structure based on the values of the property sheet data members.

```
void CEx13aView::Format(CHARFORMAT& cf)
{
    cf.cbSize = sizeof(CHARFORMAT);
    cf.dwMask = CFM_BOLD | CFM_COLOR | CFM_FACE |
                CFM_ITALIC | CFM_SIZE | CFM_UNDERLINE;
    cf.dwEffects = (m_sh.m_page2.m_bBold ? CFE_BOLD : 0) |
                   (m_sh.m_page2.m_bItalic ? CFE_ITALIC : 0) |
                   (m_sh.m_page2.m_bUnderline ? CFE_UNDERLINE : 0);
    cf.yHeight = m_sh.m_page4.m_nFontSize * 20;
    switch(m_sh.m_page3.m_nColor) {
    case -1:
    case 0:
        cf.crTextColor = RGB(0, 0, 0);
        break;
    case 1:
        cf.crTextColor = RGB(255, 0, 0);
        break;
    case 2:
        cf.crTextColor = RGB(0, 255, 0);
        break;
    }
    switch(m_sh.m_page1.m_nFont) {
    case -1:
```

(continued)

```
case 0:
    strcpy(cf.szFaceName, "Times New Roman");
    break;
case 1:
    strcpy(cf.szFaceName, "Arial");
    break;
case 2:
    strcpy(cf.szFaceName, "Courier New");
    break;
}
cf.bCharSet = 0;
cf.bPitchAndFamily = 0;
}
```

7. **Build and test the enhanced EX13A application.** Type some text, and then choose Default from the Format menu. Observe the *TRACE* messages in the Debug window as you click on property sheet tabs and click the Apply button. Try highlighting some text and then formatting the selection.

Apply Button Processing

You might be curious about the way the property sheet classes process the Apply button. In all the page classes, the overridden *OnCommand* functions enable the Apply button whenever a control sends a message to the page. This works fine for pages 1 through 3 in EX13A, but for page 4, *OnCommand* is called during the initial conversation between the spin button control and its buddy.

The *OnApply* virtual override in the *CPage1* class sends a user-defined message to the view. The function finds the view in an expedient way—by using a global variable set by the view class. A better approach would be to pass the view pointer to the sheet constructor and then to the page constructor.

The view class calls the property sheet's *DoModal* function for both default formatting and selection formatting. It sets the *m_bDefault* flag to indicate the mode. We don't need to check the return from *DoModal* because the user-defined message is sent for both the OK button and the Apply button. If the user clicks Cancel, no message is sent.

The *CMenu* Class

Up to this point, the application framework and the menu editor have shielded you from the menu class, *CMenu*. A *CMenu* object can represent each Windows menu, including the top-level menu items and associated pop-up menus. Most of the time, the menu's resource is directly attached to a frame window when the window's *Create* or *LoadFrame* function is called, and a *CMenu* object is never explicitly constructed. The *CWnd* member function *GetMenu* returns a temporary *CMenu* pointer. Once you have this pointer, you can freely access and update the menu object.

Suppose you want to switch menus after the application starts. *IDR_MAIN-FRAME* always identifies the initial menu in the resource script. If you want a second menu, you use the menu editor to create a menu resource with your own ID. Then, in your program, you construct a *CMenu* object, use the *CMenu::Load-Menu* function to load the menu from the resource, and call the *CWnd::SetMenu* function to attach the new menu to the frame window. Then you call the *Detach* member function to separate the object's *HMENU* handle so that the menu is not destroyed when the *CMenu* object goes out of scope.

You can use a resource to define a menu, and then your program can modify the menu items at runtime. If necessary, however, you can build the whole menu at runtime, without benefit of a resource. In either case, you can use *CMenu* member functions such as *ModifyMenu*, *InsertMenu*, and *DeleteMenu*. Each of these functions operates on an individual menu item identified by ID or by a relative position index.

A menu object is actually composed of a nested structure of submenus. You can use the *GetSubMenu* member function to get a *CMenu* pointer to a pop-up menu contained in the main *CMenu* object. The *CMenu::GetMenuString* function returns the menu item string corresponding to either a zero-based index or a command ID. If you use the command ID option, the menu is searched, together with any submenus.

Creating Floating Pop-Up Menus

Floating pop-up menus are one of the latest trends in user interface design. The user presses the right mouse button and a floating menu offers choices that relate to the current selection. It's easy to create these menus using the resource editor and the MFC library *CMenu::TrackPopupMenu* function. Just follow these steps:

1. Use the menu editor to insert a new, empty menu in your project's resource file.

2. Type some characters in the left top-level item, and then add your menu items in the resulting pop-up menu.

3. Use ClassWizard to add a WM_CONTEXTMENU message handler in your view class or in some other window class that receives mouse-click messages. Code the handler as shown on the following page.

```
void CMyView::OnContextMenu(CWnd *pWnd, CPoint point)
{
    CMenu menu;
    menu.LoadMenu(IDR_MYFLOATINGMENU);
    menu.GetSubMenu(0)
        ->TrackPopupMenu(TPM_LEFTALIGN | TPM_RIGHTBUTTON,
        point.x, point.y, this);
}
```

You can use ClassWizard to map the floating menu's command IDs the same way you would map the frame menu's command IDs.

Extended Command Processing

In addition to the *ON_COMMAND* message map macro, the MFC library provides an extended variation, *ON_COMMAND_EX*. The extended command message map macro provides two features not supplied by the regular command message—a command ID function parameter and the ability to reject a command at runtime, sending it to the next object in the command route. If the extended command handler returns *TRUE*, the command goes no further; if it returns *FALSE*, the application framework looks for another command handler.

The command ID parameter is useful when you want one function to handle several related command messages. You might invent some of your own uses for the rejection feature.

ClassWizard can't help you with extended command handlers, so you'll have to do the coding yourself, outside the *AFX_MSG_MAP* brackets. Assume that *IDM_ZOOM_1* and *IDM_ZOOM_2* are related command IDs defined in resource.h. Here's the class code you'll need to process both messages with one function, *OnZoom*:

```
BEGIN_MESSAGE_MAP(CMyView, CView)
    ON_COMMAND_EX(IDM_ZOOM_1, OnZoom)
    ON_COMMAND_EX(IDM_ZOOM_2, OnZoom)
END_MESSAGE_MAP()

BOOL CMyView::OnZoom(UINT nID)
{
    if (nID == IDM_ZOOM_1) {
        // code specific to first zoom command
    }
    else {
        // code specific to second zoom command
    }
    // code common to both commands
    return TRUE; // Command goes no further
}
```

Here's the function prototype:

```
afx_msg BOOL OnZoom(UINT nID);
```

Other MFC message map macros are helpful for processing ranges of commands, as you might see in dynamic menu applications. These macros include

ON_COMMAND_RANGE
ON_COMMAND_EX_RANGE
ON_UPDATE_COMMAND_UI_RANGE

If the values of *IDM_ZOOM_1* and *IDM_ZOOM_2* were consecutive, you could rewrite the *CMyView* message map as follows:

```
BEGIN_MESSAGE_MAP(CMyView, CView)
    ON_COMMAND_EX_RANGE(IDM_ZOOM_1, IDM_ZOOM_2, OnZoom)
END_MESSAGE_MAP()
```

Now *OnZoom* is called for both menu choices, and the handler can determine the choice from the integer parameter.

CHAPTER FOURTEEN

Toolbars and Status Bars

All the Microsoft Visual C++ examples up to this point have included toolbars and status bars. AppWizard generated the code that initialized these application framework elements as long as you accepted the AppWizard default options Docking Toolbar and Initial Status Bar. The default toolbar provides graphics equivalents for many of the standard application framework menu selections, and the default status bar displays menu prompts together with the keyboard state indicators CAP, NUM, and SCRL.

This chapter shows you how to customize the toolbar and the status bar for your application. You'll be able to add your own toolbar graphical buttons and control their appearance. You'll also learn how to disable the status bar's normal display of menu prompts and keyboard indicators. This allows your application to take over the status bar for its own use.

Control Bars and the Application Framework

The toolbar is an object of class *CToolBar*, and the status bar is an object of class *CStatusBar*. Both these classes are derived from class *CControlBar*, which is itself derived from *CWnd*. The *CControlBar* class supports control bar windows that are positioned inside frame windows. These control bar windows resize and reposition themselves as the parent frame moves and changes size. The application framework takes care of the construction, window creation, and destruction of the control bar objects. AppWizard generates control bar code for its derived frame class located in the files MainFrm.cpp and MainFrm.h.

In a typical SDI application, a *CToolBar* object occupies the top portion of the *CMainFrame* client area and a *CStatusBar* object occupies the bottom portion. The view occupies the remaining (middle) part of the frame.

Beginning with Microsoft Foundation Class (MFC) Library version 4.0, the toolbar has been built around the toolbar common control that first became available with Microsoft Windows 95. Thus the toolbar is fully dockable. The programming interface is much the same as it was in earlier versions of the MFC library, however. The button images are easy to work with because a special resource type is supported by the resource editor. The old global *buttons* array is gone.

Assuming that AppWizard has generated the control bar code for your application, the user can enable and disable the toolbar and the status bar individually by choosing commands from the application's View menu. When a control bar is disabled, it disappears and the view size is recalculated. Apart from the common behavior just described, toolbar and status bar objects operate independently of each other and have rather different characteristics.

In Visual C++ 6.0, a new MFC toolbar was introduced called the <u>rebar</u>. The rebar is based on the controls that come as part of Microsoft Internet Explorer 4.0 and provides a Microsoft Internet Explorer–style "sliding" toolbar. We will cover this later in this chapter.

The Toolbar

A toolbar consists of a number of horizontally (or vertically) arranged graphical buttons that might be clustered in groups. The programming interface determines the grouping. The graphical images for the buttons are stored in a single bitmap that is attached to the application's resource file. When a button is clicked, it sends a command message, as do menus and keyboard accelerators. An update command UI message handler is used to update the button's state, which in turn is used by the application framework to modify the button's graphical image.

The Toolbar Bitmap

Each button on a toolbar appears to have its own bitmap, but actually a single bitmap serves the entire toolbar. The toolbar bitmap has a tile, 15 pixels high and 16 pixels wide, for each button. The application framework supplies the button borders, and it modifies those borders, together with the button's bitmap tile color, to reflect the current button state. Figure 14-1 shows the relationship between the toolbar bitmap and the corresponding toolbar.

Figure 14-1.
A toolbar bitmap and an actual toolbar.

The toolbar bitmap is stored in the file Toolbar.bmp in the application's \res subdirectory. The bitmap is identified in the resource script (RC) file as *IDR_MAINFRAME*. You don't edit the toolbar bitmap directly; instead you use Visual C++'s special toolbar-editing facility.

Button States

Each button can assume the following states.

State	Meaning
0	Normal, unpressed state.
TBSTATE_CHECKED	Checked (down) state.
TBSTATE_ENABLED	Available for use. Button is grayed and unavailable if this state is not set.
TBSTATE_HIDDEN	Not visible.
TBSTATE_INDETERMINATE	Grayed.
TBSTATE_PRESSED	Currently selected (pressed) with the mouse.
TBSTATE_WRAP	Line break follows the button.

A button can behave in either of two ways: it can be a pushbutton, which is down only when currently selected by the mouse, or it can be a check box button, which can be toggled up and down with mouse clicks. All buttons in the standard application framework toolbar are pushbuttons.

The Toolbar and Command Messages

When the user clicks a toolbar button with the mouse, a command message is generated. This message is routed like the menu command messages you saw in Chapter 13. Most of the time, a toolbar button matches a menu option. In the standard application framework toolbar, for example, the Disk button is equivalent to the File Save menu option because both generate the *ID_FILE-_SAVE* command. The object receiving the command message doesn't need to know whether the message was produced by a click on the toolbar or by a selection from the menu.

A toolbar button doesn't have to mirror a menu item. If you don't provide the equivalent menu item, however, you are advised to define a keyboard accelerator for the button so that the user can activate the command with the keyboard or with a keyboard macro product for Microsoft Windows. You can use ClassWizard to define command and update command UI message handlers for toolbar buttons, whether or not they have corresponding menu items.

A toolbar has an associated bitmap resource and, in the RC file, a companion TOOLBAR resource that defines the menu commands associated with the buttons. Both the bitmap and the TOOLBAR resource have the same ID, typically *IDR_MAINFRAME*. The text of the AppWizard-generated TOOLBAR resource is shown below:

```
IDR_MAINFRAME TOOLBAR DISCARDABLE  16, 15
BEGIN
    BUTTON        ID_FILE_NEW
    BUTTON        ID_FILE_OPEN
    BUTTON        ID_FILE_SAVE
        SEPARATOR
    BUTTON        ID_EDIT_CUT
    BUTTON        ID_EDIT_COPY
    BUTTON        ID_EDIT_PASTE
        SEPARATOR
    BUTTON        ID_FILE_PRINT
    BUTTON        ID_APP_ABOUT
END
```

The *SEPARATOR* constants serve to group the buttons by inserting corresponding spaces on the toolbar. If the number of toolbar bitmap panes exceeds the number of resource elements (excluding separators), the extra buttons are not displayed.

When you edit the toolbar with the resource editor, you're editing both the bitmap resource and the TOOLBAR resource. You select a button image, and then you double-click on the left panel to edit the properties, including the button's ID.

Toolbar Update Command UI Message Handlers

Remember from Chapter 13 that update command UI message handlers are used to disable or add check marks to menu items. These same message handlers apply to toolbar buttons. If your update command UI message handler calls the *CCmdUI::Enable* member function with a *FALSE* parameter, the corresponding button is set to the disabled (grayed) state and no longer responds to mouse clicks.

On a menu item, the *CCmdUI::SetCheck* member function displays a check mark. For the toolbar, the *SetCheck* function implements check box buttons. If the update command UI message handler calls *SetCheck* with a parameter value of 1, the button is toggled to the down (checked) state; if the parameter is 0, the button is toggled up (unchecked).

NOTE: If the *SetCheck* parameter value is 2, the button is set to the <u>indeterminate</u> state. This state looks like the disabled state, but the button is still active and its color is a bit brighter.

The update command UI message handlers for a pop-up menu are called only when the menu is painted. The toolbar is displayed all the time, so when are its update command UI message handlers called? They're called during the application's idle processing, so the buttons can be updated continuously. If the same handler covers a menu item and a toolbar button, it is called both during idle processing and when the pop-up menu is displayed.

ToolTips

You've seen ToolTips in various Windows applications, including Visual C++. When the user positions the mouse on a toolbar button for a certain interval, text is displayed in a little ToolTip box next to the button. In Chapter 13, you learned that menu items can have associated prompt strings, which are string resource elements with matching IDs. To create a ToolTip, you simply add the tip text to the end of the menu prompt, preceded by a newline (\n) character. The resource editor lets you edit the prompt string while you are editing the toolbar images. Just double-click in the left panel.

Locating the Main Frame Window

The toolbar and status bar objects you'll be working with are attached to the application's main frame window, not to the view window. How does your view find its main frame window? In an SDI application, you can use the *CWnd::GetParentFrame* function. Unfortunately, this function won't work in an MDI application because the view's parent frame is the MDI child frame, not the MDI frame window.

If you want your view class to work in both SDI and MDI applications, you must find the main frame window through the application object. The *AfxGetApp* global function returns a pointer to the application object. You can use that pointer to get the *CWinApp* data member *m_pMainWnd*. In an MDI application, AppWizard generates code that sets *m_pMainWnd*, but in an SDI application, the framework sets *m_pMainWnd* during the view creation process. Once *m_pMainWnd* is set, you can use it in a view class to get the frame's toolbar with statements such as this:

```
CMainFrame* pFrame = (CMainFrame*) AfxGetApp()->m_pMainWnd;
CToolBar* pToolBar = &pFrame->m_wndToolBar;
```

NOTE: You'll need to cast *m_pMainWnd* from *CFrameWnd** to *CMainFrame** because *m_wndToolBar* is a member of that derived class. You'll also have to make *m_wndToolBar* public or make your class a friend of *CMainFrame*.

You can use similar logic to locate menu objects, status bar objects, and dialog objects.

NOTE: In an SDI application, the value of *m_pMainWnd* is not set when the view's *OnCreate* message handler is called. If you need to access the main frame window in your *OnCreate* function, you must use the *GetParentFrame* function.

The EX14A Toolbar Example

In this example, you will replace the standard application framework Edit Cut, Copy, and Paste toolbar buttons with three special-purpose buttons that control drawing in the view window. You will also construct a Draw menu with three corresponding menu items, as follows.

Menu Item	Function
Circle	Draws a circle in the view window
Square	Draws a square in the view window
Pattern	Toggles a diagonal line fill pattern for new squares and circles

The menu and toolbar options force the user to alternate between drawing circles and squares. After the user draws a circle, the Circle menu item and toolbar button are disabled; after the user draws a square, the Square menu item and toolbar button are disabled.

On the application's Draw menu, the Pattern menu item gets a check mark when pattern fill is active. On the toolbar, the corresponding button is a check box button that is down when pattern fill is active and up when it is not active.

Figure 14-2 shows the application in action. The user has just drawn a square with pattern fill. Notice the states of the three drawing buttons.

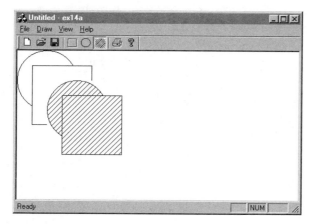

Figure 14-2.
The EX14A program in action.

The EX14A example introduces the resource editor for toolbars. You'll need to do very little C++ coding. Simply follow these steps:

1. Run AppWizard to generate \vcpp32\ex14a\ex14a. Accept all default settings but two: select Single Document and deselect Printing and Print Preview. The options and the default class names are shown here.

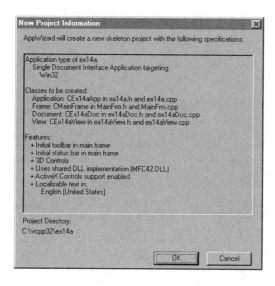

2. Use the resource editor to edit the application's main menu. In ResourceView, double-click on *IDR_MAINFRAME* under Menu. Edit the *IDR_MAINFRAME* menu resource to create a menu that looks like this (which means you'll need to change the Edit menu).

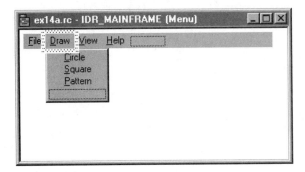

Use the following command IDs for your new menu items.

Menu	Caption	Command ID
Draw	Circle	*ID_DRAW_CIRCLE*
Draw	Square	*ID_DRAW_SQUARE*
Draw	Pattern	*ID_DRAW_PATTERN*

When you're in the Menu Item Properties dialog, add some appropriate prompt strings and ToolTips (following a newline character). The string for *ID_DRAW_CIRCLE* might be "Draw a circle\nCircle."

3. Use the resource editor to update the application's toolbar. Edit the *IDR_MAINFRAME* toolbar resource to create a bitmap that looks like this.

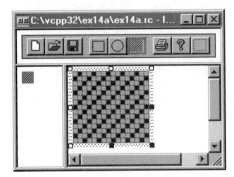

You'll be erasing the Edit Cut, Copy, and Paste tiles (fourth, fifth, and sixth from the left) and replacing them with new tiles. The toolbar editor is fairly intuitive. You simply move the buttons around with the mouse. The Delete key erases a button's pixels. If you want to eliminate a button entirely, just drag it off the toolbar. Use the rectangle and ellipse tools from the graphics toolbar. Experiment with different line widths. Save the resource file when you're done—just in case.

Assign the IDs *ID_DRAW_CIRCLE*, *ID_DRAW_SQUARE*, and *ID_DRAW_PATTERN* to the three new buttons.

4. Use ClassWizard to add *CEx14aView* view class message handlers.
Add message handlers for the following command and update command UI messages, and accept the default function names shown in the following table.

Object ID	Message	Member Function
ID_DRAW_CIRCLE	COMMAND	*OnDrawCircle*
ID_DRAW_CIRCLE	UPDATE_COMMAND_UI	*OnUpdateDrawCircle*
ID_DRAW_PATTERN	COMMAND	*OnDrawPattern*
ID_DRAW_PATTERN	UPDATE_COMMAND_UI	*OnUpdateDrawPattern*
ID_DRAW_SQUARE	COMMAND	*OnDrawSquare*
ID_DRAW_SQUARE	UPDATE_COMMAND_UI	*OnUpdateDrawSquare*

5. Add three data members to the *CEx14aView* class. Edit the file ex14aView.h, or use ClassView.

```
private:
    CRect m_rect;
    BOOL  m_bCircle;
    BOOL  m_bPattern;
```

6. Edit the ex14aView.cpp file. The *CEx14aView* constructor simply initializes the class data members. Add the following boldface code:

```
CEx14aView::CEx14aView() : m_rect(0, 0, 100, 100)
{
    m_bCircle = TRUE;
    m_bPattern = FALSE;
}
```

The *OnDraw* function draws an ellipse or a rectangle, depending on the value of the *m_bCircle* flag. The brush is plain white or a diagonal pattern, depending on the value of *m_bPattern*.

```
void CEx14aView::OnDraw(CDC* pDC)
{
    CBrush brush(HS_BDIAGONAL, 0L); // brush with diagonal pattern

    if (m_bPattern) {
        pDC->SelectObject(&brush);
    }
    else {
        pDC->SelectStockObject(WHITE_BRUSH);
    }
    if (m_bCircle) {
        pDC->Ellipse(m_rect);
    }
    else {
        pDC->Rectangle(m_rect);
    }
    pDC->SelectStockObject(WHITE_BRUSH); // Deselects brush
                                         //  if selected
}
```

The *OnDrawCircle* function handles the *ID_DRAW_CIRCLE* command message, and the *OnDrawSquare* function handles the *ID_DRAW-_SQUARE* command message. These two functions move the drawing rectangle down and to the right, and then they invalidate the rectangle, causing the *OnDraw* function to redraw it. The effect of this invalidation strategy is a diagonal cascading of alternating squares and circles. Also, the display is not buffered, so when the window is hidden or minimized, previously drawn items are not redisplayed.

```
void CEx14aView::OnDrawCircle()
{
    m_bCircle = TRUE;
    m_rect += CPoint(25, 25);
    InvalidateRect(m_rect);
}

void CEx14aView::OnDrawSquare()
{
    m_bCircle = FALSE;
    m_rect += CPoint(25, 25);
    InvalidateRect(m_rect);
}
```

The following two update command UI functions alternately enable and disable the Circle and Square buttons and corresponding menu items. Only one item can be enabled at a time.

```
void CEx14aView::OnUpdateDrawCircle(CCmdUI* pCmdUI)
{
    pCmdUI->Enable(!m_bCircle);
}

void CEx14aView::OnUpdateDrawSquare(CCmdUI* pCmdUI)
{
    pCmdUI->Enable(m_bCircle);
}
```

The *OnDrawPattern* function toggles the state of the *m_bPattern* flag.

```
void CEx14aView::OnDrawPattern()
{
    m_bPattern ^= 1;
}
```

The *OnUpdateDrawPattern* function updates the Pattern button and menu item according to the state of the *m_bPattern* flag. The toolbar button appears to move in and out, and the menu item check mark appears and disappears.

```
void CEx14aView::OnUpdateDrawPattern(CCmdUI* pCmdUI)
{
    pCmdUI->SetCheck(m_bPattern);
}
```

7. **Build and test the EX14A application.** Notice the behavior of the toolbar buttons. Try the corresponding menu items, and notice that they too are enabled, disabled, and checked as the application's state changes. Observe the ToolTip when you stop the mouse pointer on one of the new toolbar buttons.

The Status Bar

The status bar window neither accepts user input nor generates command messages. Its job is simply to display text in panes under program control. The status bar supports two types of text panes—message line panes and status indicator panes. To use the status bar for application-specific data, you must first disable the standard status bar that displays the menu prompt and keyboard status.

The Status Bar Definition

The static *indicators* array that AppWizard generates in the MainFrm.cpp file defines the panes for the application's status bar. The constant *ID_SEPARATOR* identifies a message line pane; the other constants are string resource IDs that identify indicator panes. Figure 14-3 shows the *indicators* array and its relationship to the standard framework status bar.

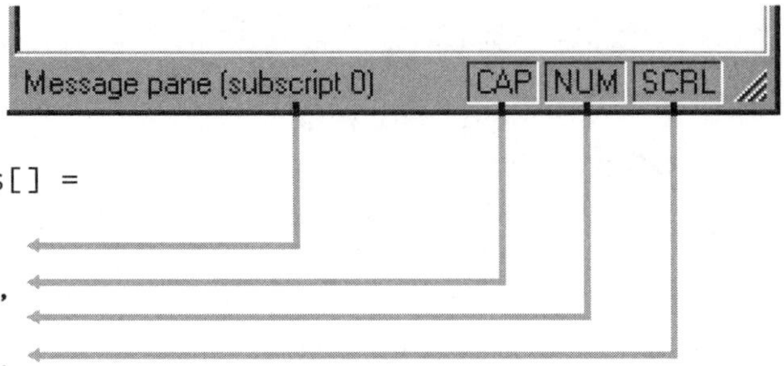


```
Static UINT indicators[] =
{
     ID_SEPARATOR,
     ID_INDICATOR_CAPS,
     ID_INDICATOR_NUM,
     ID_INDICATOR_SCRL,
};
```

Figure 14-3.
The status bar and the indicators *array.*

The *CStatusBar::SetIndicators* member function, called in the application's derived frame class, configures the status bar according to the contents of the *indicators* array.

The Message Line

A message line pane displays a string that the program supplies dynamically. To set the value of the message line, you must first get access to the status bar object and then you must call the *CStatusBar::SetPaneText* member function with a zero-based index parameter. Pane 0 is the leftmost pane, 1 is the next pane to the right, and so forth.

The following code fragment is part of a view class member function. Note that you must navigate up to the application object and then back down to the main frame window.

```
CMainFrame* pFrame = (CMainFrame*) AfxGetApp()->m_pMainWnd;
CStatusBar* pStatus = &pFrame->m_wndStatusBar;
pStatus->SetPaneText(0, "message line for first pane");
```

Normally, the length of a message line pane is exactly one-fourth the width of the display. If, however, the message line is the first (index 0) pane, it is a stretchy pane without a beveled border. Its minimum length is one-fourth the display width, and it expands if room is available in the status bar.

The Status Indicator

A status indicator pane is linked to a single resource-supplied string that is displayed or hidden by logic in an associated update command UI message handler function. An indicator is identified by a string resource ID, and that same ID is used to route update command UI messages. The Caps Lock indicator is handled in the frame class by a message map entry and a handler function equivalent to those shown below. The *Enable* function turns on the indicator if the Caps Lock mode is set.

```
ON_UPDATE_COMMAND_UI(ID_INDICATOR_CAPS, OnUpdateKeyCapsLock)

void CMainFrame::OnUpdateKeyCapsLock(CCmdUI* pCmdUI)
{
    pCmdUI->Enable(::GetKeyState(VK_CAPITAL) & 1);
}
```

The status bar update command UI functions are called during idle processing so that the status bar is updated whenever your application receives messages.

The length of a status indicator pane is the exact length of the corresponding resource string.

Taking Control of the Status Bar

In the standard application framework implementation, the status bar has the child window ID *AFX_IDW_STATUS_BAR*. The application framework looks for this ID when it wants to display a menu prompt. The update command UI handlers for the keyboard state indicators, embedded in the frame window base class, are linked to the following string IDs: *ID_INDICATOR_CAPS, ID_INDICATOR_NUM,* and *ID_INDICATOR_SCRL*. To take control of the status bar, you must use a different child window ID and you must use different indicator ID constants.

> NOTE: The only reason to change the status bar's child window ID is to prevent the framework from writing menu prompts in pane 0. If you like the menu prompts, you can disregard the following instructions.

The status bar window ID is assigned in the *CStatusBar::Create* function called by the derived frame class *OnCreate* member function. That function is contained in the MainFrm.cpp file that AppWizard generates. The window ID is the third *Create* parameter, and it defaults to *AFX_IDW_STATUS_BAR*.

To assign your own ID, you must replace this call

```
m_wndStatusBar.Create(this);
```

with this call

```
m_wndStatusBar.Create(this, WS_CHILD | WS_VISIBLE | CBRS_BOTTOM,
                      ID_MY_STATUS_BAR);
```

You must also, of course, define the *ID_MY_STATUS_BAR* constant in the resource.h file (using Visual C++'s resource symbol editor).

We forgot one thing. The standard application framework's View menu allows the user to turn the status bar on and off. That logic is pegged to the *AFX_IDW_STATUS_BAR* window ID, so you'll have to change the menu logic, too. In your derived frame class, you must write message map entries and handlers for the *ID_VIEW_STATUS_BAR* command and update command UI messages. *ID_VIEW_STATUS_BAR* is the ID of the Status Bar menu item. The derived class handlers override the standard handlers in the *CFrameWnd* base class. See the EX14B example for code details.

The EX14B Status Bar Example

The EX14B example replaces the standard application framework status bar with a new status bar that has the following text panes.

Pane Index	String ID	Type	Description
0	*ID_SEPARATOR* (0)	Message line	*x* cursor coordinate
1	*ID_SEPARATOR* (0)	Message line	*y* cursor coordinate
2	*ID_INDICATOR_LEFT*	Status indicator	Left mouse button status
3	*ID_INDICATOR_RIGHT*	Status indicator	Right mouse button status

The resulting status bar is shown in Figure 14-4. Notice that the leftmost pane stretches past its normal $\frac{1}{20}$-screen length as the displayed frame window expands.

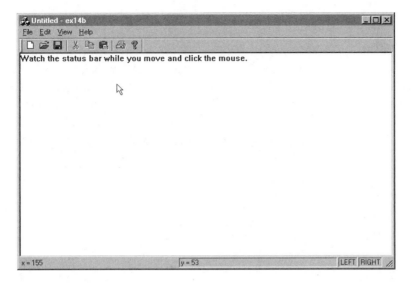

Figure 14-4.
The status bar of the EX14B example.

Follow these steps to produce the EX14B example:

1. Run AppWizard to generate \vcpp32\ex14b\ex14b. Accept all default settings but two: select Single Document and deselect Printing and Print Preview. The options and the default class names are shown here.

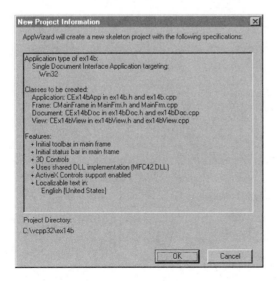

2. Use the string editor to edit the application's string table resource.
The application has a single string table resource with artificial "segment" divisions left over from the 16-bit era. Double-click on the String Table icon in the String Table folder on the ResourceView page to bring up the string editor. Then double-click on the empty entry at the end of the list. A dialog allows you to assign the ID and the string value as shown below.

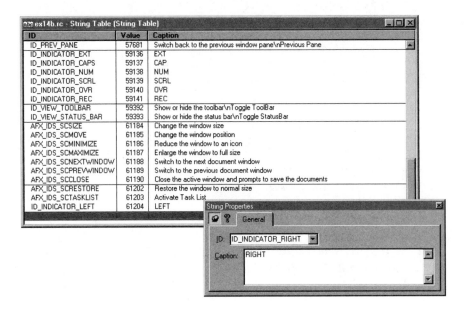

Add two strings as follows.

String ID	String Caption
ID_INDICATOR_LEFT	LEFT
ID_INDICATOR_RIGHT	RIGHT

3. Use Visual C++ to edit the application's symbols. Choose Resource Symbols from the View menu. Add the new status bar identifier, *ID_MY_STATUS_BAR*, and accept the default value.

4. Use ClassWizard to add View menu command handlers in the class *CMainFrame*. Add the following command message handlers.

Object ID	Message	Member Function
ID_VIEW_STATUS_BAR	COMMAND	*OnViewStatusBar*
ID_VIEW_STATUS_BAR	UPDATE_COMMAND_UI	*OnUpdateViewStatusBar*

5. **Add the following function prototypes to MainFrm.h.** You must add these *CMainFrame* message handler prototypes manually because ClassWizard doesn't recognize the associated command message IDs.

```
afx_msg void OnUpdateLeft(CCmdUI* pCmdUI);
afx_msg void OnUpdateRight(CCmdUI* pCmdUI);
```

Add the message handler statements <u>inside</u> the *AFX_MSG* brackets so that ClassWizard will let you access and edit the code later. While MainFrm.h is open, make *m_wndStatusBar* public rather than protected.

6. **Edit the MainFrm.cpp file.** Replace the original *indicators* array with the following boldface code:

```
static UINT indicators[] =
{
    ID_SEPARATOR,   // first message line pane
    ID_SEPARATOR,   // second message line pane
    ID_INDICATOR_LEFT,
    ID_INDICATOR_RIGHT,
};
```

Next edit the *OnCreate* member function. Replace the following statement

```
if (!m_wndStatusBar.Create(this) ||
    !m_wndStatusBar.SetIndicators(indicators,
      sizeof(indicators)/sizeof(UINT)))
{
    TRACE0("Failed to create status bar\n");
    return -1;      // fail to create
}
```

with the statement shown here:

```
if (!m_wndStatusBar.Create(this,
      WS_CHILD | WS_VISIBLE | CBRS_BOTTOM, ID_MY_STATUS_BAR) ||
    !m_wndStatusBar.SetIndicators(indicators,
      sizeof(indicators)/sizeof(UINT)))
{
    TRACE0("Failed to create status bar\n");
    return -1;      // fail to create
}
```

The modified call to *Create* uses our own status bar ID, *ID_MY-_STATUS_BAR*, instead of *AFX_IDW_STATUS_BAR* (the application framework's status bar object).

Now add the following message map entries for the class *CMain-Frame*. ClassWizard can't add these for you because it doesn't recognize the string table IDs as object IDs.

```
ON_UPDATE_COMMAND_UI(ID_INDICATOR_LEFT, OnUpdateLeft)
ON_UPDATE_COMMAND_UI(ID_INDICATOR_RIGHT, OnUpdateRight)
```

Next add the following *CMainFrame* member functions that update the two status indicators:

```
void CMainFrame::OnUpdateLeft(CCmdUI* pCmdUI)
{
    pCmdUI->Enable(::GetKeyState(VK_LBUTTON) < 0);
}

void CMainFrame::OnUpdateRight(CCmdUI* pCmdUI)
{
    pCmdUI->Enable(::GetKeyState(VK_RBUTTON) < 0);
}
```

Note that the left and right mouse buttons have virtual key codes like keys on the keyboard have. You don't have to depend on mouse-click messages to determine the button status.

Finally, edit the following View menu functions that ClassWizard originally generated in MainFrm.cpp:

```
void CMainFrame::OnViewStatusBar()
{
    m_wndStatusBar.ShowWindow((m_wndStatusBar.GetStyle() &
                              WS_VISIBLE) == 0);
    RecalcLayout();
}
void CMainFrame::OnUpdateViewStatusBar(CCmdUI* pCmdUI)
{
    pCmdUI-
>SetCheck((m_wndStatusBar.GetStyle() & WS_VISIBLE) != 0);
}
```

These functions ensure that the View menu Status Bar command is properly linked to the new status bar.

7. Edit the *OnDraw* function in Ex14bView.cpp. The *OnDraw* function displays a message in the view window. Add the following boldface code:

```
void CEx14bView::OnDraw(CDC* pDC)
{
    pDC->TextOut(0, 0,
        "Watch the status bar while you move and click the mouse.");
}
```

8. **Add a WM_MOUSEMOVE handler in the *CEx14bView* class.** Use ClassWizard to map the message to *OnMouseMove*, and then edit the function as shown below. This function gets a pointer to the status bar object and then calls the *SetPaneText* function to update the first and second message line panes.

```
void CEx14bView::OnMouseMove(UINT nFlags, CPoint point)
{
    CString str;
    CMainFrame* pFrame = (CMainFrame*) AfxGetApp()->m_pMainWnd;
    CStatusBar* pStatus = &pFrame->m_wndStatusBar;
    if (pStatus) {
        str.Format("x = %d", point.x);
        pStatus->SetPaneText(0, str);
        str.Format("y = %d", point.y);
        pStatus->SetPaneText(1, str);
    }
}
```

Finally, add the statement

```
#include "MainFrm.h"
```

near the top of the file ex14bView.cpp.

9. **Build and test the EX14B application.** Move the mouse, and observe that the left two status bar panes accurately reflect the mouse cursor's position. Try the left and right mouse buttons. Can you toggle the status bar on and off from the View menu?

> NOTE: If you want the first (index 0) status bar pane to have a beveled border like the other panes and you want the status bar to grow and resize to fit their contents, include the following two lines in the *CMainFrame::OnCreate* function, following the call to the status bar *Create* function.
>
> ```
> m_wndStatusBar.SetPaneInfo(0, 0, 0, 50);
> m_wndStatusBar.SetPaneInfo(1, 0, SBPS_STRETCH, 50);
> ```
>
> These statements change the width of the first two panes (from their default of one-fourth the display size) and make the second pane (index 1) the stretchy one.

The Internet Explorer Rebar Toolbar

As we learned in Chapter 9, Visual C++ 6.0 contains many features that are part of Internet Explorer 4.0: the Internet Explorer Common Controls. One of the new controls in the IE Common Controls is a new kind of toolbar called a <u>rebar</u>.

You're probably already familiar with the rebar if you have ever used Internet Explorer 4.0. The rebar differs from the default MFC toolbar in that it provides grippers and allows the user to "slide" its horizontal and vertical positions, whereas the MFC toolbar's position is changed via drag-and-drop docking. Rebars also allow the developer to provide many more internal control types—such as drop-down menus–than are available in *CToolBar*.

Anatomy of a Rebar

Figure 14-5 shows the various terminology used on a rebar. Each internal toolbar in a rebar is called a <u>band</u>. The raised edge where the user slides the band is called a <u>gripper</u>. Each band can also have a label.

Gripper bar   Child window (combo box)   Band 1   Label text   Band 2

Figure 14-5.
Rebar terminology.

MFC provides two classes that facilitate working with rebars:

- **CReBar**—A high-level abstraction class that provides members for adding *CToolBar* and *CDialogBar* classes to rebars as bands. *CReBar* also handles communication (such as message notifications) between the underlying control and the MFC framework.

- **CReBarCtrl**—A low-level wrapper class that wraps the IE ReBar control. This class provides numerous members for creating and manipulating rebars but does not provide the niceties that are found in *CReBar*.

Most MFC applications use *CReBar* and call the member function *GetReBarCtrl*, which returns a *CReBarCtrl* pointer to gain access to the lower-level control if needed.

The EX14C Rebar Example

Let's get familiar with the rebar by jumping into an example. This example creates an SDI application that has a rebar with two bands: a familiar toolbar band and a dialog bar band. Figure 14-6 shows the example in action.

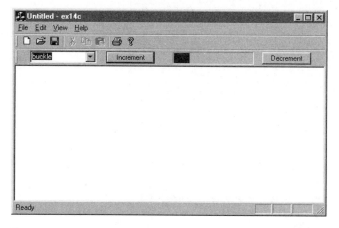

Figure 14-6.
EX14C rebar example.

Here are the steps required to create the EX14C example:

1. **Run AppWizard to generate \vcpp32\ex14c\ex14c.** Select Single Document. In Step 4, be sure you select Internet Explorer ReBars under the How Do You Want Your Toolbars To Look option. Figure 14-7 on the next page shows the correct settings. Accept all other default settings.

2. **Compile and run the application.** When you run the application, you will see that AppWizard has automatically created a rebar with two bands. One band contains a conventional toolbar and the other contains the text "TODO: layout dialog bar" in the band. Figure 14-8 on the next page shows the initial rebar control.

   At this point, you can open the MainFrm.h header file and see the code below, which declares the *CReBar* data member *m_ndReBar*.

   ```
   protected: // control bar embedded members
       CStatusBar   m_wndStatusBar;
       CToolBar     m_wndToolBar;
       CReBar       m_wndReBar;
       CDialogBar   m_wndDlgBar;
   ```

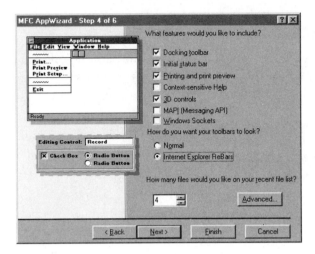

Figure 14-7.
AppWizard Step 4 settings for the rebar control.

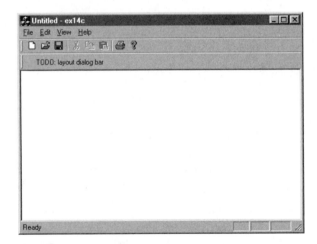

Figure 14-8.
Initial windows for EX14C example with the default rebar controls.

In the MainFrm.cpp file, you can see the code that adds the toolbar and the dialog bar to the *CReBar* object:

```
if (!m_wndReBar.Create(this) ||
    !m_wndReBar.AddBar(&m_wndToolBar) ||
    !m_wndReBar.AddBar(&m_wndDlgBar))
{
    TRACE0("Failed to create rebar\n");
    return -1;     // fail to create
}
```

3. Lay out the Dialog Bar. Open the Visual C++ resource editor. Under the Dialog heading you'll find a dialog resource for the dialog bar with the ID *IDR_MAINFRAME*. Open *IDR_MAINFRAME* and you'll see the dialog bar with the text "TODO: layout dialog bar". Let's follow App-Wizard's friendly suggestion and put some real controls into the dialog bar. First delete the static control with the "TODO" text in it. Next place a combo box in the dialog bar and enter some default data items: *one, two, buckle, my, shoe!* Now place a button on the dialog bar and change the button's text to *Increment*. Next place a progress bar with the default properties on the dialog bar. Finally place another button with the text *Decrement* on the dialog bar. When you are done laying out the dialog bar, it should look similar to Figure 14-9.

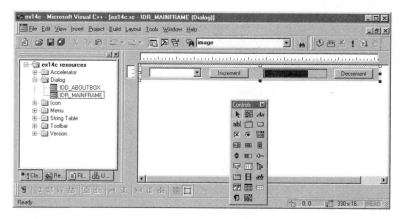

Figure 14-9.
Edited IDR_MAINFRAME *dialog bar.*

4. Associate the dialog bar with the *CMainFrame* class. Before we can program the handlers for the Increment and Decrement buttons, we need to attach the dialog bar to a class using ClassWizard. While in the resource editor, bring up ClassWizard by double-clicking on the Increment button. You will now see this dialog.

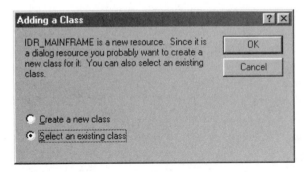

Choose Select An Existing Class. We choose this option because we want
our dialog resource to be a band in the toolbar, not a separate dialog
class. Click OK and you will see these choices.

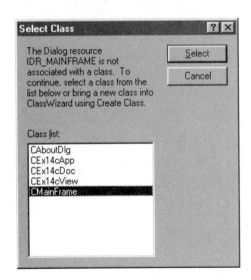

Choose *CMainFrame* from the list and click Select.
ClassWizard will prompt you with one last dialog.

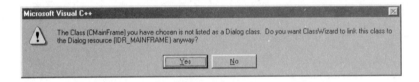

Click Yes and then exit ClassWizard. You have successfully associated the
IDR_MAINFRAME dialog bar with the *CMainFrame* class.

5. **Program the dialog bar.** To program the dialog bar, bring up the IDR-_MAINFRAME dialog resource in the resource editor again and double-click on the Increment button. ClassWizard will automatically create an *ONBUTTON1* handler for you—accept the default name for this function. Enter the following boldface code in the *OnButton1* function:

```
void CMainFrame::OnButton1()
{
    CProgressCtrl * pProgress =
        (CProgressCtrl*)m_wndDlgBar.GetDlgItem(IDC_PROGRESS1);
    pProgress->StepIt();
}
```

The *OnButton1* handler first gets a pointer to the progress control and then calls *StepIt* to increment the progress control.

Now we need to add similar code to the decrement handler. Double-click on the Decrement button in the resource editor and ClassWizard will automatically create an *OnButton2* handler. Add the following boldface code to the *OnButton2* member function:

```
void CMainFrame::OnButton2()
{
    CProgressCtrl * pProgress =
            (CProgressCtrl*)m_wndDlgBar.GetDlgItem(IDC_PROGRESS1);

    int nCurrentPos = pProgress->GetPos();

    pProgress->SetPos(nCurrentPos-10);

}
```

6. **Compile and test.** Now you can compile and run EX14C to see your custom rebar in action. The Increment button increases the progress bar and the Decrement button decreases it.

In this chapter, we learned how to use MFC's toolbar, status bar, and the new rebar control. In the next chapter, we'll look at how to extend MFC to implement a frame window that remembers its position.

CHAPTER FIFTEEN

A Reusable Frame Window Base Class

C++ promises programmers the ability to produce "software Lego blocks" that can be taken "off the shelf" and fitted easily into an application. The Microsoft Foundation Class (MFC) Library version 6.0 classes are a good example of this kind of reusable software. This chapter shows you how to build your own reusable base class by taking advantage of what the MFC library already provides.

In the process of building the reusable class, you'll learn a few more things about Microsoft Windows and the MFC library. In particular, you'll see how the application framework allows access to the Windows Registry, you'll learn more about the mechanics of the *CFrameWnd* class, and you'll get more exposure to static class variables and the *CString* class.

Why Reusable Base Classes Are Difficult to Write

In a normal application, you write code for software components that solve particular problems. It's usually a simple matter of meeting the project specification. With reusable base classes, however, you must anticipate future programming needs, both your own and those of others. You have to write a class that is general and complete yet efficient and easy to use.

This chapter's example showed me the difficulty in building reusable software. I started out intending to write a frame class that would "remember" its window size and position. When I got into the job, I discovered that existing Windows-based programs remember whether they have been minimized to the taskbar or whether they have been maximized to full screen. Then there was the oddball case of a window that was both minimized and maximized. After that, I had to worry about the toolbar and the status bar, plus the class had to work in a dynamic link library (DLL). In short, it was surprisingly difficult to write a frame class that would do everything that a programmer might expect.

In a production programming environment, reusable base classes might fall out of the normal software development cycle. A class written for one project might be extracted and further generalized for another project. There's always the temptation, though, to cut and paste existing classes without asking, "What can I factor out into a base class?" If you're in the software business for the long term, it's beneficial to start building your library of truly reusable components.

The *CPersistentFrame* Class

In this chapter, you'll be using a class named *CPersistentFrame* that is derived from the *CFrameWnd* class. This *CPersistentFrame* class supports a persistent SDI (Single Document Interface) frame window that remembers the following characteristics.

- Window size
- Window position
- Maximized status
- Minimized status
- Toolbar and status bar enablement and position

When you terminate an application that's built with the *CPersistentFrame* class, the above information is saved on disk in the Windows Registry. When the application starts again, it reads the Registry and restores the frame to its state at the previous exit.

You can use the persistent frame class in any SDI application, including the examples in this book. All you have to do is substitute *CPersistentFrame* for *CFrameWnd* in your application's derived frame class files.

The *CFrameWnd* Class and the *ActivateFrame* Member Function

Why choose *CFrameWnd* as the base class for a persistent window? Why not have a persistent view class instead? In an MFC SDI application, the main frame window is always the parent of the view window. This frame window is created first, and then the control bars and the view are created as child windows. The application framework ensures that the child windows shrink and expand appropriately as the user changes the size of the frame window. It wouldn't make sense to change the view size after the frame was created.

The key to controlling the frame's size is the *CFrameWnd::ActivateFrame* member function. The application framework calls this virtual function (declared in *CFrameWnd*) during the SDI main frame window creation process (and in response to the File New and File Open commands). The framework's job is to call the *CWnd::ShowWindow* function with the parameter *nCmdShow*. *ShowWindow* makes the frame window visible along with its menu, view window, and control bars. The *nCmdShow* parameter determines whether the window is maximized or minimized or both.

If you override *ActivateFrame* in your derived frame class, you can change the value of *nCmdShow* before passing it to the *CFrameWnd::ActivateFrame* function. You can also call the *CWnd::SetWindowPlacement* function, which sets the size and position of the frame window, and you can set the visible status of the control bars. Because all changes are made before the frame window becomes visible, no annoying flash occurs on the screen.

You must be careful not to reset the frame window's position and size after every File New or File Open command. A first-time flag data member ensures that your *CPersistentFrame::ActivateFrame* function operates only when the application starts.

The *PreCreateWindow* Member Function

PreCreateWindow, declared at the *CWnd* level, is another virtual function that you can override to change the characteristics of your window before it is displayed. The framework calls this function before it calls *ActivateFrame*. AppWizard <u>always</u> generates an overridden *PreCreateWindow* function in your project's view and frame window classes.

This function has a *CREATESTRUCT* structure as a parameter, and two of the data members in this structure are *style* and *dwExStyle*. You can change these data members before passing the structure on to the base class *PreCreateWindow* function. The *style* flag determines whether the window has a border, scroll bars, a minimize box, and so on. The *dwExStyle* flag controls other characteristics, such as always-on-top status. See the online documentation for Window Styles and Extended Window Styles for details.

The *CREATESTRUCT* member *lpszClass* is also useful to change the window's background brush, cursor, or icon. It makes no sense to change the brush or cursor in a frame window because the view window covers the client area. If you want an ugly red view window with a special cursor, for example, you can override your view's *PreCreateWindow* function like this:

```
BOOL CMyView::PreCreateWindow(CREATESTRUCT& cs)
{
    if (!CView::PreCreateWindow(cs)) {
        return FALSE;
    }
    cs.lpszClass =
        AfxRegisterWndClass(CS_DBLCLKS | CS_HREDRAW | CS_VREDRAW,
                            AfxGetApp()->LoadCursor(IDC_MYCURSOR),
                            ::CreateSolidBrush(RGB(255, 0, 0)));
    if (cs.lpszClass != NULL) {
        return TRUE;
    }
    else {
        return FALSE;
    }
}
```

If you override the *PreCreateWindow* function in your persistent frame class, windows of all derived classes will share the characteristics you programmed in the base class. Of course, derived classes can have their own overridden *PreCreateWindow* functions, but then you'll have to be careful about the interaction between the base class and derived class functions.

The Windows Registry

If you've used Win16-based applications, you've probably seen INI files. You can still use INI files in Win32-based applications, but Microsoft recommends that you use the Windows Registry instead. The Registry is a set of system files, managed by Windows, in which Windows and individual applications can store and access permanent information. The Registry is organized as a kind of hierarchical database in which string and integer data is accessed by a multipart key.

For example, a text processing application, TEXTPROC, might need to store the most recent font and point size in the Registry. Suppose that the program name forms the root of the key (a simplification) and that the application maintains two hierarchy levels below the name. The structure looks something like this.

TEXTPROC
    Text formatting
        Font = Times Roman
        Points = 10

Unicode

European languages use characters that can be encoded in 8 bits—even characters with diacritics. Most Asian languages require 16 bits for their characters. Many programs use the double-byte character set (DBCS) standard: some characters use 8 bits and others 16 bits, depending on the value of the first 8 bits. DBCS is being replaced by Unicode, in which all characters are 16-bit "wide" characters. No specific Unicode character ranges are set aside for individual languages: if a character is used in both the Chinese and the Japanese languages, for example, that character appears only once in the Unicode character set.

When you look at MFC source code and the code that AppWizard generates, you'll see the types *TCHAR*, *LPTSTR*, and *LPCTSTR* and you'll see literal strings like *_T("string")*. You are looking at Unicode macros. If you build your project without defining *_UNICODE*, the compiler generates code for ordinary 8-bit ANSI characters (*CHAR*) and pointers to 8-bit character arrays (*LPSTR*, *LPCSTR*). If you do define *_UNICODE*, the compiler generates code for 16-bit Unicode characters (*WCHAR*), pointers (*LPWSTR*, *LPCWSTR*), and literals (*L"wide string"*).

The *_UNICODE* preprocessor symbol also determines which Windows functions your program calls. Many Win32 functions have two versions. When your program calls *CreateWindowEx*, for example, the compiler generates code to call either *CreateWindowExA* (with ANSI parameters) or *CreateWindowExW* (with Unicode parameters). In Microsoft Windows NT, which uses Unicode internally, *CreateWindowExW* passes all parameters straight through, but *CreateWindowExA* converts ANSI string and character parameters to Unicode. In Microsoft Windows 95, which uses ANSI internally, *CreateWindowExW* is a stub that returns an error and *CreateWindowExA* passes the parameters straight through.

If you want to create a Unicode application, you should target it for Windows NT and use the macros throughout. You can write Unicode applications for Windows 95, but you'll do extra work to call the "A" versions of the Win32 functions. As shown in Chapters 24-30, COM calls (except DAO) always use wide characters. Although Win32 functions are available for converting between ANSI and Unicode, if you're using the *CString* class you can rely on a wide character constructor and the *AllocSysString* member function to do the conversions.

For simplicity, this book's example programs use ANSI only. The code AppWizard generated uses Unicode macros, but the code I wrote uses 8-bit literal strings and the *char*, *char**, and *const char** types.

The MFC library provides four *CWinApp* member functions, holdovers from the days of INI files, for accessing the Registry. Starting with Visual C++ version 5.0, AppWizard generates a call to *CWinApp::SetRegistryKey* in your application's *InitInstance* function as shown here.

```
SetRegistryKey(_T("Local AppWizard-Generated Applications"));
```

If you remove this call, your application will not use the Registry but will create and use an INI file in the Windows directory. The *SetRegistryKey* function's string parameter establishes the top of the hierarchy, and the following Registry functions define the bottom two levels: called heading name and entry name.

- *GetProfileInt*
- *WriteProfileInt*
- *GetProfileString*
- *WriteProfileString*

These functions treat Registry data as either *CString* objects or unsigned integers. If you need floating-point values as entries, you must use the string functions and do the conversion yourself. All the functions take a heading name and an entry name as parameters. In the example shown above, the heading name is Text Formatting and the entry names are Font and Points.

To use the Registry access functions, you need a pointer to the application object. The global function *AfxGetApp* does the job. With the previous sample Registry, the Font and Points entries were set with the following code:

```
AfxGetApp()->WriteProfileString("Text formatting", "Font",
                                "Times Roman");
AfxGetApp()->WriteProfileInt("Text formatting", "Points", 10);
```

You'll see a real Registry example in EX15A, and you'll learn to use the Windows Regedit program to examine and edit the Registry.

NOTE: The application framework stores a list of most recently used files in the Registry under the heading Recent File List.

Using the *CString* Class

The MFC *CString* class is a significant de facto extension to the C++ language. As the *Microsoft Foundation Classes and Templates* section of the online help points out, the *CString* class has many useful operators and member functions, but perhaps its most important feature is its dynamic memory allocation. You never have to worry about the size of a *CString* object. The statements on the next page represent typical uses of *CString* objects.

```
CString strFirstName("Elvis");
CString strLastName("Presley");
CString strTruth = strFirstName + " " + strLastName; // concatenation
strTruth += " is alive";
ASSERT(strTruth == "Elvis Presley is alive");
ASSERT(strTruth.Left(5) == strFirstName);
ASSERT(strTruth[2] == 'v'); // subscript operator
```

In a perfect world, C++ programs would use all *CString* objects and never use ordinary zero-terminated character arrays. Unfortunately, many runtime library functions still use character arrays, so programs must always mix and match their string representations. Fortunately, the *CString* class provides a *const char*()* operator that converts a *CString* object to a character pointer. Many of the MFC library functions have *const char** parameters. Take the global *AfxMessageBox* function, for example. Here is one of the function's prototypes:

```
int AFXAPI AfxMessageBox(LPCTSTR lpszText, UINT nType = MB_OK,
                         UINT nIDHelp = 0);
```

(Note: *LPCTSTR* is not a pointer to a *CString* object but rather is a <u>Unicode-enabled</u> replacement for *const char**.)

You can call *AfxMessageBox* this way:

```
char szMessageText[] = "Unknown error";
AfxMessageBox(szMessageText);
```

or you can call it this way:

```
CString strMessageText("Unknown error");
AfxMessageBox(strMessageText);
```

Now suppose you want to generate a formatted string. *CString::Format* does the job, as shown here:

```
int nError = 23;
CString strMessageText;
strMessageText.Format("Error number %d", nError);
AfxMessageBox(strMessageText);
```

NOTE: Suppose you want direct write access to the characters in a *CString* object. If you write code like this:

```
CString strTest("test");
strncpy(strTest, "T", 1);
```

you'll get a compile error because the first parameter of *strncpy* is declared *char**, not *const char**. The *CString::GetBuffer* function "locks down" the buffer with a specified size and returns a *char**. You must call the *ReleaseBuffer* member function later to make the string dynamic again. The correct way to capitalize the *T* is shown on the following page.

```
CString strTest("test");
strncpy(strTest.GetBuffer(5), "T", 1);
strTest.ReleaseBuffer();
ASSERT(strTest == "Test");
```

The *const char** operator takes care of converting a *CString* object to a constant character pointer; but what about conversion in the other direction? It so happens that the *CString* class has a constructor that converts a constant character pointer to a *CString* object, and it has a set of overloaded operators for these pointers. That's why statements such as the following work.

```
strTruth += " is alive";
```

The special constructor works with functions that take a *CString* reference parameter, such as *CDC::TextOut*. In the following statement, a temporary *CString* object is created on the calling program's stack and then the object's address is passed to *TextOut*:

```
pDC->TextOut(0, 0, "Hello, world!");
```

It's more efficient to use the other overloaded version of *CDC::TextOut* if you're willing to count the characters:

```
pDC->TextOut(0, 0, "Hello, world!", 13);
```

If you're writing a function that takes a string parameter, you've got some design choices. Here are some programming rules.

- If the function doesn't change the contents of the string and you're willing to use C runtime functions such as *strcpy*, use a *const char** parameter.

- If the function doesn't change the contents of the string but you want to use *CString* member functions inside the function, use a *const CString&* parameter.

- If the function changes the contents of the string, use a *CString&* parameter.

The Position of a Maximized Window

As a Windows user, you know that you can maximize a window from the system menu or by clicking a button at the top right corner of the window. You can return a maximized window to its original size in a similar fashion. It's obvious that a maximized window remembers its original size and position.

The *CWnd* function *GetWindowRect* retrieves the screen coordinates of a window. If a window is maximized, *GetWindowRect* returns the coordinates of the screen rather than the window's unmaximized coordinates. If a persistent frame class is to work for maximized windows, it has to know the window's unmaximized coordinates. *CWnd::GetWindowPlacement* retrieves the unmaximized coordinates together with some flags that indicate whether the window is currently minimized or maximized or both.

The companion *SetWindowPlacement* function lets you set the maximized and minimized status and the size and position of the window. To calculate the position of the top left corner of a maximized window, you need to account for the window's border size, obtainable from the Win32 *GetSystemMetrics* function. See Figure 15-1 for the *CPersistentFrame::ActivateFrame* code for an example of how *SetWindowPlacement* is used.

Control Bar Status and the Registry

The MFC library provides two *CFrameWnd* member functions, *SaveBarState* and *LoadBarState*, for saving and loading control bar status to and from the Registry. These functions process the size and position of the status bar and docked toolbars. They don't process the position of floating toolbars, however.

Static Data Members

The *CPersistentFrame* class stores its Registry key names in *static const char* array data members. What were the other storage choices? String resource entries won't work because the strings need to be defined with the class itself. (String resources make sense if *CPersistentFrame* is made into a DLL, however.) Global variables are generally not recommended because they defeat encapsulation. Static *CString* objects don't make sense because the characters must be copied to the heap when the program starts.

An obvious choice would have been regular data members. But static data members are better because, as constants, they are segregated into the program's read-only data section and can be mapped to multiple instances of the same program. If the *CPersistentFrame* class is part of a DLL, all processes that are using the DLL can map the character arrays. Static data members are really global variables, but they are scoped to their class so there's no chance of name collisions.

The Default Window Rectangle

You're used to defining rectangles with device or logical coordinates. A *CRect* object constructed with the statement

```
CRect rect(CW_USEDEFAULT, CW_USEDEFAULT, 0, 0);
```

has a special meaning. When Windows creates a new window with this special rectangle, it positions the window in a cascade pattern with the top left corner below and to the right of the window most recently created. The right and bottom edges of the window are always within the display's boundaries.

The *CFrameWnd* class's static *rectDefault* data member is constructed using *CW_USEDEFAULT* this way, so it contains the special rectangle. The *CPersistentFrame* class declares its own *rectDefault* default window rectangle with a fixed size and position as a static data member, thus hiding the base class member.

The EX15A Example

The EX15A program illustrates the use of a persistent frame window class, *CPersistentFrame*. Figure 15-1 shows the contents of the files Persist.h and Persist.cpp, which are included in the EX15A project on the companion CD-ROM. In this example, you'll insert the new frame class into an AppWizard-generated SDI application. EX15A is a "do-nothing" application, but you can insert the persistent frame class into any of your own SDI "do-something" applications.

PERSIST.H

```
// Persist.h

#ifndef _INSIDE_VISUAL_CPP_PERSISTENT_FRAME
#define _INSIDE_VISUAL_CPP_PERSISTENT_FRAME

class CPersistentFrame : public CFrameWnd
{ // remembers where it was on the desktop
    DECLARE_DYNAMIC(CPersistentFrame)
private:
    static const CRect s_rectDefault;
    static const char s_profileHeading[];
    static const char s_profileRect[];
    static const char s_profileIcon[];
```

Figure 15-1. *(continued)*
The CPersistentFrame *class listing.*

Figure 15-1. *continued*

```
    static const char s_profileMax[];
    static const char s_profileTool[];
    static const char s_profileStatus[];
    BOOL m_bFirstTime;
protected: // Create from serialization only
    CPersistentFrame();
    ~CPersistentFrame();
//{{AFX_VIRTUAL(CPersistentFrame)
    public:
    virtual void ActivateFrame(int nCmdShow = -1);
    protected:
    //}}AFX_VIRTUAL

    //{{AFX_MSG(CPersistentFrame)
    afx_msg void OnDestroy();
    //}}AFX_MSG

    DECLARE_MESSAGE_MAP()
};

#endif // _INSIDE_VISUAL_CPP_PERSISTENT_FRAME
```

PERSIST.CPP

```
// Persist.cpp Persistent frame class for SDI apps

#include "stdafx.h"
#include "persist.h"

#ifdef _DEBUG
#undef THIS_FILE
static char BASED_CODE THIS_FILE[] = __FILE__;
#endif
/////////////////////////////////////////////////////////////////
// CPersistentFrame

const CRect CPersistentFrame::s_rectDefault(10,  10,
                                            500, 400);  // static
const char CPersistentFrame::s_profileHeading[] = "Window size";
const char CPersistentFrame::s_profileRect[] = "Rect";
const char CPersistentFrame::s_profileIcon[] = "icon";
const char CPersistentFrame::s_profileMax[] = "max";
```

(continued)

Figure 15-1. *continued*

```
const char CPersistentFrame::s_profileTool[] = "tool";
const char CPersistentFrame::s_profileStatus[] = "status";
IMPLEMENT_DYNAMIC(CPersistentFrame, CFrameWnd)

BEGIN_MESSAGE_MAP(CPersistentFrame, CFrameWnd)
    //{{AFX_MSG_MAP(CPersistentFrame)
    ON_WM_DESTROY()
    //}}AFX_MSG_MAP
END_MESSAGE_MAP()

//////////////////////////////////////////////////////////////
CPersistentFrame::CPersistentFrame(){
    m_bFirstTime = TRUE;
}


//////////////////////////////////////////////////////////////
CPersistentFrame::~CPersistentFrame()
{
}

//////////////////////////////////////////////////////////////
void CPersistentFrame::OnDestroy()
{
    CString strText;
    BOOL bIconic, bMaximized;

    WINDOWPLACEMENT wndpl;
    wndpl.length = sizeof(WINDOWPLACEMENT);
    // gets current window position and
    //   iconized/maximized status
    BOOL bRet = GetWindowPlacement(&wndpl);
    if (wndpl.showCmd == SW_SHOWNORMAL) {
        bIconic = FALSE;
        bMaximized = FALSE;
    }
    else if (wndpl.showCmd == SW_SHOWMAXIMIZED) {
        bIconic = FALSE;
        bMaximized = TRUE;
    }
    else if (wndpl.showCmd == SW_SHOWMINIMIZED) {
        bIconic = TRUE;
        if (wndpl.flags) {
```

```
                    bMaximized = TRUE;
            }
            else {
                bMaximized = FALSE;
            }
        }
        strText.Format("%04d %04d %04d %04d",
                        wndpl.rcNormalPosition.left,
                        wndpl.rcNormalPosition.top,
                        wndpl.rcNormalPosition.right,
                        wndpl.rcNormalPosition.bottom);
        AfxGetApp()->WriteProfileString(s_profileHeading,
                                            s_profileRect, strText);
        AfxGetApp()->WriteProfileInt(s_profileHeading,
                                        s_profileIcon, bIconic);
        AfxGetApp()->WriteProfileInt(s_profileHeading,
                                        s_profileMax, bMaximized);
        SaveBarState(AfxGetApp()->m_pszProfileName);
        CFrameWnd::OnDestroy();
}

/////////////////////////////////////////////////////////////////
void CPersistentFrame::ActivateFrame(int nCmdShow)
{
        CString strText;
        BOOL bIconic, bMaximized;
        UINT flags;
        WINDOWPLACEMENT wndpl;
        CRect rect;

        if (m_bFirstTime) {
            m_bFirstTime = FALSE;
            strText = AfxGetApp()->GetProfileString(s_profileHeading,
                                                    s_profileRect);
            if (!strText.IsEmpty()) {
                rect.left = atoi((const char*) strText);
                rect.top = atoi((const char*) strText + 5);
                rect.right = atoi((const char*) strText + 10);
                rect.bottom = atoi((const char*) strText + 15);
            }
            else {
                rect = s_rectDefault;
            }
```

(continued)

Figure 15-1. *continued*

```
    bIconic = AfxGetApp()->GetProfileInt(s_profileHeading,
                                        s_profileIcon, 0);
    bMaximized = AfxGetApp()->GetProfileInt(s_profileHeading,
                                          s_profileMax, 0);
    if (bIconic) {
        nCmdShow = SW_SHOWMINNOACTIVE;
        if (bMaximized) {
            flags = WPF_RESTORETOMAXIMIZED;
        }
        else {
            flags = WPF_SETMINPOSITION;
        }
    }
    else {
        if (bMaximized) {
            nCmdShow = SW_SHOWMAXIMIZED;
            flags = WPF_RESTORETOMAXIMIZED;
        }
        else {
            nCmdShow = SW_NORMAL;
            flags = WPF_SETMINPOSITION;
        }
    }
    wndpl.length = sizeof(WINDOWPLACEMENT);
    wndpl.showCmd = nCmdShow;
    wndpl.flags = flags;
    wndpl.ptMinPosition = CPoint(0, 0);
    wndpl.ptMaxPosition =
        CPoint(-::GetSystemMetrics(SM_CXBORDER),
               -::GetSystemMetrics(SM_CYBORDER));
    wndpl.rcNormalPosition = rect;
    LoadBarState(AfxGetApp()->m_pszProfileName);
    // sets window's position and minimized/maximized status
    BOOL bRet = SetWindowPlacement(&wndpl);
}
CFrameWnd::ActivateFrame(nCmdShow);
}
```

Here are the steps for building the EX15A example program.

1. **Run AppWizard to generate \vcpp32\ex15a\ex15a.** Accept all default settings but two: select Single Document and deselect Printing and Print Preview. The options and the default class names are shown in the following illustration.

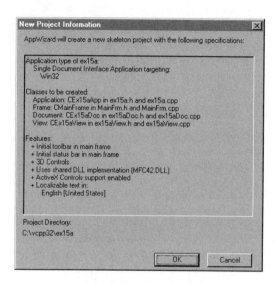

2. **Modify MainFrm.h.** You must change the base class of *CMainFrame*. To do this, simply change the line

```
class CMainFrame : public CFrameWnd
```

to

```
class CMainFrame : public CPersistentFrame
```

Also, add the line

```
#include "persist.h"
```

3. **Modify MainFrm.cpp.** Globally replace all occurrences of *CFrameWnd* with *CPersistentFrame*.

4. **Modify ex15a.cpp.** Replace the line

```
SetRegistryKey(_T("Local AppWizard-Generated Applications"));
```

with the line

```
SetRegistryKey("Programming Visual C++");
```

5. Add the Persist.cpp file to the project. You can type in the Persist.h and Persist.cpp files from Figure 15-1, or you can copy the files from the companion CD-ROM. Having the files in the \vcpp32\ex15a directory is not sufficient. You must add the names of the files to the project's project (DSP) file. Choose Add To Project from Visual C++'s Project menu, and choose Files from the submenu. Select Persist.h and Persist.cpp from the list.

6. Rebuild the ClassWizard file to include the new *CPersistentFrame* class. Use Windows Explorer to delete the ClassWizard file ex15a.clw. Back in Visual C++, choose ClassWizard from the View menu. Follow Visual C++'s instructions if it asks you to close any files. Click Yes when asked if you would like to rebuild the CLW file. The Select Source Files dialog box will appear. Make sure all of the header and source files are listed in the Files In Project box, as shown in the following illustration.

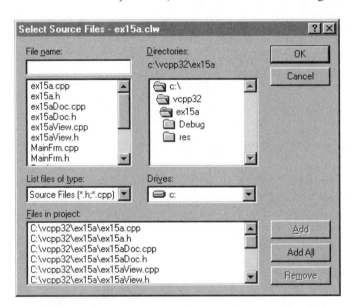

Then click OK to regenerate the CLW file. Notice that *CPersistentFrame* is now integrated into ClassWizard. You'll now be able to map messages and override virtual functions in the *CPersistentFrame* class.

7. Build and test the EX15A application. Size and move the application's frame window, and then close the application. When you restart the application, does its window open at the same location at which it was closed? Experiment with maximizing and minimizing, and then change the status and position of the control bars. Does the persistent frame remember its settings?

8. **Save the *CPersistentFrame* class as a Gallery component for future use.**   In the ClassView window, right-click on *CPersistentFrame* and select Add To Gallery. Bring up the Components And Controls Gallery by choosing Add To Project from the Project menu and then choosing Components And Controls. Notice that Visual C++ created the file Persistent Frame.ogx in a folder named \ex15a. Change this folder's name to Persistent Frame. Now you can add the *CPersistentFrame* class to any project by simply adding Persistent Frame.ogx. We will add *CPersistentFrame* to EX22A this way.

9. **Examine the Windows Registry.**   Run the Windows regedit.exe program. Navigate to the HKEY_CURRENT_USER\Software\Programming Visual C++\ex15a key. You should see data values similar to those shown in the following illustration.

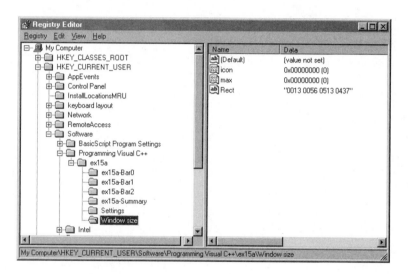

Notice the relationship between the Registry key and the *SetRegistryKey* function parameter, "*Programming Visual C++.*" If you supply an empty string as the *SetRegistryKey* parameter, the program name (ex15a, in this case) is positioned directly below the Software key.

Persistent Frames in MDI Applications

You won't get to Multiple Document Interface (MDI) applications until Chapter 18, but if you're using this book as a reference, you might want to apply the persistent frame technique to MDI applications.

The *CPersistentFrame* class, as presented in this chapter, won't work in an MDI application because the MDI main frame window's *ShowWindow* function is called, not by a virtual *ActivateFrame* function, but directly by the application class's *InitInstance* member function. If you need to control the characteristics of an MDI main frame window, add the necessary code to *InitInstance*.

The *ActivateFrame* function is called, however, for *CMDIChildWnd* objects. This means your MDI application could remember the sizes and positions of its child windows. You could store the information in the Registry, but you would have to accommodate multiple windows. You would have to modify the *CPersistentFrame* class for this purpose.

CHAPTER SIXTEEN

Separating the Document from Its View

Now you're finally going to see the interaction between documents and views. Chapter 13 gave you a preview of this interaction when it showed the routing of command messages to both view objects and document objects. In this chapter, you'll see how the document maintains the application's data and how the view presents the data to the user. You'll also learn how the document and view objects talk to each other while the application executes.

The two examples in this chapter both use the *CFormView* class as the base class for their views. The first example is as simple as possible, with the document holding only one simple object of class *CStudent*, which represents a single student record. The view shows the student's name and grade and allows editing. With the *CStudent* class, you'll get some practice writing classes to represent real-world entities. You'll also get to use the Microsoft Foundation Class (MFC) Library version 6.0 diagnostic dump functions.

The second example goes further by introducing pointer collection classes—the *CObList* and *CTypedPtrList* classes in particular. Now the document holds a collection of student records, and the view allows the sequencing, insertion, and deletion of individual records.

Document–View Interaction Functions

You already know that the document object holds the data and that the view object displays the data and allows editing. An SDI application has a document class derived from *CDocument*, and it has one or more view classes, each ultimately derived from *CView*. A complex handshaking process takes place among the document, the view, and the rest of the application framework. To understand this process, you need to know about five important member functions in the document and view classes. Two are nonvirtual base class functions that you call in your derived classes; three are virtual functions that you often override in your derived classes. Let's look at these functions one at a time.

The *CView::GetDocument* Function

A view object has one and only one associated document object. The *GetDocument* function allows an application to navigate from a view to its document. Suppose a view object gets a message that the user has entered new data into an edit control. The view must tell the document object to update its internal data accordingly. The *GetDocument* function provides the document pointer that can be used to access document class member functions or public data members.

> NOTE: The *CDocument::GetNextView* function navigates from the document to the view, but because a document can have more than one view, it's necessary to call this member function once for each view, inside a loop. You'll seldom call *GetNextView* because the application framework provides a better method of iterating through a document's views.

When AppWizard generates a derived *CView* class, it creates a special <u>type-safe</u> version of the *GetDocument* function that returns not a *CDocument* pointer but a pointer to an object of your derived class. This function is an inline function, and it looks something like this:

```
CMyDoc* GetDocument()
{
    return (CMyDoc*) m_pDocument;
}
```

When the compiler sees a call to *GetDocument* in your view class code, it uses the derived class version instead of the *CDocument* version, so you do not have to cast the returned pointer to your derived document class. Because the *CView::GetDocument* function is <u>not</u> a virtual function, a statement such as

```
pView->GetDocument(); // pView is declared CView*
```

calls the base class *GetDocument* function and thus returns a pointer to a *CDocument* object.

The *CDocument::UpdateAllViews* Function

If the document data changes for any reason, all views must be notified so that they can update their representations of that data. If *UpdateAllViews* is called from a member function of a derived document class, its first parameter, *pSender*, is *NULL*. If *UpdateAllViews* is called from a member function of a derived view class, set the *pSender* parameter to the current view, like this:

```
GetDocument()->UpdateAllViews(this);
```

The non-null parameter prevents the application framework from notifying the current view. The assumption here is that the current view has already updated itself.

The function has optional <u>hint</u> parameters that can be used to give view-specific and application-dependent information about which parts of the view to update. This is an advanced use of the function.

How exactly is a view notified when *UpdateAllViews* gets called? Take a look at the next function, *OnUpdate*.

The *CView::OnUpdate* Function

This virtual function is called by the application framework in response to your application's call to the *CDocument::UpdateAllViews* function. You can, of course, call it directly within your derived *CView* class. Typically, your derived view class's *OnUpdate* function accesses the document, gets the document's data, and then updates the view's data members or controls to reflect the changes. Alternatively, *OnUpdate* can invalidate a portion of the view, causing the view's *OnDraw* function to use document data to draw in the window. The *OnUpdate* function might look something like this:

```
void CMyView::OnUpdate(CView* pSender, LPARAM lHint, CObject* pHint)
{
    CMyDocument* pMyDoc = GetDocument();
    CString lastName = pMyDoc->GetLastName();
    m_pNameStatic->SetWindowText(lastName); // m_pNameStatic is
                                            //  a CMyView data member
}
```

The hint information is passed through directly from the call to *Update-AllViews*. The default *OnUpdate* implementation invalidates the entire window rectangle. In your overridden version, you can choose to define a smaller invalid rectangle as specified by the hint information.

If the *CDocument* function *UpdateAllViews* is called with the *pSender* parameter pointing to a specific view object, *OnUpdate* is called for all the document's views <u>except</u> the specified view.

The *CView::OnInitialUpdate* Function

This virtual *CView* function is called when the application starts, when the user chooses New from the File menu, and when the user chooses Open from the File menu. The *CView* base class version of *OnInitialUpdate* does nothing but call *OnUpdate*. If you override *OnInitialUpdate* in your derived view class, be sure that the view class calls the base class's *OnInitialUpdate* function or the derived class's *OnUpdate* function.

You can use your derived class's *OnInitialUpdate* function to initialize your view object. When the application starts, the application framework calls *OnInitialUpdate* immediately after *OnCreate* (if you've mapped *OnCreate* in your view class). *OnCreate* is called once, but *OnInitialUpdate* can be called many times.

The *CDocument::OnNewDocument* Function

The framework calls this virtual function after a document object is first constructed and when the user chooses New from the File menu in an SDI application. This is a good place to set the initial values of your document's data members. AppWizard generates an overridden *OnNewDocument* function in your derived document class. Be sure to retain the call to the base class function.

The Simplest Document–View Application

Suppose you don't need multiple views of your document but you plan to take advantage of the application framework's file support. In this case, you can forget about the *UpdateAllViews* and *OnUpdate* functions. Simply follow these steps when you develop the application:

1. In your derived document class header file (generated by AppWizard), declare your document's data members. These data members are the primary data storage for your application. You can make these data members public, or you can declare the derived view class a <u>friend</u> of the document class.

2. In your derived view class, override the *OnInitialUpdate* virtual member function. The application framework calls this function after the document data has been initialized or read from disk. (Chapter 17 discusses disk file I/O.) *OnInitialUpdate* should update the view to reflect the current document data.

3. In your derived view class, let your window message handlers, command message handlers and your *OnDraw* function read and update the document data members directly, using *GetDocument* to access the document object.

The sequence of events for this simplified document–view environment is as follows.

Application starts	*CMyDocument* object constructed
	CMyView object constructed
	View window created
	CMyView::OnCreate called (if mapped)
	CMyDocument::OnNewDocument called
	CMyView::OnInitialUpdate called
	View object initialized
	View window invalidated
	CMyView::OnDraw called
User edits data	*CMyView* functions update *CMyDocument* data members
User exits application	*CMyView* object destroyed
	CMyDocument object destroyed

The *CFormView* Class

The *CFormView* class is a useful view class that has many of the characteristics of a modeless dialog window. Like a class derived from *CDialog*, a derived *CFormView* class is associated with a dialog resource that defines the frame characteristics and enumerates the controls. The *CFormView* class supports the same dialog data exchange and validation (DDX and DDV) functions that you saw in the *CDialog* examples in Chapter 6.

> **WARNING:** If AppWizard generates a Form View dialog, the properties are set correctly, but if you use the dialog editor to make a dialog for a form view, you <u>must</u> specify the following items in the Dialog Properties dialog:
>
> Style = Child
> Border = None
> Visible = unchecked

A *CFormView* object receives notification messages directly from its controls, and it receives command messages from the application framework. This application framework command-processing ability clearly separates *CFormView* from *CDialog*, and it makes controlling the view from the frame's main menu or toolbar easy.

The *CFormView* class is derived from *CView* (actually, from *CScrollView*) and not from *CDialog*. You can't, therefore, assume that *CDialog* member functions are supported. *CFormView* does <u>not</u> have virtual *OnInitDialog*,

OnOK, and *OnCancel* functions. *CFormView* member functions do not call *UpdateData* and the DDX functions. You have to call *UpdateData* yourself at the appropriate times, usually in response to control notification messages or command messages.

Even though the *CFormView* class is not derived from the *CDialog* class, it is built around the Microsoft Windows dialog. For this reason, you can use many of the *CDialog* class member functions such as *GotoDlgCtrl* and *NextDlgCtrl*. All you have to do is cast your *CFormView* pointer to a *CDialog* pointer. The following statement, extracted from a member function of a class derived from *CFormView*, sets the focus to a specified control. *GetDlgItem* is a *CWnd* function and is thus inherited by the derived *CFormView* class.

```
((CDialog*) this)->GotoDlgCtrl(GetDlgItem(IDC_NAME));
```

AppWizard gives you the option of using *CFormView* as the base class for your view. When you select *CFormView*, AppWizard generates an empty dialog with the correct style properties set. The next step is to use ClassWizard to add control notification message handlers, command message handlers, and update command UI handlers. (The example steps beginning on page 380 show you what to do.) You can also define data members and validation criteria.

The *CObject* Class

If you study the MFC library hierarchy, you'll notice that the *CObject* class is at the top. Most other classes are derived from the *CObject* <u>root</u> class. When a class is derived from *CObject*, it inherits a number of important characteristics. The many benefits of *CObject* derivation will become clear as you read the chapters that follow.

In this chapter, you'll see how *CObject* derivation allows objects to participate in the diagnostic dumping scheme and allows objects to be elements in the collection classes.

Diagnostic Dumping

The MFC library gives you some useful tools for diagnostic dumping. You enable these tools when you select the Debug target. When you select the Win32 Release target, diagnostic dumping is disabled and the diagnostic code is not linked to your program. All diagnostic output goes to the Debug view in the debugger's Output window.

TIP: To clear diagnostic output from the debugger's Output window, position the cursor in the Output window and click the right mouse button. Then choose Clear from the pop-up menu.

The *TRACE* Macro

You've seen the *TRACE* macro used throughout the preceding examples in this book. *TRACE* statements are active whenever the constant *_DEBUG* is defined (when you select the Debug target and when the *afxTraceEnabled* variable is set to *TRUE*). *TRACE* statements work like C language *printf* statements, but they're completely disabled in the release version of the program. Here's a typical *TRACE* statement:

```
int nCount = 9;
CString strDesc("total");
TRACE("Count = %d, Description = %s\n", nCount, strDesc);
```

NOTE: The *TRACE* macro takes a variable number of parameters and is thus easy to use. If you look at the MFC source code, you won't see *TRACE* macros but rather *TRACE0*, *TRACE1*, *TRACE2*, and *TRACE3* macros. These macros take 0, 1, 2, and 3 parameters, respectively, and are leftovers from the 16-bit environment, where it was necessary to conserve space in the data segment.

The *afxDump* Object

An alternative to the *TRACE* statement is more compatible with the C++ language. The MFC *afxDump* object accepts program variables with a syntax similar to that of *cout*, the C++ output stream object. You don't need complex formatting strings; instead, overloaded operators control the output format. The *afxDump* output goes to the same destination as the *TRACE* output, but the *afxDump* object is defined only in the Debug version of the MFC library. Here is a typical stream-oriented diagnostic statement that produces the same output as the *TRACE* statement above:

```
int nCount = 9;
CString strDesc("total");
#ifdef _DEBUG
    afxDump << "Count = " << nCount
            << ", Description = " << strDesc << "\n";
#endif // _DEBUG
```

Although both *afxDump* and *cout* use the same insertion operator (<<), they don't share any code. The *cout* object is part of the Microsoft Visual C++ iostream library, and *afxDump* is part of the MFC library. Don't assume that any of the *cout* formatting capability is available through *afxDump*.

Classes that aren't derived from *CObject*, such as *CString*, *CTime*, and *CRect*, contain their own overloaded insertion operators for *CDumpContext* objects. The *CDumpContext* class, of which *afxDump* is an instance, includes the overloaded insertion operators for the native C++ data types (*int*, *double*, *char**, and so on). The *CDumpContext* class also contains insertion operators for *CObject* references and pointers, and that's where things get interesting.

The Dump Context and the *CObject* Class

If the *CDumpContext* insertion operator accepts *CObject* pointers and references, it must also accept pointers and references to derived classes. Consider a trivial class, *CAction*, that is derived from *CObject*, as shown here:

```
class CAction : public CObject
{
public:
    int m_nTime;
};
```

What happens when the following statement executes?

```
#ifdef _DEBUG
    afxDump << action; // action is an object of class CAction
#endif // _DEBUG
```

The virtual *CObject::Dump* function gets called. If you haven't overridden *Dump* for *CAction*, you don't get much except for the address of the object. If you have overridden *Dump*, however, you can get the internal state of your object. Here's a *CAction::Dump* function:

```
#ifdef _DEBUG
void CAction::Dump(CDumpContext& dc) const
{
    CObject::Dump(dc); // Always call base class function
    dc << "time = " << m_nTime << "\n";
}
#endif // _DEBUG
```

The base class (*CObject*) *Dump* function prints a line such as this:

```
a CObject at $4115D4
```

If you have called the *DECLARE_DYNAMIC* macro in your *CAction* class definition and the *IMPLEMENT_DYNAMIC* macro in your *CAction* declaration, you will see the name of the class in your dump

```
a CAction at $4115D4
```

even if your dump statement looks like this:

```
#ifdef _DEBUG
    afxDump << (CObject&) action;
#endif // _DEBUG
```

The two macros work together to include the MFC library runtime class code in your derived *CObject* class. With this code in place, your program can determine an object's class name at runtime (for the dump, for example) and it can obtain class hierarchy information.

> **N O T E :** The (*DECLARE_SERIAL, IMPLEMENT_SERIAL*) and (*DECLARE_DYNCREATE, IMPLEMENT_DYNCREATE*) macro pairs provide the same runtime class features as those provided by the (*DECLARE_DYNAMIC, IMPLEMENT_DYNAMIC*) macro pair.

Automatic Dump of Undeleted Objects

With the Debug target selected, the application framework dumps all objects that are undeleted when your program exits. This dump is a useful diagnostic aid, but if you want it to be really useful, you must be sure to delete <u>all</u> your objects, even the ones that would normally disappear after the exit. This object cleanup is good programming discipline.

> **N O T E :** The code that adds debug information to allocated memory blocks is now in the Debug version of the CRT (C runtime) library rather than in the MFC library. If you choose to dynamically link MFC, the MSVCRTD DLL is loaded along with the necessary MFC DLLs. When you add the line
>
> ```
> #define new DEBUG_NEW
> ```
>
> at the top of a CPP file, the CRT library lists the filename and line number at which the allocations were made. AppWizard puts this line at the top of all the CPP files it generates.

Window Subclassing for Enhanced Data-Entry Control

What if you want an edit control (in a dialog or a form view) that accepts only numeric characters? That's easy. You just set the Number style in the control's property sheet. If, however, you want to exclude numeric characters or change the case of alphabetic characters, you must do some programming.

The MFC library provides a convenient way to change the behavior of any standard control, including the edit control. Actually, there are several ways. You can derive your own classes from *CEdit*, *CListBox*, and so forth (with their own message handler functions) and then create control objects at runtime. Or you can register a special window class, as a Win32 programmer would do, and integrate it into the project's resource file with a text editor. Neither of these methods, however, allows you to use the dialog editor to position controls in the dialog resource.

The easy way to modify a control's behavior is to use the MFC library's window subclassing feature. You use the dialog editor to position a normal control in a dialog resource, and then you write a new C++ class that contains message handlers for the events that you want to handle yourself. Here are the steps for subclassing an edit control:

1. With the dialog editor, position an edit control in your dialog resource. Assume that it has the child window ID *IDC_EDIT1*.

2. Write a new class—for example, *CNonNumericEdit*—derived from *CEdit*. Map the WM_CHAR message and write a handler like this:

```
void CNonNumericEdit::OnChar(UINT nChar, UINT nRepCnt, UINT nFlags)
{
    if (!isdigit(nChar)) {
        CEdit::OnChar(nChar, nRepCnt, nFlags);
    }
}
```

3. In your derived dialog or form view class header, declare a data member of class *CNonNumericEdit* in this way:

```
private:
    CNonNumericEdit m_nonNumericEdit;
```

4. If you're working with a dialog class, add the following line to your *OnInitDialog* override function:

```
m_nonNumericEdit.SubclassDlgItem(IDC_EDIT1, this);
```

5. If you're working with a form view class, add the following code to your *OnInitialUpdate* override function:

```
if (m_nonNumericEdit.m_hWnd == NULL) {
    m_nonNumericEdit.SubclassDlgItem(IDC_EDIT1, this);
}
```

The *CWnd::SubclassDlgItem* member function ensures that all messages are routed through the application framework's message dispatch system before being sent to the control's built-in window procedure. This technique is called dynamic <u>subclassing</u> and is explained in more detail in Technical Note #14 in the online documentation.

The code in the preceding steps only accepts or rejects a character. If you want to change the value of a character, your handler must call *CWnd::DefWindowProc*, which bypasses some MFC logic that stores parameter values in thread object data members. Here's a sample handler that converts lowercase characters to uppercase:

```
void CUpperEdit::OnChar(UINT nChar, UINT nRepCnt, UINT nFlags)
{
    if (islower(nChar)) {
        nChar = toupper(nChar);
    }
    DefWindowProc(WM_CHAR, (WPARAM) nChar,
                  (LPARAM) (nRepCnt | (nFlags << 16)));
}
```

You can also use window subclassing to handle reflected messages, which were mentioned in Chapter 6. If an MFC window class doesn't map a message from one of its child controls, the framework reflects the message back to the control. Technical Note #62 in the online documentation explains the details.

If you need an edit control with a yellow background, for example, you can derive a class *CYellowEdit* from *CEdit* and use ClassWizard to map the =WM_CTLCOLOR message in *CYellowEdit*. (ClassWizard lists the message name with an equal sign in front to indicate that it is reflected.) The handler code, shown below, is substantially the same as the nonreflected WM_CTLCOLOR handler shown on page 128. (Member variable *m_hYellowBrush* is defined in the control class's constructor.)

```
HBRUSH CYellowEdit::CtlColor(CDC* pDC, UINT nCtlColor)
{
    pDC->SetBkColor(RGB(255, 255, 0)); // yellow
    return m_hYellowBrush;
}
```

The EX16A Example

The first of this chapter's two examples shows a very simple document–view interaction. The *CEx16aDoc* document class, derived from *CDocument*, allows for a single embedded *CStudent* object. The *CStudent* class represents a student record composed of a *CString* name and an integer grade. The *CEx16aView* view class is derived from *CFormView*. It is a visual representation of a student record that has edit controls for the name and grade. The default Enter pushbutton updates the document with data from the edit controls. Figure 16-1 shows the EX16A program window.

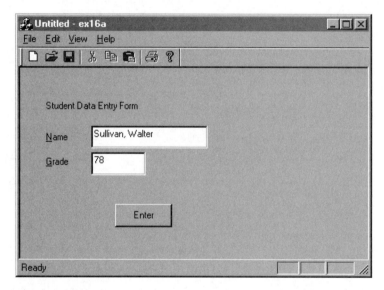

Figure 16-1.
The EX16A program in action.

Figure 16-2 shows the code for the *CStudent* class. Most of the class's features serve EX16A, but a few items carry forward to EX16B and the programs discussed in Chapter 17. For now, take note of the two data members, the default constructor, the operators, and the *Dump* function declaration. The *DECLARE_DYNAMIC* and *IMPLEMENT_DYNAMIC* macros ensure that the class name is available for the diagnostic dump.

STUDENT.H

```cpp
// student.h

#ifndef _INSIDE_VISUAL_CPP_STUDENT
#define _INSIDE_VISUAL_CPP_STUDENT
class CStudent : public CObject
{
    DECLARE_DYNAMIC(CStudent)
public:
    CString m_strName;
    int m_nGrade;

    CStudent()
    {
        m_nGrade = 0;
    }

    CStudent(const char* szName, int nGrade) : m_strName(szName)
    {
        m_nGrade = nGrade;
    }

    CStudent(const CStudent& s) : m_strName(s.m_strName)
    {
        // copy constructor
        m_nGrade = s.m_nGrade;
    }

    const CStudent& operator =(const CStudent& s)
    {
        m_strName = s.m_strName;
        m_nGrade = s.m_nGrade;
        return *this;
    }

    BOOL operator ==(const CStudent& s) const
    {
        if ((m_strName == s.m_strName) && (m_nGrade == s.m_nGrade)) {
            return TRUE;
        }
```

Figure 16-2.
The CStudent *class listing.*

(continued)

Figure 16-2. *continued*

```
        else {
            return FALSE;
        }
    }

    BOOL operator !=(const CStudent& s) const
    {
        // Let's make use of the operator we just defined!
        return !(*this == s);
    }
#ifdef _DEBUG
    void Dump(CDumpContext& dc) const;
#endif // _DEBUG
};

#endif // _INSIDE_VISUAL_CPP_STUDENT
```

STUDENT.CPP

```
#include "stdafx.h"
#include "student.h"

IMPLEMENT_DYNAMIC(CStudent, CObject)

#ifdef _DEBUG
void CStudent::Dump(CDumpContext& dc) const
{
    CObject::Dump(dc);
    dc << "m_strName = " << m_strName << "\nm_nGrade = " << m_nGrade;
}
#endif // _DEBUG
```

Follow these steps to build the EX16A example:

1. Run AppWizard to generate \vcpp32\ex16a\ex16a. In the Step 6 page, change the view's base class to *CFormView*, as shown here.

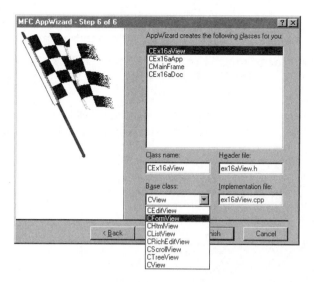

The options and the default class names are shown here.

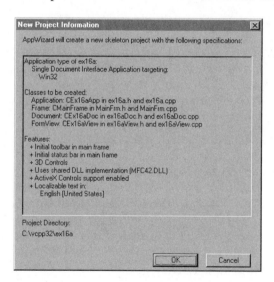

2. Use the menu editor to replace the Edit menu options. Delete the current Edit menu items and replace them with a Clear All option, as shown here.

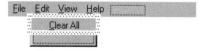

Use the default constant *ID_EDIT_CLEAR_ALL*, which is assigned by the application framework. A menu prompt automatically appears.

3. **Use the dialog editor to modify the *IDD_EX16A_FORM* dialog.** Open the AppWizard-generated dialog *IDD_EX16A_FORM*, and add controls as shown below.

Be sure that the Styles properties are set <u>exactly</u> as shown in the Dialog Properties dialog (Style = Child; Border = None) and that Visible is unchecked.

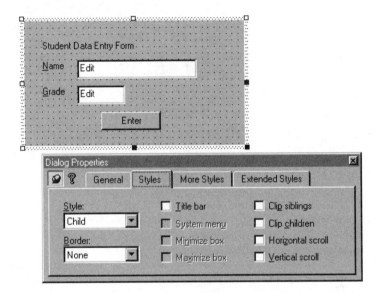

Use the following IDs for the controls.

Control	ID
Name edit control	*IDC_NAME*
Grade edit control	*IDC_GRADE*
Enter pushbutton	*IDC_ENTER*

4. **Use ClassWizard to add message handlers for *CEx16aView*.** Select the *CEx16aView* class, and then add handlers for the following messages. Accept the default function names.

Object ID	Message	Member Function
IDC_ENTER	BN_CLICKED	*OnEnter*
ID_EDIT_CLEAR_ALL	COMMAND	*OnEditClearAll*
ID_EDIT_CLEAR_ALL	UPDATE_COMMAND_UI	*OnUpdateEditClearAll*

5. Use ClassWizard to add variables for *CEx16aView*. Click on the Member Variables tab in the MFC ClassWizard dialog, and then add the following variables.

Control ID	Member Variable	Category	Variable Type
IDC_GRADE	*m_nGrade*	Value	*int*
IDC_NAME	*m_strName*	Value	*CString*

For *m_nGrade*, enter a minimum value of 0 and a maximum value of 100. Notice that ClassWizard generates the code necessary to validate data entered by the user.

6. Add a prototype for the helper function *UpdateControlsFromDoc*. In the ClassView window, right-click on *CEx16aView* and choose Add Member Function. Fill out the dialog box to add the following function:

```
private:
    void UpdateControlsFromDoc();
```

7. Edit the file Ex16aView.cpp. AppWizard generated the skeleton *OnInitialUpdate* function, and ClassView generated the skeleton *UpdateControlsFromDoc* function. *UpdateControlsFromDoc* is a private <u>helper</u> member function that transfers data from the document to the *CEx16aView* data members and then to the dialog edit controls. Edit the code as shown here:

```
void CEx16aView::OnInitialUpdate()
{   // called on startup
    UpdateControlsFromDoc();
}
void CEx16aView::UpdateControlsFromDoc()
{   // called from OnInitialUpdate and OnEditClearAll
    CEx16aDoc* pDoc = GetDocument();
```

(continued)

```
    m_nGrade = pDoc->m_student.m_nGrade;
    m_strName = pDoc->m_student.m_strName;
    UpdateData(FALSE); // calls DDX
}
```

The *OnEnter* function replaces the *OnOK* function you'd expect to see in a dialog class. The function transfers data from the edit controls to the view's data members and then to the document. Add the boldface code shown here:

```
void CEx16aView::OnEnter()
{
    CEx16aDoc* pDoc = GetDocument();
    UpdateData(TRUE);
    pDoc->m_student.m_nGrade = m_nGrade;
    pDoc->m_student.m_strName = m_strName;
}
```

In a complex multiview application, the Edit Clear All command would be routed directly to the document. In this simple example, it's routed to the view. The update command UI handler disables the menu item if the document's student object is already blank. Add the following boldface code:

```
void CEx16aView::OnEditClearAll()
{
    GetDocument()->m_student = CStudent(); // "blank" student object
    UpdateControlsFromDoc();
}
void CEx16aView::OnUpdateEditClearAll(CCmdUI* pCmdUI)
{
    pCmdUI->Enable(GetDocument()->m_student != CStudent()); // blank?
}
```

8. **Edit the EX16A project to add the files for *CStudent*.**   Choose Add To Project from the Project menu, choose Files from the submenu, and select the Student.h header and the Student.cpp source code files. Visual C++ will add the files' names to the project's DSP file so that they will be compiled when you build the project.

9. **Add a *CStudent* data member to the *CEx16aDoc* class.**   Use Class-View to add the following data member, and the *#include* will be added automatically.

```
public:
    CStudent m_student;
```

The *CStudent* constructor is called when the document object is constructed, and the *CStudent* destructor is called when the document object is destroyed.

10. Edit the Ex16aDoc.cpp file. Use the *CEx16aDoc* constructor to initialize the student object, as shown here:

```
CEx16aDoc::CEx16aDoc() : m_student("default value", 0)
{
    TRACE("Document object constructed\n");
}
```

We can't tell whether the EX16A program works properly unless we dump the document when the program exits. We'll use the destructor to call the document's *Dump* function, which calls the *CStudent::Dump* function shown here:

```
CEx16aDoc::~CEx16aDoc()
{
#ifdef _DEBUG
    Dump(afxDump);
#endif // _DEBUG
}

void CEx16aDoc::Dump(CDumpContext& dc) const
{
    CDocument::Dump(dc);
    dc << "\n" << m_student << "\n";
}
```

11. Build and test the EX16A application. Type a name and a grade, and then click Enter. Now exit the application. Does the Debug window show messages similar to those shown here?

```
a CEx16aDoc at $411580
m_strTitle = Untitled
m_strPathName =
m_bModified = 0
m_pDocTemplate = $4113A0

a CStudent at $4115D4
m_strName = Sullivan, Walter
m_nGrade = 78
```

> **NOTE:** To see these messages, you must compile the application with the Win32 Debug target selected and you must run the program from the debugger.

A More Advanced Document–View Interaction

If you're laying the groundwork for a multiview application, the document–view interaction must be more complex than the simple interaction in example EX16A. The fundamental problem is this: the user edits in view #1, so view #2 (and any other views) must be updated to reflect the changes. Now you need the *UpdateAllViews* and *OnUpdate* functions because the document is going to act as the clearinghouse for all view updates. The development steps are shown here:

1. In your derived document class header file (generated by AppWizard), declare your document's data members. If you want to, you can make these data members private and you can define member functions to access them or declare the view class as a friend of the document class.

2. In your derived view class, use ClassWizard to override the *OnUpdate* virtual member function. The application framework calls this function whenever the document data has changed for any reason. *OnUpdate* should update the view with the current document data.

3. Evaluate all your command messages. Determine whether each one is document-specific or view-specific. (A good example of a document-specific command is the Clear All command on the Edit menu.) Now map the commands to the appropriate classes.

4. In your derived view class, allow the appropriate command message handlers to update the document data. Be sure these message handlers call the *CDocument::UpdateAllViews* function before they exit. Use the type-safe version of the *CView::GetDocument* member function to access the view's document.

5. In your derived document class, allow the appropriate command message handlers to update the document data. Be sure that these message handlers call the *CDocument::UpdateAllViews* function before they exit.

The sequence of events for the complex document–view interaction is shown here.

Application starts	*CMyDocument* object constructed
	CMyView object constructed
	Other view objects constructed
	View windows created
	CMyView::OnCreate called (if mapped)
	CDocument::OnNewDocument called

CView::OnInitialUpdate called

Calls CMyView::OnUpdate

Initializes the view

User executes view command

CMyView functions update CMyDocument data members

Call CDocument::UpdateAllViews

Other views' OnUpdate functions called

User executes document command

CMyDocument functions update data members

Call CDocument::UpdateAllViews

CMyView::OnUpdate called

Other views' OnUpdate functions called

User exits application

View objects destroyed

CMyDocument object destroyed

The *CDocument::DeleteContents* Function

At some point, you'll need a function to delete the contents of your document. You could write your own private member function, but it happens that the application framework declares a virtual *DeleteContents* function for the *CDocument* class. The application framework calls your overridden *DeleteContents* function when the document is closed and as you'll see in the next chapter, at other times as well.

The *CObList* Collection Class

Once you get to know the collection classes, you'll wonder how you ever got along without them. The *CObList* class is a useful representative of the collection class family. If you're familiar with this class, it's easy to learn the other list classes, the array classes, and the map classes.

You might think that collections are something new, but the C programming language has always supported one kind of collection—the array. C arrays must be fixed in size, and they do not support insertion of elements. Many C programmers have written function libraries for other collections, including linked lists, dynamic arrays, and indexed dictionaries. For implementing collections, the C++ class is an obvious and better alternative than a C function library. A list object, for example, neatly encapsulates the list's internal data structures.

The *CObList* class supports ordered lists of pointers to objects of classes derived from *CObject*. Another MFC collection class, *CPtrList*, stores *void* pointers instead of *CObject* pointers. Why not use *CPtrList* instead? The *CObList* class offers advantages for diagnostic dumping, which you'll see in this chapter, and for serialization, which you'll see in the next chapter. One important feature of *CObList* is that it can contain <u>mixed</u> pointers. In other words, a *CObList* collection can hold pointers to both *CStudent* objects and *CTeacher* objects, assuming that both *CStudent* and *CTeacher* were derived from *CObject*.

Using the *CObList* Class for a First-In, First-Out List

One of the easiest ways to use a *CObList* object is to add new elements to the tail, or bottom, of the list and to remove elements from the head, or top, of the list. The first element added to the list will always be the first element removed from the head of the list. Suppose you're working with element objects of class *CAction*, which is your own custom class derived from *CObject*. A command-line program that puts five elements into a list and then retrieves them in the same sequence is shown here:

```
#include <afx.h>
#include <afxcoll.h>

class CAction : public CObject
{
private:
    int m_nTime;
public:
    CAction(int nTime) { m_nTime = nTime; } // Constructor stores
                                            //    integer time value
    void PrintTime() { TRACE("time = %d\n", m_nTime); }
};

int main()
{
    CAction* pAction;
    CObList actionList; // action list constructed on stack
    int i;

    // inserts action objects in sequence {0, 1, 2, 3, 4}
    for (i = 0; i < 5; i++) {
        pAction = new CAction(i);
        actionList.AddTail(pAction); // no cast necessary for pAction
    }

    // retrieves and removes action objects in sequence {0, 1, 2, 3, 4}
    while (!actionList.IsEmpty()) {
        pAction =                                 // cast required for
            (CAction*) actionList.RemoveHead(); //   return value
```

```
        pAction->PrintTime();
        delete pAction;
    }

    return 0;
}
```

Here's what's going on in the program. First a *CObList* object, *actionList*, is constructed. Then the *CObList::AddTail* member function inserts pointers to newly constructed *CAction* objects. No casting is necessary for *pAction* because *AddTail* takes a *CObject* pointer parameter and *pAction* is a pointer to a derived class.

Next the *CAction* object pointers are removed from the list of the objects deleted. A cast is necessary for the returned value of *RemoveHead* because *Remove-Head* returns a *CObject* pointer that is <u>higher</u> in the class hierarchy than *CAction*.

When you remove an object pointer from a collection, the object is not automatically deleted. The *delete* statement is necessary for deleting the *CAction* objects.

CObList Iteration—The *POSITION* Variable

Suppose you want to iterate through the elements in a list. The *CObList* class provides a *GetNext* member function that returns a pointer to the "next" list element, but using it is a little tricky. *GetNext* takes a parameter of type *POSITION*, which is a 32-bit variable. The *POSITION* variable is an internal representation of the retrieved element's position in the list. Because the *POSITION* parameter is declared as a reference (&), the function can change its value.

GetNext does the following:

1. It returns a pointer to the "current" object in the list, identified by the incoming value of the *POSITION* parameter.

2. It increments the value of the *POSITION* parameter to the next list element.

Here's what a *GetNext* loop looks like, assuming you're using the list generated in the previous example:

```
CAction* pAction;
POSITION pos = actionList.GetHeadPosition();
while (pos != NULL) {
    pAction = (CAction*) actionList.GetNext(pos);
    pAction->PrintTime();
}
```

389

Now suppose you have an interactive Windows-based application that uses toolbar buttons to sequence forward and backward through the list one element at a time. You can't use *GetNext* to retrieve the entry because *GetNext* always <u>increments</u> the *POSITION* variable and you don't know in advance whether the user is going to want the next element or the previous element. Here's a sample view class command message handler function that gets the next list entry. In the *CMyView* class, *m_actionList* is an embedded *CObList* object and the *m_position* data member is a *POSITION* variable that holds the current list position.

```
CMyView::OnCommandNext()
{
    POSITION pos;
    CAction* pAction;

    if ((pos = m_position) != NULL) {
        m_actionList.GetNext(pos);
        if (pos != NULL) { // pos is NULL at end of list
            pAction = (CAction*) m_actionList.GetAt(pos);
            pAction->PrintTime();
            m_position = pos;
        }
        else {
            AfxMessageBox("End of list reached");
        }
    }
}
```

GetNext is now called first to increment the list position, and the *CObList-::GetAt* member function is called to retrieve the entry. The *m_position* variable is updated only when we're sure we're not at the tail of the list.

The *CTypedPtrList* Template Collection Class

The *CObList* class works fine if you want a collection to contain mixed pointers. If, on the other hand, you want a type-safe collection that contains only one type of object pointer, you should look at the MFC library template pointer collection classes. *CTypedPtrList* is a good example. Templates are a relatively new C++ language element, introduced by Microsoft Visual C++ version 2.0. *CTypedPtrList* is a template class that you can use to create a list of any pointers to objects of any specified class. To make a long story short, you use the template to create a custom derived list class, using either *CPtrList* or *CObList* as a base class.

To declare an object for *CAction* pointers, you write the following line of code:

```
CTypedPtrList<CObList, CAction*> m_actionList;
```

The first parameter is the base class for the collection, and the second parameter is the type for parameters and return values. Only *CPtrList* and *CObList* are permitted for the base class because those are the only two MFC library pointer list classes. If you are storing objects of classes derived from *CObject*, you should use *CObList* as your base class; otherwise, use *CPtrList*.

By using the template as shown above, the compiler ensures that all list member functions return a *CAction* pointer. Thus, you can write the following code:

```
pAction = m_actionList.GetAt(pos); // no cast required
```

If you want to clean up the notation a little, use a *typedef* statement to generate what looks like a class, as shown here:

```
typedef CTypedPtrList<CObList, CAction*> CActionList;
```

Now you can declare *m_actionList* as follows:

```
CActionList m_actionList;
```

The Dump Context and Collection Classes

The *Dump* function for *CObList* and the other collection classes has a useful property. If you call *Dump* for a collection object, you can get a display of each object in the collection. If the element objects use the *DECLARE_DYNAMIC* and *IMPLEMENT_DYNAMIC* macros, the dump will show the class name for each object.

The default behavior of the collection *Dump* functions is to display only class names and addresses of element objects. If you want the collection *Dump* functions to call the *Dump* function for each element object, you must, somewhere at the start of your program, make the following call:

```
#ifdef _DEBUG
    afxDump.SetDepth(1);
#endif
```

Now the statement

```
#ifdef _DEBUG
    afxDump << actionList;
#endif
```

produces output such as this:

```
a CObList at $411832
with 4 elements
    a CAction at $412CD6
time = 0
    a CAction at $412632
time = 1
    a CAction at $41268E
time = 2
    a CAction at $4126EA
time = 3
```

If the collection contains mixed pointers, the virtual *Dump* function is called for the object's class and the appropriate class name is printed.

The EX16B Example

This second SDI example improves on EX16A in the following ways:

- Instead of a single embedded *CStudent* object, the document now contains a list of *CStudent* objects. (Now you see the reason for using the *CStudent* class instead of making *m_strName* and *m_nGrade* data members of the document.)

- Toolbar buttons allow the user to sequence through the list.

- The application is structured to allow the addition of extra views. The Edit Clear All command is now routed to the document object, so the document's *UpdateAllViews* function and the view's *OnUpdate* function are brought into play.

- The student-specific view code is isolated so that the *CEx16bView* class can later be transformed into a base class that contains only general-purpose code. Derived classes can override selected functions to accommodate lists of application-specific objects.

The EX16B window, shown in Figure 16-3, looks a little different from the EX16A window shown in Figure 16-1 on page 378. The toolbar buttons are enabled only when appropriate. The Next (arrow-down graphic) button, for example, is disabled when we're positioned at the bottom of the list.

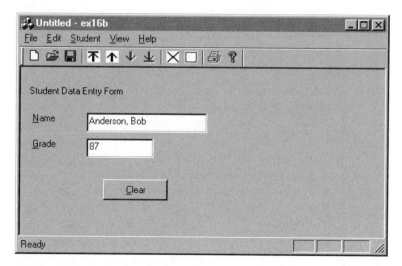

Figure 16-3.
The EX16B program in action.

The toolbar buttons function as follows.

Button	Function
⊼	Retrieves the first student record
⊻	Retrieves the last student record
↑	Retrieves the previous student record
↓	Retrieves the next student record
⊠	Deletes the current student record
☐	Inserts a new student record

The Clear button in the view window clears the contents of the Name and Grade edit controls. The Clear All command on the Edit menu deletes all the student records in the list and clears the view's edit controls.

This example deviates from the step-by-step format in the previous examples. Because there's now more code, we'll simply list selected code and the resource requirements. In the listing figures, boldface code indicates additional code or other changes that you enter in the output from AppWizard and Class-Wizard. The frequent use of *TRACE* statements lets you follow the program's execution in the debugging window.

Resource Requirements

The file ex16b.rc defines the application's resources as follows.

Toolbar

The toolbar (visible in Figure 16-3) was created by erasing the Edit Cut, Copy, and Paste tiles (fourth, fifth, and sixth from the left) and replacing them with six new patterns. The Flip Vertical command (on the Image menu) was used to duplicate some of the tiles. The ex16b.rc file defines the linkage between the command IDs and the toolbar buttons.

Student Menu

Having menu options that correspond to the new toolbar buttons isn't absolutely necessary. (ClassWizard allows you to map toolbar button commands just as easily as menu commands.) However, most applications for Microsoft Windows have menu options for all commands, so users generally expect them.

Edit Menu

On the Edit menu, the clipboard menu items are replaced by the Clear All menu item. See step 2 on page 381 for an illustration of the Edit menu.

The *IDD_STUDENT* Dialog Template

The *IDD_STUDENT* dialog template, shown here, is similar to the EX16A dialog shown in Figure 16-1 except that the Enter pushbutton has been replaced by the Clear pushbutton.

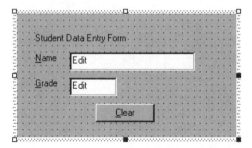

The following IDs identify the controls.

Control	ID
Name edit control	IDC_NAME
Grade edit control	IDC_GRADE
Clear pushbutton	IDC_CLEAR

The controls' styles are the same as for the EX16A program.

Code Requirements

Here's a list of the files and classes in the EX16B example.

Header File	Source Code File	Classes	Description
ex16b.h	ex16b.cpp	CEx16bApp	Application class (from AppWizard)
		CAboutDlg	About dialog
MainFrm.h	MainFrm.cpp	CMainFrame	SDI main frame
StuDoc.h	StuDoc.cpp	CStudentDoc	Student document
StuView.h	StuView.cpp	CStudentView	Student form view (derived from CFormView)
Student.h	Student.cpp	CStudent	Student record (similar to EX16A)
StdAfx.h	StdAfx.cpp		Includes the standard precompiled headers

CEx16bApp
The files ex16b.cpp and ex16b.h are standard AppWizard output.

CMainFrame
The code for the *CMainFrame* class in MainFrm.cpp is standard AppWizard output.

CStudent
This is the code from EX16A, except for the following line added at the end of Student.h:

```
typedef CTypedPtrList<CObList, CStudent*> CStudentList;
```

NOTE: Use of the MFC template collection classes requires the following statement in StdAfx.h:

```
#include <afxtempl.h>
```

CStudentDoc

AppWizard originally generated the *CStudentDoc* class. Figure 16-4 shows the code used in the EX16B example.

STUDOC.H

```
// StuDoc.h : interface of the CStudentDoc class
//
/////////////////////////////////////////////////////////////////////

#if !defined(AFX_STUDOC_H__4D011047_7E1C_11D0_8FE0_00C04FC2A0C2__INCLUDED_)
#define AFX_STUDOC_H__4D011047_7E1C_11D0_8FE0_00C04FC2A0C2__INCLUDED_

#if _MSC_VER > 1000
#pragma once
#endif // _MSC_VER > 1000

#include "student.h"

class CStudentDoc : public CDocument
{
protected: // create from serialization only
    CStudentDoc();
    DECLARE_DYNCREATE(CStudentDoc)

// Attributes
public:
    CStudentList* GetList() {
        return &m_studentList;
    }

// Operations
public:

// Overrides
    // ClassWizard generated virtual function overrides
    //{{AFX_VIRTUAL(CStudentDoc)
    public:
    virtual BOOL OnNewDocument();
    virtual void Serialize(CArchive& ar);
```

Figure 16-4. *(continued)*
The CStudentDoc *class listing.*

```
    virtual void DeleteContents();
    //}}AFX_VIRTUAL

// Implementation
public:
    virtual ~CStudentDoc();
#ifdef _DEBUG
    virtual void AssertValid() const;
    virtual void Dump(CDumpContext& dc) const;
#endif

protected:

// Generated message map functions
protected:
    //{{AFX_MSG(CStudentDoc)
    afx_msg void OnEditClearAll();
    afx_msg void OnUpdateEditClearAll(CCmdUI* pCmdUI);
    //}}AFX_MSG
    DECLARE_MESSAGE_MAP()
private:
    CStudentList m_studentList;
};

/////////////////////////////////////////////////////////////////////

//{{AFX_INSERT_LOCATION}}
// Microsoft Visual C++ will insert additional declarations
//   immediately before the previous line.

#endif // !defined(AFX_STUDOC_H__4D011047_7E1C_  ⮑
                   11D0_8FE0_00C04FC2A0C2__INCLUDED_)
```

STUDOC.CPP

```
// StuDoc.cpp : implementation of the CStudentDoc class
//

#include "stdafx.h"
#include "ex16b.h"

#include "StuDoc.h"
#ifdef _DEBUG
#define new DEBUG_NEW
#undef THIS_FILE
static char THIS_FILE[] = __FILE__;
```

(continued)

Figure 16-4. *continued*

```
#endif

/////////////////////////////////////////////////////////////////////
// CStudentDoc

IMPLEMENT_DYNCREATE(CStudentDoc, CDocument)

BEGIN_MESSAGE_MAP(CStudentDoc, CDocument)
    //{{AFX_MSG_MAP(CStudentDoc)
    ON_COMMAND(ID_EDIT_CLEAR_ALL, OnEditClearAll)
    ON_UPDATE_COMMAND_UI(ID_EDIT_CLEAR_ALL, OnUpdateEditClearAll)
    //}}AFX_MSG_MAP
END_MESSAGE_MAP()

/////////////////////////////////////////////////////////////////////
// CStudentDoc construction/destruction

CStudentDoc::CStudentDoc()
{
    TRACE("Entering CStudentDoc constructor\n");
#ifdef _DEBUG
    afxDump.SetDepth(1); // Ensure dump of list elements
#endif // _DEBUG
}

CStudentDoc::~CStudentDoc()
{
}

BOOL CStudentDoc::OnNewDocument()
{
    TRACE("Entering CStudentDoc::OnNewDocument\n");
    if (!CDocument::OnNewDocument())
        return FALSE;

    // TODO: add reinitialization code here
    // (SDI documents will reuse this document)

    return TRUE;
}
/////////////////////////////////////////////////////////////////////
// CStudentDoc serialization

void CStudentDoc::Serialize(CArchive& ar)
{
    if (ar.IsStoring())
```

```
    {
        // TODO: add storing code here
    }
    else
    {
        // TODO: add loading code here
    }
}


/////////////////////////////////////////////////////////////////////
// CStudentDoc diagnostics

#ifdef _DEBUG
void CStudentDoc::AssertValid() const
{
    CDocument::AssertValid();
}

void CStudentDoc::Dump(CDumpContext& dc) const
{
    CDocument::Dump(dc);
    dc << "\n" << m_studentList << "\n";
}
#endif //_DEBUG


/////////////////////////////////////////////////////////////////////
// CStudentDoc commands

void CStudentDoc::DeleteContents()
{
#ifdef _DEBUG
    Dump(afxDump);
#endif
    while (m_studentList.GetHeadPosition()) {
        delete m_studentList.RemoveHead();
    }
}
void CStudentDoc::OnEditClearAll()
{
    DeleteContents();
    UpdateAllViews(NULL);
}


void CStudentDoc::OnUpdateEditClearAll(CCmdUI* pCmdUI)
{
    pCmdUI->Enable(!m_studentList.IsEmpty());
}
```

ClassWizard and *CStudentDoc*

The Edit Clear All command is handled in the document class. The following message handlers were added through ClassWizard.

Object ID	Message	Member Function
ID_EDIT_CLEAR_ALL	COMMAND	*OnEditClearAll*
ID_EDIT_CLEAR_ALL	ON_UPDATE_COMMAND_UI	*OnUpdateEditClearAll*

Data Members

The document class provides for an embedded *CStudentList* object, the *m_studentList* data member, which holds pointers to *CStudent* objects. The list object is constructed when the *CStudentDoc* object is constructed, and it is destroyed at program exit. *CStudentList* is a *typedef* for a *CTypedPtrList* for *CStudent* pointers.

Constructor

The document constructor sets the depth of the dump context so that a dump of the list causes dumps of the individual list elements.

GetList

The inline *GetList* function helps isolate the view from the document. The document class must be specific to the type of object in the list—in this case, objects of the class *CStudent*. A generic list view base class, however, can use a member function to get a pointer to the list without knowing the name of the list object.

DeleteContents

The *DeleteContents* function is a virtual override function that is called by other document functions and by the application framework. Its job is to remove all student object pointers from the document's list and to delete those student objects. An important point to remember here is that SDI document objects are reused after they are closed. *DeleteContents* also dumps the student list.

Dump

AppWizard generates the *Dump* function skeleton between the lines *#ifdef _DEBUG* and *#endif*. Because the *afxDump* depth was set to 1 in the document constructor, all the *CStudent* objects contained in the list are dumped.

CStudentView

Figure 16-5 shows the code for the *CStudentView* class. This code will be carried over into the next two chapters.

STUVIEW.H

```cpp
// StuView.h : interface of the CStudentView class
//
/////////////////////////////////////////////////////////////////////

#if !defined(AFX_STUVIEW_H__4D011049_7E1C_11D0_8FE0_00C04FC2A0C2__INCLUDED_)
#define AFX_STUVIEW_H__4D011049_7E1C_11D0_8FE0_00C04FC2A0C2__INCLUDED_

#if _MSC_VER > 1000
#pragma once
#endif // _MSC_VER > 1000

class CStudentView : public CFormView
{
protected:
    POSITION     m_position; // current position in document list
    CStudentList* m_pList;    // copied from document

protected: // create from serialization only
    CStudentView();
    DECLARE_DYNCREATE(CStudentView)

public:
    //{{AFX_DATA(CStudentView)
    enum { IDD = IDD_STUDENT };
    int     m_nGrade;
    CString m_strName;
    //}}AFX_DATA

// Attributes
public:
    CStudentDoc* GetDocument();

// Operations
public:

// Overrides
    // ClassWizard generated virtual function overrides
    //{{AFX_VIRTUAL(CStudentView)
    public:
    virtual BOOL PreCreateWindow(CREATESTRUCT& cs);
    protected:
    virtual void DoDataExchange(CDataExchange* pDX); // DDX/DDV support
    virtual void OnInitialUpdate(); // called first time after construct
```

Figure 16-5. *(continued)*

The CStudentView *class listing.*

Figure 16-5. *continued*

```
    virtual void OnUpdate(CView* pSender, LPARAM lHint, CObject* pHint);
    //}}AFX_VIRTUAL

// Implementation
public:
    virtual ~CStudentView();
#ifdef _DEBUG
    virtual void AssertValid() const;
    virtual void Dump(CDumpContext& dc) const;
#endif

protected:
    virtual void ClearEntry();
    virtual void InsertEntry(POSITION position);
    virtual void GetEntry(POSITION position);

// Generated message map functions
protected:
    //{{AFX_MSG(CStudentView)
    afx_msg void OnClear();
    afx_msg void OnStudentHome();
    afx_msg void OnStudentEnd();
    afx_msg void OnStudentPrev();
    afx_msg void OnStudentNext();
    afx_msg void OnStudentIns();
    afx_msg void OnStudentDel();
    afx_msg void OnUpdateStudentHome(CCmdUI* pCmdUI);
    afx_msg void OnUpdateStudentEnd(CCmdUI* pCmdUI);
    afx_msg void OnUpdateStudentDel(CCmdUI* pCmdUI);
    //}}AFX_MSG
    DECLARE_MESSAGE_MAP()
};

#ifndef _DEBUG  // debug version in StuView.cpp
inline CStudentDoc* CStudentView::GetDocument()
   { return (CStudentDoc*)m_pDocument; }
#endif


/////////////////////////////////////////////////////////////////////////

//{{AFX_INSERT_LOCATION}}
// Microsoft Visual C++ will insert additional declarations
//   immediately before the previous line.

#endif // !defined(AFX_STUVIEW_H__4D011049_7E1C_       →
                 11D0_8FE0_00C04FC2A0C2__INCLUDED_)
```

STUVIEW.CPP

```cpp
// StuView.cpp : implementation of the CStudentView class
//

#include "stdafx.h"
#include "ex16b.h"

#include "StuDoc.h"
#include "StuView.h"

#ifdef _DEBUG
#define new DEBUG_NEW
#undef THIS_FILE
static char THIS_FILE[] = __FILE__ ;
#endif

/////////////////////////////////////////////////////////////////////
// CStudentView

IMPLEMENT_DYNCREATE(CStudentView, CFormView)
BEGIN_MESSAGE_MAP(CStudentView, CFormView)
    //{{AFX_MSG_MAP(CStudentView)
    ON_BN_CLICKED(IDC_CLEAR, OnClear)
    ON_COMMAND(ID_STUDENT_HOME, OnStudentHome)
    ON_COMMAND(ID_STUDENT_END, OnStudentEnd)
    ON_COMMAND(ID_STUDENT_PREV, OnStudentPrev)
    ON_COMMAND(ID_STUDENT_NEXT, OnStudentNext)
    ON_COMMAND(ID_STUDENT_INS, OnStudentIns)
    ON_COMMAND(ID_STUDENT_DEL, OnStudentDel)
    ON_UPDATE_COMMAND_UI(ID_STUDENT_HOME, OnUpdateStudentHome)
    ON_UPDATE_COMMAND_UI(ID_STUDENT_END, OnUpdateStudentEnd)
    ON_UPDATE_COMMAND_UI(ID_STUDENT_PREV, OnUpdateStudentHome)
    ON_UPDATE_COMMAND_UI(ID_STUDENT_NEXT, OnUpdateStudentEnd)
    ON_UPDATE_COMMAND_UI(ID_STUDENT_DEL, OnUpdateStudentDel)
    //}}AFX_MSG_MAP
END_MESSAGE_MAP()

/////////////////////////////////////////////////////////////////////
// CStudentView construction/destruction

CStudentView::CStudentView()
    : CFormView(CStudentView::IDD)
{
    TRACE("Entering CStudentView constructor\n");
    //{{AFX_DATA_INIT(CStudentView)
```

(continued)

Figure 16-5. *continued*

```
    m_nGrade = 0;
    m_strName = _T("");
    //}}AFX_DATA_INIT
    m_position = NULL;
}


CStudentView::~CStudentView()
{
}


void CStudentView::DoDataExchange(CDataExchange* pDX)
{
    CFormView::DoDataExchange(pDX);
    //{{AFX_DATA_MAP(CStudentView)
    DDX_Text(pDX, IDC_GRADE, m_nGrade);
    DDV_MinMaxInt(pDX, m_nGrade, 0, 100);
    DDX_Text(pDX, IDC_NAME, m_strName);
    DDV_MaxChars(pDX, m_strName, 20);
    //}}AFX_DATA_MAP
}
BOOL CStudentView::PreCreateWindow(CREATESTRUCT& cs)
{
    // TODO: Modify the Window class or styles here by modifying
    //   the CREATESTRUCT cs
    return CFormView::PreCreateWindow(cs);
}


void CStudentView::OnInitialUpdate()
{
    TRACE("Entering CStudentView::OnInitialUpdate\n");
    m_pList = GetDocument()->GetList();
    CFormView::OnInitialUpdate();
}


/////////////////////////////////////////////////////////////////
// CStudentView diagnostics

#ifdef _DEBUG
void CStudentView::AssertValid() const
{
    CFormView::AssertValid();
}


void CStudentView::Dump(CDumpContext& dc) const
{
```

```
    CFormView::Dump(dc);
}

CStudentDoc* CStudentView::GetDocument() // non-debug version is inline
{
    ASSERT(m_pDocument->IsKindOf(RUNTIME_CLASS(CStudentDoc)));
    return (CStudentDoc*)m_pDocument;
}
#endif //_DEBUG

/////////////////////////////////////////////////////////////////////////
// CStudentView message handlers

void CStudentView::OnClear()
{
    TRACE("Entering CStudentView::OnClear\n");
    ClearEntry();
}

void CStudentView::OnUpdate(CView* pSender, LPARAM lHint,
                            CObject* pHint)
{
    // called by OnInitialUpdate and by UpdateAllViews
    TRACE("Entering CStudentView::OnUpdate\n");
    m_position = m_pList->GetHeadPosition();
    GetEntry(m_position); // initial data for view
}

void CStudentView::OnStudentHome()
{
    TRACE("Entering CStudentView::OnStudentHome\n");
    // need to deal with list empty condition
    if (!m_pList->IsEmpty()) {
        m_position = m_pList->GetHeadPosition();
        GetEntry(m_position);
    }
}

void CStudentView::OnStudentEnd()
{
    TRACE("Entering CStudentView::OnStudentEnd\n");
    if (!m_pList->IsEmpty()) {
        m_position = m_pList->GetTailPosition();
        GetEntry(m_position);
    }
}
```

(continued)

Figure 16-5. *continued*

```
void CStudentView::OnStudentPrev()
{
    POSITION pos;
    TRACE("Entering CStudentView::OnStudentPrev\n");
    if ((pos = m_position) != NULL) {
        m_pList->GetPrev(pos);
        if (pos) {
            GetEntry(pos);
            m_position = pos;
        }
    }
}

void CStudentView::OnStudentNext()
{
    POSITION pos;
    TRACE("Entering CStudentView::OnStudentNext\n");
    if ((pos = m_position) != NULL) {
        m_pList->GetNext(pos);
        if (pos) {
            GetEntry(pos);
            m_position = pos;
        }
    }
}
void CStudentView::OnStudentIns()
{
    TRACE("Entering CStudentView::OnStudentIns\n");
    InsertEntry(m_position);
    GetDocument()->SetModifiedFlag();
    GetDocument()->UpdateAllViews(this);
}

void CStudentView::OnStudentDel()
{
    // deletes current entry and positions to next one or head
    POSITION pos;
    TRACE("Entering CStudentView::OnStudentDel\n");
    if ((pos = m_position) != NULL) {
        m_pList->GetNext(pos);
        if (pos == NULL) {
            pos = m_pList->GetHeadPosition();
            TRACE("GetHeadPos = %ld\n", pos);
            if (pos == m_position) {
                pos = NULL;
```

```
                }
            }
            GetEntry(pos);
            CStudent* ps = m_pList->GetAt(m_position);
            m_pList->RemoveAt(m_position);
            delete ps;
            m_position = pos;
            GetDocument()->SetModifiedFlag();
            GetDocument()->UpdateAllViews(this);
        }
}

void CStudentView::OnUpdateStudentHome(CCmdUI* pCmdUI)
{
    // called during idle processing and when Student menu drops down
    POSITION pos;

    // enables button if list not empty and not at home already
    pos = m_pList->GetHeadPosition();
    pCmdUI->Enable((m_position != NULL) && (pos != m_position));
}

void CStudentView::OnUpdateStudentEnd(CCmdUI* pCmdUI)
{
    // called during idle processing and when Student menu drops down
    POSITION pos;

    // enables button if list not empty and not at end already
    pos = m_pList->GetTailPosition();
    pCmdUI->Enable((m_position != NULL) && (pos != m_position));
}

void CStudentView::OnUpdateStudentDel(CCmdUI* pCmdUI)
{
    // called during idle processing and when Student menu drops down
    pCmdUI->Enable(m_position != NULL);
}

void CStudentView::GetEntry(POSITION position)
{
    if (position) {
        CStudent* pStudent = m_pList->GetAt(position);
        m_strName = pStudent->m_strName;
        m_nGrade = pStudent->m_nGrade;
    }
    else {
```

(continued)

407

Figure 16-5. *continued*

```
        ClearEntry();
    }
    UpdateData(FALSE);
}

void CStudentView::InsertEntry(POSITION position)
{
    if (UpdateData(TRUE)) {
        // UpdateData returns FALSE if it detects a user error
        CStudent* pStudent = new CStudent;
        pStudent->m_strName = m_strName;
        pStudent->m_nGrade = m_nGrade;
        m_position = m_pList->InsertAfter(m_position, pStudent);
    }
}

void CStudentView::ClearEntry()
{
    m_strName = "";
    m_nGrade = 0;
    UpdateData(FALSE);
    ((CDialog*) this)->GotoDlgCtrl(GetDlgItem(IDC_NAME));
}
```

ClassWizard and *CStudentView*

ClassWizard was used to map the *CStudentView* Clear pushbutton notification message as follows.

Object ID	Message	Member Function
IDC_CLEAR	BN_CLICKED	*OnClear*

Because *CStudentView* is derived from *CFormView*, ClassWizard supports the definition of dialog data members. The variables shown here were added with the Add Variables button.

Control ID	Member Variable	Category	Variable Type
IDC_GRADE	*m_nGrade*	Value	*int*
IDC_NAME	*m_strName*	Value	*CString*

The minimum value of the *m_nGrade* data member was set to 0, and its maximum value was set to 100. The maximum length of the *m_strName* data member was set to 20 characters.

ClassWizard maps toolbar button commands to their handlers. Here are the commands and the handler functions to which they were mapped.

Object ID	Message	Member Function
ID_STUDENT_HOME	COMMAND	*OnStudentHome*
ID_STUDENT_END	COMMAND	*OnStudentEnd*
ID_STUDENT_PREV	COMMAND	*OnStudentPrev*
ID_STUDENT_NEXT	COMMAND	*OnStudentNext*
ID_STUDENT_INS	COMMAND	*OnStudentIns*
ID_STUDENT_DEL	COMMAND	*OnStudentDel*

Each command handler has built-in error checking.

The following update command UI message handlers are called during idle processing to update the state of the toolbar buttons and, when the Student menu is painted, to update the menu items.

Object ID	Message	Member Function
ID_STUDENT_HOME	UPDATE_COMMAND_UI	*OnUpdateStudentHome*
ID_STUDENT_END	UPDATE_COMMAND_UI	*OnUpdateStudentEnd*
ID_STUDENT_PREV	UPDATE_COMMAND_UI	*OnUpdateStudentHome*
ID_STUDENT_NEXT	UPDATE_COMMAND_UI	*OnUpdateStudentEnd*
ID_STUDENT_DEL	UPDATE_COMMAND_UI	*OnUpdateCommandDel*

For example, this button,

which retrieves the first student record, is disabled when the list is empty and when the *m_position* variable is already set to the head of the list. The Previous button is disabled under the same circumstances, so it uses the same update command UI handler. The End and the Next buttons share a handler for similar reasons. Because a delay sometimes occurs in calling the update command UI functions, the command message handlers must look for error conditions.

Data Members

The *m_position* data member is a kind of cursor for the document's collection. It contains the position of the *CStudent* object that is currently displayed. The *m_pList* variable provides a quick way to get at the student list in the document.

OnInitialUpdate

The virtual *OnInitialUpdate* function is called when you start the application. It sets the view's *m_pList* data member for subsequent access to the document's list object.

OnUpdate

The virtual *OnUpdate* function is called both by the *OnInitialUpdate* function and by the *CDocument::UpdateAllViews* function. It resets the list position to the head of the list, and it displays the head entry. In this example, the *Update-AllViews* function is called only in response to the Edit Clear All command. In a multiview application, you might need a different strategy for setting the *CStudentView m_position* variable in response to document updates from another view.

Protected Virtual Functions

The following three functions are protected virtual functions that deal specifically with *CStudent* objects:

> *GetEntry*
> *InsertEntry*
> *ClearEntry*

You can transfer these functions to a derived class if you want to isolate the general-purpose list-handling features in a base class.

Testing the EX16B Application

Fill in the student name and grade fields, and then click this button

to insert the entry into the list. Repeat this action several times, using the Clear pushbutton to erase the data from the previous entry. When you exit the application, the debug output should look similar to this:

```
a CStudentDoc at $4116D0
m_strTitle = Untitled
m_strPathName =
m_bModified = 1
m_pDocTemplate = $4113F1

a CObList at $411624
with 4 elements
    a CStudent at $412770
m_strName = Fisher, Lon
m_nGrade = 67
    a CStudent at $412E80
m_strName = Meyers, Lisa
m_nGrade = 80
    a CStudent at $412880
m_strName = Seghers, John
m_nGrade = 92
    a CStudent at $4128F0
m_strName = Anderson, Bob
m_nGrade = 87
```

Two Exercises for the Reader

You might have noticed the absence of a Modify button on the toolbar. Without such a button, you can't modify an existing student record. Can you add the necessary toolbar button and message handlers? The most difficult task might be designing a graphic for the button's tile.

Recall that the *CStudentView* class is just about ready to be a general-purpose base class. Try separating the *CStudent*-specific virtual functions into a derived class. After that, make another derived class that uses a new element class other than *CStudent*.

CHAPTER SEVENTEEN

Reading and Writing Documents—SDI Applications

As you've probably noticed, every AppWizard-generated program has a File menu that contains the familiar New, Open, Save, and Save As commands. In this chapter, you'll learn how to make your application respond to read and write documents.

Here we'll stick with the Single Document Interface (SDI) application because it's familiar territory. Chapter 18 introduces the Multiple Document Interface (MDI) application, which is more flexible in its handling of documents and files. In both chapters, you'll get a heavy but necessary dose of application-framework theory; you'll learn a lot about the various helper classes that have been concealed up to this point. The going will be rough, but believe me, you must know the details to get the most out of the application framework.

This chapter's example, EX17A, is an SDI application based on the EX16B example from the previous chapter. It uses the student list document with a *CFormView*-derived view class. Now the student list can be written to and read from disk through a process called serialization. Chapter 18 shows you how to use the same view and document classes to make an MDI application.

Serialization—What Is It?

The term "serialization" might be new to you, but it's already seen some use in the world of object-oriented programming. The idea is that objects can be persistent, which means they can be saved on disk when a program exits and then can be restored when the program is restarted. This process of saving and re-storing objects is called <u>serialization</u>. In the Microsoft Foundation Class (MFC) library, designated classes have a member function named *Serialize*. When the application framework calls *Serialize* for a particular object—for example, an object of class *CStudent*—the data for the student is either saved on disk or read from disk.

In the MFC library, serialization is not a substitute for a database management system. All the objects associated with a document are <u>sequentially</u> read from or written to a single disk file. It's not possible to access individual objects at random disk file addresses. If you need database capability in your application, consider using the Microsoft Open Database Connectivity (ODBC) software or Data Access Objects (DAO). Chapters 31 and 32 show you how to use ODBC and DAO with the MFC application framework.

NOTE: There's a storage option that fits between sequential files and a database: <u>structured storage</u>, described in Chapter 27. The MFC framework already uses structured storage for container programs that support embedded objects.

Disk Files and Archives

How do you know whether *Serialize* should read or write data? How is *Serialize* connected to a disk file? With the MFC library, objects of class *CFile* represent disk files. A *CFile* object encapsulates the binary file handle that you get through the Win32 function *CreateFile*. This is <u>not</u> the buffered *FILE* pointer that you'd get with a call to the C runtime *fopen* function; rather, it's a handle to a binary file. The application framework uses this file handle for Win32 *ReadFile*, *WriteFile*, and *SetFilePointer* calls.

If your application does no direct disk I/O but instead relies on the serialization process, you can avoid direct use of *CFile* objects. Between the *Serialize* function and the *CFile* object is an archive object (of class *CArchive*), as shown in Figure 17-1.

The *CArchive* object buffers data for the *CFile* object, and it maintains an internal flag that indicates whether the archive is storing (writing to disk) or loading (reading from disk). Only one active archive is associated with a file at any one time. The application framework takes care of constructing the *CFile* and *CArchive* objects, opening the disk file for the *CFile* object and associating the archive object with the file. All you have to do (in your *Serialize* function) is load data from or store data in the archive object. The application framework calls the document's *Serialize* function during the File Open and File Save processes.

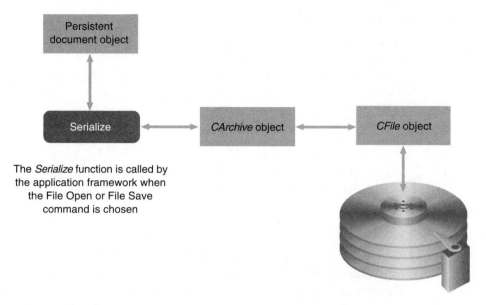

Figure 17-1.
The serialization process.

Making a Class Serializable

A serializable class must be derived directly or indirectly from *CObject*. In addition (with some exceptions), the class declaration must contain the *DECLARE_SERIAL* macro call, and the class implementation file must contain the *IMPLEMENT_SERIAL* macro call. (See the *Microsoft Foundation Class Reference* for a description of these macros.) This chapter's *CStudent* class example is modified from the class in Chapter 16 to include these macros.

Writing a *Serialize* Function

In Chapter 16, you saw a *CStudent* class, derived from *CObject*, with these data members:

```
public:
    CString m_strName;
    int     m_nGrade;
```

Now your job is to write a *Serialize* member function for *CStudent*. Because *Serialize* is a virtual member function of class *CObject*, you must be sure that the return value and parameter types match the *CObject* declaration. The *Serialize* function for the *CStudent* class is on the following page.

```
void CStudent::Serialize(CArchive& ar)
{
    TRACE("Entering CStudent::Serialize\n");
    if (ar.IsStoring()) {
        ar << m_strName << m_nGrade;
    }
    else {
        ar >> m_strName >> m_nGrade;
    }
}
```

Most serialization functions call the *Serialize* functions of their base classes. If *CStudent* were derived from *CPerson*, for example, the first line of the *Serialize* function would be

```
CPerson::Serialize(ar);
```

The *Serialize* function for *CObject* (and for *CDocument*, which doesn't override it) doesn't do anything useful, so there's no need to call it.

Notice that *ar* is a *CArchive* reference parameter that identifies the application's archive object. The *CArchive::IsStoring* member function tells us whether the archive is currently being used for storing or loading. The *CArchive* class has overloaded insertion operators (<<) and extraction operators (>>) for many of the C++ built-in types, as shown in the following table.

Type	Description
BYTE	8 bits, unsigned
WORD	16 bits, unsigned
LONG	32 bits, signed
DWORD	32 bits, unsigned
float	32 bits
double	64 bits, IEEE standard
int	32 bits, signed
short	16 bits, signed
char	8 bits, unsigned
unsigned	32 bits, unsigned

The insertion operators are overloaded for values; the extraction operators are overloaded for references. Sometimes you must use a cast to satisfy the compiler. Suppose you have a data member *m_nType* that is an enumerated type. Here's the code you would use:

```
ar << (int) m_nType;
ar >> (int&) m_nType;
```

MFC classes that are not derived from *CObject*, such as *CString* and *CRect*, have their own overloaded insertion and extraction operators for *CArchive*.

Loading from an Archive—Embedded Objects vs. Pointers

Now suppose your *CStudent* object has other objects embedded in it, and these objects are not instances of standard classes such as *CString*, *CSize*, and *CRect*. Let's add a new data member to the *CStudent* class:

```
public:
    CTranscript m_transcript;
```

Assume that *CTranscript* is a custom class, derived from *CObject*, with its own *Serialize* member function. There's no overloaded << or >> operator for *CObject*, so the *CStudent::Serialize* function now becomes

```
void CStudent::Serialize(CArchive& ar)
{
    if (ar.IsStoring()) {
        ar << m_strName << m_nGrade;
    }
    else {
        ar >> m_strName >> m_nGrade;
    }
    m_transcript.Serialize(ar);
}
```

Before the *CStudent::Serialize* function can be called to load a student record from the archive, a *CStudent* object must exist somewhere. The embedded *CTranscript* object *m_transcript* is constructed along with the *CStudent* object before the call to the *CTranscript::Serialize* function. When the virtual *CTranscript::Serialize* function does get called, it can load the archived transcript data into the embedded *m_transcript* object. If you're looking for a rule, here it is: always make a direct call to *Serialize* for embedded objects of classes derived from *CObject*.

Suppose that, instead of an embedded object, your *CStudent* object contained a *CTranscript* pointer data member such as this:

```
public:
    CTranscript* m_pTranscript;
```

You could use the *Serialize* function, as shown on the following page, but as you can see, you must construct a new *CTranscript* object yourself.

417

```
void CStudent::Serialize(CArchive& ar)
{
    if (ar.IsStoring())
        ar << m_strName << m_nGrade;
    else {
        m_pTranscript = new CTranscript;
        ar >> m_strName >> m_nGrade;
    }
    m_pTranscript->Serialize(ar);
}
```

Because the *CArchive* insertion and extraction operators are indeed overloaded for *CObject* pointers, you could write *Serialize* this way instead:

```
void CStudent::Serialize(CArchive& ar)
{
    if (ar.IsStoring())
        ar << m_strName << m_nGrade << m_pTranscript;
    else
        ar >> m_strName >> m_nGrade >> m_pTranscript;
}
```

But how is the *CTranscript* object constructed when the data is loaded from the archive? That's where the *DECLARE_SERIAL* and *IMPLEMENT-_SERIAL* macros in the *CTranscript* class come in.

When the *CTranscript* object is written to the archive, the macros ensure that the class name is written along with the data. When the archive is read, the class name is read in and an object of the correct class is dynamically constructed, under the control of code generated by the macros. Once the *CTranscript* object has been constructed, the overridden *Serialize* function for *CTranscript* can be called to do the work of reading the student data from the disk file. Finally the *CTranscript* pointer is stored in the *m_pTranscript* data member. To avoid a memory leak, you must be sure that *m_pTranscript* does not already contain a pointer to a *CTranscript* object. If the *CStudent* object was just constructed and thus was not previously loaded from the archive, the transcript pointer will be null.

The insertion and extraction operators do <u>not</u> work with embedded objects of classes derived from *CObject*, as shown here:

```
ar >> m_strName >> m_nGrade >> &m_transcript; // Don't try this
```

Serializing Collections

Because all collection classes are derived from the *CObject* class and the collection class declarations contain the *DECLARE_SERIAL* macro call, you can conveniently serialize collections with a call to the collection class's *Serialize* member function. If you call *Serialize* for a *CObList* collection of *CStudent* objects, for example, the *Serialize* function for each *CStudent* object will be called in turn. You should, however, remember the following specifics about loading collections from an archive:

■ If a collection contains pointers to objects of mixed classes (all derived from *CObject*), the individual class names are stored in the archive so that the objects can be properly constructed with the appropriate class constructor.

■ If a container object, such as a document, contains an embedded collection, loaded data is appended to the existing collection. You might need to empty the collection before loading from the archive. This is usually done in the document's virtual *DeleteContents* function, which is called by the application framework.

■ When a collection of *CObject* pointers is loaded from an archive, the following processing steps take place for each object in the collection:

  1. The object's class is identified.

  2. Heap storage is allocated for the object.

  3. The object's data is loaded into the newly allocated storage.

  4. A pointer to the new object is stored in the collection.

The EX17A example, beginning on page 428, shows serialization of an embedded collection of *CStudent* records.

The *Serialize* Function and the Application Framework

OK, so you know how to write *Serialize* functions, and you know that these function calls can be nested. But do you know when the first *Serialize* function gets called to start the serialization process? With the application framework, everything is keyed to the document (the object of a class derived from *CDocument*). When you choose Save or Open from the File menu, the application framework creates a *CArchive* object (and an underlying *CFile* object) and then calls your document class's *Serialize* function, passing a reference to the *CArchive* object. Your derived document class *Serialize* function then serializes each of its nontemporary data members.

> NOTE: If you take a close look at any AppWizard-generated document class, you'll notice that the class includes the *DECLARE-_DYNCREATE* and *IMPLEMENT_DYNCREATE* macros rather than the *DECLARE_SERIAL* and *IMPLEMENT_SERIAL* macros. The *SERIAL* macros are unneeded because document objects are never used in conjunction with the *CArchive* extraction operator or included in collections; the application framework calls the document's *Serialize* member function directly. You should include the *DECLARE_SERIAL* and *IMPLEMENT_SERIAL* macros in all other serializable classes.

The SDI Application

You've seen many SDI applications that have one document class and one view class. We'll stick to a single view class in this chapter, but we'll explore the interrelationships among the application object, the main frame window, the document, the view, the document template object, and the associated string and menu resources.

The Windows Application Object

For each of your applications, AppWizard has been quietly generating a class derived from *CWinApp*. It has also been generating a statement such as this:

```
CMyApp theApp;
```

What you're seeing here is the mechanism that starts an MFC application. The class *CMyApp* is derived from the class *CWinApp*, and *theApp* is a globally declared instance of the class. This global object is called the Windows application object.

Here's a summary of the startup steps in a Microsoft Windows MFC library application:

1. Windows loads your program into memory.

2. The global object *theApp* is constructed. (All globally declared objects are constructed immediately when the program is loaded.)

3. Windows calls the global function *WinMain*, which is part of the MFC library. (*WinMain* is equivalent to the non-Windows *main* function—each is a main program entry point.)

4. *WinMain* searches for the one and only instance of a class derived from *CWinApp*.

5. *WinMain* calls the *InitInstance* member function for *theApp*, which is overridden in your derived application class.

6. Your overridden *InitInstance* function starts the process of loading a document and displaying the main frame and view windows.

7. *WinMain* calls the *Run* member function for *theApp*, which starts the processes of dispatching window messages and command messages.

You can override another important *CWinApp* member function. The *ExitInstance* function is called when the application terminates, after all its windows are closed.

NOTE: Windows allows multiple instances of programs to run. The *InitInstance* function is called each time a program instance starts up. In Win32, each instance runs as an independent process. It's only incidental that the same code is mapped to the virtual memory address space of each process. If you want to locate other running instances of your program, you must either call the Win32 *FindWindow* function or set up a shared data section or memory-mapped file for communication.

The Document Template Class

If you look at the *InitInstance* function that AppWizard generates for your derived application class, you'll see that the following statements are featured:

```
CSingleDocTemplate* pDocTemplate;
pDocTemplate = new CSingleDocTemplate(
    IDR_MAINFRAME,
    RUNTIME_CLASS(CStudentDoc),
    RUNTIME_CLASS(CMainFrame),        // main SDI frame window
    RUNTIME_CLASS(CStudentView));
AddDocTemplate(pDocTemplate);
```

Unless you start doing fancy things with splitter windows and multiple views, this is the only time you'll actually see a document template object. In this case, it's an object of class *CSingleDocTemplate*, which is derived from *CDocTemplate*. The *CSingleDocTemplate* class applies only to SDI applications because SDI applications are limited to one document object. *AddDocTemplate* is a member function of class *CWinApp*.

The *AddDocTemplate* call, together with the document template constructor call, establishes the relationships among classes—the application class, the document class, the view window class, and the main frame window class. The

421

application object exists, of course, before template construction, but the document, view, and frame objects are <u>not</u> constructed at this time. The application framework later dynamically constructs these objects when they are needed.

This dynamic construction is a sophisticated use of the C++ language. The *DECLARE_DYNCREATE* and *IMPLEMENT_DYNCREATE* macros in a class declaration and implementation enable the MFC library to construct objects of the specified class dynamically. If this dynamic construction capability weren't present, more relationships among your application's classes would have to be hard-coded. Your derived application class, for example, would need code for constructing document, view, and frame objects of your specific derived classes. This would compromise the object-oriented nature of your program.

With the template system, all that's required in your application class is use of the *RUNTIME_CLASS* macro. Notice that the target class's declaration must be included for this macro to work.

Figure 17-2 illustrates the relationships among the various classes, and Figure 17-3 illustrates the object relationships. An SDI application can have only one template (and associated class groups), and when the SDI program is running, there can be only one document object and only one main frame window object.

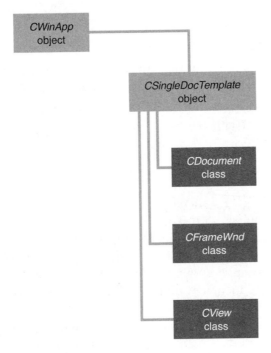

Figure 17-2.
Class relationships.

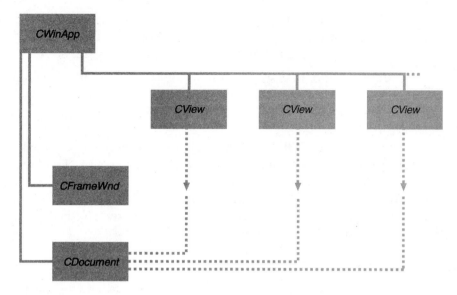

Figure 17-3.
Object relationships.

> **NOTE:** The MFC library dynamic construction capability was de-
> signed before the runtime type identification (RTTI) feature was
> added to the C++ language. The original MFC implementation goes
> beyond RTTI, and the MFC library continues to use it for dynamic
> object construction. See Appendix B for a description of MFC library
> dynamic construction.

The Document Template Resource

The first *AddDocTemplate* parameter is *IDR_MAINFRAME*, the identifier for
a string table resource. Here is the corresponding string that AppWizard generates for EX17A in the application's RC file:

```
IDR_MAINFRAME
    "ex17a\n"                  // application window caption
    "\n"                       // root for default document name
                               //  ("Untitled" used if none provided)
    "Ex17a\n"                  // document type name
    "Ex17a Files (*.17a)\n"    // document type description and filter
    ".17a\n"                   // extension for documents of this type
    "Ex17a.Document\n"         // Registry file type ID
    "Ex17a Document"           // Registry file type description
```

NOTE: The resource compiler won't accept the string concatenations as shown on the previous page. If you examine the ex17a.rc file, you'll see the substrings combined in one long string.

IDR_MAINFRAME specifies one string that is separated into substrings by newline characters (\n). The substrings show up in various places when the application executes. The string *17A* is the default document file extension specified to AppWizard.

The *IDR_MAINFRAME* ID, in addition to specifying the application's strings, identifies the application's icon, toolbar resources, and menu. AppWizard generates these resources, and you can maintain them with the resource editors.

So now you've seen how the *AddDocTemplate* call ties all the application elements together. Be aware, though, that no windows have been created yet and therefore nothing appears on the screen.

Multiple Views of an SDI Document

Providing multiple views of an SDI document is a little more complicated. You could provide a menu item that allows the user to choose a view, or you could allow multiple views in a splitter window. Chapter 20 shows you how to implement both techniques.

Creating an Empty Document— The *CWinApp::OnFileNew* Function

After your application class's *InitInstance* function calls the *AddDocTemplate* member function, it calls *OnFileNew* (indirectly through *CWinApp::Process-ShellCommand*), another important *CWinApp* member function. *OnFileNew* sorts through the web of interconnected class names and does the following:

1. Constructs the document object but does not attempt to read data from disk.

2. Constructs the main frame object (of class *CMainFrame*); also creates the main frame window but does not show it. The main frame window includes the *IDR_MAINFRAME* menu, the toolbar, and the status bar.

3. Constructs the view object; also creates the view window but doesn't show it.

4. Establishes connections among the document, main frame, and view objects. Do not confuse these object connections with the class connections established by the call to *AddDocTemplate*.

5. Calls the virtual *CDocument::OnNewDocument* member function for the document object, which calls the virtual *DeleteContents* function.

6. Calls the virtual *CView::OnInitialUpdate* member function for the view object.

7. Calls the virtual *CFrameWnd::ActivateFrame* for the frame object to show the main frame window together with the menus, view window, and control bars.

> **NOTE:** Some of the functions listed above are not called directly by *OnFileNew* but are called indirectly through the application framework.

In an SDI application, the document, main frame, and view objects are created only once, and they last for the life of the program. The *CWinApp::OnFileNew* function is called by *InitInstance*. It's also called in response to the user choosing the File New menu item. In this case, *OnFileNew* must behave a little differently. It can't construct the document, frame, and view objects because they're already constructed. Instead, it reuses the existing document object and performs steps 5, 6, and 7 above. Notice that *OnFileNew* always calls *DeleteContents* (indirectly) to empty the document.

The Document Class's *OnNewDocument* Function

You've seen the view class *OnInitialUpdate* member function and the document class *OnNewDocument* member function in Chapter 16. If an SDI application didn't reuse the same document object, you wouldn't need *OnNewDocument* because you could perform all document initialization in your document class constructor. Now you must override *OnNewDocument* to initialize your document object each time the user chooses File New or File Open. AppWizard helps you by providing a skeleton function in the derived document class it generates.

> **NOTE:** It's a good idea to minimize the work you do in constructor functions. The fewer things you do, the less chance there is for the constructor to fail—and constructor failures are messy. Functions such as *CDocument::OnNewDocument* and *CView::OnInitialUpdate* are excellent places to do initial housekeeping. If anything fails at creation time, you can pop up a message box, and in the case of *OnNewDocument*, you can return *FALSE*. Be advised that both functions can be called more than once for the same object. If you need certain instructions executed only once, declare a "first time" flag data member and then test/set it appropriately.

Connecting File Open to Your Serialization Code—The *OnFileOpen* Function

When AppWizard generates an application, it maps the File Open menu item to the *CWinApp::OnFileOpen* member function. When called, this function invokes a sequence of functions to accomplish these steps:

1. Prompts the user to select a file.

2. Calls the virtual function *CDocument::OnOpenDocument* for the already existing document object. This function opens the file, calls *CDocument::DeleteContents*, and constructs a *CArchive* object set for loading. It then calls the document's *Serialize* function, which loads data from the archive.

3. Calls the view's *OnInitialUpdate* function.

The Most Recently Used (MRU) file list is a handy alternative to the File Open menu item. The application framework tracks the four most recently used files and displays their names on the File menu. These filenames are stored in the Windows Registry between program executions.

NOTE: You can change the number of recent files tracked by supplying a parameter to the *LoadStdProfileSetting* function in the application class *InitInstance* function.

The Document Class's *DeleteContents* Function

When you load an existing SDI document object from a disk file, you must somehow erase the existing contents of the document object. The best way to do this is to override the *CDocument::DeleteContents* virtual function in your derived document class. The overridden function, as you've seen in Chapter 16, does whatever is necessary to clean up your document class's data members. In response to both the File New and File Open menu items, the *CDocument* functions *OnNewDocument* and *OnOpenDocument* both call the *DeleteContents* function, which means *DeleteContents* is called immediately after the document object is first constructed. It's called again when you close a document.

If you want your document classes to work in SDI applications, plan on emptying the document's contents in the *DeleteContents* member function rather than in the destructor. Use the destructor only to clean up items that last for the life of the object.

Connecting File Save and
File Save As to Your Serialization Code

When AppWizard generates an application, it maps the File Save menu item to the *OnFileSave* member function of the *CDocument* class. *OnFileSave* calls the *CDocument* function *OnSaveDocument*, which in turn calls your document's *Serialize* function with an archive object set for storing. The File Save As menu item is handled in a similar manner: it is mapped to the *CDocument* function *OnFileSaveAs*, which calls *OnSaveDocument*. Here the application framework does all the file management necessary to save a document on disk.

> NOTE: Yes, it is true that the File New and File Open menu options are mapped to <u>application</u> class member functions, but File Save and File Save As are mapped to <u>document</u> class member functions. File New is mapped to *OnFileNew*. The SDI version of *InitInstance* also calls *OnFileNew* (indirectly). No document object exists when the application framework calls *InitInstance*, so *OnFileNew* can't possibly be a member function of *CDocument*. When a document is saved, however, a document object certainly exists.

The Document's "Dirty" Flag

Many document-oriented applications for Windows track the user's modifications of a document. If the user tries to close a document or exit the program, a message box asks whether the user wants to save the document. The MFC application framework directly supports this behavior with the *CDocument* data member *m_bModified*. This Boolean variable is *TRUE* if the document has been modified (has become "dirty"); otherwise, it is *FALSE*.

The protected *m_bModified* flag is accessed through the *CDocument* member functions *SetModifiedFlag* and *IsModified*. The framework sets the document object's flag to *FALSE* when the document is created or read from disk and when it is saved on disk. You, the programmer, must use the *SetModifiedFlag* function to set the flag to *TRUE* when the document data changes. The virtual function *CDocument::SaveModified*, which the framework calls when the user closes the document, displays a message box if the *m_bModified* flag is set to *TRUE*. You can override this function if you need to do something else.

In the EX17A example, you'll see how a one-line update command UI function can use *IsModified* to control the state of the disk button and the corresponding menu item. When the user modifies the file, the disk button is enabled; when the user saves the file, the button changes to gray.

NOTE: In one respect, MFC SDI applications behave a little differently from other Windows SDI applications such as Notepad. Here's a typical sequence of events:

1. The user creates a document and saves it on disk under the name (for example) test.dat.

2. The user modifies the document.

3. The user chooses File Open and then specifies test.dat.

When the user chooses File Open, Notepad asks whether the user wants to save the changes made to the document (in Step 2 above). If the user answers no, the program rereads the document from disk. An MFC application, on the other hand, assumes that the changes are permanent and does not reread the file.

The EX17A Example—SDI with Serialization

The EX17A example is similar to example EX16B. The student dialog and the toolbar are the same, and the view class is the same. Serialization has been added, together with an update command UI function for File Save. The header and implementation files for the view and document classes will be reused in example EX18A in the next chapter.

All the new code (code that is different from EX16B) is listed, with additions and changes to the AppWizard-generated code and the ClassWizard code in boldface. A list of the files and classes in the EX17A example is shown in the following table.

Header File	Source Code File	Class	Description
ex17a.h	ex17a.cpp	*CEx17aApp*	Application class (from AppWizard)
		CAboutDlg	About dialog
MainFrm.h	MainFrm.cpp	*CMainFrame*	SDI main frame
StuDoc.h	StuDoc.cpp	*CStudentDoc*	Student document
StuView.h	StuView.cpp	*CStudentView*	Student form view (from EX16B)
Student.h	Student.cpp	*CStudent*	Student record
StdAfx.h	StdAfx.cpp		Precompiled headers (with afxtempl.h included)

CStudent

The EX17A Student.h file is almost the same as the file in the EX16A project. (See Figure 16-2 beginning on page 379.) The header contains the macro

```
DECLARE_SERIAL(CStudent)
```

instead of

```
DECLARE_DYNAMIC(CStudent)
```

and the implementation file contains the macro

```
IMPLEMENT_SERIAL(CStudent, CObject, 0)
```

instead of

```
IMPLEMENT_DYNAMIC(CStudent, Cobject)
```

The virtual *Serialize* function (as shown on page 417) has also been added.

CEx17aApp

The application class files, shown in Figure 17-4, contain only code generated by AppWizard. The application was generated with a default file extension and with the Microsoft Windows Explorer launch and drag-and-drop capabilities. These features are described later in this chapter.

To generate additional code, you must do the following when you first run AppWizard: in the AppWizard Step 4 page, click the Advanced button. When the Advanced Options dialog appears, you must enter the filename extension in the upper-left control, as shown here.

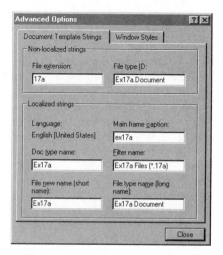

This ensures that the document template resource string contains the correct default extension and that the correct Explorer-related code is inserted into your application class *InitInstance* member function. You can change some of the other resource substrings if you want.

NOTE: The generated calls to *Enable3dControls* and *Enable3d-ControlsStatic* in *CEx17aApp::InitInstance* are not necessary with Microsoft Windows 95, Microsoft Windows 98, or Microsoft Windows NT 4.0. These two functions support an older DLL that is shipped with Microsoft Windows 3.51.

EX17A.H

```
// ex17a.h : main header file for the EX17A application
//

#if !defined(AFX_EX17A_H__1A036EA3_821A_11D0_8FE2_00C04FC2A0C2__INCLUDED_)
#define AFX_EX17A_H__1A036EA3_821A_11D0_8FE2_00C04FC2A0C2__INCLUDED_

#if _MSC_VER > 1000
#pragma once
#endif // _MSC_VER > 1000
#ifndef __AFXWIN_H__
    #error include 'stdafx.h' before including this file for PCH
#endif

#include "resource.h"        // main symbols

/////////////////////////////////////////////////////////////////////
// CEx17aApp:
// See ex17a.cpp for the implementation of this class
//

class CEx17aApp : public CWinApp
{
public:
    CEx17aApp();

// Overrides
    // ClassWizard generated virtual function overrides
    //{{AFX_VIRTUAL(CEx17aApp)
    public:
    virtual BOOL InitInstance();
    //}}AFX_VIRTUAL
```

Figure 17-4.   *(continued)*
The CEx17aApp *class listing.*

```
// Implementation

    //{{AFX_MSG(CEx17aApp)
    afx_msg void OnAppAbout();
        // NOTE - the ClassWizard will add and remove     →
                    member functions here.
        //      DO NOT EDIT what you see in these blocks   →
                    of generated code !
    //}}AFX_MSG
    DECLARE_MESSAGE_MAP()
};


/////////////////////////////////////////////////////////////////////
/

//{{AFX_INSERT_LOCATION}}
// Microsoft Visual C++ will insert additional declarations
//  immediately before the previous line.

#endif // !defined(AFX_EX17A_H__1A036EA3_821A_        →
                    11D0_8FE2_00C04FC2A0C2__INCLUDED_)
```

EX17A.CPP

```
// ex17a.cpp : Defines the class behaviors for the application.
//

#include "stdafx.h"
#include "ex17a.h"

#include "MainFrm.h"
#include "StuDoc.h"
#include "StuView.h"

#ifdef _DEBUG
#define new DEBUG_NEW
#undef THIS_FILE
static char THIS_FILE[] = __FILE__;
#endif

/////////////////////////////////////////////////////////////////////
// CEx17aApp

BEGIN_MESSAGE_MAP(CEx17aApp, CWinApp)
    //{{AFX_MSG_MAP(CEx17aApp)
```

(continued)

431

Figure 17-4. *continued*

```
    ON_COMMAND(ID_APP_ABOUT, OnAppAbout)
        // NOTE -
 the ClassWizard will add and remove mapping macros here.
        //      DO NOT EDIT what you see in these blocks of generated code!
    //}}AFX_MSG_MAP
    // Standard file based document commands
    ON_COMMAND(ID_FILE_NEW, CWinApp::OnFileNew)
    ON_COMMAND(ID_FILE_OPEN, CWinApp::OnFileOpen)
END_MESSAGE_MAP()

/////////////////////////////////////////////////////////////////////////////
// CEx17aApp construction

CEx17aApp::CEx17aApp()
{
    // TODO: add construction code here,
    // Place all significant initialization in InitInstance
}


/////////////////////////////////////////////////////////////////////////////
// The one and only CEx17aApp object

CEx17aApp theApp;
/////////////////////////////////////////////////////////////////////////////
// CEx17aApp initialization

BOOL CEx17aApp::InitInstance()
{
    AfxEnableControlContainer();

    // Standard initialization
    // If you are not using these features and wish to reduce the size
    //  of your final executable, you should remove from the following
    //  the specific initialization routines you do not need.

#ifdef _AFXDLL
    Enable3dControls();         // Call this when using MFC in a shared DLL
#else
    Enable3dControlsStatic(); // Call this when linking to MFC statically
#endif

    // Change the registry key under which our settings are stored.
    // You should modify this string to be something appropriate
    // such as the name of your company or organization.
    SetRegistryKey(_T("Local AppWizard-Generated Applications"));
```

```
        LoadStdProfileSettings();  // Load standard INI file options
                                   //   (including MRU)

        // Register the application's document templates.
        //  Document templates serve as the connection between
        //  documents, frame windows and views.

        CSingleDocTemplate* pDocTemplate;
        pDocTemplate = new CSingleDocTemplate(
            IDR_MAINFRAME,
            RUNTIME_CLASS(CStudentDoc),
            RUNTIME_CLASS(CMainFrame),          // main SDI frame window
            RUNTIME_CLASS(CStudentView));
        AddDocTemplate(pDocTemplate);

        // Enable DDE Execute open
        EnableShellOpen();
        RegisterShellFileTypes(TRUE);
        // Parse command line for standard shell commands, DDE, file open
        CCommandLineInfo cmdInfo;
        ParseCommandLine(cmdInfo);

        // Dispatch commands specified on the command line
        if (!ProcessShellCommand(cmdInfo))
            return FALSE;

        // The one and only window has been initialized,
        //   so show and update it.
        m_pMainWnd->ShowWindow(SW_SHOW);
        m_pMainWnd->UpdateWindow();

        // Enable drag/drop open
        m_pMainWnd->DragAcceptFiles();

        return TRUE;
    }


/////////////////////////////////////////////////////////////////////
// CAboutDlg dialog used for App About

class CAboutDlg : public CDialog
{
public:
    CAboutDlg();

// Dialog Data
    //{{AFX_DATA(CAboutDlg)
```

(continued)

Figure 17-4. *continued*

```
    enum { IDD = IDD_ABOUTBOX };
    //}}AFX_DATA

    // ClassWizard generated virtual function overrides
    //{{AFX_VIRTUAL(CAboutDlg)
    protected:
    virtual void DoDataExchange(CDataExchange* pDX); // DDX/DDV support
    //}}AFX_VIRTUAL

// Implementation
protected:
    //{{AFX_MSG(CAboutDlg)
        // No message handlers
    //}}AFX_MSG
    DECLARE_MESSAGE_MAP()
};
CAboutDlg::CAboutDlg() : CDialog(CAboutDlg::IDD)
{
    //{{AFX_DATA_INIT(CAboutDlg)
    //}}AFX_DATA_INIT
}

void CAboutDlg::DoDataExchange(CDataExchange* pDX)
{
    CDialog::DoDataExchange(pDX);
    //{{AFX_DATA_MAP(CAboutDlg)
    //}}AFX_DATA_MAP
}

BEGIN_MESSAGE_MAP(CAboutDlg, CDialog)
    //{{AFX_MSG_MAP(CAboutDlg)
        // No message handlers
    //}}AFX_MSG_MAP
END_MESSAGE_MAP()

// App command to run the dialog
void CEx17aApp::OnAppAbout()
{
    CAboutDlg aboutDlg;
    aboutDlg.DoModal();
}


/////////////////////////////////////////////////////////////////////
// CEx17aApp commands
```

CMainFrame

The main frame window class code, shown in Figure 17-5, is almost unchanged from the code that AppWizard generated. The overridden *ActivateFrame* function and the *WM_DROPFILES* handler exist solely for trace purposes.

MAINFRM.H

```
// MainFrm.h : interface of the CMainFrame class
//
/////////////////////////////////////////////////////////////////////

#if !defined(AFX_MAINFRM_H__1A036EA7_821A_11D0_8FE2_00C04FC2A0C2__INCLUDED_)
#define AFX_MAINFRM_H__1A036EA7_821A_11D0_8FE2_00C04FC2A0C2__INCLUDED_
#if _MSC_VER >= 1000
#pragma once
#endif // _MSC_VER >= 1000

class CMainFrame : public CFrameWnd
{
protected: // create from serialization only
    CMainFrame();
    DECLARE_DYNCREATE(CMainFrame)

// Attributes
public:

// Operations
public:

// Overrides
    // ClassWizard generated virtual function overrides
    //{{AFX_VIRTUAL(CMainFrame)
    public:
    virtual BOOL PreCreateWindow(CREATESTRUCT& cs);
    virtual void ActivateFrame(int nCmdShow = -1);
    //}}AFX_VIRTUAL

// Implementation
public:
    virtual ~CMainFrame();
#ifdef _DEBUG
    virtual void AssertValid() const;
    virtual void Dump(CDumpContext& dc) const;
#endif
```

Figure 17-5. *(continued)*
The CMainFrame *class listing.*

Figure 17-5. *continued*

```
protected:  // control bar embedded members
    CStatusBar   m_wndStatusBar;
    CToolBar     m_wndToolBar;

// Generated message map functions
protected:
    //{{AFX_MSG(CMainFrame)
    afx_msg int OnCreate(LPCREATESTRUCT lpCreateStruct);
    afx_msg void OnDropFiles(HDROP hDropInfo);
    //}}AFX_MSG
    DECLARE_MESSAGE_MAP()
};
////////////////////////////////////////////////////////////////////////

//{{AFX_INSERT_LOCATION}}
// Microsoft Visual C++ will insert additional declarations
//   immediately before the previous line.

#endif // !defined(AFX_MAINFRM_H__1A036EA7_821A_         ➞
                   11D0_8FE2_00C04FC2A0C2__INCLUDED_)
```

MAINFRM.CPP

```
// MainFrm.cpp : implementation of the CMainFrame class
//

#include "stdafx.h"
#include "ex17a.h"

#include "MainFrm.h"

#ifdef _DEBUG
#define new DEBUG_NEW
#undef THIS_FILE
static char THIS_FILE[] = __FILE__;
#endif


////////////////////////////////////////////////////////////////////////
// CMainFrame

IMPLEMENT_DYNCREATE(CMainFrame, CFrameWnd)

BEGIN_MESSAGE_MAP(CMainFrame, CFrameWnd)
    //{{AFX_MSG_MAP(CMainFrame)
    ON_WM_CREATE()
    ON_WM_DROPFILES()
```

```
    //}}AFX_MSG_MAP
END_MESSAGE_MAP()

static UINT indicators[] =
{
    ID_SEPARATOR,              // status line indicator
    ID_INDICATOR_CAPS,
    ID_INDICATOR_NUM,
    ID_INDICATOR_SCRL,
};
/////////////////////////////////////////////////////////////////////
// CMainFrame construction/destruction

CMainFrame::CMainFrame()
{
    // TODO: add member initialization code here

}

CMainFrame::~CMainFrame()
{
}

int CMainFrame::OnCreate(LPCREATESTRUCT lpCreateStruct)
{
    if (CFrameWnd::OnCreate(lpCreateStruct) == -1)
        return -1;

    if (!m_wndToolBar.Create(this) ||
        !m_wndToolBar.LoadToolBar(IDR_MAINFRAME))
    {
        TRACE0("Failed to create toolbar\n");
        return -1;      // fail to create
    }

    if (!m_wndStatusBar.Create(this) ||
        !m_wndStatusBar.SetIndicators(indicators,
          sizeof(indicators)/sizeof(UINT)))
    {
        TRACE0("Failed to create status bar\n");
        return -1;      // fail to create
    }

    // TODO: Remove this if you don't want tool tips
    //   or a resizeable toolbar
    m_wndToolBar.SetBarStyle(m_wndToolBar.GetBarStyle() |
        CBRS_TOOLTIPS | CBRS_FLYBY | CBRS_SIZE_DYNAMIC);
```

(continued)

Figure 17-5. *continued*

```
    // TODO: Delete these three lines if you don't want the toolbar to
    //   be dockable
    m_wndToolBar.EnableDocking(CBRS_ALIGN_ANY);
    EnableDocking(CBRS_ALIGN_ANY);

DockControlBar(&m_wndToolBar);
    return 0;
}

BOOL CMainFrame::PreCreateWindow(CREATESTRUCT& cs)
{
    // TODO: Modify the Window class or styles here by modifying
    //   the CREATESTRUCT cs

    return CFrameWnd::PreCreateWindow(cs);
}

/////////////////////////////////////////////////////////////////////////////
// CMainFrame diagnostics

#ifdef _DEBUG
void CMainFrame::AssertValid() const
{
    CFrameWnd::AssertValid();
}

void CMainFrame::Dump(CDumpContext& dc) const
{
    CFrameWnd::Dump(dc);
}

#endif //_DEBUG

/////////////////////////////////////////////////////////////////////////////
// CMainFrame message handlers
void CMainFrame::ActivateFrame(int nCmdShow)
{
    TRACE("Entering CMainFrame::ActivateFrame\n");
    CFrameWnd::ActivateFrame(nCmdShow);
}

void CMainFrame::OnDropFiles(HDROP hDropInfo)
{
    TRACE("Entering CMainFrame::OnDropFiles\n");
    CFrameWnd::OnDropFiles(hDropInfo);
}
```

CStudentDoc

The *CStudentDoc* class is the same as the *CStudentDoc* class from the previous chapter (shown in Figure 16-4) except for four functions: *Serialize, Delete-Contents, OnOpenDocument,* and *OnUpdateFileSave.*

Serialize

One line has been added to the AppWizard-generated function to serialize the document's student list, as shown here:

```
/////////////////////////////////////////////////////////////////////////////
// CStudentDoc serialization

void CStudentDoc::Serialize(CArchive& ar)
{
    TRACE("Entering CStudentDoc::Serialize\n");
    if (ar.IsStoring())
    {
        // TODO: add storing code here
    }
    else
    {
        // TODO: add loading code here
    }
    m_studentList.Serialize(ar);
}
```

DeleteContents

The *Dump* statement is replaced by a simple *TRACE* statement. Here is the modified code:

```
void CStudentDoc::DeleteContents()
{
    TRACE("Entering CStudentDoc::DeleteContents\n");
    while (m_studentList.GetHeadPosition()) {
        delete m_studentList.RemoveHead();
    }
}
```

OnOpenDocument

This virtual function is overridden only for the purpose of displaying a *TRACE* message, as shown on the following page.

```
BOOL CStudentDoc::OnOpenDocument(LPCTSTR lpszPathName)
{
    TRACE("Entering CStudentDoc::OnOpenDocument\n");
    if (!CDocument::OnOpenDocument(lpszPathName))
        return FALSE;

    // TODO: Add your specialized creation code here

    return TRUE;
}
```

OnUpdateFileSave

This message map function grays the File Save toolbar button when the document is in the unmodified state. The view controls this state by calling the document's *SetModifiedFlag* function, as shown here:

```
void CStudentDoc::OnUpdateFileSave(CCmdUI* pCmdUI)
{
    // Disable disk toolbar button if file is not modified
    pCmdUI->Enable(IsModified());
}
```

CStudentView

The code for the *CStudentView* class comes from the previous chapter. Figure 16-5 beginning on page 401 shows the code.

Testing the EX17A Application

Build the program and start it from the debugger, and then test it by typing some data and saving it on disk with the filename Test.17a. (You don't need to type the *.17a.*)

Exit the program, and then restart it and open the file you saved. Did the data you typed come back? Take a look at the Debug window and observe the sequence of function calls. Is the following sequence produced when you start the application and open the file?

```
Entering CStudentDoc constructor
Entering CStudentView constructor
Entering CStudentDoc::OnNewDocument
Entering CStudentDoc::DeleteContents
Entering CStudentView::OnInitialUpdate
Entering CStudentView::OnUpdate
Entering CMainFrame::ActivateFrame
Entering CStudentDoc::OnOpenDocument
```

```
Entering CStudentDoc::DeleteContents
Entering CStudentDoc::Serialize
Entering CStudent::Serialize
Entering CStudent::Serialize
Entering CStudent::Serialize
Entering CStudentView::OnInitialUpdate
Entering CStudentView::OnUpdate
Entering CMainFrame::ActivateFrame
```

Explorer Launch and Drag and Drop

In the past, PC users were accustomed to starting up a program and then selecting a disk file (sometimes called a document) that contained data the program understood. Many MS-DOS–based programs worked this way. The old Windows Program Manager improved things by allowing the user to double-click on a program icon instead of typing a program name. Meanwhile, Apple Macintosh users were double-clicking on a document icon; the Macintosh operating system figured out which program to run.

While Windows Explorer still lets users double-click on a program, it also lets users double-click on a document icon to run the document's program. But how does Explorer know which program to run? Explorer uses the Windows Registry to make the connection between document and program. The link starts with the filename extension that you typed into AppWizard, but as you'll see, there's more to it than that. Once the association is made, users can launch your program by double-clicking on its document icon or by dragging the icon from Explorer to a running instance of your program. In addition, users can drag the icon to a printer, and your program will print it.

Program Registration

In Chapter 15, you saw how MFC applications store data in the Windows Registry by calling *SetRegistryKey* from the *InitInstance* function. Independent of this *SetRegistryKey* call, your program can write file association information in a different part of the Registry on startup. To activate this feature, you must type in the filename extension when you create the application with AppWizard. (Use the Advanced button in AppWizard Step 4.) After you do that, AppWizard adds the extension as a substring in your template string and adds the following line in your *InitInstance* function:

```
RegisterShellFileTypes(TRUE);
```

Now your program adds two items to the Registry. Under the HKEY-_CLASSES_ROOT top-level key, it adds a subkey and a data string as shown here (for the EX17A example):

.17A = Ex17a.Document

The data item is the file type ID that AppWizard has chosen for you. Ex17a.Document, in turn, is the key for finding the program itself. The Registry entries for Ex17a.Document, also beneath HKEY_CLASSES_ROOT, are shown here.

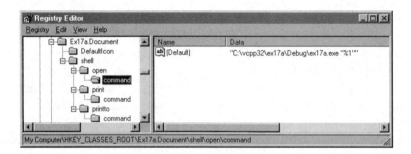

Notice that the Registry contains the full pathname of the EX17A program. Now Explorer can use the Registry to navigate from the extension to the file type ID to the actual program itself. After the extension is registered, Explorer finds the document's icon and displays it next to the filename, as shown here.

test.17a

Double-Clicking on a Document

When the user double-clicks on a document icon, Explorer executes the associated SDI program, passing in the selected filename on the command line. You might notice that AppWizard generates a call to *EnableShellOpen* in the application class *InitInstance* function. This supports execution via DDE message, the technique used by the File Manager in Windows NT 3.51. Explorer can launch your SDI application without this call.

Enabling Drag and Drop

If you want your already-running program to open files dragged from Explorer, you must call the *CWnd* function *DragAcceptFiles* for the application's main frame window. The application object's public data member *m_pMainWnd* points to the *CFrameWnd* (or *CMDIFrameWnd*) object. When the user drops a file anywhere inside the frame window, the window receives a WM_DROP-FILES message, which triggers a call to *FrameWnd::OnDropFiles*. The following line in *InitInstance*, generated by AppWizard, enables drag and drop:

```
m_pMainWnd->DragAcceptFiles();
```

Program Startup Parameters

When you choose Run from the Start menu, or when you double-click the program directly in Explorer, there is no command-line parameter. The *Init-Instance* function processes the command line with calls to *ParseCommandLine* and *ProcessShellCommand*. If the command line contains something that looks like a filename, the program immediately loads that file. Thus, you create a Windows shortcut that can run your program with a specific document file.

Experimenting with Explorer Launch and Drag and Drop

Once you have built EX17A, you can try running it from Explorer. You must execute the program directly, however, in order to write the initial entries in the Registry. Be sure that you've saved at least one 17A file to disk, and then exit EX17A. Start Explorer, and then open the \vcpp32\ex17a directory. Double-click on one of the 17A files in the panel on the right. Your program should start with the selected file loaded. Now, with both EX17A and Explorer open on the desktop, try dragging another file from Explorer to the EX17A window. The program should open the new file just as if you had chosen File Open from the EX17A menu.

You might also want to look at the EX17A entries in the Registry. Run the Regedit program (possibly named Regedt32 in Windows NT), and expand the HKEY_CLASSES_ROOT key. Look under ".17A" and "Ex17a.Document." Also expand the HKEY_CURRENT_USER (or HKEY_USERS\.DEFAULT) key, and look under "Software." You should see a Recent File List under the subkey ex17a. The EX17A program calls *SetRegistryKey* with the string *"Local AppWizard-Generated Applications"*, so the program name goes beneath the ex17a subkey.

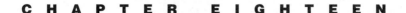

Reading and Writing Documents—MDI Applications

This chapter introduces the Microsoft Foundation Class (MFC) Library version 6.0 Multiple Document Interface (MDI) application and demonstrates how it reads and writes its document files. The MDI application appears to be the preferred MFC library program style. It's the AppWizard default, and most of the sample programs that come with Microsoft Visual C++ are MDI applications.

In this chapter, you'll learn the similarities and differences between Single Document Interface (SDI) and MDI applications, and you'll learn how to convert an SDI application to an MDI application. Be sure you thoroughly understand the SDI application described in Chapter 17 before you attack the MDI application in this chapter.

The MDI Application

Before you look at the MFC library code for MDI applications, you should be familiar with the operation of Microsoft Windows MDI programs. Take a close look at Visual C++ now. It's an MDI application whose "multiple documents" are program source code files. Visual C++ is not the most typical MDI application, however, because it collects its documents into projects. It's better to examine Microsoft Word or, better yet, a real MFC library MDI application—the kind that AppWizard generates.

A Typical MDI Application, MFC Style

This chapter's example, EX18A, is an MDI version of EX17A. Run the EX17A example to see an illustration of the SDI version after the user has selected a file. Now look at the MDI equivalent, as shown in Figure 18-1 on the following page.

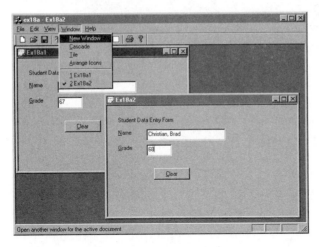

Figure 18-1.
The EX18A application with two files open and the Window menu shown.

The user has two separate document files open, each in a separate MDI child window, but only one child window is active—the lower window, which lies on top of the other child window. The application has only one menu and one toolbar, and all commands are routed to the active child window. The main window's title bar reflects the name of the active child window's document file.

The child window's minimize box allows the user to reduce the child window to an icon in the main window. The application's Window menu (shown in Figure 18-1) lets the user control the presentation through the following items.

Menu Item	Action
New Window	Opens as an additional child window for the selected document
Cascade	Arranges the existing windows in an overlapped pattern
Tile	Arranges the existing windows in a nonoverlapped, tiled pattern
Arrange Icons	Arranges minimized windows in the frame window
(document names)	Selects the corresponding child window and brings it to the top

If the user closes both child windows (and opens the File menu), the application looks like Figure 18-2.

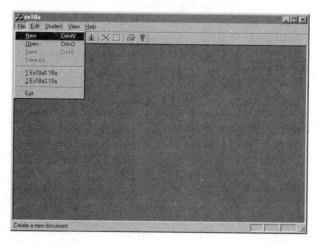

Figure 18-2.
EX18A with no child windows.

The File menu is different, most toolbar buttons are disabled, and the window caption does not show a filename. The only choices the user has are to start a new document or to open an existing document from disk.

Figure 18-3 shows the application when it first starts up and a new document is created. The single child window has been maximized.

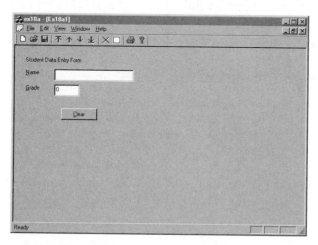

Figure 18-3.
EX18A with initial child window.

The single, empty child window has the default document name Ex18a1. This name is based on the Doc Type Name (Ex18a) that you selected in the Advanced Options dialog after clicking the Advanced button in Step 4 of App-Wizard. The first new file is Ex18a1, the second is Ex18a2, and so forth. The user normally chooses a different name when saving the document.

An MFC library MDI application, like many commercial MDI applications, starts up with a new, empty document. (Visual C++ is an exception.) If you want your application to start up with a blank frame, you can modify the argument to the *ProcessShellCommand* call in the application class file, as shown in example EX18A.

For Win32 Programmers

Starting with version 3.0, Windows directly supports MDI applications. The MFC library builds on this Windows support to create an MDI environment that parallels the SDI environment. In a Win32 MDI application, a main application frame window contains the menu and a single <u>client</u> <u>window</u>. The client window manages various child windows that correspond to documents. The MDI client window has its own preregistered window class (not to be confused with a C++ class) with a procedure that handles special messages such as WM_MDI-CASCADE and WM_MDITILE. An MDI child window procedure is similar to the window procedure for an SDI main window.

In the MFC library, the *CMDIFrameWnd* class encapsulates the functions of both the main frame window and the MDI client window. This class has message handlers for all the Windows MDI messages and thus can manage its child windows, which are represented by objects of class *CMDIChildWnd*.

The MDI Application Object

You're probably wondering how an MDI application works and what code makes it different from an SDI application. Actually, the startup sequences are pretty much the same. An application object of a class derived from class *CWinApp* has an overridden *InitInstance* member function. This *InitInstance* function is somewhat different from the SDI *InitInstance* function, starting with the call to *AddDocTemplate*.

The MDI Document Template Class

The MDI template construction call in *InitInstance* looks like this:

```
CMultiDocTemplate* pDocTemplate;
pDocTemplate = new CMultiDocTemplate(
    IDR_EX18ATYPE,
    RUNTIME_CLASS(CStudentDoc),
    RUNTIME_CLASS(CChildFrame), // custom MDI child frame
    RUNTIME_CLASS(CStudentView));
AddDocTemplate(pDocTemplate);
```

Unlike the SDI application you saw in Chapter 17, an MDI application can use multiple document types and allows the simultaneous existence of more than one document object. This is the essence of the MDI application.

The single *AddDocTemplate* call shown above permits the MDI application to support multiple child windows, each connected to a document object and a view object. It's also possible to have several child windows (and corresponding view objects) connected to the same document object. In this chapter, we'll start with only one view class and one document class. You'll see multiple view classes and multiple document classes in Chapter 20.

> NOTE: When your application is running, the document template object maintains a list of active document objects that were created from the template. The *CMultiDocTemplate* member functions *GetFirstDocPosition* and *GetNextDoc* allow you to iterate through the list. Use *CDocument::GetDocTemplate* to navigate from a document to its template.

The MDI Frame Window and the MDI Child Window

The SDI examples had only one frame window class and only one frame window object. For SDI applications, AppWizard generated a class named *CMainFrame*, which was derived from the class *CFrameWnd*. An MDI application has two frame window classes and many frame objects, as shown in the table on the next page. The MDI frame–view window relationship is shown in Figure 18-4 on the following page.

Base Class	AppWizard-Generated Class	Number of Objects	Menu and Control Bars	Contains a View	Object Constructed
CMDIFrameWnd	*CMainFrame*	1 only	Yes	No	In application class's *InitInstance* function
CMDIChildWnd	*CChildFrame*	1 per child window	No	Yes	By application framework when a new child window is opened

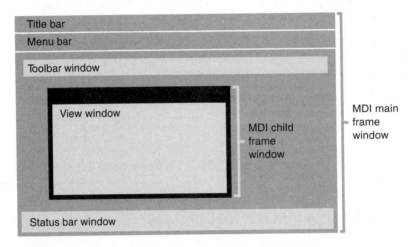

Figure 18-4.
The MDI frame–view window relationship.

In an SDI application, the *CMainFrame* object frames the application <u>and</u> contains the view object. In an MDI application, the two roles are separated. Now the *CMainFrame* object is explicitly constructed in *InitInstance*, and the *CChildFrame* object contains the view. AppWizard generates the following code:

```
CMainFrame* pMainFrame = new CMainFrame;
if (!pMainFrame->LoadFrame(IDR_MAINFRAME))
    return FALSE;
m_pMainWnd = pMainFrame;
```

(code calls ProcessShellCommand *to create child frame)*

```
pMainFrame->ShowWindow(m_nCmdShow);
pMainFrame->UpdateWindow();
```

The application framework can create the *CChildFrame* objects dynamically because the *CChildFrame* runtime class pointer is passed to the *CMultiDoc-Template* constructor.

NOTE: The MDI *InitInstance* function sets the *CWinApp* data member *m_pMainWnd* to point to the application's main frame window. This means you can access *m_pMainWnd* through the global *AfxGetApp* function anytime you need to get your application's main frame window.

The Main Frame and Document Template Resources

An MDI application (EX18A, as described later in this chapter) has two separate string and menu resources, identified by the *IDR_MAINFRAME* and *IDR_EX18ATYPE* constants. The first resource set goes with the empty main frame window; the second set goes with the occupied main frame window. Here are the two string resources with substrings broken out:

```
IDR_MAINFRAME
    "ex18a"                        // application window caption

IDR_EX18ATYPE
    "\n"                           // (not used)
    "Ex18a\n"                      // root for default document name
    "Ex18a\n"                      // document type name
    "Ex18a Files (*.18a)\n"        // document type description and filter
    ".18a\n"                       // extension for documents of this type
    "Ex18a.Document\n"             // Registry file type ID
    "Ex18a Document"               // Registry file type description
```

NOTE: The resource compiler won't accept the string concatenations as shown above. If you examine the ex18a.rc file, you'll see the substrings combined in one long string.

The application window caption comes from the *IDR_MAINFRAME* string. When a document is open, the document filename is appended. The last two substrings in the *IDR_EX18ATYPE* string support embedded launch and drag and drop.

Creating an Empty Document—
The *CWinApp::OnFileNew* Function

The MDI *InitInstance* function calls *OnFileNew* (through *ProcessShellCommand*), as did the SDI *InitInstance* function. This time, however, the main frame window has already been created. *OnFileNew*, through a call to the *CMultiDoc-Template* function *OpenDocumentFile*, now does the following:

1. Constructs a document object but does not attempt to read data from disk.

2. Constructs a child frame window object (of class *CChildFrame*). Also creates the child frame window but does not show it. In the main frame window, the *IDR_EX18ATYPE* menu replaces the *IDR_MAIN-FRAME* menu. *IDR_EX18ATYPE* also identifies an icon resource that is used when the child window is minimized within the frame.

3. Constructs a view object. Also creates the view window but does not show it.

4. Establishes connections among the document, the main frame, and view objects. Do not confuse these object connections with the class associations established by the call to *AddDocTemplate*.

5. Calls the virtual *OnNewDocument* member function for the document object.

6. Calls the virtual *OnInitialUpdate* member function for the view object.

7. Calls the virtual *ActivateFrame* member function for the child frame object to show the frame window and the view window.

The *OnFileNew* function is also called in response to the File New menu command. In an MDI application, *OnFileNew* performs exactly the same steps as it does when called from *InitInstance*.

NOTE: Some functions listed above are not called directly by *OpenDocumentFile* but are called indirectly through the application framework.

Creating an Additional View for an Existing Document

If you choose the New Window command from the Window menu, the application framework opens a new child window that is linked to the currently selected document. The associated *CMDIFrameWnd* function, *OnWindowNew*, does the following:

1. Constructs a child frame object (of class *CChildFrame*). Also creates the child frame window but does not show it.

2. Constructs a view object. Also creates the view window but does not show it.

3. Establishes connections between the new view object and the existing document and main frame objects.

4. Calls the virtual *OnInitialUpdate* member function for the view object.

5. Calls the virtual *ActivateFrame* member function for the child frame object to show the frame window and the view window.

Loading and Storing Documents

In MDI applications, documents are loaded and stored the same way as in SDI applications but with two important differences: a new document object is constructed each time a document file is loaded from disk, and the document object is destroyed when the child window is closed. Don't worry about clearing a document's contents before loading—but override the *CDocument::Delete-Contents* function anyway to make the class portable to the SDI environment.

Multiple Document Templates

An MDI application can support multiple document templates through multiple calls to the *AddDocTemplate* function. Each template can specify a different combination of document, view, and MDI child frame classes. When the user chooses New from the File menu of an application with multiple templates, the application framework displays a list box that allows the user to select a template by name as specified in the string resource (document type substring). Multiple *AddDocTemplate* calls are not supported in SDI applications because the document, view, and frame objects are constructed once for the life of the application.

> **N O T E :** When your application is running, the application object keeps a list of active document template objects. The *CWinApp* member functions *GetFirstDocTemplatePosition* and *GetNextDocTemplate* allow you to iterate through the list of templates. These functions, together with the *CDocTemplate* member functions *GetFirstDocPosition* and *GetNextDoc*, allow you to access all of the application's document objects.

If you don't want the template list box, you can edit the File menu to add a New menu item for each document type. Code the command message handlers as shown on the next page, using the document type substring from each template.

```
void CMyApp::OnFileNewStudent()
{
    OpenNewDocument("Studnt");
}
void CMyApp::OnFileNewTeacher()
{
    OpenNewDocument("Teachr");
}
```

Then add the *OpenNewDocument* helper function as follows:

```
BOOL CMyApp::OpenNewDocument(const CString& strTarget)
{
    CString strDocName;
    CDocTemplate* pSelectedTemplate;
    POSITION pos = GetFirstDocTemplatePosition();
    while (pos != NULL) {
        pSelectedTemplate = (CDocTemplate*) GetNextDocTemplate(pos);
        ASSERT(pSelectedTemplate != NULL);
        ASSERT(pSelectedTemplate->IsKindOf(
            RUNTIME_CLASS(CDocTemplate)));
        pSelectedTemplate->GetDocString(strDocName,
            CDocTemplate::docName);
        if (strDocName == strTarget) { // from template's
                                       //  string resource
            pSelectedTemplate->OpenDocumentFile(NULL);
            return TRUE;
        }
    }
    return FALSE;
}
```

Explorer Launch and Drag and Drop

When you double-click on a document icon for an MDI application in Windows Explorer, the application launches only if it was not running already; otherwise, a new child window opens in the running application for the document you selected. The *EnableShellOpen* call in the application class *InitInstance* function is necessary for this to work. Drag and drop works much the same way in an MDI application as it does in an SDI application. If you drag a file from Windows Explorer to your MDI main frame window, the program opens a new child frame (with associated document and view) just as if you'd chosen the File Open command. As with SDI applications, you must use the AppWizard Step 4 Advanced button to specify the filename extension.

The EX18A Example

This example is the MDI version of the EX17A example from the previous chapter. It uses the same document and view class code and the same resources (except the program name). The application code and main frame class code are different, however. All the new code is listed here, including the code that App-Wizard generates. A list of the files and classes in the EX18A example are shown in the table below.

Header File	Source Code File	Class	Description
ex18a.h	ex18a.cpp	*CEx18aApp*	Application class (from AppWizard)
		CAboutDlg	About dialog
MainFrm.h	MainFrm.cpp	*CMainFrame*	MDI main frame
ChildFrm.h	ChildFrm.cpp	*CChildFrame*	MDI child frame
StuDoc.h	StuDoc.cpp	*CStudentDoc*	Student document (from EX17A)
StuView.h	StuView.cpp	*CStudentView*	Student form view (from EX16B)
Student.h	Student.cpp	*CStudent*	Student record (from EX17A)
StdAfx.h	StdAfx.h		Precompiled headers (with afxtempl.h included)

CEx18aApp

In the *CEx18aApp* source code listing, the *OpenDocumentFile* member function is overridden only for the purpose of inserting a *TRACE* statement. Also, a few lines have been added before the *ProcessShellCommand* call in *Init-Instance*. They check the argument to *ProcessShellCommand* and change it if necessary to prevent the creation of any empty document window on startup. Figure 18-5, which begins on the following page, shows the source code.

EX18A.H

```
// ex18a.h : main header file for the EX18A application
//

#if !defined(AFX_EX18A_H__7B5FE267_85E9_11D0_8FE3_00C04FC2A0C2__INCLUDED_)
#define AFX_EX18A_H__7B5FE267_85E9_11D0_8FE3_00C04FC2A0C2__INCLUDED_

#if _MSC_VER > 1000
#pragma once
#endif // _MSC_VER > 1000

#ifndef __AFXWIN_H__
    #error include 'stdafx.h' before including this file for PCH
#endif
#include "resource.h"        // main symbols


/////////////////////////////////////////////////////////////////////////
// CEx18aApp:
// See ex18a.cpp for the implementation of this class
//

class CEx18aApp : public CWinApp
{
public:
    CEx18aApp();

// Overrides
    // ClassWizard generated virtual function overrides
    //{{AFX_VIRTUAL(CEx18aApp)
    public:
    virtual BOOL InitInstance();
    virtual CDocument* OpenDocumentFile(LPCTSTR lpszFileName);
    //}}AFX_VIRTUAL

// Implementation

    //{{AFX_MSG(CEx18aApp)
    afx_msg void OnAppAbout();
        // NOTE - the ClassWizard will add and remove          →
                member functions here.
        //    DO NOT EDIT what you see in these               →
                blocks of generated code !
    //}}AFX_MSG
```

Figure 18-5.   *(continued)*

The CEx18aApp *source code listing.*

```
    DECLARE_MESSAGE_MAP()
};


//////////////////////////////////////////////////////////////////

//{{AFX_INSERT_LOCATION}}
// Microsoft Visual C++ will insert additional declarations
//   immediately before the previous line.

#endif // !defined(AFX_EX18A_H__7B5FE267_85E9_          ➞
                   11D0_8FE3_00C04FC2A0C2__INCLUDED_)
```

EX18A.CPP

```
// ex18a.cpp : Defines the class behaviors for the application.
//

#include "stdafx.h"
#include "ex18a.h"

#include "MainFrm.h"
#include "ChildFrm.h"
#include "StuDoc.h"
#include "StuView.h"

#ifdef _DEBUG
#define new DEBUG_NEW
#undef THIS_FILE
static char THIS_FILE[] = __FILE__;
#endif


//////////////////////////////////////////////////////////////////
// CEx18aApp

BEGIN_MESSAGE_MAP(CEx18aApp, CWinApp)
    //{{AFX_MSG_MAP(CEx18aApp)
    ON_COMMAND(ID_APP_ABOUT, OnAppAbout)
        // NOTE - the ClassWizard will add and remove        ➞
                 mapping macros here.
        //     DO NOT EDIT what you see in these            ➞
                 blocks of generated code!
    //}}AFX_MSG_MAP
    // Standard file based document commands
    ON_COMMAND(ID_FILE_NEW, CWinApp::OnFileNew)
    ON_COMMAND(ID_FILE_OPEN, CWinApp::OnFileOpen)
END_MESSAGE_MAP()
```

(continued)

Figure 18-5. *continued*

```
/////////////////////////////////////////////////////////////////////////
// CEx18aApp construction

CEx18aApp::CEx18aApp()
{
    // TODO: add construction code here,
    // Place all significant initialization in InitInstance
}


/////////////////////////////////////////////////////////////////////////
// The one and only CEx18aApp object

CEx18aApp theApp;


/////////////////////////////////////////////////////////////////////////
// CEx18aApp initialization

BOOL CEx18aApp::InitInstance()
{
    AfxEnableControlContainer();

    // Standard initialization
    // If you are not using these features and wish to reduce the size
    //  of your final executable, you should remove from the following
    //  the specific initialization routines you do not need.

#ifdef _AFXDLL
    Enable3dControls();        // Call this when using MFC in a shared DLL
#else
    Enable3dControlsStatic();        // Call this when linking to MFC
                                     //  statically
#endif

    // Change the registry key under which our settings are stored.
    // TODO: You should modify this string to be something appropriate
    // such as the name of your company or organization.
    SetRegistryKey(_T("Local AppWizard-Generated Applications"));
    LoadStdProfileSettings();  // Load standard INI file options
                               //  (including MRU)
    // Register the application's document templates.  Document
    //  templates serve as the connection between documents, frame
    //  windows and views.

    CMultiDocTemplate* pDocTemplate;
```

```
    pDocTemplate = new CMultiDocTemplate(
        IDR_EX18ATYPE,
        RUNTIME_CLASS(CStudentDoc),
        RUNTIME_CLASS(CChildFrame), // custom MDI child frame
        RUNTIME_CLASS(CStudentView));
    AddDocTemplate(pDocTemplate);

    // create main MDI Frame window
    CMainFrame* pMainFrame = new CMainFrame;
    if (!pMainFrame->LoadFrame(IDR_MAINFRAME))
        return FALSE;
    m_pMainWnd = pMainFrame;

    // Enable drag/drop open
    m_pMainWnd->DragAcceptFiles();

    // Enable DDE Execute open
    EnableShellOpen();
    RegisterShellFileTypes(TRUE);

    // Parse command line for standard shell commands, DDE, file open
    CCommandLineInfo cmdInfo;
    ParseCommandLine(cmdInfo);

    // no empty document window on startup
    if (cmdInfo.m_nShellCommand == CCommandLineInfo::FileNew) {
        cmdInfo.m_nShellCommand = CCommandLineInfo::FileNothing;
    }

    // Dispatch commands specified on the command line
    if (!ProcessShellCommand(cmdInfo))
        return FALSE;

    // The main window has been initialized, so show and update it.
    pMainFrame->ShowWindow(m_nCmdShow);
    pMainFrame->UpdateWindow();

    return TRUE;
}
//////////////////////////////////////////////////////////////////
// CAboutDlg dialog used for App About

class CAboutDlg : public CDialog
{
public:
    CAboutDlg();
```

(continued)

459

Figure 18-5. *continued*

```
// Dialog Data
    //{{AFX_DATA(CAboutDlg)
    enum { IDD = IDD_ABOUTBOX };
    //}}AFX_DATA
    // ClassWizard generated virtual function overrides
    //{{AFX_VIRTUAL(CAboutDlg)
    protected:
    virtual void DoDataExchange(CDataExchange* pDX); // DDX/DDV
                                                     // support

    //}}AFX_VIRTUAL

// Implementation
protected:
    //{{AFX_MSG(CAboutDlg)
        // No message handlers
    //}}AFX_MSG
    DECLARE_MESSAGE_MAP()
};

CAboutDlg::CAboutDlg() : CDialog(CAboutDlg::IDD)
{
    //{{AFX_DATA_INIT(CAboutDlg)
    //}}AFX_DATA_INIT
}

void CAboutDlg::DoDataExchange(CDataExchange* pDX)
{
    CDialog::DoDataExchange(pDX);
    //{{AFX_DATA_MAP(CAboutDlg)
    //}}AFX_DATA_MAP
}

BEGIN_MESSAGE_MAP(CAboutDlg, CDialog)
    //{{AFX_MSG_MAP(CAboutDlg)
        // No message handlers
    //}}AFX_MSG_MAP
END_MESSAGE_MAP()

// App command to run the dialog
void CEx18aApp::OnAppAbout()
{
    CAboutDlg aboutDlg;
    aboutDlg.DoModal();
}
```

```
/////////////////////////////////////////////////////////////////////
// CEx18aApp message handlers

CDocument* CEx18aApp::OpenDocumentFile(LPCTSTR lpszFileName)
{
    TRACE("CEx18aApp::OpenDocumentFile\n");
    return CWinApp::OpenDocumentFile(lpszFileName);
}
```

CMainFrame

This main frame class, listed in Figure 18-6, is almost identical to the SDI version, except that it's derived from *CMDIFrameWnd* instead of *CFrameWnd*.

MAINFRM.H

```
// MainFrm.h : interface of the CMainFrame class
//
/////////////////////////////////////////////////////////////////////

#if !defined(AFX_MAINFRM_H__7B5FE26B_85E9_11D0_8FE3_          ⌐
            00C04FC2A0C2__INCLUDED_)
#define AFX_MAINFRM_H__7B5FE26B_85E9_11D0_8FE3_00C04FC2A0C2__INCLUDED_

#if _MSC_VER > 1000
#pragma once
#endif // _MSC_VER > 1000

class CMainFrame : public CMDIFrameWnd
{
    DECLARE_DYNAMIC(CMainFrame)
public:
    CMainFrame();

// Attributes
public:
// Operations
public:

// Overrides
    // ClassWizard generated virtual function overrides
    //{{AFX_VIRTUAL(CMainFrame)
    virtual BOOL PreCreateWindow(CREATESTRUCT& cs);
    //}}AFX_VIRTUAL
```

Figure 18-6. (continued)
The CMainFrame *class listing.*

Figure 18-6. *continued*

```
// Implementation
public:
    virtual ~CMainFrame();
#ifdef _DEBUG
    virtual void AssertValid() const;
    virtual void Dump(CDumpContext& dc) const;
#endif

protected:  // control bar embedded members
    CStatusBar  m_wndStatusBar;
    CToolBar    m_wndToolBar;

// Generated message map functions
protected:
    //{{AFX_MSG(CMainFrame)
    afx_msg int OnCreate(LPCREATESTRUCT lpCreateStruct);
        // NOTE - the ClassWizard will add and remove      ➙
                 member functions here.
        //     DO NOT EDIT what you see in these blocks     ➙
                 of generated code!
    //}}AFX_MSG
    DECLARE_MESSAGE_MAP()
};

/////////////////////////////////////////////////////////////////////

//{{AFX_INSERT_LOCATION}}
// Microsoft Visual C++ will insert additional declarations
//   immediately before the previous line.

#endif // !defined(AFX_MAINFRM_H__7B5FE26B_85E9_          ➙
                 11D0_8FE3_00C04FC2A0C2__INCLUDED_)
```

MAINFRM.CPP

```
// MainFrm.cpp : implementation of the CMainFrame class
//

#include "stdafx.h"
#include "ex18a.h"

#include "MainFrm.h"

#ifdef _DEBUG
#define new DEBUG_NEW
```

```
#undef THIS_FILE
static char THIS_FILE[] = __FILE__;
#endif

/////////////////////////////////////////////////////////////////
// CMainFrame

IMPLEMENT_DYNAMIC(CMainFrame, CMDIFrameWnd)
BEGIN_MESSAGE_MAP(CMainFrame, CMDIFrameWnd)
    //{{AFX_MSG_MAP(CMainFrame)
        // NOTE - the ClassWizard will add and remove          ⇥
                mapping macros here.
        //     DO NOT EDIT what you see in these blocks         ⇥
                of generated code !
    ON_WM_CREATE()
    //}}AFX_MSG_MAP
END_MESSAGE_MAP()

static UINT indicators[] =
{
    ID_SEPARATOR,            // status line indicator
    ID_INDICATOR_CAPS,
    ID_INDICATOR_NUM,
    ID_INDICATOR_SCRL,
};

/////////////////////////////////////////////////////////////////
// CMainFrame construction/destruction

CMainFrame::CMainFrame()
{
    // TODO: add member initialization code here
}
CMainFrame::~CMainFrame()
{
}

int CMainFrame::OnCreate(LPCREATESTRUCT lpCreateStruct)
{
    if (CMDIFrameWnd::OnCreate(lpCreateStruct) == -1)
        return -1;

    if (!m_wndToolBar.CreateEx(this, TBSTYLE_FLAT, WS_CHILD
        | WS_VISIBLE | CBRS_TOP | CBRS_GRIPPER | CBRS_TOOLTIPS
        | CBRS_FLYBY | CBRS_SIZE_DYNAMIC) ||
        !m_wndToolBar.LoadToolBar(IDR_MAINFRAME))
    {
```

(continued)

Figure 18-6. *continued*

```
        TRACE0("Failed to create toolbar\n");
        return -1;      // fail to create
    }
    if (!m_wndStatusBar.Create(this) ||
        !m_wndStatusBar.SetIndicators(indicators,
          sizeof(indicators)/sizeof(UINT)))
    {
        TRACE0("Failed to create status bar\n");
        return -1;      // fail to create
    }

    // TODO: Delete these three lines if you don't want the toolbar to
    //   be dockable
    m_wndToolBar.EnableDocking(CBRS_ALIGN_ANY);
    EnableDocking(CBRS_ALIGN_ANY);
    DockControlBar(&m_wndToolBar);

    return 0;
}
BOOL CMainFrame::PreCreateWindow(CREATESTRUCT& cs)
{
    if ( !CMDIFrameWnd::PreCreateWindow(cs) )
        return FALSE;
    // TODO: Modify the Window class or styles here by modifying
    //   the CREATESTRUCT cs

    return TRUE;
}
/////////////////////////////////////////////////////////////////////
// CMainFrame diagnostics

#ifdef _DEBUG
void CMainFrame::AssertValid() const
{
    CMDIFrameWnd::AssertValid();
}

void CMainFrame::Dump(CDumpContext& dc) const
{
    CMDIFrameWnd::Dump(dc);
}

#endif //_DEBUG


/////////////////////////////////////////////////////////////////////
// CMainFrame message handlers
```

CChildFrame

This child frame class, listed in Figure 18-7, lets you conveniently control the child frame window's characteristics by adding code in the *PreCreateWindow* function. You can also map messages and override other virtual functions.

CHILDFRM.H

```
// ChildFrm.h : interface of the CChildFrame class
//
/////////////////////////////////////////////////////////////////////////

#if !defined(AFX_CHILDFRM_H__7B5FE26D_85E9_11D0         ⌐
            _8FE3_00C04FC2A0C2__INCLUDED_)
#define AFX_CHILDFRM_H__7B5FE26D_85E9_11D0_8FE3_00C04FC2A0C2__INCLUDED_

#if _MSC_VER > 1000
#pragma once
#endif // _MSC_VER > 1000

class CChildFrame : public CMDIChildWnd
{
    DECLARE_DYNCREATE(CChildFrame)
public:
    CChildFrame();

// Attributes
public:

// Operations
public:

// Overrides
    // ClassWizard generated virtual function overrides
    //{{AFX_VIRTUAL(CChildFrame)
    public:
    virtual BOOL PreCreateWindow(CREATESTRUCT& cs);
    virtual void ActivateFrame(int nCmdShow = -1);
    //}}AFX_VIRTUAL

// Implementation
public:
    virtual ~CChildFrame();
#ifdef _DEBUG
    virtual void AssertValid() const;
```

Figure 18-7.
The CChildFrame *class listing.*

(continued)

465

Figure 18-7. *continued*

```
    virtual void Dump(CDumpContext& dc) const;
#endif

// Generated message map functions
protected:
    //{{AFX_MSG(CChildFrame)
        // NOTE - the ClassWizard will add and remove         ⌐
                  member functions here.
        //      DO NOT EDIT what you see in these blocks       ⌐
                  of generated code!
    //}}AFX_MSG
    DECLARE_MESSAGE_MAP()
};


/////////////////////////////////////////////////////////////////////

//{{AFX_INSERT_LOCATION}}
// Microsoft Visual C++ will insert additional declarations
//   immediately before the previous line.

#endif // !defined(AFX_CHILDFRM_H__7B5FE26D_85E9_          ⌐
                  11D0_8FE3_00C04FC2A0C2__INCLUDED_)
```

CHILDFRM.CPP

```
// ChildFrm.cpp : implementation of the CChildFrame class
//

#include "stdafx.h"
#include "ex18a.h"

#include "ChildFrm.h"

#ifdef _DEBUG
#define new DEBUG_NEW
#undef THIS_FILE
static char THIS_FILE[] = __FILE__;
#endif

/////////////////////////////////////////////////////////////////////
// CChildFrame

IMPLEMENT_DYNCREATE(CChildFrame, CMDIChildWnd)

BEGIN_MESSAGE_MAP(CChildFrame, CMDIChildWnd)
    //{{AFX_MSG_MAP(CChildFrame)
```

```
        // NOTE - the ClassWizard will add and remove        ⇁
              mapping macros here.
        //       DO NOT EDIT what you see in these blocks     ⇁
              of generated code !
    //}}AFX_MSG_MAP
END_MESSAGE_MAP()


/////////////////////////////////////////////////////////////////////
// CChildFrame construction/destruction

CChildFrame::CChildFrame()
{
    // TODO: add member initialization code here

}


CChildFrame::~CChildFrame()
{
}


BOOL CChildFrame::PreCreateWindow(CREATESTRUCT& cs)
{
    // TODO: Modify the Window class or styles here by modifying
    //  the CREATESTRUCT cs

    if ( !CMDIChildWnd::PreCreateWindow(cs) )
        return FALSE;

    return TRUE;
}


/////////////////////////////////////////////////////////////////////
// CChildFrame diagnostics

#ifdef _DEBUG
void CChildFrame::AssertValid() const
{
    CMDIChildWnd::AssertValid();
}


void CChildFrame::Dump(CDumpContext& dc) const
{
    CMDIChildWnd::Dump(dc);
}


#endif //_DEBUG
```

(continued)

Figure 18-7. *continued*

```
//////////////////////////////////////////////////////////////////////////
// CChildFrame message handlers

void CChildFrame::ActivateFrame(int nCmdShow)
{
    TRACE("Entering CChildFrame::ActivateFrame\n");
    CMDIChildWnd::ActivateFrame(nCmdShow);
}
```

Testing the EX18A Application

Do the build, run the program from Visual C++, and then make several documents. Try saving the documents on disk, closing them, and reloading them. Also, choose New Window from the Window menu. Notice that you now have two views (and child frames) attached to the same document. Now exit the program and start Windows Explorer. The files you created should show up with document icons. Double-click on a document icon and see whether the EX18A program starts up. Now, with both Windows Explorer and EX18A on the desktop, drag a document from Windows Explorer to EX18A. Was the file opened?

Printing and Print Preview

If you're depending on the Win32 API alone, printing is one of the tougher programming jobs you'll have. If you don't believe me, just skim through the 60-page chapter "Using the Printer" in Charles Petzold's *Programming Windows 95* (Microsoft Press, 1996). Other books about Microsoft Windows ignore the subject completely. The Microsoft Foundation Class (MFC) Library version 6.0 application framework goes a long way toward making printing easy. As a bonus, it adds a print preview capability that behaves like the print preview functions in commercial Windows-based programs such as Microsoft Word and Microsoft Excel.

In this chapter, you'll learn how to use the MFC library Print and Print Preview features. In the process, you'll get a feeling for what's involved in Windows printing and how it's different from printing in MS-DOS. First you'll do some wysiwyg printing, in which the printer output matches the screen display. This option requires careful use of mapping modes. Later you'll print a paginated data processing–style report that doesn't reflect the screen display at all. In that example, you will use a template array to structure your document so that the program can print any specified range of pages on demand.

Windows Printing

In the old days, programmers had to worry about configuring their applications for dozens of printers. Now Windows makes life easy because it provides all of the printer drivers you'll ever need. It also supplies a consistent user interface for printing.

Standard Printer Dialogs

When the user chooses Print from the File menu of a Windows-based application, the standard Print dialog appears, as shown in Figure 19-1 on the following page.

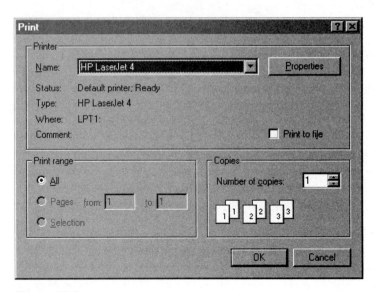

Figure 19-1.
The standard Print dialog.

If the user chooses Print Setup from the File menu, the standard Print Setup dialog appears, as shown in Figure 19-2.

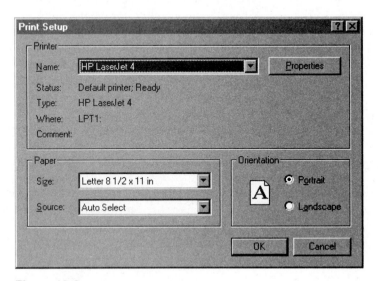

Figure 19-2.
The standard Print Setup dialog.

During the printing process, the application displays a standard printer status dialog, as shown in Figure 19-3.

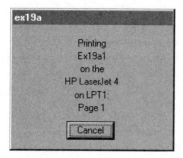

Figure 19-3.
The standard printer status dialog.

Interactive Print Page Selection

If you've worked in the data processing field, you might be used to batch-mode printing. A program reads a record and then formats and prints selected information as a line in a report. Let's say, for example, that every time 50 lines have been printed the program ejects the paper and prints a new page heading. The programmer assumes that the whole report will be printed at one time and makes no allowance for interactively printing selected pages.

As Figure 19-1 shows, page numbers are important in Windows-based printing. A program must respond to a user's page selection by calculating which information to print and then printing the selected pages. If you're aware of this page selection requirement, you can design your application's data structures accordingly.

Remember the student list from Chapter 17? What if the list included 1000 students' names and the user wanted to print page 5 of a student report? If you assumed that each student record required one print line and that a page held 50 lines, page 5 would include records 201 through 250. With an MFC list collection class, you're stuck iterating through the first 200 list elements before you can start printing. Maybe the list isn't the ideal data structure. How about an array collection instead? With the *CObArray* class (or with one of the template array classes), you can directly access the 201st student record.

Not every application has elements that map to a fixed number of print lines. Suppose the student record contained a multi-line text biography field. Because you wouldn't know how many biography lines each record included, you'd have to search through the whole file to determine the page breaks. If your program could remember those page breaks as it calculated them, its efficiency would increase.

Display Pages vs. Printed Pages

In many cases, you'll want a printed page to correspond to a display page. As you learned in Chapter 5, you cannot guarantee that objects will be printed exactly as they are displayed on screen. With TrueType fonts, however, your printed page will be pretty close. If you're working with full-size paper and you want the corresponding display to be readable, you'll certainly want a display window that is larger than the screen. Thus, a scrolling view such as the one that the *CScrollView* class provides is ideal for your printable views.

Sometimes, however, you might not care about display pages. Perhaps your view holds its data in a list box, or maybe you don't need to display the data at all. In these cases, your program can contain stand-alone print logic that simply extracts data from the document and sends it to the printer. Of course, the program must properly respond to a user's page-range request. If you query the printer to determine the paper size and orientation (portrait or landscape), you can adjust the pagination accordingly.

Print Preview

The MFC library Print Preview feature shows you on screen the <u>exact</u> page and line breaks you'll get when you print your document on a selected printer. The fonts might look a little funny, especially in the smaller sizes, but that's not a problem. Look now at the print preview window that appears on page 480.

Print Preview is an MFC library feature, not a Windows feature. Don't underestimate how much effort went into programming Print Preview. The Print Preview program examines each character individually, determining its position based on the printer's device context. After selecting an approximating font, the program displays the character in the print preview window at the proper location.

Programming for the Printer

The application framework does most of the work for printing and print preview. To use the printer effectively, you must understand the sequence of function calls and know which functions to override.

The Printer Device Context and the *CView::OnDraw* Function

When your program prints on the printer, it uses a device context object of class *CDC*. Don't worry about where the object comes from; the application framework constructs it and passes it as a parameter to your view's *OnDraw* function.

If your application uses the printer to duplicate the display, the *OnDraw* function can do double duty. If you're displaying, the *OnPaint* function calls *OnDraw* and the device context is the display context. If you're printing, *OnDraw* is called by another *CView* virtual function, *OnPrint*, with a printer device context as a parameter. The *OnPrint* function is called once to print an entire page.

In print preview mode, the *OnDraw* parameter is actually a pointer to a *CPreviewDC* object. Your *OnPrint* and *OnDraw* functions work the same regardless of whether you're printing or previewing.

The *CView::OnPrint* Function

You've seen that the base class *OnPrint* function calls *OnDraw* and that *OnDraw* can use both a display device context and a printer device context. The mapping mode should be set before *OnPrint* is called. You can override *OnPrint* to print items that you don't need on the display, such as a title page, headers, and footers. The *OnPrint* parameters are as follows:

- A pointer to the device context
- A pointer to a print information object (*CPrintInfo*) that includes page dimensions, the current page number, and the maximum page number

In your overridden *OnPrint* function, you can elect not to call *OnDraw* at all to support print logic that is totally independent of the display logic. The application framework calls the *OnPrint* function once for each page to be printed, with the current page number in the *CPrintInfo* structure. You'll soon find out how the application framework determines the page number.

Preparing the Device Context—The *CView::OnPrepareDC* Function

If you need a display mapping mode other than *MM_TEXT* (and you often do), that mode is usually set in the view's *OnPrepareDC* function. You override this function yourself if your view class is derived directly from *CView*, but it's already overridden if your view is derived from *CScrollView*. The *OnPrepareDC* function is called in *OnPaint* immediately before the call to *OnDraw*. If you're printing, the same *OnPrepareDC* function is called, this time immediately before the application framework calls *OnPrint*. Thus, the mapping mode is set before both the painting of the view and the printing of a page.

The second parameter of the *OnPrepareDC* function is a pointer to a *CPrint-Info* structure. This pointer is valid only if *OnPrepareDC* is being called prior

473

to printing. You can test for this condition by calling the *CDC* member function *IsPrinting*. The *IsPrinting* function is particularly handy if you're using *OnPrepareDC* to set different mapping modes for the display and the printer.

If you do not know in advance how many pages your print job requires, your overridden *OnPrepareDC* function can detect the end of the document and reset the *m_bContinuePrinting* flag in the *CPrintInfo* structure. When this flag is *FALSE*, the *OnPrint* function won't be called again and control will pass to the end of the print loop.

The Start and End of a Print Job

When a print job starts, the application framework calls two *CView* functions, *OnPreparePrinting* and *OnBeginPrinting*. (AppWizard generates the *On-PreparePrinting*, *OnBeginPrinting*, and *OnEndPrinting* functions for you if you select the Printing And Print Preview option.) The first function, *OnPreparePrinting*, is called before the display of the Print dialog. If you know the first and last page numbers, call *CPrintInfo::SetMinPage* and *CPrintInfo::SetMaxPage* in *OnPreparePrinting*. The page numbers you pass to these functions will appear in the Print dialog for the user to override.

The second function, *OnBeginPrinting*, is called after the Print dialog exits. Override this function to create Graphics Device Interface (GDI) objects, such as fonts, that you need for the entire print job. A program runs faster if you create a font once instead of re-creating it for each page.

The *CView* function *OnEndPrinting* is called at the end of the print job, after the last page has been printed. Override this function to get rid of GDI objects created in *OnBeginPrinting*.

The following table summarizes the important overridable *CView* print loop functions.

Function	Common Override Behavior
OnPreparePrinting	Sets first and last page numbers
OnBeginPrinting	Creates GDI objects
OnPrepareDC (for each page)	Sets mapping mode and optionally detects end of print job
OnPrint (for each page)	Does print-specific output and then calls *OnDraw*
OnEndPrinting	Deletes GDI objects

The EX19A Example—A Wysiwyg Print Program

This example displays and prints a single page of text stored in a document. The printed image should match the displayed image. The *MM_TWIPS* mapping mode is used for both printer and display. First we'll use a fixed drawing rectangle; later we'll base the drawing rectangle on the printable area rectangle supplied by the printer driver.

Here are the steps for building the example:

1. **Run AppWizard to generate \vcpp32\ex19a\ex19a.**   Accept the default options, and then rename the document and view classes and files as shown here.

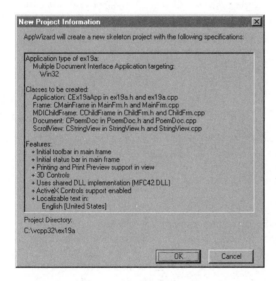

Note that this is an MDI application.

2. **Add a *CStringArray* data member to the *CPoemDoc* class.**   Edit the PoemDoc.h header file or use ClassView.

```
public:
    CStringArray m_stringArray;
```

The document data is stored in a string array. The MFC library *CString-Array* class holds an array of *CString* objects, accessible by a zero-based subscript. You need not set a maximum dimension in the declaration because the array is dynamic.

475

3. **Add a *CRect* data member to the *CStringView* class.** Edit the StringView.h header file or use ClassView:

```
private:
    CRect m_rectPrint;
```

4. **Edit three *CPoemDoc* member functions in the file PoemDoc.cpp.** AppWizard generated skeleton *OnNewDocument* and *Serialize* functions, but we'll have to use ClassWizard to override the *DeleteContents* function. We'll initialize the poem document in the overridden *OnNewDocument* function. *DeleteContents* is called in *CDocument::OnNewDocument*, so by calling the base class function first we're sure the poem won't be deleted. (The text, by the way, is an excerpt from the twentieth poem in Lawrence Ferlinghetti's book *A Coney Island of the Mind*.) Type 10 lines of your choice. You can substitute another poem or maybe your favorite Win32 function description. Add the following boldface code:

```
BOOL CPoemDoc::OnNewDocument()
{
    if (!CDocument::OnNewDocument())
        return FALSE;

    m_stringArray.SetSize(10);
    m_stringArray[0] = "The pennycandystore beyond the El";
    m_stringArray[1] = "is where I first";
    m_stringArray[2] = "                    fell in love";
    m_stringArray[3] = "                        with unreality";
    m_stringArray[4] = "Jellybeans glowed in the semi-gloom";
    m_stringArray[5] = "of that september afternoon";
    m_stringArray[6] = "A cat upon the counter moved among";
    m_stringArray[7] = "                    the licorice sticks";
    m_stringArray[8] = "                    and tootsie rolls";
    m_stringArray[9] = "            and Oh Boy Gum";

    return TRUE;
}
```

NOTE: The *CStringArray* class supports dynamic arrays, but here we're using the *m_stringArray* object as though it were a static array of 10 elements.

The application framework calls the document's virtual *DeleteContents* function when it closes the document; this action deletes the strings in the

476

array. A *CStringArray* contains actual objects, and a *CObArray* contains pointers to objects. This distinction is important when it's time to delete the array elements. Here the *RemoveAll* function actually deletes the string objects:

```
void CPoemDoc::DeleteContents()
{
    // called before OnNewDocument and when document is closed
    m_stringArray.RemoveAll();
}
```

Serialization isn't important in this example, but the following function illustrates how easy it is to serialize strings. The application framework calls the *DeleteContents* function before loading from the archive, so you don't have to worry about emptying the array. Add the following boldface code:

```
void CPoemDoc::Serialize(CArchive& ar)
{
    m_stringArray.Serialize(ar);
}
```

5. Edit the *OnInitialUpdate* function in StringView.cpp. You must override the function for all classes derived from *CScrollView*. This function's job is to set the logical window size and the mapping mode. Add the following boldface code:

```
void CStringView::OnInitialUpdate()
{
    CScrollView::OnInitialUpdate();
    CSize sizeTotal(m_rectPrint.Width(), -m_rectPrint.Height());
    CSize sizePage(sizeTotal.cx / 2,
                   sizeTotal.cy / 2);   // page scroll
    CSize sizeLine(sizeTotal.cx / 100,
                   sizeTotal.cy / 100); // line scroll
    SetScrollSizes(MM_TWIPS, sizeTotal, sizePage, sizeLine);
}
```

6. Edit the *OnDraw* function in StringView.cpp. The *OnDraw* function of class *CStringView* draws on both the display and the printer. In addition to displaying the poem text lines in 10-point roman font, it draws a border around the printable area and a crude ruler along the top and left margins. *OnDraw* assumes the *MM_TWIPS* mapping mode, in which 1 inch = 1440 units. Add the boldface code shown on the following page.

```
void CStringView::OnDraw(CDC* pDC)
{
    int        i, j, nHeight;
    CString    str;
    CFont      font;
    TEXTMETRIC tm;

    CPoemDoc* pDoc = GetDocument();
    // Draw a border -- slightly smaller to avoid truncation
    pDC->Rectangle(m_rectPrint + CRect(0, 0, -20, 20));
    // Draw horizontal and vertical rulers
    j = m_rectPrint.Width() / 1440;
    for (i = 0; i <= j; i++) {
        str.Format("%02d", i);
        pDC->TextOut(i * 1440, 0, str);
    }
    j = -(m_rectPrint.Height() / 1440);
    for (i = 0; i <= j; i++) {
        str.Format("%02d", i);
        pDC->TextOut(0, -i * 1440, str);
    }
    // Print the poem 0.5 inch down and over;
    //   use 10-point roman font
    font.CreateFont(-200, 0, 0, 0, 400, FALSE, FALSE, 0, ANSI_CHARSET,
                    OUT_DEFAULT_PRECIS, CLIP_DEFAULT_PRECIS,
                    DEFAULT_QUALITY, DEFAULT_PITCH | FF_ROMAN,
                    "Times New Roman");
    CFont* pOldFont = (CFont*) pDC->SelectObject(&font);
    pDC->GetTextMetrics(&tm);
    nHeight = tm.tmHeight + tm.tmExternalLeading;
    TRACE("font height = %d, internal leading = %d\n",
          nHeight, tm.tmInternalLeading);
    j = pDoc->m_stringArray.GetSize();
    for (i = 0; i < j; i++) {
        pDC->TextOut(720, -i * nHeight - 720, pDoc->m_stringArray[i]);
    }
    pDC->SelectObject(pOldFont);
    TRACE("LOGPIXELSX = %d, LOGPIXELSY = %d\n",
          pDC->GetDeviceCaps(LOGPIXELSX),
          pDC->GetDeviceCaps(LOGPIXELSY));
    TRACE("HORZSIZE = %d, VERTSIZE = %d\n",
          pDC->GetDeviceCaps(HORZSIZE),
          pDC->GetDeviceCaps(VERTSIZE));
}
```

7. Edit the *OnPreparePrinting* function in StringView.cpp.
This function sets the maximum number of pages in the print job. This example has only one page. It's absolutely necessary to call the base class *DoPreparePrinting* function in your overridden *OnPreparePrinting* function. Add the following boldface code:

```
BOOL CStringView::OnPreparePrinting(CPrintInfo* pInfo)
{
    pInfo->SetMaxPage(1);
    return DoPreparePrinting(pInfo);
}
```

8. Edit the constructor in StringView.cpp. The initial value of the print rectangle should be 8-by-15 inches, expressed in twips (1 inch = 1440 twips). Add the following boldface code:

```
CStringView::CStringView() : m_rectPrint(0, 0, 11520, -15120)
{
}
```

9. Build and test the application. If you run the EX19A application under Microsoft Windows NT with the lowest screen resolution, your MDI child window will look like the one shown below. (The text will be larger under higher resolutions and under Windows 95 and Windows 98.)

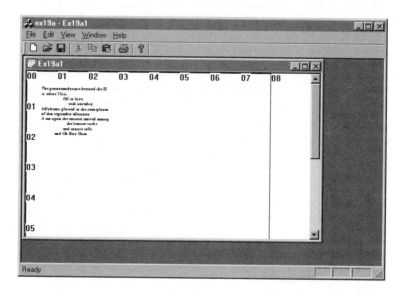

The window text is too small, isn't it? Go ahead and choose Print Preview from the File menu, and then click twice with the magnifying glass to enlarge the image. The print preview output is illustrated here.

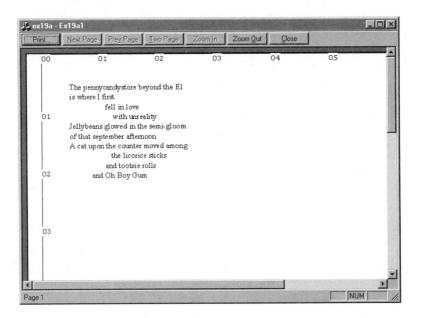

Remember "logical twips" from Chapter 5? We're going to use logical twips now to enlarge type on the display while keeping the printed text the same size. This requires some extra work because the *CScrollView* class wasn't designed for nonstandard mapping modes. You will be changing the view's base class from *CScrollView* to *CLogScrollView*, which is a class that I created by copying and modifying the MFC code in ViewScrl.cpp. The files LogScrollView.h and LogScrollView.cpp are in the \vcpp32\ex19a directory on the companion CD-ROM.

10. **Insert the *CScrollView* class into the project.** Copy the files LogScroll-View.h and LogScrollView.cpp from the companion CD-ROM if you have not done so already. Choose Add To Project from the Project menu, and then choose Files from the submenu. Select the two new files and click OK to insert them into the project.

11. **Edit the StringView.h header file.**   Add the following line at the top of the file:

```
#include "LogScrollView.h"
```

   Then change the line

```
class CStringView : public CScrollView
```

   to

```
class CStringView : public CLogScrollView
```

12. **Edit the StringView.cpp file.**   Globally replace all occurrences of *CScrollView* with *CLogScrollView*. Then edit the *OnInitialUpdate* function. Here is the edited code, which is much shorter:

```
void CStringView::OnInitialUpdate()
{
    CLogScrollView::OnInitialUpdate();
    CSize sizeTotal(m_rectPrint.Width(), -m_rectPrint.Height());
    SetLogScrollSizes(sizeTotal);
}
```

13. **Build and test the application again.**   Now the screen should look like this.

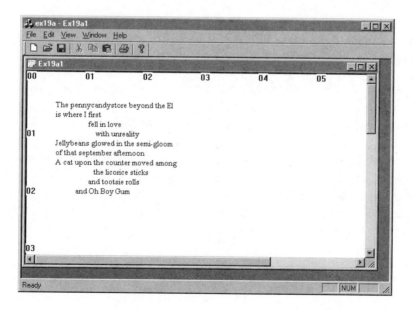

481

Reading the Printer Rectangle

The EX19A program prints in a fixed-size rectangle that's appropriate for a laser printer set to portrait mode with 8.5-by-11-inch (letter-size) paper. But what if you load European-size paper or you switch to landscape mode? The program should be able to adjust accordingly.

It's relatively easy to read the printer rectangle. Remember the *CPrintInfo* pointer that's passed to *OnPrint*? That structure has a data member *m_rectDraw* that contains the rectangle in logical coordinates. Your overridden *OnPrint* function simply stuffs the rectangle in a view data member, and *OnDraw* uses it. There's only one problem: you can't get the rectangle until you start printing, so the constructor still needs to set a default value for *OnDraw* to use before printing begins.

If you want the EX19A program to read the printer rectangle and adjust the size of the scroll view, use ClassWizard to override *OnPrint* and then code the function as follows:

```
void CStringView::OnPrint(CDC* pDC, CPrintInfo* pInfo)
{
    m_rectPrint = pInfo->m_rectDraw;
    SetLogScrollSizes(CSize(m_rectPrint.Width(),
                      -m_rectPrint.Height()));
    CLogScrollView::OnPrint(pDC, pInfo);
}
```

Template Collection Classes Revisited—The *CArray* Class

In EX16B in Chapter 16, you saw the MFC library *CTypedPtrList* template collection class, which was used to store a list of pointers to *CStudent* objects. Another collection class, *CArray*, is appropriate for the next example, EX19B. This class is different from *CTypedPtrList* in two ways. First, it's an array, with elements accessible by index, just like *CStringArray* in EX19A. Second, the array holds actual objects, not pointers to objects. In EX19B, the elements are *CRect* objects. The elements' class does not have to be derived from *CObject*, and indeed, *CRect* is not.

As in EX16B, a *typedef* makes the template collection easier to use. We use the statement

```
typedef CArray<CRect, CRect&> CRectArray;
```

to define an array class that holds *CRect* objects and whose functions take *CRect* reference parameters. (It's cheaper to pass a 32-bit pointer than to copy a 128-bit object.) To use the template array, you declare an instance of *CRectArray* and then you call *CArray* member functions such as *SetSize*. You can also use the *CArray* subscript operator to get and set elements.

The template classes *CArray*, *CList*, and *CMap* are easy to use if the element class is sufficiently simple. The *CRect* class fits that description because it contains no pointer data members. Each template class uses a global function, *Serialize-Elements*, to serialize all the elements in the collection. The default *SerializeElements* function does a <u>bitwise</u> copy of each element to and from the archive.

If your element class contains pointers or is otherwise complex, you'll need to write your own *SerializeElements* function. If you wrote this function for the rectangle array (not required), your code would look like this:

```
void AFXAPI SerializeElements(CArchive& ar, CRect* pNewRects,
    int nCount)
{
    for (int i = 0; i < nCount; i++, pNewRects++) {
        if (ar.IsStoring()) {
            ar << *pNewRects;
        }
        else {
            ar >> *pNewRects;
        }
    }
}
```

When the compiler sees this function, it uses the function to replace the *SerializeElements* function inside the template. This only works, however, if the compiler sees the *SerializeElements* prototype before it sees the template class declaration.

> **NOTE:** The template classes depend on two other global functions, *ConstructElements* and *DestructElements*. Starting with Visual C++ version 4.0, these functions call the element class constructor and destructor for each object. Therefore, there's no real need to replace them.

The EX19B Example—A Multipage Print Program

In this example, the document contains an array of 50 *CRect* objects that define circles. The circles are randomly positioned in a 6-by-6-inch area and have random diameters of as much as 0.5 inch. The circles, when drawn on the display, look like two-dimensional simulations of soap bubbles. Instead of drawing the circles on the printer, the application prints the corresponding *CRect* coordinates in numeric form, 12 to a page, with headers and footers.

1. **Run AppWizard to generate \vcpp32\ex19b\ex19b.**   Select Single Document, and accept the defaults for all the other settings. The options and the default class names are shown here.

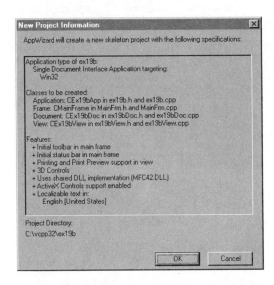

2. **Edit the StdAfx.h header file.**   You'll need to bring in the declarations for the MFC template collection classes. Add the following statement:

   ```
   #include <afxtempl.h>
   ```

3. **Edit the ex19bDoc.h header file.**   In the EX19A example, the document data consists of strings stored in a *CStringArray* collection. Because we're using a template collection for ellipse rectangles, we'll need a *typedef* statement outside the class declaration, as shown here:

```
typedef CArray<CRect, CRect&> CRectArray;
```

Next add the following public data members to the ex19bDoc.h header file:

```
public:
    enum { nLinesPerPage = 12 };
    enum { nMaxEllipses = 50 };
    CRectArray m_ellipseArray;
```

The two enumerations are object-oriented replacements for *#defines*.

4. Edit the ex19bDoc.cpp implementation file.   The overridden *OnNew Document* function initializes the ellipse array with some random values, and the *Serialize* function reads and writes the whole array. AppWizard generated the skeletons for both functions. You don't need a *DeleteContents* function because the *CArray* subscript operator writes a new *CRect* object on top of any existing one. Add the following boldface code:

```
BOOL CEx19bDoc::OnNewDocument()
{
    if (!CDocument::OnNewDocument())
        return FALSE;

    int n1, n2, n3;
    // Make 50 random circles
    srand((unsigned) time(NULL));
    m_ellipseArray.SetSize(nMaxEllipses);

    for (int i = 0; i < nMaxEllipses; i++) {
        n1 = rand() * 600 / RAND_MAX;
        n2 = rand() * 600 / RAND_MAX;
        n3 = rand() * 50  / RAND_MAX;
        m_ellipseArray[i] = CRect(n1, -n2, n1 + n3, -(n2 + n3));
    }

    return TRUE;
}


void CEx19bDoc::Serialize(CArchive& ar)
{
    m_ellipseArray.Serialize(ar);
}
```

5. **Edit the ex19bView.h header file.**   Use ClassView to add the member variable and two function prototypes listed below. ClassView will also generate skeletons for the functions in ex19bView.cpp.

```
public:
    int m_nPage;
private:
    void PrintPageHeader(CDC *pDC);
    void PrintPageFooter(CDC *pDC);
```

The *m_nPage* data member holds the document's current page number for printing. The private functions are for the header and footer subroutines.

6. **Edit the *OnDraw* function in ex19bView.cpp.**   The overridden *OnDraw* function simply draws the bubbles in the view window. Add the boldface code shown here:

```
void CEx19bView::OnDraw(CDC* pDC)
{
    int i, j;

    CEx19bDoc* pDoc = GetDocument();
    j = pDoc->m_ellipseArray.GetUpperBound();
    for (i = 0; i < j; i++) {
        pDC->Ellipse(pDoc->m_ellipseArray[i]);
    }
}
```

7. **Insert the *OnPrepareDC* function in ex19bView.cpp.**   The view class is not a scrolling view, so the mapping mode must be set in this function. Use ClassWizard to override the *OnPrepareDC* function, and then add the following boldface code:

```
void CEx19bView::OnPrepareDC(CDC* pDC, CPrintInfo* pInfo)
{
    pDC->SetMapMode(MM_LOENGLISH);
}
```

8. **Insert the *OnPrint* function in ex19bView.cpp.**   The *CView* default *OnPrint* function calls *OnDraw*. In this example, we want the printed output to be entirely different from the displayed output, so the *OnPrint* function must take care of the print output without calling *OnDraw*. *OnPrint* first sets the mapping mode to *MM_TWIPS*, and then it creates a fixed-pitch font. After printing the numeric contents of 12 *m_ellipseArray* elements, *OnPrint* deselects the font. You could have created the font once in *OnBeginPrinting*, but you wouldn't have noticed the increased

efficiency. Use ClassWizard to override the *OnPrint* function, and then add
the following boldface code:

```
void CEx19bView::OnPrint(CDC* pDC, CPrintInfo* pInfo)
{
    int        i, nStart, nEnd, nHeight;
    CString    str;
    CPoint     point(720, -1440);
    CFont      font;
    TEXTMETRIC tm;

    pDC->SetMapMode(MM_TWIPS);
    CEx19bDoc* pDoc = GetDocument();
    m_nPage = pInfo->m_nCurPage; // for PrintPageFooter's benefit
    nStart = (m_nPage - 1) * CEx19bDoc::nLinesPerPage;
    nEnd = nStart + CEx19bDoc::nLinesPerPage;
     // 14-point fixed-pitch font
    font.CreateFont(-280, 0, 0, 0, 400, FALSE, FALSE,
                    0, ANSI_CHARSET, OUT_DEFAULT_PRECIS,
                    CLIP_DEFAULT_PRECIS, DEFAULT_QUALITY,
                    DEFAULT_PITCH | FF_MODERN, "Courier New");
                    // Courier New is a TrueType font
    CFont* pOldFont = (CFont*) (pDC->SelectObject(&font));
    PrintPageHeader(pDC);
    pDC->GetTextMetrics(&tm);
    nHeight = tm.tmHeight + tm.tmExternalLeading;
    for (i = nStart; i < nEnd; i++) {
        if (i > pDoc->m_ellipseArray.GetUpperBound()) {
            break;
        }
        str.Format("%6d %6d %6d %6d %6d", i + 1,
                    pDoc->m_ellipseArray[i].left,
                    pDoc->m_ellipseArray[i].top,
                    pDoc->m_ellipseArray[i].right,
                    pDoc->m_ellipseArray[i].bottom);
        point.y -= nHeight;
        pDC->TextOut(point.x, point.y, str);
    }
    PrintPageFooter(pDC);
    pDC->SelectObject(pOldFont);
}
```

9. **Edit the *OnPreparePrinting* function in ex19bView.cpp.** The
OnPreparePrinting function (whose skeleton is generated by AppWizard)
computes the number of pages in the document and then communicates

that value to the application framework through the *SetMaxPage* function. Add the following boldface code:

```
BOOL CEx19bView::OnPreparePrinting(CPrintInfo* pInfo)
{
    CEx19bDoc* pDoc = GetDocument();
    pInfo->SetMaxPage(pDoc->m_ellipseArray.GetUpperBound() /
                      CEx19bDoc::nLinesPerPage + 1);
    return DoPreparePrinting(pInfo);
}
```

10. **Insert the page header and footer functions in ex19bView.cpp.**

These private functions, called from *OnPrint*, print the page headers and the page footers. The page footer includes the page number, stored by *OnPrint* in the view class data member *m_nPage*. The *CDC::GetTextExtent* function provides the width of the page number so that it can be right-justified. Add the boldface code shown here:

```
void CEx19bView::PrintPageHeader(CDC* pDC)
{
    CString str;

    CPoint point(0, 0);
    pDC->TextOut(point.x, point.y, "Bubble Report");
    point += CSize(720, -720);
    str.Format("%6.6s %6.6s %6.6s %6.6s %6.6s",
               "Index", "Left", "Top", "Right", "Bottom");
    pDC->TextOut(point.x, point.y, str);
}

void CEx19bView::PrintPageFooter(CDC* pDC)
{
    CString str;

    CPoint point(0, -14400); // Move 10 inches down
    CEx19bDoc* pDoc = GetDocument();
    str.Format("Document %s", (LPCSTR) pDoc->GetTitle());
    pDC->TextOut(point.x, point.y, str);
    str.Format("Page %d", m_nPage);
    CSize size = pDC->GetTextExtent(str);
    point.x += 11520 - size.cx;
    pDC->TextOut(point.x, point.y, str); // right-justified
}
```

11. **Build and test the application.** For one set of random numbers, the bubble view window looks like this.

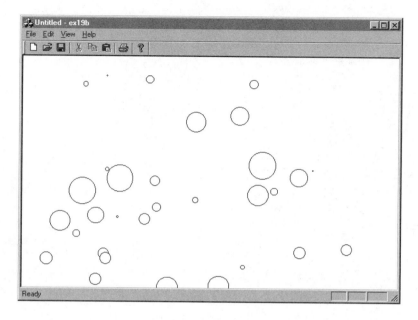

Each time you choose New from the File menu, you should see a different picture. In Print Preview, the first page of the output should look like this.

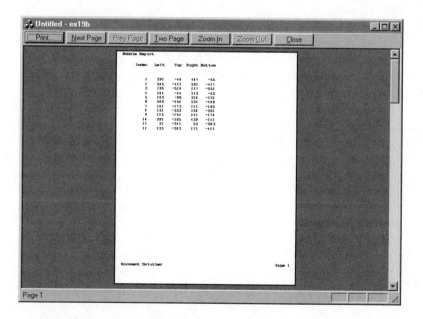

With the Print dialog, you can specify any range of pages to print.

CHAPTER TWENTY

Splitter Windows and Multiple Views

Except for the EX18A example, each program you've seen so far in this book has had only one view attached to a document. If you've used a Microsoft Windows–based word processor, you know that it's convenient to have two windows open simultaneously on various parts of a document. Both windows might contain normal views, or one window might contain a page layout view and another might contain an outline view.

With the application framework, you can use a <u>splitter</u> <u>window</u> or <u>multiple MDI child windows</u> to display multiple views. You'll learn about both presentation options here, and you'll see that it's easy to make multiple view <u>objects</u> of the same view class (the normal view) in both cases. It's slightly more difficult, however, to use two or more view <u>classes</u> in the same application (say, the outline view and the page layout view).

This chapter emphasizes the selection and presentation of multiple views. The examples depend on a document with data initialized in the *OnNewDocument* function. Look back now to Chapter 16 for a review of document–view communication.

The Splitter Window

A splitter window appears as a special type of frame window that holds several views in <u>panes</u>. The application can split the window on creation, or the user can split the window by choosing a menu command or by dragging a splitter box on the window's scroll bar. After the window has been split, the user can move the splitter bars with the mouse to adjust the relative sizes of the panes. Splitter windows can be used in both SDI and MDI applications. You can see examples of splitter windows on pages 495 and 498.

An object of class *CSplitterWnd* represents the splitter window. As far as Windows is concerned, a *CSplitterWnd* object is an actual window that fully occupies the frame window (*CFrameWnd* or *CMDIChildWnd*) client area. The view windows occupy the splitter window pane areas. The splitter window does not take part in the command dispatch mechanism. The active view window (in a splitter pane) is connected directly to its frame window.

View Options

When you combine multiview presentation methods with application models, you get a number of permutations. Here are some of them:

- **SDI application with splitter window, single view class**   This chapter's first example, EX20A, covers this case. Each splitter window pane can be scrolled to a different part of the document. The programmer determines the maximum number of horizontal and vertical panes; the user makes the split at runtime.

- **SDI application with splitter window, multiple view classes**   The EX20B example illustrates this case. The programmer determines the number of panes and the sequence of views; the user can change the pane size at runtime.

- **SDI application with no splitter windows, multiple view classes**   The EX20C example illustrates this case. The user switches view classes by making a selection from a menu.

- **MDI application with no splitter windows, single view class**   This is the standard MDI application you've seen already in Chapter 18. The New Window menu item lets the user open a new child window for a document that's open already.

- **MDI application with no splitter windows, multiple view classes**   A small change to the standard MDI application allows the use of multiple views. As example EX20D shows, all that's necessary is to add a menu item and a handler function for each additional view class available.

- **MDI application with splitter child windows**   This case is covered thoroughly in the online documentation. The SCRIBBLE example illustrates the splitting of an MDI child window.

Dynamic and Static Splitter Windows

A <u>dynamic splitter window</u> allows the user to split the window at any time by choosing a menu item or by dragging a splitter box located on the scroll bar. The panes in a dynamic splitter window generally use the same view class. The top left pane is initialized to a particular view when the splitter window is created. In a dynamic splitter window, scroll bars are shared among the views. In a window with a single horizontal split, for example, the bottom scroll bar controls both views. A dynamic splitter application starts with a single view object. When the user splits the frame, other view objects are constructed. When the user unsplits the frame, view objects are destroyed.

The panes of a <u>static</u> <u>splitter</u> <u>window</u> are defined when the window is first created and they cannot be changed. The user can move the bars but cannot unsplit or resplit the window. Static splitter windows can accommodate multiple view classes, with the configuration set at creation time. In a static splitter window, each pane has separate scroll bars. In a static splitter window application, all view objects are constructed when the frame is constructed and they are all destroyed when the frame is destroyed.

The EX20A Example— A Single View Class SDI Dynamic Splitter

In this example, the user can dynamically split the view into four panes with four separate view objects, all managed by a single view class. We'll use the document and the view code from EX19A. AppWizard lets you add a dynamic splitter window to a new application. Create an SDI project. Click the Advanced button in the AppWizard Step 4 dialog. Click on the Window Styles tab, and select Use Split Window as shown here.

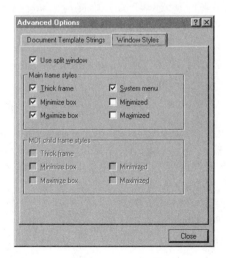

When you check the Use Split Window check box, AppWizard adds code to your *CMainFrame* class. Of course, you could add the same code to the *CMainFrame* class of an existing application to add splitter capability.

Resources for Splitting

When AppWizard generates an application with a splitter frame, it includes a Split option in the project's View menu. The *ID_WINDOW_SPLIT* command ID is mapped in the *CView* class within the MFC library.

CMainFrame

The application's main frame window class needs a splitter window data member and a prototype for an overridden *OnCreateClient* function. Here are the additions that AppWizard makes to the MainFrm.h file:

```
protected:
    CSplitterWnd m_wndSplitter;
public:
    virtual BOOL OnCreateClient(LPCREATESTRUCT lpcs,      ↴
                                CCreateContext* pContext);
```

The application framework calls the *CFrameWnd::OnCreateClient* virtual member function when the frame object is created. The base class version creates a single view window as specified by the document template. The App-Wizard-generated *OnCreateClient* override shown here (in MainFrm.cpp) creates a splitter window instead, and the splitter window creates the first view:

```
BOOL CMainFrame::OnCreateClient( LPCREATESTRUCT /*lpcs*/,
    CCreateContext* pContext)
{
    return m_wndSplitter.Create( this,
        2, 2,           // TODO: adjust the number of rows, columns
        CSize(10, 10),  // TODO: adjust the minimum pane size
        pContext);
}
```

The *CSplitterWnd Create* member function creates a dynamic splitter window, and the *CSplitterWnd* object knows the view class because its name is embedded in the *CCreateContext* structure that's passed as a parameter to *Create*.

The second and third *Create* parameters (2, 2) specify that the window can be split into a maximum of two rows and two columns. If you changed the parameters to (2, 1), you would allow only a single horizontal split. The parameters (1, 2) allow only a single vertical split. The *CSize* parameter specifies the minimum pane size.

Testing the EX20A Application

When the application starts, you can split the window by choosing Split from the View menu or by dragging the splitter boxes at the left and top of the scroll bars. Figure 20-1 shows a typical single view window with a four-way split. Multiple views share the scroll bars.

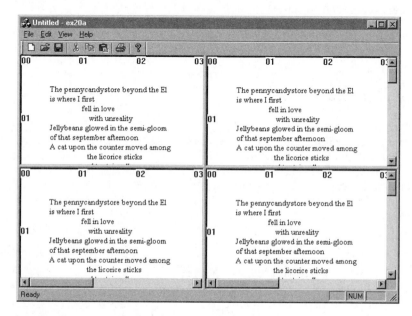

Figure 20-1.
A single view window with a four-way split.

The EX20B Example—
A Double View Class SDI Static Splitter

In EX20B, we'll extend EX20A by defining a second view class and allowing a static splitter window to show the two views. (The H and CPP files are cloned from the original view class.) This time the splitter window works a little differently. Instead of starting off as a single pane, the splitter is initialized with two panes. The user can move the bar between the panes by dragging it with the mouse or by choosing the Window Split menu item.

The easiest way to generate a static splitter application is to let AppWizard generate a dynamic splitter application and then edit the generated *CMain-Frame::OnCreateClient* function.

CHexView

The *CHexView* class was written to allow programmers to appreciate poetry. It is essentially the same code used for *CStringView* except for the *OnDraw* member function:

```
void CHexView::OnDraw(CDC* pDC)
{
    // hex dump of document strings
    int         i, j, k, l, n, nHeight;
    CString     outputLine, str;
    CFont       font;
    TEXTMETRIC tm;

    CPoemDoc* pDoc = GetDocument();
    font.CreateFont(-160, 80, 0, 0, 400, FALSE, FALSE, 0,
        ANSI_CHARSET, OUT_DEFAULT_PRECIS, CLIP_DEFAULT_PRECIS,
        DEFAULT_QUALITY, DEFAULT_PITCH | FF_SWISS, "Arial");
    CFont* pOldFont = pDC->SelectObject(&font);
    pDC->GetTextMetrics(&tm);
    nHeight = tm.tmHeight + tm.tmExternalLeading;

    j = pDoc->m_stringArray.GetSize();
    for (i = 0; i < j; i++) {
        outputLine.Format("%02x    ", i);
        l = pDoc->m_stringArray[i].GetLength();
        for (k = 0; k < l; k++) {
            n = pDoc->m_stringArray[i][k] & 0x00ff;
            str.Format("%02x ", n);
            outputLine += str;
        }
        pDC->TextOut(720, -i * nHeight - 720, outputLine);
    }
    pDC->SelectObject(pOldFont);
}
```

This function displays a hexadecimal dump of all strings in the document's *m_stringArray* collection. Notice the use of the subscript operator to access individual characters in a *CString* object.

496

CMainFrame

As in EX20A, the EX20B application's main frame window class needs a splitter window data member and a prototype for an overridden *OnCreateClient* function. You can let AppWizard generate the code by specifying Use Split Window, as in EX20A. You won't have to modify the MainFrm.h file.

The implementation file, MainFrm.cpp, needs both view class headers (and the prerequisite document header), as shown here:

```
#include "PoemDoc.h"
#include "StringView.h"
#include "HexView.h"
```

AppWizard generates dynamic splitter code in the *OnCreateClient* function, so you'll have to do some editing if you want a static splitter. Instead of calling *CSplitterWnd::Create*, you'll call the *CSplitterWnd::CreateStatic* function, which is tailored for multiple view classes. The following calls to *CSplitterWnd::CreateView* attach the two view classes. As the second and third *CreateStatic* parameters (2, 1) dictate, this splitter window contains only two panes. The horizontal split is initially 100 device units from the top of the window. The top pane is the string view; the bottom pane is the hex dump view. The user can change the splitter bar position but the view configuration cannot be changed.

```
BOOL CMainFrame::OnCreateClient( LPCREATESTRUCT /*lpcs*/,
    CCreateContext* pContext)
{
    VERIFY(m_wndSplitter.CreateStatic(this, 2, 1));
    VERIFY(m_wndSplitter.CreateView(0, 0, RUNTIME_CLASS(CStringView),
                                    CSize(100, 100), pContext));
    VERIFY(m_wndSplitter.CreateView(1, 0, RUNTIME_CLASS(CHexView),
                                    CSize(100, 100), pContext));
    return TRUE;
}
```

Testing the EX20B Application

When you start the EX20B application, the window should look like the one shown on the following page. Notice the separate horizontal scroll bars for the two views.

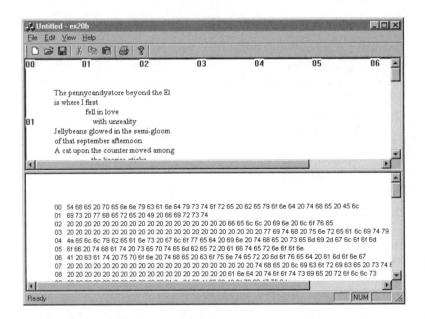

The EX20C Example—
Switching View Classes Without a Splitter

Sometimes you just want to switch view classes under program control and you don't want to be bothered with a splitter window. The EX20C example is an SDI application that switches between *CStringView* and *CHexView* in response to selections on the View menu. Starting with what AppWizard generates, all you need to do is add two new menu commands and then add some code to the *CMainFrame* class. You also need to change the *CStringView* and *CHexView* constructors from protected to public.

Resource Requirements

The following two items have been added to the View menu in the *IDR_MAIN-FRAME* menu resource.

Caption	Command ID	*CMainFrame* Function
St&ring View	*ID_VIEW_STRINGVIEW*	*OnViewStringView*
&Hex View	*ID_VIEW_HEXVIEW*	*OnViewHexView*

ClassWizard was used to add the command-handling functions (and corresponding update command UI handlers) to the *CMainFrame* class.

CMainFrame

The *CMainFrame* class gets a new private helper function, *SwitchToView*, which is called from the two menu command handlers. The *enum* parameter tells the function which view to switch to. Here are the two added items in the Main-Frm.h header file:

```
private:
    enum eView { STRING = 1, HEX = 2 };
    void SwitchToView(eView nView);
```

The *SwitchToView* function (in MainFrm.cpp) makes some low-level MFC calls to locate the requested view and to activate it. Don't worry about how it works. Just adapt it to your own applications when you want the view-switching feature. Add the following code:

```
void CMainFrame::SwitchToView(eView nView)
{
    CView* pOldActiveView = GetActiveView();
    CView* pNewActiveView = (CView*) GetDlgItem(nView);
    if (pNewActiveView == NULL) {
        switch (nView) {
        case STRING:
            pNewActiveView = (CView*) new CStringView;
            break;
        case HEX:
            pNewActiveView = (CView*) new CHexView;
            break;
        }
        CCreateContext context;
        context.m_pCurrentDoc = pOldActiveView->GetDocument();
        pNewActiveView->Create(NULL, NULL, WS_BORDER,
            CFrameWnd::rectDefault, this, nView, &context);
        pNewActiveView->OnInitialUpdate();
    }
    SetActiveView(pNewActiveView);
    pNewActiveView->ShowWindow(SW_SHOW);
    pOldActiveView->ShowWindow(SW_HIDE);
    pOldActiveView->SetDlgCtrlID(
        pOldActiveView->GetRuntimeClass() ==
        RUNTIME_CLASS(CStringView) ? STRING : HEX);
    pNewActiveView->SetDlgCtrlID(AFX_IDW_PANE_FIRST);
    RecalcLayout();
}
```

Finally, here are the menu command handlers and update command UI handlers that ClassWizard initially generated (along with message map entries and prototypes). The update command UI handlers test the current view's class.

```
void CMainFrame::OnViewStringView()
{
    SwitchToView(STRING);
}


void CMainFrame::OnUpdateViewStringView(CCmdUI* pCmdUI)
{
    pCmdUI->Enable(
        !GetActiveView()->IsKindOf(RUNTIME_CLASS(CStringView)));
}

void CMainFrame::OnViewHexView()
{
    SwitchToView(HEX);
}

void CMainFrame::OnUpdateViewHexView(CCmdUI* pCmdUI)
{
    pCmdUI->Enable(
        !GetActiveView()->IsKindOf(RUNTIME_CLASS(CHexView)));
}
```

Testing the EX20C Application

The EX20C application initially displays the *CStringView* view of the document. You can toggle between the *CStringView* and *CHexView* views by choosing the appropriate command from the View menu. Both views of the document are shown side by side in Figure 20-2.

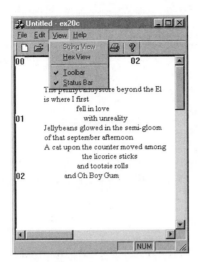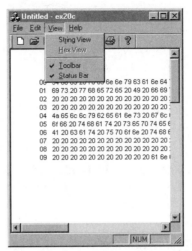

Figure 20-2.
The CStringView *view and the* CHexView *view of the document.*

The EX20D Example—
A Multiple View Class MDI Application

The final example, EX20D, uses the previous document and view classes to create a multiple view class MDI application without a splitter window. The logic is different from the logic in the other multiple view class applications. This time the action takes place in the application class in addition to the main frame class. As you study EX20D, you'll gain more insight into the use of *CDocTemplate* objects.

This example was generated with the AppWizard Context-Sensitive Help option. In Chapter 21, you'll activate the context-sensitive help capability.

If you're starting from scratch, use AppWizard to generate an ordinary MDI application with one of the view classes. Then add the second view class to the project and modify the application class files and main frame class files as described in the following sections.

Resource Requirements

The two items on the following page have been added to the Window menu in the *IDR_EX20DTYPE* menu resource.

Caption	Command ID	*CMainFrame* Function
New &String Window (replaces New Window item)	*ID_WINDOW_NEW_STRING*	*CMDIFrameWnd::OnWindowNew*
New &Hex Window	*ID_WINDOW_NEW_HEX*	*OnWindowNewHex*

ClassWizard was used to add the command-handling function *OnWindowNewHex* to the *CMainFrame* class.

CEx20dApp

In the application class header file, ex20d.h, the following data member has been added:

```
public:
    CMultiDocTemplate* m_pTemplateHex;
```

The implementation file, ex20d.cpp, contains the *#include* statements shown here:

```
#include "PoemDoc.h"
#include "StringView.h"
#include "HexView.h"
```

The *CEx20dApp InitInstance* member function has the code shown below inserted immediately after the *AddDocTemplate* function call.

```
m_pTemplateHex = new CMultiDocTemplate(
    IDR_EX20DTYPE,
    RUNTIME_CLASS(CPoemDoc),
    RUNTIME_CLASS(CChildFrame),
    RUNTIME_CLASS(CHexView));
```

The *AddDocTemplate* call generated by AppWizard established the primary document/frame/view combination for the application that is effective when the program starts. The template object above is a secondary template that can be activated in response to the New Hex Window menu item.

Now all you need is an *ExitInstance* member function that cleans up the secondary template:

```
int CEx20dApp::ExitInstance()
{
    delete m_pTemplateHex;
    return CWinApp::ExitInstance(); // saves profile settings
}
```

CMainFrame

The main frame class implementation file, MainFrm.cpp, has the *CHexView* class header (and the prerequisite document header) included:

```
#include "PoemDoc.h"
#include "HexView.h"
```

The base frame window class, *CMDIFrameWnd*, has an *OnWindowNew* function that is normally connected to the standard New Window menu item on the Window menu. The New String Window menu item is mapped to this function in EX20D. The New Hex Window menu item is mapped to the command handler function below to create new hex child windows. The function is a clone of *OnWindowNew*, adapted for the hex view-specific template defined in *InitInstance*.

```
void CMainFrame::OnWindowNewHex()
{
    CMDIChildWnd* pActiveChild = MDIGetActive();
    CDocument* pDocument;
    if (pActiveChild == NULL ||
            (pDocument = pActiveChild->GetActiveDocument()) == NULL) {
        TRACE("Warning:  No active document for WindowNew command\n");
        AfxMessageBox(AFX_IDP_COMMAND_FAILURE);
        return; // Command failed
    }

    // Otherwise, we have a new frame!
    CDocTemplate* pTemplate =
        ((CEx20dApp*) AfxGetApp())->m_pTemplateHex;
    ASSERT_VALID(pTemplate);
    CFrameWnd* pFrame =
        pTemplate->CreateNewFrame(pDocument, pActiveChild);
    if (pFrame == NULL) {
        TRACE("Warning:  failed to create new frame\n");
        AfxMessageBox(AFX_IDP_COMMAND_FAILURE);
        return; // Command failed
    }

    pTemplate->InitialUpdateFrame(pFrame, pDocument);
}
```

NOTE: The function cloning above is a useful MFC programming technique. You must first find a base class function that does almost what you want, and then copy it from the \VC98\mfc\src subdirectory into your derived class, changing it as required. The only danger of cloning is that subsequent versions of the MFC library might implement the original function differently.

Testing the EX20D Application

When you start the EX20D application, a text view child window appears. Choose New Hex Window from the Window menu. The application should look like this.

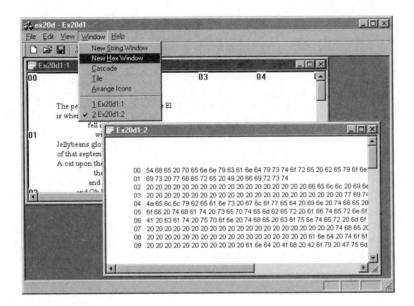

CHAPTER TWENTY-ONE

Context-Sensitive Help

Help technology is in a transition phase at the moment. The Hypertext Markup Language (HTML) format seems to be replacing rich text format (RTF). You can see this in the new Visual C++ online documentation via the MSDN viewer, which uses a new HTML-based help system called HTML Help. Microsoft is developing tools for compiling and indexing HTML files that are not shipped with Visual C++ 6.0. In the meantime, Microsoft Foundation Class (MFC) Library version 6.0 application framework programs are set up to use the WinHelp help engine included with Microsoft Windows. That means you'll be writing RTF files and your programs will be using compiled HLP files.

This chapter first shows you how to construct and process a simple stand-alone help file that has a table of contents and lets the user jump between topics. Next you'll see how your MFC library program activates WinHelp with help context IDs derived from window and command IDs keyed to an AppWizard-generated help file. Finally you'll learn how to use the MFC library help message routing system to customize the help capability.

The Windows WinHelp Program

If you've used commercial Windows-based applications, you've probably marveled at their sophisticated help screens: graphics, hyperlinks, and popups abound. At some software firms, including Microsoft, help authoring has been elevated to a profession in its own right. This section won't turn you into a help expert, but you can get started by learning to prepare a simple no-frills help file.

Rich Text Format

The original Windows SDK documentation showed you how to format help files with the ASCII file format called rich text format. We'll be using rich text format too, but we'll be working in wysiwyg mode, thereby avoiding the direct use of awkward escape sequences. You'll write with the same fonts, sizes, and styles that your user sees on the help screens. You'll definitely need a word processor that handles RTF. I've used Microsoft Word for this book, but many other word processors accommodate the RTF format.

> **NOTE:** Several commercial Windows help tools are available, including RoboHELP from Blue Sky Software and ForeHelp from the Forefront Corporation. RoboHELP is a set of templates and macros for Microsoft Word, and ForeHelp is a stand-alone package that simulates WinHelp, giving you immediate feedback as you write the help system.

Writing a Simple Help File

We're going to write a simple help file with a table of contents and three topics. This help file is designed to be run directly from WinHelp and started from Windows. No C++ programming is involved. Here are the steps:

1. **Create a \vcpp32\ex21a subdirectory.**

2. **Write the main help text file.** Use Microsoft Word (or another RTF-compatible word processor) to type text as shown here.

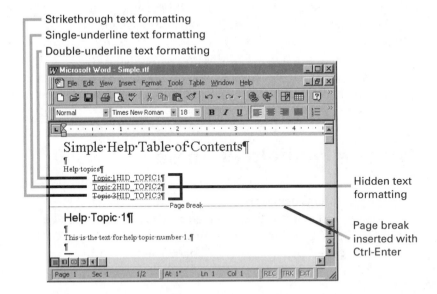

Be sure to apply the double-underline and hidden text formatting correctly and to insert the page break at the correct place.

NOTE: To see hidden text, you must turn on your word processor's hidden text viewing mode. In Word, choose Options from the Tools menu, click on the View tab, and select All in the Nonprinting Characters section.

3. Insert footnotes for the Table Of Contents screen. The Table Of Contents screen is the first topic screen in this help system. Using the specified custom footnote marks, insert the following footnotes at the beginning of the topic title.

Footnote Mark	Text	Description
#	HID_CONTENTS	Help context ID
$	SIMPLE Help Contents	Topic title

When you're finished with this step, the document should look like this.

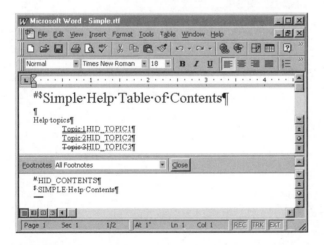

4. Insert footnotes for the Help Topic 1 screen. The Help Topic 1 screen is the second topic screen in the help system. Using the specified custom footnote marks, insert the footnotes on the following page.

Footnote Mark	Text	Description
#	HID_TOPIC1	Help context ID
$	SIMPLE Help Topic 1	Topic title
K	SIMPLE Topics	Keyword text

5. **Clone the Help Topic 1 screen.** Copy the entire Help Topic 1 section of the document—including the page break—to the clipboard, and then paste two copies of the text into the document. The footnotes are copied along with the text. In the first copy, change all occurrences of *1* to *2*. In the second copy, change all occurrences of *1* to *3*. Don't forget to change the footnotes. With Word, seeing which footnote goes with which topic can be a little difficult—be careful. When you're finished with this step, the document text (including footnotes) should look like this.

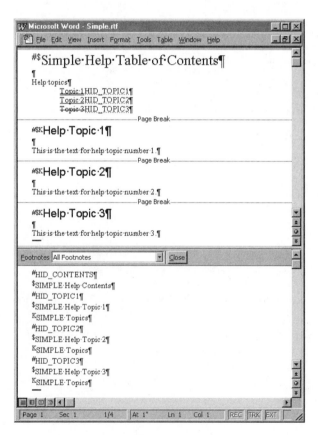

6. **Save the document.** Save the document as \vcpp32\ex21a\Simple.rtf. Specify Rich Text Format as the file type.

7. **Write a help project file.** Using Visual C++ or another text editor, create the file \vcpp32\ex21a\Simple.hpj, as follows:

```
[OPTIONS]
CONTENTS=HID_CONTENTS
TITLE=SIMPLE Application Help
COMPRESS=true
WARNING=2

[FILES]
Simple.rtf
```

This file specifies the context ID of the Table Of Contents screen and the name of the RTF file that contains the help text. Be sure to save the file in text (ASCII) format.

8. **Build the help file.** From Windows, run the Microsoft Help Workshop (HCRTF) utility (located by default in Program Files\Microsoft Visual Studio\Common\Tools). Open the file \vcpp32\ex21a\Simple.hpj, and then click the Save And Compile button.

This step runs the Windows Help Compiler with the project file Simple.hpj. The output is the help file Simple.hlp in the same directory.

NOTE: If you use Word 97 to create or edit RTF files, make sure you use version 4.02 (or later) of the HCRTF utility. Earlier versions of the HCRTF cannot process the rich text flags generated by Word 97.

9. **Run WinHelp with the new help file.** From Windows Explorer, double-click the file \vcpp32\ex21a\Simple.hlp. The Table Of Contents screen should look like this.

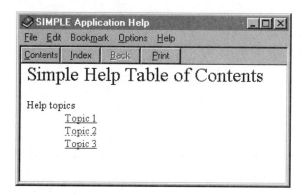

Now move the mouse cursor to Topic 1. Notice that the cursor changes from an arrow to a pointing hand. When you press the left mouse button, the Help Topic 1 screen should appear, as shown here.

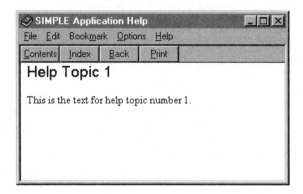

The *HID_TOPIC1* text in the Table Of Contents screen links to the corresponding context ID (the # footnote) in the topic page. This link is known as a jump.

The link to Help Topic 2 is coded as a pop-up jump. When you click on Topic 2, here's what you see.

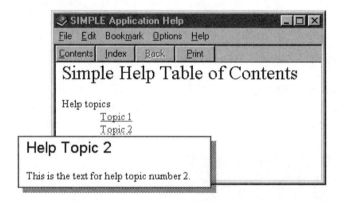

10. **Click the WinHelp Contents pushbutton.** Clicking this button should take you to the Table Of Contents screen, as shown at the beginning of step 9. WinHelp knows the ID of the Table Of Contents window because you specified it in the HPJ file.

11. **Click the WinHelp Index pushbutton.** When you click the Index button, WinHelp opens its Index dialog, which displays the help file's list of keywords. In Simple.hlp, all topics (excluding the table of contents) have

the same keyword (the K footnotes): SIMPLE Topics. When you double-click on this keyword, you see all associated topic titles (the $ footnotes), as shown here.

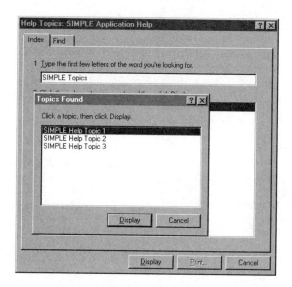

What you have here is a two-level help search hierarchy. The user can type the first few letters of the keyword and then select a topic from a list box. The more carefully you select your keywords and topic titles, the more effective your help system will be.

An Improved Table of Contents

You've been looking at the "old-style" help table of contents. The latest Win32 version of WinHelp can give you a modern tree-view table of contents. All you need is a text file with a CNT extension. Add a new file, Simple.cnt, in the \vcpp32\ex21a directory, containing this text:

```
:Base Simple.hlp
1 Help topics
2 Topic 1=HID_TOPIC1
2 Topic 2=HID_TOPIC2
2 Topic 3=HID_TOPIC3
```

Notice the context IDs that match the help file. The next time you run WinHelp with the Simple.hlp file, you'll see a new contents screen similar to the one shown on the following page.

You can also use HCRTF to edit CNT files. The CNT file is independent of the HPJ file and the RTF files. If you update your RTF files, you must make corresponding changes in your CNT file.

The Application Framework and WinHelp

You've seen WinHelp running as a stand-alone program. The application framework and WinHelp cooperate to give you context-sensitive help. Here are some of the main elements:

1. You select the Context-Sensitive Help option when you run AppWizard.

2. AppWizard generates a Help Topics item on your application's Help menu, and it creates one or more generic RTF files together with an HPJ file and a batch file that runs the Help Compiler.

3. AppWizard inserts a keyboard accelerator for the F1 key, and it maps the F1 key and the Help Topics menu item to member functions in the main frame window object.

4. When your program runs, it calls WinHelp when the user presses F1 or chooses the Help Topics menu item, passing a context ID that determines which help topic is displayed.

You now need to understand how WinHelp is called from another application and how your application generates context IDs for WinHelp.

Calling WinHelp

The *CWinApp* member function *WinHelp* activates WinHelp from within your application. If you look up *WinHelp* in the online documentation, you'll see a long list of actions that the optional second parameter controls. Ignore the second parameter and pretend that *WinHelp* has only one unsigned long integer parameter, *dwData*. This parameter corresponds to a help topic. Suppose that the SIMPLE help file is available and that your program contains the statement

```
AfxGetApp()->WinHelp(HID_TOPIC1);
```

When the statement is executed in response to the F1 key or some other event the Help Topic 1 screen appears, as it would if the user had clicked on Topic 1 in the Help Table Of Contents screen.

"Wait a minute," you say. "How does WinHelp know which help file to use?" The name of the help file matches the application name. If the executable program name is Simple.exe, the help file is named Simple.hlp.

> **NOTE:** You can force *WinHelp* to use a different help file by set-ting the *CWinApp* data member *m_pszHelpFilePath*.

"And how does WinHelp match the program constant *HID_TOPIC1* to the help file's context ID?" you ask. The help project file must contain a MAP section that maps context IDs to numbers. If your application's resource.h file defines *HID_TOPIC1* as *101*, the Simple.hpj MAP section looks like this:

```
[MAP]
HID_TOPIC1          101
```

The program's *#define* constant name doesn't have to match the help context ID; only the numbers must match. Making the names correspond, how-ever, is good practice.

Using Search Strings

For a text-based application, you might need help based on a keyword rather than a numeric context ID. In that case, use the WinHelp *HELP_KEY* or *HELP-_PARTIALKEY* option as follows:

```
CString string("find this string");
AfxGetApp()->WinHelp((DWORD) (LPCSTR) string, HELP_KEY);
```

The double cast for *string* is necessary because the first *WinHelp* parameter is multipurpose; its meaning depends on the value of the second parameter.

Calling WinHelp from the Application's Menu

AppWizard generates a Help Topics option on the Help menu, and it maps that option to *CWnd::OnHelpFinder* in the main frame window, which calls Win-Help this way:

```
AfxGetApp()->WinHelp(0L, HELP_FINDER);
```

With this call, WinHelp displays the Help Table Of Contents screen, and the user can navigate the help file through jumps and searches.

If you want the old-style table of contents, call WinHelp this way instead:

```
AfxGetApp()->WinHelp(0L, HELP_INDEX);
```

And if you want a "help on help" item, make this call:

```
AfxGetApp()->WinHelp(0L, HELP_HELPONHELP);
```

Help Context Aliases

The ALIAS section of the HPJ file allows you to equate one context ID with another. Suppose your HPJ file contained the following statements:

```
[ALIAS]
HID_TOPIC1 = HID_GETTING_STARTED

[MAP]
HID_TOPIC1          101
```

Your RTF files could use *HID_TOPIC1* and *HID_GETTING_STARTED* interchangeably. Both would be mapped to the help context 101 as generated by your application.

Determining the Help Context

You now have enough information to add a simple context-sensitive help system to an MFC program. You define F1 (the standard MFC library Help key) as a keyboard accelerator, and then you write a command handler that maps the program's help context to a *WinHelp* parameter. You could invent your own method for mapping the program state to a context ID, but why not take advantage of the system that's already built into the application framework?

The application framework determines the help context based on the ID of the active program element. These identified program elements include menu commands, frame windows, dialog windows, message boxes, and control bars. For example, a menu item might be identified as *ID_EDIT_CLEAR_ALL*. The main frame window usually has the *IDR_MAINFRAME* identifier. You might expect these identifiers to map directly to help context IDs. *IDR_MAINFRAME*, for example, would map to a help context ID of the same name. But what if a frame ID and a command ID had the same numeric value? Obviously, you need a way to prevent these overlaps.

The application framework solves the overlap problem by defining a new set of help *#define* constants that are derived from program element IDs. These help constants are the sum of the element ID and a base value, as shown in the following table.

Program Element	Element ID Prefix	Help Context ID Prefix	Base (Hexadecimal)
Menu Item or toolbar button	*ID_*, *IDM_*	*HID_*, *HIDM_*	10000
Frame or dialog	*IDR_*, *IDD_*	*HIDR_*, *HIDD*	20000
Error message box	*IDP_*	*HIDP_*	30000
Nonclient area		*H...*	40000
Control bar	*IDW_*	*HIDW_*	50000
Dispatch error messages			60000

HID_EDIT_CLEAR_ALL (0x1E121) corresponds to *ID_EDIT_CLEAR_ALL* (0xE121), and *HIDR_MAINFRAME* (0x20080) corresponds to *IDR_MAIN-FRAME* (0x80).

F1 Help

Two separate context-sensitive help access methods are built into an MFC application and are available if you have selected the AppWizard Context-Sensitive Help option. The first is standard F1 help. The user presses F1; the program makes its best guess about the help context and then calls WinHelp. In this mode, it is possible to determine the currently selected menu item or the currently selected window (frame, view, dialog, or message box).

Shift-F1 Help

The second context-sensitive help mode is more powerful than the F1 mode. With Shift-F1 help, the program can identify the following help contexts:

- A menu item selected with the mouse cursor
- A toolbar button

- A frame window

- A view window

- A specific graphics element within a view window

- The status bar

- Various nonclient elements such as the system menu control

NOTE: Shift-F1 help doesn't work with modal dialogs or message boxes.

The user activates Shift-F1 help by pressing Shift-F1 or by clicking the Context Help toolbar button, shown here.

In either case, the mouse cursor changes to

On the next mouse click, the help topic appears, with the position of the mouse cursor determining the context.

Message Box Help—The *AfxMessageBox* Function

The global function *AfxMessageBox* displays application framework error messages. This function is similar to the *CWnd::MessageBox* member function except that it has a help context ID as a parameter. The application framework maps this ID to a WinHelp context ID and then calls WinHelp when the user presses F1. If you can use the *AfxMessageBox* help context parameter, be sure to use prompt IDs that begin with *IDP_*. In your RTF file, use help context IDs that begin with *HIDP_*.

There are two versions of *AfxMessageBox*. In the first version, the prompt string is specified by a character-array pointer parameter. In the second version, the prompt ID parameter specifies a string resource. If you use the second version, your executable program will be more efficient. Both *AfxMessageBox* versions take a style parameter that makes the message box display an exclamation point, a question mark, or another graphics symbol.

Generic Help

When context-sensitive help is enabled, AppWizard assembles a series of default help topics that are associated with standard MFC library program elements. Following are some of the standard topics:

- Menu and toolbar commands (File, Edit, and so forth)
- Nonclient window elements (maximize box, title bar, and so forth)
- Status bar
- Error message boxes

These topics are contained in the files AfxCore.rtf and AfxPrint.rtf, which are copied, along with the associated bitmap files, to the application's \hlp subdirectory. Your job is to customize the generic help files.

NOTE: AppWizard generates AfxPrint.rtf only if you specify the Printing And Print Preview option.

A Help Example—No Programming Required

If you followed the instructions for EX20D in Chapter 20, you selected the AppWizard Context-Sensitive Help option. We'll now return to that example and explore the application framework's built-in help capability. You'll see how easy it is to link help topics to menu command IDs and frame window resource IDs. You edit RTF files, not CPP files.

Here are the steps for customizing the help for EX20D:

1. **Verify that the help file was built correctly.**   If you have built the EX20D project already, chances are that the help file was created correctly as part of the build process. Check this by running the application and then pressing the F1 key. You should see the generic Application Help screen with the title "Modifying the Document," as shown on the next page.

   If you do not see this screen, the MAKEHELP batch file did not run correctly. First check the last two lines of the ex20d.hpj file in the \hlp subdirectory. Are the paths correct for your Visual C++ installation? Next choose Options from the Tools menu, and click on the Directories tab. Make sure that the \VC98\bin subdirectory of your Visual C++ directory is one of the search directories for Executable Files.

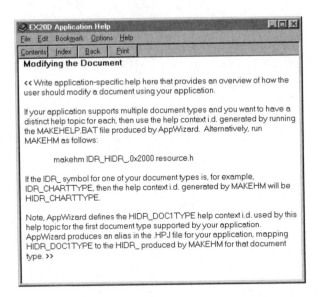

To generate the help file, highlight the ex20d.hpj file in the Workspace FileView window, and then choose Compile Ex20d.hpj from the Build menu. This runs the MAKEHELP batch file that is in your project directory. (You can also run it directly from an MS-DOS prompt.) You should observe some "file(s) copied" messages but no error messages. Rerun the EX20D program, and press F1 again.

NOTE: The Visual C++ make processor doesn't always detect all the dependencies in your help system. Sometimes you must run the MAKEHELP batch file yourself to rebuild the HLP file after making changes.

2. Test the generic help file. Try the following experiments:

- Close the Help dialog, press Alt-F and then press F1. This should open the help topic for the File New command. You can also press F1 while holding down the mouse button on the File New menu item to see the same help topic.

- Close the Help dialog, click the Context Help toolbar button (shown on page 516), and then choose Save from the File menu. Do you get the appropriate help topic?

- Click the Context Help toolbar button again, and then select the frame window's title bar. You should get an explanation of a Windows title bar.

■ Close all child windows and then press F1. You should see a main index page that is also an old-style table of contents.

3. Change the application title. The file AfxCore.rtf, in the \vcpp32\ex20d\hlp directory, contains the string *<<YourApp>>* throughout. Replace it globally with *EX20D*.

4. Change the Modifying The Document Help screen. The file AfxCore.rtf in the \vcpp32\ex20d\hlp directory contains text for the generic Application Help screen. Search for *Modifying the Document*, and then change the text to something appropriate for the application. This topic has the help context ID *HIDR_DOC1TYPE*. The generated ex20d.hpj file provides the alias *HIDR_EX20DTYPE*.

5. Add a topic for the Window New String Window menu item.
The New String Window menu item was added to EX20D and thus didn't have associated help text. Add a topic to AfxCore.rtf, as shown here.

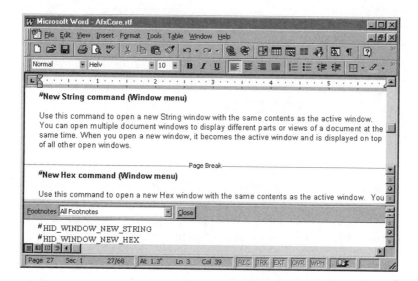

Notice the # footnote that links the topic to the context ID *HID_WIN-DOW_NEW_STRING* as defined in hlp\ex20d.hm. The program's command ID for the New String Window menu item is, of course, *ID_WINDOW_NEW_STRING*.

6. Rebuild the help file and test the application. Run the MAKEHELP batch file again, and then rerun the EX20D program. Try the two new help links.

The MAKEHELP Process

The process of building the application's HLP file is complex. Part of the complexity results from the Help Compiler's nonacceptance of statements such as

```
HID_MAINFRAME = ID_MAINFRAME + 0x20000
```

Because of the Help Compiler's nonacceptance, a special preprocessing program named makehm.exe must read the resource.h file to produce a help map file that defines the help context ID values. Below is a diagram of the entire MAKEHELP process.

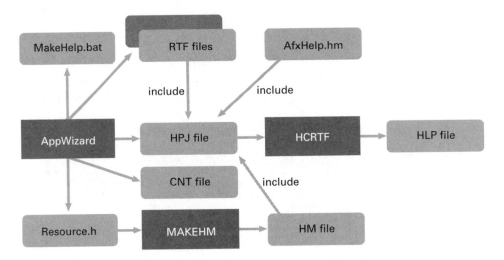

AppWizard generates the application's help project file (HPJ) and the help contents file (CNT). In the project file, the *[FILES]* section brings in RTF files and the *[MAP]* section contains #*include* statements for the generic and the application-specific help map (HM) files. The Help Workshop (HCRTF) processes the project file to produce the help file that WinHelp reads.

Help Command Processing

You've seen the components of a help file, and you've seen the effects of F1 and Shift-F1. You know how the application element IDs are linked to help context IDs. What you haven't seen is the application framework's internal processing of the help requests. Why should you be concerned? Suppose you want to provide help on a specific view window instead of a frame window. What if you need help topics linked to specific graphics items in a view window? These and other needs can be met by mapping the appropriate help messages in the view class.

Help command processing depends on whether the help request was an F1 request or a Shift-F1 request. The processing of each help request will be described separately.

F1 Processing

The F1 key is normally handled by a keyboard accelerator entry that AppWizard inserts in the RC file. The accelerator associates the F1 key with an *ID_HELP* command that is sent to the *OnHelp* member function in the *CFrameWnd* class.

> NOTE: In an active modal dialog or a menu selection in progress, the F1 key is processed by a Windows <u>hook</u> that causes the same *OnHelp* function to be called. The F1 accelerator key would otherwise be disabled.

The *CFrameWnd::OnHelp* function sends an MFC-defined WM_COMMANDHELP message to the innermost window, which is usually the view. If your view class does not map this message or if the handler returns *FALSE*, the framework routes the message to the next outer window, which is either the MDI child frame or the main frame. If you have not mapped WM_COMMANDHELP in your derived frame window classes, the message is processed in the MFC *CFrameWnd* class, which displays help for the symbol that AppWizard generates for your application or document type.

If you map the WM_COMMANDHELP message in a derived class, your handler must call *CWinApp::WinHelp* with the proper context ID as a parameter.

For any application, AppWizard adds the symbol *IDR_MAINFRAME* to your project and the HM file defines the help context ID *HIDR_MAINFRAME*, which is aliased to *main_index* in the HPJ file. The standard AfxCore.rtf file associates the main index with this context ID.

For an MDI application named SAMPLE, for example, AppWizard also adds the symbol *IDR_SAMPLETYPE* to your project and the HM file defines the help context ID *HIDR_SAMPLETYPE*, which is aliased to *HIDR_DOC1TYPE* in the HPJ file. The standard AfxCore.rtf file associates the topic "Modifying the Document" with this context ID.

Shift-F1 Processing

When the user presses Shift-F1 or clicks the Context Help toolbar button, a command message is sent to the *CFrameWnd* function *OnContextHelp*. When the user presses the mouse button again after positioning the mouse cursor, an MFC-defined WM_HELPHITTEST message is sent to the innermost window where the mouse click is detected. From that point on, the routing of this message is identical to that for the WM_COMMANDHELP message, described previously in "F1 Processing."

The *lParam* parameter of *OnHelpHitTest* contains the mouse coordinates in device units, relative to the upper-left corner of the window's client area. The *y* value is in the high-order half; the *x* value is in the low-order half. You can use these coordinates to set the help context ID specifically for an item in the view. Your *OnHelpHitTest* handler should return the correct context ID; the framework will call *WinHelp*.

A Help Command Processing Example—EX21B

EX21B is based on example EX20D from Chapter 20. It's a two-view MDI application with view-specific help added. Each of the two view classes has an *OnCommandHelp* message handler to process F1 help requests and an *OnHelp-HitTest* message handler to process Shift-F1 help requests.

Header Requirements

The compiler recognizes help-specific identifiers only if the following *#include* statement is present:

```
#include <afxpriv.h>
```

In EX21B, the statement is in the StdAfx.h file.

CStringView

The modified string view in StringView.h needs message map function prototypes for both F1 help and Shift-F1 help, as shown here:

```
afx_msg LRESULT OnCommandHelp(WPARAM wParam, LPARAM lParam);
afx_msg LRESULT OnHelpHitTest(WPARAM wParam, LPARAM lParam);
```

Here are the message map entries in StringView.cpp:

```
ON_MESSAGE(WM_COMMANDHELP, OnCommandHelp)
ON_MESSAGE(WM_HELPHITTEST, OnHelpHitTest)
```

The *OnCommandHelp* message handler member function in StringView.cpp processes F1 help requests. It responds to the message sent from the MDI main frame and displays the help topic for the string view window, as shown here:

```
LRESULT CStringView::OnCommandHelp(WPARAM wParam, LPARAM lParam)
{
    if (lParam == 0) { // context not already determined
        lParam = HID_BASE_RESOURCE + IDR_STRINGVIEW;
    }
    AfxGetApp()->WinHelp(lParam);
```

```
    return TRUE;
}
```

Finally the *OnHelpHitTest* member function handles Shift-F1 help, as shown here:

```
LRESULT CStringView::OnHelpHitTest(WPARAM wParam, LPARAM lParam)
{
    return HID_BASE_RESOURCE + IDR_STRINGVIEW;
}
```

In a more complex application, you might want *OnHelpHitTest* to set the help context ID based on the mouse cursor position.

CHexView

The *CHexView* class processes help requests the same way as the *CStringView* class does. Following is the necessary header code in HexView.h:

```
afx_msg LRESULT OnCommandHelp(WPARAM wParam, LPARAM lParam);
afx_msg LRESULT OnHelpHitTest(WPARAM wParam, LPARAM lParam);
```

Here are the message map entries in HexView.cpp:

```
ON_MESSAGE(WM_COMMANDHELP, OnCommandHelp)
ON_MESSAGE(WM_HELPHITTEST, OnHelpHitTest)
```

And here is the implementation code in HexView.cpp:

```
LRESULT CHexView::OnCommandHelp(WPARAM wParam, LPARAM lParam)
{
    if (lParam == 0) { // context not already determined
        lParam = HID_BASE_RESOURCE + IDR_HEXVIEW;
    }
    AfxGetApp()->WinHelp(lParam);
    return TRUE;
}

LRESULT CHexView::OnHelpHitTest(WPARAM wParam, LPARAM lParam)
{
    return HID_BASE_RESOURCE + IDR_HEXVIEW;
}
```

Resource Requirements

Two new symbols were added to the project's Resource.h file. Their values and corresponding help context IDs are shown on the next page.

Symbol	Value	Help Context ID	Value
IDR_STRINGVIEW	101	*HIDR_STRINGVIEW*	0x20065
IDR_HEXVIEW	102	*HIDR_HEXVIEW*	0x20066

Help File Requirements

Two topics were added to the AfxCore.rtf file with the help context IDs *HIDR-_STRINGVIEW* and *HIDR_HEXVIEW*, as shown here.

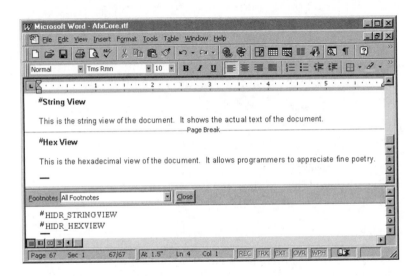

The generated ex21b.hm file, in the project's \hlp subdirectory, should look like this:

```
// MAKEHELP.BAT generated Help Map file.  Used by EX21B.HPJ.

// Commands (ID_* and IDM_*)
HID_WINDOW_NEW_STRING                    0x18003
HID_WINDOW_NEW_HEX                       0x18005

// Prompts (IDP_*)


// Resources (IDR_*)
HIDR_STRINGVIEW                          0x20065
HIDR_HEXVIEW                             0x20066
HIDR_MAINFRAME                           0x20080
HIDR_EX21BTYPE                           0x20081
```

```
// Dialogs (IDD_*)
HIDD_ABOUTBOX                           0x20064

// Frame Controls (IDW_*)
```

Testing the EX21B Application

Open a string child window and a hexadecimal child window. Test the action of F1 help and Shift-F1 help within those windows. If the help file didn't compile correctly, follow the instructions in step 1 of the help example beginning on page 517.

CHAPTER TWENTY-TWO

Dynamic Link Libraries

If you want to write modular software, you'll be very interested in dynamic link libraries (DLLs). You're probably thinking that you've been writing modular software all along because C++ classes are modular. But classes are build-time modular, and DLLs are runtime modular. Instead of programming giant EXEs that you must rebuild and test each time you make a change, you can build smaller DLL modules and test them individually. You can, for example, put a C++ class in a DLL, which might be as small as 12 KB after compiling and linking. Client programs can load and link your DLL very quickly when they run. Microsoft Windows itself uses DLLs for its major functions.

DLLs are getting easier to write. Win32 has greatly simplified the programming model, and there's more and better support from AppWizard and the Microsoft Foundation Class (MFC) library. This chapter shows you how to write DLLs in C++ and how to write client programs that use DLLs. You'll explore how Win32 maps DLLs into your processes, and you'll learn the differences between MFC library regular DLLs and MFC library extension DLLs. You'll see examples of simple DLLs of each type as well as a more complex DLL example that implements a custom control.

Fundamental DLL Theory

Before you look at the application framework's support for DLLs, you must understand how Win32 integrates DLLs into your process. You might want to review Chapter 10 to refresh your knowledge of processes and virtual memory. Remember that a process is a running instance of a program and that the program starts out as an EXE file on disk.

Basically, a DLL is a file on disk (usually with a DLL extension) consisting of global data, compiled functions, and resources, that becomes part of your process. It is compiled to load at a preferred base address, and if there's no conflict with other DLLs, the file gets mapped to the same virtual address in your process. The DLL has various <u>exported</u> functions, and the client program (the program that loaded the DLL in the first place) <u>imports</u> those functions. Windows matches up the imports and exports when it loads the DLL.

> **NOTE:** Win32 DLLs allow exported global variables as well as functions.

In Win32, each process gets its own copy of the DLL's read/write global variables. If you want to share memory among processes, you must either use a memory-mapped file or declare a <u>shared</u> <u>data</u> <u>section</u> as described in Jeffrey Richter's *Advanced Windows* (Microsoft Press, 1997). Whenever your DLL requests heap memory, that memory is allocated from the client process's heap.

How Imports Are Matched to Exports

A DLL contains a table of exported functions. These functions are identified to the outside world by their symbolic names and (optionally) by integers called <u>ordinal</u> <u>numbers</u>. The function table also contains the addresses of the functions within the DLL. When the client program first loads the DLL, it doesn't know the addresses of the functions it needs to call, but it does know the symbols or ordinals. The dynamic linking process then builds a table that connects the client's calls to the function addresses in the DLL. If you edit and rebuild the DLL, you don't need to rebuild your client program unless you have changed function names or parameter sequences.

> **NOTE:** In a simple world, you'd have one EXE file that imports functions from one or more DLLs. In the real world, many DLLs call functions inside other DLLs. Thus, a particular DLL can have both exports and imports. This is not a problem because the dynamic linkage process can handle cross-dependencies.

In the DLL code, you must explicitly declare your exported functions like this:

```
__declspec(dllexport) int MyFunction(int n);
```

(The alternative is to list your exported functions in a module-definition [DEF] file, but that's usually more troublesome.) On the client side, you need to declare the corresponding imports like this:

```
__declspec(dllimport) int MyFunction(int n);
```

If you're using C++, the compiler generates a <u>decorated</u> name for *MyFunction* that other languages can't use. These decorated names are the long names the compiler invents based on class name, function name, and parameter types. They are listed in the project's MAP file. If you want to use the plain name *MyFunction*, you have to write the declarations this way:

```
extern "C" __declspec(dllexport) int MyFunction(int n);
extern "C" __declspec(dllimport) int MyFunction(int n);
```

> **NOTE:** By default, the compiler uses the *__cdecl* argument passing convention, which means that the calling program pops the parameters off the stack. Some client languages might require the *__stdcall* convention, which replaces the Pascal calling convention, and which means that the called function pops the stack. Therefore, you might have to use the *__stdcall* modifier in your DLL export declaration.

Just having import declarations isn't enough to make a client link to a DLL. The client's project must specify the import library (LIB) to the linker, <u>and</u> the client program must actually contain a call to at least one of the DLL's imported functions. That call statement must be in an executable path in the program.

Implicit Linkage vs. Explicit Linkage

The preceding section primarily describes <u>implicit linking</u>, which is what you as a C++ programmer will probably be using for your DLLs. When you build a DLL, the linker produces a companion import LIB file, which contains every DLL's exported symbols and (optionally) ordinals, but no code. The LIB file is a surrogate for the DLL that is added to the client program's project. When you build (statically link) the client, the imported symbols are matched to the exported symbols in the LIB file, and those symbols (or ordinals) are bound into the EXE file. The LIB file also contains the DLL filename (but not its full pathname), which gets stored inside the EXE file. When the client is loaded, Windows finds and loads the DLL and then dynamically links it by symbol or by ordinal.

<u>Explicit linking</u> is more appropriate for interpreted languages such as Microsoft Visual Basic, but you can use it from C++ if you need to. With explicit linking, you don't use an import file; instead, you call the Win32 *LoadLibrary* function, specifying the DLL's pathname as a parameter. *LoadLibrary* returns an *HINSTANCE* parameter that you can use in a call to *GetProcAddress*, which converts a symbol (or an ordinal) to an address inside the DLL. Suppose you have a DLL that exports a function such as this:

```
extern "C" __declspec(dllexport) double SquareRoot(double d);
```

Here's an example of a client's explicit linkage to the function:

```
typedef double (SQRTPROC)(double);
HINSTANCE hInstance;
SQRTPROC* pFunction;
VERIFY(hInstance = ::LoadLibrary("c:\\winnt\\system32\\mydll.dll"));
VERIFY(pFunction = (SQRTPROC*)::GetProcAddress(hInstance, "SquareRoot"));
double d = (*pFunction)(81.0); // Call the DLL function
```

With implicit linkage, all DLLs are loaded when the client is loaded, but with explicit linkage, you can determine when DLLs are loaded and unloaded. Explicit linkage allows you to determine at runtime which DLLs to load. You could, for example, have one DLL with string resources in English and another with string resources in Spanish. Your application would load the appropriate DLL after the user chose a language.

Symbolic Linkage vs. Ordinal Linkage

In Win16, the more efficient ordinal linkage was the preferred linkage option. In Win32, the symbolic linkage efficiency was improved. Microsoft now recommends symbolic over ordinal linkage. The DLL version of the MFC library, however, uses ordinal linkage. A typical MFC program might link to hundreds of functions in the MFC DLL. Ordinal linkage permits that program's EXE file to be smaller because it does not have to contain the long symbolic names of its imports. If you build your own DLL with ordinal linkage, you must specify the ordinals in the project's DEF file, which doesn't have too many other uses in the Win32 environment. If your exports are C++ functions, you must use decorated names in the DEF file (or declare your functions with *extern "C"*). Here's a short extract from one of the MFC library DEF files:

```
?ReadList@CRecentFileList@@UAEXXZ @ 5458 NONAME
?ReadNameDictFromStream@CPropertySection@@QAEHPAUIStream@@@Z @ 5459 NONAME
?ReadObject@CArchive@@QAEPAVCObject@@PBUCRuntimeClass@@@Z @ 5460 NONAME
?ReadString@CArchive@@QAEHAAVCString@@@Z @ 5461 NONAME
?ReadString@CArchive@@QAEPADPADI@Z @ 5462 NONAME
?ReadString@CInternetFile@@UAEHAAVCString@@@Z @ 5463 NONAME
?ReadString@CInternetFile@@UAEPADPADI@Z @ 5464 NONAME
```

The numbers after the at (@) symbols are the ordinals. (Kind of makes you want to use symbolic linkage instead, doesn't it?)

The DLL Entry Point—*DllMain*

By default, the linker assigns the main entry point *_DllMainCRTStartup* to your DLL. When Windows loads the DLL, it calls this function, which first calls the constructors for global objects and then calls the global function *DllMain*, which you're supposed to write. *DllMain* is called not only when the DLL is attached to the process but also when it is detached (and at other times as well). Here is a skeleton *DllMain* function:

```
HINSTANCE g_hInstance;
extern "C" int APIENTRY
    DllMain(HINSTANCE hInstance, DWORD dwReason, LPVOID lpReserved)
{
    if (dwReason == DLL_PROCESS_ATTACH)
    {
        TRACE0("EX22A.DLL Initializing!\n");
        // Do initialization here
    }
    else if (dwReason == DLL_PROCESS_DETACH)
    {
        TRACE0("EX22A.DLL Terminating!\n");
        // Do cleanup here
    }
    return 1;   // ok
}
```

If you don't write a *DllMain* function for your DLL, a do-nothing version is brought in from the runtime library.

The *DllMain* function is also called when individual threads are started and terminated, as indicated by the *dwReason* parameter. Richter's book tells you all you need to know about this complex subject.

Instance Handles—Loading Resources

Each DLL in a process is identified by a unique 32-bit *HINSTANCE* value. In addition, the process itself has an *HINSTANCE* value. All these instance handles are valid only within a particular process, and they represent the starting virtual address of the DLL or EXE. In Win32, the *HINSTANCE* and *HMODULE* values are the same and the types can be used interchangeably. The process (EXE) instance handle is almost always 0x400000, and the handle for a DLL loaded at the default base address is 0x10000000. If your program uses several DLLs, each will have a different *HINSTANCE* value, either because the DLLs had different base addresses specified at build time or because the loader copied and relocated the DLL code.

Instance handles are particularly important for loading resources. The Win32 *FindResource* function takes an *HINSTANCE* parameter. EXEs and DLLs can each have their own resources. If you want a resource from the DLL, you specify the DLL's instance handle. If you want a resource from the EXE file, you specify the EXE's instance handle.

How do you get an instance handle? If you want the EXE's handle, you call the Win32 *GetModuleHandle* function with a *NULL* parameter. If you want the DLL's handle, you call the Win32 *GetModuleHandle* function with the DLL name as a parameter. Later you'll see that the MFC library has its own method of loading resources by searching various modules in sequence.

How the Client Program Finds a DLL

If you link explicitly with *LoadLibrary*, you can specify the DLL's full pathname. If you don't specify the pathname, or if you link implicitly, Windows follows this search sequence to locate your DLL:

1. The directory containing the EXE file
2. The process's current directory
3. The Windows system directory
4. The Windows directory
5. The directories listed in the Path environment variable

Here's a trap you can easily fall into. You build a DLL as one project, copy the DLL file to the system directory, and then run the DLL from a client program. So far, so good. Next you rebuild the DLL with some changes, but you forget to copy the DLL file to the system directory. The next time you run the client program, it loads the old version of the DLL. Be careful!

Debugging a DLL

Visual C++ makes debugging a DLL easy. Just run the debugger from the DLL project. The first time you do this, the debugger asks for the pathname of the client EXE file. Every time you "run" the DLL from the debugger after this, the debugger loads the EXE, but the EXE uses the search sequence to find the DLL. This means that you must either set the Path environment variable to point to the DLL or copy the DLL to a directory in the search sequence.

MFC DLLs—Extension vs. Regular

We've been looking at Win32 DLLs that have a *DllMain* function and some exported functions. Now we'll move into the world of the MFC application framework, which adds its own support layer on top of the Win32 basics. AppWizard lets you build two kinds of DLLs with MFC library support: <u>extension</u> DLLs and <u>regular</u> DLLs. You must understand the differences between these two types before you decide which one is best for your needs.

NOTE: Of course, Visual C++ lets you build a pure Win32 DLL without the MFC library, just as it lets you build a Windows program without the MFC library. This is an MFC-oriented book, however, so we'll ignore the Win32 option here.

An extension DLL supports a C++ interface. In other words, the DLL can export whole classes and the client can construct objects of those classes or derive classes from them. An extension DLL dynamically links to the code in the DLL version of the MFC library. Therefore, an extension DLL requires that your client program be dynamically linked to the MFC library (the AppWizard default) and that both the client program and the extension DLL be synchronized to the same version of the MFC DLLs (mfc42.dll, mfc42d.dll, and so on). Extension DLLs are quite small; you can build a simple extension DLL with a size of 10 KB, which loads quickly.

If you need a DLL that can be loaded by any Win32 programming environment (including Visual Basic version 6.0), you should use a regular DLL. A big restriction here is that the regular DLL can export only C-style functions. It can't export C++ classes, member functions, or overloaded functions because every C++ compiler has its own method of decorating names. You can, however, use C++ classes (and MFC library classes, in particular) inside your regular DLL.

When you build an MFC regular DLL, you can choose to statically link or dynamically link to the MFC library. If you choose static linking, your DLL will include a copy of all the MFC library code it needs and will thus be self-contained. A typical Release-build statically linked regular DLL is about 144 KB in size. If you choose dynamic linking, the size drops to about 17 KB but you'll have to ensure that the proper MFC DLLs are present on the target machine. That's no problem if the client program is already dynamically linked to the same version of the MFC library.

When you tell AppWizard what kind of DLL or EXE you want, compiler *#define* constants are set as shown in the following table.

	Dynamically Linked to Shared MFC Library	Statically Linked* to MFC Library
Regular DLL	*_AFXDLL*, *_USRDLL*	*_USRDLL*
Extension DLL	*_AFXEXT*, *_AFXDLL*	unsupported option
Client EXE	*_AFXDLL*	no constants defined

* Visual C++ Learning Edition does not support the static linking option.

If you look inside the MFC source code and header files, you'll see a ton of *#ifdef* statements for these constants. This means that the library code is compiled quite differently depending on the kind of project you're producing.

The Shared MFC DLLs and the Windows DLLs

If you build a Windows Debug target with the shared MFC DLL option, your program is dynamically linked to one or more of these (ANSI) MFC DLLs:

mfc42d.dll	Core MFC classes
mfco42d.dll	ActiveX (OLE) classes
mfcd42d.dll	Database classes (ODBC and DAO)
mfcn42d.dll	Winsock, WinInet classes

When you build a Release target, your program is dynamically linked to mfc42.dll only. Linkage to these MFC DLLs is implicit via import libraries. You might assume implicit linkage to the ActiveX and ODBC DLLs in Windows, in which case you would expect all these DLLs to be linked to your Release-build client when it loads, regardless of whether it uses ActiveX or ODBC features. However, this is not what happens. Through some creative thunking, MFC loads the ActiveX and ODBC DLLs explicitly (by calling *LoadLibrary*) when one of their functions is first called. Your client application thus loads only the DLLs it needs.

MFC Extension DLLs—Exporting Classes

If your extension DLL contains only exported C++ classes, you'll have an easy time building and using it. The steps for building the EX22A example show you how to tell AppWizard that you're building an extension DLL skeleton. That skeleton has only the *DllMain* function. You simply add your own C++ classes to the project. There's only one special thing you must do. You must add the macro *AFX_EXT_CLASS* to the class declaration, as shown here:

```
class AFX_EXT_CLASS CStudent : public CObject
```

This modification goes into the H file that's part of the DLL project, and it also goes into the H file that client programs use. In other words, the H files are exactly the same for both client and DLL. The macro generates different code depending on the situation—it exports the class in the DLL and imports the class in the client.

The MFC Extension DLL Resource Search Sequence

If you build a dynamically linked MFC <u>client</u> application, many of the MFC library's standard resources (error message strings, print preview dialog templates, and so on) are stored in the MFC DLLs (mfc42.dll, mfco42.dll, and so on), but your application has its own resources too. When you call an MFC function such as *CString::LoadString* or *CBitmap::LoadBitmap*, the framework steps in and searches first the EXE file's resources and then the MFC DLL's resources.

If your program includes an extension DLL and your EXE needs a resource, the search sequence is first the EXE file, then the extension DLL, and then the MFC DLLs. If you have a string resource ID, for example, that is unique among all resources, the MFC library will find it. If you have duplicate string IDs in your EXE file and your extension DLL file, the MFC library loads the string in the EXE file.

If the extension DLL loads a resource, the sequence is first the extension DLL, then the MFC DLLs, and then the EXE.

You can change the search sequence if you need to. Suppose you want your EXE code to search the extension DLL's resources first. Use code such as this:

```
HINSTANCE hInstResourceClient = AfxGetResourceHandle();
// Use DLL's instance handle
AfxSetResourceHandle(::GetModuleHandle("mydllname.dll"));
CString strRes;
strRes.LoadString(IDS_MYSTRING);
// Restore client's instance handle
AfxSetResourceHandle(hInstResourceClient);
```

You can't use *AfxGetInstanceHandle* instead of *::GetModuleHandle*. In an extension DLL, *AfxGetInstanceHandle* returns the EXE's instance handle, not the DLL's handle.

The EX22A Example—An MFC Extension DLL

This example makes an extension DLL out of the *CPersistentFrame* class you saw in Chapter 15. First you'll build the ex22a.dll file, and then you'll use it in a test client program, EX22B.

Here are the steps for building the EX22A example:

1. **Run AppWizard to produce \vcpp32\ex22a\ex22a.** Choose New from Visual C++'s File menu, and then click on the Projects tab as usual. Instead of selecting MFC AppWizard (exe), choose MFC AppWizard (dll), as shown on the following page.

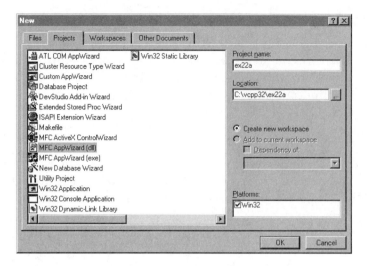

In this example, only one AppWizard screen appears. Choose MFC Extension DLL, as shown here.

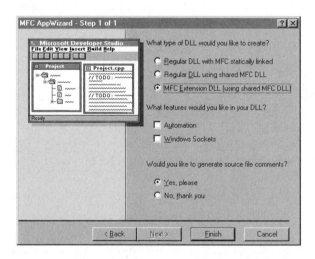

2. **Examine the ex22a.cpp file.** AppWizard generates the following code, which includes the *DllMain* function:

```
// ex22a.cpp : Defines the initialization routines for the DLL.
//

#include "stdafx.h"
#include <afxdllx.h>
```

```
#ifdef _DEBUG
#define new DEBUG_NEW
#undef THIS_FILE
static char THIS_FILE[] = __FILE__;
#endif

static AFX_EXTENSION_MODULE Ex22aDLL = { NULL, NULL };

extern "C" int APIENTRY
DllMain(HINSTANCE hInstance, DWORD dwReason, LPVOID lpReserved)
{
    // Remove this if you use lpReserved
    UNREFERENCED_PARAMETER(lpReserved);

    if (dwReason == DLL_PROCESS_ATTACH)
    {
        TRACE0("EX22A.DLL Initializing!\n");

        // Extension DLL one-time initialization
        if (!AfxInitExtensionModule(Ex22aDLL, hInstance))
            return 0;

        // Insert this DLL into the resource chain

    (generated comment lines deleted)

        new CDynLinkLibrary(Ex22aDLL);
    }
    else if (dwReason == DLL_PROCESS_DETACH)
    {
        TRACE0("EX22A.DLL Terminating!\n");
        // Terminate the library before destructors are called
        AfxTermExtensionModule(Ex22aDLL);
    }
    return 1;    // ok
}
```

3. **Insert the *CPersistentFrame* class into the project.** Choose Add To Project from the Project menu, and then choose Components And Controls from the submenu. Locate the file Persistent Frame.ogx that you created in Chapter 15 (or locate the copy on the companion CD-ROM). Click the Insert button to insert the class into the current project.

> NOTE: If you don't want to use the OGX component, you can copy the files Persist.h and Persist.cpp into your project directory and add them to the project by choosing Add To Project from the Visual C++ Project menu.

4. Edit the persist.h file. Modify the line

```
class CPersistentFrame : public CFrameWnd
```

to read

```
class AFX_EXT_CLASS CPersistentFrame : public CFrameWnd
```

5. **Build the project and copy the DLL file.** Copy the file ex22a.dll from the \vcpp32\ex22a\Debug directory to your system directory (\Windows\System or \Winnt\System32).

The EX22B Example—A DLL Test Client Program

This example starts off as a client for ex22a.dll. It imports the *CPersistentFrame* class from the DLL and uses it as a base class for the SDI frame window. Later you'll add code to load and test the other sample DLLs in this chapter.

Here are the steps for building the EX22B example:

1. **Run AppWizard to produce \vcpp32\ex22b\ex22b.** This is an ordinary MFC EXE program. Select Single Document. Otherwise, accept the default settings. Be absolutely sure that in Step 5 you accept the As A Shared DLL option.

2. **Copy the file persist.h from the \vcpp32\ex22a directory.** Note that you're copying the header file, not the CPP file.

3. **Change the *CMainFrame* base class to *CPersistentFrame* as you did in EX15A.** Replace all occurrences of *CFrameWnd* with *CPersistent-Frame* in both MainFrm.h and MainFrm.cpp. Also insert the following line into MainFrm.h:

```
#include "persist.h"
```

4. **Add the ex22a import library to the linker's input library list.** Choose Settings from Visual C++'s Project menu. Select All Configurations in the Settings For drop-down list. Then fill in the Object/Library Modules control on the Link page as shown on the facing page.

You must specify the full pathname for the ex22a.lib file unless you have a copy of that file in your project directory.

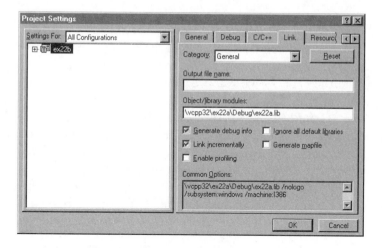

5. **Build and test the EX22B program.** If you run the program from the debugger and Windows can't find the EX22A DLL, Windows displays a message box when EX22B starts. If all goes well, you should have a persistent frame application that works exactly like the one in EX15A. The only difference is that the *CPersistentFrame* code is in an extension DLL.

MFC Regular DLLs—The *CWinApp* Derived Class

When AppWizard generates a regular DLL, the *DllMain* function is inside the framework and you end up with a class derived from *CWinApp* (and a global object of that class), just as you would with an EXE program. You can get control by overriding *CWinApp::InitInstance* and *CWinApp::ExitInstance*. Most of the time, you don't bother overriding those functions, though. You simply write the C functions and then export them with the *__declspec(dllexport)* modifier (or with entries in the project's DEF file).

Using the *AFX_MANAGE_STATE* Macro

When mfc42.dll is loaded as part of a process, it stores data in some truly global variables. If you call MFC functions from an MFC program or extension DLL, mfc42.dll knows how to set these global variables on behalf of the calling process. If you call into mfc42.dll from a regular MFC DLL, however, the global variables are not synchronized and the effects will be unpredictable. To solve this problem, insert the line

```
AFX_MANAGE_STATE(AfxGetStaticModuleState());
```

at the start of all exported functions in your regular DLL. If the MFC code is statically linked, the macro will have no effect.

The MFC Regular DLL Resource Search Sequence

When an EXE links to a regular DLL, resource loading functions inside the EXE will load the EXE's own resources. Resource loading functions inside the regular DLL will load the DLL's own resources.

If you want your EXE code to load resources from the DLL, you can use *AfxSetResourceHandle* to temporarily change the resource handle. The code will be nearly the same as that on page 535. If you're writing an application that needs to be localized, you can put language-specific strings, dialogs, menus, and so forth in an MFC regular DLL. You might, for example, include the modules English.dll, German.dll, and French.dll. Your client program would explicitly load the correct DLL and use code such as that on page 535 to load the resources, which would have the same IDs in all the DLLs.

The EX22C Example—An MFC Regular DLL

This example creates a regular DLL that exports a single square root function. First you'll build the ex22c.dll file, and then you'll modify the test client program, EX22B, to test the new DLL.

Here are the steps for building the EX22C example:

1. **Run AppWizard to produce \vcpp32\ex22c\ex22c.** Proceed as you did for EX22A, but accept Regular DLL Using Shared MFC DLL (instead of choosing MFC Extension DLL) from the one and only AppWizard page.

2. **Examine the ex22c.cpp file.** AppWizard generates the following code, which includes a derived *CWinApp* class:

```
// ex22c.cpp : Defines the initialization routines for the DLL.
//

#include "stdafx.h"
#include "ex22c.h"

#ifdef _DEBUG
#define new DEBUG_NEW
#undef THIS_FILE
static char THIS_FILE[] = __FILE__;
#endif

(generated comment lines omitted)

/////////////////////////////////////////////////////////////////////
// CEx22cApp
```

```
BEGIN_MESSAGE_MAP(CEx22cApp, CWinApp)
    //{{AFX_MSG_MAP(CEx22cApp)
        // NOTE - the ClassWizard will add and remove        →
                 mapping macros here.
        //      DO NOT EDIT what you see in these blocks      →
                 of generated code!
    //}}AFX_MSG_MAP
END_MESSAGE_MAP()


/////////////////////////////////////////////////////////////////////
// CEx22cApp construction

CEx22cApp::CEx22cApp()
{
    // TODO: add construction code here,
    // Place all significant initialization in InitInstance
}


/////////////////////////////////////////////////////////////////////
// The one and only CEx22cApp object

CEx22cApp theApp;
```

3. **Add the code for the exported *Ex22cSquareRoot* function.**   It's okay to add this code in the ex22c.cpp file, although you can use a new file if you want to:

```
extern "C" __declspec(dllexport) double Ex22cSquareRoot(double d)
{
    AFX_MANAGE_STATE(AfxGetStaticModuleState());
    TRACE("Entering Ex22cSquareRoot\n");
    if (d >= 0.0) {
        return sqrt(d);
    }
    AfxMessageBox("Can't take square root of a negative number.");
    return 0.0;
}
```

You can see that there's no problem with the DLL displaying a message box or another modal dialog. You'll need to include math.h in the file containing this code.

4. **Build the project and copy the DLL file.**   Copy the file ex22c.dll from the \vcpp32\ex22c\Debug directory to your system directory.

Updating the EX22B Example—Adding Code to Test ex22c.dll

When you first built the EX22B program, it linked dynamically to the EX22A MFC extension DLL. Now you'll update the project to implicitly link to the EX22C MFC regular DLL and to call the DLL's square root function.

Following are the steps for updating the EX22B example.

1. Add a new dialog resource and class to \vcpp32\ex22b\ex22b. Use the dialog editor to create the *IDD_EX22C* template, as shown here.

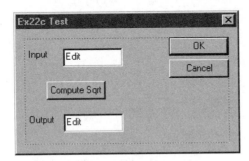

Then use ClassWizard to generate a class *CTest22cDialog*, derived from *CDialog*. The controls, data members, and message map function are shown in the following table.

Control ID	Type	Data Member	Message Map Function
IDC_INPUT	edit	*m_dInput* (double)	
IDC_OUTPUT	edit	*m_dOutput* (double)	
IDC_COMPUTE	button		*OnCompute*

2. Code the *OnCompute* function to call the DLL's exported function. Edit the ClassWizard-generated function in Test22cDialog.cpp as shown here:

```
void CTest22cDialog::OnCompute()
{
    UpdateData(TRUE);
    m_dOutput = Ex22cSquareRoot(m_dInput);
    UpdateData(FALSE);
}
```

You'll have to declare the *Ex22cSquareRoot* function as an imported function. Add the following line to the Test22cDialog.h file:

```
extern "C" __declspec(dllimport) double Ex22cSquareRoot(double d);
```

3. **Integrate the *CTest22cDialog* class into the EX22B application.**
   You'll need to add a top-level menu, Test, and an Ex22c DLL option with the ID *ID_TEST_EX22CDLL*. Use ClassWizard to map this option to a member function in the *CEx22bView* class, and then code the handler in Ex22bView.cpp as follows:

```
void CEx22bView::OnTestEx22cdll()
{
    CTest22cDialog dlg;
    dlg.DoModal();
}
```

   Of course, you'll have to add this line to the Ex22bView.cpp file:

```
#include "Test22cDialog.h"
```

4. **Add the EX22C import library to the linker's input library list.**
   Choose Settings from Visual C++'s Project menu, and then add
   \vcpp32\ex22c\Debug\ex22c.lib to the Object/Library Modules control
   on the Link page. (Use a space to separate the new entry from the existing entry.) Now the program should implicitly link to both the EX22A DLL and the EX22C DLL. As you can see, the client doesn't care whether the DLL is a regular DLL or an extension DLL. You just specify the LIB name to the linker.

5. **Build and test the updated EX22B application.** Choose Ex22c DLL from the Test menu. Type a number in the Input edit control, and then click the Compute Sqrt button. The result should appear in the Output control.

A Custom Control DLL

Programmers have been using DLLs for custom controls since the early days of Windows because custom controls are neatly self-contained. The original custom controls were written in pure C and configured as stand-alone DLLs. Today you can use the features of the MFC library in your custom controls, and you can use the wizards to make coding easier. A regular DLL is the best choice for a custom control because the control doesn't need a C++ interface and because it can be used by any development system that accepts custom controls (such as the Borland C++ compiler). You'll probably want to use the MFC dynamic linking option because the resulting DLL will be small and quick to load.

What Is a Custom Control?

You've seen ordinary controls and Microsoft Windows common controls in Chapter 6, and you've seen ActiveX controls in Chapter 8. The custom control acts like an ordinary control, such as the edit control, in that it sends WM_COMMAND notification messages to its parent window and receives user-defined messages. The dialog editor lets you position custom controls in dialog templates. That's what the "head" control palette item, shown here, is for.

You have a lot of freedom in designing your custom control. You can paint anything you want in its window (which is managed by the client application) and you can define any notification and inbound messages you need. You can use ClassWizard to map normal Windows messages in the control (WM_L-BUTTONDOWN, for example), but you must manually map the user-defined messages and manually map the notification messages in the parent window class.

A Custom Control's Window Class

A dialog resource template specifies its custom controls by their symbolic <u>window class</u> names. Don't confuse the Win32 window class with the C++ class; the only similarity is the name. A window class is defined by a structure that contains the following:

- The name of the class
- A pointer to the *WndProc* function that receives messages sent to windows of the class
- Miscellaneous attributes, such as the background brush

The Win32 *RegisterClass* function copies the structure into process memory so that any function in the process can use the class to create a window. When the dialog window is initialized, Windows creates the custom control child windows from the window class names stored in the template.

Suppose now that the control's *WndProc* function is inside a DLL. When the DLL is initialized (by a call to *DllMain*), it can call *RegisterClass* for the control. Because the DLL is part of the process, the client program can create child windows of the custom control class. To summarize, the client knows the name string of a control window class and it uses that class name to construct the child window. All the code for the control, including the *WndProc* function, is inside the DLL. All that's necessary is that the client load the DLL prior to creating the child window.

The MFC Library and the *WndProc* Function

Okay, so Windows calls the control's *WndProc* function for each message sent to that window. But you really don't want to write an old-fashioned *switch-case* statement—you want to map those messages to C++ member functions, as you've been doing all along. Now, in the DLL, you must rig up a C++ class that corresponds to the control's window class. Once you've done that, you can happily use ClassWizard to map messages.

The obvious part is the writing of the C++ class for the control. You simply use ClassWizard to create a new class derived from *CWnd*. The tricky part is wiring the C++ class to the *WndProc* function and to the application framework's message pump. You'll see a real *WndProc* in the EX22D example, but here's the pseudocode for a typical control *WndProc* function:

```
LRESULT MyControlWndProc(HWND hWnd, UINT message
                         WPARAM wParam, LPARAM lParam)
{
    if (this is the first message for this window) {
        CWnd* pWnd = new CMyControlWindowClass();
        attach pWnd to hWnd
    }
    return AfxCallWndProc(pWnd, hWnd, message, WParam, lParam);
}
```

The MFC *AfxCallWndProc* function passes messages to the framework, which dispatches them to the member functions mapped in *CMyControl-WindowClass*.

Custom Control Notification Messages

The control communicates with its parent window by sending it special WM_COMMAND notification messages with parameters, as shown here.

Parameter	Usage
(HIWORD) wParam	Notification code
(LOWORD) wParam	Child window ID
lParam	Child window handle

The meaning of the notification code is arbitrary and depends on the control. The parent window must interpret the code based on its knowledge of the control. For example, the code 77 might mean that the user typed a character while positioned on the control.

The control might send a notification message such as this:

```
GetParent()->SendMessage(WM_COMMAND,
    GetDlgCtrlID() | ID_NOTIFYCODE << 16, (LONG) GetSafeHwnd());
```

On the client side, you map the message with the MFC *ON_CONTROL* macro like this:

```
ON_CONTROL(ID_NOTIFYCODE, IDC_MYCONTROL, OnClickedMyControl)
```

Then you declare the handler function like this:

```
afx_msg void OnClickedMyControl();
```

User-Defined Messages Sent to the Control

You have already seen user-defined messages in Chapter 7. This is the means by which the client program communicates with the control. Because a standard message returns a 32-bit value if it is sent rather than posted, the client can obtain information from the control.

The EX22D Example—A Custom Control

The EX22D program is an MFC regular DLL that implements a traffic light control indicating off, red, yellow, and green states. When clicked with the left mouse button, the DLL sends a clicked notification message to its parent and responds to two user-defined messages, RYG_SETSTATE and RYG_GET-STATE. The state is an integer that represents the color. Credit goes to Richard Wilton, who included the original C-language version of this control in his book *Windows 3 Developer's Workshop* (Microsoft Press, 1991).

The EX22D project was originally generated using AppWizard, with linkage to the shared MFC DLL, just like EX22C. Figure 22-1 shows the code for the primary source file, with the added code in the *InitInstance* function in boldface. The dummy exported *Ex22dEntry* function exists solely to allow the DLL to be implicitly linked. The client program must include a call to this function. That call must be in an executable path in the program or the compiler will eliminate the call. As an alternative, the client program could call the Win32 *LoadLibrary* function in its *InitInstance* function to explicitly link the DLL.

EX22D.CPP

```
// ex22d.cpp : Defines the initialization routines for the DLL.
//

#include "stdafx.h"
#include "ex22d.h"
#include "RygWnd.h"

#ifdef _DEBUG
#define new DEBUG_NEW
#undef THIS_FILE
static char THIS_FILE[] = __FILE__;
#endif


extern "C" __declspec(dllexport) void Ex22dEntry() {} // dummy function

(generated comment lines omitted)

///////////////////////////////////////////////////////////////////////
// CEx22dApp

BEGIN_MESSAGE_MAP(CEx22dApp, CWinApp)
    //{{AFX_MSG_MAP(CEx22dApp)
        // NOTE - the ClassWizard will add and remove        ⌐
                  mapping macros here.
        //      DO NOT EDIT what you see in these blocks      ⌐
                  of generated code!
    //}}AFX_MSG_MAP
END_MESSAGE_MAP()


///////////////////////////////////////////////////////////////////////
// CEx22dApp construction

CEx22dApp::CEx22dApp()
{
    // TODO: add construction code here,
    // Place all significant initialization in InitInstance
}


///////////////////////////////////////////////////////////////////////
// The one and only CEx22dApp object

CEx22dApp theApp;
```

Figure 22-1.

(continued)

The EX22D primary source listing.

Figure 22-1. *continued*

```
BOOL CEx22dApp::InitInstance()
{
    CRygWnd::RegisterWndClass(AfxGetInstanceHandle());
    return CWinApp::InitInstance();
}
```

Figure 22-2 shows the code for the *CRygWnd* class, including the global *RygWndProc* function. (Click the Add Class button in ClassWizard to create this class.) The code that paints the traffic light isn't very interesting, so we'll concentrate on the functions that are common to most custom controls. The static *RegisterWndClass* member function actually registers the *RYG* window class and must be called as soon as the DLL is loaded. The *OnLButtonDown* handler is called when the user presses the left mouse button inside the control window. It sends the clicked notification message to the parent window. The overridden *PostNcDestroy* function is important because it deletes the *CRygWnd* object when the client program destroys the control window. The *OnGetState* and *OnSetState* functions are called in response to user-defined messages sent by the client. Remember to copy the DLL to your system directory.

RYGWND.H

```
#if !defined(AFX_RYGWND_H__1AA889D5_9788_11D0_BED2_00C04FC2A0C2__INCLUDED_)
#define AFX_RYGWND_H__1AA889D5_9788_11D0_BED2_00C04FC2A0C2__INCLUDED_

#if _MSC_VER > 1000
#pragma once
#endif // _MSC_VER > 1000
// RygWnd.h : header file
//


/////////////////////////////////////////////////////////////////////////
// CRygWnd window

#define RYG_SETSTATE WM_USER + 0
#define RYG_GETSTATE WM_USER + 1

LRESULT CALLBACK AFX_EXPORT
    RygWndProc(HWND hWnd, UINT message, WPARAM wParam, LPARAM lParam);

class CRygWnd : public CWnd
{
private:
    int m_nState; // 0=off, 1=red, 2=yellow, 3=green
```

Figure 22-2.
The CRygWnd *class listing.*

(continued)

548

```
    static CRect  s_rect;
    static CPoint s_point;
    static CRect  s_rColor[3];
    static CBrush s_bColor[4];

// Construction
public:
    CRygWnd();
public:
    static BOOL RegisterWndClass(HINSTANCE hInstance);

// Attributes
public:

// Operations
public:

// Overrides
    // ClassWizard generated virtual function overrides
    //{{AFX_VIRTUAL(CRygWnd)
    protected:
    virtual void PostNcDestroy();
    //}}AFX_VIRTUAL

// Implementation
public:
    virtual ~CRygWnd();

    // Generated message map functions
private:
    void SetMapping(CDC* pDC);
    void UpdateColor(CDC* pDC, int n);
protected:
    //{{AFX_MSG(CRygWnd)
    afx_msg void OnPaint();
    afx_msg void OnLButtonDown(UINT nFlags, CPoint point);
    //}}AFX_MSG
    afx_msg LRESULT OnSetState(WPARAM wParam, LPARAM lParam);
    afx_msg LRESULT OnGetState(WPARAM wParam, LPARAM lParam);
    DECLARE_MESSAGE_MAP()
};


/////////////////////////////////////////////////////////////////////
//{{AFX_INSERT_LOCATION}}
// Microsoft Visual C++ will insert additional declarations
//   immediately before the previous line.
```

(continued)

Figure 22-2. *continued*

```
#endif // !defined(AFX_RYGWND_H__1AA889D5_9788_        →
                   11D0_BED2_00C04FC2A0C2__INCLUDED_)
```

RYGWND.CPP

```cpp
// RygWnd.cpp : implementation file
//

#include "stdafx.h"
#include "ex22d.h"
#include "RygWnd.h"

#ifdef _DEBUG
#define new DEBUG_NEW
#undef THIS_FILE
static char THIS_FILE[] = __FILE__;
#endif

LRESULT CALLBACK AFX_EXPORT
    RygWndProc(HWND hWnd, UINT message, WPARAM wParam, LPARAM lParam)
{
    AFX_MANAGE_STATE(AfxGetStaticModuleState());

    CWnd* pWnd;

    pWnd = CWnd::FromHandlePermanent(hWnd);
    if (pWnd == NULL) {
        // Assume that client created a CRygWnd window
        pWnd = new CRygWnd();
        pWnd->Attach(hWnd);
    }
    ASSERT(pWnd->m_hWnd == hWnd);
    ASSERT(pWnd == CWnd::FromHandlePermanent(hWnd));
    LRESULT lResult = AfxCallWndProc(pWnd, hWnd, message,
                                     wParam, lParam);

    return lResult;
}


/////////////////////////////////////////////////////////////////////
// CRygWnd

// static data members
CRect   CRygWnd::s_rect(-500, 1000, 500, -1000); // outer rectangle
CPoint CRygWnd::s_point(300, 300); // rounded corners
CRect   CRygWnd::s_rColor[] = {CRect(-250, 800, 250, 300),
```

```
                                CRect(-250, 250, 250, -250),
                                CRect(-250, -300, 250, -800)};
CBrush CRygWnd::s_bColor[] = {RGB(192, 192, 192),
                              RGB(0xFF, 0x00, 0x00),
                              RGB(0xFF, 0xFF, 0x00),
                              RGB(0x00, 0xFF, 0x00)};

BOOL CRygWnd::RegisterWndClass(HINSTANCE hInstance) // static member
                                                    //  function
{
    WNDCLASS wc;
    wc.lpszClassName = "RYG"; // matches class name in client
    wc.hInstance = hInstance;
    wc.lpfnWndProc = RygWndProc;
    wc.hCursor = ::LoadCursor(NULL, IDC_ARROW);
    wc.hIcon = 0;
    wc.lpszMenuName = NULL;
    wc.hbrBackground = (HBRUSH) ::GetStockObject(LTGRAY_BRUSH);
    wc.style = CS_GLOBALCLASS;
    wc.cbClsExtra = 0;
    wc.cbWndExtra = 0;
    return (::RegisterClass(&wc) != 0);
}


//////////////////////////////////////////////////////////////////////

CRygWnd::CRygWnd()
{
    m_nState = 0;
    TRACE("CRygWnd constructor\n");
}

CRygWnd::~CRygWnd()
{
    TRACE("CRygWnd destructor\n");
}


BEGIN_MESSAGE_MAP(CRygWnd, CWnd)
    //{{AFX_MSG_MAP(CRygWnd)
    ON_WM_PAINT()
    ON_WM_LBUTTONDOWN()
    //}}AFX_MSG_MAP
    ON_MESSAGE(RYG_SETSTATE, OnSetState)
    ON_MESSAGE(RYG_GETSTATE, OnGetState)
END_MESSAGE_MAP()
```

(continued)

Figure 22-2. *continued*

```
void CRygWnd::SetMapping(CDC* pDC)
{
    CRect clientRect;
    GetClientRect(clientRect);
    pDC->SetMapMode(MM_ISOTROPIC);
    pDC->SetWindowExt(1000, 2000);
    pDC->SetViewportExt(clientRect.right, -clientRect.bottom);
    pDC->SetViewportOrg(clientRect.right / 2, clientRect.bottom / 2);
}

void CRygWnd::UpdateColor(CDC* pDC, int n)
{
    if (m_nState == n + 1) {
        pDC->SelectObject(&s_bColor[n+1]);
    }
    else {
        pDC->SelectObject(&s_bColor[0]);
    }
    pDC->Ellipse(s_rColor[n]);
}

/////////////////////////////////////////////////////////////////////////
// CRygWnd message handlers

void CRygWnd::OnPaint()
{
    int i;
    CPaintDC dc(this); // device context for painting
    SetMapping(&dc);
    dc.SelectStockObject(DKGRAY_BRUSH);
    dc.RoundRect(s_rect, s_point);
    for (i = 0; i < 3; i++) {
        UpdateColor(&dc, i);
    }
}

void CRygWnd::OnLButtonDown(UINT nFlags, CPoint point)
{
    // Notification code is HIWORD of wParam, 0 in this case
    GetParent()->SendMessage(WM_COMMAND, GetDlgCtrlID(),
        (LONG) GetSafeHwnd()); // 0
}
void CRygWnd::PostNcDestroy()
{
    TRACE("CRygWnd::PostNcDestroy\n");
    delete this; // CWnd::PostNcDestroy does nothing
}
```

```
LRESULT CRygWnd::OnSetState(WPARAM wParam, LPARAM lParam)
{
    TRACE("CRygWnd::SetState, wParam = %d\n", wParam);
    m_nState = (int) wParam;
    Invalidate(FALSE);
    return 0L;
}

LRESULT CRygWnd::OnGetState(WPARAM wParam, LPARAM lParam)
{
    TRACE("CRygWnd::GetState\n");
    return m_nState;
}
```

Revising the Updated EX22B Example— Adding Code to Test ex22d.dll

The EX22B program already links to the EX22A and EX22C DLLs. Now you'll revise the project to implicitly link to the EX22D custom control.

Here are the steps for updating the EX22B example:

1. **Add a new dialog resource and class to \vcpp32\ex22b\ex22b.** Use the dialog editor to create the *IDD_EX22D* template with a custom control with child window ID *IDC_RYG*, as shown here.

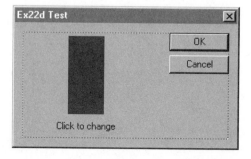

Specify *RYG* as the window class name of the custom control, as shown.

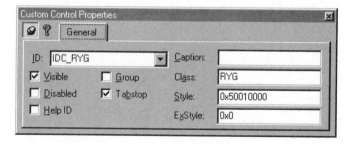

Then use ClassWizard to generate a class *CTest22dDialog*, derived from *CDialog*.

2. **Edit the Test22dDialog.h file.** Add the following private data member:

```
enum { OFF, RED, YELLOW, GREEN } m_nState;
```

Also add the following import and user-defined message IDs:

```
extern "C" __declspec(dllimport) void Ex22dEntry(); // dummy function
#define RYG_SETSTATE WM_USER + 0
#define RYG_GETSTATE WM_USER + 1
```

3. **Edit the constructor in Test22dDialog.cpp to initialize the state data member.** Add the following boldface code:

```
CTest22dDialog::CTest22dDialog(CWnd* pParent /*=NULL*/)
    : CDialog(CTest22dDialog::IDD, pParent)
{
    //{{AFX_DATA_INIT(CTest22dDialog)
        // NOTE: the ClassWizard will add member initialization here
    //}}AFX_DATA_INIT
    m_nState = OFF;
    Ex22dEntry(); // Make sure DLL gets loaded
}
```

4. **Map the control's clicked notification message.** You can't use ClassWizard here, so you must add the message map entry and handler function in the Test22dDialog.cpp file, as shown here:

```
ON_CONTROL(0, IDC_RYG, OnClickedRyg) // Notification code is 0

void CTest22dDialog::OnClickedRyg()
{
    switch(m_nState) {
    case OFF:
        m_nState = RED;
        break;
    case RED:
        m_nState = YELLOW;
        break;
    case YELLOW:
        m_nState = GREEN;
        break;
    case GREEN:
        m_nState = OFF;
        break;
    }
    GetDlgItem(IDC_RYG)->SendMessage(RYG_SETSTATE, m_nState);
    return;
}
```

When the dialog gets the clicked notification message, it sends the RYG_SETSTATE message back to the control in order to change the color. Don't forget to add this prototype in the Test22dDialog.h file:

```
afx_msg void OnClickedRyg();
```

5. Integrate the *CTest22dDialog* class into the EX22B application.
You'll need to add a second item on the Test menu, an Ex22d DLL option with ID *ID_TEST_EX22DDLL*. Use ClassWizard to map this option to a member function in the *CEx22bView* class, and then code the handler in Ex22bView.cpp as follows:

```
void CEx22bView::OnTestEx22ddll()
{
    CTest22dDialog dlg;
    dlg.DoModal();
}
```

Of course, you'll have to add the following line to Ex22bView.cpp:

```
#include "Test22dDialog.h"
```

6. Add the EX22D import library to the linker's input library list.
Choose Settings from Visual C++'s Project menu, and then add \vcpp32\ex22d\Debug\ex22d.lib to the Object/Library Modules control on the Link page. With this addition, the program should implicitly link to all three DLLs.

7. Build and test the updated EX22B application. Choose Ex22d DLL from the Test menu. Try clicking the traffic light with the left mouse button. The traffic-light color should change. The result of clicking the traffic light several times is shown here.

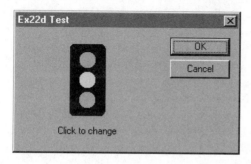

CHAPTER TWENTY-THREE

MFC Programs Without Document or View Classes

The document–view architecture is useful for many applications, but sometimes a simpler program structure is sufficient. This chapter illustrates three applications: a dialog-based program, a Single Document Interface (SDI) program, and a Multiple Document Interface (MDI) program. None of these programs uses document, view, or document–template classes, but they all use command routing and some other Microsoft Foundation Class (MFC) library features. In Visual C++ 6.0, you can create all three types of applications using AppWizard.

In each example, we'll look at how AppWizard generates code that doesn't rely on the document–view architecture and show you how to add your own code to each example.

The EX23A Example—A Dialog-Based Application

For many applications, a dialog provides a sufficient user interface. The dialog window immediately appears when the user starts the application. The user can minimize the dialog window, and as long as the dialog is not system modal, the user can freely switch to other applications.

In this example, the dialog functions as a simple calculator, as shown in Figure 23-1 on the following page. ClassWizard takes charge of defining the class data members and generating the DDX (Dialog Data Exchange) function calls—everything but the coding of the compute function. The application's resource script, ex23a.rc, defines an icon as well as the dialog.

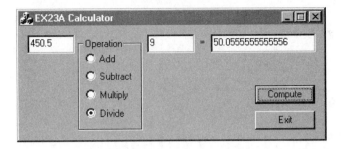

Figure 23-1.
The EX23A Calculator dialog.

AppWizard gives you the option of generating a dialog-based application. Here are the steps for building the EX23A example:

1. Run AppWizard to produce \vcpp32\ex23a\ex23a. Select the Dialog Based option in the AppWizard Step 1 dialog, as shown here.

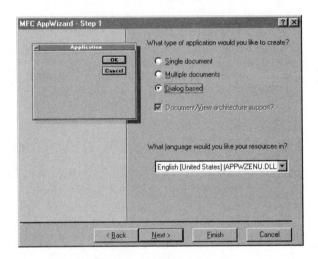

In the next dialog, enter *EX23A Calculator* as the dialog title.

2. Edit the *IDD_EX23A_DIALOG* resource. Refer to Figure 23-1 as a guide. Use the dialog editor to assign IDs to the controls shown in the table on the facing page.

Open the Properties dialog box and click on the Styles tab. Select the System Menu and Minimize Box options.

Control	ID
Left operand edit control	*IDC_LEFT*
Right operand edit control	*IDC_RIGHT*
Result edit control	*IDC_RESULT*
First radio button (group property set)	*IDC_OPERATION*
Compute pushbutton	*IDC_COMPUTE*

3. Use ClassWizard to add member variables and a command handler.
AppWizard has already generated a class *CEx23aDlg*. Add the following
data members.

Control ID	Member Variable	Type
IDC_LEFT	*m_dLeft*	*double*
IDC_RIGHT	*m_dRight*	*double*
IDC_RESULT	*m_dResult*	*double*
IDC_OPERATION	*m_nOperation*	*int*

Add the message handler *OnCompute* for the *IDC_COMPUTE* button.

4. Code the *OnCompute* member function in the ex23aDlg.cpp file.
Add the following boldface code:

```
void CEx23aDlg::OnCompute()
{
    UpdateData(TRUE);
    switch (m_nOperation) {
    case 0:  // add
        m_Result = m_dLeft + m_dRight;
        break;
    case 1:  // subtract
        m_dResult = m_dLeft - m_dRight;
        break;
    case 2:  // multiply
        m_dResult = m_dLeft * m_dRight;
        break;
    case 3:  // divide
        if (m_dRight != 0.0) {
```

(continued)

```
                m_dResult = m_dLeft / m_dRight;
            }
            else {
                AfxMessageBox("Divide by zero");
                m_dResult = 0.0;
            }
            break;
        default:
            TRACE("default; m_nOperation = %d\n", m_nOperation);
        }
        UpdateData(FALSE);
    }
```

5. **Build and test the EX23A application.** Notice that the program's icon appears in the Microsoft Windows taskbar. Verify that you can minimize the dialog window.

The Application Class *InitInstance* Function

The critical element of the EX23A application is the *CEx23aApp::InitInstance* function generated by AppWizard. A normal *InitInstance* function creates a main frame window and returns *TRUE*, allowing the program's message loop to run. The EX23A version constructs a modal dialog object, calls *DoModal*, and then returns *FALSE*. This means that the application exits after the user exits the dialog. The *DoModal* function lets the Windows dialog procedure get and dispatch messages, as it always does. Note that AppWizard does not generate a call to *CWinApp::SetRegistryKey*.

Here is the generated *InitInstance* code from ex23a.cpp:

```
BOOL CEx23aApp::InitInstance()
{
    AfxEnableControlContainer();

    // Standard initialization
    // If you are not using these features and wish to reduce the size
    //  of your final executable, you should remove from the following
    //  the specific initialization routines you do not need.

#ifdef _AFXDLL
    Enable3dControls();         // Call this when using MFC in a shared DLL
#else
    Enable3dControlsStatic(); // Call this when linking to MFC statically
#endif
```

```
CEx23aDlg dlg;
m_pMainWnd = &dlg;
int nResponse = dlg.DoModal();
if (nResponse == IDOK)
{
    // TODO: Place code here to handle when the dialog is
    //  dismissed with OK
}
else if (nResponse == IDCANCEL)
{
    // TODO: Place code here to handle when the dialog is
    //  dismissed with Cancel
}

// Since the dialog has been closed, return FALSE so that we
// exit the application, rather than start the application's
// message pump.
return FALSE;
}
```

The Dialog Class and the Program Icon

The generated *CEx23aDlg* class contains these two message map entries:

```
ON_WM_PAINT()
ON_WM_QUERYDRAGICON()
```

The associated handler functions take care of displaying the application's icon when the user minimizes the program. This code applies only to Microsoft Windows NT version 3.51, in which the icon is displayed on the desktop. You don't need the two handlers for Windows 95, Windows 98, or Windows NT 4.0 because those versions of Windows display the program's icon directly on the taskbar.

There is some icon code that you do need. It's in the dialog's handler for WM_INITDIALOG, which is generated by AppWizard. Notice the two *SetIcon* calls in the *OnInitDialog* function code below. If you checked the About box option, AppWizard generates code to add an About box to the System menu. The variable *m_hIcon* is a data member of the dialog class that is initialized in the constructor.

```
BOOL CEx23aDlg::OnInitDialog()
{
    CDialog::OnInitDialog();

    // Add "About..." menu item to system menu.

    // IDM_ABOUTBOX must be in the system command range.
    ASSERT((IDM_ABOUTBOX & 0xFFF0) == IDM_ABOUTBOX);
    ASSERT(IDM_ABOUTBOX < 0xF000);

    CMenu* pSysMenu = GetSystemMenu(FALSE);
    if (pSysMenu != NULL)
    {
        CString strAboutMenu;
        strAboutMenu.LoadString(IDS_ABOUTBOX);
        if (!strAboutMenu.IsEmpty())
        {
            pSysMenu->AppendMenu(MF_SEPARATOR);
            pSysMenu->AppendMenu(MF_STRING,
                                 IDM_ABOUTBOX, strAboutMenu);
        }
    }

    // Set the icon for this dialog.  The framework does this
    //  automatically when the application's main window
    //  is not a dialog
    SetIcon(m_hIcon, TRUE);          // Set big icon
    SetIcon(m_hIcon, FALSE);         // Set small icon

    // TODO: Add extra initialization here

    return TRUE;  //
 return TRUE  unless you set the focus to a control
}
```

The EX23B Example—An SDI Application

This SDI "Hello, world!" example builds on the code you saw way back in Chapter 2. The application has only one window, an object of a class derived from *CFrameWnd*. All drawing occurs inside the frame window and all messages are handled there.

1. Run AppWizard to produce \vcpp32\ex23b\ex23b. Select the Single Document option in the AppWizard Step 1 dialog and uncheck the Document/View Architecture Support? option, as shown here.

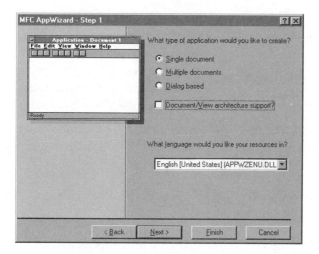

2. **Add code to paint in the dialog.** Add the following boldface code to the *CChildView::OnPaint* function in the ChildView.cpp source code file:

```
void CChildView::OnPaint()
{
    CPaintDC dc(this); // device context for painting

    dc.TextOut(0, 0, "Hello, world!");

    // Do not call CWnd::OnPaint() for painting messages
}
```

3. **Compile and run.** You now have a complete SDI application that has no dependencies on the document–view architecture.

AppWizard automatically takes out dependencies on the document–view architecture and generates an application for you with the following elements:

- **A main menu**—You can have a Windows-based application without a menu—you don't even need a resource script. But EX23B has both. The application framework routes menu commands to message handlers in the frame class.

- **An icon**—An icon is useful if the program is to be activated from Microsoft Windows Explorer. It's also useful when the application's main frame window is minimized. The icon is stored in the resource, along with the menu.

■ **Window close message command handler**—Many an application needs to do special processing when its main window is closed. If you were using documents, you could override the *CDocument::Save-Modified* function. Here, to take control of the close process, App-Wizard creates message handlers to process close messages sent as a result of user actions and by Windows itself when it shuts down.

■ **Toolbar and status bar**—AppWizard automatically generates a default toolbar and status bar for you and sets up the routing even though there are no document–view classes.

There are several interesting features in the SDI application that have no document–view support, including:

■ *CChildView* **class**—Contrary to its name, this class is actually a CWnd derivative that is declared in ChildView.h and implemented in Child-View.cpp. *CChildView* implements only a virtual *OnPaint* member function, which contains any code that you want to draw in the frame window (as illustrated in step 2 of the EX23B sample).

■ *CMainFrame* **class**—This class contains a data member, *m_wndView*, that is created and initialized in the *CMainFrame::OnCreate* member function.

■ *CMainFrame::OnSetFocus* **function**—This function makes sure the focus is translated to the *CChildView*:

```
void CMainFrame::OnSetFocus(CWnd* pOldWnd)
{
    // forward focus to the view window
    m_wndView.SetFocus();
}
```

■ *CMainFrame::OnCmdMsg* **function**—This function gives the view a chance to handle any command messages first:

```
BOOL CMainFrame::OnCmdMsg(UINT nID, int nCode, void* pExtra,
                         AFX_CMDHANDLERINFO* pHandlerInfo)
{
    // let the view have first crack at the command
    if (m_wndView.OnCmdMsg(nID, nCode, pExtra, pHandlerInfo))
        return TRUE;

    // otherwise, do default handling
    return CFrameWnd::OnCmdMsg(nID, nCode, pExtra, pHandlerInfo);
}
```

The EX23C Example—An MDI Application

Now let's create an MDI application that doesn't use the document–view architecture.

1. Run AppWizard to produce \vcpp32\ex23c\ex23c. Select the Multiple Documents option in the AppWizard Step 1 dialog and uncheck the Document/View Architecture Support? option, as shown here.

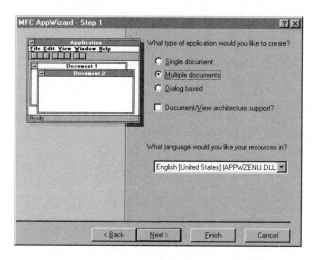

2. Add code to paint in the dialog. Add the following boldface code to the *CChildView::OnPaint* function in the ChildView.cpp source code file:

```
void CChildView::OnPaint()
{
    CPaintDC dc(this); // device context for painting

    dc.TextOut(0, 0, "Hello, world!");

    // Do not call CWnd::OnPaint() for painting messages
}
```

3 Compile and run. You now have a complete MDI application without dependencies on the document–view architecture.

As in EX23B, this example automatically creates a *CChildView* class. The main difference between EX23B and EX23C is the fact that in EX23C the *CChildView* class is created in the *CChildFrame::OnCreate* function instead of in the *CMainFrame* class.

565

In this chapter you've learned how to create three kinds of applications that do not depend on the document–view architecture. Examining how these applications are generated is also a great way to learn how MFC works. We recommend that you compare the generated results to similar applications with document–view architecture support to get a complete picture of how the document–view classes work with the rest of MFC.

PART IV

ACTIVEX: COM, AUTOMATION, AND OLE

The Component Object Model

The Component Object Model (COM) is the foundation of much of the new Microsoft ActiveX technology, and after five years it's become an integral part of Microsoft Windows. So COM is now an integral part of *Programming Visual C++*. Soon, most Windows programming will involve COM, so you'd better start learning it now. But where do you begin? You could start with the Microsoft Foundation Class classes for ActiveX Controls, Automation, and OLE, but as useful as those classes are, they obscure the real COM architecture. You've got to start with fundamental theory, and that includes COM and something called an <u>interface</u>.

This is the first of seven chapters that make up Part IV of this book. Here you'll get the theory you need for the next six chapters. You'll learn about interfaces and how the MFC library implements interfaces through its macros and <u>interface</u> <u>maps</u>.

ActiveX Technology Background

The terminology is changing as fast as the technology, and not all groups within Microsoft can agree on how to use the terms ActiveX and OLE. Think of ActiveX as something that was created when the "old" OLE collided with the Internet. ActiveX includes not only those Windows features built on COM (which you'll study in this part of the book) but also the Microsoft Internet Information Server family and the WinInet programming interface (covered in Part VI).

Yes, OLE is still here, but once again it stands for Object Linking and Embedding, just as it did in the days of OLE 1. It's just another subset of ActiveX technology that includes odds and ends such as drag and drop. Unfortunately (or fortunately, if you have existing code), the MFC source code and the Windows API have not kept current with the naming conventions. As a result, you'll see lots of occurrences of "OLE" and "Ole" in class names and in function names, even though some of those classes and functions go beyond linking and embedding. In this part of the book, you might notice references to the "server" in the code generated by AppWizard. Microsoft has now reserved this term for database servers and Internet servers; "component" is the new term for OLE servers.

Bookstore computer sections are now full of books on OLE, COM, and ActiveX. We don't claim to offer that level of detail here, but you should come away with a pretty good understanding of COM theory. We've included a closer connection to the MFC library classes than you might see in other books, with the exception of *MFC Internals* (Addison-Wesley, 1996) by George Shepherd and Scot Wingo. The net result should be good preparation for the really heavy-duty ActiveX/COM books, including Kraig Brockschmidt's *Inside OLE,* 2nd ed. (Microsoft Press, 1995) and Don Box's *Essential COM* (Addison-Wesley, 1998). A good mid-level book is Dale Rogerson's *Inside COM* (Microsoft Press, 1997).

One more thing: don't expect this stuff to be easy. Kraig Brockschmidt reported "six months of mental fog" before he started understanding these concepts. A thorough knowledge of the C++ language is the minimum prerequisite. Don't be afraid to dig in and write code. Make sure you can do the easy things before getting into advanced areas like multithreaded COM, custom marshaling, and distributed COM (DCOM).

The Component Object Model

COM is an "industry-standard" software architecture supported by Microsoft, Digital Equipment Corporation, and many other companies. It's by no means the <u>only</u> standard. Indeed, it competes directly against other standards, such as Corba from the Open Software Foundation (OSF). Some people are working to establish interoperability between COM and other architectures, but my guess is that COM will become the leading standard.

The Problem That COM Solves

The "problem" is that there's no standard way for Windows program modules to communicate with one another. "But," you say "what about the DLL with its exported functions, Dynamic Data Exchange (DDE), the Windows Clipboard, and the Windows API itself, not to mention legacy standards such as VBX and OLE 1? Aren't they good enough?" Well, no. You can't build an object-oriented operating system for the future out of these ad hoc, unrelated standards. With the Component Object Model, however, you can, and that's precisely what Microsoft is doing.

The Essence of COM

What's wrong with the old standards? A lot. The Windows API has too large a programming "surface area"—more than 350 separate functions. VBXs don't work in the 32-bit world. DDE comes with a complicated system of applications, topics, and items. How you call a DLL is totally application-specific. COM provides a unified, expandable, object-oriented communications protocol for Windows that already supports the following features:

- A standard, language-independent way for a Win32 client EXE to load and call a Win32 DLL

- A general-purpose way for one EXE to control another EXE on the same computer (the DDE replacement)

- A replacement for the VBX control, called an ActiveX control

- A powerful new way for application programs to interact with the operating system

- Expansion to accommodate new protocols such as Microsoft's OLE DB database interface

- The distributed COM (DCOM) that allows one EXE to communicate with another EXE residing on a different computer, even if the computers use different microprocessor-chip families

So what is COM? That's an easier question to ask than to answer. At DevelopMentor (a training facility for software developers), the party line is that "COM is love." That is, COM is a powerful integrating technology that allows you to mix all sorts of disparate software parts together at runtime. COM allows developers to write software that runs together regardless of issues such as thread-awareness and language choice.

COM is a protocol that connects one software module with another and then drops out of the picture. After the connection is made, the two modules can communicate through a mechanism called an <u>interface</u>. Interfaces require no statically or dynamically linked entry points or hard-coded addresses other than the few general-purpose COM functions that start the communication process. An interface (more precisely, a COM interface) is a term that you'll be seeing a lot of.

What Is a COM Interface?

Before digging into the topic of interfaces, let's re-examine the nature of inheritance and polymorphism in normal C++. We'll use a planetary-motion simulation (suitable for NASA or Nintendo) to illustrate C++ inheritance and polymorphism. Imagine a spaceship that travels through our solar system under the influence of the sun's gravity. In ordinary C++, you could declare a *CSpaceship* class and write a constructor that sets the spaceship's initial position and acceleration. Then you could write a nonvirtual member function named *Fly* that implemented Kepler's laws to model the movement of the spaceship from one position to the next—say, over a period of 0.1 second. You could also write a *Display* function that painted an image of the spaceship in a window. The most interesting feature of the *CSpaceship* class is that the interface of the C++ class (the way the client talks to the class) and the implementation are tightly bound. One of the main goals of COM is to separate a class's interface from its implementation.

If we think of this example within the context of COM, the spaceship code could exist as a separate EXE or DLL (the <u>component</u>), which is a COM module. In COM the simulation manager (the <u>client</u> program) can't call *Fly* or any *CSpaceship* constructor directly: COM provides only a standard global function to gain access to the spaceship object, and then the client and the object use interfaces to talk to one another. Before we tackle real COM, let's build a COM simulation in which both the component and the client code are statically linked in the same EXE file. For our standard global function, we'll invent a function named *GetClassObject*.

> **NOTE:** If you want to map this process back to the way MFC works, you can look at *CRuntimeClass*, which serves as a class object for *CObject*-based classes. A class object is a meta-class (either in concept or in form).

In this COM simulation, clients will use this global single abstract function (*GetClassObject*) for objects of a particular class. In real COM, clients would get a class object first and then ask the class object to manufacture the real object in much the same way MFC does dynamic creation. *GetClassObject* has the following three parameters:

```
BOOL GetClassObject(int nClsid, int nIid, void** ppvObj);
```

The first *GetClassObject* parameter, *nClsid*, is a 32-bit integer that uniquely identifies the *CSpaceship* class. The second parameter, *nIid*, is the unique identifier of the interface that we want. The third parameter is a pointer to an interface to the object. Remember that we're going to be dealing with interfaces now, (which are different from classes). As it turns out, a class can have several interfaces, so the last two parameters exist to manage interface selection. The function returns *TRUE* if the call is successful.

Now let's back up to the design of *CSpaceship*. We haven't really explained spaceship interfaces yet. A COM interface is a C++ base class (actually, a C++

struct) that declares a group of pure virtual functions. These functions completely control some aspect of derived class behavior. For *CSpaceship*, let's write an interface named *IMotion*, which controls the spaceship object's position. For simplicity's sake, we'll declare just two functions, *Fly* and *GetPosition*, and we'll keep things uncomplicated by making the position value an integer. The *Fly* function calculates the position of the spaceship, and the *GetPosition* function returns a reference to the current position. Here are the declarations:

```
struct IMotion
{
    virtual void Fly() = 0;
    virtual int& GetPosition() = 0;
};

class CSpaceship : public IMotion
{
protected:
    int m_nPosition;
public:
    CSpaceship() { m_nPosition = 0; }
    void Fly();
    int& GetPosition() { return m_nPosition; }
};
```

The actual code for the spaceship-related functions—including *GetClass-Object*—is located in the component part of the program. The client part calls the *GetClassObject* function to construct the spaceship and to obtain an *IMotion* pointer. Both parts have access to the *IMotion* declaration at compile time. Here's how the client calls *GetClassObject*:

```
IMotion* pMot;
GetClassObject(CLSID_CSpaceship, IID_IMotion, (void**) &pMot);
```

Assume for the moment that COM can use the unique integer identifiers *CLSID_CSpaceship* and *IID_IMotion* to construct a spaceship object instead of some other kind of object. If the call is successful, *pMot* points to a *CSpaceship* object that *GetClassObject* somehow constructs. As you can see, the *CSpaceship* class implements the *Fly* and *GetPosition* functions, and our main program can call them for the one particular spaceship object, as shown here:

```
int nPos = 50;
pMot->GetPosition() = nPos;
pMot->Fly();
nPos = pMot->GetPosition();
TRACE("new position = %d\n", nPos);
```

Now the spaceship is off and flying. We're controlling it entirely through the *pMot* pointer. Notice that *pMot* is technically not a pointer to a *CSpaceship* object. However, in this case, a *CSpaceship* pointer and an *IMotion* pointer are the same because *CSpaceship* is derived from *IMotion*. You can see how the virtual functions work here: it's classic C++ polymorphism.

Let's make things a little more complex by adding a second interface, *IVisual*, which handles the spaceship's visual representation. One function is enough—*Display*. Here's the whole base class:

```
struct IVisual
{
    virtual void Display() = 0;
};
```

Are you getting the idea that COM wants you to associate functions in groups? You're not imagining it. But why? Well, in your space simulation, you probably want to include other kinds of objects in addition to spaceships. Imagine that the *IMotion* and *IVisual* interfaces are being used for other classes. Perhaps a *CSun* class has an implementation of *IVisual* but does not have an implementation of *IMotion*, and perhaps a *CSpaceStation* class has other interfaces as well. If you "published" your *IMotion* and *IVisual* interfaces, perhaps other space simulation software companies would adopt them.

Think of an interface as a contract between two software modules. The idea is that interface declarations never change. If you want to upgrade your spaceship code, you don't change the *IMotion* or the *IVisual* interface; rather, you add a new interface, such as *ICrew*. The existing spaceship clients can continue to run with the old interfaces, and new client programs can use the new *ICrew* interface as well. These client programs can find out at runtime which interfaces a particular spaceship software version supports.

Consider the *GetClassObject* function as a more powerful alternative to the C++ constructor. With the ordinary constructor, you obtain one object with one batch of member functions. With the *GetClassObject* function, you obtain the object plus your choice of interfaces. As you'll see later, you start with one interface and then use that interface to get other interfaces to the same object.

So how do you program two interfaces for *CSpaceship*? You could use C++ multiple inheritance, but that wouldn't work if two interfaces had the same member function name. The MFC library uses nested classes instead, so that's what we'll use to illustrate multiple interfaces on the *CSpaceship* class. Not all C++ programmers are familiar with nested classes, so I'll offer a little help. Here's a first cut at nesting interfaces within the *CSpaceship* class:

```
class CSpaceship
{
protected:
    int m_nPosition;
    int m_nAcceleration;
    int m_nColor;
public:
    CSpaceship()
        { m_nPosition = m_nAcceleration = m_nColor = 0; }
    class XMotion : public IMotion
    {
    public:
        XMotion() { }
        virtual void Fly();
        virtual int& GetPosition();
    } m_xMotion;

    class XVisual : public IVisual
    {
    public:
        XVisual() { }
        virtual void Display();
    } m_xVisual;

    friend class XVisual;
    friend class XMotion;
};
```

NOTE: It might make sense to make *m_nAcceleration* a data member of *XMotion* and *m_nColor* a data member of *XVisual*. We'll make them data members of *CSpaceship* because that strategy is more compatible with the MFC macros, as you'll see later.

Notice that the implementations of *IMotion* and *IVisual* are contained within the "parent" *CSpaceship* class. In COM, this parent class is known as the class with <u>object identity</u>. Be aware that *m_xMotion* and *m_xVisual* are actually embedded data members of *CSpaceship*. Indeed, you could have implemented *CSpaceship* strictly with embedding. Nesting, however, brings to the party two advantages : 1) nested class member functions can access parent class data members without the need for *CSpaceship* pointer data members, and 2) the nested classes are neatly packaged along with the parent while remaining invisible outside the parent. Look at the code on the following page for the *GetPosition* member function.

```
int& CSpaceship::XMotion::GetPosition()
{
    METHOD_PROLOGUE(CSpaceship, Motion) // makes pThis
    return pThis->m_nPosition;
}
```

Notice also the double scope resolution operators, which are necessary for nested class member functions. *METHOD_PROLOGUE* is a one-line MFC macro that uses the C *offsetof* operator to retrieve the offset used in generating a *this* pointer to the parent class, *pThis*. The compiler always knows the offset from the beginning of parent class data to the beginning of nested class data. *GetPosition* can thus access the *CSpaceship* data member *m_nPosition*.

Now suppose you have <u>two</u> interface pointers, *pMot* and *pVis*, for a particular *CSpaceship* object. (Don't worry yet about how you got these pointers.) You can call interface member functions in the following manner:

```
pMot->Fly();
pVis->Display();
```

What's happening under the hood? In C++, each <u>class</u> (at least, each class that has virtual functions and is not an abstract base class) has a virtual function table, which is otherwise known as a <u>vtable</u>. In this example, that means there are vtables for *CSpaceship::XMotion* and *CSpaceship::XVisual*. For each <u>object</u>, there's a pointer to the object's data, the first element of which is a pointer to the class's vtable. The pointer relationships are shown here.

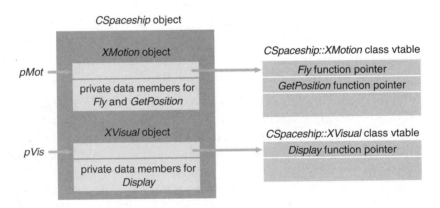

NOTE: Theoretically, it's possible to program COM in C. If you look at the Windows header files, you'll see code such as this:

```
#ifdef __cplusplus
        // C++-specific headers
#else
        /* C-specific headers */
#endif
```

In C++, interfaces are declared as C++ *structs*, often with inheritance; in C, they're declared as C *typedef structs* with no inheritance. In C++, the compiler generates vtables for your derived classes; in C, you must "roll your own" vtables, and that gets tedious. It's important to realize, however, that in neither language do the interface declarations have data members, constructors, or destructors. Therefore, you can't rely on the interface having a virtual destructor—but that's not a problem because you never invoke a destructor for an interface.

The *IUnknown* Interface and the *QueryInterface* Member Function

Let's get back to the problem of how to obtain your interface pointers in the first place. COM declares a special interface named *IUnknown* for this purpose. As a matter of fact, all interfaces are derived from *IUnknown*, which has a pure virtual member function, *QueryInterface*, that returns an interface pointer based on the interface ID you feed it.

Once the interface mechanisms are hooked up, the client needs to get an *IUnknown* interface pointer (at the very least) or a pointer to one of the derived interfaces. Here is the new interface hierarchy, with *IUnknown* at the top:

```
struct IUnknown
{
    virtual BOOL QueryInterface(int nIid, void** ppvObj) = 0;
};

struct IMotion : public IUnknown
{
    virtual void Fly() = 0;
    virtual int& GetPosition() = 0;
};

struct IVisual : public IUnknown
{
    virtual void Display() = 0;
};
```

To satisfy the compiler, we must now add *QueryInterface* implementations in both *CSpaceship::XMotion* and *CSpaceship::XVisual*. What do the vtables look like after this is done? For each derived class, the compiler builds a vtable with the base class function pointers on top, as shown here.

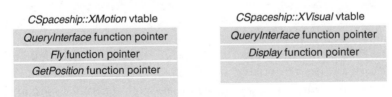

GetClassObject can get the interface pointer for a given *CSpaceship* object by getting the address of the corresponding embedded object. Here's the code for the *QueryInterface* function in *XMotion*:

```
BOOL CSpaceship::XMotion::QueryInterface(int nIid,
                                         void** ppvObj)
{
    METHOD_PROLOGUE(CSpaceship, Motion)
    switch (nIid) {
    case IID_IUnknown:
    case IID_IMotion:
        *ppvObj = &pThis->m_xMotion;
        break;
    case IID_IVisual:
        *ppvObj = &pThis->m_xVisual;
        break;
    default:
        *ppvObj = NULL;
        return FALSE;
    }
    return TRUE;
}
```

Because *IMotion* is derived from *IUnknown*, an *IMotion* pointer is a valid pointer if the caller asks for an *IUnknown* pointer.

> **NOTE:** The COM standard demands that *QueryInterface* return exactly the same *IUnknown* pointer value for *IID_IUnknown*, no matter which interface pointer you start with. Thus, if two *IUnknown* pointers match, you can assume that they refer to the same object. *IUnknown* is sometimes known as the "void*" of COM because it represents the object's identity.

Below is a *GetClassObject* function that uses the address of *m_xMotion* to obtain the first interface pointer for the newly constructed *CSpaceship* object:

```
BOOL GetClassObject(int& nClsid, int& nIid,
                    void** ppvObj)
{
    ASSERT(nClsid == CLSID_CSpaceship);
    CSpaceship* pObj = new CSpaceship();
    IUnknown* pUnk = &pObj->m_xMotion;
    return pUnk->QueryInterface(nIid, ppvObj);
}
```

Now your client program can call *QueryInterface* to obtain an *IVisual* pointer, as shown here:

```
IMotion* pMot;
IVisual* pVis;
GetClassObject(CLSID_CSpaceship, IID_IMotion, (void**) &pMot);
pMot->Fly();
pMot->QueryInterface(IID_IVisual, (void**) &pVis);
pVis->Display();
```

Notice that the client uses a *CSpaceship* object, but it <u>never</u> has an actual *CSpaceship* pointer. Thus, the client cannot directly access *CSpaceship* data members even if they're public. Notice also that we haven't tried to delete the spaceship object yet—that will come shortly.

There's a special graphical representation for interfaces and COM classes. Interfaces are shown as small circles (or <u>jacks</u>) with lines attached to their class. The *IUnknown* interface, which every COM class supports, is at the top, and the others are on the left. The *CSpaceship* class can be represented like this.

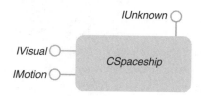

Reference Counting: The *AddRef* and *Release* Functions

COM interfaces don't have virtual destructors, so it isn't cool to write code like the following:

```
delete pMot;  // pMot is an IMotion pointer; don't do this
```

COM has a strict protocol for deleting objects; the two other *IUnknown* virtual functions, *AddRef* and *Release*, are the key. Each COM class has a data member—*m_dwRef*, in the MFC library—that keeps track of how many "users" an object has. Each time the component program returns a new interface pointer (as in *QueryInterface*), the program calls *AddRef*, which increments *m_dwRef*. When the client program is finished with the pointer, it calls *Release*. When *m_dwRef* goes to 0, the object destroys itself. Here's an example of a *Release* function for the *CSpaceship::XMotion* class:

```
DWORD CSpaceship::XMotion::Release()
{
    METHOD_PROLOGUE(CSpaceship, Motion) // makes pThis
    if (pThis->m_dwRef == 0)
        return 0;
    if (--pThis->m_dwRef == 0) {
        delete pThis; // the spaceship object
        return 0;
    }
    return pThis->m_dwRef;
}
```

In MFC COM-based programs, the object's constructor sets *m_dwRef* to 1. This means that it isn't necessary to call *AddRef* after the object is first constructed. A client program should call *AddRef*, however, if it makes a copy of an interface pointer.

Class Factories

Object-oriented terminology can get a little fuzzy sometimes. Smalltalk programmers, for example, talk about "objects" the way C++ programmers talk about "classes." The COM literature often uses the term "component object" to refer to the object plus the code associated with it. COM carries with it the notion of a "class object," which is sometimes referred to as a "class factory." To be more accurate, it should probably be called an "object factory." A COM class object represents the global static area of a specific COM class. Its analog in MFC is the *CRuntimeClass*. A class object is sometimes called a <u>class</u> <u>factory</u> because it often implements a special COM interface named *IClassFactory*. This interface, like all interfaces, is derived from *IUnknown*. *IClassFactory*'s principal member function is *CreateInstance*, which in our COM simulation is declared like this:

```
virtual BOOL CreateInstance(int& nIid, void** ppvObj) = 0;
```

Why use a class factory? We've already seen that we can't call the target class constructor directly; we have to let the component module decide how to construct objects. The component provides the class factory for this purpose and thus encapsulates the creation step, as it should. Locating and launching component modules—and thus establishing the class factory—is expensive, but constructing objects with *CreateInstance* is cheap. We can therefore allow a single class factory to create multiple objects.

What does all this mean? It means that we screwed up when we let *GetClassObject* construct the *CSpaceship* object directly. We were supposed to construct a class factory object first and then call *CreateInstance* to cause the class factory (object factory) to construct the actual spaceship object.

Let's properly construct the spaceship simulation. First we declare a new class, *CSpaceshipFactory*. To avoid complication, we'll derive the class from *IClassFactory* so that we don't have to deal with nested classes. In addition, we'll add the code that tracks references:

```
struct IClassFactory : public IUnknown
{
    virtual BOOL CreateInstance(int& nIid, void** ppvObj) = 0;
};

class CSpaceshipFactory : public IClassFactory
{
private:
    DWORD m_dwRef;
public:
    CSpaceshipFactory() { m_dwRef = 1; }
    // IUnknown functions
    virtual BOOL QueryInterface(int& nIid,
                                void** ppvObj);
    virtual DWORD AddRef();
    virtual DWORD Release();
    // IClassFactory function
    virtual BOOL CreateInstance(int& nIid,
                                void** ppvObj);
};
```

Next we'll write the *CreateInstance* member function:

```
BOOL CSpaceshipFactory::CreateInstance(int& nIid, void** ppvObj)
{
    CSpaceship* pObj = new CSpaceship();
    IUnknown* pUnk = &pObj->m_xMotion;
    return pUnk->QueryInterface(nIid, ppvObj);
}
```

Finally, on the following page is the new *GetClassObject* function, which constructs a class factory object and returns an *IClassFactory* interface pointer.

```
BOOL GetClassObject(int& nClsid, int& nIid,
                    void** ppvObj)
{
    ASSERT(nClsid == CLSID_CSpaceship);
    ASSERT((nIid == IID_IUnknown) || (nIid == IID_IClassFactory));
    CSpaceshipFactory* pObj = new CSpaceshipFactory();
    *ppObj = pObj; // IUnknown* = IClassFactory* = CSpaceship*
}
```

The *CSpaceship* and *CSpaceshipFactory* classes work together and share the same class ID. Now the client code looks like this (without error-checking logic):

```
IMotion* pMot;
IVisual* pVis;
IClassFactory* pFac;
GetClassObject(CLSID_CSpaceship, IID_IClassFactory, (void**) &pFac);
pFac->CreateInstance(IID_IMotion, &pMot);
pMot->QueryInterface(IID_IVisual, (void**) &pVis);
pMot->Fly();
pVis->Display();
```

Notice that the *CSpaceshipFactory* class implements the *AddRef* and *Release* functions. It must do this because *AddRef* and *Release* are pure virtual functions in the *IUnknown* base class. We'll start using these functions in the next iteration of the program.

The *CCmdTarget* Class

We're still a long way from real MFC COM-based code, but we can take one more step in the COM simulation before we switch to the real thing. As you might guess, some code and data can be "factored out" of our spaceship COM classes into a base class. That's exactly what the MFC library does. The base class is *CCmdTarget*, the standard base class for document and window classes. *CCmdTarget*, in turn, is derived from *CObject*. We'll use *CSimulatedCmdTarget* instead, and we won't put too much in it—only the reference-counting logic and the *m_dwRef* data member. The *CSimulatedCmdTarget* functions *ExternalAddRef* and *ExternalRelease* can be called in derived COM classes. Because we're using *CSimulatedCmdTarget*, we'll bring *CSpaceshipFactory* in line with *CSpaceship*, and we'll use a nested class for the *IClassFactory* interface.

We can also do some factoring out inside our *CSpaceship* class. The *QueryInterface* function can be "delegated" from the nested classes to the outer class helper function *ExternalQueryInterface*, which calls *ExternalAddRef*. Thus, each *QueryInterface* function increments the reference count, but *CreateInstance* calls *ExternalQueryInterface*, followed by a call to *ExternalRelease*. When the first interface pointer is returned by *CreateInstance*, the spaceship object has a reference count of 1. A subsequent *QueryInterface* call increments the count to 2, and in this case, the client must call *Release* twice to destroy the spaceship object.

One last thing—we'll make the class factory object a global object. That way we won't have to call its constructor. When the client calls *Release*, there isn't a problem because the class factory's reference count is 2 by the time the client receives it. (The *CSpaceshipFactory* constructor sets the reference count to 1, and *ExternalQueryInterface*, called by *GetClassObject*, sets the count to 2.)

The EX24A Example—A Simulated COM

Figures 24-1, 24-2, 24-3, and 24-4 show code for a working "simulated COM" program, EX24A. This is a Win32 Console Application (without the MFC library) that uses a class factory to construct an object of class *CSpaceship*, calls its interface functions, and then releases the spaceship. The Interface.h header file, shown in Figure 24-1, contains the *CSimulatedCmdTarget* base class and the interface declarations that are used by both the client and component programs. The Spaceship.h header file shown in Figure 24-2 on page 585 contains the spaceship-specific class declarations that are used in the component program. Spaceship.cpp, shown in Figure 24-3 on page 587, is the component that implements *GetClassObject*; Client.cpp, shown in Figure 24-4 on page 590, is the client that calls *GetClassObject*. What's phony here is that both client and component code are linked within the same ex24a.exe program. Thus, our simulated COM is not required to make the connection at runtime. (You'll see how that's done later in this chapter.)

INTERFACE.H

```
// definitions that make our code look like MFC code
#define BOOL    int
#define DWORD   unsigned int
#define TRUE    1
#define FALSE   0
#define TRACE   printf
#define ASSERT  assert
//----------definitions and macros-------------------------------------
#define CLSID_CSpaceship    10
#define IID_IUnknown        0
#define IID_IClassFactory   1
#define IID_IMotion         2
#define IID_IVisual         3
```

Figure 24-1.
The Interface.h file.

(continued)

Figure 24-1. *continued*

```
// this macro for 16-bit Windows only
#define METHOD_PROLOGUE(theClass, localClass) \
    theClass* pThis = ((theClass*)((char*)(this) - \
    offsetof(theClass, m_x##localClass))); \


BOOL GetClassObject(int nClsid, int nIid, void** ppvObj);

//----------interface declarations----------------------------------
struct IUnknown
{
    IUnknown() { TRACE("Entering IUnknown ctor %p\n", this); }
    virtual BOOL QueryInterface(int nIid, void** ppvObj) = 0;
    virtual DWORD Release() = 0;
    virtual DWORD AddRef() = 0;
};

struct IClassFactory : public IUnknown
{
    IClassFactory()
        { TRACE("Entering IClassFactory ctor %p\n", this); }
    virtual BOOL CreateInstance(int nIid, void** ppvObj) = 0;
};

struct IMotion : public IUnknown
{
    IMotion() { TRACE("Entering IMotion ctor %p\n", this); }
    virtual void Fly() = 0; // pure
    virtual int& GetPosition() = 0;
};
struct IVisual : public IUnknown
{
    IVisual() { TRACE("Entering IVisual ctor %p\n", this); }
    virtual void Display() = 0;
};

class CSimulatedCmdTarget // 'simulated' CSimulatedCmdTarget
{
public:
    DWORD m_dwRef;

protected:
    CSimulatedCmdTarget() {
        TRACE("Entering CSimulatedCmdTarget ctor %p\n", this);
        m_dwRef = 1; // implied first AddRef
    }
```

```
    virtual ~CSimulatedCmdTarget()
        { TRACE("Entering CSimulatedCmdTarget dtor %p\n", this); }
    DWORD ExternalRelease() {
    TRACE("Entering CSimulatedCmdTarget::ExternalRelease--RefCount = \
        %ld\n", m_dwRef);
        if (m_dwRef == 0)
            return 0;
        if(--m_dwRef == 0L) {
            TRACE("deleting\n");
            delete this;
            return 0;
        }
        return m_dwRef;
    }
    DWORD ExternalAddRef() { return ++m_dwRef; }
};
```

SPACESHIP.H

```
class CSpaceship;

//----------class declarations----------------------------------------
class CSpaceshipFactory : public CSimulatedCmdTarget
{
public:
    CSpaceshipFactory()
        { TRACE("Entering CSpaceshipFactory ctor %p\n", this); }
    ~CSpaceshipFactory()
        { TRACE("Entering CSpaceshipFactory dtor %p\n", this); }
    BOOL ExternalQueryInterface(int lRid, void** ppvObj);
    class XClassFactory : public IClassFactory
    {
    public:
        XClassFactory()
            { TRACE("Entering XClassFactory ctor %p\n", this); }
        virtual BOOL QueryInterface(int lRid, void** ppvObj);
        virtual DWORD Release();
        virtual DWORD AddRef();
        virtual BOOL CreateInstance(int lRid, void** ppvObj);
    } m_xClassFactory;
    friend class XClassFactory;
};
```

Figure 24-2. *(continued)*
The Spaceship.h file.

Figure 24-2. *continued*

```
class CSpaceship : public CSimulatedCmdTarget
{
private:
    int m_nPosition; // We can access these from
                     //  all the interfaces
    int m_nAcceleration;
    int m_nColor;
public:
    CSpaceship() {
        TRACE("Entering CSpaceship ctor %p\n", this);
        m_nPosition = 100;
        m_nAcceleration = 101;
        m_nColor = 102;
    }
    ~CSpaceship()
        { TRACE("Entering CSpaceship dtor %p\n", this); }
    BOOL ExternalQueryInterface(int lRid, void** ppvObj);
    class XMotion : public IMotion
    {
    public:
        XMotion()
            { TRACE("Entering XMotion ctor %p\n", this); }
        virtual BOOL QueryInterface(int lRid, void** ppvObj);
        virtual DWORD Release();
        virtual DWORD AddRef();
        virtual void Fly();
        virtual int& GetPosition();
    } m_xMotion;

class XVisual : public IVisual
    {
    public:
        XVisual() { TRACE("Entering XVisual ctor\n"); }
        virtual BOOL QueryInterface(int lRid, void** ppvObj);
        virtual DWORD Release();
        virtual DWORD AddRef();
        virtual void Display();
    } m_xVisual;

    friend class XVisual;  // These must be at the bottom!
    friend class XMotion;
    friend class CSpaceshipFactory::XClassFactory;
};
```

SPACESHIP.CPP

```
#include <stdio.h>
#include <stddef.h> // for offsetof in METHOD_PROLOGUE
#include <ASSERT.h>
#include "Interface.h"
#include "Spaceship.h"


CSpaceshipFactory g_factory;

//----------member functions-----------------------------------------
BOOL CSpaceshipFactory::ExternalQueryInterface(int nIid,
                                                   void** ppvObj) {
    TRACE("Entering CSpaceshipFactory::ExternalQueryInterface--nIid = \
        %d\n", nIid);
    switch (nIid) {
    case IID_IUnknown:
    case IID_IClassFactory:
        *ppvObj = &m_xClassFactory;
        break;
    default:
        *ppvObj = NULL;
        return FALSE;
    }
    ExternalAddRef();
    return TRUE;
}
BOOL CSpaceshipFactory::XClassFactory::QueryInterface(int nIid,
                                                      void** ppvObj) {
    TRACE("Entering CSpaceshipFactory::XClassFactory::\
        QueryInterface--nIid = %d\n", nIid);
    METHOD_PROLOGUE(CSpaceshipFactory, ClassFactory) // makes pThis
    return pThis->
    ExternalQueryInterface(nIid, ppvObj); // delegate to
                                          //   CSpaceshipFactory
}


BOOL CSpaceshipFactory::XClassFactory::CreateInstance(int nIid,
                                                      void** ppvObj) {
    TRACE("Entering CSpaceshipFactory::XClassFactory::CreateInstance\n");
    METHOD_PROLOGUE(CSpaceshipFactory, ClassFactory) // makes pThis
    CSpaceship* pObj = new CSpaceship();
    if (pObj->ExternalQueryInterface(nIid, ppvObj)) {
        pObj->ExternalRelease(); // balance reference count
        return TRUE;
```

Figure 24-3.
The Spaceship.cpp file.

(continued)

Figure 24-3. *continued*

```
    }
    return FALSE;
}

DWORD CSpaceshipFactory::XClassFactory::Release() {
    TRACE("Entering CSpaceshipFactory::XClassFactory::Release\n");
    METHOD_PROLOGUE(CSpaceshipFactory, ClassFactory) // makes pThis
    return pThis->ExternalRelease(); // delegate to CSimulatedCmdTarget
}

DWORD CSpaceshipFactory::XClassFactory::AddRef() {
    TRACE("Entering CSpaceshipFactory::XClassFactory::AddRef\n");
    METHOD_PROLOGUE(CSpaceshipFactory, ClassFactory) // makes pThis
    return pThis->ExternalAddRef(); // delegate to CSimulatedCmdTarget
}

BOOL CSpaceship::ExternalQueryInterface(int nIid, void** ppvObj) {
    TRACE("Entering CSpaceship::ExternalQueryInterface--nIid =
            %d\n", nIid);
    switch (nIid) {
    case IID_IUnknown:
    case IID_IMotion:
        *ppvObj = &m_xMotion; // Both IMotion and IVisual are derived
        break;                //   from IUnknown, so either pointer will do
    case IID_IVisual:
        *ppvObj = &m_xVisual;
        break;
    default:
        *ppvObj = NULL;
        return FALSE;
    }
    ExternalAddRef();
    return TRUE;
}

BOOL CSpaceship::XMotion::QueryInterface(int nIid, void** ppvObj) {
    TRACE("Entering CSpaceship::XMotion::QueryInterface--nIid = \
            %d\n", nIid);
    METHOD_PROLOGUE(CSpaceship, Motion) // makes pThis
    return pThis->ExternalQueryInterface(nIid, ppvObj); // delegate to
                                                         //   CSpaceship
}

DWORD CSpaceship::XMotion::Release() {
    TRACE("Entering CSpaceship::XMotion::Release\n");
```

```
        METHOD_PROLOGUE(CSpaceship, Motion) // makes pThis
        return pThis->ExternalRelease(); // delegate to CSimulatedCmdTarget
    }

    DWORD CSpaceship::XMotion::AddRef() {
        TRACE("Entering CSpaceship::XMotion::AddRef\n");
        METHOD_PROLOGUE(CSpaceship, Motion) // makes pThis
        return pThis->ExternalAddRef(); // delegate to CSimulatedCmdTarget
    }

    void CSpaceship::XMotion::Fly() {
        TRACE("Entering CSpaceship::XMotion::Fly\n");
        METHOD_PROLOGUE(CSpaceship, Motion) // makes pThis
        TRACE("this = %p, pThis = %p\n", this, pThis);
        TRACE("m_nPosition = %d\n", pThis->m_nPosition);
        TRACE("m_nAcceleration = %d\n", pThis->m_nAcceleration);
    }

    int& CSpaceship::XMotion::GetPosition() {
        TRACE("Entering CSpaceship::XMotion::GetPosition\n");
        METHOD_PROLOGUE(CSpaceship, Motion) // makes pThis
        TRACE("this = %p, pThis = %p\n", this, pThis);
        TRACE("m_nPosition = %d\n", pThis->m_nPosition);
        TRACE("m_nAcceleration = %d\n", pThis->m_nAcceleration);
        return pThis->m_nPosition;
    }

    BOOL CSpaceship::XVisual::QueryInterface(int nIid, void** ppvObj) {
        TRACE("Entering CSpaceship::XVisual::QueryInterface--nIid = \
            %d\n", nIid);
        METHOD_PROLOGUE(CSpaceship, Visual) // makes pThis
        return pThis->ExternalQueryInterface(nIid, ppvObj); // delegate to
                                                            //  CSpaceship
    }

    DWORD CSpaceship::XVisual::Release() {
        TRACE("Entering CSpaceship::XVisual::Release\n");
        METHOD_PROLOGUE(CSpaceship, Visual) // makes pThis
        return pThis->ExternalRelease(); // delegate to CSimulatedCmdTarget
    }

    DWORD CSpaceship::XVisual::AddRef() {
        TRACE("Entering CSpaceship::XVisual::AddRef\n");
        METHOD_PROLOGUE(CSpaceship, Visual) // makes pThis
        return pThis->ExternalAddRef(); // delegate to CSimulatedCmdTarget
    }
```

(continued)

Figure 24-3. *continued*

```
void CSpaceship::XVisual::Display() {
    TRACE("Entering CSpaceship::XVisual::Display\n");
    METHOD_PROLOGUE(CSpaceship, Visual) // makes pThis
    TRACE("this = %p, pThis = %p\n", this, pThis);
    TRACE("m_nPosition = %d\n", pThis->m_nPosition);
    TRACE("m_nColor = %d\n", pThis->m_nColor);
}


//----------simulates COM component -----------------------------------
// In real COM, this would be DllGetClassObject, which would be called
//  whenever a client called CoGetClassObject

BOOL GetClassObject(int nClsid, int nIid, void** ppvObj)
{
    ASSERT(nClsid == CLSID_CSpaceship);
    ASSERT((nIid == IID_IUnknown) || (nIid == IID_IClassFactory));
    return g_factory.ExternalQueryInterface(nIid, ppvObj);
    // Refcount is 2, which prevents accidental deletion
}
```

CLIENT.CPP

```
#include <stdio.h>
#include <stddef.h> // for offsetof in METHOD_PROLOGUE
#include <assert.h>
#include "interface.h"



//----------main program--------------------------------------------
int main() // simulates OLE client program
{
    TRACE("Entering client main\n");
    IUnknown* pUnk; // If you declare these void*, you lose type-safety
    IMotion* pMot;
    IVisual* pVis;
    IClassFactory* pClf;

    GetClassObject(CLSID_CSpaceship, IID_IClassFactory,
                   (void**) &pClf);

    pClf->CreateInstance(IID_IUnknown, (void**) &pUnk);
    pUnk->QueryInterface(IID_IMotion, (void**) &pMot); // All three
    pMot->QueryInterface(IID_IVisual, (void**) &pVis); //   pointers
                                                       //   should work
```

Figure 24-4.
The Client.cpp file.

(continued)

```
TRACE("main: pUnk = %p, pMot = %p, pDis = %p\n", pUnk, pMot, pVis);

// Test all the interface virtual functions
pMot->Fly();
int nPos = pMot->GetPosition();
TRACE("nPos = %d\n", nPos);
pVis->Display();

pClf->Release();
pUnk->Release();
pMot->Release();
pVis->Release();
return 0;
}
```

Real COM with the MFC Library

So much for simulations. Now we'll get ready to convert the spaceship example to genuine COM. You need to acquire a little more knowledge before we start, though. First you must learn about the *CoGetClassObject* function, then you must learn how COM uses the Windows Registry to load the component, and then you have to understand the difference between an <u>in-process</u> <u>component</u> (a DLL) and an <u>out-of-process</u> <u>component</u> (an EXE or a DLL running as a surrogate). Finally, you must become familiar with the MFC macros that support nested classes.

The net result will be an MFC regular DLL component that contains all the *CSpaceship* code with the *IMotion* and *IVisual* interfaces. A regular MFC library Windows application acts as the client. It loads and runs the component when the user selects a menu item.

The COM *CoGetClassObject* Function

In our simulation, we used a phony function named *GetClassObject*. In real COM, we use the global *CoGetClassObject* function. (*Co* stands for "component object.") Compare the following prototype to the *GetClassObject* function you've seen already:

```
STDAPI CoGetClassObject(REFCLSID rclsid, DWORD dwClsContext,
    COSERVERINFO* pServerInfo, REFIID riid, LPVOID* ppvObj)
```

The interface pointer goes in the *ppvObj* parameter, and *pServerInfo* is a pointer to a machine on which the class object is instantiated (*NULL* if the machine is local). The types *REFCLSID* and *REFIID* are references to 128-bit GUIDs (globally unique identifiers for COM classes and interfaces). STDAPI indicates that the function returns a 32-bit value of type *HRESULT*.

The standard GUIDs (for example, those GUIDs naming interfaces that Microsoft has already created) are defined in the Windows libraries that are dynamically linked to your program. GUIDs for custom classes and interfaces, such as those for spaceship objects, must be defined in your program in this way:

```
// {692D03A4-C689-11CE-B337-88EA36DE9E4E}
static const IID IID_IMotion =
    {0x692d03a4, 0xc689, 0x11ce, {0xb3, 0x37, 0x88, 0xea, 0x36,
    0xde, 0x9e, 0x4e}};
```

If the *dwClsContext* parameter is *CLSCTX_INPROC_SERVER*, the COM subsytem looks for a DLL. If the parameter is *CLSCTX_LOCAL_SERVER*, COM looks for an EXE. The two codes can be combined to select either a DLL or an EXE—selected in order of performance. For example, inproc servers are fastest because everybody shares the same address space. Communication EXE servers are considerably slower because the interprocess calls involve data copying as well as many thread context switches. The return value is an *HRESULT* value, which is 0 (*NOERROR*) if no error occurs.

NOTE: Another COM function, *CoCreateInstance*, combines the functionality of *CoGetClassObject* and *IClassFactory::CreateInstance*.

COM and the Windows Registry

In the EX24A example, the component was statically linked to the client, a clearly bogus circumstance. In real COM, the component is either a DLL or a separate EXE. When the client calls the *CoGetClassObject* function, COM steps in and finds the correct component, which is located somewhere on disk. How does COM make the connection? It looks up the class's unique 128-bit class ID number in the Windows Registry. Thus, the class must be registered permanently on your computer.

If you run the Windows Regedit program (Regedt32 in Microsoft Windows NT 3.51), you'll see a screen similar to the one shown in Figure 24-5. This figure shows subfolders for four class IDs, three of which are class IDs associated with DLLs (InprocServer32) and one of which is a class ID associated with an EXE (LocalServer32). The *CoGetClassObject* function looks up the class ID in the Registry and then loads the DLL or EXE as required.

What if you don't want to track those ugly class ID numbers in your client program? No problem. COM supports another type of registration database entry that translates a human-readable program ID into the corresponding class ID. Figure 24-6 shows the Registry entries. The COM function *CLSIDFromProgID* reads the database and performs the translation.

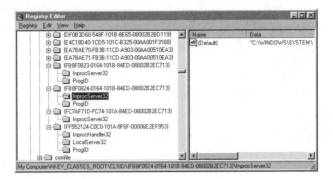

Figure 24-5.
Subfolders of four class IDs in the Registry.

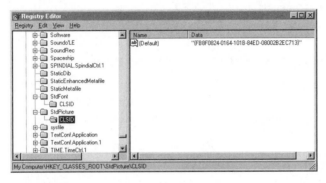

Figure 24-6.
Human-readable program IDs in the Registry.

NOTE: The first *CLSIDFromProgID* parameter is a string that holds the program ID, but it's not an ordinary string. This is your first exposure to double-byte characters in COM. All string parameters of COM functions (except Data Access Objects [DAOs]) are Unicode character string pointers of type *OLECHAR**. Your life is going to be made miserable because of the constant need to convert between double-byte strings and ordinary strings. If you need a double-byte literal string, prefix the string with an *L* character, like this:

```
CLSIDFromProgID(L"Spaceship", &clsid);
```

You'll begin learning about the MFC library's Unicode string conversion capabilities in Chapter 25.

How does the registration information get into the Registry? You can program your component application to call Windows functions that directly update the Registry. The MFC library conveniently wraps these functions with the function *COleObjectFactory::UpdateRegistryAll*, which finds all your program's global class factory objects and registers their names and class IDs.

Runtime Object Registration

You've just seen how the Windows Registry registers COM classes on disk. Class factory <u>objects</u> also must be registered. It's unfortunate that the word "register" is used in both contexts. Objects in out-of-process component modules are registered at runtime with a call to the COM *CoRegisterClassObject* function, and the registration information is maintained in memory by the Windows DLLs. If the factory is registered in a mode that permits a single instance of the component module to create multiple COM objects, COM can use an existing process when a client calls *CoGetClassObject*.

How a COM Client Calls an In-Process Component

We're beginning with a DLL component instead of an EXE component because the program interactions are simpler. I'll show pseudocode here because you're going to be using the MFC library classes, which hide much of the detail.

Client

```
CLSID clsid;
IClassFactory* pClf;
IUnknown* pUnk;
CoInitialize(NULL);  // Initialize COM
CLSIDFromProgID ("componentname", &clsid);
```

COM

```
COM uses the Registry to look up the class ID from "componentname"
```

Client

```
CoGetClassObject(clsid, CLSCTX_INPROC_SERVER, NULL,
    IID_IClassFactory, (void**) &pClf );
```

COM

```
COM uses the class ID to look for a component in memory
if (component DLL is not loaded already) {
    COM gets DLL filename from the Registry
```

COM loads the component DLL into process memory
}

DLL Component

if (component just loaded) {
    Global factory objects are constructed
    DLL's InitInstance called (MFC only)
}

COM

COM calls DLL's global exported DllGetClassObject with the CLSID
    value that was passed to CoGetClassObject

DLL Component

DllGetClassObject returns IClassFactory*

COM

COM returns IClassFactory* to client

Client

pClf->CreateInstance (NULL, IID_IUnknown, (void**) &pUnk);

DLL Component

Class factory's CreateInstance function called (called directly—through
    component's vtable)
Constructs object of "componentname" class
Returns requested interface pointer

Client

pClf->Release();
pUnk->Release();

DLL Component

"componentname" Release is called through vtable
    if (refcount == 0) {
    Object destroys itself
}

Client

    CoFreeUnusedLibraries();

COM

    COM calls DLL's global exported DllCanUnloadNow

DLL Component

    DllCanUnloadNow called if (all DLL's objects destroyed) {

      return TRUE

    }

Client

    CoUninitialize(); // COM frees the DLL if DllCanUnloadNow returns

      TRUE just prior to exit

COM

    COM releases resources

Client

    Client exits

DLL Component

    Windows unloads the DLL if it is still loaded and no other programs are
    using it

Some important points to note: first, the DLL's exported *DllGetClass-Object* function is called in response to the client's *CoGetClassObject* call. Second, the class factory interface address returned is the actual physical address of the class factory vtable pointer in the DLL. Third, when the client calls *Create-Instance*, or any other interface function, the call is direct (through the component's vtable).

The COM linkage between a client EXE and a component DLL is quite efficient—as efficient as the linkage to any C++ virtual function in the same process, plus the full C++ parameter and return type-checking at compile time. The only penalty for using ordinary DLL linkage is the extra step of looking up the class ID in the Registry when the DLL is first loaded.

How a COM Client Calls an Out-of-Process Component

The COM linkage to a separate EXE component is more complicated than the linkage to a DLL component. The EXE component is in a different process, or possibly on a different computer. Don't worry, though. Write your programs as if a direct connection existed. COM takes care of the details through its remoting architecture, which usually involves Remote Procedure Calls (RPCs).

In an RPC, the client makes calls to a special DLL called a proxy. The proxy sends a stream of data to a stub, which is inside a DLL in the component's process. When the client calls a component function, the proxy alerts the stub by sending a message to the component program, which is processed by a hidden window. The mechanism of converting parameters to and from data streams is called marshaling.

If you use standard interfaces (those interfaces defined by Microsoft) such as *IClassFactory* and *IPersist* (an interface we haven't seen yet but will appear when we examine COM persistence), the proxy and stub code, which implements marshaling, is provided by the Windows OLE32 DLL. If you invent your own interfaces, such as *IMotion* and *IVisual*, you need to write the proxies and stubs yourself. Fortunately, creating proxy and stub classes only involves defining your interfaces in Interface Definition Language (IDL) and compiling the code produced by the Microsoft Interface Definition Language (MIDL) compiler.

Here's the pseudocode interaction between an EXE client and an EXE component. Compare it to the DLL version beginning on page 594. Notice that the client-side calls are exactly the same.

Client
```
CLSID clsid;
IClassFactory* pClf;
IUnknown* pUnk;
CoInitialize(NULL);  // Initialize COM
CLSIDFromProgID("componentname", &clsid);
```

COM
```
COM uses the Registry to look up the class ID from "componentname"
```

Client
```
CoGetClassObject(clsid, CLSCTX_LOCAL_SERVER, NULL,
    IID_IClassFactory, (void**) &pClf);
```

COM
> COM uses the class ID to look for a component in memory
>> if (component EXE is not loaded already, or
>> if we need another instance) {
>> COM gets EXE filename from the Registry
>> COM loads the component EXE
>
>> }

EXE Component
> if (just loaded) {
>> Global factory objects are constructed
>> InitInstance called (MFC only)
>> CoInitialize(NULL);
>> for each factory object {
>>> CoRegisterClassObject(...);
>>> Returns IClassFactory* to COM
>>> }
>
>> }

COM
> COM returns the requested interface pointer to the client
>> (client's pointer is not the same as the component's interface pointer)

Client
> pClf->CreateInstance(NULL, IID_IUnknown, (void**) &pUnk);

EXE Component
> Class factory's CreateInstance function called
>> (called indirectly through marshaling)
>> Constructs object of "componentname" class
>> Returns requested interface pointer indirectly

Client
> pClf->Release();
> pUnk->Release();

EXE Component
> "componentname" Release is called indirectly
> if (refcount == 0) {

```
        Object destroys itself
    }
    if (all objects released) {
        Component exits gracefully
    }
```

Client

    CoUninitialize(); // just prior to exit

COM

    COM calls Release for any objects this client has failed to release

EXE Component

    Component exits

COM

    COM releases resources

Client

    Client exits

As you can see, COM plays an important role in the communication between the client and the component. COM keeps an in-memory list of class factories that are in active EXE components, but it does not keep track of individual COM objects such as the *CSpaceship* object. Individual COM objects are responsible for updating the reference count and for destroying themselves through the *AddRef/Release* mechanism. COM does step in when a client exits. If that client is using an out-of-process component, COM "listens in" on the communication and keeps track of the reference count on each object. COM disconnects from component objects when the client exits. Under certain circumstances, this causes those objects to be released. Don't depend on this behavior, however. Be sure that your client program releases all its interface pointers prior to exiting.

The MFC Interface Macros

In EX24A, you saw nested classes used for interface implementation. The MFC library has a set of macros that automate this process. For the *CSpaceship* class, derived from the real MFC *CCmdTarget* class, you use the macros on the following page inside the declaration.

```
BEGIN_INTERFACE_PART(Motion, IMotion)
    STDMETHOD_(void, Fly) ();
    STDMETHOD_(int&, GetPosition) ();
END_INTERFACE_PART(Motion)

BEGIN_INTERFACE_PART(Visual, IVisual)
    STDMETHOD_(void, Display) ();
END_INTERFACE_PART(Visual)

DECLARE_INTERFACE_MAP()
```

The *INTERFACE_PART* macros generate the nested classes, adding *X* to the first parameter to form the class name and adding *m_x* to form the embedded object name. The macros generate prototypes for the specified interface functions plus prototypes for *QueryInterface*, *AddRef*, and *Release*.

The *DECLARE_INTERFACE_MAP* macro generates the declarations for a table that holds the IDs of all the class's interfaces. The *CCmdTarget::ExternalQueryInterface* function uses the table to retrieve the interface pointers.

In the *CSpaceship* implementation file, use the following macros:

```
BEGIN_INTERFACE_MAP(CSpaceship, CCmdTarget)
    INTERFACE_PART(CSpaceship, IID_IMotion, Motion)
    INTERFACE_PART(CSpaceship, IID_IVisual, Visual)
END_INTERFACE_MAP()
```

These macros build the interface table used by *CCmdTarget::ExternalQueryInterface*. A typical interface member function looks like this:

```
STDMETHODIMP_(void) CSpaceship::XMotion::Fly()
{
    METHOD_PROLOGUE(CSpaceship, Motion)
    pThis->m_nPosition += 10;
    return;
}
```

Don't forget that you must implement all the functions for each interface, including *QueryInterface*, *AddRef*, and *Release*. Those three functions can delegate to functions in *CCmdTarget*.

> **NOTE:** The *STDMETHOD_* and *STDMETHODIMP_* macros declare and implement functions with the *__stdcall* parameter passing convention, as required by COM. These macros allow you to specify the return value as the first parameter. Two other macros, *STDMETHOD* and *STDMETHODIMP*, assume an *HRESULT* return value.

The MFC *COleObjectFactory* Class

In the simulated COM example, you saw a *CSpaceshipFactory* class that was hard-coded to generate *CSpaceship* objects. The MFC library applies its dynamic creation technology to the problem. Thus, a single class, aptly named *COle-ObjectFactory*, can create objects of any class specified at runtime. All you need to do is use macros like these in the class declaration:

```
DECLARE_DYNCREATE(CSpaceship)
DECLARE_OLECREATE(CSpaceship)
```

And use macros like these in the implementation file:

```
IMPLEMENT_DYNCREATE(CSpaceship, CCmdTarget)
// {692D03A3-C689-11CE-B337-88EA36DE9E4E}
IMPLEMENT_OLECREATE(CSpaceship, "Spaceship", 0x692d03a3, 0xc689, 0x11ce,
    0xb3, 0x37, 0x88, 0xea, 0x36, 0xde, 0x9e, 0x4e)
```

The *DYNCREATE* macros set up the standard dynamic creation mechanism as described in Appendix B. The *OLECREATE* macros declare and define a global object of class *COleObjectFactory* with the specified unique CLSID. In a DLL component, the exported *DllGetClassObject* function finds the specified class factory object and returns a pointer to it based on global variables set by the *OLECREATE* macros. In an EXE component, initialization code calls the static *COleObjectFactory::RegisterAll*, which finds all factory objects and registers each one by calling *CoRegisterClassObject*. The *RegisterAll* function is called also when a DLL is initialized. In that case, it merely sets a flag in the factory object(s).

We've really just scratched the surface of MFC's COM support. If you need more details, be sure to refer to Shepherd and Wingo's *MFC Internals* (Addison-Wesley, 1996).

AppWizard/ClassWizard Support for COM In-Process Components

AppWizard isn't optimized for creating COM DLL components, but you can fool it by requesting a regular DLL with Automation support. The following functions in the project's main source file are of interest:

```
BOOL CEx24bApp::InitInstance()
{
    COleObjectFactory::RegisterAll();
    return TRUE;
}
```

(continued)

```
STDAPI DllGetClassObject(REFCLSID rclsid, REFIID riid, LPVOID* ppv)
{
    AFX_MANAGE_STATE(AfxGetStaticModuleState());
    return AfxDllGetClassObject(rclsid, riid, ppv);
}

STDAPI DllCanUnloadNow(void)
{
    AFX_MANAGE_STATE(AfxGetStaticModule_State());
    return AfxDllCanUnloadNow();
}

STDAPI DllRegisterServer(void)
{
    AFX_MANAGE_STATE(AfxGetStaticModuleState());
    COleObjectFactory::UpdateRegistryAll();
    return S_OK;
}
```

The three global functions are exported in the project's DEF file. By calling MFC functions, the global functions do everything you need in a COM in-process component. The *DllRegisterServer* function can be called by a utility program to update the system Registry.

Once you've created the skeleton project, your next step is to use Class-Wizard to add one or more COM-creatable classes to the project. Just fill in the New Class dialog box, as shown here.

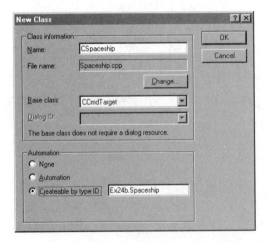

In your generated class, you end up with some Automation elements such as dispatch maps, but you can safely remove those. You can also remove the following two lines from StdAfx.h:

```
#include <afxodlgs.h>
#include <afxdisp.h>
```

MFC COM Client Programs

Writing an MFC COM client program is a no-brainer. You just use AppWizard to generate a normal application. Add the following line in StdAfx.h:

```
#include <afxole.h>
```

Then add the following line at the beginning of the application class *InitInstance* member function:

```
AfxOleInit();
```

You're now ready to add code that calls *CoGetClassObject*.

The EX24B Example—An MFC COM In-Process Component

The EX24B example is an MFC regular DLL that incorporates a true COM version of the *CSpaceship* class you saw in EX24A. AppWizard generated the ex24b.cpp and ex24b.h files, as described previously. Figure 24-7 shows the Interface.h file, which declares the *IMotion* and *IVisual* interfaces. Figures 24-8 on the following page and 24-9 on page 605 show the code for the *CSpaceship* class. Compare the code to the code in EX24A. Do you see how the use of the MFC macros reduces code size? Note that the MFC *CCmdTarget* class takes care of the reference counting and *QueryInterface* logic.

INTERFACE.H

```
struct IMotion : public IUnknown
{
    STDMETHOD_(void, Fly) () = 0;
    STDMETHOD_(int&, GetPosition) () = 0;
};

struct IVisual : public IUnknown
{
    STDMETHOD_(void, Display) () = 0;
};
```

Figure 24-7.
The Interface.h file.

SPACESHIP.H

```
void ITrace(REFIID iid, const char* str);


/////////////////////////////////////////////////////////////////
// CSpaceship command target

class CSpaceship : public CCmdTarget
{
    DECLARE_DYNCREATE(CSpaceship)

private:
    int m_nPosition; // We can access this from all the interfaces
    int m_nAcceleration;
    int m_nColor;
protected:
    CSpaceship();     // protected constructor used by dynamic creation

// Attributes
public:

// Operations
public:

// Overrides
    // ClassWizard generated virtual function overrides
    //{{AFX_VIRTUAL(CSpaceship)
    public:
    virtual void OnFinalRelease();
    //}}AFX_VIRTUAL

// Implementation
protected:
    virtual ~CSpaceship();

    // Generated message map functions
    //{{AFX_MSG(CSpaceship)
        // NOTE - the ClassWizard will add and remove member
        //   functions here.
    //}}AFX_MSG

    DECLARE_MESSAGE_MAP()
    DECLARE_OLECREATE(CSpaceship)
    BEGIN_INTERFACE_PART(Motion, IMotion)
        STDMETHOD_(void, Fly) ();
```

Figure 24-8.
The Spaceship.h file.

```
        STDMETHOD_(int&, GetPosition) ();
    END_INTERFACE_PART(Motion)

    BEGIN_INTERFACE_PART(Visual, IVisual)
        STDMETHOD_(void, Display) ();
    END_INTERFACE_PART(Visual)

    DECLARE_INTERFACE_MAP()
};
/////////////////////////////////////////////////////////////////////
```

SPACESHIP.CPP

```
#include "stdAfx.h"
#include "ex24b.h"
#include "Interface.h"
#include "Spaceship.h"

#ifdef _DEBUG
#undef THIS_FILE
static char THIS_FILE[] = __FILE__;
#endif
/////////////////////////////////////////////////////////////////////
// CSpaceship

// {692D03A4-C689-11CE-B337-88EA36DE9E4E}
static const IID IID_IMotion =
{ 0x692d03a4, 0xc689, 0x11ce,
    { 0xb3, 0x37, 0x88, 0xea, 0x36, 0xde, 0x9e, 0x4e } };

// {692D03A5-C689-11CE-B337-88EA36DE9E4E}
static const IID IID_IVisual =
{ 0x692d03a5, 0xc689, 0x11ce,
    { 0xb3, 0x37, 0x88, 0xea, 0x36, 0xde, 0x9e, 0x4e } };

IMPLEMENT_DYNCREATE(CSpaceship, CCmdTarget)
CSpaceship::CSpaceship()
{
    TRACE("CSpaceship ctor\n");
    m_nPosition = 100;
    m_nAcceleration = 101;
    m_nColor = 102;
    // To keep the application running as long as an OLE automation
    //  object is active, the constructor calls AfxOleLockApp.
```

Figure 24-9. *(continued)*

The Spaceship.cpp file.

Figure 24-9. *continued*

```
    AfxOleLockApp();
}

CSpaceship::~CSpaceship()
{
    TRACE("CSpaceship dtor\n");
    // To terminate the application when all objects created with
    //  OLE automation, the destructor calls AfxOleUnlockApp.

    AfxOleUnlockApp();
}
void CSpaceship::OnFinalRelease()
{
    // When the last reference for an automation object is released
    //  OnFinalRelease is called. This implementation deletes the
    //  object. Add additional cleanup required for your object before
    //  deleting it from memory.

    delete this;
}
BEGIN_MESSAGE_MAP(CSpaceship, CCmdTarget)
    //{{AFX_MSG_MAP(CSpaceship)
    // NOTE - ClassWizard will add and remove mapping macros here.
    //}}AFX_MSG_MAP
END_MESSAGE_MAP()

BEGIN_INTERFACE_MAP(CSpaceship, CCmdTarget)
    INTERFACE_PART(CSpaceship, IID_IMotion, Motion)
    INTERFACE_PART(CSpaceship, IID_IVisual, Visual)
END_INTERFACE_MAP()

// {692D03A3-C689-11CE-B337-88EA36DE9E4E}
IMPLEMENT_OLECREATE(CSpaceship, "Spaceship", 0x692d03a3, 0xc689,
                    0x11ce, 0xb3, 0x37, 0x88, 0xea, 0x36, 0xde,
                    0x9e, 0x4e)
STDMETHODIMP_(ULONG) CSpaceship::XMotion::AddRef()
{
    TRACE("CSpaceship::XMotion::AddRef\n");
    METHOD_PROLOGUE(CSpaceship, Motion)
    return pThis->ExternalAddRef();
}

STDMETHODIMP_(ULONG) CSpaceship::XMotion::Release()
{
    TRACE("CSpaceship::XMotion::Release\n");
    METHOD_PROLOGUE(CSpaceship, Motion)
```

```
        return pThis->ExternalRelease();
    }

STDMETHODIMP CSpaceship::XMotion::QueryInterface(
    REFIID iid, LPVOID* ppvObj)
{

    ITrace(iid, "CSpaceship::XMotion::QueryInterface");
    METHOD_PROLOGUE(CSpaceship, Motion)
    return pThis->ExternalQueryInterface(&iid, ppvObj);
}
STDMETHODIMP_(void) CSpaceship::XMotion::Fly()
{

    TRACE("CSpaceship::XMotion::Fly\n");
    METHOD_PROLOGUE(CSpaceship, Motion)
    TRACE("m_nPosition = %d\n", pThis->m_nPosition);
    TRACE("m_nAcceleration = %d\n", pThis->m_nAcceleration);
    return;
}


STDMETHODIMP_(int&) CSpaceship::XMotion::GetPosition()
{

    TRACE("CSpaceship::XMotion::GetPosition\n");
    METHOD_PROLOGUE(CSpaceship, Motion)
    TRACE("m_nPosition = %d\n", pThis->m_nPosition);
    TRACE("m_nAcceleration = %d\n", pThis->m_nAcceleration);
    return pThis->m_nPosition;
}


/////////////////////////////////////////////////////////////////////
STDMETHODIMP_(ULONG) CSpaceship::XVisual::AddRef()
{

    TRACE("CSpaceship::XVisual::AddRef\n");
    METHOD_PROLOGUE(CSpaceship, Visual)
    return pThis->ExternalAddRef();
}


STDMETHODIMP_(ULONG) CSpaceship::XVisual::Release()
{

    TRACE("CSpaceship::XVisual::Release\n");
    METHOD_PROLOGUE(CSpaceship, Visual)
    return pThis->ExternalRelease();
}


STDMETHODIMP CSpaceship::XVisual::QueryInterface(
    REFIID iid, LPVOID* ppvObj)
{

    ITrace(iid, "CSpaceship::XVisual::QueryInterface");
```

(continued)

Figure 24-9. *continued*

```
    METHOD_PROLOGUE(CSpaceship, Visual)
    return pThis->ExternalQueryInterface(&iid, ppvObj);
}
STDMETHODIMP_(void) CSpaceship::XVisual::Display()
{
    TRACE("CSpaceship::XVisual::Display\n");
    METHOD_PROLOGUE(CSpaceship, Visual)
    TRACE("m_nPosition = %d\n", pThis->m_nPosition);
    TRACE("m_nColor = %d\n", pThis->m_nColor);
}


/////////////////////////////////////////////////////////////////////////
void ITrace(REFIID iid, const char* str)
{
    OLECHAR* lpszIID;
    ::StringFromIID(iid, &lpszIID);
    CString strTemp = (LPCWSTR) lpszIID;
    TRACE("%s - %s\n", (const char*) strTemp, (const char*) str);
    AfxFreeTaskMem(lpszIID);
}


/////////////////////////////////////////////////////////////////////////
// CSpaceship message handlers
```

The EX24C Example—An MFC COM Client

The EX24C example is an MFC program that incorporates a true COM version of the client code you saw in EX24A. This is a generic AppWizard MFC Single Document Interface (SDI) EXE program with an added *#include* statement for the MFC COM headers and a call to *AfxOleInit*, which initializes the DLL. A Spaceship option on an added Test menu is mapped to the view class handler function shown in Figure 24-10. The project also contains a copy of the EX24B component's Interface.h file, shown in Figure 24-7 on page 603. You can see an *#include* statement for this file at the top of ex24cView.cpp.

```
void CEx24cView::OnTestSpaceship()
{
    CLSID clsid;
    LPCLASSFACTORY pClf;
    LPUNKNOWN pUnk;
    IMotion* pMot;
    IVisual* pVis;
```

Figure 24-10. *(continued)*
The client's command handler that loads and tests the CSpaceship *component.*

```
HRESULT hr;
if ((hr = ::CLSIDFromProgID(L"Spaceship", &clsid)) != NOERROR) {
    TRACE("unable to find Program ID -- error = %x\n", hr);
    return;
}
if ((hr = ::CoGetClassObject(clsid, CLSCTX_INPROC_SERVER,
    NULL, IID_IClassFactory, (void **) &pClf)) != NOERROR) {;
    TRACE("unable to find CLSID -- error = %x\n", hr);
    return;
}

pClf->CreateInstance(NULL, IID_IUnknown, (void**) &pUnk);
pUnk->QueryInterface(IID_IMotion, (void**) &pMot); // All three
pMot->QueryInterface(IID_IVisual, (void**) &pVis); //  pointers
                                                   //  should work
TRACE("main: pUnk = %p, pMot = %p, pDis = %p\n", pUnk, pMot, pVis);

// Test all the interface virtual functions
pMot->Fly();
int nPos = pMot->GetPosition();
TRACE("nPos = %d\n", nPos);
pVis->Display();

pClf->Release();
pUnk->Release();
pMot->Release();
pVis->Release();
AfxMessageBox("Test succeeded. See Debug window for output.");
}
```

To test the client and the component, you must first run the component to update the Registry. Several utilities can be used to do this, but you might want to try the REGCOMP program in the \vcpp32\RegComp project on the companion CD-ROM. This program prompts you to select a DLL or an OCX file, and then it calls the exported *DllRegisterServer* function.

Both client and component show their progress through *TRACE* calls, so you need the debugger. You can run either the client or the component from the debugger. If you try to run the component, you'll be prompted for the client pathname. In either case, you don't have to copy the DLL because Windows finds it through the Registry.

Containment and Aggregation vs. Inheritance

In normal C++ programming, you frequently use inheritance to factor out common behavior into a reusable base class. The *CPersistentFrame* class (discussed in Chapter 15) is an example of reusability through inheritance.

COM uses containment and aggregation instead of inheritance. Let's start with containment. Suppose you extended the spaceship simulation to include planets in addition to spaceships. Using C++ by itself, you would probably write a *COrbiter* base class that encapsulated the laws of planetary motion. With COM, you would have "outer" *CSpaceship* and *CPlanet* classes plus an "inner" *COrbiter* class. The outer classes would implement the *IVisual* interface directly, but those outer classes would <u>delegate</u> their *IMotion* interfaces to the inner class. The result would look something like this.

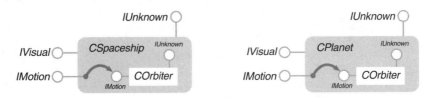

Note that the *COrbiter* object doesn't know that it's inside a *CSpaceship* or *CPlanet* object, but the outer object certainly knows that it has a *COrbiter* object embedded inside. The outer class needs to implement all its interface functions, but the *IMotion* functions, including *QueryInterface*, simply call the same *IMotion* functions of the inner class.

A more complex alternative to containment is aggregation. With aggregation, the client can have direct access to the inner object's interfaces. Shown here is the aggregation version of the space simulation.

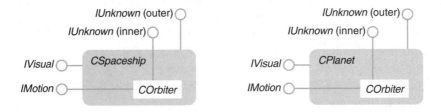

The orbiter is embedded in the spaceship and planet, just as it was in the containment case. Suppose the client obtains an *IVisual* pointer for a spaceship and then calls *QueryInterface* for an *IMotion* pointer. Using the outer *IUnknown* pointer will draw a blank because the *CSpaceship* class doesn't support *IMotion*.

The *CSpaceship* class keeps track of the inner *IUnknown* pointer (of its embedded *COrbiter* object), so the class uses that pointer to obtain the *IMotion* pointer for the *COrbiter* object.

Now suppose the client obtains an *IMotion* pointer and then calls *QueryInterface* for *IVisual*. The inner object must be able to navigate to the outer object, but how? Take a close look at the *CreateInstance* call back in Figure 24-10 on page 609. The first parameter is set to *NULL* in that case. If you are creating an aggregated (inner) object, you use that parameter to pass an *IUnknown* pointer for the outer object that you have already created. This pointer is called the <u>controlling unknown</u>. The *COrbiter* class saves this pointer in a data member and then uses it to call *QueryInterface* for interfaces that the class itself doesn't support.

The MFC library supports aggregation. The *CCmdTarget* class has a public data member *m_pOuterUnknown* that holds the outer object's *IUnknown* pointer (if the object is aggregated). The *CCmdTarget* member functions *ExternalQueryInterface*, *ExternalAddRef*, and *ExternalRelease* delegate to the outer *IUnknown* if it exists. Member functions *InternalQueryInterface*, *InternalAddRef*, and *InternalRelease* do not delegate. See Technical Note #38 in the online documentation for a description of the MFC macros that support aggregation.

CHAPTER TWENTY-FIVE

Automation

After reading Chapter 24, you should know what an interface is; you've already seen two standard COM interfaces, *IUnknown* and *IClassFactory*. Now you're ready for "applied" COM, or at least one aspect of it—Automation (formerly known as OLE Automation). You'll learn about the COM *IDispatch* interface, which enables C++ programs to communicate with Microsoft Visual Basic for Applications (VBA) programs and with programs written in other scripting languages. In addition, *IDispatch* is the key to getting your COM object onto a Web page. You'll use the MFC library implementation of *IDispatch* to write C++ Automation component and client programs. Both out-of-process components and in-process components are explored.

But before jumping into C++ Automation programming, you need to know how the rest of the world writes programs. In this chapter, you'll get some exposure to VBA as it is implemented in Microsoft Excel. You'll run your C++ components from Excel, and you'll run Excel from a C++ client program.

Connecting C++ with Visual Basic for Applications

Not all programmers for Microsoft Windows–based applications are going to be C++ programmers, especially if they have to learn the intricacies of COM theory. If you've been paying attention over the last few years, you've probably noticed a trend in which C++ programmers produce reusable modules. Programmers using higher-level languages (Visual Basic, VBA, and Web scripting languages, for example) consume those modules by integrating them into applications. You can participate in this programming model by learning how to make your software Script-friendly. Automation is one tool available now that is supported by the Microsoft Foundation Class library. ActiveX Controls are another tool for C++/VBA integration and are very much a superset of Automation because both tools use the *IDispatch* interface. Using ActiveX Controls, however, might be overkill in many situations. Many applications, including Microsoft Excel 97, can support both Automation components and ActiveX controls. You'll be able to apply all that you learn about Automation when you write and use ActiveX controls.

Two factors are responsible for Automation's success. First, VBA (or VB Script) is now the programming standard in most Microsoft applications, including Microsoft Word, Microsoft Access, and Excel, not to mention Microsoft Visual Basic itself. All these applications support Automation, which means they can be linked to other Automation-compatible components, including those written in C++ and VBA. For example, you can write a C++ program that uses the text-processing capability of Word, or you can write a C++ matrix inversion component that can be called from a VBA macro in an Excel worksheet.

The second factor connected to Automation's success is that dozens of software companies provide Automation programming interfaces for their applications, mostly for the benefit of VBA programmers. With a little effort, you can run these applications from C++. You can, for example, write an MFC program that controls Shapeware's Visio drawing program.

Automation isn't just for C++ and VBA programmers. Software-tool companies are already announcing Automation-compatible, Basic-like languages that you can license for your own programmable applications. One version of Smalltalk even supports Automation.

Automation Clients and Automation Components

A clearly defined "master–slave" relationship is always present in an Automation communication dialog. The master is the Automation client and the slave is the Automation component (server). The client initiates the interaction by constructing a component object (it might have to load the component program) or by attaching to an existing object in a component program that is already running. The client then calls interface functions in the component and releases those interfaces when it's finished.

Here are some interaction scenarios:

- A C++ Automation client uses a Microsoft or third-party application as a component. The interaction could trigger the execution of VBA code in the component application.

- A C++ Automation component is used from inside a Microsoft application (or a Visual Basic application), which acts as the Automation client. Thus, VBA code can construct and use C++ objects.

- A C++ Automation client uses a C++ Automation component.

- A Visual Basic program uses an Automation-aware application such as Excel. In this case, Visual Basic is the client and Excel is the component.

Microsoft Excel—A Better
Visual Basic than Visual Basic

At the time that the first three editions of this book were written, Visual Basic worked as an Automation client, but you couldn't use it to create an Automation component. Since version 5.0, Visual Basic lets you write components too, even ActiveX controls. We originally used Excel instead of VB because Excel was the first Microsoft application to support VBA syntax and it could serve as both a client and a component. We decided to stick with Excel because C++ programmers who look down their noses at Visual Basic might be inclined to buy Excel (if only to track their software royalties).

We strongly recommend that you get a copy of Excel 97 (or a later version). This is a true 32-bit application and a part of the Microsoft Office suite. With this version of Excel, you can write VBA code in a separate location that accesses worksheet cells in an object-oriented manner. Adding visual programming elements—such as pushbuttons—is easy. Forget all you ever knew about the old spreadsheet programs that forced you to wedge macro code inside cells.

This chapter isn't meant to be an Excel tutorial, but we've included a simple Excel workbook. (A workbook is a file that can contain multiple worksheets plus separate VBA code.) This workbook demonstrates a VBA macro that executes from a pushbutton. You can use Excel to load Demo.xls from the \vcpp32\ex25a subdirectory, or you can key in the example from scratch. Figure 25-1 on the next page shows the actual spreadsheet with the button and sample data.

In this spreadsheet, you highlight cells A4 through A9 and click the Process Col button. A VBA program iterates down the column and draws a hatched pattern on cells with numeric values greater than 10.

Figure 25-2 on the next page shows the macro code itself, which is "behind" the worksheet. In Excel 97, choose Macro from the Tools menu, and then choose Visual Basic Editor. (Alt-F11 is the shortcut.) As you can see, you're working in the standard VBA 5.0 environment at this point.

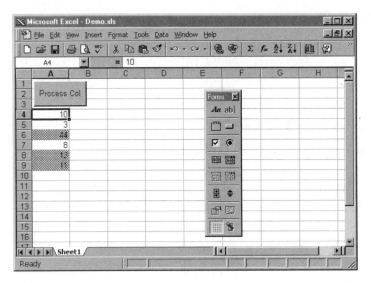

Figure 25-1.
An Excel spreadsheet that uses VBA code.

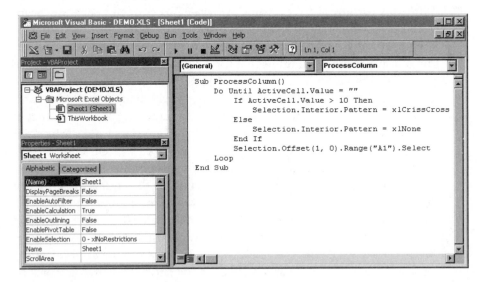

Figure 25-2.
The VBA code for the Excel spreadsheet.

If you want to create the example yourself, follow these steps:

1. Start Excel with a new workbook, press Alt-F11, and then double-click Sheet1 in the top left window.

2. Type in the macro code shown in Figure 25-2.

3. Return to the Excel window by choosing Close And Return To Microsoft Excel from the File menu. Choose Toolbars from the View menu. Check Forms to display the Forms toolbar. (You can also access the list of toolbars by right-clicking on any existing toolbar.)

4. Click the Button control, and then create the pushbutton by dragging the mouse in the upper-left corner of the worksheet. Assign the button to the *Sheet1.ProcessColumn* macro.

5. Size the pushbutton, and type the caption *Process Col*, as shown in Figure 25-1.

6. Type some numbers in the column starting at cell A4. Select the cells containing these numbers, and then click the button to test the program.

Pretty easy, isn't it?

Let's analyze an Excel VBA statement from the macro above:

```
Selection.Offset(1, 0).Range("A1").Select
```

The first element, Selection, is a <u>property</u> of an implied <u>object</u>, the Excel application. The Selection property in this case is assumed to be a *Range* object that represents a rectangular array of cells. The second element, Offset, is a property of the *Range* object that returns another *Range* object based on the two parameters. In this case, the returned *Range* object is the one-cell range that begins one row down from the original range. The third element, Range, is a property of the *Range* object that returns yet another range. This time it's the upper-left cell in the second range. Finally, the *Select* <u>method</u> causes Excel to highlight the selected cell and makes it the new Selection property of the application.

As the program iterates through the loop, the preceding statement moves the selected cell down the worksheet one row at a time. This style of programming takes some getting used to, but you can't afford to ignore it. The real value here is that you now have all the capabilities of the Excel spreadsheet and graphics engine available to you in a seamless programming environment.

Properties, Methods, and Collections

The distinction between a property and a method is somewhat artificial. Basically, a property is a value that can be both set and retrieved. You can, for example, set and get the Selection property for an Excel application. Another example is Excel's Width property, which applies to many object types. Some Excel properties are read-only; most are read/write.

Properties don't officially have parameters, but some properties are indexed. The property index acts a lot like a parameter. It doesn't have to be an integer, and it can have more than one element (row and column, for example). You'll find many indexed properties in Excel's object model, and Excel VBA can handle indexed properties in Automation components.

Methods are more flexible than properties. They can have zero or many parameters, and they can either set or retrieve object data. Most frequently they perform some action, such as showing a window. Excel's *Select* method is an example of an action method.

The Excel object model supports collection objects. If you use the Worksheets property of the *Application* object, you get back a *Sheets* collection object, which represents all the worksheets in the active workbook. You can use the Item property (with an integer index) to get a specific *Worksheet* object from a Sheets collection, or you can use an integer index directly on the collection.

The Problem That Automation Solves

You've already learned that a COM interface is the ideal way for Windows programs to communicate with one another, but you've also learned that designing your own COM interfaces is mostly impractical. Automation's general-purpose interface, *IDispatch*, serves the needs of both C++ and VBA programmers. As you might guess from your glimpse of Excel VBA, this interface involves objects, methods, and properties.

You can write COM interfaces that include functions with any parameter types and return values you specify. *IMotion* and *IVisual*, created in Chapter 24, are some examples. If you're going to let VBA programmers in, however, you can't be fast and loose anymore. You can solve the communication problem with one interface that has a member function smart enough to accommodate methods and properties as defined by VBA. Needless to say, *IDispatch* has such a function: *Invoke*. You use *IDispatch::Invoke* for COM objects that can be constructed and used in either C++ or VBA programs.

Now you're beginning to see what Automation does. It funnels all inter-module communication through the *IDispatch::Invoke* function. How does a client first connect to its component? Because *IDispatch* is merely another COM interface, all the registration logic supported by COM comes into play. Automation components can be DLLs or EXEs, and they can be accessed over a network using distributed COM (DCOM).

The *IDispatch* Interface

IDispatch is the heart of Automation. It's fully supported by COM marshaling (that is, Microsoft has already marshaled it for you), as are all the other standard COM interfaces, and it's supported well by the MFC library. At the component end, you need a COM class with an *IDispatch* interface (plus the prerequisite class factory, of course). At the client end, you use standard COM techniques to obtain an *IDispatch* pointer. (As you'll see, the MFC library and the wizards take care of a lot of these details for you.)

Remember that *Invoke* is the principal member function of *IDispatch*. If you looked up *IDispatch::Invoke* in the Visual C++ online documentation, you'd see a really ugly set of parameters. Don't worry about those now. The MFC library steps in on both sides of the *Invoke* call, using a data-driven scheme to call component functions based on dispatch map parameters that you define with macros.

Invoke isn't the only *IDispatch* member function. Another function your controller might call is *GetIDsOfNames*. From the VBA programmer's point of view, properties and methods have symbolic names, but C++ programmers prefer more efficient integer indexes. *Invoke* uses integers to specify properties and methods, so *GetIDsOfNames* is useful at the start of a program for converting each name to a number if you don't know the index numbers at compile time. You've already seen that *IDispatch* supports symbolic names for methods. In addition, the interface supports symbolic names for a method's parameters. The *GetIDsOfNames* function returns those parameter names along with the method name. Unfortunately, the MFC *IDispatch* implementation doesn't support named parameters.

Automation Programming Choices

Suppose you're writing an Automation component in C++. You've got some choices to make. Do you want an in-process component or an out-of-process component? What kind of user interface do you want? Does the component need a user interface at all? Can users run your EXE component as a stand-alone application? If the component is an EXE, will it be SDI or MDI? Can the user shut down the component program directly?

If your component is a DLL, COM linkage will be more efficient than it would be with an EXE component because no marshaling is required. Most of the time, your in-process Automation components won't have their own user interfaces, except for modal dialog boxes. If you need a component that manages its own child window, you should use an ActiveX control, and if you want to use a main frame window, use an out-of-process component. As with any 32-bit DLL, an Automation DLL is mapped into the client's process memory. If two client programs happen to request the same DLL, Windows loads and links the DLL twice. Each client is unaware that the other is using the same component.

With an EXE component, however, you must be careful to distinguish between a component program and a component object. When a client calls *IClassFactory::CreateInstance* to construct a component object, the component's class factory constructs the object, but COM might or might not need to start the component program.

Here are some scenarios:

1. The component's COM-creatable class is programmed to require a new process for each object constructed. In this case, COM starts a new process in response to the second and subsequent *Create-Instance* calls, each of which returns an *IDispatch* pointer.

2. Here's a special case of scenario 1 above, specific to MFC applications. The component class is an MFC document class in an SDI application. Each time a client calls *CreateInstance*, a new component process starts, complete with a document object, a view object, and an SDI main frame window.

3. The component class is programmed to allow multiple objects in a single process. Each time a client calls *CreateInstance*, a new component object is constructed. There is only one component process, however.

4. Here's a special case of scenario 3 above, specific to MFC applications. The component class is an MFC document class in an MDI application. There is a single component process with one MDI main frame window. Each time a client calls *CreateInstance*, a new document object is constructed, along with a view object and an MDI child frame window.

There's one more interesting case. Suppose a component EXE is running before the client needs it, and then the client decides to access a component object that already exists. You'll see this case with Excel. The user might have Excel running but minimized on the desktop, and the client needs access to Excel's one and only Application object. Here the client calls the COM function *GetActiveObject*, which provides an interface pointer for an existing component object. If the call fails, the client can create the object with *CoCreate-Instance*.

For component object deletion, normal COM rules apply. Automation objects have reference counts, and they delete themselves when the client calls *Release* and the reference count goes to 0. In an MDI component, if the Automation object is an MFC document, its destruction causes the corresponding MDI child window to close. In an SDI component, the destruction of the document object causes the component process to exit. The client is responsible for calling *Release* for each *IDispatch* interface before the client exits. For EXE components, COM will intervene if the client exits without releasing an interface, thus allowing the component process to exit. You can't always depend on this intervention, however, so be sure that your client cleans up its interfaces!

With generic COM, a client application often obtains multiple interface pointers for a single component object. Look back at the spaceship example in Chapter 24, in which the simulated COM component class had both an *IMotion* pointer and an *IVisual* pointer. With Automation, however, there's usually only a single (*IDispatch*) pointer per object. As in all COM programming, you must be careful to release all your interface pointers. In Excel, for example, many properties return an *IDispatch* pointer to new or existing objects. If you fail to release a pointer to an in-process COM component, the Debug version of the MFC library alerts you with a memory-leak dump when the client program exits.

The MFC *IDispatch* Implementation

The component program can implement its *IDispatch* interface in several ways. The most common of these pass off much of the work to the Windows COM DLLs by calling the COM function *CreateStdDispatch* or by delegating the *Invoke* call to the *ITypeInfo* interface, which involves the component's type library. A type library is a table, locatable through the Registry, which allows a client to query the component for the symbolic names of objects, methods, and properties. A client could, for example, contain a browser that allows the user to explore the component's capabilities.

The MFC library supports type libraries, but it doesn't use them in its implementation of *IDispatch*, which is instead driven by a dispatch map. MFC programs don't call *CreateStdDispatch* at all, nor do they use a type library to implement *IDispatch::GetIDsOfNames*. This means that you can't use the MFC library if you implement a multilingual Automation component—one that supports English and German property and method names, for example. (*CreateStd-Dispatch* doesn't support multilingual components either.)

Later in this chapter you'll learn how a client can use a type library, and you'll see how AppWizard and ClassWizard create and maintain type libraries for you. Once your component has a type library, a client can use it for browsing, independent of the *IDispatch* implementation.

An MFC Automation Component

Let's look at what happens in an MFC Automation component—in this case, a simplified version of the EX25C alarm clock program that is discussed later in this chapter. In the MFC library, the *IDispatch* implementation is part of the *CCmdTarget* base class, so you don't need *INTERFACE_MAP* macros. You write an Automation component class—*CClock*, for example—derived from *CCmdTarget*. This class's CPP file contains *DISPATCH_MAP* macros:

```
BEGIN_DISPATCH_MAP(CClock, CCmdTarget)
    DISP_PROPERTY(CClock, "Time", m_time, VT_DATE)
    DISP_PROPERTY_PARAM(CClock, "Figure", GetFigure,
                        SetFigure, VT_VARIANT, VTS_I2)
    DISP_FUNCTION(CClock, "RefreshWin", Refresh, VT_EMPTY, VTS_NONE)
    DISP_FUNCTION(CClock, "ShowWin", ShowWin, VT_BOOL, VTS_I2)
END_DISPATCH_MAP()
```

Looks a little like an MFC message map, doesn't it? The *CClock* class header file contains related code, shown here:

```
public:
    DATE m_time;
    afx_msg VARIANT GetFigure(short n);
    afx_msg void SetFigure(short n, const VARIANT& vaNew);
    afx_msg void Refresh();
    afx_msg BOOL ShowWin(short n);
    DECLARE_DISPATCH_MAP()
```

What does all this stuff mean? It means that the *CClock* class has the following properties and methods.

Name	Type	Description
Time	Property	Linked directly to class data member *m_time*
Figure	Property	Indexed property, accessed through member functions *GetFigure* and *SetFigure*: first parameter is the index; second (for *SetFigure*) is the string value (The figures are the "XII," "III," "VI," and "IX" that appear on the clock face.)
RefreshWin	Method	Linked to class member function *Refresh*—no parameters or return value
ShowWin	Method	Linked to class member function *ShowWin*—short integer parameter, Boolean return value

How does the MFC dispatch map relate to *IDispatch* and the *Invoke* member function? The dispatch-map macros generate static data tables that the MFC library's *Invoke* implementation can read. A controller gets an *IDispatch* pointer for *CClock* (connected through the *CCmdTarget* base class), and it calls *Invoke* with an array of pointers as a parameter. The MFC library's implementation of *Invoke*, buried somewhere inside *CCmdTarget*, uses the *CClock* dispatch map to decode the supplied pointers and either calls one of your member functions or accesses *m_time* directly.

As you'll see in the examples, ClassWizard can generate the Automation component class for you and help you code the dispatch map.

An MFC Automation Client Program

Let's move on to the client's end of the Automation conversation. How does an MFC Automation client program call *Invoke*? The MFC library provides a base class *COleDispatchDriver* for this purpose. This class has a data member, *m_lpDispatch*, which contains the corresponding component's *IDispatch* pointer. To shield you from the complexities of the *Invoke* parameter sequence, *COleDispatchDriver* has several member functions, including *InvokeHelper*, *GetProperty*, and *SetProperty*. These three functions call *Invoke* for an *IDispatch* pointer that links to the component. The *COleDispatchDriver* object incorporates the *IDispatch* pointer.

Let's suppose our client program has a class *CClockDriver*, derived from *COleDispatchDriver*, that drives *CClock* objects in an Automation component. The functions that get and set the Time property are on the following page.

```
DATE CClockDriver::GetTime()
{
    DATE result;
    GetProperty(1, VT_DATE, (void*)&result);
    return result;
}

void CClockDriver::SetTime(DATE propVal)
{
    SetProperty(1, VT_DATE, propVal);
}
```

Here are the functions for the indexed Figure property:

```
VARIANT CClockDriver::GetFigure(short i)
{
    VARIANT result;
    static BYTE parms[] = VTS_I2;
    InvokeHelper(2, DISPATCH_PROPERTYGET, VT_VARIANT,
                (void*)&result, parms, i);
    return result;
}

void CClockDriver::SetFigure(short i, const VARIANT& propVal)
{
    static BYTE parms[] = VTS_I2 VTS_VARIANT;
    InvokeHelper(2, DISPATCH_PROPERTYPUT, VT_EMPTY, NULL,
                parms, i, &propVal);
}
```

And finally, here are the functions that access the component's methods:

```
void CClockDriver::RefreshWin()
{
    InvokeHelper(3, DISPATCH_METHOD, VT_EMPTY, NULL, NULL);
}

BOOL CClockDriver::ShowWin(short i)
{
    BOOL result;
    static BYTE parms[] = VTS_I2;
    InvokeHelper(4, DISPATCH_METHOD, VT_BOOL,
                (void*)&result, parms, i);
    return result;
}
```

The function parameters identify the property or method, its return value, and its parameters. You'll learn about dispatch function parameters later, but for now take special note of the first parameter for the *InvokeHelper*, *GetProperty*, and *SetProperty* functions. This is the unique integer index, or dispatch ID (DISPID), for the property or method. Because you're using compiled C++, you can establish these IDs at compile time. If you're using an MFC Automation component with a dispatch map, the indexes are determined by the map sequence, beginning with 1. If you don't know a component's dispatch indexes, you can call the *IDispatch* member function *GetIDsOfNames* to convert the symbolic property or method names to integers.

The following illustration shows the interactions between the client (or controller) and the component.

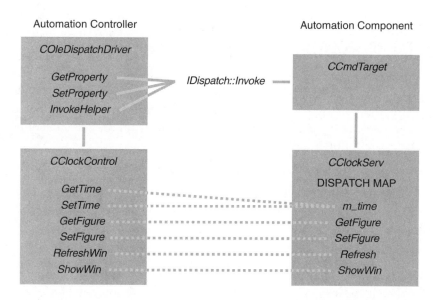

The solid lines show the actual connections through the MFC base classes and the *Invoke* function. The dotted lines represent the resulting logical connections between client class members and component class members.

Most Automation components have a binary type library file with a TLB extension. ClassWizard can access this type library file to generate a class derived from *COleDispatchDriver*. This generated controller class contains member functions for all the component's methods and properties with hard-coded dispatch IDs. Sometimes you need to do some surgery on this generated code, but that's better than writing the functions from scratch.

After you have generated your driver class, you embed an object of this class in your client application's view class (or in another class) like this:

```
CClockDriver m_clock;
```

Then you ask COM to create a clock component object with this statement:

```
m_clock.CreateDispatch("Ex25c.Document");
```

Now you're ready to call the dispatch driver functions:

```
m_clock.SetTime(COleDateTime::GetCurrentTime());
m_clock.RefreshWin();
```

When the *m_clock* object goes out of scope, its destructor releases the *IDispatch* pointer.

An Automation Client Program
Using the Compiler's *#import* Directive

Now there's an entirely new way of writing Automation client programs. Instead of using ClassWizard to generate a class derived from *COleDispatchDriver*, you use the compiler to generate header and implementation files directly from a component's type library. For the clock component, your client program contains the following statement:

```
#import"..\ex25c\debug\ex25c.tlb" rename_namespace("ClockDriv") using namespace ClockDriv;
```

The compiler then generates (and processes) two files, ex25c.tlh and ex25c.tli, in the project's Debug or Release subdirectory. The TLH file contains the *IEx25c* clock driver class declaration plus this <u>smart</u> <u>pointer</u> declaration:

```
_COM_SMARTPTR_TYPEDEF(IEx25c, __uuidof(IDispatch));
```

The *_COM_SMARTPTR_TYPEDEF* macro generates the *IEx25cPtr* pointer type, which encapsulates the component's *IDispatch* pointer. The TLI file contains inline implementations of member functions, some of which are shown in the following code:

```
inline HRESULT IEx25c::RefreshWin ( ) {
    return _com_dispatch_method(this, 0x4, DISPATCH_METHOD,
        VT_EMPTY, NULL, NULL);
}

inline DATE IEx25c::GetTime ( ) {
    DATE _result;
    _com_dispatch_propget(this, 0x1, VT_DATE, (void*)&_result);
    return _result;
}
```

```
inline void IEx25c::PutTime ( DATE _val ) {
    _com_dispatch_propput(this, 0x1, VT_DATE, _val);
}
```

Note the similarity between these functions and the *COleDispatchDriver* member functions you've already seen. The functions *_com_dispatch_method*, *_com_dispatch_propget*, and *_com_dispatch_propput* are in the runtime library.

In your Automation client program, you declare an embedded smart pointer member in your view class (or in another class) like this:

```
IEx25cPtr  m_clock;
```

Then you create a clock component object with this statement:

```
m_clock.CreateInstance(__uuidof(Document));
```

Now you're ready to use the *IEx25cPtr* class's overloaded -> operator to call the member functions defined in the TLI file:

```
m_clock->PutTime(COleDateTime::GetCurrentTime());
m_clock->RefreshWin();
```

When the *m_clock* smart pointer object goes out of scope, its destructor calls the COM *Release* function.

The *#import* directive is the future of COM programming. With each new version of Visual C++, you'll see COM features moving into the compiler, along with the document–view architecture itself.

The *VARIANT* Type

No doubt you've noticed the *VARIANT* type used in both Automation client and component functions in the previous example. *VARIANT* is an all-purpose data type that *IDispatch::Invoke* uses to transmit parameters and return values. The *VARIANT* type is the natural type to use when exchanging data with VBA. Let's look at a simplified version of the *VARIANT* definition in the Windows header files.

```
struct tagVARIANT {
    VARTYPE vt; // unsigned short integer type code
    WORD wReserved1, wReserved2, wReserved3;
    union {
        short      iVal;              // VT_I2   short integer
        long       lVal;              // VT_I4   long integer
        float      fltVal;            // VT_R4   4-byte float
        double     dblVal;            // VT_R8   8-byte IEEE float
        DATE       date;              // VT_DATE stored as dbl
```

(continued)

```
                                           //   date.time
       CY           vtCY                    // VT_CY 64-bit integer
       BSTR         bstrVal;                // VT_BSTR
       IUnknown*    punkVal;                // VT_UNKNOWN
       IDispatch*   pdispVal;               // VT_DISPATCH
       short*       piVal;                  // VT_BYREF | VT_I2
       long*        plVal;                  // VT_BYREF | VT_I4
       float*       pfltVal;                // VT_BYREF | VT_R4
       double*      pdblVal;                // VT_BYREF | VT_R8
       DATE*        pdate;                  // VT_BYREF | VT_DATE
       CY*          pvtCY;                  // VT_BYREF | VT_CY
       BSTR*        pbstrVal;               // VT_BYREF | VT_BSTR
   }
};
```

```
typedef struct tagVARIANT VARIANT;
```

As you can see, the *VARIANT* type is a C structure that contains a type code *vt*, some reserved bytes, and a big <u>union</u> of types that you already know about. If *vt* is VT_I2, for example, you would read the *VARIANT*'s value from *iVal*, which contains a 2-byte integer. If *vt* is VT_R8, you would read this value from *dblVal*, which contains an 8-byte real value.

A *VARIANT* object can contain actual data or a pointer to data. If *vt* has the VT_BYREF bit set, you must access a pointer in *piVal*, *plVal*, and so on. Note that a *VARIANT* object can contain an *IUnknown* pointer or an *IDispatch* pointer. This means that you can pass a complete COM object using an Automation call, but if you want VBA to process that object, its class should have an *IDispatch* interface.

Strings are special. The *BSTR* type is yet another way to represent character strings. A *BSTR* variable is a pointer to a zero-terminated character array with a character count in front. A *BSTR* variable could, therefore, contain binary characters, including zeros. If you had a *VARIANT* object with *vt* = VT_BSTR, memory would look like this.

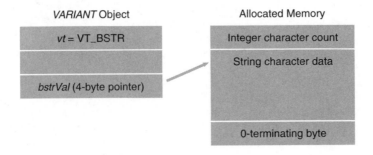

Because the string has a terminating 0, you can use *bstrVal* as though it were an ordinary *char* pointer, but you have to be very, very careful about memory cleanup. You can't simply delete the string pointer, because the allocated memory begins with the character count. Windows provides the *SysAllocString* and *SysFreeString* functions for allocating and deleting *BSTR* objects.

NOTE: *SysAllocString* is another COM function that takes a wide string pointer as a parameter. This means that all *BSTRs* contain wide characters, even if you haven't defined *_UNICODE*. Be careful.

Windows supplies some useful functions for *VARIANTs*, including those shown in the following table. If a *VARIANT* contains a *BSTR*, these functions ensure that memory is allocated and cleared properly. The *VariantInit* and *VariantClear* functions set *vt* to VT_EMPTY. All the variant functions are global functions and take a *VARIANT** parameter.

Function	Description
VariantInit	Initializes a *VARIANT*
VariantClear	Clears a *VARIANT*
VariantCopy	Frees memory associated with the destination *VARIANT* and copies the source *VARIANT*
VariantCopyInd	Frees the destination *VARIANT* and performs any indirection necessary to copy the source *VARIANT*
VariantChangeType	Changes the type of the *VARIANT*

The *COleVariant* Class

Writing a C++ class to wrap the *VARIANT* structure makes a lot of sense. Constructors can call *VariantInit*, and the destructor can call *VariantClear*. The class can have a constructor for each standard type, and it can have copy constructors and assignment operators that call *VariantCopy*. When a variant object goes out of scope, its destructor is called and memory is cleaned up automatically.

Well, the MFC team created just such a class, mostly for use in the Data Access Objects (DAO) subsystem, described in Chapter 32. It works well in Automation clients and components, however. A simplified declaration is on the following page.

```
class COleVariant : public tagVARIANT
{
// Constructors
public:
    COleVariant();

    COleVariant(const VARIANT& varSrc);
    COleVariant(const COleVariant& varSrc);

    COleVariant(LPCTSTR lpszSrc);
    COleVariant(CString& strSrc);

    COleVariant(BYTE nSrc);
    COleVariant(short nSrc, VARTYPE vtSrc = VT_I2);
    COleVariant(long lSrc, VARTYPE vtSrc = VT_I4);

    COleVariant(float fltSrc);
    COleVariant(double dblSrc);
    COleVariant(const COleDateTime& dateSrc);
// Destructor
    ~COleVariant(); // deallocates BSTR
// Operations
public:
    void Clear(); // deallocates BSTR
    VARIANT Detach(); // more later
    void ChangeType(VARTYPE vartype, LPVARIANT pSrc = NULL);
};
```

In addition, the *CArchive* and *CDumpContext* classes have comparison operators, assignment operators, conversion operators, and friend insertion/extrac-
tion operators. See the online documentation for a complete description of this
useful MFC *COleVariant* class.

Now let's see how the *COleVariant* class helps us write the component's
GetFigure function that you previously saw referenced in the sample dispatch
map. Assume that the component stores strings for four figures in a class data
member:

```
private:
    CString m_strFigure[4];
```

Here's what we'd have to do if we used the *VARIANT* structure directly:

```
VARIANT CClock::GetFigure(short n)
{
    VARIANT vaResult;
    ::VariantInit(&vaResult);
    vaResult.vt = VT_BSTR;
    // CString::AllocSysString creates a BSTR
```

```
        vaResult.bstrVal = m_strFigure[n].AllocSysString();
        return vaResult; // Copies vaResult without copying BSTR
                         //  BSTR still must be freed later
}
```

Here's the equivalent, with a *COleVariant* return value:

```
VARIANT CClock::GetFigure(short n)
{
    return COleVariant(m_strFigure[n]).Detach();
}
```

Calling the *COleVariant::Detach* function is critical here. The *GetFigure* function is constructing a temporary object that contains a pointer to a *BSTR*. That object gets bitwise-copied to the return value. If you didn't call *Detach*, the *COleVariant* destructor would free the *BSTR* memory and the calling program would get a *VARIANT* that contained a pointer to nothing.

A component's variant dispatch function parameters are declared as *const VARIANT&*. You can always cast a *VARIANT* pointer to a *COleVariant* pointer inside the function. Here's the *SetFigure* function:

```
void CClock::SetFigure(short n, const VARIANT& vaNew)
{
    COleVariant vaTemp;
    vaTemp.ChangeType(VT_BSTR, (COleVariant*) &vaNew);
    m_strFigure[n] = vaTemp.bstrVal;
}
```

> **NOTE:** Remember that all *BSTRs* contain wide characters. The *CString* class has a constructor and an assignment operator for the *LPCWSTR* (wide-character pointer) type. Thus, the *m_strFigure* string will contain single-byte characters, even though *bstrVal* points to a wide-character array.

Client dispatch function variant parameters are also typed as *const VARIANT&*. You can call those functions with either a *VARIANT* or a *COleVariant* object. Here's an example of a call to the *CClockDriver::SetFigure* function:

```
pClockDriver->SetFigure(0, COleVariant("XII"));
```

> **NOTE:** Visual C++ 5.0 added two new classes for *BSTRs* and *VARIANTs*. These classes are independent of the MFC library: *_bstr_t* and *_variant_t*. The *_bstr_t* class encapsulates the *BSTR* data type; the *_variant_t* class encapsulates the *VARIANT* type. Both classes manage resource allocation and deallocation. For more information on these classes, see the online documentation.

Parameter and Return Type Conversions for *Invoke*

All *IDispatch::Invoke* parameters and return values are processed internally as *VARIANT*s. Remember that! The MFC library implementation of *Invoke* is smart enough to convert between a *VARIANT* and whatever type you supply (where possible), so you have some flexibility in declaring parameter and return types. Suppose, for example, that your controller's *GetFigure* function specifies the return type *BSTR*. If a component returns an *int* or a *long*, all is well: COM and the MFC library convert the number to a string. Suppose your component declares a *long* parameter and the controller supplies an *int*. Again, no problem.

> **NOTE:** An MFC library Automation client specifies the expected return type as a *VT_* parameter to the *COleDispatchDriver* functions *GetProperty*, *SetProperty*, and *InvokeHelper*. An MFC library Automation component specifies the expected parameter types as *VTS_* parameters in the *DISP_PROPERTY* and *DISP_FUNCTION* macros.

Unlike C++, VBA is not a strongly typed language. VBA variables are often stored internally as *VARIANT*s. Take an Excel spreadsheet cell value, for example. A spreadsheet user can type a text string, an integer, a floating-point number, or a date/time in a cell. VBA treats the cell value as a *VARIANT* and returns a *VARIANT* object to an Automation client. If your client function declares a *VARIANT* return value, it can test *vt* and process the data accordingly.

VBA uses a date/time format that is distinct from the MFC library *CTime* class. Variables of type *DATE* hold both the date and the time in one <u>double</u> value. The fractional part represents time (.25 is 6:00 AM), and the whole part represents the date (number of days since December 30, 1899). The MFC library provides a *COleDateTime* class that makes dates easy to deal with. You could construct a date this way:

```
COleDateTime date(1998, 10, 1, 18, 0, 0);
```

The above declaration initializes the date to October 1, 1998, at 6:00 PM.

The *COleVariant* class has an assignment operator for *COleDateTime*, and the *COleDateTime* class has member functions for extracting date/time components. Here's how you print the time:

```
TRACE("time = %d:%d:%d\n",
    date.GetHour(),date.GetMinute(),date.GetSecond());
```

If you have a variant that contains a *DATE*, you use the *COleVariant::ChangeType* function to convert a date to a string, as shown here:

```
COleVariant vaTimeDate = date;
COleVariant vaTemp;
vaTemp.ChangeType(VT_BSTR, &vaTimeDate);
CString str = vaTemp.bstrVal;
TRACE("date = %s\n", str);
```

One last item concerning *Invoke* parameters: a dispatch function can have optional parameters. If the component declares trailing parameters as *VARIANTs*, the client doesn't have to supply them. If the client calls the function without supplying an optional parameter, the *VARIANT* object's *vt* value on the component end is VT_ERROR.

Automation Examples

The remainder of this chapter presents five sample programs. The first three programs are Automation components—an EXE component with no user interface, a DLL component, and a multi-instance SDI EXE component. Each of these component programs comes with a Microsoft Excel driver workbook file. The fourth sample program is an MFC Automation client program that drives the three components and also runs Excel using the *COleDispatchDriver* class. The last sample is a client program that uses the C++ #*import* directive instead of the MFC *COleDispatchDriver* class.

The EX25A Automation Component
EXE Example—No User Interface

The Visual C++ Autoclik example is a good demonstration of an MDI framework application with the document object as the Automation component. (To find the Autoclik example, look in the online documentation under Visual C++ Documentation/Samples/MFC Samples/Tutorial Samples.) The EX25A example is different from the Autoclik example because EX25A has no user interface. There is one Automation-aware class, and in the first version of the program, a single process supports the construction of multiple Automation component objects. In the second version, a new process starts up each time an Automation client creates an object.

The EX25A example represents a typical use of Automation. A C++ component implements financial transactions. VBA programmers can write User-interface–intensive applications that rely on the audit rules imposed by the Automation component. A production component program would probably use a database, but EX25A is simpler. It implements a bank account with two methods, *Deposit* and *Withdrawal*, and one read-only property, Balance. Obviously, *Withdrawal* can't permit withdrawals that make the balance negative. You can use Excel to control the component, as shown in Figure 25-3 on the next page.

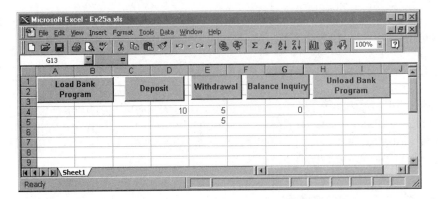

Figure 25-3.
This Excel workbook is controlling the EX25A component.

Here are the steps for creating the program from scratch:

1. **Run AppWizard to create the EX25A project in the \vcpp32\ex25a directory.**   Select the Dialog Based option (Step 1). Deselect <u>all</u> options in Step 2, and accept the remaining default settings. This is the simplest application that AppWizard can generate.

2. **Eliminate the dialog class from the project.**   Using Windows Explorer or the command-line prompt, delete the files ex25aDlg.cpp and ex25aDlg.h. Remove ex25aDlg.cpp and ex25aDlg.h from the project by deleting them from the project's Workspace window (FileView). Edit ex25a.cpp. Remove the dialog *#include*, and remove all dialog-related code from the *InitInstance* function. In ResourceView, delete the *IDD_EX25A_DIALOG* dialog resource template.

3. **Add code to enable Automation.**   Add this line in StdAfx.h:

```
#include <afxdisp.h>
```

Edit the *InitInstance* function (in Ex25a.cpp) to look like this:

```
BOOL CEx25aApp::InitInstance()
{
    AfxOleInit();
    if(RunEmbedded() || RunAutomated()) {
        // component started by COM
        COleTemplateServer::RegisterAll();
        return TRUE;
    }
    // Component is being run directly by the user
    COleObjectFactory::UpdateRegistryAll();
```

```
      AfxMessageBox("Bank server is registered");
      return FALSE;
}
```

4. Use ClassWizard to add a new class, *CBank*, as shown here.

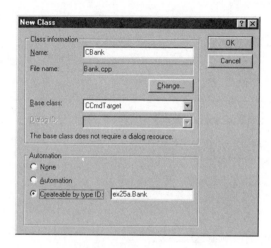

Be sure to select the Createable By Type ID option.

5. Use ClassWizard to add two methods and a property. Click on the Automation tab, and then add a Withdrawal method, as shown here.

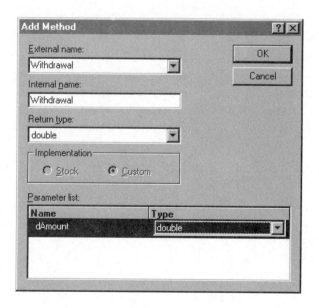

The *dAmount* parameter is the amount to be withdrawn, and the return value is the actual amount withdrawn. If you try to withdraw $100 from an account that contains $60, the amount withdrawn is $60.

Add a similar *Deposit* method that returns *void*, and then add the Balance property, as shown here.

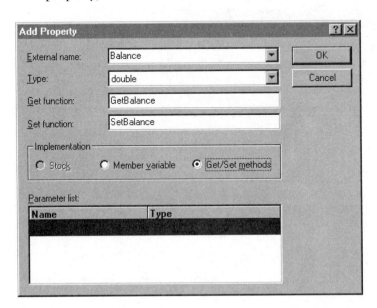

We could have chosen direct access to a component data member, but then we wouldn't have read-only access. We choose Get/Set Methods so that we can code the *SetBalance* function to do nothing.

6. **Add a public *m_dBalance* data member of type *double* to the *CBank* class.** Because we've chosen the Get/Set Methods option for the Balance property, ClassWizard doesn't generate a data member for us. You should declare *m_dBalance* in the Bank.h file and initialize *m_dBalance* to 0.0 in the *CBank* constructor located in the bank.cpp file.

7. **Edit the generated method and property functions.** Add the following boldface code:

```
double CBank::Withdrawal(double dAmount)
{
    if (dAmount < 0.0) {
        return 0.0;
    }
    if (dAmount <= m_dBalance) {
        m_dBalance -= dAmount;
```

```
        return dAmount;
    }
    double dTemp = m_dBalance;
    m_dBalance = 0.0;
    return dTemp;
}

void CBank::Deposit(double dAmount)
{
    if (dAmount < 0.0) {
        return;
    }
    m_dBalance += dAmount;
}

double CBank::GetBalance()
{
    return m_dBalance;
}

void CBank::SetBalance(double newValue)
{
    TRACE("Sorry, Dave, I can't do that!\n");
}
```

8. Build the EX25A program; run it once to register the component.

9. Set up five Excel macros in a new workbook file, ex25a.xls. Add the
following code:

```
Dim Bank As Object
Sub LoadBank()
    Set Bank = CreateObject("Ex25a.Bank")
End Sub

Sub UnloadBank()
    Set Bank = Nothing
End Sub

Sub DoDeposit()
    Range("D4").Select
    Bank.Deposit (ActiveCell.Value)
End Sub

Sub DoWithdrawal()
    Range("E4").Select
    Dim Amt
```

(continued)

```
        Amt = Bank.Withdrawal(ActiveCell.Value)
        Range("E5").Select
        ActiveCell.Value = Amt
    End Sub

    Sub DoInquiry()
        Dim Amt
        Amt = Bank.Balance()
        Range("G4").Select
        ActiveCell.Value = Amt
    End Sub
```

10. **Arrange an Excel worksheet as shown in Figure 25-3 on page 634.**
    Attach the macros to the pushbuttons (by right-clicking the pushbuttons).

11. **Test the EX25A bank component.**   Click the Load Bank Program button, and then enter a deposit value in cell D4 and click the Deposit button. Click the Balance Inquiry button, and watch the balance appear in cell G4. Enter a withdrawal value in cell E4, and click the Withdrawal button. To see the balance, click the Balance Inquiry button.

    > NOTE: Sometimes you need to click the buttons twice. The first click switches the focus to the worksheet, and the second click runs the macro. The hourglass pointer tells you the macro is working.

What's happening in this program? Look closely at the *CEx25aApp::Init-Instance* function. When you run the program directly from Windows, it displays a message box and then quits, but not before it updates the Registry. The *COleObjectFactory::UpdateRegistryAll* function hunts for global class factory objects, and the *CBank* class's *IMPLEMENT_OLECREATE* macro invocation defines such an object. (The *IMPLEMENT_OLECREATE* line was generated because you checked ClassWizard's Createable By Type ID check box when you added the *CBank* class.) The unique class ID and the program ID, *EX25A-.BANK*, are added to the Registry.

When Excel now calls *CreateObject*, COM loads the EX25A program, which contains the global factory for *CBank* objects; COM then calls the factory object's *CreateInstance* function to construct the *CBank* object and return an *IDispatch* pointer. Here's the *CBank* class declaration that Class-Wizard generated in the bank.h file, with unnecessary detail (and the method and property functions you've already seen) omitted:

```
class CBank : public CCmdTarget
{
    DECLARE_DYNCREATE(CBank)
public:
```

```
    double m_dBalance;
    CBank();    // protected constructor used by dynamic creation

// Attributes
public:

// Operations
public:

// Overrides
    // ClassWizard generated virtual function overrides
    //{{AFX_VIRTUAL(CBank)
    public:
    virtual void OnFinalRelease();
    //}}AFX_VIRTUAL

// Implementation
protected:
    virtual ~CBank();

    // Generated message map functions
    //{{AFX_MSG(CBank)
        // NOTE - the ClassWizard will add and remove member ⟶
        //   functions here.
    //}}AFX_MSG

    DECLARE_MESSAGE_MAP()
    DECLARE_OLECREATE(CBank)

    // Generated OLE dispatch map functions
    //{{AFX_DISPATCH(CBank)
    afx_msg double GetBalance();
    afx_msg void SetBalance(double newValue);
    afx_msg double Withdrawal(double dAmount);
    afx_msg void Deposit(double dAmount);
    //}}AFX_DISPATCH
    DECLARE_DISPATCH_MAP()
    DECLARE_INTERFACE_MAP()
};
```

Here is the code automatically generated by ClassWizard in bank.cpp:

```
IMPLEMENT_DYNCREATE(CBank, CCmdTarget)

CBank::CBank()
{
    EnableAutomation();
```

(continued)

```
    // To keep the application running as long as an OLE automation
    //  object is active, the constructor calls AfxOleLockApp.

    AfxOleLockApp();
}

CBank::~CBank()
{
    // To terminate the application when all objects created with
    //  OLE automation, the destructor calls AfxOleUnlockApp.

    AfxOleUnlockApp();
}

void CBank::OnFinalRelease()
{
    // When the last reference for an automation object is released,
    //  OnFinalRelease is called. This implementation deletes the
    //  object. Add additional cleanup required for your object
    //  before deleting it from memory.

    CCmdTarget::OnFinalRelease
}

BEGIN_MESSAGE_MAP(CBank, CCmdTarget)
    //{{AFX_MSG_MAP(CBank)
        // NOTE - the ClassWizard will add and remove ⟶
        //  mapping macros here.
    //}}AFX_MSG_MAP
END_MESSAGE_MAP()

BEGIN_DISPATCH_MAP(CBank, CCmdTarget)
    //{{AFX_DISPATCH_MAP(CBank)
    DISP_PROPERTY_EX(CBank, "Balance", GetBalance, SetBalance, VT_R8)
    DISP_FUNCTION(CBank, "Withdrawal", Withdrawal, VT_R8, VTS_R8)
    DISP_FUNCTION(CBank, "Deposit", Deposit, VT_EMPTY, VTS_R8)
    //}}AFX_DISPATCH_MAP
END_DISPATCH_MAP()

// Note: we add support for IID_IBank to support typesafe binding
//  from VBA.  This IID must match the GUID that is attached to the
//  dispinterface in the .ODL file.

// {A9515AB6-5B85-11D0-848F-00400526305B}
static const IID IID_IBank =
{ 0xa9515ab6, 0x5b85, 0x11d0, { 0x84, 0x8f, 0x0, 0x40, 0x5, 0x26,
    0x30, 0x5b } };
```

```
BEGIN_INTERFACE_MAP(CBank, CCmdTarget)
    INTERFACE_PART(CBank, IID_IBank, Dispatch)
END_INTERFACE_MAP()

// {632B1E4C-F287-11CE-B5E3-00AA005B1574}
IMPLEMENT_OLECREATE2(CBank, "EX25A.BANK", 0x632b1e4c, 0xf287,
    0x11ce, 0xb5, 0xe3, 0x0, 0xaa, 0x0, 0x5b, 0x15, 0x74)
```

This first version of the EX25A program runs in single-process mode, as does the Autoclik program. If a second Automation client asks for a new *CBank* object, COM calls the class factory *CreateInstance* function again and the existing process constructs another *CBank* object on the heap. You can verify this by making a copy of the ex25a.xls workbook (under a different name) and loading both the original and the copy. Click the Load Bank Program button in each workbook, and watch the Debug window. *InitInstance* should be called only once.

A small change in the EX25A program makes it behave differently. To have a new EX25A process start up each time a new component object is requested, follow these steps.

1. Add the following macro in bank.h:

```
#define IMPLEMENT_OLECREATE2(class_name, external_name, \
    l, w1, w2, b1, b2, b3, b4, b5, b6, b7, b8) \
    AFX_DATADEF COleObjectFactory class_name::factory(class_name::guid, \
    RUNTIME_CLASS(class_name), TRUE, _T(external_name)); \
    const AFX_DATADEF GUID class_name::guid = \
    { l, w1, w2, { b1, b2, b3, b4, b5, b6, b7, b8 } };
```

This macro is the same as the standard MFC *IMPLEMENT_OLE-CREATE* macro except that the original *FALSE* parameter (after the *RUNTIME_CLASS* parameter) has been changed to *TRUE*.

2. In bank.cpp, change the *IMPLEMENT_OLECREATE* macro invocation to *IMPLEMENT_OLECREATE2*.

3. Build the program and test it using Excel.   Start two Excel processes and then load the bank program from each. Use the Microsoft Windows NT Task Manager or PVIEW95 to verify that two EX25A processes are running.

> NOTE: The EX25A program on the companion CD-ROM uses the *IMPLEMENT_OLECREATE2* macro.

Debugging an EXE Component Program

When an Automation client launches an EXE component program, it sets the */Embedding* command-line parameter. If you want to debug your component, you must do the same. Choose Settings from the Visual C++ Project menu, and then enter */Embedding* in the Program Arguments box on the Debug page, as shown here.

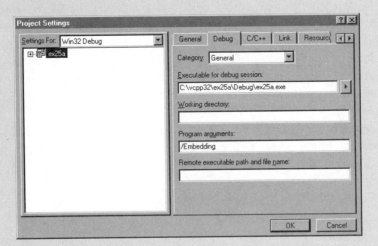

When you click the Go button on the Debug toolbar, your program will start and then wait for a client to activate it. At this point, you should start the client program from Windows (if it is not already running) and then use it to create a component object. Your component program in the debugger should then construct its object. It might be a good idea to include a *TRACE* statement in the component object's constructor.

Don't forget that your component program must be registered before the client can find it. That means you have to run it once <u>without</u> the */Embedding* flag. Many clients don't synchronize with Registry changes. If your client is running when you register the component, you may have to restart the client.

The EX25B Automation Component DLL Example

You could easily convert EX25A from an EXE to a DLL. The *CBank* class would be exactly the same, and the Excel driver would be similar. It's more interesting, though, to write a new application—this time with a minimal user interface (UI). We'll use a modal dialog box because it's the most complex UI we can conveniently use in an Automation DLL.

Parameters Passed by Reference

So far, you've seen VBA parameters passed by <u>value</u>. VBA has pretty strange rules for calling methods. If the method has one parameter, you can use parentheses; if it has more than one, you can't (unless you're using the function's return value, in which case you <u>must</u> use parentheses). Here is some sample VBA code that passes the string parameter by value:

```
Object.Method1 parm1, "text"
Object.Method2("text")
Dim s as String
s = "text"
Object.Method2(s)
```

Sometimes, though, VBA passes the address of a parameter (a reference). In this example, the string is passed by reference:

```
Dim s as String
s = "text"
Object.Method1 parm1, s
```

You can override VBA's default behavior by prefixing a parameter with *ByVal* or *ByRef*. Your component can't predict if it's getting a value or a reference—it must prepare for both. The trick is to test *vt* to see whether its *VT_BYREF* bit is set. Here's a sample method implementation that accepts a string (in a *VARIANT*) passed either by reference or value:

```
void CMyComponent::Method(long nParm1, const VARIANT& vaParm2)
{
    CString str;
    if ((vaParm2.vt & 0x7f) == VT_BSTR) {
        if ((vaParm2.vt & VT_BYREF) != 0)
            str = *(vaParm2.pbstrVal); // byref
        else
            str = vaParm2.bstrVal; // byval
    }
    AfxMessageBox(str);
}
```

If you declare a *BSTR* parameter, the MFC library does the conversion for you. Suppose your client program passed a *BSTR* reference to an out-of-process component and the component program changed the value. Because the component can't access the memory of the client process, COM must copy the string to the component and then copy it back to the client after the function returns. So before you declare reference parameters, remember that passing references through *IDispatch* is not like passing references in C++.

The EX25B program is fairly simple. An Automation component class, identified by the registered name Ex25b.Auto, has the following properties and method:

LongData	Long integer property
TextData	*VARIANT* property
DisplayDialog	Method—no parameters, *BOOL* return

DisplayDialog displays the EX25B data gathering dialog box shown in Figure 25-4. An Excel macro passes two cell values to the DLL and then updates the same cells with the updated values.

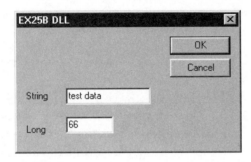

Figure 25-4.
The EX25B DLL dialog in action.

The example was first generated as an MFC AppWizard DLL with the Regular DLL Using Shared MFC DLL option and the Automation option selected. Here are the steps for building and testing the EX25B component DLL from the code installed from the companion CD-ROM:

1. **From Visual C++, open the \vcpp32\ex25b\ex25b.dsw workspace.** Build the project.

2. **Register the DLL with the RegComp utility.** You can use the Reg-Comp program in the \vcpp32\RegComp\Release directory on the companion CD-ROM; a file dialog makes it easy to select the DLL file.

3. **Start Excel, and then load the \vcpp32\ex25b\ex25b.xls workbook file.** Type an integer in cell C3, and type some text in cell D3, as shown at the top of page 646.

Debugging a DLL Component

To debug a DLL, you must tell the debugger which EXE file to load. Choose Settings from Visual C++'s Project menu, and then enter the controller's full pathname (including the EXE extension) in the Executable For Debug Session box on the Debug page.

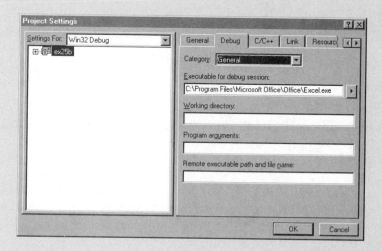

When you click the Go button on the Debug toolbar, your controller will start (loading the DLL as part of its process) and then wait for you to activate the component.

When you activate the component, your DLL in the debugger should then construct its component object. It might be a good idea to include a *TRACE* statement in the component object's constructor. Don't forget that your DLL must be registered before the client can load it.

Here's another option. If you have the source code for the client program, you can start the client program in the debugger. When the client loads the component DLL, you can see the output from the component program's *TRACE* statements.

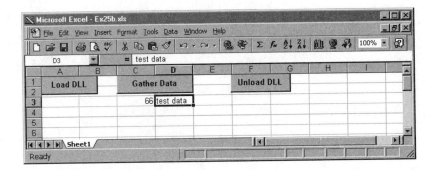

Click the Load DLL button, and then click the Gather Data button. Edit the data, click OK, and watch the new values appear in the spreadsheet.

4. **Click the Unload DLL button.** If you've started the DLL (and Excel) from the debugger, you can watch the Debug window to be sure the DLL's *ExitInstance* function is called.

Now let's look at the EX25B code. Like an MFC EXE, an MFC regular DLL has an application class (derived from *CWinApp*) and a global application object. The overridden *InitInstance* member function in ex25b.cpp looks like this:

```
BOOL CEx25bApp::InitInstance()
{
    TRACE("CEx25bApp::InitInstance\n");
    // Register all OLE server (factories) as running.  This
    //  enables the OLE libraries to create objects from other
    //  applications.
    COleObjectFactory::RegisterAll();

    return TRUE;
}
```

There's also an *ExitInstance* function for diagnostic purposes only, as well as the following code for the three standard COM DLL exported functions:

```
STDAPI DllGetClassObject(REFCLSID rclsid, REFIID riid, LPVOID* ppv)
{
    AFX_MANAGE_STATE(AfxGetStaticModuleState());
    return AfxDllGetClassObject(rclsid, riid, ppv);
}
```

```
STDAPI DllCanUnloadNow(void)
{
    AFX_MANAGE_STATE(AfxGetStaticModuleState());
    return AfxDllCanUnloadNow();
}

STDAPI DllRegisterServer(void)
{
    AFX_MANAGE_STATE(AfxGetStaticModuleState());
    COleObjectFactory::UpdateRegistryAll();
    VERIFY(AfxOleRegisterTypeLib(AfxGetInstanceHandle(),
            theTypeLibGUID, "ex25b.tlb"));
        return S_OK;
}
```

The PromptDl.cpp file contains code for the *CPromptDlg* class, but that class is a standard class derived from *CDialog*. The file PromptDl.h contains the *CPromptDlg* class header.

The *CEx25bAuto* class, the Automation component class initially generated by ClassWizard (with the Createable By Type ID option), is more interesting. This class is exposed to COM under the program ID ex25b.Auto. Figure 25-5 below shows the header file ex25bAuto.h.

EX25BAUTO.H

```
class CEx25bAuto : public CCmdTarget
{
    DECLARE_DYNCREATE(CEx25bAuto)

    CEx25bAuto(); // protected constructor used by dynamic creation

// Attributes
public:

// Operations
public:

// Overrides
    // ClassWizard generated virtual function overrides
    //{{AFX_VIRTUAL(CEx25bAuto)
    public:
    virtual void OnFinalRelease();
    //}}AFX_VIRTUAL
```

Figure 25-5.
Excerpt from the ex25bAuto.h header file.

(continued)

Figure 25-5. *continued*

```
// Implementation
protected:
    virtual ~CEx25bAuto();

    // Generated message map functions
    //{{AFX_MSG(CEx25bAuto)
        // NOTE - the ClassWizard will add and remove member
        //   functions here.
    //}}AFX_MSG

    DECLARE_MESSAGE_MAP()
    DECLARE_OLECREATE(CEx25bAuto)

    // Generated OLE dispatch map functions
    //{{AFX_DISPATCH(CEx25bAuto)
    long m_lData;
    afx_msg void OnLongDataChanged();
    VARIANT m_vaTextData;
    afx_msg void OnTextDataChanged();
    afx_msg BOOL DisplayDialog();
    //}}AFX_DISPATCH
    DECLARE_DISPATCH_MAP()
    DECLARE_INTERFACE_MAP()
};
```

Figure 25-6 shows the implementation file ex25bAuto.cpp.

EX25BAUTO.CPP

```
#include "stdafx.h"
#include "ex25b.h"
#include "Ex25bAuto.h"
#include "PromptDl.h"

#ifdef _DEBUG
#define new DEBUG_NEW
#undef THIS_FILE
static char THIS_FILE[] = __FILE__;
#endif


/////////////////////////////////////////////////////////////////////
// CEx25bAuto
```

Figure 25-6.   *(continued)*
The ex25bAuto.cpp implementation file.

```
IMPLEMENT_DYNCREATE(CEx25bAuto, CCmdTarget)

CEx25bAuto::CEx25bAuto()
{
    EnableAutomation();

    // To keep the application running as long as an OLE automation
    //  object is active, the constructor calls AfxOleLockApp.

    ::VariantInit(&m_vaTextData); // necessary initialization
    m_lData = 0;

    AfxOleLockApp();
}


CEx25bAuto::~CEx25bAuto()
{
    // To terminate the application when all objects created with
    //  with OLE automation, the destructor calls AfxOleUnlockApp.

    AfxOleUnlockApp();
}


void CEx25bAuto::OnFinalRelease()
{
    // When the last reference for an automation object is released,
    //  OnFinalRelease is called. The base class will automatically
    //  delete the object. Add additional cleanup required for your
    //  object before calling the base class.

    CCmdTarget::OnFinalRelease();
}

BEGIN_MESSAGE_MAP(CEx25bAuto, CCmdTarget)
    //{{AFX_MSG_MAP(CEx25bAuto)
        // NOTE - the ClassWizard will add and remove mapping
        //  macros here.
    //}}AFX_MSG_MAP
END_MESSAGE_MAP()

BEGIN_DISPATCH_MAP(CEx25bAuto, CCmdTarget)
    //{{AFX_DISPATCH_MAP(CEx25bAuto)
        DISP_PROPERTY_NOTIFY(CEx25bAuto, "LongData", m_lData,
            OnLongDataChanged, VT_I4)
        DISP_PROPERTY_NOTIFY(CEx25bAuto, "TextData", m_vaTextData,
```

(continued)

Figure 25-6. *continued*

```
                OnTextDataChanged, VT_VARIANT)
            DISP_FUNCTION(CEx25bAuto, "DisplayDialog", DisplayDialog,
                VT_BOOL, VTS_NONE)
        //}}AFX_DISPATCH_MAP
END_DISPATCH_MAP()

// Note: we add support for IID_IEx25bAuto to support typesafe
//   binding from VBA. This IID must match the GUID that is attached
//   to the dispinterface in the .ODL file.

// {A9515AD7-5B85-11D0-848F-00400526305B}
static const IID IID_IEx25bAuto =
{ 0xa9515ad7, 0x5b85, 0x11d0, { 0x84, 0x8f, 0x0, 0x40, 0x5, 0x26,
    0x30, 0x5b } };

BEGIN_INTERFACE_MAP(CEx25bAuto, CCmdTarget)
    INTERFACE_PART(CEx25bAuto, IID_IEx25bAuto, Dispatch)
END_INTERFACE_MAP()

// {A9515AD8-5B85-11D0-848F-00400526305B}
IMPLEMENT_OLECREATE(CEx25bAuto, "ex25b.Auto", 0xa9515ad8, 0x5b85,
    0x11d0, 0x84, 0x8f, 0x0, 0x40, 0x5, 0x26, 0x30, 0x5b)


///////////////////////////////////////////////////////////////////
// CEx25bAuto message handlers

void CEx25bAuto::OnLongDataChanged()
{
    TRACE("CEx25bAuto::OnLongDataChanged\n");
}
void CEx25bAuto::OnTextDataChanged()
{
    TRACE("CEx25bAuto::OnTextDataChanged\n");
}

BOOL CEx25bAuto::DisplayDialog()
{
    TRACE("Entering CEx25bAuto::DisplayDialog %p\n", this);
    BOOL bRet = TRUE;
    AfxLockTempMaps();   // See MFC Tech Note #3
    CWnd* pTopWnd = CWnd::FromHandle(::GetTopWindow(NULL));
    try {
        CPromptDlg dlg /*(pTopWnd)*/;
        if (m_vaTextData.vt == VT_BSTR){
            dlg.m_strData = m_vaTextData.bstrVal; // converts
                                                  //   double-byte
```

```
                                               //   character to
                                               //   single-byte
                                               //   character
        }
        dlg.m_lData = m_lData;
        if (dlg.DoModal() == IDOK) {
            m_vaTextData = COleVariant(dlg.m_strData).Detach();
            m_lData = dlg.m_lData;
            bRet = TRUE;
        }
        else {
            bRet =  FALSE;
        }
    }
    catch (CException* pe) {
        TRACE("Exception: failure to display dialog\n");
        bRet =  FALSE;
        pe->Delete();
    }
    AfxUnlockTempMaps();
    return bRet;
}
```

The two properties, LongData and TextData, are represented by class data members *m_lData* and *m_vaTextData*, both initialized in the constructor. When the LongData property was added in ClassWizard, a notification function, *OnLongDataChanged*, was specified. This function is called whenever the controller changes the property value. Notification functions apply only to properties that are represented by data members. Don't confuse this notification with the notifications that ActiveX controls give their container when a bound property changes.

The *DisplayDialog* member function, which is the *DisplayDialog* method, is ordinary except that the *AfxLockTempMaps* and *AfxUnlockTempMaps* functions are necessary for cleaning up temporary object pointers that would normally be deleted in an EXE program's idle loop.

What about the Excel VBA code? Here are the three macros and the global declarations:

```
Dim Dllcomp As Object
Private Declare Sub CoFreeUnusedLibraries Lib "OLE32" ()

Sub LoadDllComp()
    Set Dllcomp = CreateObject("Ex25b.Auto")
    Range("C3").Select
    Dllcomp.LongData = Selection.Value
```

(continued)

```
    Range("D3").Select
    Dllcomp.TextData = Selection.Value
End Sub

Sub RefreshDllComp() 'Gather Data button
    Range("C3").Select
    Dllcomp.LongData = Selection.Value
    Range("D3").Select
    Dllcomp.TextData = Selection.Value
    Dllcomp.DisplayDialog
    Range("C3").Select
    Selection.Value = Dllcomp.LongData
    Range("D3").Select
    Selection.Value = Dllcomp.TextData
End Sub

Sub UnloadDllComp()
    Set Dllcomp = Nothing
    Call CoFreeUnusedLibraries
End Sub
```

The first line in *LoadDllComp* creates a component object as identified by the registered name *Ex25b.Auto*. The *RefreshDllComp* macro accesses the component object's LongData and TextData properties. The first time you run *LoadDllComp*, it loads the DLL and constructs an *Ex25b.Auto* object. The second time you run *LoadDllComp*, something curious happens: a second object is constructed, and the original object is destroyed. If you run *LoadDllComp* from another copy of the workbook, you get two separate *Ex25b.Auto* objects. Of course, there's only one mapping of ex25b.dll in memory at any time unless you're running more than one Excel process.

Look closely at the *UnloadDllComp* macro. When the "Set Dllcomp = Nothing" statement is executed, the DLL is disconnected, but it's not unmapped from Excel's address space, which means the component's *ExitInstance* function is not called. The *CoFreeUnusedLibraries* function calls the exported *DllCanUnloadNow* function for each component DLL and, if that function returns *TRUE*, *CoFreeUnusedLibraries* frees the DLL. MFC programs call *CoFreeUnusedLibraries* in the idle loop (after a one-minute delay), but Excel doesn't. That's why *UnloadDllComp* must call *CoFreeUnusedLibraries* after disconnecting the component.

NOTE: The *CoFreeUnusedLibraries* function doesn't do anything in Windows NT 3.51 unless you have Service Pack 2 (SP2) installed.

The EX25C SDI Automation Component
EXE Example—with User Interface

This Automation component example illustrates the use of a document component class in an SDI application in which a new process is started for each object. This component program demonstrates an indexed property plus a method that constructs a new COM object.

The first Automation component example you saw, EX25A, didn't have a user interface. The global class factory constructed a *CBank* object that did the component's work. What if you want your EXE component to have a window? If you've bought into the MFC document–view architecture, you'll want the document, view, and frame, with all the benefits they provide.

Suppose you created a regular MFC application and then added a COM-creatable class such as *CBank*. How do you attach the *CBank* object to the document and view? From a *CBank* class member function, you could navigate through the application object and main frame to the current document or view, but you'd have a tough time in an MDI application if you encountered several component objects and several documents. There is a better way. You make the document class the creatable class, and you have the full support of AppWizard for this task. This is true for both MDI and SDI applications.

The MDI Autoclik example demonstrates how COM triggers the construction of new document, view, and child frame objects each time an Automation client creates a new component object. Because the EX25C example is an SDI program, Windows starts a new process each time the client creates an object. Immediately after the program starts, COM, with the help of the MFC application framework, constructs not only the Automation-aware document but also the view and the main frame window.

Now is a good time to experiment with the EX25C application, which was first generated by AppWizard with the Automation option checked. It's a Windows-based alarm clock program designed to be manipulated from an Automation client such as Excel. EX25C has the following properties and methods.

Name	Description
Time	*DATE* property that holds a *COM DATE* (*m_vaTime*)
Figure	Indexed *VARIANT* property for the four figures on the clockface (*m_strFigure[]*)
RefreshWin	Method that invalidates the view window and brings the main frame window to the top (*Refresh*)
ShowWin	Method that displays the application's main window (*ShowWin*)
CreateAlarm	Method that creates a *CAlarm* object and returns its *IDispatch* pointer (*CreateAlarm*)

Here are the steps for building and running EX25C from the companion CD-ROM:

1. **From Visual C++, open the workspace \vcpp32\ex25c\ex25c.dsw.** Build the project to produce the ex25c.exe file in the project's Debug subdirectory.

2. **Run the program once to register it.** The program is designed to be executed either as a stand-alone application or as an Automation component. When you run it from Windows or from Visual C++, it updates the Registry and displays the face of a clock with the characters XII, III, VI, and IX at the 12, 3, 6, and 9 o'clock positions. Exit the program.

3. **Load the Excel workbook file \vcpp32\ex25c\ex25c.xls.** The worksheet should look like the one shown here.

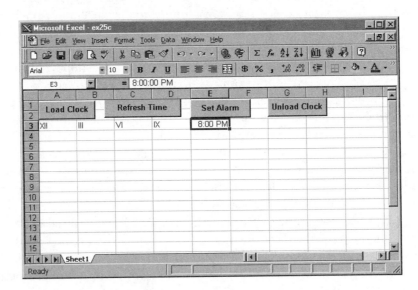

Click the Load Clock button, and then double-click the Set Alarm button. (There could be a long delay after you click the Load Clock button, depending on your system.) The clock should appear as shown on the next page, with the letter *A* indicating the alarm setting.

If you've started the component program from the debugger, you can watch the Debug window to see when *InitInstance* is called and when the document object is constructed.

If you're wondering why there's no menu, it's because of the following statement in the *CMainFrame::PreCreateWindow* function:

```
cs.hMenu = NULL;
```

4. Close the Clock program and then click the Unload Clock button. If you've started the component program from the debugger, you can watch the Debug window for a message box that indicates that the *ExitInstance* function is called.

AppWizard did most of the work of setting up the document as an Automation component. In the derived application class *CEx25cApp*, it generated a data member for the component, as shown here:

```
public:
    COleTemplateServer m_server;
```

The MFC *COleTemplateServer* class is derived from *COleObjectFactory*. It is designed to create a COM document object when a client calls *IClassFactory::CreateInstance*. The class ID comes from the global *clsid* variable defined in ex25c.cpp. The human-readable program ID (Ex25c.Document) comes from the *IDR_MAINFRAME* string resource.

In the *InitInstance* function (in ex25c.cpp), AppWizard generated the code on the following page, which connects the component object (the document) to the application's document template.

```
CSingleDocTemplate* pDocTemplate;
pDocTemplate = new CSingleDocTemplate(
    IDR_MAINFRAME,
    RUNTIME_CLASS(CEx25cDoc),
    RUNTIME_CLASS(CMainFrame),       // main SDI frame window
    RUNTIME_CLASS(CEx25cView));
AddDocTemplate(pDocTemplate);
⋮
m_server.ConnectTemplate(clsid, pDocTemplate, TRUE);
```

Now all the plumbing is in place for COM and the framework to construct the document, together with the view and frame. When the objects are constructed, however, the main window is not made visible. That's your job. You must write a method that shows the window.

The following *UpdateRegistry* call from the *InitInstance* function updates the Windows Registry with the contents of the project's *IDR_MAINFRAME* string resource:

```
m_server.UpdateRegistry(OAT_DISPATCH_OBJECT);
```

The following dispatch map in the ex25cDoc.cpp file shows the properties and methods for the *CEx25cDoc* class. Note that the Figure property is an indexed property that ClassWizard can generate if you specify a parameter. Later you'll see the code you have to write for the *GetFigure* and *SetFigure* functions.

```
BEGIN_DISPATCH_MAP(CEx25cDoc, CDocument)
    //{{AFX_DISPATCH_MAP(CEx25cDoc)
    DISP_PROPERTY_NOTIFY(CEx25cDoc, "Time", m_time, OnTimeChanged,
        VT_DATE)
    DISP_FUNCTION(CEx25cDoc, "ShowWin", ShowWin, VT_EMPTY, VTS_NONE)
    DISP_FUNCTION(CEx25cDoc, "CreateAlarm", CreateAlarm,
        VT_DISPATCH, VTS_DATE)
    DISP_FUNCTION(CEx25cDoc, "RefreshWin", Refresh, VT_EMPTY,
        VTS_NONE)
    DISP_PROPERTY_PARAM(CEx25cDoc, "Figure", GetFigure, SetFigure,
        VT_VARIANT, VTS_I2)
    //}}AFX_DISPATCH_MAP
END_DISPATCH_MAP()
```

The *ShowWin* and *RefreshWin* member functions aren't very interesting, but the *CreateAlarm* method is worth a close look. Here's the corresponding *CreateAlarm* member function:

```
LPDISPATCH CEx25cDoc::CreateAlarm(DATE time)
{
    TRACE("Entering CEx25cDoc::CreateAlarm, time = %f\n", time);
    // OLE deletes any prior CAlarm object
```

```
    m_pAlarm = new CAlarm(time);
    return m_pAlarm->GetIDispatch(FALSE);    // no AddRef here
}
```

We've chosen to have the component create an alarm object when a controller calls *CreateAlarm*. *CAlarm* is an Automation component class that we've generated with ClassWizard. It is <u>not</u> COM-creatable, which means there's no *IMPLEMENT_OLECREATE* macro and no class factory. The *CreateAlarm* function constructs a *CAlarm* object and returns an *IDispatch* pointer. (The *FALSE* parameter for *CCmdTarget::GetIDispatch* means that the reference count is not incremented; the *CAlarm* object already has a reference count of 1 when it is constructed.)

The *CAlarm* class is declared in alarm.h as follows:

```
class CAlarm : public CCmdTarget
{
    DECLARE_DYNAMIC(CAlarm)
public:
    CAlarm(DATE time);

// Attributes
public:

// Operations
public:

// Overrides
    // ClassWizard generated virtual function overrides
    //{{AFX_VIRTUAL(CAlarm)
    public:
    virtual void OnFinalRelease();
    //}}AFX_VIRTUAL

// Implementation
protected:
    virtual ~CAlarm();

    // Generated message map functions
    //{{AFX_MSG(CAlarm)
        // NOTE - the ClassWizard will add and remove member
        //   functions here.
    //}}AFX_MSG

    DECLARE_MESSAGE_MAP()
    // Generated OLE dispatch map functions
```

(continued)

```
public:
    //{{AFX_DISPATCH(CAlarm)
    DATE m_time;
    //}}AFX_DISPATCH
    DECLARE_DISPATCH_MAP()
    DECLARE_INTERFACE_MAP()
};
```

Notice the absence of the *DECLARE_DYNCREATE* macro.

Alarm.cpp contains a dispatch map, as follows:

```
BEGIN_DISPATCH_MAP(CAlarm, CCmdTarget)
    //{{AFX_DISPATCH_MAP(CAlarm)
    DISP_PROPERTY(CAlarm, "Time", m_time, VT_DATE)
    //}}AFX_DISPATCH_MAP
END_DISPATCH_MAP()
```

Why do we have a *CAlarm* class? We could have added an AlarmTime property in the *CEx25cDoc* class instead, but then we would have needed another property or method to turn the alarm on and off. By using the *CAlarm* class, what we're really doing is setting ourselves up to support multiple alarms—a <u>collection</u> of alarms.

To implement an Automation collection, we would write another class, *CAlarms,* that would contain the methods *Add, Remove,* and *Item. Add* and *Remove* are self-explanatory; *Item* returns an IDispatch pointer for a collection element identified by an index, numeric, or some other key. We would also implement a read-only Count property that returned the number of elements. The document class (which owns the collection) would have an *Alarms* method with an optional *VARIANT* parameter. If the parameter were omitted, the method would return the *IDispatch* pointer for the collection. If the parameter specified an index, the method would return an *IDispatch* pointer for the selected alarm.

> **NOTE:** If we wanted our collection to support the VBA "For Each" syntax, we'd have some more work to do. We'd add an *IEnum VARIANT* interface to the *CAlarms* class to enumerate the collection of variants and implement the *Next* member function of this interface to step through the collection. Then we'd add a *CAlarms* method named *_NewEnum* that returned an *IEnumVARIANT* interface pointer. If we wanted the collection to be general, we'd allow separate enumerator objects (with an *IEnum VARIANT* interface) and we'd implement the other *IEnumVARIANT* functions— *Skip, Reset,* and *Clone.*

The Figure property is an indexed property, which makes it interesting. The Figure property represents the four figures on the clock face—XII, III, VI, and IX. It's a *CString* array, so we can use Roman numerals. Here's the declaration in ex25cDoc.h:

```
public:
    CString m_strFigure[4];
```

And here are the *GetFigure* and *SetFigure* functions in ex25cDoc.cpp:

```
VARIANT CEx25cDoc::GetFigure(short n)
{
    TRACE("Entering CEx25cDoc::GetFigure --
            n = %d m_strFigure[n] = %s\n",
            n, m_strFigure[n]);
    return COleVariant(m_strFigure[n]).Detach();
}

void CEx25cDoc::SetFigure(short n, const VARIANT FAR& newValue)
{
    TRACE("Entering CEx25cDoc::SetFigure -- n = %d, vt = %d\n", n,
            newValue.vt);
    COleVariant vaTemp;
    vaTemp.ChangeType(VT_BSTR, (COleVariant*) &newValue);
    m_strFigure[n] = vaTemp.bstrVal; // converts double-to-single
}
```

These functions tie back to the *DISP_PROPERTY_PARAM* macro in the *CEx25cDoc* dispatch map. The first parameter is the index number, specified as a short integer by the last macro parameter. Property indexes don't have to be integers, and the index can have several components (row and column numbers, for example). The *ChangeType* call in *SetFigure* is necessary because the controller might otherwise pass numbers instead of strings.

You've just seen collection properties and indexed properties. What's the difference? A controller can't add or delete elements of an indexed property, but it can add elements to a collection and it can delete elements from a collection.

What draws the clock face? As you might expect, it's the *OnDraw* member function of the view class. This function uses *GetDocument* to get a pointer to the document object, and then it accesses the document's property data members and method member functions.

The Excel macro code appears on the following page.

```
Dim Clock As Object
Dim Alarm As Object

Sub LoadClock()
    Set Clock = CreateObject("ex25c.Document")
    Range("A3").Select
    n = 0
    Do Until n = 4
        Clock.figure(n) = Selection.Value
        Selection.Offset(0, 1).Range("A1").Select
        n = n + 1
    Loop
    RefreshClock
    Clock.ShowWin
End Sub

Sub RefreshClock()
    Clock.Time = Now()
    Clock.RefreshWin
End Sub

Sub CreateAlarm()
    Range("E3").Select
    Set Alarm = Clock.CreateAlarm(Selection.Value)
    RefreshClock
End Sub

Sub UnloadClock()
    Set Clock = Nothing
End Sub
```

Notice the Set Alarm statement in the *CreateAlarm* macro. It calls the *CreateAlarm* method to return an *IDispatch* pointer, which is stored in an object variable. If the macro is run a second time, a new alarm is created, but the original one is destroyed because its reference count goes to 0.

> WARNING: You've seen a modal dialog in a DLL (EX25B) and you've seen a main frame window in an EXE (EX25C). Be careful with modal dialogs in EXEs. It's fine to have an About dialog that is invoked directly by the component program, but it isn't a good idea to invoke a modal dialog in an out-of-process component method function. The problem is that once the modal dialog is on the screen, the user can switch back to the client program. MFC clients handle this situation with a special "Server Busy" message box, which appears right away. Excel does something similar, but it waits 30 seconds, and this could confuse the user.

The EX25D Automation Client Example

So far, you've seen C++ Automation component programs. Now you'll see a C++ Automation client program that runs all the previous components and also controls Microsoft Excel 97. The EX25D program was originally generated by AppWizard, but without any COM options. It was easier to add the COM code than it would have been to rip out the component-specific code. If you do use AppWizard to build such an Automation controller, add the following line at the end of StdAfx.h:

```
#include <afxdisp.h>
```

Then add this call at the beginning of the application's *InitInstance* function:

```
AfxOleInit();
```

To prepare EX25D, open the \vcpp32\ex25d\ex25d project and do the build. Run the application from the debugger, and you'll see a standard SDI application with a menu structure similar to that shown in Figure 25-7.

If you have built and registered all the components, you can test them from EX25D. Notice that the DLL doesn't have to be copied to the \Winnt\System32 directory because Windows finds it through the Registry. For some components, you'll have to watch the Debug window to verify that the test results are correct. The program is reasonably modular. Menu commands and update command UI events are mapped to the view class. Each component object has its own C++ controller class and an embedded data member in ex25dView.h. We'll look at each part separately after we delve into type libraries.

File	Edit	Bank Comp	DLL Comp	Clock Comp	Excel Comp	View	Help
		Load	Load	Load	Load		
		Test	Get Data	Create Alarm	Execute		
		Unload	Unload	Refresh Time			
				Unload			

Figure 25-7.
A sample menu structure for a standard SDI application.

Type Libraries and ODL Files

We've told you that type libraries aren't necessary for the MFC *IDispatch* implementation, but Visual C++ has been quietly generating and updating type libraries for all your components. What good are these type libraries? VBA can use a type library to browse your component's methods and properties, and it can use the type library for improved access to properties and methods, a process called <u>early</u> <u>binding</u> described later in this chapter. But we're building a C++ client program here, not a VBA program. It so happens that ClassWizard can read a component's type library and use the information to generate C++ code for the client to use to "drive" an Automation component.

> **NOTE:** AppWizard initializes a project's Object Description Language (ODL) file when you first create it. ClassWizard edits this file each time you generate a new Automation component class or add properties and methods to an existing class. Unlike it does with the ClassWizard (CLW) file, ClassWizard can't rebuild an ODL file from the contents of your source files. If you mess up your ODL file, you'll have to re-create it manually.

When you were adding properties and methods to your component classes, ClassWizard was updating the project's ODL file. This file is a text file that describes the component in an ODL. (Your GUID will be different if you used AppWizard to generate this project.) Here's the ODL file for the bank component:

```
// ex25a.odl : type library source for ex25a.exe

// This file will be processed by the MIDL compiler to produce the
//   type library (ex25a.tlb).

[ uuid(85D56DE4-789D-11D0-92E1-D74D1B9CCD32), version(1.0) ]
library Ex25a
{
    importlib("stdole32.tlb");

    // Primary dispatch interface for CBank

    [ uuid(99EA95E1-78A1-11D0-92E1-D74D1B9CCD32) ]
    dispinterface IBank
    {
        properties:
            // NOTE - ClassWizard will maintain property information
            //   here.
            //   Use extreme caution when editing this section.
            //{{AFX_ODL_PROP(CBank)
            [id(1)] double Balance;
            //}}AFX_ODL_PROP
```

```
        methods:
        // NOTE - ClassWizard will maintain method information here.
        // Use extreme caution when editing this section.
        //{{AFX_ODL_METHOD(CBank)
        [id(2)] double Withdrawal(double dAmount);
        [id(3)] void Deposit(double dAmount);
        //}}AFX_ODL_METHOD

    };

    // Class information for CBank

        [ uuid(99EA95E2-78A1-11D0-92E1-D74D1B9CCD32) ]
        coclass Bank
        {
            [default] dispinterface IBank;
        };

    // {{AFX_APPEND_ODL}}
};
```

The ODL file has a unique GUID type library identifier, 85D56DE4-789D-11D0-92E1-D74D1B9CCD32, and it completely describes the bank component's properties and methods under a <u>dispinterface</u> named *IBank*. In addition, it specifies the dispinterface GUID, 99EA95E1-78A1-11D0-92E1-D74D1B9CCD32, which is the same GUID that's in the interface map of the *CBank* class listed on page 639. You'll see the significance of this GUID when you read the "VBA Early Binding" section near the end of this chapter. The CLSID, 99EA95E2-78A1-11D0-92E1-D74D1B9CCD32, is what a VBA browser can actually use to load your component.

Anyway, when you build your <u>component</u> project, Visual C++ invokes the MIDL utility, which reads the ODL file and generates a binary TLB file in your project's debug or release subdirectory. Now when you develop a C++ <u>client program</u>, you can ask ClassWizard to generate a driver class from the component project's TLB file.

NOTE: The MIDL utility generates the type library in a stand-alone TLB file, and that's what Automation controllers such as Excel look for. ActiveX controls have their type libraries bound into their resources.

To actually do this, you click the ClassWizard Add Class button and then select From A Type Library from the drop-down list. You navigate to the component project's TLB file, and then ClassWizard shows you a dialog similar to the illustration below.

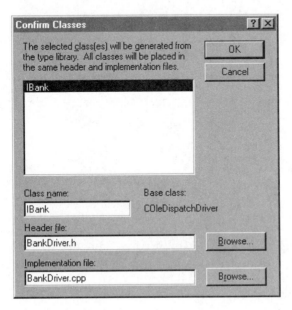

IBank is the dispinterface specified in the ODL file. You can keep this name for the class if you want, and you can specify the H and CPP filenames. If a type library contains several interfaces you can make multiple selections. You'll see the generated controller classes in the sections that follow.

The Controller Class for ex25a.exe

ClassWizard generated the *IBank* class (derived from *COleDispatchDriver*) listed in Figure 25-8. Look closely at the member function implementations. Note the first parameters of the *GetProperty*, *SetProperty*, and *InvokeHelper* function calls. These are hard-coded DISPIDs for the component's properties and methods, as determined by the component's dispatch map sequence.

> WARNING: If you use ClassWizard to delete a property and then add the property back, you'll probably change the component's dispatch IDs. That means that you'll have to regenerate or edit the controller class so that the IDs match.

BANKDRIVER.H

```
class IBank : public COleDispatchDriver
{
public:
    IBank() {} // calls COleDispatchDriver default constructor
    IBank(LPDISPATCH pDispatch) : COleDispatchDriver(pDispatch) {}
    IBank(const IBank& dispatchSrc) : COleDispatchDriver(dispatchSrc) {}

// Attributes
public:
    double GetBalance();
    void SetBalance(double);

// Operations
public:
    double Withdrawal(double dAmount);
    void Deposit(double dAmount);
};
```

BANKDRIVER.CPP

```
#include "StdAfx.h"
#include "BankDriver.h"

#ifdef _DEBUG
#define new DEBUG_NEW
#undef THIS_FILE
static char THIS_FILE[] = __FILE__;
#endif


/////////////////////////////////////////////////////////////////////
// IBank properties

double IBank::GetBalance()
{
    double result;
    GetProperty(0x1, VT_R8, (void*)&result);
    return result;
}
void IBank::SetBalance(double propVal)
{
    SetProperty(0x1, VT_R8, propVal);
}
```

Figure 25-8.   *(continued)*

The IBank *class listing.*

Figure 25-8. *continued*

```
/////////////////////////////////////////////////////////////////////
// IBank operations

double IBank::Withdrawal(double dAmount)
{
    double result;
    static BYTE parms[] =
        VTS_R8;
    InvokeHelper(0x2, DISPATCH_METHOD, VT_R8, (void*)&result, parms,
                dAmount);
    return result;
}

void IBank::Deposit(double dAmount)
{
    static BYTE parms[] =
        VTS_R8;
    InvokeHelper(0x3, DISPATCH_METHOD, VT_EMPTY, NULL, parms,
                dAmount);
}
```

The *CEx25dView* class has a data member *m_bank* of class *IBank*. The *CEx25dView* member functions for the Ex25a.Bank component are listed below. They are hooked up to options on the EX25D main menu. Of particular interest is the *OnBankoleLoad* function. The *COleDispatchDriver::CreateDispatch* function loads the component program (by calling *CoGetClassObject* and *IClassFactory::CreateInstance*) and then calls *QueryInterface* to get an *IDispatch* pointer, which it stores in the object's *m_lpDispatch* data member. The *COleDispatchDriver::ReleaseDispatch* function, called in *OnBankoleUnload*, calls *Release* on the pointer.

```
void CEx25dView::OnBankoleLoad()
{
    if(!m_bank.CreateDispatch("Ex25a.Bank")) {
        AfxMessageBox("Ex25a.Bank component not found");
        return;
    }
}

void CEx25dView::OnUpdateBankoleLoad(CCmdUI* pCmdUI)
{
    pCmdUI->Enable(m_bank.m_lpDispatch == NULL);
}

void CEx25dView::OnBankoleTest()
```

```
{
    m_bank.Deposit(20.0);
    m_bank.Withdrawal(15.0);
    TRACE("new balance = %f\n", m_bank.GetBalance());
}

void CEx25dView::OnUpdateBankoleTest(CCmdUI* pCmdUI)
{
    pCmdUI->Enable(m_bank.m_lpDispatch != NULL);
}

void CEx25dView::OnBankoleUnload()
{
    m_bank.ReleaseDispatch();
}

void CEx25dView::OnUpdateBankoleUnload(CCmdUI* pCmdUI)
{
    pCmdUI->Enable(m_bank.m_lpDispatch != NULL);
}
```

The Controller Class for ex25b.dll

Figure 25-9 shows the class header file generated by ClassWizard.

AUTODRIVER.H

```
class IEx25bAuto : public COleDispatchDriver
{
public:
    IEx25bAuto() {} // calls COleDispatchDriver default constructor
    IEx25bAuto(LPDISPATCH pDispatch) : COleDispatchDriver(pDispatch) {}
    IEx25bAuto(const IEx25bAuto& dispatchSrc) :
        COleDispatchDriver(dispatchSrc) {}

// Attributes
public:
    long GetLongData();
    void SetLongData(long);
    VARIANT GetTextData();
    void SetTextData(const VARIANT&);

// Operations
public:
    BOOL DisplayDialog();
};
```

Figure 25-9.
The Ex25bAuto *class header file.*

Notice that each property requires separate *Get* and *Set* functions in the client class, even though a data member in the component represents the property.

The view class header has a data member *m_auto* of class *IEx25bAuto*. Here are some DLL-related command handler member functions from ex25d-View.cpp:

```
void CEx25dView::OnDlloleGetdata()
{
    m_auto.DisplayDialog();
    COleVariant vaData = m_auto.GetTextData();
    ASSERT(vaData.vt == VT_BSTR);
    CString strTextData = vaData.bstrVal;
    long lData = m_auto.GetLongData();
    TRACE("CEx25dView::OnDlloleGetdata -- long = %ld, text = %s\n",
        lData, strTextData);
}

void CEx25dView::OnUpdateDlloleGetdata(CCmdUI* pCmdUI)
{
    pCmdUI->Enable(m_auto.m_lpDispatch != NULL);
}

void CEx25dView::OnDlloleLoad()
{
    if(!m_auto.CreateDispatch("Ex25b.Auto")) {
        AfxMessageBox("Ex25b.Auto component not found");
        return;
    }
    m_auto.SetTextData(COleVariant("test"));  // testing
    m_auto.SetLongData(79);  // testing
    // verify dispatch interface
    //  {A9515AD7-5B85-11D0-848F-00400526305B}
    static const IID IID_IEx25bAuto =
        { 0xa9515ad7, 0x5b85, 0x11d0, { 0x84, 0x8f, 0x0, 0x40, 0x5,
            0x26, 0x30, 0x5b } };
    LPDISPATCH p;
    HRESULT hr = m_auto.m_lpDispatch->QueryInterface(IID_IEx25bAuto,
        (void**) &p);
    TRACE("OnDlloleLoad -- QueryInterface result = %x\n", hr);
    p->Release();
}

void CEx25dView::OnUpdateDlloleLoad(CCmdUI* pCmdUI)
{
    pCmdUI->Enable(m_auto.m_lpDispatch == NULL);
}
```

```
void CEx25dView::OnDlloleUnload()
{
    m_auto.ReleaseDispatch();
}

void CEx25dView::OnUpdateDlloleUnload(CCmdUI* pCmdUI)
{
    pCmdUI->Enable(m_auto.m_lpDispatch != NULL);
}
```

The Controller Class for ex25c.exe

Figure 25-10 shows the headers for the *IEx25c* and *IAlarm* classes, which drive
the EX25C Automation component.

CLOCKDRIVER.H

```
class IEx25c : public COleDispatchDriver
{
public:
    IEx25c() {} // calls COleDispatchDriver default constructor
    IEx25c(LPDISPATCH pDispatch) : COleDispatchDriver(pDispatch) {}
    IEx25c(const IEx25c& dispatchSrc) :
        COleDispatchDriver(dispatchSrc) {}

// Attributes
public:
    DATE GetTime();
    void SetTime(DATE);

// Operations
public:
    void ShowWin();
    LPDISPATCH CreateAlarm(DATE time);
    void RefreshWin();
    void SetFigure(short n, const VARIANT& newValue);
    VARIANT GetFigure(short n);
};

class IAlarm : public COleDispatchDriver
{
public:
    IAlarm() {} // calls COleDispatchDriver default constructor
    IAlarm(LPDISPATCH pDispatch) : COleDispatchDriver(pDispatch) {}
    IAlarm(const IAlarm& dispatchSrc) :
        COleDispatchDriver(dispatchSrc) {}
```

Figure 25-10.   *(continued)*

The IEx25c *and* IAlarm *class header files.*

Figure 25-10. *continued*

```
// Attributes
public:
    DATE GetTime();
    void SetTime(DATE);

// Operations
public:
};
```

Of particular interest is the *IEx25c::CreateAlarm* member function in ClockDriver.cpp:

```
LPDISPATCH IEx25c::CreateAlarm(DATE time)
{
    LPDISPATCH result;
    static BYTE parms[] =
        VTS_DATE;
    InvokeHelper(0x3, DISPATCH_METHOD, VT_DISPATCH, (void*)&result,
        parms, time);
    return result;
}
```

This function can be called only after the clock object (document) has been constructed. It causes the EX25C component to construct an alarm object and return an *IDispatch* pointer with a reference count of 1. The *COleDispatch-Driver::AttachDispatch* function connects that pointer to the client's *m_alarm* object, but if that object already has a dispatch pointer, the old pointer is released. That's why, if you watch the Debug window, you'll see that the old EX25C instance exits immediately after you ask for a new instance. You'll have to test this behavior with the Excel driver because EX25D disables the Load menu option when the clock is running.

The view class has the data members *m_clock* and *m_alarm*. Here are the view class command handlers:

```
void CEx25dView::OnClockoleCreatealarm()
{
    CAlarmDialog dlg;
    if (dlg.DoModal() == IDOK) {
        COleDateTime dt(1995, 12, 23, dlg.m_nHours, dlg.m_nMinutes,
            dlg.m_nSeconds);
        LPDISPATCH pAlarm = m_clock.CreateAlarm(dt);
        m_alarm.AttachDispatch(pAlarm);  // releases prior object!
        m_clock.RefreshWin();
    }
}
```

```
void CEx25dView::OnUpdateClockoleCreatealarm(CCmdUI* pCmdUI)
{
    pCmdUI->Enable(m_clock.m_lpDispatch != NULL);
}

void CEx25dView::OnClockoleLoad()
{
    if(!m_clock.CreateDispatch("Ex25c.Document")) {
        AfxMessageBox("Ex25c.Document component not found");
        return;
    }
    m_clock.SetFigure(0, COleVariant("XII"));
    m_clock.SetFigure(1, COleVariant("III"));
    m_clock.SetFigure(2, COleVariant("VI"));
    m_clock.SetFigure(3, COleVariant("IX"));
    OnClockoleRefreshtime();
    m_clock.ShowWin();
}

void CEx25dView::OnUpdateClockoleLoad(CCmdUI* pCmdUI)
{
    pCmdUI->Enable(m_clock.m_lpDispatch == NULL);
}

void CEx25dView::OnClockoleRefreshtime()
{
    COleDateTime now = COleDateTime::GetCurrentTime();
    m_clock.SetTime(now);
    m_clock.RefreshWin();
}

void CEx25dView::OnUpdateClockoleRefreshtime(CCmdUI* pCmdUI)
{
    pCmdUI->Enable(m_clock.m_lpDispatch != NULL);
}

void CEx25dView::OnClockoleUnload()
{
    m_clock.ReleaseDispatch();
}

void CEx25dView::OnUpdateClockoleUnload(CCmdUI* pCmdUI)
{
    pCmdUI->Enable(m_clock.m_lpDispatch != NULL);
}
```

Controlling Microsoft Excel

The EX25D program contains code that loads Excel, creates a workbook, and reads from and writes to cells from the active worksheet. Controlling Excel is exactly like controlling an MFC Automation component, but you need to know about a few Excel peculiarities.

If you study Excel VBA, you'll notice that you can use more than 100 "objects" in your programs. All of these objects are accessible through Automation, but if you write an MFC Automation client program, you'll need to know about the objects' properties and methods. Ideally, you'd like a C++ class for each object, with member functions coded to the proper dispatch IDs.

Excel has its own type library, found in the file Excel8.olb, usually in the \Program Files\Microsoft Office\Office directory. ClassWizard can read this file—exactly as it reads TLB files—to create C++ driver classes for individual Excel objects. It makes sense to select the objects you need and then combine the classes into a single pair of files, as shown in Figure 25-11.

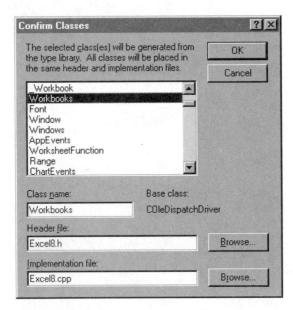

Figure 25-11.
ClassWizard can create C++ classes for the Excel objects listed in Excel8.olb.

You might need to edit the generated code to suit your needs. Let's look at an example. If you use ClassWizard to generate a driver class for the *Worksheet* object, you get a *GetRange* member function, as shown here:

```
LPDISPATCH _Worksheet::GetRange(const VARIANT& Cell1,
                                const VARIANT& Cell2)
{
    LPDISPATCH result;
    static BYTE parms[] = VTS_VARIANT VTS_VARIANT;
    InvokeHelper(0xc5, DISPATCH_PROPERTYGET, VT_DISPATCH,
        (void*)&result, parms, &Cell1, &Cell2);
    return result;
}
```

You know (from the Excel VBA documentation) that you can call the method with either a single cell (one parameter) or a rectangular area specified by two cells (two parameters). Remember: you can omit optional parameters in a call to *InvokeHelper*. Now it makes sense to add a second overloaded *GetRange* function with a single cell parameter like this:

```
LPDISPATCH _Worksheet::GetRange(const VARIANT& Cell1) // added
{
    LPDISPATCH result;
    static BYTE parms[] = VTS_VARIANT;
    InvokeHelper(0xc5, DISPATCH_PROPERTYGET, VT_DISPATCH,
        (void*)&result, parms, &Cell1);
    return result;
}
```

How do you know which functions to fix up? They're the functions you decide to use in your program. You'll have to read the Excel VBA reference manual to figure out the required parameters and return values. Perhaps someday soon someone will write a set of C++ Excel controller classes.

The EX25D program uses the Excel objects and contains the corresponding classes shown in the table below. All the code for these objects is contained in the files excel8.h and excel8.cpp.

Object/Class	View Class Data Member
_Application	*m_app*
Range	*m_range[5]*
_Worksheet	*m_worksheet*
Workbooks	*m_workbooks*
Worksheets	*m_worksheets*

The following view member function, *OnExceloleLoad*, handles the Excel Comp Load menu command. This function must work if the user already has

Excel running on the desktop. The COM *GetActiveObject* function tries to return an *IUnknown* pointer for Excel. *GetActiveObject* requires a class ID, so we must first call *CLSIDFromProgID*. If *GetActiveObject* is successful, we call *QueryInterface* to get an *IDispatch* pointer and we attach it to the view's *m_app* controller object of class *_Application*. If *GetActiveObject* is unsuccessful, we call *COleDispatchDriver::CreateDispatch*, as we did for the other components.

```
void CEx25dView::OnExceloleLoad()
{    // If Excel is already running, attach to it; otherwise, start it
    LPDISPATCH pDisp;
    LPUNKNOWN pUnk;
    CLSID clsid;
    TRACE("Entering CEx25dView::OnExcelLoad\n");
    BeginWaitCursor();
    ::CLSIDFromProgID(L"Excel.Application.8", &clsid); // from Registry
    if(::GetActiveObject(clsid, NULL, &pUnk) == S_OK) {
        VERIFY(pUnk->QueryInterface(IID_IDispatch,
                (void**) &pDisp) == S_OK);
        m_app.AttachDispatch(pDisp);
        pUnk->Release();
        TRACE(" attach complete\n");
    }
    else {
        if(!m_app.CreateDispatch("Excel.Application.8")) {
            AfxMessageBox("Excel 97 program not found");
        }
        TRACE(" create complete\n");
    }
    EndWaitCursor();
}
```

OnExceloleExecute is the command handler for the Execute item in the Excel Comp menu. Its first task is to find the Excel main window and bring it to the top. We must write some Windows code here because a method for this purpose couldn't be found. We must also create a workbook if no workbook is currently open.

We have to watch our method return values closely. The *Workbooks Add* method, for example, returns an *IDispatch* pointer for a *Workbook* object and, of course, increments the reference count. If we generated a class for *Workbook*, we could call *COleDispatchDriver::AttachDispatch* so that *Release* would be called when the *Workbook* object was destroyed. Because we don't need a *Workbook* class, we'll simply release the pointer at the end of the function. If we don't properly clean up our pointers, we might get memory-leak messages from the Debug version of MFC.

The rest of the *OnExceloleExecute* function accesses the cells in the worksheet. It's easy to get and set numbers, dates, strings, and formulas. The C++code is similar to the VBA code you would write to do the same job.

```cpp
void CEx25dView::OnExceloleExecute()
{
    LPDISPATCH pRange, pWorkbooks;

    CWnd* pWnd = CWnd::FindWindow("XLMAIN", NULL);
    if (pWnd != NULL) {
        TRACE("Excel window found\n");
        pWnd->ShowWindow(SW_SHOWNORMAL);
        pWnd->UpdateWindow();
        pWnd->BringWindowToTop();
    }

    m_app.SetSheetsInNewWorkbook(1);

    VERIFY(pWorkbooks = m_app.GetWorkbooks());
    m_workbooks.AttachDispatch(pWorkbooks);

    LPDISPATCH pWorkbook = NULL;
    if (m_workbooks.GetCount() == 0) {
        // Add returns a Workbook pointer, but we
        //   don't have a Workbook class
        pWorkbook = m_workbooks.Add(); // Save the pointer for
                                       //   later release
    }
    LPDISPATCH pWorksheets = m_app.GetWorksheets();
    ASSERT(pWorksheets != NULL);
    m_worksheets.AttachDispatch(pWorksheets);
    LPDISPATCH pWorksheet = m_worksheets.GetItem(COleVariant((short) 1));

    m_worksheet.AttachDispatch(pWorksheet);
    m_worksheet.Select();

    VERIFY(pRange = m_worksheet.GetRange(COleVariant("A1")));
    m_range[0].AttachDispatch(pRange);

    VERIFY(pRange = m_worksheet.GetRange(COleVariant("A2")));
    m_range[1].AttachDispatch(pRange);

    VERIFY(pRange = m_worksheet.GetRange(COleVariant("A3")));
    m_range[2].AttachDispatch(pRange);
```

(continued)

```
VERIFY(pRange = m_worksheet.GetRange(COleVariant("A3"),
       COleVariant("C5")));
m_range[3].AttachDispatch(pRange);

VERIFY(pRange = m_worksheet.GetRange(COleVariant("A6")));
m_range[4].AttachDispatch(pRange);

m_range[4].SetValue(COleVariant(COleDateTime
                                (1998, 4, 24, 15, 47, 8)));
// Retrieve the stored date and print it as a string
COleVariant vaTimeDate = m_range[4].GetValue();
TRACE("returned date type = %d\n", vaTimeDate.vt);
COleVariant vaTemp;
vaTemp.ChangeType(VT_BSTR, &vaTimeDate);
CString str = vaTemp.bstrVal;
TRACE("date = %s\n", (const char*) str);

m_range[0].SetValue(COleVariant("test string"));

COleVariant vaResult0 = m_range[0].GetValue();
if (vaResult0.vt == VT_BSTR) {
    CString str = vaResult0.bstrVal;
    TRACE("vaResult0 = %s\n", (const char*) str);
}

m_range[1].SetValue(COleVariant(3.14159));

COleVariant vaResult1 = m_range[1].GetValue();
if (vaResult1.vt == VT_R8) {
    TRACE("vaResult1 = %f\n", vaResult1.dblVal);
}

m_range[2].SetFormula(COleVariant("=$A2*2.0"));

COleVariant vaResult2 = m_range[2].GetValue();
if (vaResult2.vt == VT_R8) {
    TRACE("vaResult2 = %f\n", vaResult2.dblVal);
}

COleVariant vaResult2a = m_range[2].GetFormula();
if (vaResult2a.vt == VT_BSTR) {
    CString str = vaResult2a.bstrVal;
    TRACE("vaResult2a = %s\n", (const char*) str);
}

m_range[3].FillRight();
m_range[3].FillDown();
```

```
    // cleanup
    if (pWorkbook != NULL) {
        pWorkbook->Release();
    }
}
```

The EX25E Automation Client Example

This program uses the new *#import* directive to generate smart pointers. It behaves just like EX25D except that it doesn't run Excel. The *#import* statements are in the StdAfx.h file to minimize the number of times the compiler has to generate the driver classes. Here is the added code:

```
#include <afxdisp.h>

#import "..\ex25a\debug\ex25a.tlb" rename_namespace("BankDriv")
using namespace BankDriv;

#import "..\ex25b\debug\ex25b.tlb" rename_namespace("Ex25bDriv")
using namespace Ex25bDriv;

#import "..\ex25c\debug\ex25c.tlb" rename_namespace("ClockDriv")
using namespace ClockDriv;
```

And of course you'll need to call *AfxOleInit* in your application class *InitInstance* member function.

The view class header contains embedded smart pointers as shown:

```
IEx25bAutoPtr m_auto;
IBankPtr m_bank;
IEx25cPtr m_clock;
IAlarmPtr m_alarm;
```

Here is the code for the view class menu command handlers:

```
void CEx25eView::OnBankoleLoad()
{
    if(m_bank.CreateInstance(__uuidof(Bank)) != S_OK) {
        AfxMessageBox("Bank component not found");
        return;
    }
}

void CEx25eView::OnUpdateBankoleLoad(CCmdUI* pCmdUI)
{
    pCmdUI->Enable(m_bank.GetInterfacePtr() == NULL);
}
```

(continued)

```
void CEx25eView::OnBankoleTest()
{
    try {
        m_bank->Deposit(20.0);
        m_bank->Withdrawal(15.0);
        TRACE("new balance = %f\n", m_bank->GetBalance());
    } catch(_com_error& e) {
        AfxMessageBox(e.ErrorMessage());
    }
}

void CEx25eView::OnUpdateBankoleTest(CCmdUI* pCmdUI)
{
    pCmdUI->Enable(m_bank.GetInterfacePtr() != NULL);
}

void CEx25eView::OnBankoleUnload()
{
    m_bank.Release();
}

void CEx25eView::OnUpdateBankoleUnload(CCmdUI* pCmdUI)
{
    pCmdUI->Enable(m_bank.GetInterfacePtr() != NULL);
}

void CEx25eView::OnClockoleCreatealarm()
{
    CAlarmDialog dlg;
    try {
        if (dlg.DoModal() == IDOK) {
            COleDateTime dt(1995, 12, 23, dlg.m_nHours, dlg.m_nMinutes,
                dlg.m_nSeconds);
            LPDISPATCH pAlarm = m_clock->CreateAlarm(dt);
            m_alarm.Attach((IAlarm*) pAlarm);  // releases prior object!
            m_clock->RefreshWin();
        }
    } catch(_com_error& e) {
        AfxMessageBox(e.ErrorMessage());
    }
}

void CEx25eView::OnUpdateClockoleCreatealarm(CCmdUI* pCmdUI)
{
    pCmdUI->Enable(m_clock.GetInterfacePtr() != NULL);
}

void CEx25eView::OnClockoleLoad()
```

```
    {
        if(m_clock.CreateInstance(__uuidof(Document)) != S_OK) {
            AfxMessageBox("Clock component not found");
            return;
        }
        try {
            m_clock->PutFigure(0, COleVariant("XII"));
            m_clock->PutFigure(1, COleVariant("III"));
            m_clock->PutFigure(2, COleVariant("VI"));
            m_clock->PutFigure(3, COleVariant("IX"));
            OnClockoleRefreshtime();
            m_clock->ShowWin();
        } catch(_com_error& e) {
            AfxMessageBox(e.ErrorMessage());
        }
    }

void CEx25eView::OnUpdateClockoleLoad(CCmdUI* pCmdUI)
{
    pCmdUI->Enable(m_clock.GetInterfacePtr() == NULL);
}


void CEx25eView::OnClockoleRefreshtime()
{
    COleDateTime now = COleDateTime::GetCurrentTime();
    try {
        m_clock->PutTime(now);
        m_clock->RefreshWin();
    } catch(_com_error& e) {
        AfxMessageBox(e.ErrorMessage());
    }
}


void CEx25eView::OnUpdateClockoleRefreshtime(CCmdUI* pCmdUI)
{
    pCmdUI->Enable(m_clock.GetInterfacePtr() != NULL);
}


void CEx25eView::OnClockoleUnload()
{
    m_clock.Release();
}


void CEx25eView::OnUpdateClockoleUnload(CCmdUI* pCmdUI)
{
    pCmdUI->Enable(m_clock.GetInterfacePtr() != NULL);
}
```

(continued)

```
void CEx25eView::OnDlloleGetdata()
{
    try {
        m_auto->DisplayDialog();
        COleVariant vaData = m_auto->GetTextData();
        ASSERT(vaData.vt == VT_BSTR);
        CString strTextData = vaData.bstrVal;
        long lData = m_auto->GetLongData();
        TRACE("CEx25dView::OnDlloleGetdata--long = %ld, text = %s\n",
            lData, strTextData);
    } catch(_com_error& e) {
        AfxMessageBox(e.ErrorMessage());
    }
}

void CEx25eView::OnUpdateDlloleGetdata(CCmdUI* pCmdUI)
{
    pCmdUI->Enable(m_auto.GetInterfacePtr() != NULL);
}

void CEx25eView::OnDlloleLoad()
{
    if(m_auto.CreateInstance(__uuidof(Ex25bAuto)) != S_OK) {
        AfxMessageBox("Ex25bAuto component not found");
        return;
    }
}

void CEx25eView::OnUpdateDlloleLoad(CCmdUI* pCmdUI)
{
    pCmdUI->Enable(m_auto.GetInterfacePtr() == NULL);
}

void CEx25eView::OnDlloleUnload()
{
    m_auto.Release();
}

void CEx25eView::OnUpdateDlloleUnload(CCmdUI* pCmdUI)
{
    pCmdUI->Enable(m_auto.GetInterfacePtr() != NULL);
}
```

Note the use of the *try/catch* blocks in the functions that manipulate the components. These are particularly necessary for processing errors that occur when a component program stops running. In the previous example, EX25D, the MFC *COleDispatchDriver* class took care of this detail.

VBA Early Binding

When you ran the EX25A, EX25B, and EX25C components from Excel VBA, you used something called <u>late</u> binding. Normally, each time VBA accesses a property or a method, it calls *IDispatch::GetIDsOfNames* to look up the dispatch ID from the symbolic name. Not only is this inefficient, VBA can't do type-checking until it actually accesses a property or a method. Suppose, for example, that a VBA program tried to get a property value that it assumed was a number, but the component provided a string instead. VBA would give you a runtime error when it executed the Property Get statement.

With <u>early</u> binding, VBA can preprocess the Visual Basic code, converting property and method symbols to DISPIDs before it runs the component program. In so doing, it can check property types, method return types, and method parameters, giving you compile-time error messages. Where can VBA get the advance information it needs? From the component's type library, of course. It can use that same type library to allow the VBA programmer to browse the component's properties and methods. VBA reads the type library before it even loads the component program.

Registering a Type Library

You've already seen that Visual C++ generates a TLB file for each component. For VBA to locate that type library, its location must be specified in the Windows Registry. The simplest way of doing this is to write a text REG file that the Windows Regedit program can import. Here's the ex25b.reg file for the EX25B DLL component:

```
REGEDIT4

[HKEY_CLASSES_ROOT\TypeLib\{A9515ACA-5B85-11D0-848F-00400526305B}]

[HKEY_CLASSES_ROOT\TypeLib\{A9515ACA-5B85-11D0-848F-00400526305B}\1.0]
@="Ex25b"

[HKEY_CLASSES_ROOT\TypeLib\{A9515ACA-5B85-11D0-848F-00400526305B}\1.0\0]

[HKEY_CLASSES_ROOT\TypeLib\{A9515ACA-5B85-11D0-848F-00400526305B} →
    \1.0\0\win32]
@="C:\\vcpp32\\ex25b\\Debug\\ex25b.tlb"

[HKEY_CLASSES_ROOT\TypeLib\{A9515ACA-5B85-11D0-848F-00400526305B} →
    \1.0\FLAGS]
@="0"
```

(continued)

681

```
[HKEY_CLASSES_ROOT\TypeLib\{A9515ACA-5B85-11D0-848F-00400526305B} →
    \1.0\HELPDIR]
@="C:\\vcpp32\\ex25b\\Debug"

[HKEY_CLASSES_ROOT\Interface\{A9515AD7-5B85-11D0-848F-00400526305B}]
@="IEx25bAuto"

[HKEY_CLASSES_ROOT\Interface\{A9515AD7-5B85-11D0-848F-00400526305B} →
    \ProxyStubClsid]
@="{00020420-0000-0000-C000-000000000046}"

[HKEY_CLASSES_ROOT\Interface\{A9515AD7-5B85-11D0-848F-00400526305B} →
    \ProxyStubClsid32]
@="{00020420-0000-0000-C000-000000000046}"

[HKEY_CLASSES_ROOT\Interface\{A9515AD7-5B85-11D0-848F-00400526305B} →
    \TypeLib]
@="{A9515ACA-5B85-11D0-848F-00400526305B}"
"Version"="1.0"
```

Notice that this file generates subtrees under the Registry's TypeLib and Interface keys. The third entry specifies the path for the version 1.0 TLB file. The 0 subkey stands for "neutral language." If you had a multilingual application, you would have separate entries for English, French, and so forth. Browsers use the TypeLib entries, and the Interface entries are used for runtime type-checking and, for an EXE component, marshaling the dispinterface.

How a Component Can Register Its Own Type Library

When an EXE component is run stand-alone, it can call the MFC *AfxRegister-TypeLib* function to make the necessary Registry entries, as shown here:

```
VERIFY(AfxOleRegisterTypeLib(AfxGetInstanceHandle(), theTypeLibGUID,
    "ex25b.tlb"));
```

Shown here is *theTypeLibGUID*, a static variable of type *GUID*:

```
// {A9515ACA-5B85-11D0-848F-00400526305B}
static const GUID theTypeLibGUID =
{ 0xa9515aca, 0x5b85, 0x11d0, { 0x84, 0x8f, 0x00, 0x40, 0x05, 0x26,
    0x30, 0x5b } };
```

The *AfxRegisterTypeLib* function is declared in the afxwin.h header, which requires *_AFXDLL* to be defined. That means you can't use it in a regular DLL unless you copy the code from the MFC source files.

The ODL File

Now is a good time to look at the ODL file for the same project.

```
// ex25b.odl : type library source for ex25b.dll

// This file will be processed by the MIDL compiler to produce the
//  type library (ex25b.tlb)

[ uuid(A9515ACA-5B85-11D0-848F-00400526305B), version(1.0) ]

// GUID for the type library--matches TypeLib Registry key and
//  AfxOleRegisterTypeLib parameter
library Ex25b
{
    // library name for Excel's object borrower

    importlib("stdole32.tlb");
    // primary dispatch interface for CEx25bAuto

    [ uuid(A9515AD7-5B85-11D0-848F-00400526305B) ]

    // GUID from component's interface map--matches Registry Interface
    //  entry

    dispinterface IEx25bAuto
    {
        // name used in VBA Dim statement and Object list
        properties:
            // NOTE - ClassWizard will maintain property
            //  information here.
            //  Use extreme caution when editing this section.
            //{{AFX_ODL_PROP(CEx25bAuto)
            [id(1)] long LongData;
            [id(2)] VARIANT TextData;
            //}}AFX_ODL_PROP

        methods:
            // NOTE - ClassWizard will maintain method
            //  information here.
            //  Use extreme caution when editing this section.
            //{{AFX_ODL_METHOD(CEx25bAuto)
            [id(3)] boolean DisplayDialog();
            //}}AFX_ODL_METHOD
    };
```

(continued)

```
    [ uuid(A9515AD8-5B85-11D0-848F-00400526305B) ]

// component's CLSID

    coclass Ex25bAuto
    {
        [default] dispinterface IEx25bAuto;
    };

    //{{AFX_APPEND_ODL}}
};
```

As you can see, numerous connections exist among the Registry, the type library, the component, and the VBA client.

NOTE: A useful Visual C++ utility, OLEVIEW, lets you examine registered components and their type libraries.

How Excel Uses a Type Library

Let's examine the sequence of steps Excel uses to utilize your type library:

1. When Excel starts up, it reads the TypeLib section of the Registry to compile a list of all type libraries. It loads the type libraries for VBA and for the Excel object library.

2. After starting Excel, loading a workbook, and switching to the Visual Basic Editor, the user (or workbook author) chooses References from the Tools menu and checks the EX25B LIB line, as shown at the top of page 685.

   When the workbook is saved, this reference information is saved with it.

3. Now the Excel user will be able to browse through the EX25B properties and methods by choosing Object Browser from the Visual Basic Editor's View menu to view the Object Browser dialog, as shown in the middle of page 685.

4. To make use of the type library in your VBA program, you simply replace the line

   ```
   Dim DllComp as Object
   ```

   with

   ```
   Dim DllComp as IEx25bAuto
   ```

   The VBA program will exit immediately if it can't find *IEx25b-Auto* in its list of references.

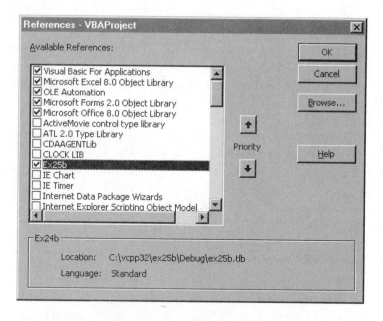

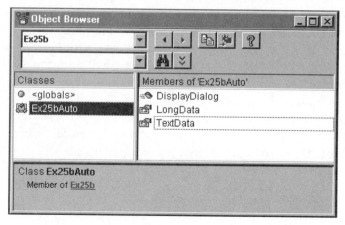

5. Immediately after VBA executes the CreateObject statement and loads the component program, it calls *QueryInterface* for *IID-_IEx25bAuto*, which is defined in the Registry, the type library, and the component class's interface map. (*IEx25bAuto* is really an *IDispatch* interface.) This is a sort of security check. If the component can't deliver this interface, the VBA program exits. Theoretically, Excel could use the CLSID in the type library to load the component program, but it uses the CLSID from the Registry instead, just as it did in late binding mode.

Why Use Early Binding?

You might think that early binding would make your Automation component run faster. You probably won't notice any speed increase, though, because the *IDispatch::Invoke* calls are the limiting factor. A typical MFC *Invoke* call from a compiled C++ client to a compiled C++ component requires about 0.5 millisecond, which is pretty gross.

The browse capability that the type library provides is probably more valuable than the compiled linkage. If you are writing a C++ controller, for example, you can load the type library through various COM functions, including *LoadTypeLib*, and then you can access it through the *ITypeLib* and *ITypeInfo* interfaces. Plan to spend some time on that project, however, because the type library interfaces are tricky.

Faster Client-Component Connections

Microsoft has recognized the limitations of the *IDispatch* interface. It's naturally slow because all data must be funneled through *VARIANT*s and possibly converted on both ends. There's a new variation called a dual interface. (A discussion of dual interfaces is beyond the scope of this book. See Kraig Brockschmidt's *Inside OLE*, 2d ed. [Microsoft Press, 1995], for more information.) In a dual interface, you define your own custom interface, derived from *IDispatch*. The *Invoke* and *GetIDsOfNames* functions are included, but so are other functions. If the client is smart enough, it can bypass the inefficient *Invoke* calls and use the specialized functions instead. Dual interfaces can support only standard Automation types, or they can support arbitrary types.

There is no direct MFC support for dual interfaces in Visual C++ 6.0, but the ACDUAL Visual C++ sample should get you started.

Uniform Data Transfer— Clipboard Transfer and OLE Drag and Drop

ActiveX technology includes a powerful mechanism for transferring data within and among Microsoft Windows–based applications. The COM *IDataObject* interface is the key element of what is known as <u>Uniform</u> <u>Data</u> <u>Transfer</u>. As you'll see, Uniform Data Transfer (UDT) gives you all sorts of options for the formatting and storage of your transferred data, going well beyond standard clipboard transfers.

Microsoft Foundation Class support is available for Uniform Data Transfer, but MFC's support for UDT is not so high-level as to obscure what's going on at the COM interface level. One of the useful applications of UDT is OLE Drag and Drop. Many developers want to use drag-and-drop capabilities in their applications, and drag-and-drop support means that programs now have a standard for information interchange. The MFC library supports drag-and-drop operations, and that, together with clipboard transfer, is the main focus of this chapter.

The *IDataObject* Interface

The *IDataObject* interface is used for clipboard transfers and drag-and-drop operations, but it's also used in compound documents, ActiveX Controls, and custom OLE features. In his book *Inside OLE,* 2d ed. (Microsoft Press, 1995) Kraig Brockschmidt says, "Think of objects as little piles of stuff." The *IDataObject* interface helps you move those piles around, no matter what kind of stuff they contain.

If you were programming at the Win32 level, you would write C++ code that supported the *IDataObject* interface. Your program would then construct <u>data</u> <u>objects</u> of this class, and you would manipulate those objects with the *IDataObject* member functions. In this chapter you'll see how to accomplish the same results by using MFC's implementation of *IDataObject*. Let's start by taking a quick look at why the OLE clipboard is an improvement on the regular Windows clipboard.

How *IDataObject* Improves on Standard Clipboard Support

There has never been much MFC support for the Windows Clipboard. If you've written programs for the clipboard already, you've used Win32 clipboard functions such as *OpenClipboard*, *CloseClipboard*, *GetClipboardData*, and *SetClipboardData*. One program copies a single data element of a specified format to the clipboard, and another program selects the data by format code and pastes it. Standard clipboard formats include global memory (specified by an *HGLOBAL* variable) and various GDI objects, such as bitmaps and metafiles (specified by their handles). Global memory can contain text as well as custom formats.

The *IDataObject* interface picks up where the Windows Clipboard leaves off. To make a long story short, you transfer a single *IDataObject* pointer to or from the clipboard instead of transferring a series of discrete formats. The underlying data object can contain a whole array of formats. Those formats can carry information about target devices, such as printer characteristics, and they can specify the data's <u>aspect</u> or view. The standard aspect is content. Other aspects include an icon for the data and a thumbnail picture.

Note that the *IDataObject* interface specifies the <u>storage</u> <u>medium</u> of a data object format. Conventional clipboard transfer relies exclusively on global memory. The *IDataObject* interface permits the transmission of a disk filename or a structured storage pointer instead. Thus, if you want to transfer a very large block of data that's already in a disk file, you don't have to waste time copying it to and from a memory block.

In case you were wondering, *IDataObject* pointers are compatible with programs that use existing clipboard transfer methods. The format codes are the same. Windows takes care of the conversion to and from the data object. Of course, if an OLE-aware program puts an *IStorage* pointer in a data object and puts the object on the clipboard, older, non-OLE-aware programs are unable to read that format.

The *FORMATETC* and *STGMEDIUM* Structures

Before you're ready for the *IDataObject* member functions, you need to examine two important COM structures that are used as parameter types: the *FORMATETC* structure and the *STGMEDIUM* structure.

FORMATETC

The *FORMATETC* structure is often used instead of a clipboard format to represent data format information. However, unlike the clipboard format, the *FORMATETC* structure includes information about a target device, the aspect or view of the data, and a storage medium indicator. Here are the members of the *FORMATETC* structure.

Type	Name	Description
CLIPFORMAT	*cfFormat*	Structure that contains clipboard formats, such as standard interchange formats (for example, *CF_TEXT*, which is a text format, and *CF_DIB*, which is an image compression format), custom formats (such as rich text format), and OLE formats used to create linked or embedded objects
DVTARGETDEVICE*	*ptd*	Structure that contains information about the target device for the data, including the device driver name (can be *NULL*)
DWORD	*dwAspect*	A *DVASPECT* enumeration constant (*DVASPECT_CONTENT*, *DVASPECT_THUMBNAIL*, and so on)
LONG	*lindex*	Usually –1
DWORD	*tymed*	Specifies type of media used to transfer the object's data (TYMED_HGLOBAL, TYMED_FILE, TYMED_ISTORAGE, and so on)

An individual data object accommodates a collection of FORMATETC elements, and the IDataObject interface provides a way to enumerate them. A useful macro for filling in a *FORMATETC* structure appears on the following page.

```
#define SETFORMATETC(fe, cf, asp, td, med, li)   \
    ((fe).cfFormat=cf, \
     (fe).dwAspect=asp, \
     (fe).ptd=td, \
     (fe).tymed=med, \
     (fe).lindex=li)
```

STGMEDIUM

The other important structure for *IDataObject* members is the *STGMEDIUM* structure. The *STGMEDIUM* structure is a global memory handle used for operations involving data transfer. Here are the members.

Type	Name	Description
DWORD	*tymed*	Storage medium value used in marshaling and unmarshaling routines
HBITMAP	*hBitmap*	Bitmap handle*
HMETAFILEPICT	*hMetaFilePict*	Metafile handle*
HENHMETAFILE	*hEnhMetaFile*	Enhanced metafile handle*
HGLOBAL	*hGlobal*	Global memory handle*
LPOLESTR	*lpszFileName*	Disk filename (double-byte)*
*ISTREAM**	*pstm*	*IStream* interface pointer*
*ISTORAGE**	*pstg*	*IStorage* interface pointer*
IUNKNOWN	*pUnkForRelease*	Used by clients to call *Release* for formats with interface pointers

* This member is part of a union, including handles, strings, and interface pointers used by the receiving process to access the transferred data.

As you can see, the *STGMEDIUM* structure specifies <u>where</u> data is stored. The *tymed* variable determines which union member is valid.

The *IDataObject* Interface Member Functions

This interface has nine member functions. Both Brockschmidt and the online documentation do a good job of describing all of these functions. Following are the functions that are important for this chapter.

HRESULT EnumFormatEtc(DWORD *dwDirection*,
IEnumFORMATETC *ppEnum*);

If you have an *IDataObject* pointer for a data object, you can use *EnumFormatEtc* to enumerate all the formats that it supports. This is an ugly API that the MFC library insulates you from. You'll learn how this happens when you examine the *COleDataObject* class.

HRESULT GetData(FORMATETC* *pFEIn*, STGMEDIUM* *pSTM*);

GetData is the most important function in the interface. Somewhere, up in the sky, is a data object, and you have an *IDataObject* pointer to it. You specify, in a *FORMATETC* variable, the exact format you want to use when you retrieve the data, and you prepare an empty *STGMEDIUM* variable to accept the results. If the data object has the format you want, *GetData* fills in the *STGMEDIUM* structure. Otherwise, you get an error return value.

HRESULT QueryGetData(FORMATETC* *pFE*);

You call *QueryGetData* if you're not sure whether the data object can deliver data in the format specified in the *FORMATETC* structure. The return value says, "Yes, I can" (*S_OK*) or "No, I can't" (an error code). Calling this function is definitely more efficient than allocating a *STGMEDIUM* variable and calling *GetData*.

HRESULT SetData(FORMATETC* *pFEIn*,
STGMEDIUM* *pSTM*, BOOL *fRelease*);

Data objects rarely support *SetData*. Data objects are normally loaded with formats in their own server module; clients retrieve data by calling *GetData*. With *SetData*, you'd be transferring data in the other direction—like pumping water from your house back to the water company.

Other *IDataObject* Member Functions—Advisory Connections

The interface contains other important functions that let you implement an <u>advisory</u> connection. When the program using a data object needs to be notified whether the object's data changes, the program can pass an *IAdviseSink* pointer to the object by calling the *IDataObject::DAdvise* function. The object then calls various *IAdviseSink* member functions, which the client program implements. You won't need advisory connections for drag-and-drop operations, but you will need them when you get to embedding in Chapter 28.

MFC Uniform Data Transfer Support

The MFC library does a lot to make data object programming easier. As you study the MFC data object classes, you'll start to see a pattern in MFC COM support. At the component end, the MFC library provides a base class that implements one or more OLE interfaces. The interface member functions call virtual functions that you override in your derived class. At the client end, the MFC library provides a class that wraps an interface pointer. You call simple member functions that use the interface pointer to make COM calls.

The terminology needs some clarification here. The data object that's been described is the actual C++ object that you construct, and that's the way Brockschmidt uses the term. In the MFC documentation, a data object is what the client program sees through an *IDataObject* pointer. A <u>data</u> <u>source</u> is the object you construct in a component program.

The *COleDataSource* Class

When you want to use a data source, you construct an object of class *COleDataSource*, which implements the *IDataObject* interface (without advisory connection support). This class builds and manages a <u>collection</u> of data formats stored in a <u>cache</u> in memory. A data source is a regular COM object that keeps a reference count. Usually, you construct and fill a data source, and then you pass it to the clipboard or drag and drop it in another location, never to worry about it again. If you decide not to pass off a data source, you can invoke the destructor, which cleans up all its formats.

Following are some of the more useful member functions of the *COleDataSource* class.

void CacheData(CLIPFORMAT *cfFormat*,
STGMEDIUM* *lpStgMedium*,
FORMATETC* *lpFormatEtc* = NULL);

This function inserts an element in the data object's cache for data transfer. The *lpStgMedium* parameter points to the data, and the *lpFormatEtc* parameter describes the data. If, for example, the *STGMEDIUM* structure specifies a disk filename, that filename gets stored inside the data object. If *lpFormatEtc* is set to *NULL*, the function fills in a *FORMATETC* structure with default values. It's safer, though, if you create your *FORMATETC* variable with the *tymed* member set.

void CacheGlobalData(CLIPFORMAT *cfFormat*, HGLOBAL *hGlobal*, FORMATETC* *lpFormatEtc* = NULL);

You call this specialized version of *CacheData* to pass data in global memory (identified by an *HGLOBAL* variable). The data source object is considered the owner of that global memory block, so you should not free it after you cache it. You can usually omit the *lpFormatEtc* parameter. The *CacheGlobalData* function does <u>not</u> make a copy of the data.

DROPEFFECT DoDragDrop(DWORD *dwEffects* = DROPEFFECT_COPY|DROPEFFECT_MOVE| DROPEFFECT_LINK, LPCRECT *lpRectStartDrag* = NULL, COleDropSource* *pDropSource* = NULL);

You call this function for drag-and-drop operations on a data source. You'll see it used in the EX26B example.

void SetClipboard(void);

The *SetClipboard* function, which you'll see in the EX26A example, calls the *OleSetClipboard* function to put a data source on the Windows Clipboard. The clipboard is responsible for deleting the data source and thus for freeing the global memory associated with the formats in the cache. When you construct a *COleDataSource* object and call *SetClipboard*, COM calls *AddRef* on the object.

The *COleDataObject* Class

This class is on the destination side of a data object transfer. Its base class is *CCmdTarget*, and it has a public member *m_lpDataObject* that holds an *IData-Object* pointer. That member must be set before you can effectively use the object. The class destructor only calls *Release* on the *IDataObject* pointer.

Following are a few of the more useful *COleDataObject* member functions.

BOOL AttachClipboard(void);

As Brockschmidt points out, OLE clipboard processing is internally complex. From your point of view, however, it's straightforward—as long as you use the *COleDataObject* member functions. You first construct an "empty" *COleData-Object* object, and then you call *AttachClipboard*, which calls the global *OleGet-Clipboard* function. Now the *m_lpDataObject* data member points back to the source data object (or so it appears), and you can access its formats.

If you call the *GetData* member function to get a format, you must remember that the clipboard owns the format and you cannot alter its contents. If the format consists of an *HGLOBAL* pointer, you must not free that memory and you cannot hang on to the pointer. If you need to have long-term access to the data in global memory, consider calling *GetGlobalData* instead.

If a non-COM-aware program copies data onto the clipboard, the *Attach-Clipboard* function still works because COM invents a data object that contains formats corresponding to the regular Windows data on the clipboard.

void BeginEnumFormats(void);
BOOL GetNextFormat(FORMATETC* *lpFormatEtc*);

These two functions allow you to iterate through the formats that the data object contains. You call *BeginEnumFormats* first, and then you call *GetNextFormat* in a loop until it returns *FALSE*.

BOOL GetData(CLIPFORMAT *cfFormat,*
STGMEDIUM* *lpStgMedium*
FORMATETC* *lpFormatEtc* = NULL);

This function calls *IDataObject::GetData* and not much more. The function returns *TRUE* if the data source contains the format you asked for. You generally need to supply the *lpFormatEtc* parameter.

HGLOBAL GetGlobalData(CLIPFORMAT *cfFormat,*
FORMATETC* *lpFormatEtc* = NULL);

Use the *GetGlobalData* function if you know your requested format is compatible with global memory. This function makes a copy of the selected format's memory block, and it gives you an *HGLOBAL* handle that you must free later. You can often omit the *lpFormatEtc* parameter.

BOOL IsDataAvailable(CLIPFORMAT *cfFormat,*
FORMATETC* *lpFormatEtc* = NULL);

The *IsDataAvailable* function tests whether the data object contains a given format.

MFC Data Object Clipboard Transfer

Now that you've seen the *COleDataObject* and *COleDataSource* classes, you'll have an easy time doing clipboard data object transfers. But why not just do clipboard transfers the old way with *GetClipboardData* and *SetClipboardData*? You could for most common formats, but if you write functions that process data objects, you can use those same functions for drag and drop.

Figure 26-1 shows the relationship between the clipboard and the *COle-DataSource* and *COleDataObject* classes. You construct a *COleDataSource* object

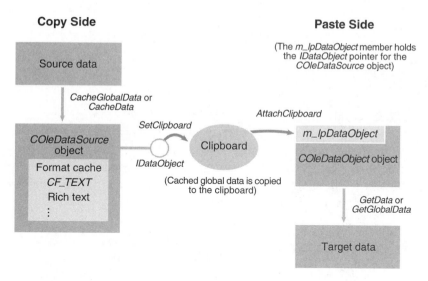

Copy Side

Paste Side

(The *m_lpDataObject* member holds the *IDataObject* pointer for the *COleDataSource* object)

Source data

CacheGlobalData or *CacheData*

AttachClipboard

SetClipboard

COleDataSource object

Clipboard

m_lpDataObject

COleDataObject object

Format cache *CF_TEXT* Rich text ⋮

IDataObject

(Cached global data is copied to the clipboard)

GetData or *GetGlobalData*

Target data

Figure 26-1.
MFC OLE clipboard processing.

on the copy side, and then you fill its cache with formats. When you call *Set-Clipboard*, the formats are copied to the clipboard. On the paste side, you call *AttachClipboard* to attach an *IDataObject* pointer to a *COleDataObject* object, after which you can retrieve individual formats.

Suppose you have a document–view application whose document has a *CString* data member *m_strText*. You want to use view class command handler functions that copy to and paste from the clipboard. Before you write those functions, write two helper functions. The first, *SaveText*, creates a data source object from the contents of *m_strText*. The function constructs a *COleData-Source* object, and then it copies the string contents to global memory. Last it calls *CacheGlobalData* to store the *HGLOBAL* handle in the data source object. Here is the *SaveText* code:

```
COleDataSource* CMyView::SaveText()
{
    CEx26fDoc* pDoc = GetDocument();
    if (!pDoc->m_strtext.IsEmpty()) {
        COleDataSource* pSource = new COleDataSource();
        int nTextSize = GetDocument()->m_strText.GetLength() + 1;
        HGLOBAL hText = ::GlobalAlloc(GMEM_SHARE, nTextSize);
        LPSTR pText = (LPSTR) ::GlobalLock(hText);
        ASSERT(pText);
        strcpy(pText, GetDocument()->m_strText);
```

(continued)

695

```
        ::GlobalUnlock(hText);
        pSource->CacheGlobalData(CF_TEXT, hText);
        return pSource;
    }
    return NULL;
}
```

The second helper function, *DoPasteText*, fills in *m_strText* from a data object specified as a parameter. We're using *COleDataObject::GetData* here instead of *GetGlobalData* because *GetGlobalData* makes a copy of the global memory block. That extra copy operation is unnecessary because we're copying the text to the *CString* object. We don't free the original memory block because the data object owns it. Here is the *DoPasteText* code:

```
// Memory is MOVEABLE, so we must use GlobalLock!
    SETFORMATETC(fmt, CF_TEXT, DVASPECT_CONTENT, NULL, TYMED_HGLOBAL, -1);
    VERIFY(pDataObject->GetData(CF_TEXT, &stg, &fmt));
    HGLOBAL hText = stg.hGlobal;
    GetDocument()->m_strText = (LPSTR) ::GlobalLock(hText);
    ::GlobalUnlock(hText);
    return TRUE;
}
```

Here are the two command handler functions:

```
void CMyView::OnEditCopy()
{
    COleDataSource* pSource = SaveText();
    if (pSource) {
        pSource->SetClipboard();
    }
}
void CMyView::OnEditPaste()
{
    COleDataObject dataObject;
    VERIFY(dataObject.AttachClipboard());
    DoPasteText(&dataObject);
    // dataObject released
}
```

The MFC *CRectTracker* Class

The *CRectTracker* class is useful in both OLE and non-OLE programs. It allows the user to move and resize a rectangular object in a view window. There are two important data members: the *m_nStyle* member determines the border, resize handle, and other characteristics; and the *m_rect* member holds the <u>device</u> coordinates for the rectangle.

The important member functions follow.

void Draw(CDC* *pDC*) const;

The *Draw* function draws the tracker, including border and resize handles, but it does not draw anything inside the rectangle. That's your job.

BOOL Track(CWnd* *pWnd*, CPoint *point*, BOOL *bAllowInvert* = FALSE, CWnd* *pWndClipTo* = NULL);

You call this function in a *WM_LBUTTONDOWN* handler. If the cursor is on the rectangle border, the user can resize the tracker by holding down the mouse button; if the cursor is inside the rectangle, the user can move the tracker. If the cursor is outside the rectangle, *Track* returns *FALSE* immediately; otherwise, *Track* returns *TRUE* only when the user releases the mouse button. That means *Track* works a little like *CDialog::DoModal*. It contains its own message dispatch logic.

int HitTest(CPoint *point*) const;

Call *HitTest* if you need to distinguish between mouse button hits inside and on the tracker rectangle. The function returns immediately with the hit status in the return value.

BOOL SetCursor(CWnd* *pWnd*, UINT *nHitTest*) const;

Call this function in your view's *WM_SETCURSOR* handler to ensure that the cursor changes during tracking. If *SetCursor* returns *FALSE*, call the base class *OnSetCursor* function; if *SetCursor* returns *TRUE*, you return *TRUE*.

CRectTracker Rectangle Coordinate Conversion

You must deal with the fact that the *CRectTracker::m_rect* member stores device coordinates. If you are using a scrolling view or have otherwise changed the mapping mode or viewport origin, you must do coordinate conversion. Here's a strategy:

1. Define a *CRectTracker* data member in your view class. Use the name *m_tracker*.

2. Define a separate data member in your view class to hold the rectangle in logical coordinates. Use the name *m_rectTracker*.

3. In your view's *OnDraw* function, set *m_rect* to the updated device coordinates, and then draw the tracker. This adjusts for any scrolling since the last *OnDraw*. Some sample code appears on the following page.

```
m_tracker.m_rect = m_rectTracker;
pDC->LPtoDP(m_tracker.m_rect); // tracker requires device
                              //   coordinates
m_tracker.Draw(pDC);
```

4. In your mouse button down message handler, call *Track*, set *m_rectTracker* to the updated logical coordinates, and call *Invalidate*, as shown here:

```
if (m_tracker.Track(this, point, FALSE, NULL)) {
    CClientDC dc(this);
    OnPrepareDC(&dc);
    m_rectTracker = m_tracker.m_rect;
    dc.DPtoLP(m_rectTracker);
    Invalidate();
}
```

The EX26A Example—A Data Object Clipboard

This example uses the *CDib* class from EX11C. Here you'll be able to move and resize the DIB image with a tracker rectangle, and you'll be able to copy and paste the DIB to and from the clipboard using a COM data object. The example also includes functions for reading DIBs from and writing DIBs to BMP files.

If you create such an example from scratch, use AppWizard without any ActiveX or Automation options and then add the following line in your StdAfx.h file:

```
#include <afxole.h>
```

Add the following call at the start of the application's *InitInstance* function:

```
AfxOleInit();
```

To prepare EX26A, open the \vcpp32\ex26a\ex26a.dsw workspace and then build the project. Run the application, and paste a bitmap into the rectangle by choosing Paste From on the Edit menu. You'll see an MDI application similar to the one shown in Figure 26-2.

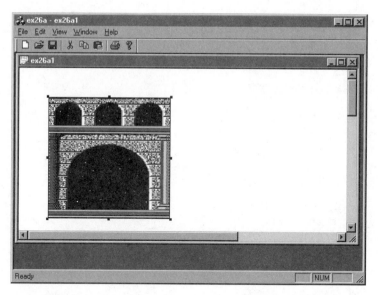

Figure 26-2.
The EX26A program in operation.

The *CMainFrame* Class

This class contains the handlers *OnQueryNewPalette* and *OnPaletteChanged* for the WM_QUERYNEWPALETTE and WM_PALETTECHANGED messages, respectively. These handlers send a user-defined WM_VIEWPALETTE-CHANGED message to all the views, and then the handler calls *CDib::UsePalette* to realize the palette. The value of *wParam* tells the view whether it should realize the palette in background or foreground mode.

The *CEx26aDoc* Class

This class is pretty straightforward. It contains an embedded *CDib* object, *m_dib*, plus a Clear All command handler. The overridden *DeleteContents* member function calls the *CDib::Empty* function.

The *CEx26aView* Class

This class contains the clipboard function command handlers, the tracking code, the DIB drawing code, and the palette message handler. Figure 26-3 shows the header and implementation files with manually entered code in boldface.

EX26AVIEW.H

```
#if !defined(AFX_EX26AVIEW_H__4F329B0F_5DF1_11D0_848F_00400526305B__INCLUDED_)
#define AFX_EX26AVIEW_H__4F329B0F_5DF1_11D0_848F_00400526305B__INCLUDED_

#if _MSC_VER > 1000
#pragma once
#endif// _MSC_VER > 1000

#define WM_VIEWPALETTECHANGED  WM_USER + 5

class CEx26aView : public CScrollView
{
    // for tracking
    CRectTracker m_tracker;
    CRect m_rectTracker; // logical coordinates
    CSize m_sizeTotal;   // document size
protected: // create from serialization only
    CEx26aView();
    DECLARE_DYNCREATE(CEx26aView)

// Attributes
public:
    CEx26aDoc* GetDocument();
// Operations
public:

// Overrides
    // ClassWizard generated virtual function overrides
    //{{AFX_VIRTUAL(CEx26aView)
    public:
    virtual void OnDraw(CDC* pDC);  // overridden to draw this view
    virtual BOOL PreCreateWindow(CREATESTRUCT& cs);
    virtual void OnPrepareDC(CDC* pDC, CPrintInfo* pInfo = NULL);
    virtual void OnInitialUpdate();
    protected:
    virtual BOOL OnPreparePrinting(CPrintInfo* pInfo);
    virtual void OnBeginPrinting(CDC* pDC, CPrintInfo* pInfo);
    virtual void OnEndPrinting(CDC* pDC, CPrintInfo* pInfo);
    //}}AFX_VIRTUAL

// Implementation
public:
    virtual ~CEx26aView();
```

Figure 26-3.   *(continued)*

The CEx26aView *class listing.*

```
#ifdef _DEBUG
    virtual void AssertValid() const;
    virtual void Dump(CDumpContext& dc) const;
#endif

protected:

// generated message map functions
protected:
    //{{AFX_MSG(CEx26aView)
    afx_msg void OnEditCopy();
    afx_msg void OnUpdateEditCopy(CCmdUI* pCmdUI);]
    afx_msg void OnEditCopyto();
    afx_msg void OnEditCut();
    afx_msg void OnEditPaste();
    afx_msg void OnUpdateEditPaste(CCmdUI* pCmdUI);
    afx_msg void OnEditPastefrom();
    afx_msg void OnLButtonDown(UINT nFlags, CPoint point);
    afx_msg BOOL OnSetCursor(CWnd* pWnd, UINT nHitTest, UINT message);
    afx_msg LONG OnViewPaletteChanged(UINT wParam, LONG lParam);
    afx_msg void OnSetFocus(CWnd* pOldWnd);
    //}}AFX_MSG
    DECLARE_MESSAGE_MAP()
private:
    BOOL DoPasteDib(COleDataObject* pDataObject);
    COleDataSource* SaveDib();
};

#ifndef _DEBUG  // debug version in Ex26aView.cpp
inline CEx26aDoc* CEx26aView::GetDocument()
    { return (CEx26aDoc*)m_pDocument; }
#endif

////////////////////////////////////////////////////////////////////////

//{{AFX_INSERT_LOCATION}}
// Microsoft Visual C++ will insert additional declarations
//   immediately before the previous line

#endif
// !defined(AFX_EX26AVIEW_H__4F329B0F_5DF1_11D0_848F_00400526305B__INCLUDED_)
```

(continued)

Figure 26-3. *continued*

EX26AVIEW.CPP

```
#include "stdafx.h"
#include "ex26a.h"

#include "cdib.h"
#include "ex26aDoc.h"
#include "ex26aView.h"

#ifdef _DEBUG
#define new DEBUG_NEW
#undef THIS_FILE
static char THIS_FILE[] = __FILE__;
#endif

/////////////////////////////////////////////////////////////////////
// CEx26aView

IMPLEMENT_DYNCREATE(CEx26aView, CScrollView)

BEGIN_MESSAGE_MAP(CEx26aView, CScrollView)
    //{{AFX_MSG_MAP(CEx26aView)
    ON_COMMAND(ID_EDIT_COPY, OnEditCopy)
    ON_UPDATE_COMMAND_UI(ID_EDIT_COPY, OnUpdateEditCopy)
    ON_COMMAND(ID_EDIT_COPYTO, OnEditCopyto)
    ON_COMMAND(ID_EDIT_CUT, OnEditCut)
    ON_COMMAND(ID_EDIT_PASTE, OnEditPaste)
    ON_UPDATE_COMMAND_UI(ID_EDIT_PASTE, OnUpdateEditPaste)
    ON_COMMAND(ID_EDIT_PASTEFROM, OnEditPastefrom)
    ON_WM_LBUTTONDOWN()
    ON_WM_SETCURSOR()
    ON_MESSAGE(WM_VIEWPALETTECHANGED, OnViewPaletteChanged)
    ON_UPDATE_COMMAND_UI(ID_EDIT_COPYTO, OnUpdateEditCopy)
    ON_UPDATE_COMMAND_UI(ID_EDIT_CUT, OnUpdateEditCopy)
    ON_WM_SETFOCUS()
    //}}AFX_MSG_MAP
    // standard printing commands
    ON_COMMAND(ID_FILE_PRINT, CScrollView::OnFilePrint)
    ON_COMMAND(ID_FILE_PRINT_DIRECT, CScrollView::OnFilePrint)
    ON_COMMAND(ID_FILE_PRINT_PREVIEW, CScrollView::OnFilePrintPreview)
END_MESSAGE_MAP()
```

```
///////////////////////////////////////////////////////////////////
// CEx26aView construction/destruction

CEx26aView::CEx26aView() : m_sizeTotal(800, 1050), // 8-by-10.5 inches
                                                   //  when printed
    m_rectTracker(50, 50, 250, 250)
{
}


CEx26aView::~CEx26aView()
{
}


BOOL CEx26aView::PreCreateWindow(CREATESTRUCT& cs)
{
    // TODO: Modify the Window class or styles here by modifying
    //  the CREATESTRUCT cs

    return CScrollView::PreCreateWindow(cs);
}


///////////////////////////////////////////////////////////////////
// CEx26aView drawing

void CEx26aView::OnDraw(CDC* pDC)
{
    CDib& dib = GetDocument()->m_dib;
    m_tracker.m_rect = m_rectTracker;
    pDC->LPtoDP(m_tracker.m_rect); // tracker wants device coordinates
    m_tracker.Draw(pDC);
    dib.Draw(pDC, m_rectTracker.TopLeft(), m_rectTracker.Size());
}


///////////////////////////////////////////////////////////////////
// CEx26aView printing

BOOL CEx26aView::OnPreparePrinting(CPrintInfo* pInfo)
{
    pInfo->SetMaxPage(1);
    return DoPreparePrinting(pInfo);
}


void CEx26aView::OnBeginPrinting(CDC* /*pDC*/, CPrintInfo* /*pInfo*/)
{
    // TODO: add extra initialization before printing
}
```

(continued)

Figure 26-3. *continued*

```
void CEx26aView::OnEndPrinting(CDC* /*pDC*/, CPrintInfo* /*pInfo*/)
{
    // TODO: add cleanup after printing
}


/////////////////////////////////////////////////////////////////////
// CEx26aView diagnostics

#ifdef _DEBUG
void CEx26aView::AssertValid() const
{
    CScrollView::AssertValid();
}

void CEx26aView::Dump(CDumpContext& dc) const
{
    CScrollView::Dump(dc);
}

CEx26aDoc* CEx26aView::GetDocument() // nondebug version is inline
{
    ASSERT(m_pDocument->IsKindOf(RUNTIME_CLASS(CEx26aDoc)));
    return (CEx26aDoc*)m_pDocument;
}
#endif //_DEBUG


/////////////////////////////////////////////////////////////////
// helper functions used for clipboard and drag-drop

BOOL CEx26aView::DoPasteDib(COleDataObject* pDataObject)
{
    // update command user interface should keep us out of
    //   here if not CF_DIB
    if (!pDataObject->IsDataAvailable(CF_DIB)) {
        TRACE("CF_DIB format is unavailable\n");
        return FALSE;
    }
    CEx26aDoc* pDoc = GetDocument();
    // Seems to be MOVEABLE memory, so we must use GlobalLock!
    //   (hDib != lpDib) GetGlobalData copies the memory, so we can
    //   hang onto it until we delete the CDib.
    HGLOBAL hDib = pDataObject->GetGlobalData(CF_DIB);
    ASSERT(hDib != NULL);
    LPVOID lpDib = ::GlobalLock(hDib);
    ASSERT(lpDib != NULL);
```

```
        pDoc->m_dib.AttachMemory(lpDib, TRUE, hDib);
        pDoc->SetModifiedFlag();
        pDoc->UpdateAllViews(NULL);
        return TRUE;
    }

COleDataSource* CEx26aView::SaveDib()
{
    CDib& dib = GetDocument()->m_dib;
    if (dib.GetSizeImage() > 0) {
        COleDataSource* pSource = new COleDataSource();
        int nHeaderSize = dib.GetSizeHeader();
        int nImageSize = dib.GetSizeImage();
        HGLOBAL hHeader = ::GlobalAlloc(GMEM_SHARE,
            nHeaderSize + nImageSize);
        LPVOID pHeader = ::GlobalLock(hHeader);
        ASSERT(pHeader != NULL);
        LPVOID pImage = (LPBYTE) pHeader + nHeaderSize;
        memcpy(pHeader, dib.m_lpBMIH, nHeaderSize);
        memcpy(pImage, dib.m_lpImage, nImageSize);
        // Receiver is supposed to free the global memory
        ::GlobalUnlock(hHeader);
        pSource->CacheGlobalData(CF_DIB, hHeader);
        return pSource;
    }
    return NULL;
}


/////////////////////////////////////////////////////////////////////
// CEx26aView message handlers

void CEx26aView::OnEditCopy()
{
    COleDataSource* pSource = SaveDib();
    if (pSource) {
        pSource->SetClipboard(); // OLE deletes data source
    }
}

void CEx26aView::OnUpdateEditCopy(CCmdUI* pCmdUI)
{
    // serves Copy, Cut, and Copy To
    CDib& dib = GetDocument()->m_dib;
    pCmdUI->Enable(dib.GetSizeImage() > 0L);
}
```

(continued)

Figure 26-3. *continued*

```
void CEx26aView::OnEditCopyto()
{
    CDib& dib = GetDocument()->m_dib;
    CFileDialog dlg(FALSE, "bmp", "*.bmp");
    if (dlg.DoModal() != IDOK) return;

    BeginWaitCursor();
    dib.CopyToMapFile(dlg.GetPathName());
    EndWaitCursor();
}

void CEx26aView::OnEditCut()
{
    OnEditCopy();
    GetDocument()->OnEditClearAll();
}
void CEx26aView::OnEditPaste()
{
    CEx26aDoc* pDoc = GetDocument();
    COleDataObject dataObject;
    VERIFY(dataObject.AttachClipboard());
    DoPasteDib(&dataObject);
    CClientDC dc(this);
    pDoc->m_dib.UsePalette(&dc);
    pDoc->SetModifiedFlag();
    pDoc->UpdateAllViews(NULL);
}

void CEx26aView::OnUpdateEditPaste(CCmdUI* pCmdUI)
{
    COleDataObject dataObject;
    BOOL bAvail = dataObject.AttachClipboard() &&
        dataObject.IsDataAvailable(CF_DIB);
    pCmdUI->Enable(bAvail);
}

void CEx26aView::OnEditPastefrom()
{
    CEx26aDoc* pDoc = GetDocument();
    CFileDialog dlg(TRUE, "bmp", "*.bmp");
    if (dlg.DoModal() != IDOK) return;
    if (pDoc->m_dib.AttachMapFile(dlg.GetPathName(), TRUE)) { // share
        CClientDC dc(this);
        pDoc->m_dib.SetSystemPalette(&dc);
        pDoc->m_dib.UsePalette(&dc);
        pDoc->SetModifiedFlag();
```

```
            pDoc->UpdateAllViews(NULL);
        }
    }

    void CEx26aView::OnPrepareDC(CDC* pDC, CPrintInfo* pInfo)
    {
        // custom MM_LOENGLISH; positive y is down
        if (pDC->IsPrinting()) {
            int nHsize = pDC->GetDeviceCaps(HORZSIZE) * 1000 / 254;
            int nVsize = pDC->GetDeviceCaps(VERTSIZE) * 1000 / 254;
            pDC->SetMapMode(MM_ANISOTROPIC);
            pDC->SetWindowExt(nHsize, nVsize);
            pDC->SetViewportExt(pDC->GetDeviceCaps(HORZRES),
                                pDC->GetDeviceCaps(VERTRES));
        }
        else {
            CScrollView::OnPrepareDC(pDC, pInfo);
        }
    }
    void CEx26aView::OnInitialUpdate()
    {
        SetScrollSizes(MM_TEXT, m_sizeTotal);
        m_tracker.m_nStyle = CRectTracker::solidLine |
            CRectTracker::resizeOutside;
        CScrollView::OnInitialUpdate();
    }


    void CEx26aView::OnLButtonDown(UINT nFlags, CPoint point)
    {
        if (m_tracker.Track(this, point, FALSE, NULL)) {
            CClientDC dc(this);
            OnPrepareDC(&dc);
            m_rectTracker = m_tracker.m_rect;
            dc.DPtoLP(m_rectTracker); // Update logical coordinates
            Invalidate();
        }
    }


    BOOL CEx26aView::OnSetCursor(CWnd* pWnd, UINT nHitTest, UINT message)
    {
        if (m_tracker.SetCursor(pWnd, nHitTest)) {
            return TRUE;
        }
        else {
            return CScrollView::OnSetCursor(pWnd, nHitTest, message);
        }
    }
```

(continued)

707

Figure 26-3. *continued*

```
LONG CEx26aView::OnViewPaletteChanged(UINT wParam, LONG lParam)
{
    TRACE("CEx26aView::OnViewPaletteChanged, HWND = %x, \
        code = %d\n", GetSafeHwnd(), wParam);
    CClientDC dc(this);
    GetDocument()->m_dib.UsePalette(&dc, wParam);
    Invalidate();
    return 0;
}

void CEx26aView::OnSetFocus(CWnd* pOldWnd)
{
    CScrollView::OnSetFocus(pOldWnd);
    AfxGetApp()->m_pMainWnd->SendMessage(WM_PALETTECHANGED,
        (UINT) GetSafeHwnd());
}
```

Several interesting things happen in the view class. In the *DoPasteDib* helper, we can call *GetGlobalData* because we can attach the returned *HGLO-BAL* variable to the document's *CDib* object. If we called *GetData*, we would have to copy the memory block ourselves. The Paste From and Copy To command handlers rely on the memory-mapped file support in the *CDib* class. The *OnPrepareDC* function creates a special printer-mapping mode that is just like MM_LOENGLISH except that positive *y* is down. One pixel on the display corresponds to 0.01 inch on the printer.

MFC Drag and Drop

Drag and drop was the ultimate justification for the data object code you've been looking at. OLE supports this feature with its *IDropSource* and *IDropTarget* interfaces plus some library code that manages the drag-and-drop process. The MFC library offers good drag-and-drop support at the view level, so we'll use it. Be aware that drag-and-drop transfers are immediate and independent of the clipboard. If the user cancels the operation, there's no "memory" of the object being dragged.

Drag-and-drop transfers should work consistently between applications, between windows of the same application, and within a window. When the user starts the operation, the cursor should change to an arrow–rectangle combination. If the user holds down the Ctrl key, the cursor turns into a plus sign (+), which indicates that the object is being copied rather than moved.

MFC also supports drag-and-drop operations for items in compound documents. This is the next level up in MFC OLE support, and it's not covered in this chapter. Look up the OCLIENT example in the online documentation under Visual C++ Samples.

The Source Side of the Transfer

When your source program starts a drag-and-drop operation for a data object, it calls *COleDataSource::DoDragDrop*. This function internally creates an object of MFC class *COleDropSource*, which implements the *IOleDropSource* interface. *DoDragDrop* is one of those functions that don't return for a while. It returns when the user drops the object or cancels the operation or when a specified number of milliseconds have elapsed.

If you're programming drag-and-drop operations to work with a *CRectTracker* object, you should call *DoDragDrop* only when the user clicks <u>inside</u> the tracking rectangle, not on its border. *CRectTracker::HitTest* gives you that information. When you call *DoDragDrop*, you need to set a flag that tells you whether the user is dropping the object into the same view (or document) that it was dragged from.

The Destination Side of the Transfer

If you want to use the MFC library's view class drag-and-drop support, you must add a data member of class *COleDropTarget* to your derived view class. This class implements the *IDropTarget* interface, and it holds an *IDropSource* pointer that links back to the *COleDropSource* object. In your view's *OnInitialUpdate* function, you call the *Register* member function for the embedded *COleDropTarget* object.

After you have made your view a drop target, you must override four *CView* virtual functions, which the framework calls during the drag-and-drop operation. Here's a summary of what they should do, assuming that you're using a tracker.

OnDragEnter	Adjusts the focus rectangle and then calls *OnDragOver*
OnDragOver	Moves the dotted focus rectangle and sets the drop effect (determines cursor shape)
OnDragLeave	Cancels the transfer operation; returns the rectangle to its original position and size
OnDrop	Adjusts the focus rectangle and then calls the *DoPaste* helper function to get formats from the data object

The Drag-and-Drop Sequence

Figure 26-4 illustrates the MFC drag-and-drop process.

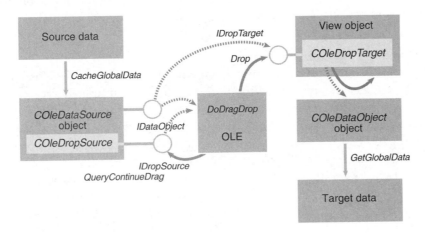

Figure 26-4.
MFC OLE drag-and-drop processing.

Here's a summary of what's going on:

1. User presses the left mouse button in the source view window.

2. Mouse button handler calls *CRectTracker::HitTest* and finds out that the cursor was inside the tracker rectangle.

3. Handler stores formats in a *COleDataSource* object.

4. Handler calls *COleDataSource::DoDragDrop* for the data source.

5. User moves the cursor to the view window of the target application.

6. OLE calls *IDropTarget::OnDragEnter* and *OnDragOver* for the *COleDropTarget* object, which calls the corresponding virtual functions in the target's view. The *OnDragOver* function is passed a *COleDataObject* pointer for the source object, which the target tests for a format it can understand.

7. *OnDragOver* returns a drop effect code, which OLE uses to set the cursor.

8. OLE calls *IDataSource::QueryContinueDrag* on the source side to find out whether the drag operation is still in progress. The MFC *COleDataSource* class responds appropriately.

9. User releases the mouse button to drop the object in the target view window.

10. OLE calls *IDropTarget::OnDrop*, which calls *OnDrop* for the target's view. Because *OnDrop* is passed a *COleDataObject* pointer, it can retrieve the desired format from that object.

11. When *OnDrop* returns in the target program, *DoDragDrop* can return in the source program.

The EX26B Example—OLE Drag and Drop

This example picks up where the EX26A example leaves off. It adds drag-and-drop support, using the existing *SaveDib* and *DoPasteDib* helper functions. All of the clipboard code is the same. You should be able to adapt EX26B to other applications that require drag and drop for data objects.

To prepare EX26B, open the \vcpp32\ex26b\ex26b.dsw workspace and build the project. Run the application, and test drag and drop between child windows and between instances of the program.

The *CEx26bDoc* Class

This class is just like the EX26A version except for an added flag data member, *m_bDragHere*. This flag is *TRUE* when a drag-and-drop operation is in progress for this document. The flag is in the document and not in the view because it is possible to have multiple views attached to the same document. It doesn't make sense to drag a DIB from one view to another when both views reflect the document's *m_dib* member.

The *CEx26bView* Class

To start with, this class has three additional data members and a constructor that initializes all the data members, as shown here:

```
CRect m_rectTrackerEnter; // original logical coordinates
COleDropTarget m_dropTarget;
CSize m_dragOffset; // device coordinates

CEx26bView::CEx26bView() : m_sizeTotal(800, 1050), // 8-by-10.5 inches
                                               //  when printed
    m_rectTracker(50, 50, 250, 250),
    m_dragOffset(0, 0),
    m_rectTrackerEnter(50, 50, 250, 250)
{
}
```

The *OnInitialUpdate* function needs one additional line to register the drop target:

```
m_dropTarget.Register(this);
```

Following are the drag-and-drop virtual override functions. Note that *OnDrop* replaces the DIB only if the document's *m_bDragHere* flag is *TRUE*, so if the user drops the DIB in the same window or in another window connected to the same document, nothing happens.

```
DROPEFFECT CEx26bView::OnDragEnter(COleDataObject* pDataObject,
    DWORD dwKeyState, CPoint point)
{
    TRACE("Entering CEx26bView::OnDragEnter, point = (%d, %d)\n",
        point.x, point.y);
    m_rectTrackerEnter = m_rectTracker; // save original coordinates
                                        // for cursor leaving
                                        // rectangle
    CClientDC dc(this);
    OnPrepareDC(&dc);
    dc.DrawFocusRect(m_rectTracker); // will be erased in OnDragOver
    return OnDragOver(pDataObject, dwKeyState, point);
}

DROPEFFECT CEx26bView::OnDragOver(COleDataObject* pDataObject,
    DWORD dwKeyState, CPoint point)
{
    if (!pDataObject->IsDataAvailable(CF_DIB)) {
        return DROPEFFECT_NONE;
    }
    MoveTrackRect(point);
    if ((dwKeyState & MK_CONTROL) == MK_CONTROL) {
        return DROPEFFECT_COPY;
    }
    // Check for force move
    if ((dwKeyState & MK_ALT) == MK_ALT) {
        return DROPEFFECT_MOVE;
    }
    // default -- recommended action is move
    return DROPEFFECT_MOVE;
}

void CEx26bView::OnDragLeave()
{
    TRACE("Entering CEx26bView::OnDragLeave\n");
    CClientDC dc(this);
```

```
    OnPrepareDC(&dc);
    dc.DrawFocusRect(m_rectTracker);
    m_rectTracker = m_rectTrackerEnter; // Forget it ever happened
}

BOOL CEx26bView::OnDrop(COleDataObject* pDataObject,
    DROPEFFECT dropEffect, CPoint point)
{
    TRACE("Entering CEx26bView::OnDrop --
 dropEffect = %d\n", dropEffect);
    BOOL bRet;
    CEx26bDoc* pDoc = GetDocument();
    MoveTrackRect(point);
    if (pDoc->m_bDragHere) {
        pDoc->m_bDragHere = FALSE;
        bRet = TRUE;
    }
    else {
        bRet = DoPasteDib(pDataObject);
    }
    return bRet;
}
```

The handler for the WM_LBUTTONDOWN message needs substantial overhaul. It must call *DoDragDrop* if the cursor is inside the rectangle and *Track* if it is on the rectangle border. The revised code is shown here:

```
void CEx26bView::OnLButtonDown(UINT nFlags, CPoint point)
{
    CEx26bDoc* pDoc = GetDocument();
    if (m_tracker.HitTest(point) == CRectTracker::hitMiddle) {
        COleDataSource* pSource = SaveDib();
        if (pSource) {
            // DoDragDrop returns only after drop is complete
            CClientDC dc(this);
            OnPrepareDC(&dc);
            CPoint topleft = m_rectTracker.TopLeft();
            dc.LPtoDP(&topleft);
            // 'point' here is not the same as the point parameter in
            //   OnDragEnter, so we use this one to compute the offset
            m_dragOffset = point - topleft;  // device coordinates
            pDoc->m_bDragHere = TRUE;
            DROPEFFECT dropEffect = pSource->DoDragDrop(
                DROPEFFECT_MOVE | DROPEFFECT_COPY, CRect(0, 0, 0, 0));
            TRACE("after DoDragDrop -- dropEffect = %ld\n", dropEffect);
            if (dropEffect == DROPEFFECT_MOVE && pDoc->m_bDragHere) {
```

(continued)

713

```
                pDoc->OnEditClearAll();
            }
            pDoc->m_bDragHere = FALSE;
            delete pSource;
        }
    }
    else {
        if (m_tracker.Track(this, point, FALSE, NULL)) {
            CClientDC dc(this);
            OnPrepareDC(&dc);
            // should have some way to prevent it going out of bounds
            m_rectTracker = m_tracker.m_rect;
            dc.DPtoLP(m_rectTracker); // update logical coordinates
        }
    }
    Invalidate();
}
```

Finally, the new *MoveTrackRect* helper function, shown here, moves the tracker's focus rectangle each time the *OnDragOver* function is called. This job was done by *CRectTracker::Track* in the EX26A example.

```
void CEx26bView::MoveTrackRect(CPoint point)
{
    CClientDC dc(this);
    OnPrepareDC(&dc);
    dc.DrawFocusRect(m_rectTracker);
    dc.LPtoDP(m_rectTracker);
    CSize sizeTrack = m_rectTracker.Size();
    CPoint newTopleft = point - m_dragOffset;  // still device
    m_rectTracker = CRect(newTopleft, sizeTrack);
    m_tracker.m_rect = m_rectTracker;
    dc.DPtoLP(m_rectTracker);
    dc.DrawFocusRect(m_rectTracker);
}
```

Windows Applications and Drag and Drop—Dobjview

I tested EX26B with the Microsoft Office 97 suite. I tried both drag-and-drop and clipboard transfers, with the results shown in the following table.

714

EX26B	Word	Excel	PowerPoint
Sends clipboard data to	x	x (no palettes)	x
Accepts clipboard data from			
Sends drag-drop data to	x		x
Accepts drag-drop data from			

When I started to investigate why these programs were so uncooperative, I discovered a useful OLE utility called Dobjview (*IDataObject* viewer). I could use Dobjview to examine a data object on the clipboard, and I could drag objects to the Dobjview window. Here's what I got when I dragged a picture from Microsoft Excel.

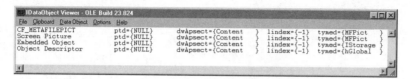

No *CF_DIB* format is present. If you want pictures from Excel, you must enhance EX26B to process metafiles. Another alternative is to rewrite the program with compound document support as described in Chapter 28. The OLE libraries contain code to display bitmaps and metafiles.

Conclusion

As you can see, MFC makes clipboard and drag-and-drop data transfer pretty easy. While you can always write all the code necessary to implement the interfaces (*IDataObject*, *IDropTarget*, and *IDropSource*), using MFC's implementations is much more convenient. While we've looked only at clipboard and drag and drop transfers through *IDataObject* in this chapter, everything you learn about the *IDataObject* interface will carry forward to your study of compound documents in the next chapter.

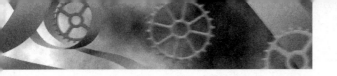

CHAPTER TWENTY SEVEN

Structured Storage

Like Automation and Uniform Data Transfer, structured storage is one of those COM features that you can use effectively by itself. Of course, it's also behind much of the ActiveX technology, particularly compound documents.

In this chapter, you'll learn to write and read compound files with the *IStorage* and *IStream* interfaces. The *IStorage* interface is used to create and manage structured storage objects. *IStream* is used to manipulate the data contained by the storage object. The *IStorage* and *IStream* interfaces, like all COM interfaces, are simply virtual function declarations. Compound files, on the other hand, are implemented by code in the Microsoft Windows OLE32 DLL. Compound files represent a Microsoft file I/O standard that you can think of as "a file system inside a file."

When you're familiar with *IStorage* and *IStream*, you'll move on to the *IPersistStorage* and *IPersistStream* interfaces. With the *IPersistStorage* and *IPersistStream* interfaces, you can program a class to save and load objects to and from a compound file. You say to an object, "Save yourself," and it knows how.

Compound Files

This book discusses four options for file I/O. You can read and write whole sequential files (like the MFC archive files you saw first in Chapter 17). You can use a database management system (as described in Chapters 31 and 32). You can write your own code for random file access. Finally, you can use <u>compound files</u>.

Think of a compound file as a whole file system within a file. Figure 27-1 shows a traditional disk directory as supported by early MS-DOS systems and by Microsoft Windows. This directory is composed of files and subdirectories, with a root directory at the top. Now imagine the same structure inside a single disk file. The files are called <u>streams</u>, and the directories are called <u>storages</u>. Each is identified by a name of up to 32 wide characters in length. A stream is a logically sequential array of bytes, and a storage is a collection of streams and sub-storages.

717

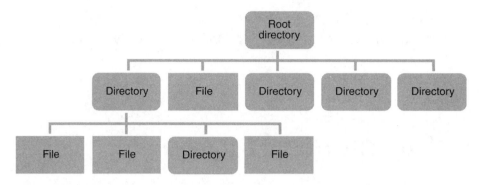

Figure 27-1.
A disk directory with files and subdirectories.

(A storage can contain other storages, just as a directory can contain sub-directories.) In a disk file, the bytes aren't necessarily stored in contiguous clusters. Similarly, the bytes in a stream aren't necessarily contiguous in their compound file. They just appear that way.

> **NOTE:** Storage and stream names cannot contain the characters /, \, :, or !. If the first character has an ASCII value of less than 32, the element is marked as managed by some agent other than the owner.

You can probably think of many applications for a compound file. The classic example is a large document composed of chapters and paragraphs within chapters. The document is so large that you don't want to read the whole thing into memory when your program starts, and you want to be able to insert and delete portions of the document. You could design a compound file with a root storage that contains substorages for chapters. The chapter substorages would contain streams for the paragraphs. Other streams could be for index information.

One useful feature of compound files is <u>transactioning</u>. When you start a transaction for a compound file, all changes are written to a temporary file. The changes are made to your file only when you commit the transaction.

Storages and the *IStorage* Interface

If you have a storage object, you can manipulate it through the *IStorage* interface. Pay attention to these functions because Microsoft Foundation Class offers no support for storage access. Following are some of the important member functions and their significant parameters.

HRESULT Commit(...);

Commits all the changes to this storage and to all elements below it.

HRESULT CopyTo(..., IStorage** *pStgDest*);

Copies a storage, with its name and all its substorages and streams (recursively), to another existing storage. Elements are merged into the target storage, replacing elements with matching names.

HRESULT CreateStorage(const WCHAR* *pName*, ..., DWORD *mode*, ..., IStorage** *ppStg*);

Creates a new substorage under this storage object.

HRESULT CreateStream(const WCHAR* *pName*, ..., DWORD *mode*, ..., IStream** *ppStream*);

Creates a new stream under this storage object.

HRESULT DestroyElement(const WCHAR* *pName*);

Destroys the named storage or stream that is under this storage object. A storage cannot destroy itself.

HRESULT EnumElements(..., IEnumSTATSTG** *ppEnumStatstg*);

Iterates through all the storages and streams under this storage object. The *IEnumSTATSTG* interface has *Next*, *Skip*, and *Clone* member functions, as do other COM enumerator interfaces.

HRESULT MoveElementTo(const WCHAR* *pName*, IStorage* *pStgDest*, const LPWSTR* *pNewName*, DWORD *flags*);

Moves an element from this storage object to another storage object.

HRESULT OpenStream(const WCHAR* *pName*, ..., DWORD *mode*, ..., IStorage** *ppStg*);

Opens an existing stream object, designated by name, under this storage object.

HRESULT OpenStorage(const WCHAR* *pName*, ..., DWORD *mode*, ..., IStorage** *ppStg*);

Opens an existing substorage object, designated by name, under this storage object.

DWORD Release(void);

Decrements the reference count. If the storage is a root storage representing a disk file, *Release* closes the file when the reference count goes to 0.

HRESULT RenameElement(const WCHAR* *pOldName*, const WCHAR* *pNewName*);

Assigns a new name to an existing storage or stream under this storage object.

HRESULT Revert(void);

Abandons a transaction, leaving the compound file unchanged.

HRESULT SetClass(CLSID& *clsid*);

Inserts a 128-bit class identifier into this storage object. This ID can then be retrieved with the *Stat* function.

HRESULT Stat(STATSTG* *pStatstg*, DWORD *flag*);

Fills in a *STATSTG* structure with useful information about the storage object, including its name and class ID.

Getting an *IStorage* Pointer

Where do you get the first *IStorage* pointer? COM gives you the global function *StgCreateDocfile* to create a new structured storage file on disk and the function *StgOpenStorage* to open an existing file. Both of these set a pointer to the file's <u>root</u> storage. Here's some code that opens an existing storage file named MyStore.stg and then creates a new substorage:

```
IStorage* pStgRoot;
IStorage* pSubStg;

if (::StgCreateDocfile(L"MyStore.stg",
    STGM_READWRITE | STGM_SHARE_EXCLUSIVE | STGM_CREATE,
    0, &pStgRoot) == S_OK) {
    if (pStgRoot->CreateStorage(L"MySubstorageName",
        STGM_READWRITE | STGM_SHARE_EXCLUSIVE | STGM_CREATE,
        0, 0, &pSubStg) == S_OK) {
        // Do something with pSubStg
        pSubStg->Release();
    }
    pStgRoot->Release();
}
```

Freeing *STATSTG* Memory

When you call *IStorage::Stat* with a *STATFLAG_DEFAULT* value for the flag parameter, COM allocates memory for the element name. You must free this memory in a manner compatible with its allocation. COM has its own allocation system that uses an <u>allocator</u> <u>object</u> with an *IMalloc* interface. You must get an

IMalloc pointer from COM, call *IMalloc::Free* for the string, and then release the allocator. The code below illustrates this.

If you want just the element size and type and not the name, you can call *Stat* with the *STATFLAG_NONAME* flag. In that case, no memory is allocated and you don't have to free it. This seems like an irritating detail, but if you don't follow the recipe, you'll have a memory leak.

Enumerating the Elements in a Storage Object

Following is some code that iterates through all the elements under a storage object, differentiating between substorages and streams. The elements are retrieved in a seemingly random sequence, independent of the sequence in which they were created; however, I've found that streams are always retrieved first. The *IEnumSTATSTG::Next* element fills in a *STATSTG* structure that tells you whether the element is a stream or a storage object.

```
IEnumSTATSTG* pEnum;
IMalloc* pMalloc;
STATSTG statstg;
extern IStorage* pStg;  // maybe from OpenStorage
::CoGetMalloc(MEMCTX_TASK, &pMalloc); // assumes AfxOleInit called
VERIFY(pStg->EnumElements(0, NULL, 0, &pEnum) == S_OK)
while (pEnum->Next(1, &statstg, NULL) == NOERROR) {
    if (statstg.type == STGTY_STORAGE) {
        if (pStg->OpenStorage(statstg.pwcsName, NULL,
            STGM_READ | STGM_SHARE_EXCLUSIVE,
            NULL, 0, &pSubStg) == S_OK) {
            // Do something with the substorage
        }
        else if (statstg.type == STGTY_STREAM) {
            // Process the stream
        }
        pMalloc->Free(statstg.pwcsName); // avoids memory leaks
    }
    pMalloc->Release();
}
```

Sharing Storages Among Processes

If you pass an *IStorage* pointer to another process, the marshaling code ensures that the other process can access the corresponding storage element and everything below it. This is a convenient way of sharing part of a file. One of the standard data object media types of the *TYMED* enumeration is *TYMED_ISTORAGE*, and this means you can pass an *IStorage* pointer on the clipboard or through a drag-and-drop operation.

Streams and the *IStream* Interface

If you have a stream object, you can manipulate it through the *IStream* interface. Streams are always located under a root storage or a substorage object. Streams grow automatically (in 512-byte increments) as you write to them. An MFC class for streams, *COleStreamFile*, makes a stream look like a *CFile* object. That class won't be of much use to us in this chapter, however.

Once you have a pointer to *IStream*, a number of functions are available to you for manipulating the stream. Here is a list of all the *IStream* functions:

HRESULT CopyTo(IStream** *pStm*, ULARGE_INTEGER *cb*, ...);
Copies *cb* bytes from this stream to the named stream. *ULARGE_INTEGER* is a structure with two 32-bit members—*HighPart* and *LowPart*.

HRESULT Clone(IStream** *ppStm*);
Creates a new stream object with its own seek pointer that references the bytes in this stream. The bytes are not copied, so changes in one stream are visible in the other.

HRESULT Commit(...);
Transactions are not currently implemented for streams.

HRESULT Read(void const* *pv*, ULONG *cb*, ULONG* *pcbRead*);
Tries to read *cb* bytes from this stream into the buffer pointed to by *pv*. The variable *pcbRead* indicates how many bytes were actually read.

DWORD Release(void);
Closes this stream.

HRESULT Revert(void);
Has no effect for streams.

HRESULT Seek(LARGE_INTEGER *dlibMove*, DWORD *dwOrigin*, ULARGE_INTEGER* *NewPosition*);
Seeks to the specified position in this stream. The *dwOrigin* parameter specifies the origin of the offset defined in the *NewPosition* parameter.

HRESULT SetSize(ULARGE_INTEGER *libNewSize*);
Extends or truncates a stream. Streams grow automatically as they are written, but calling *SetSize* can optimize performance.

HRESULT Stat(STATSTG* *pStatstg*, DWORD *flag*);

Fills in the *STATSTG* structure with useful information about the stream, including the stream name and size. The size is useful if you need to allocate memory for a read.

HRESULT Write(void const* *pv*, ULONG *cb*, ULONG* *pcbWritten*);

Tries to write *cb* bytes to this stream from the buffer pointed to by *pv*. The variable *pcbWritten* indicates how many bytes were actually written.

IStream Programming

Here is some sample code that creates a stream under a given storage object and writes some bytes from *m_buffer* to the stream:

```
extern IStorage* pStg;
IStream* pStream;
ULONG nBytesWritten;

if (pStg->CreateStream(L"MyStreamName",
    STGM_CREATE | STGM_READWRITE | STGM_SHARE_EXCLUSIVE,
    0, 0, &pStream) == S_OK) {
    ASSERT(pStream != NULL);
    pStream->Write(m_buffer, m_nLength, &nBytesWritten);
    pStream->Release();
}
```

The *ILockBytes* Interface

As already mentioned, the compound file system you've been looking at is implemented in the OLE32 DLL. The structured storage interfaces are flexible enough, however, to permit you to change the underlying implementation. The key to this flexibility is the *ILockBytes* interface. The *StgCreateDocfile* and *StgOpenStorage* global functions use the default Windows file system. You can write your own file access code that implements the *ILockBytes* interface and then call *StgCreateDocfileOnILockBytes* or *StgOpenStorageOnILockBytes* to create or open the file, instead of calling the other global functions.

Rather than implement your own *ILockBytes* interface, you can call *CreateILockBytesOnHGlobal* to create a compound file in RAM. If you wanted to put compound files inside a database, you would implement an *ILockBytes* interface that used the database's <u>blobs</u> (binary large objects).

The EX27A Example—Structured Storage

When you choose the Storage Write option in the EX27A example, the program walks through your entire disk directory looking for TXT files. As it looks, it writes a compound file (\direct.stg) on the top level of your directory structure. This file contains storages that match your subdirectories. For each TXT file that the program finds in a subdirectory, it copies the first line of text to a stream in the corresponding storage. When you choose the Storage Read option, the program reads the direct.stg compound file and prints the contents of this file in the Debug window.

If you create such an example from scratch, use AppWizard without any ActiveX or Automation options and then add the following lines in your StdAfx.h file:

```
#include <afxole.h>
#include <afxpriv.h> // for wide-character conversion
```

Then delete the following line:

```
#define VC_EXTRALEAN
```

To prepare EX27A, open the \vcpp32\ex27a\ex27a.dsw workspace and build the project. Run the program from the debugger. First choose Write from the Storage menu and wait for a "Write complete" message box. Then choose Read. Observe the output in the Debug window.

The Menu

The EX27A example has an added top-level Storage menu with Write and Read options.

The *CEx27aView* Class

This class maps the new Storage Read and Write menu commands listed above to start worker threads. The handlers are shown here:

```
void CEx27aView::OnStorageRead()
{
    CWinThread* pThread = AfxBeginThread(ReadThreadProc, GetSafeHwnd());
}


void CEx27aView::OnStorageWrite()
{
    CWinThread* pThread = AfxBeginThread(WriteThreadProc, GetSafeHwnd());
}
```

The Worker Threads

Figure 27-2 lists the code for the Storage Write and Storage Read worker threads.

THREAD.H

```
extern int g_nIndent;
extern const char* g_szBlanks;
extern const char* g_szRootStorageName;

UINT WriteThreadProc(LPVOID pParam);
UINT ReadThreadProc(LPVOID pParam);
void ReadDirectory(const char* szPath, LPSTORAGE pStg);
void ReadStorage(LPSTORAGE pStg);
```

WRITETHREAD.CPP

```
#include "StdAfx.h"
#include "Thread.h"

int g_nIndent = 0;
const char* g_szBlanks = "                                 ";
const char* g_szRootStorageName = "\\direct.stg";

UINT WriteThreadProc(LPVOID pParam)
{
    USES_CONVERSION;
    LPSTORAGE pStgRoot = NULL;
    g_nIndent = 0;
    VERIFY(::StgCreateDocfile(T2COLE(g_szRootStorageName),
            STGM_READWRITE | STGM_SHARE_EXCLUSIVE | STGM_CREATE,
            0, &pStgRoot) == S_OK);
    ReadDirectory("\\", pStgRoot);
    pStgRoot->Release();
    AfxMessageBox("Write complete");
    return 0;
}

void ReadDirectory(const char* szPath, LPSTORAGE pStg)
{
    // recursive function
    USES_CONVERSION;
    WIN32_FIND_DATA fData;
    HANDLE h;
    char szNewPath[MAX_PATH];
    char szStorageName[100];
```

Figure 27-2. *(continued)*

The Storage menu worker threads.

Figure 27-2. *continued*

```
char szStreamName[100];
char szData[81];
char* pch = NULL;
LPSTORAGE pSubStg = NULL;
LPSTREAM pStream = NULL;

g_nIndent++;
strcpy(szNewPath, szPath);
strcat(szNewPath, "*.*");
h = ::FindFirstFile(szNewPath, &fData);
if (h == (HANDLE) 0xFFFFFFFF) return;  // can't find directory
do {
    if (!strcmp(fData.cFileName, "..") ||
        !strcmp(fData.cFileName, ".") ) continue;
    while((pch = strchr(fData.cFileName, '!')) != NULL) {
        *pch = '|';
    }
    if (fData.dwFileAttributes & FILE_ATTRIBUTE_DIRECTORY) {
        // It's a directory, so make a storage
        strcpy(szNewPath, szPath);
        strcat(szNewPath, fData.cFileName);
        strcat(szNewPath, "\\");

        strcpy(szStorageName, fData.cFileName);
        szStorageName[31] = '\0';    // limit imposed by OLE
        TRACE("%0.*sStorage = %s\n", (g_nIndent - 1) * 4,
            g_szBlanks, szStorageName);
        VERIFY(pStg->CreateStorage(T2COLE(szStorageName),
            STGM_CREATE | STGM_READWRITE | STGM_SHARE_EXCLUSIVE,
            0, 0, &pSubStg) == S_OK);
        ASSERT(pSubStg != NULL);
        ReadDirectory(szNewPath, pSubStg);
        pSubStg->Release();
    }
    else {
        if ((pch = strrchr(fData.cFileName, '.')) != NULL) {
            if (!stricmp(pch, ".TXT")) {
                // It's a text file, so make a stream
                strcpy(szStreamName, fData.cFileName);
                strcpy(szNewPath, szPath);
                strcat(szNewPath, szStreamName);
                szStreamName[32] = '\0'; // OLE max length
                TRACE("%0.*sStream = %s\n", (g_nIndent - 1) * 4,
                    g_szBlanks, szNewPath);
                CStdioFile file(szNewPath, CFile::modeRead);
                // Ignore zero-length files
```

```
                    if(file.ReadString(szData, 80)) {
                        TRACE("%s\n", szData);
                        VERIFY(pStg->CreateStream(T2COLE(szStreamName),
                            STGM_CREATE | STGM_READWRITE |
                            STGM_SHARE_EXCLUSIVE,
                            0, 0, &pStream) == S_OK);
                        ASSERT(pStream != NULL);
                        // Include the null terminator in the stream
                        pStream->Write(szData, strlen(szData) + 1, NULL);
                        pStream->Release();
                    }
                }
            }
        }
    } while (::FindNextFile(h, &fData));
    g_nIndent--;
}
```

READTHREAD.CPP

```
#include "StdAfx.h"
#include "Thread.h"

UINT ReadThreadProc(LPVOID pParam)
{
    USES_CONVERSION;
    LPSTORAGE pStgRoot = NULL;
    // doesn't work without STGM_SHARE_EXCLUSIVE
    g_nIndent = 0;
    if (::StgOpenStorage(T2COLE(g_szRootStorageName), NULL,
        STGM_READ | STGM_SHARE_EXCLUSIVE,
        NULL, 0, &pStgRoot) == S_OK) {
        ASSERT(pStgRoot!= NULL);
        ReadStorage(pStgRoot);
        pStgRoot->Release();
    }
    else {
        AfxMessageBox("Storage file not available or not readable.");
    }
    AfxMessageBox("Read complete");
    return 0;
}


void ReadStorage(LPSTORAGE pStg)
// reads one storage -- recursive calls for substorages
```

(continued)

Figure 27-2. *continued*

```
{
    USES_CONVERSION;
    LPSTORAGE pSubStg = NULL;
    LPSTREAM pStream = NULL;
    LPENUMSTATSTG pEnum = NULL;
    LPMALLOC pMalloc = NULL; // for freeing statstg
    STATSTG statstg;
    ULONG nLength;
    BYTE buffer[101];

    g_nIndent++;
    ::CoGetMalloc(MEMCTX_TASK, &pMalloc); // assumes AfxOleInit
                                          //  was called
    VERIFY(pStg->EnumElements(0, NULL, 0, &pEnum) == S_OK);
    while (pEnum->Next(1, &statstg, NULL) == S_OK) {
        if (statstg.type == STGTY_STORAGE) {
            VERIFY(pStg->OpenStorage(statstg.pwcsName, NULL,
                    STGM_READ | STGM_SHARE_EXCLUSIVE,
                    NULL, 0, &pSubStg) == S_OK);
            ASSERT(pSubStg != NULL);
            TRACE("%0.*sStorage = %s\n", (g_nIndent - 1) * 4,
                    g_szBlanks, OLE2CT(statstg.pwcsName));
            ReadStorage(pSubStg);
            pSubStg->Release();
        }
        else if (statstg.type == STGTY_STREAM) {
            VERIFY(pStg->OpenStream(statstg.pwcsName, NULL,
                    STGM_READ | STGM_SHARE_EXCLUSIVE,
                    0, &pStream) == S_OK);
            ASSERT(pStream != NULL);
            TRACE("%0.*sStream = %s\n", (g_nIndent - 1) * 4,
                    g_szBlanks, OLE2CT(statstg.pwcsName));
            pStream->Read(buffer, 100, &nLength);
            buffer[nLength] = '\0';
            TRACE("%s\n", buffer);
            pStream->Release();
        }
        else {
            ASSERT(FALSE);   // LockBytes?
        }
        pMalloc->Free(statstg.pwcsName); // avoids memory leaks
    }
    pMalloc->Release();
    pEnum->Release();
    g_nIndent--;
}
```

To keep the program simple, there's no synchronization between the main thread and the two worker threads. You could run both threads at the same time if you used two separate compound files.

From your study of the Win32 threading model, you might expect that closing the main window would cause the read thread or write thread to terminate "midstream," possibly causing memory leaks. But this does not happen because MFC senses that the worker threads are using COM objects. Even though the window closes immediately, the program does not exit until all threads exit.

Both threads use recursive functions. The *ReadStorage* function reads a storage and calls itself to read the substorages. The *ReadDirectory* function reads a directory and calls itself to read the subdirectories. This function calls the Win32 functions *FindFirstFile* and *FindNextFile* to iterate through the elements in a directory. The *dwFileAttributes* member of the *WIN32_FIND_DATA* structure indicates whether the element is a file or a subdirectory. *ReadDirectory* uses the MFC *CStdioFile* class because the class is ideal for reading text.

The *USES_CONVERSION* macro is necessary to support the wide-character conversion macros *OLE2CT* and *T2COLE*. These macros are used here because the example doesn't use the *CString* class, which has built-in conversion logic.

Structured Storage and Persistent COM Objects

The EX27A program explicitly called member functions of *IStorage* and *IStream* to write and read a compound file. In the object-oriented world, objects should know how to save and load themselves to and from a compound file. That's what the *IPersistStorage* and *IPersistStream* interfaces are for. If a COM component implements these interfaces, a container program can "connect" the object to a compound file by passing the file's *IStorage* pointer as a parameter to the *Save* and *Load* member functions of the *IPersistStorage* interface. Such objects are said to be <u>persistent</u>. Figure 27-3 on the following page shows the process of calling the *IPersistStorage::Save* function.

A COM component is more likely to work with an *IStorage* interface than an *IStream* interface. If the COM object is associated with a particular storage, the COM component can manage substorages and streams under that storage once it gets the *IStorage* pointer. A COM component uses the *IStream* interface only if it stores all its data in an array of bytes. ActiveX controls implement the *IStream* interface for storing and loading property values.

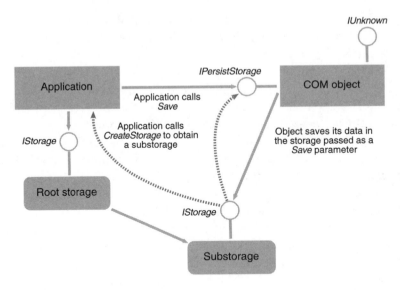

Figure 27-3.
Calling IPersistStorage::Save.

The *IPersistStorage* Interface

Both the *IPersistStorage* and *IPersistStream* interfaces are derived from *IPersist*, which contributes the *GetClassID* member function. Here's a summary of the *IPersistStorage* member functions:

HRESULT GetClassID(CLSID* *pClsid*);

Returns the COM component's 128-bit class identifier.

HRESULT InitNew(IStorage* *pStg*);

Initializes a newly created object. The component might need to use the storage for temporary data, so the container must provide an *IStorage* pointer that's valid for the life of the object. The component should call *AddRef* if it intends to use the storage. The component should not use this *IStorage* pointer for saving and loading; it should wait for *Save* and *Load* calls and then use the passed-in *IStorage* pointer to call *IStorage::Write* and *Read*.

HRESULT IsDirty(void);

Returns *S_OK* if the object has changed since it was last saved; otherwise, returns *S_FALSE*.

HRESULT Load(IStorage* *pStg*);

Loads the COM object's data from the designated storage.

HRESULT Save(IStorage* *pStg*, BOOL *fSameAsLoad*);

Saves the COM object's data in the designated storage.

The *IPersistStream* Interface

Here's a summary of the *IPersistStream* member functions:

HRESULT GetClassID(CLSID* *pClsid*);

Returns the COM component's 128-bit class identifier.

HRESULT GetMaxSize(ULARGE_INTEGER* *pcbSize*);

Returns the number of bytes needed to save the object.

HRESULT IsDirty(void);

Returns *S_OK* if the object has changed since it was last saved; otherwise, returns *S_FALSE*.

HRESULT Load(IStream* *pStm*);

Loads the COM object's data from the designated stream.

HRESULT Save(IStream* *pStm*, BOOL *fClearDirty*);

Saves the COM object's data to the designated stream. If the *fClearDirty* parameter is *TRUE*, *Save* clears the object's dirty flag.

IPersistStream Programming

The following container program code fragment creates a stream and saves a COM object's data in it. Both the *IPersistStream* pointer for the COM object and the *IStorage* pointer are set elsewhere.

```
extern IStorage* pStg;
extern IPersistStream* pPersistStream;
IStream* pStream;
if (pStg->CreateStream(L"MyStreamName",
    STGM_CREATE | STGM_READWRITE | STGM_SHARE_EXCLUSIVE,
    0, 0, &pStream) == S_OK) {
    ASSERT(pStream != NULL);
    pPersistStream->Save(pStream, TRUE);
    pStream->Release();
}
```

If you program your own COM class for use in a container, you'll need to use the MFC interface macros to add the *IPersistStream* interface. Too bad there's not an "interface wizard" to do the job.

The EX27B Example—
A Persistent DLL Component

The EX27B program, which is used by EX27C, is a COM DLL that contains the *CText* component. This is a simple COM class that implements the *IDispatch* and *IPersistStream* interfaces. The *IDispatch* interface allows access to the component's one and only property, Text, and the *IPersistStream* interface allows an object to save and load that Text property to and from a structured storage file.

To prepare EX27B, open the \vcpp32\ex27b\ex27b.dsw workspace and build the project. Use regsvr32 or REGCOMP to register the DLL.

Figure 27-4 lists the code for the *CText* class in Text.h and Text.cpp.

TEXT.H

```
#ifndef __TEXT_H__
#define __TEXT_H__
// CText command target
class CText : public CCmdTarget
{
private:
    char* m_pchText;

    DECLARE_DYNCREATE(CText)

    CText();            // protected constructor used by dynamic creation

// Attributes
public:

// Operations
public:

// Overrides
    // ClassWizard generated virtual function overrides
    //{{AFX_VIRTUAL(CText)
    public:
    virtual void OnFinalRelease();
    //}}AFX_VIRTUAL

// Implementation
protected:
    virtual ~CText();
// Generated message map functions
```

Figure 27-4. *(continued)*

The code listing for the CText *class in Text.h and Text.cpp.*

```
    //{{AFX_MSG(CText)
        // NOTE the ClassWizard will add and remove member functions here.
    //}}AFX_MSG

    DECLARE_MESSAGE_MAP()
    DECLARE_OLECREATE(CText)

    // Generated OLE dispatch map functions
    //{{AFX_DISPATCH(CText)
    afx_msg VARIANT GetText();
    afx_msg void SetText(const VARIANT FAR& newValue);
    //}}AFX_DISPATCH
    DECLARE_DISPATCH_MAP()
    DECLARE_INTERFACE_MAP()

    BEGIN_INTERFACE_PART(PersistStream, IPersistStream)
        STDMETHOD(GetClassID)(LPCLSID);
        STDMETHOD(IsDirty)();
        STDMETHOD(Load)(LPSTREAM);
        STDMETHOD(Save)(LPSTREAM, BOOL);
        STDMETHOD(GetSizeMax)(ULARGE_INTEGER FAR*);
    END_INTERFACE_PART(PersistStream)
};


/////////////////////////////////////////////////////////////////////
//{{AFX_INSERT_LOCATION}}
// Microsoft Visual C++ will insert additional declarations
//   immediately before the previous line.

#endif // __TEXT_H__
```

TEXT.CPP

```
#include "stdafx.h"
#include "ex27b.h"
#include "Text.h"

#ifdef _DEBUG
#define new DEBUG_NEW
#undef THIS_FILE
static char THIS_FILE[] =__FILE__;
#endif
/////////////////////////////////////////////////////////////////////
// CText

IMPLEMENT_DYNCREATE(CText, CCmdTarget)
```

(continued)

Figure 27-4. *continued*

```
CText::CText()
{
    EnableAutomation();

    // To keep the application running as long as an OLE automation
    //  object is active, the constructor calls AfxOleLockApp.

    AfxOleLockApp();
    m_pchText = NULL;
}


CText::~CText()
{
    // To terminate the application when all objects created
    //  with OLE automation, the destructor calls AfxOleUnlockApp.

    if(m_pchText != NULL) {
        delete [] m_pchText;
    }
    AfxOleUnlockApp();
}


void CText::OnFinalRelease()
{
    // When the last reference for an automation object is released,
    //  OnFinalRelease is called. The base class will automatically
    //  delete the object. Add additional cleanup required for your
    //  object before calling the base class.

    CCmdTarget::OnFinalRelease();
}


BEGIN_MESSAGE_MAP(CText, CCmdTarget)
    //{{AFX_MSG_MAP(CText)
        // NOTE - ClassWizard will add and remove mapping macros here.
    //}}AFX_MSG_MAP
END_MESSAGE_MAP()
BEGIN_DISPATCH_MAP(CText, CCmdTarget)
    //{{AFX_DISPATCH_MAP(CText)
    DISP_PROPERTY_EX(CText, "Text", GetText, SetText, VT_VARIANT)
    //}}AFX_DISPATCH_MAP
END_DISPATCH_MAP()

// Note: we add support for IID_IText to support typesafe binding
//  from VBA. This IID must match the GUID that is attached to the
//  dispinterface in the ODL file.
```

```
// {4EBFDD71-5F7D-11D0-848F-00400526305B}
static const IID IID_IText =
{ 0x4ebfdd71, 0x5f7d, 0x11d0, { 0x84, 0x8f, 0x0, 0x40, 0x5, 0x26,
    0x30, 0x5b } };

BEGIN_INTERFACE_MAP(CText, CCmdTarget)
    INTERFACE_PART(CText, IID_IPersistStream, PersistStream)
    INTERFACE_PART(CText, IID_IText, Dispatch)
END_INTERFACE_MAP()

// {4EBFDD72-5F7D-11D0-848F-00400526305B}
IMPLEMENT_OLECREATE(CText, "Ex27b.Text", 0x4ebfdd72, 0x5f7d,
    0x11d0, 0x84, 0x8f, 0x0, 0x40, 0x5, 0x26, 0x30, 0x5b)

/////////////////////////////////////////////////////////////////////
// CText message handlers

VARIANT CText::GetText()
{
    return COleVariant(m_pchText).Detach();
}

void CText::SetText(const VARIANT FAR& newValue)
{
    CString strTemp;
    ASSERT(newValue.vt == VT_BSTR);
    if(m_pchText != NULL) {
        delete [] m_pchText;
    }
    strTemp = newValue.bstrVal; // converts to narrow chars
    m_pchText = new char[strTemp.GetLength() + 1];
    strcpy(m_pchText, strTemp);
}
/////////////////////////////////////////////////////////////////////

STDMETHODIMP_(ULONG) CText::XPersistStream::AddRef()
{
    METHOD_PROLOGUE(CText, PersistStream)
    return (ULONG) pThis->ExternalAddRef();
}

STDMETHODIMP_(ULONG) CText::XPersistStream::Release()
{
    METHOD_PROLOGUE(CText, PersistStream)
    return (ULONG) pThis->ExternalRelease();
}
```

(continued)

Figure 27-4. *continued*

```
STDMETHODIMP CText::XPersistStream::QueryInterface(REFIID iid,
    void FAR* FAR* ppvObj)
{
    METHOD_PROLOGUE(CText, PersistStream)
    // ExternalQueryInterface looks up IID in the macro-generated tables
    return (HRESULT) pThis->ExternalQueryInterface(&iid, ppvObj);
}
/////////////////////////////////////////////////////////////////////

STDMETHODIMP CText::XPersistStream::GetClassID(LPCLSID lpClassID)
{
    TRACE("Entering CText::XPersistStream::GetClassID\n");
    METHOD_PROLOGUE(CText, PersistStream)
    ASSERT_VALID(pThis);

    *lpClassID = CText::guid;
    return NOERROR;
}

STDMETHODIMP CText::XPersistStream::IsDirty()
{
    TRACE("Entering CText::XPersistStream::IsDirty\n");
    METHOD_PROLOGUE(CText, PersistStream)
    ASSERT_VALID(pThis);

    return NOERROR;
}
STDMETHODIMP CText::XPersistStream::Load(LPSTREAM pStm)
{
    ULONG nLength;
    STATSTG statstg;
    METHOD_PROLOGUE(CText, PersistStream)
    ASSERT_VALID(pThis);
    if(pThis->m_pchText != NULL) {
        delete [] pThis->m_pchText;
    }
    // don't need to free statstg.pwcsName because of NONAME flag
    VERIFY(pStm->Stat(&statstg, STATFLAG_NONAME) == NOERROR);
    int nSize = statstg.cbSize.LowPart; // assume < 4 GB
    if(nSize > 0) {
        pThis->m_pchText = new char[nSize];
        pStm->Read(pThis->m_pchText, nSize, &nLength);
    }
    return NOERROR;
}
```

```
STDMETHODIMP CText::XPersistStream::Save(LPSTREAM pStm, BOOL fClearDirty)
{
    METHOD_PROLOGUE(CText, PersistStream)
    ASSERT_VALID(pThis);
    int nSize = strlen(pThis->m_pchText) + 1;
    pStm->Write(pThis->m_pchText, nSize, NULL);
    return NOERROR;
}

STDMETHODIMP CText::XPersistStream::GetSizeMax(ULARGE_INTEGER FAR* pcbSize)
{
    TRACE("Entering CText::XPersistStream::GetSizeMax\n");
    METHOD_PROLOGUE(CText, PersistStream)
    ASSERT_VALID(pThis);
    pcbSize->LowPart = strlen(pThis->m_pchText) + 1;
    pcbSize->HighPart = 0; // assume < 4 GB
    return NOERROR;
}
```

ClassWizard generated the *CText* class as an ordinary Automation component. The *IPersistStream* interface was added manually. Look carefully at the *XPersistStream::Load* and *XPersistStream::Save* functions. The *Load* function allocates heap memory and then calls *IStream::Read* to load the contents of the stream. The *Save* function copies the object's data to the stream by calling *IStream::Write*.

The EX27C Example—
A Persistent Storage Client Program

This program is similar to EX27A in function—indeed, the storage files are compatible. Internally, however, both worker threads use the persistent COM class *CText* (EX27B) for loading and storing text.

To prepare EX27C, open the \vcpp32\ex27c\ex27c.dsw workspace and build the project. Run the program from the debugger, first choosing Write from the Storage menu and then choosing Read. Observe the output in the Debug window.

The menu, the view class, and the application class are the same as the EX27A versions. Only the thread code is different.

Figure 27-5 on the following page lists the code for both the Write-Thread.cpp and the ReadThread.cpp files.

WRITETHREAD.CPP

```
#include "StdAfx.h"
#include "Thread.h"
#include "itext.h"

CLSID g_clsid; // for the Text server
int g_nIndent = 0;
const char* g_szBlanks = "                        ";
const char* g_szRootStorageName = "\\direct.stg";

UINT WriteThreadProc(LPVOID pParam)
{
    USES_CONVERSION;
    LPSTORAGE pStgRoot = NULL;
    g_nIndent = 0;
    ::CoInitialize(NULL);
    ::CLSIDFromProgID(L"EX27B.TEXT", &g_clsid);
    VERIFY(::StgCreateDocfile(T2COLE(g_szRootStorageName),
            STGM_READWRITE | STGM_SHARE_EXCLUSIVE | STGM_CREATE,
            0, &pStgRoot) == S_OK);
    ReadDirectory("\\", pStgRoot);
    pStgRoot->Release();
    AfxMessageBox("Write complete");
    return 0;
}
void ReadDirectory(const char* szPath, LPSTORAGE pStg)
{
    // recursive function
    USES_CONVERSION;
    WIN32_FIND_DATA fData;
    HANDLE h;
    char szNewPath[MAX_PATH];
    char szStorageName[100];
    char szStreamName[100];
    char szData[81];
    char* pch = NULL;

    LPSTORAGE pSubStg = NULL;
    LPSTREAM pStream = NULL;
    LPPERSISTSTREAM pPersistStream = NULL;

    g_nIndent++;
    strcpy(szNewPath, szPath);
    strcat(szNewPath, "*.*");
    h = ::FindFirstFile(szNewPath, &fData);
```

Figure 27-5. *(continued)*
The code listing for the two worker threads in EX27C.

```
if (h == (HANDLE) 0xFFFFFFFF) return;  // can't find directory
do {
        if (!strcmp(fData.cFileName, "..") ||
            !strcmp(fData.cFileName, ".") ) continue;
        while((pch = strchr(fData.cFileName, '!')) != NULL) {
            *pch = '|';
        }
    }
    if (fData.dwFileAttributes & FILE_ATTRIBUTE_DIRECTORY) {
        // It's a directory, so make a storage
        strcpy(szNewPath, szPath);
        strcat(szNewPath,fData.cFileName);
        strcat(szNewPath, "\\");

        strcpy(szStorageName, fData.cFileName);
        szStorageName[31] = '\0';    // limit imposed by OLE
        TRACE("%0.*sStorage = %s\n", (g_nIndent - 1) * 4,
            g_szBlanks, szStorageName);
        VERIFY(pStg->CreateStorage(T2COLE(szStorageName),
            STGM_CREATE | STGM_READWRITE | STGM_SHARE_EXCLUSIVE,
            0, 0, &pSubStg) == S_OK);
        ASSERT(pSubStg != NULL);
        ReadDirectory(szNewPath, pSubStg);
        pSubStg->Release();
    }
    else {
        if ((pch = strrchr(fData.cFileName, '.')) != NULL) {
            if (!stricmp(pch, ".TXT")) {
                // It's a text file, so make a stream
                strcpy(szStreamName, fData.cFileName);
                strcpy(szNewPath, szPath);
                strcat(szNewPath, szStreamName);
                szStreamName[32] = '\0'; // OLE max length
                TRACE("%0.*sStream = %s\n", (g_nIndent - 1) * 4,
                    g_szBlanks, szNewPath);
                CStdioFile file(szNewPath, CFile::modeRead);
                // Ignore zero-length files
                if(file.ReadString(szData, 80)) {
                    TRACE("%s\n", szData);
                    VERIFY(pStg->CreateStream(T2COLE(szStreamName),
                        STGM_CREATE | STGM_READWRITE |
                        STGM_SHARE_EXCLUSIVE,
                        0, 0, &pStream) == S_OK);
                    ASSERT(pStream != NULL);
                    // Include the null terminator in the stream
                    IText text;
                    VERIFY(text.CreateDispatch(g_clsid));
```

(continued)

739

Figure 27-5. *continued*

```
                                    text.m_lpDispatch->QueryInterface
                                        (IID_IPersistStream,
                                        (void**) &pPersistStream);
                                    ASSERT(pPersistStream != NULL);
                                    text.SetText(COleVariant(szData));
                                    pPersistStream->Save(pStream, TRUE);
                                    pPersistStream->Release();
                                    pStream->Release();
                    }
                }
            }
        }
    } while (::FindNextFile(h, &fData));
    g_nIndent--;
}
```

READTHREAD.CPP

```
#include "StdAfx.h"
#include "Thread.h"
#include "itext.h"

#ifdef _DEBUG
#define new DEBUG_NEW
#undef THIS_FILE
static char THIS_FILE[] = __FILE__;
#endif


UINT ReadThreadProc(LPVOID pParam)
{
    g_nIndent = 0;
    ::CoInitialize(NULL);
    ::CLSIDFromProgID(L"EX27B.TEXT", &g_clsid);
    LPSTORAGE pStgRoot = NULL;
    if(::StgOpenStorage(L"\\DIRECT.STG", NULL,
                        STGM_READ|STGM_SHARE_EXCLUSIVE,
                        NULL, 0, &pStgRoot) == S_OK) {
        ASSERT(pStgRoot!= NULL);
        ReadStorage(pStgRoot);
        pStgRoot->Release();
    }
    else {
        AfxMessageBox("Storage file not available or not readable.");
    }
    AfxMessageBox("Read complete");
    return 0;
}
```

```
void ReadStorage(LPSTORAGE pStg)
// reads one storage -- recursive calls for substorages
{
    LPSTORAGE pSubStg = NULL;
    LPSTREAM pStream = NULL;
    LPENUMSTATSTG pEnum = NULL;
    STATSTG statstg;
    LPPERSISTSTREAM pPersistStream = NULL;

    g_nIndent++;
    if(pStg->EnumElements(0, NULL, 0, &pEnum) != NOERROR) {
        ASSERT(FALSE);
        return;
    }
    while(pEnum->Next(1, &statstg, NULL) == NOERROR) {
        if(statstg.type == STGTY_STORAGE) {
            VERIFY(pStg->OpenStorage(statstg.pwcsName, NULL,
                    STGM_READ|STGM_SHARE_EXCLUSIVE,
                    NULL, 0, &pSubStg) == S_OK);
            ASSERT(pSubStg != NULL);
            ReadStorage(pSubStg);
            pSubStg->Release();
        }
        else if(statstg.type == STGTY_STREAM) {
            VERIFY(pStg->OpenStream(statstg.pwcsName, NULL,
                    STGM_READ|STGM_SHARE_EXCLUSIVE,
                    0, &pStream) == S_OK);
            ASSERT(pStream != NULL);
            IText text;
            VERIFY(text.CreateDispatch(g_clsid));
            text.m_lpDispatch->QueryInterface(IID_IPersistStream,
                (void**) &pPersistStream);
            ASSERT(pPersistStream != NULL);
            pPersistStream->Load(pStream);
            pPersistStream->Release();
            COleVariant va = text.GetText();
            ASSERT(va.vt == VT_BSTR);
            CString str = va.bstrVal;
            TRACE("%s\n", str);
            pStream->Release();
        }
        else {
            ASSERT(FALSE);  // LockBytes?
        }
        ::CoTaskMemFree(statstg.pwcsName);
    }
    pEnum->Release();
    g_nIndent--;
}
```

Look at the second half of the *ReadDirectory* function in the WriteThread.cpp file in Figure 27-5 beginning on page 738. For each TXT file, the program constructs a *CText* object by constructing an *IText* driver object and then calling *CreateDispatch*. Then it calls the *SetText* member function to write the first line of the file to the object. After that, the program calls *IPersistStream::Save* to write the object to the compound file. The *CText* object is deleted after the *IPersistStream* pointer is released and after the *IText* object is deleted, releasing the object's *IDispatch* pointer.

Now look at the second half of the *ReadStorage* function in the ReadThread.cpp file. Like *ReadDirectory*, it constructs an *IText* driver object and calls *CreateDispatch*. Then it calls *QueryInterface* to get the object's *IPersistStream* pointer, which it uses to call *Load*. Finally, the program calls *GetText* to retrieve the line of text for tracing.

As you've learned already, a COM component usually implements *IPersistStorage*, not *IPersistStream*. The *CText* class could have worked this way, but then the compound file would have been more complex because each TXT file would have needed both a storage element (to support the interface) and a subsidiary stream element (to hold the text).

Now get ready to take a giant leap. Suppose you have a true creatable-by-CLSID COM component that supports the *IPersistStorage* interface. Recall the *IStorage* functions for class IDs. If a storage element contains a class ID, together with all the data an object needs, COM can load the server, use the class factory to construct the object, get an *IPersistStorage* pointer, and call *Load* to load the data from a compound file. This is a preview of compound documents, which you'll see in Chapter 28.

Compound File Fragmentation

Structured storage has a dark side. Like the disk drive itself, compound files can become fragmented with frequent use. If a disk drive becomes fragmented, however, you still have the same amount of free space. With a compound file, space from deleted elements isn't always recovered. This means that compound files can keep growing even if you delete data.

Fortunately, there is a way to recover unused space in a compound file. You simply create a new file and copy the contents. The *IStorage::CopyTo* function can do the whole job in one call if you use it to copy the root storage. You can either write a stand-alone utility or build a file regeneration capability into your application.

Other Compound File Advantages

You've seen how compound files add a kind of random access capability to your programs, and you can appreciate the value of transactioning. Now consider the brave new world in which every program can read any other program's documents. We're not there yet, but we have a start. Compound files from Microsoft applications have a stream under the root storage named \005SummaryInformation. This stream is formatted as a property set, as defined for ActiveX controls. If you can decode the format for this stream, you can open any conforming file and read the summary.

Visual C++ comes with a compound file viewing utility named DocFile Viewer (Dfview.exe), which uses a tree view to display the file's storages and streams. Here is the DocFile Viewer output for the structured storage file generated by EX27A.

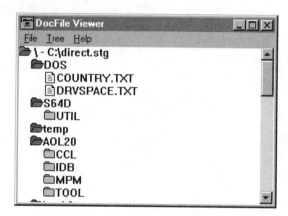

As a matter of fact, you can use DFVIEW to view the structure of any compound file. Are you starting to see the potential of this "universal file format?"

OLE Embedded Components and Containers

In this chapter, you'll get familiar with the core of Object Linking and Embedding (OLE). You'll learn how an embedded component talks to its container. This is knowledge you'll need to use ActiveX controls, in-place activation (Visual Editing), and linking, all of which are described in Adam Denning's *ActiveX Controls Inside Out* (Microsoft Press, 1997), Kraig Brockschmidt's *Inside OLE,* 2d ed. (Microsoft Press, 1995), and other books.

You'll get started with a Microsoft Foundation Class mini-server, an out-of-process OLE component program that supports in-place activation but can't run as a stand-alone program. Running this component will give you a good idea of what OLE looks like to the user, in case you don't know already. You'll also see the extensive MFC support for this kind of application. If you work at only the top MFC level, however, you won't appreciate or understand the underlying OLE mechanisms. For that, you'll have to dig deeper. Shepherd and Wingo's *MFC Internals* (Addison-Wesley, 1996) provides extensive coverage of the internal workings of MFC's OLE Document support.

Next you'll build a container program that uses the familiar parts of the MFC library but supports embedded OLE objects that can be edited in their own windows. This container can, of course, run your MFC mini-server, but you'll really start to learn OLE when you build a mini-server from scratch and watch the interactions between it and the container.

Embedding vs. In-Place Activation (Visual Editing)

Visual Editing is Microsoft's name for in-place activation. A component that supports in-place activation also supports embedding. Both in-place activation and embedding store their data in a container's document, and the container can activate both. An in-place–capable component can run inside the container application's main window, taking over the container's menu and toolbar, and it can run in its own top-level window if necessary. An embedded component can run only in its own window, and that window has a special menu that does not include file commands. Figure 28-1 shows a Microsoft Excel spreadsheet in-place activated inside a Microsoft Word document. Notice the Excel menus and toolbars.

Some container applications support only embedded components; others support both in-place and embedded components. Usually, an in-place container program allows the user to activate in-place components either in place or in their own windows. You should be getting the idea that embedding is a subset of in-place activation. This is true not only at the user level but also at the OLE implementation level. Embedding relies on two key interfaces, *IOleObject* and *IOleClientSite*, which are used for in-place activation as well.

Figure 28-1.
An Excel spreadsheet activated inside a Word document.

Mini-Servers vs. Full Servers (Components)—Linking

A mini-server can't be run as a stand-alone program; it depends on a container application to launch it. It can't do its own file I/O but depends on the container's files. A full server, on the other hand, can be run both as a stand-alone program and from a container. When it's running as a stand-alone program, it can read and write its own files, which means that it supports OLE linking. With embedding, the container document contains all the data that the component needs; with linking, the container contains only the name of a file that the component must open.

The Dark Side of Visual Editing

We're really enthusiastic about the COM architecture, and we truly believe that ActiveX Controls will take over the programming world. We're not so sure about Visual Editing, though, and we aren't alone. From our cumulative experience meeting developers around the world, we've learned that few developers are writing applications that fit the "objects embedded in a document" model. From our programming experiences, we've learned that it is tricky for containers and components to coordinate the size and scale of embedded objects. From our "user" experience, we've learned that in-place activation can be slow and awkward, although the situation is improving with faster computers.

If you don't believe us, try embedding an Excel worksheet in a Word document, as shown in Figure 28-1. Resize the worksheet in both the active mode and the nonactive mode. Notice that the two sizes don't track and that processing is slow.

Consider the need for drawing graphics. Older versions of Microsoft PowerPoint used an in-place component named Microsoft Draw. The idea was that other applications could use this component for all their graphics needs. Well, it didn't work out that way, and PowerPoint now has its own built-in drawing code. If you have old PowerPoint files with Microsoft Draw objects, you'll have a hard time converting them.

Now consider printing. Let's say you receive a Word document over the Internet from Singapore, and that document contains the metafiles for some embedded objects. You don't have the objects' component programs, however. You print the document on your trusty 1200-dpi color laser printer, and the metafiles print with it. Embedded object metafiles can be rendered for a specific printer, but it's doubtful that the person in Singapore used your printer driver when creating the document. The result is less-than-optimal output with incorrect line breaks.

We do believe, however, that the OLE embedding technology has a lot of potential. Playing sounds and movies is cool, and storing objects in a database is interesting. What you learn in this chapter will help you think of new uses for this technology.

Windows Metafiles and Embedded Objects

You're going to need a little more Windows theory before you can understand how in-place and embedded components draw in their clients' windows. We've avoided metafiles up to this point because we haven't needed them, but they've always been an integral part of Windows. Think of a metafile as a cassette tape for GDI instructions. To use a cassette, you need a player/recorder, and that's what the metafile device context (DC) is. If you specify a filename when you create the metafile DC, your metafile will be saved on disk; otherwise, it's saved in memory and you get a handle.

In the world of OLE embedding, components create metafiles and containers play them. Here's some component code that creates a metafile containing some text and a rectangle:

```
CMetaFileDC dcm; // MFC class for metafile DC
VERIFY(dcm.Create());
dcm.SetMapMode(MM_ANISOTROPIC);
dcm.SetWindowOrg(0,0);
dcm.SetWindowExt(5000, -5000);
// drawing code
dcm.Rectangle(CRect(500, -1000, 1500, -2000));
dcm.TextOut(0, 0, m_strText);
HMETAFILE hMF = dcm.Close();
ASSERT(hMF != NULL);
```

It's possible to create a metafile that uses a fixed mapping mode such as *MM_LOENGLISH*, but with OLE we'll always use the *MM_ANISOTROPIC* mode, which is not fixed. The metafile contains a *SetWindowExt* call to set the *x* and *y* extents of the window, and the program that plays the metafile calls *SetViewportExt* to set the extents of the viewport. Here's some code that you might put inside your container view's *OnDraw* function:

```
pDC->SetMapMode(MM_HIMETRIC);
pDC->SetViewportExt(5000, 5000);
pDC->PlayMetafile(hMF);
```

What's supposed to show up on the screen is a rectangle 1-by-1-cm square because the component assumes the *MM_HIMETRIC* mapping mode. It will be 1-by-1 cm as long as the viewport extent matches the window extent. If the container sets the viewport extent to (5000, 10000) instead, the rectangle will be stretched vertically but the text will be the same size because it's drawn with the nonscalable system font. If the container decided to use a mapping mode other than *MM_HIMETRIC*, it could adjust the viewport extent to retain the 1-by-1-cm size.

To reiterate, the <u>component</u> sets the window extent to the assumed size of the viewable area and draws inside that box. If the component uses a negative *y* extent, the drawing code works just as it does in *MM_HIMETRIC* mapping mode. The <u>container</u> somehow gets the component's extent size and attempts to draw the metafile in an area with those *HIMETRIC* dimensions.

Why are we bothering with metafiles? Because the container needs to draw something in the component's rectangle, even if the component program isn't running. The component creates the metafile and hands it off in a data object to the in-process OLE <u>handler</u> module on the container side of the Remote Procedure Call (RPC) link. The handler then caches the metafile and plays it on demand and also transfers it to and from the container's storage. When a component is in-place active, however, its view code is drawing directly in a window that's managed by the container.

The MFC OLE Architecture for Component Programs

We're not going into too many details here—just enough to allow you to understand the new files in the next example. You need to know about three new MFC base classes—*COleIPFrameWnd*, *COleServerDoc*, and *COleServerItem*.

When you use AppWizard to generate an OLE component, AppWizard generates a class derived from each of the base classes, in addition to an application class, a main frame class, and a view class. The *COleIPFrameWnd* class is rather like *CFrameWnd*. It's your application's main frame window, which contains the view. It has a menu associated with it, *IDR_SRVR_INPLACE*, which will be merged into the container program's menu. When your component program is running in place, it's using the in-place frame, and when it's running stand-alone or embedded, it's using the regular frame, which is an object of a class derived from *CFrameWnd*. The embedded menu is *IDR_SRVR_EMBEDDED*, and the stand-alone menu is *IDR_MAINFRAME*.

The *COleServerDoc* class is a replacement for *CDocument*. It contains added features that support OLE connections to the container. The *COleServerItem* class works with the *COleServerDoc* class. If components never supported OLE linking, the functionality of the two classes could be combined into one class.

Because stand-alone component programs do support linking, the MFC architecture dictates that both classes be present in all components. You'll see in the EX28C example that we can make our own simple mini-server without this division.

Together, the *COleServerItem* class and the *COleServerDoc* class implement a whole series of OLE interfaces, including *IOleObject*, *IDataObject*, *IPersistStorage*, and *IOleInPlaceActiveObject*. These classes make calls to the container, using interface pointers that the container passes to them. The important things to know, however, are that your derived *CView* class draws in the component's in-place–active window and that the derived *COleServerItem* class draws in the metafile on command from the container.

The EX28A Example—
An MFC In-Place–Activated Mini-Server

You don't need much OLE theory to build an MFC mini-server. This example is a good place to start, though, because you'll get an idea of how containers and components interact. This component isn't too sophisticated. It simply draws some text and graphics in a window. The text is stored in the document, and there's a dialog for updating it.

Here are the steps for creating the program from scratch:

1. Run AppWizard to create the EX28A project in the \vcpp32\ex28a directory. Select Single Document interface. Click the Mini-Server option in the AppWizard Step 3 dialog shown here.

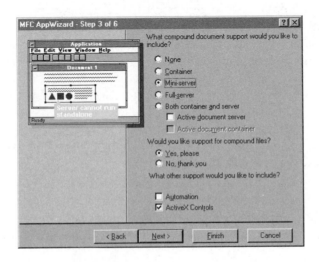

2. **Examine the generated files.** You've got the familiar application, document, main frame, and view files, but you've got two new files too.

Header	Implementation	Class	MFC Base Class
SrvrItem.h	SrvrItem.cpp	*CEx28aSrvrItem*	*COleServerItem*
IpFrame.h	IpFrame.cpp	*CInPlaceFrame*	*COleIPFrameWnd*

3. **Add a text member to the document class.** Add the following public data member in the class declaration in ex28aDoc.h:

```
CString m_strText;
```

Set the string's initial value to *Initial default text* in the document's *OnNewDocument* member function.

4. **Add a dialog to modify the text.** Insert a new dialog template with an edit control, and then use ClassWizard to generate a *CTextDialog* class derived from *CDialog*. Don't forget to include the dialog class header in ex28aDoc.cpp. Also, use ClassWizard to add a *CString* member variable named *m_strText* for the edit control.

5. **Add a new menu command in both the embedded and in-place menus.** Add a Modify menu command in both the *IDR_SRVR_EMBEDDED* and *IDR_SRVR_INPLACE* menus. To insert this menu command on the *IDR_SRVR_EMBEDDED* menu, use the resource editor to add an EX28A-EMBED menu item on the top level, and then add a Modify option on the submenu for this item. Next add an EX28A-INPLACE menu item on the top level of the *IDR_SRVR_INPLACE* menu and add a Modify option on the EX28A-INPLACE submenu.

To associate both Modify options with one *OnModify* function, use *ID_MODIFY* as the ID for the Modify option of both the *IDR_SRVR-_EMBEDDED* and *IDR_SRVR_INPLACE* menus. Then use ClassWizard to map both Modify options to the *OnModify* function in the document class. Code the Modify command handler as shown here:

```
void CEx28aDoc::OnModify()
{
    CTextDialog dlg;
    dlg.m_strText = m_strText;
    if (dlg.DoModal() == IDOK) {
        m_strText = dlg.m_strText;
```

(continued)

751

```
                        UpdateAllViews(NULL); // Trigger CEx28aView::OnDraw
                        UpdateAllItems(NULL); // Trigger CEx28aSrvrItem::OnDraw
                        SetModifiedFlag();
              }
    }
```

6. **Override the view's *OnPrepareDC* function.**   Use ClassWizard
   to generate the function, and then replace any existing code with the
   following line:

```
pDC->SetMapMode(MM_HIMETRIC);
```

7. **Edit the view's *OnDraw* function.**   The following code in ex28aView.cpp
   draws a 2-cm circle centered in the client rectangle, with the text word-
   wrapped in the window:

```
void CEx28aView::OnDraw(CDC* pDC)
{
    CEx28aDoc* pDoc = GetDocument();
    ASSERT_VALID(pDoc);
    CFont font;
    font.CreateFont(-500, 0, 0, 0, 400, FALSE, FALSE, 0,
                    ANSI_CHARSET, OUT_DEFAULT_PRECIS,
                    CLIP_DEFAULT_PRECIS, DEFAULT_QUALITY,
                    DEFAULT_PITCH | FF_SWISS, "Arial");
    CFont* pFont = pDC->SelectObject(&font);
    CRect rectClient;
    GetClientRect(rectClient);
    CSize sizeClient = rectClient.Size();
    pDC->DPtoHIMETRIC(&sizeClient);
    CRect rectEllipse(sizeClient.cx / 2 - 1000,
                      -sizeClient.cy / 2 + 1000,
                       sizeClient.cx / 2 + 1000,
                      -sizeClient.cy / 2 - 1000);
    pDC->Ellipse(rectEllipse);
    pDC->TextOut(0, 0, pDoc->m_strText);
    pDC->SelectObject(pFont);
}
```

8. **Edit the server item's *OnDraw* function.**   The following code in the
   SrvrItem.cpp file tries to draw the same circle drawn in the view's *OnDraw*
   function. You'll learn what a <u>server item</u> is shortly.

```
BOOL CEx28aSrvrItem::OnDraw(CDC* pDC, CSize& rSize)
{
    // Remove this if you use rSize
    UNREFERENCED_PARAMETER(rSize);
```

```
    CEx28aDoc* pDoc = GetDocument();
    ASSERT_VALID(pDoc);

    // TODO: set mapping mode and extent
    //  (The extent is usually the same as the size returned from
    //  OnGetExtent)
    pDC->SetMapMode(MM_ANISOTROPIC);
    pDC->SetWindowOrg(0,0);
    pDC->SetWindowExt(3000, -3000);

    CFont font;
    font.CreateFont(-500, 0, 0, 0, 400, FALSE, FALSE, 0,
                    ANSI_CHARSET, OUT_DEFAULT_PRECIS,
                    CLIP_DEFAULT_PRECIS, DEFAULT_QUALITY,
                    DEFAULT_PITCH | FF_SWISS, "Arial");
    CFont* pFont = pDC->SelectObject(&font);
    CRect rectEllipse(CRect(500, -500, 2500, -2500));
    pDC->Ellipse(rectEllipse);
    pDC->TextOut(0, 0, pDoc->m_strText);
    pDC->SelectObject(pFont);

    return TRUE;
}
```

9. **Edit the document's *Serialize* function.** The framework takes care of loading and saving the document's data from and to an OLE stream named *Contents* that is attached to the object's main storage. You simply write normal serialization code, as shown here:

```
void CEx28aDoc::Serialize(CArchive& ar)
{
    if (ar.IsStoring())
    {
        ar << m_strText;
    }
    else
    {
        ar >> m_strText;
    }
}
```

There is also a *CEx28aSrvrItem::Serialize* function that delegates to the document *Serialize* function.

10. **Build and register the EX28A application.** You must run the application directly once to update the Registry.

11. **Test the EX28A application.** You need a container program that supports in-place activation. Use Microsoft Excel 97 or a later version if you have it, or build the project in the MFC DRAWCLI sample. Choose the container's Insert Object menu item. If this option does not appear on the Insert menu, it might appear on the Edit menu instead. Then select Ex28a Document from the list.

> NOTE: You debug an embedded component the same way you debug an Automation EXE component. See the sidebar, "Debugging an EXE Component Program," on page 641 for more information.

When you first insert the EX28A object, you'll see a hatched border, which indicates that the object is in-place active. The bounding rectangle is 3-by-3-cm square, with a 2-cm circle in the center, as illustrated here.

If you click elsewhere in the container's window, the object becomes inactive, and it's shown like this.

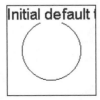

In the first case, you saw the output of the <u>view's</u> *OnDraw* function; in the second case, you saw the output of the <u>server item's</u> *OnDraw* function. The circles are the same, but the text is formatted differently because the server (component) item code is drawing on a metafile device context.

If you use the resize handles to extend the height of the object (click once on the object to see the resize handles; don't double-click), you'll stretch the circle and the font will get bigger, as shown on the next page in the figure on the left. If you reactivate the object by double-clicking on it, it's reformatted as shown on the next page in the figure on the right.

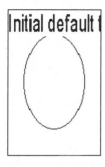 

Click elsewhere in the container's window, single-click on the object, and then choose Ex28a Object from the bottom of the Edit menu. Choose Open from the submenu. This starts the component program in embedded mode rather than in in-place mode, as shown here.

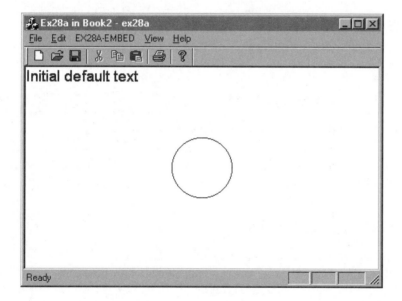

Notice that the component's *IDR_SRVR_EMBEDDED* menu is visible.

An MDI Embedded Component?

The EX28A example is an SDI mini-server. Each time a controller creates an EX28A object, a new EX28A process is started. You might expect an MDI mini-server process to support multiple component objects, each with its own document, but this is not the case. When you ask AppWizard to generate an MDI mini-server, it generates an SDI program, as in EX28A. It's theoretically possible to have a single process support multiple embedded objects in different windows, but you can't easily create such a program with the MFC library.

In-Place Component Sizing Strategy

If you look at the EX28A output on pages 754 and 755, you'll observe that the metafile image does not always match the image in the in-place frame window. We had hoped to create another example in which the two images matched. We were unsuccessful, however, when we tried to use the Microsoft Office 97 applications as containers. Each one did something a little different and unpredictable. A complicating factor is the containers' different zooming abilities.

When AppWizard generates a component program, it gives you an overridden *OnGetExtent* function in your server item class. This function returns a hard-coded size of (3000, 3000). You can certainly change this value to suit your needs, but be careful if you change it dynamically. We tried maintaining our own document data member for the component's extent, but that messed us up when the container's zoom factor changed. We thought containers would make more use of another component item virtual function, *OnSetExtent*, but they don't.

You'll be safest if you simply make your component extents fixed and assume that the container will do the right thing. Keep in mind that when the container application prints its document, it prints the component metafiles. The metafiles are more important than the in-place views.

If you control both container and component programs, however, you have more flexibility. You can build up a modular document processing system with its own sizing protocol. You can even use other OLE interfaces.

Container–Component Interactions

Analyzing the component and the container separately won't help you to understand fully how they work. You must watch them working together to understand their interactions. Let's reveal the complexity one step at a time. Consider first that you have a container EXE and a component EXE, and the container must manage the component by means of OLE interfaces.

Look back to the space simulation example in Chapter 24. The client program called *CoGetClassObject* and *IClassFactory::CreateInstance* to load the spaceship component and to create a spaceship object, and then it called *QueryInterface* to get *IMotion* and *IVisual* pointers. An embedding container program works the same way that the space simulation client works. It starts the component program based on the component's class ID, and the component program constructs an object. Only the interfaces are different.

Figure 28-2 shows a container program looking at a component. You've already seen all the interfaces except one—*IOleObject*.

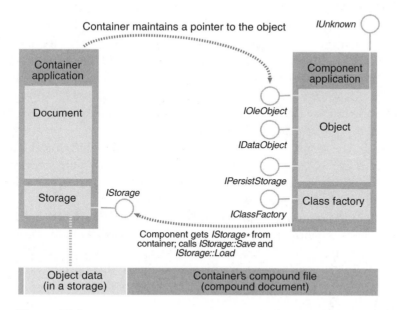

Figure 28-2.
A container program's view of the component.

Using the Component's *IOleObject* Interface

Loading a component is not the same as activating it. Loading merely starts a process, which then sits waiting for further instructions. If the container gets an *IOleObject* pointer to the component object, it can call the *DoVerb* member function with a verb parameter such as *OLEIVERB_SHOW*. The component should then show its main window and act like a Windows-based program. If you look at the *IOleObject::DoVerb* description on page 763, you'll see an *IOleClientSite** parameter. We'll consider client sites shortly, but for now you can simply set the parameter to *NULL* and most components will work okay.

Another important *IOleObject* function, *Close*, is useful at this stage. As you might expect, the container calls *Close* when it wants to terminate the component program. If the component process is currently servicing one embedded object (as is the case with MFC components), the process exits.

Loading and Saving the Component's
Native Data—Compound Documents

Figure 28-2 on the previous page demonstrates that the container manages a storage through an *IStorage* pointer and that the component implements *IPersistStorage*. That means that the component can load and save its native data when the container calls the *Load* and *Save* functions of *IPersistStorage*. You've seen the *IStorage* and *IPersistStorage* interfaces used in Chapter 27, but this time the container is going to save the component's class ID in the storage. The container can read the class ID from the storage and use it to start the component program prior to calling *IPersistStorage::Load*.

Actually, the storage is very important to the embedded object. Just as a virus needs to live in a cell, an embedded object needs to live in a storage. The storage must always be available because the object is constantly loading and saving itself and reading and writing temporary data.

A compound document appears at the bottom of Figure 28-2. The container manages the whole file, but the embedded components are responsible for the storages inside it. There's one main storage for each embedded object, and the container doesn't know or care what's inside those storages.

Clipboard Data Transfers

If you've run any OLE container programs, including Microsoft Excel, you've noticed that you can copy and paste whole embedded objects. There's a special data object format, *CF_EMBEDDEDOBJECT*, for embedded objects. If you put an *IDataObject* pointer on the clipboard and that data object contains the *CF_EMBEDDEDOBJECT* format (and the companion *CF_OBJECTDESCRIPTOR* format), another program can load the proper component program and reconstruct the object.

There's actually less here than meets the eye. The only thing inside the *CF_EMBEDDEDOBJECT* format is an *IStorage* pointer. The clipboard copy program verifies that *IPersistStorage::Save* has been called to save the embedded object's data in the storage, and then it passes off the *IStorage* pointer in a data object. The clipboard paste program gets the class ID from the source storage, loads the component program, and then calls *IPersistStorage::Load* to load the data from the source storage.

The data objects for the clipboard are generated as needed by the container program. The component's *IDataObject* interface isn't used for transferring the objects' native data.

Getting the Component's Metafile

You already know that a component program is supposed to draw in a metafile and that a container is supposed to play it. But how does the component deliver the metafile? That's what the *IDataObject* interface, shown in Figure 28-2 on page 757, is for. The container calls *IDataObject::GetData*, asking for a *CF_META-FILEPICT* format. But wait a minute. The container is supposed to get the metafile even if the component program isn't running. So now you're ready for the next complexity level.

The Role of the In-Process Handler

If the component program is running, it's in a separate process. Sometimes it's not running at all. In either case, the OLE32 DLL is linked into the container's process. This DLL is known as the <u>object</u> <u>handler</u>.

> **NOTE:** It's possible for an EXE component to have its own custom handler DLL, but most components use the "default" OLE32 DLL.

Figure 28-3 on the following page shows the new picture. The handler communicates with the component over the RPC link, marshaling all interface function calls. But the handler does more than act as the component's proxy for marshaling; it maintains a <u>cache</u> that contains the component object's metafile. The handler saves and loads the cache to and from storage, and it can fill the cache by calling the component's *IDataObject::GetData* function.

When the container wants to draw the metafile, it doesn't do the drawing itself; instead, it asks the handler to draw the metafile by calling the handler's *IViewObject2::Draw* function. The handler tries to satisfy as many container requests as it can without bothering the component program. If the handler needs to call a component function, it takes care of loading the component program if it is not already loaded.

> **NOTE:** The *IViewObject2* interface is an example of OLE's design evolution. Someone decided to add a new function—in this case, *GetExtent*—to the *IViewObject* interface. *IViewObject2* is derived from *IViewObject* and contains the new function. All new components should implement the new interface and should return an *IViewObject2* pointer when *QueryInterface* is called for either *IID_IViewObject* or *IID_IView-Object2*. This is easy with the MFC library because you write two interface map entries that link to the same nested class.

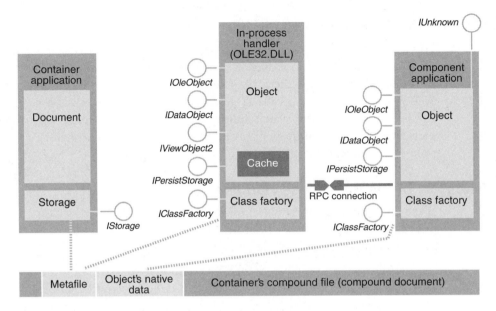

Figure 28-3.
The in-process handler and the component.

Figure 28-3 shows both object data and metafile data in the object's storage. When the container calls the handler's *IPersistStorage::Save* function, the handler writes the cache (containing the metafile) to the storage and then calls the component's *IPersistStorage::Save* function, which writes the object's native data to the same storage. The reverse happens when the object is loaded.

Component States

Now that you know what a handler is, you're ready for a description of the four states that an embedded object can assume.

State	Description
Passive	The object exists only in a storage.
Loaded	The object handler is running and has a metafile in its cache, but the EXE component program is not running.
Running	The EXE component program is loaded and running, but the window is not visible to the user.
Active	The EXE component's window is visible to the user.

The Container Interfaces

Now for the container side of the conversation. Look at Figure 28-4. The container consists of a document and one or more <u>sites</u>. The *IOleContainer* interface has functions for iterating over the sites, but we won't worry about iterating over the client sites here. The important interface is *IOleClientSite*. Each site is an object that the component accesses through an *IOleClientSite* pointer. When the container creates an embedded object, it calls *IOleObject::SetClientSite* to establish one of the two connections from component to container. The site maintains an *IOleObject* pointer to its component object.

One important *IOleClientSite* function is *SaveObject*. When the component decides it's time to save itself to its storage, it doesn't do so directly; instead, it asks the site to do the job by calling *IOleClientSite::SaveObject*. "Why the indirection?" you ask. The handler needs to save the metafile to the storage, that's why. The *SaveObject* function calls *IPersistStorage::Save* at the handler level, so the handler can do its job before calling the component's *Save* function.

Another important *IOleClientSite* function is *OnShowWindow*. The component program calls this function when it starts running and when it stops running. The client is supposed to display a hatched pattern in the embedded object's rectangle when the component program is running or active.

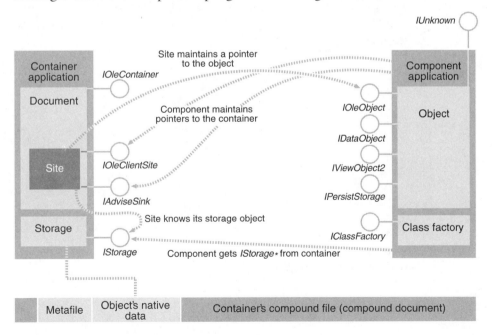

Figure 28-4.
The interaction between the container and the component.

The Advisory Connection

Figure 28-4 on the previous page shows another interface attached to the site—*IAdviseSink*. This is the container's end of the second component connection. Why have another connection? The *IOleClientSite* connection goes directly from the component to the container, but the *IAdviseSink* connection is routed through the handler. After the site has created the embedded object, it calls *IViewObject2::SetAdvise*, passing its *IAdviseSink* pointer. Meanwhile, the handler has gone ahead and established <u>two</u> advisory connections to the component. When the embedded object is created, the handler calls *IOleObject::Advise* and then calls *IDataObject::DAdvise* to notify the advise sink of changes in the data object. When the component's data changes, it notifies the handler through the *IDataObject* advisory connection. When the user saves the component's data or closes the program, the component notifies the handler through the *IOleObject* advisory connection. Figure 28-5 shows these connections.

When the handler gets the notification that the component's data has changed (the component calls *IAdviseSink::OnDataChange*), it can notify the container by calling *IAdviseSink::OnViewChange*. The container responds by calling *IViewObject2::Draw* in the handler. If the component program is not running, the handler draws its metafile from the cache. If the component program is running, the handler calls the component's *IDataObject::GetData* function to get the latest metafile, which it draws. The *OnClose* and *OnSave* notifications are passed in a similar manner.

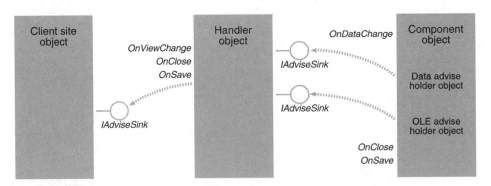

Figure 28-5.
Advisory connection details.

A Metafile for the Clipboard

As you've just learned, the container doesn't deal with the metafile directly when it wants to draw the embedded object; instead, it calls *IViewObject2::Draw*. In one case, however, the container needs direct access to the metafile. When the container copies an embedded object to the clipboard, it must copy a metafile in addition to the embedded object and the object descriptor. That's what the handler's *IDataObject* interface is for. The container calls *IDataObject::GetData*, requesting a metafile format, and it copies that format into the clipboard's data object.

An Interface Summary

Following is a summary of the important OLE interfaces we'll be using in the remaining examples in this chapter. The function lists are by no means complete, nor are the parameter lists. See MSDN Online Help or Brockschmidt's book for the complete specifications.

The *IOleObject* Interface

Embedded components implement this interface. The client site maintains an *IOleObject* pointer to an embedded object.

HRESULT Advise(IAdviseSink* *AdvSink*, DWORD* *pdwConnection*);

The handler calls this function to establish one of the two advisory connections from the component to the handler. The component usually implements *Advise* with an OLE advise holder object, which can manage multiple advisory connections.

HRESULT Close(DWORD *dwSaveOption*);

The container calls *Close* to terminate the component application but to leave the object in the loaded state. Containers call this function when the user clicks outside an in-place–active component's window. Components that support in-place activation should clean up and terminate.

HRESULT DoVerb(LONG *iVerb*, …, IOleClientSite* *pActiveSite*, …);

Components support numeric <u>verbs</u> as defined in the Registry. A sound component might support a "Play" verb, for example. Embedded components should support the *OLEIVERB_SHOW* verb, which instructs the object to show itself for editing or viewing. If the component supports in-place activation, this verb starts the Visual Editing process; otherwise, it starts the component program in a window separate from that of its container. The *OLEIVERB_OPEN* verb causes an in-place-activation–capable component to start in a separate window.

HRESULT GetExtent(DWORD *dwDrawAspect*, SIZEL* *pSizel*);

The component returns the object extent in *HIMETRIC* dimensions. The container uses these dimensions to size the rectangle for the component's metafile. Sometimes the container uses the extents that are included in the component's metafile picture.

HRESULT SetClientSite(IOleClientSite* *pClientSite*);

The container calls *SetClientSite* to enable the component to store a pointer back to the site in the container.

HRESULT SetExtent(DWORD *dwDrawAspect*, SIZEL* *pSizel*);

Some containers call this function to impose extents on the component.

HRESULT SetHostNames(LPCOLESTR *szContainerApp*, PCOLESTR *szContainerObj*);

The container calls *SetHostNames* so that the component can display the container program's name in its window caption.

HRESULT Unadvise(DWORD* *dwConnection*);

This function terminates the advisory connection set up by *Advise*.

The *IViewObject2* Interface

Embedded component <u>handlers</u> implement this interface. Handlers are a type of COM component for dealing with certain client-side aspects of linking and embedding. The default handler (the one provided by Microsoft) lives in a DLL named "OLE32.DLL." The container calls its functions, but the component program itself doesn't implement them. An *IViewObject2* interface cannot be marshaled across a process boundary because it's associated with a device context.

HRESULT Draw(DWORD *dwAspect*, ..., const LPRECTL *lprcBounds*, ...);

The container calls this function to draw the component's metafile in a specified rectangle.

HRESULT SetAdvise(DWORD *dwAspect*, ..., IAdviseSink* *pAdvSink*);

The container calls *SetAdvise* to set up the advisory connection to the handler, which in turn sets up the advisory connection to the component.

The *IOleClientSite* Interface

Containers implement this interface. There is one client site object per component object.

HRESULT GetContainer(IOleContainer** *ppContainer*);

The *GetContainer* function retrieves a pointer to the container object (document), which can be used to enumerate the container's sites.

HRESULT OnShowWindow(BOOL *fShow*);

The component program calls this function when it switches between the running and the loaded (or active) state. When the object is in the loaded state, the container should display a hatched pattern on the embedded object's rectangle.

HRESULT SaveObject(void);

The component program calls *SaveObject* when it wants to be saved to its storage. The container calls *IPersistStorage::Save*.

The *IAdviseSink* Interface

Containers implement this interface. Embedded object handlers call its functions in response to component notifications.

void OnClose(void);

Component programs call this function when they are being terminated.

void OnViewChange(DWORD dwAspect, ...);

The handler calls *OnViewChange* when the metafile has changed. Because the component program must have been running for this notification to have been sent, the handler can call the component's *IDataObject::GetData* function to get the latest metafile for its cache. The container can then draw this metafile by calling *IViewObject2::Draw*.

OLE Helper Functions

A number of global OLE functions encapsulate a sequence of OLE interface calls. Following are some that we'll use in the EX28B example:

HRESULT OleCreate(REFCLSID *rclsid*, REFIID *riid*, ...,
IOleClientSite* *pClientSite*, IStorage* *pStg*, void** *ppvObj*);

The *OleCreate* function first executes the COM creation sequence using the specified class ID. This loads the component program. Then the function calls

QueryInterface for an *IPersistStorage* pointer, which it uses to call *InitNew*, passing the *pStg* parameter. It also calls *QueryInterface* to get an *IOleObject* pointer, which it uses to call *SetClientSite* using the *pClientSite* parameter. Finally it calls *QueryInterface* for the interface specified by *riid*, which is usually *IID_IOleObject*.

HRESULT OleCreateFromData(IDataObject* *pSrcDataObj*, REFIID *riid*, ..., IOleClientSite* *pClientSite*, IStorage* *pStg*, void** *ppvObj*);

The *OleCreateFromData* function creates an embedded object from a data object. In the EX28B example, the incoming data object has the *CF_EMBEDDED-OBJECT* format with an *IStorage* pointer. The function then loads the component program based on the class ID in the storage, and then it calls *IPersistStorage::Load* to make the component load the object's native data. Along the way, it calls *IOleObject::SetClientSite*.

HRESULT OleDraw(IUnknown* *pUnk*, DWORD *dwAspect*, HDC *hdcDraw*, LPCRECT *lprcBounds*);

This function calls *QueryInterface* on *pUnk* to get an *IViewObject* pointer, and then it calls *IViewObject::Draw*, passing the *lprcBounds* parameter.

HRESULT OleLoad(IStorage* *pStg*, REFIID *riid*, IOleClientSite* *pClientSite*, void** *ppvObj*);

The *OleLoad* function first executes the COM creation sequence by using the class ID in the specified storage. Then it calls *IOleObject::SetClientSite* and *IPersistStorage::Load*. Finally, it calls *QueryInterface* for the interface specified by *riid*, which is usually *IID_IOleObject*.

HRESULT OleSave(IPersistStorage* *pPS*, IStorage* *pStg*, ...);

This function calls *IPersistStorage::GetClassID* to get the object's class ID, and then it writes that class ID in the storage specified by *pStg*. Finally it calls *IPersistStorage::Save*.

An OLE Embedding Container Application

Now that we've got a working mini-server that supports embedding (EX28A), we'll write a container program to run it. We're not going to use the MFC container support, however, because you need to see what's happening at the OLE interface level. We will use the MFC document–view architecture and the MFC interface maps, and we'll also use the MFC data object classes.

MFC Support for OLE Containers

If you did use AppWizard to build an MFC OLE container application, you'd get a class derived from *COleDocument* and a class derived from *COleClientItem*. These MFC base classes implement a number of important OLE container interfaces for embedding and in-place activation. The idea is that you have one *COleClientItem* object for each embedded object in a single container document. Each *COleClientItem* object defines a site, which is where the component object lives in the window.

The *COleDocument* class maintains a list of client items, but it's up to you to specify how to select an item and how to synchronize the metafile's position with the in-place frame position. AppWizard generates a basic container application with no support for linking, clipboard processing, or drag and drop. If you want those features, you might be better off looking at the MFC DRAWCLI and OCLIENT samples.

We will use one MFC OLE class in the container—*COleInsertDialog*. This class wraps the *OleUIInsertObject* function, which invokes the standard Insert Object dialog box. This Insert Object dialog enables the user to select from a list of registered component programs.

Some Container Limitations

Because our container application is designed for learning, we'll make some simplifications to reduce the bulk of the code. First of all, this container won't support in-place activation—it allows the user to edit embedded objects only in a separate window. Also, the container supports only one embedded item per document, and that means there's no linking support. The container uses a structured storage file to hold the document's embedded item, but it handles the storage directly, bypassing the framework's serialization system. Clipboard support is provided; drag-and-drop support is not. Outside these limitations, however, it's a pretty good container!

Container Features

So, what does the container actually do? Here's a list of features:

- As an MFC MDI application, it handles multiple documents.
- Displays the component's metafile in a sizeable, moveable tracker rectangle in the view window.
- Maintains a temporary storage for each embedded object.

- Implements the Insert Object menu option, which allows the user to select a registered component. The selected component program starts in its own window.

- Allows embedded objects to be copied (and cut) to the clipboard and pasted. These objects can be transferred to and from other containers such as Microsoft Word and Microsoft Excel.

- Allows an embedded object to be deleted.

- Tracks the component program's loaded–running transitions and hatches the tracker rectangle when the component is running or active.

- Redraws the embedded object's metafile on receipt of component change notifications.

- Saves the object in its temporary storage when the component updates the object or exits.

- Copies the embedded object's temporary storage to and from named storage files in response to Copy To and Paste From commands on the Edit menu.

The EX28B Example—An Embedding Container

Now we can move on to the working program. It's a good time to open the \vcpp32\ex28b\ex28b.dsw workspace and build the EX28B project. If you choose Insert Object from the Edit menu and select Ex28a Document, the EX28A component will start. If you change the component's data, the container and the component will look like this.

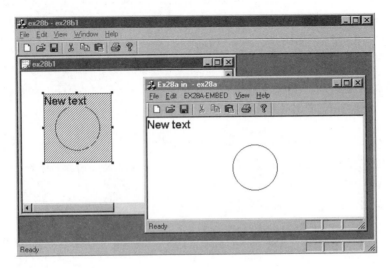

The *CEx28bView* Class

You can best understand the program by first concentrating on the view class. Look at the code in Figure 28-6, but ignore all *IOleClientSite* pointers. The container program will actually work if you pass *NULL* in every *IOleClient-Site* pointer parameter. It just won't get notifications when the metafile or the native data changes. Also, components will appear displaying their stand-alone menus instead of the special embedded menus.

EX28BVIEW.H

```
#if !defined(AFX_EX28BVIEW_H__1EAAB6E1_6011_11D0_848F_00400526305B →
__INCLUDED_)
#define AFX_EX28BVIEW_H__1EAAB6E1_6011_11D0_848F_00400526305B →
__INCLUDED_

#if _MSC_VER > 1000
#pragma once
#endif // _MSC_VER > 1000

#define CF_OBJECTDESCRIPTOR "Object Descriptor"
#define CF_EMBEDDEDOBJECT "Embedded Object"
#define SETFORMATETC(fe, cf, asp, td, med, li)  \
    ((fe).cfFormat=cf, \
    (fe).dwAspect=asp, \
    (fe).ptd=td, \
    (fe).tymed=med, \
    (fe).lindex=li)
////////////////////////////////////////////////////////////////
class CEx28bView : public CScrollView
{
public:
    CLIPFORMAT m_cfObjDesc;
    CLIPFORMAT m_cfEmbedded;
    CSize m_sizeTotal;  // document size
    CRectTracker m_tracker;
    CRect m_rectTracker; // logical coords
protected: // create from serialization only
    CEx28bView();
    DECLARE_DYNCREATE(CEx28bView)

// Attributes
public:
    CEx28bDoc* GetDocument();
```

Figure 28-6. *(continued)*
The container's CEx28bView class listing.

Figure 28-6. *continued*

```cpp
private:
    void GetSize();
    void SetNames();
    void SetViewAdvise();
    BOOL MakeMetafilePict(COleDataSource* pSource);
    COleDataSource* SaveObject();
    BOOL DoPasteObject(COleDataObject* pDataObject);
    BOOL DoPasteObjectDescriptor(COleDataObject* pDataObject);

// Overrides
    // ClassWizard generated virtual function overrides
    //{{AFX_VIRTUAL(CEx28bView)
    public:
    virtual void OnDraw(CDC* pDC);  // overridden to draw this view
    virtual BOOL PreCreateWindow(CREATESTRUCT& cs);
    virtual void OnInitialUpdate();
    protected:
    virtual BOOL OnPreparePrinting(CPrintInfo* pInfo);
    virtual void OnBeginPrinting(CDC* pDC, CPrintInfo* pInfo);
    virtual void OnEndPrinting(CDC* pDC, CPrintInfo* pInfo);
    //}}AFX_VIRTUAL

// Implementation
public:
    virtual ~CEx28bView();
#ifdef _DEBUG
    virtual void AssertValid() const;
    virtual void Dump(CDumpContext& dc) const;
#endif

protected:

// Generated message map functions
protected:
    //{{AFX_MSG(CEx28bView)
    afx_msg void OnEditCopy();
    afx_msg void OnUpdateEditCopy(CCmdUI* pCmdUI);
    afx_msg void OnEditCopyto();
    afx_msg void OnEditCut();
    afx_msg void OnEditPaste();
    afx_msg void OnUpdateEditPaste(CCmdUI* pCmdUI);
    afx_msg void OnEditPastefrom();
    afx_msg void OnEditInsertobject();
    afx_msg void OnUpdateEditInsertobject(CCmdUI* pCmdUI);
    afx_msg void OnLButtonDown(UINT nFlags, CPoint point);
    afx_msg void OnLButtonDblClk(UINT nFlags, CPoint point);
```

```
    afx_msg BOOL OnSetCursor(CWnd* pWnd, UINT nHitTest,
                             UINT message);
    //}}AFX_MSG
    DECLARE_MESSAGE_MAP()
};

#ifndef _DEBUG  // debug version in ex28bView.cpp
inline CEx28bDoc* CEx28bView::GetDocument()
    { return (CEx28bDoc*)m_pDocument; }
#endif

/////////////////////////////////////////////////////////////////////////

//{{AFX_INSERT_LOCATION}}
// Microsoft Visual C++ will insert additional declarations
//   immediately before the previous line.

#endif
//!defined(AFX_EX28BVIEW_H__1EAAB6E1_6011_11D0_848F_00400526305B →
__INCLUDED_)
```

EX28BVIEW.CPP

```
#include "stdafx.h"
#include "ex28b.h"

#include "ex28bDoc.h"
#include "ex28bView.h"

#ifdef _DEBUG
#define new DEBUG_NEW
#undef THIS_FILE
static char THIS_FILE[] = _FILE_;
#endif

/////////////////////////////////////////////////////////////////////////
// CEx28bView

IMPLEMENT_DYNCREATE(CEx28bView, CScrollView)

BEGIN_MESSAGE_MAP(CEx28bView, CScrollView)
    //{{AFX_MSG_MAP(CEx28bView)
    ON_COMMAND(ID_EDIT_COPY, OnEditCopy)
    ON_UPDATE_COMMAND_UI(ID_EDIT_COPY, OnUpdateEditCopy)
    ON_COMMAND(ID_EDIT_COPYTO, OnEditCopyto)
    ON_UPDATE_COMMAND_UI(ID_EDIT_COPYTO, OnUpdateEditCopy)
```

(continued)

Figure 28-6. *continued*

```
    ON_COMMAND(ID_EDIT_CUT, OnEditCut)
    ON_UPDATE_COMMAND_UI(ID_EDIT_CUT, OnUpdateEditCopy)
    ON_COMMAND(ID_EDIT_PASTE, OnEditPaste)
    ON_UPDATE_COMMAND_UI(ID_EDIT_PASTE, OnUpdateEditPaste)
    ON_COMMAND(ID_EDIT_PASTEFROM, OnEditPastefrom)
    ON_COMMAND(ID_EDIT_INSERTOBJECT, OnEditInsertobject)
    ON_UPDATE_COMMAND_UI(ID_EDIT_INSERTOBJECT,
                         OnUpdateEditInsertobject)
    ON_WM_LBUTTONDOWN()
    ON_WM_LBUTTONDBLCLK()
    ON_WM_SETCURSOR()
    //}}AFX_MSG_MAP
    // Standard printing commands
    ON_COMMAND(ID_FILE_PRINT, CScrollView::OnFilePrint)
    ON_COMMAND(ID_FILE_PRINT_DIRECT, CScrollView::OnFilePrint)
    ON_COMMAND(ID_FILE_PRINT_PREVIEW,
               CScrollView::OnFilePrintPreview)
END_MESSAGE_MAP()


/////////////////////////////////////////////////////////////////
// CEx28bView construction/destruction

CEx28bView::CEx28bView() : m_sizeTotal(20000, 25000),
    // 20 x 25 cm when printed
    m_rectTracker(0, 0, 0, 0)
{
    m_cfObjDesc = ::RegisterClipboardFormat(CF_OBJECTDESCRIPTOR);
    m_cfEmbedded = ::RegisterClipboardFormat(CF_EMBEDDEDOBJECT);
}


CEx28bView::~CEx28bView()
{
}


BOOL CEx28bView::PreCreateWindow(CREATESTRUCT& cs)
{
    // TODO: Modify the Window class or styles here by modifying
    //   the CREATESTRUCT cs

    return CScrollView::PreCreateWindow(cs);
}


/////////////////////////////////////////////////////////////////
// CEx28bView drawing

void CEx28bView::OnDraw(CDC* pDC)
```

```
    {
        CEx28bDoc* pDoc = GetDocument();

        if(pDoc->m_lpOleObj != NULL) {
            VERIFY(::OleDraw(pDoc->m_lpOleObj, DVASPECT_CONTENT,
                    pDC->GetSafeHdc(), m_rectTracker) == S_OK);
        }

        m_tracker.m_rect = m_rectTracker;
        pDC->LPtoDP(m_tracker.m_rect);    // device
        if(pDoc->m_bHatch) {
            m_tracker.m_nStyle |= CRectTracker::hatchInside;
        }
        else {
            m_tracker.m_nStyle &= ~CRectTracker::hatchInside;
        }
        m_tracker.Draw(pDC);
    }


    //////////////////////////////////////////////////////////////////
    // CEx28bView printing

    BOOL CEx28bView::OnPreparePrinting(CPrintInfo* pInfo)
    {
        pInfo->SetMaxPage(1);
        return DoPreparePrinting(pInfo);
    }


    void CEx28bView::OnBeginPrinting(CDC* /*pDC*/, CPrintInfo* /*pInfo*/)
    {
        // TODO: add extra initialization before printing
    }


    void CEx28bView::OnEndPrinting(CDC* /*pDC*/, CPrintInfo* /*pInfo*/)
    {
        // TODO: add cleanup after printing
    }


    //////////////////////////////////////////////////////////////////
    // CEx28bView diagnostics

    #ifdef _DEBUG
    void CEx28bView::AssertValid() const
    {
        CScrollView::AssertValid();
    }
```

(continued)

Figure 28-6. *continued*

```
void CEx28bView::Dump(CDumpContext& dc) const
{
    CScrollView::Dump(dc);
}

CEx28bDoc* CEx28bView::GetDocument() // non-debug version is inline
{
    ASSERT(m_pDocument->IsKindOf(RUNTIME_CLASS(CEx28bDoc)));
    return (CEx28bDoc*)m_pDocument;
}
#endif //_DEBUG

//////////////////////////////////////////////////////////////////////
// CEx28bView message handlers

void CEx28bView::OnInitialUpdate()
{
    TRACE("CEx28bView::OnInitialUpdate\n");
    m_rectTracker = CRect(1000, -1000, 5000, -5000);
    m_tracker.m_nStyle = CRectTracker::solidLine |
        CRectTracker::resizeOutside;
    SetScrollSizes(MM_HIMETRIC, m_sizeTotal);
    CScrollView::OnInitialUpdate();
}

void CEx28bView::OnEditCopy()
{
    COleDataSource* pSource = SaveObject();
    if(pSource) {
        pSource->SetClipboard(); // OLE deletes data source
    }
}

void CEx28bView::OnUpdateEditCopy(CCmdUI* pCmdUI)
{
    // serves Copy, Cut, and Copy To
    pCmdUI->Enable(GetDocument()->m_lpOleObj != NULL);
}

void CEx28bView::OnEditCopyto()
{
    // Copy text to an STG file (nothing special about STG ext)
    CFileDialog dlg(FALSE, "stg", "*.stg");
    if (dlg.DoModal() != IDOK) {
        return;
    }
    CEx28bDoc* pDoc = GetDocument();
```

```
    // Create a structured storage home for the object (  pStgSub).
    //  Create a root storage file, then a substorage named "sub".
    LPSTORAGE pStgRoot;
    VERIFY(::StgCreateDocfile(dlg.GetPathName().AllocSysString(),
            STGM_READWRITE|STGM_SHARE_EXCLUSIVE|STGM_CREATE,
            0, &pStgRoot) == S_OK);
    ASSERT(pStgRoot != NULL);

    LPSTORAGE pStgSub;
    VERIFY(pStgRoot->CreateStorage(CEx28bDoc::s_szSub,
            STGM_CREATE|STGM_READWRITE|STGM_SHARE_EXCLUSIVE,
            0, 0, &pStgSub) == S_OK);
    ASSERT(pStgSub != NULL);

    // Get the IPersistStorage* for the object
    LPPERSISTSTORAGE pPS = NULL;
    VERIFY(pDoc->m_lpOleObj->QueryInterface(IID_IPersistStorage,
            (void**) &pPS) == S_OK);

    // Finally, save the object in its new home in the user's file
    VERIFY(::OleSave(pPS, pStgSub, FALSE) == S_OK);
    // FALSE means different stg
    pPS->SaveCompleted(NULL);  // What does this do?
    pPS->Release();

    pStgSub->Release();
    pStgRoot->Release();
}

void CEx28bView::OnEditCut()
{
    OnEditCopy();
    GetDocument()->OnEditClearAll();
}
void CEx28bView::OnEditPaste()
{
    CEx28bDoc* pDoc = GetDocument();
    COleDataObject dataObject;
    VERIFY(dataObject.AttachClipboard());
    pDoc->DeleteContents();
    DoPasteObjectDescriptor(&dataObject);
    DoPasteObject(&dataObject);
    SetViewAdvise();
    GetSize();
    pDoc->SetModifiedFlag();
    pDoc->UpdateAllViews(NULL);
}
```

(continued)

Figure 28-6. *continued*

```
void CEx28bView::OnUpdateEditPaste(CCmdUI* pCmdUI)
{
    // Make sure that object data is available
    COleDataObject dataObject;
    if (dataObject.AttachClipboard() &&
        dataObject.IsDataAvailable(m_cfEmbedded)) {
        pCmdUI->Enable(TRUE);
    } else {
        pCmdUI->Enable(FALSE);
    }
}


void CEx28bView::OnEditPastefrom()
{
    CEx28bDoc* pDoc = GetDocument();
    // Paste from an STG file
    CFileDialog dlg(TRUE, "stg", "*.stg");
    if (dlg.DoModal() != IDOK) {
        return;
    }
    // Open the storage and substorage
    LPSTORAGE pStgRoot;
    VERIFY(::StgOpenStorage(dlg.GetPathName().AllocSysString(),
            NULL, STGM_READ|STGM_SHARE_EXCLUSIVE,
            NULL, 0, &pStgRoot) == S_OK);
    ASSERT(pStgRoot != NULL);

    LPSTORAGE pStgSub;
    VERIFY(pStgRoot->OpenStorage(CEx28bDoc::s_szSub, NULL,
            STGM_READ|STGM_SHARE_EXCLUSIVE,
            NULL, 0, &pStgSub) == S_OK);
    ASSERT(pStgSub != NULL);

    // Copy the object data from the user storage to the temporary
    //   storage
    VERIFY(pStgSub->CopyTo(NULL, NULL, NULL,
            pDoc->m_pTempStgSub) == S_OK);
    // Finally, load the object -- pClientSite not necessary
    LPOLECLIENTSITE pClientSite =
        (LPOLECLIENTSITE) pDoc->GetInterface(&IID_IOleClientSite);
    ASSERT(pClientSite != NULL);
    pDoc->DeleteContents();
    VERIFY(::OleLoad(pDoc->m_pTempStgSub, IID_IOleObject,
            pClientSite, (void**) &pDoc->m_lpOleObj) == S_OK);
    SetViewAdvise();
    pStgSub->Release();
```

```
        pStgRoot->Release();
        GetSize();
        pDoc->SetModifiedFlag();
        pDoc->UpdateAllViews(NULL);
    }

void CEx28bView::OnEditInsertobject()
{
        CEx28bDoc* pDoc = GetDocument();
        COleInsertDialog dlg;
        if(dlg.DoModal() == IDCANCEL) return;
        // no addrefs done for GetInterface
        LPOLECLIENTSITE pClientSite =
            (LPOLECLIENTSITE) pDoc->GetInterface(&IID_IOleClientSite);
        ASSERT(pClientSite != NULL);
        pDoc->DeleteContents();
        VERIFY(::OleCreate(dlg.GetClassID(), IID_IOleObject,
                OLERENDER_DRAW, NULL, pClientSite, pDoc->m_pTempStgSub,
                (void**) &pDoc->m_lpOleObj) == S_OK);
        SetViewAdvise();

        pDoc->m_lpOleObj->DoVerb(OLEIVERB_SHOW, NULL, pClientSite, 0,
            NULL, NULL); // OleRun doesn't show it
        SetNames();
        GetDocument()->SetModifiedFlag();
        GetSize();
        pDoc->UpdateAllViews(NULL);
    }

void CEx28bView::OnUpdateEditInsertobject(CCmdUI* pCmdUI)
{
        pCmdUI->Enable(GetDocument()->m_lpOleObj == NULL);
    }

void CEx28bView::OnLButtonDown(UINT nFlags, CPoint point)
{
        TRACE("**Entering CEx28bView::OnLButtonDown -- point = "
            "(%d, %d)\n", point.x, point.y);
        if(m_tracker.Track(this, point, FALSE, NULL)) {
            CClientDC dc(this);
            OnPrepareDC(&dc);
            m_rectTracker = m_tracker.m_rect;
            dc.DPtoLP(m_rectTracker); // Update logical coords
            GetDocument()->UpdateAllViews(NULL);
        }
        TRACE("**Leaving CEx28bView::OnLButtonDown\n");
    }
```

(continued)

Figure 28-6. *continued*

```
void CEx28bView::OnLButtonDblClk(UINT nFlags, CPoint point)
{
    if(m_tracker.HitTest(point) == CRectTracker::hitNothing) return;
    // Activate the object
    CEx28bDoc* pDoc = GetDocument();
    if(pDoc->m_lpOleObj != NULL) {
        LPOLECLIENTSITE pClientSite =
            (LPOLECLIENTSITE)
            pDoc->GetInterface(&IID_IOleClientSite);
        ASSERT(pClientSite != NULL);
        VERIFY(pDoc->m_lpOleObj->DoVerb(OLEIVERB_OPEN, NULL,
            pClientSite, 0,GetSafeHwnd(), CRect(0, 0, 0, 0))
            == S_OK);
        SetNames();
        GetDocument()->SetModifiedFlag();
    }
}

BOOL CEx28bView::OnSetCursor(CWnd* pWnd, UINT nHitTest, UINT message)
{
    if(m_tracker.SetCursor(pWnd, nHitTest)) {
        return TRUE;
    }
    else {
        return CScrollView::OnSetCursor(pWnd, nHitTest, message);
    }
}

//////////////////////////////////////////////////////////////////////

void CEx28bView::SetViewAdvise()
{
    CEx28bDoc* pDoc = GetDocument();
    if(pDoc->m_lpOleObj != NULL) {
        LPVIEWOBJECT2 pViewObj;
        pDoc->m_lpOleObj->QueryInterface(IID_IViewObject2,
            (void**) &pViewObj);
        LPADVISESINK pAdviseSink =
            (LPADVISESINK) pDoc->GetInterface(&IID_IAdviseSink);
        VERIFY(pViewObj->SetAdvise(DVASPECT_CONTENT, 0, pAdviseSink)
            == S_OK);
        pViewObj->Release();
    }
}

void CEx28bView::SetNames() // sets host names
```

```
    {
        CEx28bDoc* pDoc = GetDocument();
        CString strApp = AfxGetApp()->m_pszAppName;
        if(pDoc->m_lpOleObj != NULL) {
            pDoc->m_lpOleObj->SetHostNames(strApp.AllocSysString(),
            NULL);
        }
    }


    void CEx28bView::GetSize()
    {
        CEx28bDoc* pDoc = GetDocument();
        if(pDoc->m_lpOleObj != NULL) {
            SIZEL size;       // Ask the component for its size
            pDoc->m_lpOleObj->GetExtent(DVASPECT_CONTENT, &size);
            m_rectTracker.right = m_rectTracker.left + size.cx;
            m_rectTracker.bottom = m_rectTracker.top - size.cy;
        }
    }


    BOOL CEx28bView::DoPasteObject(COleDataObject* pDataObject)
    {
        TRACE("Entering CEx28bView::DoPasteObject\n");
        // Update command UI should keep us out of here if not
        //   CF_EMBEDDEDOBJECT
        if (!pDataObject->IsDataAvailable(m_cfEmbedded)) {
            TRACE("CF_EMBEDDEDOBJECT format is unavailable\n");
            return FALSE;
        }
        CEx28bDoc* pDoc = GetDocument();
        // Now create the object from the IDataObject*.
        //   OleCreateFromData will use CF_EMBEDDEDOBJECT format if
        //   available.
        LPOLECLIENTSITE pClientSite =
            (LPOLECLIENTSITE) pDoc->GetInterface(&IID_IOleClientSite);
        ASSERT(pClientSite != NULL);
        VERIFY(::OleCreateFromData(pDataObject->m_lpDataObject,
                IID_IOleObject, OLERENDER_DRAW, NULL, pClientSite,
                pDoc->m_pTempStgSub, (void**) &pDoc->m_lpOleObj) == S_OK);
        return TRUE;
    }


    BOOL CEx28bView::DoPasteObjectDescriptor(COleDataObject* pDataObject)
    {
        TRACE("Entering CEx28bView::DoPasteObjectDescriptor\n");
        STGMEDIUM stg;
```

(continued)

Figure 28-6. *continued*

```
    FORMATETC fmt;
    CEx28bDoc* pDoc = GetDocument();
    if (!pDataObject->IsDataAvailable(m_cfObjDesc)) {
        TRACE("OBJECTDESCRIPTOR format is unavailable\n");
        return FALSE;
    }
    SETFORMATETC(fmt, m_cfObjDesc, DVASPECT_CONTENT, NULL,
        TYMED_HGLOBAL, -1);
    VERIFY(pDataObject->GetDatam_cfObjDesc, &stg, &fmt));

    return TRUE;
}

// helper function used for clipboard and drag-drop
COleDataSource* CEx28bView::SaveObject()
{
    TRACE("Entering CEx28bView::SaveObject\n");
    CEx28bDoc* pDoc = GetDocument();
    if (pDoc->m_lpOleObj != NULL) {
        COleDataSource* pSource = new COleDataSource();

        // CODE FOR OBJECT DATA
        FORMATETC fmte;
        SETFORMATETC(fmte, m_cfEmbedded, DVASPECT_CONTENT, NULL,
            TYMED_ISTORAGE, -1);
        STGMEDIUM stgm;
        stgm.tymed = TYMED_ISTORAGE;
        stgm.pstg = pDoc->m_pTempStgSub;
        stgm.pUnkForRelease = NULL;
        pDoc->m_pTempStgSub->AddRef();    // must do both!
        pDoc->m_pTempStgRoot->AddRef();
        pSource->CacheData(m_cfEmbedded, &stgm, &fmte);

        // metafile needed too
        MakeMetafilePict(pSource);

        // CODE FOR OBJECT DESCRIPTION DATA
        HGLOBAL hObjDesc = ::GlobalAlloc(GMEM_SHARE,
            sizeof(OBJECTDESCRIPTOR));
        LPOBJECTDESCRIPTOR pObjDesc =
            (LPOBJECTDESCRIPTOR) ::GlobalLock(hObjDesc);
        pObjDesc->cbSize = sizeof(OBJECTDESCRIPTOR);
        pObjDesc->clsid = CLSID_NULL;
        pObjDesc->dwDrawAspect = 0;
        pObjDesc->dwStatus = 0;
        pObjDesc->dwFullUserTypeName = 0;
```

```
            pObjDesc->dwSrcOfCopy = 0;
            pObjDesc->sizel.cx = 0;
            pObjDesc->sizel.cy = 0;
            pObjDesc->pointl.x = 0;
            pObjDesc->pointl.y = 0;
            ::GlobalUnlock(hObjDesc);
            pSource->CacheGlobalData(m_cfObjDesc, hObjDesc);
            return pSource;
    }
    return NULL;
}


BOOL CEx28bView::MakeMetafilePict(COleDataSource* pSource)
{
    CEx28bDoc* pDoc = GetDocument();
    COleDataObject dataObject;
    LPDATAOBJECT pDataObj; // OLE object's IDataObject interface
    VERIFY(pDoc->m_lpOleObj->QueryInterface(IID_IDataObject,
        (void**) &pDataObj) == S_OK);
    dataObject.Attach(pDataObj);
    FORMATETC fmtem;
    SETFORMATETC(fmtem, CF_METAFILEPICT, DVASPECT_CONTENT, NULL,
        TYMED_MFPICT, -1);
    if (!dataObject.IsDataAvailable(CF_METAFILEPICT, &fmtem)) {
        TRACE("CF_METAFILEPICT format is unavailable\n");
        return FALSE;
    }
    // Just copy the metafile handle from the OLE object
    //  to the clipboard data object
    STGMEDIUM stgmm;
    VERIFY(dataObject.GetData(CF_METAFILEPICT, &stgmm, &fmtem));
    pSource->CacheData(CF_METAFILEPICT, &stgmm, &fmtem);
    return TRUE;
}
```

Study the message map and the associated command handlers. They're all relatively short, and they mostly call the OLE functions described earlier. A few private helper functions need some explanation, however.

> **NOTE:** You'll see many calls to a *GetInterface* function. This is a member of class *CCmdTarget* and returns the specified OLE interface pointer for a class in your project. It's used mostly to get the *IOleClientSite* interface pointer for your document. It's more efficient than calling *ExternalQueryInterface*, but it doesn't increment the object's reference count.

GetSize

This function calls *IOleObject::GetSize* to get the embedded object's extents, which it converts to a rectangle for storage in the tracker.

SetNames

The *SetNames* function calls *IOleObject::SetHostNames* to send the container application's name to the component.

SetViewAdvise

This function calls the embedded object's *IViewObject2::SetAdvise* function to set up the advisory connection from the component object to the container document.

MakeMetafilePict

The *MakeMetafilePict* function calls the embedded object's *IDataObject::GetData* function to get a metafile picture to copy to the clipboard data object. (A metafile picture, by the way, is a Windows *METAFILEPICT* structure instance, which contains a pointer to the metafile plus extent information.)

SaveObject

This function acts like the *SaveDib* function in the EX25A example. It creates a *COleDataSource* object with three formats: embedded object, metafile, and object descriptor.

DoPasteObjectDescriptor

The *DoPasteObjectDescriptor* function pastes an object descriptor from the clipboard but doesn't do anything with it. This function must be called prior to calling *DoPasteObject*.

DoPasteObject

This function calls *OleCreateFromData* to create an embedded object from an embedded object format on the clipboard.

The *CEx28bDoc* Class

This class implements the *IOleClientSite* and *IAdviseSink* interfaces. Because of our one-embedded-item-per-document simplification, we don't need to track separate site objects. The document <u>is</u> the site. We're using the standard MFC interface macros, and, as always, we must provide at least a skeleton function for <u>all</u> interface members.

Look carefully at the functions *XOleClientSite::SaveObject*, *XOleClientSite::OnShowWindow*, and *XAdviseSink::OnViewChange* in Figure 28-7.

They're the important ones. The other ones are less important, but they contain TRACE statements as well, so you can watch the functions as they're called by the handler. Look also at the *OnNewDocument*, *OnCloseDocument*, and *DeleteContents* functions of the *CEx28bView* class. Notice how the document is managing a temporary storage. The document's *m_pTempStgSub* data member holds the storage pointer for the embedded object, and the *m_lpOleObj* data member holds the embedded object's *IOleObject* pointer.

EX28BDOC.H

```
#if !defined(AFX_EX28BDOC_H__1EAAB6DF_6011_11D0_848F_00400526305B ⮕
__INCLUDED_)
#define AFX_EX28BDOC_H__1EAAB6DF_6011_11D0_848F_00400526305B ⮕
__INCLUDED_

#if _MSC_VER > 1000
#pragma once
#endif //_MSC_VER > 1000

void ITrace(REFIID iid, const char* str);

class CEx28bDoc : public CDocument
{
protected: // create from serialization only
    CEx28bDoc();
    DECLARE_DYNCREATE(CEx28bDoc)
    BEGIN_INTERFACE_PART(OleClientSite, IOleClientSite)
        STDMETHOD(SaveObject)();
        STDMETHOD(GetMoniker)(DWORD, DWORD, LPMONIKER*);
        STDMETHOD(GetContainer)(LPOLECONTAINER*);
        STDMETHOD(ShowObject)();
        STDMETHOD(OnShowWindow)(BOOL);
        STDMETHOD(RequestNewObjectLayout)();
    END_INTERFACE_PART(OleClientSite)

    BEGIN_INTERFACE_PART(AdviseSink, IAdviseSink)
        STDMETHOD_(void,OnDataChange)(LPFORMATETC, LPSTGMEDIUM);
        STDMETHOD_(void,OnViewChange)(DWORD, LONG);
        STDMETHOD_(void,OnRename)(LPMONIKER);
        STDMETHOD_(void,OnSave)();
        STDMETHOD_(void,OnClose)();
    END_INTERFACE_PART(AdviseSink)

    DECLARE_INTERFACE_MAP()
```

Figure 28-7. *(continued)*
The container's CEx28bDoc class listing.

Figure 28-7. *continued*

```
friend class CEx28bView;
private:
    LPOLEOBJECT m_lpOleObj;
    LPSTORAGE m_pTempStgRoot;
    LPSTORAGE m_pTempStgSub;
    BOOL m_bHatch;
    static const OLECHAR* s_szSub;
// Overrides
    // ClassWizard generated virtual function overrides
    //{{AFX_VIRTUAL(CEx28bDoc)
    public:
    virtual BOOL OnNewDocument();
    virtual void Serialize(CArchive& ar);
    virtual void OnCloseDocument();
    virtual void DeleteContents();
    protected:
    virtual BOOL SaveModified();
    //}}AFX_VIRTUAL

// Implementation
public:
    virtual ~CEx28bDoc();
#ifdef _DEBUG
    virtual void AssertValid() const;
    virtual void Dump(CDumpContext& dc) const;
#endif

protected:

// Generated message map functions
protected:
    //{{AFX_MSG(CEx28bDoc)
    afx_msg void OnEditClearAll();
    //}}AFX_MSG
    DECLARE_MESSAGE_MAP()
};

/////////////////////////////////////////////////////////////////////

//{{AFX_INSERT_LOCATION}}
// Microsoft Visual C++ will insert additional declarations
//   immediately before the previous line.

#endif
// !defined(AFX_EX28BDOC_H__1EAAB6DF_6011_11D0_848F_00400526305B →
__INCLUDED_)
```

EX28BDOC.CPP

```
#include "stdafx.h"
#include "ex28b.h"

#include "ex28bDoc.h"

#ifdef _DEBUG
#define new DEBUG_NEW
#undef THIS_FILE
static char THIS_FILE[] = __FILE__;
#endif
const OLECHAR* CEx28bDoc::s_szSub = L"sub";   // static

//////////////////////////////////////////////////////////////////
// CEx28bDoc

IMPLEMENT_DYNCREATE(CEx28bDoc, CDocument)

BEGIN_MESSAGE_MAP(CEx28bDoc, CDocument)
    //{{AFX_MSG_MAP(CEx28bDoc)
    ON_COMMAND(ID_EDIT_CLEAR_ALL, OnEditClearAll)
    //}}AFX_MSG_MAP
END_MESSAGE_MAP()

BEGIN_INTERFACE_MAP(CEx28bDoc, CDocument)
    INTERFACE_PART(CEx28bDoc, IID_IOleClientSite, OleClientSite)
    INTERFACE_PART(CEx28bDoc, IID_IAdviseSink, AdviseSink)
END_INTERFACE_MAP()

//////////////////////////////////////////////////////////////////
// implementation of IOleClientSite

STDMETHODIMP_(ULONG) CEx28bDoc::XOleClientSite::AddRef()
{
    TRACE("CEx28bDoc::XOleClientSite::AddRef\n");
    METHOD_PROLOGUE(CEx28bDoc, OleClientSite)
    return pThis->InternalAddRef();
}

STDMETHODIMP_(ULONG) CEx28bDoc::XOleClientSite::Release()
{
    TRACE("CEx28bDoc::XOleClientSite::Release\n");
    METHOD_PROLOGUE(CEx28bDoc, OleClientSite)
    return pThis->InternalRelease();
}
```

(continued)

Figure 28-7. *continued*

```
STDMETHODIMP CEx28bDoc::XOleClientSite::QueryInterface(
    REFIID iid, LPVOID* ppvObj)
{
    ITrace(iid, "CEx28bDoc::XOleClientSite::QueryInterface");
    METHOD_PROLOGUE(CEx28bDoc, OleClientSite)
    return pThis->InternalQueryInterface(&iid, ppvObj);
}


STDMETHODIMP CEx28bDoc::XOleClientSite::SaveObject()
{
    TRACE("CEx28bDoc::XOleClientSite::SaveObject\n");
    METHOD_PROLOGUE(CEx28bDoc, OleClientSite)
    ASSERT_VALID(pThis);

    LPPERSISTSTORAGE lpPersistStorage;
    pThis->m_pOleObj->QueryInterface(IID_IPersistStorage,
        (void**) &lpPersistStorage);
    ASSERT(lpPersistStorage != NULL);
    HRESULT hr = NOERROR;
    if (lpPersistStorage->IsDirty() == NOERROR)
    {
        // NOERROR == S_OK != S_FALSE, therefore object is dirty!
        hr = ::OleSave(lpPersistStorage, pThis->m_pTempStgSub,
                       TRUE);
        if (hr != NOERROR)
            hr = lpPersistStorage->SaveCompleted(NULL);

        // Mark the document as dirty if save successful
        pThis->SetModifiedFlag();
    }
    lpPersistStorage->Release();
    pThis->UpdateAllViews(NULL);
    return hr;
}


STDMETHODIMP CEx28bDoc::XOleClientSite::GetMoniker(
    DWORD dwAssign, DWORD dwWhichMoniker, LPMONIKER* ppMoniker)
{
    TRACE("CEx28bDoc::XOleClientSite::GetMoniker\n");
    return E_NOTIMPL;
}


STDMETHODIMP CEx28bDoc::XOleClientSite::GetContainer(
    LPOLECONTAINER* ppContainer)
{
    TRACE("CEx28bDoc::XOleClientSite::GetContainer\n");
```

```
        return E_NOTIMPL;
}

STDMETHODIMP CEx28bDoc::XOleClientSite::ShowObject()
{
    TRACE("CEx28bDoc::XOleClientSite::ShowObject\n");
    METHOD_PROLOGUE(CEx28bDoc, OleClientSite)
    ASSERT_VALID(pThis);
    pThis->UpdateAllViews(NULL);
    return NOERROR;
}

STDMETHODIMP CEx28bDoc::XOleClientSite::OnShowWindow(BOOL fShow)
{
    TRACE("CEx28bDoc::XOleClientSite::OnShowWindow\n");
    METHOD_PROLOGUE(CEx28bDoc, OleClientSite)
    ASSERT_VALID(pThis);
    pThis->m_bHatch = fShow;
    pThis->UpdateAllViews(NULL);
    return NOERROR;
}
STDMETHODIMP CEx28bDoc::XOleClientSite::RequestNewObjectLayout()
{
    TRACE("CEx28bDoc::XOleClientSite::RequestNewObjectLayout\n");
    return E_NOTIMPL;
}


/////////////////////////////////////////////////////////////////////
// implementation of IAdviseSink

STDMETHODIMP_(ULONG) CEx28bDoc::XAdviseSink::AddRef()
{
    TRACE("CEx28bDoc::XAdviseSink::AddRef\n");
    METHOD_PROLOGUE(CEx28bDoc, AdviseSink)
    return pThis->InternalAddRef();
}


STDMETHODIMP_(ULONG) CEx28bDoc::XAdviseSink::Release()
{
    TRACE("CEx28bDoc::XAdviseSink::Release\n");
    METHOD_PROLOGUE(CEx28bDoc, AdviseSink)
    return pThis->InternalRelease();
}
STDMETHODIMP CEx28bDoc::XAdviseSink::QueryInterface(
    REFIID iid, LPVOID* ppvObj)
```

(continued)

Figure 28-7. *continued*

```
{
    ITrace(iid, "CEx28bDoc::XAdviseSink::QueryInterface");
    METHOD_PROLOGUE(CEx28bDoc, AdviseSink)
    return pThis->InternalQueryInterface(&iid, ppvObj);
}

STDMETHODIMP_(void) CEx28bDoc::XAdviseSink::OnDataChange(
    LPFORMATETC lpFormatEtc, LPSTGMEDIUM lpStgMedium)
{
    TRACE("CEx28bDoc::XAdviseSink::OnDataChange\n");
    METHOD_PROLOGUE(CEx28bDoc, AdviseSink)
    ASSERT_VALID(pThis);

    // Interesting only for advanced containers. Forward it such
    //  that containers do not have to implement the entire
    //  interface.
}

STDMETHODIMP_(void) CEx28bDoc::XAdviseSink::OnViewChange(
    DWORD aspects, LONG /*lindex*/)
{
    TRACE("CEx28bDoc::XAdviseSink::OnViewChange\n");
    METHOD_PROLOGUE(CEx28bDoc, AdviseSink)
    ASSERT_VALID(pThis);

    pThis->UpdateAllViews(NULL);          // the really important one
}

STDMETHODIMP_(void) CEx28bDoc::XAdviseSink::OnRename(
    LPMONIKER /*lpMoniker*/)
{
    TRACE("CEx28bDoc::XAdviseSink::OnRename\n");
    // Interesting only to the OLE link object. Containers ignore
    //  this.
}

STDMETHODIMP_(void) CEx28bDoc::XAdviseSink::OnSave()
{
    TRACE("CEx28bDoc::XAdviseSink::OnSave\n");
    METHOD_PROLOGUE(CEx28bDoc, AdviseSink)
    ASSERT_VALID(pThis);

    pThis->UpdateAllViews(NULL);
}
STDMETHODIMP_(void) CEx28bDoc::XAdviseSink::OnClose()
```

```
{
    TRACE("CEx28bDoc::XAdviseSink::OnClose\n");
    METHOD_PROLOGUE(CEx28bDoc, AdviseSink)
    ASSERT_VALID(pThis);

    pThis->UpdateAllViews(NULL);
}

/////////////////////////////////////////////////////////////////////
// CEx28bDoc construction/destruction

CEx28bDoc::CEx28bDoc()
{
    m_lpOleObj = NULL;
    m_pTempStgRoot = NULL;
    m_pTempStgSub = NULL;
    m_bHatch = FALSE;
}

CEx28bDoc::~CEx28bDoc()
{
}

BOOL CEx28bDoc::OnNewDocument()
{
    TRACE("Entering CEx28bDoc::OnNewDocument\n");
    // Create a structured storage home for the object
    //  (m_pTempStgSub). This is a temporary file -- random name
    //  supplied by OLE.
    VERIFY(::StgCreateDocfile(NULL,
            STGM_READWRITE|STGM_SHARE_EXCLUSIVE|STGM_CREATE|
            STGM_DELETEONRELEASE,
            0, &m_pTempStgRoot) == S_OK);
    ASSERT(m_pTempStgRoot != NULL);

    VERIFY(m_pTempStgRoot->CreateStorage(OLESTR("sub"),
            STGM_CREATE|STGM_READWRITE|STGM_SHARE_EXCLUSIVE,
            0, 0, &m_pTempStgSub) == S_OK);
    ASSERT(m_pTempStgSub != NULL);
    return CDocument::OnNewDocument();
}

/////////////////////////////////////////////////////////////////////
// CEx28bDoc serialization
```

(continued)

789

Figure 28-7. *continued*

```
void CEx28bDoc::Serialize(CArchive& ar)
{
    // no hookup to MFC serialization
    if (ar.IsStoring())
    {
        // TODO: add storing code here
    }
    else
    {
        // TODO: add loading code here
    }
}


/////////////////////////////////////////////////////////////////////
// CEx28bDoc diagnostics

#ifdef _DEBUG
void CEx28bDoc::AssertValid() const
{
    CDocument::AssertValid();
}

void CEx28bDoc::Dump(CDumpContext& dc) const
{
    CDocument::Dump(dc);
}
#endif //_DEBUG


/////////////////////////////////////////////////////////////////////
// CEx28bDoc commands

void CEx28bDoc::OnCloseDocument()
{
    m_pTempStgSub->Release(); // must release BEFORE calling
                              //  base class
    m_pTempStgRoot->Release();
    CDocument::OnCloseDocument();
}

void CEx28bDoc::DeleteContents()
{
    if(m_lpOleObj != NULL) {
        // If object is running, close it, which releases our
        //  IOleClientSite
        m_lpOleObj->Close(OLECLOSE_NOSAVE);
```

```
        m_lpOleObj->Release(); // should be final release
                               //  (or else...)
        m_lpOleObj = NULL;
    }
}

void CEx28bDoc::OnEditClearAll()
{
    DeleteContents();
    UpdateAllViews(NULL);
    SetModifiedFlag();
    m_bHatch = FALSE;
}

BOOL CEx28bDoc::SaveModified()
{
    // Eliminate "save to file" message
    return TRUE;
}

void ITrace(REFIID iid, const char* str)
{
    OLECHAR* lpszIID;
    ::StringFromIID(iid, &lpszIID);
    CString strIID = lpszIID;
    TRACE("%s - %s\n", (const char*) strIID, (const char*) str);
    AfxFreeTaskMem(lpszIID);
}
```

The EX28C Example—
An OLE Embedded Component

You've already seen an MFC embedded component with in-place–activation capability (EX28A). Now you'll see a bare-bones component program that activates an embedded object in a separate window. It doesn't do much except display text and graphics in the window, but you'll learn a lot if you study the code. The application started as an SDI AppWizard Automation component with the document as the creatable object. The document's *IDispatch* interface was ripped out and replaced with *IOleObject*, *IDataObject*, and *IPersistStorage* interfaces. All the template server code carries through, so the document, view, and main frame objects are created when the container starts the component.

Open and build the EX28C project now. Run the application to register it, and then try it with the EX28B container or any other container program.

The *CEx28cView* Class

This class is straightforward. The only member functions of interest are the *OnDraw* function and the *OnPrepareDC* function, shown here:

```
void CEx28cView::OnDraw(CDC* pDC)
{
    CEx28cDoc* pDoc = GetDocument();
    ASSERT_VALID(pDoc);

    pDC->Rectangle(CRect(500, -1000, 1500, -2000));
    pDC->TextOut(0, 0, pDoc->m_strText);
}

void CEx28cView::OnPrepareDC(CDC* pDC, CPrintInfo* pInfo)
{
    pDC->SetMapMode(MM_HIMETRIC);

}
```

The *CEx28cDoc* Class

This class does most of the component's work and is too big to list here. Figure 28-8 lists the header file, but you'll have to go to the companion CD-ROM for the implementation code. A few of the important functions are listed here, however.

EX28CDOC.H

```
#if !defined(AFX_EX28CDOC_H__1EAAB6F5_6011_11D0_848F_00400526305B ↴
__INCLUDED_)
#define AFX_EX28CDOC_H__1EAAB6F5_6011_11D0_848F_00400526305B ↴
__INCLUDED_

#if _MSC_VER > 1000
#pragma once
#endif // _MSC_VER > 1000

extern const CLSID clsid; // defined in ex28c.cpp
void ITrace(REFIID iid, const char* str);

#define SETFORMATETC(fe, cf, asp, td, med, li)    \
    ((fe).cfFormat=cf, \
     (fe).dwAspect=asp, \
     (fe).ptd=td, \
```

Figure 28-8. *(continued)*
The component's CEx28cDoc class handler file listing.

```
        (fe).tymed=med, \
        (fe).lindex=li)

class CEx28cDoc : public CDocument
{
friend class CEx28cView;
private:
    CString m_strText;
    LPOLECLIENTSITE m_lpClientSite;
    LPOLEADVISEHOLDER m_lpOleAdviseHolder;
    LPDATAADVISEHOLDER m_lpDataAdviseHolder;
    CString m_strContainerApp;
    CString m_strContainerObj;
    HGLOBAL MakeMetaFile();

    BEGIN_INTERFACE_PART(OleObject, IOleObject)
        STDMETHOD(SetClientSite)(LPOLECLIENTSITE);
        STDMETHOD(GetClientSite)(LPOLECLIENTSITE*);
        STDMETHOD(SetHostNames)(LPCOLESTR, LPCOLESTR);
        STDMETHOD(Close)(DWORD);
        STDMETHOD(SetMoniker)(DWORD, LPMONIKER);
        STDMETHOD(GetMoniker)(DWORD, DWORD, LPMONIKER*);
        STDMETHOD(InitFromData)(LPDATAOBJECT, BOOL, DWORD);
        STDMETHOD(GetClipboardData)(DWORD, LPDATAOBJECT*);
        STDMETHOD(DoVerb)(LONG, LPMSG, LPOLECLIENTSITE, LONG,
                          HWND, LPCRECT);
        STDMETHOD(EnumVerbs)(LPENUMOLEVERB*);
        STDMETHOD(Update)();
        STDMETHOD(IsUpToDate)();
        STDMETHOD(GetUserClassID)(LPCLSID);
        STDMETHOD(GetUserType)(DWORD, LPOLESTR*);
        STDMETHOD(SetExtent)(DWORD, LPSIZEL);
        STDMETHOD(GetExtent)(DWORD, LPSIZEL);
        STDMETHOD(Advise)(LPADVISESINK, LPDWORD);
        STDMETHOD(Unadvise)(DWORD);
        STDMETHOD(EnumAdvise)(LPENUMSTATDATA*);
        STDMETHOD(GetMiscStatus)(DWORD, LPDWORD);
        STDMETHOD(SetColorScheme)(LPLOGPALETTE);
    END_INTERFACE_PART(OleObject)

    BEGIN_INTERFACE_PART(DataObject, IDataObject)
        STDMETHOD(GetData)(LPFORMATETC, LPSTGMEDIUM);
        STDMETHOD(GetDataHere)(LPFORMATETC, LPSTGMEDIUM);
        STDMETHOD(QueryGetData)(LPFORMATETC);
        STDMETHOD(GetCanonicalFormatEtc)(LPFORMATETC, LPFORMATETC);
        STDMETHOD(SetData)(LPFORMATETC, LPSTGMEDIUM, BOOL);
```

(continued)

793

Figure 28-8. *continued*

```
        STDMETHOD(EnumFormatEtc)(DWORD, LPENUMFORMATETC*);
        STDMETHOD(DAdvise)(LPFORMATETC, DWORD, LPADVISESINK, LPDWORD);
        STDMETHOD(DUnadvise)(DWORD);
        STDMETHOD(EnumDAdvise)(LPENUMSTATDATA*);
    END_INTERFACE_PART(DataObject)

    BEGIN_INTERFACE_PART(PersistStorage, IPersistStorage)
        STDMETHOD(GetClassID)(LPCLSID);
        STDMETHOD(IsDirty)();
        STDMETHOD(InitNew)(LPSTORAGE);
        STDMETHOD(Load)(LPSTORAGE);
        STDMETHOD(Save)(LPSTORAGE, BOOL);
        STDMETHOD(SaveCompleted)(LPSTORAGE);
        STDMETHOD(HandsOffStorage)();
    END_INTERFACE_PART(PersistStorage)

    DECLARE_INTERFACE_MAP()

protected: // Create from serialization only
    CEx28cDoc();
    DECLARE_DYNCREATE(CEx28cDoc)

// Overrides
    // ClassWizard generated virtual function overrides
    //{{AFX_VIRTUAL(CEx28cDoc)
    public:
    virtual BOOL OnNewDocument();
    virtual void Serialize(CArchive& ar);
    virtual void OnFinalRelease();
    virtual void OnCloseDocument();
    protected:
    virtual BOOL SaveModified();
    //}}AFX_VIRTUAL

// Implementation
public:
    virtual ~CEx28cDoc();
#ifdef _DEBUG
    virtual void AssertValid() const;
    virtual void Dump(CDumpContext& dc) const;
#endif

// Generated message map functions
public:
    //{{AFX_MSG(CEx28cDoc)
    afx_msg void OnModify();
    afx_msg void OnFileUpdate();
```

```
    afx_msg void OnUpdateFileUpdate(CCmdUI* pCmdUI);
    //}}AFX_MSG
    DECLARE_MESSAGE_MAP()
};
/////////////////////////////////////////////////////////////////////////

//{{AFX_INSERT_LOCATION}}
// Microsoft Visual C++ will insert additional
//  declarations immediately before the previous line

#endif
// !defined(AFX_EX28CDOC_H__1EAAB6F5_6011_11D0_848F_00400526305B ⮑
__INCLUDED_)
```

Here's a list of the important interface functions in ex28cDoc.cpp:

> *XOleObject::SetClientSite*
> *XOleObject::DoVerb*
> *XOleObject::Advise*
> *XDataObject::GetData*
> *XDataObject::QueryGetData*
> *XDataObject::DAdvise*
> *XPersistStorage::GetClassID*
> *XPersistStorage::InitNew*
> *XPersistStorage::Load*
> *XPersistStorage::Save*

You've seen the container code that draws a metafile. Here's the component code that creates it. The object handler calls the component's *XDataObject::GetData* function when it needs a metafile. This *GetData* implementation calls a helper function, *MakeMetaFile*, which creates the metafile picture. Compare the drawing code with the drawing code in *CEx28cView::OnDraw*.

```
STDMETHODIMP CEx28cDoc::XDataObject::GetData(
    LPFORMATETC lpFormatEtc, LPSTGMEDIUM lpStgMedium)
{
    TRACE("CEx28cDoc::XDataObject::GetData -- %d\n",
        lpFormatEtc->cfFormat);
    METHOD_PROLOGUE(CEx28cDoc, DataObject)
    ASSERT_VALID(pThis);

    if (lpFormatEtc->cfFormat != CF_METAFILEPICT) {
        return S_FALSE;
    }
    HGLOBAL hPict = pThis->MakeMetaFile();
    lpStgMedium->tymed = TYMED_MFPICT;
    lpStgMedium->hMetaFilePict = hPict;
```

(continued)

```
        lpStgMedium->pUnkForRelease = NULL;
        return S_OK;
}

HGLOBAL CEx28cDoc::MakeMetaFile
{
        HGLOBAL hPict;
        CMetaFileDC dcm;
        VERIFY(dcm.Create());
        CSize size(5000, 5000); // initial size of object in Excel & Word
        dcm.SetMapMode(MM_ANISOTROPIC);
        dcm.SetWindowOrg(0,0);
        dcm.SetWindowExt(size.cx, -size.cy);
        // drawing code
        dcm.Rectangle(CRect(500, -1000, 1500, -2000));
        CFont font;
        font.CreateFont(-500, 0, 0, 0, 400, FALSE, FALSE, 0,
                        ANSI_CHARSET, OUT_DEFAULT_PRECIS,
                        CLIP_DEFAULT_PRECIS, DEFAULT_QUALITY,
                        DEFAULT_PITCH | FF_SWISS, "Arial");
        CFont* pFont = dcm.SelectObject(&font);
        dcm.TextOut(0, 0, m_strText);
        dcm.SelectObject(pFont);

        HMETAFILE hMF = dcm.Close();
        ASSERT(hMF != NULL);
        hPict = ::GlobalAlloc(GMEM_SHARE|GMEM_MOVEABLE,
                              sizeof(METAFILEPICT));
        ASSERT(hPict != NULL);
        LPMETAFILEPICT lpPict;
        lpPict = (LPMETAFILEPICT) ::GlobalLock(hPict);
        ASSERT(lpPict != NULL);
        lpPict->mm = MM_ANISOTROPIC;
        lpPict->hMF = hMF;
        lpPict->xExt = size.cx;
        lpPict->yExt = size.cy;  // HIMETRIC height
        ::GlobalUnlock(hPict);
        return hPict;
}
```

The *XOleObject::Advise* and the *XDataObject::DAdvise* functions are similar. Both functions call global OLE functions to set up OLE advise holder objects that can manage multiple advise sinks. (In this program, there is only one
advise sink per OLE advise holder object.) The *XOleObject::Advise* function,
listed below, establishes an OLE advise holder object with the *IOleAdviseHolder*

interface. Other document functions call *IOleAdviseHolder::SendOnClose* and *SendOnSave*, which in turn call *IAdviseSink::OnClose* and *OnSave* for each attached sink.

```
STDMETHODIMP CEx28cDoc::XOleObject::Advise(
    IAdviseSink* pAdvSink, DWORD* pdwConnection)
{
    TRACE("CEx28cDoc::XOleObject::Advise\n");
    METHOD_PROLOGUE(CEx28cDoc, OleObject)
    ASSERT_VALID(pThis);
    *pdwConnection = 0;
    if (pThis->m_lpOleAdviseHolder == NULL &&
        ::CreateOleAdviseHolder(&pThis->m_lpOleAdviseHolder)
        != NOERROR) {
            return E_OUTOFMEMORY;
    }
    ASSERT(pThis->m_lpOleAdviseHolder != NULL);
    return pThis->m_lpOleAdviseHolder->Advise(pAdvSink,
                                          pdwConnection);
}
```

The framework calls the *OnModify* function when the user chooses Modify from the EX28C-MAIN menu. The user enters a string through a dialog, and the function sends the *OnDataChange* notification to the object handler's data advise sink. (Figure 28-5 on page 762 illustrates the advisory connections.)

Here is the *OnModify* function code:

```
void CEx28cDoc::OnModify()
{
    CTextDialog dlg;
    dlg.m_strText = m_strText;
    if (dlg.DoModal() == IDOK) {
        m_strText = dlg.m_strText;
        UpdateAllViews(NULL); // redraw view
        // Notify the client that the metafile has changed.
        //  Client must call IViewObject::SetAdvise.
        LPDATAOBJECT lpDataObject =
            (LPDATAOBJECT) GetInterface(&IID_IDataObject);
        HRESULT hr =
            m_lpDataAdviseHolder->SendOnDataChange(lpDataObject,
                                               0, NULL);
        ASSERT(hr == NOERROR);
        SetModifiedFlag(); // won't update without this
    }
}
```

The framework calls the *OnFileUpdate* function when the user chooses Update from the File menu. The function calls *IOleClientSite::SaveObject*, which in turn causes the container to save the metafile and the object's native data in the storage. The function also sends the *OnSave* notification back to the client's advise sink. Here is the *OnFileUpdate* function code:

```
void CEx28cDoc::OnFileUpdate()
{
    if (m_lpClientSite == NULL) return;
    VERIFY(m_lpClientSite->SaveObject() == NOERROR);
    if (m_lpOleAdviseHolder != NULL)
        m_lpOleAdviseHolder->SendOnSave();
    SetModifiedFlag(FALSE);
}
```

CHAPTER TWENTY-NINE

Introducing the Active Template Library

In this chapter, you'll take a look at the second framework (MFC being the first) now included within Microsoft Visual C++—the Active Template Library (ATL). You'll start by quickly revisiting the Component Object Model (COM) and looking at an alternative method of writing Chapter 24's *CSpaceship* object, illustrating that there is more than one way to write a COM class. (This will become important as you examine ATL's class composition methods.) Next you'll investigate the Active Template Library, focusing first on C++ templates and raw C++ smart pointers and how they might be useful in COM development. You'll cover the client side of ATL programming and examine some of ATL's smart pointers. Finally you'll check out the server side of ATL programming, reimplementing the Chapter 24 spaceship example using ATL to get a feel for ATL's architecture.

Revisiting COM

The most important concept to understand about COM programming is that it is interface-based. As you saw in Chapter 24, you don't need real COM or even Microsoft runtime support to use interface-based programming. All you need is some discipline.

Think back to the spaceship example in Chapter 24. You started out with a single class named *CSpaceship* that implemented several functions. Seasoned C++ developers usually sit down at the computer and start typing a class like this:

```
class CSpaceship {
    void Fly();
    int& GetPosition();
};
```

However, the procedure is a little different with interface-based development. Instead of writing the class directly, interface-based programming involves spelling out an interface before implementing it. In Chapter 24, the *Fly* and *GetPosition* functions were moved into an abstract base class named *IMotion*.

```
struct IMotion {
    virtual void Fly() = 0;
    virtual int& GetPosition() = 0;
};
```

Then we inherited the *CSpaceship* class from the *IMotion* interface like this:

```
class CSpaceship : IMotion {
    void Fly();
    int& GetPosition();
};
```

Notice that at this point the motion interface has been separated from its implementation. When practicing interface development, the interface comes first. You can work on the interface as you develop it, making sure it's complete while at the same time not over-bloated. But once the interface has been published (that is, once a lot of other developers have started coding to it), the interface is frozen and can never change.

This subtle distinction between class-based programming and interface-based programming seems to introduce some programming overhead. However, it turns out to be one of the key points to understanding COM. By collecting the *Fly* and the *GetPosition* functions in an interface, you've developed a binary signature. That is, by defining the interface ahead of time and talking to the class through the interface, client code has a potentially language-neutral way of talking to the class.

Gathering functions together into interfaces is itself quite powerful. Imagine you want to describe something other than a spaceship—an airplane, for example. It's certainly conceivable that an airplane would also have *Fly* and *GetPosition* functions. Interface programming provides a more advanced form of polymorphism—polymorphism at the interface level, not only at the single-function level.

Separating interface from implementation is the basis of interface-based development. The Component Object Model is centered on interface programming. COM enforces the distinction between interface and implementation. In COM, the only way client code can talk to an object is through an interface. However, gathering functions together into interfaces isn't quite enough. There's one more ingredient needed—a mechanism for discovering functionality at runtime.

The Core Interface: *IUnknown*

The key element that makes COM different from ordinary interface programming is this rule: the first three functions of every COM interface are the same. The core interface in COM, *IUnknown,* looks like this:

```
struct IUnknown {
    virtual HRESULT QueryInterface(REFIID riid, void** ppv) = 0;
    virtual ULONG AddRef() = 0;
    virtual ULONG Release() = 0;
};
```

Every COM interface derives from this interface (meaning the first three functions of every COM interface you ever see will be *QueryInterface, AddRef,* and *Release*). To turn *IMotion* into a COM interface, derive it from *IUnknown* like this:

```
struct IMotion : IUnknown {
    void Fly();
    int& GetPosition();
};
```

> **NOTE:** If you wanted these interfaces to work out-of-process, you'd have to make each function return an HRESULT. You'll see this when we cover Interface Definition Language (IDL) later in this chapter.

AddRef and *Release* deserve some mention because they are part of *IUnknown. AddRef* and *Release* allow an object to control its own lifetime if it chooses to. As a rule, clients are supposed to treat interface pointers like resources: clients acquire interfaces, use them, and release them when they are done using them. Objects learn about new references to themselves via *AddRef*. Objects learn they have been unreferenced through the *Release* function. Objects often use this information to control their lifetimes. For example, many objects self-destruct when their reference count reaches zero.

Here's how some client code might use the spaceship:

```
void UseSpaceship() {
    IMotion* pMotion = NULL;

    pMotion = GetASpaceship(); // This is a member of the
                               //  hypothetical Spaceship
                               //  API. It's presumably an
                               //  entry point into some DLL.
                               //  Returns an IMotion* and
                               //  causes an implicit AddRef.
    If(pMotion) {
```

(continued)

```
        pMotion->Fly();
        int i = pMotion->GetPosition();
        pMotion->Release(); // done with this instance of CSpaceship
    }
}
```

The other (and more important) function within *IUnknown* is the first one: *QueryInterface*. *QueryInterface* is the COM mechanism for discovering functionality at runtime. If someone gives you a COM interface pointer to an object and you don't want to use that pointer, you can use the pointer to ask the object for a different interface to the same object. This mechanism, along with the fact that interfaces remain constant once published, are the key ingredients that allow COM-based software to evolve safely over time. The result is that you can add functionality to your COM software without breaking older versions of the clients running that software. In addition, clients have a widely recognized means of acquiring that new functionality once they know about it. For example, you add functionality to the implementation of *CSpaceship* by adding a new interface named *IVisual*. Adding this interface makes sense because you can have objects in three-dimensional space that move in and out of view. You might also have an invisible object in three-dimensional space (a black hole, for example). Here's the *IVisual* interface:

```
struct IVisual : IUnknown {
    virtual void Display() = 0;
};
```

A client might use the *IVisual* interface like this:

```
void UseSpaceship() {
    IMotion* pMotion = NULL;

    pMotion = GetASpaceship(); // Implicit AddRef
    if(pMotion) {
        pMotion->Fly();
        int i = pMotion->GetPosition();

        IVisual* pVisual = NULL;
        PMotion->QueryInterface(IID_IVisual, (void**) &pVisual);
        // Implicit AddRef within QueryInterface

        if(pVisible) {
            pVisual->Display(); // uncloaking now
            pVisual->Release(); // done with this interface
        }
    }
    pMotion->Release(); // done with this instance of IMotion
}
```

Notice that the preceding code uses interface pointers very carefully: it uses them only if the interface was acquired properly, and then it releases the interface pointers when it is done using them. This is raw COM programming at the lowest level—you acquire an interface pointer, you use the interface pointer, and you release it when you're done with it.

Writing COM Code

As you can see, writing COM client code isn't a whole lot different from writing regular C++ code. However, the C++ classes that the client talks to are abstract base classes. Instead of calling *operator new* as you would in C++, you create COM objects and acquire COM interfaces by explicitly calling some sort of API function. And instead of deleting the object outright, you simply follow the COM interface rule of balancing calls to *AddRef* with calls to *Release*.

What does it take to get the COM class up and running? You saw how to do it using MFC in Chapter 24. Here's another example of implementing *CSpaceship* as a COM class. This example uses the multiple inheritance approach to writing COM classes. That is, the C++ class inherits from several interfaces and then implements the union of all the functions (including *IUnknown*, of course).

```
struct CSpaceship : IMotion, IDisplay {
    ULONG m_cRef;
    int m_nPosition;

    CSpaceship() : m_cRef(0),
                   m_nPosition(0) {
    }

    HRESULT QueryInterface(REFIID riid,
                           void** ppv);
    ULONG AddRef() {
        return InterlockedIncrement(&m_cRef);
    }
    ULONG Release() {
        ULONG cRef = InterlockedIncrement(&m_cRef);
        if(cRef == 0){
            delete this;
            return 0;
        } else
            return m_cRef;
    }
```

(continued)

```
    // IMotion functions:
    void Fly() {
        // Do whatever it takes to fly here
    }
    int GetPosition() {
        return m_nPosition;
    }

    // IVisual functions:
    void Display() {
        // Uncloak
    }
};
```

COM Classes Using Multiple Inheritance

If you're used to seeing plain C++ code, the preceding code might look a little strange to you. This is a less common form of multiple inheritance called interface inheritance. Most C++ developers are used to an implementation inheritance in which the derived class inherits everything from the base class—including the implementation. Interface inheritance simply means the derived class inherits the interfaces of the base class. The preceding code effectively adds two data members to the *CSpaceship* class—a *vptr* for each implied *vtable*.

When using the multiple inheritance approach to implementing interfaces, each interface shares *CSpaceship*'s implementation of *IUnknown*. This sharing illustrates a rather esoteric yet important concept known as COM identity. The basic idea of COM identity is that *IUnknown* is the void* of COM. *IUknown* is the one interface guaranteed to be hanging off any object, and you can always get to it. COM identity also says (in the previous example) the client can call *QueryInterface* through the *CSpaceship IMotion* interface to get the *IVisual* interface. Conversely, the client can call *QueryInterface* through the *CSpaceship IVisual* interface to get the *IMotion* interface. Finally, the client can call *QueryInterface* through *IUnknown* to acquire the *IMotion* or the *IVisual* interface, and the client can call *QueryInterface* through either *IMotion* or *IVisual* to get a pointer to *IUnknown*. To learn more about COM identity, see *Essential COM* by Don Box (Addison-Wesley, 1997) or *Inside COM* by Dale Rogerson (Microsoft Press, 1997).

Often you'll see COM classes illustrated with "lollipop" diagrams depicting the interfaces implemented by a COM class. You can see an example of a lollipop diagram on page 579 in Chapter 24.

The multiple inheritance method of implementing *CSpaceship* automatically fulfills the rules of COM identity. Note that all calls to *QueryInterface*, *AddRef*, and *Release* land in the same place in the C++ class, regardless of the interface through which they were called.

This is more or less the essence of COM. As a COM developer, your job is to create useful services and expose them through COM interfaces. At the most basic level, this means wiring up some function tables to follow COM's identity rules. You've seen two ways to accomplish this so far. (Chapter 24 showed you how to do it using nested classes and MFC. This chapter just showed you how to write a COM class using multiple inheritance in C++.) However, in addition to interface programming and writing classes to implement interfaces, there are several other pieces to the COM puzzle.

The COM Infrastructure

Once you get your mind around the concept of interface-based programming, quite a few details need implementation in order to get the class to mix in with the rest of the system. These details often overshadow the fundamental beauty of COM.

To start off with, COM classes need a place to live, so you must package them in either an EXE or a DLL. In addition, each COM class you write needs an accompanying class object (often referred to as a class factory). The way in which a COM server's class object is exposed differs depending upon how you package the COM class (in a DLL or an EXE). The server lifetime also needs to be considered. The server should stay in memory for as long as it's needed, and it should go away when it's not needed. To accomplish this, servers maintain global lock counts indicating the number of objects with extant interface pointers. Finally, well-behaved servers insert the necessary values in the Windows Registry so that client software can easily activate them.

You've spent a lot of time looking at MFC while reading this book. As you saw in Chapter 24, MFC takes care of most of the COM-based details for you. For example, *CCmdTarget* has an implementation of *IUnknown*. MFC has even created C++ classes and macros to implement class objects (such as *COleObject-Factory*, *COleTemplateServer*, *DECLARE_OLE_CREATE*, and *IMPLEMENT-_OLE_CREATE*) that will put most of the correct entries into the Registry. MFC has the easiest-to-implement, zippiest version of *IDispatch* around—all you need is a *CCmdTarget* object and ClassWizard. If you decide OLE Documents or ActiveX Documents are your thing, MFC provides standard implementations of the Object Linking and Embedding and ActiveX Document protocols. Finally, MFC remains hands-down the easiest way to write fast, powerful ActiveX controls. (You can write ActiveX controls in Microsoft Visual Basic, but you don't have quite as much flexibility). These are all great features. However, using MFC has a downside.

To get these features, you need to buy into MFC 100%. Now, that's not necessarily a bad idea. However, you should be aware of the cost of entry when you decide to use MFC. MFC is big. It has to be—it's a C++ framework with many capabilities.

A New Framework

As you can see from the examples we've looked at so far, implementing COM classes and making them available to clients involves writing a great deal of code—code that remains the same from one class implementation to another. *IUnknown* implementations are generally the same for every COM class you encounter—the main difference between them is the interfaces exposed by each class.

But just as you no longer need to understand assembly language to get software working these days, pretty soon you'll no longer need to understand all the nuances of *IUnknown* and COM's relationship to C++ to get your COM-based software up and running. You're not quite at that stage, but the Active Template Library (ATL) from Microsoft is a great first step in that direction. (However, ATL does not absolve you from learning the important concepts behind COM, such as apartments and remoting.)

Before diving into ATL, let's take a quick peek at where COM and ATL fit into the big picture.

ActiveX, OLE, and COM

COM is simply the plumbing for a series of higher-level application integration technologies consisting of such items as ActiveX Controls and OLE Documents. These technologies define protocols based on COM interfaces. For example, for a COM object to qualify as a minimal OLE Document object, that COM object has to implement at least three interfaces—*IPersistStorage, IOleObject,* and *IDataObject.* You might choose to implement the higher-level features of OLE Documents and controls. However, it makes more sense to let some sort of application framework do the grunt work. Of course, that's why there's MFC.

> NOTE: For more information about how to implement higher-level features in raw C++, see Kraig Brockschmidt's *Inside OLE,* 2d. ed. (Microsoft Press, 1995).

ActiveX, MFC, and COM

While the pure plumbing of COM is quite interesting by itself (it's simply amazing to see how COM remoting works), the higher-level features are what sell applications. MFC is a huge framework geared toward creating entire Windows applications. Inside MFC, you'll find tons of utility classes, a data management/rendering mechanism (the Document–View architecture), as well as support for OLE Documents, drag and drop, Automation, and ActiveX Controls. You probably don't want to develop an OLE Document application from scratch; you're much better off using MFC. However, if you need to create a small or medium-size COM-based service, you might want to turn away from MFC so you don't have to include all the baggage MFC maintains for the higher-level features.

You can use raw C++ to create COM components, but doing so forces you to spend a good portion of your time hacking out the boilerplate code (*IUnknown* and class objects, for example). Using MFC to write COM-based applications turns out to be a less painful way of adding the big-ticket items to your application, but it's difficult to write lightweight COM classes in MFC. ATL sits between pure C++ and MFC as a way to implement COM-based software without having to type in the boilerplate code or buy into all of MFC's architecture. ATL is basically a set of C++ templates and other kinds of support for writing COM classes.

The ATL Roadmap

If you look at the source code for ATL, you'll find ATL consists of a collection of header files and C++ source code files. Most of it resides inside ATL's Include directory. Here's a rundown of some of the ATL files and what's inside each of them.

ATLBASE.H

This file contains:

- ATL's function *typedefs*
- Structure and macro definitions
- Smart pointers for managing COM interface pointers
- Thread synchronization support classes
- Definitions for *CComBSTR*, *CComVariant*, threading, and apartment support

ATLCOM.H

This file contains:

- Template classes for class object/class factory support
- *IUnknown* implementations
- Support for tear-off interfaces
- Type information management and support
- ATL's *IDispatch* implementation

■ COM enumerator templates

■ Connection point support

ATLCONV.CPP and ATLCONV.H

These two source code files include support for Unicode conversions.

ATLCTL.CPP and ATLCTL.H

These two files contain:

■ The source code for ATL's *IDispatch* client support and event firing support

■ *CComControlBase*

■ The OLE embedding protocol support for controls

■ Property page support

ATLIFACE.IDL and ATLIFACE.H

ATLIFACE.IDL (which generates ATLIFACE.H) includes an ATL-specific interface named *IRegistrar*.

ATLIMPL.CPP

ATLIMPL.CPP implements such classes as *CComBSTR*, which is declared in ATLBASE.H.

ATLWIN.CPP and ATLWIN.H

These files provide windowing and user-interface support, including:

■ A message-mapping mechanism

■ A windowing class

■ Dialog support

STATREG.CPP and STATREG.H

ATL features a COM component named the Registrar that handles putting appropriate entries into the Registry. The code for implementing this feature is in STATREG.H and STATREG.CPP.

Let's start our excursions into ATL by examining ATL's support for client-side COM development.

Client-Side ATL Programming

There are basically two sides to ATL—client-side support and object-side support. By far the largest portion of support is on the object side because of all the code necessary to implement ActiveX controls. However, the client-side support provided by ATL turns out to be useful and interesting also. Let's take a look at the client side of ATL. Because C++ templates are the cornerstone of ATL, we'll take a little detour first to examine them.

C++ Templates

The key to understanding the Active Template Library is understanding C++ templates. Despite the intimidating template syntax, the concept of templates is fairly straightforward. C++ templates are sometimes called compiler-approved macros, which is an appropriate description. Think about what macros do: when the preprocessor encounters a macro, the preprocessor looks at the macro and expands it into regular C++ code. But the problem with macros is that they are sometimes error-prone and they are never type-safe. If you use a macro and pass an incorrect parameter, the compiler won't complain but your program might very well crash. Templates, however, are like type-safe macros. When the compiler encounters a template, the compiler expands the template just as it would a macro. But because templates are type-safe, the compiler catches any type problems before the user encounters them.

Using templates to reuse code is different from what you're used to with conventional C++ development. Components written using templates reuse code by template substitution rather than by inheriting functionality from base classes. All the boilerplate code from templates is literally pasted into the project.

The archetypal example of using a template is a dynamic array. Imagine you need an array for holding integers. Rather than declaring the array with a fixed size, you want the array to grow as necessary. So you develop the array as a C++ class. Then someone you work with gets wind of your new class and says that he or she needs the exact same functionality. However, this person wants to use floating point numbers in the array. Rather than pumping out the exact same code (except for using a different type of data), you can use a C++ template.

Here's an example of how you might use templates to solve the problem described above. The following is a dynamic array implemented as a template:

```
template <class T> class DynArray {
public:
    DynArray();
    ~DynArray(); // clean up and do memory management
```

(continued)

809

```
        int Add(T Element); // adds an element and does
                            //  memory management
        void Remove(int nIndex) // remove element and
                            //  do memory management
        T GetAt(nIndex) const;
        int GetSize();
private:
        T* TArray;
        int m_nArraysize;
};

void UseDynArray() {
        DynArray<int> intArray;
        DynArray<float> floatArray;

        intArray.Add(4);
        floatArray.Add(5.0);

        intArray.Remove(0);
        floatArray.Remove(0);

        int x = intArray.GetAt(0);
        float f = floatArray.GetAt(0);
}
```

As you can imagine, creating templates is useful for implementing boilerplate COM code, and templates are the mechanism ATL uses for providing COM support. The previous example is just one of the many uses available for templates. Not only are templates useful for applying type information to a certain kind of data structure, they're also useful for encapsulating algorithms. You'll see how when you take a closer look at ATL. Let's take a look at the Active Template Library to see what comes with it.

Smart Pointers

One of the most common uses of templates is for smart pointers. The traditional C++ literature calls C++'s built-in pointers "dumb" pointers. That's not a very nice name, but normal C++ pointers don't do much except point. It's often up to the client to perform details such as pointer initialization.

As an example, let's model two types of software developer using C++ classes. You can start by creating the classes: *CVBDeveloper* and *CCPPDeveloper*.

```
class CVBDeveloper {
public:
        CVBDeveloper() {
        }
```

```
    ~CVBDeveloper() {
        AfxMessageBox("I used VB, so I got home early.");
    }
    virtual void DoTheWork() {
        AfxMessageBox("Write them forms");
    }
};

class CCPPDeveloper {
public:
    CCPPDeveloper() {
    }
    ~CCPPDeveloper() {
        AfxMessageBox("Stay at work and fix those pointer problems");
    }
    virtual void DoTheWork() {
        AfxMessageBox("Hacking C++ code");
    }
};
```

The Visual Basic developer and the C++ developer both have functions for eliciting optimal performance. Now imagine some client code that looks like this:

```
//UseDevelopers.CPP

void UseDevelopers() {
    CVBDeveloper* pVBDeveloper;
    :
    // The VB Developer pointer needs
    //   to be initialized
    //   sometime. But what if
    //   you forget to initialize and later
    //   on do something like this:
    if(pVBDeveloper) {
        // Get ready for fireworks
        //   because pVBDeveloper is
        //   NOT NULL, it points
        //   to some random data.
        c->DoTheWork();
    }
}
```

In this case, the client code forgot to initialize the *pVBDeveloper* pointer to *NULL*. (Of course, this never happens in real life!) Because *pVBDeveloper* contains a non-*NULL* value (the value is actually whatever happened to be on the stack at the time), the test to make sure the pointer is valid succeeds when in fact you're expecting it to fail. The client gleefully proceeds, believing all is well. The client crashes, of course, because the client is "calling into darkness."

(Who knows where *pVBDeveloper* is pointing—probably to nothing that even resembles a Visual Basic developer.) Naturally, you'd like some mechanism for ensuring that the pointers are initialized. This is where smart pointers come in handy.

Now imagine a second scenario. Perhaps you'd like to plug a little extra code into your developer-type classes that performs some sort of operation common to all developers. For example, perhaps you'd like all the developers to do some design work before they begin coding. Consider the earlier VB developer and C++ developer examples. When the client calls *DoTheWork,* the developer gets right to coding without proper design, and he or she probably leaves the poor clients in a lurch. What you'd like to do is add a very generic hook to the developer classes so they make sure the design is done before beginning to code.

The C++ solution to coping with these problems is called a smart pointer. Let's find out exactly what a smart pointer is.

Giving C++ Pointers Some Brains

Remember that a smart pointer is a C++ class for wrapping pointers. By wrapping a pointer in a class (and specifically, a template), you can make sure certain operations are taken care of automatically instead of deferring mundane, boilerplate-type operations to the client. One good example of such an operation is to make sure pointers are initialized correctly so that embarrassing crashes due to randomly assigned pointers don't occur. Another good example is to make certain that boilerplate code is executed before function calls are made through a pointer.

Let's invent a smart pointer for the developer model described earlier. Consider a template-based class named *SmartDeveloper*:

```
template<class T>
class SmartDeveloper {
    T* m_pDeveloper;

public:
    SmartDeveloper(T* pDeveloper) {
        ASSERT(pDeveloper != NULL);
        m_pDeveloper = pDeveloper;
    }
    ~SmartDeveloper() {
        AfxMessageBox("I'm smart so I'll get paid.");
    }
    SmartDeveloper &
      operator=(const SmartDeveloper& rDeveloper) {
        return *this;
    }
```

```
T* operator->() const {
    AfxMessageBox("About to de-reference pointer. Make /
                  sure everything's okay. ");
    return m_pDeveloper;
}
};
```

The *SmartDeveloper* template listed above wraps a pointer—any pointer. Because the *SmartDeveloper* class is based on a template, it can provide generic functionality regardless of the type associated with the class. Think of templates as compiler-approved macros: declarations of classes (or functions) whose code can apply to any type of data.

We want the smart pointer to handle all developers, including those using VB, Visual C++, Java, and Delphi (among others). The *template <class T>* statement at the top accomplishes this. The *SmartDeveloper* template includes a pointer (*m_pDeveloper*) to the type of developer for which the class will be defined. The *SmartDeveloper* constructor takes a pointer to that type as a parameter and assigns it to *m_pDeveloper*. Notice that the constructor generates an assertion if the client passes a NULL parameter to construct *SmartDeveloper*.

In addition to wrapping a pointer, the *SmartDeveloper* implements several operators. The most important one is the "->" operator (the member selection operator). This operator is the workhorse of any smart pointer class. Overloading the member selection operator is what turns a regular class into a smart pointer. Normally, using the member selection operator on a regular C++ dumb pointer tells the compiler to select a member belonging to the class or structure being pointed to. By overriding the member selection operator, you provide a way for the client to hook in and call some boilerplate code every time that client calls a method. In the *SmartDeveloper* example, the smart developer makes sure the work area is in order before working. (This example is somewhat contrived. In real life, you might want to put in a debugging hook, for example.)

Adding the -> operator to the class causes the class to behave like C++'s built-in pointer. To behave like native C++ pointers in other ways, smart pointer classes need to implement the other standard operators such as the de-referencing and assignment operators.

Using Smart Pointers

Using smart pointers is really no different from using the regular built-in C++ pointers. Let's start by looking at a client that uses plain vanilla developer classes:

```
void UseDevelopers() {
    CVBDeveloper VBDeveloper;
    CCPPDeveloper CPPDeveloper;
```

(continued)

```
    VBDeveloper.DoTheWork();
    CPPDeveloper.DoTheWork();
}
```

No surprises here—executing this code causes the developers simply to come in and do the work. However, you want to use the smart developers— the ones that make sure the design is done before actually starting to hack. Here's the code that wraps the VB developer and C++ developer objects in the smart pointer class:

```
void UseSmartDevelopers {
    CVBDeveloper VBDeveloper;
    CCPPDeveloper CPPDeveloper;

    SmartDeveloper<CVBDeveloper> smartVBDeveloper(&VBDeveloper);
    SmartDeveloper<CCPPDeveloper> smartCPPDeveloper(&CPPDeveloper);

    smartVBDeveloper->DoTheWork();
    smartCPPDeveloper->DoTheWork();
}
```

Instead of bringing in any old developer to do the work (as in the previous example), the client asks the smart developers to do the work. The smart developers will automatically prepare the design before proceeding with coding.

Smart Pointers and COM

While the last example was fabricated to make an interesting story, smart pointers do have useful applications in the real world. One of those applications is to make client-side COM programming easier.

Smart pointers are frequently used to implement reference counting. Because reference counting is a very generic operation, hoisting client-side reference count management up into a smart pointer makes sense.

Because you're now familiar with the Microsoft Component Object Model, you understand that COM objects expose interfaces. To C++ clients, interfaces are simply pure abstract base classes, and C++ clients treat interfaces more or less like normal C++ objects. However, as you discovered in previous chapters, COM objects are a bit different from regular C++ objects. COM objects live at the binary level. As such, they are created and destroyed using language-independent means. COM objects are created via API functions calls. Most COM objects use a reference count to know when to delete themselves from memory. Once a COM object is created, a client object can refer to it in a number of ways by referencing multiple interfaces belonging to the same COM object. In addition, several different clients can talk to a single COM object. In these situations, the COM object must stay alive for as long as it is referred to. Most COM objects destroy themselves when they're no longer referred to by any clients. COM objects use reference counting to accomplish this self-destruction.

To support this reference-counting scheme, COM defines a couple of rules for managing COM interfaces from the client side. The first rule is that creating a new copy of a COM interface should result in bumping the object's reference count up by one. The second rule is that clients should release interface pointers when they have finished with them. Reference counting is one of the more difficult aspects of COM to get right—especially from the client side. Keeping track of COM interface reference counting is a perfect use of smart pointers.

For example, the smart pointer's constructor might take the live interface pointer as an argument and set an internal pointer to the live interface pointer. Then the destructor might call the interface pointer's *Release* function to release the interface so that the interface pointer will be released automatically when the smart pointer is deleted or falls out of scope. In addition, the smart pointer can help manage COM interfaces that are copied.

For example, imagine you've created a COM object and you're holding on to the interface. Suppose you need to make a copy of the interface pointer (perhaps to pass it as an out parameter). At the native COM level, you'd perform several steps. First you must release the old interface pointer. Next you need to copy the old pointer to the new pointer. Finally you must call *AddRef* on the new copy of the interface pointer. These steps need to occur regardless of the interface being used, making this process ideal for boilerplate code. To implement this process in the smart pointer class, all you need to do is override the assignment operator. The client can then assign the old pointer to the new pointer. The smart pointer does all the work of managing the interface pointer, relieving the client of the burden.

ATL's Smart Pointers

Much of ATL's support for client-side COM development resides in a pair of ATL smart pointers: *CComPtr* and *CComQIPtr*. *CComPtr* is a basic smart pointer that wraps COM interface pointers. *CComQIPtr* adds a little more smarts by associating a GUID (for use as the interface ID) with a smart pointer. Let's start by looking at *CComPtr*.

CComPtr

Here's an abbreviated version of *CComPtr* showing its most important parts:

```
template <class T>
class CComPtr {
public:
```

(continued)

```
      typedef T _PtrClass;
      CComPtr() {p=NULL;}
      CComPtr(T* lp) {
          if ((p = lp) != NULL) p->AddRef();
      }
      CComPtr(const CComPtr<T>& lp) {
          if ((p = lp.p) != NULL) p->AddRef();
      }
      ~CComPtr() {if (p) p->Release();}
      void Release() {if (p) p->Release(); p=NULL;}
      operator T*() {return (T*)p;}
      T& operator*() {_ASSERTE(p!=NULL); return *p; }
      T** operator&() { _ASSERTE(p==NULL); return &p; }
      T* operator->() { _ASSERTE(p!=NULL); return p; }
      T* operator=(T* lp){return (T*)AtlComPtrAssign(
                                  (IUnknown**)&p, lp);}
      T* operator=(const CComPtr<T>& lp) {
          return (T*)AtlComPtrAssign((IUnknown**)&p, lp.p);
      }
      T* p;
};
```

CComPtr is a fairly basic smart pointer. Notice the data member *p* of type T (the type introduced by the template parameter). *CComPtr*'s constructor performs an *AddRef* on the pointer while the destructor releases the pointer—no surprises here. *CComPtr* also has all the necessary operators for wrapping a COM interface. Only the assignment operator deserves special mention. The assignment does a raw pointer re-assignment. The assignment operator calls a function named *AtlComPtrAssign*:

```
ATLAPI_(IUnknown*) AtlComPtrAssign(IUnknown** pp, IUnknown* lp) {
    if (lp != NULL)
        lp->AddRef();
    if (*pp)
        (*pp)->Release();
    *pp = lp;
    return lp;
}
```

AtlComPtrAssign does a blind pointer assignment, *AddRef*-ing the assignee before calling *Release* on the assignor. You'll soon see a version of this function that calls *QueryInterface*.

CComPtr's main strength is that it helps you manage the reference count on a pointer to some degree.

Using *CComPtr*

In addition to helping you manage *AddRef* and *Release* operations, *CComPtr* can help you manage code layout. Looking at a bit of code will help illustrate the usefulness of *CComPtr*. Imagine that your client code needs three interface pointers to get the work done, as shown here:

```
void GetLottaPointers(LPUNKNOWN pUnk){
    HRESULT hr;
    LPPERSIST pPersist;
    LPDISPATCH pDispatch;
    LPDATAOBJECT pDataObject;
    hr = pUnk->QueryInterface(IID_IPersist, (LPVOID *)&pPersist);
    if(SUCCEEDED(hr)) {
        hr = pUnk->QueryInterface(IID_IDispatch, (LPVOID *)
                                      &pDispatch);
        if(SUCCEEDED(hr)) {
            hr = pUnk->QueryInterface(IID_IDataObject,
                                          (LPVOID *) &pDataObject);
            if(SUCCEEDED(hr)) {
                DoIt(pPersist, pDispatch, pDataObject);
                pDataObject->Release();
            }
            pDispatch->Release();
        }
        pPersist->Release();
    }
}
```

You could use the controversial *goto* statement (and risk facing derisive comments from your co-workers) to try to make your code look cleaner, like this:

```
void GetLottaPointers(LPUNKNOWN pUnk){
    HRESULT hr;
    LPPERSIST pPersist; LPDISPATCH pDispatch;
    LPDATAOBJECT pDataObject;

    hr = pUnk->QueryInterface(IID_IPersist, (LPVOID *)&pPersist);
    if(FAILED(hr)) goto cleanup;

    hr = pUnk->QueryInterface(IID_IDispatch, (LPVOID *) &pDispatch);
    if(FAILED(hr)) goto cleanup;

    hr = pUnk->QueryInterface(IID_IDataObject,
                                  (LPVOID *) &pDataObject);
    if(FAILED(hr)) goto cleanup;
```

(continued)

```
        DoIt(pPersist, pDispatch, pDataObject);

cleanup:
        if (pDataObject) pDataObject->Release();
        if (pDispatch) pDispatch->Release();
        if (pPersist) pPersist->Release();
}
```

That may not be as elegant a solution as you would like. Using *CComPtr* makes the same code a lot prettier and much easier to read, as shown here:

```
void GetLottaPointers(LPUNKNOWN pUnk){
        HRESULT hr;
        CComPtr<IUnknown> persist;
        CComPtr<IUnknown> dispatch;
        CComPtr<IUnknown> dataobject;

        hr = pUnk->QueryInterface(IID_IPersist, (LPVOID *)&persist);
        if(FAILED(hr)) return;

        hr = pUnk->QueryInterface(IID_IDispatch, (LPVOID *) &dispatch);
        if(FAILED(hr)) return;

        hr = pUnk->QueryInterface(IID_IDataObject,
                                  (LPVOID *) &dataobject);
        if(FAILED(hr)) return;

        DoIt(pPersist, pDispatch, pDataObject);

        // Destructors call release...
}
```

At this point, you're probably wondering why *CComPtr* doesn't wrap *QueryInterface*. After all, *QueryInterface* is a hot spot for reference counting. Adding *QueryInterface* support for the smart pointer requires some way of associating a GUID with the smart pointer. *CComPtr* was introduced in the first version of ATL. Rather than disrupt any existing code base, Microsoft introduced a beefed-up version of *CComPtr* named *CComQIPtr*.

CComQIPtr

Here's part of *CComQIPtr*'s definition:

```
template <class T, const IID* piid = &__uuidof(T)>
class CComQIPtr {
public:
```

```
typedef T _PtrClass;
CComQIPtr() {p=NULL;}
CComQIPtr(T* lp) {
    if ((p = lp) != NULL)
        p->AddRef();
}
CComQIPtr(const CComQIPtr<T,piid>& lp) {
    if ((p = lp.p) != NULL)
        p->AddRef();
}
CComQIPtr(IUnknown* lp) {
    p=NULL;
    if (lp != NULL)
        lp->QueryInterface(*piid, (void **)&p);
}
~CComQIPtr() {if (p) p->Release();}
void Release() {if (p) p->Release(); p=NULL;}
operator T*() {return p;}
T& operator*() {_ASSERTE(p!=NULL); return *p; }
T** operator&() { _ASSERTE(p==NULL); return &p; }
T* operator->() {_ASSERTE(p!=NULL); return p; }
T* operator=(T* lp){
    return (T*)AtlComPtrAssign((IUnknown**)&p, lp);
}
T* operator=(const CComQIPtr<T,piid>& lp) {
    return (T*)AtlComPtrAssign((IUnknown**)&p, lp.p);
}
T* operator=(IUnknown* lp) {
    return (T*)AtlComQIPtrAssign((IUnknown**)&p, lp, *piid);
}
bool operator!(){return (p == NULL);}
T* p;
};
```

What makes *CComQIPtr* different from *CComPtr* is the second template parameter, *piid*—the interfaces's GUID. This smart pointer has several constructors: a default constructor, a copy constructor, a constructor that takes a raw interface pointer of unspecified type, and a constructor that accepts an *IUnknown* interface as a parameter. Notice in this last constructor that if the developer creates an object of this type and initializes it with a plain old *IUnknown* pointer, *CComQIPtr* calls *QueryInterface* using the GUID template parameter. Also notice that the assignment to an *IUnknown* pointer calls *AtlComQIPtrAssign* to make the assignment. As you can imagine, *AtlComQIPtrAssign* performs a *QueryInterface* under the hood using the GUID template parameter.

Using *CComQIPtr*

Here's how you might use *CComQIPtr* in some COM client code:

```
void GetLottaPointers(ISomeInterface* pSomeInterface){
    HRESULT hr;
    CComQIPtr<IPersist, &IID_IPersist> persist;
    CComQIPtr<IDispatch, &IID_IDispatch> dispatch;
    CComPtr<IDataObject, &IID_IDataObject> dataobject;

    dispatch = pSomeInterface;    // implicit QI
    persist = pSomeInterface;     //  implicit QI
    dataobject = pSomeInterface; //  implicit QI

    DoIt(persist, dispatch, dataobject); // send to a function
                                         // that needs IPersist*,
                                         // IDispatch*, and
                                         // IDataObject*

    // Destructors call release...
}
```

The *CComQIPtr* is useful whenever you want the Java-style or Visual Basic–style type conversions. Notice that the code listed above didn't require any calls to *QueryInterface* or *Release*. Those calls happened automatically.

ATL Smart Pointer Problems

Smart pointers can be quite convenient in some places (as in the *CComPtr* example where we eliminated the *goto* statement). Unfortunately, C++ smart pointers aren't the panacea that programmers pray for to solve their reference-counting and pointer-management problems. Smart pointers simply move these problems to a different level.

One situation in which to be very careful with smart pointers is when converting from code that is not smart-pointer based to code that uses the ATL smart pointers. The problem is that the ATL smart pointers don't hide the *AddRef* and *Release* calls. This just means you need to take care to understand how the smart pointer works rather than be careful about how you call *AddRef* and *Release*.

For example, imagine taking this code:

```
void UseAnInterface(){
    IDispatch* pDispatch = NULL;

    HRESULT hr = GetTheObject(&pDispatch);
    if(SUCCEEDED(hr)) {
        DWORD dwTICount;
        pDispatch->GetTypeInfoCount(&dwTICount);
```

```
        pDispatch->Release();
    }
}
```

and capriciously converting the code to use a smart pointer like this:

```
void UseAnInterface() {
    CComPtr<IDispatch> dispatch = NULL;

    HRESULT hr = GetTheObject(&dispatch);
    if(SUCCEEDED(hr)) {
        DWORD dwTICount;
        dispatch->GetTypeInfoCount(&dwTICount);
        dispatch->Release();
    }
}
```

Because *CComPtr* and *CComQIPtr* do not hide calls to *AddRef* and *Release*, this blind conversion causes a problem when the release is called through the dispatch smart pointer. The *IDispatch* interface performs its own release, so the code above calls *Release* twice—the first time explicitly through the call *dispatch->Release()* and the second time implicitly at the function's closing curly bracket.

In addition, ATL's smart pointers include the implicit cast operator that allows smart pointers to be assigned to raw pointers. In this case, what's actually happening with the reference count starts to get confusing.

The bottom line is that while smart pointers make some aspect of client-side COM development more convenient, they're not foolproof. You still have to have some degree of knowledge about how smart pointers work if you want to use them safely.

Server-Side ATL Programming

We've covered ATL's client-side support. While a fair amount of ATL is devoted to client-side development aids (such as smart pointers and BSTR wrappers), the bulk of ATL exists to support COM-based servers, which we'll cover next. First you'll get an overview of ATL in order to understand how the pieces fit together. Then you'll re-implement the spaceship example in ATL to investigate ATL's Object Wizard and get a good feel for what it takes to write COM classes using ATL.

ATL and COM Classes

Your job as a COM class developer is to wire up the function tables to their implementations and to make sure *QueryInterface*, *AddRef*, and *Release* work as advertised. How you get that to happen is your own business. As far as users are concerned, they couldn't care less what methods you use. You've seen two basic approaches so far—the raw C++ method using multiple inheritance of interfaces and the MFC approach using macros and nested classes. The ATL approach to implementing COM classes is somewhat different from either of these approaches.

Compare the raw C++ approach to MFC's approach. Remember that one way of developing COM classes using raw C++ involves multiply inheriting a single C++ class from at least one COM interface and then writing all the code for the C++ class. At that point, you've got to add any extra features (such as supporting *IDispatch* or COM aggregation) by hand. The MFC approach to COM classes involves using macros that define nested classes (with one nested class implementing each interface). MFC supports *IDispatch* and COM aggregation—you don't have to do a lot to get those features up and running. However, it's very difficult to paste any new interfaces onto a COM class without a lot of typing. (As you saw in Chapter 24, MFC's COM support uses some lengthy macros.)

The ATL approach to composing COM classes requires inheriting a C++ class from several template-based classes. However, Microsoft has already done the work of implementing *IUnknown* for you through the class templates within ATL.

Let's dive right in and create the spaceship example as a COM class. As always, start by selecting New from the File in Visual C++. This opens the New dialog with the Projects tab activated, as shown in Figure 29-1. Select ATL COM AppWizard from the Projects tab. Give your project a useful name such as spaceshipsvr, and click OK.

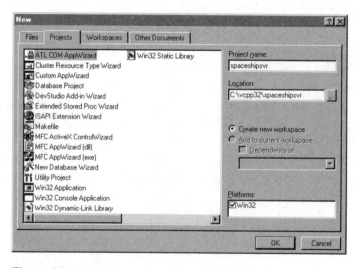

Figure 29-1.
Selecting ATL COM AppWizard from the New dialog box.

ATL COM AppWizard Options

In the Step 1 dialog, shown in Figure 29-2, you can choose the server type for your project from a list of options. The ATL COM AppWizard gives you the choice of creating a Dynamic Link Library (DLL), an Executable (EXE), or a Service (EXE). If you select the DLL option, the options for attaching the proxy/stub code to the DLL and for including MFC in your ATL project will be activated.

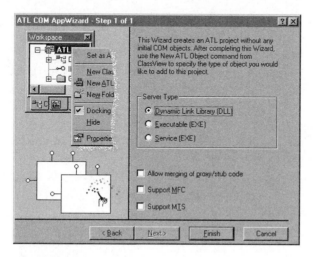

Figure 29-2.
Step 1 of the ATL COM AppWizard.

Selecting DLL as the server type produces all the necessary pieces to make your server DLL fit into the COM milieu. Among these pieces are the following well-known COM functions: *DllGetClassObject, DllCanUnloadNow, DllRegisterServer,* and *DllUnregisterServer.* Also included are the correct server lifetime mechanisms for a DLL.

If you decide you might want to run your DLL out of process as a surrogate, selecting the Allow Merging Of Proxy/Stub Code option permits you to package all your components into a single binary file. (Proxy/stub code has traditionally shipped as a separate DLL.) That way you have to distribute only a single DLL. If you decide you absolutely must include MFC in your DLL, go ahead and select the Support MFC check box. MFC support includes AfxWin.h and AfxDisp.h in your StdAfx.h file and links your project to the current version of MFC's import library. While using MFC can be very convenient and almost addictive at times, beware of dependencies you're inheriting when you include MFC. You can also select Support MTS to add support for Microsoft Transaction Server.

If you elect to produce an Executable EXE server, the ATL COM AppWizard produces code that compiles to an EXE file. The EXE will correctly register the class objects with the operating system by using *CoRegisterClassObject* and *CoRevokeClassObject*. The project will also insert the correct code for managing the lifetime of the executable server. Finally, if you choose the Service EXE option, the ATL COM AppWizard adds the necessary service-oriented code.

Using the ATL COM AppWizard to write a lightweight COM server yields several products. First, you get a project file for compiling your object. The project file ties together all the source code for the project and maintains the proper build instructions for each of the files. Second, you get some boilerplate Interface Definition Language (IDL) code. The IDL file is important because as the starting point for genuine COM development, it's one of the primary files you'll focus on when writing COM classes.

IDL is a purely declarative language for describing COM interfaces. Once a COM interface is described in an IDL file, a simple pass though the Microsoft Interface Definition Language (MIDL) compiler creates several more useful products.

These products include:

■ The pure abstract base classes needed to write COM classes

■ A type library

■ Source code for building the proxy stub DLL (necessary for standard COM remoting)

Creating a COM Class

Once you've created a COM server, you're ready to start piling COM classes into the server. Fortunately, there's an easy way to do that with the ATL Object Wizard, shown in Figure 29-3. Select New ATL Object from the Insert menu to start the ATL Object Wizard.

Using the ATL Object Wizard to generate a new object adds a C++ source file and a header file containing the new class definition and implementation to your project. In addition, the ATL Object Wizard adds an interface to the IDL code. Although the ATL Object Wizard takes care of pumping out a skeleton IDL file, you'll still need to understand IDL to some extent if you want to write effective COM interfaces (as you'll soon see).

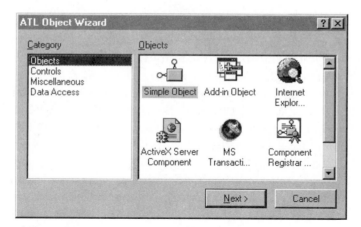

Figure 29-3.
*Using the ATL Object Wizard to insert a new ATL-based COM class
into the project.*

After you choose the type of ATL object, click Next to display the ATL
Object Wizard Properties dialog. Depending on which object you choose, the
Attributes tab of the ATL Object Wizard Properties dialog allows you to
select the threading model for your COM class, and whether you want a dual
(*IDispatch*-based) or a custom interface. The dialog also allows you to choose
how your class will support aggregation. In addition, the Object Wizard lets
you easily include the *ISupportErrorInfo* interface and connection points in
your class. Finally, you can aggregate to the Free-Threaded Marshaler if you
so choose.

Apartments and Threading

To figure out COM, you have to understand that COM is centered on the notion
of abstraction—hiding as much information as possible from the client. One
piece of information that COM hides from the client is whether the COM class
is thread-safe. The client should be able to use an object as it sees fit without
worrying about whether an object properly serializes access to itself—that
is, properly protects access to its internal data. COM defines the notion of an
apartment to provide this abstraction.

An apartment defines an execution context, or thread, that houses interface
pointers. A thread enters an apartment by calling a function from the *CoInitialize*
family: *CoInitialize, CoInitializeEx,* or *OleInitialize.* Then COM requires that
all method calls to an interface pointer be executed within the apartment that
initialized the pointer (in other words, from the same thread that called *CoCreate-
Instance*). COM defines two kinds of apartments—single-threaded apartments

and multithreaded apartments. Single-threaded apartments can house only one thread while multithreaded apartments can house several threads. While a process can have only one multithreaded apartment, it can have many single-threaded apartments. An apartment can house any number of COM objects.

A single-threaded apartment guarantees that COM objects created within it will have method calls serialized through the remoting layer, while a COM object created within a multithreaded apartment will not. A helpful way to remember the difference between apartments is to think of it this way: instantiating a COM object within the multithreaded apartment is like putting a piece of data into the global scope where multiple threads can get to it. Instantiating a COM object within a single-threaded apartment is like putting data within the scope of only one thread. The bottom line is that COM classes that want to live in the multithreaded apartment had better be thread-safe, while COM classes that are satisfied living in their own apartments need not worry about concurrent access to their data.

A COM object living within a different process space from its client has its method calls serialized automatically via the remoting layer. However, a COM object living in a DLL might want to provide its own internal protection (using critical sections, for example) rather than having the remoting layer protect it. A COM class advertises its thread safety to the world via a Registry setting. This named value lives in the Registry under the CLSID under *HKEY_CLASSES-_ROOT* like this:

```
[HKCR\CLSID\{some GUID …}\InprocServer32]
@="C:\SomeServer.DLL"
ThreadingModel=<thread model>
```

The ThreadingModel can be one of four values: *Single*, *Both*, *Free*, or *Apartment*, or it can be blank. ATL provides support for all current threading models. Here's a rundown of what each value indicates:

- *Single* or blank indicates that the class executes in the main thread only (the first single thread created by the client).

- *Both* indicates that the class is thread-safe and can execute in both the single-threaded and multithreaded apartments. This value tells COM to use the same kind of apartment as the client.

- *Free* indicates that the class is thread-safe. This value tells COM to force the object inside the multithreaded apartment.

- *Apartment* indicates that the class isn't thread-safe and must live in its own single-threaded apartment.

When you choose a threading model in the ATL Object Wizard, the wizard inserts different code into your class depending upon your selection. For example, if you select the apartment model, the Object Wizard derives your class from *CComObjectRootEx* and includes *CComSingleThreadModel* as the template parameter like this:

```
class ATL_NO_VTABLE CAtlSpaceship :
    public CComObjectRootEx<CComSingleThreadModel>,
    public CComCoClass<CAtlSpaceship, &CLSID_AtlSpaceship>,
    public IDispatchImpl<IAtlSpaceship, &IID_IAtlSpaceship,
                         &LIBID_SPACESHIPSVRLib>
{
    ⋮
};
```

The *CComSingleThreadModel* template parameter mixes in the more efficient standard increment and decrement operations for *IUnknown* (because access to the class is automatically serialized). In addition, the ATL Object Wizard causes the class to insert the correct threading model value in the Registry. If you choose the Single option in the ATL Object Wizard, the class uses the *CComSingleThreadModel* but leaves the ThreadingModel value blank in the Registry.

Choosing Both or Free causes the class to use the *CComMultiThreadModel* template parameter, which employs the thread-safe Win32 increment and decrement operations *InterlockedIncrement* and *InterlockedDecrement*. For example, a free-threaded class definition looks like this:

```
class ATL_NO_VTABLE CAtlSpaceship :
    public CComObjectRootEx< CComMultiThreadModel>,
    public CComCoClass<CAtlSpaceship, &CLSID_AtlSpaceship>,
    public IDispatchImpl<IAtlSpaceship, &IID_IAtlSpaceship,
                         &LIBID_SPACESHIPSVRLib>
{
    ⋮
};
```

Choosing Both for your threading model inserts *Both* as the data for the ThreadingModel value, while choosing Free uses the data value *Free* for the ThreadingModel value.

Connection Points and *ISupportErrorInfo*

Adding connection to your COM class is easy. Selecting the Support Connection Points check box causes the class to derive from *IConnectionPointImpl*. This option also adds a blank connection map to your class. Adding connection points (for example, an event set) to your class is simply a matter of performing the following four steps:

1. Define the callback interface in the IDL file.

2. Use the ATL proxy generator to create a proxy.

3. Add the proxy class to the COM class.

4. Add the connection points to the connection point map.

ATL also includes support for *ISupportErrorInfo*. The *ISupportErrorInfo* interface ensures that error information is propagated up the call chain correctly. OLE Automation objects that use the error-handling interfaces must implement *ISupportErrorInfo*. Selecting Support *ISupportErrorInfo* in the ATL Object Wizard dialog causes the ATL-based class to derive from *ISupportErrorInfoImpl*.

The Free-Threaded Marshaler

Selecting the Free Threaded Marshaler option aggregates the COM free-threaded marshaler to your class. The generated class does this by calling *CoCreateFree-ThreadedMarshaler* in its *FinalConstruct* function. The free-threaded marshaler allows thread-safe objects to bypass the standard marshaling that occurs whenever cross-apartment interface methods are invoked, allowing threads living in one apartment to access interface methods in another apartment as though they were in the same apartment. This process speeds up cross-apartment calls tremendously. The free-threaded marshaler does this by implementing the *IMarshal* interface. When the client asks the object for an interface, the remoting layer calls *QueryInterface*, asking for *IMarshal*. If the object implements *IMarshal* (in this case, the object implements *IMarshal* because the ATL Object Wizard also adds an entry into the class's interface to handle *Query-Interface* requests for *IMarshal*) and the marshaling request is in process, the free-threaded marshaler actually copies the pointer into the marshaling packet. That way, the client receives an actual pointer to the object. The client talks to the object directly without having to go through proxies and stubs. Of course, if you choose the Free Threaded Marshaler option, all data in your object had better be thread-safe. Just be very cautious if you check this box.

Implementing the Spaceship Class Using ATL

We'll create the spaceship class using the defaults provided by the ATL Object Wizard in the ATL Object Wizard Properties dialog. For example, the spaceship class will have a dual interface, so it will be accessible from environments such as VBScript on a Web page. In addition, the spaceship class will be an apartment model object, meaning COM will manage most of the concurrency issues. The only information you need to supply to the ATL Object Wizard is a clever name. Enter a value such as *AtlSpaceship* in the Short Name text box on the Names tab.

You don't need to set any of the other options right now. For instance, you don't need to set the Support Connection Points option because we'll cover connections in the next chapter. You can always add connection points later by typing them in by hand.

If you tell the ATL Object Wizard to create a Simple Object COM class named *ATLSpaceship*, here's the class definition it generates:

```
class ATL_NO_VTABLE CAtlSpaceship :
    public CComObjectRootEx<CComSingleThreadModel>,
    public CComCoClass<CAtlSpaceship, &CLSID_AtlSpaceship>,
    public IDispatchImpl<IAtlSpaceship, &IID_IAtlSpaceship,
                         &LIBID_SPACESHIPSVRLib>
{
    ⋮
};
```

While ATL includes quite a few COM-oriented C++ classes, those listed in the spaceship class's inheritance list above are enough to get a flavor of how ATL works.

The most generic ATL-based COM objects derive from three base classes: *CComObjectRoot, CComCoClass,* and *IDispatch. CComObjectRoot* implements *IUnknown* and manages the identity of the class. This means *CComObjectRoot* implements *AddRef* and *Release* and hooks into ATL's *QueryInterface* mechanism. *CComCoClass* manages the COM class's class object and some general error reporting. In the class definition above, *CComCoClass* adds the class object that knows how to create *CAtlSpaceship* objects. Finally, the code produced by the ATL Object Wizard includes an implementation of *IDispatch* based on the type library produced by compiling the IDL. The default *IDispatch* is based on a dual interface (which is an *IDispatch* interface followed by the functions defined in the IDL).

As you can see, using ATL to implement COM classes is different from using pure C++. The Tao of ATL differs from what you might be used to when developing normal C++ classes. With ATL, the most important part of the project is the interfaces, which are described in IDL. By adding functions to the interfaces in the IDL code, you automatically add functions to the concrete classes implementing the interfaces. The functions are added automatically because the projects are set up such that compiling the IDL file yields a C++ header file with those functions. All that's left for you to do after adding the functions in the interface is to implement those functions in the C++ class. The IDL file also provides a type library so the COM class can implement *IDispatch*. However, while ATL is useful for implementing lightweight COM services and objects, ATL is also a new means by which you can create ActiveX controls, as you'll see in the next chapter.

Basic ATL Architecture

If you've experimented at all with ATL, you've seen how it simplifies the process of implementing COM classes. The tool support is quite good—it's almost as easy to develop COM classes using Visual C++ 6.0 as it is to create MFC-based programs. Just use AppWizard to create a new ATL-based class. However, instead of using ClassWizard (as you would to handle messages and to add dialog box member variables), use ClassView to add new function definitions to an interface. Then simply fill in the functions within the C++ code generated by ClassView. The code generated by AppWizard includes all the necessary code for implementing your class, including an implementation of *IUnknown*, a server module to house your COM class, and a class object that implements *IClassFactory*.

Writing COM objects as we've just described is certainly more convenient than most other methods. But exactly what happens when you use the AppWizard to generate the code for you? Understanding how ATL works is important if you want to extend your ATL-based COM classes and servers much beyond what AppWizard and ClassView provide. For example, ATL provides support for advanced interface techniques such as tear-off interfaces. Unfortunately, there's no Wizard option for implementing a tear-off interface. Even though ATL supports it, you've got to do a little work by hand to accomplish the tear-off interface. Understanding how ATL implements *IUnknown* is helpful in this situation.

Let's examine the *CAtlSpaceship* class in a bit more detail. Here's the entire definition:

```
class ATL_NO_VTABLE CAtlSpaceship :
    public CComObjectRootEx<CComSingleThreadModel>,
    public CComCoClass<CAtlSpaceship, &CLSID_AtlSpaceship>,
    public IDispatchImpl<IAtlSpaceship, &IID_IAtlSpaceship,
                        &LIBID_SPACESHIPSVRLib>
{
public:
    CAtlSpaceship()
    {
    }

DECLARE_REGISTRY_RESOURCEID(IDR_ATLSPACESHIP)

BEGIN_COM_MAP(CAtlSpaceship)
    COM_INTERFACE_ENTRY(IAtlSpaceship)
```

```
    COM_INTERFACE_ENTRY(IDispatch)
END_COM_MAP()

// IAtlSpaceship
public:
};
```

While this is ordinary vanilla C++ source code, it differs from normal everyday C++ source code for implementing a COM object in several ways. For example, while many COM class implementations derive strictly from COM interfaces, this COM class derives from several templates. In addition, this C++ class uses several odd-looking macros. As you examine the code, you'll see ATL's implementation of *IUnknown*, as well as a few other interesting topics, such as a technique for managing *vtable* bloat and an uncommon use for templates. Let's start by taking a look at the first symbol in the wizard-generated macro code: *ATL_NO_VTABLE*.

Managing VTBL Bloat

COM interfaces are easily expressed in C++ as pure abstract base classes. Writing COM classes using multiple inheritance (there are other ways to write COM classes) is merely a matter of adding the COM interface base classes to your inheritance list and implementing the union of all the functions. Of course, this means that the memory footprint of your COM server will include a significant amount of vtable overhead for each interface implemented by your class. That's not a big deal if you have only a few interfaces and your C++ class hierarchy isn't very deep. However, implementing interfaces this way does add overhead that tends to accumulate as interfaces are added and hierarchies deepen. ATL provides a way to cut down on some of the overhead introduced by a lot of virtual functions. ATL defines the following symbol:

```
#define ATL_NO_VTABLE  __declspec(novtable)
```

Using *ATL_NO_VTABLE* prevents an object's vtable (*vtable*) from being initialized in the constructor, thereby eliminating from the linker the vtable and all the functions pointed to by the vtable for that class. This elimination can lower the size of your COM server somewhat, provided the most-derived class does not use the *novtable declspec* shown above. You'll notice the size difference in classes with deep derivation lists. One caveat, however: calling virtual functions from the constructor of any object that uses this *declspec* is unsafe because *vptr* is uninitialized.

The second line in the class declaration previously shown demonstrates that *CAtlSpaceship* derives from *CComObjectRootEx*. This is where you get to ATL's version of *IUnknown*.

ATL's *IUnknown: CComObjectRootEx*

While *CComObjectRootEx* isn't quite at the top of the ATL hierarchy, it's pretty close. The actual base class for a COM object in ATL is a class named *CCom-ObjectRootBase*. (Both class definitions are located in ATLCOM.H.) Looking at *CComObjectRootBase* reveals the code you might expect for a C++ based COM class. *CComObjectRootBase* includes a DWORD member named *m_dw-Ref* for reference counting. You'll also see *OuterAddRef*, *OuterRelease*, and *OuterQueryInterface* to support COM aggregation and tear-off interfaces. Looking at *CComObjectRootEx* reveals *InternalAddRef*, *InternalRelease*, and *InternalQueryInterface* for performing the regular native reference counting, and *QueryInterface* mechanisms for class instances with object identity.

Notice that *CAtlSpaceship*'s definition shows that the class is derived from *CComObjectRootEx* and that *CComObjectRootEx* is a parameterized template class. The listing below shows the definition of *CComObjectRootEx*.

```
template <class ThreadModel>
class CComObjectRootEx : public CComObjectRootBase
{
public:
    typedef ThreadModel _ThreadModel;
    typedef _ThreadModel::AutoCriticalSection _CritSec;
    typedef CComObjectLockT<_ThreadModel> ObjectLock;

    ULONG InternalAddRef() {
        ATLASSERT(m_dwRef != -1L);
        return _ThreadModel::Increment(&m_dwRef);
    }
    ULONG InternalRelease() {
        ATLASSERT(m_dwRef > 0);
        return _ThreadModel::Decrement(&m_dwRef);
    }

    void Lock() {m_critsec.Lock();}
    void Unlock() {m_critsec.Unlock();}
private:
    _CritSec m_critsec;
};
```

CComObjectRootEx is a template class that varies in type based on the kind of threading model class passed in as the template parameter. In fact, ATL supports several threading models: Single-Threaded Apartments (STAs), Multi-Threaded Apartments (MTAs), and Free Threading. ATL includes three pre-processor symbols for selecting the various default threading models for your project: *_ATL_SINGLE_THREADED*, *_ATL_APARTMENT_THREADED*, and *_ATL_FREE_THREADED*.

Defining the preprocessor symbol _ATL_SINGLE_THREADED in stdafx.h changes the default threading model to support only one STA-based thread. This option is useful for out-of-process servers that don't create any extra threads. Because the server supports only one thread, ATL's global state can remain unprotected by critical sections and the server is therefore more efficient. The downside is that your server can support only one thread. Defining _ATL_APART-MENT_THREADED for the preprocessor causes the default threading model to support multiple STA-based threads. This is useful for apartment model in-process servers (servers supporting the *ThreadingModel=Apartment* Registry value). Because a server employing this threading model can support multiple threads, ATL protects its global state using critical sections. Finally, defining the _ATL_FREE_THREADED preprocessor symbol creates servers compatible with any threading environment. That is, ATL protects its global state using critical sections, and each object in the server will have its own critical sections to maintain data safety.

These preprocessor symbols merely determine which threading class to plug into *CComObjectRootEx* as a template parameter. ATL provides three threading model classes. The classes provide support for the most efficient yet thread-safe behavior for COM classes within each of the three contexts listed above. The three classes are *CComMultiThreadModelNoCS*, *CComMultiThreadModel*, and *CComSingleThreadModel*. The following listing shows the three threading model classes within ATL:

```
class CComMultiThreadModelNoCS
{
public:
    static ULONG WINAPI Increment(LPLONG p)
                        {return InterlockedIncrement(p);}
    static ULONG WINAPI Decrement(LPLONG p)
                        {return InterlockedDecrement(p);}
    typedef CComFakeCriticalSection AutoCriticalSection;
    typedef CComFakeCriticalSection CriticalSection;
    typedef CComMultiThreadModelNoCS ThreadModelNoCS;
};

class CComMultiThreadModel
{
public:
    static ULONG WINAPI Increment(LPLONG p)
                        {return InterlockedIncrement(p);}
    static ULONG WINAPI Decrement(LPLONG p)
                        {return InterlockedDecrement(p);}
```

(continued)

```
    typedef CComAutoCriticalSection AutoCriticalSection;
    typedef CComCriticalSection CriticalSection;
    typedef CComMultiThreadModelNoCS ThreadModelNoCS;
};

class CComSingleThreadModel
{
public:
    static ULONG WINAPI Increment(LPLONG p) {return ++(*p);}
    static ULONG WINAPI Decrement(LPLONG p) {return --(*p);}
    typedef CComFakeCriticalSection AutoCriticalSection;
    typedef CComFakeCriticalSection CriticalSection;
    typedef CComSingleThreadModel ThreadModelNoCS;
};
```

Notice that each of these classes exports two static functions—*Increment* and *Decrement*—and various aliases for critical sections.

CComMultiThreadModel and *CComMultiThreadModelNoCS* both implement *Increment* and *Decrement* using the thread-safe Win32 *InterlockedIncrement* and *InterlockedDecrement* functions. *CComSingleThreadModel* implements *Increment* and *Decrement* using the more conventional ++ and -- operators.

In addition to implementing incrementing and decrementing differently, the three threading models also manage critical sections differently. ATL provides wrappers for two critical sections—a *CComCriticalSection* (which is a plain wrapper around the Win32 critical section API) and *CComAutoCriticalSection* (which is the same as *CComCriticalSection* with the addition of automatic initialization and cleanup of critical sections). ATL also defines a "fake" critical section class that has the same binary signature as the other critical section classes but doesn't do anything. As you can see from the class definitions, *CComMultiThreadModel* uses real critical sections while *CComMultiThreadModelNoCS* and *CComSingleThreadModel* use the fake no-op critical sections.

So now the minimal ATL class definition makes a bit more sense. *CComObjectRootEx* takes a thread model class whenever you define it. *CAtlSpaceship* is defined using the *CComSingleThreadModel* class, so it uses the *CComSingleThreadModel* methods for incrementing and decrementing as well as the fake no-op critical sections. Thus *CAtlSpaceship* uses the most efficient behavior since it doesn't need to worry about protecting data. However, you're not stuck with that model. If you want to make *CAtlSpaceship* safe for any threading environment, for example, simply redefine *CAtlSpaceship* to derive from *CComObjectRootEx* using *CComMultiThreadModel* as the template parameter. *AddRef* and *Release* calls are automatically mapped to the correct *Increment* and *Decrement* functions.

ATL and *QueryInterface*

It looks as though ATL took a cue from MFC for implementing *QueryInterface*—ATL uses a lookup table just like MFC's version. Take a look at the middle of *CAtlSpaceship*'s definition—you'll see a construct based on macros called the interface map. ATL's interface maps constitute its *QueryInterface* mechanism.

Clients use *QueryInterface* to arbitrarily widen the connection to an object. That is, when a client needs a new interface, it calls *QueryInterface* through an existing interface. The object then looks at the name of the requested interface and compares that name to all the interfaces implemented by the object. If the object implements the interface, the object hands the interface back to the client. Otherwise, *QueryInterface* returns an error indicating that no interface was found.

Traditional *QueryInterface* implementations usually consist of long if-then statements. For example, a standard implementation of *QueryInterface* for a multiple-inheritance COM class might look like this:

```
class CAtlSpaceship: public IDispatch,
                            IAtlSpaceship {
    HRESULT QueryInterface(RIID riid,
                            void** ppv) {
        if(riid == IID_IDispatch)
            *ppv = (IDispatch*) this;
        else if(riid == IID_IAtlSpaceship ||
                riid == IID_IUnknown)
            *ppv = (IAtlSpaceship *) this;
        else {
            *ppv = 0;
            return E_NOINTERFACE;
        }

        ((IUnknown*)(*ppv))->AddRef();
        return NOERROR;
    }
    // AddRef, Release, and other functions
};
```

As you'll see in a moment, ATL uses a lookup table instead of this conventional if-then statement.

ATL's lookup table begins with a macro named *BEGIN_COM_MAP*. The listing below shows the full definition of *BEGIN_COM_MAP*.

```
#define BEGIN_COM_MAP(x) public:
    typedef x _ComMapClass;
    static HRESULT WINAPI _Cache(void* pv,
                            REFIID iid,
```

(continued)

```
                              void** ppvObject,
                              DWORD dw) {
      _ComMapClass* p = (_ComMapClass*)pv;
      p->Lock();
      HRESULT hRes =
        CComObjectRootBase::_Cache(pv,
                                   iid,
                                   ppvObject,
                                   dw);
      p->Unlock();
      return hRes;
  }
  IUnknown* GetRawUnknown() {
      ATLASSERT(_GetEntries()[0].pFunc ==
          _ATL_SIMPLEMAPENTRY);
      return (IUnknown*)((int)this+_GetEntries()->dw);
  }
  _ATL_DECLARE_GET_UNKNOWN(x)
  HRESULT _InternalQueryInterface(REFIID iid,
                                  void** ppvObject) {
      return InternalQueryInterface(this,
                                    _GetEntries(),
                                    iid,
                                    ppvObject);
  }
  const static _ATL_INTMAP_ENTRY* WINAPI _GetEntries() {
  static const _ATL_INTMAP_ENTRY _entries[] = {
      DEBUG_QI_ENTRY(x)
      ⋮
#define END_COM_MAP()    {NULL, 0, 0}};\
  return _entries;}
```

Each class that uses ATL for implementing *IUnknown* specifies an interface map to provide to *InternalQueryInterface*. ATL's interface maps consist of structures containing interface ID (GUID)/DWORD/function pointer tuples. The following listing shows the type named *_ATL_INTMAP_ENTRY* that contains these tuples.

```
struct _ATL_INTMAP_ENTRY {
    const IID* piid;
    DWORD dw;
    _ATL_CREATORARGFUNC* pFunc;
};
```

The first member is the interface ID (a GUID), and the second member indicates what action to take when the interface is queried. There are three ways to interpret the third member. If *pFunc* is equal to the constant *_ATL_SIMPLE-MAPENTRY* (the value 1), *dw* is an offset into the object. If *pFunc* is non-null but not equal to 1, *pFunc* indicates a function to be called when the interface is queried. If *pFunc* is *NULL*, *dw* indicates the end of the *QueryInterface* lookup table.

Notice that *CAtlSpaceship* uses *COM_INTERFACE_ENTRY*. This is the interface map entry for regular interfaces. Here's the raw macro:

```
#define offsetofclass(base, derived)
((DWORD)(static_cast<base*>((derived*)8))-8)

#define COM_INTERFACE_ENTRY(x)\
    {&_ATL_IIDOF(x), \
    offsetofclass(x, _ComMapClass), \
    _ATL_SIMPLEMAPENTRY}
```

COM_INTERFACE_ENTRY fills the *_ATL_INTMAP_ENTRY* structure with the interface's GUID. In addition, notice how *offsetofclass* casts the *this* pointer to the right kind of interface and fills the *dw* member with that value. Finally, *COM_INTERFACE_ENTRY* fills the last field with *_ATL_SIMPLE-MAPENTRY* to indicate that *dw* points to an offset into the class.

For example, the interface map for *CAtlSpaceship* looks like this after the preprocessor is done with it:

```
const static _ATL_INTMAP_ENTRY* __stdcall _GetEntries() {
    static const _ATL_INTMAP_ENTRY _entries[] = {
        {&IID_IAtlSpaceship,
        ((DWORD)(static_cast< IAtlSpaceship*>((_ComMapClass*)8))-8),
        ((_ATL_CREATORARGFUNC*)1)},
        {&IID_IDispatch,
        ((DWORD)(static_cast<IDispatch*>((_ComMapClass*)8))-8),
        ((_ATL_CREATORARGFUNC*)1)},
        {0, 0, 0}
    };
    return _entries;
}
```

Right now, the *CAtlSpaceship* class supports two interfaces—*IAtlSpaceship* and *IDispatch*, so there are only two entries in the map.

CComObjectRootEx's implementation of *InternalQueryInterface* uses the *_GetEntries* function as the second parameter. *CComObjectRootEx::Internal-QueryInterface* uses a global ATL function named *AtlInternalQueryInterface* to look up the interface in the map. *AtlInternalQueryInterface* simply walks through the map trying to find the interface.

In addition to *COM_INTERFACE_ENTRY*, ATL includes 16 other macros for implementing composition techniques ranging from tear-off interfaces to COM aggregation. Now you'll see what it takes to beef up the *IAtlSpaceship* interface and add those two other interfaces, *IMotion* and *IVisual*. You'll also learn about the strange COM beast known as a dual interface.

Making the Spaceship Go

Now that you've got some ATL code staring you in the face, what can you do with it? This is COM, so the place to start is in the IDL file. Again, if you're a seasoned C++ developer, this is a new aspect of software development you're probably not used to. Remember that these days, software distribution and integration are becoming very important. You've been able to get away with hacking out C++ classes and throwing them into a project together because you (as a developer) know the entire picture. However, component technologies (like COM) change that. You as a developer no longer know the entire picture. Often you have only a component—you don't have the source code for the component. The only way to know how to talk to a component is through the interfaces it exposes.

Keep in mind that modern software developers use many different tools—not just C++. You've got Visual Basic developers, Java developers, Delphi developers, and C developers. COM is all about making the edges line up so that software pieces created by these various components can all integrate smoothly when they come together. In addition, distributing software remotely (either out-of-process on the same machine or even to a different machine) requires some sort of inter-process communication. That's why there's Interface Definition Language (IDL). Here's the default IDL file created by the ATL wizards with the new spaceship class:

```
import "oaidl.idl";
import "ocidl.idl";
    [
        object,
        uuid(A9D750E1-51A1-11D1-8CAA-FD10872CC837),
        dual,
        helpstring("IAtlSpaceship Interface"),
        pointer_default(unique)
    ]
    interface IAtlSpaceship : IDispatch
    {
    };


[
    uuid(A0736061-50DF-11D1-8CAA-FD10872CC837),
    version(1.0),
    helpstring("spaceshipsvr 1.0 Type Library")
]
library SPACESHIPSVRLib
{
    importlib("stdole32.tlb");
```

```
    importlib("stdole2.tlb");

    [
        uuid(A9D750E2-51A1-11D1-8CAA-FD10872CC837),
        helpstring("AtlSpaceship Class")
    ]
    coclass AtlSpaceship
    {
        [default] interface IAtlSpaceship;
    };
};
```

The key concept involved here is that IDL is a purely <u>declarative</u> language. This language defines how other clients will talk to an object. Remember—you'll eventually run this code through the MIDL compiler to get a pure abstract base class (useful for C++ clients) and a type library (useful for Visual Basic and Java clients as well as others). If you understand plain C code, you're well on your way to understanding IDL. You might think of IDL as C with footnotes. The syntax of IDL dictates that attributes will always precede what they describe. For example, attributes precede items such as interface declarations, library declarations, and method parameters.

If you look at the IDL file, you'll notice that it begins by importing oaidl.idl and ocidl.idl. Importing these files is somewhat akin to including windows.h inside one of your C or C++ files. These IDL files include definitions for all of the basic COM infrastructures (including definitions for *IUnknown* and *IDispatch*).

An open square bracket ([) follows the *import* statement. In IDL, square brackets always enclose attributes. The first element described in this IDL file is the *IAtlSpaceship* interface. However, before you can describe the interface, you need to apply some attributes to it. For example, it needs a name (a GUID), and you need to tell the MIDL compiler that this interface is COM-oriented rather than being used for standard RPC and that this is a dual interface (more on dual interfaces shortly). Next comes the actual interface itself. Notice how it appears very much like a normal C structure.

Once the interfaces are described in IDL, it is often useful to collect this information into a type library, which is what the next section of the IDL file does. Notice the type library section also begins with an open square bracket, designating that attributes are to follow. As always, the type library is a discrete "thing" in COM and as such requires a name (GUID). The library statement tells the MIDL compiler that this library includes a COM class named *AtlSpaceship* and that clients of this class can acquire the *IAtlSpaceship* interface.

Adding Methods to an Interface

Right now the *IAtlSpaceship* interface is pretty sparse. It looks like it could use a method or two. Let's add one. Notice that Visual C++ now extends Class-View to include COM interfaces. (You can tell they're COM interfaces because of the little lollipop next to the symbol.) Notice also that *CAtlSpaceship* derives from something named *IAtlSpaceship*. *IAtlSpaceship* is, of course, a COM interface. Double-clicking on *IAtlSpaceship* in ClassView brings that specific section of the IDL into the editor window, as shown in Figure 29-4.

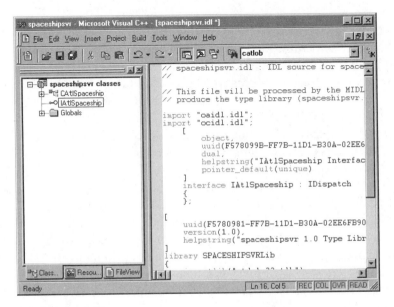

Figure 29-4.
Interfaces in ClassView.

At this point, you could begin typing the COM interface into the IDL file. If you add functions and methods this way (straight into the IDL file), you'll have to touch the AtlSpaceship.h and AtlSpaceship.cpp files and insert the methods by hand. A more effective way to add functions to the interface is through the ClassView. To edit the IDL through the ClassView, simply right-click the mouse on the interface within ClassView. Two items that appear in the context menu are Add Method and Add Property. Let's add a method named *CallStarFleet*. Figure 29-5 shows the dialog box that appears when adding a method.

To add a method, simply type the name of the method into the Method Name text box. Then type the method parameters into the Parameters text box. Here's where it helps to understand a little bit about IDL.

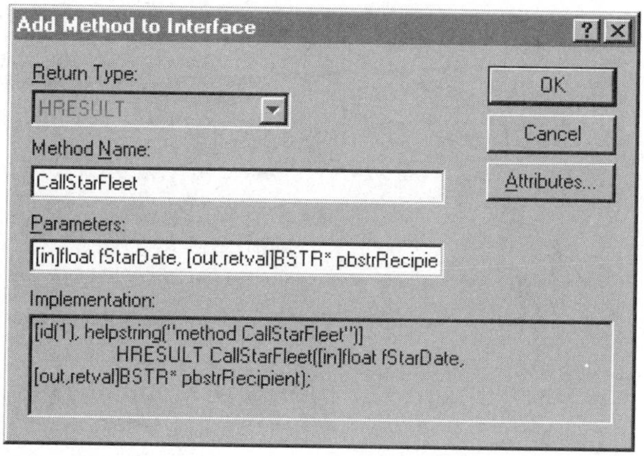

Figure 29-5.
Adding a method to an interface.

Remember that IDL's purpose is to provide completely unambiguous information about how methods can be invoked. In the standard C++ world, you could often get away with ambiguities like open-ended arrays because the caller and the callee shared the same stack frame—there was always a lot of wiggle room available. Now that method calls might eventually go over the wire, it's important to tell the remoting layer exactly what to expect when it encounters a COM interface. This is done by applying attributes to the method parameters (more square brackets).

The method call shown in Figure 29-5 (*CallStarFleet*) has two parameters in its list—a floating point number indicating the stardate and a BSTR indicating who received the communication. Notice that the method definition spells out the parameter direction. The stardate is passed into the method call, designated by the [in] attribute. A BSTR identifying the recipient is passed back as a pointer to a BSTR. The [out] attribute indicates the direction of the parameter is from the object back to the client. The [retval] attribute indicates that you can assign the result of this method to a variable in higher languages supporting this feature.

Dual Interfaces

If you read through Chapter 25, you had a chance to see the *IDispatch* interface. *IDispatch* makes it possible to expose functionality (at the binary level) to environments such as VBScript that don't have a clue about vtables. For *IDispatch* to work, the client has to go through a lot of machinations before it can call *Invoke*. The client first has to acquire the invocation tokens. Then the client has to set up the VARIANT arguments. On the object side, the object has to decode all those VARIANT parameters, make sure they're correct, put them on some sort of stack frame, and then make the function call. As you can imagine, all this work is complex and time-consuming. If you're writing a COM object and you expect some of your clients to use scripting languages and other clients to use languages like C++, you've got a dilemma. You've got to include *IDispatch* or you lock your scripting language clients out. If you provide only *IDispatch*, you make accessing your object from C++ very inconvenient. Of course, you can provide access through both *IDispatch* and a custom interface, but that involves a lot of bookkeeping work. Dual interfaces evolved to handle this problem.

A dual interface is simply *IDispatch* with functions pasted onto the end. For example, the *IMotion* interface described below is a valid dual interface:

```
interface IMotion : public IDispatch {
    virtual HRESULT Fly() = 0;
    virtual HRESULT GetPosition() = 0;
};
```

Because *IMotion* derives from *IDispatch*, the first seven functions of *IMotion* are those of *IDispatch*. Clients who understand only *IDispatch* (VBScript for instance) look at the interface as just another version of *IDispatch* and feed DISPIDs to the *Invoke* function in the hopes of invoking a function. Clients who understand vtable-style custom interfaces look at the entire interface, ignore the middle four functions (the *IDispatch* functions), and concentrate on the first three functions (*IUnknown*) and the last three functions (the ones that represent the interface's core functions). Figure 29-6 shows the vtable layout of *IMotion*.

Most raw C++ implementations load the type library right away and delegate to *ITypeInfo* to perform the nasty task of implementing *Invoke* and *GetIDsOfNames*. To get an idea of how this works, see Kraig Brockschmidt's book *Inside OLE*, 2d. ed. (Microsoft Press, 1995) or Dale Rogerson's book *Inside COM* (Microsoft Press, 1997).

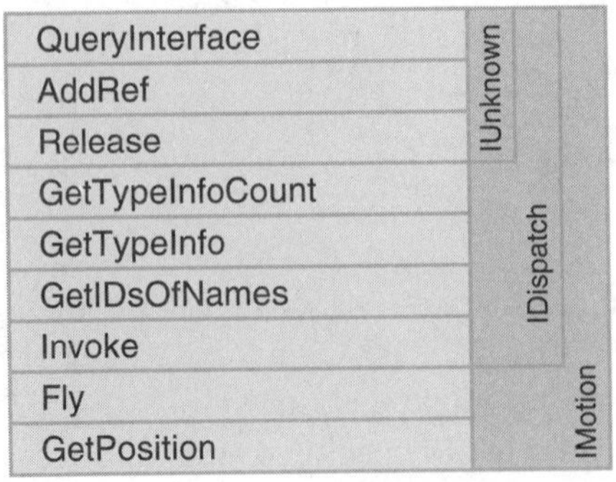

Figure 29-6.
The layout of a dual interface.

ATL and *IDispatch*

ATL's implementation of *IDispatch* delegates to the type library. ATL's implementation of *IDispatch* lives in the class *IDispatchImpl*. Objects that want to implement a dual interface include the *IDispatchImpl* template in the inheritance list like this:

```
class ATL_NO_VTABLE CAtlSpaceship :
    public CComObjectRootEx<CComSingleThreadModel>,
    public CComCoClass<CAtlSpaceship, &CLSID_AtlSpaceship>,
    public IDispatchImpl<IAtlSpaceship, &IID_IAtlSpaceship,
                         &LIBID_SPACESHIPSVRLib>,
    public IDispatchImpl<IVisual, &IID_IVisual,
                         &LIBID_SPACESHIPSVRLib>,
    public IDispatchImpl<IMotion, &IID_IMotion,
                         &LIBID_SPACESHIPSVRLib>
{
    ⋮
};
```

In addition to including the *IDispatchImpl* template class in the inheritance list, the object includes entries for the dual interface and for *IDispatch* in the interface map so that *QueryInterface* works properly:

```
BEGIN_COM_MAP(CAtlSpaceship)
    COM_INTERFACE_ENTRY(IAtlSpaceship)
    COM_INTERFACE_ENTRY(IDispatch)
END_COM_MAP()
```

As you can see, the *IDispatchImpl* template class arguments include the dual interface itself, the GUID for the interface, and the GUID representing the type library holding all the information about the interface. In addition to these template arguments, the *IDispatchImpl* class has some optional parameters not illustrated in Figure 29-6. The template parameter list also includes room for a major and minor version of the type library. Finally, the last template parameter is a class for managing the type information. ATL provides a default class named *CComTypeInfoHolder*.

In most raw C++ implementations of *IDispatch*, the class calls *LoadTypeLib* and *ITypeLib::GetTypeInfoOfGuid* in the constructor and holds on to the *ITypeInfo* pointer for the life of the class. ATL's implementation does things a little differently by using the *CComTypeInfoHolder* class to help manage the *ITypeInfo* pointer. *CComTypeInfoHolder* maintains an *ITypeInfo* pointer as a data member and wraps the critical *IDispatch*-related functions *GetIDsOfNames* and *Invoke*.

Clients acquire the dual interface by calling *QueryInterface* for *IID_IAtl-Spaceship*. (The client can also get this interface by calling *QueryInterface* for

843

IDispatch.) If the client calls *CallStartFleet* on the interface, the client accesses those functions directly (as for any other COM interface).

When a client calls *IDispatch::Invoke*, the call lands inside *IDispatchImpl's Invoke* function as you'd expect. From there, *IDispatchImpl::Invoke* delegates to the *CComTypeInfoHolder* class to perform the invocation, *CComTypeInfoHolder's Invoke*. The *CComTypeInfoHolder* class doesn't call *LoadTypeLib* until an actual call to *Invoke* or *GetIDsOfNames*. *CComTypeInfoHolder* has a member function named *GetTI* that consults the Registry for the type information (using the GUID and any major/minor version numbers passed in as a template parameter). Then *CComTypeInfoHolder* calls *ITypeLib::GetTypeInfo* to get the information about the interface. At that point, the type information holder delegates to the type information pointer. *IDispatchImpl* implements *IDispatch::GetIDsOfNames* in the same manner.

The *IMotion* and *IVisual* Interfaces

To get this COM class up to snuff with the other versions (the raw C++ version and the MFC version described in Chapter 24), you need to add the *IMotion* and *IVisual* interfaces to the project and to the class. Unfortunately, at the present time the only way to get this to happen is by typing the interfaces in by hand (the ATL AppWizard gives you only one interface by default). Open the IDL file and position the cursor near the top (somewhere after the *#import* statements but before the *library* statement), and start typing interface definitions as described in the following paragraph.

Once you get the hang of IDL, your first instinct when describing an interface should be to insert an open square bracket. Remember that in IDL, distinct items get attributes. One of the most important attributes for an interface is the name, or the GUID. In addition, at the very least the interface has to have the *object* attribute to tell the MIDL compiler you're dealing with COM at this point (as opposed to regular RPC). You also want these interfaces to be dual interfaces. The keyword "dual" in the interface attributes indicates this and inserts certain Registry entries to get the universal marshaling working correctly. After the attributes are closed off with a closing square bracket, the interface keyword kicks in to describe the interface. You'll make *IMotion* a dual interface and *IVisual* a plain custom interface to illustrate how the two different types of interfaces are attached to the *CSpaceship* class. Here are the *IMotion* and *IVisual* interfaces described in IDL:

```
[
    object,
    uuid(97B5C101-5299-11d1-8CAA-FD10872CC837),
    dual,
```

```
          helpstring("IMotion interface")
     ]
     interface IMotion : IDispatch
     {
          HRESULT Fly();
          HRESULT GetPosition([out,retval]long* nPosition);
     };


     [
          object,
          uuid(56F58464-52A4-11d1-8CAA-FD10872CC837),
          helpstring("IVisual interface")
     ]
     interface IVisual : IUnknown
     {
          HRESULT Display();
     };
```

Once the interfaces are described in IDL, you run the IDL through the MIDL compiler again. The MIDL compiler spits out a new copy of spaceshipsvr.h with the pure abstract base classes for *IMotion* and *IVisual*.

Now you need to add these interfaces to the *CSpaceship* class. There are two steps here. The first step is to create the interface part of the COM class's identity. Let's do the *IMotion* interface first. Adding the *IMotion* interface to *CSpaceship* is easy. Just use the *IDispatchImpl* template to provide an implementation of a dual interface like this:

```
class ATL_NO_VTABLE CAtlSpaceship :
    public CComObjectRootEx<CComSingleThreadModel>,
    public CComCoClass<CAtlSpaceship, &CLSID_AtlSpaceship>,
    public IDispatchImpl<IAtlSpaceship, &IID_IAtlSpaceship,
                         &LIBID_SPACESHIPSVRLib>,
    public IDispatchImpl<IMotion, &IID_IMotion,
                         &LIBID_SPACESHIPSVRLib>
{
    :
};
```

The second step involves beefing up the interface map so the client can acquire the *IMotion* interface. However, having two dual interfaces in a single COM class brings up an interesting issue. When a client calls *QueryInterface* for *IMotion*, the client should definitely get *IMotion*. However, when the client calls *QueryInterface* for *IDispatch*, which version of *IDispatch* should the client get—*IAtlSpaceship*'s dispatch interface or *IMotion*'s dispatch interface?

Multiple Dual Interfaces

Remember that all dual interfaces begin with the seven functions of *IDispatch*. A problem occurs whenever the client calls *QueryInterface* for *IID_IDispatch*. As a developer, you need to choose which version of *IDispatch* to pass out.

The interface map is where the *QueryInterface* for *IID_IDispatch* is specified. ATL has a specific macro for handling the dual interface situation. First consider the interface map for *CAtlSpaceship* so far:

```
BEGIN_COM_MAP(CAtlSpaceship)
    COM_INTERFACE_ENTRY(IAtlSpaceship)
    COM_INTERFACE_ENTRY(IDispatch)
END_COM_MAP()
```

When the client calls *QueryInterface*, ATL rips through the table trying to match the requested IID to one in the table. The interface map above handles two interfaces: *IAtlSpaceship* and *IDispatch*. If you want to add another dual interface to the *CAtlSpaceship* class, you need a different macro.

The macro handling multiple dispatch interfaces in an ATL-based COM class is named *COM_INTERFACE_ENTRY2*. To get *QueryInterface* working correctly, all you need to do is decide which version of *IDispatch* the client should get when asking for *IDispatch*, like this:

```
BEGIN_COM_MAP(CAtlSpaceship)
    COM_INTERFACE_ENTRY(IAtlSpaceship)
    COM_INTERFACE_ENTRY(IMotion)
    COM_INTERFACE_ENTRY2(IDispatch, IAtlSpaceship)
END_COM_MAP()
```

In this case, a client asking for *IDispatch* gets a pointer to *IAtlSpaceship* (whose first seven functions include the *IDispatch* functions).

Adding a nondual interface to an ATL-based COM class is even easier. Just add the interface to the inheritance list like this:

```
class ATL_NO_VTABLE CAtlSpaceship :
    public CComObjectRootEx<CComSingleThreadModel>,
    public CComCoClass<CAtlSpaceship, &CLSID_AtlSpaceship>,
    public IDispatchImpl<IAtlSpaceship, &IID_IAtlSpaceship,
                        &LIBID_SPACESHIPSVRLib>,
    public IDispatchImpl<IMotion, &IID_IMotion,
                        &LIBID_SPACESHIPSVRLib>,
    public IVisual
{
    :
};
```

Then add an interface map entry like this:

```
BEGIN_COM_MAP(CAtlSpaceship)
    COM_INTERFACE_ENTRY(IAtlSpaceship)
    COM_INTERFACE_ENTRY(IMotion)
    COM_INTERFACE_ENTRY2(IDispatch, IAtlSpaceship)
    COM_INTERFACE_ENTRY(IVisual)
END_COM_MAP()
```

Conclusion

There are a couple of key points in this chapter to remember. COM is a <u>binary</u> object model. Clients and objects agree on a binary layout (the interface). Once both parties agree on the layout, they talk together via the interface. The client is not at all concerned about how that interface is actually wired up. As long as the functions work as advertised, the client is happy. There are a number of ways to hook up COM interfaces, including multiply inheriting a single C++ class from several interfaces, using nested classes, or using a framework such as ATL.

ATL is Microsoft's framework for assembling small COM classes. ATL has two sides—some smart pointers to help with client-side coding and a complete framework for implementing COM classes. ATL implements *IUnknown*, *IDispatch*, and *IClassFactory* in templates provided through the library. In addition, ATL includes a wizard for helping you get started with a COM server and a wizard for inserting COM classes into your project.

While ATL does a lot for you, it doesn't completely excuse you from learning the basics of how COM works. In fact, you'll be able to use ATL a lot more efficiently once you understand COM. In the next chapter, we'll take a look at how to use ATL to write ActiveX controls effectively.

CHAPTER THIRTY

ATL and ActiveX Controls

If you've finished reading about COM and ATL and still wonder how COM fits into your day-to-day programming activities, you're not alone. Figuring out how to use COM in real life isn't always obvious at first glance. After all, a whole lot of extra code must be typed in just to get a COM object up and running. However, there's a very real application of COM right under your nose —ActiveX Controls. ActiveX controls are small gadgets (usually UI-oriented) written around the Component Object Model.

In Chapter 29, you examined COM classes created by using ATL. In this chapter, you'll learn how to write a certain kind of COM class—an ActiveX control. You had a chance to work with ActiveX Controls from the client side in Chapter 8. Now it's time to write your own.

There are several steps involved in creating an ActiveX control using ATL, including:

- Deciding what to draw
- Developing incoming interfaces for the control
- Developing outgoing interfaces (events) for the control
- Implementing a persistence mechanism for the control
- Providing a user interface for manipulating the control's properties

This chapter covers all these steps. Soon you'll be able to use ATL to create ActiveX controls that you (or other developers) can use within other programs.

ActiveX Controls

Even today, there's some confusion as to what really constitutes an ActiveX control. In 1994, Microsoft tacked some new interfaces onto its Object Linking and Embedding protocol, packaged them within DLLs, and called them

OLE Controls. Originally, OLE Controls implemented nearly the entire OLE Document embedding protocol. In addition, OLE Controls supported the following:

- Dynamic invocation (Automation)
- Property pages (so the user could modify the control's properties)
- Outbound callback interfaces (event sets)
- Connections (a standard way to for clients and controls to hook up the event callbacks)

When the Internet became a predominant factor in Microsoft's marketing plans, Microsoft announced its intention to plant ActiveX Controls on Web pages. At that point, the size of these components became an issue. Microsoft took its OLE Control specification, changed the name from OLE Controls to ActiveX Controls, and stated that all the features listed above were optional. This means that under the new ActiveX Control definition, a control's only requirement is that it be based on COM and that it implement *IUnknown*. Of course, for a control to be useful it really needs to implement most of the features listed above. So in the end, ActiveX Controls and OLE Controls refer to more or less the same animal.

Developers have been able to use MFC to create ActiveX controls since mid-1994. However, one of the downsides of using MFC to create ActiveX controls is that the controls become bound to MFC. Sometimes you want your controls to be smaller or to work even if the end user doesn't have the MFC DLLs on his or her system. In addition, using MFC to create ActiveX controls forces you into making certain design decisions. For example, if you decide to use MFC to write an ActiveX control, you more or less lock yourself out of using dual interfaces (unless you feel like writing a lot of extra code). Using MFC to create ActiveX controls also means the control and its property pages need to use *IDispatch* to communicate between themselves.

To avoid the problems described so far, developers can now use ATL to create ActiveX controls. ATL now includes the facilities to create full-fledged ActiveX controls, complete with every feature an ActiveX control should have. These features include incoming interfaces, persistent properties, property pages, and connection points. If you've ever written an ActiveX control using MFC, you'll see how much more flexible using ATL can be.

Using ATL to Write a Control

Although creating an ActiveX control using ATL is actually a pretty straight-forward process, using ATL ends up being a bit more burdensome than using MFC. That's because ATL doesn't include all of MFC's amenities. For example, ATL doesn't include device context wrappers. When you draw on a device context, you need to use the raw device context handle. In addition, ClassWizard doesn't understand ATL-based source code, so when you want your control to handle messages, you end up using the "TypingWizard." (That is, you end up typing the message maps in by hand.)

Despite these issues, creating an ActiveX control using ATL is a whole lot easier than creating one from scratch. Also, using ATL gives you a certain amount of flexibility you don't get when you use MFC. For example, while adding dual interfaces to your control is a tedious process with MFC, you get them for free when you use ATL. The ATL COM Object Wizard also makes adding more COM classes (even noncontrol classes) to your project very easy, while adding new controls to an MFC-based DLL is a bit more difficult.

For this chapter's example, we'll represent a small pair of dice as an ATL-based ActiveX control. The dice control will illustrate the most important facets of ActiveX Controls, including control rendering, incoming interfaces, properties, property pages, and events.

Creating the Control

As always, the easiest way to create a COM server in ATL is to use the ATL COM Object Wizard. To use the ATL COM Object Wizard, select New from the File menu. Select the Project tab in the New dialog, and highlight the ATL COM AppWizard item. Name the project something clever like *ATLDiceSvr*. As you step through AppWizard, just leave the defaults checked. Doing so will ensure that the server you create is a DLL.

Once the DLL server has been created, perform the following steps:

1. Select New ATL Object from the Insert menu to insert a new ATL object into the project.

2. In the ATL Object Wizard, select Controls from the Category list and then select Full Control from the Objects list.

3. Click Next to open the ATL Object Wizard Properties dialog. In the Short Name text box on the Names tab, give the control some clever name (like *ATLDiceObj*). The dialog box should look similar to Figure 30-1 on the following page.

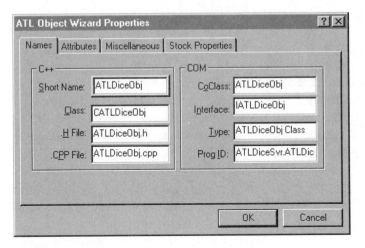

Figure 30-1.
The ATL Object Wizard Properties dialog box.

4. Select the Attributes tab. Here's where you configure the control. For example, you can

   ■ Designate the threading model for the control

   ■ Decide whether the main interface is a dual or custom interface

   ■ Indicate whether your control supports aggregation

   ■ Choose whether you want to use COM exceptions and connection points in your control

5. To make your life easier for now, select Support Connection Points. (This will save you some typing later on.) Leave everything else as the default value. Figure 30-2 shows what the Attributes tab on the ATL Object Wizard Properties dialog box looks like now.

6. Select the Miscellaneous tab. Here you have the option of applying some miscellaneous traits to your control. For example, you can give the control behaviors based on regular Microsoft Windows controls such as buttons and edit controls. You might also select other options for your control, such as having your control appear invisible at runtime or giving your control an opaque background. Figure 30-3 shows the available options.

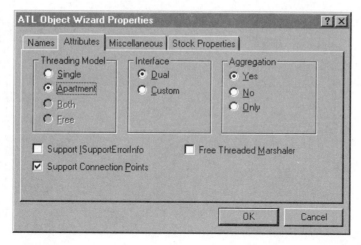

Figure 30-2.
The Attributes tab on the ATL Object Wizard Properties dialog box.

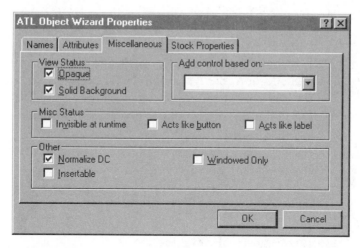

Figure 30-3.
The Miscellaneous control properties tab on the ATL Object Wizard Properties dialog box.

7. Finally, select the Stock Properties tab if you want to give your control some stock properties. Stock properties are those properties that you might expect any control to have, including background colors, border colors, foreground colors, and a caption. Figure 30-4 on the following page shows the Stock Properties tab.

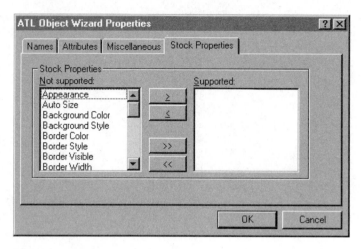

Figure 30-4.
The Stock Properties tab on the ATL Object Wizard Properties dialog box.

8. When you've finished selecting the attributes for the control, click OK.

The ATL Object Wizard adds a header file and a source file defining the new control. In addition, the ATL Object Wizard sets aside space in the IDL file to hold the control's main interface and assigns a GUID to the interface. Here's the C++ definition of the control produced by the ATL Object Wizard:

```
class ATL_NO_VTABLE CATLDiceObj :
    public CComObjectRootEx<CComSingleThreadModel>,
    public IDispatchImpl<IATLDieceObj,
                         &IID_IATLDieceObj,
                         &LIBID_ATLDICESVRLib>,
    public CComControl<CATLDiceObj>,
    public IPersistStreamInitImpl<CATLDiceObj>,
    public IOleControlImpl<CATLDiceObj>,
    public IOleObjectImpl<CATLDiceObj>,
    public IOleInPlaceActiveObjectImpl<CATLDiceObj>,
    public IViewObjectExImpl<CATLDiceObj>,
    public IOleInPlaceObjectWindowlessImpl<CATLDiceObj>,
    public IConnectionPointContainerImpl<CATLDiceObj>,
    public IPersistStorageImpl<CATLDiceObj>,
    public ISpecifyPropertyPagesImpl<CATLDiceObj>,
    public IQuickActivateImpl<CATLDiceObj>,
    public IDataObjectImpl<CATLDiceObj>,
```

```
public IProvideClassInfo2Impl<&CLSID_ATLDiceObj,
                              &DIID__DDiceEvents,
                              &LIBID_ATLDICESVRLib>,
public IPropertyNotifySinkCP<CATLDiceObj>,
public CComCoClass<CATLDiceObj, &CLSID_ATLDiceObj>
{
    ⋮
};
```

That's a pretty long inheritance list. You've already seen the template implementations of *IUnknown* and support for class objects. They exist in *CComObjectRootEx* and *CComCoClass*. You've also seen how ATL implements *IDispatch* within the *IDispatchImpl* template. However, for a basic control there are about 11 more interfaces required to make everything work. These interfaces can be categorized into several areas as shown in the following table.

Category	Interface
Interfaces for handling self-description	*IProvideClassInfo2*
Interfaces for handling persistence	*IPersistStreamInit* *IPersistStorage*
Interfaces for handling activation	*IQuickActivate* (and some of *IOleObject*)
Interfaces from the original OLE Control specification	*IOleControl*
Interfaces from the OLE Document specification	*IOleObject*
Interfaces for rendering	*IOleInPlaceActiveObject* *IViewObject* *IOleInPlaceObjectWindowless* *IDataObject*
Interfaces for helping the container manage property pages	*ISpecifyPropertyPages*
Interfaces for handling connections	*IPropertyNotifySinkCP* *IConnectionPointContainer*

NOTE: These are by and large boilerplate interfaces—ones that a COM class must implement to qualify as an ActiveX control. Most of the implementations are standard and vary only slightly (if at all) from one control to the next. The beauty of ATL is that it implements this standard behavior and gives you programmatic hooks where you can plug in your custom code. That way, you don't have to burn your eyes out by looking directly at the COM code. You can live a full and rich life without understanding exactly how these interfaces work. However, if you want to know more about the internal workings of ActiveX Controls, be sure to check out these books: *Inside OLE* by Kraig Brockschmidt (Microsoft Press, 1995), *ActiveX Controls Inside Out* by Adam Denning (Microsoft Press, 1997), and *Designing and Using ActiveX Controls* by Tom Armstrong (IDG Books Worldwide, 1997).

ATL's Control Architecture

From the highest level, an ActiveX control has two aspects to it: its external state (what it renders on the screen) and its internal state (its properties). Once an ActiveX control is hosted by some sort of container (such as a Microsoft Visual Basic form or an MFC dialog box), it maintains a symbiotic relationship with that container. The client code talks to the control through incoming COM interfaces such as *IDispatch* and OLE Document interfaces such as *IOleObject* and *IDataObject*.

The control also has the opportunity to talk back to the client. One method of implementing this two-way communication is for the client to implement an *IDispatch* interface to represent the control's event set. The container maintains a set of properties called <u>ambient properties</u> that the control can use to find out about its host. For instance, a control can camouflage itself within the container because the container makes the information stored in these properties available through a specifically named *IDispatch* interface. The container can implement an interface named *IPropertyNotifySink* to find out when the properties within a control might change. Finally, the container implements *IOleClientSite* and *IOleControlSite* as part of the control-embedding protocol.

The interfaces listed on page 855 allow the client and the object to exhibit the behaviors expected of an ActiveX control. We'll tackle some of these interfaces as we go along. The best place to begin looking at ATL-based controls is the *CComControl* class and its base classes.

CComControl

You can find the definition of *CComControl* in Microsoft's ATLCTL.H file under ATL's Include directory. *CComControl* is a template class that takes a single class parameter:

```
template <class T>
class ATL_NO_VTABLE CComControl :   public CComControlBase,
                                    public CWindowImpl<T>

{
  :
};
```

CComControl is a rather lightweight class that does little by itself—it derives functionality from *CComControlBase* and *CWindowImpl*. *CComControl* expects the template parameter to be an ATL-based COM object derived from *CComObjectRootEx*. *CComControl* requires the template parameter for various reasons, the primary reason being that from time to time the control class uses the template parameter to call back to the control's *InternalQueryInterface*.

CComControl implements several functions that make it easy for the control to call back to the client. For example, *CComControl* implements a function named *FireOnRequestEdit* to give controls the ability to tell the client that a specified property is about to change. This function calls back to the client through the client-implemented interface *IPropertyNotifySink*. *FireOnRequest-Edit* notifies all connected *IPropertyNotifySink* interfaces that the property specified by a certain *DISPID* is about to change.

CComControl also implements the *FireOnChanged* function. *FireOn-Changed* is very much like *FireOnRequestEdit* in that it calls back to the client through the *IPropertyNotifySink* interface. This function tells the clients of the control (all clients connected to the control through *IPropertyNotifySink*) that a property specified by a certain *DISPID* has already changed.

In addition to mapping the *IPropertyNotifySink* interface to some more easily understood functions, *CComControl* implements a function named *Con-trolQueryInterface*, which simply forwards on to the control's *IUnknown* interface. (This is how you can get a control's *IUnknown* interface from inside the control.) Finally, *CComControl* implements a function named *CreateControl-Window*. The default behavior for this function is to call *CWindowImpl::Create*. (Notice that *CComControl* also derives from *CWindowImpl*.) If you want to, you can override this function to do something other than create a single window. For example, you might want to create multiple windows for your control.

Most of the real functionality for *CComControl* exists within those two other classes—*CComControlBase* and *CWindowImpl*. Let's take a look at those classes now.

CComControlBase

CComControlBase is a much more substantial class than *CComControl*. To begin with, *CComControlBase* maintains all the pointers used by the control to talk back to the client. *CComControlBase* uses ATL's *CComPtr* smart pointer to include member variables that wrap the following interfaces implemented for calling back to the client:

■ A wrapper for *IOleInPlaceSite*(*m_spInPlaceSite*)

- An advise holder for the client's data advise sink (*m_spDataAdviseHolder*)

- An OLE advise holder for the client's OLE advise sink (*m_spOleAdviseHolder*)

- A wrapper for *IOleClientSite* (*m_spClientSite*)

- A wrapper for *IAdviseSink* (*m_spAdviseSink*)

CComControlBase also uses ATL's *CComDispatchDriver* to wrap the client's dispatch interface for exposing its ambient properties.

CComControlBase is also where you'll find the member variables that contain the control's sizing and positioning information: *m_sizeNatural*, *m_sizeExtent*, and *m_rcPos*. The other important data member within *CComControlBase* is the control's window handle. Most ActiveX controls are UI gadgets and as such maintain a window. *CWindowImpl* and *CWindowImplBase* handle the windowing aspects of an ATL-based ActiveX control.

CWindowImpl and *CWindowImplBase*

CWindowImpl derives from *CWindowImplBase*, which in turn derives from *CWindow* and *CMessageMap*. As a template class, *CWindowImpl* takes a single parameter upon instantiation. The template parameter is the control being created. *CWindowImpl* needs the control type because *CWindowImpl* calls back to the control during window creation. Let's take a closer look at how ATL handles windowing.

ATL Windowing

Just as *CComControl* is relatively lightweight (most work happens in *CComControlBase*), *CWindowImpl* is also relatively lightweight. *CWindowImpl* more or less handles only window creation. In fact, that's the only function explicitly defined by *CWindowImpl*. *CWindowImpl::Create* creates a new window based on the window class information managed by a class named *_ATLWNDCLASSINFO*. There's an ASCII character version and a wide character version.

```
struct _ATL_WNDCLASSINFOA
{
    WNDCLASSEXA m_wc;
    LPCSTR m_lpszOrigName;
    WNDPROC pWndProc;
    LPCSTR m_lpszCursorID;
    BOOL m_bSystemCursor;
    ATOM m_atom;
    CHAR m_szAutoName[13];
```

```
    ATOM Register(WNDPROC* p)
    {
        return AtlModuleRegisterWndClassInfoA(&_Module, this, p);
    }
};
struct _ATL_WNDCLASSINFOW
{
    WNDCLASSEXW m_wc;
    LPCWSTR m_lpszOrigName;
    WNDPROC pWndProc;
    LPCWSTR m_lpszCursorID;
    BOOL m_bSystemCursor;
    ATOM m_atom;
    WCHAR m_szAutoName[13];
    ATOM Register(WNDPROC* p)
    {
        return AtlModuleRegisterWndClassInfoW(&_Module, this, p);
    }
};
```

Then ATL uses typedefs to alias this structure to a single class named *CWndClassInfo*:

```
typedef _ATL_WNDCLASSINFOA CWndClassInfoA;
typedef _ATL_WNDCLASSINFOW CWndClassInfoW;
#ifdef UNICODE
#define CWndClassInfo CWndClassInfoW
#else
#define CWndClassInfo CWndClassInfoA
#endif
```

CWindowImpl uses a macro named *DECLARE_WND_CLASS* to add window class information to a *CWindowImpl*-derived class. *DECLARE_WND_CLASS* also adds a function named *GetWndClassInfo*. Here's the *DECLARE_WND_CLASS* macro:

```
#define DECLARE_WND_CLASS(WndClassName) \
static CWndClassInfo& GetWndClassInfo() \
{ \
    static CWndClassInfo wc = \
    { \
        { sizeof(WNDCLASSEX), CS_HREDRAW | CS_VREDRAW | CS_DBLCLKS,\
        StartWindowProc, \
        0, 0, NULL, NULL, NULL, (HBRUSH)(COLOR_WINDOW + 1), \
        NULL, WndClassName, NULL }, \
        NULL, NULL, IDC_ARROW, TRUE, 0, _T("") \
    }; \
    return wc; \
}
```

This macro expands to provide a *CWndClassInfo* structure for the control class. Because *CWndClassInfo* manages the information for a single window class, each window created through a specific instance of *CWindowImpl* will be based on the same window class.

CWindowImpl derives from *CWindowImplBaseT*. *CWindowImplBaseT* derives from *CWindowImplRoot*, which is specialized around the *CWindow* class and the *CControlWinTraits* classes like this:

```
template <class TBase = CWindow,
        class TWinTraits = CControlWinTraits>
class ATL_NO_VTABLE CWindowImplBaseT :
    public CWindowImplRoot< TBase >
{
public:
    :
};
```

CWindowImplRoot derives from *CWindow* (by default) and *CMessageMap*. *CWindowImplBaseT* manages the window procedure of a *CWindowImpl*-derived class. *CWindow* is a lightweight class that wraps window handles in the same way (but not as extensively) as MFC's *CWnd* class. *CMessageMap* is a tiny class that defines a single pure virtual function named *ProcessWindowMessage*. ATL-based message-mapping machinery assumes this function is available, so ATL-based classes that want to use message maps need to derive from *CMessageMap*. Let's take a quick look at ATL message maps.

ATL Message Maps

The root of ATL's message mapping machinery lies within the *CMessageMap* class. ATL-based controls expose message maps by virtue of indirectly deriving from *CWindowImplBase*. In MFC, by contrast, deriving from *CCmdTarget* enables message mapping. However, just as in MFC, it's not enough to derive from a class that supports message maps. The message maps actually have to be there—and those message maps are implemented via macros.

To implement a message map in an ATL-based control, use message map macros. First ATL's *BEGIN_MSG_MAP* macro goes into the control class's header file. *BEGIN_MSG_MAP* marks the beginning of the default message map. *CWindowImpl::WindowProc* uses this default message map to process messages sent to the window. The message map directs messages either to the appropriate handler function or to another message map. ATL defines another macro named *END_MSG_MAP* to mark the end of a message map. Between *BEGIN_MSG_MAP* and *END_MSG_MAP* lie some other macros for mapping window messages to member functions in the control. For example, here's a typical message map you might find in an ATL-based control:

```
BEGIN_MSG_MAP(CAFullControl)
    CHAIN_MSG_MAP(CComControl<CAFullControl>)
    DEFAULT_REFLECTION_HANDLER()
    MESSAGE_HANDLER(WM_TIMER, OnTimer);
    MESSAGE_HANDLER(WM_LBUTTONDOWN, OnLButton);
END_MSG_MAP()
```

This message map delegates most of the message processing to the control through the *CHAIN_MSG_MAP* macro and handles message reflection through the *DEFAULT_REFLECTION_HANDLER* macro. The message map also handles two window messages explicitly: WM_TIMER and WM_LBUTTONDOWN. These are standard window messages that are mapped using the *MESSAGE_HANDLER* macro. The macros simply produce a table relating window messages to member functions in the class. In addition to regular messages, message maps are capable of handling other sorts of events. Here's a rundown of the kinds of macros that can go in a message map.

Macro	Description
MESSAGE_HANDLER	Maps a Windows message to a handler function
MESSAGE_RANGE_HANDLER	Maps a contiguous range of Windows messages to a handler function
COMMAND_HANDLER	Maps a WM_COMMAND message to a handler function, based on the identifier and the notification code of the menu item, control, or accelerator
COMMAND_ID_HANDLER	Maps a WM_COMMAND message to a handler function, based on the identifier of the menu item, control, or accelerator
COMMAND_CODE_HANDLER	Maps a WM_COMMAND message to a handler function, based on the notification code
COMMAND_RANGE_HANDLER	Maps a contiguous range of WM_COMMAND messages to a handler function, based on the identifier of the menu item, control, or accelerator

(continued)

861

Macro	Description
NOTIFY_HANDLER	Maps a WM_NOTIFY message to a handler function, based on the notification code and the control identifier
NOTIFY_ID_HANDLER	Maps a WM_NOTIFY message to a handler function, based on the control identifier
NOTIFY_CODE_HANDLER	Maps a WM_NOTIFY message to a handler function, based on the notification code
NOTIFY_RANGE_HANDLER	Maps a contiguous range of WM_NOTIFY messages to a handler function, based on the control identifier

Handling messages within ATL works much the same as in MFC. ATL includes a single window procedure through which messages are routed. Technically, you can build your controls effectively without understanding everything about ATL's control architecture. However, this knowledge is sometimes helpful as you develop a control, and it's even more useful when debugging a control.

Developing the Control

Once the control is inserted into the server, you need to add some code to make the control do something. If you were to compile and load ATL's default control into a container, the results wouldn't be particularly interesting. You'd simply see a blank rectangle with the string "ATL 3.0 : ATLDiceOb." You'll want to add code to render the control, to represent the internal state of the control, to respond to events, and to generate events to send back to the container.

Deciding What to Draw

A good place to start working on a control is on its drawing code—you get instant gratification that way. This is a control that is visually represented by a couple of dice. The easiest way to render to the dice control is to draw bitmaps representing each of the six possible dice sides and then show the bitmaps on the screen. This implies that the dice control will maintain some variables to represent its state. For example, the control needs to manage the bitmaps for representing the dice as well as two numbers representing the first value shown by each die. Here is the code from ATLDICEOBJ.H that represents the state of the dice:

```
#define MAX_DIEFACES 6

HBITMAP m_dieBitmaps[MAX_DIEFACES];
unsigned short m_nFirstDieValue;
unsigned short m_nSecondDieValue;
```

Before diving headfirst into the control's drawing code, you need to do a bit of preliminary work—the bitmaps need to be loaded. Presumably each die rendered by the dice control will show any one of six dice faces, so the control needs one bitmap for each face. Figure 30-5 shows what one of the dice bitmaps looks like.

Figure 30-5.
A bitmap for the dice control.

If you draw the bitmaps one at a time, they'll have sequential identifiers in the resource.h file. Giving the bitmaps sequential identifiers will make them easier to load. Otherwise, you might need to modify the resource.h file, which contains the following identifiers:

```
#define IDB_DICE1                    207
#define IDB_DICE2                    208
#define IDB_DICE3                    209
#define IDB_DICE4                    210
#define IDB_DICE5                    211
#define IDB_DICE6                    212
```

Loading bitmaps is fairly straightforward. Cycle through the bitmap array, and load the bitmap resources. When they're stored in an array like this, grabbing the bitmap out of the array and showing it is much easier than if you didn't use an array. Here is the function that loads the bitmaps into the array:

```
BOOL CATLDiceObj::LoadBitmaps() {
    BOOL bSuccess = TRUE;

    for(int i=0; i<MAX_DIEFACES; i++) {
        DeleteObject(m_dieBitmaps[i]);
        m_dieBitmaps[i] = LoadBitmap(_Module.m_hInst,
                            MAKEINTRESOURCE(IDB_DICE1+i));
        if(!m_dieBitmaps[i]) {
            ::MessageBox(NULL,
                        "Failed to load bitmaps",
                        NULL,
                        MB_OK);
```

(continued)

```
        bSuccess = FALSE;
    }
}
return bSuccess;
}
```

The best place to call *LoadBitmaps* is from within the control's constructor, as shown in the following code. To simulate a random roll of the dice, set the control's state so that the first and second die values are random numbers between 0 and 5 (these numbers will be used when the dice control is drawn):

```
class CATLDiceObj : // big inheritance list {
    CATLDiceObj () {
        LoadBitmaps();
        srand((unsigned)time(NULL));
        m_nFirstDieValue = (rand() % (MAX_DIEFACES)) + 1;
        m_nSecondDieValue = (rand() % (MAX_DIEFACES)) + 1;
    }
```

Once the bitmaps are loaded, you'll want to render them. The dice control should include a function for showing each die face based on the current internal state of the dice. Here's where you first encounter ATL's drawing machinery.

One of the most convenient things about ATL-based controls (and MFC-based controls) is that all the drawing code happens in one place: within the control's *OnDraw* function. *OnDraw* is a virtual function of *COleControlBase*. Here's *OnDraw*'s signature:

```
virtual HRESULT OnDraw(ATL_DRAWINFO& di);
```

OnDraw takes a single parameter: a pointer to an *ATL_DRAWINFO* structure. Among other things, the *ATL_DRAWINFO* structure contains a device context on which to render your control. Here's the *ATL_DRAWINFO* structure:

```
struct ATL_DRAWINFO {
    UINT cbSize;
    DWORD dwDrawAspect;
    LONG lindex;
    DVTARGETDEVICE* ptd;
    HDC hicTargetDev;
    HDC hdcDraw;
    LPCRECTL prcBounds; //Rectangle in which to draw
    LPCRECTL prcWBounds; //WindowOrg and Ext if metafile
    BOOL bOptimize;
    BOOL bZoomed;
    BOOL bRectInHimetric;
```

```
    SIZEL ZoomNum;        //ZoomX = ZoomNum.cx/ZoomNum.cy
    SIZEL ZoomDen;
};
```

As you can see, there's a lot more information here than a simple device context. While you can count on the framework filling it out correctly for you, it's good to know where the information in the structure comes from and how it fits into the picture.

ActiveX Controls are interesting because they are drawn in two contexts. The first and most obvious context is when the control is active and it draws within the actual drawing space of the client. The other, less-obvious context in which controls are drawn is during design time (as when an ActiveX control resides in a Visual Basic form in design mode). In the first context, ActiveX Controls render themselves to a live screen device context. In the second context, ActiveX Controls render themselves to a metafile device context.

Many (though not all) ATL-based controls are composed of at least one window. So ActiveX Controls need to render themselves during the WM_PAINT message. Once the control receives the WM_PAINT message, the message routing architecture passes control to *CComControlBase::OnPaint*. (Remember, *CComControlBase* is one of the control's base classes.) *CComControlBase::OnPaint* performs several steps. The function begins by creating a painting device context (using *BeginPaint*). Then *OnPaint* creates an *ATL_DRAWINFO* structure on the stack and initializes the fields within the structure. *OnPaint* sets up *ATL_DRAWINFO* to show the entire content (the *dwDrawAspect* field is set to *DVASPECT_CONTENT*). *OnPaint* also sets the *lindex* field to –1, sets the drawing device context to the newly created painting device context, and sets up the bounding rectangle to be the client area of the control's window. Then *OnPaint* goes on to call *OnDrawAdvanced*.

The default *OnDrawAdvanced* function prepares a normalized device context for drawing. You can override this method if you want to use the device context passed by the container without normalizing it. ATL then calls your control class's *OnDraw* method.

The second context in which the *OnDraw* function is called is when the control draws on to a metafile. The control draws itself on to a metafile whenever someone calls *IViewObjectEx::Draw*. (*IViewObjectEx* is one of the interfaces implemented by the ActiveX control.) ATL implements the *IViewObjectEx* interface through the template class *IViewObjectExImpl*. *IViewObjectExImpl::Draw* is called whenever the control needs to take a snapshot of its presentation space for the container to store. In this case, the container creates a metafile device context and hands it to the control. *IViewObjectExImpl* puts an *ATL_DRAWINFO* structure on the stack and initializes. The bounding rectangle, the index, the drawing aspect, and the device contexts are all passed in as parameters by the client. The rest of the drawing is the same in this case—the control calls *OnDrawAdvanced*, which in turn calls your version of *OnDraw*.

Once you're armed with this knowledge, writing functions to render the bitmaps becomes fairly straightforward. To show the first die face, create a memory-based device context, select the object into the device context, and *BitBlt* the memory device context into the real device context. Here's the code:

```
void CATLDiceObj::ShowFirstDieFace(ATL_DRAWINFO& di) {

    BITMAP bmInfo;
    GetObject(m_dieBitmaps[m_nFirstDieValue-1],
                        sizeof(bmInfo), &bmInfo);

    SIZE size;

    size.cx = bmInfo.bmWidth;
    size.cy = bmInfo.bmHeight;

    HDC hMemDC;
    hMemDC = CreateCompatibleDC(di.hdcDraw);

    HBITMAP hOldBitmap;
    HBITMAP hbm = m_dieBitmaps[m_nFirstDieValue-1];
    hOldBitmap = (HBITMAP)SelectObject(hMemDC, hbm);

    if (hOldBitmap == NULL)
        return;       // destructors will clean up

    BitBlt(di.hdcDraw,
            di.prcBounds->left+1,
            di.prcBounds->top+1,
            size.cx,
            size.cy,
            hMemDC, 0,
            0,
            SRCCOPY);

    SelectObject(di.hdcDraw, hOldBitmap);
    DeleteDC(hMemDC);
}
```

Showing the second die face is more or less the same process—just make sure that the dice are represented separately. For example, you probably want to change the call to *BitBlt* so that the two dice bitmaps are shown side by side.

```
void CATLDiceObj::ShowSecondDieFace(ATL_DRAWINFO& di) {
    //
    // This code is exactly the same as ShowFirstDieFace
    //   except the second die is positioned next to the first die.
    //
    BitBlt(di.hdcDraw,
           di.prcBounds->left+size.cx + 2,
           di.prcBounds->top+1,
           size.cx,
           size.cy,
           hMemDC, 0,
           0, SRCCOPY);
    // The rest is the same as in ShowFirstDieFace
}
```

The last step is to call these two functions whenever the control is asked to render itself—during the control's *OnDraw* function. *ShowFirstDieFace* and *ShowSecondDieFace* will show the correct bitmap based on the state of *m_nFirstDieValue* and *m_nSecondDieValue*:

```
HRESULT CATLDiceObj::OnDraw(ATL_DRAWINFO& di) {
    ShowFirstDieFace(di);
    ShowSecondDieFace(di);
    return S_OK;
}
```

At this point, if you compile and load this control into some ActiveX Control container (like a Visual Basic form or an MFC-based dialog), you'll see two die faces staring back at you. Now it's time to add some code to enliven the control and roll the dice.

Responding to Window Messages

Just looking at two dice faces isn't that much fun. You want to make the dice work. A good way to get the dice to appear to jiggle is to use a timer to generate events and then respond to the timer by showing a new pair of dice faces. Setting up a Windows timer in the control means adding a function to handle the timer message and adding a macro to the control's message map. Start by using ClassView to add a handler for WM_TIMER. Right-click on the CAtl-DiceOb symbol in ClassView, and select Add Windows Message Handler from the context menu. This adds a prototype for the *OnTimer* function and an entry into the message map to handle the WM_TIMER message. Add some code to the *OnTimer* function to handle the WM_TIMER message. The *OnTimer* function should look like the code shown at the top of the next page.

```
LRESULT CATLDiceObj::OnTimer(UINT msg, WPARAM wParam,
                             LPARAM lParam, BOOL& bHandled) {

    if(m_nTimesRolled > 15) {
        m_nTimesRolled = 0;
        KillTimer(1);
    } else {
        m_nFirstDieValue = (rand() % (MAX_DIEFACES)) + 1;
        m_nSecondDieValue = (rand() % (MAX_DIEFACES)) + 1;
        FireViewChange();
        m_nTimesRolled++;
    }
    bHandled = TRUE;
    return 0;
}
```

This function responds to the timer message by generating two random numbers, setting up the control's state to reflect these two new numbers, and then asking the control to refresh itself by calling *FireViewChange*. Notice the function kills the timer as soon as the dice have rolled a certain number of times. Also notice that the message handler tells the framework that it successfully handled the function by setting the *bHandled* variable to TRUE.

Notice there's an entry for WM_TIMER in the control's message map. Because WM_TIMER is just a plain vanilla window message, it's represented with a standard *MESSAGE_HANDLER* macro as follows:

```
BEGIN_MSG_MAP(CATLDiceObj)
    CHAIN_MSG_MAP(CComControl<CATLDiceObj>)
    DEFAULT_REFLECTION_HANDLER()
    MESSAGE_HANDLER(WM_TIMER, OnTimer);
END_MSG_MAP()
```

As you can tell from this message map, the dice control already handles the gamut of Windows messages through the *CHAIN_MSG_MAP* macro. However, now the pair of dice has the ability to simulate rolling by responding to the timer message. Setting a timer causes the control to repaint itself with a new pair of dice numbers every quarter of a second or so. Of course, there needs to be some way to start the dice rolling. Because this is an ActiveX control, it's reasonable to allow client code to start rolling the dice via a call to a function in one of its incoming interfaces. Use ClassView to add a *RollDice* function to the main interface. Do this by right-clicking on the *IATLDiceObj* interface appearing in ClassView on the left side of the screen and selecting Add Method from the pop-up menu. Then add a *RollDice* function. Microsoft Visual C++ adds a function named *RollDice* to your control. Implement *RollDice* by setting the timer for a reasonably short interval and then returning S_OK. Add the following boldface code:

```
STDMETHODIMP CATLDiceObj::RollDice()
{
    SetTimer(1, 250);
    return S_OK;
}
```

If you load the dice into an ActiveX control container, you'll now be able to browse and call the control's methods and roll the dice.

In addition to using the incoming interface to roll the dice, the user might reasonably expect to roll the dice by double-clicking the control. To enable this behavior, just add a message handler to trap the mouse-button-down message by adding a function to handle a left-mouse double click.

```
LRESULT CATLDiceObj::OnLButtonDblClick(UINT uMsg,
                                       WPARAM wParam,
                                       LPARAM lParam,
                                       BOOL& bHandled) {
    RollDice();
    bHandled = TRUE;
    return 0;
}
```

Then be sure you add an entry to the message map to handle the WM_LBUT-TONDOWN message:

```
BEGIN_MSG_MAP(CATLDiceObj)
    // Other message handlers
    MESSAGE_HANDLER(WM_LBUTTONDBLCLK, OnLButtonDblClick)
END_MSG_MAP()
```

When you load the dice control into a container and double-click on it, you should see the dice roll. Now that you've added rendering code and given the control the ability to roll, it's time to add some properties.

Adding Properties and Property Pages

You've just seen that ActiveX controls have an external presentation state. (The presentation state is the state reflected when the control draws itself.) In addition, most ActiveX controls also have an internal state. The control's internal state is a set of variables exposed to the outside world via interface functions. These internal variables are also known as properties.

For example, imagine a simple grid implemented as an ActiveX control. The grid has an external presentation state and a set of internal variables for describing the state of the grid. The properties of a grid control would probably include the number of rows in the grid, the number of columns in the grid, the color of the lines composing the grid, the type of font used, and so forth.

As you saw in Chapter 29, adding properties to an ATL-based class means adding member variables to the class and then using ClassWizard to create *get* and *put* functions to access these properties. For example, two member variables that you might add to the dice control include the dice color and the number of times the dice are supposed to roll before stopping. Those two properties could easily be represented as a pair of short integers as shown here:

```
class ATL_NO_VTABLE CATLDiceObj :
    ⋮
{
    ⋮
    short m_nDiceColor;
    short m_nTimesToRoll;
    ⋮
};
```

To make these properties accessible to the client, you need to add *get* and *put* functions to the control. Right-clicking on the interface symbol in ClassView brings up a context menu, giving you a choice to Add Property, which will present you with the option of adding these functions. Adding DiceColor and TimesToRoll properties to the control using ClassView will add four new functions to the control: *get_DiceColor*, *put_DiceColor*, *get_TimesToRoll*, and *put_TimesToRoll*.

The *get_DiceColor* function should retrieve the state of *m_nDiceColor*:

```
STDMETHODIMP CATLDiceObj::get_DiceColor(short * pVal)
{
    *pVal = m_nDiceColor;
    return S_OK;
}
```

To make the control interesting, *put_DiceColor* should change the colors of the dice bitmaps and redraw the control immediately. This example uses red and blue dice as well as the original black and white dice. To make the control show the new color bitmaps immediately after the client sets the dice color, the *put_DiceColor* function should load the new bitmaps according to new color, and redraw the control:

```
STDMETHODIMP CATLDiceObj::put_DiceColor(short newVal)
{
    if(newVal < 3 && newVal >= 0)
        m_nDiceColor = newVal;
    LoadBitmaps();
    FireViewChange();
    return S_OK;
}
```

Of course, this means that *LoadBitmaps* needs to load the bitmaps based on the state of *m_nDiceColor*, so we need to add the following boldface code to our existing *LoadBitmaps* function:

```
BOOL CATLDiceObj::LoadBitmaps() {
    int i;
    BOOL bSuccess = TRUE;
    int nID = IDB_DICE1;

    switch(m_nDiceColor) {
        case 0:
            nID = IDB_DICE1;
            break;

        case 1:
            nID = IDB_BLUEDICE1;
            break;

        case 2:
            nID = IDB_REDDICE1;
            break;

    }

    for(i=0; i<MAX_DIEFACES; i++) {
        DeleteObject(m_dieBitmaps[i]);
        m_dieBitmaps[i] = LoadBitmap(_Module.m_hInst,
                                    MAKEINTRESOURCE(nID+i));
        if(!m_dieBitmaps[i]) {
            ::MessageBox(NULL,
                        "Failed to load bitmaps",
                        NULL, MB_OK);
            bSuccess = FALSE;
        }
    }
    return bSuccess;
}
```

Just as the dice color property reflects the color of the dice, the number of times the dice rolls should be reflected by the state of the TimesToRoll property. The *get_TimesToRoll* function needs to read the *m_nTimesToRoll* member, and the *put_TimesToRoll* function needs to modify *m_nTimesToRoll*. Add the boldface code on the following page.

```
STDMETHODIMP CATLDiceObj::get_TimesToRoll(short * pVal)
{
    *pVal = m_nTimesToRoll;
    return S_OK;
}

STDMETHODIMP CATLDiceObj::put_TimesToRoll(short newVal)
{
    m_nTimesToRoll = newVal;
    return S_OK;
}
```

Finally, instead of hard-coding the number of times the dice rolls, use the *m_nTimesToRoll* variable to determine when to kill the timer.

```
LRESULT CATLDiceObj::OnTimer(UINT msg, WPARAM wParam,
                             LPARAM lParam, BOOL& bHandled) {

    if(m_nTimesRolled > m_nTimesToRoll) {
        m_nTimesRolled = 0;
        KillTimer(1);
        Fire_DiceRolled(m_nFirstDieValue, m_nSecondDieValue);
        if(m_nFirstDieValue == m_nSecondDieValue)
            Fire_Doubles(m_nFirstDieValue);
        if(m_nFirstDieValue == 1 && m_nSecondDieValue == 1)
            Fire_SnakeEyes();
    } else {
        m_nFirstDieValue = (rand() % (MAX_DIEFACES)) + 1;
        m_nSecondDieValue = (rand() % (MAX_DIEFACES)) + 1;
        FireViewChange();
        m_nTimesRolled++;
    }

    bHandled = TRUE;
    return 0;
}
```

Now these two properties are exposed to the outside world. When the client code changes the color of the dice, the control loads a new set of bitmaps and redraws the control with the new dice faces. When the client code changes the number of times to roll, the dice control uses that information to determine the number of times the dice control should respond to the WM_TIMER message. So the next question is, "How are these properties accessed by the client code?" One way is through a control's property pages.

Property Pages

Since ActiveX controls are usually UI gadgets meant to be mixed into much larger applications, they often find their homes within places such as Visual Basic forms and MFC form views and dialogs. When a control is instantiated, the client code can usually reach into the control and manipulate its properties by calling certain functions on the control's incoming interface functions. However, when an ActiveX control is in design mode, accessing the properties through the interface functions isn't always practical. It would be unkind to tool developers to force them to go through the interface functions all the time just to tweak some properties in the control. Why should the tool vendor who is creating the client have to provide UI for managing control properties? That's what property pages are for. Property pages are sets of dialogs implemented by the control for manipulating properties. That way, the tool vendors don't have to keep re-creating dialog boxes for tweaking the properties of an ActiveX control.

How Property Pages Are Used   Property pages are usually used in one of two ways. The first way is through the control's *IOleObject* interface. The client can call *IOleObject*'s *DoVerb* function, passing in the properties verb identifier (named *OLEIVERB_PROPERTIES* and defined as the number −7) to ask the control to show its property pages. The control then displays a dialog, or property frame, that contains all of the control's property pages. For example, Figure 30-6 shows the Property Pages dialog containing the property pages for the Microsoft FlexGrid 6.0 control.

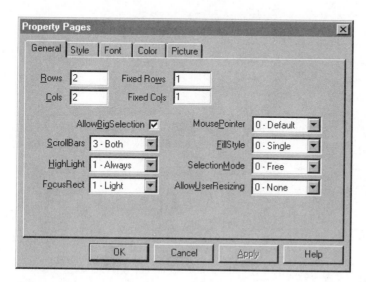

Figure 30-6.
The Microsoft FlexGrid 6.0 control executing the properties verb.

873

Property pages are a testament to the power of COM. As it turns out, each single property page is a separate COM object (named using a GUID and registered like all the other COM classes on your system). When a client asks an ActiveX control to show its property pages via the properties verb, the control passes its own list of property page GUIDs into a system API function named *OleCreatePropertyFrame*. *OleCreatePropertyFrame* enumerates the property page GUIDs, calling *CoCreateInstance* for each property page. The property frame gets a copy of an interface so that the frame can change the properties within the control. *OleCreatePropertyFrame* calls back to the control when the user clicks the OK or Apply button.

The second way clients use property pages is when the client asks the control for a list of property page GUIDs. Then the client calls *CoCreateInstance* on each property page and installs each property page in its own frame. In Figure 30-7 you can see an example of how Visual C++ uses the Microsoft Flex-Grid property pages in its own property dialog frame.

This second method is by far the most common way for a control's property pages to be used. Notice that the property sheet in Figure 30-7 contains a General tab in addition to the control's property pages, and that the General tab shown in Figure 30-6 has been renamed the Control tab. The General property page in Figure 30-7 belongs to Visual C++. The Control, Style, Font, Color, and Picture property pages belong to the control (even though they're being shown within the context of Visual C++).

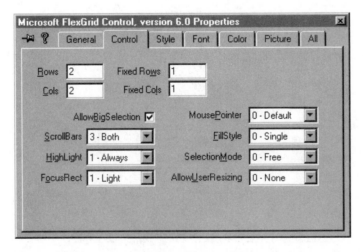

Figure 30-7.
Microsoft Visual C++ inserting the Microsoft FlexGrid 6.0 property pages into its own dialog box for editing resource properties.

For a property page to work correctly, the control that the property page is associated with needs to implement *ISpecifyPropertyPages* and the property page object needs to implement an interface named *IPropertyPage*. With this in mind, let's examine exactly how ATL implements property pages.

Adding a Property Page to Your Control   You can use the Visual Studio ATL Object Wizard to create property pages in your ATL project. To create a property page, perform the following steps:

1. Select New ATL Object from the Visual C++ Insert menu.

2. From the ATL Object Wizard dialog, select Controls from the Category list.

3. Select Property Page from the Objects list.

4. Click Next.

5. Fill in the required information on the ATL Object Wizard Properties dialog, and click OK.

ATL's Object Wizard generates a dialog template and includes it as part of a control's resources. In the dice control example, the two properties you're concerned with are the color of the dice and the number of times to roll the dice. The dialog template created by ATL's Object Wizard is blank, so you'll want to add a couple of controls to represent these properties. In this example, the user will be able to select the dice color from a combo box and enter the number of times the dice should roll in an edit control, as shown in Figure 30-8.

Figure 30-8.
The property page dialog template.

The ATL Object Wizard also creates a C++ class for you that implements the interface necessary for the class to behave as a property page. In addition to generating this C++ class, the ATL Object Wizard makes the class part of the project. The ATL Object Wizard adds the new property page class to the IDL file within the coclass section. In addition, the ATL Object Wizard appends the property page to the object map so that *DllGetClassObject* can find the property page class. Finally the ATL Object Wizard adds a new Registry script (so that the DLL makes the correct Registry entries when the control is registered). Here is the header file created by the ATL Object Wizard for a property page named DiceMainPropPage:

```
#include "resource.h"        // main symbols

class ATL_NO_VTABLE CDiceMainPropPage :
    public CComObjectRootEx<CComSingleThreadModel>,
    public CComCoClass<CDiceMainPropPage, &CLSID_DiceMainPropPage>,
    public IPropertyPageImpl<CDiceMainPropPage>,
    public CDialogImpl<CDiceMainPropPage>
{
public:
    CDiceMainPropPage()
    {
        m_dwTitleID = IDS_TITLEDiceMainPropPage;
        m_dwHelpFileID = IDS_HELPFILEDiceMainPropPage;
        m_dwDocStringID = IDS_DOCSTRINGDiceMainPropPage;
    }

    enum {IDD = IDD_DICEMAINPROPPAGE};

DECLARE_REGISTRY_RESOURCEID(IDR_DICEMAINPROPPAGE)

DECLARE_PROTECT_FINAL_CONSTRUCT()

BEGIN_COM_MAP(CDiceMainPropPage)
    COM_INTERFACE_ENTRY(IPropertyPage)
END_COM_MAP()

BEGIN_MSG_MAP(CDiceMainPropPage)
    CHAIN_MSG_MAP(IPropertyPageImpl<CDiceMainPropPage>)
END_MSG_MAP()

STDMETHOD(Apply)(void)
{
    ATLTRACE(_T("CDiceMainPropPage::Apply\n"));
    for (UINT i = 0; i < m_nObjects; i++)
    {
        // Do something interesting here
        // ICircCtl* pCirc;
        // m_ppUnk[i]->QueryInterface(IID_ICircCtl, (void**)&pCirc);
        // pCirc->put_Caption(CComBSTR("something special"));
```

```
        // pCirc->Release();
    }
    m_bDirty = FALSE;
    return S_OK;
}
};
```

Examining this property page listing reveals that ATL's property page classes are composed of several ATL templates: *CComObjectRootEx* (to implement *IUnknown*), *CComCoClass* (the class object for the property page), *IPropertyPageImpl* (for implementing *IPropertyPage*), and *CDialogImpl* (for implementing the dialog-specific behavior).

As with most other COM classes created by ATL's Object Wizard, most of the code involved in getting a property page to work is boilerplate code. Notice that besides the constructor and some various maps, the only other function is one named *Apply*.

Before getting into the mechanics of implementing a property page, it's helpful to take a moment to understand how the property page architecture works. The code you need to type in to get the property pages working will then make more sense.

When the client decides it's time to show some property pages, a modal dialog frame needs to be constructed. The frame is constructed by either the client or by the control itself. If the property pages are being shown via the *DoVerb* function, the control constructs the frame. If the property pages are being shown within the context of another application—as when Visual C++ shows the control's property pages within the IDE—the client constructs the dialog frame. The key to the dialog frame is that it holds property page sites (small objects that implement *IPropertyPageSite*) for each property page.

The client code (the modal dialog frame, in this case) then enumerates through a list of GUIDs, calling *CoCreateInstance* on each one of them and asking for the *IPropertyPage* interface. If the COM object produced by *CoCreateInstance* is a property page, it implements the *IPropertyPage* interface. The dialog frame uses the *IPropertyPage* interface to talk to the property page. Here's the declaration of the *IPropertyPage* interface:

```
interface IPropertyPage : public IUnknown {
    HRESULT SetPageSite(IPropertyPageSite *pPageSite) = 0;
    HRESULT Activate(HWND hWndParent,
                     LPCRECT pRect,
                     BOOL bModal) = 0;
    HRESULT Deactivate( void) = 0;
    HRESULT GetPageInfo(PROPPAGEINFO *pPageInfo) = 0;
```

(continued)

```
HRESULT SetObjects(ULONG cObjects,
                        IUnknown **ppUnk) = 0;
HRESULT Show(UINT nCmdShow) = 0;
HRESULT Move(LPCRECT pRect) = 0;
HRESULT IsPageDirty( void) = 0;
HRESULT Apply( void) = 0;
HRESULT Help(LPCOLESTR pszHelpDir) = 0;
HRESULT TranslateAccelerator(MSG *pMsg) = 0;
};
```

Once a property page has been created, the property page and the client code need some channels to communicate back and forth with the control. After the property dialog frame successfully calls *QueryInterface* for *IPropertyPage* on the property page objects, the frame calls *IPropertyPage::SetPageSite* on each *IPropertyPage* interface pointer it holds, passing in an *IPropertyPageSite* interface pointer. The property page sites within the property frame provide a way for each property page to call back to the frame. The property page site provides information to the property page and receives notifications from the page when changes occur. Here's the *IPropertyPageSite* interface:

```
interface IPropertyPageSite : public IUnknown {
    public:
        virtual HRESULT OnStatusChange(DWORD dwFlags) = 0;
        virtual HRESULT GetLocaleID(LCID *pLocaleID) = 0;
        virtual HRESULT GetPageContainer(IUnknown *ppUnk) = 0;
        virtual HRESULT TranslateAccelerator(MSG *pMsg) = 0;
};
```

In addition to the frame and control connecting to each other through *IPropertyPage* and *IPropertyPageSite*, each property page needs a way to talk back to the control. This is usually done when the dialog frame calls *IProperty-Page::SetObjects*, passing in the control's *IUnknown*. Figure 30-9 illustrates the property page architecture.

Now that you see how ActiveX Control property pages work in general, understanding how they work within ATL will be a lot easier. You'll see how ATL's property pages work—in cases when the client code exercises the control's properties verb as well as in cases when environments like Visual C++ integrate a control's property pages into the IDE.

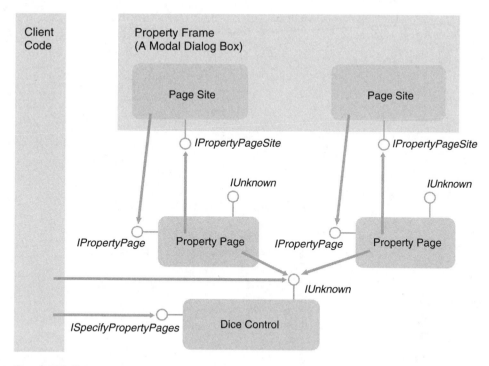

Figure 30-9.
How the property pages, the property frame, and the property page sites communicate.

ATL and the Properties Verb   The first way in which an ActiveX control shows its property pages is when the client invokes the properties verb by calling *IOleObject::DoVerb* using the constant *OLEIVERB_PROPERTIES*. When the client calls *DoVerb* in an ATL-based control, the call ends up in the function *CComControlBase::DoVerbProperties,* which simply calls *OleCreateProperty-Frame,* passing in its own *IUnknown* pointer and the list of property page GUIDs. *OleCreatePropertyFrame* takes the list of GUIDs, calling *CoCreate-Instance* on each one to create the property pages, and arranges them within the dialog frame. *OleCreatePropertyFrame* uses each property page's *IProp-ertyPage* interface to manage the property page, as described on page 874.

ATL Property Maps   Of course, understanding how *OleCreatePropertyFrame* works from within the ATL-based control begs the next question: where does the list of property pages actually come from? ATL uses macros to generate lists of property pages called <u>property maps</u>. Whenever you add a new property page to an ATL-based control, you need to set up the list of property pages through these macros. ATL includes several macros for implementing property maps: *BEGIN_PROPERTY_MAP, PROP_ENTRY, PROP_ENTRY_EX, PROP__PAGE,* and *END_PROPERTY_MAP.* Here are those macros in the raw:

```
struct ATL_PROPMAP_ENTRY
{
    LPCOLESTR szDesc;
    DISPID dispid;
    const CLSID* pclsidPropPage;
    const IID* piidDispatch;
    DWORD dwOffsetData;
    DWORD dwSizeData;
    VARTYPE vt;
};

#define BEGIN_PROPERTY_MAP(theClass) \
    typedef _ATL_PROP_NOTIFY_EVENT_CLASS __ATL_PROP_NOTIFY_EVENT_CLASS; \
        typedef theClass _PropMapClass; \
    static ATL_PROPMAP_ENTRY* GetPropertyMap()\
    {\
        static ATL_PROPMAP_ENTRY pPropMap[] = \
        {

#define PROP_PAGE(clsid) \
    {NULL, NULL, &clsid, &IID_NULL},

#define PROP_ENTRY(szDesc, dispid, clsid) \
    {OLESTR(szDesc), dispid, &clsid, &IID_IDispatch},

#define PROP_ENTRY_EX(szDesc, dispid, clsid, iidDispatch) \
    {OLESTR(szDesc), dispid, &clsid, &iidDispatch},

#define END_PROPERTY_MAP() \
        {NULL, 0, NULL, &IID_NULL} \
    }; \
    return pPropMap; \
}
```

When you decide to add property pages to a COM class using ATL's property page macros, according to the ATL documentation you should put these macros into your class's header file. For example, if you want to add property pages to the dice control, you'd add the following code to the C++ class:

```
class ATL_NO_VTABLE CATLDiceObj :
    ⋮
{
    ⋮
```

```
BEGIN_PROP_MAP(CATLDiceObj)
    PROP_ENTRY("Caption goes here…", 2,
                CLSID_MainPropPage)
    PROP_ENTRY_EX("Caption goes here…", 3,
                CLSID_SecondPropPage,
                DIID_SecondDualInterface)
    PROP_PAGE(CLSID_StockColorPage)
END_PROPERTY_MAP()

};
```

ATL's property map macros set up the list of GUIDs representing property pages. ATL's property maps are composed of an array of *ATL_PROP-MAP_ENTRY* structures. The *BEGIN_PROPERTY_MAP* macro declares a static variable of this structure. The *PROP_PAGE* macro inserts a GUID into the list of property pages. *PROP_ENTRY* inserts a property page GUID into the list as well as associating a specific control property with the property page. The final macro, *PROP_ENTRY_EX*, lets you associate a certain dual interface to a property page. When client code invokes the control's properties verb, the control just rips through this list of GUIDs and hands the list over to the *Ole-CreatePropertyFrame* so that the property can create the property pages.

Property Pages and Development Tools   Executing the properties verb isn't the only way for an ActiveX control to show its property pages. As we mentioned before, folks who write tools such as Visual Basic and Visual C++ might want programmatic access to a control's property pages. For example, when using MFC to work on a dialog box containing an ActiveX control, right-clicking on the control to view the properties gives you a dialog frame produced by Visual C++ (as opposed to the dialog frame produced by *OleCreatePropertyFrame*).

Visual C++ uses the control's *ISpecifyPropertyPages* interface to get the list of GUIDs (the list generated by the property page macros). Here's the *ISpecifyPropertyPages* interface definition:

```
interface ISpecifyPropertyPages : public IUnknown {
    HRESULT GetPages(CAUUID *pPages);
};

typedef struct tagCAUUID
{
    ULONG       cElems;
    GUID FAR*   pElems;
} CAUUID;
```

ATL implements the *ISpecifyPropertyPages::GetPages* function by cycling through the list of GUIDS (produced by the property map macros) and returning them within the *CAUUID* structure. Environments like Visual C++ use each GUID in a call to *CoCreateInstance* to create a new property page. The property page site and the property page exchange interfaces. The property page site holds on to the property page's *IPropertyPage* interface, and the property page holds on to the property site's *IPropertyPageSite* interface. After the dialog frame constructs the property pages, it needs to reflect the current state of the ActiveX control through the dialog controls. For that you need to override the property page's *Show* method.

Showing the Property Page　The property page's *Show* method is called whenever the property page is about to be shown. A good thing for a property page to do at this time is fetch the values from the ActiveX control and populate the property page's controls. Remember that the property page holds on to an array of unknown pointers. (They're held in the *IPropertyPageImpl*'s *m_ppUnk* array.) To access the ActiveX control's properties, you need to call *QueryInterface* on the unknown pointers and ask for the interface that exposes the properties. In this case, the interface is *IATLDiceObj*. Once the property page has the interface, it can use the interface to fetch the properties and plug the values into the dialog box controls. Here's the overridden *Show* method:

```
#include "atldicesrvr.h"

class ATL_NO_VTABLE CDiceMainPropPage :
    public CComObjectRootEx<CComSingleThreadModel>,
    public CComCoClass<CDiceMainPropPage, &CLSID_DiceMainPropPage>,
    public IPropertyPageImpl<CDiceMainPropPage>,
    public CDialogImpl<CDiceMainPropPage>
{
    ⋮
STDMETHOD(Show)( UINT nCmdShow ) {
        HRESULT hr;

        USES_CONVERSION;

        if(nCmdShow == SW_SHOW ||
           nCmdShow == SW_SHOWNORMAL) {
          for (UINT i = 0; i < m_nObjects; i++)
          {
                CComQIPtr< IATLDieceObj,
                        &IID_IATLDieceObj > pATLDiceObj(m_ppUnk[i]);
                short nColor = 0;

                if FAILED(pATLDiceObj->get_DiceColor(&nColor))
                {
```

```
                    CComPtr<IErrorInfo> pError;
                    CComBSTR            strError;
                    GetErrorInfo(0, &pError);
                    pError->GetDescription(&strError);
                    MessageBox(OLE2T(strError),
                        _T("Error"), MB_ICONEXCLAMATION);
                    return E_FAIL;
                }
                HWND hWndComboBox = GetDlgItem(IDC_COLOR);
                ::SendMessage(hWndComboBox,
                            CB_SETCURSEL,
                            nColor, 0);

                short nTimesToRoll = 0;
                if FAILED(
                    pATLDiceObj->get_TimesToRoll(&nTimesToRoll))
                {
                    CComPtr<IErrorInfo> pError;
                    CComBSTR            strError;
                    GetErrorInfo(0, &pError);
                    pError->GetDescription(&strError);
                    MessageBox(OLE2T(strError),
                        _T("Error"), MB_ICONEXCLAMATION);
                    return E_FAIL;
                }
                SetDlgItemInt(IDC_TIMESTOROLL, nTimesToRoll, FALSE);
            }
        }
        m_bDirty = FALSE;
        hr = IPropertyPageImpl<CDiceMainPropPage>::Show(nCmdShow);
        return hr;
    }
};
```

In addition to adding code to prepare to show the dialog box, you need to add code allowing users to set the control's properties. Whenever the user changes a property, the property dialog activates the Apply button, indicating that the user can apply the newly set properties. When the user presses the Apply button, control jumps to the property page's *Apply* function so you need to insert some code in here to make the Apply button work.

Handling the Apply Button   After the user finishes manipulating the properties, he or she clicks either the Apply button or the OK button to save the changes. In response, the client code asks the property page to apply the new properties to the control. Remember that the ActiveX control and the property page are separate COM objects, so they need to communicate via interfaces. Here's how the process works.

When you create a property page using the ATL Object Wizard, ATL overrides the *Apply* function from *IPropertyPage* for you. The property page site uses this function for notifying the property page of changes that need to be made to the control. When the property page's *Apply* function is called, it's time to synch up the state of the property page with the state of the control. Remember, the control's *IUnknown* interface was passed into the property page early in the game via a call to *IPropertyPage::SetObjects*. (The interface pointers are stored in the property page's *m_ppUnk* array.) Most property pages respond to the *Apply* function by setting the state of the ActiveX control properties through the interface provided. In the case of our example ATL-based property page, this means examining the value in the combo box and the edit box and setting the new values inside the control itself, like this:

```
#include "atldicesrvr.h"

class ATL_NO_VTABLE CDiceMainPropPage :
    public CComObjectRootEx<CComSingleThreadModel>,
    public CComCoClass<CDiceMainPropPage, &CLSID_DiceMainPropPage>,
    public IPropertyPageImpl<CDiceMainPropPage>,
    public CDialogImpl<CDiceMainPropPage>
{
    ⋮
    STDMETHOD(Apply)(void)
    {
        USES_CONVERSION;
        ATLTRACE(_T("CDiceMainPropPage::Apply\n"));
        for (UINT i = 0; i < m_nObjects; i++)
        {
            CComQIPtr<IATLDieceObj,
                    &IID_IATLDieceObj> pATLDiceObj(m_ppUnk[i]);
            HWND hWndComboBox = GetDlgItem(IDC_COLOR);
            short nColor  = (short)::SendMessage(hWndComboBox,
                                                CB_GETCURSEL,
                                                0, 0);
            if(nColor >= 0 && nColor <= 2) {
                if FAILED(pATLDiceObj->put_DiceColor(nColor))
                {
                    CComPtr<IErrorInfo> pError;
                    CComBSTR            strError;
                    GetErrorInfo(0, &pError);
                    pError->GetDescription(&strError);
                    MessageBox(OLE2T(strError),
                        _T("Error"),
                        MB_ICONEXCLAMATION);
```

```
                return E_FAIL;
            }
        }
        short nTimesToRoll = (short)GetDlgItemInt
                                    (IDC_TIMESTOROLL);
        if FAILED(pATLDiceObj->put_TimesToRoll(nTimesToRoll))
        {
            CComPtr<IErrorInfo> pError;
            CComBSTR            strError;
            GetErrorInfo(0, &pError);
            pError->GetDescription(&strError);
            MessageBox(OLE2T(strError),
                    _T("Error"),
                    MB_ICONEXCLAMATION);
            return E_FAIL;
        }
    }
    m_bDirty = FALSE;
    return S_OK;
}
```

Property Persistence

Once you have added properties to the control, it's logical that you might want to have those properties persist with their container. For example, imagine Hasbro buys your dice control to include in its new Windows version of Monopoly. The game vendor uses your dice control within one of the Monopoly dialog boxes and configures the control so that the dice are blue and they roll 23 times before stopping. If the dice control had a sound property, the Monopoly authors could configure the dice to emit a beep every time they roll. When someone plays the game and rolls the dice, that person will see a pair of blue dice that roll 23 times before stopping and they will hear the dice make a sound while they roll. Remember that these properties are all properties of the control. If you're using the control in an application, chances are good you'll want these properties to be saved with the application.

Fortunately, adding persistence support to your control is almost free when you use the ATL property macros. You've already seen how to add the property pages to the control DLL using the property map macros. As it turns out, these macros also make the properties persistent.

You can find ATL's code for handling the persistence of a control's properties within the *CComControlBase* class. *CComControlBase* has a member function named *IPersistStreamInit_Save* that handles saving a control's properties to a stream provided by the client. Whenever the container calls *IPersistStreamInit::Save*, ATL ends up calling *IPersistStreamInit_Save* to do the actual work.

IPersistStreamInit_Save works by retrieving the control's property map—the list of properties maintained by the control. (Remember that the *BEGIN-_PROPERTY_MAP* macro adds a function named *GetPropertyMap* to the control.) The first item written out by *IPersistStreamInit_Save* is the control's extents (its size on the screen). *IPersistStreamInit_Save* then cycles through the property map to write the contents of the property map out to the stream. For each property, the control calls *QueryInterface* on itself to get its own *dispatch* interface. As *IPersistStreamInit_Save* goes through the list of properties, the control calls *IDispatch::Invoke* on itself to get the property based on the *DISPID* associated with the property. (The property's *DISPID* is included as part of the property map structure.) The property comes back from *IDispatch::Invoke* as a Variant, and *IPersistStreamInit_Save* writes the property to the stream provided by the client.

Bidirectional Communication (Events)

Now that the dice control has properties and property pages and renders itself to a device context, the last thing to do is to add some events to the control. Events provide a way for the control to call back to the client code and inform the client code of certain events as they occur.

For example, the user can roll the dice. Then when the dice stop rolling, the client application can fish the dice values out of the control. However, another way to implement the control is to set it up so that the control notifies the client application when the dice have rolled using an event. Here you'll see how to add some events to the dice control. We'll start by understanding how ActiveX Control events work.

How Events Work When a control is embedded in a container (such as a Visual Basic form or an MFC-based dialog box), one of the steps the client code takes is to establish a connection to the control's event set. That is, the client implements an interface that has been described by the control and makes that interface available to the control. That way, the control can talk back to the container.

Part of developing a control involves defining an interface that the control can use to call back to the client. For example, if you're developing the control using MFC, ClassWizard will define the interface and produce some functions you can call from within the control to fire events back to the client. If you're developing the control in ATL, you can accomplish the same result by defining the event callback interface in the control's IDL and using ClassView to create a set of callback proxy functions for firing the events to the container. When the callback interface is defined by the control, the container needs to implement that interface and hand it over to the control. The client and the control do this through the *IConnectionPointContainer* and *IConnectionPoint* interfaces.

IConnectionPointContainer is the interface a COM object implements to indicate that it supports connections. *IConnectionPointContainer* represents a collection of connections available to the client. Within the context of ActiveX Controls, one of these connections is usually the control's main event set. Here's the *IConnectionPointContainer* interface:

```
interface IConnectionPointContainer : IUnknown {
    HRESULT FindConnectionPoint(REFIID riid,
                                IConnectionPoint **ppcp) = 0;
    HRESULT EnumConnectionPoints(IEnumConnectionsPoint **ppec) = 0;
};
```

IConnectionPointContainer represents a collection of *IConnectionPoint* interfaces. Here's the *IConnectionPoint* interface:

```
interface IConnectionPoint : IUnknown {
    HRESULT GetConnectionInterface(IID *pid) = 0;
    HRESULT GetConnectionPointContainer(
                        IConnectionPointContainer **ppcpc) = 0;
    HRESULT Advise(IUnknown *pUnk, DWORD *pdwCookie) = 0;
    HRESULT Unadvise(dwCookie) = 0;
    HRESULT EnumConnections(IEnumConnections **ppec) = 0;
}
```

The container creates the control by calling *CoCreateInstance* on the control. As the control and the container are establishing the interface connections between themselves, one of the interfaces the container asks for is *IConnectionPointContainer* (that is, the container calls *QueryInterface* asking for *IID_IConnectionPointContainer*). If the control supports connection points (the control answers "Yes" when queried for *IConnectionPointContainer*), the control uses *IConnectionPointContainer::FindConnectionPoint* to get the *IConnectionPoint* interface representing the main event set. The container knows the GUID representing the main event set by looking at the control's type information as the control is inserted into the container.

If the container can establish a connection point to the control's main event set (that is, *IConnectionPointContainer::FindConnectionPoint* returns an *IConnectionPoint* interface pointer), the container uses *IConnectionPoint::Advise* to subscribe to the callbacks. Of course, to do this the container needs to implement the callback interface defined by the control (which the container can learn about by using the control's type library). Once the connection is established, the control can call back to the container whenever the control fires off an event. Here's what it takes to make events work within an ATL-based ActiveX control.

Adding Events to the Dice Control There are several steps to adding event sets to your control. Some of them are hidden by clever wizardry. First, use IDL to describe the events. Second, add a proxy that encapsulates the connection points and event functions. Finally, fill out the control's connection map so that the client and the object have a way to connect to each other. Let's examine each step in detail.

When using ATL to write an ActiveX control, IDL is the place to start adding events to your control. The event callback interface is described within the IDL so the client knows how to implement the callback interface correctly. The IDL is compiled into a type library that the client will use to figure out how to implement the callback interface. For example, if you wanted to add events indicating the dice were rolled, doubles were rolled, and snake eyes were rolled, you'd describe the callback interface like this in the control's IDL file:

```
library ATLDICESRVRLib
{
    importlib("stdole32.tlb");
    importlib("stdole2.tlb");

    [
        uuid(21C85C43-0BFF-11d1-8CAA-FD10872CC837),
        helpstring("Events created from rolling dice")
    ]
    dispinterface _IATLDiceObjEvents {
        properties:
        methods:
            [id(1)] void DiceRolled([in]short x, [in] short y);
            [id(2)] void Doubles([in] short x);
            [id(3)] void SnakeEyes();
    }

    [
        uuid(6AED4EBD-0991-11D1-8CAA-FD10872CC837),
        helpstring("ATLDiceObj Class")
    ]
    coclass ATLDiceObj
    {
        [default] interface IATLDieceObj;
        [default, source] dispinterface _IATLDiceObjEvents;
    };
```

The control's callback interface is defined as a dispatch interface (note the *dispinterface* keyword) because that's the most generic kind of interface available. When it comes to callback interfaces, most environments understand only

IDispatch. The code on the previous page describes a callback interface to be implemented by the client (if the client decides it wants to receive these callbacks). We added this dice events interface by hand. The Object Wizard will put one in for you. It might have a different name than the one we have listed. (For example, the Wizard is likely to put in an interface named *IATLObjEvents.*)

Implementing the Connection Point   After you've described the callback interface within the IDL and compiled the control, the control's type information will contain the callback interface description so that the client will know how to implement the callback interface. However, you don't yet have a convenient way to fire these events from the control. You could, of course, call back to the client by setting up calls to *IDispatch::Invoke* by hand. However, a better way to do this is to set up a proxy (a set of functions wrapping calls to *IDispatch*) to handle the hard work for you. To generate a set of functions that you can call to fire events in the container, use the Implement Connection Point menu option from ClassView.

In ClassView, click the right mouse button while the cursor is hovering over the CATLDiceObj symbol. This brings up the context menu for the CATLDiceObj item. Choose Implement Connection Point from the menu to bring up the Implement Connection Point dialog box. This dialog box asks you to locate the type information describing the interface you expect to use when calling back to the container (the _*IATLDiceObjEvents* interface, in this case). By default, this dialog box looks at your control's type library. The dialog box reads the type library and shows the interfaces found within it. Choose _*IATLDiceObjEvents* and click OK. Doing so creates a C++ class that wraps the dice events interface. Given the above interface definition, here's the code generated by the Implement Connection Point dialog box:

```
template <class T>
class CProxy_IATLDieceObjEvents :
public IConnectionPointImpl<T,
                          &DIID__IATLDieceObjEvents,
                          CComDynamicUnkArray>
{
    //Warning this class may be recreated by the wizard.
public:
};

{
    //Warning this class may be recreated by the wizard.
public:
    VOID Fire_Doubles(SHORT x)
```

(continued)

```
{
    T* pT = static_cast<T*>(this);
    int nConnectionIndex;
    CComVariant* pvars = new CComVariant[1];
    int nConnections = m_vec.GetSize();

    for (nConnectionIndex = 0;
         nConnectionIndex < nConnections;
         nConnectionIndex++)
    {
        pT->Lock();
        CComPtr<IUnknown> sp = m_vec.GetAt(nConnectionIndex);
        pT->Unlock();
        IDispatch* pDispatch =
            reinterpret_cast<IDispatch*>(sp.p);
        if (pDispatch != NULL)
        {
            pvars[0].vt = VT_I2;
            pvars[0].iVal= x;
            DISPPARAMS disp = { pvars, NULL, 1, 0 };
            pDispatch->Invoke(0x1, IID_NULL,
                              LOCALE_USER_DEFAULT,
                              DISPATCH_METHOD, &disp,
                              NULL, NULL, NULL);
        }
    }
    delete[] pvars;
}
VOID Fire_DiceRolled(SHORT x, SHORT y)
{
    T* pT = static_cast<T*>(this);
    int nConnectionIndex;
    CComVariant* pvars = new CComVariant[2];
    int nConnections = m_vec.GetSize();

    for (nConnectionIndex = 0;
         nConnectionIndex < nConnections;
         nConnectionIndex++)
    {
        pT->Lock();
        CComPtr<IUnknown> sp = m_vec.GetAt(nConnectionIndex);
        pT->Unlock();
        IDispatch* pDispatch =
            reinterpret_cast<IDispatch*>(sp.p);
        if (pDispatch != NULL)
        {
            pvars[1].vt = VT_I2;
            pvars[1].iVal= x;
```

```
                pvars[0].vt = VT_I2;
                pvars[0].iVal= y;
                DISPPARAMS disp = { pvars, NULL, 2, 0 };
                pDispatch->Invoke(0x2, IID_NULL,
                                LOCALE_USER_DEFAULT,
                                DISPATCH_METHOD, &disp,
                                NULL, NULL, NULL);
            }
        }
        delete[] pvars;

    }
    VOID Fire_SnakeEyes()
    {
        T* pT = static_cast<T*>(this);
        int nConnectionIndex;
        int nConnections = m_vec.GetSize();

        for (nConnectionIndex = 0;
             nConnectionIndex < nConnections;
             nConnectionIndex++)
        {
            pT->Lock();
            CComPtr<IUnknown> sp = m_vec.GetAt(nConnectionIndex);
            pT->Unlock();
            IDispatch* pDispatch =
                reinterpret_cast<IDispatch*>(sp.p);
            if (pDispatch != NULL)
            {
                DISPPARAMS disp = { NULL, NULL, 0, 0 };
                pDispatch->Invoke(0x3, IID_NULL,
                                LOCALE_USER_DEFAULT,
                                DISPATCH_METHOD, &disp,
                                NULL, NULL, NULL);
            }
        }

    }
};
```

The C++ class generated by the connection point generator serves a dual purpose. First, it acts as the specific connection point. (Notice that it derives from *IConnectionPointImpl*.) Second, the class serves as a proxy to the interface implemented by the container. For example, if you want to call over to the client and tell the client that doubles were rolled, you'd simply call the proxy's *Fire_Doubles* function. Notice how the proxy wraps the *IDispatch* call so that you don't have to get your hands messy dealing with variants by yourself.

Establishing the Connection and Firing the Events   The final step in setting up the event set is to add the connection point to the dice control and turn
on the *IConnectionPointContainer* interface. The connection point dialog box
added the *CProxy_IATLDiceObjEvents* class to the dice control's inheritance list,
which provides the *IConnectionPoint* implementation inside the control. An ATL
class named *IConnectionPointContainerImpl* provides the implementation
of *IConnectionPointContainer*. These two interfaces should be in the dice
control's inheritance list like this:

```
class CATLDiceObj :
    public CComObjectRootEx<CComSingleThreadModel>,
    public CStockPropImpl<CATLDiceObj, IATLDieceObj,
                          &IID_IATLDieceObj,
                          &LIBID_ATLDICESRVRLib>,
    public CComControl<CATLDiceObj>,
    public IPersistStreamInitImpl<CATLDiceObj>,
    public IOleControlImpl<CATLDiceObj>,
    public IOleObjectImpl<CATLDiceObj>,
    public IOleInPlaceActiveObjectImpl<CATLDiceObj>,
    public IViewObjectExImpl<CATLDiceObj>,
    public IOleInPlaceObjectWindowlessImpl<CATLDiceObj>,
    public IConnectionPointContainerImpl<CATLDiceObj>,
    public IPersistStorageImpl<CATLDiceObj>,
    public ISpecifyPropertyPagesImpl<CATLDiceObj>,
    public IQuickActivateImpl<CATLDiceObj>,
    public IDataObjectImpl<CATLDiceObj>,
    public IProvideClassInfo2Impl<&CLSID_ATLDiceObj,
                          &DIID__IATLDiceObjEvents,
                          &LIBID_ATLDICESRVRLib>,
    public IPropertyNotifySinkCP<CATLDiceObj>,
    public CComCoClass<CATLDiceObj, &CLSID_ATLDiceObj>,
    public CProxy_DDiceEvents< CATLDiceObj >
{
    ⋮
};
```

Having these classes in the inheritance list inserts the machinery in your
control that makes connection points work. Whenever you want to fire an event
to the container, all you need to do is call one of the functions in the proxy. For
example, a good time to fire these events is from within the control's *OnTimer*
method, firing a DiceRolled event whenever the timer stops, firing a SnakeEyes
event whenever both die faces have the value 1, and firing a Doubles event when
both die faces are equal:

```
CATLDiceObj::OnTimer(UINT msg, WPARAM wParam,
                     LPARAM lParam, BOOL& bHandled) {

    if(m_nTimesRolled > m_nTimesToRoll) {
        m_nTimesRolled = 0;
        KillTimer(1);
        Fire_DiceRolled(m_nFirstDieValue, m_nSecondDieValue);
        if(m_nFirstDieValue == m_nSecondDieValue)
            Fire_Doubles(m_nFirstDieValue);
        if(m_nFirstDieValue == 1 &&
           m_nSecondDieValue == 1)
            Fire_SnakeEyes();
    } else {
        m_nFirstDieValue = (rand() % (MAX_DIEFACES)) + 1;
        m_nSecondDieValue = (rand() % (MAX_DIEFACES)) + 1;
        FireViewChange();
        m_nTimesRolled++;
    }
        bHandled = TRUE;
        return 0;
}
```

Finally, notice the connection map contains entries for the control's connection points:

```
BEGIN_CONNECTION_POINT_MAP(CATLDiceObj)
    CONNECTION_POINT_ENTRY(DIID__IATLDiceObjEvents)
    CONNECTION_POINT_ENTRY(IID_IPropertyNotifySink)
END_CONNECTION_POINT_MAP()
```

The control uses this map to hand back connection points as the client requests them.

Using the Control

So how do you use the control once you've written it? The beauty of COM is that as long as the client and the object agree on their shared interfaces, they don't need to know anything else about each other. All the interfaces implemented within the dice control are well understood by a number of programming environments. You've already seen how to use ActiveX Controls within an MFC-based dialog box. The control you just wrote will work fine within an MFC-based dialog box—just use the Add To Project menu option under the Project menu. Select Registered ActiveX Controls and insert the ATLDiceObj component into your project. Visual C++ will read the dice control's type information and insert all the necessary COM glue to make the dialog box and the control talk together. (This includes all the OLE embedding interfaces as well as the connection and event interfaces.) In addition, you could just as easily use this control from within a Visual Basic form. When working on a Visual Basic project, select References from the Project menu and insert the dice control into the Visual Basic project.

Conclusion

ActiveX Controls are one of the most widely used applications of COM in the real world today. To summarize, ActiveX controls are just COM objects that happen to implement a number of standard interfaces that environments like Visual C++ and Visual Basic understand how to use. These interfaces deal with rendering, persistence, and events, allowing you to drop these components into the aforementioned programming environments and use them right away.

In the past, MFC was the only practical way to implement ActiveX Controls. However, these days ATL provides a reasonable way of implementing ActiveX Controls, provided you're willing to follow ATL's rules. For example, if you buy into the ATL architecture for writing controls, you'll have to dip down into Windows and start working with window handles and device context handles in their raw forms. However, the tradeoff is often worthwhile, because ATL provides more flexibility when developing ActiveX controls. For example, dual interfaces are free when using ATL, whereas they're a real pain to implement in MFC.

PART V

DATABASE
MANAGEMENT

Database Management with Microsoft ODBC

Microcomputers became popular, in part, because businesspeople saw them as a low-cost means of tracking inventory, processing orders, printing payroll checks, and so forth. Business applications required fast access to individual records in a large database. One of the first microcomputer database tools was dBASE II, a single-user product with its own programming language and file format. Today Windows programmers have a wide choice of programmable database management systems (DBMS's), including Inprise Paradox, Microsoft Access, Microsoft FoxPro, and Powersoft PowerBuilder. Most of these products can access both local data and remote data on a central computer. The latter case requires the addition of <u>database</u> <u>server</u> software such as ORACLE or Microsoft SQL Server.

> **NOTE:** Microsoft SQL Server is included with the Enterprise Edition of Visual C++.

How do you, as an MFC programmer, fit into the picture? Visual C++ contains all the components you'll need to write C++ database applications for Microsoft Windows. Indeed, the product contains two separate client-side database access systems: Open Database Connectivity (ODBC) and Data Access Objects (DAO). In addition, Visual C++ now contains wrapper templates for interacting with data directly through OLE DB. This chapter covers the ODBC standard, which consists of an extensible set of dynamic link libraries (DLLs) that provide a standard database application programming interface. ODBC is based on a standardized version of Structured Query Language (SQL). With ODBC and SQL, you can write database access code that is independent of any database product.

Visual C++ includes tools and MFC classes for ODBC, and that's the subject of this chapter. You'll learn the basics of ODBC, and you'll see four sample programs: one that uses the ODBC rowset with support from the MFC

CRecordset class (EX31A), one that uses the MFC *CRecordView* class (EX31B), one that uses multiple recordsets (EX31C), and one that uses the *CRecordset* class without binding (EX31D).

The Advantages of Database Management

The serialization process, introduced in Chapters 17 and 18, ties a document object to a disk file. All the document's data must be read into memory when the document is opened, and all the data must be written back to disk when an updated document is closed. Obviously, you can't serialize a document that's bigger than the available virtual memory. Even if the document is small enough to fit in memory, you might not need to read and write all the data every time the program runs.

You could program your own random access disk file, thus inventing your own DBMS, but you probably have enough work to do already. Besides, using a real DBMS gives you many advantages, including the following:

- **Use of standard file formats**—Many people think of dBASE/Xbase DBF files when they think of database formats. This is only one database file format, but it's a popular one. A lot of data is distributed in DBF files, and many programs can read and write in this format. Lately, the Microsoft Access MDB format has become popular, too. With the MDB format, all of a database's tables and indexes can be contained in a single disk file.

- **Indexed file access**—If you need quick access to records by key (a customer name, for example), you need indexed file access. You could always write your own B-tree file access routines, but that's a tedious job that's been done already. All DBMS's contain efficient indexed access routines.

- **Data integrity safeguards**—Many professional DBMS products have procedures for protecting their data. One example is transaction processing. A transaction encompasses a series of related changes. If the entire transaction can't be processed, it is rolled back so that the database reverts to its original state before the transaction.

- **Multiuser access control**—If your application doesn't need multiuser access now, it might in the future. Most DBMS's provide record locking to prevent interference among simultaneous users. Some multiuser DBMS's use the client–server model, which means that most processing is handled on a single database server computer; the workstations handle the user interface. Other multiuser DBMSs handle database processing on the workstations, and they control each workstation's access to shared files.

Structured Query Language

You could not have worked in the software field without at least hearing about Structured Query Language (SQL), a standard database access language with its own grammar. In the SQL world, a database is a collection of tables that consist of rows and columns. Many DBMS products support SQL, and many programmers know SQL. The SQL standard is continually evolving, and SQL grammar varies among products. SQL extensions, such as <u>blob</u> (binary large object) capability, allow storage of pictures, sound, and complex data structures.

The ODBC Standard

The Microsoft Open Database Connectivity (ODBC) standard defines not only the rules of SQL grammar but also the C-language programming interface to any SQL database. It's now possible for a single compiled C or C++ program to access any DBMS that has an ODBC driver. The ODBC Software Development Kit (SDK), included with Visual C++, contains 32-bit drivers for DBF files, Microsoft Access MDB databases, Microsoft Excel XLS files, Microsoft FoxPro files, ASCII text files, and Microsoft SQL Server databases.

Other database companies, including Oracle, Informix, Progress, Ingres, and Centura Software, provide ODBC drivers for their own DBMS's. If you develop an MFC program with the dBASE/Xbase driver, for example, you can run the same program with an Access database driver. No recompilation is necessary—the program simply loads a different DLL.

Not only can C++ programs use ODBC but other DBMS programming environments can also take advantage of this new standard. You could write a C++ program to update a SQL Server database, and then you could use an off-the-shelf ODBC-compatible report writer to format and print the data. ODBC thus separates the user interface from the actual database-management process. You no longer have to buy your interface tools from the same company that supplies the database engine.

Some people have criticized ODBC because it doesn't let programmers take advantage of the special features of some particular DBMS's. Well, that's the whole point! Programmers only need to learn one application programming interface (API), and they can choose their software components based on price, performance, and support. No longer will developers be locked into buying all their tools from their database suppliers.

What's the future of ODBC? That's a difficult question. Microsoft is driving the standard, but it isn't actually "selling" ODBC; it's giving ODBC away for the purpose of promoting other products. Other companies are selling their own proprietary ODBC libraries. Meanwhile, Microsoft has introduced OLE-based DAO, which relies on the Jet database engine from Microsoft Access. (Chapter 32 describes DAO and compares its features with the features of ODBC.) And if that isn't enough, Microsoft is in the process of introducing OLE DB, an alternative to ODBC based on the Component Object Model (COM). Chapter 33 covers Visual C++'s new templates for wrapping OLE DB consumer and provider code.

The ODBC Architecture

ODBC's unique DLL-based architecture makes the system fully modular. A small top-level DLL, ODBC32.DLL, defines the API. ODBC32.DLL loads database-specific DLLs, known as drivers, during program execution. With the help of the Windows Registry (maintained by the ODBC Administrator module in the Windows Control Panel), ODBC32.DLL tracks which database-specific DLLs are available and thus allows a single program to access data in several DBMSs simultaneously. A program could, for example, keep some local tables in DBF format and use other tables controlled by a database server. Figure 31-1 shows the 32-bit ODBC DLL hierarchy.

Note from this figure that many standard database formats can be accessed through the Microsoft Access Jet database engine, a redistributable module packaged with Visual C++. If, for example, you access a DBF file through the Jet engine, you're using the same code that Microsoft Access uses.

ODBC SDK Programming

If you program directly at the ODBC C-language API level, you must know about three important ODBC elements: the environment, the connection, and the statement. All three are accessed through handles.

First you need an environment that establishes the link between your program and the ODBC system. An application usually has only one environment handle.

Next you need one or more connections. The connection references a specific driver and data source combination. You might have several connections to subdirectories that contain DBF files, and you might have connections to several SQL servers on the same network. A specific ODBC connection can be hardwired into a program, or the user can be allowed to choose from a list of available drivers and data sources.

900

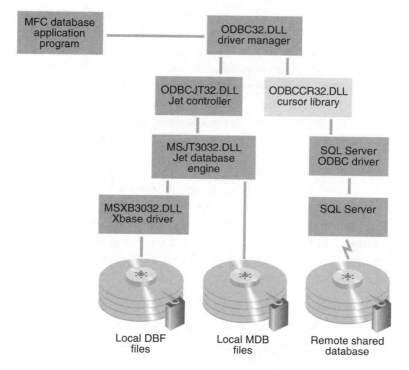

Figure 31-1.
32-bit ODBC architecture.

ODBC32.DLL has a built-in Windows dialog box that lists the connections that are defined in the Registry (under HKEY_LOCAL_MACHINE-\SOFTWARE\ODBC). Once you have a connection, you need a SQL statement to execute. The statement might be a query, such as this:

SELECT FNAME, LNAME, CITY FROM AUTHORS
WHERE STATE = 'UT' ORDER BY LNAME

Or the statement could be an update statement, such as this:

UPDATE AUTHORS SET PHONE = '801 232-5780'
WHERE ID = '357-86-4343'

Because query statements need a program loop to process the returned rows, your program might need several statements active at the same time. Many ODBC drivers allow multiple active statement handles per connection.

Look again at the SQL statement above. Suppose there were 10 authors in Utah. ODBC lets you define the query result as a block of data, called a <u>rowset</u>, which is associated with an SQL statement. Through the ODBC SDK function

SQLExtendedFetch, your program can move forward and backward through the 10 selected records by means of an ODBC <u>cursor</u>. This cursor is a programmable pointer into the rowset.

What if, in a multiuser situation, another program modified (or deleted) a Utah author record while your program was stepping through the rowset? With an ODBC Level 2 driver, the rowset would probably be dynamic and ODBC could update the rowset whenever the database changed. A dynamic rowset is called a <u>dynaset</u>. The Jet engine supports ODBC Level 2, and thus it supports dynasets.

Visual C++ includes the ODBC cursor library module ODBCCR32.DLL, which supports static rowsets (called <u>snapshots</u>) for Level 1 drivers. With a snapshot, a *SELECT* statement causes ODBC to make what amounts to a local copy of the 10 author records and build an in-memory list of pointers to those records. These records are guaranteed not to change once you've scrolled through them; in a multiuser situation, you might need to requery the database periodically to rebuild the snapshot.

The MFC ODBC Classes—
CRecordset and *CDatabase*

With the MFC classes for Windows, you use C++ objects instead of window handles and device context handles; with the MFC ODBC classes, you use objects instead of connection handles and statement handles. The environment handle is stored in a global variable and is not represented by a C++ object. The two principal ODBC classes are *CDatabase* and *CRecordset*. Objects of class *CDatabase* represent ODBC connections to data sources, and objects of class *CRecordset* represent scrollable rowsets. The Visual C++ documentation uses the term "recordset" instead of "rowset" to be consistent with Microsoft Visual Basic and Microsoft Access. You seldom derive classes from *CDatabase*, but you generally derive classes from *CRecordset* to match the columns in your database tables.

For the author query in the previous section, you would derive (with the help of ClassWizard) a *CAuthorSet* class from *CRecordset* that had data members for first name, last name, city, state, and zip code. Your program would construct a *CAuthorSet* object (typically embedded in the document) and call its inherited *Open* member function. Using the values of parameters and data members, *CRecordset::Open* constructs and opens a *CDatabase* object; this function issues an SQL *SELECT* statement and then moves to the first record. Your program would then call other *CRecordset* member functions to position the ODBC cursor and exchange data between the database fields and the *CAuthorSet* data members. When the *CAuthorSet* object is deleted, the recordset is closed and, under certain conditions, the database is closed and deleted. Figure 31-2 shows the relationships between the C++ objects and the ODBC components.

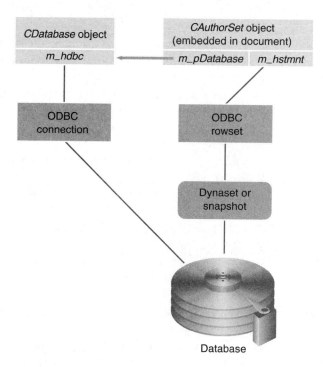

Figure 31-2.
MFC ODBC class database relationships.

It's important to recognize that the *CAuthorSet* object contains data members that represent only one row in a table, the so-called "current record." The *CRecordset* class, together with the underlying ODBC rowset code, manages the database dynaset or snapshot.

NOTE: It's possible to have several active dynasets or snapshots per data source, and you can use multiple data sources within the same program.

The important *CRecordset* member functions discussed in this chapter are summarized in the table on the following page.

Function	Description
Open	Opens the recordset
AddNew	Prepares to add a new record to the table
Update	Completes an *AddNew* or *Edit* operation by saving the new or edited data in the data source
Delete	Deletes the current record from the recordset
Edit	Prepares to implement changes on the current record
IsBOF	Determines whether the recordset has been positioned before the first record
IsEOF	Determines whether the recordset has been positioned after the last record
MoveNext	Sets the current record to the next record or to the next rowset
MoveFirst	Sets the current record to the first record in the recordset
MoveLast	Sets the current record to the last record or to the last rowset
MovePrev	Sets the current record to the previous record or to the previous rowset
GetDefaultConnect	Gets the default connect string for the data source on which the recordset is based
GetDefaultSQL	Gets the default SQL string
DoFieldExchange	Exchanges data between the recordset data fields and the corresponding record on the data source
GetStatus	Gets the index of the current record in the recordset and the final count status
GetRecordCount	Determines the highest-numbered record yet encountered as the user moves through the records
GetODBCFieldCount	Gets the number of fields in the recordset object
GetODBCFieldInfo	Gets information about the fields in the recordset

Counting the Rows in a Recordset

It's difficult to know how many records are contained in an ODBC recordset. ODBC doesn't provide an accurate count of the rows in a recordset until you've read past the end. Until that time, the count returned from the *CRecordset::GetRecordCount* member function is a "high-water mark" that returns only the last row accessed by *CRecordset::MoveNext*. The *CRecordset::GetStatus* function returns a *CRecordsetStatus* object, which has a member *m_bRecordCountFinal* that indicates whether the count is final.

The *CRecordset::MoveLast* function does not register the record count for you, even for dynasets. If you want to know how many records are included in a recordset, loop through the whole table with *MoveNext* calls. (A faster alternative is to use the COUNT function.) If your program adds or deletes a record or if another user adds or deletes a record, the record count is not adjusted.

Processing ODBC Exceptions

Many MFC ODBC calls don't return an error code but instead throw a *CDBException* object, which contains a string describing the error. Suppose you are trying to delete a record from a table in an Access database. Access might be enforcing referential integrity rules, which means that you're not allowed to delete that row because a row in another table depends on it. If you call *CRecordset::Delete*, you'll see an ODBC error message box that came from the MFC base classes.

You certainly appreciate the error message, but now ODBC has "lost its place" in the recordset, and there is no longer a current record. Your program needs to detect the error so that it won't call functions that depend on a current record, such as *CRecordset::MoveNext*. You must handle the exception in this way:

```
try {
    m_pSet->Delete();
}
catch(CDBException* e) {
    AfxMessageBox(e->m_strError);
    e->Delete();
    m_pSet->MoveFirst(); // lost our place!
    UpdateData(FALSE);
    return;
}
m_pSet->MoveNext();
```

The Student Registration Database

The Visual C++ Enroll tutorial uses a ready-made sample Access database (STDREG32.MDB) that tracks students, classes, and instructors. (See Tutorial Samples under Visual C++ Documentation\Samples\MFC Samples\Database Samples in the online documentation.) Figure 31-3 shows the four database tables and the relationships among them. The boldfaced fields are indexed fields, and the 1–? relationships represent referential integrity constraints. If there's at least one section for the course MATH101, for example, Access prevents the user from deleting the MATH101 course record.

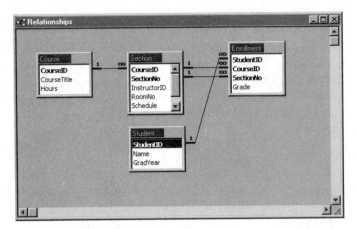

Figure 31-3.
The Student Registration database schema.

The EX31A Recordset Example

You can use AppWizard to generate a complete forms-oriented database application, and that's what the Enroll tutorial is all about. If customers or users wanted a straightforward business database application like that, however, they probably wouldn't call in a Visual C++ programmer; instead, they might use a less technical tool, such as Microsoft Access. Visual C++ and the MFC ODBC classes are more appropriate for a complex application that might have an incidental need for database access. You can also use the classes to make your own general-purpose database query tool.

The EX31A program isolates the database access code from user interface code so that you can see how to add ODBC database capability to any MFC application. You'll be using ClassWizard to generate a *CRecordset* class, but you won't be using the *CRecordView* class that AppWizard generates when you ask for a database view application.

The EX31A application is fairly simple. It displays the rows from the student database table in a scrolling view, as shown in the screen on page 912. The student table is part of the Student Registration (Microsoft Access 97) sample database that's included with Visual C++.

Here are the steps for building the EX31A example:

1. **Copy the Student Registration database to your hard disk.** You can find the file stdreg32.mdb in the \Samples\VC98\Mfc\Database\Stdreg directory on the Visual C++ MSDN CD-ROM. Copy it to the new project directory on your hard disk, and make sure the copy does not have its read-only attribute set.

2. Run the ODBC Data Source Administrator to install the Student Registration data source. Click the ODBC icon in the Windows Control Panel. The Visual C++ Setup program should have already installed the required ODBC drivers on your hard disk. If you are running Windows 95, click the Drivers button to see whether the Microsoft Access driver is available. If you're running Windows 98, click the Drivers tab to see whether the Microsoft Access driver is available. (If the Microsoft Access driver is not available, rerun Visual C++ Setup.) Click the Add button (in Windows 98, the Add button is on the User DSN tab), choose Microsoft Access Driver in the Add Data Source dialog box (in Windows 98, select the Microsoft Access Driver in the Create New Data Source dialog box and click the Finish button), and fill in the ODBC Microsoft Access 97 Setup dialog box as shown here.

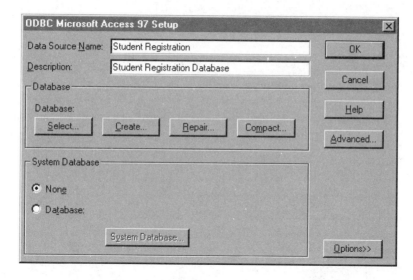

Set the database to point to stdreg32.mdb using the Select button. Finally, click the OK button.

NOTE: If you are using Microsoft Windows NT version 4.0, click on the ODBC icon in the Windows Control Panel and then click on the ODBC Drivers tab to see whether the Microsoft Access Driver is available. On the User DSN tab, click the Add button, choose Microsoft Access Driver in the Create New Data Source dialog box, click the Finish button, and then fill in the dialog box as shown above.

3. **Run AppWizard to produce \vcpp32\ex31a\.** Specify an SDI application (Step 1 dialog box) with *CScrollView* as the view's class type (Step 6 dialog box). Select the Header Files Only option from the AppWizard Step 2 dialog box, as shown here.

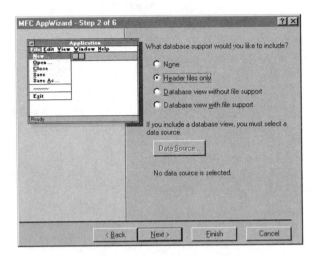

4. **Use ClassWizard to create the *CEx31aSet* recordset class.** Choose New from the Add Class menu, and then fill in the New Class dialog box as shown here.

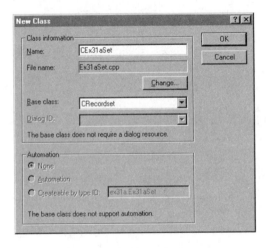

5. Select the Student Registration database's Student table for the CEx31aSet class. When you click the OK button in the New Class dialog box, ClassWizard displays the Database Options dialog box. Select the Student Registration data source, and select the Dynaset option as shown here.

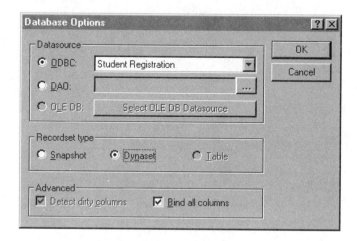

After you select the data source, ClassWizard prompts you to select a table. Select Student, as shown here.

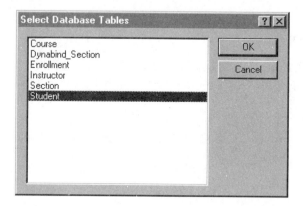

6. Examine the data members that ClassWizard generates. Click on the Member Variables tab for the newly generated *CEx31aSet* class. ClassWizard should have generated data members based on student column names, as shown on the next page.

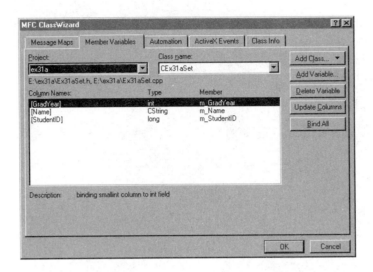

7. **Declare an embedded recordset object in ex31aDoc.h.** Add the following public data member in the *CEx31aDoc* class declaration:

```
CEx31aSet m_ex31aSet;
```

8. **Edit the ex31aDoc.cpp file.** Add the line

```
#include "ex31aSet.h"
```

just before the line

```
#include "ex31aDoc.h"
```

9. **Declare a recordset pointer in ex31aView.h.** Add the following private data member in the *CEx31aView* class declaration:

```
CEx31aSet* m_pSet;
```

10. **Edit the *OnDraw* and *OnInitialUpdate* functions in ex31aView.cpp.** Add the following boldface code:

```
void CEx31aView::OnDraw(CDC* pDC)
{
    TEXTMETRIC tm;
    pDC->GetTextMetrics(&tm);
    int nLineHeight=tm.tmHeight+tm.tmExternalLeading;
    CPoint pText(0,0);

    int y = 0;
    CString str;
```

```
        if (m_pSet->IsBOF()) { // detects empty recordset
            return;
        }
        m_pSet->MoveFirst();   // fails if recordset is empty
        while (!m_pSet->IsEOF()) {
            str.Format("%ld", m_pSet->m_StudentID);
            pDC->TextOut(pText.x, pText.y, str);
            pDC->TextOut(pText.x+1000, pText.y, m_pSet->m_Name);
            str.Format("%d", m_pSet->m_GradYear);
            pDC->TextOut(pText.x+4000, pText.y, str);
            m_pSet->MoveNext();
            pText.y -= nLineHeight;
        }
    }
}
void CEx31aView::OnInitialUpdate()
{
    CScrollView::OnInitialUpdate();
    CSize sizeTotal(8000, 10500);

    SetScrollSizes(MM_HIENGLISH, sizeTotal);

    m_pSet = &GetDocument()->m_ex31aSet;
    // Remember that documents/views are reused in SDI applications!
    if (m_pSet->IsOpen()) {
        m_pSet->Close();
    }
    m_pSet->Open();
}
```

Also in ex31aView.cpp, add the line

```
#include "ex31aSet.h"
```

just before the line

```
#include "ex31aDoc.h"
```

11. **Edit the ex31a.cpp file.** Add the line

```
#include "ex31aSet.h"
```

just before the line

```
#include "ex31aDoc.h"
```

12. **Build and test the EX31A application.** Does the resulting screen look like the one shown on the next page?

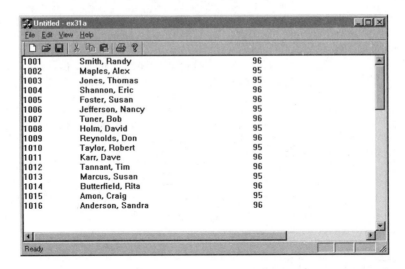

Adding ODBC Capability to an MFC Application

If you need to add ODBC capability to an existing MFC application, make the following changes to the project:

1. Add the following line at the end of StdAfx.h:

   ```
   #include <afxdb.h>
   ```

2. Edit the RC file in text mode. After the line

   ```
   "#include ""afxprint.rc""" // printing/
   print preview resources\r\n"
   ```

   add the line

   ```
   "#include ""afxdb.rc"""    // database resources\r\n"
   ```

   And after the line

   ```
   #include "afxprint.rc"     // printing/
   print preview resources
   ```

   add the line

   ```
   #include "afxdb.rc"        // database resources
   ```

The EX31A Program Elements

Let's take a look at the major elements in the EX31A program.

Connecting the Recordset Class to the Application

When ClassWizard generates the *CEx31aSet* class, it adds the CPP and H files to the project—and that's all it does. It's up to you to link the recordset to your view and to your document. By embedding a *CEx31aSet* object inside the *CEx31aDoc* class, you ensure that the recordset object will be constructed when the application starts.

The view could always get the recordset from the document, but it's more efficient if the view has its own recordset pointer. Notice how the view's *OnInitialUpdate* function sets the *m_pSet* data member.

> **NOTE:** If you run AppWizard with either of the Database View options, AppWizard generates a class derived from *CRecordset*, a class derived from *CRecordView* (for ODBC), and all the necessary linkage as just described. We're not using AppWizard in this mode because we don't want a form-based application.

The *CEx31aView* Class's *OnInitialUpdate* Member Function

The job of the *CEx31aView::OnInitialUpdate* function is to open the recordset that's associated with the view. The recordset constructor was called with a *NULL* database pointer parameter, so the *CRecordset::Open* function knows it must construct a *CDatabase* object and link that database one to one with the recordset. But how does *Open* know what data source and table to use? It calls two *CRecordset* virtual functions, *GetDefaultConnect* and *GetDefaultSQL*. Class-Wizard generates implementations of these functions in your derived recordset class, as shown here:

```
CString CEx31aSet::GetDefaultConnect()
{
    return _T("ODBC;DSN=Student Registration");
}


CString CEx31aSet::GetDefaultSQL()
{
    return _T("[Student]");
}
```

> **NOTE:** ClassWizard and AppWizard place brackets around all column and table [names]. These brackets are necessary only if the names contain embedded blanks.

GetDefaultSQL is a pure virtual function, so the derived class must implement it. *GetDefaultConnect*, on the other hand, has a base class implementation that opens an ODBC dialog box, which in turn prompts the user for the data source name.

Because documents and views are reused in SDI applications, the *OnInitialUpdate* function must close any open recordset before it opens a new recordset. The *CRecordSet::IsOpen* member function is used to test this.

The *CEx31aView* Class's *OnDraw* Member Function

As in any document–view application, the *CEx31aView::OnDraw* function is called every time the view is invalidated and once for every printed page. Here *OnDraw* inefficiently slogs through every row in the recordset and paints its column values with the *CDC::TextOut* function. The principal *CRecordset* member functions it calls are *MoveFirst* and *MoveNext*. *MoveFirst* will fail if the recordset is empty, so the initial call to *CRecordset::IsBOF* is necessary to detect the beginning-of-file condition. The *CRecordset::IsEOF* call detects the end-of-file condition for the recordset and terminates the row loop.

Remember that ClassWizard generated *CEx31aSet* class data members for the recordset's columns. This means that the recordset class and now the view class are both hard-coded for the student record. The *CRecordset* member functions call a pure virtual function, *DoFieldExchange*, that ClassWizard generates based on the data members *m_StudentID*, *m_Name*, and *m_GradYear*. Here is the code for this example's derived recordset class:

```
void CEx31aSet::DoFieldExchange(CFieldExchange* pFX)
{
    //{{AFX_FIELD_MAP(CEx31aSet)
    pFX->SetFieldType(CFieldExchange::outputColumn);
    RFX_Long(pFX, _T("[StudentID]"), m_StudentID);
    RFX_Text(pFX, _T("[Name]"), m_Name);
    RFX_Int(pFX, _T("[GradYear]"), m_GradYear);
    //}}AFX_FIELD_MAP
}
```

Each SQL data type has a record field exchange (RFX) function. RFX functions are quite complex and are called many times during database processing. You might think at first that the RFX functions are like the *CDialog* DDX functions and thus actually transfer data between the database and the data members. This is not the case. The primary purpose of the RFX functions is to <u>bind</u> the database columns to the data members so that the underlying ODBC functions, such as *SQLExtendedFetch*, can transfer the column data. To this end, the *DoFieldExchange* function is called from *CRecordSet::Open*. *DoFieldExchange* is also called by the *Move* functions for the purpose of reallocating strings and clearing status bits.

Because the *DoFieldExchange* function is so tightly integrated with MFC database processing, you are advised not to call this function directly in your programs.

Filter and Sort Strings

SQL query statements can have an ORDER BY clause and a WHERE clause. The *CRecordset* class has a public data member *m_strSort* that holds the text of the ORDER BY clause (excluding the words "ORDER BY"). Another public data member, *m_strFilter*, holds the text of the WHERE clause (excluding the word "WHERE"). You can set the values of these strings prior to opening the recordset.

Joining Two Database Tables

Most database programmers know that a <u>join</u> is one big logical table composed of fields from two or more related tables. In the Student Registration database, you could join the Student table with the Enrollment table to get a list of students and the classes they are enrolled in.

Joins are easy to do with Visual C++ because ClassWizard lets you add tables to an existing recordset. A few additional programming tasks are needed, though. Here are the steps for joining the Enrollment table to the Student table in EX31A.

1. Use ClassWizard to access the *CEx31aSet* class on the Member Variables tab. Click the Update Columns button, and then select the Enrollment table from the Student Registration database. If you get a warning message indicating that the data source does not contain all the columns that the recordset classes need, click the Yes button to continue. Then click the Bind All button to add the data members for the Enrollment fields.

2. Edit the *CEx31aSet::GetDefaultSQL* function, as shown here, to access the Student and Enrollment tables:

```
CString CEx31aSet::GetDefaultSQL()
{
    return _T("[Student],[Enrollment]");
}
```

3. Two StudentID fields are now in the joined table. In the *CEx31aSet-::DoFieldExchange* function, edit the StudentID line to qualify the field with a table name:

```
RFX_Long(pFX, _T("[Student].[StudentID]"), m_StudentID);
```

4. In the *CEx31aView::OnInitialUpdate* function, set the recordset's *m_strFilter* string as follows:

```
m_pSet->m_strFilter = "[Student].[StudentID] =
    [Enrollment].[StudentID]";
```

5. In the *CEx31aView::OnDraw* function, add code to display the new Enrollment fields. Here is a sample:

```
pDC->TextOut(pText.x+5000, pText.y, m_pSet->m_CourseID);
```

The MFC *CRecordView* Class

The *CRecordView* class is a form view class that's attached to a recordset. Figure 31-4 illustrates an MFC record view application. The toolbar buttons enable the user to step forward and backward through a database table.

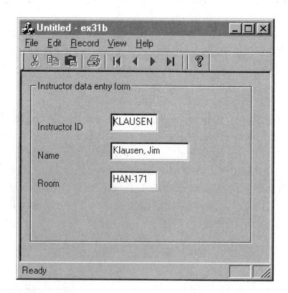

Figure 31-4.
An MFC application based on the CRecordView *class.*

Like the *CFormView* class, the *CRecordView* class depends on a dialog template resource. The *CFormView* class has data members that correspond to the controls in the dialog box, but the *CRecordView* class accesses data members in a <u>foreign</u> <u>object</u>, namely the attached *CRecordset* object. When the user enters data in the controls, the record view's DDX (Dialog Data Exchange) code moves the data into the recordset's data members, which are bound to database columns by the recordset's RFX (Record Field Exchange) code.

When you specify a database view application, AppWizard generates a class derived from *CRecordView* together with an empty dialog template. AppWizard also generates a class derived from *CRecordset*, so it must ask you for a database table name. At runtime, the record view object and the recordset object are connected. Your job is to add controls to the dialog template and match the controls to recordset data members—no C++ programming is required to create a working form-based database application.

AppWizard generates a read-only, view-based database application. If you want to modify, add, and delete records, you must do some coding. The default behavior of the resulting application matches the behavior of Visual Basic and Access, which is a little weird. A record is added or modified only when the user moves out of it. If that's what you want, you can pattern your applications after the ENROLL sample program in the \\Samples\VC98\Mfc\Tutorial-\Enroll directory on the Visual C++ MSDN CD-ROM.

The EX31B Record View Example

The EX31B example is an "add-change-delete" application that's different from the Access model. The user must explicitly add, update, and delete records. Even if you prefer the Access-style behavior, you can learn a lot about the *CRecordView* class by going through the steps in the EX31B example.

Here are the steps for building the EX31B example:

1. **Run AppWizard to produce \vcpp32\ex31b.** As you move through the AppWizard steps, select Single Document Interface (Step 1 dialog box) and Database View Without File Support (Step 2). In the Step 2 dialog box, also click the Data Source button and choose the ODBC datasource named Student Registration. Choose Dynaset as the Recordset Type, then select the Instructor table. Finally, deselect Printing And Print Preview (Step 4). The options and the default class names are shown on the next page.

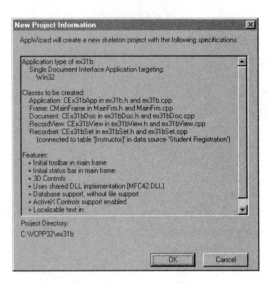

2. **Add edit controls to the *IDD_EX31B_FORM* template.** Use the IDs *IDC_ID*, *IDC_NAME*, and *IDC_ROOM*, and position the controls as shown here.

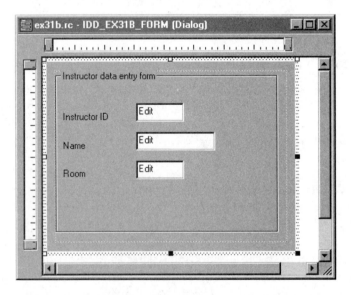

3. **Use ClassWizard to link the edit controls to the recordset data members.** To add a data member, click on the Member Variables tab and choose the ID corresponding to the edit box for each variable. Click

the Add Variable button, and click the arrow in the Member Variable Name combo box to display a list of variables. Select only the appropriate variable, as shown here.

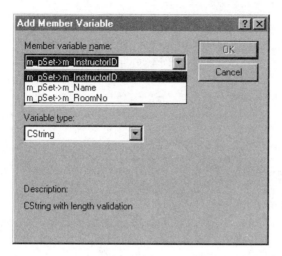

When you're finished adding variable names for each edit box, you'll see a screen like the one shown here.

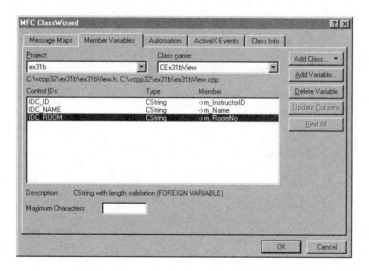

4. **Build and test the EX31B application.** You should have a working read-only database application that looks like Figure 31-4 on page 916. Use the toolbar buttons to sequence through the instructor records.

5. **Back up your database.** Now you're going to include the logic to add, change, and delete records. It's a good idea to make a copy of the STD-REG32.MDB file first. That way you have something to refer back to after you delete all the records.

6. **Add menu commands.** Add the following items to the Record pop-up menu in the *IDR_MAINFRAME* menu. Also, use ClassWizard to map the commands to the specified *CEx31bView* class members.

Menu Command	Command ID	Command Handler	Update Command UI Handler
Add Record	*ID_RECORD_ADD*	*OnRecordAdd*	
Clear Fields	*ID_RECORD_CLEAR-FIELDS*	*OnRecordClearfields*	
Delete Record	*ID_RECORD_DELETE*	*OnRecordDelete*	*OnUpdate-RecordDelete*
Update Record	*ID_RECORD_UPDATE*	*OnRecordUpdate*	*OnUpdate-RecordUpdate*

7. **Add and override the *OnMove* function in the *CEx31bView* class.** The *CRecordView::OnMove* function does the work of updating the database when the user moves out of a record. Because we don't want this behavior, we must override the function as follows:

```
BOOL CEx31bView::OnMove(UINT nIDMoveCommand)
{
    switch (nIDMoveCommand)
    {
    case ID_RECORD_PREV:
        m_pSet->MovePrev();
        if (!m_pSet->IsBOF())
            break;

    case ID_RECORD_FIRST:
        m_pSet->MoveFirst();
        break;

    case ID_RECORD_NEXT:
        m_pSet->MoveNext();
        if (!m_pSet->IsEOF())
            break;
```

```
            if (!m_pSet->CanScroll()) {
                // Clear screen since we're sitting on EOF
                m_pSet->SetFieldNull(NULL);
                break;
            }

        case ID_RECORD_LAST:
            m_pSet->MoveLast();
            break;

        default:
            // unexpected case value
            ASSERT(FALSE);
    }

    // Show results of Move operation
    UpdateData(FALSE);
    return TRUE;
}
```

Also, add the declaration for this overridden function to the ex31bView.h header file.

8. **Edit the menu command handlers.** The following functions call various *CRecordset* member functions to edit the database. To add a record, you must call *CRecordset::AddNew*, followed by *Update*. To modify a record, you must call *CRecordset::Edit*, followed by *Update*. When you add a new record to the database, you should call *CRecordset::MoveLast* because the new record is always added to the end of the dynaset.

> NOTE: If you have a sorted recordset (or if your ODBC driver doesn't put added records in the recordset), you should call *CRecordset::Requery* to completely regenerate the recordset. In that case, there's no convenient way to position the cursor on the newly added record, and that's a basic problem with SQL.

Add the following boldface code:

```
void CEx31bView::OnRecordAdd()
{
    m_pSet->AddNew();
    UpdateData(TRUE);
    if (m_pSet->CanUpdate()) {
        m_pSet->Update();
    }
    if (!m_pSet->IsEOF()) {
        m_pSet->MoveLast();
    }
```

(continued)

921

```
    m_pSet->Requery(); // for sorted sets
    UpdateData(FALSE);
}

void CEx31bView::OnRecordClearfields()
{
    m_pSet->SetFieldNull(NULL);
    UpdateData(FALSE);
}

void CEx31bView::OnRecordDelete()
{
    CRecordsetStatus status;
    try {
        m_pSet->Delete();
    }
    catch(CDBException* e) {
        AfxMessageBox(e->m_strError);
        e->Delete();
        m_pSet->MoveFirst(); // lost our place!
        UpdateData(FALSE);
        return;
    }
    m_pSet->GetStatus(status);
    if (status.m_lCurrentRecord == 0) {
        // We deleted last of 2 records
        m_pSet->MoveFirst();
    }
    else {
        m_pSet->MoveNext();
    }
    UpdateData(FALSE);
}

void CEx31bView::OnUpdateRecordDelete(CCmdUI* pCmdUI)
{
    pCmdUI->Enable(!m_pSet->IsEOF());
}

void CEx31bView::OnRecordUpdate()
{
    m_pSet->Edit();
    UpdateData(TRUE);
    if (m_pSet->CanUpdate()) {
        m_pSet->Update();
    }
// should requery if key field changed
}
```

```
void CEx31bView::OnUpdateRecordUpdate(CCmdUI* pCmdUI)
{
    pCmdUI->Enable(!m_pSet->IsEOF());
}
```

9. **Build and test the EX31B application again.** Now you can add, change, and delete records. Observe what happens if you try to add a record with a duplicate key. You get an error message that comes from an exception handler inside the framework. You can add try/catch logic in *OnRecordAdd* to customize the error processing.

Multiple Recordsets

Both the EX31A and EX31B examples relied on a single recordset. In many cases, you'll need simultaneous access to multiple recordsets. Suppose you're writing a program that lets the user add Section records, but you want the user to select a valid CourseID and InstructorID. You'll need auxiliary Course and Instructor recordsets in addition to the primary Section recordset.

In the previous examples, the view object contained an embedded recordset that was created with the *CRecordset* default constructor, which caused the creation of a *CDatabase* object. The view's *OnInitialUpdate* function called *CRecordset::Open*, which called the virtual *CRecordset::GetDefaultConnect* function, opened the database, and then called the virtual *CRecordset::GetDefault-SQL* function. The problem with this scenario is that there can be only one recordset per database because the database is <u>embedded</u> in the recordset.

To get multiple recordsets, you have to do things differently—you must create the *CDatabase* object first. Then you can construct as many recordsets as you want, passing a *CDatabase* pointer as a parameter to the *CRecordset* constructor. You start by embedding a *CDatabase* object in the document in place of the *CRecordset* object. You also include a pointer to the primary recordset. Here are the document data members:

```
CEx31bSet* m_pEx31bSet;
CDatabase m_database;
```

In your overridden *CDocument::OnNewDocument* function, you construct the primary recordset on the heap, passing the address of the *CDatabase* object to the recordset constructor. Here's the code you insert:

```
if (m_pEx31bSet == NULL) {
    m_pEx31bSet = new CEx31bSet(&m_database);
    CString strConnect = m_pEx31bSet->GetDefaultConnect();
    m_database.Open(NULL, FALSE, FALSE, strConnect, FALSE);
}
```

The *CRecordView::OnInitialUpdate* function still opens the recordset, but this time *CRecordset::Open* does not open the database. (It's already open.) Now the code for setting the view's *m_pSet* data member is a little different:

```
m_pSet = GetDocument()->m_pEx31bSet;
```

Figure 31-5 shows the new relationship between the document, the view, and the primary recordset. Also shown are possible auxiliary recordsets.

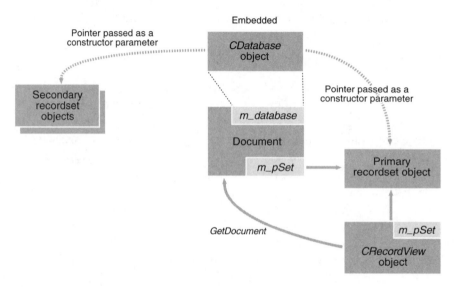

Figure 31-5.
Object relationships for multiple recordsets.

The EX31C Multiple Recordset Example

The EX31C program is similar to EX31B except that the new database–recordset relationships are implemented and an auxiliary recordset allows listing of the sections an instructor teaches. The EX31C window looks like the screen on the facing page.

Build the EX31C project, and test the application. Sequence through the instructor records, and watch the Sections Taught list change.

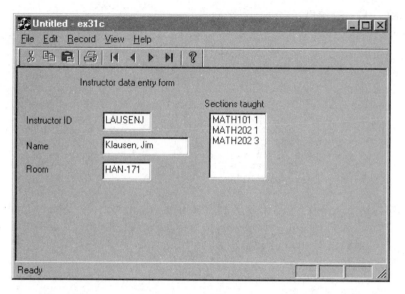

As you can see, there's a new list-box control in the form dialog box. Also, there's one short helper function in the view class, *LoadListbox*, which loads the list box with the rows in the Section recordset, as shown here:

```
void CEx31cView::LoadListbox()
{
    CEx31cDoc* pDoc = GetDocument();
    CListBox* pLB = (CListBox*) GetDlgItem(IDC_SECTIONS);
    CSectionSet sect(&pDoc->m_database);  // db passed via constructor

    sect.m_strFilter.Format("InstructorID = '%s'",
        (LPCSTR) m_pSet->m_InstructorID);

    sect.Open();
    pLB->ResetContent();
    while (!sect.IsEOF()) {
        pLB->AddString(sect.m_CourseID + " " + sect.m_SectionNo);
        sect.MoveNext();
    }
    // sect closed by CRecordset destructor
}
```

Notice that this function sets up a filter string based on the value of the *InstructorID* field in the primary recordset. *LoadListbox* is called from these member functions: *OnInitDialog*, *OnMove*, *OnUpdate*, *OnRecordAdd*, and *OnRecordDelete*.

Parameterized Queries

The EX31C example sets up and executes a new query each time it accesses the auxiliary recordset. It's more efficient, however, if you set up a single parameterized query, which enables ODBC to bind to a parameter in your program. You can simply change the value of that parameter and re-execute the query.

Here are the steps for querying the section set for all the sections a selected instructor teaches.

1. Add a parameter data member to the section recordset class:

   ```
   CString m_InstructorIDParam;
   ```

2. Add the following line to the section recordset constructor, which sets the value of the inherited *m_nParams* data member to the total number of query parameters, in this case 1:

   ```
   m_nParams = 1;
   ```

3. Add the following code to the section recordset *DoFieldExchange* function:

   ```
   pFX->SetFieldType(CFieldExchange::param);
   RFX_Text(pFX, "Param", m_InstructorIDParam); // Any name will do
   ```

4. Add the following code to the view class prior to calling *Open* for the section recordset:

   ```
   sect.m_strFilter = "InstructorID = ?";
   sect.m_InstructorIDParam = m_pSet->m_InstructorID;
   ```

ODBC Multithreading

ODBC itself supports multithreaded programming, but not all ODBC drivers do. In particular, the Access driver you've used for the preceding examples does not support multithreading, but the Microsoft SQL Server driver does. Even if your ODBC driver does not support multithreading, you can put all your database access code in a worker thread if you want to. (Multithreaded programming and worker threads are described in Chapter 12.)

Bulk Row Fetches

If you're using Microsoft SQL Server or another client–server DBMS, you can speed up your database access by using the bulk row–fetch feature of ODBC that is now supported by the *CRecordset* class. As the name implies, your program fetches multiple records from the data source instead of only one record at a time. The data source is bound to elements in an array that is attached to an object of a class derived from *CRecordset*. Currently, no MFC support exists for adding, changing, or deleting records from a bulk-fetch–enabled recordset. (See the InfoView article "Recordset: Fetching Records in Bulk (ODBC)" for details.)

Using Recordsets Without Binding

All three of the examples in this chapter used recordset classes derived from *CRecordset*. The data members of those classes were bound to database columns at recordset creation time using the ODBC binding mechanism. When the programs called *CRecordset::Move*, the ODBC driver copied data directly from the data source into the data members.

ODBC has always supported unbound data access through the functions *SQLGetData* and *SQLPutData*. Now the *CRecordset* class supports read-only unbound data access through its *GetFieldValue* member function. One overloaded version of this function retrieves the value of a field specified by name and then stores it in an object of class *CDBVariant*. This class is similar to the *COleVariant* class described in Chapter 25, but it does not use any OLE code and it doesn't have as many overloaded operators and member functions. The *COleVariant* class has a data member, *m_dwType*, followed by a union. If the type code is DBVT_LONG, for example, you access an integer in the union member *m_lVal*.

You can use *CRecordset::GetFieldValue* for circumstances in which you don't know the database schema at design time. Your "dynamic database" program constructs an object of class *CRecordset*, and you access the column values with code like this:

```
void CEx31dView::DrawDataRow(CDC* pDC, int y)
{
    int x = 0;
    CString strTime, str;
    CEx31dDoc* pDoc = GetDocument();
    for (int i = 0; i < pDoc->m_nFields; i++) {
        CDBVariant var; // must declare this inside the loop
        m_pSet->GetFieldValue(i, var);
        switch (var.m_dwType) {
        case DBVT_STRING:
            str = *var.m_pstring; // narrow characters
            break;
        case DBVT_SHORT:
            str.Format("%d", (int) var.m_iVal);
```

(continued)

```
                break;
            case DBVT_LONG:
                str.Format("%d", var.m_lVal);
                break;
            case DBVT_SINGLE:
                str.Format("%10.2f", (double) var.m_fltVal);
                break;
            case DBVT_DOUBLE:
                str.Format("%10.2f", var.m_dblVal);
                break;
            case DBVT_DATE:
                str.Format("%d/%d/%d", var.m_pdate->month, var.m_pdate->day,
                    var.m_pdate->year);
                break;
            case DBVT_BOOL:
                str = (var.m_boolVal == 0) ? "FALSE" : "TRUE";
                break;
            case DBVT_NULL:
                str = "----";
                break;
            default:
                str.Format("Unk type %d\n", var.m_dwType);
                TRACE("Unknown type %d\n", var.m_dwType);
            }
            pDC->TextOut(x, y, str);
            x += pDoc->m_arrayFieldSize[i] * m_nCharWidth;
    }
}
```

The code above is excerpted from a sample program EX31D, which is on the CD-ROM included with this book. That program uses the *CRowView* code from the DAO example, EX32A, described in the next chapter. The programs EX31D and EX32A are similar in architecture and function. EX31D uses ODBC, and EX32A uses DAO.

Although MFC gives you the *CRecordset* functions *GetODBCFieldCount* and *GetODBCFieldInfo* to get field lengths and types, you must call the ODBC function *SQLTables* to get a "table of tables." The *CTables* class in the EX31D project encapsulates this table.

Database Management with Microsoft Data Access Objects

In Chapter 31, you saw database management programming with the Microsoft Foundation Class (MFC) Library and Microsoft Open Database Connectivity (ODBC). In this chapter, you'll see a completely different database programming approach—the MFC Data Access Objects (DAO) classes and the underlying DAO software. Actually, the approach is not so different. Instead of the ODBC classes *CDatabase* and *CRecordset*, you'll be using *CDaoDatabase* and *CDaoRecordset*. The ODBC and DAO classes are so similar (many member function names are the same) that you can convert ODBC applications, such as the examples in Chapter 31, to DAO applications simply by changing class names and little else. Thus, you can look at DAO as a sort of replacement for ODBC. But as you'll see, DAO goes far beyond ODBC.

This chapter merely scratches the surface of DAO, highlighting its features and outlining the differences between DAO and ODBC. Along the way, it explains the relationships between DAO, COM, the Microsoft Jet database engine, Visual Basic for Applications (VBA), and the MFC library. Finally, it presents a dynamic database example.

DAO, COM, and the Microsoft Jet Database Engine

One feature of DAO is a set of COM interfaces, which, like all COM interfaces, are nothing more than specifications—sets of pure virtual function declarations. These interfaces have names such as *DAOWorkspace*, *DAODatabase*, and *DAORecordset*. (Notice that these interface names don't begin with the letter *I* as do most other interface names.)

The other feature of DAO is the implementation of those interfaces. Microsoft supplies the COM module DAO350.DLL, which connects to the same Jet database engine DLL that serves the Microsoft Access database product. As a Visual C++ developer, you have royalty-free redistribution rights to these DLLs. At the moment, the only DAO implementation available with Jet is DAO350.DLL, but nothing prevents other database software companies from providing their own DAO implementations.

DAO and VBA

In Chapter 25, you learned about Automation. A VBA Automation controller (such as Microsoft Excel or Microsoft Visual Basic) can load any Automation component and then use it to create objects. Once the objects are created, the component can get and set properties and can call methods. The components you created in Chapter 25 all communicated through the COM *IDispatch* interface. But VBA can use interfaces other than *IDispatch* to communicate with a component.

If you look in the Windows Registry under HKEY_CLASSES_ROOT-\TypeLib, you'll find the class ID {00025E01-0000-0000-C000-000000000046} and the pathname for DAO350.DLL, which contains the DAO type library. If you select this item as a VBA reference (by pressing Alt-F11 in Excel and then choosing Object Browser from the Visual Basic View menu, for example), your VBA programs can use the DAO objects and you can browse the DAO library, as shown here.

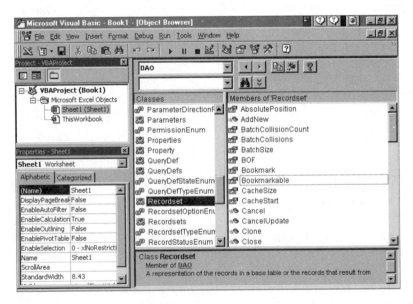

Like *IDispatch* servers, the Microsoft DAO component implements objects that have properties and methods.

DAO and MFC

The MFC library has the following five DAO database classes.

Class	Use
CDaoWorkspace	An interface for managing a single user's database session
CDaoDatabase	An interface for working with a database
CDaoRecordset	An interface for working with a set of records (such as table-type recordsets, dynaset-type recordsets, or snapshot-type recordsets)
CDaoTableDef	An interface for manipulating a definition of a base table or an attached table
CDaoQueryDef	An interface for querying a database

These classes more or less wrap the COM interfaces with corresponding names. (*CDaoRecordset* wraps *DAORecordset*, for example.) The *CDaoWorkspace* class actually wraps two interfaces, *DAOWorkspace* and *DAODBEngine*. The MFC wrapping is fairly complete, so you need to make direct COM DAO calls only when you need access to certain database security features. If you use the MFC library, all reference counting is taken care of; if you call DAO directly, you must be sure to call *Release* on your interfaces.

Both AppWizard and ClassWizard fully support DAO. You can use AppWizard to generate a complete form-based application that works like EX31B in Chapter 31, and you can use ClassWizard to generate a table-specific class that is derived from *CDaoRecordset*.

What Databases Can You Open with DAO?

The following four database options are supported by DAO:

- **Opening an Access database (MDB file)**—An MDB file is a self-contained database that includes query definitions, security information, indexes, relationships, and of course the actual data tables. You simply specify the MDB file's pathname.

- **Opening an ODBC data source directly**—There's a significant limitation here. You can't open an ODBC data source that uses the Jet engine as a driver; you can use only data sources that have their own ODBC driver DLLs.

■ Opening an ISAM-type (indexed sequential access method) data source (a group of dBASE, FoxPro, Paradox, Btrieve, Excel, or text files) through the Jet engine—Even if you've set up an ODBC data source that uses the Jet engine to access one of these file types, you must open the file as an ISAM-type data source, not as an ODBC data source.

■ Attaching external tables to an Access database—This is actually the preferred way of using DAO to access ODBC data. First you use Access to attach the ODBC tables to an MDB file, and then you use DAO to open the MDB file as in the first option. You can also use Access to attach ISAM files to an MDB file.

Using DAO in ODBC Mode— Snapshots and Dynasets

You've already heard that DAO goes far beyond ODBC, but let's take things one step at a time. We'll start with DAO snapshots and dynasets, which behave pretty much the same way in DAO as they do in ODBC. You can use snapshots and dynasets with ODBC data sources, ISAM-type files, and Access tables. You write programs using the MFC library classes *CDaoDatabase* and *CDaoRecordset*, which are very similar to the ODBC classes *CDatabase* and *CRecordset*. There are a few notable differences, however:

■ The *CDaoRecordset::GetRecordCount* function works differently from the *CRecordset::GetRecordCount* function. For attached tables and ODBC data sources, *CDaoRecordset::GetRecordCount* always returns –1. For Access tables and ISAM-type files, it returns the number of records actually read, which is the final count for the recordset only if you have moved to the last record. Unfortunately, DAO has no equivalent for the ODBC *CRecordset::GetStatus* function, so you can't test a DAO recordset to find out whether the record count is indeed final.

■ With DAO, you can get and set the absolute position of the current record in a dynaset or a snapshot, you can get and set a percent position, you can find a record containing a matching string, and you can use bookmarks to mark records for later retrieval.

■ DAO makes it easy to get and set column values without binding. Because values are passed as *VARIANT*s, you can build dynamic applications that adjust to the database schema at runtime.

932

One important thing to remember about snapshot recordsets is that the record count never changes. With dynasets, the record count changes only if you delete or add records in the dynaset. If another user deletes a record, that record is marked as deleted in your dynaset; if another user adds a record, you don't see that record in your dynaset. If you add a record to a dynaset, that record is added at the end of the dynaset, regardless of the sort order.

DAO Table-Type Recordsets

DAO introduces a new type of recordset unknown in the ODBC universe. A table-type recordset (supported by the *CDaoRecordset* class) is a direct view of an entire database table. You can use a table-type recordset only with a table in an Access database. Table-type recordsets have the following characteristics that distinguish them from snapshots and dynasets:

■ The *CDaoRecordset::GetRecordCount* function returns an approximate record count that reflects records added or deleted by other users.

■ You can't use the *CDaoRecordset* functions that access a record's absolute position or percent position.

■ The *CDaoRecordset::Seek* function lets you position to a record by key value. You first call the *CDaoRecordset::SetCurrentIndex* function to select the index.

■ If you add a record to a table-type recordset, the record is added in its proper place using the sort order that is determined by the current index.

The table-type recordset is a significant departure from ODBC and SQL. You can now select an individual record without first issuing a query. You can find a record with one index and then move sequentially using a different index. It's like dBASE or FoxPro programming!

DAO *QueryDef*s and *TableDef*s

If you're working with an Access database, you can store parameterized queries in the database, using the MFC *CDaoQueryDef* class. Also, you can use the *CDaoTableDef* class to define tables at runtime, which is more convenient than using a SQL CREATE statement.

DAO Multithreading

The Microsoft Access Jet engine is not multithreaded, and that means that DAO is not multithreaded. Furthermore, you must confine all DAO calls to your application's main thread.

Displaying Database Rows in a Scrolling Window

You've seen all the general DAO theory you're going to get here. Now you're ready for a practical example. Before you dig into the code for EX32A, however, you need to study the general problem of displaying database rows in a scrolling window. If this were an easy problem to solve, there would probably be an MFC *CScrollDatabaseView* class. But there isn't, so we'll write our own class. Actually, it's not that difficult if we make some simplifying assumptions about the database. First, our scrolling row–view class will be based on a dynaset, and that means that it can accommodate <u>any</u> table, including those in ODBC data sources and ISAM-type files. Second, we'll specify read-only access, which means that the number of rows in the dynaset can't change.

Scrolling Alternatives

There are lots of ways to implement scrolling with Visual C++. If you look at the DAOVIEW MFC sample database program on the Visual C++ CD-ROM, you'll see the use of the MFC *CListView* class, which encapsulates the Windows list view common control. The trouble with this approach is that you must copy all the selected rows into the control, which can be slow, and more significantly, you can't see updates that other programs are making in the same table. The list view is a de facto snapshot of a database table.

We'll base our scrolling view on the MFC *CScrollView* class, and our code will be smart enough to retrieve only those records that are needed for the client area of the window. The only limitation here is the logical size of the scrolling window. In Microsoft Windows 95, the limits are ±32,767, and that restricts the number of rows we can display. If the distance between rows is 14 units, we can display only up to 2340 rows.

A Row–View Class

If you've read other books about programming for Windows, you know that authors spend lots of time on the problem of scrolling lists. This is a tricky programming exercise that must be repeated over and over. Why not encapsulate a scrolling list in a base class? All the ugly details would be hidden, and you could get on with the business of writing your application.

The *CRowView* class, adapted from the class of the identical name in the CHKBOOK MFC advanced sample program on the Visual C++ CD-ROM, does the job. Through its use of virtual callback functions, it serves as a model for other derivable base classes. *CRowView* has some limitations, and it's not built to industrial-strength specifications, but it works well in the DAO example. Figure 32-1 shows the header file listing.

ROWVIEW.H

```
// rowview.h : interface of the CRowView class
//
// This class implements the behavior of a scrolling view that presents
//   multiple rows of fixed-height data. A row view is similar to an
//   owner-draw list box in its visual behavior; but unlike list boxes,
//   a row view has all of the benefits of a view (as well as scroll view),
//   including perhaps most importantly printing and print preview.
/////////////////////////////////////////////////////////////////////////////

class CRowView : public CScrollView
{
DECLARE_DYNAMIC(CRowView)
protected:
// Construction/destruction
    CRowView();
    virtual ~CRowView();

// Attributes
protected:
    int m_nRowWidth;            // width of row in logical units
    int m_nRowHeight;           // height of row in logical units
    int m_nCharWidth;           // avg char width in logical units
    int m_nPrevSelectedRow;     // index of the most recently selected row
    int m_nPrevRowCount;        // most recent row count, before update
    int m_nRowsPerPrintedPage;  // how many rows fit on a printed page

// Operations-Attributes
protected:
    virtual void UpdateRow(int nInvalidRow); // called by derived class
                                             //   OnUpdate
    virtual void CalculateRowMetrics(CDC* pDC)
        { GetRowWidthHeight(pDC, m_nRowWidth, m_nRowHeight,
            m_nCharWidth); }
    virtual void UpdateScrollSizes();
    virtual CRect RowToWndRect(CDC* pDC, int nRow);
```

Figure 32-1.
The CRowView *header file listing.*

(continued)

Figure 32-1. *continued*

```
virtual int RowToYPos(int nRow);
    virtual void RectLPtoRowRange(const CRect& rectLP, int& nFirstRow,
        int& nLastRow, BOOL bIncludePartiallyShownRows);
    virtual int LastViewableRow();

// Overridables
protected:
    virtual void GetRowWidthHeight(CDC* pDC, int& nRowWidth,
        int& nRowHeight, int& nCharWidth) = 0;
    virtual int GetActiveRow() = 0;
    virtual int GetRowCount() = 0;
    virtual void OnDrawRow(CDC* pDC, int nRow, int y, BOOL bSelected) = 0;
    virtual void ChangeSelectionNextRow(BOOL bNext) = 0;
    virtual void ChangeSelectionToRow(int nRow) = 0;

// Implementation
protected:
    // standard overrides of MFC classes
    virtual void OnInitialUpdate();
    virtual void OnDraw(CDC* pDC);  // overridden to draw this view
    virtual void OnPrepareDC(CDC* pDC, CPrintInfo* pInfo = NULL);
    virtual BOOL OnPreparePrinting(CPrintInfo* pInfo);
    virtual void OnBeginPrinting(CDC* pDC, CPrintInfo* pInfo);
    virtual void OnPrint(CDC* pDC, CPrintInfo* pInfo);

// Generated message map functions
protected:
    //{{AFX_MSG(CRowView)
    afx_msg void OnKeyDown(UINT nChar, UINT nRepCnt, UINT nFlags);
    afx_msg void OnSize(UINT nType, int cx, int cy);
    afx_msg void OnLButtonDown(UINT nFlags, CPoint point);
    //}}AFX_MSG
    DECLARE_MESSAGE_MAP()
};
```

Dividing the Work Between Base and Derived Classes

Because the *CRowView* class (itself derived from *CScrollView*) is designed to be a base class, it is as general as possible. *CRowView* relies on its derived class to access and paint the row's data. The EX32A example's document class obtains its row data from a scrollable DAO database, but the CHKBOOK example uses a random access disk file. The *CRowView* class serves both examples effectively. It supports the concept of a selected row that is highlighted in the view. Through the *CRowView* virtual member functions, the derived class is alerted when the user changes the selected row.

The *CRowView* Pure Virtual Member Functions

Classes derived from *CRowView* must implement the following pure virtual member functions:

- **■ *GetRowWidthHeight*—**This function returns the character width and height of the currently selected font and the width of the row, based on average character widths. As the device context switches between printer and display, the returned font metric values change accordingly.

- **■ *GetActiveRow*—**The base class calls this function frequently, so if another view changes the selected row, this view can track it.

- **■ *ChangeSelectionNextRow*, *ChangeSelectionToRow*—**These two functions serve to alert the derived class that the user has changed the selected row. The derived class can then update the document (and other views) if necessary.

- **■ *OnDrawRow*—**The *OnDrawRow* function is called by the function *CRowView::OnDraw* to draw a specific row.

Other *CRowView* Functions

Three other *CRowView* functions are available to be called by derived classes and the application framework:

- **■ *UpdateRow*—**This public function triggers a view update when the row selection changes. Normally, only the newly selected row and the deselected row are invalidated, and this means that the final invalid rectangle spans both rows. If the total number of rows has changed, *UpdateRow* calls *UpdateScrollSizes*.

- **■ *UpdateScrollSizes*—**This is a virtual function, so you can override it if necessary. The *CRowView* implementation updates the size of the view, which invalidates the visible portion. *UpdateScrollSizes* is called by *OnSize* and by *OnUpdate* (after the user executes a new query).

- **■ *OnPrint*—**The *CRowView* class overrides this function to cleverly adjust the viewport origin and clipping rectangle so that *OnDraw* can paint on the printed page exactly as it does in the visible portion of a window.

The MFC Dialog Bar

You haven't seen the *CDialogBar* class yet because it hasn't made sense to use it. (A dialog bar is a child of the frame window that is arranged according to a dialog template resource and that routes commands in a manner similar to that of a toolbar.) It fits well in the DAO example, however. (See Figure 32-2 on page 940.) The dialog bar contains an edit control for the SQL query string, and it has a pushbutton to re-execute the query. The button sends a command message that can be handled in the view, and it can be disabled by an update command UI handler. Most dialog bars reside at the top of the frame window, immediately under the toolbar. It's surprisingly easy to add a dialog bar to an application. You don't even need a new derived class. Here are the steps:

1. Use the resource editor to lay out the dialog bar. Apply the following styles:

   Style = Child
   Border = None
   Visible = Unchecked

   You can choose a horizontally oriented bar for the top or bottom of the frame, or you can choose a vertically oriented bar for the left or right side of the frame. Add any controls you need, including buttons and edit controls.

2. Declare an embedded *CDialogBar* object in your derived main frame class declaration, as shown here:

   ```
   CDialogBar m_wndMyBar;
   ```

3. Add dialog bar object creation code to your main frame class *OnCreate* member function, as shown here:

   ```
   if (!m_wndMyBar.Create(this, IDD_MY_BAR, CBRS_TOP,
       ID_MY_BAR)) {
       TRACE("Failed to create dialog bar\n");
       return -1;
   }
   ```

IDD_MY_BAR is the dialog resource ID assigned in the resource editor. The *CBRS_TOP* style tells the application framework to place the dialog bar at the top of the frame window. *ID_MY_BAR* is the dialog bar's control window ID, which should be within the range 0xE800 through 0xE820 to ensure that the Print Preview window preempts the dialog bar.

Programming a Dynamic Recordset

If you use AppWizard to create a DAO database application, AppWizard generates a class derived from *CDaoRecordset* with a *DoFieldExchange* function that binds data members to the columns in a specific database table. For a dynamic recordset class, however, you need to determine the column names and data types at runtime. The EX31A example shows how to do this with ODBC.

With DAO, the procedure is similar. You simply construct a *CDaoRecordset* object and call the *GetFieldValue* member function, which returns a *VARIANT* representing the column value. Other member functions tell you the number of columns in the table and the name, type, and width of each column.

> NOTE: If a field *VARIANT* contains a *BSTR*, assume the string contains 8-bit characters. This is an exception to the rule that all *BSTR*s contain wide characters.

The EX32A Example

Now we'll put everything together and build another working program—an MDI application that connects to any DAO data source. The application dynamically displays tables in scrolling view windows, and it allows the user to type in the SQL QUERY statement, which is stored in the document along with data source and table information. AppWizard generates the usual MDI main frame, document, application, and view classes, and we change the view class base to *CRowView* and add the DAO-specific code. Figure 32-2 on the following page shows the EX32A program in operation.

The document's File menu includes the following commands:

DAO Open MDB
DAO Open ISAM
DAO Open ODBC

The user must choose one of these commands after opening a document. As you will see, the code for opening the database is different depending on the data source type.

You can learn a lot about this application by looking at the three-view window in Figure 32-2. The two view windows in the upper part of the main window are tied to the same document, and the lower view window is tied to another document. The dialog bar shows the SQL statement associated with the active view window.

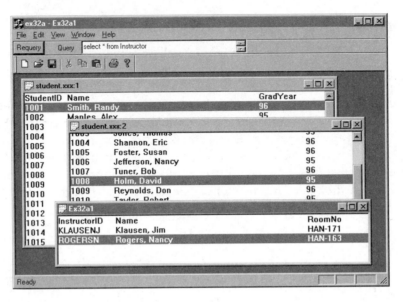

Figure 32-2.
The EX32A program in operation.

The EX32A example includes source code listings and resource requirements. Here is a table of the files and classes.

Header File	Source Code File	Class	Description
Ex32a.h	Ex32a.cpp	*CEx32aApp*	Main application
MainFrm.h	MainFrm.cpp	*CMainFrame*	MDI main frame
ChildFrm.h	ChildFrm.cpp	*CChildFrame*	MDI child frame
Ex32aDoc.h	Ex32aDoc.cpp	*CEx32aDoc*	EX32A document
Ex32aView.h	Ex32aView.cpp	*CEx32aView*	Scrolling database view class
Rowview.h	Rowview.cpp	*CRowView*	Row view base class
Tablesel.h	Tablesel.cpp	*CTableSelect*	Table selection dialog class
IsamSelect.h	IsamSelect.cpp	*CIsamSelect*	ISAM-type data source selection dialog class
StdAfx.h	StdAfx.cpp		Precompiled headers

Now we'll go through the application's classes one at a time, excluding *CRowView*. You'll see the important data members and the principal member functions.

CEx32aApp

The application class is the unmodified output from AppWizard. Nothing special here.

CMainFrame and CChildFrame

These classes are the standard output from AppWizard except for the addition of the dialog bar created in the *CMainFrame::OnCreate* member function.

CEx32aDoc

The document class manages the database connections and recordsets. Each document object can support one main recordset attached to one data source. A document object can have several views attached. Data sources (represented by *CDaoDatabase* objects) are not shared among document objects; each document has its own.

Data Members

The important *CEx32aDoc* data members are listed in the following table.

Data Member	Description
m_pRecordset	Pointer to the document's recordset object
m_database	Document's embedded *CDaoDatabase* object
m_strDatabase	Database pathname (MDB file)
m_strConnect	ODBC connection string or ISAM connection string
m_strQuery	Entire SQL SELECT statement
m_bConnected	Flag that is *TRUE* when the document is connected to a recordset
m_nFields	Number of fields (columns) in the recordset
m_nRowCount	Number of records (rows) in the recordset
m_nDatabaseType	*enum {UNK, MDB, ISAM, ODBC}*

OnOpenDocument

This overridden *CDocument* function is called when the user loads a document from disk. The document contains the name of the database and the query string, so the program can open the database and run the query upon loading.

```
BOOL CEx32aDoc::OnOpenDocument(LPCTSTR lpszPathName)
{
    if (!CDocument::OnOpenDocument(lpszPathName))
        return FALSE;
    PutQuery();
    switch (m_nDatabaseType) {
    case UNK:
        break;
    case MDB:
        DaoOpenMdb();
        break;
    case ISAM:
        DaoOpenIsam();
        break;
    case ODBC:
        DaoOpenOdbc();
        break;
    }
    return TRUE;
}
```

OnCloseDocument

This overridden *CDocument* function closes the database if one is connected:

```
void CEx32aDoc::OnCloseDocument()
{
    m_strQuery.Empty();
    PutQuery();
    if (m_bConnected) {
        delete m_pRecordset; // Destructor calls Close
        m_database.Close();
        m_bConnected = FALSE;
        m_pRecordset = NULL;
        m_nRowCount = 0;
    }
    CDocument::OnCloseDocument();
}
```

OnFileDaoOpenOdbc and DaoOpenOdbc

These functions are called in response to the user choosing the DAO Open ODBC command from the File menu. *DaoOpenOdbc*, which is also called by *OnOpenDocument*, calls *CDaoDatabase::Open* with the connect parameter string. The string *"ODBC;"* causes the ODBC data source selection dialog to be displayed. Notice the use of the *try/catch* block to detect SQL processing errors.

```
void CEx32aDoc::OnFileDaoOpenOdbc()
{
    m_strConnect.Empty();
    m_strQuery.Empty();
    DaoOpenOdbc();
}


void CEx32aDoc::DaoOpenOdbc()
{
    // can't open ODBC using Access driver
    if (m_strConnect.IsEmpty()) {
        m_strConnect = "ODBC;";
    }
    BeginWaitCursor();
    try {
        // nonexclusive, read-only
        m_database.Open("", FALSE, TRUE, m_strConnect);
    }
    catch (CDaoException* e) {
        ::DaoErrorMsg(e);
        EndWaitCursor();
        e->Delete();
        return;
    }
    m_strConnect = m_database.GetConnect();
    TRACE("database name = %s, connect = %s\n",
        (const char*) m_strDatabase,
        (const char*) m_strConnect);
    OpenRecordset();
    m_nDatabaseType = ODBC;
    EndWaitCursor();
}
```

OnFileDaoOpenIsam and *DaoOpenIsam*

These functions are called in response to the user choosing the DAO Open ISAM command from the File menu. *DaoOpenIsam*, which is also called by *OnOpenDocument*, gets a directory name from the user (through the *CIsamSelect* class) and then calls *CDaoDatabase::Open* with the connect parameter string. The *CIsamSelect::m_strIsam* string specifies the type of file. Example strings are *"dBASE III"*, *"FoxPro 2.6"*, and *"Excel 8.0"*.

```
void CEx32aDoc::OnFileDaoOpenIsam()
{
    m_strConnect.Empty();
    m_strQuery.Empty();
    DaoOpenIsam();
}

void CEx32aDoc::DaoOpenIsam()
{
    BeginWaitCursor();
    if (m_strConnect.IsEmpty()) {
        CIsamSelect isamDlg;
        if (isamDlg.DoModal() != IDOK) {
            return;
        }
        m_strConnect = isamDlg.m_strIsam + ";DATABASE=" +
            isamDlg.m_strDirectory;
        TRACE("m_strConnect = %s\n", (const char*) m_strConnect);
    }
    try {
        // nonexclusive, read-only
        m_database.Open("", FALSE, TRUE, m_strConnect);
    }
    catch(CDaoException* e) {
        ::DaoErrorMsg(e);
        EndWaitCursor();
        e->Delete();
        return;
    }
    m_strConnect = m_database.GetConnect();
    TRACE("database name = %s, connect = %s\n",
        (const char*) m_strDatabase, (const char*) m_strConnect);
    OpenRecordset();
    m_nDatabaseType = ISAM;
    EndWaitCursor();
}
```

OnFileDaoOpenMdb and *DaoOpenMdb*

These functions are called in response to the user choosing the DAO Open MDB command from the File menu. *DaoOpenMdb*, which is also called by *OnOpen-Document*, uses the MFC *CFileDialog* class to get an MDB file pathname from the user. Compare the *CDaoDatabase::Open* call with the calls in the two preceding functions. Notice that the MDB pathname is passed as the first parameter.

```
void CEx32aDoc::OnFileDaoOpenMdb()
{
    m_strDatabase.Empty();
    m_strQuery.Empty();
    DaoOpenMdb();
}

void CEx32aDoc::DaoOpenMdb()
{
    if (m_strDatabase.IsEmpty()) {
        CFileDialog dlg(TRUE, ".mdb", "*.mdb");
        if (dlg.DoModal() == IDCANCEL) return;
        m_strDatabase = dlg.GetPathName();
    }
    BeginWaitCursor();
    try {
        // nonexclusive, read-only
        m_database.Open(m_strDatabase, FALSE, TRUE);
    }
    catch (CDaoException* e) {
        ::DaoErrorMsg(e);
        EndWaitCursor();
        e->Delete();
        return;
    }
    m_strDatabase = m_database.GetName();
    TRACE("database name = %s, connect = %s\n",
        (const char*) m_strDatabase, (const char*) m_strConnect);
    OpenRecordset();
    m_nDatabaseType = MDB;
    EndWaitCursor();
}
```

OnFileDaoDisconnect

This function closes the DAO database, enabling the document to be saved.

```
void CEx32aDoc::OnFileDaoDisconnect()
{
    if (m_bConnected) {
        delete m_pRecordset; // Destructor calls Close
        m_database.Close();
        m_bConnected = FALSE;
        m_pRecordset = NULL;
        m_nRowCount = 0;
        UpdateAllViews(NULL);
    }
}
```

OpenRecordset

This helper function is called by *DaoOpenOdbc*, *DaoOpenIsam*, and *DaoOpenMdb*. The *CTableSelect* class allows the user to select a table name, which is used to construct a SELECT statement. Calls to *CDaoRecordset::MoveLast* and *CDaoRecordset::GetAbsolutePosition* set the record count for ODBC, ISAM, and MDB data sources.

```
void CEx32aDoc::OpenRecordset()
{
    GetQuery();
    if (m_strQuery.IsEmpty()) {
        CTableSelect tableDlg(&m_database);
        if (tableDlg.DoModal() != IDOK) {
            m_database.Close();  // escape route
            return;
        }
        m_strQuery.Format("select * from [%s]", tableDlg.m_strSelection);
        PutQuery();
    }

    m_pRecordset = new CDaoRecordset(&m_database);
    try {
        m_pRecordset->Open(dbOpenDynaset, m_strQuery, dbReadOnly);
    }
    catch (CDaoException* e) {
        ::DaoErrorMsg(e);
        UpdateAllViews(NULL);
        m_bConnected = FALSE;
        e->Delete();
        return;
    }
    if (!m_pRecordset->IsBOF()) {
        // might be expensive for a really big table
        // View adjusts its m_nRowCount if you supply a big value here
        m_pRecordset->MoveLast(); // to validate record count
    }
    m_nRowCount = m_pRecordset->GetAbsolutePosition() + 2;
    TRACE("m_nRowCount = %d\n", m_nRowCount);
    GetFieldSpecs();
    UpdateAllViews(NULL);
    m_bConnected = TRUE;
}
```

> **N O T E :** The MFC *CDaoRecordset* class has *m_strFilter* and *m_strSort* data members, as does the ODBC *CRecordset* class. You can't use these strings, however, if your recordset doesn't have bound fields; you must construct the entire SELECT statement as shown above.

OnRequery

This message handler is called in response to the user clicking the Requery button on the dialog bar. This message handler reads the query string value and regenerates the recordset. Note that the *CDaoRecordset::Requery* function doesn't handle an updated SELECT statement, so we close and reopen the recordset instead.

```cpp
void CEx32aDoc::OnRequery()
{
    GetQuery();
    // Requery won't work because we're changing the SQL statement
    BeginWaitCursor();
    if(m_pRecordset->IsOpen()) {
        m_pRecordset->Close();
    }
    try {
        m_pRecordset->Open(dbOpenDynaset, m_strQuery, dbReadOnly);
    }
    catch (CDaoException* e) {
        ::DaoErrorMsg(e);
        m_nRowCount = 0;
        UpdateAllViews(NULL);
        EndWaitCursor();
        e->Delete();
        return;
    }
    if (!m_pRecordset->IsBOF()) {
        m_pRecordset->MoveLast(); // to validate record count
    }
    m_nRowCount = m_pRecordset->GetAbsolutePosition() + 2;
    TRACE("m_nRowCount = %d\n", m_nRowCount);
    GetFieldSpecs();
    UpdateAllViews(NULL);
    EndWaitCursor();
}
```

PutQuery and GetQuery

These utility functions move the document's query string to and from the edit control on the dialog bar.

Serialize

The *Serialize* function reads and writes the *m_strConnect*, *m_strDatabase*, and *m_strQuery* data members.

CEx32aView

This class is derived from *CRowView* and implements the virtual functions.

Data Members

The *CEx32aView* class uses the integer variable *m_nSelectedRow* to track the currently selected row. The recordset pointer is held in *m_pSet*.

OnUpdate

This virtual *CView* function is called through the application framework when the view is created and when the document's contents change in response to a database open or requery event. If several views are active for a given document, all views reflect the current query but each can maintain its own current row and scroll position. *OnUpdate* also sets the value of the *m_pSet* data member. This can't be done in *OnInitialUpdate* because the recordset is not open at that point.

GetRowWidthHeight, GetActiveRow, ChangeSelectionNextRow, and ChangeSelectionToRow

These functions are implementations of the *CRowView* class pure virtual functions. They take care of drawing a specified query result row, and they track the current selection.

GetRowCount

This virtual function, which is called from *CRowView*, simply returns the record count value stored in the document.

OnDrawRow and DrawDataRow

The *OnDrawRow* virtual function is called from *CRowView* member functions to perform the actual work of drawing a designated row. *OnDrawRow* reads the recordset's current row and then calls the *CDaoRecordset::Move* function to position the cursor and read the data. The *try/catch* block detects catastrophic errors resulting from unreadable data. The *DrawDataRow* helper function steps through the columns and prints the values. Notice that *OnDrawRow* displays "**RECORD DELETED**" when it encounters a record that has been deleted by another user since the dynaset was first created. *OnDrawRow* and *DrawDataRow* are shown here:

```
void CEx32aView::OnDrawRow(CDC* pDC, int nRow, int y, BOOL bSelected)
{
    int x = 0;
    int i;
    CEx32aDoc* pDoc = GetDocument();
```

```
    if (m_pSet == NULL) return;

    if (nRow == 0) {     // title row
        for (i = 0; i < pDoc->m_nFields; i++) {
            pDC->TextOut(x, y, pDoc->m_arrayFieldName[i]);
            x += pDoc->m_arrayFieldSize[i] * m_nCharWidth;
        }
    }
    else {
        try {
            m_pSet->SetAbsolutePosition(nRow - 1); //
adjust for title row
            // SetAbsolutePosition doesn't throw exception until AFTER
            //   end of set
            if (m_pSet->GetAbsolutePosition() == (nRow - 1)) {
                DrawDataRow(pDC, y);
            }
        }
        catch (CDaoException* e) {
            // might be a time delay before delete is seen in this program
            if (e->m_pErrorInfo->m_lErrorCode == 3167) {
                pDC->TextOut(0, y, "**RECORD DELETED**");
            }
            else {
                m_pSet->MoveLast(); // in case m_nRowCount is too big
                pDoc->m_nRowCount = m_pSet->GetAbsolutePosition() + 2;
            }
            e->Delete();
        }
    }
}

void CEx32aView::DrawDataRow(CDC* pDC, int y)
{
    int x = 0;
    CString strTime;

    COleVariant var;
    CString str;
    CEx32aDoc* pDoc = GetDocument();
    for (int i = 0; i < pDoc->m_nFields; i++) {
        var = m_pSet->GetFieldValue(i);
        switch (var.vt) {
            case VT_BSTR:
                str = (LPCSTR) var.bstrVal; // narrow characters in DAO
                break;
```

(continued)

```
            case VT_I2:
                str.Format("%d", (int) var.iVal);
                break;
            case VT_I4:
                str.Format("%d", var.lVal);
                break;
            case VT_R4:
                str.Format("%10.2f", (double) var.fltVal);
                break;
            case VT_R8:
                str.Format("%10.2f", var.dblVal);
                break;
            case VT_CY:
                str = COleCurrency(var).Format();
                break;
            case VT_DATE:
                str = COleDateTime(var).Format();
                break;
            case VT_BOOL:
                str = (var.boolVal == 0) ? "FALSE" : "TRUE";
                break;
            case VT_NULL:
                str =  "----";
                break;
            default:
                str.Format("Unk type %d\n", var.vt);
                TRACE("Unknown type %d\n", var.vt);
        }
        pDC->TextOut(x, y, str);
        x += pDoc->m_arrayFieldSize[i] * m_nCharWidth;
    }
}
```

OnInitialUpdate and *OnTimer*

Because we're working with a dynaset, we want to show database changes made by other programs. The timer handler calls *CWnd::Invalidate*, which causes all records in the client area to be refreshed, as shown here:

```
void CEx32aView::OnInitialUpdate()
{
    CRowView::OnInitialUpdate();
}


void CEx32aView::OnTimer(UINT nIDEvent)
{
    Invalidate(); // Update view from database
}
```

CTableSelect

This is a ClassWizard-generated dialog class that contains a list box used for selecting the table. For the student registration database, the dialog looks like the one shown below.

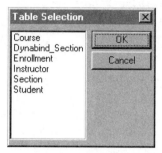

Data Members

The *CTableSelect* data members are as follows.

Data Member	Description
m_pDatabase	Pointer to the recordset's *CDaoDatabase* object
m_strSelection	ClassWizard-generated variable that corresponds to the list-box selection

Constructor

The constructor takes a database pointer parameter, which it uses to set the *m_pDatabase* data member, as shown here:

```
CTableSelect::CTableSelect(CDaoDatabase* pDatabase,
    CWnd* pParent /*=NULL*/)
    : CDialog(CTableSelect::IDD, pParent)
{
    //{{AFX_DATA_INIT(CTableSelect)
    m_strSelection = "";
    //}}AFX_DATA_INIT
    m_pDatabase = pDatabase;
}
```

OnInitDialog

This self-contained function creates, opens, and reads the data source's list of tables and puts the table name strings in the dialog's list box, as shown here:

```
BOOL CTableSelect::OnInitDialog()
{
    CListBox* pLB = (CListBox*) GetDlgItem(IDC_LIST1);
    int nTables = m_pDatabase->GetTableDefCount();
    TRACE("CTableSelect::OnInitDialog, nTables = %d\n", nTables);
    CDaoTableDefInfo tdi;
    for (int n = 0; n < nTables; n++) {
        m_pDatabase->GetTableDefInfo(n, tdi);
        TRACE("table name = %s\n", (const char*) tdi.m_strName);
        if (tdi.m_strName.Left(4) != "MSys") {
            pLB->AddString(tdi.m_strName);
        }
    }
    return CDialog::OnInitDialog();
}
```

OnDblclkList1

It's handy for the user to choose a list-box entry with a double click. This function is mapped to the appropriate list-box notification message, as shown here:

```
void CTableSelect::OnDblclkList1()
{
    OnOK();  // Double-clicking on list-box item exits dialog
}
```

CIsamSelect

This ClassWizard-generated dialog class contains a list box and an edit control used for selecting the ISAM-type data source. The user must type the directory for the files, as shown here.

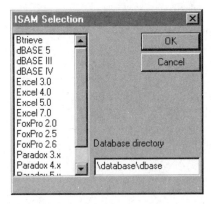

Data Members

The *CIsamSelect* class data members are as follows.

Data Member	Definition
m_strIsam	ClassWizard-generated variable that corresponds to the list-box selection
m_strDirectory	ClassWizard-generated variable that corresponds to the edit control contents

OnInitDialog

This function sets the initial values of the list box, which are the options from the "Connect Property" topic in Books Online, as shown here:

```
BOOL CIsamSelect::OnInitDialog()
{
    CListBox* pLB = (CListBox*) GetDlgItem(IDC_LIST1);
    pLB->AddString("dBASE III");
    pLB->AddString("dBASE IV");
    pLB->AddString("dBASE 5");
    pLB->AddString("Paradox 3.x");
    pLB->AddString("Paradox 4.x");
    pLB->AddString("Paradox 5.x");
    pLB->AddString("Btrieve");
    pLB->AddString("FoxPro 2.0");
    pLB->AddString("FoxPro 2.5");
    pLB->AddString("FoxPro 2.6");
    pLB->AddString("Excel 3.0");
    pLB->AddString("Excel 4.0");
    pLB->AddString("Excel 5.0");
    pLB->AddString("Excel 7.0");
    pLB->AddString("Text");
    CDialog::OnInitDialog();

    return TRUE;  // Return TRUE unless you set the focus to a control.
                  // EXCEPTION: OCX Property Pages should return FALSE.
}
```

The EX32A Resource File

This application uses a dialog bar, so you'll need a dialog resource for it. Figure 32-2 on page 940 shows the dialog bar. The dialog resource ID is *IDD-_QUERY_BAR*. The controls are listed on the next page.

Control	ID
Button	*IDC_REQUERY*
Edit	*IDC_QUERY*

The following styles are set:

Style = Child
Border = None
Visible = Unchecked

There's also a table selection dialog template, *IDD_TABLE_SELECT*, which has a list-box control with ID *IDC_LIST1* and an ISAM selection dialog template, *IDD_ISAM_SELECT*. The File menu has the following four added items.

Menu Item	Command ID
DAO Open MDB	*ID_FILE_DAOOPEN_MDB*
DAO Open ISAM	*ID_FILE_DAOOPEN_ISAM*
DAO Open ODBC	*ID_FILE_DAOOPEN_ODBC*
DAO Disconnect	*ID_FILE_DAODISCONNECT*

Running the EX32A Program

You can run the EX32A program with any DAO data source, but try the student registration database (STDREG32.MDB) from the Visual C++ CD-ROM first. To test the multiuser capabilities of the program, run it simultaneously with EX31B. Use EX31B to change and delete instructor records while displaying the instructor table in EX32A.

CHAPTER   THIRTY · THREE

The OLE DB Templates

Chapters 31 and 32 covered two alternative ways to manage databases using the Microsoft Foundation Class Library version 6.0 and Microsoft Visual C++ 6.0—using ODBC and using DAO. Microsoft has defined another way to access data—through a technology called OLE DB. This chapter covers the new OLE DB templates—Visual C++ 6.0's support for accessing data through OLE DB directly. While ODBC is designed to provide access primarily to Structured Query Language (SQL) data in a multiplatform environment, OLE DB is designed to provide access to all types of data within a system. OLE DB uses the Component Object Model (COM) to accomplish this. OLE DB is fairly flexible: it covers all the SQL functionality defined in ODBC as well as defining interfaces suitable for gaining access to other-than-SQL types of data.

This chapter covers the highlights of the new OLE DB templates. OLE DB data access is divided into two major pieces: <u>consumers</u> and <u>providers</u>. We'll take a look at the basic OLE DB architecture and then examine how the consumer templates work. Then we'll look at how the provider side templates work.

Why OLE DB?

OLE DB exists to provide a uniform way to access all sorts of disparate data sources. For example, imagine all the types of data sources you might find in a typical organization. These might include sources as varied as production systems, file systems, spreadsheets, personal databases (such as Xbase and Btrieve), and e-mail. The problem is that each of these sources requires its own protocol: if you want to access data from a specific source, you need to learn the protocol for managing the data source. (Ugh!) OLE DB is the middle layer that makes accessing data from different sources uniform. With OLE DB, client-side developers need to concentrate on only a few details to get access to data (instead of needing to know tons of different database access protocols).

The most important thing to realize about OLE DB is that it is built upon COM. In other words, OLE DB is a set of ActiveX interfaces for accessing data through COM. The OLE DB interfaces are general enough to provide a uniform means of accessing data, regardless of the method that is used to store the data. For example, developers use the same OLE DB interfaces to get to data without being concerned as to whether data is stored in a DBMS or a non-DBMS information source. At the same time, OLE DB lets developers continue to take advantage of the benefits of the underlying database technology (like speed and flexibility) without having to move data around just to access those benefits.

At the highest level, the OLE DB architecture consists of consumers and providers. A consumer is any bit of system or application code that uses an OLE DB interface. This includes OLE DB components themselves. A provider is any software component that exposes an OLE DB interface.

There are two types of OLE DB providers: <u>data providers</u> and <u>service providers</u>. The names are pretty self-explanatory. Data providers own data and expose that data in a tabular form as a rowset. (A rowset is just an abstraction for exposing data in a tabular form.) Some good examples of data providers include relational Database Management Systems (DBMS's), storage managers, spreadsheets, and Indexed Sequential Access Method (ISAM) databases.

A service provider is any OLE DB component that does not own data but encapsulates some service by massaging data through OLE DB interfaces. In one sense, a service component is both a consumer and a provider. For example, a heterogeneous query processor is a service component. In one case where a consumer tries to join data from tables in two different data sources, as a consumer the query processor retrieves rows from rowsets created over each of the base tables. As a provider, the query processor creates a rowset from these rows and returns it to the consumer.

To sum up, there are many different kinds of data and numerous ways of accessing that data in the real world. However, many developers understand how to manipulate data using standard database-management techniques. OLE DB defines an architecture that "component-izes" data access. As a component database-management system, OLE DB offers greater efficiency than traditional database-management systems by separating database functionality into the roles of consumers and producers. Because data consumers generally require only a portion of the database-management functionality, OLE DB separates that functionality, thereby reducing client-side resource overhead.

By the same token, OLE DB reduces the burden on the provider side since providers need to worry only about providing data (and don't have to concern themselves with any client-side junk). For example, OLE DB allows a simple tabular data provider to implement functionality native to its data store yet provide a singular access protocol to get to the data. That way, a minimal implementation of a provider can choose to use only the interfaces that expose data as tables. This opens up the opportunity for the development of completely different query-processor components that can consume tabular information from any provider that exposes its data through OLE DB. In addition, SQL DBMS's can expose their functionality in a more layered manner by using the OLE DB interfaces.

Basic OLE DB Architecture

In addition to defining a basic relationship between consumers and providers, OLE DB defines the following components that make up the OLE DB architecture (each component is a COM object):

- **Enumerators**   Enumerators search for available data sources. Consumers that are not hardwired for a particular data source employ enumerators to search for a data source to use.

- **Data source objects**   Data source objects contain the machinery to connect to a data source, such as a file or a DBMS. A data source object generates sessions.

- **Sessions**   Sessions represent connections to a database. For example, sessions provide a context for database transactions. A single data source object can create multiple sessions. Sessions generate transactions, commands, and rowsets.

- **Transaction objects**   Transaction objects are used for managing database transactions in order to maintain database security.

- **Commands**   Commands execute text commands, such as a SQL statement. If the text command specifies a rowset, such as a SQL SELECT statement, the command generates rowsets. A single session can create multiple commands.

- **Rowsets**   Rowsets expose data in a tabular format. A special case of a rowset is an index. Rowsets can be created from the session or the command.

- **Errors**   Errors can be created by any interface on any OLE DB object. They contain additional information about an error, including an optional custom error object.

Here's an example of how you might apply these components to create an OLE DB consumer. If you aren't sure where the data source is, you might first use an enumerator to find a data source. Once you've located a data source, you create a session with it. The session lets you access the data as rowsets as well as create commands that generate rowsets.

The upside of using the OLE DB architecture is that you get a terrific, homogenous way to access heterogeneous data sources. The downside is that you have to implement a bunch of COM interfaces to make that happen. That's why the OLE DB templates exist.

Basic OLE DB Template Architecture

Now that you understand the basic architecture behind OLE DB, it's time to take a look at a specific implementation of the OLE DB interfaces (provided by the new OLE DB consumer and provider templates). Like most other COM-based technologies, OLE DB involves implementing a bunch of interfaces. Of course, just as with ActiveX Controls, you can choose to implement them by hand (often an inefficient approach—unless you're just trying to understand the technology inside-out), or you can find someone else to do most of the dirty work. While OLE DB is a rich and powerful data access technology, getting it up and running by hand is a somewhat tedious task.

Just as Visual C++ provides a template library (ATL) for implementing ActiveX Controls, Visual C++ also provides a template library that helps you manage OLE DB. The OLE DB template support provides classes that implement many of the commonly used OLE DB interfaces. In addition, Visual C++ provides great wizard support for generating code to apply to common scenarios.

From a high level, you can divide the classes in this template library into the two groups defined by OLE DB itself: the consumer classes and the provider classes. The consumer classes help you implement database client (consumer) applications, while the provider classes help you implement database server (provider) applications. Remember that OLE DB consumers are applications that call the COM interfaces exposed by OLE DB service providers (or regular providers) to access data. OLE DB providers are COM servers that provide data and services in a form that a consumer can understand.

OLE DB Consumer Template Architecture

Microsoft has kept the top layer classes in the OLE DB Consumer Templates as close to the OLE DB specification as possible. That is, OLE DB templates don't define another object model. Their purpose is simply to wrap the existing OLE DB object model. For each of the consumer-related components listed on page 957, you'll find a corresponding C++ template class. This design philosophy leverages the flexibility of OLE DB and allows more advanced features—such as multiple accessors on rowsets—to be available through the OLE DB Templates.

The OLE DB Templates are small and flexible. They are implemented using C++ templates and multiple inheritance. Because OLE DB templates are close to the metal (they wrap only the existing OLE DB architecture), each class mirrors an existing OLE DB component. For example, *CDataSource* corresponds to the data source object in OLE DB.

The OLE DB Consumer Template architecture can be divided into three parts: the general data source support classes, classes for supporting data access and rowset operations, and classes for handling tables and commands. Here's a quick summary of these classes.

General Data Source Support

A data source is the most fundamental concept to remember when talking about data access using OLE DB. That is, where is the data coming from? Of course, the OLE DB templates have support for data sources. General data source support comprises three classes as shown in this table.

Class	Use
CDataSource	This class represents the data source component and manages the connection to a data source.
CEnumerator	This class provides a way to select a provider by cycling through a list of providers. Its functionality is equivalent to the *SQLBrowseConnect* and *SQLDriverConnect* functions.
CSession	This class handles transactions. You can use this class to create rowsets, commands, and many other objects. A *CDataSource* object creates a *CSession* object using the *CSession::Open* method.

Data Access and Rowset Support

The OLE DB templates provide binding and rowset support through several classes. The accessor classes talk to the data source while the rowset manages the data in tabular form. The data access and rowset components are implemented through the *CAccessorRowset* class. *CAccessorRowset* is a template class that's specialized on an accessor and a rowset. This class can handle multiple accessors of different types.

The OLE DB Template library defines the accessors in the table on the following page.

Class	Use
CAccessor	This class is used when a record is statically bound to a data source—it contains the pre-existing data buffer and understands the data format up front. *CAccessor* is used when you know the structure and the type of the database ahead of time.
CDynamicAccessor	This class is used for retrieving data from a source whose structure is not known at design time. This class uses *IColumnsInfo::GetColumnInfo* to get the database column information. *CDynamicAccessor* creates and manages the data buffer.
CDynamicParameterAccessor	This class is similar to *CDynamicAccessor* except that it's used with commands. When used to prepare commands, *CDynamic-ParameterAccessor* can get parameter information from the *ICommandWithParameters* interface, which is especially useful for handling unknown command types.
CManualAccessor	This class lets you access whatever data types you want as long as the provider can convert the type. *CManualAccessor* handles both result columns and command parameters.

Along with the accessors, the OLE DB templates define three types of rowsets: single fetching, bulk, and array. These are fairly self-explanatory descriptions. Clients use a function named *MoveNext* to navigate through the data. The difference between the single fetching, bulk, and array rowsets lies in the number of row handles retrieved when *MoveNext* is called. Single fetching rowsets retrieve a single rowset for each call to *MoveNext* while bulk rowsets fetch multiple rows. Array rowsets provide a convenient array syntax for fetching data. The OLE DB Templates provide the single row-fetching capability by default.

Table and Command Support

The final layer in the OLE DB Template consumer architecture consists of two more classes: table and command classes (*CTable* and *CCommand*). These classes are used to open the rowset, execute commands, and initiate bindings. Both classes derive from *CAccessorRowset*

The *CTable* class is a minimal class implementation that opens a table on a data source (which you can specify programmatically). Use this class when you need bare-bones access to a source, since *CTable* is designed for simple providers that do not support commands.

Other data sources also support commands. For those sources, you'll want to use the OLE DB Templates' *CCommand* class. As its name implies, *CCommand* is used mostly for executing commands. This class has a function named *Open* that executes singular commands. This class also has a function named *Prepare* for setting up a command to execute multiple times.

When using the *CCommand* class, you'll specialize it with three template arguments: an accessor, a rowset, and a third template argument (which defaults to *CNoMultipleResults*). If you specify *CMultipleResults* for this third argument, the *CCommand* class will support the *IMultipleResults* interface for a command that returns multiple rowsets.

OLE DB Provider Template Architecture

Remember that OLE DB is really just a set of interfaces that specify a protocol for managing data. OLE DB defines several interfaces (some mandatory and others optional) for the following types of objects: data source, session, rowset, and command. Here's a description of each followed by a code snippet that shows how the templates bring in the correct functionality for each component.

- **Data source object** A data source object wraps most aspects of data access. For example, a data source consists of actual data and its associated database management system (DBMS), the platform on which the DBMS exists, and the network used to access that platform. A data source is just a COM object that implements a bunch of interfaces, as shown in Table 33-1.

Interface	Required?	Implemented?
IDBInitialize	Mandatory	Yes
IDBCreateSession	Mandatory	Yes
IDBProperties	Mandatory	Yes
IPersist	Mandatory	Yes
IDBDataSourceAdmin	Optional	No
IDBInfo	Optional	No
IPersistFile	Optional	No
ISupportErrorInfo	Optional	No

Table 33-1.
Data source object interfaces requirements.

NOTE: Tables in this section were compiled from the Microsoft Visual Studio MSDN Online Help.

Here's a code snippet showing the code that is inserted by the ATL Object Wizard when you create a data source for an OLE DB provider:

```
class ATL_NO_VTABLE CAProviderSource :
    public CComObjectRootEx<CComSingleThreadModel>,
    public CComCoClass<CAProviderSource, &CLSID_AProvider>,
    public IDBCreateSessionImpl<CAProviderSource, CAProviderSession>,
    public IDBInitializeImpl<CAProviderSource>,
    public IDBPropertiesImpl<CAProviderSource>,
    public IPersistImpl<CAProviderSource>,
    public IInternalConnectionImpl<CAProviderSource> {
};
```

Notice that this is a normal COM class (with ATL's *IUnknown* implementation). The OLE DB data source object brings in implementations of the *IDBCreateSession*, *IDBInitialize*, *IDBProperties*, and *IPersist* interfaces through inheritance. Notice how the templates are specialized on the *CAProviderSource* and *CAProviderSession* classes. If you decide to add more functionality to your class, you can do so by inheriting from one of the OLE DB interface implementation classes.

■ **Command object** Providers that support building and executing queries expose a command object. Command objects specify, prepare, and execute a Database Manipulation Language (DML) query or Data Definition Language (DDL) definition and its associated properties. For example, the command object translates a SQL-type command into an operation specific to the data source. Compared to ODBC, the command corresponds to the general functionality of an ODBC statement in an unexecuted state. A single session can be associated with multiple commands. Table 33-2 shows the interfaces used in a command object.

Here's a code snippet showing the code inserted by the ATL Object Wizard to implement a command object when you create an OLE DB provider:

```
class ATL_NO_VTABLE CAProviderCommand :
    public CComObjectRootEx<CComSingleThreadModel>,
    public IAccessorImpl<CAProviderCommand>,
    public ICommandTextImpl<CAProviderCommand>,
    public ICommandPropertiesImpl<CAProviderCommand>,
    public IObjectWithSiteImpl<CAProviderCommand>,
```

```
        public IConvertTypeImpl<CAProviderCommand>,
        public IColumnsInfoImpl<CAProviderCommand> {
};
```

As with the data source, notice that this is just a regular COM class. This class brings in the required interfaces through inheritance. (For example, *IAccessor* comes in through the *IAccessorImpl* template.) A command object uses *IAccessor* to specify parameter bindings. Consumers call *IAccessor::CreateAccessor,* passing an array of *DBBINDING* structures. *DBBINDING* contains information on the column bindings (type, length, and so on). The provider receives the structures and determines how the data should be transferred and whether conversions are necessary.

The *ICommandText* interface provides a way to specify a text command. The *ICommandProperties* interface handles all of the command properties.

The command class is the heart of the data provider. Most of the action happens within this class.

Interface	Required?	Implemented?
IAccessor	Mandatory	Yes
IColumnsInfo	Mandatory	Yes
ICommand	Mandatory	Yes
ICommandProperties	Mandatory	Yes
ICommandText	Mandatory	Yes
IConvertType	Mandatory	Yes
IColumnsRowset	Optional	No
ICommandPrepare	Optional	No
ICommandWithParameters	Optional	No
ISupportErrorInfo	Optional	No

Table 33-2.
Command object interfaces requirements.

■ **Session object**   Session objects define the scope of a transaction and generate rowsets from the data source. Session objects also generate command objects. The command object executes commands on the rowset. For providers that support commands, the session acts as a command factory. Compared to ODBC, the session object and the data source object encapsulate the functionality of the

ODBC connection. Calling *IDBCreateSession::CreateSession* creates a session from the data source object. A single data source object can be associated with many sessions. Table 33-3 shows the interfaces found on a session object.

Interface	Required?	Implemented?
IGetDataSource	Mandatory	Yes
IOpenRowset	Mandatory	Yes
ISessionProperties	Mandatory	Yes
IDBCreateCommand	Optional	Yes
IDBSchemaRowset	Optional	Yes
IIndexDefinition	Optional	No
ISupportErrorInfo	Optional	No
ITableDefinition	Optional	No
ITransactionJoin	Optional	No
ITransactionLocal	Optional	No
ITransactionObject	Optional	No

Table 33-3.
Session object interfaces requirements.

Here's a code snippet showing the code inserted by the ATL Object Wizard to implement a session object when you create an OLE DB provider:

```
class ATL_NO_VTABLE CAProviderSession :
    public CComObjectRootEx<CComSingleThreadModel>,
    public IGetDataSourceImpl<CAProviderSession>,
    public IOpenRowsetImpl<CAProviderSession>,
    public ISessionPropertiesImpl<CAProviderSession>,
    public IObjectWithSiteSessionImpl<CAProviderSession>,
    public IDBSchemaRowsetImpl<CAProviderSession>,
    public IDBCreateCommandImpl<CAProviderSession, CAProviderCommand>
{
};
```

■ **Rowset object**   A rowset object represents tabular data. At the raw OLE DB level, rowsets are generated by calling *IOpenRowset::Open-Rowset* on the session. For providers that support commands, rowsets are used to represent the results of row-returning queries. In addition to *IOpenRowset::OpenRowset*, there are a number of other methods in OLE DB that return rowsets. For example, the schema functions return rowsets. Compared to ODBC, a rowset encapsulates the general functionality of an ODBC statement in the executed state. Single sessions can be associated with multiple rowsets. In addition, single command objects can be associated with multiple rowsets. Table 33-4 shows the interfaces associated with the rowset object.

Interface	Required?	Implemented?
IAccessor	Mandatory	Yes
IColumnsInfo	Mandatory	Yes
IConvertType	Mandatory	Yes
IRowset	Mandatory	Yes
IRowsetInfo	Mandatory	Yes
IColumnsRowset	Optional	No
IConnectionPointContainer	Optional	Yes, through ATL
IRowsetChange	Optional	No
IRowsetIdentity	Required for Level 0	Yes
IRowsetLocate	Optional	No
IRowsetResynch	Optional	No
IRowsetScroll	Optional	No
IRowsetUpdate	Optional	No
ISupportErrorInfo	Optional	No

Table 33-4.
Rowset object interfaces requirements.

Here's a code snippet showing the code inserted by the ATL Object Wizard to implement a rowset object when you create an OLE DB provider:

```
class CAProviderWindowsFile:
    public WIN32_FIND_DATA
{
public:
BEGIN_PROVIDER_COLUMN_MAP(CAProviderWindowsFile)
```

(continued)

```
        PROVIDER_COLUMN_ENTRY("FileAttributes", 1, dwFileAttributes)
        PROVIDER_COLUMN_ENTRY("FileSizeHigh", 2, nFileSizeHigh)
        PROVIDER_COLUMN_ENTRY("FileSizeLow", 3, nFileSizeLow)
        PROVIDER_COLUMN_ENTRY("FileName", 4, cFileName)
        PROVIDER_COLUMN_ENTRY("AltFileName", 5, cAlternateFileName)
    END_PROVIDER_COLUMN_MAP()
};

class CAProviderRowset :
public CRowsetImpl<CAProviderRowset,
                    CAProviderWindowsFile,
                    CAProviderCommand> {

}
```

The wizard-generated rowset object implements the *IAccessor, IRowset*, and *IRowsetInfo* interfaces, among others. *IAccessorImpl* binds both output columns. The *IRowset* interface fetches rows and data. The *IRowsetInfo* interface handles the rowset properties. The *CWindowsFile* class represents the user record class. The class generated by the Wizard is really just a placeholder. It doesn't do very much. When you decide on the column format of your data provider, this is the class you'll modify.

How the Provider Parts Work Together

The use for the first part of the architecture—the data source—should be obvious. Every provider must include a data source object. When a consumer application needs data, the consumer calls *CoCreateInstance* to create the data source object and start the provider. Within the provider, it's the data source object's job to create a session object using the *IDBCreateSession* interface. The consumer uses this interface to connect to the data source object. In comparing this to how ODBC works, the data source object is equivalent to ODBC's HENV and the session object is the equivalent of ODBC's HDBC.

The command object does most of the work. To make the data provider actually do something, you'll modify the command class's *Execute* function.

Like most COM-based protocols, the OLE DB protocol makes sense once you've examined it for a little while. Also, like most COM-based protocols, the OLE DB protocol involves a good amount of code to get going—code that could be easily implemented by some sort of framework. That's what the Data Consumer and Data Provider templates are all about. The rest of the chapter shows you what you need to do to create Data Consumers and Data Providers.

Creating an OLE DB Consumer

Creating an OLE DB consumer is pretty straightforward—most of the support comes through the ATL Object Wizard. You can see an example of a consumer in the ex33a folder on the companion CD. Here are the steps for creating a consumer using the ATL Object Wizard:

1. Create an application or a control to drive the data consumption. For example, you might want to create an ActiveX control.

2. While inside the IDE, use the ATL Object Wizard to insert a data consumer. Do this by either selecting New ATL Object from the Insert menu or by right-clicking on the project icon in ClassView and selecting New ATL Object from the context menu to start the ATL Object Wizard.

3. From the ATL Object Wizard, select the Data Access category of objects. Then select Consumer and click Next. This will cause the ATL Object Wizard Properties dialog, shown in Figure 33-1, to appear. There will be only one page in it, for naming the class and selecting the data source.

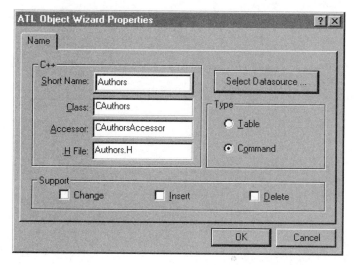

Figure 33-1.
The ATL Object Wizard Properties.

4. Click Select Datasource to configure the data consumer. Once you've picked out a data source, choose OK. The ATL Object Wizard will create an OLE DB Consumer template ready for you to use.

As an example, we took the BIBLIO.MDB database (a Microsoft Access database) that comes in the Visual Studio VB98 directory and made a data consumer out of it. The BIBLIO database includes the titles and the authors of various programming texts. Using the ATL Object Wizard to create the OLE DB Consumer template for the authors in the database yielded these classes:

```
// Authors.H : Declaration of the CAuthors class

#ifndef __AUTHORS_H_
#define __AUTHORS_H_

class CAuthorsAccessor
{
public:
    LONG m_AuID;
    TCHAR m_Author[51];
    SHORT m_YearBorn;

BEGIN_COLUMN_MAP(CAuthorsAccessor)
    COLUMN_ENTRY(1, m_AuID)
    COLUMN_ENTRY(2, m_Author)
    COLUMN_ENTRY(3, m_YearBorn)
END_COLUMN_MAP()

DEFINE_COMMAND(CAuthorsAccessor, _T("SELECT * FROM Authors"))
};

class CAuthors : public CCommand<CAccessor<CAuthorsAccessor> >
{
public:
    HRESULT Open()
    {
        HRESULT   hr;

        hr = OpenDataSource();
        if (FAILED(hr))
            return hr;

        return OpenRowset();
    }
    HRESULT OpenDataSource()
    {
        HRESULT     hr;
        CDataSource db;
        CDBPropSet  dbinit(DBPROPSET_DBINIT);

        dbinit.AddProperty(DBPROP_AUTH_CACHE_AUTHINFO, true);
        dbinit.AddProperty(DBPROP_AUTH_ENCRYPT_PASSWORD, false);
```

```
        dbinit.AddProperty(DBPROP_AUTH_MASK_PASSWORD, false);
        dbinit.AddProperty(DBPROP_AUTH_PASSWORD, OLESTR(""));
        dbinit.AddProperty(DBPROP_AUTH_PERSIST_ENCRYPTED, false);
        dbinit.AddProperty(DBPROP_AUTH_PERSIST_SENSITIVE_AUTHINFO,
                           false);
        dbinit.AddProperty(DBPROP_AUTH_USERID, OLESTR("Admin"));
        dbinit.AddProperty(DBPROP_INIT_DATASOURCE,
                           OLESTR("c:\\biblio.mdb"));
        dbinit.AddProperty(DBPROP_INIT_MODE, (long)16);
        dbinit.AddProperty(DBPROP_INIT_PROMPT, (short)4);
        dbinit.AddProperty(DBPROP_INIT_PROVIDERSTRING, OLESTR
                           (";COUNTRY=0;CP=1252;LANGID=0x0409"));
        dbinit.AddProperty(DBPROP_INIT_LCID, (long)1033);
        hr = db.Open(_T("Microsoft.Jet.OLEDB.3.51"), &dbinit);
        if (FAILED(hr))
            return hr;

        return m_session.Open(db);
    }
    HRESULT OpenRowset()
    {
        return CCommand<CAccessor<CAuthorsAccessor>
               >::Open(m_session, _T("Authors"));
    }
    Csession   m_session;
};

#endif // __AUTHORS_H_
```

The *CAuthorsAccessor* class defines the structure of the author record. Notice that the class includes an author ID field, a name field, and a field indicating when the author was born.

The *CAuthors* class represents the actual data consumer class that connects to the database. Notice that it's derived from *CCommand*. Remember that command objects represent a command (such as a SQL statement) and generate rowsets. The COLUMN_MAP represents data returned in the rowset. The PARAM_MAP represents parameter data for a command.

The column maps and the parameter maps represent the user's view of the accessor. As with many data structures in ATL and MFC, these maps are built up with macros. Here's how the maps work: when running against a database, the data that comes back is contained in a contiguous block of memory. OLE DB templates work with this block of memory to extract the data. The data members in the entries represent offsets into that block of memory. The entries in the maps filter out the data from the database. That way, you as a developer do not have to worry about doing anything funky like performing pointer arithmetic on the block to get information.

Using the OLE DB Consumer Code

Using the database consumer class is just about as easy as creating it. Here's how to take advantage of the database consumer class:

1. Declare an instance of *CAuthors* wherever you need to use it:

```
class CUseAuthors : public CDialog {
    CAuthors m_authors;
       ⋮
};
```

2. Open the Authors database by calling *Open* on the database consumer object:

```
CUseAuthors::OnInitDialog() {
    m_authors.Open();
}
```

3. Use member functions to navigate through and manipulate the database. Here's a short sampling of some of the things you can do:

```
CUseAuthors::OnNext() {
    m_authors.MoveNext();
}
CUseAuthors::OnFirst() {
    m_authors.MoveFirst();
}
CUseAuthors::OnLast() {
    m_authors.MoveLast();
}
CUseAuthors::OnInsert() {
    m_authors.Insert();
}
```

4. As you navigate through the database, the data ends up in the member variables. For example, if you want to find out the name of the next author in the database, the code would look like this:

```
m_authors.MoveNext();
m_strAuthorName = m_authors.m_Author;
```

As you can see, using the templates greatly simplifies getting the data out of the database. All you need to do is find the database, point the ATL Object Wizard there, and get the Wizard to generate your code. Then the accessor class has functions useful for moving around the database and fetching the data. The other half of the OLE DB Template equation is the data provider. Here's a rundown of how to work with providers.

Creating an OLE DB Provider

It's pretty obvious how OLE DB consumers are useful. You just ask a wizard to create a wrapper for you, and you get a fairly easy way to access the data in a database. However, it might be a bit less obvious why you'd want to create an OLE DB provider.

Why Write an OLE DB Provider?

Writing an OLE DB allows you to insert a layer between a client of some data and the actual data itself. Here are just a few reasons you might want to write a provider.

- Writing an OLE DB provider means clients don't necessarily touch the data directly. Therefore, you can add additional capabilities to your data, such as query processing.

- In some cases, writing an OLE DB provider gives you the opportunity to increase data access performance by controlling how the data is manipulated.

- Adding an OLE DB provider layer increases the potential audience of your data. For example, if you have a proprietary data format that can be accessed by only one programming language, you have a single point of failure. OLE DB providers give you a way to open that proprietary format to a wider variety of programmers, regardless of the programming language they use.

Writing an OLE DB Provider

Working with the OLE DB Providers is similar to working with the Consumers. The wizards do a lot of the work for you. You just need to know how to work with the generated classes. The steps for creating an OLE DB Provider are listed here.

1. The first step is to decide what you want the provider to do. Remember the philosophy behind OLE DB: it's all about providing a singular way to access multiple data sources. For example, you might want to write a provider that recursively enumerates the contents of a structured storage file. Or you might want a provider that sifts through e-mail folders and allows clients database-style access to your e-mail system. The possibilities are nearly endless.

2. Just as you did when writing a data consumer, use the ATL Object Wizard to create a provider. Just start the ATL Object Wizard from ClassView or from the Insert menu. Select the Data Access objects category, and choose Provider. The ATL Object Wizard will ask you to provide a name for your object and will allow you to modify the default names for the files it will create.

3. After you click OK, the ATL Object Wizard creates the code for a provider, including a data source, a rowset, and a session. In addition to these objects, a provider supports one or more properties, which are defined in property maps within the files created by the OLE DB Provider Template Wizard. When the Wizard creates the files, it inserts maps for the properties belonging to the OLE DB property group defined for the object or objects included in those files. For example, the header file containing the data source object also contains the property map for the DataSource properties. The session header file contains the property map for the Session properties. Finally, the rowset and command objects reside in a single header file, which includes properties for the command object.

For example, here's what the ATL Object Wizard produces for an OLE DB provider named AProvider. First the ATL Object Wizard creates a data source object, which lives in a file named AProviderDS.H:

```
class ATL_NO_VTABLE CAProviderSource :
    public CComObjectRootEx<CComSingleThreadModel>,
    public CComCoClass<CAProviderSource, &CLSID_AProvider>,
    public IDBCreateSessionImpl<CAProviderSource, CAProviderSession>,
    public IDBInitializeImpl<CAProviderSource>,
    public IDBPropertiesImpl<CAProviderSource>,
    public IPersistImpl<CAProviderSource>,
    public IInternalConnectionImpl<CAProviderSource>
{
public:
    HRESULT FinalConstruct()
    {
        return FInit();
    }
DECLARE_REGISTRY_RESOURCEID(IDR_APROVIDER)
BEGIN_PROPSET_MAP(CAProviderSource)
    BEGIN_PROPERTY_SET(DBPROPSET_DATASOURCEINFO)
        PROPERTY_INFO_ENTRY(ACTIVESESSIONS)
        PROPERTY_INFO_ENTRY(DATASOURCEREADONLY)
        PROPERTY_INFO_ENTRY(BYREFACCESSORS)
        PROPERTY_INFO_ENTRY(OUTPUTPARAMETERAVAILABILITY)
```

```
        PROPERTY_INFO_ENTRY(PROVIDEROLEDBVER)
        PROPERTY_INFO_ENTRY(DSOTHREADMODEL)
        PROPERTY_INFO_ENTRY(SUPPORTEDTXNISOLEVELS)
        PROPERTY_INFO_ENTRY(USERNAME)
    END_PROPERTY_SET(DBPROPSET_DATASOURCEINFO)
    BEGIN_PROPERTY_SET(DBPROPSET_DBINIT)
        PROPERTY_INFO_ENTRY(AUTH_PASSWORD)
        PROPERTY_INFO_ENTRY(AUTH_PERSIST_SENSITIVE_AUTHINFO)
        PROPERTY_INFO_ENTRY(AUTH_USERID)
        PROPERTY_INFO_ENTRY(INIT_DATASOURCE)
        PROPERTY_INFO_ENTRY(INIT_HWND)
        PROPERTY_INFO_ENTRY(INIT_LCID)
        PROPERTY_INFO_ENTRY(INIT_LOCATION)
        PROPERTY_INFO_ENTRY(INIT_MODE)
        PROPERTY_INFO_ENTRY(INIT_PROMPT)
        PROPERTY_INFO_ENTRY(INIT_PROVIDERSTRING)
        PROPERTY_INFO_ENTRY(INIT_TIMEOUT)
    END_PROPERTY_SET(DBPROPSET_DBINIT)
    CHAIN_PROPERTY_SET(CAProviderCommand)
END_PROPSET_MAP()
BEGIN_COM_MAP(CAProviderSource)
    COM_INTERFACE_ENTRY(IDBCreateSession)
    COM_INTERFACE_ENTRY(IDBInitialize)
    COM_INTERFACE_ENTRY(IDBProperties)
    COM_INTERFACE_ENTRY(IPersist)
    COM_INTERFACE_ENTRY(IInternalConnection)
END_COM_MAP()
public:
};
```

In addition to the data object, the ATL Object Wizard produces a command object and a rowset that both live within AProviderRS.H:

```
class ATL_NO_VTABLE CAProviderCommand :
    public CComObjectRootEx<CComSingleThreadModel>,
    public IAccessorImpl<CAProviderCommand>,
    public ICommandTextImpl<CAProviderCommand>,
    public ICommandPropertiesImpl<CAProviderCommand>,
    public IObjectWithSiteImpl<CAProviderCommand>,
    public IConvertTypeImpl<CAProviderCommand>,
    public IColumnsInfoImpl<CAProviderCommand>
{
public:
BEGIN_COM_MAP(CAProviderCommand)
    COM_INTERFACE_ENTRY(ICommand)
    COM_INTERFACE_ENTRY(IObjectWithSite)
    COM_INTERFACE_ENTRY(IAccessor)
```

(continued)

973

```
        COM_INTERFACE_ENTRY(ICommandProperties)
        COM_INTERFACE_ENTRY2(ICommandText, ICommand)
        COM_INTERFACE_ENTRY(IColumnsInfo)
        COM_INTERFACE_ENTRY(IConvertType)
    END_COM_MAP()
    // ICommand
    public:
        HRESULT FinalConstruct()
        {
            HRESULT hr = CConvertHelper::FinalConstruct();
            if (FAILED (hr))
                return hr;
            hr = IAccessorImpl<CAProviderCommand>::FinalConstruct();
            if (FAILED(hr))
                return hr;
            return CUtlProps<CAProviderCommand>::FInit();
        }
        void FinalRelease()
        {
            IAccessorImpl<CAProviderCommand>::FinalRelease();
        }
        HRESULT WINAPI Execute(IUnknown * pUnkOuter,
                               REFIID riid, DBPARAMS * pParams,
                               LONG * pcRowsAffected,
                               IUnknown ** ppRowset);
        static ATLCOLUMNINFO* GetColumnInfo(CAProviderCommand* pv,
                                            ULONG* pcInfo)

        {
            return CAProviderWindowsFile::GetColumnInfo(pv,pcInfo);
        }
    BEGIN_PROPSET_MAP(CAProviderCommand)
        BEGIN_PROPERTY_SET(DBPROPSET_ROWSET)
            PROPERTY_INFO_ENTRY(IAccessor)
            PROPERTY_INFO_ENTRY(IColumnsInfo)
            PROPERTY_INFO_ENTRY(IConvertType)
            PROPERTY_INFO_ENTRY(IRowset)
            PROPERTY_INFO_ENTRY(IRowsetIdentity)
            PROPERTY_INFO_ENTRY(IRowsetInfo)
            PROPERTY_INFO_ENTRY(IRowsetLocate)
            PROPERTY_INFO_ENTRY(BOOKMARKS)
            PROPERTY_INFO_ENTRY(BOOKMARKSKIPPED)
            PROPERTY_INFO_ENTRY(BOOKMARKTYPE)
            PROPERTY_INFO_ENTRY(CANFETCHBACKWARDS)
            PROPERTY_INFO_ENTRY(CANHOLDROWS)
            PROPERTY_INFO_ENTRY(CANSCROLLBACKWARDS)
            PROPERTY_INFO_ENTRY(LITERALBOOKMARKS)
            PROPERTY_INFO_ENTRY(ORDEREDBOOKMARKS)
```

```
        END_PROPERTY_SET(DBPROPSET_ROWSET)
END_PROPSET_MAP()
};

class RAProviderRowset : public CRowsetImpl<RAProviderRowset,
                                            CWindowsFile,
                                            CAProviderCommand>
{
public:
    HRESULT Execute(DBPARAMS * pParams, LONG* pcRowsAffected)
    {
        USES_CONVERSION;
        BOOL bFound = FALSE;
        HANDLE hFile;
        LPTSTR  szDir = (m_strCommandText == _T("")) ? _T("*.*") :
                        OLE2T(m_strCommandText);
        CAProviderWindowsFile wf;
        hFile = FindFirstFile(szDir, &wf);
        if (hFile == INVALID_HANDLE_VALUE)
            return DB_E_ERRORSINCOMMAND;
        LONG cFiles = 1;
        BOOL bMoreFiles = TRUE;
        while (bMoreFiles)
        {
            if (!m_rgRowData.Add(wf))
                return E_OUTOFMEMORY;
            bMoreFiles = FindNextFile(hFile, &wf);
            cFiles++;
        }
        FindClose(hFile);
        if (pcRowsAffected != NULL)
            *pcRowsAffected = cFiles;
        return S_OK;
    }
};
```

The ATL Object Wizard produces a session object in a file named AProviderSess.H as shown in this code:

```
class ATL_NO_VTABLE CAProviderSession :
    public CComObjectRootEx<CComSingleThreadModel>,
    public IGetDataSourceImpl<CAProviderSession>,
    public IOpenRowsetImpl<CAProviderSession>,
    public ISessionPropertiesImpl<CAProviderSession>,
    public IObjectWithSiteSessionImpl<CAProviderSession>,
    public IDBSchemaRowsetImpl<CAProviderSession>,
```

(continued)

975

```
        public IDBCreateCommandImpl<CAProviderSession, CAProviderCommand>
{
public:
    CAProviderSession()
    {
    }
    HRESULT FinalConstruct()
    {
        return FInit();
    }
    STDMETHOD(OpenRowset)(IUnknown *pUnk, DBID *pTID,
                          DBID *pInID, REFIID riid,
                          ULONG cSets, DBPROPSET rgSets[],
                          IUnknown **ppRowset)
    {
        CAProviderRowset* pRowset;
        return CreateRowset(pUnk, pTID, pInID, riid,
                            cSets, rgSets, ppRowset, pRowset);
    }
BEGIN_PROPSET_MAP(CAProviderSession)
    BEGIN_PROPERTY_SET(DBPROPSET_SESSION)
        PROPERTY_INFO_ENTRY(SESS_AUTOCOMMITISOLEVELS)
    END_PROPERTY_SET(DBPROPSET_SESSION)
END_PROPSET_MAP()
BEGIN_COM_MAP(CAProviderSession)
    COM_INTERFACE_ENTRY(IGetDataSource)
    COM_INTERFACE_ENTRY(IOpenRowset)
    COM_INTERFACE_ENTRY(ISessionProperties)
    COM_INTERFACE_ENTRY(IObjectWithSite)
    COM_INTERFACE_ENTRY(IDBCreateCommand)
    COM_INTERFACE_ENTRY(IDBSchemaRowset)
END_COM_MAP()
BEGIN_SCHEMA_MAP(CAProviderSession)
    SCHEMA_ENTRY(DBSCHEMA_TABLES, CAProviderSessionTRSchemaRowset)
    SCHEMA_ENTRY(DBSCHEMA_COLUMNS, CAProviderSessionColSchemaRowset)
    SCHEMA_ENTRY(DBSCHEMA_PROVIDER_TYPES, CAProviderSessionPTSchemaRowset)
END_SCHEMA_MAP()
};
class CAProviderSessionTRSchemaRowset :
    public CRowsetImpl< CAProviderSessionTRSchemaRowset,
                        CTABLESRow, CAProviderSession>
{
public:
    HRESULT Execute(LONG* pcRowsAffected, ULONG, const VARIANT*)
    {
        USES_CONVERSION;
        CAProviderWindowsFile wf;
        CTABLESRow trData;
```

```
            lstrcpyW(trData.m_szType, OLESTR("TABLE"));
            lstrcpyW(trData.m_szDesc, OLESTR("The Directory Table"));
            HANDLE hFile = INVALID_HANDLE_VALUE;
            TCHAR szDir[MAX_PATH + 1];
            DWORD cbCurDir = GetCurrentDirectory(MAX_PATH, szDir);
            lstrcat(szDir, _T("\\*.*"));
            hFile = FindFirstFile(szDir, &wf);
            if (hFile == INVALID_HANDLE_VALUE)
                return E_FAIL; // User doesn't have a c:\ drive
            FindClose(hFile);
            lstrcpynW(trData.m_szTable, T2OLE(szDir),
                    SIZEOF_MEMBER(CTABLESRow, m_szTable));
            if (!m_rgRowData.Add(trData))
                return E_OUTOFMEMORY;
            *pcRowsAffected = 1;
            return S_OK;
        }
};
class CAProviderSessionColSchemaRowset :
    public CRowsetImpl< CAProviderSessionColSchemaRowset,
                        CCOLUMNSRow, CAProviderSession>
{
public:
    HRESULT Execute(LONG* pcRowsAffected, ULONG, const VARIANT*)
    {
        USES_CONVERSION;
        CAProviderWindowsFile wf;
        HANDLE hFile = INVALID_HANDLE_VALUE;
            TCHAR szDir[MAX_PATH + 1];
        DWORD cbCurDir = GetCurrentDirectory(MAX_PATH, szDir);
        lstrcat(szDir, _T("\\*.*"));
        hFile = FindFirstFile(szDir, &wf);
        if (hFile == INVALID_HANDLE_VALUE)
            return E_FAIL; // User doesn't have a c:\ drive
        FindClose(hFile);// szDir has got the tablename
        DBID dbid;
        memset(&dbid, 0, sizeof(DBID));
        dbid.uName.pwszName = T2OLE(szDir);
        dbid.eKind = DBKIND_NAME;
        return InitFromRowset <RowsetArrayType> (m_rgRowData,
                                                 &dbid,
                                                 NULL,
                                                 m_spUnkSite,
                                                 pcRowsAffected);
    }
};
```

(continued)

```
class CAProviderSessionPTSchemaRowset :
    public CRowsetImpl<CAProviderSessionPTSchemaRowset,
                       CPROVIDER_TYPERow, CAProviderSession>
{
public:
    HRESULT Execute(LONG* pcRowsAffected, ULONG, const VARIANT*)
    {
        return S_OK;
    }
};
```

Modifying the Provider Code

As with most Wizard-generated code, the OLE DB Provider code generated
by the ATL Object Wizard is just boilerplate code—it doesn't do very much.
You need to take several steps to turn this boilerplate code into a real OLE DB
Provider. The two critical pieces that need to be added to a provider are the user
record and code to manage a data set and to set the data up as rows and columns.

■ **The user record** The ATL Object Wizard provides a default user
record named CAProviderWindowsFile. You don't really want to use
this user record. You'll probably scrap it and replace it with something useful in your domain. As a simple example, imagine you want
to write an OLE DB Provider that enumerates the compound file.
Your user record might look like this:

```
struct CStgInfo {
BEGIN_PROVIDER_COLUMN_MAP(CStgInfo)
    PROVIDER_COLUMN_ENTRY("StgName", 1, szName)
    PROVIDER_COLUMN_ENTRY("Size", 2, cbSizeLow)
    PROVIDER_COLUMN_ENTRY("Size", 2, cbSizeHigh)

END_PROVIDER_COLUMN_MAP()

    OLECHAR szName[256];
    long cbSizeLow;
    long cbSizeHigh;
};
```

This structure contains the data fields for the name and size of
the substorage. The provider column map macros map the data into
columns. You could actually derive the structure from a *STATSTG*
structure (used to enumerate structured storages). You just need to
add entries to the provider column map to handle the members.

■ **Code to open the data set**   The other important addition to the
provider is the code necessary to open the data set. This happens in
the rowset's *Execute* function. There are many different kinds of
functionality that can go on here. For example, if you want to enumerate the top-level substorages in a compound file, you'd first open
the storage and then enumerate the contents as shown in the following code snippet:

```
class RStgInfoProviderRowset :
    public CRowsetImpl<RStgInfoProviderRowset,
                       CStgInfo,
                       CStgInfoProviderCommand>
{
public:
    HRESULT Execute(DBPARAMS * pParams, LONG* pcRowsAffected)
    {
        USES_CONVERSION;
        LPTSTR  szFile =
                m_strCommandText == _T("")) ? _T("") :
                    OLE2T(m_strCommandText);

        IStorage* pStg = NULL;

        HRESULT hr = StgOpenStorage(szFile, NULL,
                                    STGM_READ|STGM_SHARE_EXCLUSIVE,
                                    NULL, NULL, &pStg);

        if(FAILED(hr))
            return DB_E_ERRORSINCOMMAND;

        LONG cStgs = 0;

        IEnumSTATSTG* pEnumSTATSTG;

        hr = pStg->EnumElements(0, 0, 0, &pEnumSTATSTG);

        if(pEnumSTATSTG) {

            STATSTG rgSTATSTG[100];
            ULONG nFetched;

            hr = pEnumSTATSTG->Next(100, rgSTATSTG, &nFetched);

            for(ULONG i = 0; i < nFetched; i++) {
                CStgInfo stgInfo;
```

(continued)

```
                         stgInfo.cbSizeLow = rgSTATSTG[i].cbSize.LowPart;
                         stgInfo.cbSizeHigh = rgSTATSTG[i].cbSize.HighPart;

                         wcsncpy(stgInfo.szName,
                                 rgSTATSTG[i].pwcsName,
                                 255);

                         CoTaskMemFree(rgSTATSTG[i].pwcsName);

                         if (!m_rgRowData.Add(stgInfo))
                             return E_OUTOFMEMORY;
                         cStgs++;
                     }
                     pEnumSTATSTG->Release();
                 }

             if(pStg)
                 pStg->Release();

             if (pcRowsAffected != NULL)
                 *pcRowsAffected = cStgs;
             return S_OK;
         }
     }
```

When some client code tries to open the OLE DB data provider, the call ends up inside this function. This function simply opens the structured storage file passed in as the command text and uses the standard structured storage enumerator to find the top-level substorages. Then the *Execute* function stores the name of the substorage and the size of the substorage in an array. The OLE DB provider uses this array to fulfill requests for the column data.

Enhancing the Provider

Of course, there's a lot you can do to beef up this OLE DB provider. We've barely scratched the surface of what you can do with a provider. When the ATL Object Wizard pumps out the default provider, it's a read-only provider. That is, users cannot change the contents of the data. In addition, the OLE DB templates provide support for locating rowsets and setting bookmarks. In most cases, enhancing the provider is a matter of tacking on implementations of COM interfaces provided by the OLE DB templates.

Conclusion

With so many disparate data sources available today, the only way you can hope to manage access to that data is through some sort of homogeneous mechanism such as OLE DB. The high-level OLE DB architecture is divided into two parts: consumers and providers. Consumers use the data that is made available through providers.

As with most other COM-based architectures, OLE DB involves developers in the task of implementing a good many interfaces—a number of which are boilerplate in nature. The OLE DB Templates available through Visual C++ make creating OLE DB consumers and providers much easier.

You can create a simple consumer by pointing the ATL Object Wizard at a data source when you generate a consumer object. The ATL Object Wizard will examine the data source and create the client-side proxy to the database. From there, you can use the standard navigation functions available through the OLE DB Consumer Templates.

Writing a provider is somewhat more involved (if you want the provider to do anything useful). While the wizards give you a good start, they generate only a simple provider that enumerates the files in a directory. However, the Provider Templates contain a full complement of OLE DB support. With this support, you can create OLE DB providers that implement rowset location strategies, data reading and writing, and bookmarking.

PART VI

PROGRAMMING FOR THE INTERNET

CHAPTER THIRTY-FOUR

TCP/IP, Winsock, and WinInet

As a C++ programmer, you're going to be asked to do more than create Web pages. You'll be the one who makes the Internet reach its true potential and who creates distributed applications that haven't even been imagined yet. To be successful, you'll have to understand how the Internet works and how to write programs that can access other computers on the Internet.

In this section, you'll start with a primer on the Transmission Control Protocol/Internet Protocol (TCP/IP) that's used throughout the Internet, and then you'll move up one level to see the workings of HyperText Transport Protocol (HTTP). Then it's time to get something running. You'll assemble your own intranet (a local version of the Internet) and study an HTTP client–server program based on Winsock, the fundamental API for TCP/IP. Finally you'll move on to WinInet, which is a higher level API than Winsock and part of Microsoft's ActiveX technology.

To COM or Not to COM

Surely you've read about ActiveX Controls for the Internet. You've probably encountered concepts such as composite monikers and anti-monikers, which are part of the Microsoft Component Object Model (COM). If you were overwhelmed, don't worry—it's possible to program for the Internet without COM, and that's a good place to start. This chapter and the next chapter are mostly COM-free. In Chapter 36, you'll be writing a COM-based ActiveX document server, but MFC effectively hides the COM details so you can concentrate on Winsock and WinInet programming. It's not that ActiveX controls aren't important, but we can't do them justice in this book. We'll defer to Adam Denning's book on this subject, *ActiveX Controls Inside Out* (Microsoft Press, 1997). Your study of this book's COM material and Internet material will prepare you well for Adam's book.

Internet Primer

You can't write a good Winsock program without understanding the concept of a <u>socket</u>, which is used to send and receive packets of data across the network. To fully understand sockets, you need a thorough knowledge of the underlying Internet protocols. This section contains a concentrated dose of Internet theory. It should be enough to get you going, but you might want to refer to one of the TCP/IP textbooks if you want more theory.

Network Protocols—Layering

All networks use <u>layering</u> for their transmission protocols, and the collection of layers is often called a <u>stack</u>. The application program talks to the top layer, and the bottom layer talks to the network. Figure 34-1 shows you the stack for a local area network (LAN) running TCP/IP. Each layer is logically connected to the corresponding layer at the other end of the communications channel. The <u>server</u> program, as shown at the right in Figure 34-1, continuously listens on one end of the channel, while the <u>client</u> program, as shown on the left, periodically connects with the server to exchange data. Think of the server as an HTTP-based World Wide Web server, and think of the client as a browser program running on your computer.

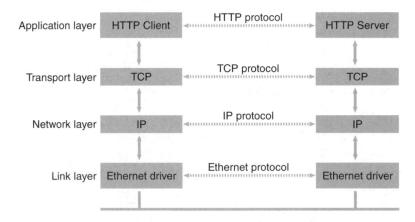

Figure 34-1.
The stack for a LAN running TCP/IP.

The Internet Protocol

The Internet Protocol (IP) layer is the best place to start in your quest to understand TCP/IP. The IP protocol defines packets called <u>datagrams</u> that are fundamental units of Internet communication. These packets, typically less than

1000 bytes in length, go bouncing all over the world when you open a Web page, download a file, or send e-mail. Figure 34-2 shows a simplified layout of an IP datagram.

Notice that the IP datagram contains 32-bit addresses for both the source and destination computers. These IP addresses uniquely identify computers on the Internet and are used by routers (specialized computers that act like telephone switches) to direct the individual datagrams to their destinations. The routers don't care about what's inside the datagrams—they're only interested in that datagram's destination address and total length. Their job is to resend the datagram as quickly as possible.

The IP layer doesn't tell the sending program whether a datagram has successfully reached its destination. That's a job for the next layer up the stack. The receiving program can look only at the checksum to determine whether the IP datagram header was corrupted.

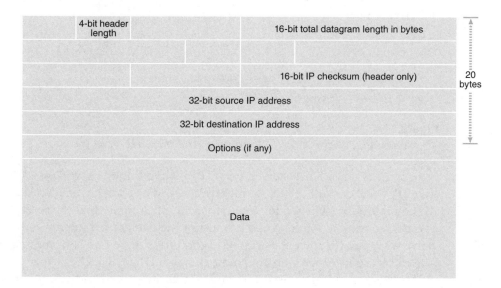

Figure 34-2.
A simple IP datagram layout.

The User Datagram Protocol

The TCP/IP protocol should really be called TCP/UDP/IP because it includes the User Datagram Protocol (UDP), which is a peer of TCP. All IP-based transport protocols store their own headers and data inside the IP data block. First let's look at the UDP layout in Figure 34-3 on the next page.

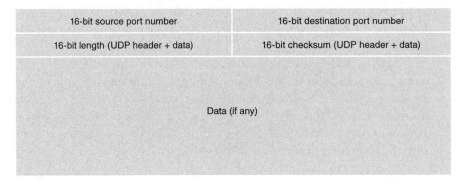

Figure 34-3.
A simple UDP layout.

A complete UDP/IP datagram is shown in Figure 34-4.

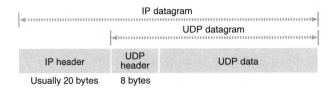

Figure 34-4.
The relationship between the IP datagram and the UDP datagram.

UDP is only a small step up from IP, but applications never use IP directly. Like IP, UDP doesn't tell the sender when the datagram has arrived. That's up to the application. The sender could, for example, require that the receiver send a response, and the sender could retransmit the datagram if the response didn't arrive within, say, 20 seconds. UDP is good for simple one-shot messages and is used by the Internet Domain Name System (DNS), which is explained later in this chapter. (UDP is used for transmitting live audio and video, for which some lost or out-of-sequence data is not a big problem.)

Figure 34-3 shows that the UDP header <u>does</u> convey some additional information—namely the source and destination <u>port</u> <u>numbers</u>. The application programs on each end use these 16-bit numbers. For example, a client program might send a datagram addressed to port 1700 on the server. The server program is listening for any datagram that includes 1700 in its destination port number, and when the server finds one, it can respond by sending another datagram back to the client, which is listening for a datagram that includes 1701 in its destination port number.

IP Address Format—Network Byte Order

You know that IP addresses are 32-bits long. You might think that 2^{32} (more than 4 billion) uniquely addressed computers could exist on the Internet, but that's not true. Part of the address identifies the LAN on which the host computer is located, and part of it identifies the host computer within the network. Most IP addresses are Class C addresses, which are formatted as shown in Figure 34-5.

Figure 34-5.
The layout of a Class C IP address.

This means that slightly more than 2 million networks can exist, and each of those networks can have 2^8 (256) addressable host computers. The Class A and Class B IP addresses, which allow more host computers on a network, are all used up.

> NOTE: The Internet "powers-that-be" have recognized the shortage of IP addresses, so they have proposed a new standard, the IP Next Generation (IPng) protocol. IPng defines a new IP datagram format that uses 128-bit addresses instead of 32-bit addresses. With IPng, you'll be able, for example, to assign a unique Internet address to each light switch in your house, so you can switch off your bedroom light from your portable computer from anywhere in the world. IPng implementation doesn't yet have a schedule.

By convention, IP addresses are written in dotted-decimal format. The four parts of the address refer to the individual byte values. An example of a Class C IP address is 194.128.198.201. In a computer with an Intel CPU, the address bytes are stored low-order-to-the-left, in so-called little-endian order. In most other computers, including the UNIX machines that first supported the Internet, bytes are stored high-order-to-the-left, in big-endian order. Because the Internet imposes a machine-independent standard for data interchange, all multibyte numbers must be transmitted in big-endian order. This means that programs running on Intel-based machines must convert between network byte order (big-endian) and host byte order (little-endian). This rule applies to 2-byte port numbers as well as to 4-byte IP addresses.

The Transmission Control Protocol

You've learned about the limitations of UDP. What you really need is a protocol that supports error-free transmission of large blocks of data. Obviously, you want the receiving program to be able to reassemble the bytes in the exact sequence in which they are transmitted, even though the individual datagrams might arrive in the wrong sequence. TCP is that protocol, and it's the principal transport protocol for all Internet applications, including HTTP and File Transfer Protocol (FTP). Figure 34-6 shows the layout of a TCP <u>segment</u>. (It's not called a datagram.) The TCP segment fits inside an IP datagram, as shown in Figure 34-7.

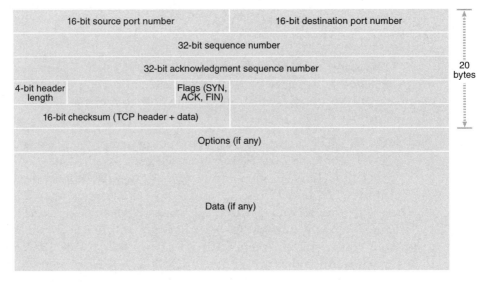

Figure 34-6.
A simple layout of a TCP segment.

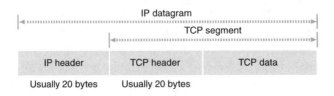

Figure 34-7.
The relationship between an IP datagram and a TCP segment.

The TCP protocol establishes a full-duplex, point-to-point connection between two computers, and a program at each end of this connection uses its own port. The combination of an IP address and a port number is called a socket. The connection is first established with a three-way handshake. The initiating program sends a segment with the *SYN* flag set, the responding program sends a segment with both the *SYN* and *ACK* flags set, and then the initiating program sends a segment with the *ACK* flag set.

After the connection is established, each program can send a stream of bytes to the other program. TCP uses the sequence number fields together with *ACK* flags to control this flow of bytes. The sending program doesn't wait for each segment to be acknowledged but instead sends a number of segments together and then waits for the first acknowledgment. If the receiving program has data to send back to the sending program, it can piggyback its acknowledgment and outbound data together in the same segments.

The sending program's sequence numbers are not segment indexes but rather indexes into the byte stream. The receiving program sends back the sequence numbers (in the acknowledgment number field) to the sending program, thereby ensuring that all bytes are received and assembled in sequence. The sending program resends unacknowledged segments.

Each program closes its end of the TCP connection by sending a segment with the *FIN* flag set, which must be acknowledged by the program on the other end. A program can no longer receive bytes on a connection that has been closed by the program on the other end.

Don't worry about the complexity of the TCP protocol. The Winsock and WinInet APIs hide most of the details, so you don't have to worry about *ACK* flags and sequence numbers. Your program calls a function to transmit a block of data, and Windows takes care of splitting the block into segments and stuffing them inside IP datagrams. Windows also takes care of delivering the bytes on the receiving end, but that gets tricky, as you'll see later in this chapter.

The Domain Name System

When you surf the Web, you don't use IP addresses. Instead, you use human-friendly names like *microsoft.com* or *www.cnn.com*. A significant portion of Internet resources is consumed when host names (such as *microsoft.com*) are translated into IP addresses that TCP/IP can use. A distributed network of name server (domain server) computers performs this translation by processing DNS queries. The entire Internet namespace is organized into domains, starting with an unnamed root domain. Under the root is a series of top-level domains such as *com, edu, gov, and org.*

NOTE: Do not confuse Internet domains with Microsoft Windows NT domains. The latter are logical groups of networked computers that share a common security database.

Servers and Domain Names

Let's look at the server end first. Suppose a company named SlowSoft has two host computers connected to the Internet, one for World Wide Web (WWW) service and the other for FTP service. By convention, these host computers are named *www.slowsoft.com* and *ftp.slowsoft.com*, respectively, and both are members of the second-level domain slowsoft, which SlowSoft has registered with an organization called InterNIC. (See *http://ds.internic.net.*)

Now SlowSoft must designate two (or more) host computers as its name servers. The name servers for the *com* domain each have a database entry for the *slowsoft* domain, and that entry contains the names and IP addresses of SlowSoft's two name servers. Each of the two *slowsoft* name servers has database entries for both of SlowSoft's host computers. These servers might also have database entries for hosts in other domains, and they might have entries for name servers in third-level domains. Thus, if a name server can't provide a host's IP address directly, it can redirect the query to a lower-level name server. Figure 34-8 illustrates SlowSoft's domain configuration.

NOTE: A top-level name server runs on its own host computer. InterNIC manages (at last count) nine computers that serve the root domain and top-level domains. Lower-level name servers could be programs running on host computers anywhere on the Net. SlowSoft's Internet service provider (ISP), ExpensiveNet, can furnish one of SlowSoft's name servers. If the ISP is running Windows NT Server, the name server is usually the DNS program that comes bundled with the operating system. That name server might be designated *ns1.expensivenet.com.*

Clients and Domain Names

Now for the client side. A user types *http://www.slowsoft.com* in the browser. (The *http://* prefix tells the browser to use the HTTP protocol when it eventually finds the host computer.) The browser must then resolve *www.slowsoft.com* into an IP address, so it uses TCP/IP to send a DNS query to the default gateway IP address for which TCP/IP is configured. This default gateway address identifies a local name server, which might have the needed host IP address in its cache. If not, the local name server relays the DNS query up to one of the root name servers. The root server looks up *slowsoft* in its database and sends the query back down to one of SlowSoft's designated name servers. In the process, the IP address for *www.slowsoft.com* will be cached for later use if it was not cached already. If you want to go the other way, name servers are also capable of converting an IP address to a name.

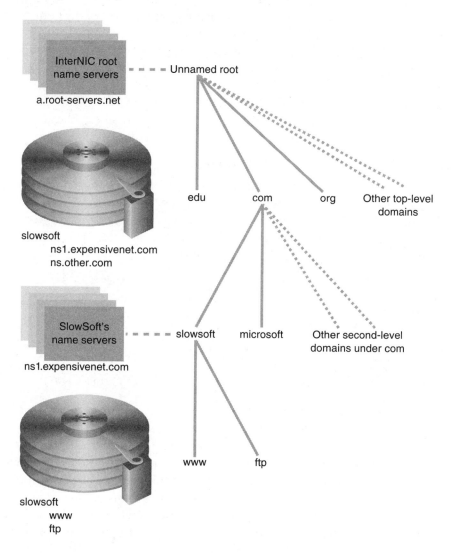

Figure 34-8.
SlowSoft's domain configuration.

HTTP Basics

You're going to be doing some Winsock programming soon, but just sending raw byte streams back and forth isn't very interesting. You need to use a higher-level protocol in order to be compatible with existing Internet servers and browsers. HTTP is a good place to start because it's the protocol of the popular World Wide Web and it's relatively simple.

HTTP is built on TCP, and this is the way it works: First a server program <u>listens</u> on port 80. Then some client program (typically a browser) <u>connects</u> to the server (*www.slowsoft.com*, in this case) after receiving the server's IP address from a name server. Using its own port number, the client sets up a two-way TCP connection to the server. As soon as the connection is established, the client sends a <u>request</u> to the server, which might look like this:

```
GET /customers/newproducts.html HTTP/1.0
```

The server identifies the request as a GET, the most common type, and it concludes that the client wants a file named newproducts.html that's located in a server directory known as /customers (which might or might not be \customers on the server's hard disk). Immediately following are <u>request</u> <u>headers</u>, which mostly describe the client's capabilities.

```
Accept: image/gif, image/x-xbitmap, image/jpeg, image/pjpeg, image/x-
jg, */*
Accept-Language: en
UA-pixels: 1024x768
UA-color: color8
UA-OS: Windows NT
UA-CPU: x86
User-Agent: Mozilla/2.0 (compatible; MSIE 3.0; AK; Windows NT)
Host: www.slowsoft.com
Connection: Keep-Alive
If-Modified-Since: Wed, 26 Mar 1997 20:23:04 GMT
(blank line)
```

The If-Modified-Since header tells the server not to bother to transmit newproducts.html unless the file has been modified since March 26, 1997. This implies that the browser already has a dated copy of this file stored in its cache. The blank line at the end of the request is crucial; it provides the only way for the server to tell that it is time to stop receiving and start transmitting, and that's because the TCP connection stays open.

Now the server springs into action. It sends newproducts.html, but first it sends an OK response:

```
HTTP/1.0 200 OK
```

immediately followed by some <u>response</u> <u>header</u> lines:

```
Server: Microsoft-IIS/2.0
Date: Thu, 03 Mar 1997 17:33:12 GMT
Content-Type: text/html
Accept-Ranges: bytes
Last-Modified: Wed, Mar 26 1997 20:23:04 GMT
Content-Length: 407
(blank line)
```

The contents of newproducts.html immediately follow the blank line:

```
<html>
<head><title>SlowSoft's New Products</title></head>
<body><body background="/images/clouds.jpg">
<h1><center>Welcome to SlowSoft's New Products List
</center></h1><p>
Unfortunately, budget constraints have prevented SlowSoft from
 introducing any new products this year. We suggest you keep
 enjoying the old products.<p>
<a href="default.htm">SlowSoft's Home Page</a><p>
</body>
</html>
```

You're looking at elementary HyperText Markup Language (HTML) code here, and the resulting Web page won't win any prizes. We won't go into details because dozens of HTML books are already available. From these books, you'll learn that HTML <u>tags</u> are contained in angle brackets and that there's often an "end" tag (with a / character) for every "start" tag. Some tags, such as <a> (hypertext <u>a</u>nchor), have <u>attributes</u>. In the example above, the line

```
<a href="default.htm">SlowSoft's Home Page</a><p>
```

creates a <u>link</u> to another HTML file. The user clicks on "SlowSoft's Home Page," and the browser requests default.htm from the original server.

Actually, newproducts.html references two server files, default.htm and /images/clouds.jpg. The clouds.jpg file is a JPEG file that contains a background picture for the page. The browser downloads each of these files as a separate transaction, establishing and closing a separate TCP connection each time. The server just dishes out files to any client that asks for them. In this case, the server doesn't know or care whether the same client requested newproducts.html and clouds.jpg. To the server, clients are simply IP addresses and port numbers. In fact, the port number is different for each request from a client. For example, if ten of your company's programmers are surfing the Web via your company's proxy server (more on proxy servers later), the server sees the same IP address for each client.

NOTE: Web pages use two graphics formats, <u>GIF</u> and <u>JPEG</u>. GIF files are compressed images that retain all the detail of the original uncompressed image but are usually limited to 256 colors. They support transparent regions and animation. JPEG files are smaller, but they don't carry all the detail of the original file. GIF files are often used for small images such as buttons, and JPEG files are often used for photographic images for which detail is not critical. Visual C++ can read, write, and convert both GIF and JPEG files, but the Win32 API cannot handle these formats unless you supply a special compression/decompression module.

The HTTP standard includes a PUT request type that enables a client program to upload a file to the server. Client programs and server programs seldom implement PUT.

FTP Basics

The File Transfer Protocol handles the uploading and downloading of server files plus directory navigation and browsing. A Windows command-line program called ftp (it doesn't work through a Web proxy server) lets you connect to an FTP server using UNIX-like keyboard commands. Browser programs usually support the FTP protocol (for downloading files only) in a more user-friendly manner. You can protect an FTP server's directories with a user-name/password combination, but both strings are passed over the Internet as clear text. FTP is based on TCP. Two separate connections are established between the client and server, one for control and one for data.

Internet vs. Intranet

Up to now, we've been assuming that client and server computers were connected to the worldwide Internet. The fact is you can run exactly the same client and server software on a local <u>intranet</u>. An intranet is often implemented on a company's LAN and is used for distributed applications. Users see the familiar browser interface at their client computers, and server computers supply simple Web-like pages or do complex data processing in response to user input.

An intranet offers a lot of flexibility. If, for example, you know that all your computers are Intel-based, you can use ActiveX controls and ActiveX document servers that provide ActiveX document support. If necessary, your server and client computers can run custom TCP/IP software that allows communication beyond HTTP and FTP. To secure your company's data, you can separate your intranet completely from the Internet or you can connect it through a <u>firewall</u>, which is another name for a proxy server.

Build Your Own $99 Intranet

Building a Microsoft Windows-based intranet is easy and cheap. Microsoft Windows 95, Microsoft Windows 98, and Microsoft Windows NT all contain the necessary networking capabilities. If you don't want to spend the $99, you can build a free intranet within a single computer. All the code in this chapter will run on this one-computer configuration.

NT File System vs. File Allocation Table

With Windows 95 and Windows 98, you are restricted to one file system, File Allocation Table (FAT—actually VFAT for long filenames). With Windows NT, you choose between NT File System (NTFS) and FAT at setup time. Your intranet will be much more secure if you choose NTFS because NTFS allows you to set user permissions for individual directories and files. Users log on to a Windows server (or to an attached workstation) supplying a user name and password.

Intranet and Internet clients participate in this operating-system security scheme because the server can log them on as though they were local users. Thus you can restrict access to any server directory or file to specific users who must supply passwords. If those user workstations are Windows network clients (as would be the case with a LAN-based intranet), the user name and password are passed through from the user's logon.

Network Hardware

You obviously need more than one computer to make a network. While your main development computer is probably a Pentium, a Pentium Pro, or a Pentium II, chances are you have at least one old computer hanging around. If it's at least a 486, it makes sense to connect it to your main computer for intranet testing and file backups.

You will need a network board for each computer, but 10-megabit-per-second Ethernet boards now cost less than $50 each. Choose a brand that either comes with its own drivers for Windows 95, Windows 98, and Windows NT, or is already supported by those operating systems. To see a list of supported boards, click on the Network icon in the Control Panel and then click the Add button to add an Adapter.

Most network boards have connectors for both thin coaxial (coax) and 10BaseT twisted pair. With 10BaseT, you must buy a <u>hub</u>, which costs several hundred dollars and needs a power supply. Thin coax requires only coaxial cable (available in precut lengths with connectors) plus terminator plugs. With coax, you daisy-chain your computers together and put terminators on each end of the chain.

Follow the instructions that come with the network board. In most cases you'll have to run an MS-DOS program that writes to the electrically erasable/ programmable read-only memory (EEPROM) on the board. Write down the values you select—you'll need them later.

Configuring Windows for Networking

After clicking on the Network icon in the Control Panel, you select protocols, adapters (network boards), and services. The screens that appear depend on whether you're using Windows 95, Windows 98, or Windows NT. You must select TCP/IP as one of your protocols if you want to run an intranet. You must also install the Windows driver for your network board, ensuring that the IRQ and I/O address values match what you put into the board's EEPROM. You must also assign an IP address to each of your network boards. If you're not connected directly to the Internet, you can choose any unique address you want.

That's actually enough configuring for an intranet, but you'll probably want to use your network for sharing files and printers, too. For Windows NT, install Client And Server Services and bind them to TCP/IP. For Windows 95 and Windows 98, install Client For Microsoft Networks and File And Printer Sharing For Microsoft Networks. If you have an existing network with another protocol installed (Novell IPX/SPX or Microsoft NetBEUI, for example), you can continue to use that protocol on the network along with TCP/IP. In that case, Windows file and print sharing will use the existing protocol and your intranet will use TCP/IP. If you want one computer to share another computer's resources, you must enable sharing from Microsoft Windows Explorer (for disk directories) or from the Printers folder (for printers).

Host Names for an Intranet—The HOSTS File

Both Internet and intranet users expect their browsers to use host names, not IP addresses. There are various methods of resolving names to addresses, including your own DNS server, which is an installable component of Windows NT Server. The easiest way of mapping Internet host names to IP addresses, however, is to use the HOSTS file. On Windows NT, this is a text file in the \Winnt\System32\DRIVERS\ETC directory. On Windows 95 and Windows 98, it's in the \WINDOWS directory, in a prototype HOSTS.SAM file that's already there. Just copy that file to HOSTS, and make the entries with Notepad. Make sure that you copy the edited HOSTS file to all computers in the network.

Testing Your Intranet—The Ping Program

You can use the Windows Ping program to test your intranet. From the command line, type *ping* followed by the IP address (dotted-decimal format) or the host name of another computer on the network. If you get a positive response, you'll know that TCP/IP is configured correctly. If you get no response or an error message, proceed no further. Go back and troubleshoot your network connections and configuration.

An Intranet for One Computer—The TCP/IP Loopback Address

The first line in the HOSTS file should be

```
127.0.0.1        localhost
```

This is the standard <u>loopback</u> IP address. If you start a server program to listen on this address, client programs running on the same machine can connect to localhost to get a TCP/IP connection to the server program. This works whether or not you have network boards installed.

Winsock

Winsock is the lowest level Windows API for TCP/IP programming. Part of the code is located in wsock32.dll (the exported functions that your program calls), and part is inside the Windows kernel. You can write both internet server programs and internet client programs using the Winsock API. This API is based on the original Berkely Sockets API for UNIX. A new and much more complex version, Winsock 2, is included for the first time with Windows NT 4.0, but we'll stick with the old version because it's the current standard for both Windows NT, Windows 95, and Windows 98.

Synchronous vs. Asynchronous Winsock Programming

Winsock was introduced first for Win16, which did not support multithreading. Consequently, most developers used Winsock in the <u>asynchronous</u> mode. In that mode, all sorts of hidden windows and *PeekMessage* calls enabled single-threaded programs to make Winsock send and receive calls without blocking, thus keeping the user interface (UI) alive. Asynchronous Winsock programs were complex, often implementing "state machines" that processed callback functions, trying to figure out what to do next based on what had just happened. Well, we're not in 16-bit land anymore, so we can do modern multithreaded programming. If this scares you, go back and review Chapter 12. Once you get used to multithreaded programming, you'll love it.

In this chapter, we will make the most of our Winsock calls from worker threads so that the program's main thread is able to carry on with the UI. The worker threads contain nice, sequential logic consisting of blocking Winsock calls.

The MFC Winsock Classes

We try to use MFC classes where it makes sense to use them, but the MFC developers informed us that the *CAsyncSocket* and *CSocket* classes were not appropriate for 32-bit synchronous programming. The Visual C++ online help says you can use *CSocket* for synchronous programming, but if you look at the source code you'll see some ugly message-based code left over from Win16.

The Blocking Socket Classes

Since we couldn't use MFC, we had to write our own Winsock classes. *CBlockingSocket* is a thin wrapping of the Winsock API, designed only for synchronous use in a worker thread. The only fancy features are exception-throwing on errors and time-outs for sending and receiving data. The exceptions help you write cleaner code because you don't need to have error tests after every Winsock call. The time-outs (implemented with the Winsock *select* function) prevent a communication fault from blocking a thread indefinitely.

CHttpBlockingSocket is derived from *CBlockingSocket* and provides functions for reading HTTP data. *CSockAddr* and *CBlockingSocketException* are helper classes.

The *CSockAddr* Helper Class

Many Winsock functions take socket address parameters. As you might remember, a socket address consists of a 32-bit IP address plus a 16-bit port number. The actual Winsock type is a 16-byte *sockaddr_in* structure, which looks like this:

```
struct sockaddr_in {
    short    sin_family;
    u_short sin_port;
    struct   in_addr sin_addr;
    char     sin_zero[8];
};
```

The IP address is stored as type *in_addr*, which looks like this:

```
struct in_addr {
    union {
        struct { u_char s_b1,s_b2,s_b3,s_b4; } S_un_b;
        struct { u_short s_w1,s_w2; } S_un_w;
        u_long S_addr;
    } S_un;
}
```

These are ugly structures, so we'll derive a programmer-friendly C++ class from *sockaddr_in*. The file \vcpp32\ex34a\Blocksock.h on the CD-ROM contains the following code for doing this, with inline functions included:

```
class CSockAddr : public sockaddr_in {
public:
    // constructors
    CSockAddr()
    {
        sin_family = AF_INET;
        sin_port = 0;
        sin_addr.s_addr = 0;
    } // Default
    CSockAddr(const SOCKADDR& sa) { memcpy(this, &sa,
        sizeof(SOCKADDR)); }
    CSockAddr(const SOCKADDR_IN& sin) { memcpy(this, &sin,
        sizeof(SOCKADDR_IN)); }
    CSockAddr(const ULONG ulAddr, const USHORT ushPort = 0)
    // parms are host byte ordered
    {
        sin_family = AF_INET;
        sin_port = htons(ushPort);
        sin_addr.s_addr = htonl(ulAddr);
    }
    CSockAddr(const char* pchIP, const USHORT ushPort = 0)
    // dotted IP addr string
    {
        sin_family = AF_INET;
        sin_port = htons(ushPort);
        sin_addr.s_addr = inet_addr(pchIP);
    } // already network byte ordered
    // Return the address in dotted-decimal format
    CString DottedDecimal()
        { return inet_ntoa(sin_addr); }
    // constructs a new CString object
    // Get port and address (even though they're public)
    USHORT Port() const
        { return ntohs(sin_port); }
    ULONG IPAddr() const
        { return ntohl(sin_addr.s_addr); }
    // operators added for efficiency
    const CSockAddr& operator=(const SOCKADDR& sa)
    {
        memcpy(this, &sa, sizeof(SOCKADDR));
        return *this;
    }
    const CSockAddr& operator=(const SOCKADDR_IN& sin)
```

(continued)

```
    {
        memcpy(this, &sin, sizeof(SOCKADDR_IN));
        return *this;
    }
    operator SOCKADDR()
        { return *((LPSOCKADDR) this); }
    operator LPSOCKADDR()
        { return (LPSOCKADDR) this; }
    operator LPSOCKADDR_IN()
        { return (LPSOCKADDR_IN) this; }
};
```

As you can see, this class has some useful constructors and conversion operators, which make the *CSockAddr* object interchangeable with the type *sockaddr_in* and the equivalent types *SOCKADDR_IN*, *sockaddr*, and *SOCKADDR*. There's a constructor and a member function for IP addresses in dotted-decimal format. The internal socket address is in network byte order, but the member functions all use host byte order parameters and return values. The Winsock functions *htonl*, *htons*, *ntohs*, and *ntohl* take care of the conversions between network and host byte order.

The *CBlockingSocketException* Class

All the *CBlockingSocket* functions throw a *CBlockingSocketException* object when Winsock returns an error. This class is derived from the MFC *CException* class and thus overrides the *GetErrorMessage* function. This function gives the Winsock error number and a character string that *CBlockingSocket* provided when it threw the exception.

The *CBlockingSocket* Class

Figure 34-9 shows an excerpt from the header file for the *CBlockingSocket* class.

BLOCKSOCK.H

```
class CBlockingSocket : public CObject
{
    DECLARE_DYNAMIC(CBlockingSocket)
public:
    SOCKET m_hSocket;
    CBlockingSocket();  { m_hSocket = NULL; }
    void Cleanup();
    void Create(int nType = SOCK_STREAM);
    void Close();
    void Bind(LPCSOCKADDR psa);
```

Figure 34-9. *(continued)*

Excerpt from the header file for the CBlockingSocket *class.*

```
void Listen();
void Connect(LPCSOCKADDR psa);
BOOL Accept(CBlockingSocket& s, LPCSOCKADDR psa);
int Send(const char* pch, const int nSize, const int nSecs);
int Write(const char* pch, const int nSize, const int nSecs);
int Receive(char* pch, const int nSize, const int nSecs);
int SendDatagram(const char* pch, const int nSize, LPCSOCKADDR psa,
    const int nSecs);
int ReceiveDatagram(char* pch, const int nSize, LPCSOCKADDR psa,
    const int nSecs);
void GetPeerAddr(LPCSOCKADDR psa);
void GetSockAddr(LPCSOCKADDR psa);
static CSockAddr GetHostByName(const char* pchName,
    const USHORT ushPort = 0);
static const char* GetHostByAddr(LPCSOCKADDR psa);
operator SOCKET();
    { return m_hSocket; }
};
```

Following is a list of the *CBlockingSocket* member functions, starting with the constructor:

- **Constructor**—The *CBlockingSocket* constructor makes an uninitialized object. You must call the *Create* member function to create a Windows socket and connect it to the C++ object.

- **Create**—This function calls the Winsock *socket* function and then sets the *m_hSocket* data member to the returned 32-bit *SOCKET* handle.

Parameter	Description
nType	Type of socket; should be *SOCK_STREAM* (the default value) or *SOCK_DGRAM*

- **Close**—This function closes an open socket by calling the Winsock *closesocket* function. The *Create* function must have been called previously. The destructor does not call this function because it would be impossible to catch an exception for a global object. Your server program can call *Close* anytime for a socket that is listening.

- **Bind**—This function calls the Winsock *bind* function to bind a previously created socket to a specified socket address. Prior to calling *Listen*, your server program calls *Bind* with a socket address containing the listening port number and server's IP address. If you supply

INADDR_ANY as the IP address, Winsock deciphers your computer's IP address.

Parameter	Description
psa	A *CSockAddr* object or a pointer to a variable of type *sockaddr*

- **Listen**—This TCP function calls the Winsock *listen* function. Your server program calls *Listen* to begin listening on the port specified by the previous *Bind* call. The function returns immediately.

- **Accept**—This TCP function calls the Winsock *accept* function. Your server program calls *Accept* immediately after calling *Listen*. *Accept* returns when a client connects to the socket, sending back a new socket (in a *CBlockingSocket* object that you provide) that corresponds to the new connection.

Parameter	Description
s	A reference to an existing *CBlockingSocket* object for which *Create* has not been called
psa	A *CSockAddr* object or a pointer to a variable of type *sockaddr* for the connecting socket's address
Return value	*TRUE* if successful

- **Connect**—This TCP function calls the Winsock *connect* function. Your client program calls *Connect* after calling *Create*. *Connect* returns when the connection has been made.

Parameter	Description
psa	A *CSockAddr* object or a pointer to a variable of type *sockaddr*

- **Send**—This TCP function calls the Winsock *send* function after calling *select* to activate the time-out. The number of bytes actually transmitted by each *Send* call depends on how quickly the program at the other end of the connection can receive the bytes. *Send* throws an exception if the program at the other end closes the socket before it reads all the bytes.

Parameter	Description
pch	A pointer to a buffer that contains the bytes to send
nSize	The size (in bytes) of the block to send
nSecs	Time-out value in seconds
Return value	The actual number of bytes sent

■ **Write**—This TCP function calls *Send* repeatedly until all the bytes are sent or until the receiver closes the socket.

Parameter	Description
pch	A pointer to a buffer that contains the bytes to send
nSize	The size (in bytes) of the block to send
nSecs	Time-out value in seconds
Return value	The actual number of bytes sent

■ **Receive**—This TCP function calls the Winsock *recv* function after calling *select* to activate the time-out. This function returns only the bytes that have been received. For more information, see the description of the *CHttpBlockingSocket* class in the next section.

Parameter	Description
pch	A pointer to an existing buffer that will receive the incoming bytes
nSize	The maximum number of bytes to receive
nSecs	Time-out value in seconds
Return value	The actual number of bytes received

■ **SendDatagram**—This UDP function calls the Winsock *sendto* function. The program on the other end needs to call *ReceiveDatagram*. There is no need to call *Listen*, *Accept*, or *Connect* for datagrams. You must have previously called *Create* with the parameter set to *SOCK_DGRAM*.

Parameter	Description
pch	A pointer to a buffer that contains the bytes to send
nSize	The size (in bytes) of the block to send
psa	The datagram's destination address; a *CSockAddr* object or a pointer to a variable of type *sockaddr*
nSecs	Time-out value in seconds
Return value	The actual number of bytes sent

■ **ReceiveDatagram**—This UDP function calls the Winsock *recvfrom* function. The function returns when the program at the other end of the connection calls *SendDatagram*. You must have previously called *Create* with the parameter set to *SOCK_DGRAM*.

Parameter	Description
pch	A pointer to an existing buffer that will receive the incoming bytes
nSize	The size (in bytes) of the block to send
psa	The datagram's destination address; a *CSockAddr* object or a pointer to a variable of type *sockaddr*
nSecs	Time-out value in seconds
Return value	The actual number of bytes received

■ **GetPeerAddr**—This function calls the Winsock *getpeername* function. It returns the port and IP address of the socket on the other end of the connection. If you are connected to the Internet through a Web proxy server, the IP address is the proxy server's IP address.

Parameter	Description
psa	A *CSockAddr* object or a pointer to a variable of type *sockaddr*

■ **GetSockAddr**—This function calls the Winsock *getsockname* function. It returns the socket address that Winsock assigns to this end of the connection. If the other program is a server on a LAN, the IP address is the address assigned to this computer's network board. If the other program is a server on the Internet, your service provider assigns the IP address when you dial in. In both cases, Winsock assigns the port number, which is different for each connection.

Parameter	Description
psa	A *CSockAddr* object or a pointer to a variable of type *sockaddr*

■ *GetHostByName*—This static function calls the Winsock function *gethostbyname*. It queries a name server and then returns the socket address corresponding to the host name. The function times out by itself.

Parameter	Description
pchName	A pointer to a character array containing the host name to resolve
ushPort	The port number (default value 0) that will become part of the returned socket address
Return value	The socket address containing the IP address from the DNS plus the port number *ushPort*

■ *GetHostByAddr*—This static function calls the Winsock *gethostbyaddr* function. It queries a name server and then returns the host name corresponding to the socket address. The function times out by itself.

Parameter	Description
psa	A *CSockAddr* object or a pointer to a variable of type *sockaddr*
Return value	A pointer to a character array containing the host name; the caller should not delete this memory

■ *Cleanup*—This function closes the socket if it is open. It doesn't throw an exception, so you can call it inside an exception *catch* block.

■ *operator SOCKET*—This overloaded operator lets you use a *CBlockingSocket* object in place of a *SOCKET* parameter.

The *CHttpBlockingSocket* Class

If you call *CBlockingSocket::Receive*, you'll have a difficult time knowing when to stop receiving bytes. Each call returns the bytes that are stacked up at your end of the connection at that instant. If there are no bytes, the call blocks, but if the sender closed the socket, the call returns zero bytes.

In the HTTP section beginning on page 994, you learned that the client sends a request terminated by a blank line. The server is supposed to send the response headers and data as soon as it detects the blank line, but the client needs to analyze the response headers before it reads the data. This means that as long as a TCP connection remains open, the receiving program must process the received data as it comes in. A simple but inefficient technique would be to call *Receive* for 1 byte at a time. A better way is to use a buffer.

The *CHttpBlockingSocket* class adds buffering to *CBlockingSocket*, and it provides two new member functions. Here is part of the \vcpp32\ex34A\Block-sock.h file:

```
class CHttpBlockingSocket : public CBlockingSocket
{
public:
    DECLARE_DYNAMIC(CHttpBlockingSocket)
    enum {nSizeRecv = 1000}; // max receive buffer size (> hdr line
                             //  length)
    CHttpBlockingSocket();
    ~CHttpBlockingSocket();
    int ReadHttpHeaderLine(char* pch, const int nSize, const int nSecs);
    int ReadHttpResponse(char* pch, const int nSize, const int nSecs);
private:
    char* m_pReadBuf; // read buffer
    int m_nReadBuf; // number of bytes in the read buffer
};
```

The constructor and destructor take care of allocating and freeing a 1000-character buffer. The two new member functions are as follows:

■ *ReadHttpHeaderLine*—This function returns a single header line, terminated with a <cr><lf> pair. *ReadHttpHeaderLine* inserts a terminating zero at the end of the line. If the line buffer is full, the terminating zero is stored in the last position.

Parameter	Description
pch	A pointer to an existing buffer that will receive the incoming line (zero-terminated)
nSize	The size of the *pch* buffer
nSecs	Time-out value in seconds
Return value	The actual number of bytes received, excluding the terminating zero

■ *ReadHttpResponse*—This function returns the remainder of the server's response received when the socket is closed or when the buffer is full. Don't assume that the buffer contains a terminating zero.

Parameter	Description
pch	A pointer to an existing buffer that will receive the incoming data
nSize	The maximum number of bytes to receive
nSecs	Time-out value in seconds
Return value	The actual number of bytes received

A Simplified HTTP Server Program

Now it's time to use the blocking socket classes to write an HTTP server program. All the frills have been eliminated, but the code actually works with a browser. This server doesn't do much except return some hard-coded headers and HTML statements in response to any GET request. (See the EX34A program later in this chapter for a more complete HTTP server.)

Initializing Winsock

Before making any Winsock calls, the program must initialize the Winsock library. The following statements in the application's *InitInstance* member function do the job:

```
WSADATA wsd;
WSAStartup(0x0101, &wsd);
```

Starting the Server

The server starts in response to some user action, such as a menu choice. Here's the command handler:

```
CBlockingSocket g_sListen; // one-and-only global socket for listening
void CSocketView::OnInternetStartServer()
{
    try {
        CSockAddr saServer(INADDR_ANY, 80);
        g_sListen.Create();
        g_sListen.Bind(saServer);
        g_sListen.Listen();
        AfxBeginThread(ServerThreadProc, GetSafeHwnd());
    }
    catch(CBlockingSocketException* e) {
        g_sListen.Cleanup();
        // Do something about the exception
        e->Delete();
    }
}
```

Pretty simple, really. The handler creates a socket, starts listening on it, and then starts a worker thread that waits for some client to connect to port 80. If something goes wrong, an exception is thrown. The global *g_sListen* object lasts for the life of the program and is capable of accepting multiple simultaneous connections, each managed by a separate thread.

The Server Thread

Now let's look at the *ServerThreadProc* function:

```
UINT ServerThreadProc(LPVOID pParam)
{
    CSockAddr saClient;
    CHttpBlockingSocket sConnect;
    char request[100];
    char headers[] = "HTTP/1.0 200 OK\r\n"
        "Server: Inside Visual C++ SOCK01\r\n"
        "Date: Thu, 05 Sep 1996 17:33:12 GMT\r\n"
        "Content-Type: text/html\r\n"
        "Accept-Ranges: bytes\r\n"
        "Content-Length: 187\r\n"
        "\r\n"; // the important blank line
    char html[] =
        "<html><head><title>Inside Visual C++ Server</title></head>\r\n"
        "<body><body background=\"/samples/images/usa1.jpg\">\r\n"
        "<h1><center>This is a custom home page</center></h1><p>\r\n"
        "</body></html>\r\n\r\n";
```

```
    try {
        if(!g_sListen.Accept(sConnect, saClient)) {
            // Handler in view class closed the listening socket
            return 0;
        }
        AfxBeginThread(ServerThreadProc, pParam);
        // read request from client
        sConnect.ReadHttpHeaderLine(request, 100, 10);
        TRACE("SERVER: %s", request); // Print the first header
        if(strnicmp(request, "GET", 3) == 0) {
            do { // Process the remaining request headers
                sConnect.ReadHttpHeaderLine(request, 100, 10);
                TRACE("SERVER: %s", request); // Print the other headers
            } while(strcmp(request, "\r\n"));
            sConnect.Write(headers, strlen(headers), 10); // response hdrs
            sConnect.Write(html, strlen(html), 10); // HTML code
        }
        else {
            TRACE("SERVER: not a GET\n");
            // don't know what to do
        }
        sConnect.Close(); // Destructor doesn't close it
    }
    catch(CBlockingSocketException* e) {
        // Do something about the exception
        e->Delete();
    }
    return 0;
}
```

The most important function call is the *Accept* call. The thread blocks until a client connects to the server's port 80, and then *Accept* returns with a new socket, *sConnect*. The current thread immediately starts another thread.

In the meantime, the current thread must process the client's request that just came in on *sConnect*. It first reads all the request headers by calling *Read-HttpHeaderLine* until it detects a blank line. Then it calls *Write* to send the response headers and the HTML statements. Finally, the current thread calls *Close* to close the connection socket. End of story for this connection. The next thread is sitting, blocked at the *Accept* call, waiting for the next connection.

Cleaning Up

To avoid a memory leak on exit, the program must ensure that all worker threads have been terminated. The simplest way to do this is to close the listening socket. This forces any thread's pending *Accept* to return *FALSE*, causing the thread to exit.

```
try {
    g_sListen.Close();
    Sleep(340); // Wait for thread to exit
    WSACleanup(); // Terminate Winsock
}
catch(CUserException* e) {
    e->Delete();
}
```

A problem might arise if a thread were in the process of fulfilling a client request. In that case, the main thread should positively ensure that all threads have terminated before exiting.

A Simplified HTTP Client Program

Now for the client side of the story—a simple working program that does a <u>blind</u> <u>GET</u> request. When a server receives a GET request with a slash, as shown below, it's supposed to deliver its default HTML file:

```
GET / HTTP/1.0
```

If you typed *http://www.slowsoft.com* in a browser, the browser sends the blind GET request.

This client program can use the same *CHttpBlockingSocket* class you've already seen, and it must initialize Winsock the same way the server did. A command handler simply starts a client thread with a call like this:

```
AfxBeginThread(ClientSocketThreadProc, GetSafeHwnd());
```

Here's the client thread code:

```
CString g_strServerName = "localhost"; // or some other host name
UINT ClientSocketThreadProc(LPVOID pParam)
{
    CHttpBlockingSocket sClient;
    char* buffer = new char[MAXBUF];
    int nBytesReceived = 0;
    char request[] = "GET / HTTP/1.0\r\n";
    char headers[] = // Request headers
        "User-Agent: Mozilla/1.22 (Windows; U; 32bit)\r\n"
        "Accept: */*\r\n"
        "Accept: image/gif\r\n"
        "Accept: image/x-xbitmap\r\n"
        "Accept: image/jpeg\r\n"
        "\r\n"; // need this
    CSockAddr saServer, saClient;
    try {
        sClient.Create();
```

```
        saServer = CBlockingSocket::GetHostByName(g_strServerName, 80);
        sClient.Connect(saServer);
        sClient.Write(request, strlen(request), 10);
        sClient.Write(headers, strlen(headers), 10);
        do { // Read all the server's response headers
            nBytesReceived = sClient.ReadHttpHeaderLine(buffer, 100, 10);
        } while(strcmp(buffer, "\r\n")); // through the first blank line
        nBytesReceived = sClient.ReadHttpResponse(buffer, 100, 10);
        if(nBytesReceived == 0) {
            AfxMessageBox("No response received");
        }
        else {
            buffer[nBytesReceived] = '\0';
            AfxMessageBox(buffer);
        }
    }
    catch(CBlockingSocketException* e) {
        // Log the exception
        e->Delete();
    }
    sClient.Close();
    delete [] buffer;
    return 0; // The thread exits
}
```

This thread first calls *CBlockingSocket::GetHostByName* to get the server computer's IP address. Then it creates a socket and calls *Connect* on that socket. Now there's a two-way communication channel to the server. The thread sends its GET request followed by some request headers, reads the server's response headers, and then reads the response file itself, which it assumes is a text file. After the thread displays the text in a message box, it exits.

Building a Web Server with *CHttpBlockingSocket*

If you need a Web server, your best bet is to buy one or to use the Microsoft Internet Information Server (IIS) that comes bundled with Windows NT Server. Of course, you'll learn more if you build your own server and you'll also have a useful diagnostic tool. And what if you need features that IIS can't deliver? Suppose you want to add Web server capability to an existing Windows application, or suppose you have a custom ActiveX control that sets up its own non-HTTP TCP connection with the server. Take a good look at the server code in EX34A, which works under Windows NT, Windows 95, and Windows 98. It might work as a foundation for your next custom server application.

EX34A Server Limitations

The server part of the EX34A program honors GET requests for files, and it has logic for processing POST requests. (POST requests are described in Chapter 35.) These are the two most common HTTP request types. EX34A will not, however, launch Common Gateway Interface (CGI) scripts or load Internet Server Application Programming Interface (ISAPI) DLLs. (You'll learn more about ISAPI in Chapter 35.) EX34A makes no provision for security, and it doesn't have FTP capabilities. Other than that, it's a great server! If you want the missing features, just write the code for them yourself.

EX34A Server Architecture

You'll soon see that EX34A combines an HTTP server, a Winsock HTTP client, and two WinInet HTTP clients. All three clients can talk to the built-in server or to any other server on the Internet. Any client program, including the Telnet utility and standard browsers such as Microsoft Internet Explorer 4.0, can communicate with the EX34A server. You'll examine the client sections a little later in this chapter.

EX34A is a standard MFC SDI document–view application with a view class derived from *CEditView*. The main menu includes Start Server and Stop Server menu choices as well as a Configuration command that brings up a tabbed dialog for setting the home directory, the default file for blind GETs, and the listening port number (usually 80).

The Start Server command handler starts a global socket listening and then launches a thread, as in the simplified HTTP server described previously. Look at the *ServerThreadProc* function included in the file \vcpp32\ex34a\Server-Thread.cpp of the EX34A project on the companion CD-ROM. Each time a server thread processes a request, it logs the request by sending a message to the *CEditView* window. It also sends messages for exceptions, such as bind errors.

The primary job of the server is to deliver files. It first opens a file, storing a *CFile* pointer in *pFile*, and then it reads 5 KB (*SERVERMAXBUF*) blocks and writes them to the socket *sConnect*, as shown in the code below:

```
char* buffer = new char[SERVERMAXBUF];
DWORD dwLength = pFile->GetLength();
nBytesSent = 0;
DWORD dwBytesRead = 0;
UINT uBytesToRead;
while(dwBytesRead < dwLength) {
    uBytesToRead = min(SERVERMAXBUF, dwLength - dwBytesRead);
    VERIFY(pFile->Read(buffer, uBytesToRead) == uBytesToRead);
    nBytesSent += sConnect.Write(buffer, uBytesToRead, 10);
    dwBytesRead += uBytesToRead;
}
```

The server is programmed to respond to a GET request for a phony file named Custom. It generates some HTML code that displays the client's IP address, port number, and a sequential connection number. This is one possibility for server customization.

The server normally listens on a socket bound to address *INADDR_ANY*. This is the server's default IP address determined by the Ethernet board or assigned during your connection to your ISP. If your server computer has several IP addresses, you can force the server to listen to one of them by filling in the Server IP Address in the Advanced Configuration page. You can also change the server's listening port number on the Server page. If you choose port 90, for example, browser users would connect to *http://localhost:90*.

The leftmost status bar indicator pane displays "Listening" when the server is running.

Using the Win32 *TransmitFile* Function

If you have Windows NT 4.0, you can make your server more efficient by using the Win32 *TransmitFile* function in place of the *CFile::Read* loop in the code excerpt shown on page 1010. *TransmitFile* sends bytes from an open file directly to a socket and is highly optimized. The EX34A *ServerThreadProc* function contains the following line:

```
if (::TransmitFile(sConnect, (HANDLE) pFile >m_hFile, dwLength, 0,
    NULL, NULL, TF_DISCONNECT))
```

If you have Windows NT, uncomment the line

```
#define USE_TRANSMITFILE
```

at the top of ServerThread.cpp to activate the *TransmitFile* logic.

Building and Testing EX34A

Open the \vcpp32\ex34a project in Visual C++, and then build the project. A directory under EX34A, called Website, contains some HTML files and is set up as the EX34A server's home directory, which appears to clients as the server's root directory.

> NOTE: If you have another HTTP server running on your computer, stop it now. If you have installed IIS along with Windows NT Server, it is probably running now, so you must run the Internet Service Manager program from the Microsoft Internet Server menu. Select the WWW Service line, and then click the stop button (the one with the square). EX34A reports a bind error (10048) if another server is already listening on port 80.

Run the program from the debugger, and then choose Start Server from the Internet menu. Now go to your Web browser and type *localhost*. You should see the Welcome To The Inside Visual C++ Home Page complete with all graphics. The EX34A window should look like this.

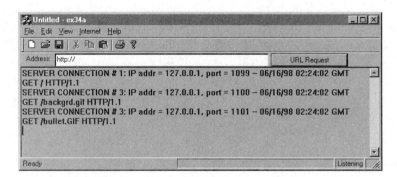

Look at the Visual C++ debug window for a listing of the client's request headers.

If you click the browser's Refresh button, you might notice EX34A error messages like this:

```
WINSOCK ERROR--SERVER: Send error #10054 -- 10/05/96 04:34:10 GMT
```

This tells you that the browser read the file's modified date from the server's response header and figured out that it didn't need the data because it already had the file in its cache. The browser then closed the socket, and the server detected an error. If the EX34A server were smarter, it would have checked the client's If-Modified-Since request header before sending the file.

Of course, you can test the server on your $99 intranet. Start the server on one computer, and then run the browser from another, typing in the server's host name as it appears in the HOSTS file.

Using Telnet

The Telnet utility is included with Windows 95, Windows 98, and Windows NT. It's useful for testing server programs such as EX34A. With Telnet, you're sending one character at a time, which means that the server's *CBlockingSocket::Receive* function is receiving one character at a time. The Telnet window is shown on the facing page.

The first time you run Telnet, choose Preferences from the Terminal menu and turn on Local Echo. Each time thereafter, choose Remote System from the Connect menu and then type your server name and port number 80. You can type a GET request (followed by a double carriage return), but you'd better type fast because the EX34A server's *Receive* calls are set to time-out after 10 seconds.

Building a Web Client with *CHttpBlockingSocket*

If you had written your own Internet browser program a few years ago, you could have made a billion dollars by now. But these days, you can download browsers for free, so it doesn't make sense to write one. It <u>does</u> make sense, however, to add Internet access features to your Windows applications. Winsock is not the best tool if you need HTTP or FTP access only, but it's a good learning tool.

The EX34A Winsock Client

The EX34A program implements a Winsock client in the file \vcpp32\ex34a-\ClientSockThread.cpp on the CD-ROM. The code is similar to the code for the simplified HTTP client on page 1012. The client thread uses global variables set by the Configuration property sheet, including server filename, server host name, server IP address and port, and client IP address. The client IP address is necessary only if your computer supports multiple IP addresses. When you run the client, it connects to the specified server and issues a GET request for the file that you specified. The Winsock client logs error messages in the EX34A main window.

EX34A Support for Proxy Servers

If your computer is connected to a LAN at work, chances are it's not exposed directly to the Internet but rather connected through a <u>proxy</u> <u>server</u>, sometimes called a <u>firewall</u>. There are two kinds of proxy servers: Web and Winsock. Web proxy servers, sometimes called CERN proxies, support only the HTTP, FTP, and gopher protocols. (The gopher protocol, which predates HTTP, allows character-mode terminals to access Internet files.) A Winsock client program must be specially adapted to use a Web proxy server. A Winsock proxy server is more flexible and thus can support protocols such as RealAudio. Instead of modifying your client program source code, you link to a special Remote Winsock DLL that can communicate with a Winsock proxy server.

The EX34A client code can communicate through a Web proxy if you check the Use Proxy check box in the Client Configuration page. In that case, you must know and enter the name of your proxy server. From that point on, the client code connects to the proxy server instead of to the real server. All GET and POST requests must then specify the full Uniform Resource Locator (URL) for the file.

If you were connected directly to SlowSoft's server, for example, your GET request might look like this:

```
GET /customers/newproducts.html HTTP/1.0
```

But if you were connected through a Web proxy server, the GET would look like this:

```
GET http://slowsoft.com/customers/newproducts.html HTTP/1.0
```

Testing the EX34A Winsock Client

The easiest way to test the Winsock client is by using the built-in Winsock server. Just start the server as before, and then choose Request (Winsock) from the Internet menu. You should see some HTML code in a message box. You can also test the client against IIS, the server running in another EX34A process on the same computer, the EX34A server running on another computer on the Net, and an Internet server. Ignore the "Address" URL on the dialog bar for the time being; it's for one of the WinInet clients. You must enter the server name and filename in the Client page of the Configuration dialog.

WinInet

WinInet is a higher-level API than Winsock, but it works only for HTTP, FTP, and gopher client programs in both asynchronous and synchronous modes. You can't use it to build servers. The WININET DLL is independent of the WIN-SOCK32 DLL. Microsoft Internet Explorer 3.0 (IE3) uses WinInet, and so do ActiveX controls.

WinInet's Advantages over Winsock

WinInet far surpasses Winsock in the support it gives to a professional-level client program. Following are just some of the WinInet benefits:

- **Caching**—Just like IE3, your WinInet client program caches HTML files and other Internet files. You don't have to do a thing. The second time your client requests a particular file, it's loaded from a local disk instead of from the Internet.

- **Security**—WinInet supports basic authentication, Windows NT challenge/response authentication, and the Secure Sockets Layer (SSL). Authentication is described in Chapter 35.

- **Web proxy access**—You enter proxy server information through the Control Panel (click on the Internet icon), and it's stored in the Registry. WinInet reads the Registry and uses the proxy server when required.

- **Buffered I/O**—WinInet's read function doesn't return until it can deliver the number of bytes you asked for. (It returns immediately, of course, if the server closes the socket.) Also, you can read individual text lines if you need to.

- **Easy API**—Status callback functions are available for UI update and cancellation. One function, *CInternetSession::OpenURL*, finds the server's IP address, opens a connection, and makes the file ready for reading, all in one call. Some functions even copy Internet files directly to and from disk.

- **User friendly**—WinInet parses and formats headers for you. If a server has moved a file to a new location, it sends back the new URL in an HTTP Location header. WinInet seamlessly accesses the new server for you. In addition, WinInet puts a file's modified date in the request header for you.

The MFC WinInet Classes

WinInet is a modern API available only for Win32. The MFC wrapping is quite good, which means we didn't have to write our own WinInet class library. Yes, MFC WinInet supports blocking calls in multithreaded programs, and by now you know that makes us happy.

The MFC classes closely mirror the underlying WinInet architecture, and they add exception processing. These classes are summarized in the sections on the following pages.

CInternetSession

You need only one *CInternetSession* object for each thread that accesses the Internet. After you have your *CInternetSession* object, you can establish HTTP, FTP, or gopher connections or you can open remote files directly by calling the *OpenURL* member function. You can use the *CInternetSession* class directly, or you can derive a class from it in order to support status callback functions.

The *CInternetSession* constructor calls the WinInet *InternetOpen* function, which returns an *HINTERNET* session handle that is stored inside the *CInternetSession* object. This function initializes your application's use of the WinInet library, and the session handle is used internally as a parameter for other WinInet calls.

CHttpConnection

An object of class *CHttpConnection* represents a "permanent" HTTP connection to a particular host. You know already that HTTP doesn't support permanent connections and that FTP doesn't either. (The connections last only for the duration of a file transfer.) WinInet gives the appearance of a permanent connection because it remembers the host name.

After you have your *CInternetSession* object, you call the *GetHttpConnection* member function, which returns a pointer to a *CHttpConnection* object. (Don't forget to delete this object when you are finished with it.)

The *GetHttpConnection* member function calls the WinInet *InternetConnect* function, which returns an *HINTERNET* connection handle that is stored inside the *CHttpConnection* object and used for subsequent WinInet calls.

CFtpConnection, CGopherConnection

These classes are similar to *CHttpConnection*, but they use the FTP and gopher protocols. The *CFtpConnection* member functions *GetFile* and *PutFile* allow you to transfer files directly to and from your disk.

CInternetFile

With HTTP, FTP, or gopher, your client program reads and writes byte streams. The MFC WinInet classes make these byte streams look like ordinary files. If you look at the class hierarchy, you'll see that *CInternetFile* is derived from *CStdioFile*, which is derived from *CFile*. Therefore, *CInternetFile* and its derived classes override familiar *CFile* functions such as *Read* and *Write*. For FTP files, you use *CInternetFile* objects directly, but for HTTP and gopher files, you use objects of the derived classes *CHttpFile* and *CGopherFile*. You don't construct a *CInternetFile* object directly, but you call *CFtpConnection::OpenFile* to get a *CInternetFile* pointer.

If you have an ordinary *CFile* object, it has a 32-bit *HANDLE* data member that represents the underlying disk file. A *CInternetFile* object uses the same *m_hFile* data member, but that data member holds a 32-bit <u>Internet</u> <u>file</u> <u>handle</u> of type *HINTERNET*, which is not interchangeable with a *HANDLE*. The *CInternetFile* overridden member functions use this handle to call WinInet functions such as *InternetReadFile* and *InternetWriteFile*.

CHttpFile

This Internet file class has member functions that are unique to HTTP files, such as *AddRequestHeaders*, *SendRequest*, and *GetFileURL*. You don't construct a *CHttpFile* object directly, but you call the *CHttpConnection::OpenRequest* function, which calls the WinInet function *HttpOpenRequest* and returns a *CHttpFile* pointer. You can specify a GET or POST request for this call.

Once you have your *CHttpFile* pointer, you call the *CHttpFile::Send-Request* member function, which actually sends the request to the server. Then you call *Read*.

CFtpFileFind, CGopherFileFind

These classes let your client program explore FTP and gopher directories.

CInternetException

The MFC WinInet classes throw *CInternetException* objects that your program can process with try/catch logic.

Internet Session Status Callbacks

WinInet and MFC provide callback notifications as a WinInet operation progresses, and these status callbacks are available in both synchronous (blocking) and asynchronous modes. In synchronous mode (which we're using exclusively here), your WinInet calls block even though you have status callbacks enabled.

Callbacks are easy in C++. You simply derive a class and override selected virtual functions. The base class for WinInet is *CInternetSession*. Now let's derive a class named *CCallbackInternetSession*:

```
class CCallbackInternetSession : public CInternetSession
{
public:
    CCallbackInternetSession( LPCTSTR pstrAgent = NULL, DWORD dwContext = 1,
        DWORD dwAccessType = PRE_CONFIG_INTERNET_ACCESS,
        LPCTSTR pstrProxyName = NULL, LPCTSTR pstrProxyBypass = NULL,
        DWORD dwFlags = 0 ) { EnableStatusCallback() }
protected:
    virtual void OnStatusCallback(DWORD dwContext, DWORD dwInternalStatus,
        LPVOID lpvStatusInformation, DWORD dwStatusInformationLength);
};
```

The only coding that's necessary is a constructor and a single overridden function, *OnStatusCallback*. The constructor calls *CInternetSession::Enable-StatusCallback* to enable the status callback feature. Your WinInet client program makes its various Internet blocking calls, and when the status changes, *OnStatusCallback* is called. Your overridden function quickly updates the UI and returns, and then the Internet operation continues. For HTTP, most of the callbacks originate in the *CHttpFile::SendRequest* function.

What kind of events trigger callbacks? A list of the codes passed in the *dwInternalStatus* parameter is shown here.

Code Passed	Action Taken
INTERNET_STATUS_RESOLVING_NAME	Looking up the IP address of the supplied name. The name is now in *lpvStatusInformation*.
INTERNET_STATUS_NAME_RESOLVED	Successfully found the IP address. The IP address is now in *lpvStatusInformation*.
INTERNET_STATUS_CONNECTING_TO_SERVER	Connecting to the socket.
INTERNET_STATUS_CONNECTED_TO_SERVER	Successfully connected to the socket.
INTERNET_STATUS_SENDING_REQUEST	Send the information request to the server.
INTERNET_STATUS_REQUEST_SENT	Successfully sent the information request to the server.
INTERNET_STATUS_RECEIVING_RESPONSE	Waiting for the server to respond to a request.
INTERNET_STATUS_RESPONSE_RECEIVED	Successfully received a response from the server.
INTERNET_STATUS_CLOSING_CONNECTION	Closing the connection to the server.
INTERNET_STATUS_CONNECTION_CLOSED	Successfully closed the connection to the server.
INTERNET_STATUS_HANDLE_CREATED	Program can now close the handle.
INTERNET_STATUS_HANDLE_CLOSING	Successfully terminated this handle value.
INTERNET_STATUS_REQUEST_COMPLETE	Successfully completed the asynchronous operation.

You can use your status callback function to interrupt a WinInet operation. You could, for example, test for an event set by the main thread when the user cancels the operation.

A Simplified WinInet Client Program

And now for the WinInet equivalent of our Winsock client program that implements a blind GET request. Because you're using WinInet in blocking mode, you must put the code in a worker thread. That thread is started from a command handler in the main thread:

```
AfxBeginThread(ClientWinInetThreadProc, GetSafeHwnd());
```

Here's the client thread code:

```
CString g_strServerName = "localhost"; // or some other host name
UINT ClientWinInetThreadProc(LPVOID pParam)
{
    CInternetSession session;
    CHttpConnection* pConnection = NULL;
    CHttpFile* pFile1 = NULL;
    char* buffer = new char[MAXBUF];
    UINT nBytesRead = 0;
    try {
        pConnection = session.GetHttpConnection(g_strServerName, 80);
        pFile1 = pConnection->OpenRequest(1, "/"); // blind GET
        pFile1->SendRequest();
        nBytesRead = pFile1->Read(buffer, MAXBUF - 1);
        buffer[nBytesRead] = '\0'; // necessary for message box
        char temp[10];
        if(pFile1->Read(temp, 10) != 0) {
            // makes caching work if read complete
            AfxMessageBox("File overran buffer -- not cached");
        }
        AfxMessageBox(buffer);
    }
    catch(CInternetException* e) {
        // Log the exception
        e->Delete();
    }
    if(pFile1) delete pFile1;
    if(pConnection) delete pConnection;
    delete [] buffer;
    return 0;
}
```

The second *Read* call needs some explanation. It has two purposes. If the first *Read* doesn't read the whole file, that means that it was longer than

MAXBUF −1. The second *Read* will get some bytes, and that lets you detect the overflow problem. If the first *Read* reads the whole file, you still need the second *Read* to force WinInet to cache the file on your hard disk. Remember that WinInet tries to read all the bytes you ask it to—through the end of the file. Even so, you need to read 0 bytes after that.

Building a Web Client with the MFC WinInet Classes

There are two ways to build a Web client with WinInet. The first method, using the *CHttpConnection* class, is similar to the simplified WinInet client on the preceding page. The second method, using *CInternetSession::OpenURL*, is even easier. We'll start with the *CHttpConnection* version.

The EX34A WinInet Client #1—Using *CHttpConnection*

The EX34A program implements a WinInet client in the file \vcpp32\ex34a-\ClientInetThread.cpp on the CD-ROM. Besides allowing the use of an IP address as well as a host name, the program uses a status callback function. That function, *CCallbackInternetSession::OnStatusCallback* in the file \vcpp32\ex34a-\utility.cpp, puts a text string in a global variable *g_pchStatus*, using a critical section for synchronization. The function then posts a user-defined message to the application's main window. The message triggers an Update Command UI handler (called by *CWinApp::OnIdle*), which displays the text in the second status bar text pane.

Testing the WinInet Client #1

To test the WinInet client #1, you can follow the same procedure you used to test the Winsock client. Note the status bar messages as the connection is made. Note that the file appears more quickly the second time you request it.

The EX34A WinInet Client #2—Using *OpenURL*

The EX34A program implements a different WinInet client in the file Client-UrlThread.cpp on the companion CD-ROM. This client uses the "Address" URL (that you type to access the Internet site). Here's the actual code:

```
CString g_strURL = "http:// ";

UINT ClientUrlThreadProc(LPVOID pParam)
{
```

```
char* buffer = new char[MAXBUF];
UINT nBytesRead = 0;

CInternetSession session; // can't get status callbacks for OpenURL
CStdioFile* pFile1 = NULL; // could call ReadString to get 1 line
try {
    pFile1 = session.OpenURL(g_strURL, 0, INTERNET_FLAG_TRANSFER_BINARY
        |INTERNET_FLAG_KEEP_CONNECTION);
     // If OpenURL fails, we won't get past here
    nBytesRead = pFile1->Read(buffer, MAXBUF - 1);
    buffer[nBytesRead] = '\0'; // necessary for message box
    char temp[100];
    if(pFile1->Read(temp, 100) != 0) {
        // makes caching work if read complete
        AfxMessageBox("File overran buffer -- not cached");
    }
    ::MessageBox(::GetTopWindow(::GetDesktopWindow()), buffer,
        "URL CLIENT", MB_OK);
}
catch(CInternetException* e) {
    LogInternetException(pParam, e);
    e->Delete();
}
if(pFile1) delete pFile1;
delete [] buffer;
return 0;
}
```

Note that *OpenURL* returns a pointer to a *CStdioFile* object. You can use that pointer to call *Read* as shown, or you can call *ReadString* to get a single line. The file class does all the buffering. As in the previous WinInet client, it's necessary to call *Read* a second time to cache the file. The *OpenURL INTERNET_FLAG_KEEP_CONNECTION* parameter is necessary for Windows NT challenge/response authentication, which is described in Chapter 35. If you added the flag *INTERNET_FLAG_RELOAD*, the program would bypass the cache just as the browser does when you click the Refresh button.

Testing the WinInet Client #2

You can test the WinInet client #2 against any HTTP server. You run this client by typing in the URL address, not by using the menu. You must include the protocol (http:// or ftp://) in the URL address. Type *http://localhost*. You should see the same HTML code in a message box. No status messages appear here because the status callback doesn't work with *OpenURL*.

Asynchronous Moniker Files

Just when you thought you knew all the ways to download a file from the Internet, you're going to learn about another one. With asynchronous moniker files, you'll be doing all your programming in your application's main thread without blocking the user interface. Sounds like magic, doesn't it? The magic is inside the Windows URLMON DLL, which depends on WinInet and is used by Microsoft Internet Explorer. The MFC *CAsyncMonikerFile* class makes the programming easy, but you should know a little theory first.

Monikers

A <u>moniker</u> is a "surrogate" COM object that holds the name (URL) of the "real" object, which could be an embedded component but more often is just an Internet file (HTML, JPEG, GIF, and so on). Monikers implement the *IMoniker* interface, which has two important member functions: *BindToObject* and *BindToStorage*. The *BindToObject* function puts an object into the running state, and the *BindToStorage* function provides an *IStream* or an *IStorage* pointer from which the object's data can be read. A moniker has an associated *IBindStatusCallback* interface with member functions such as *OnStartBinding* and *OnDataAvailable*, which are called during the process of reading data from a URL.

The callback functions are called in the thread that created the moniker. This means that the URLMON DLL must set up an invisible window in the calling thread and send the calling thread messages from another thread, which uses WinInet functions to read the URL. The window's message handlers call the callback functions.

The MFC *CAsyncMonikerFile* Class

Fortunately, MFC can shield you from the COM interfaces described above. The *CAsyncMonikerFile* class is derived from *CFile*, so it acts like a regular file. Instead of opening a disk file, the class's *Open* member function gets an *IMoniker* pointer and encapsulates the *IStream* interface returned from a call to *BindToStorage*. Furthermore, the class has virtual functions that are tied to the member functions of *IBindStatusCallback*. Using this class is a breeze; you construct an object or a derived class and call the *Open* member function, which returns immediately. Then you wait for calls to overridden virtual functions such as *OnProgress* and *OnDataAvailable*, named, not coincidentally, after their *IBindStatusCallback* equivalents.

Using the *CAsyncMonikerFile* Class in a Program

Suppose your application downloads data from a dozen URLs but has only one class derived from *CAsyncMonikerFile*. The overridden callback functions must figure out where to put the data. That means you must associate each derived class object with some UI element in your program. The steps listed below illustrate one of many ways to do this. Suppose you want to list the text of an HTML file in an edit control that's part of a form view. This is what you can do:

1. Use ClassWizard to derive a class from *CAsyncMonikerFile*.

2. Add a character pointer data member *m_buffer*. Invoke *new* for this pointer in the constructor; invoke *delete* in the destructor.

3. Add a public data member *m_edit* of class *CEdit*.

4. Override the *OnDataAvailable* function thus:

```
void CMyMonikerFile::OnDataAvailable(DWORD dwSize, DWORD bscfFlag)
{
    try {
        UINT nBytesRead = Read(m_buffer, MAXBUF - 1);
        TRACE("nBytesRead = %d\n", nBytesRead);
        m_buffer[nBytesRead] = '\0'; // necessary for edit control
        // The following two lines add text to the edit control
        m_edit.SendMessage(EM_SETSEL, (WPARAM) 999999, 1000000);
        m_edit.SendMessage(EM_REPLACESEL, (WPARAM) 0,
            (LPARAM) m_buffer);
    }
    catch(CFileException* pe) {
        TRACE("File exception %d\n, pe->m_cause");
        pe->Delete();
    }
}
```

5. Embed an object of your new moniker file class in your view class.

6. In you view's *OnInitialUpdate* function, attach the *CEdit* member to the edit control like this:

```
m_myEmbeddedMonikerFile.m_edit.SubClassDlgItem(ID_MYEDIT, this);
```

7. In your view class, open the moniker file like this:

```
m_myEmbeddedMonikerFile.Open("http://host/filename");
```

For a large file, *OnDataAvailable* will be called several times, each time adding text to the edit control. If you override *OnProgress* or *OnStopBinding* in your derived moniker file class, your program can be alerted when the transfer is finished. You can also check the value of *bscfFlag* in *OnDataAvailable* to determine whether the transfer is completed. Note that everything here is in your main thread and—most important—the moniker file object must exist for as long as the transfer is in progress. That's why it's a data member of the view class.

Asynchronous Moniker Files vs. WinInet Programming

In the WinInet examples earlier in this chapter, you started a worker thread that made blocking calls and sent a message to the main thread when it was finished. With asynchronous moniker files, the same thing happens—the transfer takes place in another thread, which sends messages to the main thread. You just don't see the other thread. There is one very important difference, however, between asynchronous moniker files and WinInet programming: with blocking WinInet calls, you need a separate thread for each transfer; with asynchronous moniker files, only one extra thread handles all transfers together. For example, if you're writing a browser that must download 50 bitmaps simultaneously, using asynchronous moniker files saves 49 threads, which makes the program much more efficient.

Of course, you have some extra control with WinInet, and it's easier to get information from the response headers, such as total file length. Your choice of programming tools, then, depends on your application. The more you know about your options, the better your choice will be.

Programming the Microsoft Internet Information Server

In Chapter 34, you used a "homemade" Web based on the Winsock APIs. In this chapter, you'll learn how to use and extend Microsoft Internet Information Server (IIS) 4.0, which is bundled with Microsoft Windows NT Server 4.0. IIS is actually three separate servers—one for HTTP (for the World Wide Web), one for FTP, and one for gopher. This chapter tells you how to write HTTP server extensions using the Microsoft IIS application programming interface (ISAPI) that is part of Microsoft ActiveX technology. You'll examine two kinds of extensions: an ISAPI server extension and an ISAPI filter, both of which are DLLs. An ISAPI server extension can perform Internet business transactions such as order entry. An ISAPI filter intercepts data traveling to and from the server and thus can perform specialized logging and other tasks.

IIS Alternatives

The exercises in this chapter assume that you have Windows NT Server 4.0 and IIS. If you are running Windows NT Workstation, you can use Peer Web Services, which supports fewer connections and doesn't allow virtual servers. If you are running Microsoft Windows 95 or Windows 98, you can use Personal Web Server, which is packaged with Microsoft FrontPage. Internet Information Server, Peer Web Services, and Personal Web Server can all use ISAPI extension DLLs. See your server's documentation for operating details.

Microsoft IIS

Microsoft IIS is a high-performance Internet/intranet server that takes advantage of Windows NT features such as I/O completion ports, the Win32 function *TransmitFile*, file-handle caching, and CPU scaling for threads.

Installing and Controlling IIS

When you install Windows NT Server 4.0, you are given the option of installing IIS. If you selected IIS at setup, the server will be running whenever Windows NT is running. IIS is a special kind of Win32 program called a <u>service</u> (actually three services—WWW, HTTP, and gopher—in one program called inetinfo.exe), which won't appear in the taskbar. You can control IIS from the Services icon in the Control Panel, but you'll probably want to use the Internet Service Manager program instead.

Running Internet Service Manager

You can run Internet Service Manager from the Microsoft Internet Server menu that's accessible on the Start menu.

> NOTE: You can also run an HTML-based version of Internet Service Manager remotely from a browser. That version allows you to change service parameters, but it won't let you turn services on and off.

Figure 35-1 shows the Microsoft Internet Service Manager screen with the World Wide Web (WWW) running and FTP services stopped.

You can select a service by clicking on its icon at the left. The triangle and square buttons on the toolbar of the screen allow you to turn the selected service on or off.

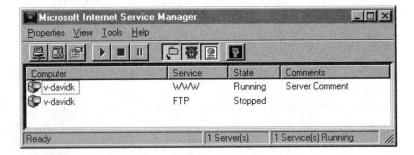

Figure 35-1.
The Microsoft Internet Service Manager screen.

IIS Security

After you double-click on the WWW service icon of the Microsoft Internet Service Manager screen, you'll see a property sheet. The Service page lets you configure IIS security. When a client browser requests a file, the server impersonates a local user for the duration of the request and that user name determines which files the client can access. Which local user does the server impersonate? Most often, it's the one you see in the Username field, shown in Figure 35-2.

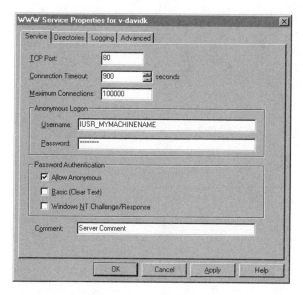

Figure 35-2.
The WWW Service Properties screen.

Most Web page visitors don't supply a user name and password, so they are considered <u>anonymous</u> <u>users</u>. Those users have the same rights they would have if they had logged on to your server locally as IUSR_MYMACHINE-NAME. That means that IUSR_MYMACHINENAME must appear in the list of users that is displayed when you run User Manager or User Manager For Domains (from the Administrative Tools menu), and the passwords must match. The IIS Setup program normally defines this anonymous user for you. You can define your own WWW anonymous user name, but you must be sure that the entry on the Service page matches the entry in the computer's (or Windows NT domain's) user list.

Note also the Password Authentication options. For the time being, stick to the Allow Anonymous option only, which means that all Web users are logged on as IUSR_MYMACHINENAME. Later in this chapter, we'll explain Windows NT Challenge/Response.

IIS Directories

Remember SlowSoft's Web site from Chapter 34? If you requested the URL http://slowsoft.com/newproducts.html, the newproducts.html file would be displayed from the slowsoft.com <u>home directory</u>. Each server needs a home directory, even if that directory contains only subdirectories. The home directory does not need to be the server computer's root directory, however. As shown in Figure 35-3, the WWW home directory is really \WebHome, so clients read the disk file \WebHome\newproducts.html.

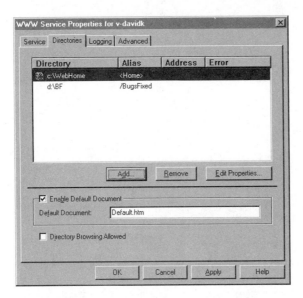

Figure 35-3.
The \WebHome WWW home directory screen.

Your server could get by with a home directory only, but the IIS <u>virtual directory</u> feature might be useful. Suppose SlowSoft wanted to allow Web access to the directory \BF on the D drive. The screen above shows a virtual /BugsFixed directory that maps to D:\BF. Clients would access files with a URL similar to this: http://slowsoft.com/BugsFixed/file1.html.

> NOTE: If your computer was configured for multiple IP addresses (see the Control Panel Network icon), IIS would allow you to define <u>virtual Web servers</u>. Each virtual server would have its own home directory (and virtual directories) attached to a specified IP address, making it appear as though you had several server computers. Unfortunately, the IIS Web server listens on all the computer's IP addresses, so you can't run IIS simultaneously with the EX34A server with both listening on port 80.

As described in Chapter 34, browsers can issue a blind request. As Figure 35-3 shows, Internet Service Manager lets you specify the file that a blind request selects, usually Default.htm. If you select the Directory Browsing Allowed option of the Directories page on the service property screen, browser clients can see a hypertext list of files in the server's directory instead.

IIS Logging

IIS is capable of making log entries for all connections. You control logging from the Internet Service Manager's Logging property page. You can specify text log files, or you can specify logging to an SQL/ODBC database. Log entries consist of date, time, client IP address, file requested, query string, and so forth.

Testing IIS

It's easy to test IIS with a browser or with any of the EX35A clients. Just make sure that IIS is running and that the EX35A server is not running. The default IIS home directory is \Winnt\System32\inetsrv\wwwroot, and some HTML files are installed there. If you're running a single machine, you can use the localhost host name. For a network, use a name from the Hosts file. If you can't access the server from a remote machine, run ping to make sure the network is configured correctly. Don't try to build and run ISAPI DLLs until you have successfully tested IIS on your computer.

ISAPI Server Extensions

An ISAPI server extension is a program (implemented as a DLL loaded by IIS) that runs in response to a GET or POST request from a client program (browser). The browser can pass parameters to the program, which are often values that the browser user types into edit controls, selects from list boxes, and so forth. The ISAPI server extension typically sends back HTML code based on those parameter values. You'll better understand this process when you see an example.

Common Gateway Interface and ISAPI

Internet server programs were first developed for UNIX computers, so the standards were in place long before Microsoft introduced IIS. The Common Gateway Interface (CGI) standard, actually part of HTTP, evolved as a way for browser programs to interact with scripts or separate executable programs running on the server. Without altering the HTTP/CGI specifications, Microsoft designed IIS to allow any browser to load and run a server DLL. DLLs are part of the IIS process and thus are faster than scripts that might need to load separate executable programs. Because of your experience, you'll probably find it easier to write an ISAPI DLL in C++ than to write a script in PERL, the standard Web scripting language for servers.

CGI shifts the programming burden to the server. Using CGI <u>parameters</u>, the browser sends small amounts of information to the server computer, and the server can do absolutely anything with this information, including access a database, generate images, and control peripheral devices. The server sends a file (HTML or otherwise) back to the browser. The file can be read from the server's disk, or it can be generated by the program. No ActiveX controls or Java applets are necessary, and the browser can be running on any type of computer.

A Simple ISAPI Server Extension GET Request

Suppose an HTML file contains the following tag:

```
<a href="scripts/maps.dll?State=Idaho">Idaho Weather Map</a><p>
```

When the user clicks on *Idaho Weather Map*, the browser sends the server a CGI GET request like this:

```
GET scripts/maps.dll?State=Idaho HTTP/1.0
```

IIS then loads maps.dll from its scripts (virtual) directory, calls a <u>default function</u> (often named *Default*), and passes it the *State* parameter *Idaho*. The DLL then goes to work generating a JPG file containing the up-to-the-minute satellite weather map for Idaho and sends it to the client.

If maps.dll had more than one function, the tag could specify the function name like this:

```
<a href="scripts/maps.dll?GetMap?State=Idaho&Res=5">Idaho Weather Map</a><p>
```

In this case, the function *GetMap* is called with two parameters, *State* and *Res*.

You'll soon learn how to write an ISAPI server similar to maps.dll, but first you'll need to understand <u>HTML</u> <u>forms</u>, because you don't often see CGI GET requests by themselves.

HTML Forms—GET vs. POST

In the HTML code for the simple CGI GET request above, the state name was hard-coded in the tag. Why not let the user select the state from a drop-down list? For that, you need a form, and here's a simple one that can do the job.

```
<html>
<head><title>Weathermap HTML Form</title>
</head>
<body>
<h1><center>Welcome to the Satellite Weathermap Service</center></h1>
<form action="scripts/maps.dll?GetMap" method=GET>
    <p>Select your state:
    <select name="State">
        <option> Alabama
        <option> Alaska
        <option> Idaho
        <option> Washington
    </select>
<p><input type="submit"><input type="reset">
</form>
</body></html>
```

If you looked at this HTML file with a browser, you would see the form shown in Figure 35-4.

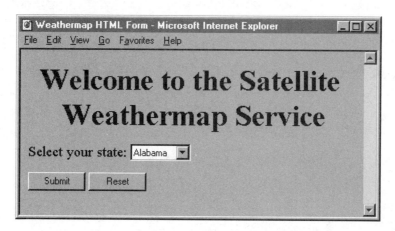

Figure 35-4.
The Weathermap HTML Form window.

The select tag provides the state name from a list of four states, and the all-important "submit" input tag displays the pushbutton that sends the form data to the server in the form of a CGI GET request that looks like this:

```
GET scripts/maps.dll?GetMap?State=Idaho HTTP/1.0
(various request headers)
(blank line)
```

Unfortunately, some early versions of the Netscape browser omit the function name in form-originated GET requests, giving you two choices: provide only a default function in your ISAPI DLL, and use the POST method inside a form instead of the GET method.

If you want to use the POST option, change one HTML line in the form on the previous page to the following:

```
<form action="scripts/maps.dll?GetMap" method=POST>
```

Now here's what the browser sends to the server:

```
POST scripts/maps.dll?GetMap
(various request headers)
(blank line)
State=Idaho
```

Note that the parameter value is in the last line instead of in the request line.

> **NOTE:** ISAPI DLLs are usually stored in a separate virtual directory on the server because these DLLs must have <u>execute permission</u> but do not need <u>read permission</u>. Clicking the Edit Properties button shown in Figure 35-3 will allow you to access these permissions from the Internet Service Manager, or you can double-click on a directory to change its properties.

Writing an ISAPI Server Extension DLL

Visual C++ gives you a quick start for writing ISAPI server extensions. Just select ISAPI Extension Wizard from the Projects list. After you click the OK button, your first screen looks like Figure 35-5.

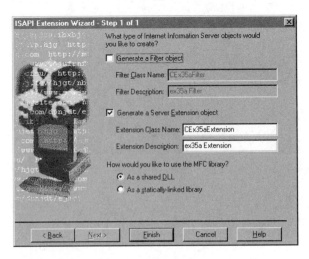

Figure 35-5.
The Step 1 page of the ISAPI Extension Wizard.

Check the Generate A Server Extension Object box, and you've got a do-nothing DLL project with a class derived from the MFC *CHttpServer* class and a *Default* member function. Now it's time for a little programming.

You must write your ISAPI functions as members of the derived *CHttp-Server* class, and you must write <u>parse</u> <u>map</u> macros to link them to IIS. There's no "parse map wizard," so you have to do some coding. It's okay to use the *Default* function, but you need a *GetMap* function too. First insert these lines into the wizard-generated parse map:

```
ON_PARSE_COMMAND(GetMap, CWeatherExtension, ITS_PSTR)
ON_PARSE_COMMAND_PARAMS("State")
```

Then write the *GetMap* function:

```
void CWeatherExtension::GetMap(CHttpServerContext* pCtxt, LPCTSTR pstrState)
{
    StartContent(pCtxt);
    WriteTitle(pCtxt);
    *pCtxt << "Visualize a weather map for the state of ";
    *pCtxt << pstrState;
    EndContent(pCtxt);
}
```

This function doesn't actually generate the weather map (what did you expect?), but it does display the selected state name in a custom HTML file. The *CHttpServer::StartContent* and *CHttpServer::EndContent* functions write the HTML boilerplate, and *CHttpServer::WriteTitle* calls the virtual *CHttpServer-::GetTitle* function, which you need to override:

```
LPCTSTR CWeatherExtension::GetTitle() const
{
    return "Your custom weather map"; // for browser's title window
}
```

The MFC *CHttpServerContext* class has an overloaded << operator, which you use to put text in the HTML file you're building. Behind the scenes, an attached object of the MFC class *CHtmlStream* represents the output to the server's socket.

The MFC ISAPI Server Extension Classes

Now is a good time to review the three MFC classes that are used to create an MFC ISAPI server extension. Remember that these classes are for ISAPI server extensions <u>only</u>. Don't even think of using them in ordinary Winsock or WinInet applications.

CHttpServer

With the help of the ISAPI Extension Wizard, you derive a class from *CHttp-Server* for each ISAPI server extension DLL that you create. You need one member function for each extension function (including the default function), and you need an overridden *GetTitle* function. The framework calls your extension functions in response to client requests, using the connections established in the parse map. The ISAPI Extension Wizard provides an overridden *Get-ExtensionVersion* function, which you seldom edit unless you need initialization code to be executed when the DLL is loaded.

One of the *CHttpServer* member functions that you're likely to call is *AddHeader*, which adds special response headers, such as Set-Cookie, before the response is sent to the server. (More on cookies later.)

CHttpServerContext

There's one *CHttpServer* object per DLL, but there is one *CHttpServerContext* object for each server transaction request. Your extension functions each provide a pointer to one of these objects. You don't derive from *CHttpServerContext*, so you can't easily have variables for individual transactions. Because different IIS threads can manage transactions, you have to be careful to perform synchronization for any data members of your *CHttpServer* class or global variables.

You've already seen the use of the *StartContent*, *EndContent*, and *Write-Title* functions of the *CHttpServer* class plus the overloaded >> operator. You might also need to call the *CHttpServerContext::GetServerVariable* function to read information sent by the client in the request headers.

CHtmlStream

Most of the time, you don't use the *CHtmlStream* class directly. The *CHttpServerContext* class has a *CHtmlStream* data member, *m_pStream*, that's hooked up to the >> operator and serves as the output for HTML data. You could access the *CHtmlStream* object and call its *Write* member function if you needed to send binary data to the client. Because objects of the *CHtmlStream* class accumulate bytes in memory before sending them to the client, you need an alternative approach if your DLL relays large files directly from disk.

A Practical ISAPI Server Extension—ex35a.dll

The weather map server isn't interesting enough to make into a real project. You'll probably find the EX35A example more to your taste. It's a real Internet commerce application—a pizza-ordering program. Imagine a computer-controlled pizza oven and a robot arm that selects frozen pizzas. (Microsoft Internet Explorer 17.0 is supposed to be able to deliver the hot pizzas directly from your clients' monitors, but in the meantime, you'll have to hire some delivery drivers.)

The First Step—Getting the Order

Junior sales trainees are constantly admonished to "get the order." That's certainly necessary in any form of commerce, including the Internet. When the hungry customer hyperlinks to your site (by clicking on a picture of a pizza, of course), he or she simply downloads an HTML file that looks like this:

```
<html>
<head><title>Inside Visual C++ HTML Form 1</title>
</head>
<body>
<h1><center>Welcome to CyberPizza</center></h1>
<p> Enter your order.
<form action="scripts/ex35a.dll?ProcessPizzaForm" method=POST>
    <p> Your Name: <input type="text" name="name" value="">
    <p> Your Address: <input type="text" name="address" value="">
    <p> Number of Pies: <input type="text" name="quantity" value=1>
    <p>Pizza Size:
        <menu>
            <li><input type="radio" name="size" value=8>8-inch
            <li><input type="radio" name="size" value=10>10-inch
            <li><input type="radio" name="size" value=12 checked>12-inch
            <li><input type="radio" name="size" value=14>14-inch
        </menu>
    <p> Toppings:
    <p>
        <input type="checkbox" name="top1" value="Pepperoni" checked>
            Pepperoni
        <input type="checkbox" name="top2" value="Onions"> Onions
        <input type="checkbox" name="top3" value="Mushrooms"> Mushrooms
        <input type="checkbox" name="top4" value="Sausage"> Sausage
    <p>
        <em>(you can select multiple toppings)</em>
    <p><input type="submit" value="Submit Order Now"><input type="reset">
</form>
</body></html>
```

Figure 35-6 on the following page shows how the order form appears in the browser.

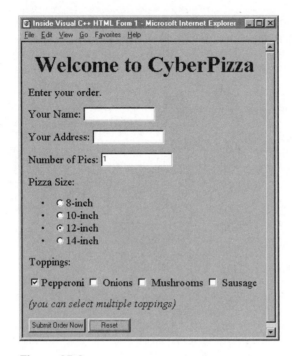

Figure 35-6.
The CyberPizza order form.

So far, no ISAPI DLL is involved. When the customer clicks the Submit Order Now button, the action begins. Here's what the server sees:

```
POST scripts/ex35a.dll?ProcessPizzaForm HTTP/1.0
(request headers)
(blank line)
name=Walter+Sullivan&address=Redmond%2C+WA&quantity=2&size=12&top1=Pepperoni
    &top3=Mushrooms
```

Looks like Walter Sullivan has ordered two 12-inch pepperoni and mushroom pizzas. The browser inserts a + sign in place of a space, the *%2C* is a comma, and the *&* is the parameter separator. Now let's look at the parse map entries in ex35a.cpp:

```
ON_PARSE_COMMAND(ProcessPizzaForm, CEx35aExtension,
    ITS_PSTR ITS_PSTR ITS_I4 ITS_PSTR ITS_PSTR ITS_PSTR ITS_PSTR ITS_PSTR)
ON_PARSE_COMMAND_PARAMS("name address quantity size top1=~ top2=~ top3=~ ⤳
    top4=~")
```

Optional Parameters

When you write your parse map statements, you must understand the browser's rules for sending parameter values from a form. In the EX35A pizza form, the browser always sends parameters for text fields, even if the user enters no data. If the user left the Name field blank, for example, the browser would send *name=&*. For check box fields, however, it's a different story. The browser sends the check box parameter value only if the user checks the box. The parameters associated with check boxes are thus defined as <u>optional</u> <u>parameters</u>.

If your parse macro for parameters looked like this

```
ON_PARSE_COMMAND_PARAMS("name address quantity size top1 top2 top3 ⬏
    top4")
```

there would be trouble if the customer didn't check all the toppings. The HTTP request would simply fail, and the customer would have to search for another pizza site. The =~ symbols in the ex35a.cpp code designate the last four parameters as optional, with default values ~. If the Toppings option is checked, the form transmits the value; otherwise, it transmits a ~ character, which the DLL can test for. Optional parameters must be listed last.

The DLL's *ProcessPizzaForm* function reads the parameter values and produces an HTML confirmation form, which it sends to the customer. Here is part of the function's code:

```
    *pCtxt << "<form action=\"ex35a.dll?ConfirmOrder\" method=POST>";
    *pCtxt << "<p><input type=\"hidden\" name=\"name\" value=\"";
    *pCtxt << pstrName << "\">"; // xref to original order
    *pCtxt << "<p><input type=\"submit\" value=\"Confirm and charge my ⬏
        credit card\">";
    *pCtxt << "</form>";
    // Store this order in a disk file or database, referenced by name
}
else {
    *pCtxt << "You forgot to enter name or address. Back up and try ⬏
        again. ";
}
EndContent(pCtxt);
```

The resulting browser screen is shown in Figure 35-7.

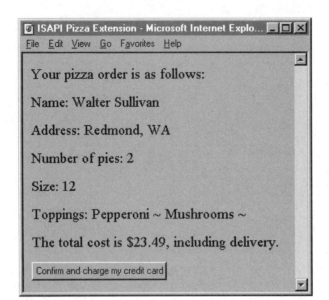

Figure 35-7.
The pizza confirmation browser screen.

As you can see, we took a shortcut computing the price. To accept, the customer clicks the submit button named Confirm And Charge My Credit Card.

The Second Step—Processing the Confirmation

When the user clicks the Confirm And Charge My Credit Card button, the browser sends a second POST request to the server, specifying that the *CEx35a-Extension::ConfirmOrder* function be called. But now you have to solve a big problem. Each HTTP connection (request/response) is independent of all others. How are you going to link the confirmation request with the original order? Although there are different ways to do this, the most common approach is to send some text back with the confirmation in a <u>hidden</u> <u>input</u> <u>tag</u>. When the confirmation parameter values come back, the server uses the hidden text to match the confirmation to the original order, which it has stored somewhere on its hard disk.

In the EX35A example, the customer's name is used in the hidden field, although it might be safer to use some combination of the name, date, and time. Here's the HTML code that *CEx35aExtension::ProcessPizzaForm* sends to the customer as part of the confirmation form:

```
<input type="hidden" name="name" value="Walter Sullivan">
```

Here's the code for the *CEx35aExtension::ConfirmOrder* function:

```
void CEx35aExtension::ConfirmOrder(CHttpServerContext* pCtxt,
    LPCTSTR pstrName)
{
    StartContent(pCtxt);
    WriteTitle(pCtxt);
    *pCtxt << "<p>Our courteous delivery person will arrive within 30 ↴
        minutes. ";
    *pCtxt << "<p>Thank you, " << pstrName << ", for using CyberPizza. ";
    // Now retrieve the order from disk by name, and then make the pizza.
    //  Be prepared to delete the order after a while if the customer
    //  doesn't confirm.
    m_cs.Lock(); // gotta be threadsafe
    long int nTotal = ++m_nTotalPizzaOrders;
    m_cs.Unlock();
    *pCtxt << "<p>Total pizza orders = " << nTotal;
    EndContent(pCtxt);
}
```

The customer's name comes back in the *pstrName* parameter, and that's what you use to retrieve the original order from disk. The function also keeps track of the total number of orders, using a critical section (*m_cs*) to ensure thread synchronization.

Building and Testing ex35a.dll

If you have copied the code from the companion CD-ROM, your project is located in \vcpp32\ex35a. Building the project adds a DLL to the Debug subdirectory. You must copy this DLL to a directory that the server can find and copy PizzaForm.html also. You can use the scripts and wwwroot subdirectories already under \Winnt\System32\inetsrv, or you can set up new virtual directories.

> **NOTE:** If you make changes to the EX35A DLL in the Visual C++ project, be sure to use Internet Service Manager (Figure 35-1) to turn off the WWW service (because the old DLL stays loaded), copy the new DLL to the scripts directory, and then turn the WWW service on again. The revised DLL will be loaded as soon as the first client requests it.

If everything has been installed correctly, you should be able to load PizzaForm.html from the browser and then order some pizza. Enjoy!

Debugging the EX35A DLL

The fact that IIS is a Windows NT service complicates debugging ISAPI DLLs. Services normally run as part of the operating system, controlled by the service manager database. They have their own window station, and they run on their own invisible desktop. This involves some of the murkier parts of Windows NT, and not much published information is available.

However, you can use these steps to debug your EX35A DLL (or any ISAPI DLL):

1. Use the Internet Service Manager to stop <u>all</u> IIS services.

2. Choose Settings from the EX35A project Build menu, and in the Project Settings dialog, type in the data as shown.

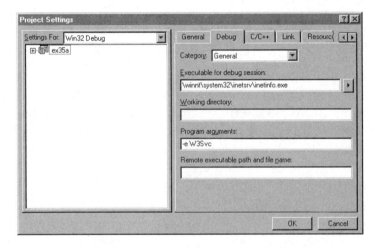

3. Start User Manager or User Manager For Domains (Administrative Tools menu). Choose User Rights from the Policies menu, check Show Advanced User Rights, select the right Act As Part Of The Operating System, and add your user group as shown on the facing page.

4. Repeat step 3 to set the right for Generate Security Audits.

5. Log back on to Windows NT to activate the new permission. (Don't forget this step.)

6. Make sure that the current EX35A DLL file has been copied into the scripts directory.

7. Start debugging. You can set breakpoints, step through code, and see the output of *TRACE* messages.

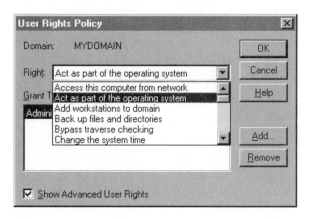

ISAPI Database Access

Your ISAPI server extension could use ODBC to access an SQL database. Before you write pages of ODBC code, however, check out the Internet Database Connector described in the IIS documentation. The Internet Database Connector is a ready-to-run DLL, Httpodbc.dll, that collects SQL query parameters and formats the output. You control the process by writing an IDC file that describes the data source and an HTX file that is a template for the resulting HTML file. No C++ programming is necessary.

The Internet Database Connector is for queries only. If you want to update a database, you must write your own ISAPI server extension with ODBC calls. Make sure your ODBC driver is multithreaded, as is the latest SQL server driver.

Using HTTP Cookies to Link Transactions

Now that you've wolfed down the pizza, it's time for some dessert. However, the cookies that we'll be digesting in this section are not made with chocolate chips. Cookies are used to store information on our customers' hard disks. In the EX35A example, the server stores the customer name in a hidden field of the confirmation form. That works fine for linking the confirmation to the order, but it doesn't help you track how many pizzas Walter ordered this year. If you notice that Walter consistently orders pepperoni pizzas, you might want to send him some e-mail when you have a surplus of pepperoni.

How Cookies Work

With cookies, you assign Walter a customer ID number with his first order and make him keep track of that number on his computer. The server assigns the number by sending a response header such as this one:

```
Set-Cookie: customer_id=12345; path=/; expires=Monday,
    02-Sep-99 00:00:00 GMT
```

The string *customer_id* is the arbitrary <u>cookie</u> <u>name</u> you have assigned, the / value for *path* means that the browser sends the cookie value for any request to your site (named CyberPizza.com), and the expiration date is necessary for the browser to store the cookie value.

When the browser sees the *Set-Cookie* response header, it creates (or replaces) an entry in its cookies.txt file as follows:

```
customer_id
12345
cyberpizza.com/
0
2096697344
0
2093550622
35
*
```

Thereafter, when the browser requests anything from CyberPizza.com, the browser sends a request header like this:

```
Cookie: customer_id=12345
```

How an ISAPI Server Extension Processes Cookies

Your ISAPI server extension function makes a call like this one to store the cookie at the browser:

```
AddHeader(pCtxt, "Set-Cookie: session_id=12345; path=/;"
    " expires=Monday, " 02-Sep-99 00:00:00 GMT\r\n");
```

To retrieve the cookie, another function uses code like this:

```
char strCookies[200];
DWORD dwLength = 200;
pCtxt->GetServerVariable("HTTP_COOKIE", strCookies, &dwLength);
```

The *strCookies* variable should now contain the text *customer_id=12345*.

Problems with Cookies

There was an uproar some time ago when Internet users first discovered that companies were storing data on the users' PCs. New browser versions now ask permission before storing a cookie from a Web site. Customers could thus refuse to accept your cookie, they could erase their cookies.txt file, or this file could become full. If you decide to use cookies at your Web site, you'll just have to deal with those possibilities.

WWW Authentication

Up to now, your IIS has been set to allow anonymous logons, which means that anyone in the world can access your server without supplying a user name or password. All users are logged on as IUSR_MYMACHINENAME and can access any files for which that user name has permissions.

NOTE: As stated in Chapter 34, you should be using NTFS on your server for maximum security.

Basic Authentication

The simplest way to limit server access is to enable basic authentication. Then, if a client makes an anonymous request, the server sends back the response

```
HTTP/1.0 401 Unauthorized
```

together with a response header like this:

```
WWW-Authenticate: Basic realm="xxxx"
```

The client prompts the user for a user name and password, and then it resends the request with a request header something like this:

```
Authorization: Basic 2rc234ldfd8kdr
```

The string that follows Basic is a pseudoencrypted version of the user name and password, which the server decodes and uses to impersonate the client.

The trouble with basic authentication is that intruders can pick up the user name and password and use it to gain access to your server. IIS and most browsers support basic authentication, but it's not very effective.

Windows NT Challenge/Response Authentication

Windows NT challenge/response authentication is often used for intranets running on Microsoft networks, but you can use it on the Internet as well. IIS supports it (see Figure 35-2), but not all browsers do.

If the server has challenge/response activated, a client making an ordinary request gets this response header:

```
WWW-Authenticate: NTLM
Authorization: NTLM T1RMTVNTUAABAAAAA5IAA ...
```

The string after *NTLM* is the well-encoded user name—the password is never sent over the network. The server issues a <u>challenge</u>, with a response header like this:

```
WWW-Authenticate: NTLM RPTUFJTgAAAAA ...
```

The client, which knows the password, does some math on the challenge code and the password and then sends back a response in a request header like this:

```
Authorization: NTLM AgACAAgAAAAAAAAAA ...
```

The server, which has looked up the client's password from the user name, runs the same math on the password and challenge code. It then compares the client's response code against its own result. If the client's and the server's results match, the server honors the client's request by impersonating the client's user name and sending the requested data.

When the client resends the request, the challenge/response dialog is performed over a single-socket connection with keep-alive capability as specified in the Connection request header.

WinInet fully supports Windows NT challenge/response authentication. Thus, Internet Explorer 4.0 and the EX34A WinInet clients support it. If the client computer is logged on to a Windows NT domain, the user name and password are passed through. If the client is on the Internet, WinInet prompts for the user name and password. If you're writing WinInet code, you must use the *INTERNET_FLAG_KEEP_CONNECTION* flag in all *CHttpConnection::OpenRequest* and *CInternetSession::OpenURL* calls, as EX34A illustrates.

The Secure Sockets Layer

Windows NT challenge/response authentication controls only who logs on to a server. Anyone snooping on the Net can read the contents of the TCP/IP segments. The secure sockets layer (SSL) goes one step further and encodes the actual requests and responses (with a performance hit, of course). Both IIS and WinInet support SSL. (The secure sockets layer is described in the IIS documentation.)

ISAPI Filters

An ISAPI server extension DLL is loaded the first time a client references it in a GET or POST request. An ISAPI filter DLL is loaded (based on a Registry entry) when the WWW service is started. The filter is then in the loop for all HTTP requests, so you can read and/or change any data that enters or leaves the server.

Writing an ISAPI Filter DLL

The ISAPI Extension Wizard makes writing filters as easy as writing server extensions. Choose Generate A Filter Object, and Step 2 looks like this.

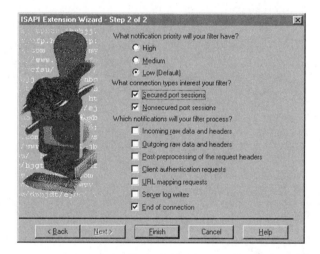

The list of options under Which Notifications Will Your Filter Process? refers to seven places where your filter can get control during the processing of an HTTP request. You check the boxes, and the wizard generates the code.

The MFC ISAPI Filter Classes

There are two MFC classes for ISAPI filters, *CHttpFilter* and *CHttpFilterContext*.

CHttpFilter

With the help of the ISAPI Extension Wizard, you derive a class from *CHttp-Filter* for each ISAPI filter you create. There's just one object of this class. The class has virtual functions for each of seven notifications. The list of filters in the order in which IIS calls them is on the following page.

```
virtual DWORD OnReadRawData(CHttpFilterContext* pCtxt,
                           PHTTP_FILTER_RAW_DATA pRawData);
virtual DWORD OnPreprocHeaders(CHttpFilterContext* pCtxt,
                           PHTTP_FILTER_PREPROC_HEADERS pHeaderInfo);
virtual DWORD OnUrlMap(CHttpFilterContext* pCtxt,
                       PHTTP_FILTER_URL_MAP pMapInfo);
virtual DWORD OnAuthentication(CHttpFilterContext* pCtxt,
                           PHTTP_FILTER_AUTHENT pAuthent);
virtual DWORD OnSendRawData(CHttpFilterContext* pCtxt,
                           PHTTP_FILTER_RAW_DATA pRawData);
virtual DWORD OnLog(CHttpFilterContext* pfc, PHTTP_FILTER_LOG pLog);
virtual DWORD OnEndOfNetSession(CHttpFilterContext* pCtxt);
```

If you override a function, you get control. It would be inefficient, however, if IIS made virtual function calls for every notification for each transaction. Another virtual function, *GetFilterVersion*, is called once when the filter is loaded. The ISAPI Extension Wizard always overrides this function for you, and it sets flags in the function's *pVer* parameter, depending on which notifications you want. Here's a simplified sample with all the flags set:

```
BOOL CMyFilter::GetFilterVersion(PHTTP_FILTER_VERSION pVer)
{
    CHttpFilter::GetFilterVersion(pVer);
    pVer->dwFlags |= SF_NOTIFY_ORDER_LOW | SF_NOTIFY_NONSECURE_PORT |
        SF_NOTIFY_LOG | SF_NOTIFY_AUTHENTICATION |
        SF_NOTIFY_PREPROC_HEADERS | SF_NOTIFY_READ_RAW_DATA |
        SF_NOTIFY_SEND_RAW_DATA | SF_NOTIFY_URL_MAP |
        SF_NOTIFY_END_OF_NET_SESSION;
    return TRUE;
}
```

If you had specified URL mapping requests only, the wizard would have set only the *SF_NOTIFY_URL_MAP* flag and it would have overridden only *OnUrlMap*. IIS would not call the other virtual functions, even if they were overridden in your derived class.

CHttpFilterContext

An object of this second MFC class exists for each server transaction, and each of the notification functions gives you a pointer to that object. The *CHttp-FilterContext* member functions you might call are *GetServerVariable*, *Add-ResponseHeaders*, and *WriteClient*.

A Sample ISAPI Filter—ex35b.dll, ex35c.exe

It was hard to come up with a cute application for ISAPI filters. The one we thought up, ex35b.dll, is a useful visual logging utility. IIS, of course, logs all transactions to a file (or database), but you must stop the server before you can see the log file entries. With this example, you have a real-time transaction viewer that you can customize.

Choosing the Notification

Start by looking at the list of *CHttpFilter* virtual member functions on page 1050. Observe the calling sequence and the parameters. For the EX35B logging application, we chose *OnReadRawData* because it allowed full access to the incoming request and header text (from *pRawData*) and to the source and destination IP addresses (from *pCtxt->GetServerVariable*).

Sending Transaction Data to the Display Program

The ISAPI filter DLL can't display the transactions directly because it runs (as part of the IIS service process) on an invisible desktop. You need a separate program that displays text in a window, and you need a way to send data from the DLL to the display program. There are various ways to send the data across the process boundary. A conversation with Jeff Richter, the Windows guru who wrote *Advanced Windows* (Microsoft Press, 1997), led to the data being put in shared memory. Then a user-defined message, WM_SENDTEXT, is posted to the display program. These messages can queue up, so IIS can keep going independently of the display program.

We declared two handle data members in *CEx35bFilter::m_hProcessDest* and *CEx35bFilter::m_hWndDest*. We added code at the end of the *GetFilterVersion* function to set these data members to the display program's process ID and main window handle. The code finds the display program's main window by its title, ex35b, and then it gets the display program's process ID.

```
m_hProcessDest = NULL;
if((m_hWndDest = ::FindWindow(NULL, "ex35b")) != NULL) {
    DWORD dwProcessId;
    GetWindowThreadProcessId(m_hWndDest, &dwProcessId);
    m_hProcessDest = OpenProcess(PROCESS_DUP_HANDLE, FALSE, dwProcessId);
    SendTextToWindow("EX35B filter started\r\n");
}
```

At the top of the following page is a helper function, *SendTextToWindow*, which sends the WM_SENDTEXT message to the display program.

```
void CEx35bFilter::SendTextToWindow(char* pchData)
{
    if(m_hProcessDest != NULL) {
        int nSize = strlen(pchData) + 1;
        HANDLE hMMFReceiver;
        HANDLE hMMF = ::CreateFileMapping((HANDLE) 0xFFFFFFFF, NULL,
            PAGE_READWRITE, 0, nSize, NULL);
        ASSERT(hMMF != NULL);
        LPVOID lpvFile = ::MapViewOfFile(hMMF, FILE_MAP_WRITE, 0, 0, nSize);
        ASSERT(lpvFile != NULL);
        memcpy((char*) lpvFile, pchData, nSize);
        ::DuplicateHandle(::GetCurrentProcess(), hMMF, m_hProcessDest,
            &hMMFReceiver, 0, FALSE, DUPLICATE_SAME_ACCESS |
            DUPLICATE_CLOSE_SOURCE);
        ::PostMessage(m_hWndDest, WM_SENDTEXT, (WPARAM) 0,
            (LPARAM) hMMFReceiver);
        ::UnmapViewOfFile(lpvFile);
    }
}
```

The *DuplicateHandle* function makes a copy of EX35B's map handle, which it sends to the EX35C program in a message parameter. The EX35C process ID, determined in *GetFilterVersion*, is necessary for the *DuplicateHandle* call. Here is the filter's *OnReadRawData* function, which calls *SendTextTo-Window*:

```
DWORD CEx35bFilter::OnReadRawData(CHttpFilterContext* pCtxt,
    PHTTP_FILTER_RAW_DATA pRawData)
{
    TRACE ("CEx35bFilter::OnReadRawData\n");
    // sends time/date, from IP, to IP, request data to a window
    char pchVar[50] = "";
    char pchOut[2000];
    DWORD dwSize = 50;
    BOOL bRet;
    CString strGmt = CTime::GetCurrentTime().FormatGmt("%m/%d/%y %H:%M:%S →
        GMT");
    strcpy(pchOut, strGmt);
    bRet = pCtxt->GetServerVariable("REMOTE_ADDR", pchVar, &dwSize);
    if(bRet && dwSize > 1) {
        strcat(pchOut, ", From ");
        strcat(pchOut, pchVar);
    }
    bRet = pCtxt->GetServerVariable("SERVER_NAME", pchVar, &dwSize);
    if(bRet && dwSize > 1) {
        strcat(pchOut, ", To ");
        strcat(pchOut, pchVar);
    }
```

```
    strcat(pchOut, "\r\n");
    int nLength = strlen(pchOut);
    // Raw data is not zero-terminated
    strncat(pchOut, (const char*) pRawData->pvInData, pRawData->cbInData);
    nLength += pRawData->cbInData;
    pchOut[nLength] = '\0';
    SendTextToWindow(pchOut);
    return SF_STATUS_REQ_NEXT_NOTIFICATION;
}
```

The Display Program

The display program, ex35c.exe, isn't very interesting. It's a standard AppWizard *CRichEditView* program with a WM_SENDTEXT handler in the main frame class:

```
LONG CMainFrame::OnSendText(UINT wParam, LONG lParam)
{
    TRACE("CMainFrame::OnSendText\n");
    LPVOID lpvFile = ::MapViewOfFile((HANDLE) lParam, FILE_MAP_READ, 0, 0,
        0);
    GetActiveView()->SendMessage(EM_SETSEL, (WPARAM) 999999, 1000000);
    GetActiveView()->SendMessage(EM_REPLACESEL, (WPARAM) 0,
        (LPARAM) lpvFile);
    ::UnmapViewOfFile(lpvFile);
    ::CloseHandle((HANDLE) lParam);

    return 0;
}
```

This function just relays the text to the view.

The EX35C *CMainFrame* class overrides *OnUpdateFrameTitle* to eliminate the document name from the main window's title. This ensures that the DLL can find the EX35C window by name.

The view class maps the WM_RBUTTONDOWN message to implement a context menu for erasing the view text. Apparently rich edit view windows don't support the WM_CONTEXTMENU message.

Building and Testing the EX35B ISAPI Filter

Build both the EX35B and EX35C projects, and then start the EX35C program. To specify loading of your new filter DLL, you must manually update the Registry. Run the Regedit application, and then double-click on *Filter DLLs* in \HKEY_LOCAL_MACHINE\SYSTEM\CurrentControlSet\Services\W3SVC\Parameters. Add the full pathname of the DLL separated from other DLL names with a comma.

There's one more thing to do. You must change the IIS mode to allow the service to interact with the EX35C display program. To do this, click on the Services icon in the Control Panel, double-click on World Wide Web Publishing Service, and then check Allow Service To Interact With Desktop. Finally, use Internet Service Manager to stop and restart the WWW service to load the filter DLL. When you use the browser to retrieve pages from the server, you should see output like this.

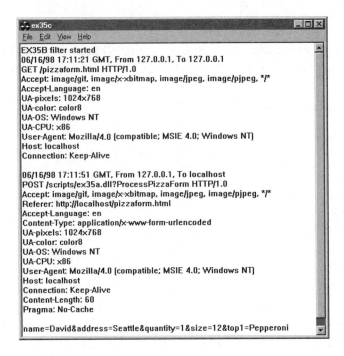

You can use the same steps for debugging an ISAPI filter that you used for an ISAPI server extension.

CHAPTER THIRTY-SIX

ActiveX Document Servers and the Internet

An ActiveX document is a special file that you can download from a Web server. When the browser sees an ActiveX document file, it automatically loads the corresponding ActiveX document server program from your hard disk, and that program takes over the whole browser window to display the contents of the document. The Microsoft Internet Explorer browser is not the only ActiveX document container program. The Microsoft Office Binder program also runs ActiveX document server programs, storing the several ActiveX documents in a single disk file.

> NOTE: In the COM world, an ActiveX document server program is called a server because it implements a COM component. The container program (Internet Explorer or Office Binder) creates and controls that COM component. In the Internet world, the same program looks like a client because it can request information from a remote host (Microsoft Internet Information Server).

In this chapter, you'll learn about ActiveX document servers and ActiveX documents and you'll build two ActiveX document servers that work over the Internet in conjunction with Internet Explorer. Pay attention to this technology now because you'll be seeing a lot more of it as Microsoft Windows evolves.

ActiveX Document Theory

It's helpful to put ActiveX documents within the context of COM and OLE, which you already understand if you've read the other chapters in this book. You can, however, get started with ActiveX document servers without fully understanding all the COM concepts covered in Part VI.

ActiveX Document Servers vs. OLE Embedded Servers

As you saw in Chapter 28, an OLE embedded server program runs in a child window of an OLE container application and occupies a rectangular area in a page of the container's document (see Figure 28-1). Unless an embedded server program is classified as a mini-server, it can run stand-alone also. In embedded mode, the server program's data is held in a storage inside the container application's file. The embedded server program takes over the container program's menu and toolbar when the user activates it by double-clicking on its rectangle.

In contrast to an embedded server, an ActiveX document server takes over a whole frame window in its container application, and the document is always active. An ActiveX server application, running inside a container's frame window, runs pretty much the same way it would in stand-alone mode. You can see this for yourself if you have Microsoft Office 97. Office includes an ActiveX container program called Binder (accessible from the Office shortcut bar), and the Office applications (Microsoft Word, Microsoft Excel, and so on) have ActiveX server capability. Figure 36-1 shows a Word document and an Excel chart inside the same binder.

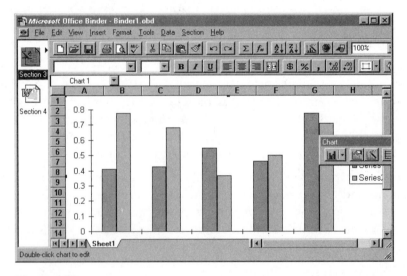

Figure 36-1.
A Word document and an Excel chart inside a Microsoft Office Binder window.

Like an embedded server, the ActiveX document server saves its data in a storage inside the ActiveX container's file. When the Office user saves the Binder program from the File menu, Binder writes a single OBD file to disk; the file contains one storage for the Word document and another for the Excel spreadsheet. You can see this file structure yourself with the DFVIEW utility, as shown in Figure 36-2.

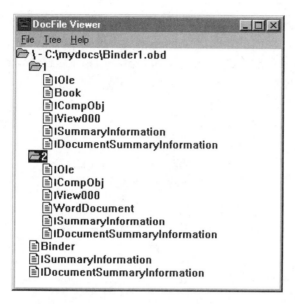

Figure 36-2.
A file structure displayed by the DocFile Viewer.

Running an ActiveX Document Server from Internet Explorer

Running an ActiveX document server from Internet Explorer is more fun than running one from Microsoft Office Binder (Internet Explorer refers to Internet Explorer 3.0 or greater). Rather than load a storage only from an OBD file, the server program can load its storage from the other side of the world. You just type in a URL, such as *http://www.DaliLama.in/SecretsOfTheUniverse.doc*, and a Microsoft Word document opens inside your Browse window, taking over the browser's menu and toolbar. That's assuming, of course, that you have installed the Microsoft Word program. If not, a Word document viewer is available, but it must be on your hard disk before you download the file.

An ActiveX document server won't let you save your changes back to the Internet host, but it will let you save them on your own hard disk. In other words, File Save is disabled but File Save As is enabled.

If you have Microsoft Office, try running Word or Excel in Internet Explorer now. The EX34A server is quite capable of delivering documents or worksheets to your browser, assuming that they are accessible from its home directory. Note that Internet Explorer recognizes documents and worksheets not by their file extensions but by the CLSID inside the files. You can prove this for yourself by renaming a file prior to accessing it.

ActiveX Document Servers vs. ActiveX Controls

Both ActiveX document servers and ActiveX controls can run with and without the Internet. Both are compiled programs that can run inside a browser. The following table lists some of the differences between the two.

	ActiveX Document Server	ActiveX Control
Module type	EXE	Most often a DLL
Can run stand-alone	Yes	No
Code automatically downloaded and registered by a WWW browser	No	Yes
Can be embedded in an HTML file	No	Yes
Occupies the entire browser window	Yes	Sometimes
Can be several pages	Yes	Not usually
Can read/write disk files	Yes	Not usually

OLE Interfaces for ActiveX Document Servers and Containers

ActiveX document servers implement the same interfaces as OLE embedded servers, including *IOleObject*, *IOleInPlaceObject*, and *IOleInPlaceActiveObject*. ActiveX document containers implement *IOleClientSite*, *IOleInPlaceFrame*, and *IOleInPlaceSite*. The menu negotiation works the same as it does for Visual Editing.

Some additional interfaces are implemented, however. ActiveX document servers implement *IOleDocument*, *IOleDocumentView*, *IOleCommandTarget*, and *IPrint*. ActiveX document containers implement *IOleDocumentSite*. The architecture allows for multiple views of the same document—sort of like the MFC document–view architecture—but most ActiveX document servers implement only one view per document.

The critical function in an OLE embedded server is *IOleObject::DoVerb*, which is called by the container when the user double-clicks on an embedded object or activates it through the menu. For an ActiveX document server, however, the critical function is *IOleDocumentView::UIActivate*. (Before calling this function, the container calls *IOleDocument::CreateView*, but generally the server just returns an interface pointer to the single document–view object.) *UIActivate* finds the container site and frame window, sets that window as the server's parent, sets the server's window to cover the container's frame window, and then activates the server's window.

> **NOTE:** It's important to realize that the COM interaction takes place between the container program (Internet Explorer or Binder) and the ActiveX document server (your program), which are both running on the client computer. We know of no cases in which remote procedure calls (RPCs) are made over the Internet. That means that the remote host (the server computer) does not use COM interfaces to communicate with clients, but it can deliver data in the form of storages.

MFC Support for ActiveX Document Servers

MFC allows you to create your own ActiveX document server programs. In addition, Visual C++ 6.0 now allows you to write ActiveX document containers. To get a server program, create a new MFC AppWizard EXE project and then check the Active Document Server check box, as shown in Figure 36-3. To create a container program, just make sure the Active Document Container check box is marked.

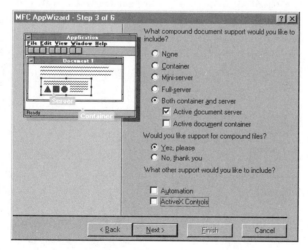

Figure 36-3.
Step 3 of the MFC AppWizard.

Here's a rundown of the classes involved in MFC's ActiveX Document Server

Architecture.

COleServerDoc

As it is for any COM component, your ActiveX document server's document class is derived from *COleServerDoc*, which implements *IPersistStorage*, *IOleObject*, *IDataObject*, *IOleInPlaceObject*, and *IOleInPlaceActiveObject*.

> **N O T E :**   The COM interfaces and MFC classes discussed here were named before Microsoft introduced ActiveX technology. An ActiveX document server was formerly known as a document object server or a doc object server, so those are the names you'll see in the source code and in some online documentation.

CDocObjectServerItem

This class is derived from the *COleServerItem* class used in embedded servers. Your ActiveX document server program has a class derived from *CDocObjectServerItem*, but that class isn't used when the program is running in ActiveX document mode.

CDocObjectServer

This class implements the new ActiveX server interfaces. Your application creates an object of class *CDocObjectServer* and attaches it to the *COleServerDoc* object. If you look at *COleServerDoc::GetDocObjectServer* in your derived document class, you'll see the construction code. Thereafter, the document object and attached *CDocObjectServer* object work together to provide ActiveX document server functionality. This class implements both *IOleDocument* and *IOleDocumentView*, which means that you can have only one view per document in an MFC ActiveX document server. You generally don't derive classes from *CDocObjectServer*.

COleDocIPFrameWnd

This class is derived from *COleIPFrameWnd*. Your application has a frame window class derived from *COleDocIPFrameWnd*. The framework constructs an object of that class when the application starts in embedded server mode or in ActiveX document server mode. In ActiveX document server mode, the server's window completely covers the container's frame window and has its own menu resource attached, with the identifier *IDR_SRVR_INPLACE* (for an SDI application).

ActiveX Document Server Example EX36A

You could construct the EX36A example in two phases. The first phase is a plain ActiveX document server that loads a file from its container. The view base class is *CRichEditView*, which means the program loads, edits, and stores text plus embedded objects. In the second phase, the application is enhanced to download a separate text file from the Internet one line at a time, demonstrating that ActiveX document servers can make arbitrary WinInet calls.

EX36A Phase 1—A Simple Server

The EX36A example on the book's CD-ROM is complete with the text download feature from Phase 2. You can exercise its Phase 1 capabilities by building it, or you can create a new application with AppWizard. If you do use AppWizard, you should refer to Figure 36-3 to see the AppWizard EXE project dialog and select the appropriate options. All other options are the default options, except those for selecting SDI (Step 1), setting the project's filename extension to *36a* using the Advanced button in Step 4, and changing the view's base class (*CRichEditView*—on the wizard's last page). You don't have to write any C++ code at all.

Be sure to run the program once in stand-alone mode to register it. While the program is running in stand-alone mode, type some text (and insert some OLE embedded objects) and then save the document as test.36a in your Internet server's home directory (\scripts or \wwwroot directory). Try loading test.36a from Internet Explorer and from Office Binder. Use Binder's Section menu for loading and storing EX36A documents to and from disk files.

You should customize the document icons for your ActiveX document servers because those icons show up on the right side of an Office Binder window.

Debugging an ActiveX Document Server

If you want to debug your program in ActiveX document server mode, click on the Debug tab in the Build Settings dialog. Set Program Arguments to */Embedding*, and then start the program. Now start the container program and use it to "start" the server, which has in fact already started in the debugger and is waiting for the container.

EX36A Phase 2—Adding WinInet Calls

The EX36A example on the CD-ROM includes two dialog bar objects, one for the main frame window and another for the in-place frame window. Both are attached to the same resource template, *IDD_DIALOGBAR*, which contains an edit control that accepts a text file URL plus start and stop buttons that display green and red bitmaps. If you click the green button (handled by the *OnStart* member function of the *CEx36aView* class), you'll start a thread that reads the text file one line at a time. The thread code from the file UrlThread.cpp is shown here:

```
CString g_strURL = "http:// ";
volatile BOOL g_bThreadStarted = FALSE;
CEvent g_eKill;

UINT UrlThreadProc(LPVOID pParam)
{
    g_bThreadStarted = TRUE;
    CString strLine;
    CInternetSession session;
    CStdioFile* pFile1 = NULL;

    try {
        pFile1 = session.OpenURL(g_strURL, 0, INTERNET_FLAG_TRANSFER_BINARY
            | INTERNET_FLAG_KEEP_CONNECTION); // needed for Windows NT
                                              //   c/r authentication
        // Keep displaying text from the URL until the Kill event is
        //   received
        while(::WaitForSingleObject(g_eKill.m_hObject, 0) != WAIT_OBJECT_0) {
            // one line at a time
            if(pFile1->ReadString(strLine) == FALSE) break;
            strLine += '\n';
            ::SendMessage((HWND) pParam, EM_SETSEL, (WPARAM) 999999,
                1000000);
            ::SendMessage((HWND) pParam, EM_REPLACESEL, (WPARAM) 0,
                        (LPARAM) (const char*) strLine);
            Sleep(250); // Deliberately slow down the transfer
        }
    }
    catch(CInternetException* e) {
        LogInternetException(pParam, e);
        e->Delete();
    }
    if(pFile1 != NULL) delete pFile1; // closes the file--prints a warning
    g_bThreadStarted = FALSE;
    // Post any message to update the toolbar buttons
    ::PostMessage((HWND) pParam, EM_SETSEL, (WPARAM) 999999, 1000000);
    TRACE("Post thread exiting normally\n");
    return 0;
}
```

This code uses the *CStdioFile* pointer to *pFile1* returned from *OpenURL*. The *ReadString* member function reads one line at a time, and each line is sent to the rich edit view window. When the main thread sets the "kill" event (the red button), the URL thread exits.

Before you test EX36A, make sure that the server (EX34A or IIS) is running and that you have a text file in the server's home directory. Test the EX36A program first in stand-alone mode by entering the text file URL in the dialog bar. Next try running the program in server mode from Internet Explorer. Enter *test.36a* (the document you created when you ran EX36A in stand-alone mode) in Internet Explorer's Address field to load the server.

> **NOTE:** We considered using the *CAsyncMonikerFile* class (see page 1026) instead of the MFC *WinInet* classes to read the text file. We stuck with WinInet, however, because the program could use the *CStdioFile* class *ReadString* member function to "pull" individual text lines from the server when it wanted them. The *CAsyncMonikerFile* class would have "pushed" arbitrary blocks of characters into the program (by calling the overridden *OnDataAvailable* function) as soon as the characters had been received.

Displaying Bitmaps on Buttons

Chapter 11 describes the *CBitmapButton* class for associating a group of bitmaps with a pushbutton. Microsoft Windows 95, Microsoft Windows 98, and Microsoft Windows NT 4.0 support an alternative technique that associates a single bitmap with a button. First you apply the Bitmap style (on the button's property sheet) to the button, and then you declare a variable of class *CBitmap* that will last at least as long as the button is enabled. Then you make sure that the *CButton::SetBitmap* function is called just after the button is created.

Here is the code for associating a bitmap with a button, from the EX36A MainFrm.cpp and IpFrame.cpp files:

```
m_bitmapGreen.LoadBitmap(IDB_GREEN);
HBITMAP hBitmap = (HBITMAP) m_bitmapGreen.GetSafeHandle();
((CButton*) m_wndDialogBar.GetDlgItem(IDC_START))-
>SetBitmap(hBitmap);
```

If your button was in a dialog, you could put similar code in the *OnInitDialog* member function and declare a *CBitmap* member in the class derived from *CDialog*.

1063

ActiveX Document Server Example EX36B

Look at the pizza form example from Chapter 35 (EX35A). Note that the server (the ISAPI DLL) processes the order only when the customer clicks the Submit Order Now button. This is okay for ordering pizzas because you're probably happy to accept money from anyone, no matter what kind of browser is used.

For a form-based intranet application, however, you can be more selective. You can dictate what browser your clients have, and you can distribute your own client software on the net. In that environment, you can make data entry more sophisticated, allowing, for example, the client computer to validate each entry as the user types it. That's exactly what's happening in EX36B, which is another ActiveX document server, of course. EX36B is a form-based employee time-sheet entry program that works inside Internet Explorer (as shown in Figure 36-4) or works as a stand-alone application. Looks like a regular HTML form, doesn't it? It's actually an MFC form view, but the average user probably won't know the difference. The Name field is a drop-down combo box, however—which is different from the select field you would see in an HTML form—because the user can type in a value if necessary. The Job Number field has a spin button control that helps the user select the value. These aren't necessarily the ideal controls for time-sheet entry, but the point here is that you can use any Windows controls you want, including tree controls, list controls, trackbars, and ActiveX controls, and you can make them interact any way you want.

Figure 36-4.
Employee time-sheet entry form.

Field Validation in an MFC Form View

<u>Problem</u>: MFC's standard validation scheme validates data only when *CWnd::UpdateData(TRUE)* is called, usually when the user exits the dialog. Applications often need to validate data the moment the user leaves a field (edit control, list box, and so on). The problem is complex because Windows permits the user to freely jump between fields in any sequence by using the mouse. Ideally, standard MFC DDX-/DDV (data exchange/validation) code should be used for field validation, and the standard *DoDataExchange* function should be called when the user finishes the transaction.

<u>Solution</u>: Derive your field validation form view classes from the class *CValidForm*, derived from *CFormView*, with this header:

```
// valform.h
#ifndef _VALIDFORM
#define _VALIDFORM

#define WM_VALIDATE WM_USER + 5

class CValidForm : public CFormView
{
DECLARE_DYNAMIC(CValidForm)
private:
    BOOL m_bValidationOn;
public:
    CValidForm(UINT ID);
    // override in derived dlg to perform validation
    virtual void ValidateDlgItem(CDataExchange* pDX, UINT ID);
    //{{AFX_VIRTUAL(CValidForm)
    protected:
    virtual BOOL OnCommand(WPARAM wParam, LPARAM lParam);
    //}}AFX_VIRTUAL

    //{{AFX_MSG(CValidForm)
    afx_msg LONG OnValidate(UINT wParam, LONG lParam);
    //}}AFX_MSG
    DECLARE_MESSAGE_MAP()
};
#endif // _VALIDFORM
```

This class has one virtual function, *ValidateDlgItem*, which accepts the control ID as the second parameter. The derived form view class implements this function to call the DDX/DDV functions for the

(continued)

appropriate field. Here is a sample *ValidateDlgItem* implementation for a form view that has two numeric edit controls:

```
void CMyForm::ValidateDlgItem(CDataExchange* pDX, UINT uID)
{
    switch (uID) {
    case IDC_EDIT1:
        DDX_Text(pDX, IDC_EDIT1, m_nEdit1);
        DDV_MinMaxInt(pDX, m_nEdit1, 0, 10);
        break;
    case IDC_EDIT2:
        DDX_Text(pDX, IDC_EDIT2, m_nEdit2);
        DDV_MinMaxInt(pDX, m_nEdit2, 20, 30);
        break;
    default:
        break;
    }
}
```

Notice the similarity to the wizard-generated *DoDataExchange* function:

```
void CAboutDlg::DoDataExchange(CDataExchange* pDX)
{
    //{{AFX_DATA_MAP(CMyForm)
    DDX_Text(pDX, IDC_EDIT1, m_nEdit1);
    DDV_MinMaxInt(pDX, m_nEdit1, 0, 10);
    DDX_Text(pDX, IDC_EDIT2, m_nEdit2);
    DDV_MinMaxInt(pDX, m_nEdit2, 20, 30);
    //}}AFX_DATA_MAP
}
```

How does it work? The *CValidForm* class traps the user's attempt to move away from a control. When the user presses the Tab key or clicks on another control, the original control sends a killfocus command message (a control notification message) to the parent window, the exact format depending on the kind of control. An edit control, for example, sends an EN_KILLFOCUS command. When the form window receives this killfocus message, it invokes the DDX/DDV code that is necessary for that field, and if there's an error, the focus is set back to that field.

There are some complications, however. First, we want to allow the user to freely switch the focus to another application—we're not interested in trapping the killfocus message in that case. Next, we must be careful how we set the focus back to the control that produced the error.

We can't just call *SetFocus* in direct response to the killfocus message; instead we must allow the killfocus process to complete. We can achieve this by posting a user-defined WM_VALIDATE message back to the form window. The WM_VALIDATE handler calls our *ValidateDlgItem* virtual function after the focus has been moved to the next field. Also, we must ignore the killfocus message that results when we switch back from the control that the user tried to select, and we must allow the IDCANCEL button to abort the transaction without validation.

Most of the work here is done in the view's virtual *OnCommand* handler, which is called for all control notification messages. We could, of course, individually map each control's killfocus message in our derived form view class, but that would be too much work. Here is the *OnCommand* handler:

```
BOOL CValidForm::OnCommand(WPARAM wParam, LPARAM lParam)
{
    // specific for WIN32 -- wParam/lParam processing different for
    //  WIN16
    TRACE("CValidForm::OnCommand, wParam = %x, lParam = %x\n",
        wParam, lParam);
    TRACE("m_bValidationOn = %d\n", m_bValidationOn);
    if(m_bValidationOn) {    // might be a killfocus
        UINT notificationCode = (UINT) HIWORD( wParam );
        if((notificationCode == EN_KILLFOCUS)  ||
           (notificationCode == LBN_KILLFOCUS) ||
           (notificationCode == CBN_KILLFOCUS) ) {
            CWnd* pFocus = CWnd::GetFocus(); // static function call
            // if we're changing focus to another control in the
            //  same form
            if( pFocus && (pFocus->GetParent() == this) ) {
                if(pFocus->GetDlgCtrlID() != IDCANCEL) {
                    // and focus not in Cancel button
                    // validate AFTER drawing finished
                    BOOL rtn = PostMessage( WM_VALIDATE, wParam );
                    TRACE("posted message, rtn = %d\n", rtn);
                }
            }
        }
    }
    return CFormView::OnCommand(wParam, lParam); // pass it on
}
```

Note that *m_bValidationOn* is a Boolean data member in *CValid-Form*.

(continued)

Finally, here is the *OnValidate* message handler, mapped to the user-defined WM_VALIDATE message:

```
LONG CValidForm::OnValidate(UINT wParam, LONG lParam)
{
    TRACE("Entering CValidForm::OnValidate\n");
    CDataExchange dx(this, TRUE);
    m_bValidationOn = FALSE;    // temporarily off
    UINT controlID = (UINT) LOWORD( wParam );
    try {
        ValidateDlgItem(&dx, controlID);
    }
    catch(CUserException* pUE) {
        pUE->Delete();
        TRACE("CValidForm caught the exception\n");
        // fall through -- user already alerted via message box
    }
    m_bValidationOn = TRUE;
    return 0;       // goes no further
}
```

Instructions for use:

1. Add valform.h and valform.cpp to your project.

2. Insert the following statement in your view class header file:

   ```
   #include "valform.h"
   ```

3. Change your view class base class from *CFormView* to *CValidForm*.

4. Override *ValidateDlgItem* for your form's controls as shown above.

That's all.

For dialogs, follow the same steps, but use valid.h and valid.cpp. Derive your dialog class from *CValidDialog* instead of from *CDialog*.

Generating POST Requests Under Program Control

The heart of the EX36B program is a worker thread that generates a POST request and sends it to a remote server. The server doesn't care whether the POST request came from an HTML form or from your program. It could process the POST request with an ISAPI DLL, with a PERL script, or with a Common Gateway Interface (CGI) executable program.

Here's what the server receives when the user clicks the EX36B Submit button:

```
POST scripts/ex35a.dll?ProcessTimesheet HTTP/1.0
(request headers)
(blank line)
Period=12&Name=Dunkel&Hours=6.5&Job=5
```

And here's the thread code from PostThread.cpp:

```cpp
// PostThread.cpp (uses MFC WinInet calls)

#include <stdafx.h>
#include "PostThread.h"

#define MAXBUF 50000

CString g_strFile = "/scripts/ex35a.dll";
CString g_strServerName = "localhost";
CString g_strParameters;

UINT PostThreadProc(LPVOID pParam)
{
    CInternetSession session;
    CHttpConnection* pConnection = NULL;
    CHttpFile* pFile1 = NULL;
    char* buffer = new char[MAXBUF];
    UINT nBytesRead = 0;
    DWORD dwStatusCode;
    BOOL bOkStatus = FALSE;
    try {
        pConnection = session.GetHttpConnection(g_strServerName,
            (INTERNET_PORT) 80);
        pFile1 = pConnection->OpenRequest(0, g_strFile +
            "?ProcessTimesheet", // POST request
            NULL, 1, NULL, NULL, INTERNET_FLAG_KEEP_CONNECTION |
            INTERNET_FLAG_RELOAD); // no cache
        pFile1->SendRequest(NULL, 0,
            (LPVOID) (const char*) g_strParameters,
            g_strParameters.GetLength());
        pFile1->QueryInfoStatusCode(dwStatusCode);
        if(dwStatusCode == 200) { // OK status
            // doesn't matter what came back from server -- we're looking
            //  for OK status
            bOkStatus = TRUE;
            nBytesRead = pFile1->Read(buffer, MAXBUF - 1);
            buffer[nBytesRead] = '\0'; // necessary for TRACE
            TRACE(buffer);
            TRACE("\n");
        }
    }
```

(continued)

```
catch(CInternetException* pe) {
    char text[100];
    pe->GetErrorMessage(text, 99);
    TRACE("WinInet exception %s\n", text);
    pe->Delete();
}
if(pFile1) delete pFile1; // does the close -- prints a warning
if(pConnection) delete pConnection; // Why does it print a warning?
delete [] buffer;
::PostMessage((HWND) pParam, WM_POSTCOMPLETE, (WPARAM) bOkStatus, 0);
return 0;
}
```

The main thread assembles the *g_strParameters* string based on what the user typed, and the worker thread sends the POST request using the *CHttpFile::SendRequest* call. The thread then calls *QueryInfoStatusCode* to find out if the server sent back an OK response. Before exiting, the thread posts a message to the main thread, using the *bOkStatus* value in *wParam* to indicate success or failure.

The EX36B View Class

The *CEx36bView* class is derived from *CValidForm*, as described in the sidebar that starts on page 1065. *CEx36bView* collects user data and starts the post thread when the user clicks the Submit button after all fields have been successfully validated. Field validation is independent of the internet application. You could use *CValidForm* in any MFC form view application.

Here is the code for the overridden *ValidateDlgItem* member function, which is called whenever the user moves from one control to another:

```
void CEx36bView::ValidateDlgItem(CDataExchange* pDX, UINT uID)
{
    ASSERT(this);
    TRACE("CEx36bView::ValidateDlgItem\n");
    switch (uID) {
    case IDC_EMPLOYEE:
        DDX_CBString(pDX, IDC_EMPLOYEE, m_strEmployee);
        // need custom DDV for empty string
        DDV_MaxChars(pDX, m_strEmployee, 10);
        if(m_strEmployee.IsEmpty()) {
            AfxMessageBox("Must supply an employee name");
            pDX->Fail();
        }
        break;
    case IDC_HOURS:
        DDX_Text(pDX, IDC_HOURS, m_dHours);
```

```
        DDV_MinMaxDouble(pDX, m_dHours, 0.1, 100.);
        break;
    case IDC_JOB:
        DDX_Text(pDX, IDC_JOB, m_nJob);
        DDV_MinMaxInt(pDX, m_nJob, 1, 20);
        break;
    default:
        break;
    }
    return;
}
```

The *OnSubmit* member function is called when the user clicks the Submit button. *CWnd::UpdateData* returns *TRUE* only when all the fields have been successfully validated. At that point, the function disables the Submit button, formats *g_strParameters*, and starts the post thread.

```
void CEx36bView::OnSubmit()
{
    if(UpdateData(TRUE) == TRUE) {
        GetDlgItem(IDC_SUBMIT)->EnableWindow(FALSE);
        CString strHours, strJob, strPeriod;
        strPeriod.Format("%d", m_nPeriod);
        strHours.Format("%3.2f", m_dHours);
        strJob.Format("%d", m_nJob);
        g_strParameters = "Period=" + strPeriod + "&Employee=" +
            m_strEmployee + "&Hours=" +strHours + "&Job=" +
            strJob + "\r\n";
        TRACE("parameter string = %s", g_strParameters);
        AfxBeginThread(PostThreadProc, GetSafeHwnd(),
            THREAD_PRIORITY_NORMAL);
    }
}
```

The *OnCancel* member function is called when the user clicks the Reset button. The *CValidForm* logic requires that the button's control ID be *IDCANCEL*.

```
void CEx36bView::OnCancel()
{
    CEx36bDoc* pDoc = GetDocument();
    m_dHours = 0;
    m_strEmployee = "" ;
    m_nJob = 0;
    m_nPeriod = pDoc->m_nPeriod;
    UpdateData(FALSE);
}
```

The *OnPostComplete* handler is called in response to the user-defined WM_POSTCOMPLETE message sent by the post thread:

```
LONG CEx36bView::OnPostComplete(UINT wParam, LONG lParam)
{
    TRACE("CEx36bView::OnPostComplete - %d\n", wParam);
    if(wParam == 0) {
        AfxMessageBox("Server did not accept the transaction");
    }
    else
        OnCancel();
    GetDlgItem(IDC_SUBMIT)->EnableWindow(TRUE);
    return 0;
}
```

This function displays a message box if the server didn't send an OK response. It then enables the Submit button, allowing the user to post another time-sheet entry.

Building and Testing EX36B

Build the /vcpp36/ex36b project, and then run it once in stand-alone mode to register it and to write a document file called test.36b in your WWW root directory. Make sure the EX35A DLL is available in the scripts directory (with execute permission) because that DLL contains an ISAPI function, *Process-Timesheet*, which handles the server end of the POST request. Be sure that you have IIS or some other ISAPI-capable server running.

Now run Internet Explorer and load test.36b from your server. The EX36B program should be running in the Browse window, and you should be able to enter time-sheet transactions.

ActiveX Document Servers vs. VB Script

It's possible to insert VB Script (or JavaScript) code into an HTML file. We're not experts on VB Script, but we've seen some sample code. You could probably duplicate the EX36B time-sheet application with VB Script, but you would be limited to the standard HTML input elements. It would be interesting to see how a VB Script programmer would solve the problem. (In any case, you're a C++ programmer, not a Visual Basic programmer, so you might as well stick to what you know.)

Going Further with ActiveX Document Servers

EX36A used a worker thread to read a text file from an Internet server. It used the MFC WinInet classes, and it assumed that a standard HTTP server was available. An ActiveX document server could just as easily make Winsock calls using the *CBlockingSocket* class from Chapter 34. That would imply that you were going beyond the HTTP and FTP protocols. You could, for example, write a custom internet server program that listened on port 81. (That server could run concurrently with IIS if necessary.) Your ActiveX document server could use a custom TCP/IP protocol to get binary data from an open socket. The server could use this data to update its window in real-time, or it could send the data to another device, such as a sound board.

CHAPTER THIRTY-SEVEN

Introducing Dynamic HTML

Dynamic HyperText Markup Language (DHTML) is a new and exciting technology—introduced as part of Microsoft Internet Explorer 4.0 (IE4)—that provides serious benefits to Webmasters and developers. DHTML could ultimately change the way we think about developing Windows applications. Why the buzz about DHTML?

It began with the IE4 "HTML display engine"—sometimes called Trident in Microsoft literature. As part of the design of Internet Explorer 4, Microsoft made Trident a COM component that exposes many of its internal objects that are used for displaying HTML pages in Internet Explorer 4. This feature allows you to traverse the portions of an HTML page in script or code, as if the HTML page were a data structure. Gone are the days of having to parse HTML or write grotesque Common Gateway Interface (CGI) scripts to get to data in a form. The real power of DHTML, however, is not this ability to access the HTML objects but the ability to actually change and manipulate the HTML page on the fly—thus the name Dynamic HTML.

Once you grasp the concept of DHTML, a million possible applications come to mind. For Webmasters, DHTML means that much of the logic that manipulates a Web page can live in scripts that are downloaded to the client. C++ developers can embed DHTML in their applications and use it as an embedded Web client or as a super-flexible, dynamic "form" that their application changes on the fly. Microsoft Visual J++ developers (who use Windows Foundation Classes [WFC]) can actually program DHTML on the server while an Internet Explorer client responds to the commands—an excellent alternative to CGI and potentially more powerful than Active Server Pages (ASP) server-side scripting.

Unfortunately, DHTML is so powerful and extensive that it requires a separate book to fill you in on all of the copious details. For example, to really leverage DHTML you need to understand all of the possible elements of an HTML page: forms, lists, style sheets, and so on. *Inside Dynamic HTML* by Scott Isaacs (Microsoft Press, 1997) is a great resource for learning the details of DHTML.

Instead of covering all aspects of DHTML, we will briefly introduce you to the DHTML object model, show you how to work with the model from the scripting angle (as a reference), and then show you how to work with the model from both the Microsoft Foundation Class Library version 4.21 (MFC) and the Active Template Library (ATL). These features are all made possible by the excellent DHTML support introduced in Visual C++ 6.0.

The DHTML Object Model

If you've been heads down on a Visual C++ project and haven't yet had time to take a peek at HTML, the first thing you should know is that HTML is an ASCII markup language format. Here is the code for a very basic HTML page:

```
<html>
<head>
<title>
This is an example very basic HTML page!
</title>
</head>
<body>
<h1>This is some text with H1!
</h1>
<h3>
This is some text with H3!
</h3>
</body>
</html>
```

This basic HTML "document" is composed of the following elements:

- **A head (or header)** In this example, the header contains a title: "This is an example very basic HTML page!"

- **The body of the document** The body in this example contains two text elements. The first has the heading 1 (h1) style and reads, "This is some text with H1!" The second text element has the heading 3 (h3) style and reads, "This is some text with H3!"

The end result is an HTML page that—when displayed in Internet Explorer 4—looks like Figure 37-1.

When Internet Explorer 4 loads this sample HTML page, it creates an internal representation that you can traverse, read, and manipulate through the DHTML object model. Figure 37-2 on page 1078 shows the basic hierarchy of the DHTML object model.

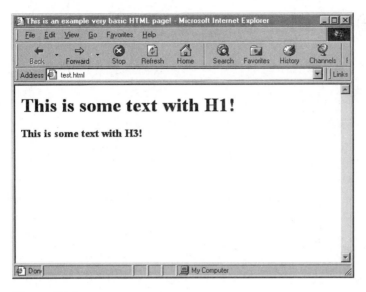

Figure 37-1.
A very basic HTML page, as seen in Internet Explorer 4.

At the root of the object model is the *window* object. This object can be used from a script to perform some action, such as popping up a dialog box. Here's an example of some JScript that accesses the window object:

```
<SCRIPT LANGUAGE="JScript">
function about()
{
    window.showModalDialog("about.htm","",
        "dialogWidth:25em;dialogHeight13em")
}
</SCRIPT>
```

When the *about* script function is called, it will call the *showModalDialog* function in the *window* DHTML object to display a dialog. This example also illustrates how scripts access the object model—through globally accessible objects that map directly to the corresponding object in the DTHML object model.

The window object has several "subobjects" that allow you to further manipulate portions of Internet Explorer 4. The *document* object is what we will spend most of our time on in this chapter because it gives us programmatic access to the various elements of the currently loaded HTML document. On page 1079, some JScript shows how to create basic dynamic content that changes the document object.

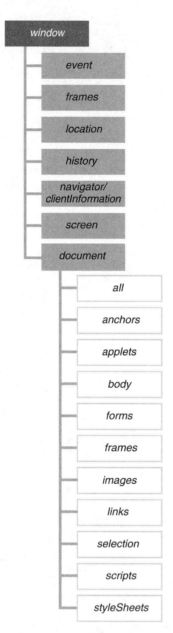

Figure 37-2.
Basic hierarchy of the DHTML object model.

```
<HTML>
<HEAD>
<TITLE>Welcome!</TITLE>
<SCRIPT LANGUAGE="JScript">
function changeMe() {
    document.all.MyHeading.outerHTML =
        "<H1 ID=MyHeading>Dynamic HTML is magic!</H1>";
    document.all.MyHeading.style.color = "green";
    document.all.MyText.innerText = "Presto Change-o! ";
    document.all.MyText.align = "center";
    document.body.insertAdjacentHTML("BeforeEnd",
        "<P ALIGN=\"center\">Open Sesame!</P>");
}
</SCRIPT>
<BODY onclick="changeMe()">
<H3 ID=MyHeading> Dynamic HTML demo!</H3>
<P ID=MyText>Click anywhere to see the power of DHTML!</P>
</BODY>
</HTML>
```

This script changes the *MyHeading* and *MyText* objects in the HTML documents on the fly. Not only does it change the text, it also changes attributes of the elements such as color and alignment. If you want to see this script in action, you can find it in the ex37_1.html file on the companion CD.

Before we further deconstruct the DHTML object model, let's examine the DHTML concept of a <u>collection</u>. Collections in DHTML are logically equivalent to C++ data structures such as linked lists. In fact, access to the DHTML object model is performed largely by iterating through collections searching for a particular HTML element and then potentially iterating through another subcollection to get to yet another element. Elements contain several methods, such as *contains* and *length*, that you use to traverse the elements.

For example, one of the subelements of the *document* object is a collection named *all* that contains all of the document's elements. In fact, most of the subobjects of the *document* object are collections. The following script (ex37_2.html) shows how to iterate through the *all* collection and list the various items of a document.

```
<HTML>
<HEAD><TITLE>Iterating through the all collection.</TITLE>
<SCRIPT LANGUAGE="JScript">
function listAllElements() {
    var tag_names = "";
    for (i=0; i<document.all.length; i++)
        tag_names = tag_names + document.all(i).tagName + " ";
    alert("This document contains: " + tag_names);
}
```

(continued)

```
</SCRIPT>
</HEAD>
<BODY onload="listAllElements()">
<H1>DHTML Rocks!</H1>
<P>This document is <B>very</B> short.
</BODY>
</HTML>
```

Notice how easy it is to retrieve items with script. (The syntax calls for parentheses, similar to accessing an array in C++.) Also notice that each element in an HTML document has properties such as tagName that allow you to programmatically "search" for various elements. For example, if you wanted to write a script that filtered out all bold items, you would scan the *all* collection for an element with tagName equal to *B*.

Now you have the basics of the DHTML object model down and you understand how to access them through scripts from the Webmaster's perspective. Let's look at how Visual C++ lets us work with DHTML from an application developer's perspective.

Visual C++ and DHTML

Visual C++ 6.0 supports DHTML through both MFC and ATL. Both MFC and ATL give you complete access to the DHTML object model. Unfortunately, access to the object model from languages like C++ is done through OLE Automation (*IDispatch*) and in many cases isn't as cut-and-dried as some of the scripts we looked at earlier.

The DHTML object model is exposed to C++ developers through a set of COM objects with the prefix IHTML (*IHTMLDocument, IHTMLWindow, IHTMLElement, IHTMLBodyElement*, and so on). In C++, once you obtain the document interface, you can use any of the *IHTMLDocument2* interface methods to obtain or to modify the document's properties.

You can access the *all* collection by calling the *IHTMLDocument2::get_all* method. This method returns an *IHTMLElementCollection* collection interface that contains all the elements in the document. You can then iterate through the collection using the *IHTMLElementCollection::item* method (similar to the parentheses in the script above). The *IHTMLElementCollection::item* method supplies you with an *IDispatch* pointer that you can call *QueryInterface* on, requesting the *IID_IHTMLElement* interface. This call to *QueryInterface* will give you an *IHTMLElement* interface pointer that you can use to get or set information for the HTML element.

Most elements also provide a specific interface for working with that particular element type. These element-specific interface names take the format of

IHTMLXXXXElement, where *XXXX* is the name of the element (*IHTMLBody-Element*, for example). You must call *QueryInterface* on the *IHTMLElement* object to request the element-specific interface you need. This might sound confusing (because it can be!). But don't worry—the MFC and ATL sections in this chapter contain plenty of samples that demonstrate how it all ties together. You'll be writing DHTML code in no time.

MFC and DHTML

MFC's support for DHTML starts with a new *CView* derivative, *CHtmlView*. *CHtmlView* allows you to embed an HTML view inside frame windows or splitter windows, where with some DHTML work it can act as a dynamic form. Example EX37A demonstrates how to use the new *CHtmlView* class in a vanilla MDI application.

Follow these steps to create the EX37A example:

1. **Run AppWizard and create \vcpp32\ex37a\ex37a.** Choose New from Visual C++'s File menu. Then click the Projects tab, and select MFC App-Wizard (exe). Accept all defaults, except in Step 6 choose CHtmlView as the Base Class, as shown here.

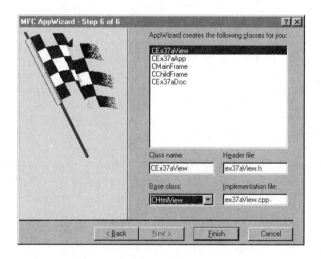

2. **Edit the URL to be loaded.** In the *CEx37aView::OnInitialUpdate* function, you will see this line:

```
Navigate2(_T("http://www.microsoft.com/visualc/"),NULL,NULL);
```

You can edit this line to have the application load a local page or a URL other than the Visual C++ page.

3. **Compile and run.** Figure 37-3 shows the application running with the default Web page.

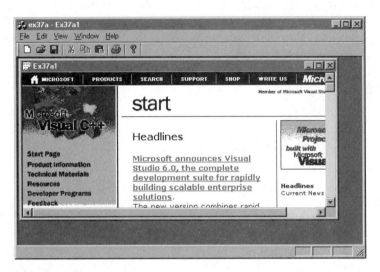

Figure 37-3.
The EX37A example.

Now let's create a sample that really shows how to use DHTML with MFC. EX37B creates a *CHtmlView* object and a *CListView* object separated by a splitter. The example then uses DHTML to enumerate the HTML elements in the *CHtmlView* object and displays the results in the *CListView* object. The end result will be a DHTML explorer that you can use to view the DHTML object model of any HTML file.

Here are the steps to create EX37B:

1. **Run AppWizard and create \vcpp32\ex37b\ex37b.** Choose New from Visual C++'s File menu. Then click the Projects tab, and select MFC AppWizard (exe). Accept all the defaults but three: select Single Document, select Windows Explorer in Step 5, and select *CHtmlView* as the Base Class in Step 6. The options that you should see after finishing the wizard are shown in the graphic on the facing page.

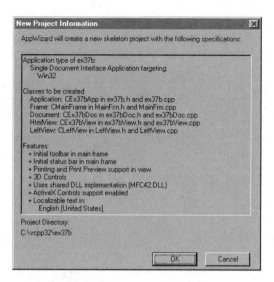

2. **Change the *CLeftView* to be a *CListView* derivative.** By default, App-Wizard makes the *CLeftView* of the splitter window a *CTreeView* deriva-tive. Open the LeftView.h file, and do a global search for *CTreeView* and replace it with *CListView*. Open LeftView.cpp, and do the same find and re-place. (Hint: Use Edit/Replace/Replace All.)

3. **Edit the URL to be loaded.** In the *CEx37bView::OnInitialUpdate* func-tion, change the URL to res://ie4tour.dll/welcome.htm.

4. **Add a *DoDHTMLExplore* function to *CMainFrame*.** First add the fol-lowing declaration to the MainFrm.h file:

```
virtual void DoDHTMLExplore(void);
```

Now add the implementation for *DoHTMLExplore* to MainFrm.cpp.

```
void CMainFrame::DoDHTMLExplore(void)
{

    CLeftView *pListView =
        (CLeftView *)m_wndSplitter.GetPane(0,0);

    CEx37bView * pDHTMLView =
        (CEx37bView *)m_wndSplitter.GetPane(0,1);

    //Clear the listview
    pListView->GetListCtrl().DeleteAllItems();
```

(continued)

```
IDispatch* pDisp = pDHTMLView->GetHtmlDocument();

if (pDisp != NULL )
{
    IHTMLDocument2* pHTMLDocument2;
    HRESULT hr;

    hr = pDisp->QueryInterface( IID_IHTMLDocument2,
            (void**)&pHTMLDocument2 );
    if (hr == S_OK)
    {
        IHTMLElementCollection* pColl = NULL;

        hr = pHTMLDocument2->get_all( &pColl );
        if (hr == S_OK && pColl != NULL)
        {
            LONG celem;
            hr = pColl->get_length( &celem );

            if ( hr == S_OK )
            {
                for ( int i=0; i< celem; i++ )
                {
                    VARIANT varIndex;
                    varIndex.vt = VT_UINT;
                    varIndex.lVal = i;
                    VARIANT var2;
                    VariantInit( &var2 );
                    IDispatch* pDisp;

                    hr = pColl->item( varIndex, var2, &pDisp );
                    if ( hr == S_OK )
                    {
                        IHTMLElement* pElem;

                        hr = pDisp->QueryInterface(
                            IID_IHTMLElement,
                            (void **)&pElem);
                        if ( hr == S_OK )
                        {
                            BSTR bstr;
                            hr = pElem->get_tagName(&bstr);
                            CString strTag = bstr;
                            IHTMLImgElement* pImgElem;
```

```
                                    //Is it an image element?
                                    hr = pDisp->QueryInterface(
                                        IID_IHTMLImgElement,
                                        (void **)&pImgElem );
                                    if ( hr == S_OK )
                                    {
                                        pImgElem->get_href(&bstr);
                                        strTag += " - ";
                                        strTag += bstr;
                                        pImgElem->Release();
                                    }
                                    else
                                    {
                                        IHTMLAnchorElement* pAnchElem;

                                        //Is it an anchor?
                                        hr = pDisp->QueryInterface(
                                            IID_IHTMLAnchorElement,
                                            (void **)&pAnchElem );
                                        if ( hr == S_OK )
                                        {
                                            pAnchElem->get_href(&bstr);
                                            strTag += " - ";
                                            strTag += bstr;
                                            pAnchElem->Release();
                                        }
                                    }//end of else

                                    pListView->GetListCtrl().InsertItem(
                                        pListView->GetListCtrl()
                                        .GetItemCount(), strTag);
                                    pElem->Release();
                                }
                                pDisp->Release();
                            }
                        }
                    }
                    pColl->Release();
                }
                pHTMLDocument2->Release();
            }
            pDisp->Release();
        }
    }
```

Here are the steps that this function takes to "explore" the HTML document using DHTMLs:

- ❑ First *DoHTMLExplore* gets pointers to the *CListView* and *CHtmlView* views in the splitter window.

- ❑ Then it makes a call to *GetHtmlDocument* to get an *IDispatch* pointer to the DHTML *document* object.

- ❑ Next *DoHTMLExplore* gets the *IHTMLDocument2* interface.

- ❑ With the *IHTMLDocument2* interface, *DoHTMLExplore* retrieves the *all* collection and iterates through it. In each iteration, *DoHTML-Explore* checks the element type. If the element is an image or an anchor, *DoHTMLExplore* retrieves additional information such as the link for the image. The *all* collection loop then places the textual description of the HTML element in the *CListView* object.

5. Make sure that Mainfrm.cpp includes mshtml.h. Add the following line to the top of Mainfrm.cpp so that the *DoHTMLExplore* code will compile.

```
#include <mshtml.h>
```

6. Add a call to *DoHTMLExplore*. For this example, we will change the *CEx37bApp::OnAppAbout* function to call the *DoDHTMLExplore* function in the ex37b.cpp file. Replace the existing code with the following boldface code:

```
void CEx37bApp::OnAppAbout()
{
    CMainFrame * pFrame = (CMainFrame*)AfxGetMainWnd();
    pFrame->DoDHTMLExplore();

}
```

7. Customize the list view. In the *CLeftView::PreCreateWindow* function (LeftView.cpp), add this line:

```
cs.style |= LVS_LIST;
```

8. Compile and run. Compile and run the sample. Press the "?" toolbar item, or choose Help/About to invoke the explore function.

Figure 37-4 shows the EX37B example in action.

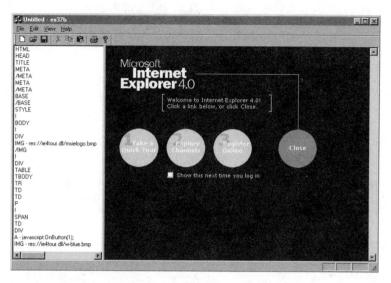

Figure 37-4.
The EX37B example in action.

Now that you've seen how to use DHTML and MFC, let's look at how ATL implements DHMTL support.

ATL and DHTML

ATL's support for DHTML comes in the form of an HTML object that can be embedded in any ATL ActiveX control. EX37C creates an ATL control that illustrates DHTML support.

To create the example, follow these steps:

1. **Run the ATL COM AppWizard and create \vcpp32\ex37c\ex37c.**
   Choose New from Visual C++'s File menu. Then click the Projects tab, and select ATL COM AppWizard. Choose Executable as the server type.

2. **Insert an HTML control.** In ClassView, right-click on the ex37c classes item and select New ATL Object. Select Controls and HTML Control as shown in the graphic on the following page.

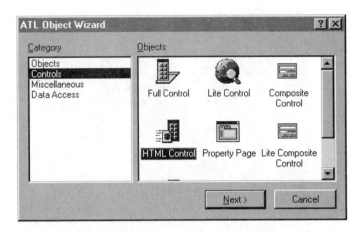

3. Click Next and fill in the C++ Short Name as shown here.

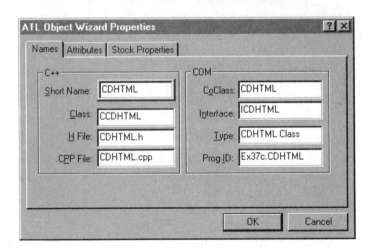

NOTE: If you look at the *IDHTMLUI* object, you will see this stock implementation of the *OnClick* handler:

```
STDMETHOD(OnClick)(IDispatch* pdispBody, VARIANT varColor)
{
    CComQIPtr<IHTMLBodyElement> spBody(pdispBody);
    if (spBody != NULL)
        spBody->put_bgColor(varColor);
    return S_OK;
}
```

The default *OnClick* handler uses *QueryInterface* on the *IDispatch* pointer to get the *IHTMLBodyElement* object. The handler then calls the *put_bgColor* method to change the background color.

4. Compile, load, and run the control to see the ATL DHTML code in action. After you build the project, select ActiveX Control Test Container from the Tools menu. In the test container, select Insert New Control from the Edit menu and choose CDHTML Class from the list box. Figure 37-5 shows the resulting ActiveX control that uses DHTML to change the background when the user clicks the button.

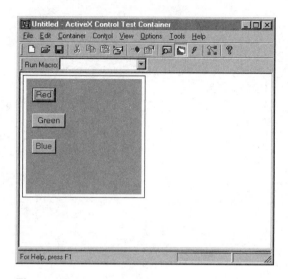

Figure 37-5.
EX37C ActiveX control.

For More Information...

We hope this introduction to DHTML has you thinking of some ways to use this exciting new technology in your Visual C++ applications. The possibilities are endless: completely dynamic applications, applications that update from the Internet, client/server ActiveX controls, and many more.

If you would like to learn more about DHTML, we suggest the following resources:

- *Inside Dynamic HTML* by Scott Isaacs (Microsoft Press, 1997)

- *Dynamic HTML in Action* by William J. Pardi and Eric M. Schurman (Microsoft Press, 1998)

- The Internet SDK (an excellent resource on DHTML and other Microsoft technologies)

- *www.microsoft.com* (several areas discuss DHTML)

Visual C++ for Windows CE

In early 1997, Microsoft released a new version of the Windows family of operating systems named Windows CE. Original equipment managers (OEMs) are the target audience for Windows CE. OEMs create small, portable devices—such as handheld computers—and embedded systems. A myriad of different operating systems, a lack of strong development tools, and a maze of user interfaces have plagued both the portable-device and embedded system markets. In the past, these problems limited the use of these systems and restricted the availability of inexpensive software applications.

> NOTE: At the time of this writing, Windows CE support for Visual C++ 6.0 was not available. All screen shots and sample programs in this chapter were created using Visual C++ for Windows CE 5.0.

Microsoft hopes that Windows CE can do for the embedded and handheld markets what Windows did for the desktop PC industry. Based on the target audience, you can probably guess that Windows CE has different design goals than Windows 98 and Windows NT. One goal was modularity: if an OEM is using Windows CE in an embedded device for a refrigerator, the keyboard and graphics output modules are not required. The OEM does not pay a penalty for modules not used by the application of Windows CE.

To date, there have been two major releases of Windows CE. The first release was primarily for Handheld PCs (H/PCs) and was limited to noncolor applications. Windows CE 1.0 lacked many advanced Win32 features such as COM and ActiveX, large chunks of GDI, and many Windows controls. Windows CE 2.0 was released in late 1997 and added support for a variety of new device types, color, COM and ActiveX technology, and also a Java virtual machine.

Before we look at the details of the Win32 support in Windows CE, let's examine some of the existing device types to get a feel for possible Windows CE applications.

Windows CE Devices

Currently the best known Windows CE devices are the H/PCs such as those available from HP, Sharp, Casio and a variety of vendors. Figure 38-1 shows a typical H/PC machine.

Figure 38-1.
A typical Handheld PC.

H/PCs currently have display resolutions anywhere from 480 by 240 pixels to as large as 640 by 240 pixels. They typically have a keyboard, infrared port, serial port, and microphone. The standard software on these devices includes: Pocket Word, Pocket Excel, Internet Explorer, Outlook Express, and other scaled-down Microsoft productivity applications.

A smaller device called a Palm-size PC (P/PC) shown in Figure 38-2 is completely pen-based and does not have a keyboard. Screen sizes are also smaller (240 by 320 pixels) and only gray-scale displays are currently available for P/PCs.

Figure 38-2.
A Palm-size PC.

NOTE: At the time of this book's publication, MFC is not supported on the Palm-size PC platform. The SDK for Palm-size PCs and embedded development is also not included with the Visual C++ for Windows CE product. These SDKs must be downloaded from the Microsoft Web site (*www.microsoft.com/windowsce*).

Perhaps the most exciting Windows CE devices now reaching the market are <u>embedded</u> applications. For example, the CD player from Clarion shown in Figure 38-3 features a GUI, voice recognition, cellular phone support, and a variety of other features that are changing the way we think about electronic devices and appliances. Unlike Windows 95, which supports only Intel processors, and Windows NT, which supports only the Intel and Alpha processors, Windows CE supports a myriad of embeddable 32-bit processors such as the MIPS chip, Hitachi chips, and a variety of other chip sets. This flexibility dramatically increases the potential reach of Windows CE in the embedded market.

Figure 38-3.
An automotive CD player powered by Window CE.

Because all of these devices are based on Windows CE, you can write applications for them using a subset of the familiar Win32 APIs that you have learned throughout this book. Before we investigate Visual C++ programming for Windows CE, let's take a look at the subset of Win32 implemented by Windows CE.

Windows CE vs. Windows 98 and Windows NT

Each Windows CE platform (H/PC, Palm-size PC, and embedded) supports various subsets of the Win32 API based on which Windows CE modules are loaded. The "core" functionality is fairly static among devices—GDI, windows, and controls and so on, but some user input functions are different. (On a Palm-size PC, for example, it doesn't make sense to have keyboard functions.)

The Win32 support in Windows CE matches the primary design goal of Windows CE: keep everything as small as possible. Whenever a duplicate Win32 call exists, Windows CE provides only the most general API function. For example, instead of implementing both *TextOut* and *ExtTextOut*, Windows CE supports only the more flexible *ExtTextOut*, because in this single API you have the functionality of both.

Another interesting aspect of the Win32 Windows CE implementation is that only Unicode functions and strings are supported. You need to be sure to wrap your Windows CE MFC strings with the *_T* macro.

At the GDI layer, Windows CE supports a relatively small subset of the implementations found in Windows 95, Windows 98, and Windows NT. The key groups of GDI Win32_API functions not implemented in Windows CE are mapping modes, arcs, chords, metafiles, and Bézier curves. When you draw lines, you must use *PolyLine* because *MoveTo* and *LineTo* are not supported. Cursor and mouse handling in Windows CE can also be different from what you are accustomed to on larger systems.

Version 2.0 of Windows CE adds many key features that allow for parity with its big brothers, such as color support, TrueType font support, printing, and memory DCs. Many other nuances of the various GDI implementations are well documented in the Windows CE SDK, which is shipped as part of the Visual C++ for Windows CE product.

Windows CE also has some major differences in windowing. Perhaps the largest difference is the fact that only SDI applications are supported. Thus, porting existing MDI applications to Windows CE is relatively difficult. Another interesting windowing fact is that Windows CE windows are not resizable. Since there are a wide variety of screen resolutions, you should programmatically size windows based on the resolution of the display, instead of using static layouts.

Most of the standard Windows 95, Windows 98, and Internet Explorer 4.0 common controls are available on Windows CE, except for the following: the rich edit control, the IP control, *ComboBoxEx* controls, and the hot key control. Windows CE actually introduces a new common control—the command bar. Command bars implement a hybrid menu bar and toolbar that occupies considerably less space than the standard menu bar and toolbar configuration found in most desktop applications. Figure 38-4 shows an example of a Windows CE command bar.

Figure 38-4.
A Windows CE command bar.

ActiveX and COM are supported in Windows CE 2.0, but only for in-process COM objects such as ActiveX controls. Multithreading, memory management, exception handling, and most other areas of Win32 are fully supported —with a few caveats—by Windows CE.

Now that you're familiar with the basics of Windows CE, let's take a look at the Visual C++ development environment for this new operating system.

Visual C++ for Windows CE

Visual C++ for Windows CE is an add-on to Visual C++. When you install C++ for Windows CE, it extends the Visual C++ environment by adding several Windows CE–specific features:

- An Intel-based Windows CE emulation environment
- New targets for each of the Windows CE supported processors (MIPS/SH and the emulation environment)
- New AppWizards for Windows CE applications
- A Windows CE compatible port of MFC
- A Windows CE compatible port of ATL
- Tools for remote execution and debugging of Windows CE applications on actual devices

One interesting aspect of Visual C++ for Windows CE is the fact that it also supports the older 1.0 and 1.01 versions of Windows CE. Figure 38-5 shows the Windows CE operating system and processor configuration bars that have been added to Visual C++.

While the environment lets you remotely run and debug your applications on a connected Windows CE device, it also includes a very powerful Windows CE emulation environment. The Windows CE emulator (WCE) is an Intel-based software-only version of Windows CE that runs on your desktop and gives you the convenience of being able to run and test your applications on your development machine. Of course, to ensure that your applications work correctly, you still need to test on real devices, but the emulator takes much of the pain out of the early compile and debug stages of Windows CE development. Figure 38-6 shows the emulation environment in action.

There are four Windows CE–specific AppWizards that ship with Visual C++ for WCE:

- **WCE ATL COM AppWizard**—An ATL-based COM object project
- **WCE MFC ActiveX ControlWizard**—An MFC ActiveX control project
- **WCE MFC AppWizard (dll)**—An MFC DLL project
- **WCE MFC AppWizard (exe)**—An MFC executable project

Configuration selector
(includes MIPS/SH/Windows
CE emulator)

Windows CE
OS target
selector

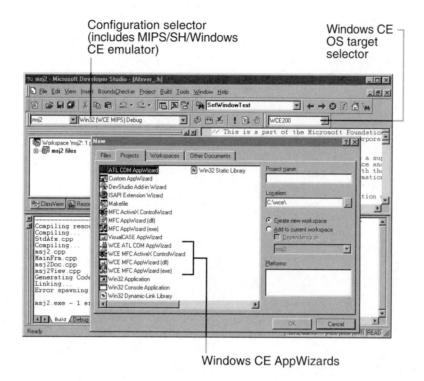

Windows CE AppWizards

Figure 38-5.
Visual C++ for the Windows CE environment.

Figure 38-6
The Windows CE emulator.

The WCE AppWizards are basically the same as their big brother Win32 counterparts, except that they have different features that take advantage of the Windows CE operating system, such as the Windows CE help environment.

Figure 38-7 shows the first three steps of the Windows CE MFC executable AppWizard. Notice that there are only two project types: SDI and dialog-based. Notice also the variety of Windows CE–specific options that you can choose from.

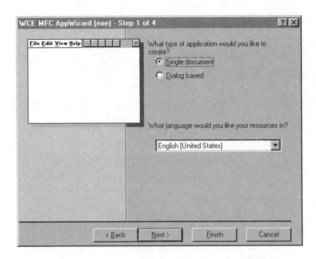

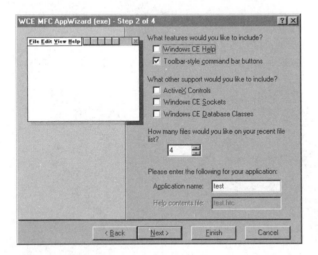

Figure 38-7.
The Windows CE MFC AppWizard.

(continued)

Figure 38-7. *continued*

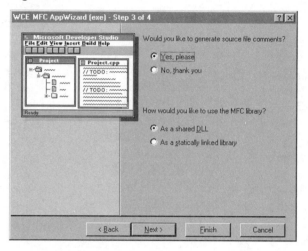

MFC for Windows CE

Visual C++ for Windows CE ships with a smaller version of MFC named Mini MFC. To get a feel for which MFC classes are and are not supported, see Figure 38-8 on the following page—the MFC for Windows CE hierarchy chart. The grayed out classes are not supported on Windows CE.

Several classes have been added to Mini MFC, including classes for command bars, object store, and socket classes. Windows CE functions provide the command bars in the Mini MFC *CFrameWnd* class.

Instead of implementing a file metaphor, Windows CE provides an object store. Several new MFC classes were added to give the Windows CE developer access to the object store:

- *CCeDBDatabase*—Encapsulates a database in the object store

- *CCeDBEnum*—Enumerates the databases in the object store

- *CCeDBProp*—Encapsulates a database property (Database properties are data items consisting of an application-defined property identifier, a data-type identifier, and the data value.)

- *CCeDBRecord*—Provides access to a record in the database

In addition to these data store classes, a new class *CCeSocket* is provided. *CCeSocket* implements an asynchronous *CSocket* derivative.

MFC for Windows CE Class Hierarchy Chart

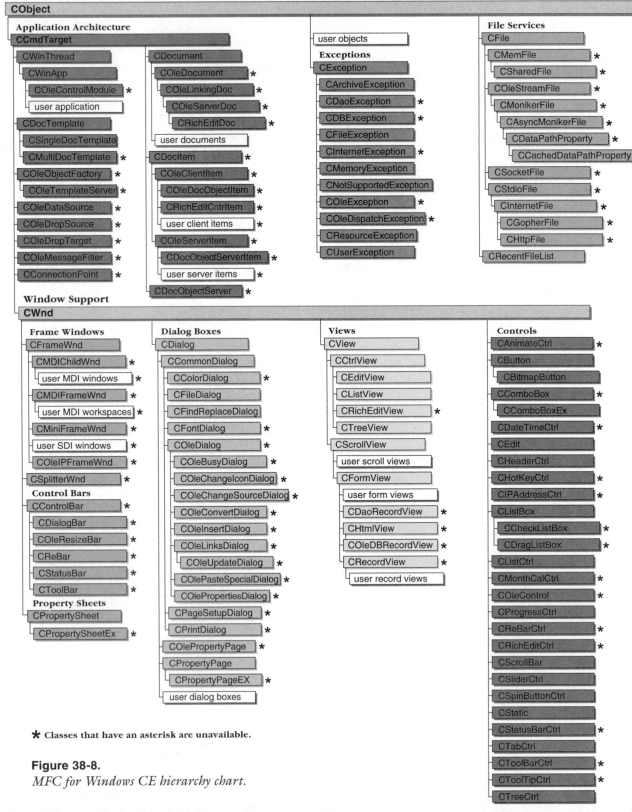

★ Classes that have an asterisk are unavailable.

Figure 38-8.
MFC for Windows CE hierarchy chart.

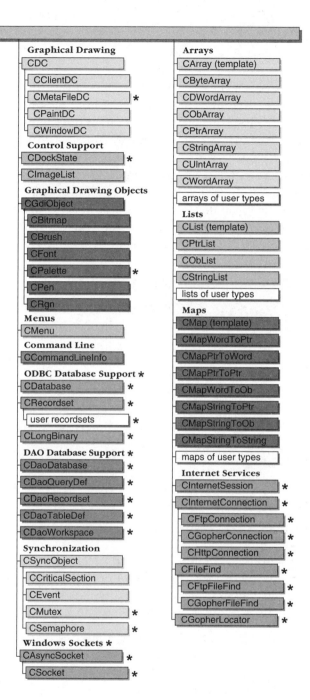

Graphical Drawing
- CDC
  - CClientDC
  - CMetaFileDC *
  - CPaintDC
  - CWindowDC

Control Support
- CDockState *
- CImageList

Graphical Drawing Objects
- CGdiObject
  - CBitmap
  - CBrush
  - CFont
  - CPalette *
  - CPen
  - CRgn

Menus
- CMenu

Command Line
- CCommandLineInfo

ODBC Database Support *
- CDatabase *
- CRecordset *
  - user recordsets *
- CLongBinary *

DAO Database Support *
- CDaoDatabase *
- CDaoQueryDef *
- CDaoRecordset *
- CDaoTableDef *
- CDaoWorkspace *

Synchronization
- CSyncObject
  - CCriticalSection
  - CEvent
  - CMutex *
  - CSemaphore *

Windows Sockets *
- CAsyncSocket *
  - CSocket *

Arrays
- CArray (template)
- CByteArray
- CDWordArray
- CObArray
- CPtrArray
- CStringArray
- CUIntArray
- CWordArray
- arrays of user types

Lists
- CList (template)
- CPtrList
- CObList
- CStringList
- lists of user types

Maps
- CMap (template)
- CMapWordToPtr
- CMapPtrToWord
- CMapPtrToPtr
- CMapWordToOb
- CMapStringToPtr
- CMapStringToOb
- CMapStringToString
- maps of user types

Internet Services
- CInternetSession *
- CInternetConnection *
  - CFtpConnection *
  - CGopherConnection *
  - CHttpConnection *
- CFileFind *
  - CFtpFileFind *
  - CGopherFileFind *
- CGopherLocator *

Classes Not Derived from CObject

Internet Server API
- CHtmlStream *
- CHttpFilter *
- CHttpFilterContext *
- CHttpServer *
- CHttpServerContext *

Runtime Object Model Support
- CArchive
- CDumpContext
- CRuntimeClass

Simple Value Types
- CPoint
- CRect
- CSize
- CString
- CTime
- CTimeSpan

Structures
- CCreateContext
- CMemoryState *
- COleSafeArray *
- CPrintInfo *

Support Classes
- CCmdUI
  - COleCmdUI *
- CDaoFieldExchange *
- CDataExchange
- CDBVariant *
- CFieldExchange *
- COleDataObject *
- COleDispatchDriver *
- CPropExchange *
- CRectTracker
- CWaitCursor

Typed Template Collections
- CTypedPtrArray
- CTypedPtrList
- CTypedPtrMap

OLE Type Wrappers *
- CFontHolder *
- CPictureHolder *

OLE Automation Types
- COleCurrency *
- COleDateTime *
- COleDateTimeSpan *
- COleVariant *

Synchronization
- CMultiLock *
- CSingleLock

Using Mini MFC

Let's look at a couple of examples to get a feel for the Mini version of MFC. In example EX38A, we will create a basic SDI application that draws some text in the view and displays a dialog when the user presses the left mouse button (or taps the screen on a Windows CE machine). EX38A is similar to the EX06A example, so you can compare the steps in creating a similar application for Windows 98, Windows NT, and Windows CE. For this example, you will create a simulated expense-tracking application for Windows CE—a perfect candidate for portable computing. For demonstration purposes, we will focus on creating a dialog that allows the user to enter expense information. Figure 38-9 shows the application running in the emulation environment.

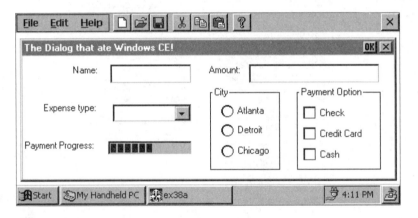

Figure 38-9.
The EX38A expense-tracking application.

Here are the steps to create the EX38A example:

1. **Run the MFC Executable for Windows CE AppWizard to produce \vcpp32\ex38a\ex38a.** Select the WCE MFC AppWizard project type and accept all the defaults. The options and the default class names are shown on the facing page.

2. **Select the WCE x86em Debug configuration.** Choose the Set Active Configuration command from the Set menu and then select Ex38a—Win32 (WCE x86em) Debug—from the list. Click OK. This configuration will allow you to work with the desktop emulator instead of working remotely with a connected Windows CE device. (If you have a connected Windows CE device you can select its configuration instead. For example, select Ex38a—Win32 [WCE SH] Debug if you have a connected HP 620LX.)

3. Use the dialog editor to create a dialog resource. Choose Resource from the Insert menu, select Dialog, and then click New. The dialog editor assigns the ID *IDD_DIALOG1* to the new dialog. Change the dialog caption to *The Dialog that ate Windows CE!* You can resize the dialog to be wider but not much taller. (Windows CE displays are much wider than they are tall.)

4. Remove the OK and CANCEL buttons and add an OK caption button. Since screen real estate is at a premium in Windows CE, we can save a good deal of space in our dialog by deleting the OK and CANCEL buttons. For Cancel functionality, users can use the close button that is part of the dialog caption. Windows CE also supports an OK caption button that you can create by setting the dialog's property bar. To set the property, open the properties editor for the dialog, click the Extended Styles tab, and then check the Caption Bar OK (WCE Only) option as shown here.

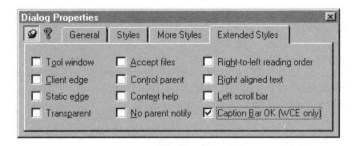

(You might also need to set the dialog's Visible property on the More Styles tab.)

5. **Add the dialog's controls.** Add the following controls shown in Figure 38-9 and accept the default names:

❑ A static control and an edit control for a name

❑ A static control and an edit control for an amount

❑ A static control and a drop-down combo box for an expense type

❑ A City group box with three radio buttons labeled Atlanta, Detroit, and Chicago

❑ A Payment Option group box with three check boxes labeled Check, Credit Card, and Cash

6. **Add the *CEx38aDialog* class.** After adding the controls, double-click on the dialog. ClassWizard detects that you have created a dialog resource and asks whether you want to create a class for the dialog. Click OK and accept the defaults to create the *CEx06aDialog* class.

7. **Program the controls.** Use ClassWizard to create the following member variables in the dialog class:

❑ *m_pComboBox*—A member variable used to configure the expense type combo box

❑ *m_pProgressCtrl*—A member variable for the progress control

NOTE: If you need a refresher on how to program modal dialogs, please refer to Chapter 6.

Next, add the following code to the *CEx38aDialog::OnInitDialog* handler to initialize the controls:

```
BOOL CWindowsCEDlg::OnInitDialog()
{
    CDialog::OnInitDialog();
    m_pComboBox.AddString(_T("Travel"));
    m_pComboBox.AddString(_T("Meal"));
    m_pComboBox.AddString(_T("Cab Fare"));
    m_pComboBox.AddString(_T("Entertainment"));
    m_pComboBox.AddString(_T("Other"));
    m_pProgressCtrl.SetPos(50);

    return TRUE;
}
```

Notice that you must use the _T macro whenever you have inline strings.

8. **Connect the dialog to the View.** In ClassWizard, select the *CEx38a-View* class and use ClassWizard to add the *OnLButtonDown* member function.

9. **Write the code for the *OnLButtonDown* handler.** Add the boldface code below:

```
void CEx38aView::OnLButtonDown(UINT nFlags, CPoint point)
{
    CWindowsCEDlg dlg;
    dlg.DoModal();
    CView::OnLButtonDown(nFlags, point);
}
```

10. **Add code to the virtual *OnDraw* function in file ex38aView.cpp.** The *CDC::TextOut* function used in previous examples is not supported on Windows CE, so we need to use the *CDC::DrawText* function as shown here:

```
void CEx38aView::OnDraw(CDC* pDC)
{
    CRect rect;
    GetClientRect(rect);

    pDC->SetTextColor(::GetSysColor(COLOR_WINDOWTEXT));
    pDC->SetBkMode(TRANSPARENT);

    pDC->DrawText(_T("Press the left mouse button here."),
        rect, DT_SINGLELINE);
}
```

11. **Add the ex38aDialog.h header file to ex38aView.cpp.** Insert the include statement

```
#include "ex38aDialog.h"
```

at the top of the ex38aView.cpp source file, after the statement

```
#include "ex38aView.h"
```

12. **Build and run the application.** The EX38A application should appear as shown in Figure 38-10 on the following page. If everything works satisfactorily, you can change the configuration for a real Windows CE device. Then you can run (or debug) the application remotely on the device to ensure it works in a real-world situation.

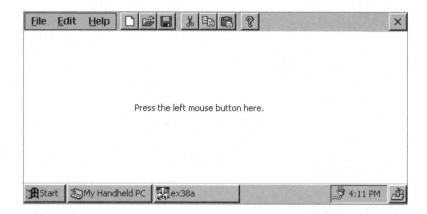

Figure 38-10.
The EX38A application running in the Windows CE emulator.

As you can tell from the EX38A application, programming for Windows CE is very similar to programming for Windows 98 and Windows NT.

Many Windows CE developers are interested in porting existing applications to the Windows CE environment. The next section shows you how to tackle this problem.

Porting an Existing MFC Application to Windows CE

In example EX38B we will port an existing application (EX06B from Chapter 6) from Windows 98 and Windows NT to Windows CE.

> NOTE: We chose the EX06B sample because it is an SDI application. If you are porting an MDI application to Windows CE, we recommend that you first convert it into an SDI application (or a series of SDI applications, if you have several views) and then port it to Windows CE.

Here are the steps for converting EX06B:

1. **Run the MFC AppWizard to produce \vcpp32\ex38b\ex38b.** Select the WCE MFC AppWizard project type and accept all defaults. (You might have thought that we could copy the EX06B workspace and then add a Windows CE configuration. However, it is actually easier to start with a WCE MFC AppWizard project instead because there are many complicated build settings that the wizard automatically sets up for you.)

2. **Using Windows Explorer, copy the EX06B files to the EX38B directory.** Be sure to copy the following files: Ex06bDialog.h, Ex06bDialog.cpp, Ex06bDoc.h, Ex06bDoc.cpp, ex06bView.h, and ex06bView.cpp.

3. **Insert the new files into the project.**   Choose the Add To Project/Files command from the Project menu and insert the files from step 2 into the project.

4. **Copy the dialog and Icon resources from EX06B.**   Choose Open from the File menu and select \vcpp32\ex06b\ex06b\ex06b.rc. Drag and drop IDD_DIALOG1 from ex06b.rc into the EX38B project. Next, drag and drop the color icon resources (IDI_BLACK, IDI_BLUE, and so on) from the ex06b.rc file into the EX38B project.

5. **Build the application and repair any compiler errors or warnings.**
   Now that you have moved the key files that you need (the document, view, and dialog classes) from the EX06B application to the Windows CE EX38B application, try to build the project. You should see a number of errors that can be fixed with the following steps:

   ❑ Change all references to the file ex06b.h to ex38b.h

   ❑ Make sure that all inline strings use the _*T* macro. For example, in Ex06bDialog.cpp the line

   ```
   TRACE("updating trackbar data members\n");
   ```

   should be changed to use the _*T* macro as follows:

   ```
   TRACE(_T("updating trackbar data members\n"));
   ```

   ❑ Convert any other non-Unicode strings to Unicode. (This is the most frequently encountered porting problem.)

   ❑ *Ex06bView::OnDraw* uses the unsupported *CDC::TextOut* member function. Change it to use *DrawText* as follows:

   ```
   CRect rect;
   GetClientRect(rect);

   pDC->SetTextColor(::GetSysColor(COLOR_WINDOWTEXT));
   pDC->SetBkMode(TRANSPARENT);

   pDC->DrawText(_T("Press the left mouse button here."),
       rect, DT_SINGLELINE);
   ```

6. **Replace the wizard-generated view with the real view.**   Open the ex38b.cpp file and do a global search and replace:

   ❑ Change CEx38bDoc to CEx06bDoc

   ❑ Change CEx38bView to CEx06bView

   Also, make sure that ex38b.cpp #includes both the ex06bView.h and ex06bDoc.h header files.

7. **Using the dialog editor, adjust the dialog's layout for Windows CE.**
As it stands, the dialog is far too tall for Windows CE. You can rearrange it by following these steps:

❑ Remove the OK and CANCEL buttons and use the OK window button (see step 4 in the EX38A example).

❑ Move the progress bar controls, sliders, and spinners closer together at the top of the dialog.

❑ Move the list control and tree control closer together. To save vertical space, move the current selection static controls to the left of both the tree and list control.

❑ Size the dialog to fit on a smaller screen.

8. **Clean up the project.** Now you can remove the document and view classes created by the MFC AppWizard by selecting the files in FileView and pressing the Delete key.

9. **Build and test.** In eight easy steps, you have converted a small MFC application from Windows 98 and Windows NT to Windows CE.
Figure 38-11 below shows EX38B running in emulation mode for Windows CE.

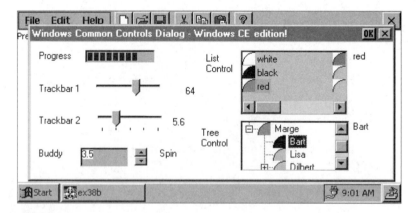

Figure 38-11.
The EX38B application running in the Windows CE emulator.

ATL and Windows CE

In addition to Mini MFC, Visual C++ for Windows CE also provides a Windows CE–friendly version of ATL. ATL is already a lightweight framework, so Microsoft didn't need to reduce the feature set for size constraints. However, there are some areas of COM not covered by Windows CE 2.0 that impact the feature set of ATL for Windows CE.

Windows CE doesn't support the apartment-threading model, so ATL for Windows CE doesn't implement the *CComApartment*, *CComAutoThread-Module*, *CComClassFactoryAutoThread*, or *CComSimpleThreadAllocator* classes.

Windows CE also doesn't support asynchronous monikers, so ATL for Windows CE doesn't implement the *IBindStatusCallbackImpl* or *CBindStatus-Callback* classes. A variety of other ATL class member functions that behave differently on Windows CE are documented in the Visual C++ for Windows CE documentation.

In addition to ATL, a Windows CE version of the ATL Wizard is provided. Figure 38-12 shows that the wizard has only one option: to use MFC or not.

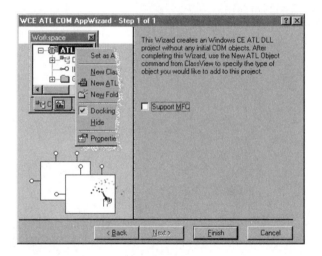

Figure 38-12.
The WCE ATL COM AppWizard.

When you write ActiveX controls for Windows CE, remember that they are binary objects and therefore processor-dependent. Depending on the devices you plan to support, you might have to provide several versions of the control (MIPS or SH, for example).

For More Information on Windows CE...

Windows CE is an exciting new environment for Windows developers to explore. The ability to leverage your knowledge of Windows, Win32, and Visual C++ makes Windows CE an extremely appealing and easy-to-work-with environment. *Programming Windows CE* by Doug Boling (Microsoft Press, 1998) is an excellent resource for learning the details of Windows CE.

Microsoft is developing Windows CE and related technologies at an incredible pace. To stay up to date, we recommend using the Web. Keep an eye on these sites:

- *http://www.microsoft.com/windowsce*. This site provides news and information about the Windows CE operating system, devices, and development tools. You can sign up for a useful newsletter here.

- *http://www.microsoft.com/msdn*. The Microsoft Developer Network (MSDN) has tons of Windows CE articles. They are all online and searchable.

Message Map Functions in the Microsoft Foundation Class Library

HANDLERS FOR WM_COMMAND MESSAGES

Map Entry	Function Prototype
ON_COMMAND(<id>, <memberFxn>)	afx_msg void memberFxn();
ON_COMMAND_EX(<id>, <memberFxn>)	afx_msg BOOL memberFxn(UINT);
ON_COMMAND_EX_RANGE(<id>,<idLast>, <memberFxn>)	afx_msg BOOL memberFxn(UINT);
ON_COMMAND_RANGE(<id>, <idLast>, <memberFxn>)	afx_msg void memberFxn(UINT);
ON_UPDATE_COMMAND_UI(<id>, <memberFxn>)	afx_msg void memberFxn(CCmdUI*);
ON_UPDATE_COMMAND_UI_RANGE (<id>, <idLast>, <memberFxn>)	afx_msg void memberFxn(CCmdUI*);
ON_UPDATE_COMMAND_UI_REFLECT (<memberFxn>)	afx_msg void memberFxn(CCmdUI*);

HANDLERS FOR CHILD WINDOW NOTIFICATION MESSAGES

Map Entry	Function Prototype
Generic Control Notification Codes	
ON_CONTROL(<wNotifyCode>, <id>, <memberFxn>)	afx_msg void memberFxn();
ON_CONTROL_RANGE(<wNotifyCode>, <id>, <idLast>, <memberFxn>)	afx_msg void memberFxn(UINT);
ON_CONTROL_REFLECT(<wNotifyCode>, <memberFxn>)	afx_msg void memberFxn();
ON_CONTROL_REFLECT_EX (<wNotifyCode>, <memberFxn>)	afx_msg BOOL memberFxn();
ON_NOTIFY(<wNotifyCode>, <id>, <memberFxn>)	afx_msg void memberFxn(NMHDR*, LRESULT*);
ON_NOTIFY_EX(<wNotifyCode>, <id>, <memberFxn>)	afx_msg BOOL memberFxn(UINT, NMHDR*, LRESULT*);
ON_NOTIFY_EX_RANGE(<wNotifyCode>, <id>, <idLast>, <memberFxn>)	afx_msg BOOL memberFxn(UINT, NMHDR*, LRESULT*);
ON_NOTIFY_RANGE(<wNotifyCode>, <id>, <idLast>, <memberFxn>)	afx_msg void memberFxn(UINT, NMHDR*, LRESULT*);
ON_NOTIFY_REFLECT(<wNotifyCode>, <memberFxn>)	afx_msg void memberFxn(NMHDR*, LRESULT*);
ON_NOTIFY_REFLECT_EX(<wNotifyCode>, <memberFxn>)	afx_msg BOOL memberFxn(NMHDR*, LRESULT*);
User Button Notification Codes	
ON_BN_CLICKED(<id>, <memberFxn>)	afx_msg void memberFxn();
ON_BN_DOUBLECLICKED(<id>, <memberFxn>)	afx_msg void memberFxn();
ON_BN_KILLFOCUS(<id>, <memberFxn>)	afx_msg void memberFxn();
ON_BN_SETFOCUS(<id>, <memberFxn>)	afx_msg void memberFxn();
Combo Box Notification Codes	
ON_CBN_CLOSEUP(<id>, <memberFxn>)	afx_msg void memberFxn();
ON_CBN_DBLCLK(<id>, <memberFxn>)	afx_msg void memberFxn();
ON_CBN_DROPDOWN(<id>, <memberFxn>)	afx_msg void memberFxn();
ON_CBN_EDITCHANGE(<id>, <memberFxn>)	afx_msg void memberFxn();
ON_CBN_EDITUPDATE(<id>, <memberFxn>)	afx_msg void memberFxn();
ON_CBN_ERRSPACE(<id>, <memberFxn>)	afx_msg void memberFxn();

HANDLERS FOR CHILD WINDOW NOTIFICATION MESSAGES

Map Entry	Function Prototype
ON_CBN_KILLFOCUS(<id>, <memberFxn>)	afx_msg void memberFxn();
ON_CBN_SELCHANGE(<id>, <memberFxn>)	afx_msg void memberFxn();
ON_CBN_SELENDCANCEL(<id>, <memberFxn>)	afx_msg void memberFxn();
ON_CBN_SELENDOK(<id>, <memberFxn>)	afx_msg void memberFxn();
ON_CBN_SETFOCUS(<id>, <memberFxn>)	afx_msg void memberFxn();

Check List Box Notification Codes

ON_CLBN_CHKCHANGE(<id>, <memberFxn>)	afx_msg void memberFxn();

Edit Control Notification Codes

ON_EN_CHANGE(<id>, <memberFxn>)	afx_msg void memberFxn();
ON_EN_ERRSPACE(<id>, <memberFxn>)	afx_msg void memberFxn();
ON_EN_HSCROLL(<id>, <memberFxn>)	afx_msg void memberFxn();
ON_EN_KILLFOCUS(<id>, <memberFxn>)	afx_msg void memberFxn();
ON_EN_MAXTEXT(<id>, <memberFxn>)	afx_msg void memberFxn();
ON_EN_SETFOCUS(<id>, <memberFxn>)	afx_msg void memberFxn();
ON_EN_UPDATE(<id>, <memberFxn>)	afx_msg void memberFxn();
ON_EN_VSCROLL(<id>, <memberFxn>)	afx_msg void memberFxn();

List Box Notification Codes

ON_LBN_DBLCLK(<id>, <memberFxn>)	afx_msg void memberFxn();
ON_LBN_ERRSPACE(<id>, <memberFxn>)	afx_msg void memberFxn();
ON_LBN_KILLFOCUS(<id>, <memberFxn>)	afx_msg void memberFxn();
ON_LBN_SELCANCEL(<id>, <memberFxn>)	afx_msg void memberFxn();
ON_LBN_SELCHANGE(<id>, <memberFxn>)	afx_msg void memberFxn();
ON_LBN_SETFOCUS(<id>, <memberFxn>)	afx_msg void memberFxn();

Static Control Notification Codes

ON_STN_CLICKED(<id>, <memberFxn>)	afx_msg void memberFxn();
ON_STN_DBLCLK(<id>, <memberFxn>)	afx_msg void memberFxn();
ON_STN_DISABLE(<id>, <memberFxn>)	afx_msg void memberFxn();
ON_STN_ENABLE(<id>, <memberFxn>)	afx_msg void memberFxn();

HANDLERS FOR WINDOW NOTIFICATION MESSAGES

Map Entry	Function Prototype
ON_WM_ACTIVATE()	afx_msg void OnActivate(UINT, CWnd*, BOOL);
ON_WM_ACTIVATEAPP()	afx_msg void OnActivateApp(BOOL, HTASK);
ON_WM_ASKCBFORMATNAME()	afx_msg void OnAskCbFormatName(UINT, LPTSTR);
ON_WM_CANCELMODE()	afx_msg void OnCancelMode();
ON_WM_CAPTURECHANGED()	afx_msg void OnCaptureChanged(CWnd*);
ON_WM_CHANGECBCHAIN()	afx_msg void OnChangeCbChain(HWND, HWND);
ON_WM_CHAR()	afx_msg void OnChar(UINT, UINT, UINT);
ON_WM_CHARTOITEM()	afx_msg int OnCharToItem(UINT, CListBox*, UINT);
ON_WM_CHARTOITEM_REFLECT()	afx_msg int CharToItem(UINT, UINT);
ON_WM_CHILDACTIVATE()	afx_msg void OnChildActivate();
ON_WM_CLOSE()	afx_msg void OnClose();
ON_WM_COMPACTING()	afx_msg void OnCompacting(UINT);
ON_WM_COMPAREITEM()	afx_msg int OnCompareItem(int, LPCOMPAREITEMSTRUCT);
ON_WM_COMPAREITEM_REFLECT()	afx_msg int CompareItem (LPCOMPAREITEMSTRUCT);
ON_WM_CONTEXTMENU()	afx_msg void OnContextMenu(CWnd*, CPoint);
ON_WM_COPYDATA()	afx_msg BOOL OnCopyData(CWnd*, COPYDATASTRUCT*);
ON_WM_CREATE()	afx_msg int OnCreate(LPCREATESTRUCT);
ON_WM_CTLCOLOR()	afx_msg HBRUSH OnCtlColor(CDC*, CWnd*, UINT);
ON_WM_CTLCOLOR_REFLECT()	afx_msg HBRUSH CtlColor(CDC*, UINT);
ON_WM_DEADCHAR()	afx_msg void OnDeadChar(UINT, UINT, UINT);
ON_WM_DELETEITEM()	afx_msg void OnDeleteItem(int, LPDELETEITEMSTRUCT);
ON_WM_DELETEITEM_REFLECT()	afx_msg void DeleteItem (LPDELETEITEMSTRUCT)
ON_WM_DESTROY()	afx_msg void OnDestroy();
ON_WM_DESTROYCLIPBOARD()	afx_msg void OnDestroyClipboard();
ON_WM_DEVICECHANGE()	afx_msg BOOL OnDeviceChange(UINT, DWORD);
ON_WM_DEVMODECHANGE()	afx_msg void OnDevModeChange(LPTSTR);

HANDLERS FOR WINDOW NOTIFICATION MESSAGES

Map Entry	Function Prototype
ON_WM_DRAWCLIPBOARD()	afx_msg void OnDrawClipboard();
ON_WM_DRAWITEM()	afx_msg void OnDrawItem(int, LPDRAWITEMSTRUCT);
ON_WM_DRAWITEM_REFLECT()	afx_msg void DrawItem (LPDRAWITEMSTRUCT);
ON_WM_DROPFILES()	afx_msg void OnDropFiles(HDROP);
ON_WM_ENABLE()	afx_msg void OnEnable(BOOL);
ON_WM_ENDSESSION()	afx_msg void OnEndSession(BOOL);
ON_WM_ENTERIDLE()	afx_msg void OnEnterIdle(UINT, CWnd*);
ON_WM_ENTERMENULOOP()	afx_msg void OnEnterMenuLoop(BOOL);
ON_WM_ERASEBKGND()	afx_msg BOOL OnEraseBkgnd(CDC*);
ON_WM_EXITMENULOOP()	afx_msg void OnExitMenuLoop(BOOL);
ON_WM_FONTCHANGE()	afx_msg void OnFontChange();
ON_WM_GETDLGCODE()	afx_msg UINT OnGetDlgCode();
ON_WM_GETMINMAXINFO()	afx_msg void OnGetMinMaxInfo (MINMAXINFO*);
ON_WM_HELPINFO()	afx_msg BOOL OnHelpInfo(HELPINFO*);
ON_WM_HSCROLL()	afx_msg void OnHScroll(UINT, UINT, CScrollBar*);
ON_WM_HSCROLL_REFLECT()	afx_msg void HScroll(UINT, UINT);
ON_WM_HSCROLLCLIPBOARD()	afx_msg void OnHScrollClipboard(CWnd*, UINT, UINT);
ON_WM_ICONERASEBKGND()	afx_msg void OnIconEraseBkgnd(CDC*);
ON_WM_INITMENU()	afx_msg void OnInitMenu(CMenu*);
ON_WM_INITMENUPOPUP()	afx_msg void OnInitMenuPopup(CMenu*, UINT, BOOL);
ON_WM_KEYDOWN()	afx_msg void OnKeyDown(UINT, UINT, UINT);
ON_WM_KEYUP()	afx_msg void OnKeyUp(UINT, UINT, UINT);
ON_WM_KILLFOCUS()	afx_msg void OnKillFocus(CWnd*);
ON_WM_LBUTTONDBLCLK()	afx_msg void OnLButtonDblClk(UINT, CPoint);
ON_WM_LBUTTONDOWN()	afx_msg void OnLButtonDown(UINT, CPoint);
ON_WM_LBUTTONUP()	afx_msg void OnLButtonUp(UINT, CPoint);
ON_WM_MBUTTONDBLCLK()	afx_msg void OnMButtonDblClk(UINT, CPoint);
ON_WM_MBUTTONDOWN()	afx_msg void OnMButtonDown(UINT, CPoint);

(continued)

HANDLERS FOR WINDOW NOTIFICATION MESSAGES *continued*

Map Entry	Function Prototype
ON_WM_MBUTTONUP()	afx_msg void OnMButtonUp(UINT, CPoint);
ON_WM_MDIACTIVATE()	afx_msg void OnMDIActivate(BOOL, CWnd*, CWnd*);
ON_WM_MEASUREITEM()	afx_msg void OnMeasureItem(int, LPMEASUREITEMSTRUCT);
ON_WM_MEASUREITEM_REFLECT()	afx_msg void MeasureItem (LPMEASUREITEMSTRUCT);
ON_WM_MENUCHAR()	afx_msg LRESULT OnMenuChar(UINT, UINT, CMenu*);
ON_WM_MENUSELECT()	afx_msg void OnMenuSelect(UINT, UINT, HMENU);
ON_WM_MOUSEACTIVATE()	afx_msg int OnMouseActivate(CWnd*, UINT, UINT);
ON_WM_MOUSEMOVE()	afx_msg void OnMouseMove(UINT, CPoint);
ON_WM_MOUSEWHEEL()	afx_msg BOOL OnMouseWheel(UINT, short, CPoint);
ON_WM_MOVE()	afx_msg void OnMove(int, int);
ON_WM_MOVING()	afx_msg void OnMoving(UINT, LPRECT);
ON_WM_NCACTIVATE()	afx_msg BOOL OnNcActivate(BOOL);
ON_WM_NCCALCSIZE()	afx_msg void OnNcCalcSize(BOOL, NCCALCSIZE_PARAMS*);
ON_WM_NCCREATE()	afx_msg BOOL OnNcCreate (LPCREATESTRUCT);
ON_WM_NCDESTROY()	afx_msg void OnNcDestroy();
ON_WM_NCHITTEST()	afx_msg UINT OnNcHitTest(CPoint);
ON_WM_NCLBUTTONDBLCLK()	afx_msg void OnNcLButtonDblClk(UINT, CPoint);
ON_WM_NCLBUTTONDOWN()	afx_msg void OnNcLButtonDown(UINT, CPoint);
ON_WM_NCLBUTTONUP()	afx_msg void OnNcLButtonUp(UINT, CPoint);
ON_WM_NCMBUTTONDBLCLK()	afx_msg void OnNcMButtonDblClk(UINT, CPoint);
ON_WM_NCMBUTTONDOWN()	afx_msg void OnNcMButtonDown(UINT, CPoint);
ON_WM_NCMBUTTONUP()	afx_msg void OnNcMButtonUp(UINT, CPoint);
ON_WM_NCMOUSEMOVE()	afx_msg void OnNcMouseMove(UINT, CPoint);
ON_WM_NCPAINT()	afx_msg void OnNcPaint();
ON_WM_NCRBUTTONDBLCLK()	afx_msg void OnNcRButtonDblClk(UINT, CPoint);

HANDLERS FOR WINDOW NOTIFICATION MESSAGES

Map Entry	Function Prototype
ON_WM_NCRBUTTONDOWN()	afx_msg void OnNcRButtonDown(UINT, CPoint);
ON_WM_NCRBUTTONUP()	afx_msg void OnNcRButtonUp(UINT, CPoint);
ON_WM_PAINT()	afx_msg void OnPaint();
ON_WM_PAINTCLIPBOARD()	afx_msg void OnPaintClipboard(CWnd*, HGLOBAL);
ON_WM_PALETTECHANGED()	afx_msg void OnPaletteChanged(CWnd*);
ON_WM_PALETTEISCHANGING()	afx_msg void OnPaletteIsChanging(CWnd*);
ON_WM_PARENTNOTIFY()	afx_msg void OnParentNotify(UINT, LPARAM);
ON_WM_PARENTNOTIFY_REFLECT()	afx_msg void ParentNotify(UINT, LPARAM);
ON_WM_QUERYDRAGICON()	afx_msg HCURSOR OnQueryDragIcon();
ON_WM_QUERYENDSESSION()	afx_msg BOOL OnQueryEndSession();
ON_WM_QUERYNEWPALETTE()	afx_msg BOOL OnQueryNewPalette();
ON_WM_QUERYOPEN()	afx_msg BOOL OnQueryOpen();
ON_WM_RBUTTONDBLCLK()	afx_msg void OnRButtonDblClk(UINT, CPoint);
ON_WM_RBUTTONDOWN()	afx_msg void OnRButtonDown(UINT, CPoint);
ON_WM_RBUTTONUP()	afx_msg void OnRButtonUp(UINT, CPoint);
ON_WM_RENDERALLFORMATS()	afx_msg void OnRenderAllFormats();
ON_WM_RENDERFORMAT()	afx_msg void OnRenderFormat(UINT);
ON_WM_SETCURSOR()	afx_msg BOOL OnSetCursor(CWnd*, UINT, UINT);
ON_WM_SETFOCUS()	afx_msg void OnSetFocus(CWnd*);
ON_WM_SETTINGCHANGE()	afx_msg void OnSettingChange(UINT, LPCTSTR);
ON_WM_SHOWWINDOW()	afx_msg void OnShowWindow(BOOL, UINT);
ON_WM_SIZE()	afx_msg void OnSize(UINT, int, int);
ON_WM_SIZECLIPBOARD()	afx_msg void OnSizeClipboard(CWnd*, HGLOBAL);
ON_WM_SIZING()	afx_msg void OnSizing(UINT, LPRECT);
ON_WM_SPOOLERSTATUS()	afx_msg void OnSpoolerStatus(UINT, UINT);
ON_WM_STYLECHANGED()	afx_msg void OnStyleChanged(int, LPSTYLESTRUCT);
ON_WM_STYLECHANGING()	afx_msg void OnStyleChanging(int, LPSTYLESTRUCT);
ON_WM_SYSCHAR()	afx_msg void OnSysChar(UINT, UINT, UINT);
ON_WM_SYSCOLORCHANGE()	afx_msg void OnSysColorChange();

(continued)

HANDLERS FOR WINDOW NOTIFICATION MESSAGES *continued*

Map Entry	Function Prototype
ON_WM_SYSCOMMAND()	afx_msg void OnSysCommand(UINT, LPARAM);
ON_WM_SYSDEADCHAR()	afx_msg void OnSysDeadChar(UINT, UINT, UINT);
ON_WM_SYSKEYDOWN()	afx_msg void OnSysKeyDown(UINT, UINT, UINT);
ON_WM_SYSKEYUP()	afx_msg void OnSysKeyUp(UINT, UINT, UINT);
ON_WM_TCARD()	afx_msg void OnTCard(UINT, DWORD);
ON_WM_TIMECHANGE()	afx_msg void OnTimeChange();
ON_WM_TIMER()	afx_msg void OnTimer(UINT);
ON_WM_VKEYTOITEM()	afx_msg int OnVKeyToItem(UINT, CListBox*, UINT);
ON_WM_VKEYTOITEM_REFLECT()	afx_msg int VKeyToItem(UINT, UINT);
ON_WM_VSCROLL()	afx_msg void OnVScroll(UINT, UINT, CScrollBar*);
ON_WM_VSCROLL_REFLECT()	afx_msg void VScroll(UINT, UINT);
ON_WM_VSCROLLCLIPBOARD()	afx_msg void OnVScrollClipboard(CWnd*, UINT, UINT);
ON_WM_WINDOWPOSCHANGED()	afx_msg void OnWindowPosChanged (WINDOWPOS*);
ON_WM_WINDOWPOSCHANGING()	afx_msg void OnWindowPosChanging (WINDOWPOS*);
ON_WM_WININICHANGE()	afx_msg void OnWinIniChange(LPCTSTR);

USER-DEFINED MESSAGE CODES

Map Entry	Function Prototype
ON_MESSAGE(<message>, <memberFxn>)	afx_msg LRESULT memberFxn(WPARAM, LPARAM);
ON_REGISTERED_MESSAGE (<nMessageVariable>,<memberFxn>)	afx_msg LRESULT memberFxn(WPARAM, LPARAM);
ON_REGISTERED_THREAD-MESSAGE(<nMessageVariable>, <memberFxn>)	afx_msg void memberFxn(WPARAM, LPARAM);
ON_THREAD_MESSAGE (<message>, <memberFxn>)	afx_msg void memberFxn(WPARAM, LPARAM);

MFC Library Runtime Class Identification and Dynamic Object Creation

Long before runtime type information (RTTI) was added to the C++ language specification, the MFC library designers realized that they needed runtime access to an object's class name and to the position of the class in the hierarchy. Also, the document–view architecture (and, later, COM class factories) demanded that objects be constructed from a class specified at runtime. So the MFC team created an integrated macro-based class identification and dynamic creation system that depends on the universal *CObject* base class. And in spite of the fact that the Visual C++ version 6.0 compiler supports the ANSI RTTI syntax, the MFC library continues to use the original system, which actually has more features.

This appendix explains how the MFC library implements the class identification and dynamic creation features. You'll see how the *DECLARE_DYNAMIC*, *DECLARE_DYNCREATE*, and associated macros work, and you'll learn about the *RUNTIME_CLASS* macro and the *CRuntimeClass* structure.

Getting an Object's Class Name at Runtime

If you wanted only an object's class name, you'd have an easy time, assuming that all your classes were derived from a common base class, *CObject*. Here's how you'd get the class name:

```
class CObject
{
public:
    virtual char* GetClassName() const { return NULL; }
};
```

(continued)

```
class CMyClass : public CObject
{
public:
    static char s_lpszClassName[];
    virtual char* GetClassName() const { return s_lpszClassName; }
};
char CMyClass::s_szClassName[] = "CMyClass";
```

Each derived class would override the virtual *GetClassName* function, which would return a static string. You would get an object's actual class name even if you used a *CObject* pointer to call *GetClassName*. If you needed the class name feature in many classes, you could save yourself some work by writing macros. A *DECLARE_CLASSNAME* macro might insert the static data member and the *GetClassName* function in the class declaration, and an *IMPLEMENT_CLASSNAME* macro might define the class name string in the implementation file.

The MFC *CRuntimeClass* Structure and the *RUNTIME_CLASS* Macro

In a real MFC program, an instance of the *CRuntimeClass* structure replaces the static *s_lpszClassName* data member shown above. This structure has data members for the class name and the object size; it also contains a pointer to a special static function, *CreateObject*, that's supposed to be implemented in the target class. Here's a simplified version of *CRuntimeClass*:

```
struct CRuntimeClass
{
    char m_lpszClassName[21];
    int m_nObjectSize; // used for memory validation
    CObject* (*m_pfnCreateObject)();
    CObject* CreateObject();
};
```

> NOTE: The real MFC *CRuntimeClass* structure has additional data members and functions that navigate through the class's hierarchy. This navigation feature is not supported by the official C++ RTTI implementation.

This structure supports not only class name retrieval but also dynamic creation. Each class you derive from *CObject* has a <u>static</u> *CRuntimeClass* data member, provided that you use the MFC *DECLARE_DYNAMIC*, *DECLARE_DYNCREATE*, or *DECLARE_SERIAL* macro in the declaration and the corresponding *IMPLEMENT* macro in the implementation file. The name of the static data member is, by convention, *class<class_name>*. If your class were named *CMyClass*, the *CRuntimeClass* data member would be named *classCMyClass*.

If you want a pointer to a <u>class's</u> static *CRuntimeClass* object, you use the MFC *RUNTIME_CLASS* macro, defined as follows:

```
#define RUNTIME_CLASS(class_name) (&class_name::class##class_name)
```

Here's how you use the macro to get the name string from a class name:

```
ASSERT(RUNTIME_CLASS(CMyClass)->m_lpszClassName == "CMyClass");
```

If you want the class name string from an <u>object</u>, you call the virtual *CObject::GetRuntimeClass* function. The function simply returns a pointer to the class's static *CRuntimeClass* object, just as earlier the *GetClassName* function returned the name string. Here's the function you'd write for *CMyClass*:

```
virtual CRuntimeClass* GetRuntimeClass()
    const { return &classCMyClass; }
```

And here's how you'd call it:

```
ASSERT(pMyObject->GetRuntimeClass()->m_lpszClassName == "CMyClass");
```

Dynamic Creation

You've already learned that the *DECLARE* and *IMPLEMENT* macros add a static *CRuntimeClass* object to a class. If you use the *DECLARE_DYN-CREATE* or *DECLARE_SERIAL* macro (and the corresponding *IMPLE-MENT* macro), you get an additional static member function *CreateObject* (distinct from *CRuntimeClass::CreateObject*) in your class. Here's an example:

```
CObject* CMyClass::CreateObject()
{
    return new CMyClass;
}
```

Obviously, *CMyClass* needs a default constructor. This constructor is declared protected in wizard-generated classes that support dynamic creation.

Now look at the code for the *CRuntimeClass::CreateObject* function:

```
CObject* CRuntimeClass::CreateObject()
{
    return (*m_pfnCreateObject)();
}
```

This function makes an indirect call to the *CreateObject* function in the target class. Here's how you would dynamically construct an object of class *CMyClass*:

```
CRuntimeClass* pRTC = RUNTIME_CLASS(CMyObject);
CMyClass* pMyObject = (CMyClass*)pRTC->CreateObject();
```

Now you know how document templates work. A document template object has three *CRuntimeClass** data members initialized at construction to point to the static *CRuntimeClass* data members for the document, frame, and view classes. When *CWinApp::OnFileNew* is called, the framework calls the *CreateObject* functions for the three stored pointers.

A Sample Program

Here is the code for a command-line program that dynamically constructs objects of two classes. Note that this isn't real MFC code—the *CObject* class is a simplified version of the MFC library *CObject* class. You can find this code in the dyncreat.cpp file in the \vcpp32\appendb folder.

```
#include <stdio.h>

#define RUNTIME_CLASS(class_name) (&class_name::class##class_name)

class CObject;

struct CRuntimeClass
{
    char m_lpszClassName[21];
    int m_nObjectSize;
    CObject* (*m_pfnCreateObject)();
    CObject* CreateObject();
};

// not a true abstract class because there are no pure
//  virtual functions, but user can't create CObject objects
//  because of the protected constructor
class CObject
{
public:
    // not pure because derived classes don't necessarily
    // implement it
    virtual CRuntimeClass* GetRuntimeClass() const { return NULL; }

    // We never construct objects of class CObject, but in MFC we
    //  use this to get class hierarchy information
```

```
    static CRuntimeClass classCObject;          // DYNAMIC
     virtual ~CObject() {};  // gotta have it
protected:
    CObject() { printf("CObject constructor\n"); }
};

CRuntimeClass CObject::classCObject = { "CObject",
    sizeof(CObject), NULL };

CObject* CRuntimeClass::CreateObject()
{
    return (*m_pfnCreateObject)(); // indirect function call
}

class CAlpha : public CObject
{
public:
    virtual CRuntimeClass* GetRuntimeClass()
        const { return &classCAlpha; }
    static CRuntimeClass classCAlpha;          // DYNAMIC
    static CObject* CreateObject();             // DYNCREATE
protected:
    CAlpha() { printf("CAlpha constructor\n"); }
};

CRuntimeClass CAlpha::classCAlpha = { "CAlpha",
    sizeof(CAlpha), CAlpha::CreateObject };

CObject* CAlpha::CreateObject() // static function
{
    return new CAlpha;
}

class CBeta : public CObject
{
public:
    virtual CRuntimeClass* GetRuntimeClass()
        const { return &classCBeta; }
    static CRuntimeClass classCBeta;           // DYNAMIC
    static CObject* CreateObject();             // DYNCREATE
protected:
    CBeta() { printf("CBeta constructor\n"); }
};

CRuntimeClass CBeta::classCBeta = { "CBeta",
    sizeof(CBeta), CBeta::CreateObject };
```

(continued)

```
CObject* CBeta::CreateObject() // static function
{
    return new CBeta;
}

int main()
{
    printf("Entering dyncreate main\n");

    CRuntimeClass* pRTCAlpha = RUNTIME_CLASS(CAlpha);
    CObject* pObj1 = pRTCAlpha->CreateObject();
    printf("class of pObj1 = %s\n",
        pObj1->GetRuntimeClass()->m_lpszClassName);

    CRuntimeClass* pRTCBeta = RUNTIME_CLASS(CBeta);
    CObject* pObj2 = pRTCBeta->CreateObject();
    printf("class of pObj2 = %s\n",
        pObj2->GetRuntimeClass()->m_lpszClassName);

    delete pObj1;
    delete pObj2;
    return 0;
}
```

INDEX

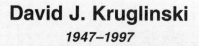

David J. Kruglinski
1947–1997

David Kruglinski was a self-taught and talented programmer, writer, teacher, and outdoorsman.

His programming career began while attending Purdue University in 1966, and he began writing applications for microcomputers in 1976 after a friend fished an 8080 board out of a garbage bin.

David wrote the first edition of this award-winning and highly acclaimed text for Microsoft Press in 1992. A best-selling title, the book is now in its fifth edition.

David's skills as a writer and programmer landed him a contract position on the Microsoft Foundation Class Library version 1.0 documentation team in mid-1991. Much of the MFC reference, especially many of the most basic classes, such as *CString*, still show David's expert touch. He left the Microsoft Languages group to pursue *Inside Visual C++* about the time Microsoft C/C++ 7.0 shipped in 1992.

David's association with MFC and the Visual C++ language made him highly regarded as an authority on both technologies. He started a successful software tools company and worked as a consultant and instructor for Microsoft Visual C++. In between his extensive travels to teach, lecture, attend conferences, and pilot his paraglider, David followed the latest software developments through his many contacts at Microsoft.

A world traveler and outdoorsman who enjoyed hiking and climbing, David was never without his "wing." He began paragliding in the late 1980s, and during the past few years he had gained an international reputation as an excellent pilot. A daring and unconventional flyer, David enjoyed soaring over mountain peaks and valleys at spectacular sites across the globe, from Europe to South America. He set site records for his time in the air and for the distances and heights he traveled.

"Downwind Dave" Kruglinski died while paragliding in the Methow Valley, Okanogan County, Washington, on April 17, 1997. He was 49 years old.

Photo by Denton D. Meier

Scott Wingo and George Shepherd

Scot Wingo has been working with C++ and MFC since the 1.0 days of both. His first job out of North Carolina State University's Master in Computer Engineering program was with Bristol Technology, Inc., a company that provides Windows to UNIX portability tools. In mid-1995, Scot left Bristol to cofound Stingray Software, the leading provider of MFC/ATL class libraries such as Objective Grid and Objective Toolkit. In early 1998, Stingray was acquired by Rogue Wave Software, and now Scot serves as vice president in charge of the Stingray division.

Between the Bristol and Stingray gigs, Scot wrote the first version of the world-famous MFC FAQ and also cowrote (with George Shepherd) *MFC Internals* (Addison-Wesley, 1996)—the only book that details how MFC works internally. Along with George Shepherd, Scot Wingo has become a regular columnist for *Dr. Dobbs, Microsoft Systems Journal,* and *Visual C++ Developer's Journal.*

When George Shepherd isn't developing the Windows development tools with Stingray Software, he's delivering training sessions with DevelopMentor, the best training company around. George cowrote *MFC Internals* (Addison-Wesley, 1996) with Scot Wingo. George prefers to play his Paul Reed Smith between compiles.

MICROSOFT LICENSE AGREEMENT

(Programming Microsoft Visual C++, Fifth Edition - Book Companion CD)

IMPORTANT—READ CAREFULLY: This Microsoft End-User License Agreement ("EULA") is a legal agreement between you (either an individual or an entity) and Microsoft Corporation for the Microsoft product identified above, which includes computer software and may include associated media, printed materials, and "on-line" or electronic documentation ("SOFTWARE PRODUCT"). Any component included within the SOFTWARE PRODUCT that is accompanied by a separate End-User License Agreement shall be governed by such agreement and not the terms set forth below. By installing, copying, or otherwise using the SOFTWARE PRODUCT, you agree to be bound by the terms of this EULA. If you do not agree to the terms of this EULA, you are not authorized to install, copy, or otherwise use the SOFTWARE PRODUCT; you may, however, return the SOFTWARE PRODUCT, along with all printed materials and other items that form a part of the Microsoft product that includes the SOFTWARE PRODUCT, to the place you obtained them for a full refund.

SOFTWARE PRODUCT LICENSE

The SOFTWARE PRODUCT is protected by United States copyright laws and international copyright treaties, as well as other intellectual property laws and treaties. The SOFTWARE PRODUCT is licensed, not sold.

1. GRANT OF LICENSE. This EULA grants you the following rights:

a. **Software Product.** You may install and use one copy of the SOFTWARE PRODUCT on a single computer. The primary user of the computer on which the SOFTWARE PRODUCT is installed may make a second copy for his or her exclusive use on a portable computer.

b. **Storage/Network Use.** You may also store or install a copy of the SOFTWARE PRODUCT on a storage device, such as a network server, used only to install or run the SOFTWARE PRODUCT on your other computers over an internal network; however, you must acquire and dedicate a license for each separate computer on which the SOFTWARE PRODUCT is installed or run from the storage device. A license for the SOFTWARE PRODUCT may not be shared or used concurrently on different computers.

c. **License Pak.** If you have acquired this EULA in a Microsoft License Pak, you may make the number of additional copies of the computer software portion of the SOFTWARE PRODUCT authorized on the printed copy of this EULA, and you may use each copy in the manner specified above. You are also entitled to make a corresponding number of secondary copies for portable computer use as specified above.

d. **Sample Code.** Solely with respect to portions, if any, of the SOFTWARE PRODUCT that are identified within the SOFTWARE PRODUCT as sample code (the "SAMPLE CODE"):

i. **Use and Modification.** Microsoft grants you the right to use and modify the source code version of the SAMPLE CODE, *provided* you comply with subsection (d)(iii) below. You may not distribute the SAMPLE CODE, or any modified version of the SAMPLE CODE, in source code form.

ii. **Redistributable Files.** Provided you comply with subsection (d)(iii) below, Microsoft grants you a nonexclusive, royalty-free right to reproduce and distribute the object code version of the SAMPLE CODE and of any modified SAMPLE CODE, other than SAMPLE CODE (or any modified version thereof) designated as not redistributable in the Readme file that forms a part of the SOFTWARE PRODUCT (the "Non-Redistributable Sample Code"). All SAMPLE CODE other than the Non-Redistributable Sample Code is collectively referred to as the "REDISTRIBUTABLES."

iii. **Redistribution Requirements.** If you redistribute the REDISTRIBUTABLES, you agree to: (i) distribute the REDISTRIBUTABLES in object code form only in conjunction with and as a part of your software application product; (ii) not use Microsoft's name, logo, or trademarks to market your software application product; (iii) include a valid copyright notice on your software application product; (iv) indemnify, hold harmless, and defend Microsoft from and against any claims or lawsuits, including attorney's fees, that arise or result from the use or distribution of your software application product; and (v) not permit further distribution of the REDISTRIBUTABLES by your end user. Contact Microsoft for the applicable royalties due and other licensing terms for all other uses and/or distribution of the REDISTRIBUTABLES.

2. DESCRIPTION OF OTHER RIGHTS AND LIMITATIONS.

- **Limitations on Reverse Engineering, Decompilation, and Disassembly.** You may not reverse engineer, decompile, or disassemble the SOFTWARE PRODUCT, except and only to the extent that such activity is expressly permitted by applicable law notwithstanding this limitation.

- **Separation of Components.** The SOFTWARE PRODUCT is licensed as a single product. Its component parts may not be separated for use on more than one computer.

- **Rental.** You may not rent, lease, or lend the SOFTWARE PRODUCT.

- **Support Services.** Microsoft may, but is not obligated to, provide you with support services related to the SOFTWARE PRODUCT ("Support Services"). Use of Support Services is governed by the Microsoft policies and programs described in the user manual, in "on-line" documentation, and/or in other Microsoft-provided materials. Any supplemental software code provided to you as part of the Support Services shall be considered part of the SOFTWARE PRODUCT and subject to the terms and conditions of this EULA. With respect to technical information you provide to Microsoft as part of the Support Services, Microsoft may use such information for its business purposes, including for product support and development. Microsoft will not utilize such technical information in a form that personally identifies you.

- **Software Transfer.** You may permanently transfer all of your rights under this EULA, provided you retain no copies, you transfer all of the SOFTWARE PRODUCT (including all component parts, the media and printed materials, any upgrades, this EULA, and, if applicable, the Certificate of Authenticity), **and** the recipient agrees to the terms of this EULA.

- **Termination.** Without prejudice to any other rights, Microsoft may terminate this EULA if you fail to comply with the terms and conditions of this EULA. In such event, you must destroy all copies of the SOFTWARE PRODUCT and all of its component parts.

3. **COPYRIGHT.** All title and copyrights in and to the SOFTWARE PRODUCT (including but not limited to any images, photographs, animations, video, audio, music, text, SAMPLE CODE, REDISTRIBUTABLES, and "applets" incorporated into the SOFTWARE PRODUCT) and any copies of the SOFTWARE PRODUCT are owned by Microsoft or its suppliers. The SOFTWARE PRODUCT is protected by copyright laws and international treaty provisions. Therefore, you must treat the SOFTWARE PRODUCT like any other copyrighted material **except** that you may install the SOFTWARE PRODUCT on a single computer provided you keep the original solely for backup or archival purposes. You may not copy the printed materials accompanying the SOFTWARE PRODUCT.

4. **U.S. GOVERNMENT RESTRICTED RIGHTS.** The SOFTWARE PRODUCT and documentation are provided with RESTRICTED RIGHTS. Use, duplication, or disclosure by the Government is subject to restrictions as set forth in subparagraph (c)(1)(ii) of the Rights in Technical Data and Computer Software clause at DFARS 252.227-7013 or subparagraphs (c)(1) and (2) of the Commercial Computer Software—Restricted Rights at 48 CFR 52.227-19, as applicable. Manufacturer is Microsoft Corporation/One Microsoft Way/Redmond, WA 98052-6399.

5. **EXPORT RESTRICTIONS.** You agree that you will not export or re-export the SOFTWARE PRODUCT, any part thereof, or any process or service that is the direct product of the SOFTWARE PRODUCT (the foregoing collectively referred to as the "Restricted Components"), to any country, person, entity, or end user subject to U.S. export restrictions. You specifically agree not to export or re-export any of the Restricted Components (i) to any country to which the U.S. has embargoed or restricted the export of goods or services, which currently include, but are not necessarily limited to, Cuba, Iran, Iraq, Libya, North Korea, Sudan, and Syria, or to any national of any such country, wherever located, who intends to transmit or transport the Restricted Components back to such country; (ii) to any end user who you know or have reason to know will utilize the Restricted Components in the design, development, or production of nuclear, chemical, or biological weapons; or (iii) to any end user who has been prohibited from participating in U.S. export transactions by any federal agency of the U.S. government. You warrant and represent that neither the BXA nor any other U.S. federal agency has suspended, revoked, or denied your export privileges.

DISCLAIMER OF WARRANTY

NO WARRANTIES OR CONDITIONS. MICROSOFT EXPRESSLY DISCLAIMS ANY WARRANTY OR CONDITION FOR THE SOFTWARE PRODUCT. THE SOFTWARE PRODUCT AND ANY RELATED DOCUMENTATION IS PROVIDED "AS IS" WITHOUT WARRANTY OR CONDITION OF ANY KIND, EITHER EXPRESS OR IMPLIED, INCLUDING, WITHOUT LIMITATION, THE IMPLIED WARRANTIES OF MERCHANTABILITY, FITNESS FOR A PARTICULAR PURPOSE, OR NONINFRINGEMENT. THE ENTIRE RISK ARISING OUT OF USE OR PERFORMANCE OF THE SOFTWARE PRODUCT REMAINS WITH YOU.

LIMITATION OF LIABILITY. TO THE MAXIMUM EXTENT PERMITTED BY APPLICABLE LAW, IN NO EVENT SHALL MICROSOFT OR ITS SUPPLIERS BE LIABLE FOR ANY SPECIAL, INCIDENTAL, INDIRECT, OR CONSEQUENTIAL DAMAGES WHATSOEVER (INCLUDING, WITHOUT LIMITATION, DAMAGES FOR LOSS OF BUSINESS PROFITS, BUSINESS INTERRUPTION, LOSS OF BUSINESS INFORMATION, OR ANY OTHER PECUNIARY LOSS) ARISING OUT OF THE USE OF OR INABILITY TO USE THE SOFTWARE PRODUCT OR THE PROVISION OF OR FAILURE TO PROVIDE SUPPORT SERVICES, EVEN IF MICROSOFT HAS BEEN ADVISED OF THE POSSIBILITY OF SUCH DAMAGES. IN ANY CASE, MICROSOFT'S ENTIRE LIABILITY UNDER ANY PROVISION OF THIS EULA SHALL BE LIMITED TO THE GREATER OF THE AMOUNT ACTUALLY PAID BY YOU FOR THE SOFTWARE PRODUCT OR US$5.00; PROVIDED, HOWEVER, IF YOU HAVE ENTERED INTO A MICROSOFT SUPPORT SERVICES AGREEMENT, MICROSOFT'S ENTIRE LIABILITY REGARDING SUPPORT SERVICES SHALL BE GOVERNED BY THE TERMS OF THAT AGREEMENT. BECAUSE SOME STATES AND JURISDICTIONS DO NOT ALLOW THE EXCLUSION OR LIMITATION OF LIABILITY, THE ABOVE LIMITATION MAY NOT APPLY TO YOU.

MISCELLANEOUS

This EULA is governed by the laws of the State of Washington USA, except and only to the extent that applicable law mandates governing law of a different jurisdiction.

Should you have any questions concerning this EULA, or if you desire to contact Microsoft for any reason, please contact the Microsoft subsidiary serving your country, or write: Microsoft Sales Information Center/One Microsoft Way/ Redmond, WA 98052-6399.

Register Today!

Return this *Programming Microsoft® Visual C++®, Fifth Edition*
registration card today

Microsoft·Press
mspress.microsoft.com

OWNER REGISTRATION CARD

1-57231-857-0

PROGRAMMING MICROSOFT® VISUAL C++®,
FIFTH EDITION

FIRST NAME   MIDDLE INITIAL   LAST NAME

INSTITUTION OR COMPANY NAME

ADDRESS

CITY   STATE   ZIP

(   )

E-MAIL ADDRESS   PHONE NUMBER

For information about Microsoft Press®
products, visit our Web site at
mspress.microsoft.com

Microsoft®*Press*